Head First
Android Development

> Wouldn't it be dreamy if there were a book on developing Android apps that was easier to understand than the space shuttle flight manual? I guess it's just a fantasy...

Dawn Griffiths
David Griffiths

Beijing · Boston · Farnham · Sebastopol · Tokyo

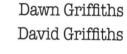
O'REILLY®

Head First Android Development

by Dawn Griffiths and David Griffiths

Published by O'Reilly Media, Inc., 1005 Gravenstein Highway North, Sebastopol, CA 95472.

O'Reilly Media books may be purchased for educational, business, or sales promotional use. Online editions are also available for most titles (*http://oreilly.com/safari*). For more information, contact our corporate/institutional sales department: (800) 998-9938 or *corporate@oreilly.com*.

Series Creators:	Kathy Sierra, Bert Bates
Editor:	Dawn Schanafelt
Cover Designer:	Karen Montgomery
Production Editor:	Kristen Brown
Proofreader:	Rachel Monaghan
Indexer:	Angela Howard
Page Viewers:	Mum and Dad, Rob and Lorraine

Printing History:

June 2015: First Edition.
August 2017: Second Edition

Mum and Dad →

← Rob and Lorraine

No kittens were harmed in the making of this book, but several pizzas were eaten.

ISBN: 978-1-491-97405-6

[M]   [2017-09-08]

To our friends and family. Thank you so much for all your love and support.

Authors of Head First Android Development

Dawn Griffiths

David Griffiths

Dawn Griffiths started life as a mathematician at a top UK university, where she was awarded a first-class honors degree in mathematics. She went on to pursue a career in software development and has over 20 years' experience working in the IT industry.

Before writing *Head First Android Development*, Dawn wrote three other Head First books (*Head First Statistics*, *Head First 2D Geometry*, and *Head First C*). She also created the video course *The Agile Sketchpad* with her husband, David, to teach key concepts and techniques in a way that keeps your brain active and engaged.

When Dawn's not working on Head First books or creating videos, you'll find her honing her Tai Chi skills, reading, running, making bobbin lace, or cooking. She particularly enjoys spending time with her wonderful husband, David.

David Griffiths began programming at age 12, when he saw a documentary on the work of Seymour Papert. At age 15, he wrote an implementation of Papert's computer language LOGO. After studying pure mathematics at university, he began writing code for computers and magazine articles for humans. He's worked as an Agile coach, a developer, and a garage attendant, but not in that order. He can write code in over 10 languages and prose in just one, and when not writing, coding, or coaching, he spends much of his spare time traveling with his lovely wife—and coauthor—Dawn.

Before writing *Head First Android Development*, David wrote three other Head First books—*Head First Rails*, *Head First Programming*, and *Head First C*—and created *The Agile Sketchpad* video course with Dawn.

You can follow us on Twitter at *https://twitter.com/HeadFirstDroid* and visit the book's website at *https://tinyurl.com/HeadFirstAndroid*.

Table of Contents (Summary)

Table of Contents (the real thing)

Intro

Your brain on Android. Here *you* are trying to *learn* something, while here your *brain* is, doing you a favor by making sure the learning doesn't *stick*. Your brain's thinking, "Better leave room for more important things, like which wild animals to avoid and whether naked snowboarding is a bad idea." So how *do* you trick your brain into thinking that your life depends on knowing how to develop Android apps?

I wonder how I can trick my brain into remembering this stuff...

getting started

Diving In

1

Android has taken the world by storm.

Everybody wants a smartphone or tablet, and Android devices are hugely popular. In this book, we'll teach you how to **develop your own apps**, and we'll start by getting you to build a basic app and run it on an Android Virtual Device. Along the way, you'll meet some of the basic components of all Android apps, such as **activities** and **layouts**. **All you need is a little Java know-how...**

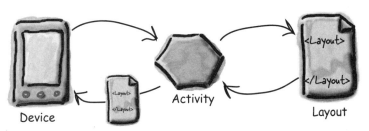

Device   Activity   Layout

building interactive apps

Apps That Do Something

Most apps need to respond to the user in some way.

In this chapter, you'll see how you can make your apps **a bit more interactive**. You'll learn how to get your app to *do* something in response to the user, and **how to get your activity and layout talking to each other** like best buddies. Along the way, we'll take you a bit **deeper into how Android actually works** by introducing you to **R**, the hidden gem that glues everything together.

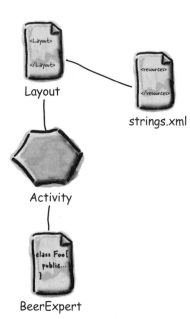

Layout

strings.xml

Activity

BeerExpert

multiple activities and intents

State Your Intent

3

Most apps need more than one activity.

So far we've just looked at single-activity apps, which is fine for simple apps. But when things get more complicated, just having the one activity won't cut it. We're going to show you **how to build apps with multiple activities**, and how you can get your apps talking to each other using *intents*. We'll also look at how you can use intents to **go beyond the boundaries of your app** and **make activities in other apps on your device perform *actions***. Things are about to get a whole lot more powerful...

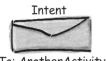

Intent

To: AnotherActivity

CreateMessageActivity

Hey, user. Which activity do you want to use this time?

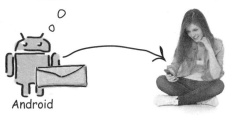

Android

User

the activity lifecycle

Being an Activity

4

Activities form the foundation of every Android app.

So far you've seen how to create activities, and made one activity start another using an intent. But *what's really going on beneath the hood?* In this chapter, we're going to dig a little deeper into **the activity lifecycle**. What happens when an activity is **created** and **destroyed**? Which methods get called when an activity is **made visible and appears in the foreground**, and which get called when the activity **loses the focus and is hidden**? And **how do you save and restore your activity's state**? Read on to find out.

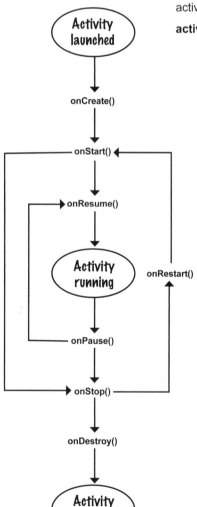

views and view groups

Enjoy the View

5

You've seen how to arrange GUI components using a linear layout, but so far we've only scratched the surface.

In this chapter we'll **look a little deeper** and show you how linear layouts *really work*. We'll introduce you to the **frame layout**, a simple layout used to stack views, and we'll also take a tour of the **main GUI components** and **how you use them**. By the end of the chapter, you'll see that even though they all look a little different, all layouts and GUI components have *more in common than you might think*.

Frame layouts let your views overlap one another. This is useful for displaying text on top of images, for example.

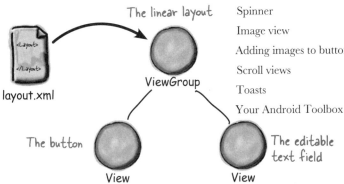

layout.xml

The linear layout

ViewGroup

The button

View

The editable text field

View

constraint layouts

Put Things in Their Place

6

Let's face it, you need to know how to create great layouts.

If you're building apps you want people to *use*, you need to make sure they **look exactly the way you want**. So far you've seen how to use linear and frame layouts, but *what if your design is more complex?* To deal with this, we'll introduce you to Android's new **constraint layout**, a type of layout you *build visually using a blueprint*. We'll show you how **constraints** let you position and size your views, *irrespective of screen size and orientation*. Finally, you'll find out how to save time by making Android Studio **infer and add constraints** on your behalf.

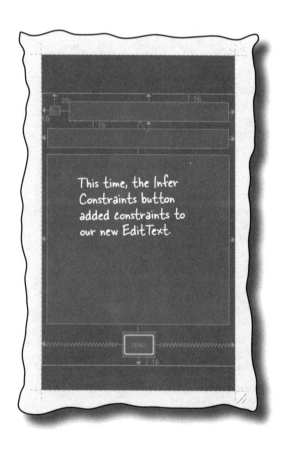

This time, the Infer Constraints button added constraints to our new EditText.

list views and adapters

Getting Organized

7

Want to know how best to structure your Android app?

You've learned about some of the basic building blocks that are used to create apps, and now **it's time to get organized**. In this chapter, we'll show you how you can take a bunch of ideas and **structure them into an awesome app**. You'll learn how **lists of data** can form the core part of your app design, and how **linking them together** can create a **powerful and easy-to-use app**. Along the way, you'll get your first glimpse of using **event listeners** and **adapters** to make your app more dynamic.

Display a start screen with a list of options.

Display a list of the drinks we sell.

Show details of each drink.

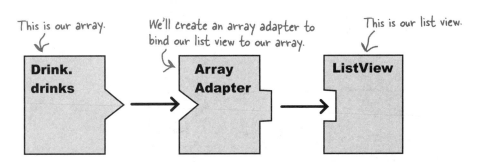

This is our array.

We'll create an array adapter to bind our list view to our array.

This is our list view.

Drink. drinks   →   **Array Adapter**   →   **ListView**

support libraries and app bars

Taking Shortcuts

8

Everybody likes a shortcut.

And in this chapter you'll see how to add shortcuts to your apps using **app bars**. We'll show you how to start activities by *adding actions* to your app bar, how to share content with other apps using the *share action provider*, and how to navigate up your app's hierarchy by implementing *the app bar's Up button*. Along the way we'll introduce you to the powerful **Android Support Libraries**, which are key to making your apps look fresh on older versions of Android.

Activity
onCreate(Bundle)
onStart()
onRestart()
onResume()
onPause()
onStop()
onDestroy()
onSaveInstanceState()

FragmentActivity

AppCompatActivity

YourActivity
onCreate(Bundle)
yourMethod()

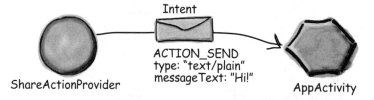

Intent

ACTION_SEND
type: "text/plain"
messageText: "Hi!"

ShareActionProvider   AppActivity

fragments

Make It Modular

9

You've seen how to create apps that work in the same way no matter what device they're running on.

But what if you want your app to look and behave differently depending on whether it's running on a *phone* or a *tablet*? In this case you need **fragments**, modular code components that can be **reused by different activities**. We'll show you how to create **basic fragments** and **list fragments**, how to **add them to your activities**, and how to get your fragments and activities to **communicate** with one another.

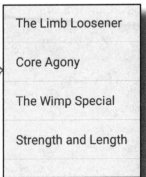

Hmmm, a <fragment> element. I need to know what goes here.

activity_detail

A list fragment comes complete with its own list view so you don't need to add it yourself. You just need to provide the list fragment with data.

The Limb Loosener

Core Agony

The Wimp Special

Strength and Length

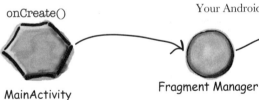

onCreate()

MainActivity

Fragment Manager

WorkoutDetail Fragment

10

fragments for larger interfaces

Different Size, Different Interface

So far we've only run our apps on devices with a small screen. But what if your users have tablets? In this chapter you'll see how to create **flexible user interfaces** by making your app **look and behave differently** depending on the device it's running on. We'll show you how to control the behavior of your app when you press the Back button by introducing you to the **back stack** and **fragment transactions**. Finally, you'll find out how to **save and restore the state** of your fragment.

The device screen's large, so I'll use the large version of the layout.

Android

layout-large

activity_main.xml

MainActivity

I'm committed. Make it so!

FragmentTransaction

Tablet

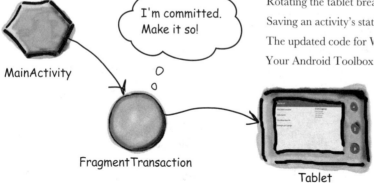

dynamic fragments

Nesting Fragments

11

So far you've seen how to create and use static fragments.

But what if you want your fragments to be more **dynamic**? Dynamic fragments have a lot in common with dynamic activities, but there are crucial differences you need to be able to deal with. In this chapter you'll see how to **convert dynamic activities** into **working dynamic fragments**. You'll find out how to use **fragment transactions** to help **maintain your fragment state**. Finally, you'll discover how to **nest one fragment inside another**, and how the **child fragment manager** helps you control unruly back stack behavior.

Whenever I see android:onClick, I assume it's all about **me**. **My** methods run, not the fragment's.

Activity

I display workout details, and I also display the stopwatch.

The transaction to add StopwatchFragment is nested inside the transaction to add WorkoutDetailFragment.

Workout Details Stopwatch

design support library

Swipe Right

Ever wondered how to develop apps with a rich, slick UI?

With the release of the **Android Design Support Library**, it became much easier to create apps with an intuitive UI. In this chapter, we'll show you around some of the highlights. You'll see how to add *tabs* so that your users can *navigate around your app more easily*. You'll discover how to **animate your toolbars** so that they can *collapse or scroll on a whim*. You'll find out how to add *floating action buttons* for common user actions. Finally, we'll introduce you to *snackbars*, a way of displaying short, informative messages to the user that they can interact with.

We'll get the toolbar to scroll when the user scrolls the content in TopFragment.

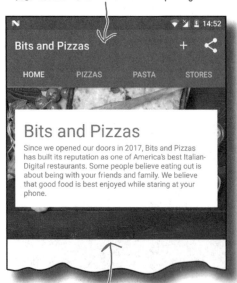

We'll add this scrollable content to TopFragment.

recycler views and card views

Get Recycling

13

You've already seen how the humble list view is a key part of most apps. But compared to some of the *material design* components we've seen, it's somewhat plain. In this chapter, we'll introduce you to the **recycler view**, a more advanced type of list that gives you *loads more flexibility* and *fits in with the material design ethos*. You'll see how to create **adapters** tailored to your data, and how to completely change the look of your list with *just two lines of code*. We'll also show you how to use **card views** to give your data a *3D material design* appearance.

ViewHolder

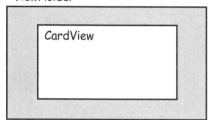

Each of our ViewHolders will contain a CardView. We created the layout for this CardView earlier in the chapter.

14

navigation drawers

Going Places

You've already seen how tabs help users navigate your apps.

But if you need a *large number* of them, or want to *split them into sections*, the **navigation drawer** is your new BFF. In this chapter, we'll show you how to create a navigation drawer that *slides out from the side of your activity at a single touch.* You'll learn how to give it a header using a **navigation view**, and provide it with a **structured set of menu items** to take the user to all the major hubs of your app. Finally, you'll discover how to set up a **navigation view listener** so that the drawer *responds to the slightest touch and swipe.*

This is the CatChat app.

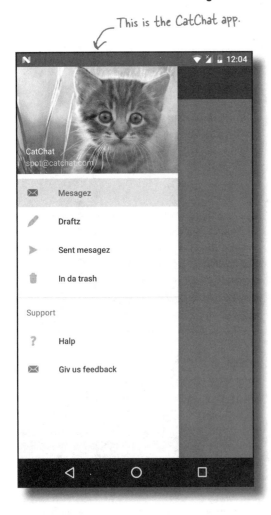

SQLite databases

15

Fire Up the Database

If you're recording high scores or saving tweets, your app will need to store data. And on Android you usually keep your data safe inside a **SQLite database**. In this chapter, we'll show you how to **create a database, add tables to it, and prepopulate it with data**, all with the help of the friendly **SQLite helper**. You'll then see how you can cleanly roll out **upgrades** to your database structure, and how to **downgrade** it if you need to undo any changes.

Your database, sir. Will that be all?

onCreate()

SQLite helper

Name: "starbuzz"
Version: 1

SQLite database

basic cursors

Getting Data Out

16

So how do you connect your app to a SQLite database?

So far you've seen how to create a SQLite database using a SQLite helper. The next step is to get your activities to access it. In this chapter, we'll focus on how you read data from a database. You'll find out **how to use cursors to get data from the database**. You'll see **how to navigate cursors,** and **how to get access to their data**. Finally, you'll discover how to use **cursor adapters** to bind cursors to list views.

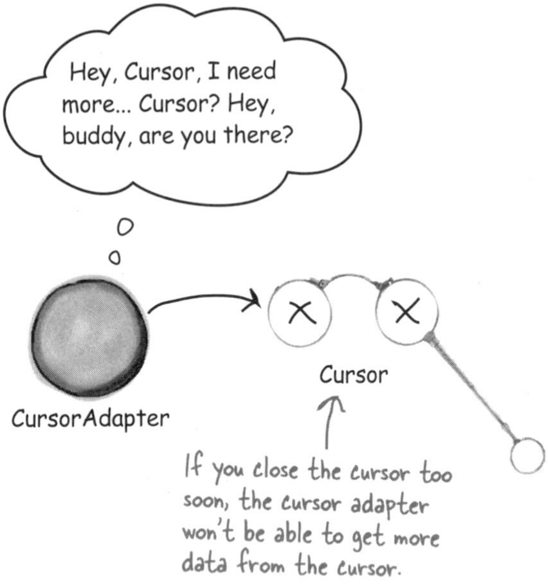

Hey, Cursor, I need more... Cursor? Hey, buddy, are you there?

CursorAdapter

Cursor

If you close the cursor too soon, the cursor adapter won't be able to get more data from the cursor.

cursors and asynctasks

Staying in the Background

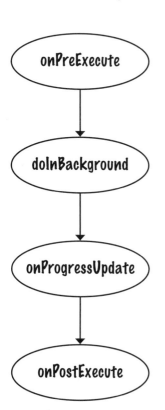

In most apps, you'll need your app to update its data.

So far you've seen how to create apps that read data from a SQLite database. But what if you want to update the app's data? In this chapter you'll see how to get your app to **respond to user input** and **update values in the database**. You'll also find out how to **refresh the data that's displayed** once it's been updated. Finally, you'll see how writing efficient **multithreaded code** with **AsyncTask**s will keep your app speedy.

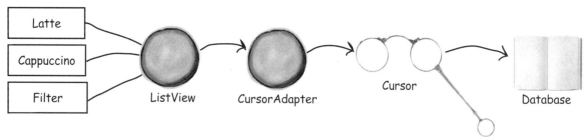

started services

18

At Your Service

There are some operations you want to keep on running, irrespective of which app has the focus. If you start downloading a file, for instance, *you don't want the download to stop when you switch to another app.* In this chapter we'll introduce you to **started services**, components that *run operations in the background.* You'll see how to create a started service using the `IntentService` class, and find out how its lifecycle fits in with that of an activity. Along the way, you'll discover how to **log messages**, and *keep users informed* using Android's built-in **notification service**.

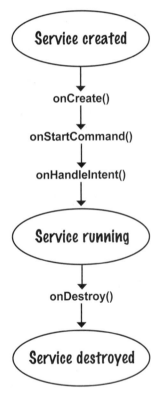

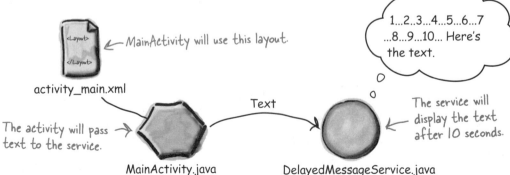

← MainActivity will use this layout.

activity_main.xml

The activity will pass → text to the service.

MainActivity.java

Text

1...2..3...4...5...6...7 ...8...9...10... Here's the text.

The service will → display the text after 10 seconds.

DelayedMessageService.java

bound services and permissions

Bound Together

Started services are great for background operations, but what if you need a service that's more interactive? In this chapter you'll discover how to create a **bound service**, *a type of service your activity can interact with*. You'll see how to **bind** to the service when you need it, and how to **unbind** from it when you're done to save resources. You'll find out how to use **Android's Location Services** to get *location updates from your device GPS*. Finally, you'll discover how to use **Android's permission model**, including *handling runtime permission requests*.

19

Are we nearly there yet?

OdometerService

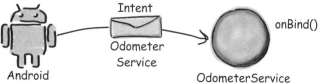

Intent

Odometer Service

Android

onBind()

OdometerService

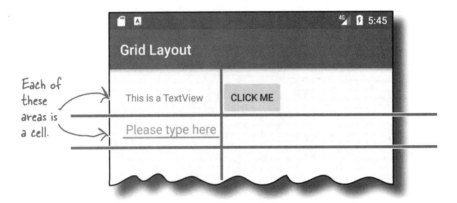

art

The Android Runtime

Ever wonder how Android apps can run on so many kinds of devices? Android apps run in a virtual machine called the **Android runtime (ART)**, not the Oracle Java Virtual Machine (JVM). This means that your apps are quicker to start on small, low-powered devices and run more efficiently. In this appendix, we'll look at how ART works.

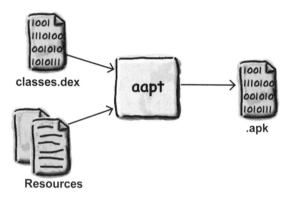

adb

The Android Debug Bridge

In this book, we've focused on using an IDE for all your Android needs. But there are times when using a command-line tool can be plain useful, like those times when Android Studio can't see your Android device but you just *know* it's there. In this chapter, we'll introduce you to the **Android Debug Bridge (or adb)**, a command-line tool you can use to communicate with the emulator or Android devices.

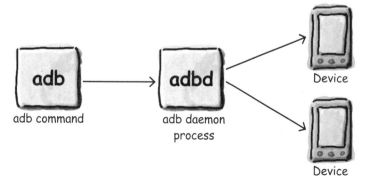

V the android emulator

Speeding Things Up

Ever felt like you were spending all your time waiting for the emulator? There's no doubt that using the Android emulator is useful. It allows you to see how your app will run on devices other than the physical ones you have access to. But at times it can feel a little...sluggish. In this appendix, we'll explain why the emulator can seem slow. Even better, we'll give you a few tips we've learned for **speeding it up**.

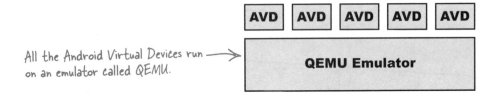

All the Android Virtual Devices run on an emulator called QEMU.
AVD
AVD
AVD
AVD
AVD
QEMU Emulator

vi leftovers

The Top Ten Things (we didn't cover)

Even after all that, there's still a little more.

There are just a few more things we think you need to know. We wouldn't feel right about ignoring them, and we really wanted to give you a book you'd be able to lift without extensive training at the local gym. Before you put down the book, **read through these tidbits**.

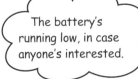

The battery's running low, in case anyone's interested.
Android

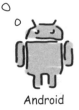

how to use this book

Intro

In this section, we answer the burning question:
"So why DID they put that in a book on Android?"

Who is this book for?

If you can answer "yes" to all of these:

1 Do you already know how to program in Java?

2 Do you want to master Android app development, create the next big thing in software, make a small fortune, and retire to your own private island? ←

OK, maybe that one's a little far-fetched. But you gotta start somewhere, right?

3 Do you prefer actually doing things and applying the stuff you learn over listening to someone in a lecture rattle on for hours on end?

this book is for you.

Who should probably back away from this book?

If you can answer "yes" to any of these:

1 Are you looking for a quick introduction or reference book to developing Android apps?

2 Would you rather have your toenails pulled out by 15 screaming monkeys than learn something new? Do you believe an Android book should cover *everything*, especially all the obscure stuff you'll never use, and if it bores the reader to tears in the process, then so much the better?

this book is ***not*** for you.

[Note from Marketing: this book is for anyone with a credit card or a PayPal account]

We know what you're thinking

"How can *this* be a serious book on developing Android apps?"

"What's with all the graphics?"

"Can I actually *learn* it this way?"

We know what your *brain* is thinking

Your brain craves novelty. It's always searching, scanning, *waiting* for something unusual. It was built that way, and it helps you stay alive.

So what does your brain do with all the routine, ordinary, normal things you encounter? Everything it *can* to stop them from interfering with the brain's *real* job—recording things that *matter*. It doesn't bother saving the boring things; they never make it past the "this is obviously not important" filter.

How does your brain *know* what's important? Suppose you're out for a day hike and a tiger jumps in front of you—what happens inside your head and body?

Neurons fire. Emotions crank up. *Chemicals surge.*

And that's how your brain knows…

This must be important! Don't forget it!

But imagine you're at home or in a library. It's a safe, warm, tiger-free zone. You're studying. Getting ready for an exam. Or trying to learn some tough technical topic your boss thinks will take a week, ten days at the most.

Just one problem. Your brain's trying to do you a big favor. It's trying to make sure that this *obviously* unimportant content doesn't clutter up scarce resources. Resources that are better spent storing the really *big* things. Like tigers. Like the danger of fire. Like how you should never have posted those party photos on your Facebook page. And there's no simple way to tell your brain, "Hey brain, thank you very much, but no matter how dull this book is, and how little I'm registering on the emotional Richter scale right now, I really *do* want you to keep this stuff around."

Your brain thinks THIS is important.

Great. Only 900 more dull, dry, boring pages.

Your brain thinks THIS isn't worth saving.

We think of a "Head First" reader as a <u>learner</u>.

So what does it take to *learn* something? First, you have to *get* it, then make sure you don't *forget* it. It's not about pushing facts into your head. Based on the latest research in cognitive science, neurobiology, and educational psychology, *learning* takes a lot more than text on a page. We know what turns your brain on.

Some of the Head First learning principles:

Make it visual. Images are far more memorable than words alone, and make learning much more effective (up to 89% improvement in recall and transfer studies). It also makes things more understandable. **Put the words within or near the graphics** they relate to, rather than on the bottom or on another page, and learners will be up to *twice* as likely to solve problems related to the content.

Use a conversational and personalized style. In recent studies, students performed up to 40% better on post-learning tests if the content spoke directly to the reader, using a first-person, conversational style rather than taking a formal tone. Tell stories instead of lecturing. Use casual language. Don't take yourself too seriously. Which would *you* pay more attention to: a stimulating dinner-party companion, or a lecture?

Get the learner to think more deeply. In other words, unless you actively flex your neurons, nothing much happens in your head. A reader has to be motivated, engaged, curious, and inspired to solve problems, draw conclusions, and generate new knowledge. And for that, you need challenges, exercises, and thought-provoking questions, and activities that involve both sides of the brain and multiple senses.

Get—and keep—the reader's attention. We've all had the "I really want to learn this, but I can't stay awake past page one" experience. Your brain pays attention to things that are out of the ordinary, interesting, strange, eye-catching, unexpected. Learning a new, tough, technical topic doesn't have to be boring. Your brain will learn much more quickly if it's not.

Touch their emotions. We now know that your ability to remember something is largely dependent on its emotional content. You remember what you care about. You remember when you *feel* something. No, we're not talking heart-wrenching stories about a boy and his dog. We're talking emotions like surprise, curiosity, fun, "what the…?", and the feeling of "I rule!" that comes when you solve a puzzle, learn something everybody else thinks is hard, or realize you know something that "I'm more technical than . thou" Bob from Engineering *doesn't*.

Metacognition: thinking about thinking

If you really want to learn, and you want to learn more quickly and more deeply, pay attention to how you pay attention. Think about how you think. Learn how you learn.

Most of us did not take courses on metacognition or learning theory when we were growing up. We were *expected* to learn, but rarely *taught* to learn.

But we assume that if you're holding this book, you really want to learn how to develop Android apps. And you probably don't want to spend a lot of time. If you want to use what you read in this book, you need to *remember* what you read. And for that, you've got to *understand* it. To get the most from this book, or *any* book or learning experience, take responsibility for your brain. Your brain on *this* content.

The trick is to get your brain to see the new material you're learning as Really Important. Crucial to your well-being. As important as a tiger. Otherwise, you're in for a constant battle, with your brain doing its best to keep the new content from sticking.

I wonder how I can trick my brain into remembering this stuff...

So just how *DO* you get your brain to treat Android development like it was a hungry tiger?

There's the slow, tedious way, or the faster, more effective way. The slow way is about sheer repetition. You obviously know that you *are* able to learn and remember even the dullest of topics if you keep pounding the same thing into your brain. With enough repetition, your brain says, "This doesn't *feel* important to him, but he keeps looking at the same thing *over* and *over* and *over*, so I suppose it must be."

The faster way is to do **anything that increases brain activity,** especially different *types* of brain activity. The things on the previous page are a big part of the solution, and they're all things that have been proven to help your brain work in your favor. For example, studies show that putting words *within* the pictures they describe (as opposed to somewhere else in the page, like a caption or in the body text) causes your brain to try to makes sense of how the words and picture relate, and this causes more neurons to fire. More neurons firing = more chances for your brain to *get* that this is something worth paying attention to, and possibly recording.

A conversational style helps because people tend to pay more attention when they perceive that they're in a conversation, since they're expected to follow along and hold up their end. The amazing thing is, your brain doesn't necessarily *care* that the "conversation" is between you and a book! On the other hand, if the writing style is formal and dry, your brain perceives it the same way you experience being lectured to while sitting in a roomful of passive attendees. No need to stay awake.

But pictures and conversational style are just the beginning…

Here's what WE did

We used **pictures**, because your brain is tuned for visuals, not text. As far as your brain's concerned, a picture really *is* worth a thousand words. And when text and pictures work together, we embedded the text *in* the pictures because your brain works more effectively when the text is *within* the thing it refers to, as opposed to in a caption or buried in the body text somewhere.

We used **redundancy**, saying the same thing in *different* ways and with different media types, and *multiple senses*, to increase the chance that the content gets coded into more than one area of your brain.

We used concepts and pictures in **unexpected** ways because your brain is tuned for novelty, and we used pictures and ideas with at least *some* **emotional** *content*, because your brain is tuned to pay attention to the biochemistry of emotions. That which causes you to *feel* something is more likely to be remembered, even if that feeling is nothing more than a little **humor**, **surprise**, or **interest.**

We used a personalized, **conversational style**, because your brain is tuned to pay more attention when it believes you're in a conversation than if it thinks you're passively listening to a presentation. Your brain does this even when you're *reading*.

We included **activities**, because your brain is tuned to learn and remember more when you **do** things than when you *read* about things. And we made the exercises challenging-yet-doable, because that's what most people prefer.

We used **multiple learning styles**, because *you* might prefer step-by-step procedures, while someone else wants to understand the big picture first, and someone else just wants to see an example. But regardless of your own learning preference, *everyone* benefits from seeing the same content represented in multiple ways.

We include content for **both sides of your brain**, because the more of your brain you engage, the more likely you are to learn and remember, and the longer you can stay focused. Since working one side of the brain often means giving the other side a chance to rest, you can be more productive at learning for a longer period of time.

And we included **stories** and exercises that present **more than one point of view,** because your brain is tuned to learn more deeply when it's forced to make evaluations and judgments.

We included **challenges**, with exercises, and by asking **questions** that don't always have a straight answer, because your brain is tuned to learn and remember when it has to *work* at something. Think about it—you can't get your *body* in shape just by *watching* people at the gym. But we did our best to make sure that when you're working hard, it's on the *right* things. That **you're not spending one extra dendrite** processing a hard-to-understand example, or parsing difficult, jargon-laden, or overly terse text.

We used **people**. In stories, examples, pictures, and the like, because, well, *you're* a person. And your brain pays more attention to *people* than it does to *things*.

Cut this out and stick it on your refrigerator.

Here's what YOU can do to bend your brain into submission

So, we did our part. The rest is up to you. These tips are a starting point; listen to your brain and figure out what works for you and what doesn't. Try new things.

---

1 Slow down. The more you understand, the less you have to memorize.

Don't just *read*. Stop and think. When the book asks you a question, don't just skip to the answer. Imagine that someone really *is* asking the question. The more deeply you force your brain to think, the better chance you have of learning and remembering.

2 Do the exercises. Write your own notes.

We put them in, but if we did them for you, that would be like having someone else do your workouts for you. And don't just *look* at the exercises. **Use a pencil.** There's plenty of evidence that physical activity *while* learning can increase the learning.

3 Read "There Are No Dumb Questions."

That means all of them. They're not optional sidebars, ***they're part of the core content!*** Don't skip them.

4 Make this the last thing you read before bed. Or at least the last challenging thing.

Part of the learning (especially the transfer to long-term memory) happens *after* you put the book down. Your brain needs time on its own, to do more processing. If you put in something new during that processing time, some of what you just learned will be lost.

5 Talk about it. Out loud.

Speaking activates a different part of the brain. If you're trying to understand something, or increase your chance of remembering it later, say it out loud. Better still, try to explain it out loud to someone else. You'll learn more quickly, and you might uncover ideas you hadn't known were there when you were reading about it.

6 Drink water. Lots of it.

Your brain works best in a nice bath of fluid. Dehydration (which can happen before you ever feel thirsty) decreases cognitive function.

7 Listen to your brain.

Pay attention to whether your brain is getting overloaded. If you find yourself starting to skim the surface or forget what you just read, it's time for a break. Once you go past a certain point, you won't learn faster by trying to shove more in, and you might even hurt the process.

8 Feel something.

Your brain needs to know that this *matters*. Get involved with the stories. Make up your own captions for the photos. Groaning over a bad joke is *still* better than feeling nothing at all.

9 Write a lot of code!

There's only one way to learn to develop Android apps: **write a lot of code**. And that's what you're going to do throughout this book. Coding is a skill, and the only way to get good at it is to practice. We're going to give you a lot of practice: every chapter has exercises that pose a problem for you to solve. Don't just skip over them—a lot of the learning happens when you solve the exercises. We included a solution to each exercise—don't be afraid to **peek at the solution** if you get stuck! (It's easy to get snagged on something small.) But try to solve the problem before you look at the solution. And definitely get it working before you move on to the next part of the book.

Read me

This is a learning experience, not a reference book. We deliberately stripped out everything that might get in the way of learning whatever it is we're working on at that point in the book. And the first time through, you need to begin at the beginning, because the book makes assumptions about what you've already seen and learned.

We assume you're new to Android, but not to Java.

We're going to be building Android apps using a combination of Java and XML. We assume that you're familiar with the Java prorgamming language. If you've never done any Java programming *at all*, then you might want to read *Head First Java* before you start on this one.

We start off by building an app in the very first chapter.

Believe it or not, even if you've never developed for Android before, you can jump right in and start building apps. You'll also learn your way around Android Studio, the official IDE for Android development.

The examples are designed for learning.

As you work through the book, you'll build a number of different apps. Some of these are very small so you can focus on a specific part of Android. Other apps are larger so you can see how different components fit together. We won't complete every part of every app, but feel free to experiment and finish them yourself. It's all part of the learning experience. The source code for all the apps is here: *https://tinyurl.com/HeadFirstAndroid*.

The activities are NOT optional.

The exercises and activities are not add-ons; they're part of the core content of the book. Some of them are to help with memory, some are for understanding, and some will help you apply what you've learned. ***Don't skip the exercises.***

The redundancy is intentional and important.

One distinct difference in a Head First book is that we want you to *really* get it. And we want you to finish the book remembering what you've learned. Most reference books don't have retention and recall as a goal, but this book is about *learning*, so you'll see some of the same concepts come up more than once.

The Brain Power exercises don't have answers.

For some of them, there is no right answer, and for others, part of the learning experience of the Brain Power activities is for you to decide if and when your answers are right. In some of the Brain Power exercises, you will find hints to point you in the right direction.

The technical review team

Andy

Jacqui

Technical reviewers:

Andy Parker is currently working as a development manager, but has been a research physicist, teacher, designer, reviewer, and team leader at various points in his career. Through all of his roles, he has never lost his passion for creating top quality, well-designed, and well-engineered software. Nowadays, he spends most of his time managing great Agile teams and passing on his wide range of experience to the next generation of developers.

Jacqui Cope started coding to avoid school netball practice. Since then she has gathered 30 years' experience working with a variety of financial software systems, from coding in COBOL to test management. Recently she has gained her MSc in Computer Security and has moved into software Quality Assurance in the higher education sector.

In her spare time, Jacqui likes to cook, walk in the countryside, and watch *Doctor Who* from behind the sofa.

Acknowledgments

Our editor:

Heartfelt thanks to our wonderful editor **Dawn Schanafelt** for picking up the reins on the second edition. She has truly been amazing, and a delight to work with. She made us feel valued and supported every step of the way, and gave us invaluable feedback and insight exactly when we needed it. We've appreciated all the many times she told us our sentences had all the right words, but not necessarily in the right order.

Thanks also to **Bert Bates** for teaching us to throw away the old rulebook and for letting us into his brain.

Dawn Schanafelt

The O'Reilly team:

A big thank you goes to **Mike Hendrickson** for having confidence in us and asking us to write the first edition of the book; **Heather Scherer** for her behind-the-scenes organization skills and herding; the **early release team** for making early versions of the book available for download; and the **design team** for all their extra help. Finally, thanks go to the **production team** for expertly steering the book through the production process and for working so hard behind the scenes.

Family, friends, and colleagues:

Writing a Head First book is a rollercoaster of a ride, even when it's a second edition, and this one's been no exception. We've truly valued the kindness and support of our family and friends along the way. Special thanks go to **Ian**, **Steve**, **Colin**, **Angela**, **Paul B**, **Chris**, **Michael**, **Mum**, **Dad**, **Carl**, **Rob**, and **Lorraine**.

The without-whom list:

Our technical review team did a great job of keeping us straight, and making sure that what we covered was spot on. We're also grateful to **Ingo Krotzky** for his valuable feedback on the early release of this book, and all the people who gave us feedback on the first edition. We think the book's much, much better as a result.

Finally, our thanks to **Kathy Sierra** and **Bert Bates** for creating this extraordinary series of books.

O'Reilly Safari®

Safari (formerly Safari Books Online) is a membership-based training and reference platform for enterprise, government, educators, and individuals.

Members have access to thousands of books, training videos, Learning Paths, interactive tutorials, and curated playlists from over 250 publishers, including O'Reilly Media, Harvard Business Review, Prentice Hall Professional, Addison-Wesley Professional, Microsoft Press, Sams, Que, Peachpit Press, Adobe, Focal Press, Cisco Press, John Wiley & Sons, Syngress, Morgan Kaufmann, IBM Redbooks, Packt, Adobe Press, FT Press, Apress, Manning, New Riders, McGraw-Hill, Jones & Bartlett, and Course Technology, among others.

For more information, please visit *http://oreilly.com/safari*.

1 getting started

Diving In

Android has taken the world by storm.

Everybody wants a smartphone or tablet, and Android devices are hugely popular. In this book, we'll teach you how to **develop your own apps**, and we'll start by getting you to build a basic app and run it on an Android Virtual Device. Along the way, you'll meet some of the basic components of all Android apps, such as **activities** and **layouts**. **All you need is a little Java know-how...**

Welcome to Androidville

Android is the world's most popular mobile platform. At the last count, there were over *two billion* active Android devices worldwide, and that number is growing rapidly.

Android is a comprehensive open source platform based on Linux and championed by Google. It's a powerful development framework that includes everything you need to build great apps using a mix of Java and XML. What's more, it enables you to deploy those apps to a wide variety of devices—phones, tablets, and more.

So what makes up a typical Android app?

We're going to build our Android apps using a mixture of Java and XML. We'll explain things along the way, but you'll need to have a fair understanding of Java to get the most out of this book.

Layouts define what each screen looks like

A typical Android app is composed of one or more screens. You define what each screen looks like using a **layout** to define its appearance. Layouts are usually defined in XML, and can include GUI components such as buttons, text fields, and labels.

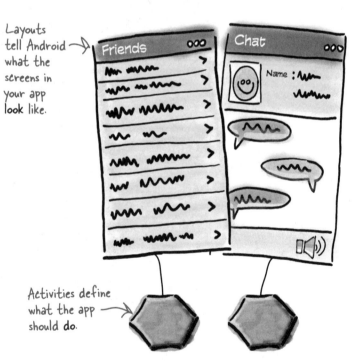

Layouts tell Android what the screens in your app look like.

Activities define what the app does

Layouts only define the *appearance* of the app. You define what the app *does* using one or more **activities**. An activity is a special Java class that decides which layout to use and tells the app how to respond to the user. As an example, if a layout includes a button, you need to write Java code in the activity to define what the button should do when you press it.

Activities define what the app should **do**.

Sometimes extra resources are needed too

In addition to activities and layouts, Android apps often need extra resources such as image files and application data. You can add any extra files you need to the app.

Android apps are really just a bunch of files in particular directories. When you build your app, all of these files get bundled together, giving you an app you can run on your device.

Resources can include sound and image files.

The Android platform dissected

The Android platform is made up of a number of different components. It includes core applications such as Contacts, a set of APIs to help you control what your app looks like and how it behaves, and a whole load of supporting files and libraries. Here's a quick look at how they all fit together:

Don't worry if this seems like a lot to take in.

We're just giving you an overview of what's included in the Android platform. We'll explain the different components in more detail as and when we need to.

Android comes with a set of core applications such as Contacts, Phone, Calendar, and a browser.

When you build apps, you have access to the same APIs used by the core applications. You use these APIs to control what your app looks like and how it behaves.

Underneath the application framework lies a set of C and C++ libraries. These libraries get exposed to you through the framework APIs.

Underneath everything else lies the Linux kernel. Android relies on the kernel for drivers, and also core services such as security and memory management.

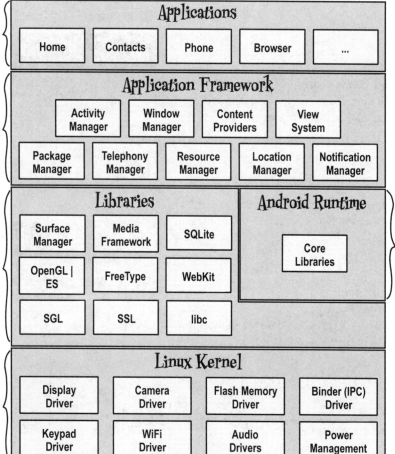

The Android runtime comes with a set of core libraries that implement most of the Java programming language. Each Android app runs in its own process.

The great news is that all of the powerful Android libraries are exposed through the APIs in the application framework, and it's these APIs that you use to create great Android apps. All you need to begin is some Java knowledge and a great idea for an app.

Here's what we're going to do

So let's dive in and create a basic Android app. There are just a few things we need to do:

1 **Set up a development environment.**
We need to install Android Studio, which includes all the tools you need to develop Android apps.

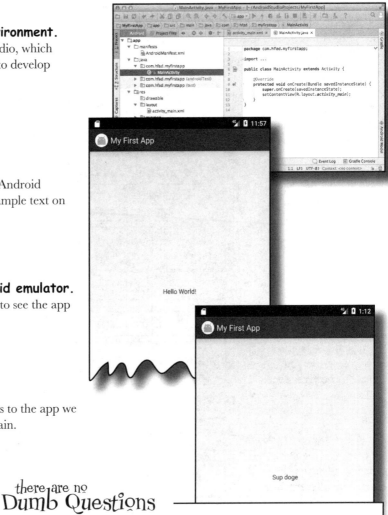

2 **Build a basic app.**
We'll build a simple app using Android Studio that will display some sample text on the screen.

3 **Run the app in the Android emulator.**
We'll use the built-in emulator to see the app up and running.

4 **Change the app.**
Finally, we'll make a few tweaks to the app we created in step 2, and run it again.

there are no Dumb Questions

Q: Are all Android apps developed in Java?

A: You can develop Android apps in other languages, too. Most developers use Java, so that's what we're covering in this book.

Q: How much Java do I need to know for Android app development?

A: You really need experience with Java SE (Standard Edition). If you're feeling rusty, we suggest getting a copy of *Head First Java* by Kathy Sierra and Bert Bates.

Q: Do I need to know about Swing and AWT?

A: Android doesn't use Swing or AWT, so don't worry if you don't have Java desktop GUI experience.

Your development environment

You are here.

getting **started**

☐ **Set up environment**
☐ **Build app**
☐ **Run app**
☐ **Change app**

Java is the most popular language used to develop Android applications. Android devices don't run *.class* and *.jar* files. Instead, to improve speed and battery performance, Android devices use their own optimized formats for compiled code. That means that you can't use an ordinary Java development environment—you also need special tools to convert your compiled code into an Android format, to deploy them to an Android device, and to let you debug the app once it's running.

All of these come as part of the **Android SDK**. Let's take a look at what's included.

The Android SDK

The Android Software Development Kit contains the libraries and tools you need to develop Android apps. Here are some of the main points:

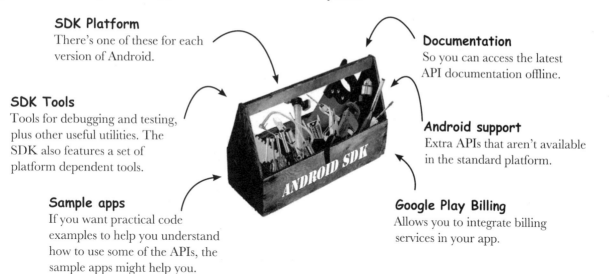

SDK Platform
There's one of these for each version of Android.

SDK Tools
Tools for debugging and testing, plus other useful utilities. The SDK also features a set of platform dependent tools.

Sample apps
If you want practical code examples to help you understand how to use some of the APIs, the sample apps might help you.

Documentation
So you can access the latest API documentation offline.

Android support
Extra APIs that aren't available in the standard platform.

Google Play Billing
Allows you to integrate billing services in your app.

Android Studio is a special version of IntelliJ IDEA

IntelliJ IDEA is one of the most popular IDEs for Java development. Android Studio is a version of IDEA that includes a version of the Android SDK and extra GUI tools to help you with your app development.

In addition to providing you with an editor and access to the tools and libraries in the Android SDK, Android Studio gives you templates you can use to help you create new apps and classes, and it makes it easy to do things such as package your apps and run them.

Install Android Studio

→ ☐ **Set up environment**
☐ **Build app**
☐ **Run app**
☐ **Change app**

Before we go any further, you need to install Android Studio on your machine. We're not including the installation instructions in this book as they can get out of date pretty quickly, but you'll be fine if you follow the online instructions.

← *We're using Android Studio version 2.3. You'll need to use this version or above to get the most out of this book.*

First, check the Android Studio system requirements here:

http://developer.android.com/sdk/index.html#Requirements ←

Google sometimes changes their URLs. If these URLs don't work, search for Android Studio and you should find them.

Then follow the Android Studio installation instructions here:

https://developer.android.com/sdk/installing/index.html?pkg=studio

Once you've installed Android Studio, open it and follow the instructions to add the latest SDK tools and Support Libraries.

When you're done, you should see the Android Studio welcome screen. You're now ready to build your first Android app.

This is the Android Studio welcome screen. It includes a set of options for things you can do. →

Welcome to Android Studio

Android Studio
Version 2.3

☼ Start a new Android Studio project

☐ Open an existing Android Studio project

⬇ Check out project from Version Control ▾

☑ Import project (Eclipse ADT, Gradle, etc.)

☑ Import an Android code sample

⚙ Configure ▾   Get Help ▾

there are no Dumb Questions

Q: You say we're going to use Android Studio to build the Android apps. Do I have to?

A: Strictly speaking, you don't *have* to use Android Studio to build Android apps. All you need is a tool that will let you write and compile Java code, plus a few other tools to convert the compiled code into a form that Android devices can run.

Android Studio is the official Android IDE, and the Android team recommends using it. But quite a lot of people use IntelliJ IDEA instead.

Q: Can I write Android apps without using an IDE?

A: It's possible, but it's more work. Most Android apps are now created using a build tool called *Gradle*. Gradle projects can be created and built using a text editor and a command line.

Q: A build tool? So is gradle like ANT?

A: It's similar, but Gradle is much more powerful than ANT. Gradle can compile and deploy code, just like ANT, but it also uses Maven to download any third-party libraries your code needs. Gradle also uses Groovy as a scripting language, which means you can easily create quite complex builds with Gradle.

Q: Most apps are built using Gradle? I thought you said most developers use Android Studio.

A: Android Studio provides a graphical interface to Gradle, and also to other tools for creating layouts, reading logs, and debugging.

You can find out more about Gradle in Appendix II.

Build a basic app

Now that you've set up your development environment, you're ready to create your first Android app. Here's what the app will look like:

This is the name of the application. →

This is a very simple app, but that's all you need for your very first Android app.

There'll be a small piece of sample text right here that Android Studio will put in for us.

How to build the app

Whenever you create a new app, you need to create a new project for it. Make sure you have Android Studio open, and follow along with us.

1. Create a new project

The Android Studio welcome screen gives you a number of options. We want to create a new project, so click on the option for "Start a new Android Studio project."

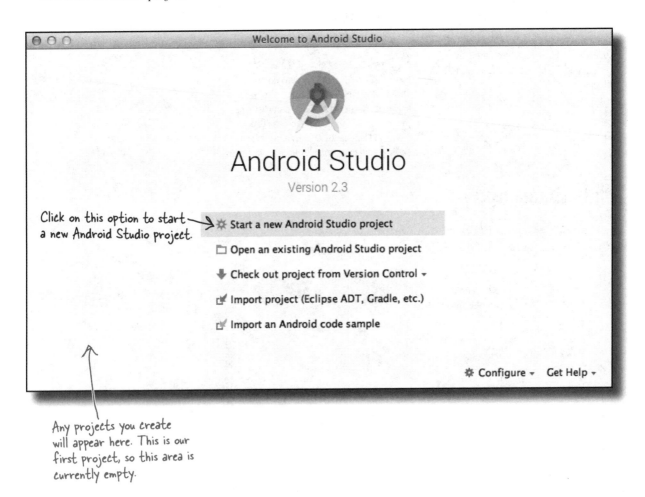

Click on this option to start a new Android Studio project.

Any projects you create will appear here. This is our first project, so this area is currently empty.

How to build the app (continued)

2. Configure the project

You now need to configure the app by telling Android Studio what you want to call it, what company domain to use, and where you would like to store the files.

Android Studio uses the company domain and application name to form the name of the package that will be used for your app. As an example, if you give your app a name of "My First App" and use a company domain of "hfad.com", Android Studio will derive a package name of com.hfad.myfirstapp. The package name is really important in Android, as it's used by Android devices to uniquely identify your app.

Enter an application name of "My First App", enter a company domain of "hfad.com", uncheck the option to include C++ support, and accept the default project location. Then click on the Next button.

Watch it!

> **The package name must stay the same for the lifetime of your app.**
>
> *It's a unique identifier for your app and used to manage multiple versions of the same app.*

Some versions of Android Studio may have an extra option asking if you want to include Kotlin support. Uncheck this option if it's there.

The wizard forms the package name by combining the application name and the company domain.

The application name is shown in the Google Play Store and various other places, too.

```
○ ○ ○                          Create New Project

   New Project
   Android Studio

   Configure your new project

   Application name:   My First App
   Company domain:     hfad.com
   Package name:       com.hfad.myfirstapp                              Edit
                       ☐ Include C++ support

   Project location:   /Users/dawng/AndroidStudioProjects/MyFirstApp    ...



                          Cancel    Previous    Next    Finish
```

Use a company domain of hfad.com.

Uncheck the option to include C++ support. If prompted, also uncheck the option to include Kotlin support.

All of the files for your project will be stored here.

How to build the app (continued)

Set up environment
Build app
Run app
Change app

3. Specify the minimum SDK

You now need to indicate the minimum SDK of Android your app will use. API levels increase with every new version of Android. Unless you only want your app to run on the very newest devices, you'll probably want to specify one of the older APIs.

Here, we're choosing a minimum SDK of API level 19, which means it will be able to run on most devices. Also, we're only going to create a version of our app to run on phones and tablets, so we'll leave the other options unchecked.

← There's more about the different API levels on the next page.

When you've done this, click on the Next button.

The minimum required SDK is the lowest version your app will support. Your app will run on devices with this level API or higher. It won't run on devices with a lower API.

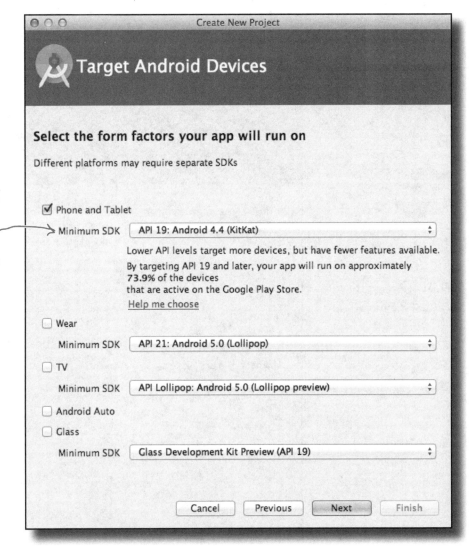

Android Versions Up Close

You've probably heard a lot of things about Android that sound tasty, like Jelly Bean, KitKat, Lollipop, and Nougat. So what's with all the confectionary?

Android versions have a version number and a codename. The version number gives the precise version of Android (e.g., 7.0), while the codename is a more generic "friendly" name that may cover several versions of Android (e.g., Nougat). The API level refers to the version of the APIs used by applications. As an example, the equivalent API level for Android version 7.1.1 is 25.

Version	Codename	API level
1.0		1
1.1		2
1.5	Cupcake	3
1.6	Donut	4
2.0–2.1	Eclair	5–7
2.2.x	Froyo	8
2.3–2.3.7	Gingerbread	9–10
3.0 - 3.2	Honeycomb	11–13
4.0–4.0.4	Ice Cream Sandwich	14–15
4.1 - 4.3	Jelly Bean	16–18
4.4	KitKat	19–20
5.0–5.1	Lollipop	21–22
6.0	Marshmallow	23
7.0	Nougat	24
7.1–7.1.2	Nougat	25

Hardly anyone uses these versions anymore.

Most devices use one of these APIs.

When you develop Android apps, you really need to consider which versions of Android you want your app to be compatible with. If you specify that your app is only compatible with the very latest version of the SDK, you might find that it can't be run on many devices. You can find out the percentage of devices running particular versions here: *https://developer.android.com/about/dashboards/index.html*.

Activities and layouts from 50,000 feet

☑ Set up environment
→ **Build app**
 Run app
 Change app

The next thing you'll be prompted to do is add an activity to your project. Every Android app is a collection of screens, and each screen is composed of an activity and a layout.

An **activity** is **a single, defined thing that your user can do**. You might have an activity to compose an email, take a photo, or find a contact. Activities are usually associated with one screen, and they're written in Java.

A **layout** describes **the appearance of the screen.** Layouts are written as XML files and they tell Android how the different screen elements are arranged.

Let's look in more detail at how activities and layouts work together to create a user interface:

Layouts define how the user interface is presented.

Activities define actions.

① The device launches your app and creates an activity object.

② The activity object specifies a layout.

③ The activity tells Android to display the layout onscreen.

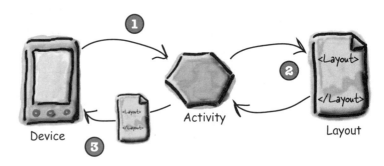

④ The user interacts with the layout that's displayed on the device.

⑤ The activity responds to these interactions by running application code.

⑥ The activity updates the display...

⑦ ...which the user sees on the device.

Now that you know a bit more about what activities and layouts are, let's go through the last couple of steps in the Create New Project wizard and get it to create an activity and layout.

How to build the app (continued)

4. Add an activity

The next screen lets you choose among a series of templates you can use to create an activity and layout. We're going to create an app with an empty activity and layout, so choose the Empty Activity option and click the Next button.

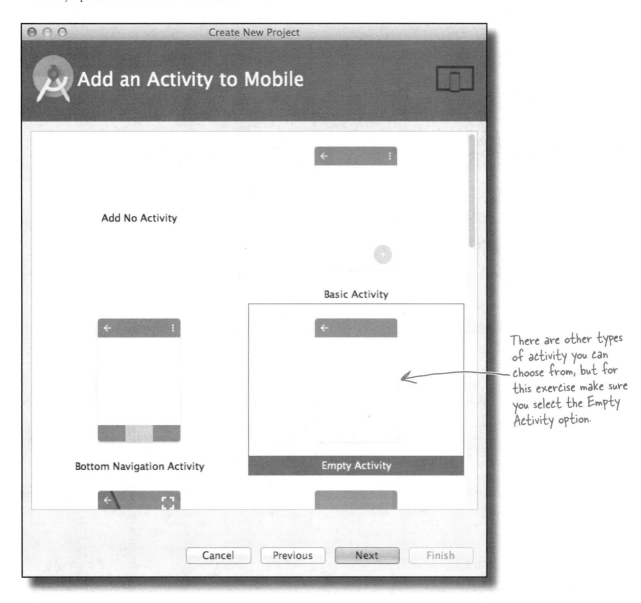

There are other types of activity you can choose from, but for this exercise make sure you select the Empty Activity option.

How to build the app (continued)

Set up environment
Build app
Run app
Change app

5. Customize the activity

You will now be asked what you want to call the screen's activity and layout. Enter an activity name of "MainActivity", make sure the option to generate a layout file is checked, enter a layout name of "activity_main", and then uncheck the Backwards Compatibility (AppCompat) option. The activity is a Java class, and the layout is an XML file, so the names we've given here will create a Java class file called *MainActivity.java* and an XML file called *activity_main.xml*.

When you click on the Finish button, Android Studio will build your app.

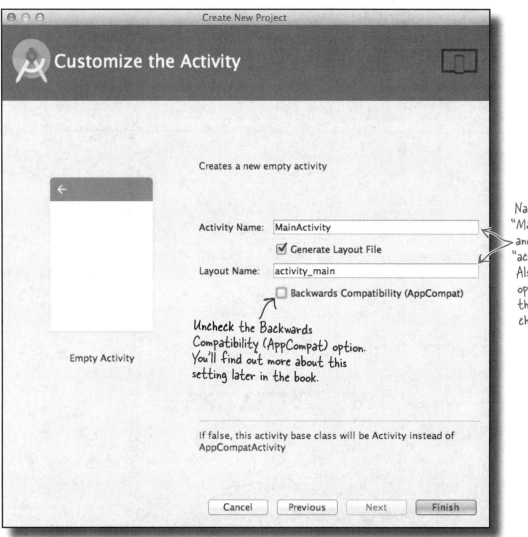

Name the activity "MainActivity" and the layout "activity_main". Also make sure the option to generate the layout is checked.

Uncheck the Backwards Compatibility (AppCompat) option. You'll find out more about this setting later in the book.

You've just created your first Android app

So what just happened?

⭐ **The Create New Project wizard created a project for your app, configured to your specifications.**
You defined which versions of Android the app should be compatible with, and the wizard created all of the files and folders needed for a basic valid app.

⭐ **The wizard created an activity and layout with template code.**
The template code includes layout XML and activity Java code, with sample "Hello World!" text in the layout.

When you finish creating your project by going through the wizard, Android Studio automatically displays the project for you.

Here's what our project looks like (don't worry if it looks complicated—we'll break it down over the next few pages):

This is the project in Android Studio.

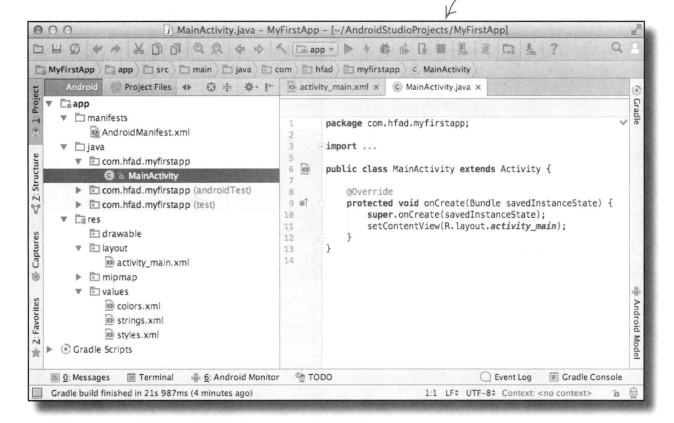

Android Studio creates a complete folder structure for you

An Android app is really just a bunch of valid files in a particular folder structure, and Android Studio sets all of this up for you when you create a new app. The easiest way of looking at this folder structure is with the explorer in the leftmost column of Android Studio.

The explorer contains all of the projects that you currently have open. To expand or collapse folders, just click on the arrows to the left of the folder icons.

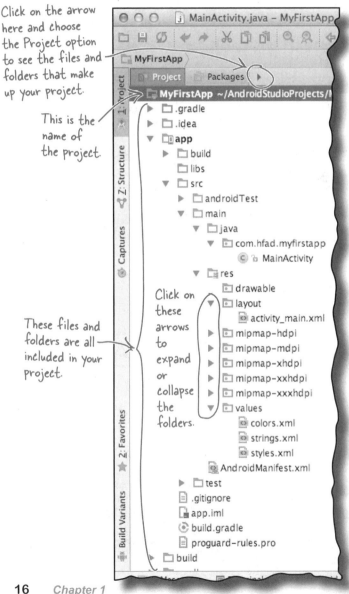

Click on the arrow here and choose the Project option to see the files and folders that make up your project.

This is the name of the project.

These files and folders are all included in your project.

Click on these arrows to expand or collapse the folders.

The folder structure includes different types of files

If you browse through the folder structure, you'll see that the wizard has created various types of files and folders for you:

Java and XML source files
These are the activity and layout files for your app.

Android-generated Java files
There are some extra Java files you don't need to touch that Android Studio generates for you automatically.

Resource files
These include default image files for icons, styles your app might use, and any common String values your app might want to look up.

Android libraries
In the wizard, you specified the minimum SDK version you want your app to be compatible with. Android Studio makes sure your app includes the relevant Android libraries for that version.

Configuration files
The configuration files tell Android what's actually in the app and how it should run.

Let's take a closer look at some of the key files and folders in Androidville.

Useful files in your project

Android Studio projects use the Gradle build system to compile and deploy apps. Gradle projects have a standard structure. Here are some of the key files and folders you'll be working with:

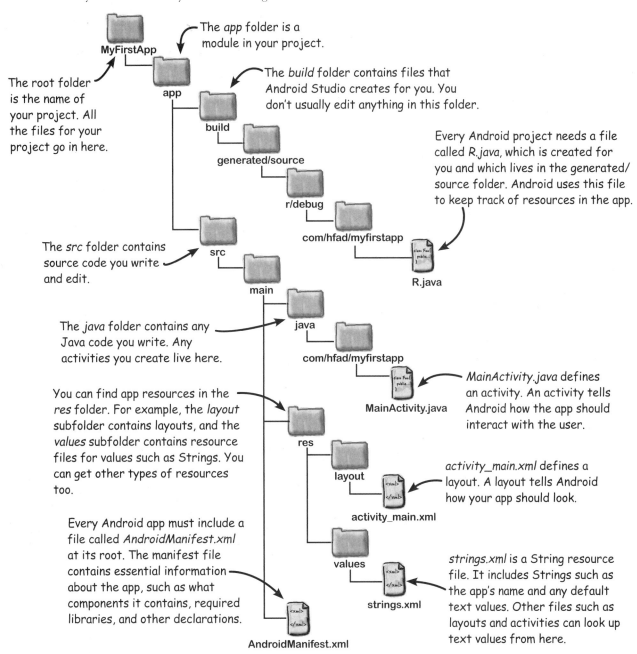

The *app* folder is a module in your project.

The root folder is the name of your project. All the files for your project go in here.

The *build* folder contains files that Android Studio creates for you. You don't usually edit anything in this folder.

Every Android project needs a file called *R.java*, which is created for you and which lives in the generated/source folder. Android uses this file to keep track of resources in the app.

The *src* folder contains source code you write and edit.

The *java* folder contains any Java code you write. Any activities you create live here.

You can find app resources in the *res* folder. For example, the *layout* subfolder contains layouts, and the *values* subfolder contains resource files for values such as Strings. You can get other types of resources too.

MainActivity.java defines an activity. An activity tells Android how the app should interact with the user.

activity_main.xml defines a layout. A layout tells Android how your app should look.

Every Android app must include a file called *AndroidManifest.xml* at its root. The manifest file contains essential information about the app, such as what components it contains, required libraries, and other declarations.

strings.xml is a String resource file. It includes Strings such as the app's name and any default text values. Other files such as layouts and activities can look up text values from here.

Set up environment
Build app
Run app
Change app

Edit code with the Android Studio editors

You view and edit files using the Android Studio editors. Double-click
on the file you want to work with, and the file's contents will appear in
the middle of the Android Studio window.

The code editor

Most files get displayed in
the code editor, which is
just like a text editor, but
with extra features such
as color coding and code
checking.

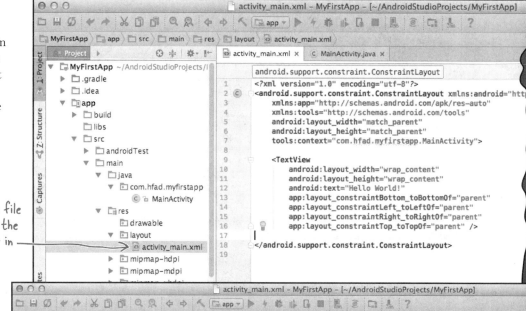

*Double-click on the file
in the explorer and the
file contents appear in
the editor panel.*

The design editor

If you're editing a
layout, you have an
extra option. Rather
than edit the XML
(such as that shown on
the next page), you can
use the design editor,
which allows you to
drag GUI components
onto your layout, and
arrange them how you
want. The code editor
and design editor give
different views of the
same file, so you can
switch back and forth
between the two.

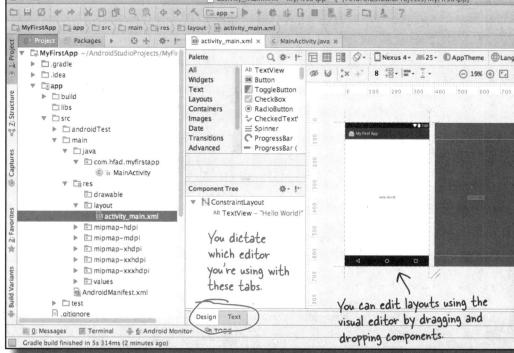

*You dictate
which editor
you're using with
these tabs.*

*You can edit layouts using the
visual editor by dragging and
dropping components.*

Here's the code from an example layout file (**not the one Android Studio generated for us**). We know you've not seen layout code before, but just see if you can match each of the descriptions at the bottom of the page to the correct lines of code. We've done one to get you started.

activity_main.xml

```xml
<?xml version="1.0" encoding="utf-8"?>
<LinearLayout xmlns:android="http://schemas.android.com/apk/res/android"
    xmlns:tools="http://schemas.android.com/tools"
    android:layout_width="match_parent"
    android:layout_height="match_parent"
    android:paddingLeft="16dp"
    android:paddingRight="16dp"
    android:paddingTop="16dp"
    android:paddingBottom="16dp"
    android:orientation="vertical"
    tools:context="com.hfad.myfirstapp.MainActivity">

    <TextView
        android:layout_width="wrap_content"
        android:layout_height="wrap_content"
        android:text="Hello World!" />
</LinearLayout>
```

Add padding to the screen margins.

Include a `<TextView>` GUI component for displaying text.

Make the GUI component just large enough for its content.

Display the String "Hello World!"

Make the layout the same width and height as the screen size on the device.

Here's the code from an example layout file (**not the one Android Studio generated for us**). We know you've not seen layout code before, but just see if you can match each of the descriptions at the bottom of the page to the correct lines of code. We've done one to get you started.

activity_main.xml

```xml
<?xml version="1.0" encoding="utf-8"?>
<LinearLayout xmlns:android="http://schemas.android.com/apk/res/android"
    xmlns:tools="http://schemas.android.com/tools"
    android:layout_width="match_parent"
    android:layout_height="match_parent"
    android:paddingLeft="16dp"
    android:paddingRight="16dp"
    android:paddingTop="16dp"
    android:paddingBottom="16dp"
    android:orientation="vertical"
    tools:context="com.hfad.myfirstapp.MainActivity">

    <TextView
        android:layout_width="wrap_content"
        android:layout_height="wrap_content"
        android:text="Hello World!" />
</LinearLayout>
```

Add padding to the screen margins.

Include a `<TextView>` GUI component for displaying text.

Make the GUI component just large enough for its content.

Display the String "Hello World!"

Make the layout the same width and height as the screen size on the device.

WHAT'S MY PURPOSE?

Now let's see if you can do the same thing for some activity code. **This is example code, and not necessarily the code that Android Studio will have generated for you**. Match the descriptions below to the correct lines of code.

MainActivity.java

```
package com.hfad.myfirstapp;

import android.os.Bundle;
import android.app.Activity;

public class MainActivity extends Activity {

    @Override
    protected void onCreate(Bundle savedInstanceState) {
        super.onCreate(savedInstanceState);
        setContentView(R.layout.activity_main);
    }
}
```

This is the package name.

These are Android classes used in **MainActivity**.

Specify which layout to use.

Implement the **onCreate()** method from the **Activity** class. This method is called when the activity is first created.

MainActivity extends the Android class **android.app.Activity**.

Now let's see if you can do the same thing for some activity code. **This is example code, and not necessarily the code that Android Studio will have generated for you**. Match the descriptions below to the correct lines of code.

MainActivity.java

```
package com.hfad.myfirstapp;

import android.os.Bundle;
import android.app.Activity;

public class MainActivity extends Activity {

    @Override
    protected void onCreate(Bundle savedInstanceState) {
        super.onCreate(savedInstanceState);
        setContentView(R.layout.activity_main);
    }
)
```

This is the package name.

These are Android classes used in MainActivity.

Specify which layout to use.

Implement the onCreate() method from the Activity class. This method is called when the activity is first created.

MainActivity extends the Android class android.app.Activity.

Run the app in the Android emulator

So far you've seen what your Android app looks like in Android Studio and got a feel for how it hangs together. But what you *really* want to do is see it running, right?

You have a couple of options when it comes to running your apps. The first option is to run them on a physical device. But what if you don't have one with you, or you want to see how your app looks on a type of device you don't have?

In that case, you can use the **Android emulator** that's built into the Android SDK. The emulator enables you to set up one or more **Android virtual devices** (AVDs) and then run your app in the emulator *as though it's running on a physical device.*

The Android emulator allows you to run your app on an Android virtual device (AVD), which behaves just like a physical Android device. You can set up numerous AVDs, each emulating a different type of device.

So what does the emulator look like?

Here's an AVD running in the Android emulator. It looks just like a phone running on your computer.

The emulator recreates the exact hardware environment of an Android device: from its CPU and memory through to the sound chips and the video display. The emulator is built on an existing emulator called QEMU (pronounced "queue em you"), which is similar to other virtual machine applications you may have used, like VirtualBox or VMWare.

The exact appearance and behavior of the AVD depends on how you've set up the AVD in the first place. The AVD here is set up to mimic a Nexus 5X, so it will look and behave just like a Nexus 5X on your computer.

Let's set up an AVD so that you can see your app running in the emulator.

Once you've set up an AVD, you'll be able to see your app running on it. Android Studio launches the emulator for you.

Create an Android Virtual Device

There are a few steps you need to go through in order to set up an AVD within Android Studio. We'll set up a Nexus 5X AVD running API level 25 so that you can see how your app looks and behaves running on this type of device. The steps are pretty much identical no matter what type of virtual device you want to set up.

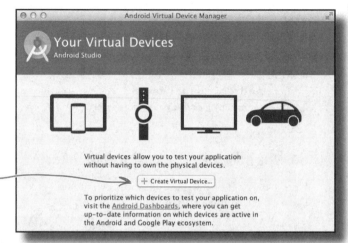

Set up environment
Build app
Run app
Change app

Open the Android Virtual Device Manager

The AVD Manager allows you to set up new AVDs, and view and edit ones you've already created. Open it by selecting Android on the Tools menu and choosing AVD Manager.

If you have no AVDs set up already, you'll be presented with a screen prompting you to create one. Click on the "Create Virtual Device" button.

Click on this button to create an AVD.

Select the hardware

On the next screen, you'll be prompted to choose a device definition. This is the type of device your AVD will emulate. You can choose a variety of phone, tablet, wear, or TV devices.

We're going to see what our app looks like running on a Nexus 5X phone. Choose Phone from the Category menu and Nexus 5X from the list. Then click the Next button.

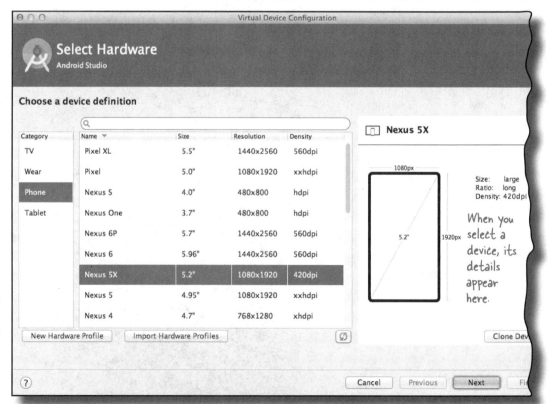

When you select a device, its details appear here.

Creating an AVD (continued)

Select a system image

Next, you need to select a system image. The system image gives you an installed version of the Android operating system. You can choose the version of Android you want to be on your AVD.

You need to choose a system image for an API level that's compatible with the app you're building. As an example, if you want your app to work on a minimum of API level 19, choose a system image for *at least* API level 19. We want our AVD to run API level 25, so choose the system image with a release name of Nougat and a target of Android 7.1.1 (API level 25). Then click on the Next button.

If you don't have this system image installed, you'll be given the option to download it.

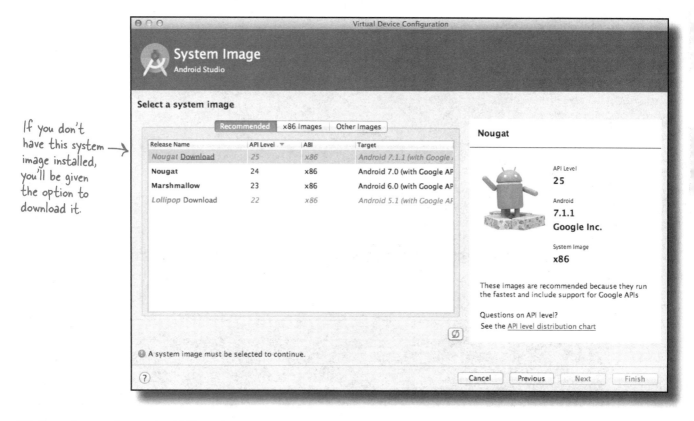

We'll continue setting up the AVD on the next page.

Creating an AVD (continued)

Set up environment
Build app
Run app
Change app

Verify the AVD configuration

On the next screen, you'll be asked to verify the AVD configuration. This screen summarizes the options you chose over the last few screens, and gives you the option of changing them. Accept the options, and click on the Finish button.

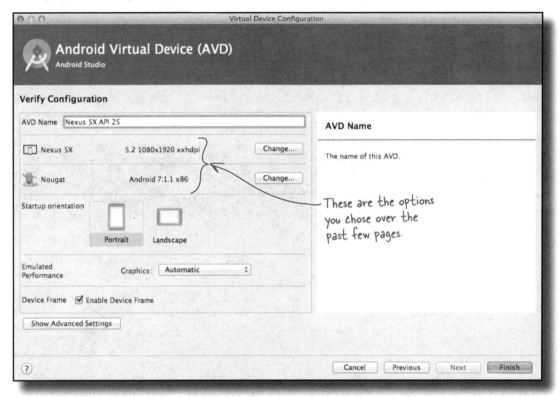

The AVD Manager will create the AVD for you, and when it's done, display it in the AVD Manager list of devices. You may now close the AVD Manager.

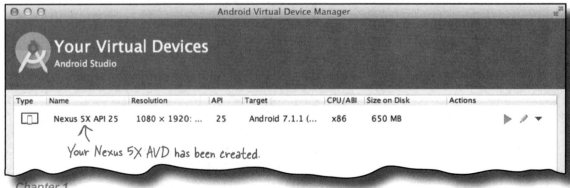

Run the app in the emulator

Now that you've set up your AVD, let's run the app on it. To do this, choose the "Run 'app'" command from the Run menu. When you're asked to choose a device, select the Nexus 5X AVD you just created. Then click OK.

The AVD can take a few minutes to appear, so while we wait, let's take a look at what happens when you choose Run.

Compile, package, deploy, and run

The Run command doesn't just run your app. It also handles all the preliminary tasks that are needed for the app to run:

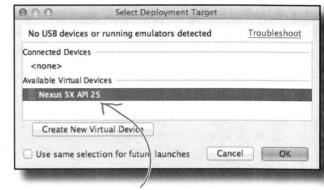

This is the AVD we just created.

Libraries Resources

Java file   Bytecode   APK file

▶ Run

Emulator

Emulator

An APK file is an Android application package. It's basically a JAR or ZIP file for Android applications.

① The Java source files get compiled to bytecode.

② An Android application package, or APK file, gets created.
The APK file includes the compiled Java files, along with any libraries and resources needed by your app.

③ Assuming there's not one already running, the emulator gets launched and then runs the AVD.

④ Once the emulator has been launched and the AVD is active, the APK file is uploaded to the AVD and installed.

⑤ The AVD starts the main activity associated with the app.
Your app gets displayed on the AVD screen, and it's all ready for you to test out.

be patient

☑ Set up environment
☑ Build app
→ ☐ Run app
☐ Change app

You can watch progress in the console

It can sometimes take quite a while for the emulator to launch with your AVD—often *several minutes*. If you like, you can watch what's happening using the Android Studio console. The console gives you a blow-by-blow account of what the build system is doing, and if it encounters any errors, you'll see them highlighted in the text.

We suggest finding something else to do while waiting for the emulator to start. Like quilting, or cooking a small meal.

You can find the console at the bottom of the Android Studio screen (click on the Run option at the bottom of the screen if it doesn't appear automatically):

Here's the output from our console window when we ran our app:

```
03/13 10:45:41: Launching app      ← Install the app.
$ adb install-multiple -r /Users/dawng/AndroidStudioProjects/MyFirstApp/app/build/intermediates/
split-apk/debug/dep/dependencies.apk /Users/dawng/AndroidStudioProjects/MyFirstApp/app/build/
intermediates/split-apk/debug/slices/slice_1.apk /Users/dawng/AndroidStudioProjects/MyFirstApp/
app/build/intermediates/split-apk/debug/slices/slice_2.apk /Users/dawng/AndroidStudioProjects/
MyFirstApp/app/build/intermediates/split-apk/debug/slices/slice_0.apk /Users/dawng/
AndroidStudioProjects/MyFirstApp/app/build/intermediates/split-apk/debug/slices/slice_3.apk /Users/
dawng/AndroidStudioProjects/MyFirstApp/app/build/intermediates/split-apk/debug/slices/slice_6.apk /
Users/dawng/AndroidStudioProjects/MyFirstApp/app/build/intermediates/split-apk/debug/slices/slice_4.
apk /Users/dawng/AndroidStudioProjects/MyFirstApp/app/build/intermediates/split-apk/debug/slices/
slice_5.apk /Users/dawng/AndroidStudioProjects/MyFirstApp/app/build/intermediates/split-apk/debug/
slices/slice_7.apk /Users/dawng/AndroidStudioProjects/MyFirstApp/app/build/intermediates/split-apk/
debug/slices/slice_8.apk /Users/dawng/AndroidStudioProjects/MyFirstApp/app/build/intermediates/
split-apk/debug/slices/slice_9.apk /Users/dawng/AndroidStudioProjects/MyFirstApp/app/build/outputs/
apk/app-debug.apk

Split APKs installed

$ adb shell am startservice com.hfad.myfirstapp/com.android.tools.fd.runtime.InstantRunService

$ adb shell am start -n "com.hfad.myfirstapp/com.hfad.myfirstapp.MainActivity" -a android.intent.
action.MAIN -c android.intent.category.LAUNCHER

Connected to process 2685 on device Nexus_5X_API_25 [emulator-5554]
```

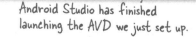

Android Studio has finished launching the AVD we just set up.

The emulator launches our app by starting the main activity for it. This is the activity the wizard created for us.

Test drive

So let's look at what actually happens onscreen when you run your app.

First, the emulator fires up in a separate window. The emulator takes a while to load the AVD, but then you see what looks like an actual Android device.

The emulator launches...

...and here's the AVD home screen. It looks and behaves just like a real Nexus 5X device.

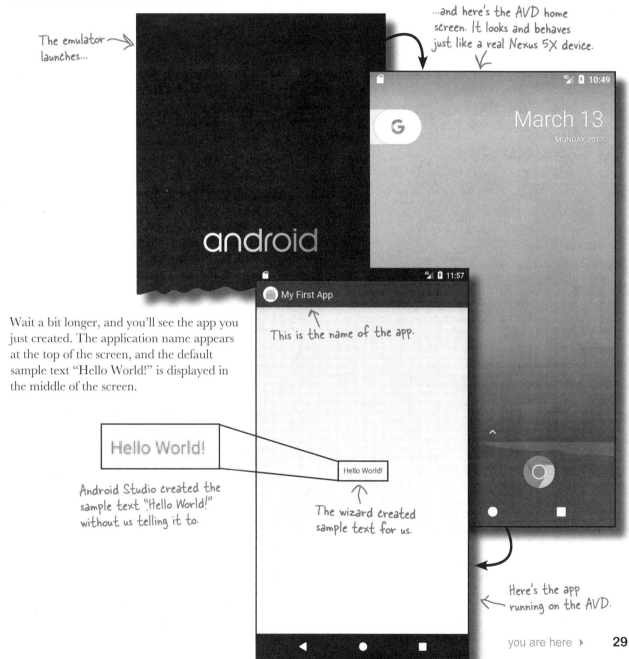

Wait a bit longer, and you'll see the app you just created. The application name appears at the top of the screen, and the default sample text "Hello World!" is displayed in the middle of the screen.

This is the name of the app.

Hello World!

Android Studio created the sample text "Hello World!" without us telling it to.

The wizard created sample text for us.

Here's the app running on the AVD.

What just happened?

Set up environment
Build app
Run app
Change app

Let's break down what happens when you run the app:

① Android Studio launches the emulator, loads the AVD, and installs the app.

② When the app gets launched, an activity object is created from MainActivity.java.

③ The activity specifies that it uses the layout activity_main.xml.

④ The activity tells Android to display the layout on the screen. The text "Hello World!" gets displayed.

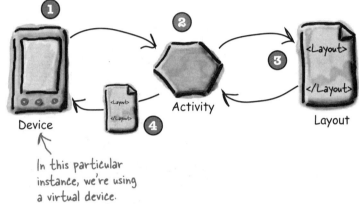

Device

Activity

Layout

In this particular instance, we're using a virtual device.

---

there are no Dumb Questions

Q: You mentioned that when you create an APK file, the Java source code gets compiled into bytecode and added to the APK. Presumably you mean it gets compiled into Java bytecode, right?

A: It does, but that's not the end of the story. Things work a little differently on Android.

The big difference with Android is that your code doesn't actually run inside an ordinary Java VM. It runs on the Android runtime (ART) instead, and on older devices it runs in a predecessor to ART called Dalvik. This means that you write your Java source code and compile it into *.class* files using the Java compiler, and then the *.class* files get stitched into one or more files in DEX format, which is smaller, more efficient bytecode. ART then runs the DEX code. You can find more details about this in Appendix III.

Q: That sounds complicated. Why not just use the normal Java VM?

A: ART can convert the DEX bytecode into native code that can run directly on the CPU of the Android device. This makes the app run a lot faster, and use a lot less battery power.

Q: Is a Java virtual machine really that much overhead?

A: Yes. Because on Android, each app runs inside its own process. If it used ordinary JVMs, it would need a lot more memory.

Q: Do I need to create a new AVD every time I create a new app?

A: No, once you've created the AVD you can use it for any of your apps. You may find it useful to create multiple AVDs in order to test your apps in different situations. As an example, in addition to a phone AVD you might want to create a tablet AVD so you can see how your app looks and behaves on larger devices.

- [x] Set up environment
- [x] Build app
- [x] Run app
- [ ] **Change app**

Refine the app

Over the past several pages, you've built a basic Android app and seen it running in the emulator. Next, we're going to refine the app.

At the moment, the app displays the sample text "Hello World!" that the wizard put in as a placeholder. You're going to change that text to say something else instead. So what do we need to change in order to achieve that? To answer that, let's take a step back and look at how the app is currently built.

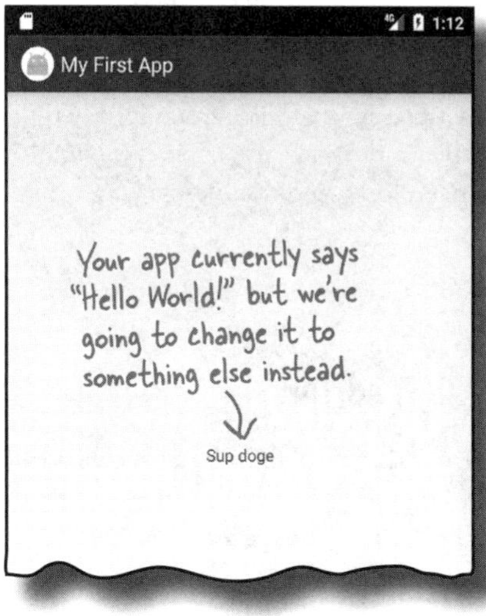
1:12
My First App
Your app currently says "Hello World!" but we're going to change it to something else instead.
Sup doge

The app has one activity and one layout

When we built the app, we told Android Studio how to configure it, and the wizard did the rest. The wizard created an activity for us, and also a default layout.

The activity controls what the app does

Android Studio created an activity for us called *MainActivity.java*. The activity specifies what the app **does** and how it should respond to the user.

The layout controls the app's appearance

MainActivity.java specifies that it uses the layout Android Studio created for us called *activity_main.xml*. The layout specifies what the app **looks like**.

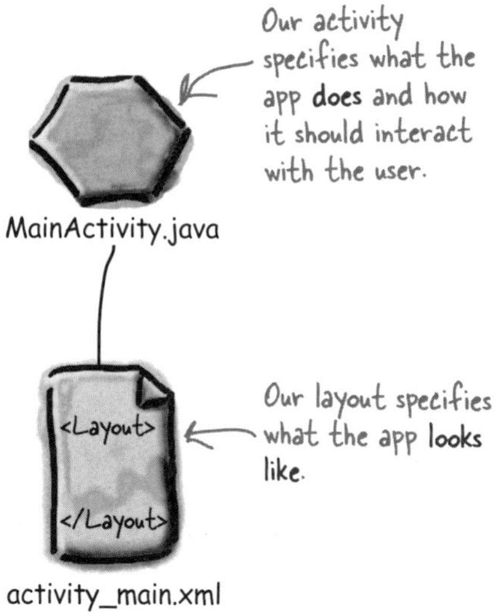
Our activity specifies what the app does and how it should interact with the user.
MainActivity.java
<Layout>
</Layout>
Our layout specifies what the app looks like.
activity_main.xml

We want to change the appearance of the app by changing the text that's displayed. This means that we need to deal with the Android component that controls what the app looks like, so we need to take a closer look at the *layout*.

What's in the layout?

We want to change the sample "Hello World!" text that Android Studio created for us, so let's start with the layout file *activity_main.xml*. If it isn't already open in an editor, open it now by finding the file in the *app/src/main/res/layout* folder in the explorer and double-clicking on it.

If you can't see the folder structure in the explorer, try switching to Project view.

Click on this arrow to change how the files and folders are shown.

The design editor

As you learned earlier, there are two ways of viewing and editing layout files in Android Studio: through the **design editor** and through the **code editor**.

When you choose the design option, you can see that the sample text "Hello World!" appears in the layout as you might expect. But what's in the underlying XML?

Let's see by switching to the code editor.

The design editor

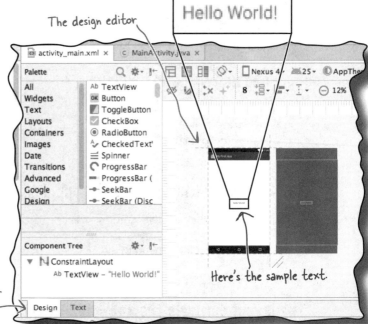

Here's the sample text.

You can see the design editor by choosing "Design" here.

The code editor

When you choose the code editor option, the content of *activity_main.xml* is displayed. Let's take a closer look at it.

The code editor

```xml
<?xml version="1.0" encoding="utf-8"?>
<android.support.constraint.ConstraintLayout xmlns:android=
    xmlns:app="http://schemas.android.com/apk/res-auto"
    xmlns:tools="http://schemas.android.com/tools"
    android:layout_width="match_parent"
    android:layout_height="match_parent"
    tools:context="com.hfad.myfirstapp.MainActivity">

    <TextView
        android:layout_width="wrap_content"
        android:layout_height="wrap_content"
        android:text="Hello World!"
        app:layout_constraintBottom_toBottomOf="parent"
        app:layout_constraintLeft_toLeftOf="parent"
        app:layout_constraintRight_toRightOf="parent"
        app:layout_constraintTop_toTopOf="parent" />

</android.support.constraint.ConstraintLayout>
```

To see the code editor, click on "Text" in the bottom tab.

activity_main.xml has two elements

Below is the code from *activity_main.xml* that Android Studio generated for us. We've left out some of the details you don't need to think about just yet; we'll cover them in more detail through the rest of the book.

Here's our code:

```xml
<?xml version="1.0" encoding="utf-8"?>
<android.support.constraint.ConstraintLayout
    ... >
    <TextView
        android:layout_width="wrap_content"
        android:layout_height="wrap_content"
        android:text="Hello World!"
        ... />
</android.support.constraint.ConstraintLayout>
```

This element determines how components should be displayed, in this case the "Hello World!" text.

> Android Studio gave us more XML here, but you don't need to think about that yet.

This is the <TextView> element.

We've left out some of the <TextView> XML too.

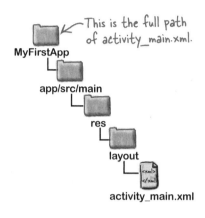

This is the full path of activity_main.xml.

MyFirstApp

app/src/main

res

layout

activity_main.xml

As you can see, the code contains two elements.

The first is an `<android.support.constraint.ConstraintLayout>` element. This is a type of layout element that tells Android how to display components on the device screen. There are various types of layout element available for you to use, and you'll find out more about these later in the book.

The most important element for now is the second element, the `<TextView>`. This element is used to display text to the user, in our case the sample text "Hello World!"

The key part of the code within the `<TextView>` element is the line starting with `android:text`. This is a text property describing the text that should be displayed:

> **Don't worry if your layout code looks different from ours.**
>
> Android Studio may give you slightly different XML depending on which version you're using. You don't need to worry about this, because from the next chapter onward you'll learn how to roll your own layout code, and replace a lot of what Android Studio gives you.

```xml
<TextView
    android:layout_width="wrap_content"
    android:layout_height="wrap_content"
    android:text="Hello World!"
    ... />
```

The <TextView> element describes the text in the layout.

This is the text that's being displayed.

Let's change the text to something else.

Update the text displayed in the layout

The key part of the <TextView> element is this line:

```
android:text="Hello World!" />
```

android:text means that this is the text property of
the <TextView> element, so it specifies what text should be
displayed in the layout. In this case, the text that's being displayed
is "Hello World!"

Display the text.... ➤ *..."Hello World!"*

```
android:text="Hello World!" />
```

To update the text that's displayed in the layout, simply change
the value of the text property from "Hello World!" to
"Sup doge". The new code for the <TextView> should look
like this:

*We've left out some
of the code, as all
we're doing for now
is changing the text
that's displayed.*

```
        ...
<TextView
    android:layout_width="wrap_content"
    android:layout_height="wrap_content"
    android:text="Hello World!Sup doge"
    ... />
        ...
```

*Change the text here from
"Hello World!" to "Sup doge".*

MyFirstApp

app/src/main

res

layout

activity_main.xml

Once you've updated the file, go to the File menu and choose the
Save All option to save your change.

there are no Dumb Questions

Q: My layout code looks different from yours. Is that OK?

A: Yes, that's fine. Android Studio may generate slightly different
code if you're using a different version than us, but that doesn't
really matter. From now on you'll be learning how to create your
own layout code, and you'll replace a lot of what Android Studio
gives you.

**Q: Am I right in thinking we're hardcoding the text that's
displayed?**

A: Yes, purely so that you can see how to update text in
the layout. There's a better way of displaying text values than
hardcoding them in your layouts, but you'll have to wait for the next
chapter to learn what it is.

**Q: The folders in my project explorer pane look different
from yours. Why's that?**

A: Android Studio lets you choose alternate views for how to
display the folder hierarchy, and it defaults to the "Android" view.
We prefer the "Project" view, as it reflects the underlying folder
structure. You can change your explorer to the "Project" view by
clicking on the arrow at the top of the explorer pane, and selecting
the "Project" option.

*We're
using the
Project
view.*

*Click on
this arrow
to change
the explorer
view.*

MyFirstApp
Project   Packages ▶
▼ MyFirstApp ~/AndroidStudio
  ▶ ☐ .gradle
  ▶ ☐ .idea
  ▼ ☐ app

Take the app for a test drive

Once you've edited the file, try running your app in the emulator again by choosing the "Run 'app'" command from the Run menu. You should see that your app now says "Sup doge" instead of "Hello World!"

Here's the updated version of our app. →

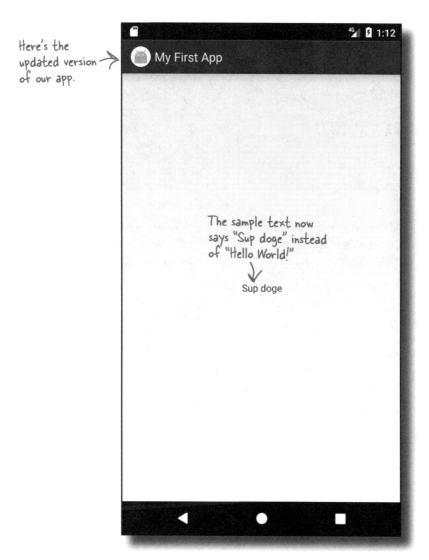

The sample text now says "Sup doge" instead of "Hello World!"

↓

Sup doge

You've now built and updated your first Android app.

Your Android Toolbox

You've got Chapter 1 under your belt and now you've added Android basic concepts to your toolbox.

You can download the full code for the chapter from https://tinyurl.com/HeadFirstAndroid.

BULLET POINTS

- Versions of Android have a version number, API level, and code name.

- Android Studio is a special version of IntelliJ IDEA that interfaces with the Android Software Development Kit (SDK) and the Gradle build system.

- A typical Android app is composed of activities, layouts, and resource files.

- Layouts describe what your app looks like. They're held in the *app/src/main/res/layout* folder.

- Activities describe what your app does, and how it interacts with the user. The activities you write are held in the *app/src/main/java* folder.

- *AndroidManifest.xml* contains information about the app itself. It lives in the *app/src/main* folder.

- An AVD is an Android Virtual Device. It runs in the Android emulator and mimics a physical Android device.

- An APK is an Android application package. It's like a JAR file for Android apps, and contains your app's bytecode, libraries, and resources. You install an app on a device by installing the APK.

- Android apps run in separate processes using the Android runtime (ART).

- The `<TextView>` element is used for displaying text.

2 building interactive apps

Apps That Do Something

Most apps need to respond to the user in some way.

In this chapter, you'll see how you can make your apps **a bit more interactive**. You'll learn how to get your app to *do* something in response to the user, and **how to get your activity and layout talking to each other** like best buddies. Along the way, we'll take you a bit **deeper into how Android actually works** by introducing you to **R**, the hidden gem that glues everything together.

Let's build a Beer Adviser app

In Chapter 1, you saw how to create an app using the Android Studio New Project wizard, and how to change the text displayed in the layout. But when you create an Android app, you're usually going to want the app to *do* something.

In this chapter, we're going to show you how to create an app that the user can interact with: a Beer Adviser app. In the app, users can select the types of beer they enjoy, click a button, and get back a list of tasty beers to try out.

Here's how the app will be structured:

① **The layout specifies what the app will look like.**
It includes three GUI components:

- A drop-down list of values called a spinner, which allows the user to choose which type of beer they want.
- A button that when pressed will return a selection of beer types.
- A text field that displays the types of beer.

② **The file strings.xml includes any String resources needed by the layout—for example, the label of the button specified in the layout and the types of beer.**

③ **The activity specifies how the app should interact with the user.**
It takes the type of beer the user chooses, and uses this to display a list of beers the user might be interested in. It achieves this with the help of a custom Java class.

④ **The custom Java class contains the application logic for the app.**
It includes a method that takes a type of beer as a parameter, and returns a list of beers of this type. The activity calls the method, passes it the type of beer, and uses the response.

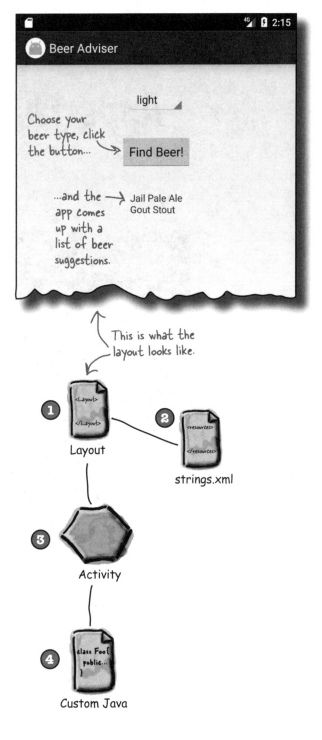

Here's what we're going to do

So let's get to work. There are a few steps you need to go through to build the Beer Adviser app (we'll tackle these throughout the rest of the chapter):

① **Create a project.**

You're creating a brand-new app, so you'll need to create a new project. Just like before, you'll need to create an empty activity with a layout.

← We'll show you the details of how to do this on the next page.

② **Update the layout.**

Once you have the app set up, you need to amend the layout so that it includes all the GUI components your app needs.

③ **Connect the layout to the activity.**

The layout only creates the visuals. To add smarts to your app, you need to connect the layout to the Java code in your activity.

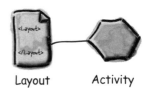

Layout   Activity

④ **Write the application logic.**

You'll add a Java custom class to the app, and use it to make sure users get the right beer based on their selection.

Layout

Create the project

☐ **Create project**
☐ **Update layout**
☐ **Connect activity**
☐ **Write logic**

Let's begin by creating the new app (the steps are similar to those we used in the previous chapter):

1 Open Android Studio and choose "Start a new Android Studio project" from the welcome screen. This starts the wizard you saw in Chapter 1.

2 When prompted, enter an application name of "Beer Adviser" and a company domain of "hfad.com", making your package name com.hfad. beeradviser. Make sure you uncheck the option to include C++ support.

If your version of Android Studio has an option to include Kotlin support, uncheck this option too.

3 We want the app to work on most phones and tablets, so choose a minimum SDK of API 19, and make sure the option for "Phone and Tablet" is selected. This means that any phone or tablet that runs the app must have API 19 installed on it as a minimum. Most Android devices meet this criterion.

4 Choose an empty activity for your default activity. Call the activity "FindBeerActivity" and the accompanying layout "activity_find_beer". Make sure the option to generate the layout is selected and you uncheck the Backwards Compatibility (AppCompat) option.

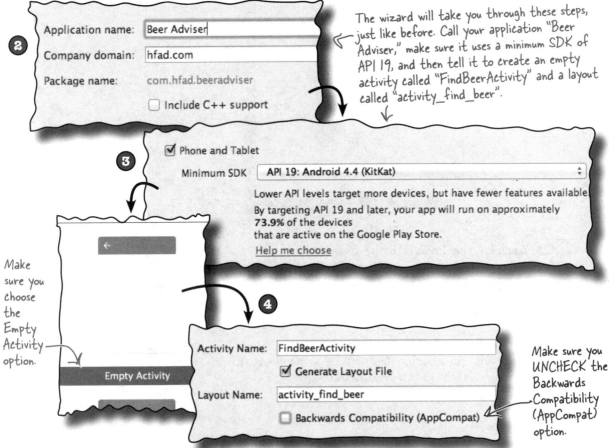

2 Application name: Beer Adviser
Company domain: hfad.com
Package name: com.hfad.beeradviser
☐ Include C++ support

The wizard will take you through these steps, just like before. Call your application "Beer Adviser," make sure it uses a minimum SDK of API 19, and then tell it to create an empty activity called "FindBeerActivity" and a layout called "activity_find_beer".

3 ☑ Phone and Tablet
Minimum SDK API 19: Android 4.4 (KitKat)
Lower API levels target more devices, but have fewer features available.
By targeting API 19 and later, your app will run on approximately **73.9%** of the devices that are active on the Google Play Store.
Help me choose

Make sure you choose the Empty Activity option.
Empty Activity

4 Activity Name: FindBeerActivity
☑ Generate Layout File
Layout Name: activity_find_beer
☐ Backwards Compatibility (AppCompat)

Make sure you UNCHECK the Backwards Compatibility (AppCompat) option.

We've created a default activity and layout

When you click on the Finish button, Android Studio creates a new project containing an activity called *FindBeerActivity.java* and a layout called *activity_find_beer.xml*.

Let's start by changing the layout file. To do this, switch to the Project view of Android Studio's explorer, go to the *app/src/main/ res/layout* folder, and open the file *activity_find_beer.xml*. Then switch to the text version of the code to open the code editor, and replace the code in *activity_find_beer.xml* with the following (we've bolded all the new code):

Click on the Text tab to open the code editor.

We're replacing the code Android Studio generated for us.

```xml
<?xml version="1.0" encoding="utf-8"?>
<LinearLayout
    xmlns:android="http://schemas.android.com/apk/res/android"
    xmlns:tools="http://schemas.android.com/tools"
    android:layout_width="match_parent"
    android:layout_height="match_parent"
    android:padding="16dp"
    android:orientation="vertical"
    tools:context="com.hfad.beeradviser.FindBeerActivity">

    <TextView
        android:id="@+id/textView"
        android:layout_width="wrap_content"
        android:layout_height="wrap_content"
        android:text="This is a text view" />
</LinearLayout>
```

These elements relate to the layout as a whole. They determine the layout width and height, any padding in the layout margins, and whether components should be laid out vertically or horizontally.

<TextView ← This is used to display text.

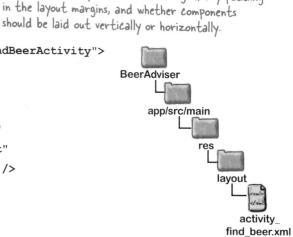

BeerAdviser
app/src/main
res
layout
activity_
find_beer.xml

We've just changed the code Android Studio gave us so that it uses a `<LinearLayout>`. This is used to display GUI components next to each other, either vertically or horizontally. If it's vertically, they're displayed in a single column, and if it's horizontally, they're displayed in a single row. You'll find out more about how this works as we go through the chapter.

Any changes you make to a layout's XML are reflected in Android Studio's design editor, which you can see by clicking on the Design tab. We'll look at this in more detail on the next page.

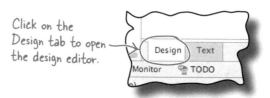

Click on the Design tab to open the design editor.

A closer look at the design editor

Create project
Update layout
Connect activity
Write logic

The design editor presents you with a more visual way of editing your layout code than editing XML. It features two different views of the layouts design. One shows you how the layout will look on an actual device, and the other shows you a blueprint of its structure:

If Android Studio doesn't show you both views of the layout, click on the "Show Design + Blueprint" icon in the design editor's toolbar.

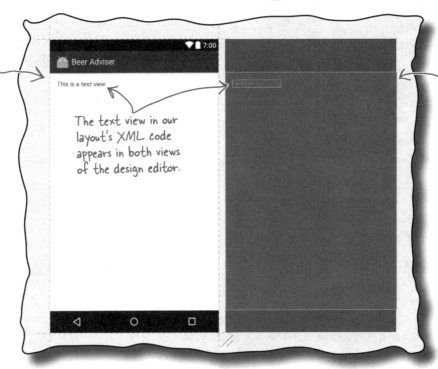

This view of the design gives you an idea of how your layout will look on an actual device.

The text view in our layout's XML code appears in both views of the design editor.

This is the blueprint view, which focuses more on the layout's structure.

To the left of the design editor, there's a palette that contains components you can drag to your layout. We'll use this next.

This list shows you the different categories of component you can add to your layout. You can click on them to filter the components displayed in the palette.

You can increase the size of the palette by clicking on this area and dragging it downward.

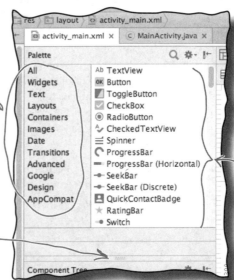

These are the components You'll find out more about them later in the book.

Add a button using the design editor

We're going to add a button to our layout using the design editor. Find the `Button` component in the palette, click on it, and then drag it into the design editor so that it's positioned above the text view. The button appears in the layout's design:

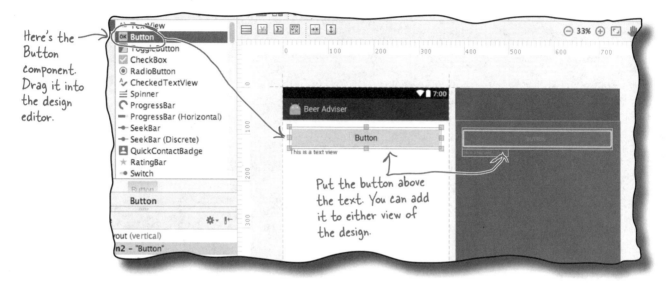

Here's the Button component. Drag it into the design editor.

Put the button above the text. You can add it to either view of the design.

Changes in the design editor are reflected in the XML

Dragging GUI components to the layout like this is a convenient way of updating the layout. If you switch to the code editor, you'll see that adding the button via the design editor has added some lines of code to the file:

There's a new <Button> element that describes the new button you've dragged to the layout. We'll look at this in more detail over the next few pages.

The code the design editor adds depends on where you place the button, so don't worry if your code looks different from ours.

```
. . .
<Button
    android:id="@+id/button"
    android:layout_width="match_parent"
    android:layout_height="wrap_content"
    android:text="Button" />

<TextView
    android:id="@+id/textView"
    android:layout_width="wrap_content"
    android:layout_height="wrap_content"
    android:text="This is a text view" />
. . .
```

BeerAdviser
app/src/main
res
layout
activity_find_beer.xml

activity_find_beer.xml has a new button

The editor added a new `<Button>` element to *activity_find_beer.xml*:

```
<Button
        android:id="@+id/button"
        android:layout_width="match_parent"
        android:layout_height="wrap_content"
        android:text="Button" />
```

A button in Androidville is a pushbutton that the user can press to trigger an action. The `<Button>` element includes properties controlling its size and appearance. These properties aren't unique to buttons—other GUI components including text views have them too.

Buttons and text views are subclasses of the same Android View class

There's a very good reason why buttons and text views have properties in common—they both inherit from the same Android **View** class. You'll find out more about this later in the book, but for now, here are some of the more common properties.

android:id

This gives the component an identifying name. The `id` property enables you to control what components do via activity code:

```
android:id="@+id/button"
```

android:layout_width, android:layout_height

These properties specify the width and height of the component. `"wrap_content"` means it should be just big enough for the content, and `"match_parent"` means it should be as wide as the layout containing it:

```
android:layout_width="match_parent"
android:layout_height="wrap_content"
```

android:text

This tells Android what text the component should display. In the case of `<Button>`, it's the text that appears on the button:

```
android:text="Button"
```

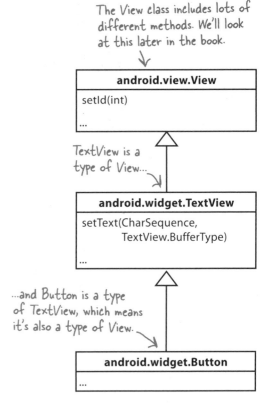

The View class includes lots of different methods. We'll look at this later in the book.

TextView is a type of View...

...and Button is a type of TextView, which means it's also a type of View.

A closer look at the layout code

Let's take a closer look at the layout code, and break it down so that you can see what it's actually doing (don't worry if your code looks a little different, just follow along with us):

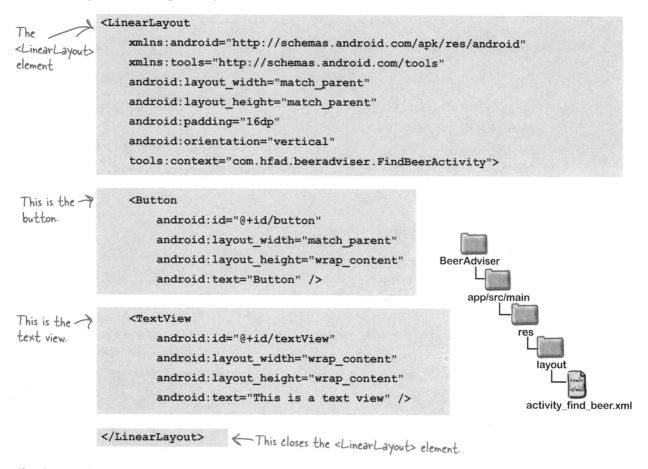

The *<LinearLayout>* element

```
<LinearLayout
    xmlns:android="http://schemas.android.com/apk/res/android"
    xmlns:tools="http://schemas.android.com/tools"
    android:layout_width="match_parent"
    android:layout_height="match_parent"
    android:padding="16dp"
    android:orientation="vertical"
    tools:context="com.hfad.beeradviser.FindBeerActivity">
```

This is the button.

```
<Button
    android:id="@+id/button"
    android:layout_width="match_parent"
    android:layout_height="wrap_content"
    android:text="Button" />
```

This is the text view.

```
<TextView
    android:id="@+id/textView"
    android:layout_width="wrap_content"
    android:layout_height="wrap_content"
    android:text="This is a text view" />
```

BeerAdviser
  app/src/main
    res
      layout
        activity_find_beer.xml

```
</LinearLayout>
```
←This closes the *<LinearLayout>* element.

The LinearLayout element

The first element in the layout code is <LinearLayout>. The <LinearLayout> element tells Android that the different GUI components in the layout should be displayed next to each other in a single row or column.

← There are other ways of laying out your GUI components too. You'll find out more about these later in the book.

You specify the orientation using the android:orientation attribute. In this example we're using:

```
android:orientation="vertical"
```

so the GUI components are displayed in a single vertical column.

A closer look at the layout code (continued)

Create project
Update layout
Connect activity
Write logic

The `<LinearLayout>` contains two elements: a `<Button>` and a `<TextView>`.

The Button element

The first element is the `<Button>`:

```
        ...
        <Button
            android:id="@+id/button"
            android:layout_width="match_parent"
            android:layout_height="wrap_content"
            android:text="Button" />
        ...
```

As this is the first element inside the `<LinearLayout>`, it appears first in the layout at the top of the screen. It has a `layout_width` of `"match_parent"`, which means that it should be as wide as its parent element, the `<LinearLayout>`. Its `layout_height` has been set to `"wrap_content"`, which means it should be tall enough to display its text.

The TextView element

The final element inside the `<LinearLayout>` is the `<TextView>`:

```
        ...
        <TextView
            android:id="@+id/textView"
            android:layout_width="wrap_content"
            android:layout_height="wrap_content"
            android:text="This is a text view" />
        ...
```

As this is the second element and we've set the linear layout's orientation to `"vertical"`, it's displayed underneath the button (the first element). Its `layout_width` and `layout_height` are set to `"wrap_content"` so that it takes up just enough space to contain its text.

> Using a linear layout means that GUI components are displayed in a single row or column.

The button is displayed at the top as it's the first element in the XML.

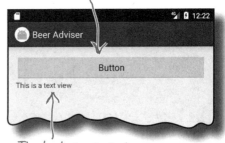

The text view is displayed underneath the button as it comes after it in the XML.

Changes to the XML...

You've seen how adding components to the design editor adds them to the layout XML. The opposite applies too—any changes you make to the layout XML are applied to the design.

Try this now. Update your *activity_find_beer.xml* code with the following changes (highlighted in bold):

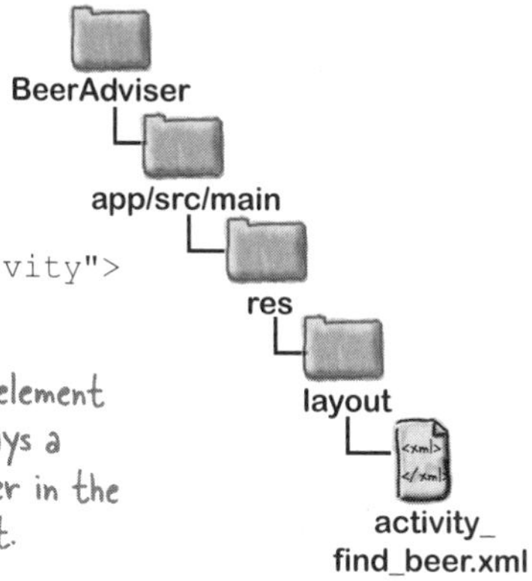

```
<?xml version="1.0" encoding="utf-8"?>
<LinearLayout
    xmlns:android="http://schemas.android.com/apk/res/android"
    xmlns:tools="http://schemas.android.com/tools"
    android:layout_width="match_parent"
    android:layout_height="match_parent"
    android:padding="16dp"
    android:orientation="vertical"
    tools:context="com.hfad.beeradviser.FindBeerActivity">
```

A spinner is the Android name for a drop-down list of values. It allows you to choose a single value from a selection.

```
<Spinner
    android:id="@+id/color"
    android:layout_width="wrap_content"
    android:layout_height="wrap_content"
    android:layout_marginTop="40dp"
    android:layout_gravity="center"
    android:layout_margin="16dp" />
```

This element displays a spinner in the layout.

BeerAdviser
app/src/main
res
layout
activity_find_beer.xml

```
<Button
    android:id="@+id/button find_beer"
```
Change the button's ID to "find_beer". We'll use this later.
```
    android:layout_width="match parent wrap_content"
    android:layout_height="wrap_content"
```
Change the button's width so it's as wide as its content.

Center the button horizontally and give it a margin.
```
    android:layout_gravity="center"
    android:layout_margin="16dp"
    android:text="Button" />
```

```
<TextView
    android:id="@+id/textView brands"
```
Change the text view's ID to "brands".
```
    android:layout_width="wrap_content"
    android:layout_height="wrap_content"
```
Center the text view and apply a margin.
```
    android:layout_gravity="center"
    android:layout_margin="16dp"
    android:text="This is a text view" />
</LinearLayout>
```

Do this!

Update the contents of *activity_find_beer.xml* with the changes shown here.

...are reflected in the design editor

Create project
Update layout
Connect activity
Write logic

Once you've changed the layout XML, switch to the design editor. Instead of a layout containing a button with a text view underneath it, you should now see a spinner, button, and text view centered in a single column.

A **spinner** is the Android term for a drop-down list of values. When you press it, it expands to show you the list so that you can pick a single value.

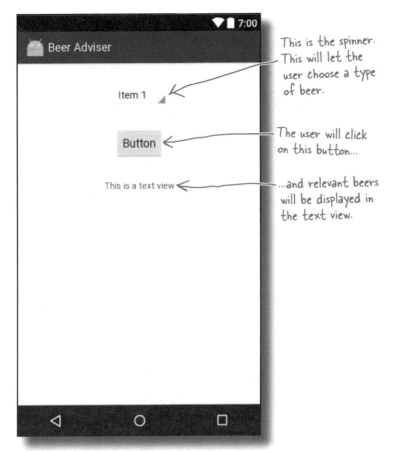

This is the spinner. This will let the user choose a type of beer.

The user will click on this button...

...and relevant beers will be displayed in the text view.

A spinner provides a drop-down list of values. It allows you to choose a single value from a set of values.

GUI components such as buttons, spinners, and text views have very similar attributes, as they are all types of View. Behind the scenes, they all inherit from the same Android View class.

We've shown you how to add GUI components to the layout with the aid of the design editor, and also by adding them through XML. In general, you're more likely to hack the XML for simple layouts to get the results you want without using the design editor. This is because editing the XML directly gives you more direct control over the layout.

Let's take the app for a test drive

We still have more work to do on the app, but let's see how it's looking so far. Save the changes you've made by choosing File→Save All, then choose the "Run 'app'" command from the Run menu. When prompted, select the option to launch the emulator.

Wait patiently for the app to load, and eventually it should appear.

Try pressing the spinner. It's not immediately obvious, but when you press it, the spinner presents you with a drop-down list of values—it's just at this point we haven't added any values to it.

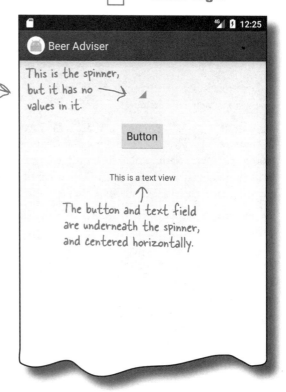

This is the spinner, but it has no values in it.

Button

This is a text view

The button and text field are underneath the spinner, and centered horizontally.

Here's what we've done so far

Here's a quick recap of what we've done so far:

1 **We've created a layout that specifies what the app looks like.**
It includes a spinner, a button, and a text view.

2 **The activity specifies how the app should interact with the user.**
Android Studio has created an activity for us, but we haven't done anything with it yet.

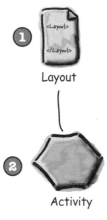

Layout

Activity

The next thing we'll do is look at replacing the hardcoded String values for the text view and button text.

---

there are no Dumb Questions

Q: My layout looks slightly different in the AVD compared with how it looks in the design editor. Why's that?

A: The design editor does its best to show you how the layout will look on a device, but it's not always accurate depending on what version of Android Studio you're using. How the layout looks in the AVD reflects how the layout will look on a physical device.

Hardcoding text makes localization hard

☑ **Create project**
→ ☐ **Update layout**
☐ **Connect activity**
☐ **Write logic**

So far, we've hardcoded the text we want to appear in our text views and buttons using the `android:text` property:

Display the text... ...*"Hello World!"*

`android:text="Hello World!" />`

While this is fine when you're just learning, hardcoding text isn't the best approach.

Suppose you've created an app that's a big hit on your local Google Play Store. You don't want to limit yourself to just one country or language—you want to make it available internationally and for different languages. But if you've hardcoded all of the text in your layout files, sending your app international will be difficult.

It also makes it much harder to make global changes to the text. Imagine your boss asks you to change the wording in the app because the company's changed its name. If you've hardcoded all of the text, this means that you need to edit a whole host of files in order to change the text.

Put the text in a String resource file

A better approach is to put your text values into a String resource file called *strings.xml*.

Having a String resource file makes it much easier to internationalize your app. Rather than having to change hardcoded text values in a whole host of different activity and layout files, you can simply replace the *strings.xml* file with an internationalized version.

This approach also makes it much easier to make global changes to text across your whole application as you only need to edit one file. If you need to make changes to the text in your app, you only need to edit *strings.xml*.

How do you use String resources?

In order to use a String resource in your layout, there are two things you need to do:

1 Create the String resource by adding it to strings.xml.

2 Use the String resource in your layout.

Let's see how this is done.

Put String values in strings.xml rather than hardcoding them. strings.xml is a resource file used to hold name/value pairs of Strings. Layouts and activities can look up String values using their names.

Create the String resource

We're going to create two String resources, one for the text that appears on the button, and another for the default text that appears in the text view.

To do this, use Android Studio's explorer to find the file *strings. xml* in the *app/src/main/res/values* folder. Then open it by double-clicking on it.

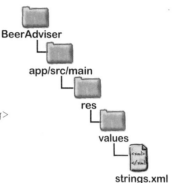

The file should look something like this:

```
<resources>
    <string name="app_name">Beer Adviser</string>
</resources>
```

strings.xml contains one string resource named "app_name", which has a value of Beer Adviser. Android Studio created this String resource for us automatically when we created the project.

This indicates that this is a String resource.

```
<string name="app_name">Beer Adviser</string>
```

This String resource has a name of "app_name", and a value of "Beer Adviser".

We're first going to add a new resource called "find_beer" that has a value of Find Beer! To do this, edit *strings.xml* so that you add it as a new line like this:

```
<resources>
    <string name="app_name">Beer Adviser</string>
    <string name="find_beer">Find Beer!</string>
</resources>
```

← This adds a new String resource called "find_beer".

Then add a new resource named "brands" with a value of No beers selected:

```
<resources>
    <string name="app_name">Beer Adviser</string>
    <string name="find_beer">Find Beer!</string>
    <string name="brands">No beers selected</string>
</resources>
```

← This will be the default text in the text view.

Once you've updated the file, go to the File menu and choose the Save All option to save your changes. Next, we'll use the String resources in our layout.

Use the String resource in your layout

Create project
Update layout
Connect activity
Write logic

You use String resources in your layout using code like this:

```
android:text="@string/find_beer" />
```

You've seen the `android:text` part of the code before; it specifies what text should be displayed. But what does `"@string/find_beer"` mean?

Let's start with the first part, `@string`. This is just a way of telling Android to look up a text value from a String resource file. In our case, this is the file *strings.xml* that you just edited.

The second part, `find_beer`, tells Android to **look up the value of a resource with the name find_beer**. So `"@string/find_beer"` means "look up the String resource with the name `find_beer`, and use the associated text value."

Display the text...

...for the String resource find_beer.

```
android:text="@string/find_beer" />
```

We want to change the button and text view elements in our layout XML so that they use the two String resources we've just added.

Go back to the layout file *activity_find_beer.xml* file, and make the following code changes:

★ Change the line:
```
android:text="Button"
```
to:
```
android:text="@string/find_beer"
```

★ Change the line:
```
android:text="TextView"
```
to:
```
android:text="@string/brands"
```

You can see the code on the next page.

Android Studio sometimes displays the values of references in the code editor in place of actual code.

As an example, it may display the text `"Find Beer!"` instead of the real code `"@string/find_beer"`. Any such substitutions should be highlighted in the code editor. If you click on them, or hover over them with your mouse, the true code will be revealed.

```
<TextView
    android:text="Hello world!"
    android:text="@string/hello_world"
    android:layout_height="wrap_content" />
```

The code for activity_find_beer.xml

Here's the updated code for *activity_find_beer.xml* (changes are in bold); update your version of the file to match ours.

```
...
    <Spinner
        android:id="@+id/color"
        android:layout_width="wrap_content"
        android:layout_height="wrap_content"
        android:layout_marginTop="40dp"
        android:layout_gravity="center"
        android:layout_margin="16dp" />

    <Button
        android:id="@+id/find_beer"
        android:layout_width="wrap_content"
        android:layout_height="wrap_content"
        android:layout_gravity="center"
        android:layout_margin="16dp"
        android:text="Button@string/find_beer" />
    <TextView
        android:id="@+id/brands"
        android:layout_width="wrap_content"
        android:layout_height="wrap_content"
        android:layout_gravity="center"
        android:layout_margin="16dp"
        android:text="This is a text view@string/brands" />
</LinearLayout>
```

We didn't need to change the spinner. We'll look at how you add values to it over the next few pages.

BeerAdviser
app/src/main
res
layout
activity_find_beer.xml

Delete the hardcoded text.

This will display the value of the find_beer String resource on the button.

Delete this hardcoded text too.

This will display the value of the brands String resource in the text view.

When you're done, save your changes.

We've put a summary of adding and using String resources on the next page.

String Resource Files Up Close

strings.xml is the default resource file used to hold name/value pairs of Strings so that they can be referenced throughout your app. It has the following format:

The <resources> element identifies the contents of the file as resources.

The <string> element identifies the name/value pairs as Strings.

```
<resources>
        <string name="app_name">Beer Adviser</string>
        <string name="find_beer">Find Beer!</string>
        <string name="brands">No beer selected</string>
</resources>
```

There are two things that allow Android to recognize *strings.xml* as being a String resource file:

⭐ **The file is held in the folder** *app/src/main/res/values*.
XML files held in this folder contain simple values, such as Strings and colors.

⭐ **The file has a <resources> element, which contains one or more <string> elements.**
The format of the file itself indicates that it's a resource file containing Strings. The <resources> element tells Android that the file contains resources, and the <string> element identifies each String resource.

This means that you don't need to call your String resource file *strings.xml*; if you want, you can call it something else, or split your Strings into multiple files.

Each name/value pair takes the form:

```
<string name="string_name">string_value</string>
```

where string_name is the identifier of the String, and string_value is the String value itself.

A layout can retrieve the value of the String using:

```
"@string/string_name"
```

"@string" tells Android to look for a String resource of this name.

This is the name of the String whose value we want to return.

Time for a test drive

Let's see how the app's looking now. Save the changes you've made, then choose the "Run 'app'" command from the Run menu. When prompted, select the option to launch the emulator.

This time when we run the app, the text for the button and the text view has changed to the String values we added to *strings.xml*. The button says "Find Beer!" and the text view says "No beers selected."

The text on the button and the text view has been changed.

Here's what we've done so far

Here's a quick recap of where we've got to:

① **We've created a layout that specifies what the app looks like.**
It includes a spinner, a button, and a text view.

② **The file strings.xml includes the String resources we need.**
We've added a label for the button, and default text for the list of suggested beer brands to try.

③ **The activity specifies how the app should interact with the user.**
Android Studio has created an activity for us, but we haven't done anything with it yet.

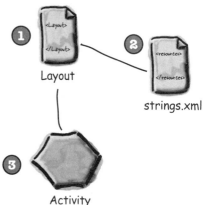

Layout

strings.xml

Activity

Next we'll look at how you add a list of beers to the spinner.

---

there are no Dumb Questions

Q: Do I absolutely have to put my text values in a String resource file such as *strings.xml*?

A: It's not mandatory, but Android gives you warning messages if you hardcode text values. Using a String resource file might seem like a lot of effort at first, but it makes things like localization much easier. It's also easier to use String resources to start off with, rather than patching them in afterward.

Q: How does separating out the String values help with localization?

A: Suppose you want your application to be in English by default, but in French if the device language is set to French. Rather than hardcode different languages into your app, you can have one String resource file for English text, and another resource file for French text.

Q: How does the app know which String resource file to use?

A: Put your default English Strings resource file in the *app/src/main/res/values* folder as normal, and your French resource file in a new folder called *app/src/main/res/values-fr*. If the device is set to French, it will use the Strings in the *app/src/main/res/values-fr* folder. If the device is set to any other language, it will use the Strings in *app/src/main/res/values*.

Add values to the spinner

Create project
Update layout
Connect activity
Write logic

At the moment, the layout includes a spinner, but it doesn't have anything in it. Whenever you use a spinner, you need to get it to display a list of values so that the user can choose the value they want.

We can give the spinner a list of values in pretty much the same way that we set the text on the button and the text view: by using a **resource**. So far, we've used *strings.xml* to specify individual String values. For the spinner, all we need to do is specify an *array* of String values, and get the spinner to reference it.

Resources are noncode assets, such as images or Strings, used by your app.

Adding an array resource is similar to adding a String

As you already know, you can add a String resource to *strings.xml* using:

```
<string name="string_name">string_value</string>
```

where `string_name` is the identifier of the String, and `string_value` is the String value itself.

To add an array of Strings, you use the following syntax:

```
<string-array name="string_array_name">        ← This is the name of the array.
    <item>string_value1</item>  ⎫
    <item>string_value2</item>  ⎬ These are the values in the array. You
    <item>string_value3</item>  ⎭ can add as many as you need.
    ...
</string-array>
```

where `string_array_name` is the name of the array, and `string_value1`, `string_value2`, `string_value3` are the individual String values that make up the array.

Let's add a `string-array` resource to our app that can be used by the spinner.

Add the string-array to strings.xml

To add the `string-array`, open up *strings.xml*, and add the
array like this:

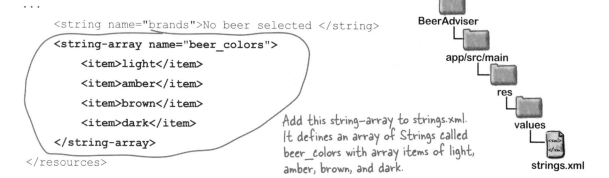

```
...
    <string name="brands">No beer selected </string>
    <string-array name="beer_colors">
        <item>light</item>
        <item>amber</item>
        <item>brown</item>
        <item>dark</item>
    </string-array>
</resources>
```

Add this string-array to strings.xml.
It defines an array of Strings called
beer_colors with array items of light,
amber, brown, and dark.

BeerAdviser
app/src/main
res
values
strings.xml

Get the spinner to reference a string-array

A layout can reference a `string-array` using similar syntax to how
it would retrieve the value of a String. Rather than use:

> `"@string/string_name"`

you use the syntax:

> `"@array/array_name"`

Use @string to reference a String, and
@array to reference an array.

where `array_name` is the name of the array.

Let's use this in the layout. Go to the layout file *activity_find_beer.xml*
and add an `entries` attribute to the spinner like this:

```
    ...
    <Spinner
        android:id="@+id/color"
        android:layout_width="wrap_content"
        android:layout_height="wrap_content"
        android:layout_marginTop="40dp"
        android:layout_gravity="center"
        android:layout_margin="16dp"
        android:entries="@array/beer_colors" />
    ...
```

This means "the entries for the
spinner come from array beer_colors".

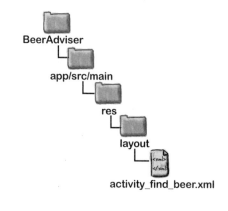

BeerAdviser
app/src/main
res
layout
activity_find_beer.xml

Those are all the changes you need in order to get the spinner to
display a list of values. Let's see what it looks like.

Test drive the spinner

☑ Create project
☑ **Update layout**
☐ Connect activity
☐ Write logic

So let's see what impact these changes have had on our app. Save your changes, then run the app. You should get something like this:

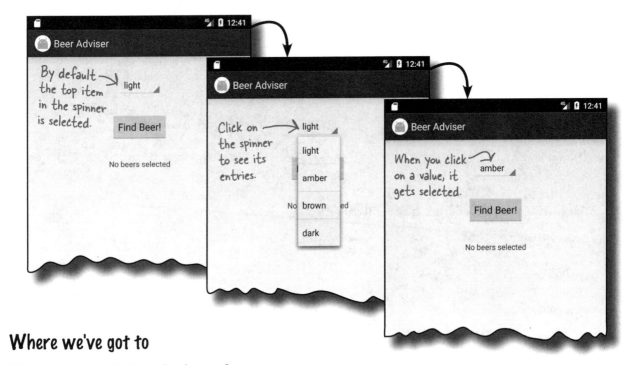

By default the top item in the spinner is selected.

Click on the spinner to see its entries.

When you click on a value, it gets selected.

Where we've got to

Here's a reminder of what we've done so far:

① **We've created a layout that specifies what the app looks like.**
It includes a spinner, a button, and a text view.

② **The file strings.xml includes the String resources we need.**
We've added a label for the button, default text for the suggested beer brands, and an array of values for the spinner.

③ **The activity specifies how the app should interact with the user.**
Android Studio has created an activity for us, but we haven't done anything with it yet.

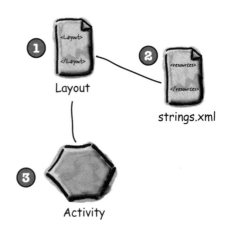

Layout

strings.xml

Activity

So what's next?

We need to make the button do something

What we need to do next is make the app react to the value we select in the spinner when the Find Beer button is clicked. We want our app to behave something like this:

① The user chooses a type of beer from the spinner.

② The user clicks the Find Beer button, and the layout specifies which method to call in the activity.

③ The method in the activity retrieves the value of the selected beer in the spinner and passes it to the getBrands() method in a Java custom class called BeerExpert.

④ BeerExpert's getBrands() method finds matching brands for the type of beer and returns them to the activity as an ArrayList of Strings.

⑤ The activity gets a reference to the layout text view and sets its text value to the list of matching beers.

After all those steps are completed, the list is displayed on the device.

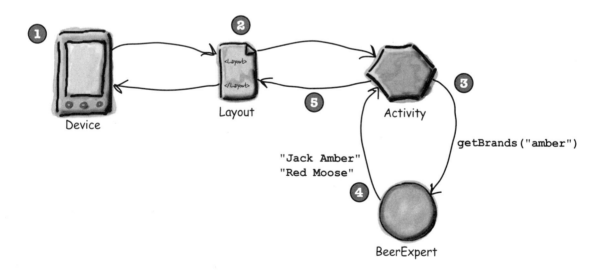

Let's start by getting the button to call a method.

Make the button call a method

Create project
Update layout
Connect activity
Write logic

Whenever you add a button to a layout, it's likely you'll want it to do something when the user clicks on it. To make this happen, you need to get the button to call a method in your activity.

To get our button to call a method in the activity when it's clicked, we need to make changes to two files:

⭐ **Change the layout file activity_find_beer.xml.**
We'll specify which method in the activity will get called when the button is clicked.

⭐ **Change the activity file FindBeerActivity.java.**
We need to write the method that gets called.

Let's start with the layout.

Use onClick to say which method the button calls

It only takes one line of XML to tell Android which method a button should call when it's clicked. All you need to do is add an `android:onClick` attribute to the `<button>` element, and tell it the name of the method you want to call:

android:onClick="method_name" ← *This means "when the component is clicked, call the method in the activity called method_name".*

Let's try this now. Go to the layout file *activity_find_beer.xml*, and add a new line of XML to the `<button>` element to say that the method `onClickFindBeer()` should be called when the button is clicked:

```
. . .
    <Button
        android:id="@+id/find_beer"
        android:layout_width="wrap_content"
        android:layout_height="wrap_content"
        android:layout_gravity="center"
        android:layout_margin="16dp"
        android:text="@string/find_beer"
        android:onClick="onClickFindBeer" />
. . .
```

When the button is clicked, call the method onClickFindBeer() in the activity. We'll create the method in the activity over the next few pages.

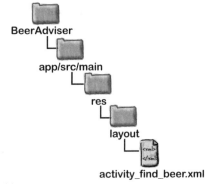

BeerAdviser
app/src/main
res
layout
activity_find_beer.xml

Once you've made these changes, save the file.

Now that the layout knows which method to call in the activity, we need to write the method. Let's take a look at the activity.

What activity code looks like

When we first created a project for our app, we asked the wizard to create an empty activity called FindBeerActivity. The code for this activity is held in a file called *FindBeerActivity.java*. Open this file by going to the *app/ src/main/java* folder and double-clicking on it.

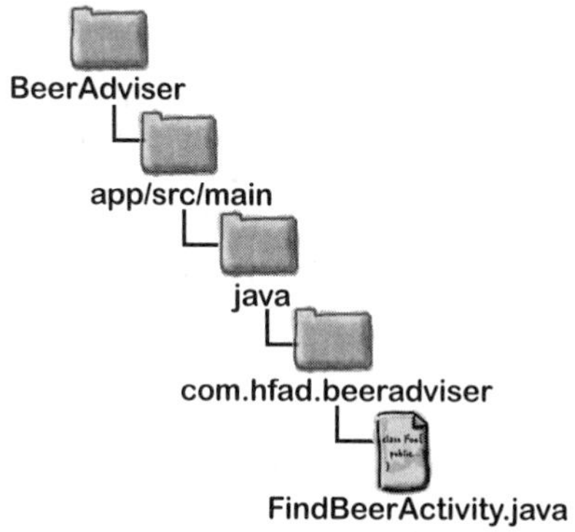

When you open the file, you'll see that Android Studio has generated some Java code for you. Rather than taking you through all the code that Android Studio may (or may not) have created, we want you to replace the code that's currently in *FindBeerActivity.java* with the code shown here:

```
package com.hfad.beeradviser;

import android.app.Activity;
import android.os.Bundle;

public class FindBeerActivity extends Activity {

    @Override
    protected void onCreate(Bundle savedInstanceState) {
        super.onCreate(savedInstanceState);
        setContentView(R.layout.activity_find_beer);
    }
}
```

Make sure class extends the Android Activity class.

This is the onCreate() method. It's called when the activity is first created.

setContentView() tells Android which layout the activity uses. In this case, it's activity_find_beer.

BeerAdviser

app/src/main

java

com.hfad.beeradviser

FindBeerActivity.java

The above code is all you need to create a basic activity. As you can see, it's a class that extends the android.app.Activity class, and implements an onCreate() method.

All activities (not just this one) have to extend the Activity class or one of its subclasses. The Activity class contains a bunch of methods that transform your Java class from a plain old Java class into a full-fledged, card-carrying Android activity.

All activities also need to implement the onCreate() method. This method gets called when the activity object gets created, and it's used to perform basic setup such as what layout the activity is associated with. This is done via the setContentView() method. In the example above, setContentView(R.layout.activity_find_beer) tells Android that this activity uses activity_find_beer as its layout.

On the previous page, we added an onClick attribute to the button in our layout and gave it a value of onClickFindBeer. We need to add this method to our activity so it will be called when the button gets clicked. This will enable the activity to respond when the user touches the button in the user interface.

Do this!

Replace the code in your version of *FindBeerActivity.java* with the code shown on this page.

Add an onClickFindBeer() method to the activity

☑ Create project
☑ Update layout
Connect activity
Write logic

The onClickFindBeer() method needs to have a particular signature, or otherwise it won't get called when the button specified in the layout gets clicked. The method needs to take the following form:

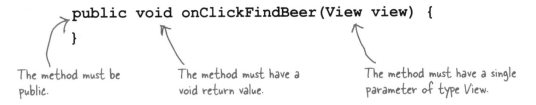

```
public void onClickFindBeer(View view) {

}
```

The method must be public.

The method must have a void return value.

The method must have a single parameter of type View.

If the method doesn't take this form, then it won't respond when the user presses the button. This is because behind the scenes, Android looks for a public method with a void return value, with a method name that matches the method specified in the layout XML.

The View parameter in the method may seem unusual at first glance, but there's a good reason for it being there. The parameter refers to the GUI component that triggers the method (in this case, the button). As we mentioned earlier, GUI components such as buttons and text views are all types of View.

So let's update our activity code. Add the onClickFindBeer() method below to your activity code (*FindBeerActivity.java*):

If you want a method to respond to a button click, it must be public, have a void return type, and take a single View parameter.

We're using this class, so we need to import it.

```
...
import android.view.View;
```

Add the onClickFindBeer() method to FindBeerActivity.java.

```
public class FindBeerActivity extends Activity {
    ...
    //Called when the user clicks the button
    public void onClickFindBeer(View view) {

    }
}
```

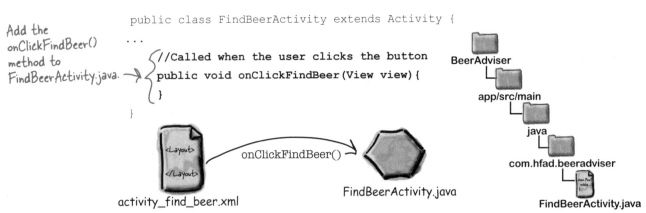

activity_find_beer.xml → onClickFindBeer() → FindBeerActivity.java

BeerAdviser
app/src/main
java
com.hfad.beeradviser
FindBeerActivity.java

onClickFindBeer() needs to <u>do</u> something

Now that we've created the `onClickFindBeer()` method in our activity, the next thing we need to do is get the method to do something when it runs. Specifically, we need to get our app to display a selection of different beers that match the beer type the user has selected.

In order to achieve this, we first need to get a reference to both the spinner and text view GUI components in the layout. This will allow us to retrieve the value of the chosen beer type from the spinner, and display text in the text view.

Use findViewById() to get a reference to a view

We can get references for our two GUI components using a method called `findViewById()`. This method takes the ID of the GUI component as a parameter, and returns a `View` object. You then cast the return value to the correct type of GUI component (for example, a `TextView` or a `Button`).

Here's how you'd use `findViewById()` to get a reference to the text view with an ID of `brands`:

We want the view with an ID of brands.

```
TextView brands = (TextView) findViewById(R.id.brands);
```

brands is a TextView, so we have to cast it as one.

Take a closer look at how we specified the ID of the text view. Rather than pass in the name of the text view, we passed in an ID of the form `R.id.brands`. So what does this mean? What's R?

R.java is a special Java file that gets generated by Android Studio whenever you create or build your app. It lives within the *app/build/ generated/source/r/debug* folder in your project in a package with the same name as the package of your app. Android uses *R.java* to keep track of the resources used within the app, and among other things it enables you to get references to GUI components from within your activity code.

If you open up *R.java*, you'll see that it contains a series of inner classes, one for each type of resource. Each resource of that type is referenced within the inner class. As an example, *R.java* includes an inner class called `id`, and the inner class includes a `static final brands` value. Android added this code to *R.java* when we used the code `"@+id/brands"` in our layout. The line of code:

```
(TextView) findViewById(R.id.brands);
```

uses the value of `brands` to get a reference to the `brands` text view.

R is a special Java class that enables you to retrieve references to resources in your app.

Relax

***R.java* gets generated for you.**

You never change any of the code within this file, but it's useful to know it's there.

☑ **Create project**
☑ **Update layout**
☑ **Connect activity**
→ ☐ **Write logic**

Once you have a view, you can access its methods

The `findViewById()` method provides you with a Java version of your GUI component. This means that you can get and set properties in the GUI component using the methods exposed by the Java class. Let's take a closer look.

Setting the text in a text view

As you've seen, you can get a reference to a text view in Java using:

```
TextView brands = (TextView) findViewById(R.id.brands);
```

When this line of code gets called, it creates a `TextView` object called `brands`. You are then able to call methods on this `TextView` object.

Let's say you wanted to set the text displayed in the `brands` text view to "Gottle of geer". The `TextView` class includes a method called `setText()` that you can use to change the text property. You use it like this:

```
brands.setText("Gottle of geer");
```

← Set the text on the brands TextView to "Gottle of geer".

Retrieving the selected value in a spinner

You can get a reference to a spinner in a similar way to how you get a reference to a text view. You use the `findViewById()` method as before, but this time you cast the result as a spinner:

```
Spinner color = (Spinner) findViewById(R.id.color);
```

This gives you a `Spinner` object whose methods you can now access. As an example, here's how you retrieve the currently selected item in the spinner, and convert it to a String:

```
String.valueOf(color.getSelectedItem())
```

← This gets the selected item in the spinner and converts it to a String.

The code:

```
color.getSelectedItem()
```

actually returns a generic Java object. This is because spinner values can be something other than Strings, such as images. In our case, we know the values are all Strings, so we can use `String.valueOf()` to convert the selected item from an `Object` to a `String`.

Update the activity code

You now know enough to write some code in the onClickFindBeer()
method. Rather than write all the code we need in one go, let's start by
reading the selected value from the spinner, and displaying it in the text view.

Activity Magnets

Somebody used fridge magnets to write a new **onClickFindBeer()**
method for us to slot into our activity. Unfortunately, a freak kitchen whirlwind
has dislodged the magnets. Can you piece the code back together again?

The code needs to retrieve the type of beer selected in the spinner, and then
display the type of beer in the text view.

```
//Called when the button gets clicked
public void onClickFindBeer(............................. view) {

    //Get a reference to the TextView
    ............................... brands = .............................  ...................................... (.................................... );

    //Get a reference to the Spinner
    Spinner ........................ = ...........................  ...................................... (............................... );

    //Get the selected item in the Spinner
    String ............................ = String.valueOf(color. ...................................................... );

    //Display the selected item
    brands. ............................ (beerType);
}
```

TextView

color

findViewById

setText

R.id.color

(TextView)

R.view.brands

R.id.brands

findView

Button

findView

View

R.view.color

findViewById

(Spinner)

getSelectedItem()

beerType

You won't
need to use
all of the
magnets.

Activity Magnets Solution

Somebody used fridge magnets to write a new
onClickFindBeer() method for us to slot into our activity.
Unfortunately, a freak kitchen whirlwind has dislodged the magnets.
Can you piece the code back together again?

The code needs to retrieve the type of beer selected in the spinner,
and then display the type of beer in the text view.

```java
//Called when the button gets clicked
public void onClickFindBeer( View view) {

    //Get a reference to the TextView
    TextView brands = (TextView) findViewById( R.id.brands );

    //Get a reference to the Spinner
    Spinner color = (Spinner) findViewById( R.id.color );

    //Get the selected item in the Spinner
    String beerType = String.valueOf(color. getSelectedItem() );

    //Display the selected item
    brands. setText (beerType);
}
```

R.view.brands

findView

Button

findView

R.view.color

You didn't need to use these magnets.

The first version of the activity

Our cunning plan is to build the activity in stages and test it as we go along. In the end, the activity will take the selected value from the spinner, call a method in a custom Java class, and then display matching types of beer. For this first version, our goal is just to make sure that we correctly retrieve the selected item from the spinner.

Here is our activity code, including the method you pieced together on the previous page. Apply these changes to *FindBeerActivity.java*, then save them:

```java
package com.hfad.beeradviser;

import android.app.Activity;
import android.os.Bundle;
import android.view.View;
import android.widget.Spinner;
import android.widget.TextView;

public class FindBeerActivity extends Activity {

    @Override
    protected void onCreate(Bundle savedInstanceState) {
        super.onCreate(savedInstanceState);
        setContentView(R.layout.activity_find_beer);
    }

    //Called when the button gets clicked
    public void onClickFindBeer(View view) {
        //Get a reference to the TextView
        TextView brands = (TextView) findViewById(R.id.brands);
        //Get a reference to the Spinner
        Spinner color = (Spinner) findViewById(R.id.color);
        //Get the selected item in the Spinner
        String beerType = String.valueOf(color.getSelectedItem());
        //Display the selected item
        brands.setText(beerType);
    }
}
```

We're using these extra classes so we need to import them.

BeerAdviser
app/src/main
java
com.hfad.beeradviser
FindBeerActivity.java

← We've not changed this method.

findViewById returns a View. You need to cast it to the right type of View.

getSelectedItem returns an Object. You need to turn it into a String.

What the code does

Before we take the app for a test drive, let's look at what the code actually does.

① **The user chooses a type of beer from the spinner and clicks on the Find Beer button. This calls the public void onClickFindBeer(View) method in the activity.**

The layout specifies which method in the activity should be called when the button is clicked via the button's `android:onClick` property.

Layout   FindBeerActivity

② **The activity gets references to the Spinner and TextView GUI components using calls to the findViewById() method.**

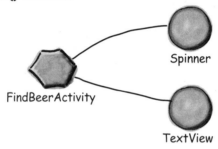

FindBeerActivity   Spinner

TextView

③ **The activity retrieves the currently selected value of the spinner (in this case amber), and converts it to a String.**

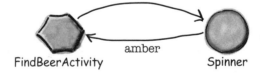

amber

FindBeerActivity   Spinner

④ **The activity then sets the text property of the TextView to reflect the currently selected item in the spinner.**

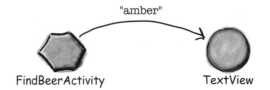

"amber"

FindBeerActivity   TextView

Test drive the changes

Make the changes to the activity file, save it, and then run your app. This time when we click on the Find Beer button, it displays the value of the selected item in the spinner.

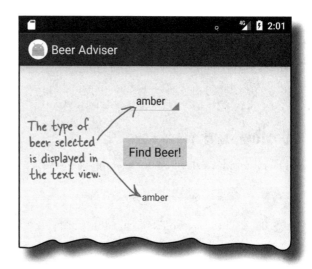

The type of beer selected is displayed in the text view.

---
there are no
Dumb Questions

Q: I added a String to my *strings.xml* file, but I can't see it in *R.java*. Why isn't it there?

A: Android Studio, generates *R.java* when you save any changes you've made. If you've added a resource but can't see it in *R.java*, check that your changes have been saved.

R.java also gets updated when the app gets built. The app builds when you run the app, so running the app will also update *R.java*.

Q: The values in the spinner look like they're static as they're set to the values in the **string-array**. Can I change these values programmatically?

A: You can, but that approach is more complicated than just using static values. We'll show you later in the book how you can have complete control over the values displayed in components such as spinners.

Q: What type of object is returned by **getSelectedItem()**?

A: It's declared as type `Object`. Because we used a `string-array` for the values, the actual value returned in this case is a String.

Q: What do you mean "in this case"—isn't it always?

A: You can do more complicated things with spinners than just display text. As an example, the spinner might display an icon next to each value. As `getSelectedItem()` returns an object, it gives you a bit more flexibility than just returning a String.

Q: Does the name of **onClickFindBeer** matter?

A: All that matters is that the name of the method in the activity code matches the name used in the button's `onClick` attribute in the layout.

Q: Why did we have to replace the activity code that Android Studio created for us?

A: IDEs such as Android Studio include functions and utilities that can save you a lot of time. They generate a lot of code for you, and sometimes this can be useful. But when you're learning a new language or development area such as Android, we think it's best to learn about the fundamentals of the language rather than what the IDE generates for you. This way you'll develop a greater understanding of the language.

Build the custom Java class

As we said at the beginning of the chapter, the Beer Adviser app decides which beers to recommend with the help of a custom Java class. This Java class is written in plain old Java, with no knowledge of the fact it's being used by an Android app.

Custom Java class spec

The custom Java class should meet the following requirements:

⭐ The package name should be com.hfad.beeradviser.

⭐ The class should be called BeerExpert.

⭐ It should expose one method, getBrands(), that takes a preferred beer color (as a String), and return a List<String> of recommended beers.

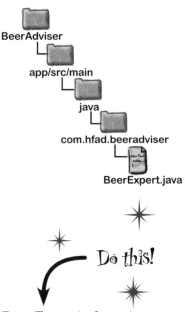

We need to create a Java class that the activity can use to find out which beer brands to suggest.

Build and test the Java class

Java classes can be extremely complicated and involve calls to complex application logic. You can either build and test your own version of the class, or use our sophisticated version of the class shown here:

```java
package com.hfad.beeradviser;

import java.util.ArrayList;
import java.util.List;

public class BeerExpert {
    List<String> getBrands(String color) {
        List<String> brands = new ArrayList<>();
        if (color.equals("amber")) {
            brands.add("Jack Amber");
            brands.add("Red Moose");
        } else {
            brands.add("Jail Pale Ale");
            brands.add("Gout Stout");
        }
        return brands;
    }
}
```

This is pure Java code; nothing Androidy about it.

Do this!

Add the BeerExpert class to your project. Select the *com.hfad.beeradviser* package in the *app/src/main/java* folder, go to File→New...→Java Class, name the file "BeerExpert", and make sure the package name is "com.hfad.beeradviser". This creates the *BeerExpert.java* file.

Enhance the activity to call the custom Java class so that we can get REAL advice

In version two of the activity we need to enhance the `onClickFindBeer()` method to call the `BeerExpert` class for beer recommendations. The code changes needed are plain old Java. You can try to write the code and run the app on your own, or you can follow along with us. But before we show you the code changes, try the exercise below; it'll help you create some of the activity code you'll need.

Sharpen your pencil

Enhance the activity so that it calls the `BeerExpert` `getBrands()` method and displays the results in the text view.

```
package com.hfad.beeradviser;

import android.app.Activity;
import android.os.Bundle;
import android.view.View;
import android.widget.Spinner;
import android.widget.TextView;
import java.util.List;       ← We added this line for you.

public class FindBeerActivity extends Activity {
    private BeerExpert expert = new BeerExpert();   ← You'll need to use the BeerExpert
...                                                   class to get the beer recommendations,
                                                      so we added this line for you too.
    //Called when the button gets clicked
    public void onClickFindBeer(View view) {
        //Get a reference to the TextView
        TextView brands = (TextView) findViewById(R.id.brands);
        //Get a reference to the Spinner
        Spinner color = (Spinner) findViewById(R.id.color);
        //Get the selected item in the Spinner
        String beerType = String.valueOf(color.getSelectedItem());
        //Get recommendations from the BeerExpert class
```

┌───┐
│   │
│   │
│   │
│   │
│   │
│   │
│   │
└───┘

```
    }
}
```
↑ You need to update the onClickFindBeer() method.

Sharpen your pencil
Solution

Enhance the activity so that it calls the `BeerExpert` `getBrands()` method and displays the results in the text view.

```java
package com.hfad.beeradviser;

import android.app.Activity;
import android.os.Bundle;
import android.view.View;
import android.widget.Spinner;
import android.widget.TextView;
import java.util.List;

public class FindBeerActivity extends Activity {
    private BeerExpert expert = new BeerExpert();
...
    //Called when the button gets clicked
    public void onClickFindBeer(View view) {
        //Get a reference to the TextView
        TextView brands = (TextView) findViewById(R.id.brands);
        //Get a reference to the Spinner
        Spinner color = (Spinner) findViewById(R.id.color);
        //Get the selected item in the Spinner
        String beerType = String.valueOf(color.getSelectedItem());
        //Get recommendations from the BeerExpert class
```

List<String> brandsList = expert.getBrands(beerType); ← Get a List of brands.

StringBuilder brandsFormatted = new StringBuilder(); ← Build a String using
the values in the List.

for (String brand : brandsList) {

    brandsFormatted.append(brand).append('\n'); ← Display each brand
    on a new line.

}

//Display the beers

brands.setText(brandsFormatted); ← Display the results in
the text view.

↖
Using the BeerExpert requires pure Java code, so don't worry if your code looks a little different than ours.

```java
    }
}
```

Activity code version 2

Here's our full version of the activity code. Apply the changes shown here to your version of *FindBeerActivity.java*, make sure you've added the BeerExpert class to your project, and then save your changes:

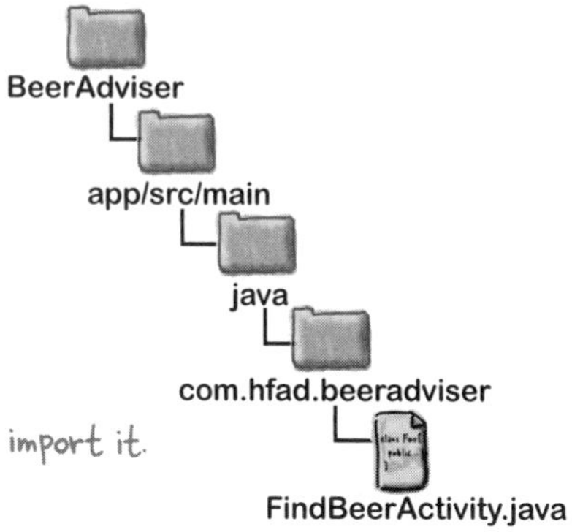

```java
package com.hfad.beeradviser;

import android.app.Activity;
import android.os.Bundle;
import android.view.View;
import android.widget.Spinner;
import android.widget.TextView;
import java.util.List;    // We're using this extra class so we need to import it.

public class FindBeerActivity extends Activity {
    private BeerExpert expert = new BeerExpert();
                                          // Add an instance of BeerExpert as a private variable.

    @Override
    protected void onCreate(Bundle savedInstanceState) {
        super.onCreate(savedInstanceState);
        setContentView(R.layout.activity_find_beer);
    }


    //Called when the button gets clicked
    public void onClickFindBeer(View view) {
        //Get a reference to the TextView
        TextView brands = (TextView) findViewById(R.id.brands);
        //Get a reference to the Spinner
        Spinner color = (Spinner) findViewById(R.id.color);
        //Get the selected item in the Spinner
        String beerType = String.valueOf(color.getSelectedItem());
        //Get recommendations from the BeerExpert class
        List<String> brandsList = expert.getBrands(beerType);    // Use the BeerExpert class to get a List of brands.
        StringBuilder brandsFormatted = new StringBuilder();
        for (String brand : brandsList) {
            brandsFormatted.append(brand).append('\n');    // Build a String, displaying each brand on a new line.
        }
        //Display the beers
        brands.setText(brandsFormatted);    // Display the String in the TextView.
        brands.setText(beerType);    // Delete this line.
    }
}
```

BeerAdviser
app/src/main
java
com.hfad.beeradviser
FindBeerActivity.java

What happens when you run the code

① **When the user clicks on the Find Beer button, the onClickFindBeer() method in the activity gets called.**
The method creates a reference to the spinner and text view, and gets the currently selected value from the spinner.

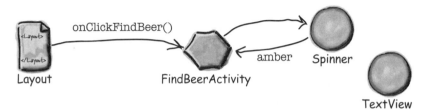

② **onClickFindBeer() calls the getBrands() method in the BeerExpert class, passing in the type of beer selected in the spinner.**
The getBrands() method returns a list of brands.

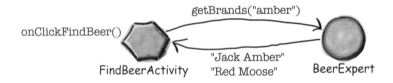

③ **The onClickFindBeer() method formats the list of brands and uses it to set the text property in the text view.**

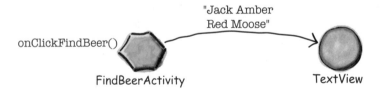

Test drive your app

building *interactive* **apps**
- [x] **Create project**
- [x] **Update layout**
- [x] **Connect activity**
- [x] **Write logic**

Once you've made the changes to your app, go ahead
and run it. Try selecting different types of beer and
clicking on the Find Beer button.

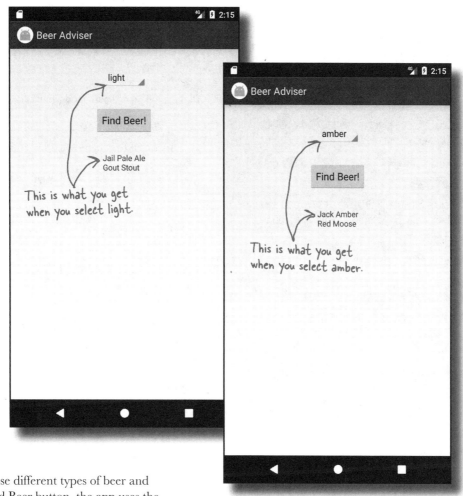

*This is what you get
when you select light.*

*This is what you get
when you select amber.*

When you choose different types of beer and
click on the Find Beer button, the app uses the
BeerExpert class to provide you with a selection
of suitable beers.

CHAPTER 2

Your Android Toolbox

You've got Chapter 2 under your belt and now you've added building interactive Android apps to your toolbox.

You can download the full code for the chapter from https://tinyurl.com/HeadFirstAndroid.

BULLET POINTS

- The `<Button>` element is used to add a button.

- The `<Spinner>` element is used to add a spinner, which is a drop-down list of values.

- All GUI components are types of view. They inherit from the Android `View` class.

- *strings.xml* is a String resource file. It's used to separate out text values from the layouts and activities, and supports localization.

- Add a String to *strings.xml* using:

    ```
    <string name="name">Value</string>
    ```

- Reference a String in the layout using:

    ```
    "@string/name"
    ```

- Add an array of String values to *strings.xml* using:

    ```
    <string-array name="array">
        <item>string1</item>
        . . .
    </string-array>
    ```

- Reference a `string-array` in the layout using:

    ```
    "@array/array_name"
    ```

- Make a button call a method when clicked by adding the following to the layout:

    ```
    android:onClick="clickMethod"
    ```

    There needs to be a corresponding method in the activity:

    ```
    public void clickMethod(View view){
    }
    ```

- *R.java* is generated for you. It enables you to get references for layouts, GUI components, Strings, and other resources in your Java code.

- Use `findViewById()` to get a reference to a view.

- Use `setText()` to set the text in a view.

- Use `getSelectedItem()` to get the selected item in a spinner.

- Add a custom class to an Android project by going to File menu→New...→Java Class.

3 multiple activities and intents

State Your Intent

> I sent an intent asking who could handle my ACTION_CALL, and was offered all **sorts** of activities to choose from.

Most apps need more than one activity.

So far we've just looked at single-activity apps, which is fine for simple apps. But when things get more complicated, just having the one activity won't cut it. We're going to show you **how to build apps with multiple activities**, and how you can get your activities talking to each other using *intents*. We'll also look at how you can use intents to **go beyond the boundaries of your app** and **make activities in other apps on your device perform** *actions*. Things are about to get a whole lot more powerful...

Apps can contain more than one activity

Earlier in the book, we said that an activity is a single, defined thing that your user can do, such as displaying a list of recipes. If your app is simple, this may be all that's needed.

But a lot of the time, you'll want users to do *more* than just one thing—for example, adding recipes as well as displaying a list of them. If this is the case, you'll need to use multiple activities: one for displaying the list of recipes and another for adding a single recipe.

The best way of understanding how this works is to see it in action. You're going to build an app containing two activities. The first activity will allow you to type a message. When you click on a button in the first activity, it will launch the second activity and pass it the message. The second activity will then display the message.

An activity is a single focused thing your user can do. If you chain multiple activities together to do something more complex, it's called a task.

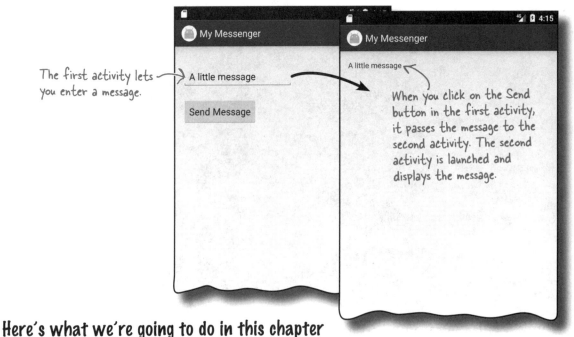

The first activity lets you enter a message.

When you click on the Send button in the first activity, it passes the message to the second activity. The second activity is launched and displays the message.

Here's what we're going to do in this chapter

1. Create an app with a single activity and layout.

2. Add a second activity and layout.

3. Get the first activity to call the second activity.

4. Get the first activity to pass data to the second activity.

Here's the app structure

The app contains two activities and two layouts.

1 **When the app gets launched, it starts activity CreateMessageActivity.**
This activity uses the layout *activity_create_message.xml*.

2 **When the user clicks a button in CreateMessageActivity, ReceiveMessageActivity is launched.**
This activity uses layout *activity_receive_message.xml*.

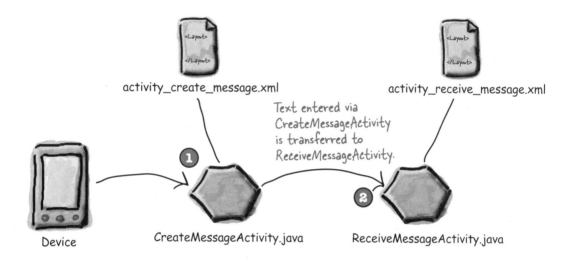

activity_create_message.xml

activity_receive_message.xml

Text entered via CreateMessageActivity is transferred to ReceiveMessageActivity.

Device

CreateMessageActivity.java

ReceiveMessageActivity.java

Get started: create the project

You create a project for the app in exactly the same way you did in previous chapters. Create a new Android Studio project for an application named "My Messenger" with a company domain of "hfad.com", making the package name com.hfad.mymessenger. The minimum SDK should be API 19 so that it will work on most devices. You'll need an empty activity named "CreateMessageActivity" with a layout named "activity_create_message" so that your code matches ours. **Make sure that you untick the Backwards Compatibility (AppCompat) option when you create the activity.**

On the next page, we'll update the activity's layout.

Create 1st activity
Create 2nd activity
Call 2nd activity
Pass data

Update the layout

Here's the XML for the *activity_create_message.xml* file. We're using a
`<LinearLayout>` to display components in a single column, and we've
added `<Button>` and `<EditText>` elements to it. The `<EditText>`
element gives you an editable text field you can use to enter data.

Change your *activity_create_message.xml* file to match the XML here:

This is the editable text field. If it's empty, it gives the user a hint about what text they should enter in it.

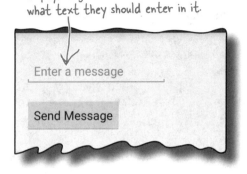

```xml
<?xml version="1.0" encoding="utf-8"?>
<LinearLayout
    xmlns:android="http://schemas.android.com/apk/res/android"
    xmlns:tools="http://schemas.android.com/tools"
    android:layout_width="match_parent"
    android:layout_height="match_parent"
    android:padding="16dp"
    android:orientation="vertical"
    tools:context="com.hfad.mymessenger.CreateMessageActivity">

    <EditText
        android:id="@+id/message"
        android:layout_width="wrap_content"
        android:layout_height="wrap_content"
        android:layout_marginTop="20dp"
        android:hint="@string/hint"
        android:ems="10" />

    <Button
        android:id="@+id/send"
        android:layout_width="wrap_content"
        android:layout_height="wrap_content"
        android:layout_marginTop="20dp"
        android:onClick="onSendMessage"
        android:text="@string/send" />

</LinearLayout>
```

We're using a linear layout with a vertical orientation.

MyMessenger
app/src/main
res
layout
activity_create_message.xml

This creates an editable text field.

The hint attribute gives the user a hint of what text they should type into the text field. We need to add it as a String resource.

This describes how wide the <EditText> should be. It should be wide enough to accommodate 10 letter Ms.

This is a String resource we need to create.

Clicking on the button runs the onSendMessage() method in the activity.

The `<EditText>` element defines an editable text field for entering text. It inherits from the same Android View class as the other GUI components we've seen so far.

Update strings.xml...

We used two String resources in our layout on the previous page. The button has a text value of @string/send that appears on the button, and the editable text field has a hint value of @string/hint that tells the user what to enter in the field. This means we need to add Strings called "send" and "hint" to *strings.xml* and give them values. Do this now:

```
<resources>
    ...
    <string name="send">Send Message</string>
    <string name="hint">Enter a message</string>
</resources>
```

The text "Send Message" will appear on the button.

The text "Enter a message" will appear as a hint in the text field if it's empty.

MyMessenger
app/src/main
res
values
strings.xml

...and add the method to the activity

This line in the <Button> element:

```
android:onClick="onSendMessage"
```

means that the onSendMessage() method in the activity will fire when the button is clicked. Let's add this method to the activity now.

Open up the *CreateMessageActivity.java* file and replace the code Android Studio created for you with the following:

```
package com.hfad.mymessenger;

import android.app.Activity;
import android.os.Bundle;
import android.view.View;

public class CreateMessageActivity extends Activity {

    @Override
    protected void onCreate(Bundle savedInstanceState) {
        super.onCreate(savedInstanceState);
        setContentView(R.layout.activity_create_message);
    }

    //Call onSendMessage() when the button is clicked
    public void onSendMessage(View view) {
    }
}
```

Make sure your activity extends the Activity class.

The onCreate() method gets called when the activity is created.

This method will get called when the button's clicked. We'll complete the method body as we work our way through the rest of the chapter.

MyMessenger
app/src/main
java
com.hfad.mymessenger
CreateMessage
Activity.java

Now that you've created the first activity, let's move on to the second.

Create the second activity and layout

Create 1st activity
Create 2nd activity
Call 2nd activity
Pass data

Android Studio has a wizard that lets you add extra activities and layouts to your apps. It's like a scaled-down version of the wizard you use to create an app, and you use it whenever you want to create a new activity.

To create the new activity, switch to the Project view of Android Studio's explorer, click on the *com.hfad.mymessenger* package in the *app/src/main/java* folder, choose File → New → Activity, and choose the option for Empty Activity. You will be presented with a new screen where you can choose options for your new activity.

Some versions of Android Studio may ask you what the source language of your activity should be. If prompted, select the option for Java.

Every time you create a new activity and layout, you need to name them. Name the new activity "ReceiveMessageActivity" and the layout "activity_receive_message". Make sure that the option to generate a layout is checked, and the Launcher Activity and Backwards Compatibility (AppCompat) options are unchecked. Finally, confirm that the package name is com.hfad.mymessenger, and when you're done, click on the Finish button.

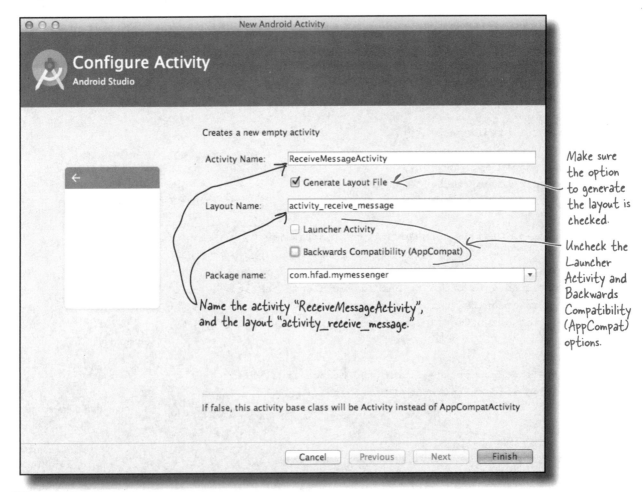

Configure Activity
Android Studio

Creates a new empty activity

Activity Name: ReceiveMessageActivity

☑ Generate Layout File

Layout Name: activity_receive_message

☐ Launcher Activity

☐ Backwards Compatibility (AppCompat)

Package name: com.hfad.mymessenger

If false, this activity base class will be Activity instead of AppCompatActivity

Cancel   Previous   Next   Finish

Make sure the option to generate the layout is checked.

Uncheck the Launcher Activity and Backwards Compatibility (AppCompat) options.

Name the activity "ReceiveMessageActivity", and the layout "activity_receive_message."

What just happened?

When you clicked on the Finish button, Android Studio created a shiny new activity file for you, along with a new layout. If you look in the explorer, you should see that a new file called *ReceiveMessageActivity.java* has appeared in the *app/src/main/java* folder, and a file called *activity_receive_message.xml* has appeared under *app/src/main/res/layout*.

Each activity uses a different layout. `CreateMessageActivity` uses the layout *activity_create_message.xml*, and `ReceiveMessageActivity` uses the layout *activity_receive_message.xml*:

Your explorer window may look different than ours because we've switched to the Project view.

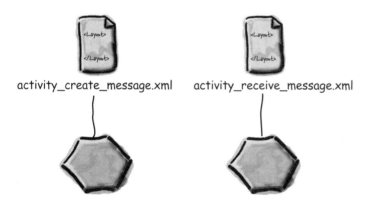

activity_create_message.xml   activity_receive_message.xml

CreateMessageActivity.java   ReceiveMessageActivity.java

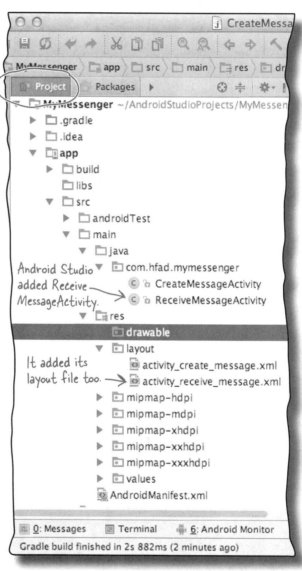

Android Studio added Receive MessageActivity.

It added its layout file too.

Behind the scenes, Android Studio also made a configuration change to the app in a file called *AndroidManifest.xml*. Let's take a closer look.

Create 1st activity
Create 2nd activity
Call 2nd activity
Pass data

Welcome to the Android manifest file

Every Android app must include a file called *AndroidManifest.xml*. You can find it in the *app/src/main* folder of your project. The *AndroidManifest.xml* file contains essential information about your app, such as what activities it contains, required libraries, and other declarations. Android creates the file for you when you create the app. If you think back to the settings you chose when you created the project, some of the file contents should look familiar.

Here's what our copy of *AndroidManifest.xml* looks like:

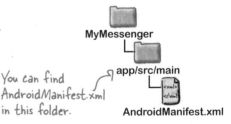

MyMessenger

app/src/main

You can find AndroidManifest.xml in this folder.

AndroidManifest.xml

```xml
<?xml version="1.0" encoding="utf-8"?>
<manifest xmlns:android="http://schemas.android.com/apk/res/android"
    package="com.hfad.mymessenger">
```
← This is the package name we specified.

```xml
    <application
        android:allowBackup="true"
        android:icon="@mipmap/ic_launcher"
        android:label="@string/app_name"
        android:roundIcon="@mipmap/ic_launcher_round"
        android:supportsRtl="true"
        android:theme="@style/AppTheme">
```
← Android Studio gave our app default icons.

The theme affects the appearance of the app. We'll look at this later.

Watch it!

If you develop Android apps without an IDE, you'll need to create this file manually.

This is the first activity, CreateMessageActivity.
```xml
        <activity android:name=".CreateMessageActivity">
            <intent-filter>
                <action android:name="android.intent.action.MAIN" />
                <category android:name="android.intent.category.LAUNCHER" />
            </intent-filter>
        </activity>
```
This bit specifies that it's the main activity of the app.

This says the activity can be used to launch the app.

```xml
        <activity android:name=".ReceiveMessageActivity"></activity>
```
This is the second activity, ReceiveMessageActivity. Android Studio added this code when we added the second activity.

```xml
    </application>

</manifest>
```

Every activity needs to be declared

All activities need to be declared in *AndroidManifest.xml*. If an activity isn't declared in the file, the system won't know it exists. And if the system doesn't know it exists, the activity will never run.

You declare an activity in the manifest by including an `<activity>` element inside the `<application>` element. In fact, *every* activity in your app needs a corresponding `<activity>` element. Here's the general format:

> *If I'm not included in AndroidManifest.xml, then as far as the system's concerned, I don't exist and will never run.*

Activity

```
<application   ←  Each activity needs to be declared
    ...            inside the <application> element.
    ...>
    <activity
        android:name=".MyActivityClassName"   ←  This line is mandatory; just
                                                  replace MyActivityClassName
        ...   ←  The activity may have            with the name of your
        ...>     other properties too.            activity.
        ...
    </activity>
    ...
</application>
```

The following line is mandatory and is used to specify the class name of the activity, in this example `"MyActivityClassName"`:

```
android:name=".MyActivityClassName"
```

`MyActivityClassName` is the name of the class. It's prefixed with a "." because Android combines the class name with the name of the package to derive the *fully qualified* class name.

The activity declaration may include other properties too, such as security permissions, and whether it can be used by activities in other apps.

Watch it!

The second activity in our app was automatically declared because we added it using the Android Studio wizard.

If you add extra activities manually, you'll need to edit AndroidManifest.xml yourself. The same may be true if you use another IDE besides Android Studio.

An intent is a type of message

Create 1st activity

Create 2nd activity

Call 2nd activity

Pass data

So far we've created an app with two activities in it, and each activity has its own layout. When the app is launched, our first activity, `CreateMessageActivity`, will run. What we need to do next is get `CreateMessageActivity` to call `ReceiveMessageActivity` when the user clicks the Send Message button.

Whenever you want an activity to start a second activity, you use an **intent**. You can think of an intent as an "intent to do something." It's a type of message that allows you to bind separate objects (such as activities) together at runtime. If one activity wants to start a second activity, it does it by sending an intent to Android. Android will then start the second activity and pass it the intent.

You can create and send an intent using just a couple of lines of code. You start by creating the intent like this:

```
Intent intent = new Intent(this, Target.class);
```

The first parameter tells Android which object the intent is from: you can use the word `this` to refer to the current activity. The second parameter is the class name of the activity that needs to receive the intent.

Once you've created the intent, you pass it to Android like this:

```
startActivity(intent);
```

This tells Android to start the activity specified by the intent.

Once Android receives the intent, it checks that everything's OK and tells the activity to start. If it can't find the activity, it throws an **ActivityNotFoundException**.

> You start an activity by creating an intent and using it in the startActivity() method.

The intent specifies the activity you want to receive it. It's like putting an address on an envelope.

Intent

To: AnotherActivity

startActivity() starts the activity specified in the intent..

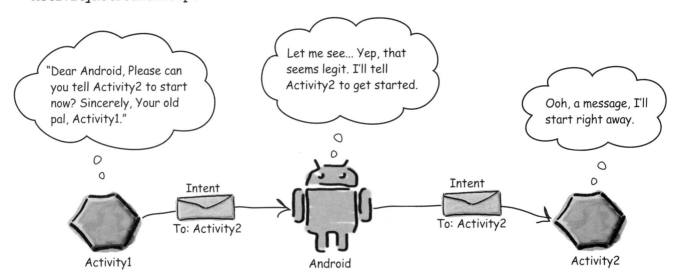

"Dear Android, Please can you tell Activity2 to start now? Sincerely, Your old pal, Activity1."

Let me see... Yep, that seems legit. I'll tell Activity2 to get started.

Ooh, a message, I'll start right away.

Activity1   Intent   To: Activity2   Android   Intent   To: Activity2   Activity2

Use an intent to start the second activity

Let's put this into practice and use an intent to call
ReceiveMessageActivity. We want to launch the activity
when the user clicks on the Send Message button, so we'll add
the two lines of code we discussed on the previous page to our
onSendMessage() method.

Make the changes highlighted below:

```
package com.hfad.mymessenger;

import android.app.Activity;
import android.content.Intent;
import android.os.Bundle;
import android.view.View;
```

← We need to import the Intent class android.content.Intent as we're using it in onSendMessage().

```
public class CreateMessageActivity extends Activity {

    @Override
    protected void onCreate(Bundle savedInstanceState) {
        super.onCreate(savedInstanceState);
        setContentView(R.layout.activity_create_message);
    }

    //Call onSendMessage() when the button is clicked
    public void onSendMessage(View view) {
        Intent intent = new Intent(this, ReceiveMessageActivity.class);
        startActivity(intent);
    }

}
```

← Start activity ReceiveMessageActivity.

MyMessenger
app/src/main
java
com.hfad.mymessenger
**CreateMessage
Activity.java**

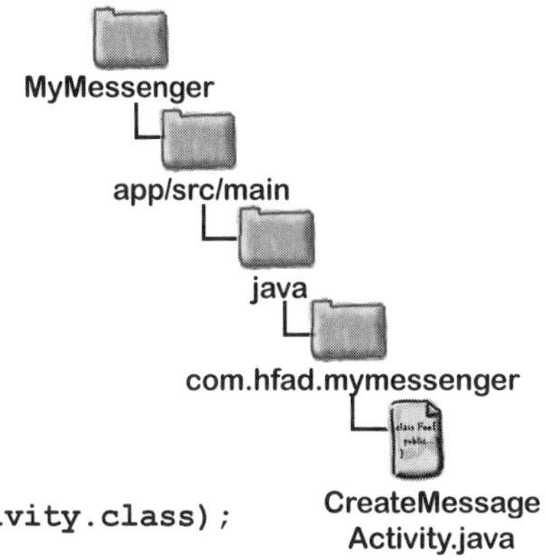

So what happens now when we run the app?

What happens when you run the app

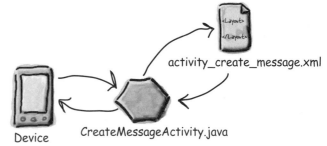

Create 1st activity
Create 2nd activity
Call 2nd activity
Pass data

Before we take the app out for a test drive, let's go over how the app we've developed so far will function:

1 **When the app gets launched, the main activity, CreateMessageActivity, starts.**
When it starts, the activity specifies that it uses layout *activity_create_message.xml*. This layout gets displayed in a new window.

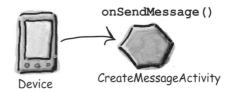

activity_create_message.xml

Device   CreateMessageActivity.java

---

2 **The user types in a message and then clicks on the button.**
The onSendMessage() method in CreateMessageActivity responds to the click.

onSendMessage()

Device   CreateMessageActivity

---

3 **The onSendMessage() method uses an intent to tell Android to start activity ReceiveMessageActivity.**
Android checks that the intent is valid, and then it tells ReceiveMessageActivity to start.

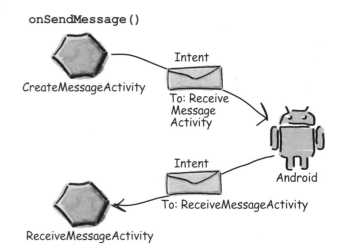

onSendMessage()

CreateMessageActivity

Intent

To: Receive Message Activity

Android

Intent

To: ReceiveMessageActivity

ReceiveMessageActivity

The story continues...

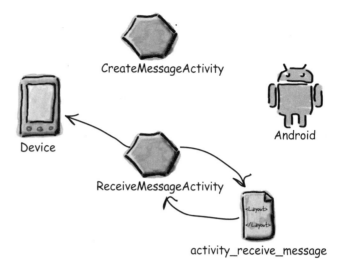

④ When ReceiveMessageActivity starts, it specifies that it uses layout *activity_receive_message.xml* and this layout gets displayed in a new window.

Test drive the app

Save your changes, and then run the app. `CreateMessageActivity` starts, and when you click on the Send Message button, it launches `ReceiveMessageActivity`.

Create 1st activity
Create 2nd activity
Call 2nd activity
Pass data

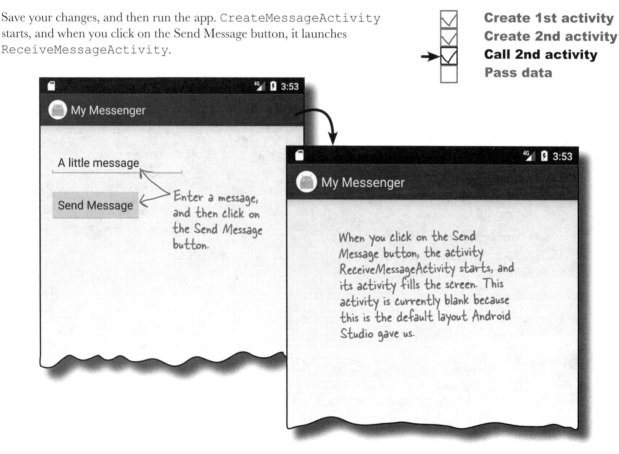

A little message

Send Message ← *Enter a message, and then click on the Send Message button.*

When you click on the Send Message button, the activity ReceiveMessageActivity starts, and its activity fills the screen. This activity is currently blank because this is the default layout Android Studio gave us.

Pass text to a second activity

Create 1st activity
Create 2nd activity
Call 2nd activity
Pass data

So far we've coded `CreateMessageActivity` to start `ReceiveMessageActivity` when the Send Message button is pressed. Next, we'll get `CreateMessageActivity` to pass text to `ReceiveMessageActivity` so that `ReceiveMessageActivity` can display it. In order to accomplish this, we'll do three things:

1 Tweak the layout *activity_receive_message.xml* so that it can display the text. At the moment it's simply the default layout the wizard gave us.

2 Update *CreateMessageActivity.java* so that it gets the text the user inputs, and then adds the text to the intent before it sends it.

3 Update *ReceiveMessageActivity.java* so that it displays the text sent in the intent.

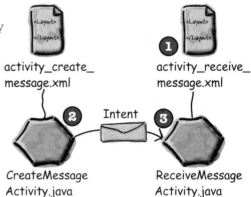

activity_create_message.xml

activity_receive_message.xml

2 Intent **3**

CreateMessage Activity.java

ReceiveMessage Activity.java

Let's start with the layout

We'll begin by changing the *activity_receive_message.xml* code Android Studio created for us so that it uses a `<LinearLayout>`. Update your version of the code so that it matches ours:

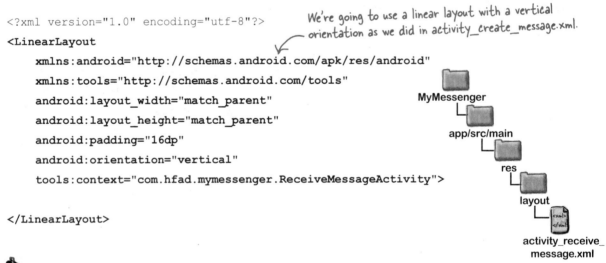

```xml
<?xml version="1.0" encoding="utf-8"?>
<LinearLayout
    xmlns:android="http://schemas.android.com/apk/res/android"
    xmlns:tools="http://schemas.android.com/tools"
    android:layout_width="match_parent"
    android:layout_height="match_parent"
    android:padding="16dp"
    android:orientation="vertical"
    tools:context="com.hfad.mymessenger.ReceiveMessageActivity">

</LinearLayout>
```

We're going to use a linear layout with a vertical orientation as we did in activity_create_message.xml.

MyMessenger

app/src/main

res

layout

activity_receive_message.xml

Exercise

We need to change the layout so that it includes a text view. The text view needs to have an ID of "message" so that we can reference it in our activity code. How should we change the layout's code? Think about this before looking at the next page.

Update the text view properties

We need to add a `<TextView>` element to the layout, and give it an ID of "message." This is because you have to add an ID to any GUI components you need to reference in your activity code, and we need to reference the text view so that we can update the text it displays.

We've updated our code so that it includes a new text view. Update your *activity_receive_message.xml* code so that it reflects ours (we've bolded our changes):

```xml
<?xml version="1.0" encoding="utf-8"?>
<LinearLayout
    xmlns:android="http://schemas.android.com/apk/res/android"
    xmlns:tools="http://schemas.android.com/tools"
    android:layout_width="match_parent"
    android:layout_height="match_parent"
    android:padding="16dp"
    android:orientation="vertical"
    tools:context="com.hfad.mymessenger.ReceiveMessageActivity">

    <TextView
        android:id="@+id/message"
        android:layout_width="wrap_content"
        android:layout_height="wrap_content" />
</LinearLayout>
```

This adds the text view.

This line gives the text view an ID of "message".

MyMessenger
app/src/main
res
layout
activity_receive_message.xml

We've not specified default text for the text view, as the only text we'll ever want to display in the text view is the message passed to it by `CreateMessageActivity`.

Now that we've updated the layout, we can get to work on the activities. Let's start by looking at how we can use an intent to pass a message to `ReceiveMessageActivity`.

there are no Dumb Questions

Q: Do I have to use intents? Can't I just construct an instance of the second activity in the code for my first activity?

A: That's a good question, but no, that's not the "Android way" of doing things. One of the reasons is that passing intents to Android tells Android the sequence in which activities are started. This means that when you click on the Back button on your device, Android knows exactly where to take you back to.

putExtra() puts extra info in an intent

Create 1st activity
Create 2nd activity
Call 2nd activity
Pass data

You've seen how you can create a new intent using:

```
Intent intent = new Intent(this, Target.class);
```

You can add extra information to this intent that can be picked up by the activity you're targeting so it can react in some way. To do this, you use the putExtra() method like so:

intent.putExtra("message", value);

where message is a String name for the value you're passing in, and value is the value. The putExtra() method is overloaded so value has many possible types. As an example, it can be a primitive such as a boolean or int, an array of primitives, or a String. You can use putExtra() repeatedly to add numerous extra data to the intent. If you do this, make sure you give each one a unique name.

putExtra() lets you put extra information in the message you're sending.

Intent

To: ReceiveMessageActivity
message: "Hello!"

There are many different options for the type of value. You can see them all in the Google Android documentation. Android Studio will also give you a list as you type code in.

How to retrieve extra information from an intent

The story doesn't end there. When Android tells ReceiveMessageActivity to start, ReceiveMessageActivity needs some way of retrieving the extra information that CreateMessageActivity sent to Android in the intent.

There are a couple of useful methods that can help with this. The first of these is:

getIntent();

getIntent() returns the intent that started the activity, and you can use this to retrieve any extra information that was sent along with it. How you do this depends on the type of information that was sent. As an example, if you know the intent includes a String value named "message", you would use the following:

Intent

To: ReceiveMessageActivity
message: "Hello!"

```
Intent intent = getIntent();
String string = intent.getStringExtra("message");
```
← Get the intent.

← Get the String passed along with the intent that has a name of "message".

You're not just limited to retrieving String values. As an example, you can use:

int intNum = intent.getIntExtra("name", default_value);

to retrieve an int with a name of name. default_value specifies what int value you should use as a default.

```
package com.hfad.mymessenger;

import android.app.Activity;
import android.os.Bundle;
import android.content.Intent;
import android.view.View;

............................................................................................................

public class CreateMessageActivity extends Activity {

    @Override
    protected void onCreate(Bundle savedInstanceState) {
        super.onCreate(savedInstanceState);
        setContentView(R.layout.activity_create_message);
    }

    //Call onSendMessage() when the button is clicked
    public void onSendMessage(View view) {

        ............................................................................................................

        ............................................................................................................

        Intent intent = new Intent(this, ReceiveMessageActivity.class);

        ............................................................................................................

        startActivity(intent);
    }
}
```

Pool Puzzle

Your **job** is to take code snippets from the pool and place them into the blank lines in *CreateMessageActivity.java*. You may **not** use the same code snippet more than once, and you won't need to use all the code snippets. Your **goal** is to make the activity retrieve text from the message <EditText> and add it to the intent.

Note: each thing from the pool can only be used once!

EditText

EditText

import   putExtra

messageView   putExtraString   "message"   =

String

getText()   findViewById   =

R.id.message   messageView   messageText

android.widget.EditText   messageText   intent

(;

(; .

( )   .

,   ;

) ;)

toString()   .

```
package com.hfad.mymessenger;

import android.app.Activity;
import android.os.Bundle;
import android.content.Intent;
import android.view.View;
import android.widget.EditText;
```

You need to import the EditText class.

Pool Puzzle Solution

Your **job** is to take code snippets from the pool and place them into the blank lines in *CreateMessageActivity.java*. You may **not** use the same code snippet more than once, and you won't need to use all the code snippets. Your **goal** is to make the activity retrieve text from the message <EditText> and add it to the intent.

```
public class CreateMessageActivity extends Activity {

    @Override
    protected void onCreate(Bundle savedInstanceState) {
        super.onCreate(savedInstanceState);
        setContentView(R.layout.activity_create_message);
    }

    //Call onSendMessage() when the button is clicked
    public void onSendMessage(View view) {
        EditText messageView = (EditText) findViewById(R.id.message);
        String messageText = messageView.getText().toString();
        Intent intent = new Intent(this, ReceiveMessageActivity.class);
        intent.putExtra("message", messageText);
        startActivity(intent);
    }
}
```

Get the text from the editable text field with an ID of "message."

Add the text to the intent, giving it a name of "message".

This code snippet wasn't needed. → putExtraString

Update the CreateMessageActivity code

multiple activities *and* intents
- [✓] Create 1st activity
- [✓] Create 2nd activity
- [✓] Call 2nd activity
- [ ] **Pass data**

We updated our code for *CreateMessageActivity.java* so that it takes the text the user enters on the screen and adds it to the intent. Here's the full code (make sure you update your code to include these changes, shown in bold):

```
package com.hfad.mymessenger;

import android.app.Activity;
import android.os.Bundle;
import android.content.Intent;
import android.view.View;
import android.widget.EditText;

public class CreateMessageActivity extends Activity {

    @Override
    protected void onCreate(Bundle savedInstanceState) {
        super.onCreate(savedInstanceState);
        setContentView(R.layout.activity_create_message);
    }

    //Call onSendMessage() when the button is clicked
    public void onSendMessage(View view) {
        EditText messageView = (EditText) findViewById(R.id.message);
        String messageText = messageView.getText().toString();
        Intent intent = new Intent(this, ReceiveMessageActivity.class);
        intent.putExtra(ReceiveMessageActivity.EXTRA_MESSAGE, messageText);
        startActivity(intent);
    }
}
```

You need to import the EditText class android.widget.EditText as you're using it in your activity code.

> MyMessenger
> > app/src/main
> > > java
> > > > com.hfad.mymessenger
> > > > > **CreateMessage Activity.java**

Get the text that's in the EditText.

Start ReceiveMessageActivity with the intent.

Create an intent, then add the text to the intent. We're using a constant for the name of the extra information so that we know CreateMessageActivity and ReceiveMessageActivity are using the same String. We'll add this constant to ReceiveMessageActivity on the next page, so don't worry if Android Studio says it doesn't exist.

Now that CreateMessageActivity has added extra information to the intent, we need to retrieve that information and use it.

Get ReceiveMessageActivity to use the information in the intent

☑ **Create 1st activity**
☑ **Create 2nd activity**
☑ **Call 2nd activity**
→ ☐ **Pass data**

Now that we've changed `CreateMessageActivity` to add text to the intent, we'll update `ReceiveMessageActivity` so that it uses that text.

We're going to get `ReceiveMessageActivity` to display the message in its text view when the activity gets created. Because the activity's `onCreate()` method gets called as soon as the activity is created, we'll add the code to this method.

To get the message from the intent, we'll first get the intent using the `getIntent()` method, then get the value of the message using `getStringExtra()`.

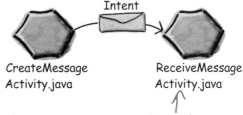

Intent

CreateMessage
Activity.java

ReceiveMessage
Activity.java

We need to make ReceiveMessageActivity deal with the intent it receives.

Here's the full code for *ReceiveMessageActivity.java* (replace the code that Android Studio generated for you with this code, and then save all your changes):

```java
package com.hfad.mymessenger;

import android.app.Activity;
import android.os.Bundle;
import android.content.Intent;
import android.widget.TextView;

public class ReceiveMessageActivity extends Activity {

    public static final String EXTRA_MESSAGE = "message";

    @Override
    protected void onCreate(Bundle savedInstanceState) {
        super.onCreate(savedInstanceState);
        setContentView(R.layout.activity_receive_message);
        Intent intent = getIntent();
        String messageText = intent.getStringExtra(EXTRA_MESSAGE);
        TextView messageView = (TextView) findViewById(R.id.message);
        messageView.setText(messageText);
    }
}
```

We need to import these classes.

Make sure your activity extends the Activity class.

This is the name of the extra value we're passing in the intent.

Get the intent, and get the message from it using getStringExtra().

Add the text to the message text view.

MyMessenger

└ **app/src/main**

└ **java**

└ **com.hfad.mymessenger**

ReceiveMessage Activity.java

Before we take the app for a test drive, let's run through what the current code does.

What happens when the user clicks the Send Message button

① **When the user clicks on the button, the onSendMessage() method is called.**

Code within the onSendMessage() method creates an intent to start activity ReceiveMessageActivity, adds a message to the intent, and passes it to Android with an instruction to start the activity.

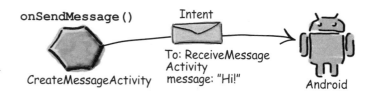

② **Android checks that the intent is OK, and then tells ReceiveMessageActivity to start.**

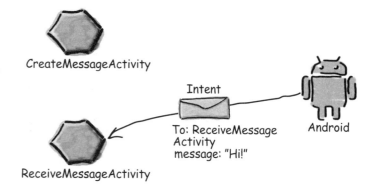

③ **When ReceiveMessageActivity starts, it specifies that it uses layout activity_receive_message.xml, and this gets displayed on the device.**

The activity also updates the layout so that it displays the extra text included in the intent.

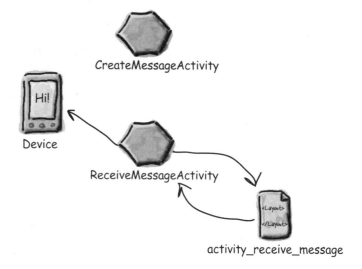

Test drive the app

Make sure you've updated the two activities, save your changes, and then run the app. `CreateMessageActivity` starts, and when you enter some text and then click on the Send Message button, it launches `ReceiveMessageActivity`. The text you entered is displayed in the text view.

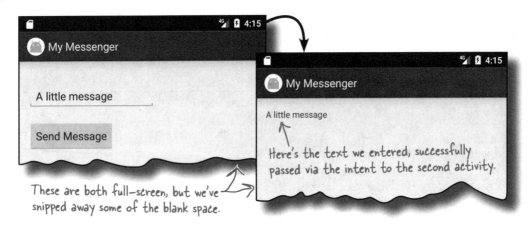

These are both full-screen, but we've snipped away some of the blank space.

Here's the text we entered, successfully passed via the intent to the second activity.

We can change the app to send messages to other people

Now that we have an app that sends a message to another activity, we can change it so that it can send messages to other people. We can do this by integrating with the message sending apps already on the device. Depending on what apps the user has, we can get our app to send messages via Gmail, Google+, Facebook, Twitter...

> Hey, hold it right there! That sounds like a freaky amount of work to get our app working with all those other apps. And how the heck do I know what apps people have on their devices anyway?

It's not as hard as it sounds thanks to the way Android is designed to work.

Remember right at the beginning of the chapter when we said that tasks are multiple activities chained together? Well, **you're not just limited to using the activities within your app**. You can go beyond the boundaries of your app to use activities within *other* apps as well.

98 Chapter 3

How Android apps work

As you've seen, all Android apps are composed of one or more activities, along with other components such as layouts. Each activity is a single defined focused thing the user can do. As an example, apps such as Gmail, Google+, Facebook, and Twitter all have activities that enable you to send messages, even though they may achieve this in different ways.

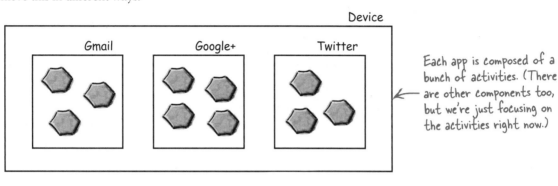

Each app is composed of a bunch of activities. (There are other components too, but we're just focusing on the activities right now.)

Intents can start activities in other apps

You've already seen how you can use an intent to start a second activity within the same app. The first activity passes an intent to Android, Android checks it, and then Android tells the second activity to start.

The same principle applies to activities in other apps. You get an activity in your app to pass an intent to Android, Android checks it, and then Android tells the second activity to start *even though it's in another app*. As an example, we can use an intent to start the activity in Gmail that sends messages, and pass it the text we want to send. That means that instead of writing our own activities to send emails, we can use the existing Gmail app.

You can create an intent to start another activity even if the activity is within another app.

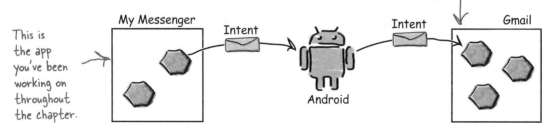

This is the app you've been working on throughout the chapter.

This means that you can build apps that perform powerful tasks by chaining together activities across the device.

But we don't know what apps are on the user's device

There are three questions we need answers to before we can call activities in other apps:

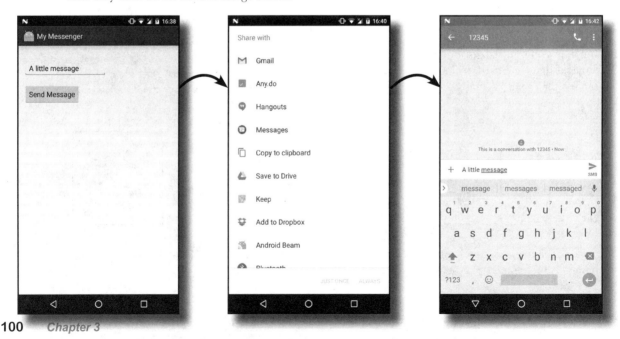

How do we know which activities are available on the user's device?

How do we know which of these activities are appropriate for what we want to do?

How do we know how to use these activities?

The great news is that we can solve all of these problems using **actions**. Actions are a way of telling Android what standard operations activities can perfom. As an example, Android knows that all activities registered for a send action are capable of sending messages.

Let's explore how to create intents that use actions to return a set of activities that you can use in a standard way—for example, to send messages.

Here's what you're going to do

1 **Create an intent that specifies an action.**
The intent will tell Android you want to use an activity that can send a message. The intent will include the text of the message.

2 **Allow the user to choose which app to use.**
Chances are, there'll be more than one app on the user's device capable of sending messages, so the user will need to pick one. We want the user to be able to choose one every time they click on the Send Message button.

Create an intent that specifies an action

So far you've seen how to create an intent that launches a specific activity using:

```
Intent intent = new Intent(this, ReceiveMessageActivity.class);
```

We've told the intent which class it's intended for, but what if we don't know?

This intent is an example of an **explicit intent**; you explicitly tell Android which class you want it to run.

If there's an action you want done but you don't care which activity does it, you create an **implicit intent**. You tell Android what sort of action you want it to perform, and you leave the details of which activity performs it to Android.

How to create the intent

You create an intent that specifies an action using the following syntax:

```
Intent intent = new Intent(action);
```

where `action` is the type of activity action you want to perform. Android provides you with a number of standard actions you can use. As an example, you can use `Intent.ACTION_DIAL` to dial a number, `Intent.ACTION_WEB_SEARCH` to perform a web search, and `Intent.ACTION_SEND` to send a message. So, if you want to create an intent that specifies you want to send a message, you use:

```
Intent intent = new Intent(Intent.ACTION_SEND);
```

Adding extra information

Once you've specified the action you want to use, you can add extra information to it. We want to pass some text with the intent that will form the body of the message we're sending. To do this, you use the following lines of code:

```
intent.setType("text/plain");
intent.putExtra(Intent.EXTRA_TEXT, messageText);
```

These attributes relate to Intent.ACTION_SEND. They're not relevant for all actions.

where `messageText` is the text you want to send. This tells Android that you want the activity to be able to handle data with a MIME data-type of `text/plain`, and also tells it what the text is.

You can make extra calls to the `putExtra()` method if there's additional information you want to add. As an example, if you want to specify the subject of the message, you can use:

```
intent.putExtra(Intent.EXTRA_SUBJECT, subject);
```

If subject isn't relevant to a particular app, it will just ignore this information. Any apps that know how to use it will do so.

where `subject` is the subject of the message.

You can find out more about the sorts of activity actions you can use and the extra information they support in the Android developer reference material: http://tinyurl.com/n57qb5.

Specify action
Create chooser

Change the intent to use an action

We'll update *CreateMessageActivity.java* so that we create an implicit
intent that uses a send action. Make the changes highlighted below,
and save your work:

```java
package com.hfad.mymessenger;

import android.app.Activity;
import android.os.Bundle;
import android.content.Intent;
import android.view.View;
import android.widget.EditText;

public class CreateMessageActivity extends Activity {

    @Override
    protected void onCreate(Bundle savedInstanceState) {
        super.onCreate(savedInstanceState);
        setContentView(R.layout.activity_create_message);
    }

    //Call onSendMessage() when the button is clicked
    public void onSendMessage(View view) {
        EditText messageView = (EditText)findViewById(R.id.message);
        String messageText = messageView.getText().toString();
        Intent intent = new Intent(this, ReceiveMessageActivity.class);
        intent.putExtra(ReceiveMessageActivity.EXTRA_MESSAGE, messageText);
        Intent intent = new Intent(Intent.ACTION_SEND);
        intent.setType("text/plain");
        intent.putExtra(Intent.EXTRA_TEXT, messageText);
        startActivity(intent);
    }
}
```

MyMessenger
  └ app/src/main
      └ java
          └ com.hfad.mymessenger
              └ CreateMessage
                 Activity.java

Remove these two lines.

Instead of creating an intent that's
explicitly for ReceiveMessageActivity, we're
creating an intent that uses a send action.

Now that you've updated your code, let's break down
what happens when the user clicks on the Send
Message button.

What happens when the code runs

① **When the onSendMessage() method is called, an intent gets created. The startActivity() method passes this intent to Android.**

The intent specifies an action of ACTION_SEND, and a MIME type of text/plain.

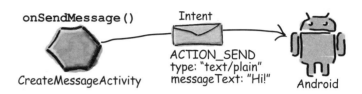

② **Android sees that the intent can only be passed to activities able to handle ACTION_SEND and text/plain data. Android checks all the activities on the user's device, looking for ones that are able to receive the intent.**

If no actions are able to handle the intent, an ActivityNotFoundException is thrown.

Aha, an implicit intent. I need to find all the activities that can handle ACTION_SEND, and data of type text/plain, and have a category of DEFAULT.

③a **If just one activity is able to receive the intent, Android tells that activity to start and passes it the intent.**

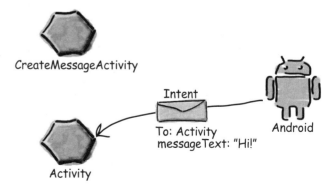

The story continues...

Specify action
Create chooser

3b If more than one activity is able to receive the intent, Android displays an activity chooser dialog and asks the user which one to use.

CreateMessageActivity

Hey, user. All of these activities can send a message for you. Which one do you want?

Android

User

---

4 **When the user chooses the activity she wants to use, Android tells the activity to start and passes it the intent.** The activity displays the extra text contained in the intent in the body of a new message.

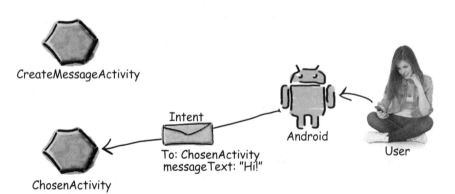

CreateMessageActivity

Intent

To: ChosenActivity
messageText: "Hi!"

Android

User

ChosenActivity

In order to pass the intent to an activity, Android must first know which activities are capable of receiving the intent. On the next couple of pages we'll look at how it does this.

The intent filter tells Android which activities can handle which actions

When Android is given an intent, it has to figure out which activity, or activities, can handle it. This process is known as **intent resolution**.

When you use an *explicit* intent, intent resolution is straightforward. The intent explicitly says which component the intent is directed at, so Android has clear instructions about what to do. As an example, the following code explicitly tells Android to start `ReceiveMessageActivity`:

```
Intent intent = new Intent(this, ReceiveMessageActivity.class);
startActivity(intent);
```

When you use an *implicit* intent, Android uses the information in the intent to figure out which components are able to receive it. It does this by checking the intent filters in every app's copy of *AndroidManifest.xml*.

An **intent filter** specifies what types of intent each component can receive. As an example, here's the entry for an activity that can handle an action of `ACTION_SEND`. The activity is able to accept data with MIME types of `text/plain` or `image`:

```
<activity android:name="ShareActivity">
    <intent-filter>
        <action android:name="android.intent.action.SEND"/>
        <category android:name="android.intent.category.DEFAULT"/>
        <data android:mimeType="text/plain"/>
        <data android:mimeType="image/*"/>
    </intent-filter>
</activity>
```

This is just an example; there's no activity called "ShareActivity" in our project.

This tells Android the activity can handle ACTION_SEND.

The intent filter must include a category of DEFAULT or it won't be able to receive implicit intents.

These are the types of data the activity can handle.

The intent filter also specifies a **category**. The category supplies extra information about the activity such as whether it can be started by a web browser, or whether it's the main entry point of the app. An intent filter ***must*** include a category of `android.intent.category.DEFAULT` if it's to receive implicit intents. If an activity has no intent filter, or it doesn't include a category name of `android.intent.category.DEFAULT`, it means that the activity can't be started with an implicit intent. It can only be started with an *explicit* intent using the full name (including the package) of the component.

Specify action
Create chooser

How Android uses the intent filter

When you use an implicit intent, Android compares the information given in the intent with the information given in the intent filters specified in every app's *AndroidManifest.xml* file.

Android first considers intent filters that include a category of `android.intent.category.DEFAULT`:

```
<intent-filter>
    <category android:name="android.intent.category.DEFAULT"/>
    ...
</intent-filter>
```

Intent filters without this category will be omitted, as they can't receive implicit intents.

Android then matches intents to intent filters by comparing the action and MIME type contained in the intent with those of the intent filters. As an example, if an intent specifies an action of `Intent.ACTION_SEND` using:

> It will also look at the category of the intent filter if one is supplied by the intent. However, this feature isn't used very often, so we don't cover how to add categories to intents.

```
Intent intent = new Intent(Intent.ACTION_SEND);
```

Android will only consider activities that specify an intent filter with an action of `android.intent.action.SEND` like this:

```
<intent-filter>
    <action android:name="android.intent.action.SEND"/>
    ...
</intent-filter>
```

Similarly, if the intent MIME type is set to `text/plain` using:

```
intent.setType("text/plain");
```

Android will only consider activities that can accommodate this type of data:

```
<intent-filter>
    <data android:mimeType="text/plain"/>
    ...
</intent-filter>
```

If the MIME type is left out of the intent, Android tries to infer the type based on the data the intent contains.

Once Android has finished comparing the intent to the component's intent filters, it sees how many matches it finds. If Android finds a single match, it starts the component (in our case, the activity) and passes it the intent. If it finds multiple matches, it asks the user to pick one.

BE the Intent

Your job is to play like you're the intent on the right and say which of the activities described below are compatible with your action and data. Say why, or why not, for each one.

Here's the intent.

```java
Intent intent = new Intent(Intent.ACTION_SEND);
intent.setType("text/plain");
intent.putExtra(Intent.EXTRA_TEXT, "Hello");
```

```xml
<activity android:name="SendActivity">
    <intent-filter>
        <action android:name="android.intent.action.SEND"/>
        <category android:name="android.intent.category.DEFAULT"/>
        <data android:mimeType="*/*"/>
    </intent-filter>
</activity>
```

```xml
<activity android:name="SendActivity">
    <intent-filter>
        <action android:name="android.intent.action.SEND"/>
        <category android:name="android.intent.category.MAIN"/>
        <data android:mimeType="text/plain"/>
    </intent-filter>
</activity>
```

```xml
<activity android:name="SendActivity">
    <intent-filter>
        <action android:name="android.intent.action.SENDTO"/>
        <category android:name="android.intent.category.MAIN"/>
        <category android:name="android.intent.category.DEFAULT"/>
        <data android:mimeType="text/plain"/>
    </intent-filter>
</activity>
```

BE the Intent Solution

Your job is to play like you're the intent on the right and say which of the activities described below are compatible with your action and data. Say why, or why not, for each one.

```java
Intent intent = new Intent(Intent.ACTION_SEND);
intent.setType("text/plain");
intent.putExtra(Intent.EXTRA_TEXT, "Hello");
```

This activity accepts ACTION_SEND and can handle data of any MIME type, so it can respond to the intent.

```xml
<activity android:name="SendActivity">
    <intent-filter>
        <action android:name="android.intent.action.SEND"/>
        <category android:name="android.intent.category.DEFAULT"/>
        <data android:mimeType="*/*"/>
    </intent-filter>
</activity>
```

This activity doesn't have a category of DEFAULT so can't receive the intent.

```xml
<activity android:name="SendActivity">
    <intent-filter>
        <action android:name="android.intent.action.SEND"/>
        <category android:name="android.intent.category.MAIN"/>
        <data android:mimeType="text/plain"/>
    </intent-filter>
</activity>
```

This activity can't accept ACTION_SEND intents, only ACTION_SENDTO (which allows you to send a message to someone specified in the intent's data).

```xml
<activity android:name="SendActivity">
    <intent-filter>
        <action android:name="android.intent.action.SENDTO"/>
        <category android:name="android.intent.category.MAIN"/>
        <category android:name="android.intent.category.DEFAULT"/>
        <data android:mimeType="text/plain"/>
    </intent-filter>
</activity>
```

You need to run your app on a REAL device

So far we've been running our apps using the emulator. The emulator only includes a small number of apps, and there may well be just one app that can handle `ACTION_SEND`. In order to test our app properly, we need to run it on a physical device where we know there'll be more than one app that can support our action—for example, an app that can send emails and an app that can send text messages.

Here's how you go about getting your app to run on a physical device.

1. Enable USB debugging on your device

On your device, open "Developer options" (in Android 4.0 onward, this is hidden by default). To enable "Developer options," go to Settings → About Phone and tap the build number seven times. When you return to the previous screen, you should now be able to see "Developer options."

Yep, seriously. →

Within "Developer options," turn on USB debugging.

You need to enable USB debugging. →

2. Set up your system to detect your device

If you're using a Mac, you can skip this step.

If you're using Windows, you need to install a USB driver. You can find the latest instructions here:

http://developer.android.com/tools/extras/oem-usb.html

If you're using Ubuntu Linux, you need to create a `udev` rules file. You can find the latest instructions on how to do this here:

http://developer.android.com/tools/device.html#setting-up

3. Plug your device into your computer with a USB cable

Your device may ask you if you want to accept an RSA key that allows USB debugging with your computer. If it does, you can check the "Always allow from this computer" option and choose OK to enable this.

→ **Specify action**
Create chooser

Running your app on a real device (continued)

4. Stop your app running on the emulator

Before you can run your app on a different device, you need to stop it running on the current one (in this case the emulator). To do this, choose Run → "Stop 'app'", or click on the "Stop 'app'" button in the toolbar.

Click on this button in Android Studio's toolbar to stop the app running on the current device.

5. Run your app on the physical device

Run the app by choosing Run → "Run 'app'". Android Studio will ask you to choose which device you want to run your app on, so select your device from the list of available devices and click OK. Android Studio will install the app on your device and launch it.

Here's our physical device. ——

Here's our virtual device.

And here's the app running on the physical device

You should find that your app looks about the same as when you ran it through the emulator. You'll probably find that your app installs and runs quicker too.

Now that you know how to run the apps you create on your own device, you're all set to test the latest changes to your app.

Test drive the app

Try running the app using the emulator, and then using your own device. The results you get will depend on how many activities you have on each that support using the Send action with text data.

If you have one activity

Clicking on the Send Message button will take you straight to that app.

We only have one activity available on the emulator that can send messages with text data, so when we click on the Send Message button, Android starts that activity.

Here's the message.

If you have more than one activity

Android displays a chooser and asks you to pick which one you want to use. It also asks you whether you want to use this activity just once or always. If you choose always, the next time you click on the Send Message button it uses the same activity by default.

We have lots of suitable activities available on our physical device. We decided to use the built-in Messages app. We selected the "always" option—great if we always want to use the same app, not so great if we want to use a different one each time.

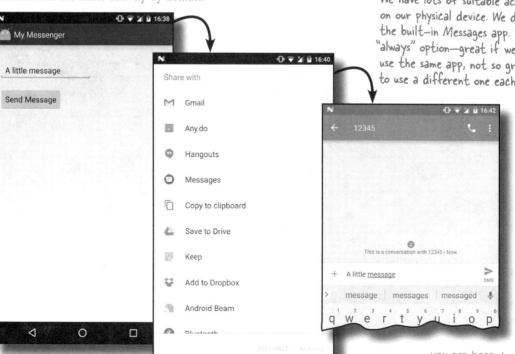

What if you ALWAYS want your users to choose an activity?

You've just seen that if there's more than one activity on your device that's capable of receiving your intent, Android automatically asks you to choose which activity you want to use. It even asks you whether you want to use this activity all the time or just on this occasion.

There's just one problem with this default behavior: what if you want to *guarantee* that users can choose an activity every time they click on the Send Message button? If they've chosen the option to always use Gmail, for instance, they won't be asked if they want to use Twitter next time.

Fortunately, there's a way around this. You can create a chooser that asks users to pick an activity without giving them the option to always use that activity.

> createChooser() allows you to specify a title for the chooser dialog, and doesn't give the user the option of selecting an activity to use by default. It also lets the user know if there are no matching activities by displaying a message.

Intent.createChooser() displays a chooser dialog

You can achieve this using the `Intent.createChooser()` method, which takes the intent you've already created and wraps it in a chooser dialog. When you use this method, the user isn't given the option of choosing a default activity—they get asked to choose one every time.

You call the `createChooser()` method like this:

This is the intent you created earlier.

```
Intent chosenIntent = Intent.createChooser(intent, "Send message via...");
```

You can pass in a title for the chooser that gets displayed at the top of the screen.

The method takes two parameters: an intent and an optional `String` title for the chooser dialog window. The `Intent` parameter needs to describe the types of activity you want the chooser to display. You can use the same intent we created earlier, as this specifies that we want to use `ACTION_SEND` with textual data.

The `createChooser()` method returns a brand-new `Intent`. This is a new explicit intent that's targeted at the activity chosen by the user. It includes any extra information supplied by the original intent, including any text.

To start the activity the user chose, you need to call:

```
startActivity(chosenIntent);
```

Over the next couple of pages we'll take a closer look at what happens when you call the `createChooser()` method.

What happens when you call createChooser()

Here's what happens when you run the following two lines of code:

```
Intent chosenIntent = Intent.createChooser(intent, "Send message via...");
startActivity(chosenIntent);
```

1 **The createChooser() method gets called.**

The method includes an intent that specifies the action and MIME type that's required.

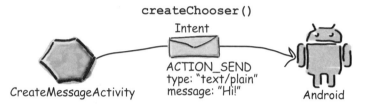

createChooser()
Intent

ACTION_SEND
type: "text/plain"
message: "Hi!"

CreateMessageActivity

Android

---

2 **Android checks which activities are able to receive the intent by looking at their intent filters.**

It matches on the actions, type of data, and categories they can support.

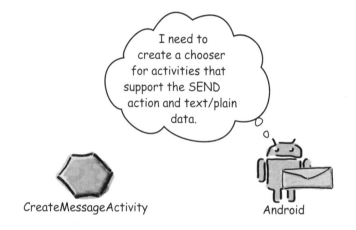

I need to create a chooser for activities that support the SEND action and text/plain data.

CreateMessageActivity

Android

---

3 **If more than one activity is able to receive the intent, Android displays an activity chooser dialog and asks the user which one to use.**

It doesn't give the user the option of always using a particular activity, and it displays "Send message via..." in the title.

If no activities are found, Android still displays the chooser but shows a message telling the user there are no apps that can perform the action.

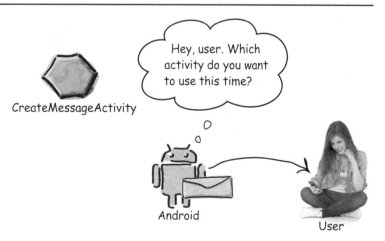

Hey, user. Which activity do you want to use this time?

CreateMessageActivity

Android

User

The story continues...

④ When the user chooses which activity she wants to use, Android returns a new explicit intent describing the chosen activity.

The new intent includes any extra information that was included in the original intent, such as any text.

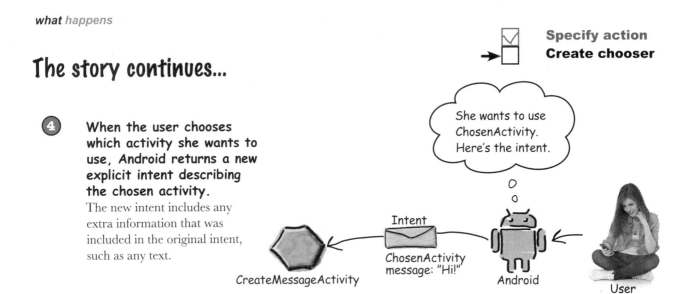

⑤ The activity asks Android to start the activity specified in the intent.

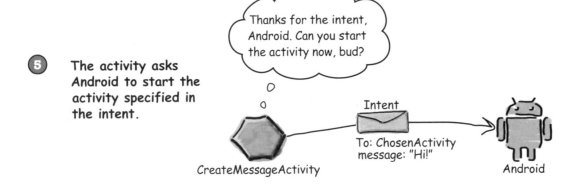

⑥ Android starts the activity specified by the intent, and then passes it the intent.

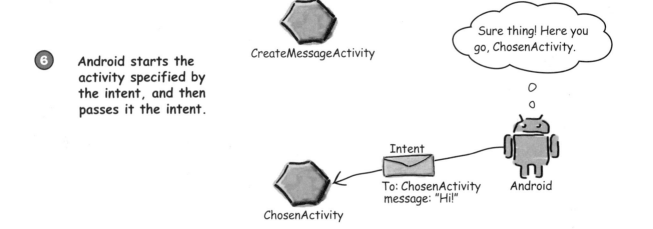

Change the code to create a chooser

Let's change the code so that the user gets asked which activity they want to use to send a message every time they click on the Send Message button. We'll add a String resource to *strings.xml* for the chooser dialog title, and we'll update the onSendMessage() method in *CreateMessageActivity.java* so that it calls the createChooser() method.

Update strings.xml...

We want the chooser dialog to have a title of "Send message via...". Add a String called "chooser" to *strings.xml*, and give it the value Send message via... (make sure to save your changes):

```
...
<string name="chooser">Send message via...</string>
...
```
This will be displayed in the chooser dialog.

MyMessenger
app/src/main
res
values
strings.xml

...and update the onSendMessage() method

We need to change the onSendMessage() method so that it retrieves the value of the chooser String resource in *strings.xml*, calls the createChooser() method, and then starts the activity the user chooses. Update your code as follows:

MyMessenger
app/src/main
java
com.hfad.mymessenger
CreateMessage
Activity.java

```
...
    //Call onSendMessage() when the button is clicked
    public void onSendMessage(View view) {
        EditText messageView = (EditText)findViewById(R.id.message);
        String messageText = messageView.getText().toString();
        Intent intent = new Intent(Intent.ACTION_SEND);
        intent.setType("text/plain");
        intent.putExtra(Intent.EXTRA_TEXT, messageText);
        String chooserTitle = getString(R.string.chooser);
        Intent chosenIntent = Intent.createChooser(intent, chooserTitle);
        startActivity(intent);
        startActivity(chosenIntent);
    }
...
```

Delete this line. → ~~startActivity(intent);~~

Get the chooser title.

Display the chooser dialog.

← Start the activity that the user selected.

The getString() method is used to get the value of a String resource. It takes one parameter, the ID of the resource (in our case, this is R.string.chooser):

```
getString(R.string.chooser);
```
← If you look in R.java, you'll find chooser in the inner class called string.

Now that we've updated the app, let's run the app to see our chooser in action.

Test drive the app

Save your changes, then try running the app again on the device or the emulator.

If you have one activity

Clicking on the Send Message button will take you straight to that activity just like before.

> There's no change here—
> Android continues to take
> you straight to the activity.

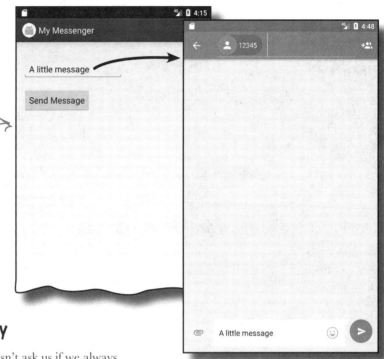

If you have more than one activity

Android displays a chooser, but this time it doesn't ask us if we always want to use the same activity. It also displays the value of the chooser String resource in the title.

> Here's the chooser we created
> with createChooser(). It no longer
> gives us the option of using a
> particular activity every time.

If you have NO matching activities

If you have no activities on your device that are capable of sending messages, the `createChooser()` method lets you know by displaying a message.

If you want to replicate this for yourself, try running the app in the emulator, and disable the built-in Messenger app that's on there.

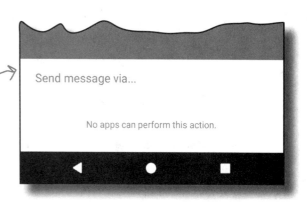

Send message via...

No apps can perform this action.

---

there are no Dumb Questions

Q: So I can run my apps in the emulator or on a physical device. Which is best?

A: Each one has its pros and cons.

If you run apps on your physical device, they tend to load a lot quicker than using the emulator. This approach is also useful if you're writing code that interacts with the device hardware.

The emulator allows you to run apps against many different versions of Android, screen resolutions, and device specifications. It saves you from buying lots of different devices. The key thing is to make sure you test your apps thoroughly using a mixture of the emulator and physical devices before releasing them to a wider audience.

Q: Should I use implicit or explicit intents?

A: It comes down to whether you need Android to use a specific activity to perform your action, or whether you just want the action done. As an example, suppose you wanted to send an email. If you don't care which email app the user uses to send it, just as long as the email gets sent, you'd use an implicit intent. On the other hand, if you needed to pass an intent to a particular activity in your app, you'd need to use an explicit intent to explicitly say which activity needs to receive the intent.

Q: You mentioned that an activity's intent filter can specify a category as well as an action. What's the difference between the two?

A: An action specifies what an activity can do, and the category gives extra detail. We've not gone into details about adding categories because you don't often need to specify a category when you create an intent.

Q: You say that the `createChooser()` method displays a message in the chooser if there are no activities that can handle the intent. What if I'd instead used the default Android chooser and passed an implicit intent to `startActivity()`?

A: If the `startActivity()` method is given an intent where there are no matching activities, an `ActivityNotFoundException` is thrown. You can check whether any activities on the device are able to receive the intent by calling the intent's `resolveActivity()` method and checking its return value. If its return value is null, no activities on the device are able to receive the intent, so you shouldn't call `startActivity()`.

Your Android Toolbox

You've got Chapter 3 under your belt and now you've added multi-activity apps and intents to your toolbox.

You can download the full code for the chapter from https://tinyurl.com/HeadFirstAndroid.

BULLET POINTS

- A **task** is two or more activities chained together.

- The `<EditText>` element defines an editable text field for entering text. It inherits from the Android `View` class.

- You can add a new activity in Android Studio by choosing File → New... → Activity.

- Each activity you create must have an entry in *AndroidManifest.xml*.

- An **intent** is a type of message that Android components use to communicate with one another.

- An explicit intent specifies the component the intent is targeted at. You create an explicit intent using `Intent intent = new Intent(this, Target.class);`.

- To start an activity, call `startActivity(intent)`. If no activities are found, it throws an `ActivityNotFoundException`.

- Use the `putExtra()` method to add extra information to an intent.

- Use the `getIntent()` method to retrieve the intent that started the activity.

- Use the `get*Extra()` methods to retrieve extra information associated with the intent. `getStringExtra()` retrieves a String, `getIntExtra()` retrieves an int, and so on.

- An activity action describes a standard operational action an activity can perform. For example, to send a message, use `Intent.ACTION_SEND`.

- To create an implicit intent that specifies an action, use `Intent intent = new Intent(action);`.

- To describe the type of data in an intent, use the `setType()` method.

- Android resolves intents based on the named component, action, type of data, and categories specified in the intent. It compares the contents of the intent with the intent filters in each app's *AndroidManifest.xml*. An activity must have a category of `DEFAULT` if it is to receive an implicit intent.

- The `createChooser()` method allows you to override the default Android activity chooser dialog. It lets you specify a title for the dialog, and doesn't give the user the option of setting a default activity. If no activities can receive the intent it is passed, it displays a message. The `createChooser()` method returns an `Intent`.

- You retrieve the value of a String resource using `getString(R.string.stringname);`.

4 the activity lifecycle

Being an Activity *

...so I told him that if he didn't onStop() soon, I'd onDestroy() him with a cattle prod.

Activities form the foundation of every Android app.

So far you've seen how to create activities, and made one activity start another using an intent. But *what's really going on beneath the hood?* In this chapter, we're going to dig a little deeper into **the activity lifecycle**. What happens when an activity is **created** and **destroyed**? Which methods get called when an activity is **made visible and appears in the foreground**, and which get called when the activity **loses the focus and is hidden**? And **how do you save and restore your activity's state**? Read on to find out.

How do activities really work?

So far you've seen how to create apps that interact with the user, and apps that use multiple activities to perform tasks. Now that you have these core skills under your belt, it's time to take a deeper look at how activities *actually work*. Here's a recap of what you know so far, with a few extra details thrown in.

⭐ **An app is a collection of activities, layouts, and other resources.**
One of these activities is the main activity for the app.

Each app has a main activity, as specified in the file AndroidManifest.xml.

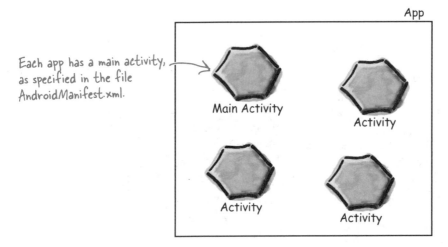

⭐ **By default, each app runs within its own process.**
This helps keep your apps safe and secure. You can read more about this in Appendix III (which covers the Android runtime, a.k.a. ART) at the back of this book.

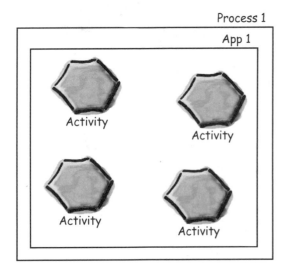

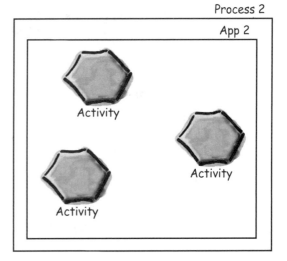

Your app can start an activity in another application by passing an intent with startActivity().
The Android system knows about all the device's installed apps and their activities, and uses the intent to start the correct activity.

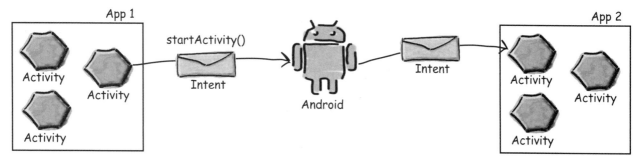

 When an activity needs to start, Android checks whether there's already a process for that app.
If one exists, Android runs the activity in that process. If one doesn't exist, Android creates one.

 When Android starts an activity, it calls its onCreate() method.
onCreate() is always run whenever an activity gets created.

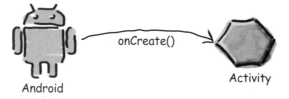

But there are still lots of things we don't yet know about how activities function. How long does an activity live for? What happens when your activity disappears from the screen? Is it still running? Is it still in memory? And what happens if your app gets interrupted by an incoming phone call? We want to be able to control the behavior of our activities in a *whole range of different circumstances*, but how?

The Stopwatch app

In this chapter, we're going to take a closer look at how activities work under the hood, common ways in which your apps can break, and how you can fix them using the activity lifecycle methods. We're going to explore the lifecycle methods using a simple Stopwatch app as an example.

The Stopwatch app consists of a single activity and a single layout. The layout includes a text view showing you how much time has passed, a Start button that starts the stopwatch, a Stop button that stops it, and a Reset button that resets the timer value to 0.

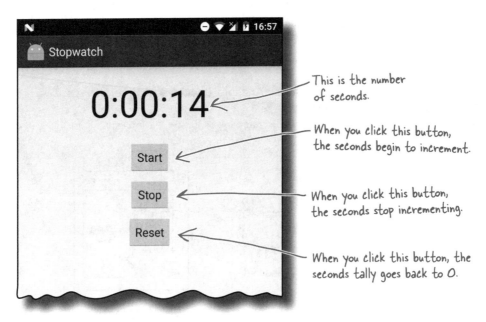

This is the number of seconds.

When you click this button, the seconds begin to increment.

When you click this button, the seconds stop incrementing.

When you click this button, the seconds tally goes back to 0.

Create a new project for the Stopwatch app

You have enough experience under your belt to build the app without much guidance from us. We're going to give you just enough code so you can build the app yourself, and then you can see what happens when you try to run it.

Start off by creating a new Android project for an application named "Stopwatch" with a company domain of "hfad.com", making the package name com.hfad.stopwatch. The minimum SDK should be API 19 so it can run on most devices. You'll need an empty activity called "StopwatchActivity" and a layout called "activity_stopwatch". **Make sure you uncheck the Backwards Compatibility (AppCompat) checkbox.**

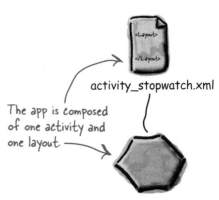

activity_stopwatch.xml

The app is composed of one activity and one layout.

StopwatchActivity.java

Add String resources

We're going to use three String values in our stopwatch layout, one for the text value of each button. These values are String resources, so they need to be added to *strings.xml*. Add the String values below to your version of *strings.xml*:

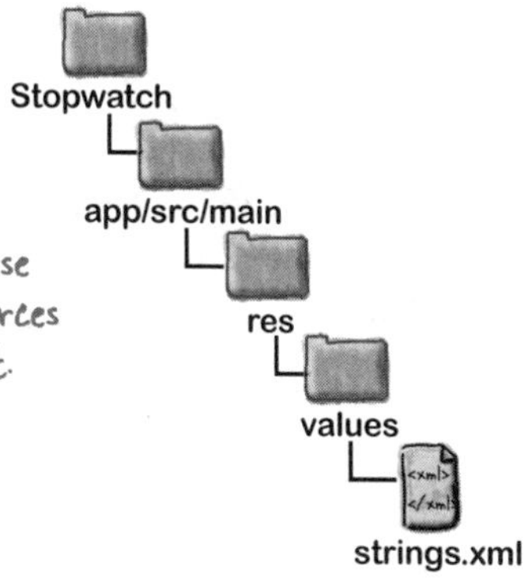

```
...
    <string name="start">Start</string>
    <string name="stop">Stop</string>
    <string name="reset">Reset</string>
...
```

We'll use these String resources in our layout.

Stopwatch
app/src/main
res
values
strings.xml

Next, let's update the code for our layout.

Update the stopwatch layout code

Here's the XML for the layout. It describes a single text view that's used to display the timer, and three buttons to control the stopwatch. Replace the XML currently in *activity_stopwatch.xml* with the XML shown here:

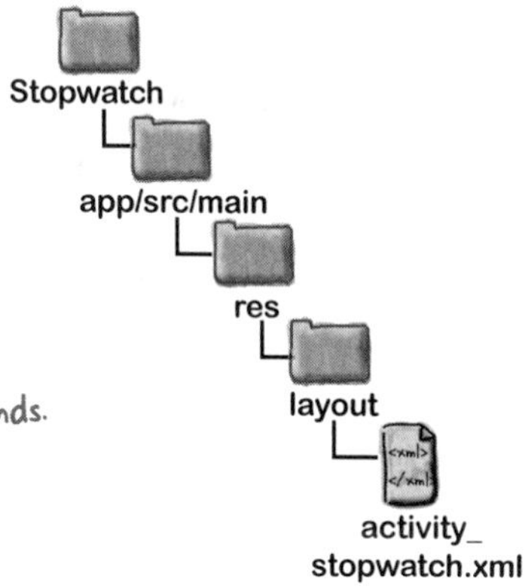

```xml
<?xml version="1.0" encoding="utf-8"?>
<LinearLayout
    xmlns:android="http://schemas.android.com/apk/res/android"
    xmlns:tools="http://schemas.android.com/tools"
    android:layout_width="match_parent"
    android:layout_height="match_parent"
    android:orientation="vertical"
    android:padding="16dp"
    tools:context=".StopwatchActivity">

    <TextView
        android:id="@+id/time_view"
        android:layout_width="wrap_content"
        android:layout_height="wrap_content"
        android:layout_gravity="center_horizontal"
        android:textAppearance="@android:style/TextAppearance.Large"
        android:textSize="56sp" />
```

Stopwatch
app/src/main
res
layout
activity_
stopwatch.xml

We'll use this text view to display the number of seconds.

These attributes make the stopwatch timer nice and big.

The layout code continues over the page.

The layout code (continued)

```xml
<Button
    android:id="@+id/start_button"          ← This code is for the Start button.
    android:layout_width="wrap_content"
    android:layout_height="wrap_content"
    android:layout_gravity="center_horizontal"
    android:layout_marginTop="20dp"
    android:onClick="onClickStart"           ← When it gets clicked, the
    android:text="@string/start" />            Start button calls the
                                               onClickStart() method.
<Button
    android:id="@+id/stop_button"           ← This is for the Stop button.
    android:layout_width="wrap_content"
    android:layout_height="wrap_content"
    android:layout_gravity="center_horizontal"
    android:layout_marginTop="8dp"
    android:onClick="onClickStop"            ← When it gets clicked, the
    android:text="@string/stop" />             Stop button calls the
                                               onClickStop() method.

<Button
    android:id="@+id/reset_button"          ← This is for the Reset button.
    android:layout_width="wrap_content"
    android:layout_height="wrap_content"
    android:layout_gravity="center_horizontal"
    android:layout_marginTop="8dp"
    android:onClick="onClickReset"           ← When it gets clicked, the
    android:text="@string/reset" />            Reset button calls the
                                               onClickReset() method.
</LinearLayout>
```

Stopwatch
 └ app/src/main
    └ res
       └ layout
          └ activity_stopwatch.xml

The layout is now done! Next, let's move on to the activity.

Do this!

Make sure you update the layout and *strings. xml* in your app before continuing.

How the activity code will work

The layout defines three buttons that we'll use to control the stopwatch. Each button uses its onClick attribute to specify which method in the activity should run when the button is clicked. When the Start button is clicked, the onClickStart() method gets called, when the Stop button is clicked the onClickStop() method gets called, and when the Reset button is clicked the onClickReset() method gets called. We'll use these methods to start, stop, and reset the stopwatch.

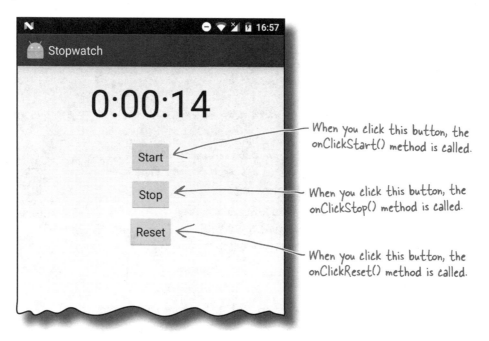

When you click this button, the onClickStart() method is called.

When you click this button, the onClickStop() method is called.

When you click this button, the onClickReset() method is called.

We'll update the stopwatch using a method we'll create called runTimer(). The runTimer() method will run code every second to check whether the stopwatch is running, and, if it is, increment the number of seconds and display the number of seconds in the text view.

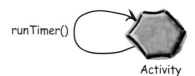

runTimer()

Activity

To help us with this, we'll use two private variables to record the state of the stopwatch. We'll use an int called seconds to track how many seconds have passed since the stopwatch started running, and a boolean called running to record whether the stopwatch is currently running.

We'll start by writing the code for the buttons, and then we'll look at the runTimer() method.

Add code for the buttons

When the user clicks on the Start button, we'll set the `running` variable to `true` so that the stopwatch will start. When the user clicks on the Stop button, we'll set `running` to `false` so that the stopwatch stops running. If the user clicks on the Reset button, we'll set `running` to `false` and `seconds` to 0 so that the stopwatch is reset and stops running.

To do all that, replace the contents of *StopwatchActivity.java* with the code below:

Start → running=true

Stop → running=false

Reset → running=false / seconds=0

```java
package com.hfad.stopwatch;

import android.app.Activity;
import android.os.Bundle;
import android.view.View;
```

Make sure your activity extends the Activity class.

Stopwatch

app/src/main

java

com.hfad.stopwatch

Stopwatch Activity.java

```java
public class StopwatchActivity extends Activity {

    private int seconds = 0;
    private boolean running;
```

Use the seconds and running variables to record the number of seconds passed and whether the stopwatch is running.

```java
    @Override
    protected void onCreate(Bundle savedInstanceState) {
        super.onCreate(savedInstanceState);
        setContentView(R.layout.activity_stopwatch);
    }


    //Start the stopwatch running when the Start button is clicked.
    public void onClickStart(View view) {
        running = true;
    }
```

This gets called when the Start button is clicked.

Start the stopwatch.

```java
    //Stop the stopwatch running when the Stop button is clicked.
    public void onClickStop(View view) {
        running = false;
    }
```

This gets called when the Stop button is clicked.

Stop the stopwatch.

```java
    //Reset the stopwatch when the Reset button is clicked.
    public void onClickReset(View view) {
        running = false;
        seconds = 0;
    }
}
```

This gets called when the Reset button is clicked.

Stop the stopwatch and set the seconds to 0.

The runTimer() method

The next thing we need to do is create the runTimer() method.
This method will get a reference to the text view in the layout; format
the contents of the seconds variable into hours, minutes, and
seconds; and then display the results in the text view. If the running
variable is set to true, it will increment the seconds variable.

The code for the runTimer() method is below. We'll add it to
StopwatchActivity.java in a few pages:

```
private void runTimer() {
    final TextView timeView = (TextView) findViewById(R.id.time_view);        ← Get the text view.
    ...
    int hours = seconds/3600;
    int minutes = (seconds%3600)/60;
    int secs = seconds%60;                                    ← Format the seconds into
    String time = String.format(Locale.getDefault(),            hours, minutes, and seconds.
                "%d:%02d:%02d", hours, minutes, secs);          This is plain Java code.
    timeView.setText(time);        ← Set the text view text.
    if (running) {
        seconds++;        ← If running is true, increment
    }                       the seconds variable.
    ...
}
```

We've left out a bit of code here. We'll look at it on the next page.

Stopwatch
└ app/src/main
  └ java
    └ com.hfad.stopwatch
      └ Stopwatch Activity.java

We need this code to keep looping so that it increments the seconds
variable and updates the text view every second. We need to do this in
such a way that we don't block the main Android thread.

In non-Android Java programs, you can perform tasks like this
using a background thread. In Androidville, that approach
won't work—only the main Android thread can update the
user interface, and if any other thread tries to do so, you get a
CalledFromWrongThreadException.

The solution is to use a Handler. We'll look at this technique on the
next page.

Handlers allow you to schedule code

A `Handler` is an Android class you can use to schedule code that should be run at some point in the future. You can also use it to post code that needs to run on a different thread than the main Android thread. In our case, we're going to use a `Handler` to schedule the stopwatch code to run every second.

To use the `Handler`, you wrap the code you wish to schedule in a `Runnable` object, and then use the `Handler post()` and `postDelayed()` methods to specify when you want the code to run. Let's take a closer look at these mehods.

The post() method

The `post()` method posts code that needs to be run as soon as possible (which is usually almost immediately). This method takes one parameter, an object of type `Runnable`. A `Runnable` object in Androidville is just like a `Runnable` in plain old Java: a job you want to run. You put the code you want to run in the `Runnable`'s `run()` method, and the `Handler` will make sure the code is run as soon as possible. Here's what the method looks like:

```
final Handler handler = new Handler();
handler.post(Runnable);
```
← *You put the code you want to run in the Runnable's run() method.*

The postDelayed() method

The `postDelayed()` method works in a similar way to the `post()` method except that you use it to post code that should be run in the future. The `postDelayed()` method takes two parameters: a `Runnable` and a `long`. The `Runnable` contains the code you want to run in its `run()` method, and the `long` specifies the number of milliseconds you wish to delay the code by. The code will run as soon as possible after the delay. Here's what the method looks like:

```
final Handler handler = new Handler();
handler.postDelayed(Runnable, long);
```
← *Use this method to delay running code by a specified number of milliseconds.*

On the next page, we'll use these methods to update the stopwatch every second.

The full runTimer() code

To update the stopwatch, we're going to repeatedly schedule code using the Handler with a delay of 1 second each time. Each time the code runs, we'll increment the seconds variable and update the text view.

Here's the full code for the runTimer() method, which we'll add to *StopwatchActivity.java* in a couple of pages:

```java
private void runTimer() {
    final TextView timeView = (TextView)findViewById(R.id.time_view);
    final Handler handler = new Handler();    ←— Create a new Handler.
    handler.post(new Runnable() {    ←— Call the post() method, passing in a new Runnable. The post()
        @Override                        method processes code without a delay, so the code in the
        public void run() {              Runnable will run almost immediately.
            int hours = seconds/3600;
            int minutes = (seconds%3600)/60;
            int secs = seconds%60;                          The Runnable run()
            String time = String.format(Locale.getDefault(), ←— method contains the code
                    "%d:%02d:%02d", hours, minutes, secs);     you want to run—in our
            timeView.setText(time);                            case, the code to update
            if (running) {                                     the text view.
                seconds++;
            }
            handler.postDelayed(this, 1000);  ←— Post the code in the Runnable to be run again
        }                                        after a delay of 1,000 milliseconds. As this line
    });                                          of code is included in the Runnable run() method,
}                                                it will keep getting called.
```

Using the post() and postDelayed() methods in this way means that the code will run as soon as possible after the required delay, which in practice means almost immediately. While this means the code will lag slightly over time, it's accurate enough for the purposes of exploring the lifecycle methods in this chapter.

We want the runTimer() method to start running when StopwatchActivity gets created, so we'll call it in the activity onCreate() method:

```java
protected void onCreate(Bundle savedInstanceState) {
    ...
    runTimer();
}
```

We'll show you the full code for StopwatchActivity on the next page.

The full StopwatchActivity code

Here's the full code for *StopwatchActivity.java*. Update your code to match our changes below.

```
package com.hfad.stopwatch;

import android.app.Activity;
import android.os.Bundle;
import android.view.View;
import java.util.Locale;
import android.os.Handler;
import android.widget.TextView;
```

We're using these extra classes so we need to import them.

```
public class StopwatchActivity extends Activity {
    //Number of seconds displayed on the stopwatch.
    private int seconds = 0;
    //Is the stopwatch running?
    private boolean running;
```

Use the seconds and running variables to record the number of seconds passed and whether the stopwatch is running.

```
    @Override
    protected void onCreate(Bundle savedInstanceState) {
        super.onCreate(savedInstanceState);
        setContentView(R.layout.activity_stopwatch);
        runTimer();
    }
```

We're using a separate method to update the stopwatch. We're starting it when the activity is created.

```
    //Start the stopwatch running when the Start button is clicked.
    public void onClickStart(View view) {
        running = true;
    }
```

This gets called when the Start button is clicked.

Start the stopwatch.

```
    //Stop the stopwatch running when the Stop button is clicked.
    public void onClickStop(View view) {
        running = false;
    }
```

This gets called when the Stop button is clicked.

Stop the stopwatch.

The folder structure:

Stopwatch
→ app/src/main
→ java
→ com.hfad.stopwatch
→ Stopwatch
Activity.java

The activity code (continued)

```
//Reset the stopwatch when the Reset button is clicked.
public void onClickReset(View view) {
    running = false;
    seconds = 0;
}
```

This gets called when the Reset button is clicked.

Stop the stopwatch and set the seconds to 0.

Stopwatch

app/src/main

java

com.hfad.stopwatch

Stopwatch Activity.java

```
//Sets the number of seconds on the timer.
private void runTimer() {
    final TextView timeView = (TextView)findViewById(R.id.time_view);
    final Handler handler = new Handler();
    handler.post(new Runnable() {
        @Override
        public void run() {
            int hours = seconds/3600;
            int minutes = (seconds%3600)/60;
            int secs = seconds%60;
            String time = String.format(Locale.getDefault(),
                    "%d:%02d:%02d", hours, minutes, secs);
            timeView.setText(time);
            if (running) {
                seconds++;
            }
            handler.postDelayed(this, 1000);
        }
    });
}
```

Get the text view.

Use a Handler to post code.

Format the seconds into hours, minutes, and seconds.

Set the text view text.

If running is true, increment the seconds variable.

Post the code again with a delay of 1 second.

Let's look at what happens when the code runs.

Do this!

Make sure you update your activity code to reflect these changes.

What happens when you run the app

① **The user decides she wants to run the app.**
On her device, she clicks on the app's icon.

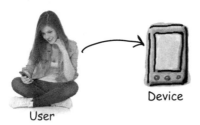

User   Device

② **An intent is constructed to start this activity using startActivity(intent).**
The *AndroidManifest.xml* file for the app specifies which activity to use as the launch activity.

AndroidManifest.xml   Android

③ **Android checks to see whether there's already a process running for the app, and if not, creates a new process.**
It then creates a new activity object—in this case, for StopwatchActivity.

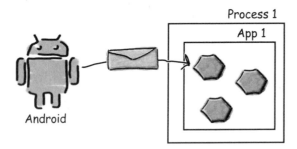

Android

Process 1

App 1

The story continues

④ **The onCreate() method in the activity gets called.**
The method includes a call to setContentView(), specifying a layout, and then starts the stopwatch with runTimer().

⑤ **When the onCreate() method finishes, the layout gets displayed on the device.**
The runTimer() method uses the seconds variable to determine what text to display in the text view, and uses the running variable to determine whether to increment the number of seconds. As running is initially false, the number of seconds isn't incremented.

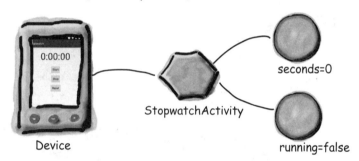

---
there are no
Dumb Questions

Q: Why does Android run each app inside a separate process?

A: For security and stability. This approach prevents one app from accessing the data of another. It also means if one app crashes, it won't take others down with it.

Q: Why have an onCreate() method in our activity? Why not just put that code inside a constructor?

A: Android needs to set up the environment for the activity after it's constructed. Once the environment is ready, Android calls onCreate(). That's why code to set up the screen goes inside onCreate() instead of a constructor.

Q: Couldn't I just write a loop in onCreate() to keep updating the timer?

A: No, onCreate() needs to finish before the screen will appear. An endless loop would prevent that from happening.

Q: runTimer() looks really complicated. Do I really need to do all this?

A: It's a little complex, but whenever you need to post code that runs in a loop, the code will look similar to runTimer().

Test drive the app

When we run the app in the emulator, the app works great. We can start, stop, and reset the stopwatch without any problems at all—the app works just as you'd expect.

> These buttons work as you'd expect. The Start button starts the stopwatch, the Stop button stops it, and the Reset button sets the stopwatch back to 0.

But there's just one problem...

When we ran the app on a physical device, the app worked OK until someone rotated the device. When the device was rotated, the stopwatch set itself back to 0.

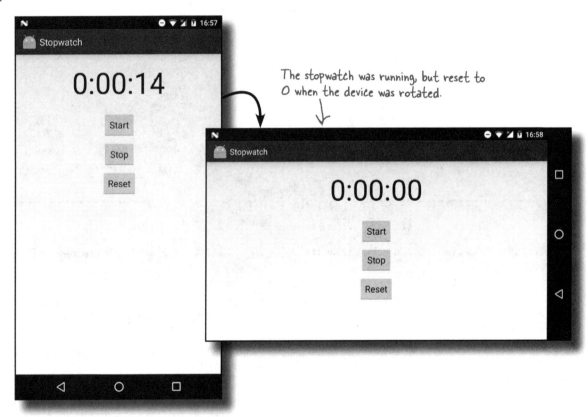

> The stopwatch was running, but reset to 0 when the device was rotated.

In Androidville, it's surprisingly common for apps to break when you rotate the device. Before we fix the problem, let's take a closer look at what caused it.

What just happened?

So why did the app break when the user rotated the screen?
Let's take a closer look at what really happened.

1 **The user starts the app, and clicks on the Start button to set the stopwatch going.**

The runTimer() method starts incrementing the number of seconds displayed in the time_view text view using the seconds and running variables.

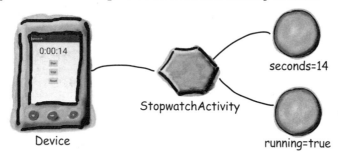

2 **The user rotates the device.**

Android sees that the screen orientation and screen size has changed, and it destroys the activity, including any variables used by the runTimer() method.

3 **StopwatchActivity is then recreated.**

The onCreate() method runs again, and the runTimer() method gets called. As the activity has been recreated, the seconds and running variables are set to their default values.

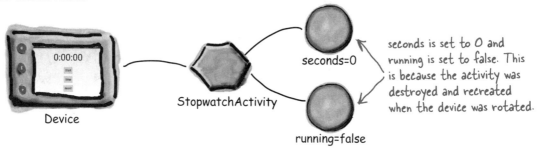

seconds is set to 0 and running is set to false. This is because the activity was destroyed and recreated when the device was rotated.

Rotating the screen changes the device configuration

When Android runs your app and starts an activity, it takes into account the **device configuration**. By this we mean the configuration of the physical device (such as the screen size, screen orientation, and whether there's a keyboard attached) and also configuration options specified by the user (such as the locale).

Android needs to know what the device configuration is when it starts an activity because the configuration can impact what resources are needed for the application. A different layout might need to be used if the device screen is landscape rather than portrait, for instance, and a different set of String values might need to be used if the locale is France.

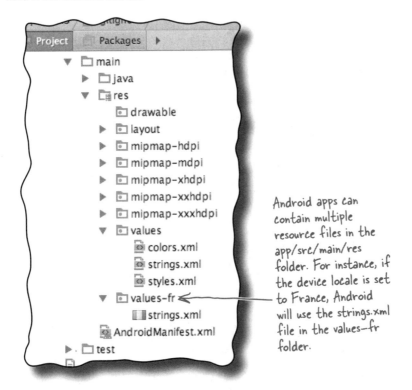

Android apps can contain multiple resource files in the app/src/main/res folder. For instance, if the device locale is set to France, Android will use the strings.xml file in the values-fr folder.

The device configuration includes options specified by the user (such as the locale), and options relating to the physical device (such as the orientation and screen size). A change to any of these options results in the activity being destroyed and then recreated.

When the device configuration changes, anything that displays a user interface needs to be updated to match the new configuration. If you rotate your device, Android spots that the screen orientation and screen size have changed, and classes this as a change to the device configuration. It destroys the current activity, and then recreates it so that resources appropriate to the new configuration get picked up.

The states of an activity

When Android creates and destroys an activity, the activity moves from being launched to running to being destroyed.

The main state of an activity is when it's *running* or *active*. An activity is running when it's in the foreground of the screen, it has the focus, and the user can interact with it. The activity spends most of its life in this state. An activity starts running after it has been launched, and at the end of its life, the activity is *destroyed*.

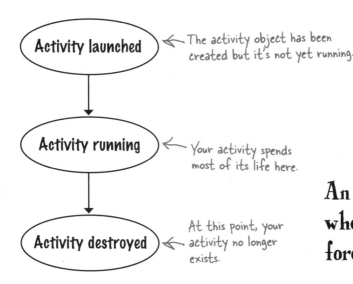

Activity launched ← The activity object has been created but it's not yet running.

Activity running ← Your activity spends most of its life here.

Activity destroyed ← At this point, your activity no longer exists.

An activity is running when it's in the foreground of the screen.

When an activity moves from being launched to being destroyed, it triggers key activity lifecycle methods: the `onCreate()` and `onDestroy()` methods. These are lifecycle methods that your activity inherits, and which you can override if necessary.

The `onCreate()` method gets called immediately after your activity is launched. This method is where you do all your normal activity setup such as calling `setContentView()`. You should always override this method. If you *don't* override it, you won't be able to tell Android what layout your activity should use.

The `onDestroy()` method is the final call you get before the activity is destroyed. There are a number of situations in which an activity can get destroyed—for example, if it's been told to finish, if the activity is being recreated due to a change in device configuration, or if Android has decided to destroy the activity in order to save space.

We'll take a closer look at how these methods fit into the activity states on the next page.

onCreate() gets called when the activity is first created, and it's where you do your normal activity setup.

onDestroy() gets called just before your activity gets destroyed.

The activity lifecycle: from create to destroy

Here's an overview of the activity lifecycle from birth to death. As you'll see later in the chapter, we've left out some of the details, but at this point we're just focusing on the onCreate() and onDestroy() methods.

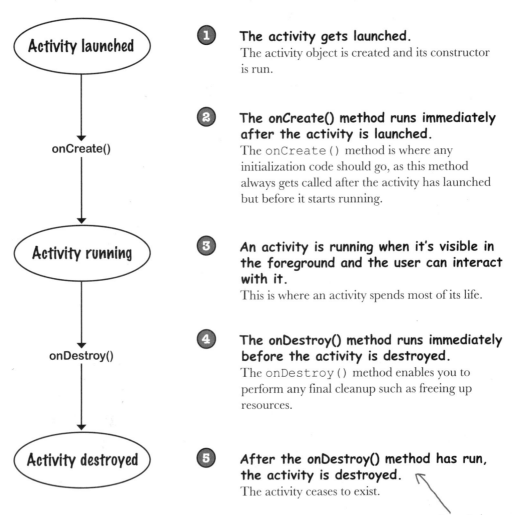

1 **The activity gets launched.**
The activity object is created and its constructor is run.

2 **The onCreate() method runs immediately after the activity is launched.**
The onCreate() method is where any initialization code should go, as this method always gets called after the activity has launched but before it starts running.

3 **An activity is running when it's visible in the foreground and the user can interact with it.**
This is where an activity spends most of its life.

4 **The onDestroy() method runs immediately before the activity is destroyed.**
The onDestroy() method enables you to perform any final cleanup such as freeing up resources.

5 **After the onDestroy() method has run, the activity is destroyed.**
The activity ceases to exist.

If your device is extremely low on memory, onDestroy() might not get called before the activity is destroyed.

The onCreate() and onDestroy() methods are two of the activity lifecycle methods. So where do these methods come from?

Your activity inherits the lifecycle methods

As you saw earlier in the book, your activity extends the `android.app.Activity` class. It's this class that gives your activity access to the Android lifecycle methods. Here's a diagram showing the class hierarchy:

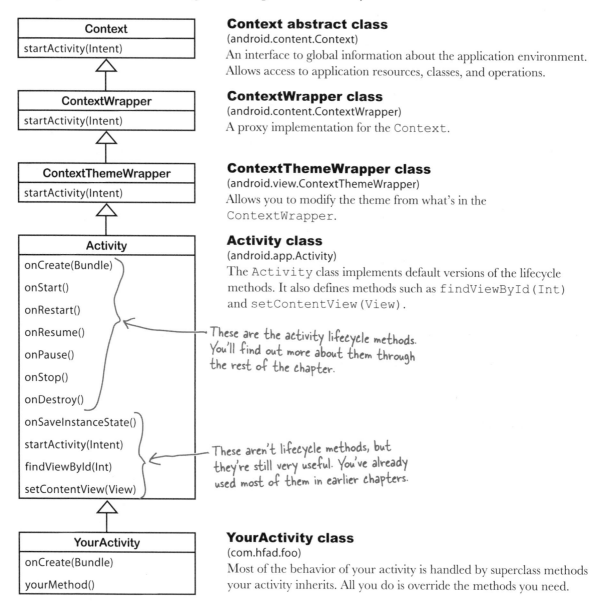

Context abstract class
(android.content.Context)
An interface to global information about the application environment. Allows access to application resources, classes, and operations.

ContextWrapper class
(android.content.ContextWrapper)
A proxy implementation for the `Context`.

ContextThemeWrapper class
(android.view.ContextThemeWrapper)
Allows you to modify the theme from what's in the `ContextWrapper`.

Activity class
(android.app.Activity)
The `Activity` class implements default versions of the lifecycle methods. It also defines methods such as `findViewById(Int)` and `setContentView(View)`.

These are the activity lifecycle methods. You'll find out more about them through the rest of the chapter.

These aren't lifecycle methods, but they're still very useful. You've already used most of them in earlier chapters.

YourActivity class
(com.hfad.foo)
Most of the behavior of your activity is handled by superclass methods your activity inherits. All you do is override the methods you need.

Now that you know more about the activity lifecycle methods, let's see how you deal with device configuration changes.

Save the current state...

As you saw, our app went wrong when the user rotated the screen. The activity was destroyed and recreated, which meant that local variables used by the activity were lost. So how do we get around this issue?

The best way of dealing with configuration changes is to save the current state of the activity, and then reinstate it in the onCreate() method of the activity.

To save the activity's current state, you need to implement the onSaveInstanceState() method. This method gets called before the activity gets destroyed, which means you get an opportunity to save any values you want to retain before they get lost.

The onSaveInstanceState() method takes one parameter, a Bundle. A Bundle allows you to gather together different types of data into a single object:

```
public void onSaveInstanceState(Bundle savedInstanceState) {

}
```

The onCreate() method gets passed the Bundle as a parameter. This means that if you add the values of the running and seconds variables to the Bundle, the onCreate() method will be able to pick them up when the activity gets recreated. To do this, you use Bundle methods to add name/value pairs to the Bundle. These methods take the form:

```
bundle.put*("name", value)
```

where bundle is the name of the Bundle, * is the type of value you want to save, and name and value are the name and value of the data. As an example, to add the seconds int value to the Bundle, you'd use:

```
bundle.putInt("seconds", seconds);
```

You can save multiple name/value pairs of data to the Bundle.

Here's our onSaveInstanceState() method in full (we'll add it to *StopwatchActivity.java* a couple of pages ahead):

```
@Override
public void onSaveInstanceState(Bundle savedInstanceState) {
    savedInstanceState.putInt("seconds", seconds);
    savedInstanceState.putBoolean("running", running);
}
```

Save the values of the seconds and running variables to the Bundle.

Once you've saved variable values to the Bundle, you can use them in our onCreate() method.

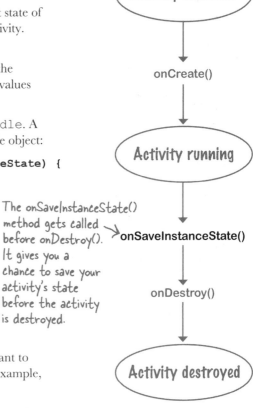

Activity launched

onCreate()

Activity running

The onSaveInstanceState() method gets called before onDestroy(). It gives you a chance to save your activity's state before the activity is destroyed. → **onSaveInstanceState()**

onDestroy()

Activity destroyed

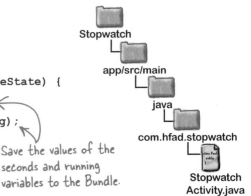

Stopwatch

app/src/main

java

com.hfad.stopwatch

Stopwatch Activity.java

...then restore the state in onCreate()

As we said earlier, the onCreate() method takes one parameter, a Bundle. If the activity's being created from scratch, this parameter will be null. If, however, the activity's being recreated and there's been a prior call to onSaveInstanceState(), the Bundle object used by onSaveInstanceState() will get passed to the activity:

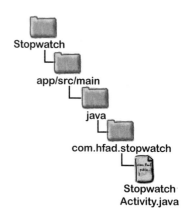

Stopwatch

app/src/main

java

com.hfad.stopwatch

Stopwatch
Activity.java

```
protected void onCreate(Bundle savedInstanceState) {
    ...
}
```

You can get values from Bundle by using methods of the form:

bundle.get*("name"); — Instead of *, use Int, String, and so on, to specify the type of data you want to get.

where bundle is the name of the Bundle, * is the type of value you want to get, and name is the name of the name/value pair you specified on the previous page. As an example, to get the seconds value from the Bundle, you'd use:

int seconds = bundle.getInt("seconds");

Putting all of this together, here's what our onCreate() method now looks like (we'll add this to *StopwatchActivity.java* on the next page):

```
protected void onCreate(Bundle savedInstanceState) {
    super.onCreate(savedInstanceState);
    setContentView(R.layout.activity_stopwatch);
    if (savedInstanceState != null) {
        seconds = savedInstanceState.getInt("seconds");
        running = savedInstanceState.getBoolean("running");
    }
    runTimer();
}
```

Retrieve the values of the seconds and running variables from the Bundle.

We'll look at the full code to save and restore StopwatchActivity's state on the next page.

The updated StopwatchActivity code

We've updated our `StopwatchActivity` code so that
if the user rotates the device, its state gets saved via the
`onSaveInstanceState()` method, and restored via the
`onCreate()` method. Update your version of *StopwatchActivity.java*
to include our changes (below in bold):

```
...

public class StopwatchActivity extends Activity {
    //Number of seconds displayed on the stopwatch.
    private int seconds = 0;
    //Is the stopwatch running?
    private boolean running;

    @Override
    protected void onCreate(Bundle savedInstanceState) {
        super.onCreate(savedInstanceState);
        setContentView(R.layout.activity_stopwatch);
        if (savedInstanceState != null) {
            seconds = savedInstanceState.getInt("seconds");
            running = savedInstanceState.getBoolean("running");
        }
        runTimer();
    }

    @Override
    public void onSaveInstanceState(Bundle savedInstanceState) {
        savedInstanceState.putInt("seconds", seconds);
        savedInstanceState.putBoolean("running", running);
    }
    ...
```

Restore the activity's state by getting values from the Bundle.

Save the state of the variables in the activity's onSaveInstanceState() method.

We've left out some of the activity code, as we don't need to change it.

So how does this work in practice?

Stopwatch → app/src/main → java → com.hfad.stopwatch → Stopwatch Activity.java

What happens when you run the app

1 **The user starts the app, and clicks on the Start button to set the stopwatch going.**
The runTimer() method starts incrementing the number of seconds displayed in the time_view text view.

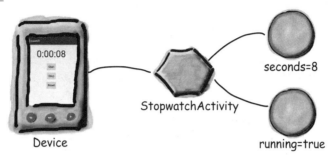

2 **The user rotates the device.**
Android views this as a configuration change, and gets ready to destroy the activity. Before the activity is destroyed, onSaveInstanceState() gets called. The onSaveInstanceState() method saves the seconds and running values to a Bundle.

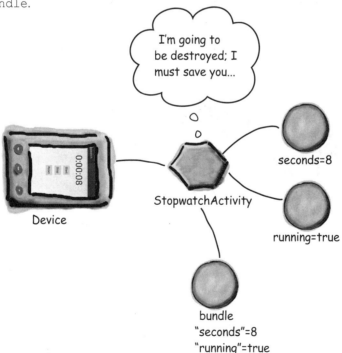

The story continues

3 **Android destroys the activity, and then recreates it.**
The onCreate() method gets called, and the Bundle gets passed to it.

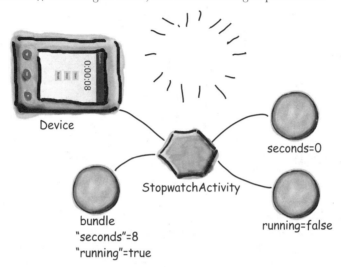

4 **The Bundle contains the values of the seconds and running variables as they were before the activity was destroyed.**
Code in the onCreate() method sets the current variables to the values in the Bundle.

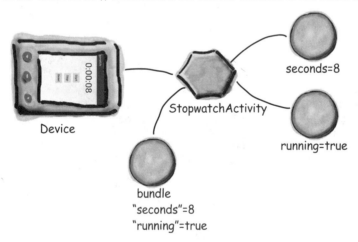

5 **The runTimer() method gets called, and the timer picks up where it left off.**
The running stopwatch gets displayed on the device and continues to increment.

Test drive the app

Make the changes to your activity code, then run the app. When you click on the Start button, the timer starts, and it continues when you rotate the device.

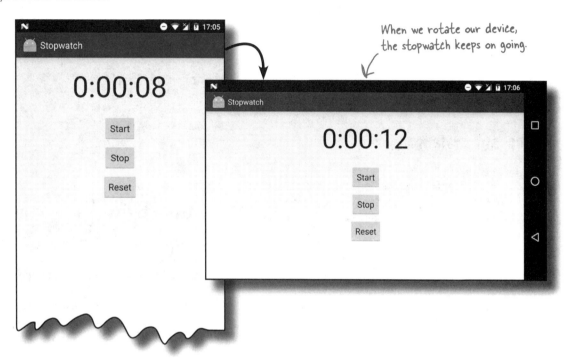

When we rotate our device, the stopwatch keeps on going.

---

there are no
Dumb Questions

Q: Why does Android want to recreate an activity just because I rotated the screen?

A: The `onCreate()` method is normally used to set up the screen. If your code in `onCreate()` depended upon the screen configuration (for example, if you had different layouts for landscape and portrait), then you would want `onCreate()` to be called every time the configuration changed. Also, if the user changed their locale, you might want to recreate the UI in the local language.

Q: Why doesn't Android automatically store every instance variable automatically? Why do I have to write all of that code myself?

A: You might not want every instance variable stored. For example, you might have a variable that stores the current screen width. You would want that variable to be recalculated the next time `onCreate()` is called.

Q: Is a `Bundle` some sort of Java map?

A: No, but it's designed to work like a `java.util.Map`. A `Bundle` has additional abilities compared to a `Map`. `Bundle`s can be sent between processes, for example. That's really useful, because it allows the Android OS to stay in touch with the state of an activity.

There's more to an activity's life than create and destroy

So far we've looked at the create and destroy parts of the activity lifecycle (and a little bit in between), and you've seen how to deal with configuration changes such as screen orientation. But there are other events in an activity's life that you might want to deal with to get the app to behave in the way you want.

As an example, suppose the stopwatch is running and you get a phone call. Even though the stopwatch isn't visible, it will continue running. But what if you want the stopwatch to stop while it's ← hidden, and resume once the app is visible again?

Even if you don't really want your stopwatch to behave like this, just play along with us. It's a great excuse to look at more lifecycle methods.

Start, stop, and restart

Fortunately, it's easy to handle actions that relate to an activity's visibility if you use the right lifecycle methods. In addition to the `onCreate()` and `onDestroy()` methods, which deal with the overall lifecycle of the activity, there are other lifecycle methods that deal with an activity's visibility.

Specifically, there are three key lifecycle methods that deal with when an activity becomes visible or invisible to the user: `onStart()`, `onStop()`, and `onRestart()`. Just as with `onCreate()` and `onDestroy()`, your activity inherits them from the Android `Activity` class.

`onStart()` gets called when your activity becomes visible to the user.

`onStop()` gets called when your activity has stopped being visible to the user. This might be because it's completely hidden by another activity that's appeared on top of it, or because the activity is going to be destroyed. If `onStop()` is called because the activity's going to be destroyed, `onSaveInstanceState()` gets called before `onStop()`.

`onRestart()` gets called after your activity has been made invisible, before it gets made visible again.

We'll take a closer look at how these fit in with the `onCreate()` and `onDestroy()` methods on the next page.

An activity has a state of stopped if it's completely hidden by another activity and isn't visible to the user. The activity still exists in the background and maintains all state information.

The activity lifecycle: the visible lifetime

Let's build on the lifecycle diagram you saw earlier in the chapter, this time including the onStart(), onStop(), and onRestart() methods (the bits you need to focus on are in bold):

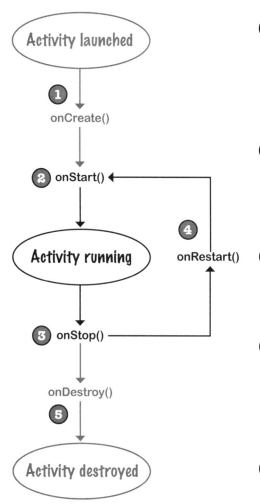

1 **The activity gets launched, and the onCreate() method runs.**
Any activity initialization code in the onCreate() method runs. At this point, the activity isn't yet visible, as no call to onStart() has been made.

2 **The onStart() method runs. It gets called when the activity is about to become visible.**
After the onStart() method has run, the user can see the activity on the screen.

3 **The onStop() method runs when the activity stops being visible to the user.**
After the onStop() method has run, the activity is no longer visible.

4 **If the activity becomes visible to the user again, the onRestart() method gets called followed by onStart().**
The activity may go through this cycle many times if the activity repeatedly becomes invisible and then visible again.

5 **Finally, the activity is destroyed.**
The onStop() method will get called before onDestroy().

We need to implement two more lifecycle methods

There are two things we need to do to update our Stopwatch app. First, we need to implement the activity's onStop() method so that the stopwatch stops running when the app isn't visible. Once we've done that, we need to implement the onStart() method so that the stopwatch starts again when the app is visible. Let's start with the onStop() method.

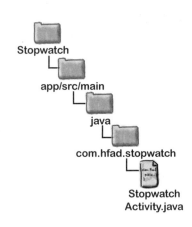

Stopwatch
└ app/src/main
  └ java
    └ com.hfad.stopwatch
      └ Stopwatch
        Activity.java

Implement onStop() to stop the timer

You override the onStop() method in the Android Activity class by adding the following method to your activity:

```
@Override
protected void onStop() {
    super.onStop();   ⟵ This calls the onStop() method
    ...                  in the activity's superclass,
}                        android.app.Activity.
```

The line of code:

```
super.onStop();
```

calls the onStop() method in the Activity superclass. You need to add this line of code whenever you override the onStop() method to make sure that the activity gets to perform any other actions in the superclass onStop() method. If you bypass this step, Android will generate an exception. This applies to all of the lifecycle methods. If you override any of the Activity lifecycle methods in your activity, you must call the superclass method or Android will give you an exception.

We need to get the stopwatch to stop when the onStop() method is called. To do this, we need to set the value of the running boolean to false. Here's the complete method:

```
@Override
protected void onStop() {
    super.onStop();
    running = false;
}
```

So now the stopwatch stops when the activity is no longer visible. The next thing we need to do is get the stopwatch to start again when the activity becomes visible.

> **When you override any activity lifecycle method in your activity, you need to call the Activity superclass method. If you don't, you'll get an exception.**

Sharpen your pencil

Now it's your turn. Change the activity code so that if the stopwatch was running before **onStop()** was called, it starts running again when the activity regains the focus. Hint: you may need to add a new variable.

```java
public class StopwatchActivity extends Activity {
    private int seconds = 0;
    private boolean running;

    @Override
    protected void onCreate(Bundle savedInstanceState) {
        super.onCreate(savedInstanceState);
        setContentView(R.layout.activity_stopwatch);
        if (savedInstanceState != null) {
            seconds = savedInstanceState.getInt("seconds");
            running = savedInstanceState.getBoolean("running");
        }
        runTimer();
    }

    @Override
    public void onSaveInstanceState(Bundle savedInstanceState) {
        savedInstanceState.putInt("seconds", seconds);
        savedInstanceState.putBoolean("running", running);
    }

    @Override
    protected void onStop() {
        super.onStop();
        running = false;
    }
```

Here's the first part of the activity code. You'll need to implement the onStart() method and change other methods slightly too.

Sharpen your pencil
Solution

Now it's your turn. Change the activity code so that if the stopwatch was running before **onStop()** was called, it starts running again when the activity regains the focus. Hint: you may need to add a new variable.

```
public class StopwatchActivity extends Activity {
    private int seconds = 0;
    private boolean running;
    private boolean wasRunning;
```

We added a new variable, wasRunning, to record whether the stopwatch was running before the onStop() method was called so that we know whether to set it running again when the activity becomes visible again.

```
    @Override
    protected void onCreate(Bundle savedInstanceState) {
        super.onCreate(savedInstanceState);
        setContentView(R.layout.activity_stopwatch);
        if (savedInstanceState != null) {
            seconds = savedInstanceState.getInt("seconds");
            running = savedInstanceState.getBoolean("running");
            wasRunning = savedInstanceState.getBoolean("wasRunning");
        }
        runTimer();
    }
```

We'll restore the state of the wasRunning variable if the activity is recreated.

```
    @Override
    public void onSaveInstanceState(Bundle savedInstanceState) {
        savedInstanceState.putInt("seconds", seconds);
        savedInstanceState.putBoolean("running", running);
        savedInstanceState.putBoolean("wasRunning", wasRunning);
    }
```

Save the state of the wasRunning variable.

```
    @Override
    protected void onStop() {
        super.onStop();
        wasRunning = running;
        running = false;
    }
```

Record whether the stopwatch was running when the onStop() method was called.

```
    @Override
    protected void onStart() {
        super.onStart();
        if (wasRunning) {
            running = true;
        }
    }
}
```

Implement the onStart() method. If the stopwatch was running, set it running again.

The updated StopwatchActivity code

We've updated our activity code so that if the stopwatch was running before it lost the focus, it starts running again when it gets the focus back. Make the following changes (in bold) to your version of *StopwatchActivity.java*:

```java
public class StopwatchActivity extends Activity {
    private int seconds = 0;
    private boolean running;
    private boolean wasRunning;

    @Override
    protected void onCreate(Bundle savedInstanceState) {
        super.onCreate(savedInstanceState);
        setContentView(R.layout.activity_stopwatch);
        if (savedInstanceState != null) {
            seconds = savedInstanceState.getInt("seconds");
            running = savedInstanceState.getBoolean("running");
            wasRunning = savedInstanceState.getBoolean("wasRunning");
        }
        runTimer();
    }

    @Override
    public void onSaveInstanceState(Bundle savedInstanceState) {
        savedInstanceState.putInt("seconds", seconds);
        savedInstanceState.putBoolean("running", running);
        savedInstanceState.putBoolean("wasRunning", wasRunning);
    }

    @Override
    protected void onStop() {
        super.onStop();
        wasRunning = running;
        running = false;
    }

    @Override
    protected void onStart() {
        super.onStart();
        if (wasRunning) {
            running = true;
        }
    }
    ...
}
```

A new variable, wasRunning, records whether the stopwatch was running before the onStop() method was called.

Restore the state of the wasRunning variable if the activity is recreated.

Save the state of the wasRunning variable.

Record whether the stopwatch was running when the onStop() method was called.

Implement the onStart() method. If the stopwatch was running, we'll set it running again.

We've left out some of the activity code as we don't need to change it.

Stopwatch

app/src/main

java

com.hfad.stopwatch

Stopwatch Activity.java

What happens when you run the app

① **The user starts the app, and clicks the Start button to set the stopwatch going.**
The `runTimer()` method starts incrementing the number of seconds displayed in the `time_view` text view.

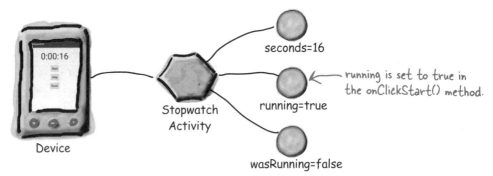

seconds=16

running=true

running is set to true in the onClickStart() method.

Stopwatch
Activity

Device

wasRunning=false

② **The user navigates to the device's home screen so the Stopwatch app is no longer visible.**
The `onStop()` method gets called, `wasRunning` is set to `true`, `running` is set to `false`, and the number of seconds stops incrementing.

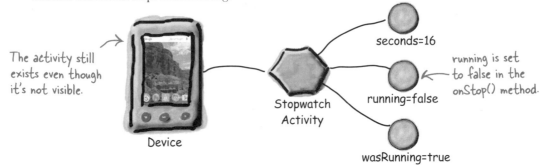

The activity still exists even though it's not visible.

seconds=16

running=false

running is set to false in the onStop() method.

Stopwatch
Activity

Device

wasRunning=true

③ **The user navigates back to the Stopwatch app.**
The `onStart()` method gets called, `running` is set to `true`, and the number of seconds starts incrementing again.

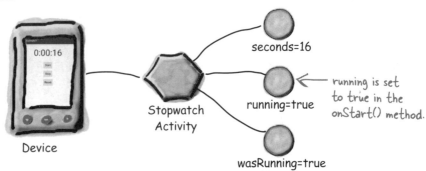

seconds=16

running=true

running is set to true in the onStart() method.

Stopwatch
Activity

Device

wasRunning=true

Test drive the app

Save the changes to your activity code, then run the app. When
you click on the Start button the timer starts: it stops when the
app is no longer visible, and it starts again when the app becomes
visible again.

We set our stopwatch
going, then switched to
the device's home screen.

The stopwatch
paused while the
app wasn't visible.

The stopwatch started again
when we went back to it.

---

there are no Dumb Questions

Q: Could we have used the `onRestart()` method
instead of `onStart()` to set the stopwatch running again?

A: `onRestart()` is used when you only want code to
run when an app becomes visible after having previously been
invisible. It doesn't run when the activity becomes visible for the
first time. In our case, we wanted the app to still work when we
rotated the device.

Q: Why should that make a difference?

A: When you rotate the device, the activity is destroyed and
a new one is created in its place. If we'd put code to set the
stopwatch running again in the `onRestart()` method
instead of `onStart()`, it wouldn't have run when the activity
was recreated. The `onStart()` method gets called in both
situations.

What if an app is only partially visible?

So far you've seen what happens when an activity gets created and destroyed, and you've also seen what happens when an activity becomes visible, and when it becomes invisible. But there's one more situation we need to consider: when an activity is visible but doesn't have the focus.

When an activity is visible but doesn't have the focus, the activity is paused. This can happen if another activity appears on top of your activity that isn't full-size or that's transparent. The activity on top has the focus, but the one underneath is still visible and is therefore paused.

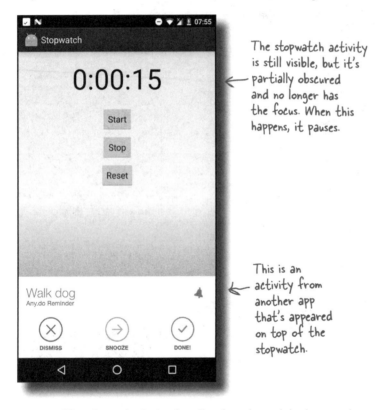

The stopwatch activity is still visible, but it's partially obscured and no longer has the focus. When this happens, it pauses.

This is an activity from another app that's appeared on top of the stopwatch.

An activity has a state of paused if it's lost the focus but is still visible to the user. The activity is still alive and maintains all its state information.

There are two lifecycle methods that handle when the activity is paused and when it becomes active again: `onPause()` and `onResume()`. `onPause()` gets called when your activity is visible but another activity has the focus. `onResume()` is called immediately before your activity is about to start interacting with the user. If you need your app to react in some way when your activity is paused, you need to implement these methods.

You'll see on the next page how these methods fit in with the rest of the lifecycle methods you've seen so far.

The activity lifecycle: the foreground lifetime

Let's build on the lifecycle diagram you saw earlier in the chapter, this time including the onResume() and onPause() methods (the new bits are in bold):

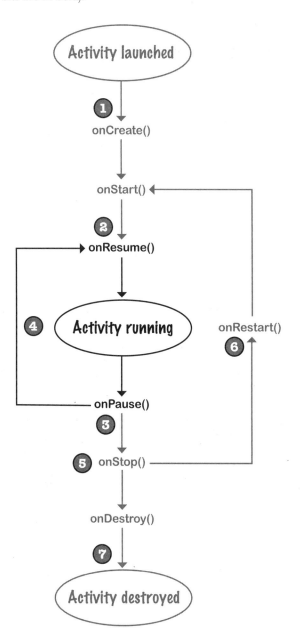

① **The activity gets launched, and the onCreate() and onStart() methods run.**
At this point, the activity is visible, but it doesn't have the focus.

② **The onResume() method runs. It gets called when the activity is about to move into the foreground.**
After the onResume() method has run, the activity has the focus and the user can interact with it.

③ **The onPause() method runs when the activity stops being in the foreground.**
After the onPause() method has run, the activity is still visible but doesn't have the focus.

④ **If the activity moves into the foreground again, the onResume() method gets called.**
The activity may go through this cycle many times if the activity repeatedly loses and then regains the focus.

⑤ **If the activity stops being visible to the user, the onStop() method gets called.**
After the onStop() method has run, the activity is no longer visible.

⑥ **If the activity becomes visible to the user again, the onRestart() method gets called, followed by onStart() and onResume().**
The activity may go through this cycle many times.

⑦ **Finally, the activity is destroyed.**
As the activity moves from running to destroyed, the onPause() and onStop() methods get called before the activity is destroyed.

Earlier on you talked about how the activity is destroyed and a new one is created when the user rotates the device. What happens if the activity is paused when the device is rotated? Does the activity go through the same lifecycle methods?

That's a great question, so let's look at this in more detail before getting back to the Stopwatch app.

The original activity goes through all its lifecycle methods, from onCreate() to onDestroy(). A new activity is created when the original is destroyed. As this new activity isn't in the foreground, only the onCreate() and onStart() lifecycle methods get called. Here's what happens when the user rotates the device when the activity doesn't have the focus::

Original Activity

(Activity launched)

1 onCreate()

onStart()

onResume()

(Activity running)

2 onPause()

3 onStop()

onDestroy()

(Activity destroyed)

1 **The user launches the activity.**
The activity lifecycle methods onCreate(), onStart(), and onResume() get called.

2 **Another activity appears in front of it.**
The activity's onPause() method gets called.

3 **The user rotates the device.**
Android sees this as a configuration change. The onStop() and onDestroy() methods get called, and Android destroys the activity. A new activity is created in its place.

4 **The activity is visible but not in the foreground.**
The onCreate() and onStart() methods get called. As the activity is visible but doesn't have the focus, onResume() isn't called.

Replacement Activity

(Activity launched)

4 onCreate()

onStart()

I see, the replacement activity doesn't reach a state of "running" because it's not in the foreground. But what if you navigate away from the activity completely so it's not even visible? If the activity's stopped, do onResume() and onPause() get called before onStop()?

Activities can go straight from onStart() to onStop() and bypass onPause() and onResume().

If you have an activity that's visible, but never in the foreground and never has the focus, the onPause() and onResume() methods **never get called**.

The onResume() method gets called when the activity appears in the foreground and has the focus. If the activity is only visible behind other activities, the onResume() method doesn't get called.

Similarly, the onPause() method gets called only when the activity is no longer in the foreground. If the activity is never in the foreground, this method won't get called.

If an activity stops or gets destroyed before it appears in the foreground, the onStart() method is followed by the onStop() method. onResume() and onPause() are bypassed.

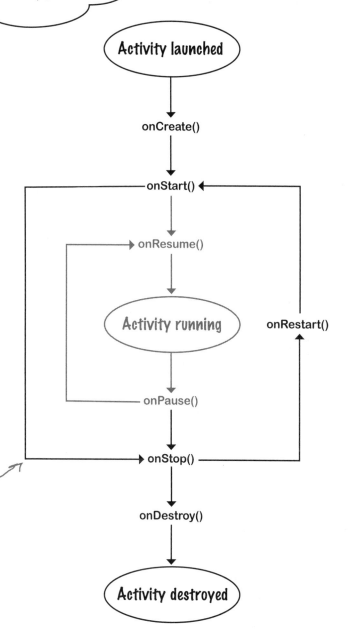

Activity launched

onCreate()

onStart()

onResume()

Activity running

onPause()

onRestart()

onStop()

onDestroy()

Activity destroyed

Stop the stopwatch if the activity's paused

Let's get back to the Stopwatch app.

So far we've made the stopwatch stop if the Stopwatch app isn't visible, and made it start again when the app becomes visible again. We did this by overriding the `onStop()` and `onStart()` methods like this:

```
@Override
protected void onStop() {
    super.onStop();
    wasRunning = running;
    running = false;
}

@Override
protected void onStart() {
    super.onStart();
    if (wasRunning) {
        running = true;
    }
}
```

Stopwatch

app/src/main

java

com.hfad.stopwatch

Stopwatch Activity.java

Let's get the app to have the same behavior if the app is only partially visible. We'll get the stopwatch to stop if the activity is paused, and start again when the activity is resumed. So what changes do we need to make to the lifecycle methods?

We want the Stopwatch app to stop running when the activity is paused, and start it again (if it was running) when the activity is resumed. In other words, we want it to behave the same as when the activity is stopped or started. This means that instead of repeating the code we already have in multiple methods, we can use one method when the activity is paused or stopped, and another method when the activity is resumed or started.

Implement the onPause() and onResume() methods

We'll start with when the activity is resumed or started.

When the activity is resumed, the activity's `onResume()` lifecycle method is called. If the activity is started, the activity's `onResume()` method is called after calling `onStart()`. The `onResume()` method is called irrespective of whether the activity is resumed or started, which means that if we move our `onStart()` code to the `onResume()` method, our app will behave the same irrespective of whether the activity is resumed or started. This means we can remove our `onStart()` method, and replace it with the `onResume()` method like this:

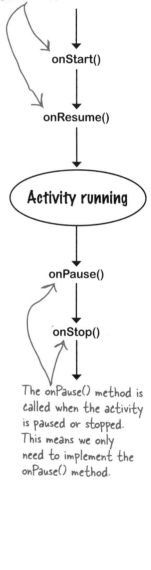

The onResume() method is called when the activity is started or resumed. As we want the app to do the same thing irrespective of whether it's started or resumed, we only need to implement the onResume() method.

onStart()

onResume()

Activity running

onPause()

onStop()

The onPause() method is called when the activity is paused or stopped. This means we only need to implement the onPause() method.

```
@Override
protected void onStart() {
    super.onStart();
    if (wasRunning) {
        running = true;
    }
}
```
← Delete the onStart() method.

```
@Override
protected void onResume() {      ←  Add the
    super.onResume();               onResume()
    if (wasRunning) {               method.
        running = true;
    }
}
```

Stopwatch
app/src/main
java
com.hfad.stopwatch
Stopwatch
Activity.java

We can do something similar when the activity is paused or stopped.

When the activity is paused, the activity's `onPause()` lifecycle method is called. If the activity is stopped, the activity's `onPause()` method is called prior to calling `onStop()`. The `onPause()` method is called irrespective of whether the activity is paused or stopped, which means we can move our `onStop()` code to the `onPause()` method:

```
@Override
protected void onStop() {
    super.onStop();
    wasRunning = running;
    running = false;
}
```
← Delete the onStop() method.

```
@Override
protected void onPause() {      ←  Add the
    super.onPause();               onPause()
    wasRunning = running;         method.
    running = false;
}
```

Stopwatch
app/src/main
java
com.hfad.stopwatch
Stopwatch
Activity.java

The complete StopwatchActivity code

Here's the full *StopwatchActivity.java* code for the finished app (with changes in bold):

```
package com.hfad.stopwatch;

import android.app.Activity;
import android.os.Bundle;
import android.view.View;
import java.util.Locale;
import android.os.Handler;
import android.widget.TextView;


public class StopwatchActivity extends Activity {
    //Number of seconds displayed on the stopwatch.
    private int seconds = 0;
    //Is the stopwatch running?
    private boolean running;
    private boolean wasRunning;


    @Override
    protected void onCreate(Bundle savedInstanceState) {
        super.onCreate(savedInstanceState);
        setContentView(R.layout.activity_stopwatch);
        if (savedInstanceState != null) {
            seconds = savedInstanceState.getInt("seconds");
            running = savedInstanceState.getBoolean("running");
            wasRunning = savedInstanceState.getBoolean("wasRunning");
        }
        runTimer();
    }


    @Override
    public void onSaveInstanceState(Bundle savedInstanceState) {
        savedInstanceState.putInt("seconds", seconds);
        savedInstanceState.putBoolean("running", running);
        savedInstanceState.putBoolean("wasRunning", wasRunning);
    }
```

Use seconds, running, and wasRunning respectively to record the number of seconds passed, whether the stopwatch is running, and whether the stopwatch was running before the activity was paused.

Get the previous state of the stopwatch if the activity's been destroyed and recreated.

Save the state of the stopwatch if it's about to be destroyed.

The activity code continues over the page.

The activity code (continued)

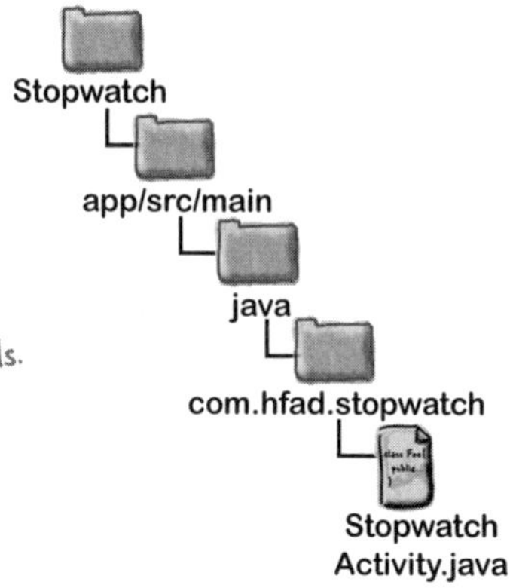

```
@Override
protected void onStop() {
    super.onStop();
    wasRunning = running;
    running = false;
}

@Override
protected void onStart() {
    super.onStart();
    if (wasRunning) {
        running = true;
    }
}
```

↳ Delete these two methods.

```
@Override
protected void onPause() {
    super.onPause();
    wasRunning = running;
    running = false;
}
```
← If the activity's paused, stop the stopwatch.

```
@Override
protected void onResume() {
    super.onResume();
    if (wasRunning) {
        running = true;
    }
}
```
← If the activity's resumed, start the stopwatch again if it was running previously.

```
//Start the stopwatch running when the Start button is clicked.
public void onClickStart(View view) {
    running = true;
}
```
↖ This gets called when the Start button is clicked.

Stopwatch

app/src/main

java

com.hfad.stopwatch

Stopwatch
Activity.java

The activity code continues over the page.

The activity code (continued)

```
//Stop the stopwatch running when the Stop button is clicked.
public void onClickStop(View view) {
    running = false;
}
```

← This gets called when the Stop button is clicked.

```
//Reset the stopwatch when the Reset button is clicked.
public void onClickReset(View view) {
    running = false;
    seconds = 0;
}
```

← This gets called when the Reset button is clicked.

The runTimer() method uses a Handler to increment the seconds and update the text view.

```
//Sets the number of seconds on the timer.
private void runTimer() {
    final TextView timeView = (TextView)findViewById(R.id.time_view);
    final Handler handler = new Handler();
    handler.post(new Runnable() {
        @Override
        public void run() {
            int hours = seconds/3600;
            int minutes = (seconds%3600)/60;
            int secs = seconds%60;
            String time = String.format(Locale.getDefault(),
                    "%d:%02d:%02d", hours, minutes, secs);
            timeView.setText(time);
            if (running) {
                seconds++;
            }
            handler.postDelayed(this, 1000);
        }
    });
}
```

Stopwatch

app/src/main

java

com.hfad.stopwatch

Stopwatch
Activity.java

Let's go through what happens when the code runs.

What happens when you run the app

1 **The user starts the app, and clicks on the Start button to set the stopwatch going.**
The runTimer() method starts incrementing the number of seconds displayed in the time_view text view.

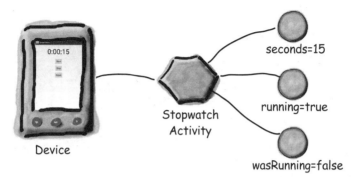

seconds=15

running=true

Stopwatch
Activity

wasRunning=false

Device

2 **Another activity appears in the foreground, leaving StopwatchActivity partially visible.**
The onPause() method gets called, wasRunning is set to true, running is set to false, and the number of seconds stops incrementing.

The activity is paused, as it's visible but not in the foreground.

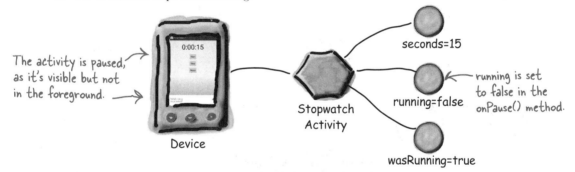

seconds=15

running is set to false in the onPause() method.

running=false

Stopwatch
Activity

Device

wasRunning=true

3 **When StopwatchActivity returns to the foreground, the onResume() method gets called, running is set to true, and the number of seconds starts incrementing again.**

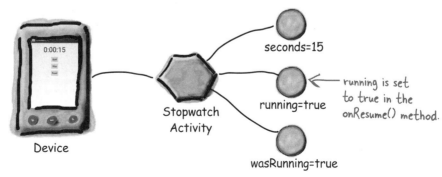

seconds=15

running is set to true in the onResume() method.

running=true

Stopwatch
Activity

Device

wasRunning=true

Test drive the app

Save the changes to your activity code, then run the app. When you click on the Start button, the timer starts; it stops when the app is partially obscured by another activity; and it starts again when the app is back in the foreground.

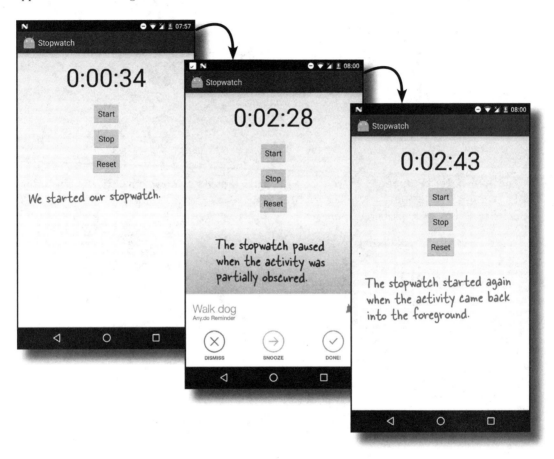

We started our stopwatch.

The stopwatch paused when the activity was partially obscured.

The stopwatch started again when the activity came back into the foreground.

BE the Activity

On the right, you'll see some activity code. Your job is to play like you're the activity and say which code will run in each of the situations below. We've labeled the code we want you to consider. We've done the first one to start you off.

User starts the activity and starts using it.

Code segments A, G, D. The activity is created, then made visible, then receives the focus.

User starts the activity, starts using it, then switches to another app.

— This one's tough.

User starts the activity, starts using it, rotates the device, switches to another app, then goes back to the activity.

```java
...
class MyActivity extends Activity{

    protected void onCreate(
            Bundle savedInstanceState) {
        //Run code A
        ...
    }

    protected void onPause() {
        //Run code B
        ...
    }

    protected void onRestart() {
        //Run code C
        ...
    }

    protected void onResume() {
        //Run code D
        ...
    }

    protected void onStop() {
        //Run code E
        ...
    }

    protected void onRecreate() {
        //Run code F
        ...
    }

    protected void onStart() {
        //Run code G
        ...
    }

    protected void onDestroy() {
        //Run code H
        ...
    }

}
```

BE the Activity Solution

On the right, you'll see some activity code. Your job is to play like you're the activity and say which code will run in each of the situations below. We've labeled the code we want you to consider. We've done the first one to start you off.

User starts the activity and starts using it.

Code segments A, G, D. The activity is created, then made visible, then receives the focus.

User starts the activity, starts using it, then switches to another app.

Code segments A, G, D, B, E. The activity is created, then made visible, then receives the focus. When the user switches to another app, it loses the focus and is no longer visible to the user.

User starts the activity, starts using it, rotates the device, switches to another app, then goes back to the activity.

Code segments A, G, D, B, E, H, A, G, D, B, E, C, G, D. First, the activity is created, made visible, and receives the focus. When the device is rotated, the activity loses the focus, stops being visible, and is destroyed. It's then created again, made visible, and receives the focus. When the user switches to another app and back again, the activity loses the focus, loses visibility, becomes visible again, and regains the focus.

```java
...
class MyActivity extends Activity{

    protected void onCreate(
            Bundle savedInstanceState) {
      A  //Run code A
        ...
    }

    protected void onPause() {
      B  //Run code B
        ...
    }

    protected void onRestart() {
      C  //Run code C
        ...
    }

    protected void onResume() {
      D  //Run code D
        ...
    }

    protected void onStop() {
      E  //Run code E
        ...
    }
```

There's no lifecycle method called onRecreate().

```java
    protected void onRecreate() {
      F  //Run code F
        ...
    }

    protected void onStart() {
      G  //Run code G
        ...
    }

    protected void onDestroy() {
      H  //Run code H
        ...
    }
}
```

Your handy guide to the lifecycle methods

Method	When it's called	Next method
onCreate()	When the activity is first created. Use it for normal static setup, such as creating views. It also gives you a `Bundle` that contains the previously saved state of the activity.	`onStart()`
onRestart()	When your activity has been stopped but just before it gets started again.	`onStart()`
onStart()	When your activity is becoming visible. It's followed by `onResume()` if the activity comes into the foreground, or `onStop()` if the activity is made invisible.	`onResume()` or `onStop()`
onResume()	When your activity is in the foreground.	`onPause()`
onPause()	When your activity is no longer in the foreground because another activity is resuming. The next activity isn't resumed until this method finishes, so any code in this method needs to be quick. It's followed by `onResume()` if the activity returns to the foreground, or `onStop()` if it becomes invisible.	`onResume()` or `onStop()`
onStop()	When the activity is no longer visible. This can be because another activity is covering it, or because this activity is being destroyed. It's followed by `onRestart()` if the activity becomes visible again, or `onDestroy()` if the activity is being destroyed.	`onRestart()` or `onDestroy()`
onDestroy()	When your activity is about to be destroyed or because the activity is finishing.	None

Your Android Toolbox

You've got Chapter 4 under
your belt and now you've
added the activity lifecycle to
your toolbox.

You can download
the full code for
the chapter from
https://tinyurl.com/
HeadFirstAndroid.

BULLET POINTS

- Each app runs in its own process by default.

- Only the main thread can update the user interface.

- Use a `Handler` to schedule code or post code to a different thread.

- A device configuration change results in the activity being destroyed and recreated.

- Your activity inherits the lifecycle methods from the `android.app.Activity` class. If you override any of these methods, you need to call up to the method in the superclass.

- `onSaveInstanceState(Bundle)` enables your activity to save its state before the activity gets destroyed. You can use the `Bundle` to restore state in `onCreate()`.

- You add values to a `Bundle` using `bundle.put*("name", value)`. You retrieve values from the bundle using `bundle.get*("name")`.

- `onCreate()` and `onDestroy()` deal with the birth and death of the activity.

- `onRestart()`, `onStart()`, and `onStop()` deal with the visibility of the activity.

- `onResume()` and `onPause()` handle when the activity gains and loses the focus.

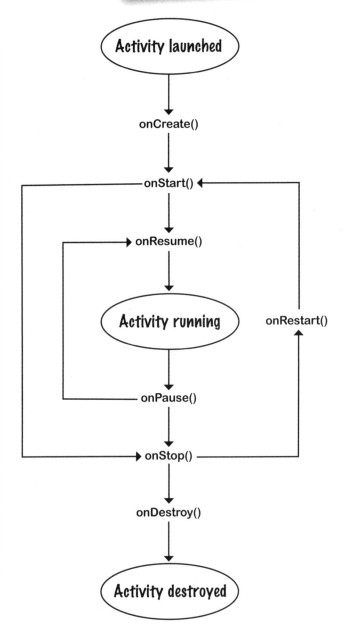

5 views and view groups

Enjoy the View

...and here's a layout
I prepared earlier.

You've seen how to arrange GUI components using a linear layout, but so far we've only scratched the surface.

In this chapter we'll **look a little deeper** and show you how linear layouts *really work*. We'll introduce you to the **frame layout**, a simple layout used to stack views, and we'll also take a tour of the **main GUI components** and **how you use them**. By the end of the chapter, you'll see that even though they all look a little different, all layouts and GUI components have *more in common than you might think*.

Your user interface is made up of layouts and GUI components

As you already know, a layout defines what a screen looks like, and you define it using XML. Layouts usually contain GUI components such as buttons and text fields. Your user interacts with these to make your app do something.

All the apps you've seen in the book so far have used linear layouts, where GUI components are arranged in a single column or row. In order to make the most out of them, however, we need to spend a bit of time looking at how they work, and how to use them effectively.

These are all examples of linear layouts.

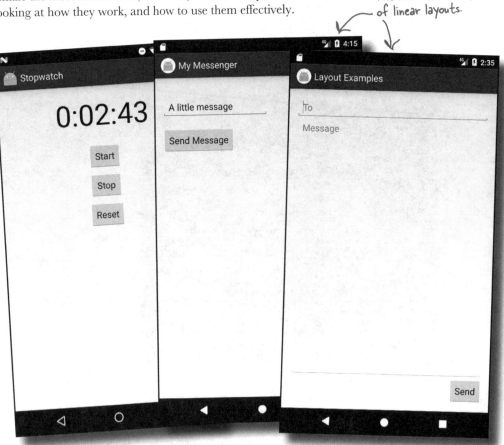

In this chapter, we're going to take a closer look at linear layouts, introduce you to their close relative the frame layout, and show you other GUI components you can use to make your app more interactive.

Let's start with linear layouts.

LinearLayout displays views in a single row or column

As you already know, a linear layout displays its views next to each other, either vertically or horizontally. If it's vertically, the views are displayed in a single column. If it's horizontally, the views are displayed in a single row.

You define a linear layout using the <LinearLayout> element like this:

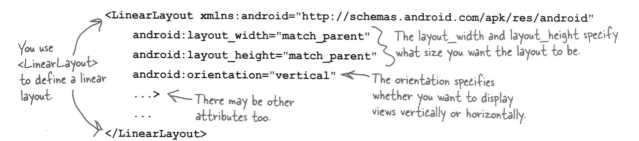

```
<LinearLayout xmlns:android="http://schemas.android.com/apk/res/android"
    android:layout_width="match_parent"
    android:layout_height="match_parent"
    android:orientation="vertical"
    ...>
    ...
</LinearLayout>
```

You use <LinearLayout> to define a linear layout.

The layout_width and layout_height specify what size you want the layout to be.

There may be other attributes too.

The orientation specifies whether you want to display views vertically or horizontally.

The xmlns:android attribute is used to specify the Android namespace, and you must always set it to "http://schemas.android.com/apk/res/android".

You MUST set the layout's width and height

The android:layout_width and android:layout_height attributes specify how wide and high you want the layout to be. **These attributes are mandatory for all types of layout and view**.

You can set android:layout_width and android:layout_height to "wrap_content", "match_parent" or a specific size such as 8dp—that's 8 density-independent pixels. "wrap_content" means that you want the layout to be just big enough to hold all of the views inside it, and "match_parent" means that you want the layout to be as big as its parent—in this case, as big as the device screen minus any padding (there's more about padding in a couple of pages). You will usually set the layout width and height to "match_parent".

You may sometimes see android:layout_width and android:layout_height set to "fill_parent". "fill_parent" was used in older versions of Android, and it's now replaced by "match_parent". "fill_parent" is deprecated.

Geek Bits

What are density-independent pixels?

Some devices create very sharp images by using very tiny pixels. Other devices are cheaper to produce because they have fewer, larger pixels. You use density-independent pixels (dp) to avoid creating interfaces that are overly small on some devices, and overly large on others. A measurement in density-independent pixels is roughly the same size across all devices.

LinearLayout
FrameLayout

Orientation is vertical or horizontal

You specify the direction in which you wish to arrange views using the `android:orientation` attribute.

As you've seen in earlier chapters, you arrange views vertically using:

`android:orientation="vertical"`

This displays the views in a single column.

You arrange views horizontally in a single row using:

`android:orientation="horizontal"`

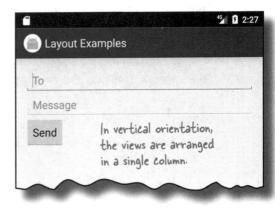

In vertical orientation, the views are arranged in a single column.

When the orientation is horizontal, views are displayed from left to right by default. This is great for languages that are read from left to right, but what if the user has set the language on their device to one that's read from right to left?

For apps where the minimum SDK is *at least* API 17, you can get views to rearrange themselves depending on the language setting on the device. If the user's language is read from right to left, you can get the views to arrange themselves starting from the right.

To do this, you declare that your app supports languages that are read from right to left in your *AndroidManifest.xml* file like this:

```
<manifest ...>
    <application
        ...
        android:supportsRtl="true">
        ...
    </application>
</manifest>
```

MyApp

app/src/main

AndroidManifest.xml

Android Studio may add this line of code for you. It must go inside the <application> tag.

`supportsRtl` means "supports right-to-left languages."

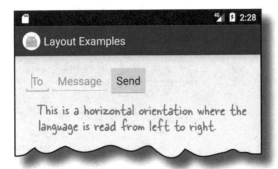

This is a horizontal orientation where the language is read from left to right.

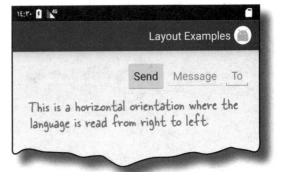

This is a horizontal orientation where the language is read from right to left.

Padding adds space

If you want there to be a bit of space around the edge of the layout, you can set **padding** attributes. These attributes tell Android how much padding you want between each of the layout's sides and its parent. Here's how you would tell Android you want to add padding of 16dp to all edges of the layout:

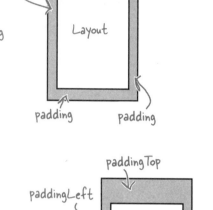

padding

padding

Layout

padding

padding

```
<LinearLayout ...
    android:padding="16dp" >   ←This adds the same padding
        ...                       to all edges of the layout.
</LinearLayout>
```

If you want to add different amounts of padding to different edges, you can specify the edges individually. Here's how you would add padding of 32dp to the top of the layout, and 16dp to the other edges:

```
<LinearLayout ...
    android:paddingBottom="16dp"
    android:paddingLeft="16dp"
    android:paddingRight="16dp"    Add padding to the individual edges.
    android:paddingTop="32dp" >
        ...
</LinearLayout>
```

paddingTop

paddingLeft

Layout

paddingBottom

paddingRight

If your app supports right-to-left languages, you can use:

> **android:paddingStart="16dp"**

and:

> **android:paddingEnd="16dp"**

to add padding to the start and end edges of the layout instead of their left and right edges.

android:PaddingStart adds padding to the start edge of the layout. The start edge is on the left for languages that are read from left to right, and the right edge for languages that are read from right to left.

android:PaddingEnd adds padding to the end edge of the layout. The end edge is on the right for languages that are read from left to right, and the left edge for languages that are read from right to left.

Watch it!

You can only use start and end properties with API 17 or above.

If you want your app to work on older versions of Android, you must use the left and right properties instead.

LinearLayout
FrameLayout

Add a dimension resource file for consistent padding across layouts

In the example on the previous page, we hardcoded the padding and set it to 16dp. An alternative approach is to specify the padding in a *dimension resource file* instead. Doing so makes it easier to maintain the padding dimensions for all the layouts in your app.

To use a dimension resource file, you first need to add one to ← your project. To do this, first select the *app/src/main/res/values* folder in Android Studio, then go to File menu and choose New→Values resource file. When prompted, enter a name of "dimens" and click on the OK button. This creates a new resource file called *dimens.xml*.

Android Studio may have already added this file for you, but it depends on which version of Android Studio you're using.

Once you've created the dimension resource file, you add dimensions to it using the <dimen> element. As an example, here's how you would add dimensions for the horizontal and vertical margins to *dimens.xml*:

```xml
<?xml version="1.0" encoding="utf-8"?>
<resources>
    <dimen name="activity_horizontal_margin">16dp</dimen>
    <dimen name="activity_vertical_margin">16dp</dimen>
</resources>
```

This creates two dimension resources.

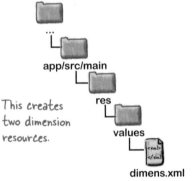

app/src/main

res

values

dimens.xml

You use the dimensions you create by setting the padding attributes in your layout file to the name of a dimension resource like this:

```xml
<LinearLayout ...
    android:paddingLeft="@dimen/activity_horizontal_margin"
    android:paddingRight="@dimen/activity_horizontal_margin"
    android:paddingTop="@dimen/activity_vertical_margin"
    android:paddingBottom="@dimen/activity_vertical_margin">
```

The paddingLeft and paddingRight attributes are set to @dimen/activity_horizontal_margin.

The paddingTop and paddingBottom attributes are set to @dimen/activity_vertical_margin.

With that kind of setup, at runtime, Android looks up the values of the attributes in the dimension resource file and applies the values it finds there.

A linear layout displays views in the order they appear in the layout XML

When you define a linear layout, you add views to the layout in the order in which you want them to appear. So, if you want a text view to appear above a button in a linear layout, you *must* define the text view first:

```
<LinearLayout ... >
    <TextView
        android:layout_width="wrap_content"
        android:layout_height="wrap_content"
        android:text="@string/text_view1" />

    <Button
        android:layout_width="wrap_content"
        android:layout_height="wrap_content"
        android:text="@string/click_me" />
</LinearLayout>
```

If you define the text view above the button in the XML, the text view will appear above the button when displayed.

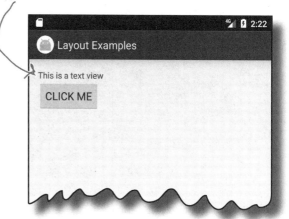

You specify the width and height of any views using `android:layout_width` and `android:layout_height`. The code:

```
android:layout_width="wrap_content"
```

means that you want the view to be just wide enough for its content to fit inside it—for example, the text displayed on a button or in a text view. The code:

```
android:layout_width="match_parent"
```

means that you want the view to be as wide as the parent layout.

If you need to refer to a view elsewhere in your code, you need to give it an ID. As an example, you'd give the text view an ID of `"text_view"` using the code:

```
    ...
    <TextView
        android:id="@+id/text_view"
        ... />
    ...
```

android:layout_width and android:layout_height are mandatory attributes for all views, no matter which layout you use.

They can take the values wrap_content, match_parent, or a specific dimension value such as 16dp.

Use margins to add distance between views

When you position a view using a linear layout, the layout doesn't leave much of a gap between views. You can increase the size of the gap by adding one or more **margins** to the view.

As an example, suppose you wanted to put one view below another, but add 48dp of extra space between the two. To do that, you'd add a margin of 48dp to the top of the bottom view:

```
LinearLayout ... >
    <Button
        android:id="@+id/button_click_me"
        ... />


    <Button
        android:id="@+id/button_below"
        android:layout_width="wrap_content"
        android:layout_height="wrap_content"
        android:layout_marginTop="48dp"
        android:text="@string/button_below" />
</LinearLayout>
```

Adding a margin to the top of the bottom button adds extra space between the two views.

Here's a list of the margins you can use to give your views extra space. Add the attribute to the view, and set its value to the size of margin you want:

```
android:attribute="8dp"
```

Attribute	What it does	
layout_marginTop	Adds extra space to the top of the view.	
layout_marginBottom	Adds extra space to the bottom of the view.	
layout_marginLeft, layout_marginStart	Adds extra space to the left (or start) of the view.	
layout_marginRight, layout_marginEnd	Adds extra space to the right (or end) of the view.	
layout_margin	Adds equal space to each side of the view.	

Let's change up a basic linear layout

At first glance, a linear layout can seem basic and inflexible. After all, all it does is arrange views in a particular order. To give you more flexibility, you can tweak your layout's appearance using some more of its attributes. To show you how this works, we're going to transform a basic linear layout.

The layout is composed of two editable text fields and a button. To start with, these text fields are simply displayed vertically on the screen like this:

We're going to change the layout so that the button is displayed in the end corner of the layout, and one of the editable text fields takes up any remaining space.

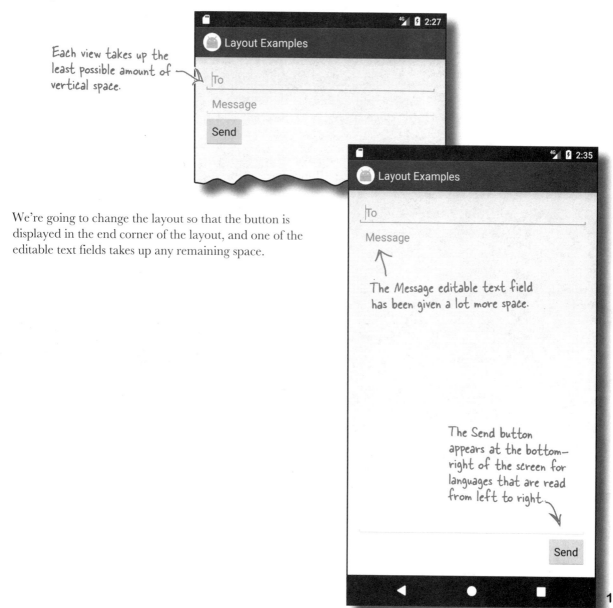

Each view takes up the least possible amount of vertical space.

The Message editable text field has been given a lot more space.

The Send button appears at the bottom-right of the screen for languages that are read from left to right.

Here's the starting point for the linear layout

The linear layout contains two editable text fields and a button. The button is labeled "Send," and the editable text fields contain hint text values of "To" and "Message."

Hint text in an editable text field is text that's displayed when the field is empty. It's used to give users a hint as to what sort of text they should enter. You define hint text using the android:hint attribute:

```
<LinearLayout xmlns:android="http://schemas.android.com/apk/res/android"
    xmlns:tools="http://schemas.android.com/tools"
    android:layout_width="match_parent"
    android:layout_height="match_parent"
    android:padding="16dp"
    android:orientation="vertical"
    tools:context="com.hfad.views.MainActivity" >

    <EditText
        android:layout_width="match_parent"
        android:layout_height="wrap_content"
        android:hint="@string/to" />

    <EditText
        android:layout_width="match_parent"
        android:layout_height="wrap_content"
        android:hint="@string/message" />

    <Button
        android:layout_width="wrap_content"
        android:layout_height="wrap_content"
        android:text="@string/send" />

</LinearLayout>
```

The editable text fields are as wide as the parent layout.

android:hint displays a hint to the user as to what they should type in the editable text field.

The values of these Strings are defined in strings.xml as usual.

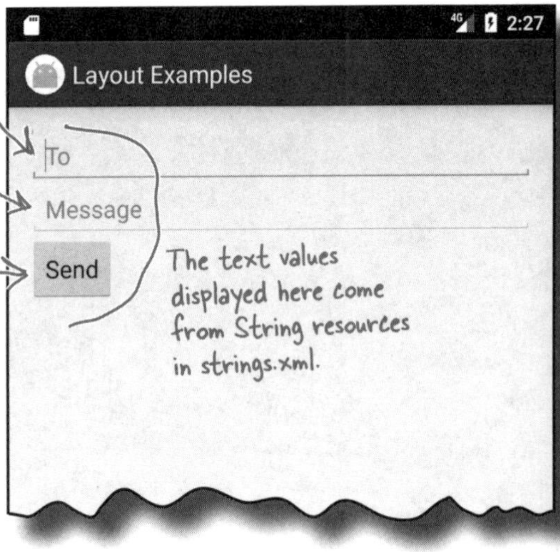

The text values displayed here come from String resources in strings.xml.

Layout Examples

To

Message

Send

All of these views take up just as much vertical space in the layout as they need for their contents. So how do we make the Message text field taller?

Make a view streeeeetch by adding weight

All of the views in our basic layout take up just as much vertical space as they need for their content. But what we actually want is to make the Message text field stretch to take up any vertical space in the layout that's not being used by the other views.

We want to make the Message text field stretch vertically so that it fills any spare space in the layout.

In order to do this, we need to allocate some **weight** to the Message text field. Allocating weight to a view is a way of telling it to stretch to take up extra space in the layout.

You assign weight to a view using:

```
android:layout_weight="number"
```

where `number` is some number greater than 0.

When you allocate weight to a view, the layout first makes sure that each view has enough space for its content: each button has space for its text, each editable text field has space for its hint, and so on. Once it's done that, the layout takes any extra space, and divides it proportionally between the views with a weight of 1 or greater.

Adding weight to one view

We need the Message editable text field to take up any extra
space in the layout. To do this, we'll set its layout_weight
attribute to 1. As this is the only view in the layout with a weight
value, this will make the text field stretch vertically to fill the
remainder of the screen. Here's the code:

```
<LinearLayout ... >
    <EditText
        android:layout_width="match_parent"
        android:layout_height="wrap_content"
        android:hint="@string/to" />

    <EditText
        android:layout_width="match_parent"
        android:layout_height="0dp"
        android:layout_weight="1"
        android:hint="@string/message" />

    <Button
        android:layout_width="wrap_content"
        android:layout_height="wrap_content"
        android:text="@string/send" />
</LinearLayout>
```

*This <EditText> and the <Button>
have no layout_weight attribute set.
They'll take up as much room as their
content needs, but no more.*

*This view is the only
one with any weight.
It will expand to
fill the space that's
not needed by any
of the other views.*

*The height of the view will be determined by
the linear layout based on the layout_weight.
Setting the layout_height to "0dp" is more
efficient than setting it to "wrap_content",
as this way Android doesn't have to work out
the value of "wrap_content".*

Giving the Message editable text field a weight of 1 means that it
takes up all of the extra space that's not used by the other views
in the layout. This is because neither of the other two views has
been allocated any weight in the layout XML.

*The Message view has a weight
of 1. As it's the only view with
its weight attribute set, it
expands to take up any extra
vertical space in the layout.*

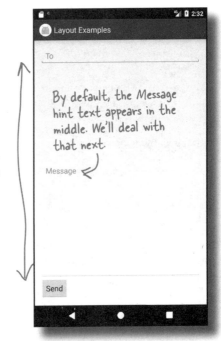

*By default, the Message
hint text appears in the
middle. We'll deal with
that next.*

Adding weight to multiple views

In this example, we only had one view with a weight attribute set. But what if we had *more* than one?

Suppose we gave the To text field a weight of 1, and the Message text field a weight of 2, like this:

```
<LinearLayout ... >

    ...

    <EditText
        android:layout_width="match_parent"
        android:layout_height="0dp"
        android:layout_weight="1"
        android:hint="@string/to" />

    <EditText
        android:layout_width="match_parent"
        android:layout_height="0dp"
        android:layout_weight="2"
        android:hint="@string/message" />

    ...

</LinearLayout>
```

To figure out how much extra space each view takes up, start by adding together the layout_weight attributes for each view. In our case, this is 1+2=3. The amount of extra space taken up by each view will be the view's weight divided by the total weight. The To view has a weight of 1, so this means it will take up 1/3 of the remaining space in the layout. The Message view has a weight of 2, so it will take up 2/3 of the remaining space.

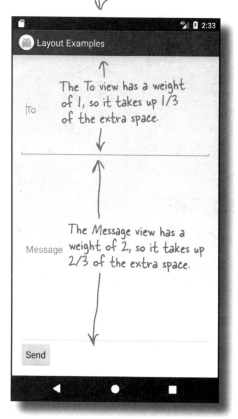

This is just an example; we're not really going to change the layout so that it looks like this.

The To view has a weight of 1, so it takes up 1/3 of the extra space.

The Message view has a weight of 2, so it takes up 2/3 of the extra space.

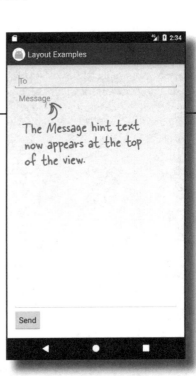

Gravity controls the position of a view's contents

The next thing we need to do is move the hint text inside the Message text field. At the moment, it's centered vertically inside the view. We need to change it so that the text appears at the top of the text field. We can achieve this using the android:gravity attribute.

The android:gravity attribute lets you specify how you want to position the contents of a view inside the view—for example, how you want to position text inside a text field. If you want the text inside a view to appear at the top, the following code will do the trick:

```
android:gravity="top"
```

We'll add an android:gravity attribute to the Message text field so that the hint text moves to the top of the view:

```
<LinearLayout ... >
    ...
    <EditText
        android:layout_width="match_parent"
        android:layout_height="0dp"
        android:layout_weight="1"
        android:gravity="top"
        android:hint="@string/message" />
    ...
</LinearLayout>
```

Displays the text inside the text field at the top of the text field

Test drive

Adding the android:gravity attribute to the Message text field moves the hint text to the top of the view, just like we want.

You'll find a list of the other values you can use with the android:gravity attribute on the next page.

182   Chapter 5

Values you can use with the android:gravity attribute

Here are some more of the values you can use with the `android:gravity` attribute. Add the attribute to your view, and set its value to one of the values below:

```
android:gravity="value"
```

android:gravity lets you say where you want the view's contents to appear inside the view.

Value	What it does
top	Puts the view's contents at the top of the view.
bottom	Puts the view's contents at the bottom of the view.
left	Puts the view's contents at the left of the view.
right	Puts the view's contents at the right of the view.
start	Puts the view's contents at the start of the view.
end	Puts the view's contents at the end of the view.
center_vertical	Centers the view's contents vertically.
center_horizontal	Centers the view's contents horizontally.
center	Centers the view's contents vertically and horizontally.
fill_vertical	Makes the view's contents fill the view vertically.
fill_horizontal	Makes the view's contents fill the view horizontally.
fill	Makes the view's contents fill the view vertically and horizontally.

start and end are only available if you're using API 17 or above.

You can also apply multiple gravities to a view by separating each value with a " | ". To sink a view's contents to the bottom-end corner, for example, use:

```
android:gravity="bottom|end"
```

LinearLayout
FrameLayout

layout_gravity controls the position of a view within a layout

There's one final change we need to make to our layout. The Send button currently appears in the bottom-left corner. We need to move it over to the end instead (the bottom-right corner for left-to-right languages). To do this, we'll use the `android:layout_gravity` attribute.

The `android:layout_gravity` attribute lets you specify where you want a view in a linear layout to appear in its enclosing space. You can use it to push a view to the right, for instance, or center the view horizontally. To move our button to the end, we'd need to add the following to the button's code:

```
android:layout_gravity="end"
```

> We'll move the button to the end so it appears on the right for left-to-right languages, and on the left for right-to-left languages.
>
> ──────────────→ Send

> *Wait a sec. I thought you said that gravity was used to say where you wanted to put the view's contents, not the view itself?*

Linear layouts have two attributes that sound similar to one another, gravity and layout_gravity.

A couple of pages ago, we used the `android:gravity` attribute to position the Message text inside a text view. This is because the `android:gravity` attribute lets you say where you want a view's **contents** to appear.

`android:layout_gravity` deals with the **placement of the view itself**, and lets you control where views appear in their available space. In our case, we want the view to move to the end of its available space, so we're using:

```
android:layout_gravity="end"
```

There's a list of some of the other values you can use with the `android:layout_gravity` attribute on the next page.

More values you can use with the android:layout_gravity attribute

Here are some of the values you can use with the
`android:layout_gravity` attribute. Add the attribute
to your view, and set its value to one of the values below:

You can apply multiple layout_gravity values by
separating each one with a "|". As an example,
use android:layout_gravity="bottom|end" to
move a view to the bottom-end corner of its
available space.

android:layout_gravity="value"

Value	What it does
top, bottom, left, right	Puts the view at the top, bottom, left, or right of its available space.
start, end	Puts the view at the start or end of its available space.
center_vertical, center_horizontal	Centers the view vertically or horizontally in its available space.
center	Centers the view vertically and horizontally in its available space.
fill_vertical, fill_horizontal	Grows the view so that it fills its available space vertically or horizontally.
fill	Grows the view so that it fills its available space vertically and horizontally.

android:layout_gravity lets you say where you
want views to appear in their available space.

android:layout_gravity deals with the placement
of the view itself, whereas android:gravity
controls how the view's contents are displayed.

The full linear layout code

Here's the full code for the linear layout:

```
<LinearLayout xmlns:android="http://schemas.android.com/apk/res/android"
    xmlns:tools="http://schemas.android.com/tools"
    android:layout_width="match_parent"
    android:layout_height="match_parent"
    android:padding="16dp"
    android:orientation="vertical"
    tools:context="com.hfad.views.MainActivity" >

    <EditText
        android:layout_width="match_parent"
        android:layout_height="wrap_content"
        android:hint="@string/to" />

    <EditText
        android:layout_width="match_parent"
        android:layout_height="0dp"
        android:layout_weight="1"
        android:gravity="top"
        android:hint="@string/message" />

    <Button
        android:layout_width="wrap_content"
        android:layout_height="wrap_content"
        android:layout_gravity="end"
        android:text="@string/send" />

</LinearLayout>
```

android:gravity is different from android:layout_gravity. android:gravity relates to the contents of the view, while android:layout_gravity relates to the view itself.

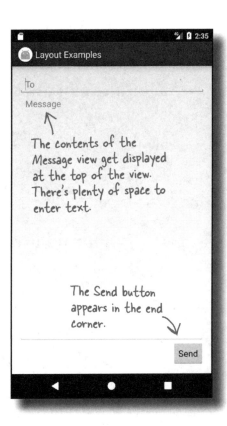

The contents of the Message view get displayed at the top of the view. There's plenty of space to enter text.

The Send button appears in the end corner.

LinearLayout: a summary

Here's a summary of how you create linear layouts.

How you specify a linear layout

You specify a linear layout using `<LinearLayout>`. You must specify the layout's width, height, and orientation, but padding is optional:

```
<LinearLayout xmlns:android="http://schemas.android.com/apk/res/android"
    android:layout_width="match_parent"
    android:layout_height="match_parent"
    android:orientation="vertical"
    ...>
    ...
</LinearLayout>
```

Views get displayed in the order they're listed in the code

When you define a linear layout, you add views to the layout in the order in which you want them to appear.

Stretch views using weight

By default, all views take up just as much space as necessary for their content. If you want to make one or more of your views take up more space, you can use the `weight` attribute to make it stretch:

```
android:layout_weight="1"
```

Use gravity to specify where a view's contents appear within a view

The `android:gravity` attribute lets you specify how you want to position the contents of a view—for example, how you want to position text inside a text field.

Use layout_gravity to specify where a view appears in its available space

The `android:layout_gravity` attribute lets you specify where you want a view in a linear layout to appear in its parent layout. You can use it to push a view to the end, for instance, or center the view horizontally.

That's everything we've covered on linear layouts. Next we'll take a look at the **frame layout**.

LinearLayout
FrameLayout

Frame layouts stack their views

As you've already seen, linear layouts arrange their views in a single row or column. Each view is allocated its own space on the screen, and they don't overlap one another.

Sometimes, however, you *want* your views to overlap. As an example, suppose you want to display an image with some text overlaid on top of it. You wouldn't be able to achieve this just using a linear layout.

If you want a layout whose views can overlap, a simple option is to use a **frame layout**. Instead of displaying its views in a single row or column, it stacks them on top of each other. This allows you to, for example, display text on top of an image.

Frame layouts let your views overlap one another. This is useful for displaying text on top of images, for example.

How you define a frame layout

You define a frame layout using the <FrameLayout> element like this:

You use <FrameLayout> to define a frame layout.

```
<FrameLayout xmlns:android="http://schemas.android.com/apk/res/android"
    android:layout_width="match_parent"
    android:layout_height="match_parent"
    ...>

    ...

</FrameLayout>
```

These are the same attributes we used for our linear layout.

←—This is where you add any views you wish to stack in the frame layout.

Just like a linear layout, the android:layout_width and android:layout_height attributes are mandatory and specify the layout's width and height.

Create a new project

To see how frame layouts work, we're going to use one to overlay text on an image. Create a new Android Studio project for an application named "Duck" with a company name of "hfad.com", making the package name com.hfad.duck. The minimum SDK should be API 19 so that it will work on most devices. You'll need an empty activity called "MainActivity" with a layout called "activity_main" so that your code matches ours. **Make sure you uncheck the Backwards Compatibility (AppCompat) option when you create the activity.**

Add an image to your project

We're going to use an image called *duck.jpg* in our layout, so we need to add it to our project.

To do this, you first need to create a *drawable* resource folder (if Android Studio hasn't already created it for you). This is the default folder for storing image resources in your app. Switch to the Project view of Android Studio's explorer, select the *app/src/main/res* folder, go to the File menu, choose the New... option, then click on the option to create a new Android resource directory. When prompted, choose a resource type of "drawable", name the folder "drawable", and click on OK.

Once you've created the *drawable* folder, download the file *duck.jpg* from *https://git.io/v9oet*, then add it to the *app/src/main/res/drawable* folder.

We're going to change *activity_main.xml* so that it uses a frame layout containing an image view (a view that displays an image) and a text view. To do this, replace the code in your version of *activity_main.xml* with ours below:

← duck.jpg

```xml
<?xml version="1.0" encoding="utf-8"?>
<FrameLayout xmlns:android="http://schemas.android.com/apk/res/android"
        xmlns:tools="http://schemas.android.com/tools"
        android:layout_width="match_parent"
        android:layout_height="wrap_content"
        tools:context="com.hfad.duck.MainActivity">

    <ImageView
        android:layout_width="match_parent"
        android:layout_height="wrap_content"
        android:scaleType="centerCrop"
        android:src="@drawable/duck"/>

    <TextView
        android:layout_width="wrap_content"
        android:layout_height="wrap_content"
        android:padding="16dp"
        android:textSize="20sp"
        android:text="It's a duck!" />
</FrameLayout>
```

We're using a frame layout.

This adds an image to the frame layout. You'll find out more about image views later in the chapter.

This crops the image's edges so it fits in the available space.

This line tells Android to use the image named "duck" located in the drawable folder.

This adds a text view to the frame layout.

We've increased the size of the text.

In a real-world duck app, you'd want to add this text as a String resource.

Duck
app/src/main
res
layout
activity_main.xml

Then run your app, and we'll look at what the code does on the next page.

A frame layout stacks views in the order they appear in the layout XML

When you define a frame layout, you add views to the layout in the order in which you want them to be stacked. The first view is displayed first, the second is stacked on top of it, and so on. In our case, we've added an image view followed by a text view, so the text view appears on top of the image view:

```
<FrameLayout ...>
    <ImageView
        android:layout_width="match_parent"
        android:layout_height="wrap_content"
        android:scaleType="centerCrop"
        android:src="@drawable/duck"/>

    <TextView
        android:layout_width="wrap_content"
        android:layout_height="wrap_content"
        android:padding="16dp"
        android:textSize="20sp"
        android:text="It's a duck!" />
</FrameLayout>
```

This is the image view.

This is the text view.

Position views in the layout using layout_gravity

By default, any views you add to a frame layout appear in the top-left corner. You can change the position of these views using the android:layout_gravity attribute, just as you could with a linear layout. As an example, here's how you would move the text view to the bottom-end corner of the image:

```
...
    <TextView
        android:layout_width="wrap_content"
        android:layout_height="wrap_content"
        android:padding="16dp"
        android:layout_gravity="bottom|end"
        android:textSize="20sp"
        android:text="It's a duck!" />
</FrameLayout>
```

This sinks the text to the bottom-end corner.

You can nest layouts

One of the disadvantages of using a frame layout is that it's easy for views to overlap one another when you don't want them to. As an example, you may want to display two text views in the bottom-end corner, one above the other:

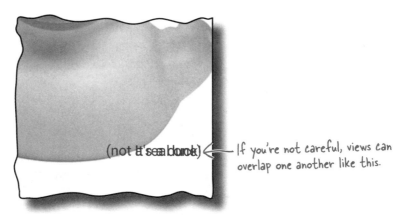

(not a real duck) ← If you're not careful, views can overlap one another like this.

It's possible to solve this problem by adding margins or padding to the text views. A neater solution, however, is to add them to a linear layout, which you then nest inside the frame layout. Doing this allows you to arrange the two text views linearly, then position them as a group inside the frame layout:

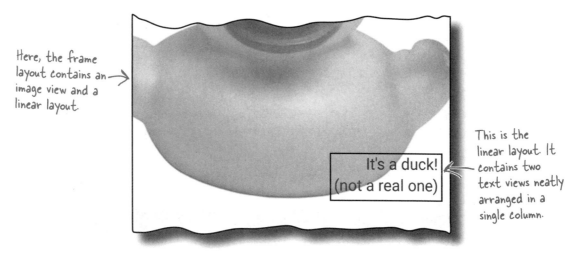

Here, the frame layout contains an image view and a linear layout.

It's a duck! (not a real one) ← This is the linear layout. It contains two text views neatly arranged in a single column.

We'll show you the full code for how to do this on the next page.

The full code to nest a layout

Here's the full code to nest a linear layout in a frame layout.
Update your version of *activity_main.xml* to include our changes,
then run your app to see how it looks.

LinearLayout
FrameLayout

Duck

app/src/main

res

layout

activity_
main.xml

```xml
<?xml version="1.0" encoding="utf-8"?>
<FrameLayout xmlns:android="http://schemas.android.com/apk/res/android"
    xmlns:tools="http://schemas.android.com/tools"
    android:layout_width="match_parent"
    android:layout_height="wrap_content"
    tools:context="com.hfad.duck.MainActivity">

    <ImageView
    android:layout_width="match_parent"
    android:layout_height="wrap_content"
    android:scaleType="centerCrop"
    android:src="@drawable/duck"/>
```

We're adding a linear layout that's just big enough to contain its text views.

```xml
    <LinearLayout
        android:layout_width="wrap_content"
        android:layout_height="wrap_content"
        android:orientation="vertical"
        android:layout_gravity="bottom|end"
        android:gravity="end"
        android:padding="16dp" >
```

Move each text view in the linear layout to the end of its available space.

This line sinks the linear layout to the bottom-end corner of the frame layout.

It's a duck!
(not a real one)

```xml
        <TextView
            android:layout_width="wrap_content"
            android:layout_height="wrap_content"
            android:textSize="20sp"
            android:text="It's a duck!"   />

        <TextView
            android:layout_width="wrap_content"
            android:layout_height="wrap_content"
            android:textSize="20sp"
            android:text="(not a real one)" />
    </LinearLayout>
</FrameLayout>
```

FrameLayout: a summary

Here's a summary of how you create frame layouts.

How you specify a frame layout

You specify a frame layout using <FrameLayout>. You must specify the layout's width and height:

```
<FrameLayout xmlns:android="http://schemas.android.com/apk/res/android"
    android:layout_width="match_parent"
    android:layout_height="match_parent"
    ...>

    ...

</FrameLayout>
```

Views are stacked in the order they appear

When you define a frame layout, you add views to the layout in the order in which you want them to be stacked. The first view you add is displayed on the bottom of the stack, the next view is stacked on top of it, and so on.

Use layout_gravity to specify where a view appears

The android:layout_gravity attribute lets you specify where you want a view in a frame layout to appear. You can use it to push a view to the end, for instance, or sink it to the bottom-end corner.

Now that you've seen how to use two simple Android layouts, a linear layout and a frame layout, have a go at the following exercise.

BE the Layout

Three of the five screens below were
made from layouts on the next page.
Your job is to match each of the three
layouts to the screen that
the layout would produce.

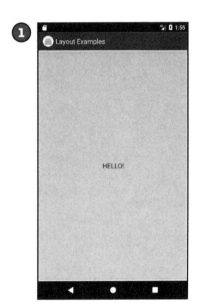

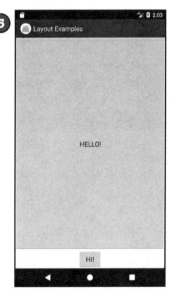

A
```
<LinearLayout xmlns:android=
        "http://schemas.android.com/apk/res/android"
    xmlns:tools="http://schemas.android.com/tools"
    android:layout_width="match_parent"
    android:layout_height="match_parent"
    android:orientation="vertical"
    tools:context="com.hfad.views.MainActivity" >
    <Button
        android:layout_width="match_parent"
        android:layout_height="match_parent"
        android:text="HELLO!" />
</LinearLayout>
```

B
```
<LinearLayout xmlns:android=
        "http://schemas.android.com/apk/res/android"
    xmlns:tools="http://schemas.android.com/tools"
    android:layout_width="match_parent"
    android:layout_height="match_parent"
    android:orientation="vertical"
    tools:context="com.hfad.views.MainActivity" >
    <Button
        android:layout_width="match_parent"
        android:layout_height="0dp"
        android:layout_weight="1"
        android:text="HELLO!" />
    <Button
        android:layout_width="wrap_content"
        android:layout_height="wrap_content"
        android:text="HI!" />
</LinearLayout>
```

C
```
<LinearLayout  xmlns:android=
        "http://schemas.android.com/apk/res/android"
    xmlns:tools="http://schemas.android.com/tools"
    android:layout_width="match_parent"
    android:layout_height="match_parent"
    android:orientation="vertical"
    tools:context="com.hfad.views.MainActivity" >
    <Button
        android:layout_width="wrap_content"
        android:layout_height="wrap_content"
        android:text="HELLO!" />
    <Button
        android:layout_width="wrap_content"
        android:layout_height="wrap_content"
        android:text="HI!" />
</LinearLayout>
```

BE the Layout Solution

Three of the five screens below were made from layouts on the next page. Your job is to match each of the three layouts to the screen that the layout would produce.

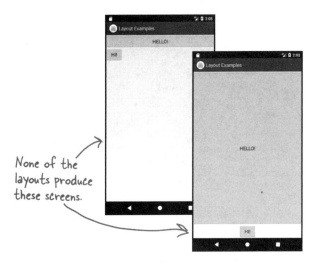

None of the layouts produce these screens.

A

```xml
<LinearLayout xmlns:android=
        "http://schemas.android.com/apk/res/android"
    xmlns:tools="http://schemas.android.com/tools"
    android:layout_width="match_parent"
    android:layout_height="match_parent"
    android:orientation="vertical"
    tools:context="com.hfad.views.MainActivity" >
    <Button
        android:layout_width="match_parent"
        android:layout_height="match_parent"
        android:text="HELLO!" />
</LinearLayout>
```

This has one button that fills the screen.

B

```xml
<LinearLayout xmlns:android=
        "http://schemas.android.com/apk/res/android"
    xmlns:tools="http://schemas.android.com/tools"
    android:layout_width="match_parent"
    android:layout_height="match_parent"
    android:orientation="vertical"
    tools:context="com.hfad.views.MainActivity" >
    <Button
        android:layout_width="match_parent"
        android:layout_height="0dp"
        android:layout_weight="1"
        android:text="HELLO!" />
    <Button
        android:layout_width="wrap_content"
        android:layout_height="wrap_content"
        android:text="HI!" />
</LinearLayout>
```

This button fills the screen, leaving space for another one underneath it.

```
<LinearLayout   xmlns:android=
        "http://schemas.android.com/apk/res/android"
    xmlns:tools="http://schemas.android.com/tools"
    android:layout_width="match_parent"
    android:layout_height="match_parent"
    android:orientation="vertical"
    tools:context="com.hfad.views.MainActivity" >
    <Button
        android:layout_width="wrap_content"
        android:layout_height="wrap_content"
        android:text="HELLO!" />
    <Button
        android:layout_width="wrap_content"
        android:layout_height="wrap_content"
        android:text="HI!" />
</LinearLayout>
```

Both buttons have their layout_width and layout_height properties set to "wrap_content", so they take up just enough space to display their contents.

Layouts and GUI components have a lot in common

You may have noticed that all layout types have attributes in common. Whichever type of layout you use, you must specify the layout's width and height using the android:layout_ width and android:layout_height attributes. And this requirement isn't just limited to layouts—the android:layout_width and android:layout_ height are mandatory for all GUI components too.

This is because **all layouts and GUI components are subclasses of the Android View class**. Let's look at this in more detail.

GUI components are a type of View

You've already seen that GUI components are all types of views—behind the scenes, they are all subclasses of the `android.view.View` class. This means that all of the GUI components in your user interface have attributes and behavior in common. They can all be displayed on the screen, for instance, and you get to say how tall or wide they should be. Each of the GUI components you use in your user interface takes this basic functionality and extends it.

android.view.View is the base class of all the GUI components you use to develop your apps.

android.widget.TextView is a direct subclass of the View class.

A spinner is a type of View that you saw in Chapter 2. We'll revisit it later in this chapter.

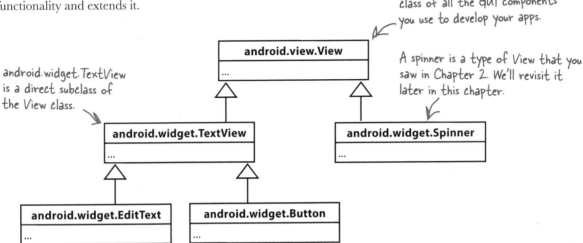

Layouts are a type of View called a ViewGroup

It's not just the GUI components that are a type of view. Under the hood, a layout is a special type of view called a **view group**. All layouts are subclasses of the `android.view.ViewGroup` class. A view group is a type of view that can contain other views.

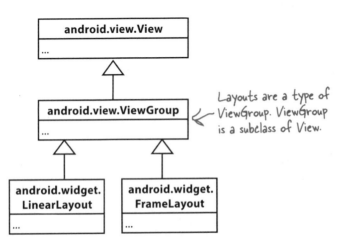

Layouts are a type of ViewGroup. ViewGroup is a subclass of View.

A GUI component is a type of view, an object that takes up space on the screen.

A layout is a type of view group, which is a special type of view that can contain other views.

What being a view buys you

A `View` object occupies rectangular space on the screen. It includes the functionality all views need in order to lead a happy helpful life in Androidville. Here are some of the qualities of views that we think are the most important:

Getting and setting properties

Each view is a Java object behind the scenes, and that means you can get and set its properties in your activity code. As an example, you can retrieve the value selected in a spinner or change the text in a text view. The exact properties and methods you can access depend on the type of view.

To help you get and set view properties, each view can have an ID associated with it so that you can refer to it in your code.

Size and position

You specify the width and height of views so that Android knows how big they need to be. You can also say whether any padding is needed around the view.

Once your view has been displayed, you can retrieve the position of the view, and its actual size on the screen.

Focus handling

Android handles how the focus moves depending on what the user does. This includes responding to any views that are hidden, removed, or made visible.

Event handling and listeners

Views can respond to events. You can also create listeners so that your app can react to things happening in the view. As an example, all views can react to getting or losing the focus, and a button (and all of its subclasses) can react to being clicked.

As a view group is also a type of view, this means that all layouts and GUI components share this common functionality.

Here are some of the View methods you can use in your activity code. As these are in the base View class, they're common to all views and view groups.

android.view.View
getId()
getHeight()
getWidth()
setVisibility(int)
findViewById(int)
isClickable()
isFocused()
requestFocus()
...

A layout is really a hierarchy of Views

The layout you define using XML gives you a *hierarchical tree of views and view groups*. As an example, here's a linear layout containing a button and an editable text field. The linear layout is a view group, and the button and text field are both views. The view group is the view's parent, and the views are the view group's children:

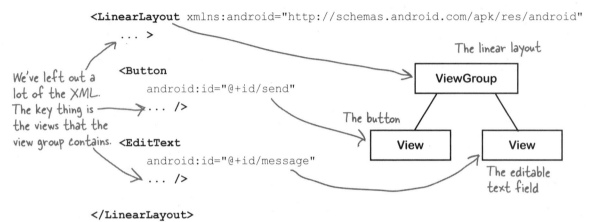

```
<LinearLayout xmlns:android="http://schemas.android.com/apk/res/android"
    ... >
```

We've left out a lot of the XML. The key thing is the views that the view group contains.

```
    <Button
        android:id="@+id/send"
        ... />

    <EditText
        android:id="@+id/message"
        ... />

</LinearLayout>
```

The linear layout

ViewGroup

The button

View

View

The editable text field

Behind the scenes, when you build your app, the layout XML is converted to a `ViewGroup` object containing a tree of `View`s. In the example above, the button gets translated to a `Button` object, and the text view gets translated to a `TextView` object. `Button` and `TextView` are both subclasses of `View`.

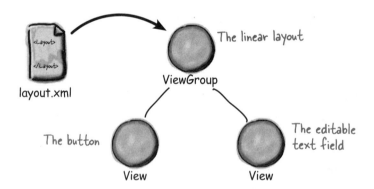

layout.xml

The linear layout

ViewGroup

The button

View

The editable text field

View

This is the reason why you can manipulate the views in your layout using Java code. Behind the scenes, all of the views are rendered to Java `View` objects.

Playing with views

Let's look at the most common GUI components. You've already seen some of these, but we'll review them anyway. We won't show you the whole API for each of these—just selected highlights to get you started.

Text view

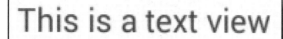

A text view is used for displaying text.

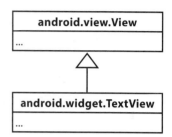

Defining it in XML

You define a text view in your layout using the `<TextView>` element. You use `android:text` to say what text you want it to display, usually by using a String resource:

```xml
<TextView
    android:id="@+id/text_view"
    android:layout_width="wrap_content"
    android:layout_height="wrap_content"
    android:text="@string/text" />
```

The `TextView` API includes many attributes to control the text view's appearance, such as the text size. To change the text size, you use the `android:textSize` attribute like this:

```xml
android:textSize="16sp"
```

You specify the text size using scale-independent pixels (sp). Scale-independent pixels take into account whether users want to use large fonts on their devices. A text size of 16sp will be physically larger on a device configured to use large fonts than on a device configured to use small fonts.

Using it in your activity code

You can change the text displayed in your text view using code like this:

```java
TextView textView = (TextView) findViewById(R.id.text_view);
textView.setText("Some other String");
```

Editable text view

This is like a text view, but editable.

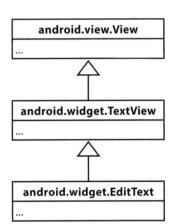

Defining it in XML

You define an editable text view in XML using the `<EditText>` element. You use the `android:hint` attribute to give a hint to the user as to how to fill in the field.

```
<EditText
    android:id="@+id/edit_text"
    android:layout_width="wrap_content"
    android:layout_height="wrap_content"
    android:hint="@string/edit_text" />
```

You can use the `android:inputType` attribute to define what type of data you're expecting the user to enter so that Android can help. As an example, if you're expecting the user to enter numbers, you can use:

```
android:inputType="number"
```

to provide them with a number keypad. Here are some more of our favorites:

You can find the entire list in the online Android developer documentation at https://developer.android.com/reference/android/widget/TextView.html#attr_android:inputType.

Value	What it does
phone	Provides a phone number keypad.
textPassword	Displays a text entry keypad, and your input is concealed.
textCapSentences	Capitalizes the first word of a sentence.
textAutoCorrect	Automatically corrects the text being input.

You can specify multiple input types using the | character. As an example, to capitalize the first word of a sentence and automatically correct any misspellings, you'd use:

```
android:inputType="textCapSentences|textAutoCorrect"
```

Using it in your activity code

You can retrieve the text entered in an editable text view like this:

```
EditText editText = (EditText) findViewById(R.id.edit_text);
String text = editText.getText().toString();
```

Button

Buttons are usually used to make your app do something when they're clicked.

Defining it in XML

You define a button in XML using the <Button> element. You use the android:text attribute to say what text you want the button to display:

```
<Button
    android:id="@+id/button"
    android:layout_width="wrap_content"
    android:layout_height="wrap_content"
    android:text="@string/button_text" />
```

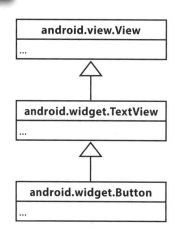

Using it in your activity code

You get the button to respond to the user clicking it by using the android:onClick attribute in the layout XML, and setting it to the name of the method you want to call in your activity code:

```
android:onClick="onButtonClicked"
```

You then define the method in your activity like this:

```
/** Called when the button is clicked */
public void onButtonClicked(View view) {
    // Do something in response to button click
}
```

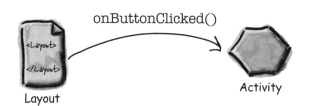

Toggle button

A toggle button allows you to choose between two states by clicking a button.

This is what the toggle button looks like when it's off.

When you click the toggle button, it changes to being on.

Defining it in XML

You define a toggle button in XML using the `<ToggleButton>` element. You use the `android:textOn` and `android:textOff` attributes to say what text you want the button to display depending on the state of the button:

```
<ToggleButton
    android:id="@+id/toggle_button"
    android:layout_width="wrap_content"
    android:layout_height="wrap_content"
    android:textOn="@string/on"
    android:textOff="@string/off" />
```

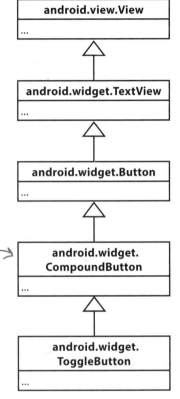

A compound button is a button with two states, checked and unchecked. A toggle button is an implementation of a compound button.

Using it in your activity code

You get the toggle button to respond to the user clicking it by using the `android:onClick` attribute in the layout XML. You give it the name of the method you want to call in your activity code:

```
android:onClick="onToggleButtonClicked"
```

This is exactly the same as calling a method when a normal button gets clicked.

You then define the method in your activity like this:

```
/** Called when the toggle button is clicked */
public void onToggleButtonClicked(View view) {
    // Get the state of the toggle button.
    boolean on = ((ToggleButton) view).isChecked();
    if (on) {
        // On
    } else {
        // Off
    }
}
```

This returns true if the toggle button is on, and false if the toggle button is off.

Switch

A switch is a slider control that acts in the same way as a toggle button.

This is the switch →  ← This is the
when it's off.   switch when
                                                                  it's on.

Defining it in XML

You define a switch in XML using the `<Switch>` element. You use the
`android:textOn` and `android:textOff` attributes to say what text
you want the switch to display depending on the state of the switch:

```
<Switch
    android:id="@+id/switch_view"
    android:layout_width="wrap_content"
    android:layout_height="wrap_content"
    android:textOn="@string/on"
    android:textOff="@string/off" />
```

Using it in your activity code

You get the switch to respond to the user clicking it by using the
`android:onClick` attribute in the layout XML, and setting it to the
name of the method you want to call in your activity code:

```
android:onClick="onSwitchClicked"
```

You then define the method in your activity like this:

```
/** Called when the switch is clicked */
public void onSwitchClicked(View view) {
    // Is the switch on?
    boolean on = ((Switch) view).isChecked();

    if (on) {
        // On
    } else {
        // Off
    }
}
```

This code is very similar to that
used with the toggle button.

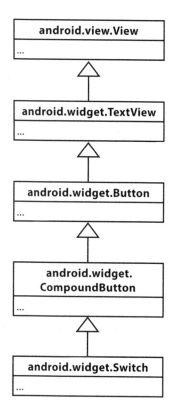

Checkboxes

Checkboxes let you display multiple options to users. They can then select whichever options they want. Each of the checkboxes can be checked or unchecked independently of any others.

Here we have two checkboxes. Users can choose milk, sugar, both milk and sugar, or neither.

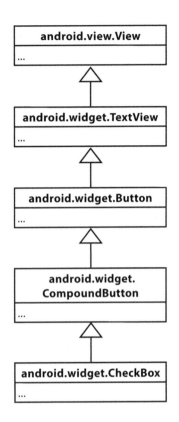

Defining them in XML

You define each checkbox in XML using the <CheckBox> element. You use the android:text attribute to display text for each option:

```
<CheckBox android:id="@+id/checkbox_milk"
    android:layout_width="wrap_content"
    android:layout_height="wrap_content"
    android:text="@string/milk" />


<CheckBox android:id="@+id/checkbox_sugar"
    android:layout_width="wrap_content"
    android:layout_height="wrap_content"
    android:text="@string/sugar" />
```

Using them in your activity code

You can find whether a particular checkbox is checked using the isChecked() method. It returns true if the checkbox is checked:

```
CheckBox checkbox = (CheckBox) findViewById(R.id.checkbox_milk);
boolean checked = checkbox.isChecked();
if (checked) {
    //do something
}
```

Checkboxes (continued)

Just like buttons, you can respond to the user clicking a checkbox by using the android:onClick attribute in the layout XML, and setting it to the name of the method you want to call in your activity code:

```
<CheckBox android:id="@+id/checkbox_milk"
    android:layout_width="wrap_content"
    android:layout_height="wrap_content"
    android:text="@string/milk"
    android:onClick="onCheckboxClicked"/>


<CheckBox android:id="@+id/checkbox_sugar"
    android:layout_width="wrap_content"
    android:layout_height="wrap_content"
    android:text="@string/sugar"
    android:onClick="onCheckboxClicked"/>
```

In this case, the onCheckboxClicked() method will get called no matter which checkbox gets clicked. We could have specified a different method for each checkbox if we'd wanted to.

You then define the method in your activity like this:

```
public void onCheckboxClicked(View view) {
    // Has the checkbox that was clicked been checked?
    boolean checked = ((CheckBox) view).isChecked();

    // Retrieve which checkbox was clicked
    switch(view.getId()) {
        case R.id.checkbox_milk:
            if (checked)
                // Milky coffee
            else
                // Black as the midnight sky on a moonless night
            break;
        case R.id.checkbox_sugar:
            if (checked)
                // Sweet
            else
                // Keep it bitter
            break;
    }
}
```

Radio buttons

These let you display multiple options to the user. The user can select a single option.

Use radio buttons to restrict the user's choice to just one option.

Defining them in XML

You start by defining a radio group, a special type of view group, using the <RadioGroup> tag. Within this, you then define individual radio buttons using the <RadioButton> tag:

```
<RadioGroup android:id="@+id/radio_group"
    android:layout_width="match_parent"
    android:layout_height="wrap_content"
    android:orientation="vertical">

    <RadioButton android:id="@+id/radio_cavemen"
        android:layout_width="wrap_content"
        android:layout_height="wrap_content"
        android:text="@string/cavemen" />

    <RadioButton android:id="@+id/radio_astronauts"
        android:layout_width="wrap_content"
        android:layout_height="wrap_content"
        android:text="@string/astronauts" />

</RadioGroup>
```

You can choose to display the radio buttons in a horizontal or vertical list.

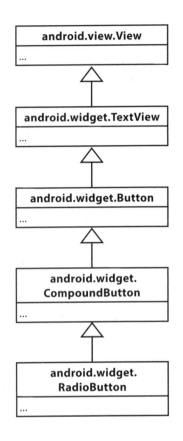

Using them in your activity code

You can find which radio button is selected using the getCheckedRadioButtonId() method:

```
RadioGroup radioGroup = (RadioGroup) findViewById(R.id.radioGroup);
int id = radioGroup.getCheckedRadioButtonId();
if (id == -1){
    //no item selected
}
else{
    RadioButton radioButton = findViewById(id);
}
```

Radio buttons (continued)

You can respond to the user clicking a radio button by using the `android:onClick` attribute in the layout XML, and setting it to the name of the method you want to call in your activity code:

```xml
<RadioGroup android:id="@+id/radio_group"
    android:layout_width="match_parent"
    android:layout_height="wrap_content"
    android:orientation="vertical">

    <RadioButton android:id="@+id/radio_cavemen"
        android:layout_width="wrap_content"
        android:layout_height="wrap_content"
        android:text="@string/cavemen"
        android:onClick="onRadioButtonClicked" />

    <RadioButton android:id="@+id/radio_astronauts"
        android:layout_width="wrap_content"
        android:layout_height="wrap_content"
        android:text="@string/astronauts"
        android:onClick="onRadioButtonClicked" />
</RadioGroup>
```

The radio group containing the radio buttons is a subclass of LinearLayout. You can use the same attributes with a radio group as you can with a linear layout.

You then define the method in your activity like this:

```java
public void onRadioButtonClicked(View view) {
    RadioGroup radioGroup = (RadioGroup) findViewById(R.id.radioGroup);
    int id = radioGroup.getCheckedRadioButtonId();
    switch(id) {
        case R.id.radio_cavemen:
            // Cavemen win
            break;
        case R.id.radio_astronauts:
            // Astronauts win
            break;
    }
}
```

Spinner

As you've already seen, a spinner gives you a drop-down list of values from which only one can be selected.

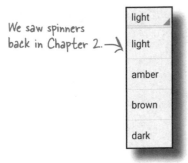

We saw spinners back in Chapter 2.

An AdapterView is a view that can use an adapter. You'll find out about adapters later in the book.

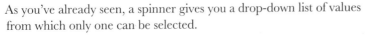

android.view.View
...

android.view.ViewGroup
...

android.widget. AdapterView
...

This is an abstract base class for Spinner widgets.

android.widget. AbsSpinner
...

There are other ways of populating the spinner, which you'll see later in the book.

android.widget.Spinner
...

Defining it in XML

You define a spinner in XML using the `<Spinner>` element. You add a static array of entries to the spinner by using the `android:entries` attribute and setting it to an array of Strings.

```
<Spinner
    android:id="@+id/spinner"
    android:layout_width="wrap_content"
    android:layout_height="wrap_content"
    android:entries="@array/spinner_values" />
```

You can add an array of Strings to *strings.xml* like this:

```
<string-array name="spinner_values">
    <item>light</item>
    <item>amber</item>
    <item>brown</item>
    <item>dark</item>
</string-array>
```

Using it in your activity code

You can get the value of the currently selected item by using the `getSelectedItem()` method and converting it to a `String`:

```
Spinner spinner = (Spinner) findViewById(R.id.spinner);
String string = String.valueOf(spinner.getSelectedItem());
```

Image view

You use an image view to display an image:

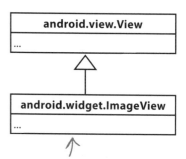

An image view contains an image. →

The ImageView class is a direct subclass of View.

Adding an image to your project

You first need to create a *drawable* resource folder, the default folder for storing image resources in your app. To do this, select the *app/src/main/res* folder in your project, go to the File menu, choose the New... option, then click on the option to create a new Android resource directory. When prompted, choose a resource type of "drawable", name the folder "drawable", and click on OK. You then need to add your image to the *app/src/main/res/drawable* folder.

If you want, you can use different image files depending on the screen density of the device. This means you can display higher-resolution images on higher-density screens, and lower-resolution images on lower-density screens. To do this, you create different *drawable* folders in *app/src/main/res* for the different screen densities. The name of the folder relates to the screen density of the device:

`drawable-ldpi`	Low-density screens, around 120 dpi.
`drawable-mdpi`	Medium-density screens, around 160 dpi.
`drawable-hdpi`	High-density screens, around 240 dpi.
`drawable-xhdpi`	Extra-high-density screens, around 320 dpi.
`drawable-xxhdpi`	Extra-extra-high-density screens, around 480 dpi.
`drawable-xxxhdpi`	Extra-extra-extra high-density screens, around 640 dpi.

Depending on what version of Android Studio you're running, the IDE may create some of these folders for you automatically.

You then put different resolution images in each of the *drawable** folders, making sure that each of the image files has the same name. Android decides which image to use at runtime, depending on the screen density of the device it's running on. As an example, if the device has an extra-high-density screen, it will use the image located in the *drawable-xhdpi* folder.

If an image is added to just one of the folders, Android will use the same image file for all devices. If you want your app to use the same image regardless of screen density, you'd normally put it in the *drawable* folder.

Image view: the layout XML

You define an image view in XML using the <ImageView> element.
You use the android:src attribute to specify what image you want to
display, and the android:contentDescription attribute to add a
String description of the image so that your app is more accessible:

```
<ImageView
    android:layout_width="200dp"
    android:layout_height="100dp"
    android:src="@drawable/starbuzz_logo"
    android:contentDescription="@string/starbuzz_logo" />
```

The android:src attribute takes a value of the form "@drawable/
image_name", where image_name is the name of the image
(without its extension). Image resources are prefixed with @drawable,
which tells Android that it's an image resource located in one or more
of the *drawable** folders.

Using image views in your activity code

You can set the image source and description in your activity code using
the setImageResource() and setContentDescription()
methods:

```
ImageView photo = (ImageView) findViewById(R.id.photo);
int image = R.drawable.starbuzz_logo;
String description = "This is the logo";
photo.setImageResource(image);
photo.setContentDescription(description);
```

This code looks for the image resource called starbuzz_logo in the
*drawable** folders, and sets it as the source of an image view with an ID
of photo. When you need to refer to an image resource in your activity
code, you use R.drawable.image_name where
image_name is the name of the image (without its extension).

Adding images to buttons

In addition to displaying images in image views, you can also display images on buttons.

Displaying text and an image on a button

To display text on a button with an image to the right of it, use the android:drawableRight attribute and specify the image to be used:

```
<Button
    android:layout_width="wrap_content"
    android:layout_height="wrap_content"
    android:drawableRight="@drawable/android"
    android:text="@string/click_me" />
```

Display the android image resource on the right side of the button.

You can also use drawableStart and drawableEnd to support right-to-left languages.

If you want to display the image on the left, use the android:drawableLeft attribute:

```
<Button
    android:layout_width="wrap_content"
    android:layout_height="wrap_content"
    android:drawableLeft="@drawable/android"
    android:text="@string/click_me" />
```

Use the android:drawableBottom attribute to display the image underneath the text:

```
<Button
    android:layout_width="wrap_content"
    android:layout_height="wrap_content"
    android:drawableBottom="@drawable/android"
    android:text="@string/click_me" />
```

The android:drawableTop attribute displays the image above the text:

```
<Button
    android:layout_width="wrap_content"
    android:layout_height="wrap_content"
    android:drawableTop="@drawable/android"
    android:text="@string/click_me" />
```

Image button

An image button is just like a button, except it contains an image and no text.

Defining it in XML

You define an image button in XML using the <ImageButton> element. You use the android:src attribute to say what image you want the image button to display:

```
<ImageButton
    android:id="@+id/button"
    android:layout_width="wrap_content"
    android:layout_height="wrap_content"
    android:src="@drawable/button_icon" />
```

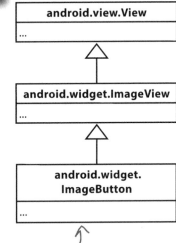

The ImageButton class extends the ImageView class, not the Button class.

Using it in your activity code

You get the image button to respond to the user clicking it by using the android:onClick attribute in the layout XML, and setting it to the name of the method you want to call in your activity code:

```
android:onClick="onButtonClicked"
```

You then define the method in your activity like this:

```
/** Called when the image button is clicked */
public void onButtonClicked(View view) {
    // Do something in response to button click
}
```

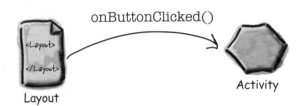

Scroll view

If you add lots of views to your layouts, you may have problems on devices with smaller screens—most layouts don't come with scrollbars to allow you to scroll down the page. As an example, when we added seven large buttons to a linear layout, we couldn't see all of them.

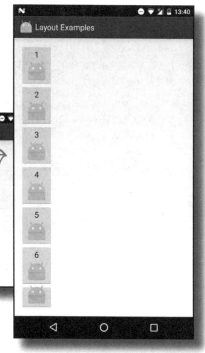

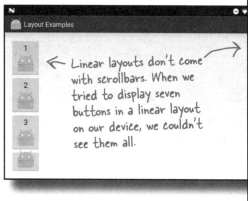

← Linear layouts don't come with scrollbars. When we tried to display seven buttons in a linear layout on our device, we couldn't see them all.

To add a vertical scrollbar to your layout, you surround your existing layout with a **`<ScrollView>`** element like this:

```
<ScrollView xmlns:android="http://schemas.android.com/apk/res/android"
    xmlns:tools="http://schemas.android.com/tools"
    android:layout_width="match_parent"
    android:layout_height="match_parent"
    tools:context="com.hfad.views.MainActivity" >
```

Move these attributes from the original layout to the `<ScrollView>`, as the `<ScrollView>` is now the root element.

```
    <LinearLayout
        android:layout_width="match_parent"
        android:layout_height="match_parent"
        android:paddingBottom="16dp"
        android:paddingLeft="16dp"
        android:paddingRight="16dp"
        android:paddingTop="16dp"
        android:orientation="vertical" >
        ...
    </LinearLayout>
</ScrollView>
```

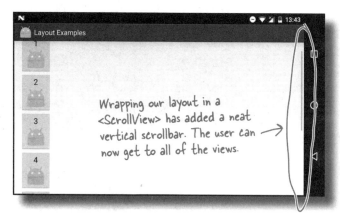

Wrapping our layout in a `<ScrollView>` has added a neat vertical scrollbar. The user can now get to all of the views. →

To add a horizontal scrollbar to your layout, wrap your existing layout inside a **`<HorizontalScrollView>`** element instead.

Toasts

There's one final widget we want to show you in this chapter: a toast. A toast is a simple pop-up message you can display on the screen.

Toasts are purely informative, as the user can't interact with them. While a toast is displayed, the activity stays visible and interactive. The toast automatically disappears when it times out.

Using it in your activity code

You create a toast using activity code only. You can't define one in your layout.

To create a toast, you call the `Toast.makeText()` method, and pass it three parameters: a `Context` (usually `this` for the current activity), a `CharSequence` that's the message you want to display, and an `int` duration. Once you've created the toast, you call its `show()` method to display it.

Here's the code you would use to create a toast that appears on screen for a short duration:

```
CharSequence text = "Hello, I'm a Toast!";
int duration = Toast.LENGTH_SHORT;

Toast toast = Toast.makeText(this, text, duration);
toast.show();
```

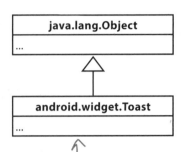

A toast isn't actually a type of view. It's a useful way of displaying a short message to the user, though, so we're sneaking it into this chapter.

A toast is a message that pops up like toast in a toaster.

By default, the toast appears at the bottom of the screen.

Hello, I'm a Toast!

Exercise

It's time for you to try out some of the views we've introduced you to this chapter. Create a layout that will create this screen:

You probably won't want to write the code here, but why not experiment in the IDE?

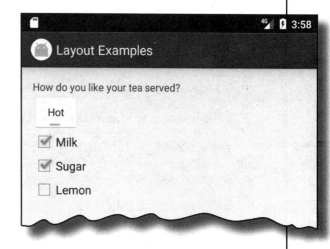

Exercise Solution

Here's one of the many ways in which you can create the layout. Don't worry if your code looks different, as there are many different solutions.

```
<LinearLayout xmlns:android="http://schemas.android.com/apk/res/android"

    xmlns:tools="http://schemas.android.com/tools"

    android:layout_width="match_parent"

    android:layout_height="match_parent"

    android:padding="16dp"

    android:orientation="vertical"

    tools:context="com.hfad.layoutexamples.MainActivity" >


    <TextView

        android:layout_width="wrap_content"

        android:layout_height="wrap_content"

        android:text="How do you like your tea served?" />

    <ToggleButton

        android:layout_width="wrap_content"

        android:layout_height="wrap_content"

        android:textOn="Hot"

        android:textOff="Cold" />
```

We used a toggle button to display whether the drink should be served hot or cold.

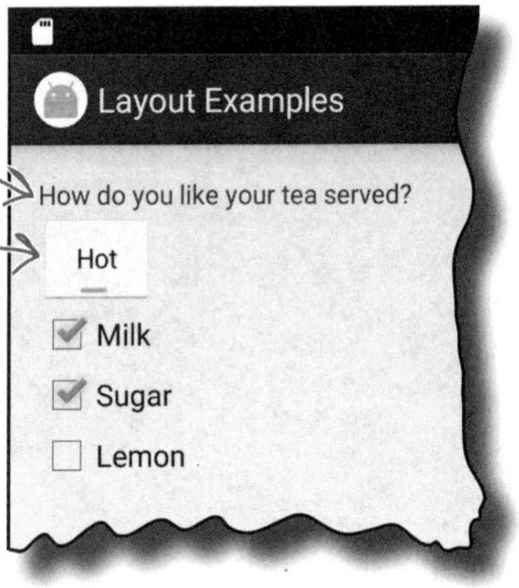

Layout Examples

How do you like your tea served?

Hot

☑ Milk

☑ Sugar

☐ Lemon

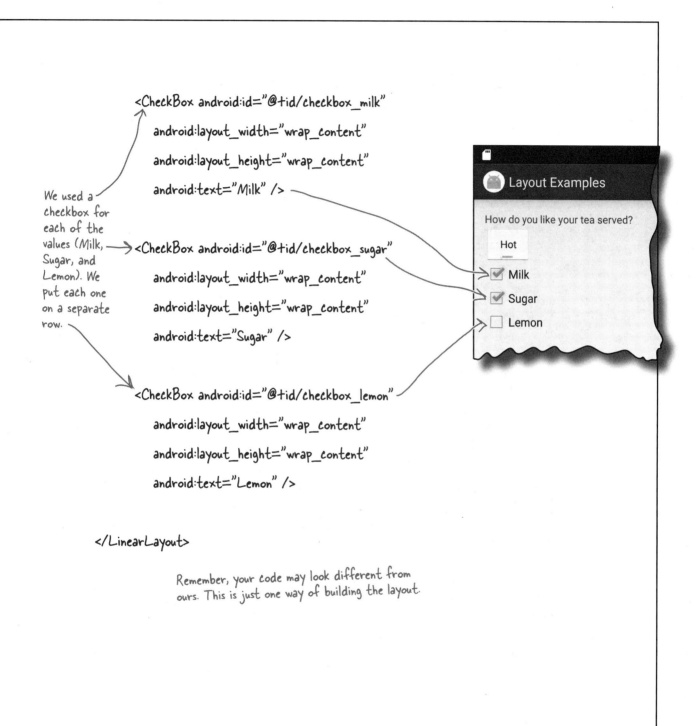

```
<CheckBox android:id="@+id/checkbox_milk"
    android:layout_width="wrap_content"
    android:layout_height="wrap_content"
    android:text="Milk" />
```

We used a checkbox for each of the values (Milk, Sugar, and Lemon). We put each one on a separate row.

```
<CheckBox android:id="@+id/checkbox_sugar"
    android:layout_width="wrap_content"
    android:layout_height="wrap_content"
    android:text="Sugar" />
```

```
<CheckBox android:id="@+id/checkbox_lemon"
    android:layout_width="wrap_content"
    android:layout_height="wrap_content"
    android:text="Lemon" />
```

```
</LinearLayout>
```

Remember, your code may look different from ours. This is just one way of building the layout.

Your Android Toolbox

You've got Chapter 5 under your belt and now you've added views and view groups to your toolbox.

You can download the full code for the chapter from https://tinyurl.com/HeadFirstAndroid.

BULLET POINTS

- GUI components are all types of view. They are all subclasses of the `android.view.View` class.

- All layouts are subclasses of the `android.view.ViewGroup` class. A view group is a type of view that can contain multiple views.

- The layout XML file gets converted to a `ViewGroup` containing a hierarchical tree of views.

- A linear layout lists views either horizontally or vertically. You specify the direction using the `android:orientation` attribute.

- A frame layout stacks views.

- Use `android:padding*` attributes to specify how much padding you want around a view.

- In a linear layout, use `android:layout_weight` if you want a view to use up extra space in the layout.

- `android:layout_gravity` lets you say where you want views to appear in their available space.

- `android:gravity` lets you say where you want the contents to appear inside a view.

- `<ToggleButton>` defines a toggle button that allows you to choose between two states by clicking a button.

- `<Switch>` defines a switch control that behaves in the same way as a toggle button. It requires API level 14 or above.

- `<CheckBox>` defines a checkbox.

- To define a group of radio buttons, first use `<RadioGroup>` to define the radio group. Then put individual radio buttons in the radio group using `<RadioButton>`.

- Use `<ImageView>` to display an image.

- `<ImageButton>` defines a button with no text, just an image.

- Add scrollbars using `<ScrollView>` or `<HorizontalScrollView>`.

- A `Toast` is a pop-up message.

6 constraint layouts

Put Things in Their Place

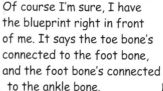

Of course I'm sure, I have the blueprint right in front of me. It says the toe bone's connected to the foot bone, and the foot bone's connected to the ankle bone.

Let's face it, you need to know how to create great layouts.

If you're building apps you want people to **use**, you need to make sure they **look exactly the way you want**. So far you've seen how to use linear and frame layouts, but *what if your design is more complex?* To deal with this, we'll introduce you to Android's new **constraint layout**, a type of layout you **build visually using a blueprint**. We'll show you how **constraints** let you position and size your views, *irrespective of screen size and orientation*. Finally, you'll find out how to save time by making Android Studio **infer and add constraints** on your behalf.

Nested layouts can be inefficient

You've seen how to build a simple user interface using linear layouts and frame layouts, but what if you need to create something more complex? While complex UIs are possible if you nest your linear and frame layouts deep enough, they can slow down your app and make your code hard to read and maintain.

As an example, suppose you wanted to create a layout containing two rows, each containing two items. One possibility would be to create this layout using three linear layouts: one linear layout at the root, and one nested linear layout for each row:

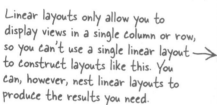

Linear layouts only allow you to display views in a single column or row, so you can't use a single linear layout to construct layouts like this. You can, however, nest linear layouts to produce the results you need.

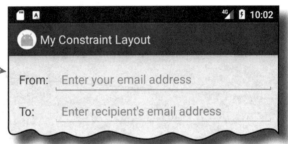

For this layout, you could use one linear layout at the root, and one nested linear layout for each row.

When Android displays a layout on the device screen, it creates a hierarchy of views based on the layout components which helps it figure out where each view should be placed. If the layout contains nested layouts, the hierarchy is more complex, and Android may need to make more than one pass through the hierarchy:

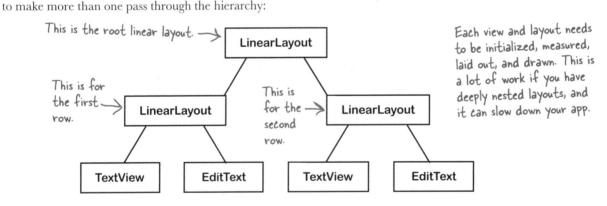

This is the root linear layout.

This is for the first row.

This is for the second row.

Each view and layout needs to be initialized, measured, laid out, and drawn. This is a lot of work if you have deeply nested layouts, and it can slow down your app.

While the above hierarchy is still relatively simple, imagine if you needed more views, more nested layouts, and a deeper hierarchy. This could lead to bottlenecks in your app's performance, and leave you with a mass of code that's difficult to read and maintain.

If you have a more complex UI that requires you to nest multiple layouts, it's usually better to **use a different type of layout**.

Introducing the constraint layout

In this chapter we're going to focus on using a new type of layout called a **constraint layout**. This type of layout is more complex than a linear or frame layout, but it's a lot more flexible. It's also much more efficient for complex UIs as it gives you a flatter view hierarchy, which means that Android has less processing to do at runtime.

You design constraint layouts VISUALLY

Another advantage of using constraint layouts is that they're specifically designed to work with Android Studio's design editor. Unlike linear and frame layouts where you usually hack direct in XML, you build constraint layouts *visually*. You drag and drop GUI components onto the design editor's blueprint tool, and give it instructions for how each view should be displayed.

To see this in action, we're going to take you on a tour of using a constraint layout, then build the following UI:

> To build constraint layouts using the visual tools, you need Android Studio 2.3 or above. If you're using an older version, check for updates.

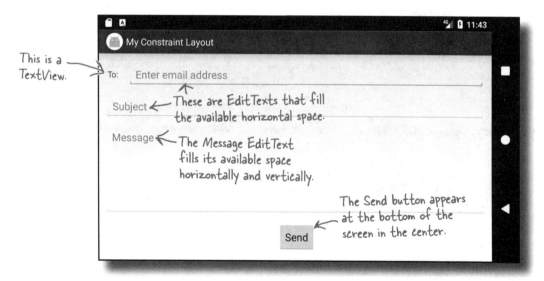

This is a TextView.

These are EditTexts that fill the available horizontal space.

The Message EditText fills its available space horizontally and vertically.

The Send button appears at the bottom of the screen in the center.

Create a new project

We'll start by creating a new Android Studio project for an application named "My Constraint Layout" with a company domain of "hfad.com", making the package name `com.hfad.myconstraintlayout`. The minimum SDK should be API 19 so that it will work on most devices. You'll need an empty activity called "MainActivity" with a layout called "activity_main" so that your code matches ours. **Make sure you uncheck the Backwards Compatibility (AppCompat) option when you create the activity.**

Make sure your project includes the Constraint Layout Library

Unlike the other layouts you've seen so far, constraint layouts come in their own library, which you need to add to your project as a dependency before you can use it. Adding a library as a dependency means that the library gets included in your app, and downloaded to the user's device.

It's likely that Android Studio added the Constraint Layout Library to your project automatically, but let's check. In Android Studio, choose File→Project Structure. Then click on the app module and choose Dependencies. You'll be presented with the following screen:

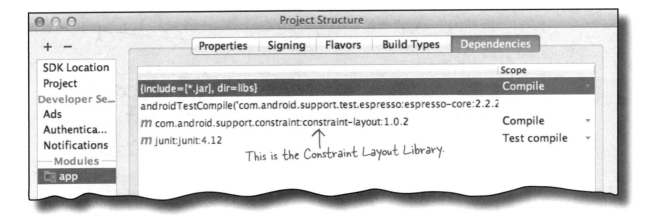

This is the Constraint Layout Library.

If Android Studio has already added the Constraint Layout Library for you, you will see it listed as "com.android.support.constraint:constraint-layout," as shown above.

If the library hasn't been added for you, you will need to add it yourself. To do this, click on the "+" button at the bottom or right side of the Project Structure screen. Choose the Library Dependency option, and select the Constraint Layout Library option from the list. If you don't see it listed, type the following text into the search box:

```
com.android.support.constraint:constraint-layout:1.0.2
```

You only need to type this in if the Constraint Layout Library hasn't already been added to your project as a dependency.

When you click on the OK button, the Constraint Layout Library should be added to the list of dependencies. Click on OK again to save your changes and close the Project Structure window.

Now that we know that our project contains the Constraint Layout Library, let's add the String resources we'll need for our layout.

Add the String resources to strings.xml

Each of the views in our layout will display text values or hints, so we'll add these as String resources. Add the String values below to *strings.xml*:

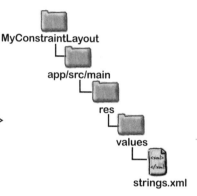

```
. . .

    <string name="to_label">To:</string>
    <string name="email_hint">Enter email address</string>
    <string name="subject_hint">Subject</string>
    <string name="message_hint">Message</string>
    <string name="send_button">Send</string>

. . .
```

Now that we've added our String resources, we'll update the layout.

Change activity_main.xml to use a constraint layout

We're going to use a constraint layout. To do this (and to make sure that your layout matches ours), update your code in *activity_main.xml* to match the code below (our changes are in bold):

```
<?xml version="1.0" encoding="utf-8"?>
<android.support.constraint.ConstraintLayout
    xmlns:android="http://schemas.android.com/apk/res/android"
    xmlns:app="http://schemas.android.com/apk/res-auto"
    xmlns:tools="http://schemas.android.com/tools"
    android:layout_width="match_parent"
    android:layout_height="match_parent"
    tools:context="com.hfad.myconstraintlayout.MainActivity">

</android.support.constraint.ConstraintLayout>
```

This is how you define a constraint layout.

If Android Studio added any extra views for you, delete them.

This defines a constraint layout to which we can add views. We'll do this using the design editor's blueprint tool.

Use the blueprint tool

To use the blueprint tool, first switch to the design view of your layout code by clicking on the Design tab. Then click on the Show Blueprint button in the design editor's toolbar to display the blueprint. Finally, drag a Button widget from the design editor's palette to the blueprint. This adds a button to your layout:

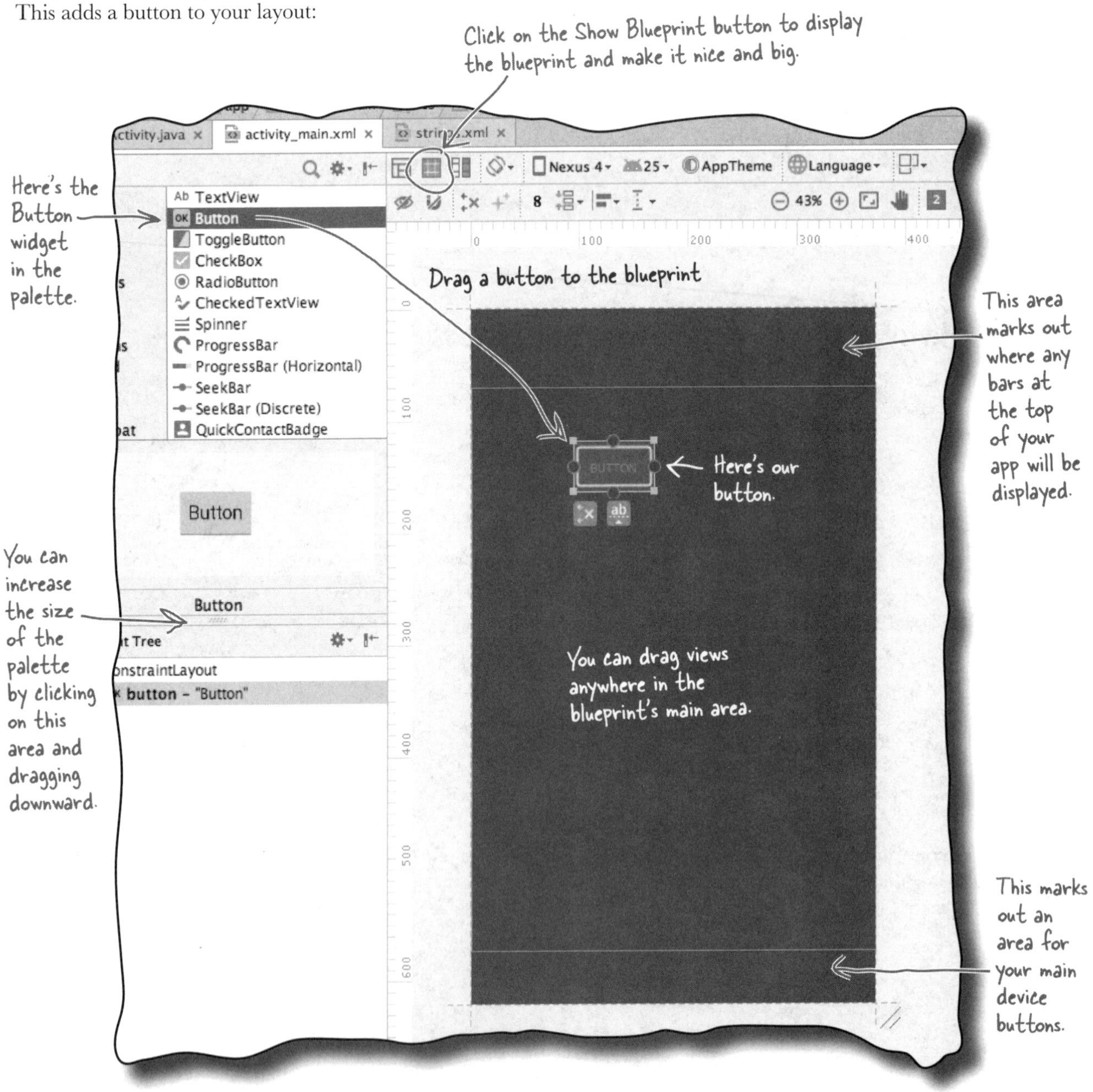

Click on the Show Blueprint button to display the blueprint and make it nice and big.

Here's the Button widget in the palette.

Drag a button to the blueprint

This area marks out where any bars at the top of your app will be displayed.

Here's our button.

You can drag views anywhere in the blueprint's main area.

You can increase the size of the palette by clicking on this area and dragging downward.

This marks out an area for your main device buttons.

Position views using constraints

With a constraint layout, you don't specify where views should be positioned by dropping them on the blueprint in a particular place. Instead, you specify placement by defining **constraints**. A **constraint** is a connection or attachment that tells the layout where the view should be positioned. For example, you can use a constraint to attach a view to the start edge of the layout, or underneath another view.

We'll add a horizontal constraint to the button

To see how this works, let's add a constraint to attach our button to the left edge of the layout.

First, make sure the button's selected by clicking it. When you select a view, a bounding box is drawn around it, and handles are added to its corners and sides. The square handles in the corners let you resize the view, and the round handles on the sides let you add constraints:

When you select a view, a bounding box is drawn around it.

Use the square handles at the corners to resize the view.

Use the round handles on the sides to add constraints.

To add a constraint, you click on one of the view's constraint handles and drag it to whatever you want to attach it to. In our case, we're going to attach the left edge of the button to the left edge of the layout, so click on the left constraint handle and drag it to the left edge of the blueprint:

Click on the round handle on the button's left side, and drag it to the left edge of the blueprint.

This adds the constraint, and pulls the button over to the left:

The button slides to the edge of the blueprint when you add the constraint.

That's how you add a horizontal constraint. We'll add a vertical constraint to the button next.

Add a vertical constraint

Let's add a second constraint to the button to attach it to the top of the layout. To do this, click on the button's top constraint handle, and drag it to the top of the blueprint's main area. This adds the second constraint, and the button slides to the top of the main area.

Each view in a constraint layout must have at least two constraints—a horizontal constraint and a vertical one—in order to specify where it should be positioned. If you omit the horizontal constraint, the view is displayed next to the start edge of the layout at runtime. If you omit the vertical constraint, the view is displayed at the top of the layout. **This is irrespective of where the view is positioned in the blueprint.**

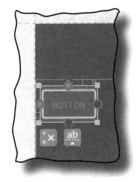

Click on the round handle on the button's top edge, and drag it to the top of the blueprint.

The button slides to the top of the blueprint's main area.

Changing the view's margins

When you add a constraint to a view, the design editor automatically adds a margin on the same edge as the constraint. You can set the size of the default margin in the design editor's toolbar by changing the number in the Default Margin box:

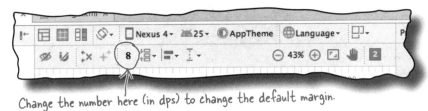

Change the number here (in dps) to change the default margin.

Changing the size of the default margin specifies the size of any *new* margins that get added. The size of any existing margins remain unchanged, but you can change these using the property window.

The property window is displayed in a separate panel at the side of the design editor. When you select a view, it displays a diagram featuring the view's constraints and the size of its margins. To change the size of a margin, you change the number next to the relevant side of the view.

You can also change the size of a view's margins by clicking and dragging the view in the blueprint. This technique has the same effect as changing the size of the margin in the property window, but it's harder to be precise.

Try changing the size of both margins using each method before looking at the next page.

This is the property window.

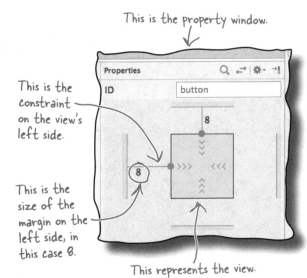

This is the constraint on the view's left side.

This is the size of the margin on the left side, in this case 8.

This represents the view.

Changes to the blueprint are reflected in the XML

When you add views to the blueprint and specify constraints, these changes are reflected in the layout's underlying XML. To see this, switch to the text view of your code. Your code should look something like this (but don't worry if it's slightly different):

```xml
<?xml version="1.0" encoding="utf-8"?>
<android.support.constraint.ConstraintLayout
    ...>
```

The design editor's added a button.

```xml
<Button
    android:id="@+id/button"
    android:layout_width="wrap_content"
    android:layout_height="wrap_content"
    android:layout_marginLeft="8dp"
    android:layout_marginTop="32dp"
    android:text="Button"
    app:layout_constraintLeft_toLeftOf="parent"
    app:layout_constraintTop_toTopOf="parent" />
```

These are all attributes you've seen before.

These lines only apply to constraint layouts.

```xml
</android.support.constraint.ConstraintLayout>
```

MyConstraintLayout

app/src/main

res

layout

activity_
main.xml

As you can see, our XML now includes a button. Most of the code for the button should look familiar to you, as it's material we covered in Chapter 5. The button's width, height, and margins are specified in exactly the same way as before. The only unfamiliar code is the two lines that specify the view's constraints on its left and top edges:

```xml
<Button>
    ...
    app:layout_constraintLeft_toLeftOf="parent"
    app:layout_constraintTop_toTopOf="parent" />
```

These lines describe the constraints on the button's left and top edges.

Similar code is generated if you add constraints to the button's remaining edges.

Next, switch your code back to design view, and we'll look at other techniques for positioning your views in a constraint layout.

How to center views

So far you've seen how you can use constraints to attach a view to the edge of its layout. This works well if you want to position a view in the top-left corner, for example, but what if you want to position it in the center?

To position views in the center of its layout, you add constraints to opposite sides of the view. Let's see how this works by centering our button horizontally.

Make sure the button is selected, then click on the constraint handle on its right edge, and drag it to the right edge of the layout:

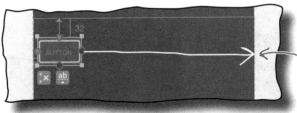

Click on the constraint handle on the button's right edge, and drag it to the right edge of the blueprint.

This adds a constraint to the view's right edge. As the button now has two horizontal constraints, one on each side, the button is pulled to the center, and the two opposing constraints are displayed in the blueprint as springs:

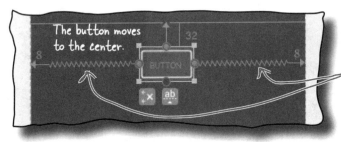

The button moves to the center.

Constraints on opposite sides of a view are displayed as springs.

As the button is now attached to both sides of the layout, it's displayed in the center irrespective of screen size or orientation. You can experiment with this by running the app, or changing the size of the blueprint by dragging the blueprint's bottom-right corner:

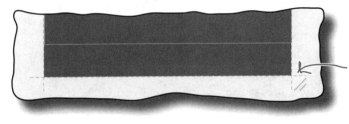

You can resize the blueprint by clicking and dragging its bottom-right corner.

Adjust a view's position by updating its bias

Once you've added constraints to opposite sides of your view, you can control where it should be positioned relative to each side by changing its **bias**. This tells Android what the proportionate length of the constraint should be on either side of the view.

To see this in action, let's change our button's horizontal bias so that it's positioned off-center. First, make sure the button's selected, then look in the view's property window. Underneath the diagram of the view, you should see a slider with a number in it. This represents the view's horizontal bias as a percentage:

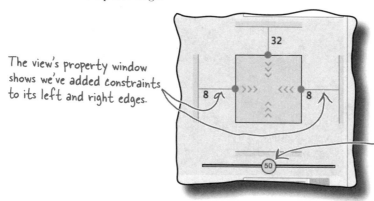

The view's property window shows we've added constraints to its left and right edges.

This slider is for the view's horizontal bias. It currently displays 50 as the view is displayed halfway between its horizontal constraints.

To change the value of the bias, simply move the slider. If you move the slider to the left, for example, it moves the button in the blueprint to the left too:

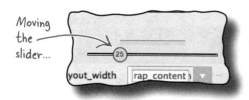

Moving the slider...

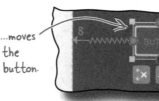

...moves the button.

You can also move the button by clicking and dragging it, but that technique is less accurate.

The view maintains this relative position irrespective of screen size and orientation.

When you add a bias to a view in the design editor, this is reflected in the underlying XML. If you change the horizontal bias of your view to 25%, for example, the following code gets added to the view's XML:

```
app:layout_constraintHorizontal_bias="0.25"
```

Now that you know how bias works, let's look at how you specify a view's size.

How to change a view's size

With a constraint layout, you have several different options for specifying a view's size:

⭐ Make it a fixed size by specifying a specific width and height.

⭐ Use `wrap_content` to make the view just big enough to display its contents.

⭐ Tell it to match the size of its constraints (if you've added constraints to opposite sides of the view).

⭐ Specify a ratio for the width and height so that, for example, the view's width is twice the size of its height.

We'll go through these options one-by-one.

1. Make the view a fixed size

There are a couple of ways of using the design editor to make the view a fixed size. One way is to simply resize the view in the blueprint by clicking and dragging the square resizing handles on its corners. The other way is to type values into the `layout_width` and `layout_height` fields in the properties window:

You can resize a view using the square resizing handles on its corners.

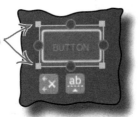

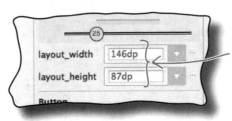

You can also hardcode the width and height in the view's property window.

In general, **making your view a fixed size is a bad idea**, as it means the view can't grow or shrink to fit the size of its contents or the size of the screen.

2. Make it just big enough

To make the view just large enough to display its contents, change the view's `layout_width` and `layout_height` properties to `wrap_content`. You do this in the view's property window as shown here:

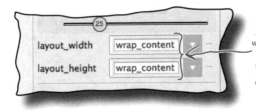

Setting the width and height to "wrap_content" makes it just large enough to display its contents, just as it does in other layouts.

3. Match the view's constraints

If you've added constraints to opposite sides of your view, you can make the view as wide as its constraints. You do this by setting its width and/or height to 0dp: set its width to 0dp to get the view to match the size of its horizontal constraints, and set its height to 0dp to get it to match the size of its vertical constraints.

In our case, we've added constraints to the left and right sides of our button, so we can get the button to match the size of these constraints. To do this, go to the view's property window, and change the `layout_width` property to 0dp. In the blueprint, the button should expand to fill the available horizontal space (allowing for any margins):

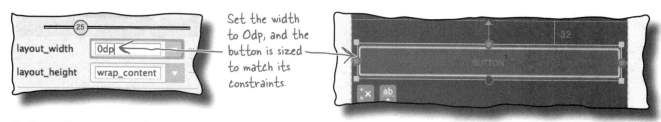

Set the width to 0dp, and the button is sized to match its constraints.

4. Specify the width:height ratio

Finally, you can specify an aspect ratio for the view's width and height. To do this, change the view's `layout_width` *or* `layout_height` to 0dp as you did above, then click in the top-left corner of the view diagram that's displayed in the property window. This should display a ratio field, which you can then update:

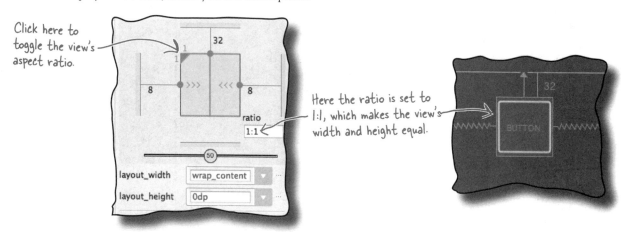

Click here to toggle the view's aspect ratio.

Here the ratio is set to 1:1, which makes the view's width and height equal.

Now that you've seen how to resize a view, try experimenting with the different techniques before having a go at the exercise on the next page.

BE the Constraint

Your job is to play like you're the constraint layout and draw the constraints that are needed to produce each layout. You also need to specify the layout_width, layout_height, and bias (when needed) for each view. We've completed the first one for you.

You need to add the views and constraints to each blueprint.

A

This is how we want the screen to look.

A button appears in the top-right corner.

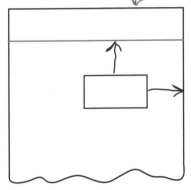

layout_width: wrap_content
layout_height: wrap_content

B

A button's centered at the bottom of the screen.

Button

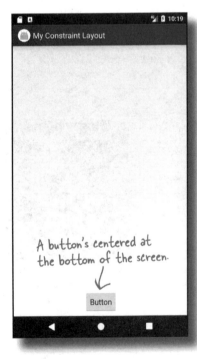

The button fills the available space.

C

D

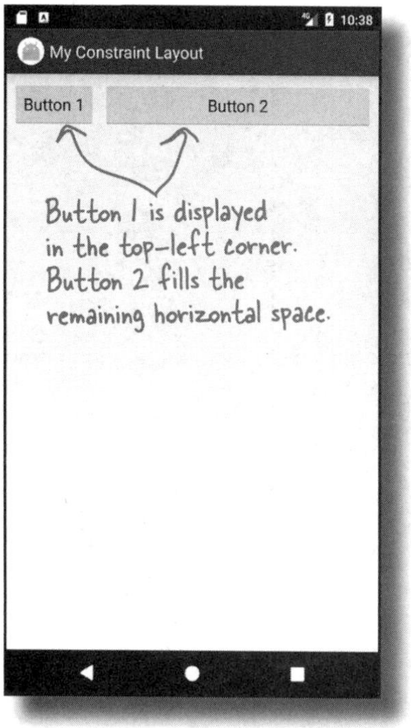

Button 1 is displayed
in the top-left corner.
Button 2 fills the
remaining horizontal space.

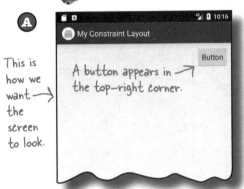

BE the Constraint Solution

Your job is to play like you're the constraint layout and draw the constraints that are needed to produce each layout. You also need to specify the layout_width, layout_height, and bias (when needed) for each view. We've completed the first one for you.

A

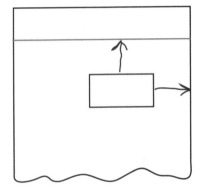

This is how we want the screen to look.

A button appears in the top-right corner.

layout_width: wrap_content
layout_height: wrap_content

B

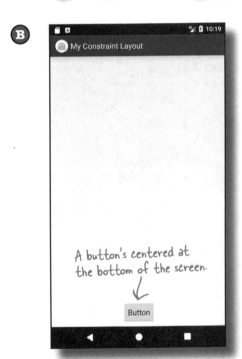

A button's centered at the bottom of the screen.

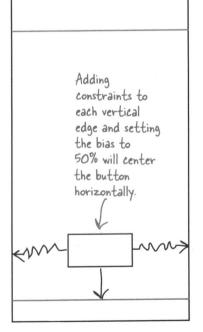

Adding constraints to each vertical edge and setting the bias to 50% will center the button horizontally.

layout_width: wrap_content
layout_height: wrap_content
bias: 50%

The button fills the available space.

 C

 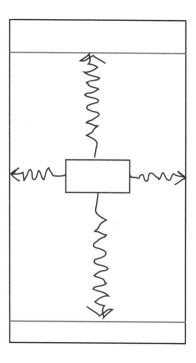

The button needs to stretch in all directions, so it requires constraints on all edges, and its width and height need to be set to 0dp.

layout_width: 0dp
layout_height: 0dp

 D

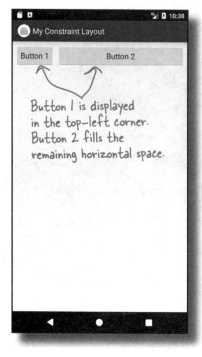 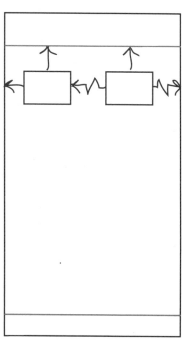

Button 1 is displayed in the top-left corner. Button 2 fills the remaining horizontal space.

Button 1:
layout_width: wrap_content
layout_height: wrap_content

Button 2:
layout_width: 0dp
layout_height: wrap_content

To make Button 2 fill the remaining horizontal space, we add constraints to each vertical edge and set its width to 0dp. Its left edge is attached to Button 1's right edge.

How to align views

So far you've seen how to position and size a single view. Next, let's examine how you align it with another view.

First, click on the Show Constraints button in the design edit toolbar to display all the constraints in the blueprint (not just the ones for the selected view). Then drag a second button from the palette to the blueprint, and place it underneath the first:

This is the Show Constraints button. Clicking on it shows (or hides) all the constraints in the layout.

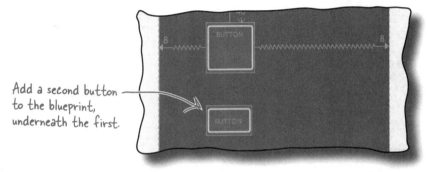

Add a second button to the blueprint, underneath the first.

To display the second button underneath the first when the app runs, we need to add a constraint to the second button's top edge, and attach it to the first button's bottom edge. To do this, select the second button, and draw a constraint from its top edge to the bottom edge of the other button:

This adds a constraint attaching the top of one button to the bottom edge of the other.

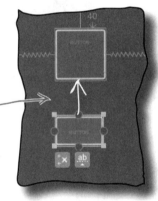

To align the left edges of both buttons, select both buttons by holding down the Shift key when you select each one, then click on the Align Left Edges button in the design editor toolbar:

Clicking on this button gives you different options for aligning views.

Aligning the view's left edges adds another constraint.

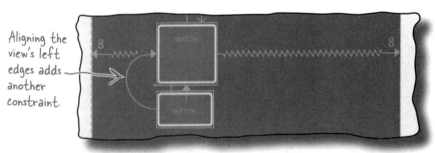

This adds a constraint from the left edge of the second button to the left edge of the first, and this constraint aligns the view's edges.

Let's build a real layout

You now know enough about constraint layouts to start building a real one. Here's the layout we're going to create:

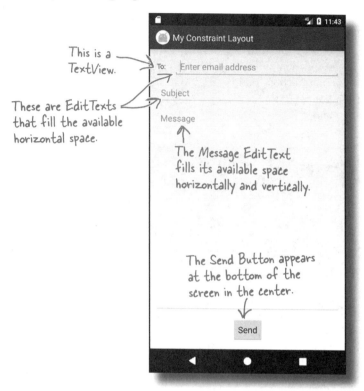

This is a TextView.

These are EditTexts that fill the available horizontal space.

The Message EditText fills its available space horizontally and vertically.

The Send Button appears at the bottom of the screen in the center.

We'll build it from scratch in *activity_main.xml*, so before we get started, delete any views that are already in the layout so that the blueprint's empty, and make sure your *activity_main.xml* code looks like this:

```xml
<?xml version="1.0" encoding="utf-8"?>
<android.support.constraint.ConstraintLayout
    xmlns:android="http://schemas.android.com/apk/res/android"
    xmlns:app="http://schemas.android.com/apk/res-auto"
    xmlns:tools="http://schemas.android.com/tools"
    android:layout_width="match_parent"
    android:layout_height="match_parent"
    tools:context="com.hfad.myconstraintlayout.MainActivity">

</android.support.constraint.ConstraintLayout>
```

MyConstraintLayout

app/src/main

res

layout

activity_main.xml

First, add the top line of views

We're going to start by adding the views we want to appear at the top of the layout: a text view and an editable text field.

To do this, switch to the design editor if you haven't already done so, then drag a TextView from the palette to the top-left corner of the blueprint. Next, drag an E-mail component to the blueprint so it's positioned to the right of the text view. This is an editable text field that uses Android's email keyboard for data entry. Manually resize the E-mail component so that it lines up with the text view and fills any remaining horizontal space:

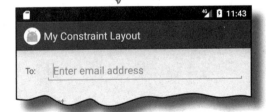

The top line of the layout features a TextView label and an EditText for the email address.

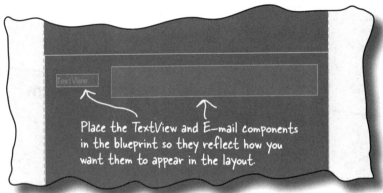

Place the TextView and E-mail components in the blueprint so they reflect how you want them to appear in the layout.

Notice that we haven't added any constraints to either view yet, and we've positioned them where we want them to appear when the layout's displayed on a device. There's a good reason for this: to save us some work, **we're going to get the design editor to figure out the constraints.**

Get the design editor to infer the constraints

As you already know, a constraint layout uses constraints to determine where its views should be positioned. The great news is that the design editor has an Infer Constraints button that's designed to work out what it thinks the constraints should be, and add them. To use this feature, simply click on the Infer Constraints button in the design editor's toolbar:

This is the Infer Constraints button. Click it now.

The Infer Constraints feature guesses which constraints to add

When you click on the Infer Constraints button, the design editor tries to figure out what the constraints should be and adds them for you. It's not completely foolproof, as it can't read your mind (as far as we know) to determine how you want the layout to behave on a real device. It simply guesses based on each view's position in the blueprint.

Here are the changes the design editor made for us when we clicked on the Infer Constraints button (yours may look different if you positioned your views differently):

Clicking on the Infer Constraints button added constraints to both views.

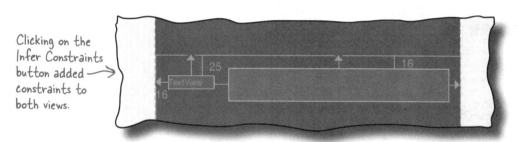

You can check the details of each constraint by selecting each view in turn and looking at its values in the property window.

If you don't like what the Infer Constraints feature has done, you can undo the changes it's made by choosing Undo Infer Constraints from the Edit menu, or adjust individual constraints.

We're going to tweak our views before adding more items to the blueprint. First, select the text view in the blueprint, then edit its properties in the properties panel to give it an ID of to_label and a text value of "@string/to_label". This does the same thing as adding the following lines of code to the <TextView> element in the XML:

When you update the ID, don't worry if Android Studio displays a message telling you it's going to make changes to the code. We want it to do this because we're changing the view's ID.

Update this property to change the TextView's text value.

```
android:id="@+id/to_label"
android:text="@string/to_label"
```

Android Studio adds these lines of code when you change the view's ID and text value.

TextView	
text	@string/to_label
� text	

Next, select the E-mail component EditText, and change its ID to email_address, its layout_height to "wrap_content", and its hint to "@string/email_hint". This does the same thing as adding these lines to the <EditText> element in the XML:

```
android:id="@+id/email_address"
android:layout_height="wrap_content"
android:hint="@string/email_hint"
```

Android Studio adds these lines of code when you change the view's layout_height and hint value.

Now that we've added the first line of views to the blueprint, let's add some more.

Add the next line to the blueprint...

The next row of the layout contains an editable text field for the message subject. Drag a Plain Text component from the palette to the blueprint, and position it underneath the two items we've already added. This adds an `EditText` to the blueprint. Then change the component's size and position so that it lines up with the other views and fills the horizontal space:

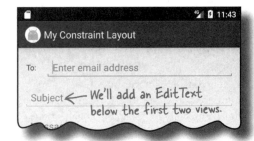

To: Enter email address

Subject ← We'll add an EditText below the first two views.

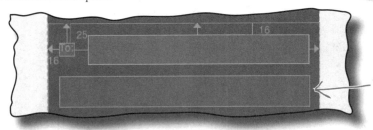

The Plain Text component adds an EditText to the layout.

Then click on the Infer Constraints button again. The design editor adds more constraints, this time positioning the new component:

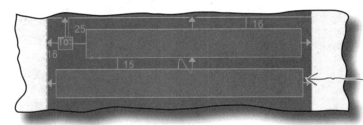

The design editor adds constraints to the new EditText when we click on the Infer Constraints button.

Select the new view in the blueprint, and then change its ID to `subject`, its `layout_height` to `"wrap_content"`, and its hint to `"@string/subject_hint"`, and delete any text in the `text` property that the design editor may have added.

...and then add the button

Next, we'll add a button to the bottom of the layout. Drag a Button component to the bottom of the blueprint and center it horizontally. When you click on the Infer Constraints button this time, the design editor adds these constraints to it:

Send

The button goes at the bottom of the layout, centered horizontally.

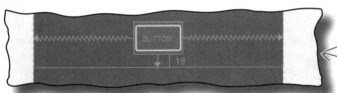

Remember, when you click on the Infer Constraints button in your layout, it may give you different results than shown here.

Change the button's ID to `send_button` and its text to `"@string/send_button"`.

Finally, add a view for the message

We have one more view to add to our layout, an editable text field that we want to be able to grow to fill any remaining space. Drag a Plain Text component from the palette to the middle of the blueprint, change its size so that it fills the entire area, and then click on the Infer Constraints button:

We want the Message EditText to fill the remaining area.

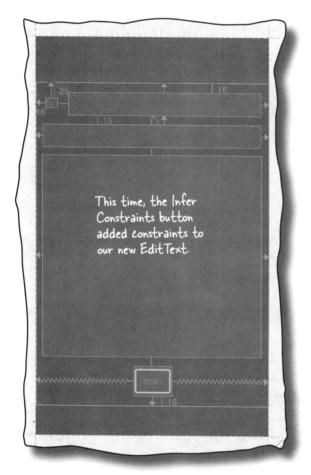

This time, the Infer Constraints button added constraints to our new EditText.

Note that we could have added all these views in one go, and clicked the Infer Constraints button when we reached the end. We've found, however, that building it up step-by-step gives the best results. Why not experiment and try this out for yourself?

Select the new component in the blueprint, then change its ID to `message`, its hint to `"@string/message_hint"`, and its gravity to `top`, and delete any text in the `text` property that the design editor may have added.

You may need to click on the "View all properties" button to see the gravity property.

Let's take the app for a test drive and see what the layout looks like.

Test drive the app

When we run the app, MainActivity's layout looks almost exactly how we want it to. When we rotate the device, the button stays centered, the email and subject editable text fields expand to fill the horizontal space, and the message view fills the remaining area:

Test your constraint layout on a variety of device sizes and orientations to make sure it behaves the way you want. If it doesn't, you may need to change the properties of some of your views and their constraints.

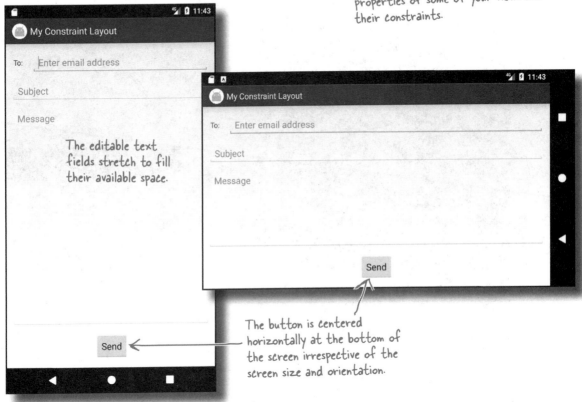

The editable text fields stretch to fill their available space.

The button is centered horizontally at the bottom of the screen irrespective of the screen size and orientation.

Remember that your layout may look and behave differently than ours depending on what constraints the design editor added when you clicked on the Infer Constraints button. The feature isn't perfect, but it usually takes you most of the way there, and you can undo or update any changes it makes.

Your Android Toolbox

You've got Chapter 6 under your belt and now you've added constraint layouts to your toolbox.

You can download the full code for the chapter from https://tinyurl.com/HeadFirstAndroid.

BULLET POINTS

- Constraint layouts are designed to work with Android Studio's design editor. They have their own library and can be used in apps where the minimum SDK is API level 9 or above.

- Position views by adding constraints. Each view needs at least one horizontal and one vertical constraint.

- Center views by adding constraints to opposite sides of the view. Change the view's bias to update its position between the constraints.

- You can change a view's size to match its constraints if the view has constraints on opposing sides.

- You can specify a width:height aspect ratio for the view's size.

- Clicking on the Infer Constraints button adds constraints to views based on their position in the blueprint.

there are no Dumb Questions

Q: Is a constraint layout my only option if I want to create complex layouts?

A: There are other types of layout as well, such as relative and grid layouts, but the constraint layout does everything that these do. Also it's designed to work with Android Studio's design editor, which makes building constraint layouts much easier.

If you're interested in finding out more about relative and grid layouts, they're covered in Appendix I at the back of the book.

Q: Why do constraint layouts have a separate library?

A: Constraint layouts are a fairly recent addition to Android compared to other types of layout. They're in a separate library so that they can be added to apps that support older versions of Android. You'll find out more about backward compatibility in later chapters.

Q: Can I still edit constraint layouts using XML?

A: Yes, but as they're designed to be edited visually, we've concentrated on building them using the design editor.

Q: I tried using the Infer Constraints feature but it didn't give me the results I wanted. Why not?

A: The Infer Constraints feature can only make guesses based on where you position views in the blueprint, so it may not always give you the results you want. You can, however, edit the changes the Infer Constraints feature makes to your app.

7 list views and adapters

Getting Organized

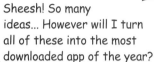

Sheesh! So many ideas... However will I turn all of these into the most downloaded app of the year?

Want to know how best to structure your Android app?

You've learned about some of the basic building blocks that are used to create apps, and now **it's time to get organized**. In this chapter, we'll show you how you can take a bunch of ideas and **structure them into an awesome app**. You'll learn how **lists of data** can form the core part of your app design, and how **linking them together** can create a **powerful and easy-to-use app**. Along the way, you'll get your first glimpse of using **event listeners** and **adapters** to make your app more dynamic.

Every app starts with ideas

When you first come up with an idea for an app, you'll have lots of thoughts about what the app should contain.

As an example, the guys at Starbuzz Coffee want a new app to entice more customers to their stores. These are some of the ideas they came up with for what the app should include:

These are all ideas that users of the app will find useful. But how do you take all of these ideas and organize them into an intuitive, well-structured app?

Organize your ideas:
top-level, category, and detail/edit activities

A useful way to bring order to these ideas is to organize them into three different types of activity: **top-level** activities, **category** activities, and **detail/edit** activities.

Top-level activities

A top-level activity contains the things that are most important to the user, and gives them an easy way of navigating to those things. In most apps, the first activity the user sees will be a top-level activity.

Category activities

Category activities show the data that belongs to a particular category, often in a list. These type of activities are often used to help the user navigate to detail/edit activities. An example of a category activity is a list of all the drinks available at Starbuzz.

Detail/edit activities

Detail/edit activities display details for a particular record, let the user edit the record, or allow the user to enter new records. An example of a detail/edit activity would be an activity that shows the user the details of a particular drink.

Once you've organized your activities, you can use them to construct a hierarchy showing how the user will navigate between activities.

Display a start screen with a list of options.

Display a menu showing all the food you can buy.

Show a list of all our stores.

Display a list of the drinks we sell.

Show details of each drink.

Show details of an item of food.

Display the address and opening times of each store.

Exercise

Think of an app you'd like to create. What activities should it include? Organize these activities into top-level activities, category activities, and detail/edit activities.

Navigating through the activities

When you organize the ideas you have into top-level, category, and detail/edit activities, you can use this organization scheme to figure out how to navigate through your app. In general, you want your users to navigate from top-level activities to detail/edit activities via category activities.

Top-level activities go at the top

These are the activities your user will encounter first, so they go at the top.

Category activities go between top-level and detail/edit activities

Your users will navigate from the top-level activity to the category activities. In complex apps, you might have several layers of categories and subcategories.

Detail/edit activities

These form the bottom layer of the activity hierarchy. Users will navigate to these from the category activities.

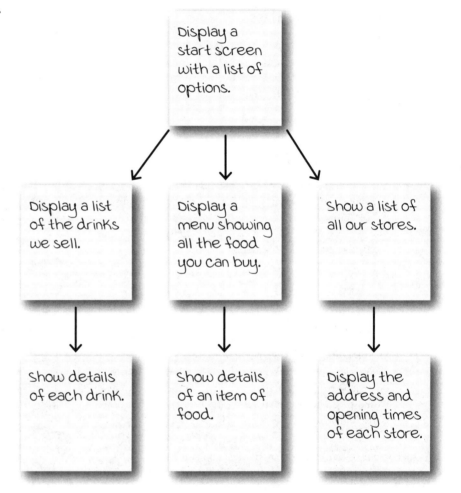

Display a start screen with a list of options.

Display a list of the drinks we sell.

Display a menu showing all the food you can buy.

Show a list of all our stores.

Show details of each drink.

Show details of an item of food.

Display the address and opening times of each store.

As an example, suppose a user wanted to look at details of one of the drinks that Starbuzz serves. To do this, she would launch the app, and be presented with the top-level activity start screen showing her a list of options. The user would click on the option to display a list of drinks. To see details of a particular drink, she would then click on her drink of choice in the list.

Use list views to navigate to data

When you structure your app in this way, you need a way of navigating between your activities. A common approach is to use **list views**. A list view allows you to display a list of data that you can then use to navigate through the app.

As an example, on the previous page, we said we'd have a category activity that displays a list of the drinks sold by Starbuzz. Here's what the activity might look like:

This is a list view containing a list of drinks. →

The activity uses a list view to display all the drinks that are sold by Starbuzz. To navigate to a particular drink, the user clicks on one of the drinks, and the details of that drink are displayed.

If you click on the Latte option in the list view, you get shown the details for the latte. →

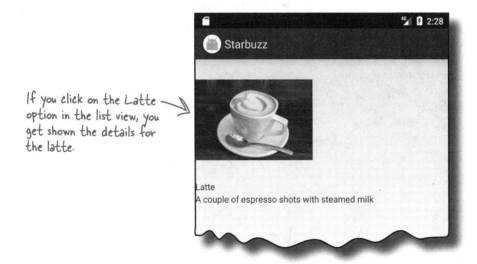

We're going to spend the rest of this chapter showing you how to use list views to implement this approach, using the Starbuzz app as an example.

We're going to build part of the Starbuzz app

Rather than build all the category and detail/edit activities required for the entire Starbuzz app, **we'll focus on just the drinks.** We're going to build a top-level activity that the user will see when they launch the app, a category activity that will display a list of drinks, and a detail/edit activity that will display details of a single drink.

The top-level activity

When the user launches the app, she will be presented with the top-level activity, the main entry point of the app. This activity includes an image of the Starbuzz logo, and a navigational list containing entries for Drinks, Food, and Stores.

When the user clicks on an item in the list, the app uses her selection to navigate to a separate activity. As an example, if the user clicks on Drinks, the app starts a category activity relating to drinks.

The drink category activity

This activity is launched when the user chooses Drinks from the navigational list in the top-level activity. The activity displays a list of all the drinks that are available at Starbuzz. The user can click on one of these drinks to see more details of it.

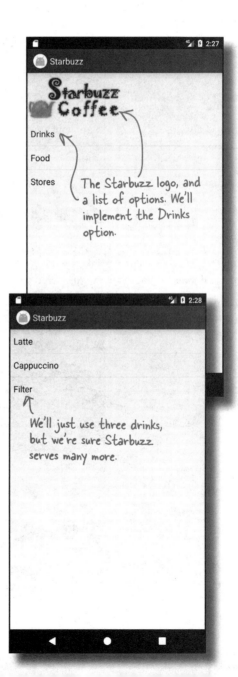

The Starbuzz logo, and a list of options. We'll implement the Drinks option.

We'll just use three drinks, but we're sure Starbuzz serves many more.

The drink detail activity

The drink detail activity is launched when the user clicks on one of the drinks listed by the drink category activity.

This activity displays details of the drink the user has selected: its name, an image of it, and a description.

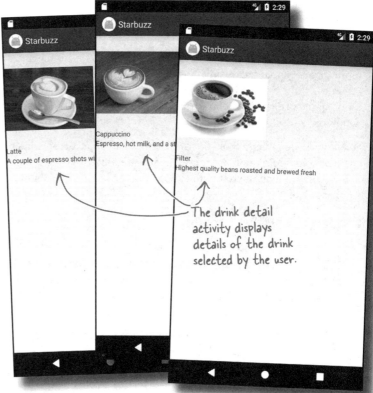

The drink detail activity displays details of the drink selected by the user.

How the user navigates through the app

The user navigates from the top-level activity to the drink category activity by clicking on the Drinks item in the top-level activity. She then navigates to the drink detail activity by clicking on a drink.

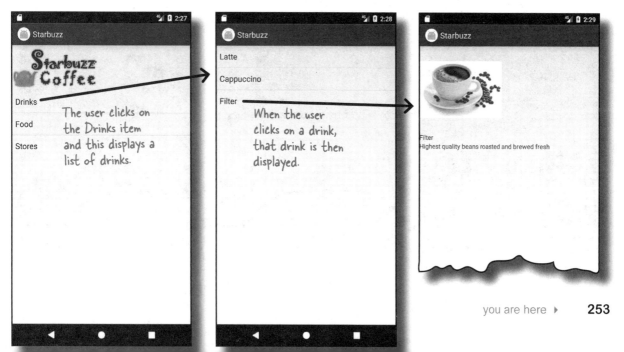

The user clicks on the Drinks item and this displays a list of drinks.

When the user clicks on a drink, that drink is then displayed.

The Starbuzz app structure

The app contains three activities. TopLevelActivity is the app's top-level activity and allows the user to navigate through the app. DrinkCategoryActivity is a category activity; it contains a list of all the drinks. The third activity, DrinkActivity, displays details of a given drink.

For now, we're going to hold the drink data in a Java class. In a later chapter, we're going to move it into a database, but for now we want to focus on building the rest of the app without teaching you about databases too.

Here's how the app will work:

1 When the app gets launched, it starts activity TopLevelActivity.
This activity uses layout *activity_top_level.xml*. The activity displays a list of options for Drinks, Food, and Stores.

2 The user clicks on Drinks in TopLevelActivity, which launches activity DrinkCategoryActivity.
This activity uses layout *activity_drink_category.xml* and displays a list of drinks. It gets information about the drinks from the *Drink.java* class file.

3 The user clicks on a drink in DrinkCategoryActivity, which launches activity DrinkActivity.
The activity uses layout *activity_drink.xml*. This activity also gets details about the drinks from the *Drink.java* class file.

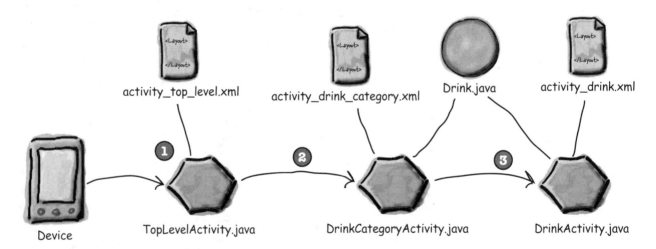

Here's what we're going to do

There are a number of steps we'll go through to build the app:

(1) **Add the Drink class and image resources.**
This class contains details of the available drinks, and we'll use images of the drinks and Starbuzz logo in the app.

(2) **Create TopLevelActivity and its layout.**
This activity is the entry point for the app. It needs to display the Starbuzz logo and include a navigational list of options. TopLevelActivity needs to launch DrinkCategoryActivity when the Drinks option is clicked.

(3) **Create DrinkCategoryActivity and its layout.**
This activity contains a list of all the drinks that are available. When a drink is clicked, it needs to launch DrinkCategory.

(4) **Create DrinkActivity and its layout.**
This activity displays details of the drink the user clicked on in DrinkCategoryActivity.

Create the project

You create the project for the app in exactly the same way you did in the previous chapters.

Create a new Android project for an application named "Starbuzz" with a company domain of "hfad.com", making the package name com.hfad.starbuzz. The minimum SDK should be API 19. You'll need an empty activity called "TopLevelActivity" and a layout called "activity_top_level". **Make sure you uncheck the Backwards Compatibility (AppCompat) checkbox.**

→ Add resources
TopLevelActivity
DrinkCategoryActivity
DrinkActivity

The Drink class

We'll start by adding the `Drink` class to the app. *Drink.java* is a pure Java class file that activities will get their drink data from. The class defines an array of three drinks, where each drink is composed of a name, description, and image resource ID. Switch to the Project view of Android Studio's explorer, select the *com.hfad.starbuzz* package in the *app/src/main/java* folder, then go to File→New...→Java Class. When prompted, name the class "Drink", and make sure the package name is `com.hfad.starbuzz`. Then replace the code in *Drink.java* with the following, and save your changes.

```java
package com.hfad.starbuzz;

public class Drink {
    private String name;
    private String description;
    private int imageResourceId;

    //drinks is an array of Drinks
    public static final Drink[] drinks = {
        new Drink("Latte", "A couple of espresso shots with steamed milk",
                R.drawable.latte),
        new Drink("Cappuccino", "Espresso, hot milk, and a steamed milk foam",
                R.drawable.cappuccino),
        new Drink("Filter", "Highest quality beans roasted and brewed fresh",
                R.drawable.filter)
    };

    //Each Drink has a name, description, and an image resource
    private Drink(String name, String description, int imageResourceId) {
        this.name = name;
        this.description = description;
        this.imageResourceId = imageResourceId;
    }

    public String getDescription() {
        return description;
    }

    public String getName() {
        return name;
    }

    public int getImageResourceId() {
        return imageResourceId;
    }

    public String toString() {
        return this.name;
    }
}
```

Each Drink has a name, description, and image resource ID. The image resource ID refers to drink images we'll add to the project on the next page.

drinks is an array of three Drinks.

These are images of the drinks. We'll add these next.

The Drink constructor

These are getters for the private variables.

The String representation of a Drink is its name.

Starbuzz
└ app/src/main
  └ java
    └ com.hfad.starbuzz
      └ Drink.java

The image files

The Drink code includes three image resources for its drinks with IDs of R.drawable.latte, R.drawable.cappuccino, and R.drawable.filter. These are so we can show the user images of the drinks. R.drawable.latte refers to an image file called *latte*, R.drawable.cappuccino refers to an image file called *cappuccino*, and R.drawable.filter refers to a file called *filter*.

We need to add these image files to the project, along with an image of the Starbuzz logo so that we can use it in our top-level activity. First, create the *app/src/main/res/drawable* folder in your Starbuzz project (if it doesn't already exist). To do this, make sure you've switched to the Project view of Android Studio's explorer, select the *app/src/main/res* folder, go to the File menu, choose the New... option, then click on the option to create a new Android resource directory. When prompted, choose a resource type of "drawable", name the folder "drawable", and click on OK.

← *Android Studio may have already added this folder for you. If so, you don't need to recreate it.*

Once your project includes the *drawable* folder, download the files *starbuzz-logo.png*, *cappuccino.png*, *filter.png*, and *latte.png* from *https://git.io/v9oet*. Finally, add each file to the *app/src/main/res/drawable* folder.

When you add images to your apps, you need to decide whether to display different images for different density screens. In our case, we're going to use the same resolution image irrespective of screen density, so we've put a single copy of the images in one folder. If you decide to cater to different screen densities in your own apps, put images for the different screen densities in the appropriate *drawable** folders as described in Chapter 5.

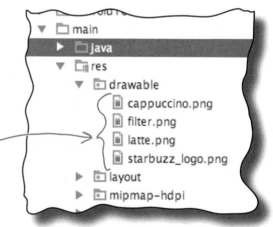

Here are the four image files. You need to create the drawable folder, then add the image files to it.

When you save images to your project, Android assigns each of them an ID in the form R.drawable.image_name (where image_name is the name of the image). As an example, the file *latte.png* is given an ID of R.drawable.latte, which matches the value of the latte's image resource ID in the Drink class.

Drink

name: "Latte"

description: "A couple of expresso shots with steamed milk"

imageResourceId: R.drawable.latte

The image latte.png is given an ID of R.drawable.latte.

R.drawable.latte

Now that we've added the Drink class and image resources to the project, let's work on the activities. We'll start with the top-level activity.

☑ Add resources
TopLevelActivity
DrinkCategoryActivity
DrinkActivity

The top-level layout contains an image and a list

When we created our project, we called our default activity *TopLevelActivity.java*, and its layout *activity_top_level.xml*. We need to change the layout so it displays an image and a list.

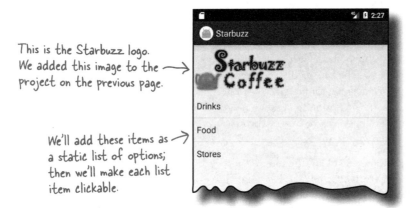

This is the Starbuzz logo. We added this image to the project on the previous page.

We'll add these items as a static list of options; then we'll make each list item clickable.

You saw how to display images in Chapter 5 using an image view. In this case, we need an image view that displays the Starbuzz logo, so we'll create one that uses *starbuzz_logo.png* as its source.

Here's the code to define the image view in the layout:

We're going to add this to activity_top_level.xml. We'll show you the full code soon.

```xml
<ImageView
    android:layout_width="200dp"
    android:layout_height="100dp"
    android:src="@drawable/starbuzz_logo"
    android:contentDescription="@string/starbuzz_logo" />
```

These are the dimensions we want the image to have.

The source of the image is the starbuzz_logo.png file we added to the app.

Adding a content description makes your app more accessible.

When you use an image view in your app, you use the `android:contentDescription` attribute to add a description of the image; this makes your app more accessible. In our case, we're using a String value of `"@string/starbuzz_logo"`, so add this to *strings.xml*:

```xml
<resources>

    . . .

    <string name="starbuzz_logo">Starbuzz logo</string>
</resources>
```

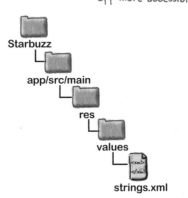

Starbuzz

app/src/main

res

values

strings.xml

That's everything we need to add the image to the layout, so let's move on to the list.

Use a list view to display the list of options

As we said earlier, a list view allows you to display a vertical list of data that people can use to navigate through the app. We're going to add a list view to the layout that displays the list of options, and later on we'll use it to navigate to a different activity.

How to define a list view in XML

You add a list view to your layout using the **<ListView>** element. You then add an array of entries to the list view by using the `android:entries` attribute and setting it to an array of Strings. The array of Strings then gets displayed in the list view as a list of text views.

Here's how you add a list view to your layout that gets its values from an array of Strings named `options`:

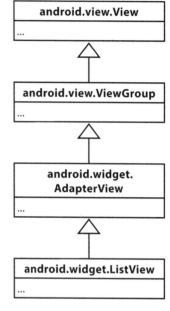

We're going to add this to activity_ top_level.xml on the next page.

```
<ListView    ←—This defines the list view.
    android:id="@+id/list_options"
    android:layout_width="match_parent"
    android:layout_height="wrap_content"
    android:entries="@array/options" />
```

The values in the list view are defined by the options array.

You define the array in exactly the same way that you did earlier in the book, by adding it to *strings.xml* like this:

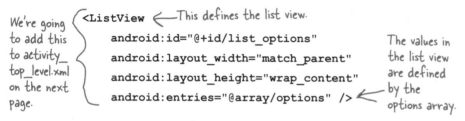

```
<resources>
    ...
    <string-array name="options">
        <item>Drinks</item>
        <item>Food</item>
        <item>Stores</item>
    </string-array>
</resources>
```

This populates the list view with three values: Drinks, Food, and Stores.

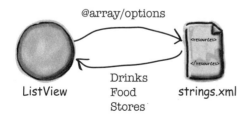

@array/options

ListView   Drinks   strings.xml
            Food
            Stores

The entries attribute populates the list view with values from the options array. Each item in the list view is a text view.

Drinks

Food

Stores

The full top-level layout code

Here's the full layout code for our *activity_top_level.xml*; make sure you update your code to match ours:

```xml
<?xml version="1.0" encoding="utf-8"?>
<LinearLayout xmlns:android="http://schemas.android.com/apk/res/android"
    xmlns:tools="http://schemas.android.com/tools"
    android:layout_width="match_parent"
    android:layout_height="match_parent"
    android:orientation="vertical"
    tools:context="com.hfad.starbuzz.TopLevelActivity" >

    <ImageView
        android:layout_width="200dp"
        android:layout_height="100dp"
        android:src="@drawable/starbuzz_logo"
        android:contentDescription="@string/starbuzz_logo" />

    <ListView
        android:id="@+id/list_options"
        android:layout_width="match_parent"
        android:layout_height="wrap_content"
        android:entries="@array/options" />

</LinearLayout>
```

We're using a linear layout with a vertical orientation. This will display our list view directly underneath the Starbuzz logo. ← android:orientation="vertical"

Starbuzz → app/src/main → res → layout → activity_top_level.xml

Test drive

Make sure you've applied all the changes to *activity_top_level.xml*, and also updated *strings.xml*. When you run the app, you should see the Starbuzz logo displayed on the device screen with the list view underneath it. The list view displays the three values from the options array.

If you click on any of the options in the list, nothing happens, as we haven't told the list view to respond to clicks yet. The next thing we'll do is see how you get list views to respond to clicks and launch a second activity.

These are the values in the options array.

Get list views to respond to clicks with a listener

You make the items in a list view respond to clicks by implementing an **event listener.**

An event listener allows you to listen for events that take place in your app, such as when views get clicked, when they receive or lose the focus, or when the user presses a hardware key on their device. By implementing an event listener, you can tell when your user performs a particular action—such as clicking on an item in a list view—and respond to it.

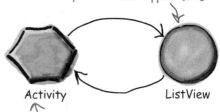

The ListView needs to know the Activity cares what happens to it.

Activity   ListView

The ListView tells the Activity when an item gets clicked so the Activity can react.

OnItemClickListener listens for item clicks

When you want to get items in a list view to respond to clicks, you need to create an OnItemClickListener and implement its onItemClick() method. The OnItemClickListener listens for when items are clicked, and the onItemClick() method lets you say how your activity should respond to the click. The onItemClick() method includes several parameters that you can use to find out which item was clicked, such as a reference to the view item that was clicked, the item's position in the list view (starting at 0), and the row ID of the underlying data.

We want to start DrinkCategoryActivity when the first item in the list view is clicked—the item at position 0. If the item at position 0 is clicked, we need to create an intent to start DrinkCategoryActivity. Here's the code to create the listener; we'll add it to *TopLevelActivity.java* on the next page:

> OnItemClickListener is a nested class within the AdapterView class. A ListView is a subclass of AdapterView.

```java
AdapterView.OnItemClickListener itemClickListener = new AdapterView.OnItemClickListener(){
    public void onItemClick(AdapterView<?> listView,    ← The view that was clicked (in this case,
                            View itemView,                   the list view).
                            int position,
                            long id) {
        if (position == 0) {
            Intent intent = new Intent(TopLevelActivity.this, DrinkCategoryActivity.class);
            startActivity(intent);
        }
    }
};
```

Drinks is the first item in the list view, so it's at position 0.

These parameters give you info about which item was clicked in the list view, such as the item's view and its position.

The intent is coming from TopLevelActivity.

It needs to launch DrinkCategoryActivity.

Once you've created the listener, you need to add it to the list view.

Add resources
TopLevelActivity
DrinkCategoryActivity
DrinkActivity

Set the listener to the list view

Once you've created the OnClickItemListener, you need
to attach it to the list view. You do this using the ListView
setOnItemClickListener() method, which takes one argument,
the listener itself:

```
AdapterView.OnItemClickListener itemClickListener = new AdapterView.OnItemClickListener(){
    public void onItemClick(AdapterView<?> listView,
        ...
    }
};
ListView listView = (ListView) findViewById(R.id.list_options);
listView.setOnItemClickListener(itemClickListener);
```

We'll add this to TopLevelActivity. The full code is listed
on the next couple of pages so you can see it in context.

This is the listener we just created.

Adding the listener to the list view is crucial, as it's this step that notifies
the listener when the user clicks on items in the list view. If you don't do
this, the items in your list view won't be able to respond to clicks.

You've now seen everything you need in order to get the
TopLevelActivity list view to respond to clicks.

The full TopLevelActivity.java code

Here's the complete code for *TopLevelActivity.java*. Replace the
code the wizard created for you with the code below and on the
next page, then save your changes:

```
package com.hfad.starbuzz;

import android.app.Activity;
import android.os.Bundle;
import android.content.Intent;
import android.widget.AdapterView;
import android.widget.ListView;
import android.view.View;

public class TopLevelActivity extends Activity {
```

We're using all these classes,
so we need to import them.

Make sure your activity
extends the Activity class.

Starbuzz
app/src/main
java
com.hfad.starbuzz
TopLevel
Activity.java

TopLevelActivity.java (continued)

```java
@Override
protected void onCreate(Bundle savedInstanceState) {
    super.onCreate(savedInstanceState);
    setContentView(R.layout.activity_top_level);
    //Create an OnItemClickListener
    AdapterView.OnItemClickListener itemClickListener =
                        new AdapterView.OnItemClickListener() {
        public void onItemClick(AdapterView<?> listView,
                                View itemView,
                                int position,
                                long id) {
            if (position == 0) {
                Intent intent = new Intent(TopLevelActivity.this,
                                DrinkCategoryActivity.class);
                startActivity(intent);
            }
        }
    };
    //Add the listener to the list view
    ListView listView = (ListView) findViewById(R.id.list_options);
    listView.setOnItemClickListener(itemClickListener);
}
}
```

Create the listener.

Implement its onItemClick() method.

Launch DrinkCategoryActivity if the user clicks on the Drinks item. We'll create this activity next, so don't worry if Android Studio says it doesn't exist.

Add the listener to the list view.

Starbuzz
 └ app/src/main
   └ java
     └ com.hfad.starbuzz
       └ TopLevel Activity.java

What the TopLevelActivity.java code does

1 The onCreate() method in TopLevelActivity creates an onItemClickListener and links it to the activity's ListView.

TopLevelActivity   ListView   onItemClickListener

2 When the user clicks on an item in the list view, the onItemClickListener's onItemClick() method gets called.

If the Drinks item is clicked, the onItemClickListener creates an intent to start DrinkCategoryActivity.

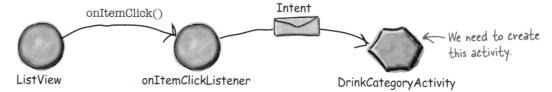

onItemClick()   Intent

We need to create this activity.

ListView   onItemClickListener   DrinkCategoryActivity

Where we've got to

So far we've added *Drink.java* to our app and created
`TopLevelActivity` and its layout.

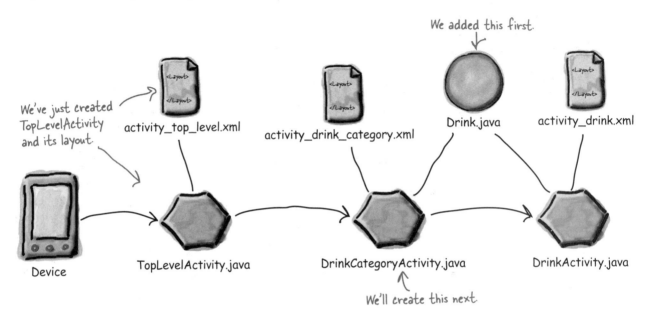

We added this first.

We've just created
TopLevelActivity
and its layout.

activity_top_level.xml

activity_drink_category.xml

Drink.java

activity_drink.xml

Device

TopLevelActivity.java

DrinkCategoryActivity.java

DrinkActivity.java

We'll create this next.

The next thing we need to do is create
`DrinkCategoryActivity` and its layout so that it
gets launched when the user clicks on the Drinks option in
`TopLevelActivity`.

---

there are no Dumb Questions

Q: Why did we have to create an event listener to get items in the list view to respond to clicks? Couldn't we have just used its `android:onClick` attribute in the layout code?

A: You can only use the `android:onClick` attribute in activity layouts for buttons, or any views that are subclasses of `Button` such as `CheckBoxes` and `RadioButtons`.

The `ListView` class isn't a subclass of `Button`, so using the `android:onClick` attribute won't work. That's why you have to implement your own listener.

Here's some activity code from a separate project. When the user clicks on an item in a list view, the code is meant to display the text of that item in a text view (the text view has an ID of `text_view` and the list view has an ID of `list_view`). Does the code do what it's meant to? If not, why not?

```
package com.hfad.ch06ex;

import android.app.Activity;
import android.os.Bundle;
import android.widget.AdapterView;
import android.widget.ListView;
import android.widget.TextView;
import android.view.View;

public class MainActivity extends Activity {

    @Override
    protected void onCreate(Bundle savedInstanceState) {
        super.onCreate(savedInstanceState);
        setContentView(R.layout.activity_main);
        final TextView textView = (TextView) findViewById(R.id.text_view);
        AdapterView.OnItemClickListener itemClickListener =
                new AdapterView.OnItemClickListener(){
                    public void onItemClick(AdapterView<?> listView,
                                            View v,
                                            int position,
                                            long id) {
                        TextView item = (TextView) v;
                        textView.setText(item.getText());
                    }
                };
        ListView listView = (ListView) findViewById(R.id.list_view);
    }
}
```

Exercise Solution

Here's some activity code from a separate project. When the user clicks on an item in a list view, the code is meant to display the text of that item in a text view (the text view has an ID of `text_view` and the list view has an ID of `list_view`). Does the code do what it's meant to? If not, why not?

```java
package com.hfad.ch06ex;

import android.app.Activity;
import android.os.Bundle;
import android.widget.AdapterView;
import android.widget.ListView;
import android.widget.TextView;
import android.view.View;

public class MainActivity extends Activity {

    @Override
    protected void onCreate(Bundle savedInstanceState) {
        super.onCreate(savedInstanceState);
        setContentView(R.layout.activity_main);
        final TextView textView = (TextView) findViewById(R.id.text_view);
        AdapterView.OnItemClickListener itemClickListener =
                new AdapterView.OnItemClickListener(){
                    public void onItemClick(AdapterView<?> listView,
                                            View v,
                                            int position,
                                            long id) {
                        TextView item = (TextView) v;
                        textView.setText(item.getText());
                    }
                };
        ListView listView = (ListView) findViewById(R.id.list_view);
    }
}
```

This is the item in the ListView that was clicked. → `TextView item = (TextView) v;`

It's a TextView, so we can get its text using getText(). → `textView.setText(item.getText());`

The code doesn't work as intended because the line of code

listView.setOnItemClickListener(itemClickListener);

is missing from the end of the code. Apart from that, the code's fine.

A category activity displays the data for a single category

As we said earlier, `DrinkCategoryActivity` is an example of a category activity. A category activity is one that shows the data that belongs to a particular category, often in a list. You use the category activity to navigate to details of the data.

We're going to use `DrinkCategoryActivity` to display a list of drinks. When the user clicks on one of the drinks, we'll show them the details of that drink.

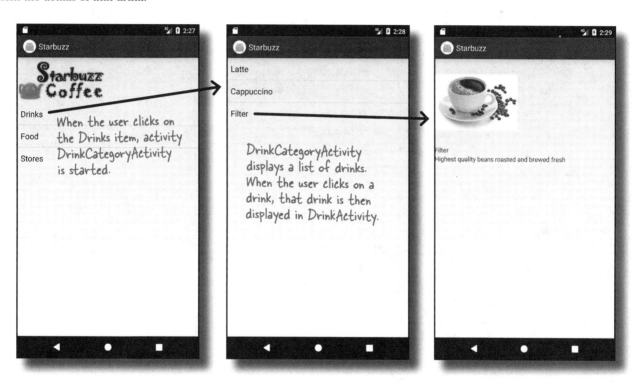

When the user clicks on the Drinks item, activity DrinkCategoryActivity is started.

DrinkCategoryActivity displays a list of drinks. When the user clicks on a drink, that drink is then displayed in DrinkActivity.

Create DrinkCategoryActivity

To work on the next step in our checklist, we'll create an activity with a single list view that displays a list of all the drinks. Select the *com.hfad.starbuzz* package in the *app/src/main/java* folder, then go to File→New...→Activity→Empty Activity. Name the activity "DrinkCategoryActivity", name the layout "activity_drink_category", make sure the package name is `com.hfad.starbuzz` and **uncheck the Backwards Compatibility (AppCompat) checkbox.**

We'll update the layout code on the next page.

Some versions of Android Studio may ask you what the source language of your activity should be. If prompted, select the option for Java.

Update activity_drink_category.xml

Add resources
TopLevelActivity
DrinkCategoryActivity
DrinkActivity

Here's the code for *activity_drink_category.xml*. As you can see, it's a simple linear layout with a list view. Update your version of *activity_drink_category.xml* to reflect ours below:

```xml
<?xml version="1.0" encoding="utf-8"?>
<LinearLayout xmlns:android="http://schemas.android.com/apk/res/android"
    xmlns:tools="http://schemas.android.com/tools"
    android:layout_width="match_parent"
    android:layout_height="match_parent"
    android:orientation="vertical"
    tools:context="com.hfad.starbuzz.DrinkCategoryActivity">

    <ListView
        android:id="@+id/list_drinks"
        android:layout_width="match_parent"
        android:layout_height="wrap_content" />

</LinearLayout>
```

This layout only needs to contain a ListView.

Starbuzz
app/src/main
res
layout
activity_drink_category.xml

There's one key difference between the list view we're creating here, and the one we created in *activity_top_activity.xml*: there's no `android:entries` attribute here. But why?

In *activity_top_activity.xml*, we used the `android:entries` attribute to bind data to the list view. This worked because the data was held as a static String array resource. The array was described in *strings.xml*, so we could easily refer to it using:

```
android:entries="@array/options"
```

where `options` is the name of the String array.

Using `android:entries` works fine if the data is a static array in *strings.xml*. But what if it isn't? What if the data is held in an array you've programmatically created in Java code, or held in a database? In that case, the `android:entries` attribute won't work.

If you need to bind your list view to data held in something other than a String array resource, you need to take a different approach; you need to write activity code to bind the data. In our case, we need to bind our list view to the `drinks` array in the `Drink` class.

For nonstatic data, use an adapter

If you need to display data in a list view that comes from a source other than *strings.xml* (such as a Java array or database), you need to use an **adapter**. An adapter acts as a bridge between the data source and the list view:

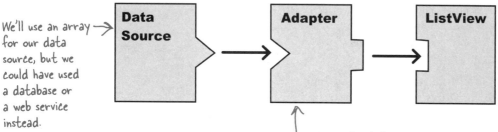

We'll use an array for our data source, but we could have used a database or a web service instead.

The adapter bridges the gap between the list view and the data source. Adapters allow list views to display data from a variety of sources.

There are several different types of adapter. For now, we're going to focus on **array adapters**.

An array adapter is a type of adapter that's used to bind arrays to views. You can use it with any subclass of the `AdapterView` class, which means you can use it with both list views and spinners.

In our case, we're going to use an array adapter to display data from the `Drink.drinks` array in the list view.

> **An adapter acts as a bridge between a view and a data source. An ArrayAdapter is a type of adapter that specializes in working with arrays.**

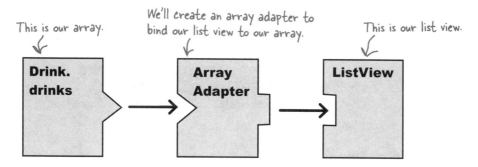

This is our array.

We'll create an array adapter to bind our list view to our array.

This is our list view.

We'll see how this works on the next page.

Connect list views to arrays with an array adapter

You use an array adapter by initializing it and then attaching it to the list view.

To initialize the array adapter, you first specify what type of data is contained in the array you want to bind to the list view. You then pass the array adapter three parameters: a `Context` (usually the current activity), a layout resource that specifies how to display each item in the array, and the array itself.

Here's the code to create an array adapter that displays drink data from the `Drink.drinks` array (you'll add this code to *DrinkCategoryActivity.java* on the next page):

```
ArrayAdapter<Drink> listAdapter = new ArrayAdapter<>(
        this,
        android.R.layout.simple_list_item_1,
        Drink.drinks);
```

"this" refers to the current activity. The Activity class is a subclass of Context.

The array

This is a built-in layout resource. It tells the array adapter to display each item in the array in a single text view.

You then attach the array adapter to the list view using the `ListView setAdapter()` method:

```
ListView listDrinks = (ListView) findViewById(R.id.list_drinks);
listDrinks.setAdapter(listAdapter);
```

Behind the scenes, the array adapter takes each item in the array, converts it to a `String` using its `toString()` method, and puts each result into a text view. It then displays each text view as a single row in the list view.

These are the drinks from the drinks array. Each row in the list view is a single text view, each one displaying a separate drink.

Add the array adapter to DrinkCategoryActivity

We'll change the *DrinkCategoryActivity.java* code so that the list view uses an array adapter to get drinks data from the Drink class. We'll put the code in the onCreate() method so that the list view gets populated when the activity gets created.

Here's the full code for the activity (update your copy of *DrinkCategoryActivity.java* to reflect ours, then save your changes):

```java
package com.hfad.starbuzz;

import android.app.Activity;
import android.os.Bundle;
import android.widget.ArrayAdapter;
import android.widget.ListView;

public class DrinkCategoryActivity extends Activity {

    @Override
    protected void onCreate(Bundle savedInstanceState) {
        super.onCreate(savedInstanceState);
        setContentView(R.layout.activity_drink_category);
        ArrayAdapter<Drink> listAdapter = new ArrayAdapter<>(
                this,
                android.R.layout.simple_list_item_1,
                Drink.drinks);
        ListView listDrinks = (ListView) findViewById(R.id.list_drinks);
        listDrinks.setAdapter(listAdapter);
    }

}
```

We're using these classes so we need to import them.

Make sure your activity extends the Activity class.

This populates the list view with data from the drinks array.

Starbuzz

app/src/main

java

com.hfad.starbuzz

DrinkCategory
Activity.java

These are all the changes needed to get your list view to display a list of the drinks from the Drink class. Let's go through what happens when the code runs.

What happens when you run the code

1 When the user clicks on the Drinks option, DrinkCategoryActivity is launched.
Its layout has a `LinearLayout` that contains a `ListView`.

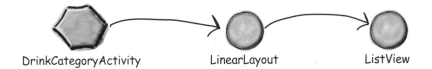

DrinkCategoryActivity   LinearLayout   ListView

2 DrinkCategoryActivity creates an ArrayAdapter<Drink>, an array adapter that deals with arrays of Drink objects.

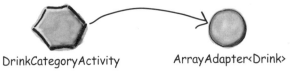

DrinkCategoryActivity   ArrayAdapter<Drink>

3 The array adapter retrieves data from the drinks array in the Drink class.
It uses the `Drink.toString()` method to return the name of each drink.

Drink.toString()

DrinkCategoryActivity   ArrayAdapter<Drink>   Drink.drinks

4 DrinkCategoryActivity makes the ListView use the array adapter via the setAdapter() method.
The list view uses the array adapter to display a list of the drink names.

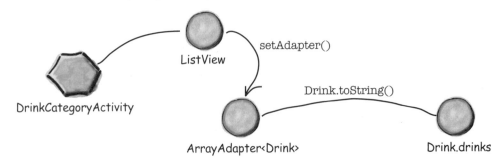

ListView

setAdapter()

Drink.toString()

DrinkCategoryActivity

ArrayAdapter<Drink>   Drink.drinks

Test drive the app

When you run the app, `TopLevelActivity` gets displayed as before. When you click on the Drinks item, `DrinkCategoryActivity` is launched. It displays the names of all the drinks from the `Drink` Java class.

Click on the Drinks item → to see a list of drinks.

On the next page we'll review what we've done in the app so far, and what's left for us to do.

App review: where we are

☑ Add resources
☑ **TopLevelActivity**
→ ☐ **DrinkCategoryActivity**
DrinkActivity

So far we've added *Drink.java* to our app, and created activities `TopLevelActivity` and `DrinkCategoryActivity` along with their layouts.

We've created Drink.java.

activity_top_level.xml   activity_drink_category.xml   Drink.java   activity_drink.xml

Device   TopLevelActivity.java   DrinkCategoryActivity.java   DrinkActivity.java

We've created these activities and their layouts.

We haven't created DrinkActivity yet.

Here's what our app currently does:

1   **When the app gets launched, it starts activity TopLevelActivity.**
The activity displays a list of options for Drinks, Food, and Stores.

2   **The user clicks on Drinks in TopLevelActivity.**
This launches activity `DrinkCategoryActivity`, which displays a list of drinks.

3   **DrinkCategoryActivity gets the values for its list of drinks from the *Drink.java* class file.**

The next thing we'll do is get `DrinkCategoryActivity` to launch `DrinkActivity`, passing it details of whichever drink was clicked.

Pool Puzzle

Your **goal** is to create an activity that binds a Java array of colors to a spinner. Take code snippets from the pool and place them into the blank lines in the activity. You may **not** use the same snippet more than once, and you won't need to use all the snippets.

← *Remember, we covered spinners in Chapter 5.*

...

We're not using this activity in our app.

```java
public class MainActivity extends Activity {

    String[] colors = new String[] {"Red", "Orange", "Yellow", "Green", "Blue"};

    @Override
    protected void onCreate(Bundle savedInstanceState) {
        super.onCreate(savedInstanceState);
        setContentView(R.layout.activity_main);
        Spinner spinner = (............) findViewById(R.id.spinner);
        ArrayAdapter<............> adapter = new ArrayAdapter<>(
                .........'
                android.R.layout.simple_spinner_item,
                colors);
        spinner.................(adapter);
    }
}
```

↖ *This displays each value in the array as a single row in the spinner.*

Note: each snippet from the pool can only be used once!

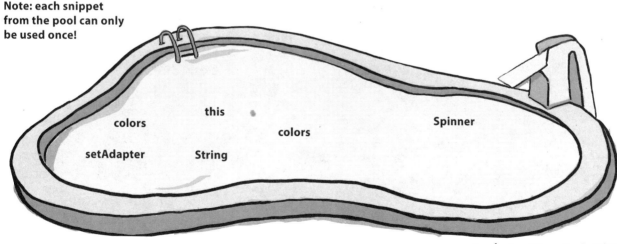

colors

this

Spinner

colors

setAdapter

String

→ Answers on page 287.

How we handled clicks in TopLevelActivity

Add resources
TopLevelActivity
DrinkCategoryActivity
DrinkActivity

Earlier in this chapter, we needed to get
TopLevelActivity to react to the user clicking on the
first item in the list view, the Drinks option, by starting
DrinkCategoryActivity. To do that, we had to
create an OnItemClickListener, implement its
onItemClick() method, and assign it to the list view.
Here's a reminder of the code:

```
AdapterView.OnItemClickListener itemClickListener =          Create the listener.
                              new AdapterView.OnItemClickListener(){
    public void onItemClick(AdapterView<?> listView,          The list view
                      View itemView,
                      int position,          The item view that was clicked, its position in
                      long id) {             the list, and the row ID of the underlying data.
        if (position == 0) {
            Intent intent = new Intent(TopLevelActivity.this,
                              DrinkCategoryActivity.class);
            startActivity(intent);
        }
    }
};
ListView listView = (ListView) findViewById(R.id.list_options);
listView.setOnItemClickListener(itemClickListener);          Add the listener to the list view.
```

We had to set up an event listener in this way because list
views aren't hardwired to respond to clicks in the way that
buttons are.

So how should we get DrinkCategoryActivity to
handle user clicks?

Pass the ID of the item that was clicked by adding it to an intent

When you use a category activity to display items in a list view, you'll usually use the `onItemClick()` method to start another activity that displays details of the item the user clicked. To do this, you create an intent that starts the second activity. You then add the ID of the item that was clicked as extra information so that the second activity can use it when the activity starts.

In our case, we want to start `DrinkActivity` and pass it the ID of the drink that was selected. `DrinkActivity` will then be able to use this information to display details of the right drink. Here's the code for the intent:

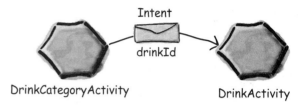

Intent

drinkId

DrinkCategoryActivity   DrinkActivity

DrinkCategoryActivity needs to start DrinkActivity.

```
Intent intent = new Intent(DrinkCategoryActivity.this, DrinkActivity.class);
intent.putExtra(DrinkActivity.EXTRA_DRINKID, (int) id);
startActivity(intent);
```

We're using a constant for the name of the extra information in the intent so that we know DrinkCategoryActivity and DrinkActivity are using the same String. We'll add this constant to DrinkActivity when we create the activity.

Add the ID of the item that was clicked to the intent. This is the index of the drink in the drinks array.

It's common practice to pass the ID of the item that was clicked because it's the ID of the underlying data. If the underlying data is an array, the ID is the index of the item in the array. If the underlying data comes from a database, the ID is the ID of the record in the table. Passing the ID of the item in this way means that it's easier for the second activity to get details of the data, and then display it.

That's everything we need to make `DrinkCategoryActivity` start `DrinkActivity` and tell it which drink was selected. The full activity code is on the next page.

The full DrinkCategoryActivity code

Add resources
TopLevelActivity
DrinkCategoryActivity
DrinkActivity

Here's the full code for *DrinkCategoryActivity.java* (add the new method to your code, then save your changes):

```java
package com.hfad.starbuzz;

import android.app.Activity;
import android.os.Bundle;
import android.widget.ArrayAdapter;
import android.widget.ListView;
import android.view.View;
import android.content.Intent;
import android.widget.AdapterView;
```

— We're using these extra classes so we need to import them.

Starbuzz → **app/src/main** → **java** → **com.hfad.starbuzz** → **DrinkCategory Activity.java**

```java
public class DrinkCategoryActivity extends Activity {

    @Override
    protected void onCreate(Bundle savedInstanceState) {
        super.onCreate(savedInstanceState);
        setContentView(R.layout.activity_drink_category);
        ArrayAdapter<Drink> listAdapter = new ArrayAdapter<>(
                this,
                android.R.layout.simple_list_item_1,
                Drink.drinks);
        ListView listDrinks = (ListView) findViewById(R.id.list_drinks);
        listDrinks.setAdapter(listAdapter);
```

Create a listener to listen for clicks. ↙

```java
        //Create the listener
        AdapterView.OnItemClickListener itemClickListener =
                new AdapterView.OnItemClickListener(){
                    public void onItemClick(AdapterView<?> listDrinks,
                                            View itemView,
                                            int position,
                                            long id) {
                        //Pass the drink the user clicks on to DrinkActivity
                        Intent intent = new Intent(DrinkCategoryActivity.this,
                                            DrinkActivity.class);
                        intent.putExtra(DrinkActivity.EXTRA_DRINKID, (int) id);
                        startActivity(intent);
                    }
                };
```

This gets called when an item ↗ in the list view is clicked.

When the user clicks on a drink, pass its ID to DrinkActivity and start it.

We'll add DrinkActivity next, so don't worry if Android Studio says it doesn't exist.

```java
        //Assign the listener to the list view
        listDrinks.setOnItemClickListener(itemClickListener);
    }
}
```

A detail activity displays data for a single record

As we said earlier, DrinkActivity is an example of a detail activity. A detail activity displays details for a particular record, and you generally navigate to it from a category activity.

We're going to use DrinkActivity to display details of the drink the user selects. The Drink class includes the drink's name, description, and image resource ID, so we'll display this data in our layout. We'll include an image view for the drink image resource, and text views for the drink name and description.

To create the activity, select the *com.hfad.starbuzz* package in the *app/src/main/ java* folder, then go to File→New...→Activity→Empty Activity. Name the activity "DrinkActivity", name the layout "activity_drink", make sure the package name is com.hfad.starbuzz, and **uncheck the Backwards Compatibility (AppCompat) checkbox.** Then replace the contents of *activity_drink.xml* with this:

Make sure you create the new activity.

If prompted for the activity's source language, select the option for Java.

```xml
<?xml version="1.0" encoding="utf-8"?>
<LinearLayout xmlns:android="http://schemas.android.com/apk/res/android"
    xmlns:tools="http://schemas.android.com/tools"
    android:layout_width="match_parent"
    android:layout_height="match_parent"
    android:orientation="vertical"
    tools:context="com.hfad.starbuzz.DrinkActivity" >

    <ImageView
        android:id="@+id/photo"
        android:layout_width="190dp"
        android:layout_height="190dp" />

    <TextView
        android:id="@+id/name"
        android:layout_width="wrap_content"
        android:layout_height="wrap_content" />

    <TextView
        android:id="@+id/description"
        android:layout_width="match_parent"
        android:layout_height="wrap_content" />
</LinearLayout>
```

Starbuzz
app/src/main
res
layout
activity_drink.xml

Now that you've created the layout of your detail activity, we can populate its views.

Add resources

TopLevelActivity

DrinkCategoryActivity

DrinkActivity

Retrieve data from the intent

As you've seen, when you want a category activity to start a detail activity, you have to make items in the category activity list view respond to clicks. When an item is clicked, you create an intent to start the detail activity. You pass the ID of the item the user clicked as extra information in the intent.

When the detail activity is started, it can retrieve the extra information from the intent and use it to populate its views. In our case, we can use the information in the intent that started DrinkActivity to retrieve details of the drink the user clicked.

When we created DrinkCategoryActivity, we added the ID of the drink the user clicked as extra information in the intent. We gave it the label DrinkActivity.EXTRA_DRINKID, which we need to define as a constant in *DrinkActivity.java*:

```
public static final String EXTRA_DRINKID = "drinkId";
```

As you saw in Chapter 3, you can retrieve the intent that started an activity using the getIntent() method. If this intent has extra information, you can use the intent's get*() methods to retrieve it. Here's the code to retrieve the value of EXTRA_DRINKID from the intent that started DrinkActivity:

```
int drinkId = (Integer)getIntent().getExtras().get(EXTRA_DRINKID);
```

Once you've retrieved the information from the intent, you can use it to get the data you need to display in your detail record.

In our case, we can use drinkId to get details of the drink the user selected. drinkId is the ID of the drink, the index of the drink in the drinks array. This means that you can get details about the drink the user clicked on using:

```
Drink drink = Drink.drinks[drinkId];
```

This gives us a Drink object containing all the information we need to update the views attributes in the activity:

drink

name="Latte"
description="A couple of espresso shots with steamed milk"
imageResourceId=R.drawable.latte

Update the views with the data

When you update the views in your detail activity, you need to make sure that the values they display reflect the data you've derived from the intent.

Our detail activity contains two text views and an image view. We need to make sure that each of these is updated to reflect the details of the drink.

name
description
imageResourceId

drink

Drink Magnets

See if you can use the magnets below to populate the DrinkActivity views with the correct data.

```
...
//Get the drink from the intent
int drinkId = (Integer)getIntent().getExtras().get(EXTRA_DRINKID);
Drink drink = Drink.drinks[drinkId];


//Populate the drink name
TextView name = (TextView)findViewById(R.id.name);

name.................(drink.getName());


//Populate the drink description
TextView description = (TextView)findViewById(R.id.description);

description.................(drink.getDescription());


//Populate the drink image
ImageView photo = (ImageView)findViewById(R.id.photo);

photo.....................(drink.getImageResourceId());

photo.............................(drink.getName());
...
```

setText

setContent

setContentDescription

setImageResourceId

setImageResource

setText

Drink Magnets Solution

See if you can use the magnets below to populate the
DrinkActivity views with the correct data.

```
...
//Get the drink from the intent
int drinkId = (Integer)getIntent().getExtras().get(EXTRA_DRINKID);
Drink drink = Drink.drinks[drinkId];


//Populate the drink name
TextView name = (TextView)findViewById(R.id.name);

name.  setText  (drink.getName());
```

Use setText()
to set the text
in a text view.

```
//Populate the drink description
TextView description = (TextView)findViewById(R.id.description);

description.  setText  (drink.getDescription());



//Populate the drink image
ImageView photo = (ImageView)findViewById(R.id.photo);
```

You set the source
of the image using
setImageResource().

```
photo.  setImageResource  (drink.getImageResourceId());
```

This is needed
to make the app
more accessible.

```
photo.  setContentDescription  (drink.getName());
...
```

You didn't need to use these.

`setContent`

`setImageResourceId`

The DrinkActivity code

Here's the full code for *DrinkActivity.java* (replace the code the wizard gave you with the code below, then save your changes):

```
package com.hfad.starbuzz;

import android.app.Activity;
import android.os.Bundle;
import android.widget.ImageView;
import android.widget.TextView;

public class DrinkActivity extends Activity {

    public static final String EXTRA_DRINKID = "drinkId";

    @Override
    protected void onCreate(Bundle savedInstanceState) {
        super.onCreate(savedInstanceState);
        setContentView(R.layout.activity_drink);

        //Get the drink from the intent
        int drinkId = (Integer)getIntent().getExtras().get(EXTRA_DRINKID);
        Drink drink = Drink.drinks[drinkId];

        //Populate the drink name
        TextView name = (TextView)findViewById(R.id.name);
        name.setText(drink.getName());

        //Populate the drink description
        TextView description = (TextView)findViewById(R.id.description);
        description.setText(drink.getDescription());

        //Populate the drink image
        ImageView photo = (ImageView)findViewById(R.id.photo);
        photo.setImageResource(drink.getImageResourceId());
        photo.setContentDescription(drink.getName());
    }
}
```

We're using these classes so we need to import them.

Make sure your activity extends the Activity class.

Add EXTRA_DRINKID as a constant.

Use the drinkId to get details of the drink the user chose.

Populate the views with the drink data.

Starbuzz
└ app/src/main
  └ java
    └ com.hfad.starbuzz
      └ DrinkActivity.java

What happens when you run the app

☑ Add resources
☑ **TopLevelActivity**
☑ **DrinkCategoryActivity**
→ ☐ **DrinkActivity**

1 When the user starts the app, it launches TopLevelActivity.

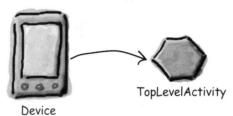

Device   TopLevelActivity

2 The onCreate() method in TopLevelActivity creates an
onItemClickListener and links it to the activity's ListView.

TopLevelActivity   ListView   onItemClickListener

3 When the user clicks on an item in the ListView, the
onItemClickListener's onItemClick() method gets called.

If the Drinks item was clicked, the onItemClickListener creates an intent to start
DrinkCategoryActivity.

onItemClick()   Intent

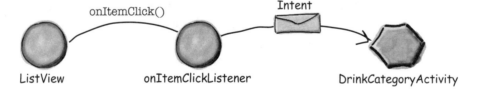

ListView   onItemClickListener   DrinkCategoryActivity

4 DrinkCategoryActivity displays a single ListView.

The DrinkCategoryActivity list view uses an ArrayAdapter<Drink> to
display a list of drink names.

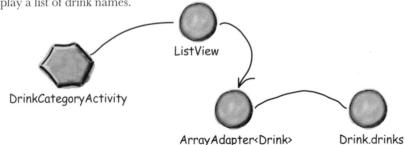

ListView

DrinkCategoryActivity

ArrayAdapter<Drink>   Drink.drinks

The story continues

⑤ When the user chooses a drink from DrinkCategoryActivity's ListView, onItemClickListener's onItemClick() method gets called.

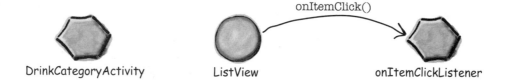

DrinkCategoryActivity   ListView   onItemClickListener

⑥ The onItemClick() method creates an intent to start DrinkActivity, passing along the drink ID as extra information.

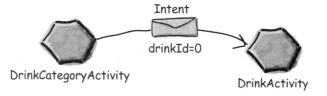

DrinkCategoryActivity   DrinkActivity

⑦ **DrinkActivity launches.**
It retrieves the drink ID from the intent, and gets details for the correct drink from the Drink class. It uses this information to update its views.

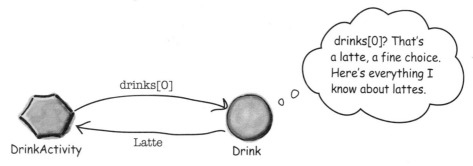

DrinkActivity   Drink

Test drive the app

When you run the app, `TopLevelActivity` gets displayed.

> We've implemented the Drinks part of the app. The other items won't do anything if you click on them.

When you click on the Drinks item, `DrinkCategoryActivity` is launched. It displays all the drinks from the `Drink` java class.

When you click on one of the drinks, `DrinkActivity` is launched and details of the selected drink are displayed.

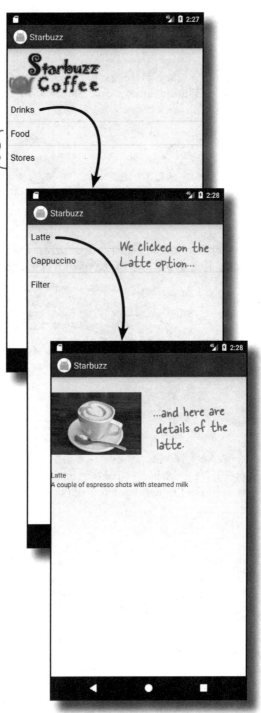

> We clicked on the Latte option...

> ...and here are details of the latte.

Using these three activities, you can see how to structure your app into top-level activities, category activities, and detail/edit activities. In Chapter 15, we'll revisit the Starbuzz app to explain how you can retrieve the drinks from a database.

Pool Puzzle Solution

Your **goal** is to create an activity that binds a Java array of colors to a spinner. Take code snippets from the pool and place them into the blank lines in the activity. You may **not** use the same snippet more than once, and you won't need to use all the snippets.

. . .

```java
public class MainActivity extends Activity {

    String[] colors = new String[] {"Red", "Orange", "Yellow", "Green", "Blue"};

    @Override
    protected void onCreate(Bundle savedInstanceState) {
        super.onCreate(savedInstanceState);
        setContentView(R.layout.activity_main);
        Spinner spinner = ( Spinner ) findViewById(R.id.spinner);
        ArrayAdapter< String > adapter = new ArrayAdapter<>(
                this ,
                android.R.layout.simple_spinner_item,
                colors);
        spinner. setAdapter (adapter);
    }
}
```

We're using an array of type String.

Use setAdapter() to get the spinner to use the array adapter.

You didn't need to use these code snippets.

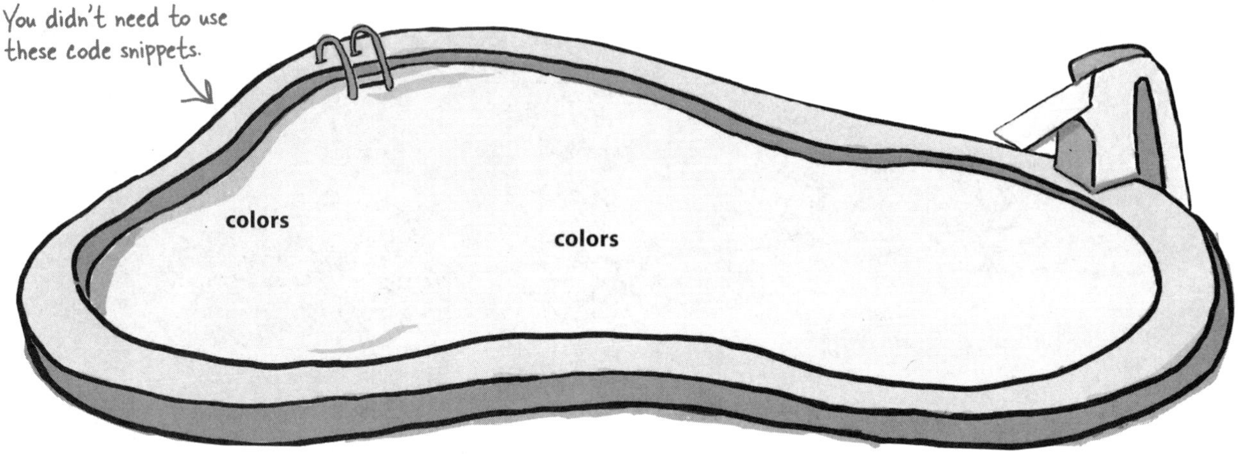

colors

colors

Your Android Toolbox

You've got Chapter 7 under your belt and now you've added list views and app design to your toolbox.

You can download the full code for the chapter from https://tinyurl.com/HeadFirstAndroid.

BULLET POINTS

- Sort your ideas for activities into top-level activities, category activities, and detail/edit activities. Use the category activities to navigate from the top-level activities to the detail/edit activities.

- A list view displays items in a list. Add it to your layout using the `<ListView>` element.

- Use `android:entries` in your layout to populate the items in your list views from an array defined in *strings.xml*.

- An adapter acts as a bridge between an `AdapterView` and a data source. `ListView`s and `Spinner`s are both types of `AdapterView`.

- An `ArrayAdapter` is an adapter that works with arrays.

- Handle click events on `Button`s using `android:onClick` in the layout code. Handle click events elsewhere by creating a listener and implementing its click event.

8 support libraries and app bars

Taking Shortcuts

Everybody likes a shortcut.

And in this chapter you'll see how to add shortcuts to your apps using **app bars**. We'll show you how to start activities by *adding actions* to your app bar, how to share content with other apps using the *share action provider*, and how to navigate up your app's hierarchy by implementing *the app bar's Up button*. Along the way we'll introduce you to the powerful **Android Support Libraries**, which are key to making your apps look fresh on older versions of Android.

Great apps have a clear structure

In the previous chapter, we looked at ways of structuring an app to create the best user experience. Remember that one way of creating an app is to organize the screens into three types:

Top-level screens

This is usually the first activity in your app that your user sees.

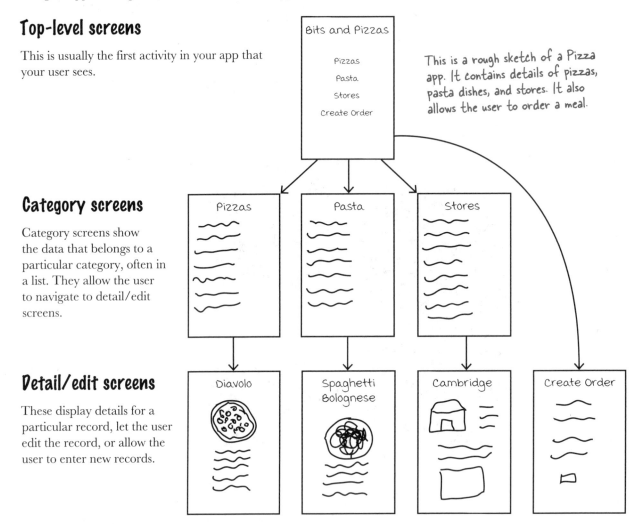

This is a rough sketch of a Pizza app. It contains details of pizzas, pasta dishes, and stores. It also allows the user to order a meal.

Category screens

Category screens show the data that belongs to a particular category, often in a list. They allow the user to navigate to detail/edit screens.

Detail/edit screens

These display details for a particular record, let the user edit the record, or allow the user to enter new records.

They also have great shortcuts

If a user's going to use your app a lot, they'll want quick ways to get around. We're going to look at navigational views that will give your user shortcuts around your app, providing more space in your app for actual content. Let's begin by taking a closer look at the top-level screen in the above Pizza app.

Different types of navigation

In the top-level screen of the Pizza app, there's a list of options for places in the app the user can go to.

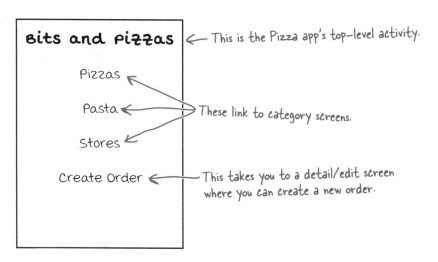

Bits and pizzas ← This is the Pizza app's top-level activity.

Pizzas
Pasta
Stores
} These link to category screens.

Create Order ← This takes you to a detail/edit screen where you can create a new order.

The top three options link to category activities; the first presents the user with a list of pizzas, the second a list of pasta, and the third a list of stores. They allow the user to navigate around the app. ← These are like the navigation options we looked at in Chapter 7.

The fourth option links to a detail/edit activity that allows the user to create an order. This option enables the user to perform an **action**.

In Android apps, you can add actions to the **app bar**. The app bar is the bar you often see at the top of activities; it's sometimes known as the **action bar**. You generally put your app's most important actions in the app bar so that they're prominent at the top of the screen.

In the Pizza app, we can make it easy for the user to place an order wherever they are in the app by making sure there's an app bar at the top of every activity that includes a Create Order button. This way the user will have access to it wherever they are.

Let's look at how you create app bars.

This is an app bar.

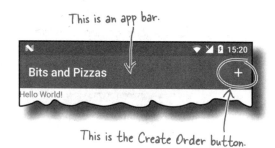

This is the Create Order button.

Here's what we're going to do

There are a few things we're going to cover in this chapter.

1 **Add a basic app bar.**
We'll create an activity called `MainActivity`
and add a basic app bar to it by applying a theme.

This is the app bar we'll add.

2 **Replace the basic app bar with a toolbar.**
To use the latest app bar features, you need to replace the basic app bar with
a toolbar. This looks the same as the basic app bar, but you can use it to do
more things.

3 **Add a Create Order action.**
We'll create a new activity called `OrderActivity`, and add an action to
`MainActivity`'s app bar that opens it.

4 **Implement the Up button.**
We'll implement the Up button on `OrderActivity`'s app bar so that
users have an easy way of navigating back to `MainActivity`.

The Up button features a button that (confusingly) points to the left.

5 **Add a share action provider.**
We'll add a share action provider to `MainActivity`'s app bar so that users
can share text with other apps and invite their friends to join them for pizza.

You'll find out what action providers are later in the chapter.

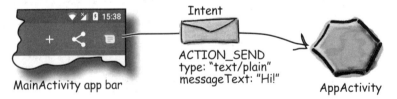

Let's start by looking at how you add a basic app bar.

support libraries and app bars

→ ☐ **Basic app bar**
☐ Toolbar
☐ Action
☐ Up button
☐ Share action

Add an app bar by applying a theme

An app bar has a number of uses:

⭐ Displaying the app or activity name so that the user knows where in the app they are. As an example, an email app might use the app bar to indicate whether the user is in their inbox or junk folder.

⭐ Making key actions prominent in a way that's predictable—for example, sharing content or performing searches.

⭐ Navigating to other activities to perform an action.

To add a basic app bar, you need to use a **theme** that includes an app bar. A theme is a style that's applied to an activity or application so that your app has a consistent look and feel. It controls such things as the color of the activity background and app bar, and the style of the text.

Android comes with a number of built-in themes that you can use in your apps. Some of these, such as the Holo themes, were introduced in early releases of Android, and others, such as the Material themes, were introduced much later to give apps a more modern appearance.

The Holo themes have been in Android since API level 11.

The Material themes were introduced in API level 21.

These themes look a bit different from the one on the previous page, as they haven't had any extra styling applied to them. You'll find out how to add styling later in the chapter.

But there's a problem. You want your apps to look as modern and up-to-date as possible, but you can only use themes from the version of Android they were released in. As an example, you can't use the native Material themes on devices that are running a version of Android older than Lollipop, as the Material themes were introduced with API level 21.

The problem isn't just limited to themes. Every new release of Android introduces new features that people want to see in their apps, such as new GUI components. But not everyone upgrades to the latest version of Android as soon as it comes out. In fact, most people are at least one version of Android behind.

So how can you use the latest Android features and themes in your apps if most people aren't using the latest version? How can you give your users a consistent user experience irrespective of what version of Android they're using without making your app look old-fashioned?

Basic app bar
Toolbar
Action
Up button
Share action

Support libraries allow you to use new features in older versions of Android

The Android team solved this problem by coming up with the idea of **Support Libraries**.

The Android Support Libraries provide backward compatibility with older versions of Android. They sit outside the main release of Android, and contain new Android features that developers can use in the apps they're building. The Support Libraries mean that you can give users on older devices the same experience as users on newer devices *even if they're using different versions of Android.*

Here are some of the Support Libraries that are available for you to use:

v4 Support Library
Includes the largest set of features, such as support for application components and user interface features.

v7 AppCompat Library
Includes support for app bars.

v7 Cardview Library
Adds support for the `CardView` widget, allowing you to show information inside cards.

Constraint Layout Library
Allows you to create constraint layouts. You used features from this library in Chapter 6.

v7 RecyclerView Library
Adds support for the `RecyclerView` widget.

Design Support Library
Adds support for extra components such as tabs and navigation drawers.

These are just some of the Support Libraries.

Each library includes a specific set of features.

The v7 AppCompat Library contains a set of up-to-date themes that can be used with older versions of Android: in practice, they can be used with nearly all devices, as most people are using API level 19 or above. We're going to use the v7 AppCompat Library by applying one of the themes it contains to our app. This will add an app bar that will look up-to-date and work the same on all versions of Android that we're targeting. Whenever you want to use one of the Support Libraries, you first need to add it to your app. We'll look at how you do this after we've created the project.

support libraries and app bars

Basic app bar
Toolbar
Action
Up button
Share action

Create the Pizza app

We'll start by creating a prototype of the Pizza app. Create a new Android project for an application named "Bits and Pizzas" with a company domain of "hfad.com", making the package name `com.hfad.bitsandpizzas`. The minimum SDK should be API level 19 so that it works with most devices. You'll need an empty activity called "MainActivity" and a layout called "activity_main". Make sure you ***check*** **the Backwards Compatibility (AppCompat) checkbox** (you'll see why a few pages ahead).

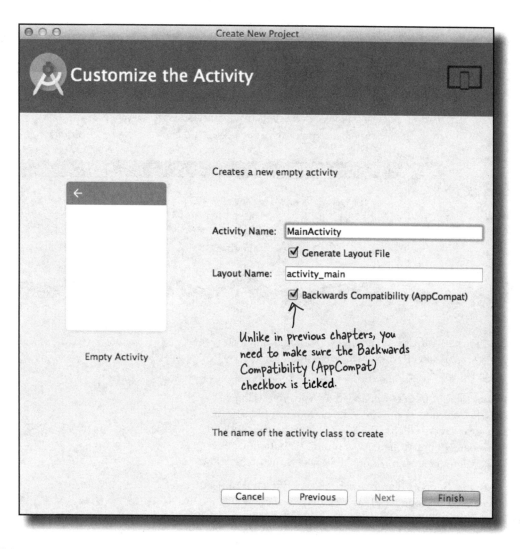

Next, we'll look at how you add a Support Library to the project.

Basic app bar
Toolbar
Action
Up button
Share action

Add the v7 AppCompat Support Library

We're going to use one of the themes from the v7 AppCompat Library, so we need to add the library to our project as a dependency. Doing so means that the library gets included in your app, and downloaded to the user's device.

To manage the Support Library files that are included in your project, choose File→Project Structure. Then click on the app module and choose Dependencies. You'll be presented with the following screen:

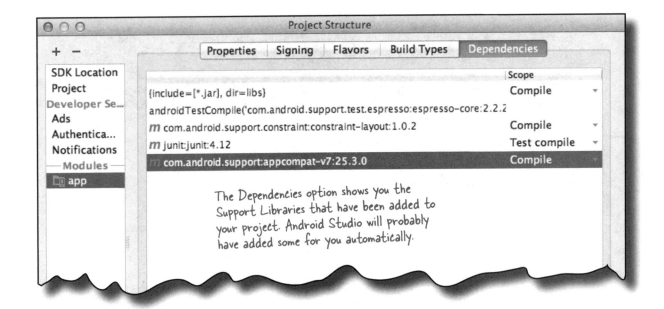

The Dependencies option shows you the Support Libraries that have been added to your project. Android Studio will probably have added some for you automatically.

Android Studio may have already added the AppCompat Support Library for you automatically. If so, you will see it listed as appcompat-v7, as shown above.

If the AppCompat Library hasn't been added for you, you will need to add it yourself. Click on the "+" button at the bottom or right side of the Project Structure screen. Choose the Library Dependency option, select the appcompat-v7 library, then click on the OK button. Click on OK again to save your changes and close the Project Structure window.

Once the AppCompat Support Library has been added to your project, you can use its resources in your app. In our case, we want to apply one of its themes in order to give `MainActivity` an app bar. Before we do that, however, we need to look at the type of activity we're using for `MainActivity`.

AppCompatActivity lets you use AppCompat themes

So far, all of the activities we've created have extended the `Activity` class. This is the base class for all activities, and it's what makes your activity an activity. If you want to use the AppCompat themes, however, you need to use a special kind of activity, called an **AppCompatActivity**, instead.

The `AppCompatActivity` class is a subclass of `Activity`. It lives in the AppCompat Support Library, and it's designed to work with the AppCompat themes. **Your activity needs to extend the `AppCompatActivity` class instead of the `Activity` class whenever you want an app bar that provides backward compatibility with older versions of Android**.

As `AppCompatActivity` is a subclass of the `Activity` class, everything you've learned about activities so far still applies. `AppCompatActivity` works with layouts in just the same way, and inherits all the lifecycle methods from the `Activity` class. The main difference is that, compared to `Activity`, `AppCompatActivity` contains extra smarts that allow it to work with the themes from the AppCompat Support Library.

Here's a diagram showing the `AppCompatActivity` class hierarchy:

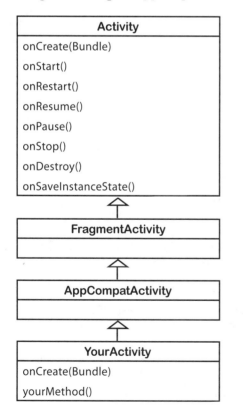

Activity class
(android.app.Activity)
The `Activity` class implements default versions of the lifecycle methods.

FragmentActivity class
(android.support.v4.app.FragmentActivity)
The base class for activities that need to use support fragments. You'll find out about fragments in the next chapter.

AppCompatActivity class
(android.support.v7.app.AppCompatActivity)
The base class for activities that use the Support Library app bar.

YourActivity class
(com.hfad.foo)

We'll make sure `MainActivity` extends `AppCompatActivity` on the next page.

MainActivity needs to be an AppCompatActivity

Basic app bar
Toolbar
Action
Up button
Share action

We want to use one of the AppCompat themes, so we need to make sure our activities extend the `AppCompatActivity` class instead of the `Activity` class. Happily, this should already be the case if you checked the Backwards Compatibility (AppCompat) checkbox when you first created the activity. Open the file *MainActivity.java*, then make sure your code matches ours below:

```java
package com.hfad.bitsandpizzas;

import android.support.v7.app.AppCompatActivity;
import android.os.Bundle;


public class MainActivity extends AppCompatActivity {

    @Override
    protected void onCreate(Bundle savedInstanceState) {
        super.onCreate(savedInstanceState);
        setContentView(R.layout.activity_main);
    }

}
```

The AppCompatActivity class lives in the v7 AppCompat Support Library.

Make sure your activity extends AppCompatActivity.

BitsAndPizzas

app/src/main

java

com.hfad.bitsandpizzas

MainActivity.java

Now that we've confirmed that our activity extends `AppCompatActivity`, we can add an app bar by applying a theme from the AppCompat Support Library. You apply a theme in the app's *AndroidManifest.xml* file, so we'll look at this file next.

---

there are no Dumb Questions

Q: What versions of Android can the Support Libraries be used with?

A: It depends on the version of the Support Library. Prior to version 24.2.0, Libraries prefixed with v4 could be used with API level 4 and above, and those prefixed with v7 could be used with API level 7 and above. When version 24.2.0 of the Support Libraries was released, the minimum API for all Support Libraries became API level 9. The minimum API level is likely to increase in the future.

Q: In earlier chapters, Android Studio gave me activities that already extended `AppCompatActivity`. Why's that?

A: When you create an activity in Android Studio, the wizard includes a checkbox asking if you want to create a Backwards Compatible (AppCompat) activity. If you left this checked in earlier chapters, Android Studio would have generated activities that extend `AppCompatActivity`.

Q: I've seen code that extends `ActionBarActivity`. What's that?

A: In older versions of the AppCompat Support Library, you used the `ActionBarActivity` class to add app bars. This was deprecated in version 22.1 in favor of `AppCompatActivity`.

AndroidManifest.xml can change your app bar's appearance

As you've seen earlier in the book, an app's *AndroidManifest.xml* file provides essential information about the app, such as what activities it contains. It also includes a number of attributes that have a direct impact on your app bars.

Here's the *AndroidManifest.xml* code Android Studio created for us (we've highlighted the key areas):

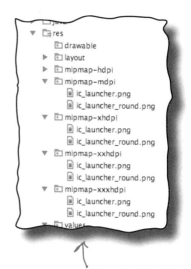

```xml
<?xml version="1.0" encoding="utf-8"?>
<manifest xmlns:android="http://schemas.android.com/apk/res/android"
    package="com.hfad.bitsandpizzas">
    <application
        android:allowBackup="true"
        android:icon="@mipmap/ic_launcher"
        android:roundIcon="@mipmap/ic_launcher_round"
        android:label="@string/app_name"
        android:supportsRtl="true"
        android:theme="@style/AppTheme">
        <activity android:name=".MainActivity">
            ...
        </activity>
    </application>
</manifest>
```

App icons. Android Studio provides icons by default.

The user-friendly name of the app

The theme

The **android:icon** attribute assigns an icon to the app. The icon is used as the launcher icon for the app, and if the theme you're using displays an icon in the app bar, it will use this icon. **android:roundIcon** may be used instead on devices running Android 7.1 or above.

The icon is a **mipmap** resource. A mipmap is an image that can be used for application icons, and they're held in *mipmap** folders in *app/src/main/res*. Just as with drawables, you can add different images for different screen densities by adding them to an appropriately named *mipmap* folder. As an example, an icon in the *mipmap-hdpi* folder will be used by devices with high-density screens. You refer to mipmap resources in your layout using @ mipmap.

The **android:label** attribute describes a user-friendly label that gets displayed in the app bar. In the code above, it's used in the `<application>` tag to apply a label to the entire app. You can also add it to the `<activity>` tag to assign a label to a single activity.

The **android:theme** attribute specifies the theme. Using this attribute in the `<application>` element applies the theme to the entire app. Using it in the `<activity>` element applies the theme to a single activity.

We'll look at how you apply the theme on the next page.

Android Studio automatically added icons to our mipmap* folders when we created the project.

How to apply a theme

When you want to apply a theme to your app, you have two main options:

★ Hardcode the theme in *AndroidManifest.xml*.

★ Apply the theme using a style.

Let's look at these two approaches.

1. Hardcoding the theme

To hardcode the theme in *AndroidManifest.xml*, you update the
`android:theme` attribute in the file to specify the name of the
theme you want to use. As an example, to apply a theme with a
light background and a dark app bar, you'd use:

```
<application

    ...

    android:theme="Theme.AppCompat.Light.DarkActionBar">
```

This approach works well if you want to apply a basic theme
without making any changes to it.

*This is a simple way of applying a
basic theme, but it means you can't,
for example, change its colors.*

2. Using a style to apply the theme

Most of the time, you'll want to apply the theme using a style, as
this approach enables you to tweak the theme's appearance. You
may want to override the theme's main colors to reflect your app's
brand, for example.

To apply a theme using a style, you update the `android:theme`
attribute in *AndroidManifest.xml* to the name of a style resource
(which you then need to create). In our case, we're going
to use a style resource named AppTheme, so update the
`android:theme` attribute in your version of *AndroidManifest.xml*
to the following:

```
<application

    ...

    android:theme="@style/AppTheme">
```

*Android Studio may have already added this
to your version of AndroidManifest.xml.*

BitsAndPizzas

app/src/main

AndroidManifest.xml

The `@style` prefix tells Android that the theme the app's using is
a style that's defined in a **style resource file**. We'll look at this
next.

support libraries *and app bars*

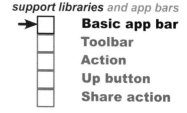

Basic app bar
Toolbar
Action
Up button
Share action

Define styles in a style resource file

The style resource file holds details of any themes and styles you want to use in your app. When you create a project in Android Studio, the IDE will usually create a default style resource file for you called *styles.xml* located in the *app/src/main/res/values* folder.

If Android Studio hasn't created the file, you'll need to add it yourself. Switch to the Project view of Android Studio's explorer, highlight the *app/src/main/res/values* folder, go to the File menu, and choose New. Then choose the option to create a new Values resource file, and when prompted, name the file "styles". When you click on OK, Android Studio will create the file for you.

A basic style resource file looks like this:

```
<resources>
    <style name="AppTheme" parent="Theme.AppCompat.Light.DarkActionBar">

    </style>
</resources>
```

This is the theme used in the app.

←*There may be extra code here to customize the theme. We'll look at this a couple of pages ahead.*

BitsAndPizzas
app/src/main
res
values
styles.xml

A style resource file can contain one or more styles. Each style is defined through the <style> element.

Each style must have a name, which you define with the name attribute; for example:

```
name="AppTheme"
```

In the code above, the style has a name of "AppTheme", and *AndroidManifest.xml* can refer to it using "@style/AppTheme".

The parent attribute specifies where the style should inherit its properties from; for example:

```
parent="Theme.AppCompat.Light.DarkActionBar"
```

This gives the app a theme of **"Theme.AppCompat.Light. DarkActionBar"**, which gives activities a light background, with a dark app bar. We'll look at some more of Android's available themes on the next page.

The app bar has a dark background with white text.

Bits and Pizzas

Hello World!

The main activity background is light.

Theme gallery

Android comes with a whole bunch of built-in themes that you can use in your apps. Here are just a few of them:

Theme.AppCompat.Light

This has a light background and app bar.

Theme.AppCompat

This has a dark background and a dark app bar.

Theme.AppCompat.Light.NoActionBar

This has a light background and no app bar.

Theme.AppCompat.NoActionBar

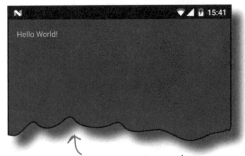

This has a dark background and no app bar.

Theme.AppCompat.Light.DarkActionBar

This has a light background and the app bar is dark.

There's also a DayNight theme, which uses one set of colors in the day, and another set at night.

The theme determines the basic appearance of the app, such as the color of the app bar and any views. But what if you want to modify the app's appearance?

support libraries *and app bars*

→ ☐ **Basic app bar**
☐ **Toolbar**
☐ **Action**
☐ **Up button**
☐ **Share action**

Customize the look of your app

You can use customize the look of your app by overriding the properties of an existing theme in the style resource file. For example, you can change the color of the app bar, the status bar, and any UI controls. You override the theme by adding `<item>` elements to the `<style>` to describe each modification you want to make.

We're going to override three of the colors used by our theme. To do this, make sure that your version of *styles.xml* matches ours below:

```
<resources>
    <!-- Base application theme. -->
    <style name="AppTheme" parent="Theme.AppCompat.Light.DarkActionBar">
        <!-- Customize your theme here. -->
        <item name="colorPrimary">@color/colorPrimary</item>
        <item name="colorPrimaryDark">@color/colorPrimaryDark</item>
        <item name="colorAccent">@color/colorAccent</item>
    </style>
</resources>
```

These three lines of code modify the theme by changing three of the colors.

BitsAndPizzas → app/src/main → res → values → styles.xml

The above code includes three modifications, each one described by a separate `<item>`. Each `<item>` has a `name` attribute that indicates what part of the theme you want to change, and a value that specifies what you want to change it to, like this:

```
<item name="colorPrimary">@color/colorPrimary</item>
```

This will change the colorPrimary part of the theme so it has a value of @color/colorPrimary.

`name="colorPrimary"` refers to the main color you want to use for your app. This color gets used for your app bar, and to "brand" your app with a particular color.

`name="colorPrimaryDark"` is a darker variant of your main color. It gets used as the color of the status bar.

`name="colorAccent"` refers to the color of any UI controls such as editable text views or checkboxes.

You set a new color for each of these areas by giving each `<item>` a value. The value can either be a hardcoded hexadecimal color value, or a reference to a color resource. We'll look at color resources on the next page.

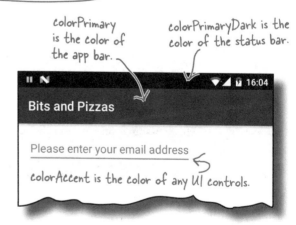

colorPrimary is the color of the app bar.

colorPrimaryDark is the color of the status bar.

Bits and Pizzas

Please enter your email address

colorAccent is the color of any UI controls.

There are a whole host of other theme properties you can change, but we're not going to cover them here. To find out more, visit https://developer. android.com/guide/topics/ui/themes.html.

Basic app bar

Toolbar

Action

Up button

Share action

Define colors in a color resource file

A color resource file is similar to a String resource file except that it contains colors instead of Strings. Using a color resource file makes it easy to make changes to the color scheme of your app, as all the colors you want to use are held in one place.

The color resource file is usually called *colors.xml*, and it's located in the *app/src/main/res/values* folder. When you create a project in Android Studio, the IDE will usually create this file for you.

If Android Studio hasn't created the file, you'll need to add it yourself. Switch to the Project view of Android Studio's explorer, highlight the *app/src/main/res/values* folder, go to the File menu, and choose New. Then choose the option to create a new Values resource file, and when prompted, name the file "colors". When you click on OK, Android Studio will create the file for you.

Next, open *colors.xml* and make sure that your version of the file matches ours below:

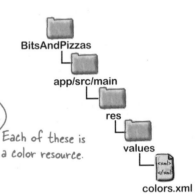

```xml
<?xml version="1.0" encoding="utf-8"?>
<resources>
    <color name="colorPrimary">#3F51B5</color>
    <color name="colorPrimaryDark">#303F9F</color>
    <color name="colorAccent">#FF4081</color>
</resources>
```

Each of these is a color resource.

The code above defines three color resources. Each one has a name and a value. The value is a hexadecimal color value:

This says it's a color resource.

```xml
<color name="colorPrimary">#3F51B5</color>
```

The color resource has a name of "colorPrimary", and a value of #3F51B5 (blue).

The style resource file looks up colors from the color resource file using `@color/colorName`. For example:

```xml
<item name="colorPrimary">@color/colorPrimary</item>
```

overrides the primary color used in the theme with the value of `colorPrimary` in the color resource file.

Now that we've seen how to add an app bar by applying a theme, let's update `MainActivity`'s layout and take the app for a test drive.

support libraries and app bars

→ Basic app bar
  Toolbar
  Action
  Up button
  Share action

The code for activity_main.xml

For `MainActivity`'s layout, we're going to display some default text in a linear layout. Here's the code to do that; update your version of *activity_main.xml* to match ours below:

```xml
<?xml version="1.0" encoding="utf-8"?>
<LinearLayout
    xmlns:android="http://schemas.android.com/apk/res/android"
    xmlns:tools="http://schemas.android.com/tools"
    android:layout_width="match_parent"
    android:layout_height="match_parent"
    android:orientation="vertical"
    android:padding="16dp"
    tools:context="com.hfad.bitsandpizzas.MainActivity">

    <TextView
        android:layout_width="wrap_content"
        android:layout_height="wrap_content"
        android:text="Hello World!" />
</LinearLayout>
```

BitsAndPizzas
  app/src/main
    res
      layout
        activity_main.xml

We're just displaying some basic placeholder text in MainActivity's layout because right now we want you to focus on app bars.

Test drive the app

When you run the app, `MainActivity` gets displayed. At the top of the activity there's an app bar.

This is the app bar. The default color's been overridden so that it's blue.

Bits and Pizzas

Hello World!

The background is light, as we've used a theme of Theme.AppCompat.Light.DarkActionBar. This theme also gives us dark text in the main body of the activity, and white text in the app bar.

The status bar's default color has been overridden so it's a darker shade of blue than the app bar.

That's everything you need to apply a basic app bar in your activities. Why not experiment with changing the theme and colors? Then when you're ready, turn the page and we'll move on to the next step.

ActionBar vs. Toolbar

So far, you've seen how to add a basic app bar to the activities in your app by applying a theme that includes an app bar. Adding an app bar in this way is easy, but it has one disadvantage: *it doesn't necessarily include all the latest app bar features.*

Behind the scenes, any activity that acquires an app bar via a theme uses the `ActionBar` class for its app bar. The most recent app bar features, however, have been added to the `Toolbar` class in the AppCompat Support Library instead. This means that if you want to use the most recent app bar features in your app, you need to use the `Toolbar` class from the Support Library.

Using the `Toolbar` class also gives you more flexibility. A toolbar is a type of view that you add to your layout just as you would any other type of view, and this makes it much easier to position and control than a basic app bar.

A toolbar looks just like the app bar you had previously, but it gives you more flexibility and includes the most recent app bar features.

How to add a toolbar

We're going to change our activity so that it uses a toolbar from the Support Library for its app bar. Whenever you want to use the `Toolbar` class from the Support Library, there are a number of steps you need to perform:

1 **Add the v7 AppCompat Support Library as a dependency.**
This is necessary because the `Toolbar` class lives in this library.

2 **Make sure your activity extends the AppCompatActivity class.**
Your activity must extend `AppCompatActivity` (or one of its subclasses) in order to use the Support Library toolbar.

3 **Remove the existing app bar.**
You do this by changing the theme to one that doesn't include an app bar.

4 **Add a toolbar to the layout.**
The toolbar is a type of view, so you can position it where you want and control its appearance.

5 **Update the activity to set the toolbar as the activity's app bar.**
This allows the activity to respond to the toolbar.

We'll go through these steps now.

Checklist (top right):
- ☑ **Basic app bar**
- → ☐ **Toolbar**
- ☐ **Action**
- ☐ **Up button**
- ☐ **Share action**

support libraries and app bars

Basic app bar
Toolbar
Action
Up button
Share action

1. Add the AppCompat Support Library

Before you can use the `Toolbar` class from the Support Library in your activities, you need to make sure that the v7 AppCompat Support Library has been added to your project as a dependency. In our particular case, the library has already been added to our project, as we needed it for the AppCompat themes.

To double-check that the Support Library is there, in Android Studio choose File→Project Structure, click on the app module, and choose Dependencies. You should see the v7 AppCompat Library listed as shown below:

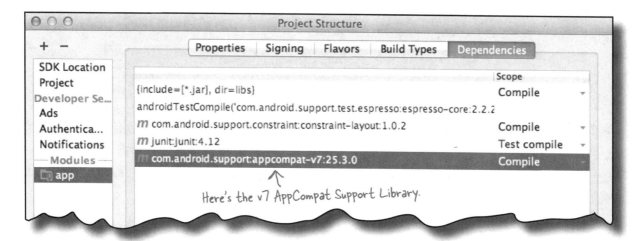

Here's the v7 AppCompat Support Library.

2. Extend the AppCompatActivity class

When you want to use a theme from the AppCompat Library, you have to make sure that your activities extend the `AppCompatActivity` class. This is also the case if you want to use a toolbar from the Support Library as your app bar.

We've already completed this step because, earlier in this chapter, we changed *MainActivity.java* to use `AppCompatActivity`:

```
...
import android.support.v7.app.AppCompatActivity;

public class MainActivity extends AppCompatActivity {
    ...
}
```

Our MainActivity already extends AppCompatActivity.

BitsAndPizzas
app/src/main
java
com.hfad.bitsandpizzas
MainActivity.java

The next thing we need to do is remove the existing app bar.

3. Remove the app bar

You remove the existing app bar in exactly the same way that you add one—by applying a **theme**.

When we wanted to add an app bar to our app, we applied a theme that displayed one. To do this, we used the theme attribute in *AndroidManifest.xml* to apply a style called AppTheme:

```
<manifest xmlns:android="http://schemas.android.com/apk/res/android"
    package="com.hfad.bitsandpizzas">
    <application

        ...

        android:theme="@style/AppTheme">

        ...                      This looks up the theme from styles.xml.
    </application>
</manifest>
```

BitsAndPizzas

app/src/main

AndroidManifest.xml

The theme was then defined in *styles.xml* like this:

This is the theme we're using. It displays a dark app bar.

```
<resources>
    <style name="AppTheme" parent="Theme.AppCompat.Light.DarkActionBar">

        ...

    </style>
</resources>
```

BitsAndPizzas

app/src/main

res

values

styles.xml

The theme Theme.AppCompat.Light.DarkActionBar gives your activity a light background with a dark app bar. To remove the app bar, we're going to change the theme to Theme.AppCompat.Light.**NoActionBar** instead. Your activity will look the same as it did before except that no app bar will be displayed.

To change the theme, update *styles.xml* like this:

```
<resources>
    <style name="AppTheme" parent="Theme.AppCompat.Light.DarkNoActionBar">

        ...    ← We customized the theme by
    </style>      overriding some of the colors.
    </resources>   You can leave this code in place.
```

Change the theme from DarkActionBar to NoActionBar. This removes the app bar.

Now that we've removed the current app bar, we can add the toolbar.

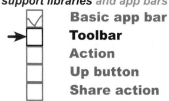

4. Add a toolbar to the layout

As we said earlier, a toolbar is a view that you add to your layout. Toolbar code looks like this:

```
<android.support.v7.widget.Toolbar          ← This defines the toolbar.
    android:id="@+id/toolbar"                ← Give the toolbar an ID so you can refer to it in your activity code.
    android:layout_width="match_parent"      ← Set the toolbar's size.
    android:layout_height="?attr/actionBarSize"
    android:background="?attr/colorPrimary"  ← These control the app bar's appearance.
    android:theme="@style/ThemeOverlay.AppCompat.Dark.ActionBar" />
```

You start by defining the toolbar using:

```
<android.support.v7.widget.Toolbar    ← This is the full path of the Toolbar
    ... />                              class in the Support Library.
```

where `android.support.v7.widget.Toolbar` is the fully qualified path of the `Toolbar` class in the Support Library.

Once the toolbar has been defined, you then use other view attributes to give it an ID, and specify its appearance. As an example, to make the toolbar as wide as its parent and as tall as the default app bar size from the underlying theme, you'd use:

```
android:layout_width="match_parent"
android:layout_height="?attr/actionBarSize"
```

The toolbar is as wide as its parent, and as tall as the default app bar.

The `?attr` prefix means that you want to use an attribute from the current theme. In this particular case, `?attr/actionBarSize` is the height of an app bar that's specified in our theme.

You can also change your toolbar's appearance so that it has a similar appearance to the app bar that we had before. To do this, you can change the background color, and apply a **theme overlay** like this:

```
android:background="?attr/colorPrimary"      ← Make the toolbar's background the same
                                               color as the app bar we had previously.
android:theme="@style/ThemeOverlay.AppCompat.Dark.ActionBar"
```

This gives the toolbar the same appearance as the app bar we had before. We have to use a theme overlay, as the NoActionBar theme doesn't style app bars in the same way as the DarkActionBar theme did.

A theme overlay is a special type of theme that alters the current theme by overwriting some of its attributes. We want our toolbar to look like our app bar did when we used a theme of `Theme.AppCompat.Light.DarkActionBar`, so we're using a theme overlay of `ThemeOverlay.AppCompat.Dark.ActionBar`.

On the next page we'll add the toolbar to the layout.

we're not doing this (in our app)

Basic app bar
Toolbar
Action
Up button
Share action

Add the toolbar to the layout...

If your app contains a single activity, you can add the toolbar to your layout just as you would any other view. Here is an example of the sort of code you would use in this situation (we're using a different approach, so don't update your layout with the code below):

```xml
<?xml version="1.0" encoding="utf-8"?>
<LinearLayout xmlns:android="http://schemas.android.com/apk/res/android"
    xmlns:tools="http://schemas.android.com/tools"
    android:layout_width="match_parent"
    android:layout_height="match_parent"
    android:orientation="vertical"
    tools:context="com.hfad.bitsandpizzas.MainActivity">

    <android.support.v7.widget.Toolbar
        android:id="@+id/toolbar"
        android:layout_width="match_parent"
        android:layout_height="?attr/actionBarSize"
        android:background="?attr/colorPrimary"
        android:theme="@style/ThemeOverlay.AppCompat.Dark.ActionBar" />

    <TextView
        android:layout_width="wrap_content"
        android:layout_height="wrap_content"
        android:text="Hello World!" />
</LinearLayout>
```

The code here doesn't include any padding. This is so that the toolbar fills the screen horizontally.

This code displays the toolbar at the top of the activity.

BitsAndPizzas
app/src/main
res
layout
activity_main.xml

Later in the chapter we'll add a second activity to our app, so we're not using this approach. So you don't need to change your layout code to match this example.

We're using a linear layout, so the text view will be positioned below the toolbar.

This code displays the toolbar at the top of the activity. We've positioned the text view Android Studio gave us so that it's displayed underneath the toolbar. Remember that a toolbar is a view like any other view, so you need to take this into account when you're positioning your other views.

Adding the toolbar code to your layout works well if your app contains a single activity, as it means that all the code relating to your activity's appearance is in a single file. It works less well, however, if your app contains multiple activities. If you wanted to display a toolbar in multiple activities, you would need to define the toolbar in the layout of each activity. This means that if you wanted to change the style of the toolbar in some way, you'd need to edit *every single layout file*.

So what's the alternative?

310 *Chapter 8*

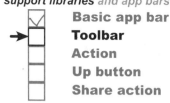

...or define the toolbar as a separate layout

An alternative approach is to define the toolbar in a separate layout, and then include the toolbar layout in each activity. This means that you only need to define the toolbar once, and if you want to change the style of your toolbar, you only need to edit one file.

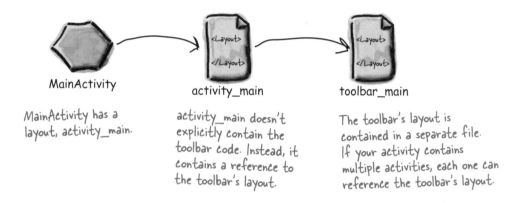

MainActivity has a layout, activity_main.

activity_main doesn't explicitly contain the toolbar code. Instead, it contains a reference to the toolbar's layout.

The toolbar's layout is contained in a separate file. If your activity contains multiple activities, each one can reference the toolbar's layout.

We're going to use this approach in our app. Start by creating a new layout file. Switch to the Project view of Android Studio's explorer, highlight the *app/src/res/main/layout* folder in Android Studio, then go to the File menu and choose New → Layout resource file. When prompted, give the layout file a name of "toolbar_main" and then click on OK. This creates a new layout file called *toolbar_main.xml*.

Next, open *toolbar_main.xml*, and replace any code Android Studio has created for you with the following:

```
<android.support.v7.widget.Toolbar
    xmlns:android="http://schemas.android.com/apk/res/android"
    android:layout_width="match_parent"
    android:layout_height="?attr/actionBarSize"
    android:background="?attr/colorPrimary"
    android:theme="@style/ThemeOverlay.AppCompat.Dark.ActionBar" />
```

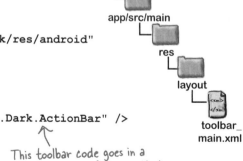

This toolbar code goes in a separate layout file so multiple activities can reference it.

This code is almost identical to the toolbar code you've already seen. The main difference is that we've left out the toolbar's id attribute, as we'll define this in the activity's main layout file *activity_main.xml* instead.

On the next page we'll look at how you include the toolbar layout in *activity_main.xml*.

Include the toolbar in the activity's layout

Basic app bar
Toolbar
Action
Up button
Share action

You can display one layout inside another using the <include> tag.
This tag must contain a layout attribute that specifies the name of the
layout you want to include. As an example, here's how you would use
the <include> tag to include the layout *toolbar_main.xml*:

```
<include
      layout="@layout/toolbar_main" />
```

The @layout tells Android to look for
a layout called toolbar_main.

We want to include the toolbar_main layout in *activity_main.xml*.
Here's our code; update your version of *activity_main.xml* to match ours:

```
<?xml version="1.0" encoding="utf-8"?>
<LinearLayout
    xmlns:android="http://schemas.android.com/apk/res/android"
    xmlns:tools="http://schemas.android.com/tools"
    android:layout_width="match_parent"
    android:layout_height="match_parent"
    android:orientation="vertical"
    android:padding="16dp"
    tools:context="com.hfad.bitsandpizzas.MainActivity">

    <include
        layout="@layout/toolbar_main"
        android:id="@+id/toolbar" />

    <TextView
        android:layout_width="wrap_content"
        android:layout_height="wrap_content"
        android:text="Hello World!" />
</LinearLayout>
```

Remove the padding so that the
toolbar fills the screen horizontally.

Include the toolbar_main layout.

We're giving the toolbar an ID so we
can refer to it in our activity code.

BitsAndPizzas

app/src/main

res

layout

activity_
main.xml

Now that we've added the toolbar to the layout, there's one more
change we need to make.

support libraries and app bars

Basic app bar
Toolbar
Action
Up button
Share action

5. Set the toolbar as the activity's app bar

The final thing we need to do is tell `MainActivity` to use the toolbar as its app bar.

So far we've only added the toolbar to the layout. While this means that the toolbar gets displayed at the top of the screen, the toolbar doesn't yet have any app bar functionality. As an example, if you were to run the app at this point, you'd find that the title of the app isn't displayed in the toolbar as it was in the app bar we had previously.

To get the toolbar to behave like an app bar, we need to call the `AppCompatActivity`'s `setSupportActionBar()` method in the activity's `onCreate()` method, which takes one parameter: the toolbar you want to set as the activity's app bar.

Here's the code for *MainActivity.java*; update your code to match ours:

If you don't update your activity code after adding a toolbar to your layout, your toolbar will just appear as a plain strip with nothing in it.

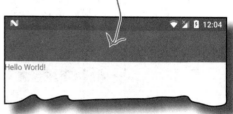

```java
package com.hfad.bitsandpizzas;

import android.support.v7.app.AppCompatActivity;
import android.os.Bundle;
import android.support.v7.widget.Toolbar;

public class MainActivity extends AppCompatActivity {

    @Override
    protected void onCreate(Bundle savedInstanceState) {
        super.onCreate(savedInstanceState);
        setContentView(R.layout.activity_main);
        Toolbar toolbar = (Toolbar) findViewById(R.id.toolbar);
        setSupportActionBar(toolbar);
    }
}
```

We're using the Toolbar class, so we need to import it.

Get a reference to the toolbar, and set it as the activity's app bar.

We need to use setSupportActionBar(), as we're using the toolbar from the Support Library.

BitsAndPizzas
└ app/src/main
  └ java
    └ com.hfad.bitsandpizzas
      └ MainActivity.java

That's all the code that you need to replace the activity's basic app bar with a toolbar. Let's see how it looks.

test drive

Test drive the app

When you run the app, a new toolbar is displayed in place of the basic app bar we had before. It looks similar to the app bar, but as it's based on the Support Library `Toolbar` class, it includes all the latest Android app bar functionality.

N   ▼ ✗ 🔋 12:15

Bits and Pizzas

Hello World!

← Here's our new toolbar. It looks like the app bar we had before, but it gives you more flexibility.

You've seen how to add an app bar, and how to replace the basic app bar with a toolbar. Over the next few pages we'll look at how to add extra functionaility to the app bar.

---

there are no Dumb Questions

Q: You've mentioned app bars, action bars, and toolbars. Is there a difference?

A: An app bar is the bar that usually appears at the top of your activities. It's sometimes called an action bar because in earlier versions of Android, the only way of implementing an app bar was via the `ActionBar` class.

The `ActionBar` class is used behind the scenes when you add an app bar by applying a theme. If your app doesn't rely on any new app bar features, this may be sufficient for your app.

An alternative way of adding an app bar is to implement a toolbar using the `Toolbar` class. The result looks similar to the default theme-based app bar, but it includes newer features of Android.

Q: I've added a toolbar to my activity, but when I run the app, it just looks like a band across the top of the screen. It doesn't even include the app name. Why's that?

A: First, check *AndroidManifest.xml* and make sure that your app has been given a label. This is where the app bar gets the app's name from.

Also, check that your activity calls the `setSupportActionBar()` method in its `onCreate()` method, as this sets the toolbar as the activity's app bar. Without it, the name of the app or activity won't get displayed in the toolbar.

Q: I've seen the <include> tag in some of the code that Android Studio has created for me. What does it do?

A: The `<include>` tag is used to include one layout inside another. Depending on what version of Android Studio you're using and what type of project you create, Android Studio may split your layout code into one or more separate layouts.

support libraries *and app bars*

Basic app bar
Toolbar
Action
Up button
Share action

Add actions to the app bar

In most of the apps you create, you'll probably want to add actions to the app bar. These are buttons or text in the app bar that you click on to make something happen. We're going to add a "Create Order" button to the app bar. When you click on it, it will start a new activity we'll create called `OrderActivity`:

We'll create a new Create Order action that will start OrderActivity.

Create OrderActivity

We'll start by creating `OrderActivity`. Select the *com.hfad. bitsandpizzas* package in the *app/src/main/java* folder, then go to File→New...→Activity→Empty Activity. Name the activity "OrderActivity", name the layout "activity_order", make sure the package name is `com.hfad.bitsandpizzas`, and ***check the Backwards Compatibility (AppCompat) checkbox.***

If prompted for the activity's source language, select the option for Java.

✏️ Sharpen your pencil

We want `OrderActivity` to display the same toolbar as `MainActivity`. See if you can complete the code for *activity_order.xml* below to display the toolbar.

```xml
<?xml version="1.0" encoding="utf-8"?>
<LinearLayout xmlns:android="http://schemas.android.com/apk/res/android"
    xmlns:tools="http://schemas.android.com/tools"
    android:layout_width="match_parent"
    android:layout_height="match_parent"
    android:orientation="vertical"
    tools:context="com.hfad.bitsandpizzas.OrderActivity">
    ..................................................................................
    ..................................................................................
    ..................................................................................

</LinearLayout>
```

The code for adding the toolbar needs to go here.

Sharpen your pencil
Solution

We want `OrderActivity` to display the same toolbar as `MainActivity`. See if you can complete the code for *activity_order.xml* below to display the toolbar.

```
<?xml version="1.0" encoding="utf-8"?>
<LinearLayout xmlns:android="http://schemas.android.com/apk/res/android"
    xmlns:tools="http://schemas.android.com/tools"
    android:layout_width="match_parent"
    android:layout_height="match_parent"
    android:orientation="vertical"
    tools:context="com.hfad.bitsandpizzas.OrderActivity">

    <include
        layout="@layout/toolbar_main"

        android:id="@+id/toolbar" />
```

← This is the same code that we had in MainActivity. It includes the toolbar_main layout in activity_order.

```
</LinearLayout>
```

Update activity_order.xml

We'll start by updating *activity_order.xml* so that it displays a toolbar. The toolbar will use the same layout we created earlier.

Here's our code; update yours so that it matches ours:

```
<?xml version="1.0" encoding="utf-8"?>
<LinearLayout xmlns:android="http://schemas.android.com/apk/res/android"
    xmlns:tools="http://schemas.android.com/tools"
    android:layout_width="match_parent"
    android:layout_height="match_parent"
    android:orientation="vertical"
    tools:context="com.hfad.bitsandpizzas.OrderActivity">

    <include      ← Add the toolbar layout we created earlier.
        layout="@layout/toolbar_main"
        android:id="@+id/toolbar" />

</LinearLayout>
```

BitsAndPizzas
app/src/main
res
layout
activity_order.xml

Update OrderActivity.java

Next we'll update `OrderActivity` so that it uses the toolbar we set up in the layout as its app bar. To do this, we need to call the `setSupportActionBar()` method, passing in the toolbar as a parameter, just as we did before.

Here's the full code for *OrderActivity.java*; update your version of the code so that it matches ours:

```java
package com.hfad.bitsandpizzas;

import android.support.v7.app.AppCompatActivity;
import android.os.Bundle;
import android.support.v7.widget.Toolbar;

public class OrderActivity extends AppCompatActivity {

    @Override                    Make sure the activity extends AppCompatActivity.
    protected void onCreate(Bundle savedInstanceState) {
        super.onCreate(savedInstanceState);
        setContentView(R.layout.activity_order);
        Toolbar toolbar = (Toolbar) findViewById(R.id.toolbar);
        setSupportActionBar(toolbar);
    }
}                Set the toolbar as the activity's app bar.
```

BitsAndPizzas
app/src/main
java
com.hfad.bitsandpizzas
OrderActivity.java

Add a String resource for the activity's title

Before we move on to creating an action to start `OrderActivity`, there's one more change we're going to make. We want to make it obvious to users when `OrderActivity` gets started, so we're going to change the text that's displayed in `OrderActivity`'s app bar to make it say "Create Order" rather than the name of the app.

To do this, we'll start by adding a String resource for the activity's title. Open the file *strings.xml* in the *app/src/main/res/values* folder, then add the following resource:

```xml
<string name="create_order">Create Order</string>
```
← We'll use this to display "Create Order" in OrderActivity's app bar.

BitsAndPizzas
app/src/main
res
values
strings.xml

We'll update the text that gets displayed in the app bar on the next page.

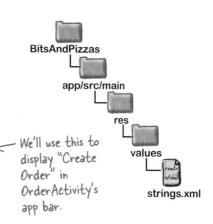

Change the app bar text by adding a label

As you saw earlier in the chapter, you tell Android what text to display in the app bar by using the `label` attribute in file *AndroidManifest.xml*.

Here's our current code for *AndroidManifest.xml*. As you can see, the code includes a `label` attribute of `@string/app_name` inside the `<application>` element. This means that the name of the app gets displayed in the app bar for the entire app.

```xml
<?xml version="1.0" encoding="utf-8"?>
<manifest xmlns:android="http://schemas.android.com/apk/res/android"
    package="com.hfad.bitsandpizzas">
    <application
        android:allowBackup="true"
        android:icon="@mipmap/ic_launcher"
        android:roundIcon="@mipmap/ic_launcher_round"
        android:label="@string/app_name"
        android:supportsRtl="true"
        android:theme="@style/AppTheme">

        <activity android:name=".MainActivity">
            ...
        </activity>

        <activity android:name=".OrderActivity">
        </activity>

    </application>
</manifest>
```

The label attribute tells Android what text to display in the app bar.

BitsAndPizzas
app/src/main
AndroidManifest.xml

This is the entry for MainActivity that we had before.

This is the entry for OrderActivity. Android added this for us when we created the new activity.

We want to override the label for `OrderActivity` so that the text "Create Order" gets displayed in the app bar whenever `OrderActivity` has the focus. To do this, we'll add a new `label` attribute to `OrderActivity`'s `<activity>` element to display the new text:

```xml
<activity
    android:name=".OrderActivity"
    android:label="@string/create_order">
</activity>
```

Adding a label to an activity means that for this activity, the activity's label gets displayed in its app bar instead of the app's label.

We'll show you this code in context on the next page.

support libraries *and app bars*

☑ Basic app bar
☑ Toolbar
→ ☐ **Action**
☐ **Up button**
☐ **Share action**

The code for AndroidManifest.xml

Here's our code for *AndroidManifest.xml*. Update your code to reflect our changes.

```xml
<?xml version="1.0" encoding="utf-8"?>
<manifest xmlns:android="http://schemas.android.com/apk/res/android"
    package="com.hfad.bitsandpizzas">
    <application
        ...
        android:label="@string/app_name"
        ...>

        <activity android:name=".MainActivity">
            ...
        </activity>

        <activity android:name=".OrderActivity"
            android:label="@string/create_order">
        </activity>

    </application>
</manifest>
```

The app's label is the default label for the entire app.

We don't need to change the code for MainActivity. MainActivity has no label of its own, so it will use the label in the `<application>` element.

Adding a label to OrderActivity overrides the app's label for this activity. It means that different text gets displayed in the app bar.

BitsAndPizzas

app/src/main

AndroidManifest.xml

That's everything we need for `OrderActivity`. Next we'll look at how you add an action to the app bar so that we can start it.

How to add an action to an app bar

To add an action to the app bar, you need to do four things:

1 **Add resources for the action's icon and text.**

2 **Define the action in a menu resource file.**
This tells Android what actions you want on the app bar.

3 **Get the activity to add the menu resource to the app bar.**
You do this by implementing the `onCreateOptionsMenu()` method.

4 **Add code to say what the action should do when clicked.**
You do this by implementing the `onOptionsItemSelected()` method.

We'll start by adding the action's icon and text resources.

1. Add the action's resources

When you add an action to an app bar, you generally assign it an icon and a short text title. The icon usually gets displayed if the action appears in the main area of the app bar. If the action doesn't fit in the main area, it's automatically moved to the app bar overflow, and the title appears instead.

We'll start with the icon.

Add the icon

If you want to display your action as an icon, you can either create your own icon from scratch or use one of the icons provided by Google. You can find the Google icons here: *https://material.io/icons/*.

We're going to use the "add" icon `ic_add_white_24dp`, and we'll add a version of it to our project's *drawable** folders, one for each screen density. Android will decide at runtime which version of the icon to use depending on the screen density of the device.

First, switch to the Project view of Android Studio's explorer if you haven't done so already, highlight the *app/src/main/res* folder, and then create folders called *drawable-hdpi*, *drawable-mdpi*, *drawable-xhdpi*, *drawable-xxhdpi*, and *drawable-xxxhdpi* if they're not already there. Then go to *https://git.io/v9oet*, and download the *ic_add_white_24dp.png* Bits and Pizzas images. Add the image in the *drawable-hdpi* folder to the *drawable-hdpi* folder in your project, then repeat this process for the other folders.

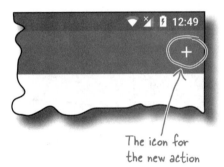

This is the app bar's overflow. Android moves actions into the overflow that don't fit on the main area of the app bar.

The icon for the new action

Add the action's title as a String resource

In addition to adding an icon for the action, we'll also add a title. This will get used if Android displays the action in the overflow area of the app bar, for example if there's no space for the action in the main area of the app bar.

We'll create the title as a String resource. Open the file *strings.xml* in the *app/src/main/res/values* folder, then add the following String resource:

```
<string name="create_order_title">Create Order</string>
```

Now that we've added resources for the action's icon and title, we can create the menu resource file.

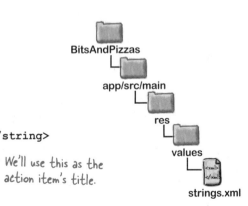

We'll use this as the action item's title.

support libraries *and app bars*

Basic app bar
Toolbar
Action
Up button
Share action

2. Create the menu resource file

A menu resource file tells Android what actions you want to appear on the app bar. Your app can contain multiple menu resource files. For example, you can create a separate menu resource file for each set of actions; this is useful if you want different activities to display different actions on their app bars.

We're going to create a new menu resource file called *menu_main.xml* in the folder *app/src/main/res/menu*. All menu resource files go in this folder.

← Android Studio may have already created this file for you. If it has, simply replace its contents with the code below.

To create the menu resource file, select the *app/src/main/res* folder, go to the File menu, and choose New. Then choose the option to create a new Android resource file. You'll be prompted for the name of the resource file and the type of resource. Give it a name of "menu_main" and a resource type of "Menu", and make sure that the directory name is *menu*. When you click on OK, Android Studio will create the file for you , and add it to the *app/src/main/res/menu* folder.

Here's the code to add the new action. Replace the contents of *menu_main.xml* with the code below:

```xml
<?xml version="1.0" encoding="utf-8"?>
<menu xmlns:android="http://schemas.android.com/apk/res/android"
    xmlns:app="http://schemas.android.com/apk/res-auto">
    <item android:id="@+id/action_create_order"
        android:title="@string/create_order_title"
        android:icon="@drawable/ic_add_white_24dp"
        android:orderInCategory="1"
        app:showAsAction="ifRoom" />
</menu>
```

The <menu> element identifies the file as a menu resource file.

The <item> element defines the action.

BitsAndPizzas
app/src/main
res
menu
menu_main.xml

The menu resource file has a <menu> element at its root. Inside the <menu> element, you get a number of <item> elements, each one describing a separate action. In this particular case, we have a single action.

You use attributes of <item> to describe each action. The code creates an action with an id of action_create_order. This is so that we can refer to the action in our activity code, and respond to the user clicking on it.

The action includes a number of other attributes that determine how the action appears on the app bar, such as its icon and text. We'll look at these on the next page.

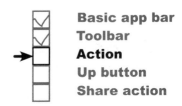

Basic app bar
Toolbar
Action
Up button
Share action

Control the action's appearance

Whenever you create an action to be displayed on the app bar, it's likely you'll want to display it as an icon. The icon can be any drawable resource. You set the icon using the `icon` attribute:

    android:icon="@drawable/ic_add_white_24dp"

This is the name of the drawable resource we want to use as the icon.

Sometimes Android can't display the action's icon. This may be because the action has no icon, or because the action is displayed in the app bar overflow instead of in the main area. For this reason, it's a good idea to set an action's title so that the action can display a short piece of text instead of an icon. You set the action's title using the `title` attribute:

    android:title="@string/create_order_title"

The title doesn't always get displayed, but it's a good idea to include it in case the action appears in the overflow.

If your app bar contains multiple actions, you might want to specify the order in which they appear. To do this, you use the `orderInCategory` attribute, which takes an integer value that reflects the action's order. Actions with a lower number will appear before actions with a higher number.

    android:orderInCategory="1"

An action with an orderInCategory of 1 will appear before an action with an orderInCategory of 10.

Finally, the `showAsAction` attribute is used to say how you want the item to appear in the app bar. As an example, you can use it to get an item to appear in the overflow area rather than the main part of the app bar, or to place an item on the main app bar only if there's room. The `showAsAction` attribute can take the following values:

"ifRoom"	Place the item in the app bar if there's space. If there's not space, put it in the overflow.
"withText"	Include the item's title text.
"never"	Put the item in the overflow area, and never in the main app bar.
"always"	Always place the item in the main area of the app bar. This value should be used sparingly; if you apply this to many items, they may overlap each other.

There are other attributes for controlling an action's appearance, but these are the most common ones.

In our example, we want the action to appear on the main area of the app bar if there's room, so we're using:

    app:showAsAction="ifRoom"

Our menu resource file is now complete. The next thing we need to do is implement the `onCreateOptionsMenu()` method in our activity.

support libraries and app bars

☑ **Basic app bar**
☑ **Toolbar**
→ ☐ **Action**
☐ **Up button**
☐ **Share action**

3. Add the menu to the app bar with the onCreateOptionsMenu() method

Once you've created the menu resource file, you add the actions it contains to an activity's app bar by implementing the activity's `onCreateOptionsMenu()` method. This method runs when the app bar's menu gets created. It takes one parameter, a `Menu` object that's a Java representation of the menu resource file.

Here's our `onCreateOptionsMenu()` method for *MainActivity.java* (update your code to reflect our changes):

```java
package com.hfad.bitsandpizzas;

import android.view.Menu;
...


public class MainActivity extends AppCompatActivity {

    ...

    @Override
    public boolean onCreateOptionsMenu(Menu menu) {
        // Inflate the menu; this adds items to the app bar.
        getMenuInflater().inflate(R.menu.menu_main, menu);
        return super.onCreateOptionsMenu(menu);
    }
}
```

← The onCreateOptionsMenu() method uses the Menu class.

Implementing this method adds any items in the menu resource file to the app bar.

All onCreateOptionsMenu() methods generally look like this.

BitsAndPizzas

app/src/main

java

com.hfad.bitsandpizzas

MainActivity.java

The line:

```java
getMenuInflater().inflate(R.menu.menu_main, menu);
```

This is the menu resource file.

This is a Menu object that's a Java representation of the menu resource file.

inflates your menu resource file. This means that it creates a `Menu` object that's a Java representation of your menu resource file, and any actions the menu resource file contains are translated to `MenuItems`. These are then added to the app bar.

There's one more thing we need to do: get our action to start `OrderActivity` when it's clicked. We'll do that on the next page.

4. React to action item clicks with the onOptionsItemSelected() method

To make your activity react when an action in the app bar is clicked, you implement the onOptionsItemSelected() method in your activity:

The MenuItem object is the action on the app bar that was clicked.

```
@Override
public boolean onOptionsItemSelected(MenuItem item) {
    switch (item.getItemId()) {
        ...
        default:
            return super.onOptionsItemSelected(item);
    }
}
```

Get the action's ID.

The onOptionsItemSelected() method runs whenever an action gets clicked. It takes one parameter, a MenuItem object that represents the action on the app bar that was clicked. You can use the MenuItem's getItemId() method to get the ID of the action so that you can perform an appropriate action, such as starting a new activity.

We want to start OrderActivity when our action is clicked. Here's the code for the onOptionsItemSelected() method that will do this:

```
@Override
public boolean onOptionsItemSelected(MenuItem item) {
    switch (item.getItemId()) {
        case R.id.action_create_order:
            //Code to run when the Create Order item is clicked
            Intent intent = new Intent(this, OrderActivity.class);
            startActivity(intent);
            return true;
        default:
            return super.onOptionsItemSelected(item);
    }
}
```

This intent is used to start OrderActivity when the Create Order action is clicked.

Returning true tells Android you've dealt with the item being clicked.

The full code for *MainActivity.java* is on the next page.

support libraries and app bars

☑ **Basic app bar**
☑ **Toolbar**
→ ☐ **Action**
☐ **Up button**
☐ **Share action**

The full MainActivity.java code

Here's the full code for *MainActivity.java*. Update your code so that it matches ours. We've highlighted our changes.

```java
package com.hfad.bitsandpizzas;

import android.support.v7.app.AppCompatActivity;
import android.os.Bundle;
import android.support.v7.widget.Toolbar;
import android.view.Menu;
import android.view.MenuItem;
import android.content.Intent;

public class MainActivity extends AppCompatActivity {

    @Override
    protected void onCreate(Bundle savedInstanceState) {
        super.onCreate(savedInstanceState);
        setContentView(R.layout.activity_main);
        Toolbar toolbar = (Toolbar) findViewById(R.id.toolbar);
        setSupportActionBar(toolbar);
    }

    @Override
    public boolean onCreateOptionsMenu(Menu menu) {
        getMenuInflater().inflate(R.menu.menu_main, menu);
        return super.onCreateOptionsMenu(menu);
    }

    @Override
    public boolean onOptionsItemSelected(MenuItem item) {
        switch (item.getItemId()) {
            case R.id.action_create_order:
                Intent intent = new Intent(this, OrderActivity.class);
                startActivity(intent);
                return true;
            default:
                return super.onOptionsItemSelected(item);
        }
    }
}
```

These classes are used by the onOptionsItemSelected() method so we need to import them.

This method gets called when an action on the app bar is clicked.

BitsAndPizzas

app/src/main

java

com.hfad.bitsandpizzas

MainActivity.java

Let's see what happens when we run the app.

Test drive the app

When you run the app, a new Create Order action is displayed in the `MainActivity` app bar. When you click on the action item, it starts `OrderActivity`.

Here's the Create Order action.

Clicking on the Create Order action starts OrderActivity. The text "Create Order" gets displayed in the app bar.

But how do we get back to MainActivity?

To return to `MainActivity` from `OrderActivity`, we currently need to click on the Back button on our device. But what if we want to get back to it from the app bar?

One option would be to add an action to `OrderActivity`'s app bar that starts `MainActivity`, but there's a better way. We can get `OrderActivity` to return to `MainActivity` by enabling the Up button on `OrderActivity`'s app bar.

Enable Up navigation

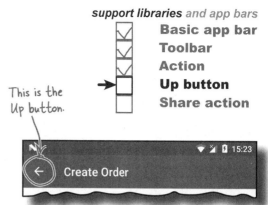

support libraries and *app bars*

Basic app bar
Toolbar
Action
Up button
Share action

This is the
Up button.

If you have an app that contains a hierarchy of activities, you
can enable the Up button on the app bar to let users navigate
through the app using hierarchical relationships. As an example,
`MainActivity` in our app includes an action on its app bar that
starts a second activity, `OrderActivity`. If we enable the Up
button on `OrderActivity`'s app bar, the user will be able to
return to `MainActivity` by clicking on this button.

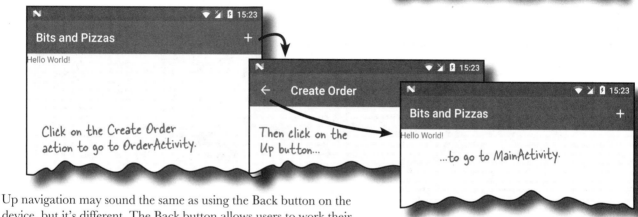

Click on the Create Order
action to go to OrderActivity.

Then click on the
Up button...

...to go to MainActivity.

Up navigation may sound the same as using the Back button on the
device, but it's different. The Back button allows users to work their
way back through the history of activities they've been to. The Up
button, on the other hand, is purely based on the app's hierarchical
structure. If your app contains a lot of activities, implementing the
Up button gives your users a quick and easy way to return to an
activity's parent without having to keep pressing the Back button.

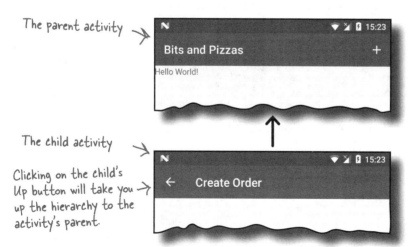

The parent activity →

The child activity →

Clicking on the child's
Up button will take you →
up the hierarchy to the
activity's parent.

**Use the Back button
to navigate back to
the previous activity.**

**Use the Up button to
navigate up the app's
hierarchy.**

We're going to enable the Up button on `OrderActivity`'s app
bar. When you click on it, it will display `MainActivity`.

Set an activity's parent

Basic app bar
Toolbar
Action
Up button
Share action

The Up button enables the user to navigate up a hierarchy of activities in the app. You declare this hierarchy in *AndroidManifest.xml* by specifying the parent of each activity. As an example, we want the user to be able to navigate from `OrderActivity` to `MainActivity` when they press the Up button, so this means that `MainActivity` is the parent of `OrderActivity`.

For API level 16 and above, you specify the parent activity using the `android:parentActivityName` attribute. For older versions of Android, you need to include a `<meta-data>` element that includes the name of the parent activity. Here are both approaches in our *AndroidManifest.xml*:

```xml
<?xml version="1.0" encoding="utf-8"?>
<manifest xmlns:android="http://schemas.android.com/apk/res/android"
    package="com.hfad.bitsandpizzas">

    <application
        android:allowBackup="true"
        android:icon="@mipmap/ic_launcher"
        android:roundIcon="@mipmap/ic_launcher_round"
        android:label="@string/app_name"
        android:supportsRtl="true"
        android:theme="@style/AppTheme">
        <activity android:name=".MainActivity">
            <intent-filter>
                <action android:name="android.intent.action.MAIN" />
                <category android:name="android.intent.category.LAUNCHER" />
            </intent-filter>
        </activity>
        <activity
            android:name=".OrderActivity"
            android:label="@string/create_order"
            android:parentActivityName=".MainActivity">
            <meta-data
                android:name="android.support.PARENT_ACTIVITY"
                android:value=".MainActivity" />
        </activity>
    </application>

</manifest>
```

BitsAndPizzas

app/src/main

AndroidManifest.xml

Apps at API level 16 or above use this line. It says that OrderActivity's parent is MainActivity.

You only need to add the <meta-data> element if you're supporting apps below API level 16. We've only included it so you can see what it looks like, but including it in your code won't do any harm.

Finally, we need to enable the Up button in `OrderActivity`.

support libraries and app bars

☑ **Basic app bar**
☑ **Toolbar**
☑ **Action**
→ ☐ **Up button**
☐ **Share action**

Adding the Up button

You enable the Up button from within your activity code. You first get a reference to the app bar using the activity's `getSupportActionBar()` method. This returns an object of type `ActionBar`. You then call the `ActionBar` `setDisplayHomeAsUpEnabled()` method, passing it a value of `true`.

Watch it!

If you enable the Up button for an activity, you MUST specify its parent.

If you don't, you'll get a null pointer exception when you call the setDisplayHomeAsUpEnabled() method.

```java
ActionBar actionBar = getSupportActionBar();
actionBar.setDisplayHomeAsUpEnabled(true);
```

We want to enable the Up button in `OrderActivity`, so we'll add the above code to the `onCreate()` method in *OrderActivity. java*. Here's our full activity code:

```java
package com.hfad.bitsandpizzas;

import android.support.v7.app.AppCompatActivity;
import android.os.Bundle;
import android.support.v7.widget.Toolbar;
import android.support.v7.app.ActionBar;
```

We're using the ActionBar class, so we need to import it. It comes from the AppCompat Support Library.

```java
public class OrderActivity extends AppCompatActivity {

    @Override
    protected void onCreate(Bundle savedInstanceState) {
        super.onCreate(savedInstanceState);
        setContentView(R.layout.activity_order);
        Toolbar toolbar = (Toolbar) findViewById(R.id.toolbar);
        setSupportActionBar(toolbar);
        ActionBar actionBar = getSupportActionBar();
        actionBar.setDisplayHomeAsUpEnabled(true);
    }
}
```

BitsAndPizzas
app/src/main
java
com.hfad.bitsandpizzas
OrderActivity.java

You need to use getSupportActionBar(), as we're using the toolbar from the Support Library.

This enables the Up button. Even though we're using a toolbar for our app bar, we need to use the ActionBar class for this method.

That's all the changes we need to make to enable the Up button. Let's see what happens when we run the app.

Test drive the app

When you run your app and click on the Create Order action item, `OrderActivity` is displayed as before.

`OrderActivity` displays an Up button in its app bar. When you click on the Up button, it displays its hierarchical parent `MainActivity`.

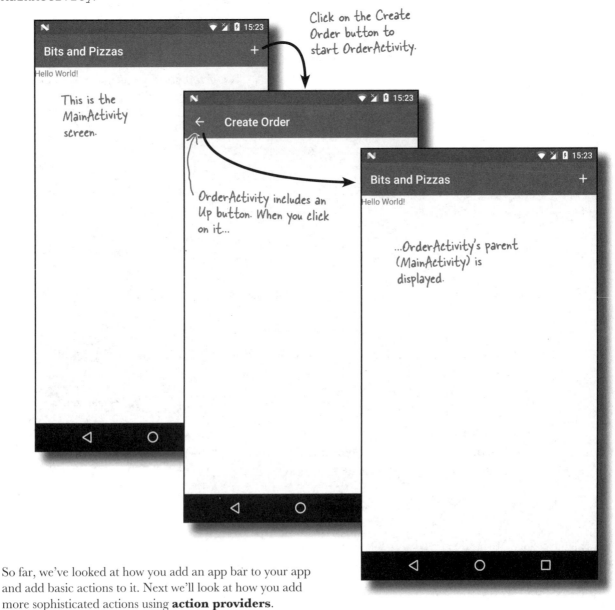

Click on the Create Order button to start OrderActivity.

This is the MainActivity screen.

OrderActivity includes an Up button. When you click on it...

...OrderActivity's parent (MainActivity) is displayed.

So far, we've looked at how you add an app bar to your app and add basic actions to it. Next we'll look at how you add more sophisticated actions using **action providers**.

Sharing content on the app bar

support libraries and app bars

Basic app bar
Toolbar
Action
Up button
Share action

The next thing we'll look at is how to add an action provider to your app bar. An action provider is an action that defines its own appearance and behavior.

We're going to concentrate on using the share action provider, which allows users to share content in your app with other apps such as Gmail. As an example, you could use it to let users send details of a particular pizza to one of their contacts.

The share action provider defines its own icon, so you don't have to add it yourself. When you click on it, it provides you with a list of apps you can use to share content. It adds a separate icon for the most commonly used app you choose to share content with.

This is what the share action looks like on the app bar. When you click on it, it gives you a list of apps that you can use to share content.

The share action also displays an icon for the app you most commonly share content with, in this case the Messenger app. This may not be visible at first.

You share the content with an intent

To get the share action provider to share content, you pass it an intent that defines the content you want to share, and its type. As an example, if you define an intent that passes text with an `ACTION_SEND` action, the share action will offer you a list of apps on your device that are capable of sharing text.

Here's how the share action works (you'll see this in action over the next two pages):

① **Your activity creates an intent and passes it to the share action provider.**
The intent describes the content that needs to be shared, its type, and an action.

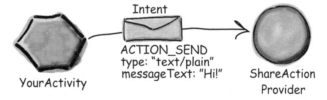

② **When the user clicks on the share action, the share action uses the intent to present the user with a list of apps that can deal with the intent.**
The user chooses an app, and the share action provider passes the intent to the app's activity that can handle it.

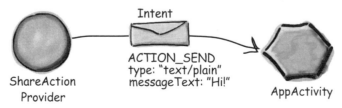

Add a share action provider to menu_main.xml

Basic app bar
Toolbar
Action
Up button
Share action

You add a share action to the app bar by including it in the menu resource file.

To start, add a new `action_share` String to *strings.xml*. We'll use this String to add a title to the share action in case it appears in the overflow:

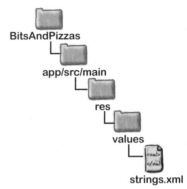

```
<string name="action_share">Share</string>
```

You add the share action to the menu resource file using the `<item>` element as before. This time, however, you need to specify that you're using a share action provider. You do this by adding an attribute of `app:actionProviderClass` and setting it to `android.support.v7.widget.ShareActionProvider`.

Here's the code to add the share action; update your copy of *menu_main.xml* to match ours:

```xml
<?xml version="1.0" encoding="utf-8"?>
<menu xmlns:android="http://schemas.android.com/apk/res/android"
    xmlns:app="http://schemas.android.com/apk/res-auto">

    <item android:id="@+id/action_create_order"
        android:title="@string/create_order_title"
        android:icon="@drawable/ic_add_white_24dp"
        android:orderInCategory="1"
        app:showAsAction="ifRoom" />

    <item android:id="@+id/action_share"
        android:title="@string/action_share"
        android:orderInCategory="2"
        app:showAsAction="ifRoom"
        app:actionProviderClass="android.support.v7.widget.ShareActionProvider" />

</menu>
```

Display the share action provider in the app bar if there's room.

This is the share action provider class. It comes from the AppCompat Support Library.

As we mentioned earlier, when you add a share action to your menu resource file, there's no need to include an icon. The share action provider already defines one.

Now that we've added the share action to the app bar, let's specify what content to share.

Specify the content with an intent

To get the share action to share content when it's clicked, you need to tell it what to share in your activity code. You do this by passing the share action provider an intent using its setShareIntent() method. Here's how you'd get the share action to share some default text when it's clicked:

We're using these extra classes, so we need to import them.

```
package com.hfad.bitsandpizzas;

...
import android.support.v7.widget.ShareActionProvider;
import android.support.v4.view.MenuItemCompat;

public class MainActivity extends AppCompatActivity {

    private ShareActionProvider shareActionProvider;

    ...
    @Override
    public boolean onCreateOptionsMenu(Menu menu) {
        getMenuInflater().inflate(R.menu.menu_main, menu);
        MenuItem menuItem = menu.findItem(R.id.action_share);
        shareActionProvider =
                    (ShareActionProvider) MenuItemCompat.getActionProvider(menuItem);
        setShareActionIntent("Want to join me for pizza?");
        return super.onCreateOptionsMenu(menu);
    }

    private void setShareActionIntent(String text) {
        Intent intent = new Intent(Intent.ACTION_SEND);
        intent.setType("text/plain");
        intent.putExtra(Intent.EXTRA_TEXT, text);
        shareActionProvider.setShareIntent(intent);
    }
}
```

Add a ShareActionProvider private variable.

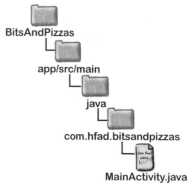

Get a reference to the share action provider and assign it to the private variable. Then call the setShareActionIntent() method.

We created the setShareActionIntent() method. It creates an intent, and passes it to the share action provider using its setShareIntent() method.

You need to call the share action provider's setShareIntent() method whenever the content you wish to share has changed. As an example, if you're flicking through images in a photo app, you need to make sure you share the current photo.

We'll show you our full activity code on the next page, and then we'll see what happens when the app runs.

The full MainActivity.java code

Basic app bar
Toolbar
Action
Up button
Share action

Here's the full activity code for *MainActivity.java*. Update your code to reflect ours.

```java
package com.hfad.bitsandpizzas;

import android.support.v7.app.AppCompatActivity;
import android.os.Bundle;
import android.support.v7.widget.Toolbar;
import android.view.Menu;
import android.view.MenuItem;
import android.content.Intent;
import android.support.v7.widget.ShareActionProvider;
import android.support.v4.view.MenuItemCompat;
```

We're using these extra classes, so we need to import them.

```java
public class MainActivity extends AppCompatActivity {

    private ShareActionProvider shareActionProvider;

    @Override
    protected void onCreate(Bundle savedInstanceState) {
        super.onCreate(savedInstanceState);
        setContentView(R.layout.activity_main);
        Toolbar toolbar = (Toolbar) findViewById(R.id.toolbar);
        setSupportActionBar(toolbar);
    }
```

BitsAndPizzas
app/src/main
java
com.hfad.bitsandpizzas
MainActivity.java

```java
    @Override
    public boolean onCreateOptionsMenu(Menu menu) {
        getMenuInflater().inflate(R.menu.menu_main, menu);
        MenuItem menuItem = menu.findItem(R.id.action_share);
        shareActionProvider =
                (ShareActionProvider) MenuItemCompat.getActionProvider(menuItem);
        setShareActionIntent("Want to join me for pizza?");
        return super.onCreateOptionsMenu(menu);
    }
}
```

← This is the default text that the share action should share.

The code continues on the next page. ⟶

The MainActivity.java code (continued)

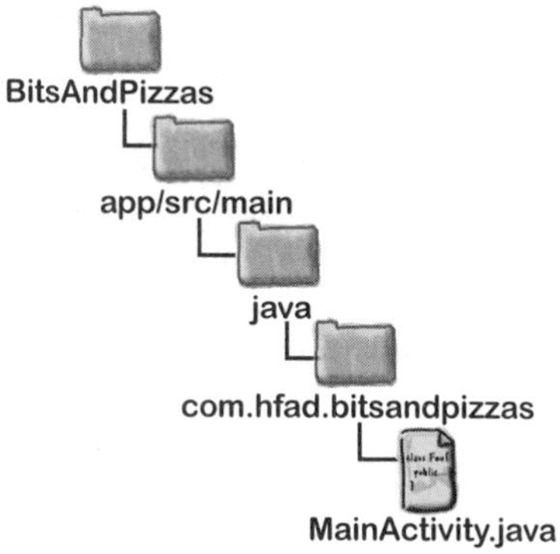

```java
private void setShareActionIntent(String text) {
    Intent intent = new Intent(Intent.ACTION_SEND);
    intent.setType("text/plain");
    intent.putExtra(Intent.EXTRA_TEXT, text);
    shareActionProvider.setShareIntent(intent);
}

@Override
public boolean onOptionsItemSelected(MenuItem item) {
    switch (item.getItemId()) {
        case R.id.action_create_order:
            //Code to run when the Create Order item is clicked
            Intent intent = new Intent(this, OrderActivity.class);
            startActivity(intent);
            return true;
        default:
            return super.onOptionsItemSelected(item);
    }
}
```

↑
This sets the default text
in the share action provider.

BitsAndPizzas
app/src/main
java
com.hfad.bitsandpizzas
MainActivity.java

On the next page we'll check what happens when the
code runs by taking the app for a test drive.

Test drive the app

☐ Basic app bar
☐ Toolbar
☐ Action
☐ Up button
→ ☑ **Share action**

When you run the app, the share action is displayed in the app bar:

The share action provider also added the Messenger icon to our app bar. We usually share this app's content with the Messenger app, so the share action gave us a shortcut.

This is the share action icon.

When you click on the share action, it gives you a list of apps to choose from that can accept the intent you want to share:

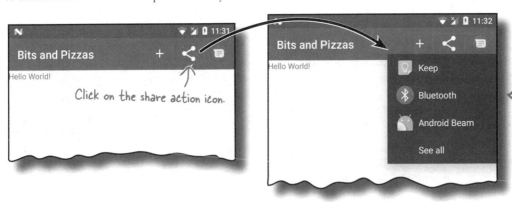

Click on the share action icon.

The intent we passed to the share action provider says we want to share text using ACTION_SEND. It displays a list of apps that can do this.

When you choose an app to share content with, the app gets launched and the default text is shared with it:

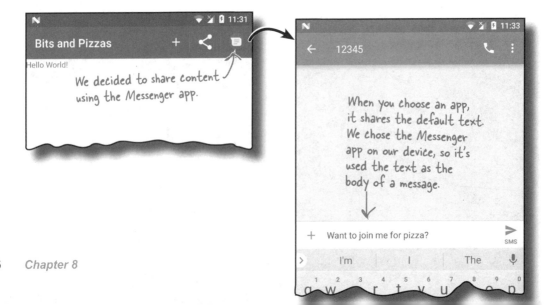

We decided to share content using the Messenger app.

When you choose an app, it shares the default text. We chose the Messenger app on our device, so it's used the text as the body of a message.

Want to join me for pizza?

Your Android Toolbox

You've got Chapter 8 under your belt and now you've added Android Support Libraries and app bars to your toolbox.

You can download the full code for the chapter from https://tinyurl.com/HeadFirstAndroid.

BULLET POINTS

- You add a basic app bar by applying a theme that contains one.

- The Android Support Libraries provide backward compatibility with older versions of Android.

- The `AppCompatActivity` class is a type of activity that resides in the v7 AppCompat Support Library. In general, your activity needs to extend the `AppCompatActivity` class whenever you want an app bar that provides backward compatibility with older versions of Android.

- The `android:theme` attribute in *AndroidManifest.xml* specifies which theme to apply.

- You define styles in a style resource file using the `<style>` element. The `name` attribute gives the style a name. The `parent` attribute specifies where the style should inherit its properties from.

- The latest app bar features are in the `Toolbar` class in the v7 AppCompat Support Library. You can use a toolbar as your app bar.

- Add actions to your app bar by adding them to a menu resource file.

- Add the items in the menu resource file to the app bar by implementing the activity's `onCreateOptionsMenu()` method.

- You determine what items should do when clicked by implementing the activity's `onOptionsItemSelected()` method.

- Add an Up button to your app bar to navigate up the app's hierarchy. Specify the hierarchy in *AndroidManifest.xml*. Use the `ActionBar setDisplayHomeAsUpEnabled()` method to enable the Up button.

- You can share content by adding the share action provider to your app bar. Add it by including it in your menu resource file. Call its `setShareIntent()` method to pass it an intent describing the content you wish to share.

9 fragments

Make It Modular

Doing the same job in different places... I guess that makes me a fragment.

You've seen how to create apps that work in the same way no matter what device they're running on.

But what if you want your app to look and behave differently depending on whether it's running on a *phone* or a *tablet*? In this case you need **fragments**, modular code components that can be **reused by different activities**. We'll show you how to create **basic fragments** and **list fragments**, how to **add them to your activities**, and how to get your fragments and activities to **communicate** with one another.

Your app needs to look great on ALL devices

One of the great things about Android development is that you can put the exact same app on devices with completely different screen sizes and processors, and have them run in exactly the same way. But that doesn't mean that they always have to *look* exactly the same.

On a phone:

Take a look at this image of an app on a phone. It displays a list of workouts, and when you click on one, you are shown the details of that workout.

Click on an item in a list, and it launches a second activity.

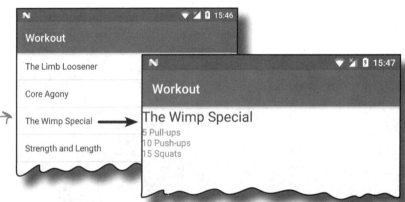

On a tablet:

On a larger device, like a tablet, you have a lot more screen space available, so it would be good if all the information appeared on the same screen. On the tablet, the list of workouts only goes partway across the screen, and when you click on an item, the details appear on the right.

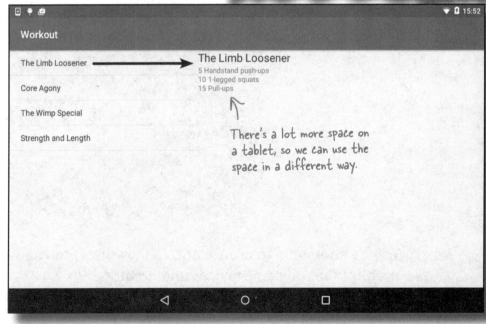

There's a lot more space on a tablet, so we can use the space in a different way.

To make the phone and tablet user interfaces look different from each other, you can use separate layouts for large devices and small devices.

Your app may need to behave differently too

It's not enough to simply have different layouts for different devices. You also need *different Java code* to run alongside the layouts so that the app can behave differently depending on the device. In our Workout app, for instance, we need to provide **one activity for tablets**, and **two activities for phones**.

On a phone:

Here we have two activities: one for the list and one for the details.

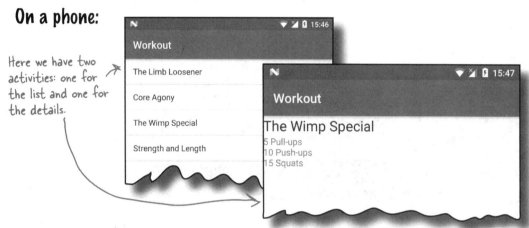

On a tablet:

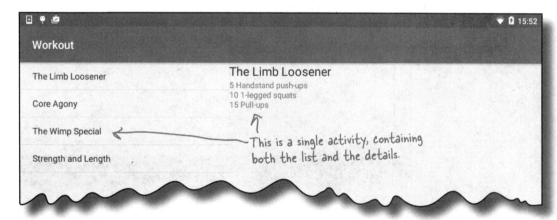

This is a single activity, containing both the list and the details.

But that means you might duplicate code

The second activity that runs only on phones will need to insert the details of a workout into the layout. But that code will also need to be available in the main activity for when the app is running on a tablet. *The same code needs to be run by multiple activities.*

Rather than duplicate the code in the two activities, we can use **fragments**. So what's a fragment?

Fragments allow you to reuse code

Fragments are like reusable components or subactivities. A fragment is used to control part of a screen, and can be reused between screens. This means we can create a fragment for the list of workouts, and a fragment to display the details of a single workout. These fragments can then be shared between layouts.

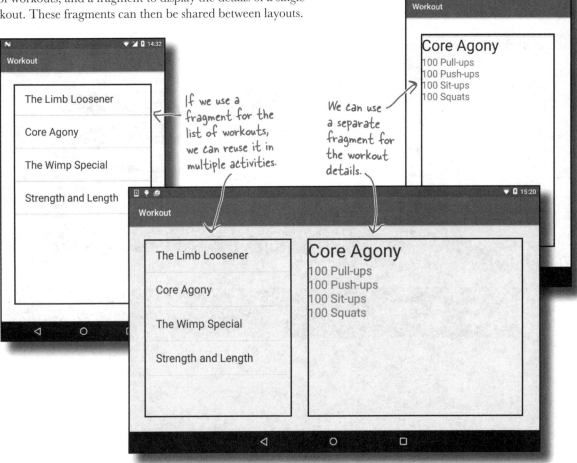

If we use a fragment for the list of workouts, we can reuse it in multiple activities.

We can use a separate fragment for the workout details.

A fragment has a layout

Just like an activity, a fragment has an associated layout. If you design it carefully, the fragment's Java code can be used to control everything within the interface. If the fragment code contains all that you need to control its layout, it greatly increases the chances that you'll be able to reuse it elsewhere in the app.

We're going to show you how to create and use fragments by building the Workout app.

The phone version of the app

We're going to build the phone version of the app in this chapter, and reuse the fragments we create to build the tablet version of the app in Chapter 10. Here's how the phone version of the app will work:

Don't worry if the app structure looks complex.

We'll work through it step by step over the course of this chapter.

① **When the app gets launched, it starts MainActivity.**
MainActivity uses *activity_main.xml* for its layout, and contains a fragment called WorkoutListFragment.

② **WorkoutListFragment displays a list of workouts.**

③ **When the user clicks on one of the workouts, DetailActivity starts.**
DetailActivity uses *activity_detail.xml* for its layout, and contains a fragment called WorkoutDetailFragment.

④ **WorkoutDetailFragment uses fragment_workout_detail.xml for its layout.**
It displays the details of the workout the user has selected.

⑤ **WorkoutListFragment and WorkoutDetailFragment get their workout data from *Workout.java*.**
Workout.java contains an array of Workouts.

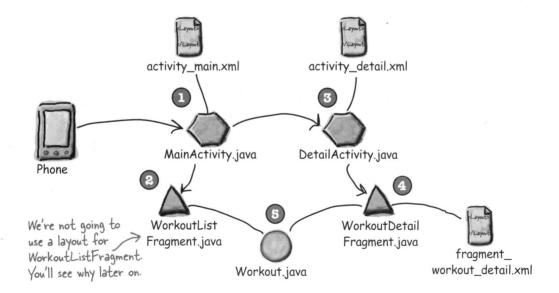

activity_main.xml

activity_detail.xml

① MainActivity.java

③ DetailActivity.java

Phone

We're not going to use a layout for WorkoutListFragment. You'll see why later on.

② WorkoutList Fragment.java

⑤ Workout.java

④ WorkoutDetail Fragment.java

fragment_ workout_detail.xml

We'll go through the steps for creating this app on the next page.

Here's what we're going to do

There are three main steps we'll go through to build the app:

1 **Create WorkoutDetailFragment.**
WorkoutDetailFragment displays the details of a specific workout. We'll start by creating two activities, MainActivity and DetailActivity, and then we'll add WorkoutDetailFragment to DetailActivity. We'll also get MainActivity to launch DetailActivity when a button is pressed. We'll also add a plain old Java class, *Workout.java*, that will provide the data for WorkoutDetailFragment.

2 **Create WorkoutListFragment.**
WorkoutListFragment displays a list of workouts. We'll add this fragment to MainActivity.

3 **Coordinate the fragments to display the correct workout.**
When the user clicks on an item in WorkoutListFragment, we'll start DetailActivity and get WorkoutDetailFragment to display details of the workout the user selected.

Let's get started.

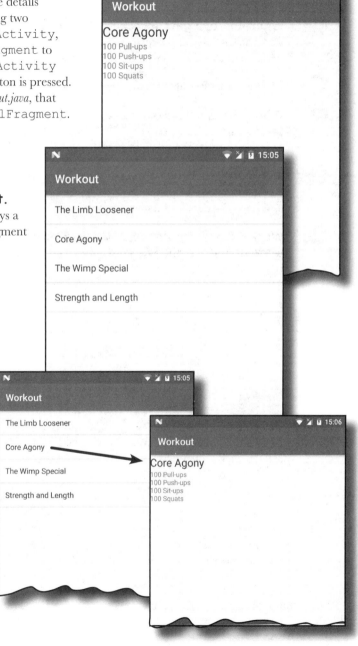

Create the project and activities

We're going to start by creating a project that contains two activities, `MainActivity` and `DetailActivity`. `MainActivity` will be used for the fragment that displays a list of workouts, and `DetailActivity` will be used for the fragment that displays details of one particular workout.

To do this, first create a new Android project with an empty activity for an application named "Workout" with a company domain of "hfad.com", making the package name `com.hfad.workout`. The minimum SDK should be API 19 so that it works on most devices. Name the activity "MainActivity" and name the layout "activity_main". **Make sure you check the Backwards Compatibility (AppCompat) checkbox.**

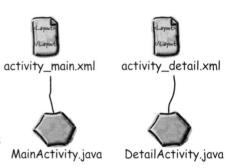

activity_main.xml   activity_detail.xml

MainActivity.java   DetailActivity.java

Next, create a second empty activity by highlighting the *com.hfad.workout* package in the *app/src/main/java* folder, and going to File→New...→Activity→ Empty Activity. Name the activity "DetailActivity", name the layout "activity_ detail", make sure the package name is `com.hfad.workout`, and **check the Backwards Compatibility (AppCompat) checkbox.**

If prompted for the activity's source language, select the option for Java.

Add the AppCompat Support Library

We're going to be using activities and fragments from the v7 AppCompat Library, which means you need to make sure the library has been added to your project as a dependency. To do this, go to the File menu and choose Project Structure. Then click on the app module and choose Dependencies.

This is the v7 AppCompat Support Library.

If Android Studio has already added the v7 AppCompat Support Library to your project, you'll see it listed in the list of dependencies. If it's not there, you'll need to add it yourself. To do this, click on the "+" button at the bottom or right side of the screen. When prompted, choose the Library Dependency option, then select the appcompat-v7 library from the list of options. Finally, use the OK buttons to save your changes.

Once you've made sure the v7 AppCompat Support Library has been added, you can close the Project Structure window. On the next page we'll update `MainActivity`.

WorkoutDetailFragment
WorkoutListFragment
Coordinate fragments

Add a button to MainActivity's layout

We're going to add a button to `MainActivity` that will start `DetailActivity`. This is because we're going to work on the fragment for `DetailActivity` first, and adding a button to `MainActivity` will give us an easy way of navigating from `MainActivity` to `DetailActivity`.

We'll start by adding the button to the layout. Open file *activity_main. xml*, then update your code so that it matches ours below:

```xml
<?xml version="1.0" encoding="utf-8"?>
<LinearLayout xmlns:android="http://schemas.android.com/apk/res/android"
    xmlns:tools="http://schemas.android.com/tools"
    android:layout_width="match_parent"
    android:layout_height="match_parent"
    android:padding="16dp"
    android:orientation="vertical"
    tools:context="com.hfad.workout.MainActivity">

    <Button
        android:layout_width="wrap_content"
        android:layout_height="wrap_content"
        android:onClick="onShowDetails"
        android:text="@string/details_button" />

</LinearLayout>
```

This is the button we're adding.

The button calls the onShowDetails() method in MainActivity when it's clicked. We need to write this method.

Workout
└ app/src/main
  └ res
    └ layout
      └ activity_main.xml

The button uses a String resource for its text, so we need to add it to the String resource file. Open file *strings.xml*, then add the following String resource:

```xml
<resources>
    ...
    <string name="details_button">Show details</string>
</resources>
```

This text will be displayed on the button.

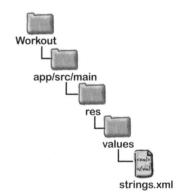

Workout
└ app/src/main
  └ res
    └ values
      └ strings.xml

When the button is clicked, we've specified that `MainActivity`'s `onShowDetails()` method should be called. We'll write the code for this method next.

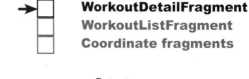

Make the button respond to clicks

We need to get `MainActivity`'s button to start
`DetailActivity` when it's clicked. To do this, we'll add
a method called `onShowDetails()` to `MainActivity`.
The method will start `DetailActivity` using an intent,
just as we've done in previous chapters.

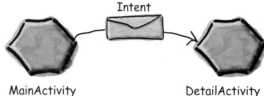

MainActivity   Intent   DetailActivity

Here's the full code for *MainActivity.java*. Update your code so
that it matches ours.

```java
package com.hfad.workout;

import android.support.v7.app.AppCompatActivity;
import android.os.Bundle;
import android.view.View;
import android.content.Intent;
```

The activity extends
AppCompatActivity.

```java
public class MainActivity extends AppCompatActivity {

    @Override
    protected void onCreate(Bundle savedInstanceState) {
        super.onCreate(savedInstanceState);
        setContentView(R.layout.activity_main);
    }

    public void onShowDetails(View view) {
        Intent intent = new Intent(this, DetailActivity.class);
        startActivity(intent);
    }
}
```

This method is called when the button is
clicked. It starts DetailActivity.

Workout
└ app/src/main
   └ java
      └ com.hfad.workout
         └ MainActivity.java

That's everything we need to get `MainActivity` to start
`DetailActivity`. On the next page we'll add a new
fragment to our project called `WorkoutDetailFragment`
that we'll then add to `DetailActivity`.

How to add a fragment to your project

We're going to add a new fragment called `WorkoutDetailFragment` to the project to display details of a single workout. You add a new fragment in a similar way to how you add a new activity: by switching to the Project view of Android Studio's explorer, highlighting the *com.hfad. workout* package in the *app/src/main/java* folder, going to the File menu, and choosing New...→Fragment→Fragment (Blank).

You will be asked to choose options for your new fragment. Name the fragment "WorkoutDetailFragment", check the option to create layout XML for it, and give the fragment layout a name of "fragment_workout_ detail". Uncheck the options to include fragment factory methods and interface callbacks; these options generate extra code that you don't need to use. When you're done, click on the Finish button.

We suggest looking at the extra code Android generates for you after you've finished this book. You might find some of it useful depending on what you want to do.

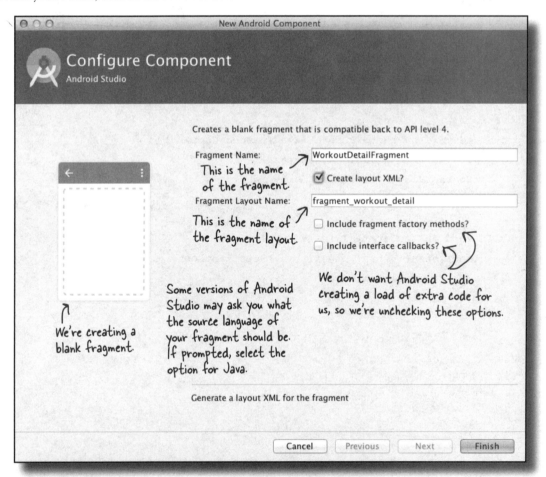

This is the name of the fragment.

This is the name of the fragment layout.

We're creating a blank fragment.

Some versions of Android Studio may ask you what the source language of your fragment should be. If prompted, select the option for Java.

We don't want Android Studio creating a load of extra code for us, so we're unchecking these options.

When you click on the Finish button, Android Studio creates your new fragment and adds it to the project.

What fragment code looks like

When you create a fragment, Android Studio creates two files for you: Java code for the fragment itself, and XML code for the fragment's layout. The Java code describes the fragment's behavior, and the layout describes the fragment's appearance.

We'll look at the Java code first. Go to the *com.hfad.workout* package in the *app/src/main/java* folder and open the file *WorkoutDetailFragment.java* that Android Studio just created for us. Then replace the code that Android Studio generated with the code below:

```java
package com.hfad.workout;

import android.support.v4.app.Fragment;
import android.os.Bundle;
import android.view.LayoutInflater;
import android.view.View;
import android.view.ViewGroup;

public class WorkoutDetailFragment extends Fragment {

    @Override
    public View onCreateView(LayoutInflater inflater, ViewGroup container,
                             Bundle savedInstanceState) {
        return inflater.inflate(R.layout.fragment_workout_detail, container, false);
    }
}
```

We're using the Fragment class from the Android Support Library.

WorkoutDetailFragment extends the Fragment class.

This is the onCreateView() method. It's called when Android needs the fragment's layout.

This tells Android which layout the fragment uses (in this case, it's fragment_workout_detail).

Workout
└ app/src/main
  └ java
    └ com.hfad.workout
      └ WorkoutDetail
        Fragment.java

The above code creates a basic fragment. As you can see, the code for a fragment looks very similar to activity code.

To create a fragment, you first need to extend the `Fragment` class or one of its subclasses. We're using fragments from the Support Library, so our fragment needs to extend the `android.support.v4.app.Fragment` class. This is because the Support Library fragments are backward compatible with earlier versions of Android, and contain the latest fragment features.

The fragment implements the `onCreateView()` method, which gets called each time Android needs the fragment's layout, and it's where you say which layout the fragment uses. The `onCreateView()` method is optional, but as you need to implement it whenever you're creating a fragment with a layout, you'll need to implement it nearly every time you create a fragment. We'll look at this method in more detail on the next page.

The fragment's onCreateView() method

The onCreateView() method returns a View object that represents the fragment's user interface. It gets called when Android is ready to instantiate the user interface, and it takes three parameters:

> The onCreateView() method gets called when Android needs the fragment's layout.

```
public View onCreateView(LayoutInflater inflater,
                         ViewGroup container,
                         Bundle savedInstanceState) {

}
```

The first parameter is a LayoutInflator that you can use to inflate the fragment's layout. Inflating the layout turns your XML views into Java objects.

The second parameter is a ViewGroup. This is the ViewGroup in the activity's layout that will contain the fragment.

The final parameter is a Bundle. This is used if you've previously saved the fragment's state, and want to reinstate it.

You specify the fragment's layout using the LayoutInflator's inflate() method:

```
public View onCreateView(LayoutInflater inflater,
                         ViewGroup container,
                         Bundle savedInstanceState) {
    return inflater.inflate(R.layout.fragment_workout_detail,
                 container,
                 false);
}
```

> This inflates the fragment's layout from XML to Java objects.

This is the fragment equivalent of calling an activity's setContentView() method. You use it to say what layout the fragment should use, in this case R.layout.fragment_workout_detail.

The inflate() method's container argument specifies the ViewGroup in the activity that the fragment's layout needs to be inserted into. It gets passed to the fragment as the second parameter in the fragment's onCreateView() method.

Now that you've seen the fragment's code, let's have a look at its layout.

Watch it!

All fragments must have a public no-argument constructor.

Android uses it to reinstantiate the fragment when needed, and if it's not there, you'll get a runtime exception.

*In practice, you only need to add a public no-argument constructor to your fragment code if you include **another** constructor with one or more arguments. This is because if a Java class contains no constructors, the Java compiler automatically adds a public no-argument constructor for you.*

Fragment layout code looks just like activity layout code

As we said earlier, fragments use layout files to describe their appearance.
Fragment layout code looks just like activity layout code, so when you
write your own fragment layout code, you can use any of the views and
layouts you've already been using to write activity layout code.

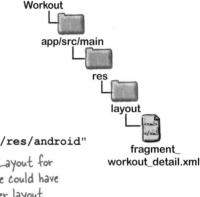

We're going to update our layout code so that our fragment contains two
text views, one for the workout title and one for the workout description.

Open the file *fragment_workout_detail.xml* in the *app/src/res/layout* folder,
and replace its contents with the code below:

```xml
<LinearLayout xmlns:android="http://schemas.android.com/apk/res/android"
    android:layout_height="match_parent"
    android:layout_width="match_parent"
    android:orientation="vertical">
```

We're using a LinearLayout for
our fragment, but we could have
used any of the other layout
types we've looked at instead.

We'll display
the workout
title and
description in
two separate
TextViews.

```xml
    <TextView
        android:layout_width="wrap_content"
        android:layout_height="wrap_content"
        android:textAppearance="?android:attr/textAppearanceLarge"
        android:text="@string/workout_title"
        android:id="@+id/textTitle" />
```

This makes the text large.

Static String resources.

```xml
    <TextView
        android:layout_width="wrap_content"
        android:layout_height="wrap_content"
        android:text="@string/workout_description"
        android:id="@+id/textDescription" />

</LinearLayout>
```

For now we're using static String resources for the title and description
of the workout so that we can see our fragment working. Open *strings.xml*,
and add the following String resources:

```xml
<resources>
    ...
    <string name="workout_title">Title</string>
    <string name="workout_description">Description</string>
</resources>
```

We'll use these to display
default text in our fragment.

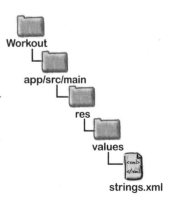

That's everything we need for our fragment. On the next page we'll look
at how you add the fragment to an activity.

WorkoutDetailFragment
WorkoutListFragment
Coordinate fragments

Add a fragment to an activity's layout

We're going to add our `WorkoutDetailFragment` to `DetailActivity` so that the fragment gets displayed in the activity's layout. To do this, we're going to add a `<fragment>` element to `DetailActivity`'s layout.

The `<fragment>` element is a view that specifies the name of the fragment you want to display. It looks like this:

```
<fragment
    android:name="com.hfad.workout.WorkoutDetailFragment"
    android:layout_width="match_parent"
    android:layout_height="match_parent" />
```

← This is the full name of the fragment class.

You specify the fragment using the `android:name` attribute and giving it a value of the fully qualified name of the fragment. In our case, we want to display a fragment called `WorkoutDetailFragment` that's in the `com.hfad.workout` package, so we use:

```
android:name="com.hfad.workout.WorkoutDetailFragment"
```

When Android creates the activity's layout, it replaces the `<fragment>` element with the `View` object returned by the fragment's `onCreateView()` method. This view is the fragment's user interface, so the `<fragment>` element is really a placeholder for where the fragment's layout should be inserted.

You add the `<fragment>` element to your layout in the same way that you add any other element. As an example, here's how you'd add the fragment to a linear layout:

```
<?xml version="1.0" encoding="utf-8"?>
<LinearLayout xmlns:android="http://schemas.android.com/apk/res/android"
    android:orientation="vertical"
    android:layout_width="match_parent"
    android:layout_height="match_parent">

    <fragment
        android:name="com.hfad.workout.WorkoutDetailFragment"
        android:layout_width="match_parent"
        android:layout_height="match_parent" />
</LinearLayout>
```

This adds the fragment
← to the activity's layout.

Workout
└ app/src/main
  └ res
    └ layout
      └ activity_detail.xml

If your layout only contains a single fragment with no other views, however, you can simplify your layout code.

Simplify the layout

If the layout code for your activity comprises a single fragment contained within a layout element with no other views, you can simplify your layout code by removing the root layout element.

Each layout file you create must have a single root element that's either a view or view group. This means that if your layout contains multiple items, these items must be contained within a view group such as a linear layout.

If your layout contains a single fragment, the <fragment> element can be the layout file's root. This is because the <fragment> element is a type of view, and Android replaces it with the layout of the fragment at runtime.

In our code example on the previous page, we showed you a fragment contained within a linear layout. As there are no other views in the layout, we can remove the linear layout so that our code looks like this:

A layout file requires a single view or view group as its root element. If your activity only contains a fragment, the fragment itself can be the root element.

```xml
<?xml version="1.0" encoding="utf-8"?>
<fragment
    xmlns:android="http://schemas.android.com/apk/res/android"
    android:name="com.hfad.workout.WorkoutDetailFragment"
    android:layout_width="match_parent"
    android:layout_height="match_parent" />
```

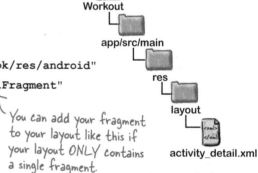

You can add your fragment to your layout like this if your layout ONLY contains a single fragment.

This code does exactly the same thing as the code on the previous page, but it's much shorter.

That's the only code we need for DetailActivity's layout, so replace the code you have in your version of *activity_detail.xml*, with the code above and save your changes.

On the next page we'll look at the code for the activity itself.

WorkoutDetailFragment
WorkoutListFragment
Coordinate fragments

Support Library fragments need activities that extend FragmentActivity

When you add a fragment to an activity, you usually need to write code that controls any interactions between the fragment and the activity. You'll see examples of this later in the chapter.

Currently, `WorkoutDetailFragment` only contains static data. `DetailActivity` only has to display the fragment, and doesn't need to interact with it, so this means that we don't need to write any extra activity code to control the interaction.

There's one important point to be aware of, however. When you're using fragments from the Support Library, as we are here, you must make sure that **any activity you want to use them with extends the FragmentActivity class, or one of its subclasses**. The `FragmentActivity` class is designed to work with Support Library fragments, and if your activity doesn't extend this class, your code will break.

In practice, this isn't a problem. This is because the `AppCompatActivity` class is a subclass of `FragmentActivity`, so as long as your activity extends the `AppCompatActivity` class, your Support Library fragments will work.

Here's the code for *DetailActivity.java*. Update your code so that it matches ours below:

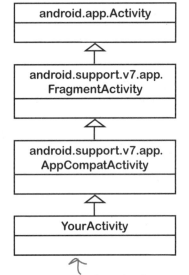

As long as your activity extends FragmentActivity, or one of its subclasses such as AppCompatActivity, you can use fragments from the Support Library.

```
package com.hfad.workout;

import android.support.v7.app.AppCompatActivity;
import android.os.Bundle;

public class DetailActivity extends AppCompatActivity {

    @Override
    protected void onCreate(Bundle savedInstanceState) {
        super.onCreate(savedInstanceState);
        setContentView(R.layout.activity_detail);
    }
}
```

DetailActivity extends AppCompatActivity.

Workout
└ app/src/main
  └ java
    └ com.hfad.workout
      └ DetailActivity.java

That's everything we need to display the `WorkoutDetailFragment` in our activity. Let's see what happens when we run the app.

What the code does

Before we take the app for a test drive, let's go through what
happens when the code runs.

1 **When the app is launched, activity MainActivity gets created.**
The user clicks on the button in MainActivity to start DetailActivity.

Device   MainActivity   DetailActivity

2 **DetailActivity's onCreate() method runs.**
The onCreate() method specifies that *activity_detail.xml* should be used for
DetailActivity's layout.

onCreate()

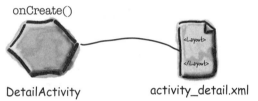

DetailActivity   activity_detail.xml

3 **activity_detail.xml sees that it includes a <fragment> element that refers
to WorkoutDetailFragment.**

activity_detail.xml

> Hmmm, a
> <fragment> element.
> I need to know what
> goes here.

4 **WorkoutDetailFragment's onCreateView() method is called.**
The onCreateView() method specifies that *fragment_workout_detail.xml* should be used for
WorkoutDetailFragment's layout. It inflates the layout to a View object.

onCreateView()

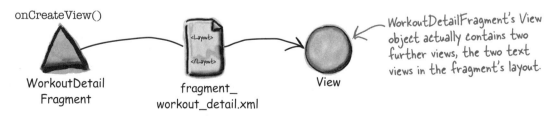

WorkoutDetail
Fragment

fragment_
workout_detail.xml

View

*WorkoutDetailFragment's View
object actually contains two
further views, the two text
views in the fragment's layout.*

The story continues

WorkoutDetailFragment
WorkoutListFragment
Coordinate fragments

⑤ activity_detail.xml's Views are inflated to View Java objects.
DetailActivity layout uses WorkoutDetailFragment's View object in place of the
<fragment> element in its layout's XML.

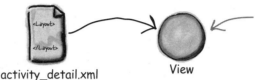

activity_detail.xml   View

*activity_detail.xml only contains the
<fragment> element. This means that
when it's inflated, it only contains
WorkoutDetailFragment's View object.*

⑥ Finally, DetailActivity is displayed on the device.
Its layout contains the fragment WorkoutDetailFragment.

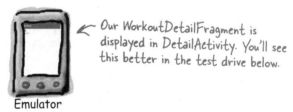

Emulator

*← Our WorkoutDetailFragment is
displayed in DetailActivity. You'll see
this better in the test drive below.*

Test drive the app

When we run our app, MainActivity gets launched.

When we click on MainActivity's button, it starts
DetailActivity. DetailActivity contains
WorkoutDetailFragment, and we see this on the device.

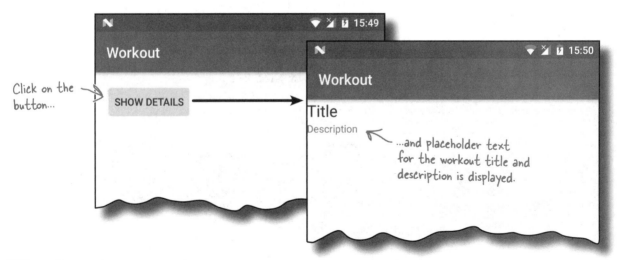

*Click on the
button...*

SHOW DETAILS

Workout

Title
Description

*...and placeholder text
for the workout title and
description is displayed.*

BE the Layout

Your job is to play like you're the layout and say whether each of these layouts is valid or invalid and why. Assume that any fragments or String resources referred to in the layout already exist.

A
```xml
<?xml version="1.0" encoding="utf-8"?>
<fragment
    xmlns:android="http://schemas.android.com/apk/res/android"
    android:name="com.hfad.workout.WorkoutDetailFragment"
    android:layout_width="match_parent"
    android:layout_height="match_parent" />
```

B
```xml
<?xml version="1.0" encoding="utf-8"?>
<fragment
    xmlns:android="http://schemas.android.com/apk/res/android"
    android:name="com.hfad.workout.WorkoutDetailFragment"
    android:layout_width="match_parent"
    android:layout_height="match_parent" />
<Button
    android:layout_width="wrap_content"
    android:layout_height="wrap_content"
    android:text="@string/details_button" />
```

C
```xml
<?xml version="1.0" encoding="utf-8"?>
<Button
    xmlns:android="http://schemas.android.com/apk/res/android"
    android:layout_width="wrap_content"
    android:layout_height="wrap_content"
    android:text="@string/details_button" />
```

BE the Layout Solution
Your job is to play like you're the layout and say whether each of these layouts is valid or invalid and why. Assume that any fragments or String resources referred to in the layout already exist.

A

This layout is valid, as it consists of a single fragment.

```xml
<?xml version="1.0" encoding="utf-8"?>
<fragment
    xmlns:android="http://schemas.android.com/apk/res/android"
    android:name="com.hfad.workout.WorkoutDetailFragment"
    android:layout_width="match_parent"
    android:layout_height="match_parent" />
```

B

```xml
<?xml version="1.0" encoding="utf-8"?>
<fragment
    xmlns:android="http://schemas.android.com/apk/res/android"
    android:name="com.hfad.workout.WorkoutDetailFragment"
    android:layout_width="match_parent"
    android:layout_height="match_parent" />
<Button
    android:layout_width="wrap_content"
    android:layout_height="wrap_content"
    android:text="@string/details_button" />
```

This layout is invalid. A layout must have a single View or ViewGroup as its root element. To make this layout valid, you would need to put the fragment and Button in a ViewGroup.

C

```xml
<?xml version="1.0" encoding="utf-8"?>
<Button
    xmlns:android="http://schemas.android.com/apk/res/android"
    android:layout_width="wrap_content"
    android:layout_height="wrap_content"
    android:text="@string/details_button" />
```

This layout is valid as it has a single View, in this case a Button, as its root element.

Get the fragment and activity to interact

So far we've looked at how you add a basic fragment to an activity. The next thing we'll look at is how you get the fragment and activity to interact.

To do this, we'll start by changing `WorkoutDetailFragment` so that it displays details of a workout instead of the placeholder text we have currently.

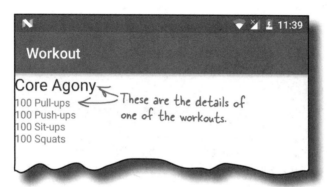

Workout

Core Agony ← These are the details of
100 Pull-ups ← one of the workouts.
100 Push-ups
100 Sit-ups
100 Squats

The first thing we'll do is update the fragment's layout to remove the static text that's currently displayed. Open file *fragment_workout_detail.xml*, then update the code to match our changes below:

```xml
<LinearLayout xmlns:android="http://schemas.android.com/apk/res/android"
    ...
    <TextView
        android:layout_width="wrap_content"
        android:layout_height="wrap_content"
        android:textAppearance="?android:attr/textAppearanceLarge"
        android:text="@string/workout_title"
        android:id="@+id/textTitle" />

    <TextView
        android:layout_width="wrap_content"
        android:layout_height="wrap_content"
        android:text="@string/workout_description"
        android:id="@+id/textDescription" />
</LinearLayout>
```

Delete both these lines.

Workout
└ app/src/main
  └ res
    └ layout
      └ fragment_workout_detail.xml

On the next page we'll add a new class to our project to hold the workout data.

The Workout class

We're going to hold our workout data in a file called *Workout.java*, which is a pure Java class file that the app will get workout data from. The class defines an array of four workouts, where each workout is composed of a name and description. Select the *com.hfad.workout* package in the *app/src/main/java* folder in your project, then go to File→New...→Java Class. When prompted, name the class "Workout", and make sure the package name is com.hfad.workout. Then replace the code in *Workout.java* with the following, and save your changes.

```java
package com.hfad.workout;

public class Workout {
    private String name;
    private String description;

    public static final Workout[] workouts = {
            new Workout("The Limb Loosener",
                    "5 Handstand push-ups\n10 1-legged squats\n15 Pull-ups"),
            new Workout("Core Agony",
                    "100 Pull-ups\n100 Push-ups\n100 Sit-ups\n100 Squats"),
            new Workout("The Wimp Special",
                    "5 Pull-ups\n10 Push-ups\n15 Squats"),
            new Workout("Strength and Length",
                    "500 meter run\n21 x 1.5 pood kettleball swing\n21 x pull-ups")
    };

    //Each Workout has a name and description
    private Workout(String name, String description) {
        this.name = name;
        this.description = description;
    }

    public String getDescription() {
        return description;
    }

    public String getName() {
        return name;
    }

    public String toString() {
        return this.name;
    }
}
```

Each Workout has a name and description.

workouts is an array of four Workouts.

These are getters for the private variables.

The String representation of a Workout is its name.

Workout
└ app/src/main
  └ java
    └ com.hfad.workout
      └ Workout.java

The data will be used by the fragment to display details of a particular workout. We'll look at this next.

Pass the workout ID to the fragment

When you have an activity that uses a fragment, the activity will usually need to talk to the fragment in some way. As an example, if you have a fragment that displays detail records, you need the activity to tell the fragment which record it needs to display details of.

In our case, we need `WorkoutDetailFragment` to display details of a particular workout. To do this, we'll add a simple setter method to the fragment that sets the value of the workout ID. The activity will then be able to use this method to set the workout ID. Later on, we'll use the workout ID to update the fragment's views.

Here's the revised code for `WorkoutDetailFragment` (update your code with our changes):

```
package com.hfad.workout;

import android.support.v4.app.Fragment;
import android.os.Bundle;
import android.view.LayoutInflater;
import android.view.View;
import android.view.ViewGroup;

public class WorkoutDetailFragment extends Fragment {
    private long workoutId;
```
← This is the ID of the workout the user chooses. Later, we'll use it to set the values of the fragment's views with the workout details.

```
    @Override
    public View onCreateView(LayoutInflater inflater, ViewGroup container,
                             Bundle savedInstanceState) {
        return inflater.inflate(R.layout.fragment_workout_detail, container, false);
    }

    public void setWorkout(long id) {
        this.workoutId = id;
    }
}
```
← This is a setter method for the workout ID. The activity will use this method to set the value of the workout ID.

Workout
app/src/main
java
com.hfad.workout
WorkoutDetail
Fragment.java

We need to get the `DetailActivity` to call the fragment's `setWorkout()` method and pass it the ID of a particular workout. In order to do this, the activity must get a reference to the fragment. But how?

WorkoutDetailFragment
WorkoutListFragment
Coordinate fragments

Use the fragment manager to manage fragments

Before an activity can talk to its fragment, the activity first needs to get a reference to the fragment. You get a reference to an activity's fragments using the activity's **fragment manager**. The fragment manager is used to keep track of and deal with any fragments used by the activity.

There are two methods for getting a reference to the fragment manager, getFragmentManager() and getSupportFragmentManager(). The getSupportFragmentManager() method gets a reference to the fragment manager that deals with fragments from the Support Library like ours, and the getFragmentManager() method gets a reference to the fragment manager that deals with fragments that use the native Android fragment class instead. You then use the fragment manager's findFragmentById() method to get a reference to the fragment.

We're using fragments from the Support Library, so we're going to use the getSupportFragmentManager() method like this:

getSupportFragmentManager().findFragmentById(R.id.fragment_id)

This is the ID of the fragment in the activity's layout.

findFragmentById() is a bit like findViewById() except you use it to get a reference to a fragment.

We're going to use DetailActivity's fragment manager to get a reference to its WorkoutDetailFragment. In order to do this, we first need to assign an ID to the fragment.

You assign an ID to an activity's fragment in the activity's layout. Open the file *activity_detail.xml*, then add an ID to the activity's fragment by adding the line of code highlighted below:

```xml
<?xml version="1.0" encoding="utf-8"?>
<fragment xmlns:android="http://schemas.android.com/apk/res/android"
    android:name="com.hfad.workout.WorkoutDetailFragment"
    android:id="@+id/detail_frag"
    android:layout_width="match_parent"
    android:layout_height="match_parent" />
```

Add an ID to the fragment.

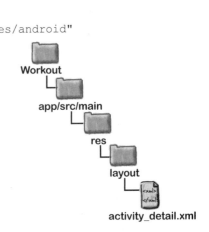

Workout

app/src/main

res

layout

activity_detail.xml

The above code gives the fragment an ID of detail_frag. On the next page we'll use the ID to get a reference to the fragment.

Get the activity to set the workout ID

To get a reference to the fragment, we need to add the
following code:

```
WorkoutDetailFragment frag = (WorkoutDetailFragment)
        getSupportFragmentManager().findFragmentById(R.id.detail_frag);
```

We can then call the fragment's `setWorkout()` method to
tell the fragment which workout we want it to display details for.
For now, we'll hardcode which workout we want it to display so
that we can see it working. Later on, we'll change the code so
that the user can select which workout she wants to see.

Here's our revised code for *DetailActivity.java*. Update your code
to reflect our changes:

```
package com.hfad.workout;

import android.support.v7.app.AppCompatActivity;
import android.os.Bundle;

public class DetailActivity extends AppCompatActivity {

    @Override
    protected void onCreate(Bundle savedInstanceState) {
        super.onCreate(savedInstanceState);
        setContentView(R.layout.activity_detail);
        WorkoutDetailFragment frag = (WorkoutDetailFragment)
                getSupportFragmentManager().findFragmentById(R.id.detail_frag);
        frag.setWorkout(1);
    }
}
```

Workout

app/src/main

java

com.hfad.workout

DetailActivity.java

We're going to get WorkoutDetailFragment to display
details of a workout here to check that it's working.

This gets us a reference to
WorkoutDetailFragment. Its id in
the activity's layout is detail_frag.

As you can see, we've got a reference to the fragment after
calling `setContentView()`. Getting the reference here is
really important, because before this point, the fragment won't
have been created.

The next thing we need to do is get the fragment to update its
views when the fragment is displayed to the user. Before we can
do this, we need to understand the fragment's lifecycle so that
we add our code to the correct method in the fragment.

WorkoutDetailFragment
WorkoutListFragment
Coordinate fragments

Activity states revisited

Just like an activity, a fragment has a number of key lifecycle methods that get called at particular times. It's important to know what these methods do and when they get called so your fragment works in just the way you want.

Fragments are contained within and controlled by activities, so the fragment lifecycle is closely linked to the activity lifecycle. Here's a reminder of the different states an activity goes through, and on the next page we'll show you how these relate to fragments.

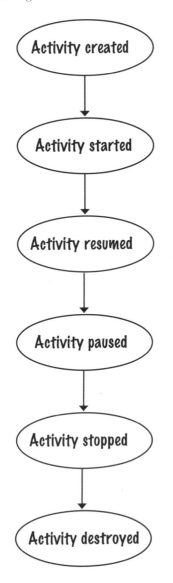

The activity is created when its onCreate() method runs.
At this point, the activity is initialized, but isn't visible.

The activity is started when its onStart() method runs.
The activity is visible, but doesn't have the focus.

The activity is resumed when its onResume() method runs.
The activity is visible, and has the focus.

The activity is paused when its onPause() method runs.
The activity is still visible, but no longer has the focus.

The activity is stopped when its onStop() method runs.
The activity is no longer visible, but still exists.

The activity is destroyed when its onDestroy() method runs.
The activity no longer exists.

The fragment lifecycle

A fragment's lifecycle is very similar to an activity's, but it has a few
extra steps. This is because it needs to interact with the lifecycle of
the activity that contains it. Here are the fragment lifecycle methods,
along with where they fit in with the different activity states.

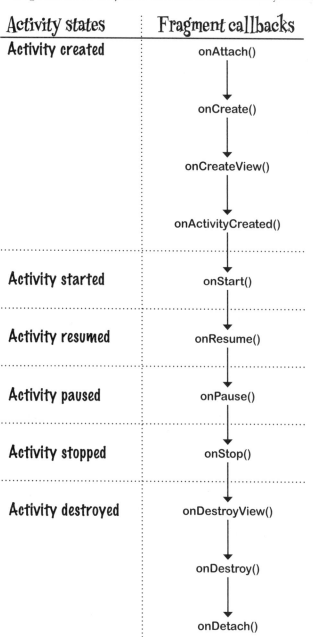

Activity states	Fragment callbacks
Activity created	onAttach()
	onCreate()
	onCreateView()
	onActivityCreated()
Activity started	onStart()
Activity resumed	onResume()
Activity paused	onPause()
Activity stopped	onStop()
Activity destroyed	onDestroyView()
	onDestroy()
	onDetach()

onAttach(Context)
This happens when the fragment is associated with a
context, in this case an activity.

onCreate(Bundle)
This is very similar to the activity's `onCreate()` method.
It can be used to do the initial setup of the fragment.

onCreateView(LayoutInflater, ViewGroup, Bundle)
Fragments use a layout inflater to create their view at this
stage.

onActivityCreated(Bundle)
Called when the `onCreate()` method of the activity
has completed.

onStart()
Called when the fragment is about to become visible.

onResume()
Called when the fragment is visible and actively running.

onPause()
Called when the fragment is no longer interacting with
the user.

onStop()
Called when the fragment is no longer visible to the user.

onDestroyView()
Gives the fragment the chance to clear away any
resources that were associated with its view.

onDestroy()
In this method, the fragment can clear away any other
resources it created.

onDetach()
Called when the fragment finally loses contact with the
activity.

Fragments inherit lifecycle methods

As you saw earlier, our fragment extends the Android `fragment` class. This class gives our fragment access to the fragment lifecycle methods. Here's a diagram showing the class hierarchy.

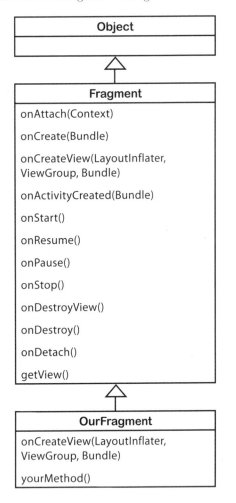

Object class
(java.lang.Object)

Fragment class
(android.support.v4.app.Fragment)
The `Fragment` class implements default versions of the lifecycle methods. It also defines other methods that fragments need, such as `getView()`.

OurFragment class
(com.hfad.foo)
Most of the behavior of our fragment is handled by superclass methods our fragment inherits. All you do is override the methods you need.

Even though fragments have a lot in common with activities, the `Fragment` class doesn't extend the `Activity` class. This means that some methods that are available to activities aren't available to fragments.

Note that the `Fragment` class doesn't implement the `Context` class. Unlike an activity, a fragment isn't a type of context and therefore doesn't have direct access to global information about the application environment. Instead, fragments must access this information using the context of other objects such as its parent activity.

Now that you understand the fragment's lifecycle better, let's get back to getting `WorkoutDetailFragment` to update its views.

Set the view's values in the fragment's onStart() method

We need to get `WorkoutDetailFragment` to update its views with details of the workout. We need to do this when the activity becomes visible, so we'll use the fragment's `onStart()` method. Update your code to match ours:

```java
package com.hfad.workout;

import android.support.v4.app.Fragment;
import android.os.Bundle;
import android.view.LayoutInflater;
import android.view.View;
import android.view.ViewGroup;
import android.widget.TextView;
```
We're using this class in the onStart() method.

```java
public class WorkoutDetailFragment extends Fragment {
    private long workoutId;

    @Override
    public View onCreateView(LayoutInflater inflater, ViewGroup container,
                             Bundle savedInstanceState) {
        return inflater.inflate(R.layout.fragment_workout_detail, container, false);
    }

    @Override
    public void onStart() {
        super.onStart();
        View view = getView();
        if (view != null) {
            TextView title = (TextView) view.findViewById(R.id.textTitle);
            Workout workout = Workout.workouts[(int) workoutId];
            title.setText(workout.getName());
            TextView description = (TextView) view.findViewById(R.id.textDescription);
            description.setText(workout.getDescription());
        }
    }

    public void setWorkout(long id) {
        this.workoutId = id;
    }
}
```

The getView() method gets the fragment's root View. We can then use this to get references to the workout title and description text views.

Workout
app/src/main
java
com.hfad.workout
WorkoutDetail Fragment.java

As we said on the previous page, fragments are distinct from activities, and therefore don't have all the methods that an activity does. Fragments don't include a `findViewById()` method, for instance. To get a reference to a fragment's views, we first have to get a reference to the fragment's root view using the `getView()` method, and use that to find its child views.

Now that we've got the fragment to update its views, let's take the app for a test drive.

You should always call up to the superclass when you implement any fragment lifecycle methods.

What happens when the code runs

Before we run the app, let's go through what happens when the code runs.

1 **When the app is launched, MainActivity gets created.**
The user clicks on the button in `MainActivity` to start `DetailActivity`.

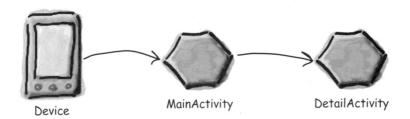

Device   MainActivity   DetailActivity

2 **DetailActivity's onCreate() method runs.**
The `onCreate()` method specifies that *activity_detail.xml* should be used for `DetailActivity`'s layout. *activity_detail.xml* includes a `<fragment>` element with an ID of `detail_frag` that refers to the fragment `WorkoutDetailFragment`.

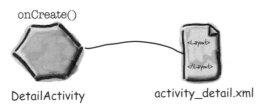

onCreate()

DetailActivity   activity_detail.xml

3 **WorkoutDetailFragment's onCreateView() method runs.**
The `onCreateView()` method specifies that *fragment_workout_detail.xml* should be used for `WorkoutDetailFragment`'s layout. It inflates the layout to a `View` object.

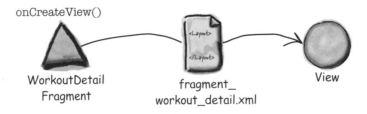

onCreateView()

WorkoutDetail
Fragment   fragment_
workout_detail.xml   View

The story continues

4 **activity_detail.xml's Views are inflated to View Java objects.**
DetailActivity uses WorkoutDetailFragment's View object in place of the
`<fragment>` element in its layout's XML, and gives it an ID of detail_frag.

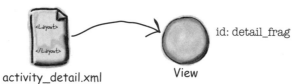

activity_detail.xml   View

id: detail_frag

5 **DetailActivity's onCreate() method continues to run.**
DetailActivity gets a reference to WorkoutDetailFragment by asking the fragment
manager for the fragment with an ID of detail_frag.

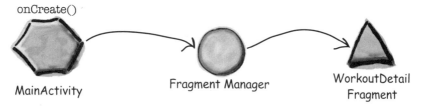

onCreate()

MainActivity   Fragment Manager   WorkoutDetail Fragment

5 **DetailActivity calls WorkoutDetailFragment's setWorkout() method.**
DetailActivity passes WorkoutDetailFragment a workout ID of 1. The fragment
sets its workoutId variable to 1.

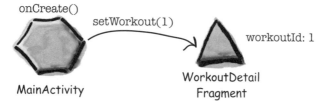

onCreate()

setWorkout(1)

MainActivity   WorkoutDetail Fragment

workoutId: 1

6 **The fragment uses the value of the workout ID in its onStart() method to
set the values of its views.**

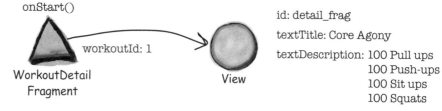

onStart()

workoutId: 1

WorkoutDetail Fragment   View

id: detail_frag

textTitle: Core Agony

textDescription: 100 Pull ups
100 Push-ups
100 Sit ups
100 Squats

Let's take the app for a test drive.

Test drive the app

When we run the app, `MainActivity` is launched.

When we click on `MainActivity`'s button, it starts `DetailActivity`. `DetailActivity` contains `WorkoutDetailFragment`, and the fragment displays details of the Core Agony workout.

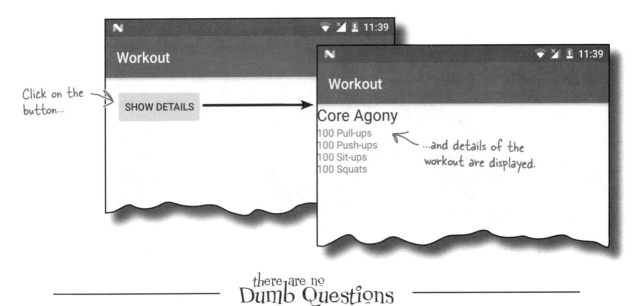

Click on the button...

...and details of the workout are displayed.

there are no

Dumb Questions

Q: Why can't an activity get a fragment by calling the `findViewById()` method?

A: Because `findViewById()` always returns a `View` object and, surprisingly, fragments aren't views.

Q: Why isn't `findFragmentById()` an activity method like `findViewById()` is?

A: That's a good question. Fragments weren't available before API 11, so it uses the fragment manager as a way to add a whole bunch of useful code for managing fragments, without having to pack lots of extra code into the activity base class.

Q: Why don't fragments have a `findViewById()` method?

A: Because fragments aren't views or activities. Instead, you need to use the fragment's `getView()` method to get a reference to the fragment's root view, and then call the view's `findViewById()` method to get its child views.

Q: Activities need to be registered in *AndroidManifest.xml* so that the app can use them. Do fragments?

A: No. Activities need to be registered in *AndroidManifest.xml*, but fragments don't.

Where we've got to

Here's a reminder of the structure of the app, and what we want it to do:

① **When the app gets launched, it starts MainActivity.**
MainActivity uses *activity_main.xml* for its layout, and contains a fragment called WorkoutListFragment.

② **WorkoutListFragment displays a list of workouts.**

③ **When the user clicks on one of the workouts, DetailActivity starts.**
DetailActivity uses *activity_detail.xml* for its layout, and contains a fragment called WorkoutDetailFragment.

④ **WorkoutDetailFragment uses fragment_workout_detail.xml for its layout.**
It displays the details of the workout the user has selected.

⑤ **WorkoutListFragment and WorkoutDetailFragment get their workout data from *Workout.java*.**
Workout.java contains an array of Workouts.

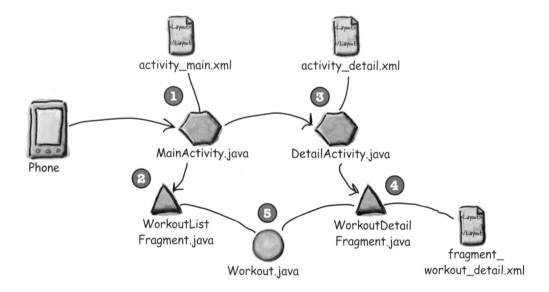

So far we've created both activities and their layouts, *WorkoutDetailFragment.java* and its layout, and also *Workout.java*. The next thing we need to look at is WorkoutListFragment.

We need to create a fragment with a list

We need to create a second fragment, `WorkoutListFragment`, that contains a list of the different workouts that the user can choose from. Using a fragment for this means that later on, we'll be able to use it to create different user interfaces for phones and tablets.

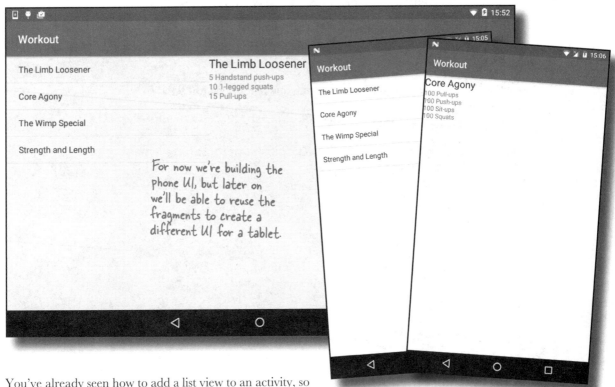

For now we're building the phone UI, but later on we'll be able to reuse the fragments to create a different UI for a tablet.

You've already seen how to add a list view to an activity, so we could do something similar for the fragment. But rather than create a new fragment with a layout that contains a single list view, we're going to use a different approach that involves a new type of fragment called a **list fragment**.

A list fragment is a fragment that contains only a list

A list fragment is a type of fragment that specializes in working with a list. It's automatically bound to a list view, so you don't need to create one yourself. Here's what one looks like:

A list fragment comes complete with its own list view so you don't need to add it yourself. You just need to provide the list fragment with data.

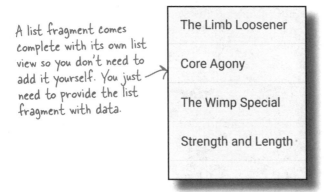

ListFragment is a subclass of Fragment.

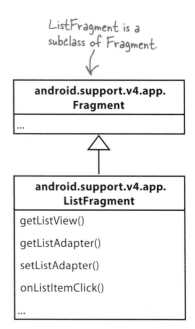

There are a couple of major advantages in using a list fragment to display categories of data:

⭐ **You don't need to create your own layout.**
List fragments define their own layout programmatically, so there's no XML layout for you to create or maintain. The layout the list fragment generates includes a single list view. You access this list view in your fragment code using the list fragment's `getListView()` method. You need this in order to specify what data should be displayed in the list view.

⭐ **You don't have to implement your own event listener.**
The `ListFragment` class automatically implements an event listener that listens for when items in the list view are clicked. Instead of creating your own event listener and binding it to the list view, you just need to implement the list fragment's `onListItemClick()` method. This makes it easier to get your fragment to respond when the user clicks on items in the list view. You'll see this in action later on.

So what does the list fragment code look like?

> **A list fragment is a type of fragment that specializes in working with a list view. It has a default layout that contains the list view.**

WorkoutDetailFragment
WorkoutListFragment
Coordinate fragments

How to create a list fragment

You add a list fragment to your project in the same way you add a normal fragment. Highlight the *com.hfad.workout* package in the *app/src/main/java* folder, then go to File→New...→Fragment→Fragment (Blank). Name the fragment "WorkoutListFragment", and then uncheck the options to create layout XML, and also the options to include fragment factory methods and interface callbacks (list fragments define their own layouts programmatically, so you don't need Android Studio to create one for you). When you click on the Finish button, Android Studio creates a new list fragment in a file called *WorkoutListFragment.java* in the *app/src/main/java* folder.

Here's what the basic code looks like to create a list fragment. As you can see, it's very similar to that of a normal fragment. Replace the code in *WorkoutListFragment.java* with the code below:

```java
package com.hfad.workout;

import android.os.Bundle;
import android.support.v4.app.ListFragment;
import android.view.LayoutInflater;
import android.view.View;
import android.view.ViewGroup;

public class WorkoutListFragment extends ListFragment {

    @Override
    public View onCreateView(LayoutInflater inflater, ViewGroup container,
                             Bundle savedInstanceState) {
        return super.onCreateView(inflater, container, savedInstanceState);
    }
}
```

ment that is compatible back to API level 4.

WorkoutListFragment

☐ Create layout XML?

☐ Include fragment factory methods?

☐ Include interface callbacks?

Uncheck these options, as we don't need them. If prompted for the fragment's source language, select the option for Java.

Workout
app/src/main
java
com.hfad.workout
WorkoutList Fragment.java

The activity needs to extend ListFragment, not Fragment.

Calling the superclass onCreateView() method gives you the default layout for the ListFragment.

The above code creates a basic list fragment called `WorkoutListFragment`. As it's a list fragment, it needs to extend the `ListFragment` class rather than `Fragment`.

The `onCreateView()` method is optional. It gets called when the fragment's view gets created. We're including it in our code as we want to populate the fragment's list view with data as soon as it gets created. If you don't need your code to do anything at this point, you don't need to include the `onCreateView()` method.

The next thing we need to do is add data to the list view in the `onCreateView()` method.

there are no Dumb Questions

Q: When we create a list fragment, why do we choose the option for Fragment (Blank) instead of Fragment (List)?

A: The Fragment (List) option produces code that's more complex, most of which we don't need to use. The code generated by the Fragment (Blank) is simpler.

Adapters revisited

As we said in Chapter 7, you can connect data to a list view using an adapter. The adapter acts as a bridge between the data and the list view. This is still the case when your list view is in a fragment, or a list fragment:

Our data's in an array, but we could have used a database or a web service instead.

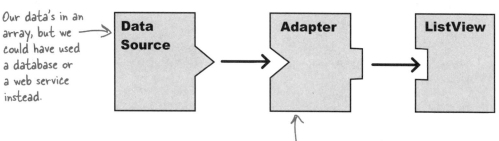

The adapter bridges the gap between the list view and the data source. Adapters allow list views to display data from a variety of sources.

We want to supply the list view in `WorkoutListFragment` with an array of workout names, so we'll use an array adapter to bind the array to the list view as before. As you may recall, an array adapter is a type of adapter that's used to bind arrays to views. You can use it with any subclass of the `AdapterView` class, which means you can use it with both list views and spinners.

In our case, we're going to use an array adapter to display an array of data from the `Workout` class in the list view.

> **An adapter acts as a bridge between a view and a data source. An array adapter is a type of adapter that specializes in working with arrays.**

This is the array.

We'll create an array adapter to bind our list view to an array.

This is our list view.

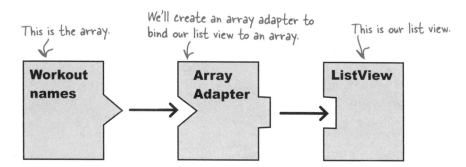

We'll see how this works on the next page.

Our previous array adapter

As we said in Chapter 7, you use an array adapter by initializing it and attaching it to the list view.

To initialize the array adapter, you first specify what type of data is contained in the array you want to bind to the list view. You then pass it three parameters: a Context (usually the current activity), a layout resource that specifies how to display each item in the array, and the array itself.

Here's the code we used in Chapter 7 to create an array adapter to displays Drink data from the Drink.drinks array:

```
ArrayAdapter<Drink> listAdapter = new ArrayAdapter<>(
        this,
        android.R.layout.simple_list_item_1,
        Drink.drinks);
```

The current context. In our Chapter 7 scenario, it was the current activity. → this,

The array ← Drink.drinks);

This is a built-in layout resource. It tells the array adapter to display each item in the array in a single text view.

There's a big difference between the situation we had back in Chapter 7 and the situation we have now. Back in Chapter 7, we used the array adapter to display data in an activity. But this time, we want to display data in a fragment. What difference does this make?

A fragment isn't a subclass of Context

As you saw earlier in the book, the Activity class is a subclass of the Context class. This means that all of the activities you create have access to global information about the app's environment.

But the Fragment class *isn't* a subclass of the Context class. It has no access to global information, and you can't use this to pass the current context to the array adapter. Instead, you need to get the current context in some other way.

One way is to use another object's getContext() method to get a reference to the current context. If you create the adapter in the fragment's onCreateView() method, you can use the getContext() method of the onCreateView() LayoutInflator parameter to get the context instead.

Once you've created the adapter, you bind it to the ListView using the fragment's setListAdapter() method:

```
setListAdapter(listAdapter);
```

We'll show you the full code on the next page.

The updated WorkoutListFragment code

We've updated our *WorkoutListFragment.java* code so that it
populates the list view with the names of the workouts. Apply
these changes to your code, then save your changes:

```
package com.hfad.workout;

import android.os.Bundle;
import android.support.v4.app.ListFragment;
import android.view.LayoutInflater;
import android.view.View;
import android.view.ViewGroup;
import android.widget.ArrayAdapter;
```

We're using this class in the onCreateView() method.

```
public class WorkoutListFragment extends ListFragment {

    @Override
    public View onCreateView(LayoutInflater inflater, ViewGroup container,
                             Bundle savedInstanceState) {
        String[] names = new String[Workout.workouts.length];
        for (int i = 0; i < names.length; i++) {
            names[i] = Workout.workouts[i].getName();
        }
```

Create an array adapter.

Create a String array of the workout names.

```
        ArrayAdapter<String> adapter = new ArrayAdapter<>(
                inflater.getContext(), android.R.layout.simple_list_item_1,
                names);
        setListAdapter(adapter);
```

Get the context from the layout inflater.

Bind the array adapter to the list view.

```
        return super.onCreateView(inflater, container, savedInstanceState);
    }
}
```

Now that the WorkoutListFragment contains a list of
workouts, let's add it to MainActivity.

Workout
  └ app/src/main
       └ java
           └ com.hfad.workout
                └ WorkoutList
                  Fragment.java

Display WorkoutListFragment in the MainActivity layout

We're going to add our new WorkoutListFragment to MainActivity's *layout activity_main.xml*. The layout currently displays a button that we're using to navigate from MainActivity to DetailActivity:

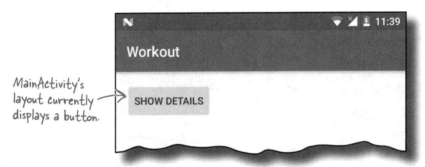

MainActivity's layout currently displays a button.

We want to remove the button, and display WorkoutListFragment in its place. Here's what the new version of the layout will look like:

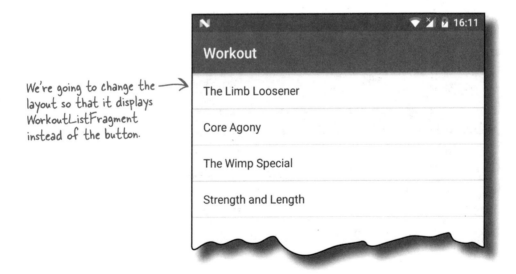

We're going to change the layout so that it displays WorkoutListFragment instead of the button.

What will the code be like? Have a go at the exercise on the next page.

Layout Magnets

Somebody put a new version of *activity_main.xml* on our fridge door. Unfortunately some of the magnets fell off when we shut the door too hard. Can you piece the layout back together again? (You won't need to use all of the magnets below.)

The layout needs to display `WorkoutListFragment`.

```
<?xml version="1.0" encoding="utf-8"?>


<.............................. xmlns:android="http://schemas.android.com/apk/res/android"


    ..............................="".............................................................."


    android:layout_width="match_parent"


    android:layout_height="match_parent"/>
```

fragment   android:fragment   Fragment

LinearLayout   com.hfad.workout.

WorkoutListFragment   android:name

Layout Magnets Solution

Somebody put a new version of *activity_main.xml* on our fridge door. Unfortunately some of the magnets fell off when we shut the door too hard. Can you piece the layout back together again? (You won't need to use all of the magnets below.)

The layout needs to display WorkoutListFragment.

```
<?xml version="1.0" encoding="utf-8"?>
```

← You declare a fragment with the <fragment> element.

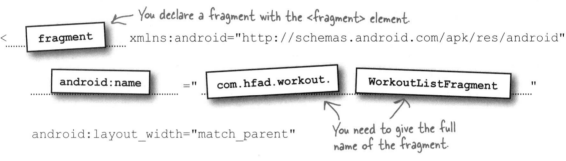

```
<    fragment        xmlns:android="http://schemas.android.com/apk/res/android"

        android:name    ="    com.hfad.workout.        WorkoutListFragment    "
```

You need to give the full name of the fragment.

```
        android:layout_width="match_parent"

        android:layout_height="match_parent"/>
```

`android:fragment`   `Fragment`

`LinearLayout`   ← You didn't need to use these magnets.

The code for activity_main.xml

As we want `MainActivity`'s layout to only contain a single fragment, we can replace nearly all of the code we currently have.

Here's the updated code for *activity_main.xml*. As you can see, it's much shorter than the original version. Update your version of the code to reflect our changes.

Our layout only contains a single fragment, so we can get rid of the LinearLayout.

```xml
<?xml version="1.0" encoding="utf-8"?>
<LinearLayout xmlns:android="http://schemas.android.com/apk/res/android"
    xmlns:tools="http://schemas.android.com/tools"
    android:layout_width="match_parent"
    android:layout_height="match_parent"
    android:padding="16dp"
    android:orientation="vertical"
    tools:context="com.hfad.workout.MainActivity">

    <Button                              We no longer need this button.
        android:layout_width="wrap_content"
        android:layout_height="wrap_content"
        android:onClick="onShowDetails"
        android:text="@string/details_button" />
</LinearLayout>
```

Here's the fragment.

```xml
<fragment xmlns:android="http://schemas.android.com/apk/res/android"
    android:name="com.hfad.workout.WorkoutListFragment"
    android:layout_width="match_parent"
    android:layout_height="match_parent"/>
```

Workout

app/src/main

res

layout

activity_main.xml

We'll go through what happens when this code runs over the next couple of pages.

What happens when the code runs

Here's a runthrough of what happens when we run the app.

1 **When the app is launched, MainActivity gets created.**
MainActivity's onCreate() method runs. This specifies that *activity_main.xml* should be used for MainActivity's layout. *activity_main.xml* includes a <fragment> element that refers to WorkoutListFragment.

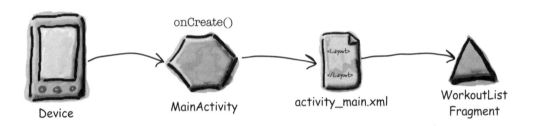

2 **WorkoutListFragment is a ListFragment, so it uses a ListView as its layout.**

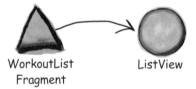

3 **WorkoutListFragment creates an ArrayAdapter<String>, an array adapter that deals with arrays of String objects.**

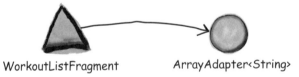

4 **The ArrayAdapter<String> retrieves data from the names array.**

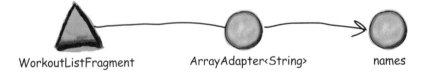

The story continues

⑤ **WorkoutListFragment attaches the array adapter to the ListView using the setListAdapter() method.**

The list view uses the array adapter to display a list of the workout names.

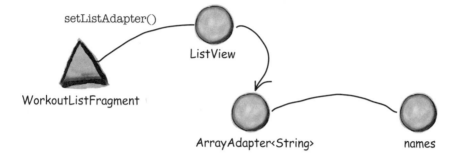

setListAdapter()

ListView

WorkoutListFragment

ArrayAdapter<String>

names

Test drive the app

When we run the app, `MainActivity` gets launched.

`MainActivity`'s layout contains the fragment `WorkoutListFragment`. The fragment contains a list of the workout names, and this is displayed in the activity.

WorkoutDetailFragment
→ **WorkoutListFragment**
Coordinate fragments

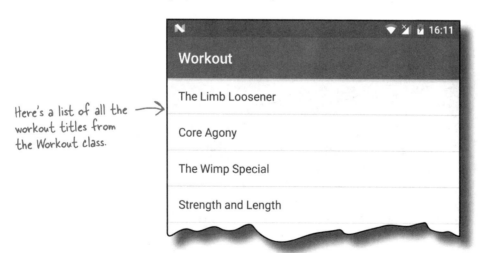

Here's a list of all the workout titles from the Workout class.

That looks great, but when we click on one of the workouts, nothing happens. We need to update the code so that when we click on one of the workouts, details of that workout are displayed.

Connect the list to the detail

There are a few ways that we can start `DetailActivity` and display the details of the workout that was clicked. We'll use this technique:

1 Add code to `WorkoutListFragment` that waits for a workout to be clicked.

2 When that code runs, call some code in *MainActivity.java* that will start `DetailActivity`, passing it the ID of the workout.

3 Get `DetailActivity` to pass the ID to `WorkoutDetailFragment` so that the fragment can display details of the correct workout.

We don't want to write code in `WorkoutListFragment` that talks *directly* to `MainActivity`. Can you think why?

The answer is *reuse*. We want our fragments to know as little as possible about the environment that contains them so that we can reuse them elsewhere. The more a fragment needs to know about the activity using it, the less reusable it is.

> Wait a minute! You're saying you don't want the fragment to know about the activity that contains it? But I thought you said the fragment has to call code in MainActivity. Won't that mean we can't use it in another activity?

We need to use an *interface* to decouple the fragment from the activity.

We have two objects that need to talk to each other—the fragment and the activity—and we want them to talk without one side knowing too much about the other. The way we do that in Java is with an *interface*. When we define an interface, we're saying *what the minimum requirements are for one object to talk usefully to another*. That means that we'll be able to get the fragment to talk to any activity, so long as that activity implements the interface.

We need to decouple the fragment by using an interface

We're going to create an interface called **Listener**. If MainActivity implements the interface, WorkoutListFragment will be able to tell MainActivity when one of its items has been clicked. To do this, we'll need to make changes to WorkoutListFragment and MainActivity.

What WorkoutListFragment needs to do

We'll start with the code for WorkoutListFragment. There are a few changes we need to make, in this order.

1 **Define the interface.**
We'll define the listener's interface in WorkoutListFragment. We're defining the interface here, as its purpose is to allow WorkoutListFragment to communicate with any activity.

2 **Register the listener (in this case MainActivity) when WorkoutListFragment gets attached to it.**
This will give WorkoutListFragment a reference to MainActivity.

3 **Tell the listener when an item gets clicked.**
MainActivity will then be able to respond to the click.

You need to go through similar steps to these whenever you have a fragment that needs to communicate with the activity it's attached to.

We'll go through each change individually, then show you the full code.

1. Define the listener interface

We want any activities that implement the listener interface to respond to item clicks, so we'll define a method for the interface, itemClicked(). The itemClicked() method has one parameter, the ID of the item that's clicked.

Here's the interface: *— We'll call the interface Listener.*

```
interface Listener {
    void itemClicked(long id);
};
```

Any activities that implement the Listener interface must include this method. We'll use it to get the activity to respond to items in the fragment being clicked.

Next we'll look at how you register the listener on the next page.

2. Register the listener

We need to save a reference to the activity WorkoutListFragment gets attached to. This activity will implement the Listener interface, so we'll add the following private variable to WorkoutListFragment:

```
private Listener listener;
```

We need to set this variable when WorkoutListFragment gets attached to an activity. If you look back at the fragment lifecycle, when a fragment gets attached to an activity, the fragment's onAttach() method is called. We'll use this method to set the value of the listener:

```
public void onAttach(Context context) {
    super.onAttach(context);
    this.listener = (Listener)context;
}
```

← This is the context (in this case, the activity) the fragment is attached to.

3. Respond to clicks

When an item in WorkoutListFragment gets clicked, we want to call the listener's itemClicked() method. This is the method we defined in the interface on the previous page. But how can we tell when an item's been clicked?

Whenever an item gets clicked in a list fragment, the list fragment's onListItemClick() method gets called. Here's what it looks like:

```
public void onListItemClick(ListView listView,    ← The list view
                            View itemView,
                            int position,        The item in the list view that was
                            long id) {           clicked, its position, and its ID

    //Do something
}
```

The onListItemClick() method has four parameters: the list view, the item in the list that was clicked, its position, and the row ID of the underlying data. This means we can use the method to pass the listener the ID of the workout the user clicked on:

```
public void onListItemClick(ListView listView, View itemView, int position, long id) {
    if (listener != null) {
        listener.itemClicked(id);    ← Call the itemClicked() method in the activity, passing
    }                                  it the ID of the workout the user selected.
}
```

The code for WorkoutListFragment.java

Here's the full code for *WorkoutListFragment.java* code (apply these changes to your code, then save your work):

```java
package com.hfad.workout;

import android.os.Bundle;
import android.support.v4.app.ListFragment;
import android.view.LayoutInflater;
import android.view.View;
import android.view.ViewGroup;
import android.widget.ArrayAdapter;
import android.content.Context;
import android.widget.ListView;

public class WorkoutListFragment extends ListFragment {

    static interface Listener {
        void itemClicked(long id);
    };

    private Listener listener;

    @Override
    public View onCreateView(LayoutInflater inflater, ViewGroup container,
                             Bundle savedInstanceState) {
        String[] names = new String[Workout.workouts.length];
        for (int i = 0; i < names.length; i++) {
            names[i] = Workout.workouts[i].getName();
        }
        ArrayAdapter<String> adapter = new ArrayAdapter<>(
                inflater.getContext(), android.R.layout.simple_list_item_1,
                names);
        setListAdapter(adapter);
        return super.onCreateView(inflater, container, savedInstanceState);
    }

    @Override
    public void onAttach(Context context) {
        super.onAttach(context);
        this.listener = (Listener)context;
    }

    @Override
    public void onListItemClick(ListView listView, View itemView, int position, long id) {
        if (listener != null) {
            listener.itemClicked(id);
        }
    }
}
```

Import these classes. *(annotation pointing to the two import lines)*

Add the listener to the fragment. *(annotation)*

This is called when the fragment gets attached to the activity. Remember, the Activity class is a subclass of Context. *(annotation pointing to onAttach)*

Tell the listener when an item in the ListView is clicked. *(annotation pointing to listener.itemClicked(id))*

Workout

app/src/main

java

com.hfad.workout

WorkoutList Fragment.java

MainActivity needs to implement the interface

Next we need to make MainActivity implement the Listener interface we just created. The interface specifies an itemClicked() method, so we'll make the method start DetailActivity, passing it the ID of the workout the user selected.

Here's the full code for *MainActivity.java*. Update your code so that it matches ours.

```
package com.hfad.workout;

import android.support.v7.app.AppCompatActivity;
import android.os.Bundle;
import android.view.View;
import android.content.Intent;

public class MainActivity extends AppCompatActivity
                    implements WorkoutListFragment.Listener {
```

Implement the listener interface defined in WorkoutListFragment.

Workout
app/src/main
java
com.hfad.workout
MainActivity.java

```
    @Override
    protected void onCreate(Bundle savedInstanceState) {
        super.onCreate(savedInstanceState);
        setContentView(R.layout.activity_main);
    }

    public void onShowDetails(View view) {
        Intent intent = new Intent(this, DetailActivity.class);
        startActivity(intent);
    }
```

This is the method called by MainActivity's button. We've removed the button, so we no longer need this method.

This method is defined by the interface, so we need to implement it.

```
    @Override
    public void itemClicked(long id) {
        Intent intent = new Intent(this, DetailActivity.class);
        intent.putExtra(DetailActivity.EXTRA_WORKOUT_ID, (int)id);
        startActivity(intent);
    }
}
```

Pass the ID of the workout to DetailActivity. EXTRA_WORKOUT_ID is the name of a constant we'll define in DetailActivity.

Those are all the changes we need to make to MainActivity. There's just one more code change we need to make to our app.

DetailActivity needs to pass the ID to WorkoutDetailFragment

So far, `WorkoutListFragment` passes the ID of the workout that was clicked to `MainActivity`, and `MainActivity` passes it to `DetailActivity`. We need to make one more change, which is to pass the ID from `DetailActivity` to `WorkoutDetailActivity`.

Here's the updated code for `DetailActivity` that does this. Update your version of *DetailActivity.java* to reflect our changes:

```java
package com.hfad.workout;

import android.support.v7.app.AppCompatActivity;
import android.os.Bundle;

public class DetailActivity extends AppCompatActivity {

    public static final String EXTRA_WORKOUT_ID = "id";

    @Override
    protected void onCreate(Bundle savedInstanceState) {
        super.onCreate(savedInstanceState);
        setContentView(R.layout.activity_detail);
        WorkoutDetailFragment frag = (WorkoutDetailFragment)
                getSupportFragmentManager().findFragmentById(R.id.detail_frag);
        frag.setWorkout(1);
        int workoutId = (int) getIntent().getExtras().get(EXTRA_WORKOUT_ID);
        frag.setWorkout(workoutId);
    }
}
```

We're using a constant to pass the ID from MainActivity to DetailActivity to avoid hardcoding this value.

Workout
└ **app/src/main**
　└ **java**
　　└ **com.hfad.workout**
　　　└ **DetailActivity.java**

We're no longer hardcoding an ID of 1, so remove this line.

Get the ID from the intent, and pass it to the fragment via its setWorkout() method.

Over the next couple of pages we'll examine what happens when the code runs.

What happens when the code runs

Here's a runthrough of what happens when we run the app.

1 **When the app is launched, MainActivity gets created.**
WorkoutListFragment is attached to MainActivity, and
WorkoutListFragment's onAttach() method runs.

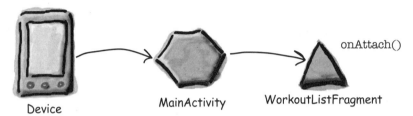

2 **WorkoutListFragment registers MainActivity as a Listener.**

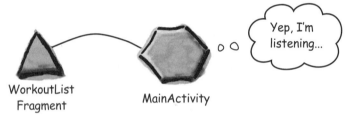

3 **When an item is clicked in WorkoutListFragment, the fragment's onListItemClick() method is called.**
This calls MainActivity's itemClicked() method, passing it the ID of the workout that was clicked, in this example 1.

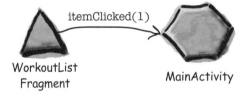

4 **MainActivity's itemClicked() method starts DetailActivity, passing it the value of the workout ID in an intent.**

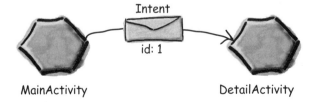

The story continues...

5 **DetailActivity calls WorkoutDetailFragment's setWorkout() method, passing it the value of the workout ID.**

WorkoutDetailFragment uses the workout ID, in this case 1, to display the workout title and description in its views.

setWorkout(1)

DetailActivity   WorkoutDetailFragment

textTitle: Core Agony

textDescription: 100 Pull ups
               100 Push-ups
               100 Sit ups
               100 Squats

Test drive the app

When we run the app, MainActivity gets launched. It displays a list of workouts in its fragment, WorkoutListFragment.

☑ **WorkoutDetailFragment**
☑ **WorkoutListFragment**
→ ☑ **Coordinate fragments**

When you click on one of the workouts, DetailActivity is displayed. It shows details of the workout that we selected.

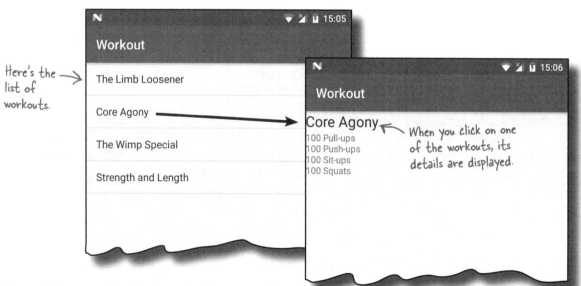

Here's the list of workouts.

When you click on one of the workouts, its details are displayed.

That's everything we need to do to use the fragments we've created in a user interface for a phone. In the next chapter, you'll see how to reuse the fragments, and create a different user interface that will work better for tablets.

Your Android Toolbox

You've got Chapter 9 under
your belt and now you've
added fragments to your
toolbox.

Fragment lifecycle methods

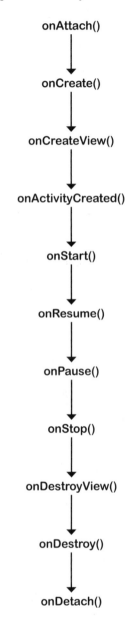

onAttach()

↓

onCreate()

↓

onCreateView()

↓

onActivityCreated()

↓

onStart()

↓

onResume()

↓

onPause()

↓

onStop()

↓

onDestroyView()

↓

onDestroy()

↓

onDetach()

CHAPTER 9

BULLET POINTS

- A fragment is used to control part of a screen. It can be reused across multiple activities.

- A fragment has an associated layout.

- The `onCreateView()` method gets called each time Android needs the fragment's layout.

- Add a fragment to an activity's layout using the `<fragment>` element and adding a `name` attribute.

- The fragment lifecycle methods tie in with the states of the activity that contains the fragment.

- The `Fragment` class doesn't extend the `Activity` class or implement the `Context` class.

- Fragments don't have a `findViewById()` method. Instead, use the `getView()` method to get a reference to the root view, then call the view's `findViewById()` method.

- A list fragment is a fragment that comes complete with a `ListView`. You create one by subclassing `ListFragment`.

You can download the full code for the chapter from https://tinyurl.com/HeadFirstAndroid.

10 fragments for larger interfaces

Different Size, Different Interface

They're using a tablet? Maybe we should rethink the UI...

So far we've only run our apps on devices with a small screen.

But what if your users have tablets? In this chapter you'll see how to create **flexible user interfaces** by making your app **look and behave differently** depending on the device it's running on. We'll show you how to control the behavior of your app when you press the Back button by introducing you to the **back stack** and **fragment transactions**. Finally, you'll find out how to **save and restore the state** of your fragment.

The Workout app looks the same on a phone and a tablet

In the previous chapter, we created a version of the Workout app designed to work on a phone.

As a reminder, when the app launches, it displays `MainActivity`. This contains a fragment, `WorkoutListFragment`, that displays a list of workouts. When the user clicks on one of the workouts, `DetailActivity` starts, and displays details of the workout in its fragment, `WorkoutDetailFragment`.

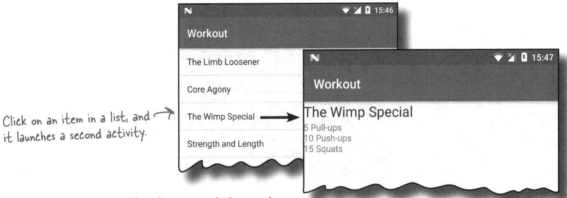

Click on an item in a list, and it launches a second activity.

When we run the app on a tablet, the app works in exactly the same way. As the screen size is larger, however, there's lots of empty space in the user interface that we could make better use of.

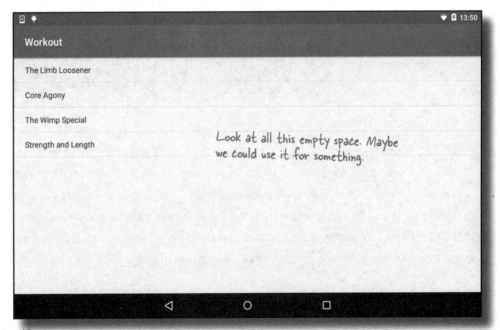

Look at all this empty space. Maybe we could use it for something.

Designing for larger interfaces

One way in which we could better use the empty space is to display details of the workout to the right of the list of workouts. When the user clicks on one of the workouts, details of that workout could be displayed on the same screen without us having to start a second activity:

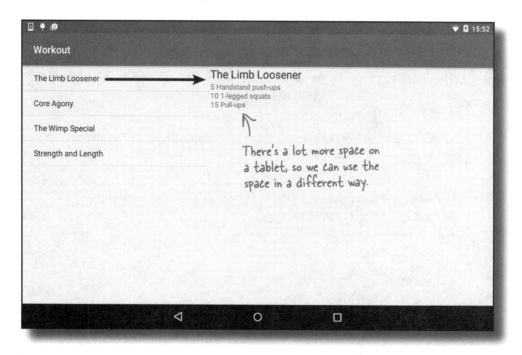

We don't want to change our app completely though. We still want our app to work as it does currently if it's running on a phone.

We're going to get our app to adapt to the type of device it's running on. If the app's running on a phone, we'll display details of the workout in a separate activity (this is the app's current behavior). If the app's running on a tablet, we'll display details of the workout next to the list of workouts.

Before we get started, let's remind ourselves how the app's currently structured.

The phone version of the app

The phone version of the app we built in Chapter 9 works in the following way:

① **When the app gets launched, it starts MainActivity.**
MainActivity uses *activity_main.xml* for its layout, and contains a fragment called WorkoutListFragment.

② **WorkoutListFragment displays a list of workouts.**

③ **When the user clicks on one of the workouts, DetailActivity starts.**
DetailActivity uses *activity_detail.xml* for its layout, and contains a fragment called WorkoutDetailFragment.

④ **WorkoutDetailFragment uses fragment_workout_detail.xml for its layout.**
It displays the details of the workout the user has selected.

⑤ **WorkoutListFragment and WorkoutDetailFragment get their workout data from *Workout.java.***
Workout.java contains an array of Workouts.

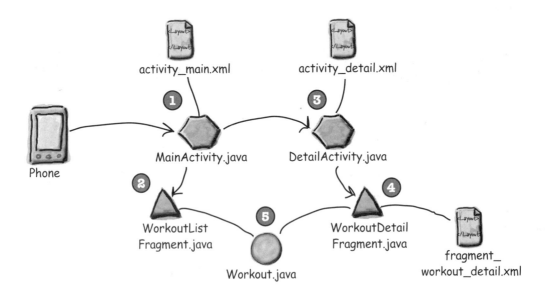

So how does it need to work differently on a tablet?

The tablet version of the app

Here's how the app will work when it runs on a tablet:

① **When the app gets launched, it starts MainActivity as before.**
MainActivity uses *activity_main.xml* for its layout.

② **MainActivity's layout displays two fragments, WorkoutListFragment and WorkoutDetailFragment.**

③ **WorkoutListFragment displays a list of workouts.**
It's a list fragment, so it has no extra layout file.

④ **When the user clicks on one of the workouts, its details are displayed in WorkoutDetailFragment.**
WorkoutDetailFragment uses *fragment_workout_detail.xml* for its layout.

⑤ **Both fragments get their workout data from *Workout.java* as before.**

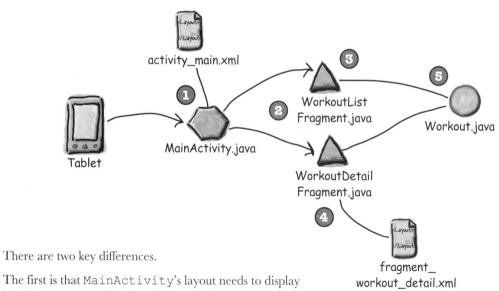

There are two key differences.

The first is that MainActivity's layout needs to display both fragments, not just WorkoutListFragment.

The second difference is that we no longer need to start DetailActivity when the user clicks on one of the workouts. Instead, we need to display WorkoutDetailFragment in MainActivity.

We'll go through the steps for how to change the app on the next page.

Here's what we're going to do

There are a number of steps we'll go through to change the app:

① **Create a tablet AVD (Android Virtual Device).**
We're going to create a new UI for a tablet, so we'll create a new tablet AVD to run it on. This will allow us to check how the app looks and behaves on a device with a larger screen.

② **Create a new tablet layout.**
We'll reuse the fragments we've already created in a new layout that's designed to work on devices with larger screens. We'll display details of the first workout in the first instance so that we can see the fragments side by side.

At first, we'll hardcode the app so it displays the Limb Loosener workout.

③ **Display details of the workout the user selects.**
We'll update the app so that when the user clicks on one of the workouts, we'll display the details of the workout the user selected.

Later in the chapter, we'll change the code so that it displays details of the workout the user clicks on.

Do this!

We're going to update the Workout app in this chapter, so open your original Workout project from Chapter 9 in Android Studio.

Create a tablet AVD

Before we get into changing the app, we're going to create a new Nexus 7 AVD running API level 25 so that you can see how the app looks and behaves when it's running on a tablet. The steps are nearly the same as when you created a Nexus 5X AVD back in Chapter 1.

Open the Android Virtual Device Manager

You create AVDs using the AVD Manager. Open the AVD Manager by selecting Android on the Tools menu and choosing AVD Manager.

You'll be presented with a screen showing you a list of the AVDs you've already set up. Click on the Create Virtual Device button at the bottom of the screen.

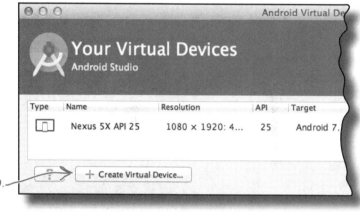

Click on the Create Virtual Device button to create an AVD.

Select the hardware

On the next screen, you'll be prompted to choose a device definition, the type of device your AVD will emulate.

We're going to see what our app looks like running on a Nexus 7 tablet. Choose Tablet from the Category menu and Nexus 7 from the list. Then click the Next button.

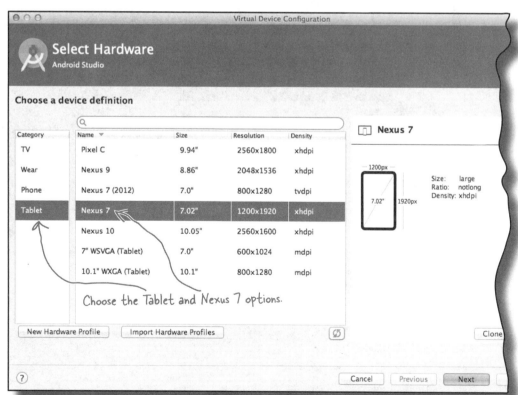

Choose the Tablet and Nexus 7 options.

Creating a tablet AVD (continued)

Select a system image

Next, you need to select a system image. The system image gives you an installed version of the Android operating system. You can choose the version of Android you want to be on your AVD.

You need to choose a system image for an API level that's compatible with the app you're building. As an example, if you want your app to work on a minimum of API level 19, choose a system image for *at least* API level 19. As in Chapter 1, we want our AVD to run API level 25, so choose the system image with a release name of Nougat and a target of Android 7.1.1, the version number of API level 25. Then click on the Next button.

We'll choose the same system image as we did in Chapter 1. →

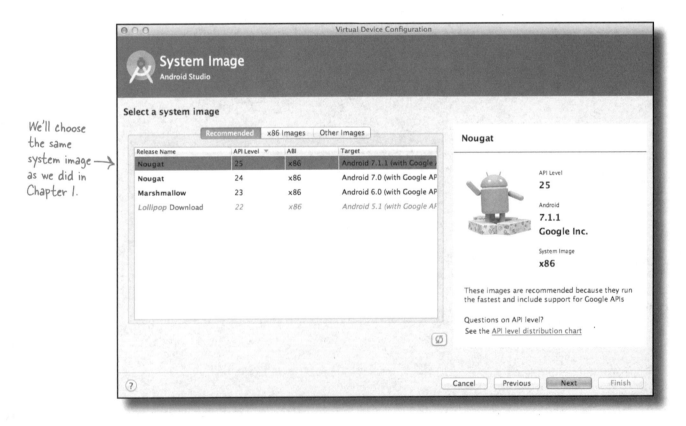

Creating a tablet AVD (continued)

Verify the AVD configuration

On the next screen, you'll be asked to verify the AVD configuration. This screen summarizes the options you chose over the last few screens, and gives you the option of changing them. Change the screen startup orientation to Landscape, then click on the Finish button.

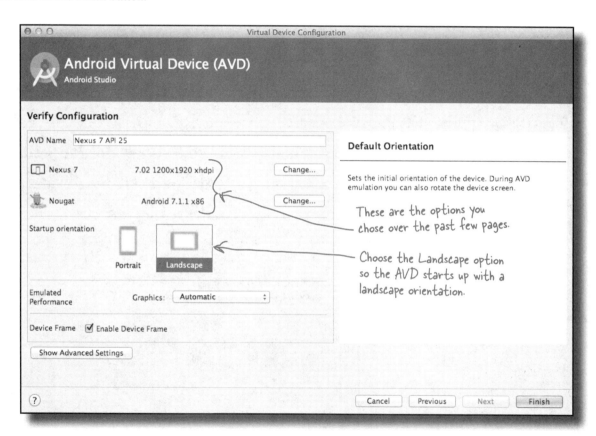

The AVD Manager will create the Nexus 7 AVD for you, and when it's done, display it in its list of devices. You may now close the AVD Manager.

Now that we've created our tablet AVD, we can get to work on updating the Workout app. We want to change the app so that `MainActivity` uses one layout when it's running on a phone, and another layout when it's running on a tablet. But how can we do this?

Put screen-specific resources in screen-specific folders

Create AVD
Create layout
Show workout

Earlier in the book, you saw how you could get different devices to use image resources appropriate to their screen size by putting different-sized images in the different *drawable** folders. As an example, you put images intended for devices with high-density screens in the *drawable-hdpi* folder.

You can do something similar with other resources such as layouts, menus, and values. If you want to create multiple versions of the same resource for different screen specs, you need to create multiple resource folders with an appropriate name, then add the resource to that folder. The device will then load the resource at runtime from the folder that's the closest match to its screen spec.

If you want to have one layout for large screen devices such as tablets, and another layout for smaller devices such as phones, you put the layout for the tablet in the *app/src/main/res/layout-large* folder, and the layout for the phone in the *app/src/main/res/layout* folder. When the app runs on a phone, it will use the layout in the *layout* folder. If it's run on a tablet, it will use the layout in the *layout-large* folder instead.

Android uses the names of your resource folders to decide which resources it should use at runtime.

Layouts in the layout folder can be used by any device, but layouts in the layout-large folder will only be used by devices with a large screen.

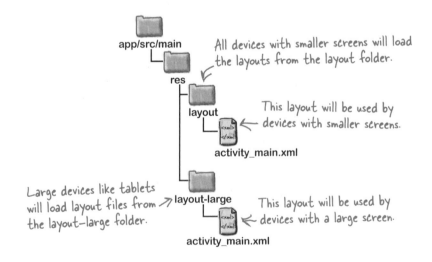

app/src/main

All devices with smaller screens will load the layouts from the layout folder.

res

layout

This layout will be used by devices with smaller screens.

activity_main.xml

Large devices like tablets will load layout files from the layout-large folder. layout-large

This layout will be used by devices with a large screen.

activity_main.xml

On the next page, we'll show you all the different options you can use for your resource folder names.

The different folder options

You can put all kinds of resources (drawables or images, layouts, menus, and values) in different folders to specify which types of device they should be used with. The screen-specific folder name can include screen size, density, orientation and aspect ratio, with each part separated by hyphens. As an example, if you want to create a layout that will only be used by very large tablets in landscape mode, you would create a folder called *layout-xlarge-land* and put the layout file in that folder. Here are the different options you can use for the folder names:

You **must** specify a resource type.

Resource type	Screen size	Screen density	Orientation	Aspect ratio
drawable	-small	-ldpi	-land	-long
layout	-normal	-mdpi	-port	-notlong
menu	-large	-hdpi		
mipmap	-xlarge	-xhdpi		
values		-xxhdpi		
		-xxxhdpi		
		-nodpi		
		-tvdpi		

Screen density is based on dots per inch.

long is for screens that have a very high value for height.

A mipmap resource is used for application icons. Older versions of Android Studio use drawables instead.

This is for density-independent resources. Use -nodpi for any image resources you don't want to scale (e.g., a folder called drawable-nodpi).

Android decides at runtime which resources to use by checking the spec of the device and looking for the best match. If there's no exact match, it will use resources designed for a smaller screen than the current one. If resources are only available for screens *larger* than the current one, Android won't use them and the app will crash.

If you only want your app to work on devices with particular screen sizes, you can specify this in *AndroidManifest.xml* using the `<supports-screens>` attribute. As an example, if you don't want your app to run on devices with small screens, you'd use:

```
<supports-screens android:smallScreens="false"/>
```

Using the different folder names above, you can create layouts that are tailored for phones and tablets.

For more information on the settings on this page, see:

https://developer.android.com/guide/practices/screens_support.html.

BE the Folder Structure

Below you'll see the code for an
activity. You want to display one
layout when it runs on devices with
large-sized screens, and
another layout when
it runs on devices with
smaller-sized screens.
Which of these folder
structures will allow you to do that?

← Here's the activity.

```java
import android.app.Activity;
import android.os.Bundle;

public class MainActivity extends Activity {

    @Override
    protected void onCreate(Bundle savedInstanceState) {
        super.onCreate(savedInstanceState);
        setContentView(R.layout.activity_main);
        ...
    }
}
```

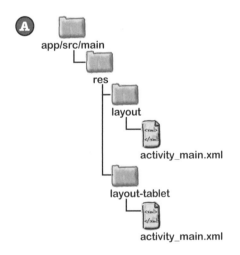

A

app/src/main
└── res
    ├── layout
    │   └── activity_main.xml
    └── layout-tablet
        └── activity_main.xml

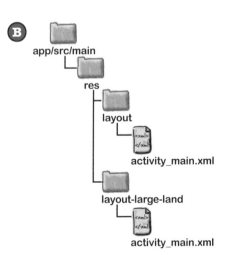

B

app/src/main
└── res
    ├── layout
    │   └── activity_main.xml
    └── layout-large-land
        └── activity_main.xml

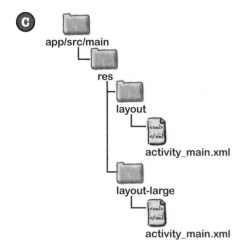

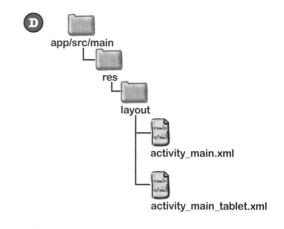

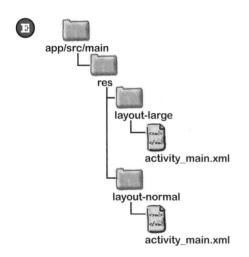

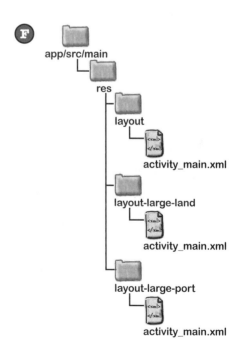

BE the Folder Structure Solution

Below you'll see the code for an activity. You want to display one layout when it runs on devices with large-sized screens, and another layout when it runs on devices with smaller-sized screens. Which of these folder structures will allow you to do that?

```java
import android.app.Activity;
import android.os.Bundle;

public class MainActivity extends Activity {

    @Override
    protected void onCreate(Bundle savedInstanceState) {
        super.onCreate(savedInstanceState);
        setContentView(R.layout.activity_main);
        ...
    }
}
```

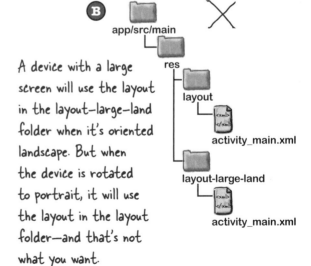

A

app/src/main
res
layout
activity_main.xml
layout-tablet
activity_main.xml

Android doesn't recognize the folder name layout-tablet. activity_main.xml in the layout folder will be displayed on all devices.

B

app/src/main
res
layout
activity_main.xml
layout-large-land
activity_main.xml

A device with a large screen will use the layout in the layout-large-land folder when it's oriented landscape. But when the device is rotated to portrait, it will use the layout in the layout folder—and that's not what you want.

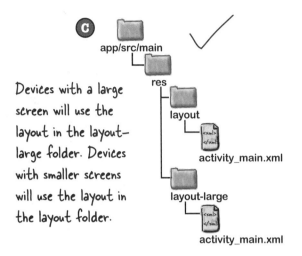

Devices with a large screen will use the layout in the layout-large folder. Devices with smaller screens will use the layout in the layout folder.

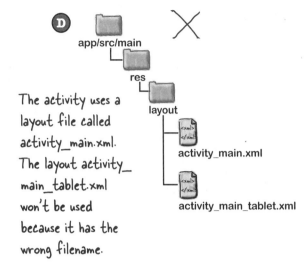

The activity uses a layout file called activity_main.xml. The layout activity_main_tablet.xml won't be used because it has the wrong filename.

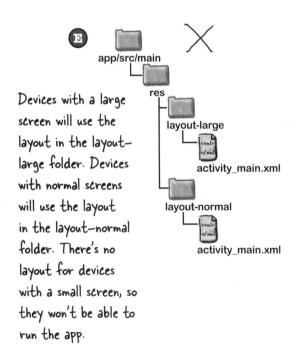

Devices with a large screen will use the layout in the layout-large folder. Devices with normal screens will use the layout in the layout-normal folder. There's no layout for devices with a small screen, so they won't be able to run the app.

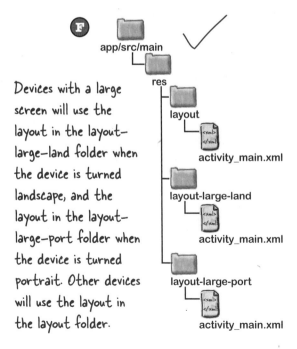

Devices with a large screen will use the layout in the layout-large-land folder when the device is turned landscape, and the layout in the layout-large-port folder when the device is turned portrait. Other devices will use the layout in the layout folder.

Tablets use layouts in the layout-large folder

To get the tablet version of our app up and running, we need to copy our existing activity layout file *activity_main.xml* into the *app/src/main/res/layout-large* folder and then update that version of the file. This layout will then only be used by devices with a large screen.

If the *app/src/main/res/layout-large* folder doesn't exist in your Android Studio project, you'll need to create it. To do this, switch to the Project view of Android Studio's explorer, highlight the *app/src/main/res* folder, and choose File→New...→Directory. When prompted, give the folder a name of "layout-large". When you click on the OK button, Android Studio will create the new *app/src/main/res/layout-large* folder.

To copy the *activity_main.xml* layout file, highlight the file in the explorer, and choose the Copy command from the Edit menu. Then highlight the new *layout-large* folder, and choose the Paste command from the Edit menu. Android Studio will copy the *activity_main.xml* file into the *app/src/main/res/layout-large* folder.

If you open the file you just pasted, it should look like this:

```xml
<?xml version="1.0" encoding="utf-8"?>
<fragment xmlns:android="http://schemas.android.com/apk/res/android"
    android:name="com.hfad.workout.WorkoutListFragment"
    android:layout_width="match_parent"
    android:layout_height="match_parent"/>
```

This is exactly the same layout that we had before. It contains a single fragment, `WorkoutListFragment`, that displays a list of workouts. The next thing we need to do is update the layout so that it displays two fragments side by side, `WorkoutListFragment` and `WorkoutDetailFragment`.

Here's the folder Android Studio created.

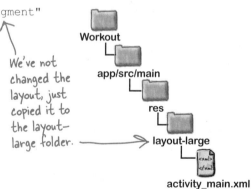

We've not changed the layout, just copied it to the layout-large folder.

The layout-large version of the layout needs to display two fragments

We're going to change the version of *activity_main.xml* in the *layout-large* folder so that it contains the two fragments. To do this, we'll add the fragments to a linear layout with the orientation set to `horizontal`. We'll adjust the width of the fragments so that `WorkoutListFragment` takes up two-fifths of the available space, and `WorkoutDetailFragment` takes up three-fifths.

Our version of *activity_main.xml* is below. Update your code to reflect our changes. Make sure that you only edit the tablet version of the layout that's in the *layout-large* folder.

> *We're putting the fragments in a LinearLayout with a horizontal orientation so the two fragments will be displayed alongside each other.*

```xml
<?xml version="1.0" encoding="utf-8"?>
<LinearLayout xmlns:android="http://schemas.android.com/apk/res/android"
    android:orientation="horizontal"
    android:layout_width="match_parent"
    android:layout_height="match_parent">

    <fragment
        android:name="com.hfad.workout.WorkoutListFragment"
        android:id="@+id/list_frag"
        android:layout_width="0dp"
        android:layout_weight="2"
        android:layout_height="match_parent"/>

    <fragment
        android:name="com.hfad.workout.WorkoutDetailFragment"
        android:id="@+id/detail_frag"
        android:layout_width="0dp"
        android:layout_weight="3"
        android:layout_height="match_parent"/>

</LinearLayout>
```

> *Our layout already includes WorkoutListFragment.*

> *The fragments need IDs so that Android doesn't lose track of where to put each fragment.*

> *We're adding WorkoutDetailFragment to MainActivity's layout.*

Workout
 └ app/src/main
    └ res
       └ layout-large
          └ activity_main.xml

We'll run through what happens when the code runs on the next page.

What the updated code does

Before we take the app for a test drive, let's go through what happens when the code runs.

① **When the app is launched, MainActivity gets created.**
MainActivity's onCreate() method runs. This specifies that *activity_main.xml* should be used for MainActivity's layout.

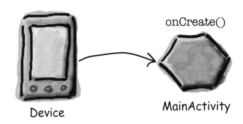

Device   MainActivity

②a **If the app's running on a tablet, it uses the version of activity_main.xml that's in the layout-large folder.**
The layout displays WorkoutListFragment and WorkoutDetailFragment side by side.

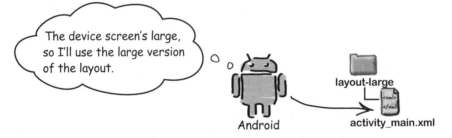

②b **If the app's running on a device with a smaller screen, it uses the version of activity_main.xml that's in the layout folder.**
The layout displays WorkoutListFragment on its own.

Test drive the app

When you run the app on a phone, the app looks just as it did before. `MainActivity` displays a list of workout names, and when you click on one of the workouts, `DetailActivity` starts and displays its details.

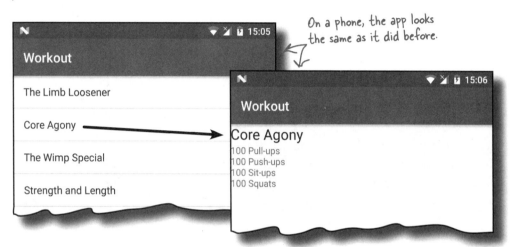

On a phone, the app looks the same as it did before.

When you run the app on a tablet, `MainActivity` displays a list of workout names on the left, and details of the first workout appear next to it.

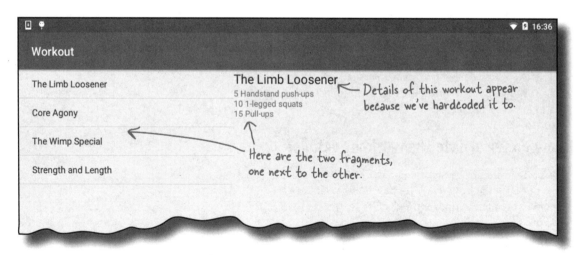

Details of this workout appear because we've hardcoded it to.

Here are the two fragments, one next to the other.

When you click on one of the workouts, `DetailActivity` still gets displayed. We need to change our code so that if the app's running on a tablet, `DetailActivity` no longer starts. Instead, we need to display details of the workout the user selects in `MainActivity`, and not just the first workout.

We need to change the itemClicked() code

Create AVD
Create layout
Show workout

We need to change the code that decides what to do when items in `WorkoutListFragment` are clicked. This means that we need to change the `itemClicked()` method in `MainActivity`. Here's the current code:

```
...

public class MainActivity extends AppCompatActivity
                    implements WorkoutListFragment.Listener {
...
    @Override
    public void itemClicked(long id) {
        Intent intent = new Intent(this, DetailActivity.class);
        intent.putExtra(DetailActivity.EXTRA_WORKOUT_ID, (int)id);
        startActivity(intent);
    }
}
```

Workout
└ app/src/main
  └ java
    └ com.hfad.workout
      └ MainActivity.java

This is the itemClicked() method we wrote in the previous chapter. It starts DetailActivity, and passes it the ID of the workout that was clicked.

The current code starts `DetailActivity` whenever the user clicks on one of the workouts. We need to change the code so that this only happens if the app's running on a device with a small screen such as a phone. If the app's running on a device with a large screen, when the user picks a workout we need to display the details of the workout shown to the right of the list of workouts in `WorkoutDetailFragment`.

But how do we update the workout details?

The `WorkoutDetailFragment` updates its views when it is started. But once the fragment is displayed onscreen, how do we get the fragment to update the details?

You might be thinking that we could play with the fragment's lifecycle so that we get it to update. Instead, **we'll replace the detail fragment with a *brand-new* detail fragment, each time we want its text to change**.

There's a really good reason why...

You want fragments to work with the Back button

Suppose you have a user that runs the app on a phone. When they click on a workout, details of that workout are displayed in a separate activity. If the user clicks on the Back button, they're returned to the list of workouts:

Then suppose the user runs the app on a tablet, and clicks on one workout, followed by a second workout. If they click on the Back button, they're probably going to expect to be returned to the first workout they chose:

In every app we've built so far, when we've clicked on the Back button, we've been returned to the previous activity. This is standard Android behavior, and something that Android has handled for us automatically. If we're running this particular app on a tablet, however, we don't want the Back button to return us to the previous *activity*. We want it to return us to the previous *fragment state*.

Welcome to the back stack

When you go from activity to activity in your app, Android keeps track of each activity you've visited by adding it to the **back stack**. The back stack is a log of the places you've visited on the device, each place recorded as a separate transaction.

A back stack scenario

1 Suppose you start by visiting a fictitious activity in your app, `Activity1`. Android records your visit to `Activity1` on the back stack as a transaction.

2 You then go to `Activity2`. Your visit to `Activity2` is added to the top of the back stack as a separate transaction.

3 You then go to `Activity3`. `Activity3` is added to the top of the back stack.

4 When you click on the Back button, `Activity3` pops off the top of the back stack. Android displays `Activity2`, as this activity is now at the top of the back stack.

5 If you click on the Back button again, `Activity2` pops off the top of the back stack, and `Activity1` is displayed.

Back stack transactions don't have to be activities

We've shown you how the back stack works with activities, but the truth is, it doesn't just apply to activities. It applies to any sort of transaction, including changes to fragments.

These are two different fragment transactions for WorkoutDetailFragment. The top one displays details of the Core Agony workout, and the bottom one displays details of the Wimp Special.

This means that *fragment* changes can be reversed when you click on the Back button, just like *activity* changes can.

When you click on the Back button, the transaction that contains details of the Core Agony is popped off the top of the back stack. Details of the Wimp Special are displayed.

So how can we record changes to fragments as separate transactions on the back stack?

Don't update—instead, replace

We're going to replace the entire `WorkoutDetailFragment` with a new instance of it each time the user selects a different workout. Each new instance of `WorkoutDetailFragment` will be set up to display details of the workout the user selects. That way, we can add each fragment replacement to the back stack as a separate transaction. Each time the user clicks on the Back button, the most recent transaction will be popped off the top of the stack, and the user will see details of the previous workout they selected.

To do this, we first need to know how to replace one fragment with another. We'll look at this on the next page.

> **Android builds the back stack as you navigate from one activity to another. Each activity is recorded in a separate transaction.**

Use a frame layout to replace fragments programmatically

To replace one fragment with another in `MainActivity`'s tablet user interface, we need to begin by making a change to the *activity_main.xml* layout file in the *layout-large* folder. Instead of inserting `WorkoutDetailFragment` directly using the `<fragment>` element, we'll use a frame layout. ← *We covered frame layouts in Chapter 5.*

We'll add the fragment to the frame layout programmatically. Whenever an item in the `WorkoutListFragment` list view gets clicked, we'll replace the contents of the frame layout with a new instance of `WorkoutDetailFragment` that displays details of the correct workout.

Here's our new version of the code for *activity_main.xml* in the *layout-large* folder. Update your code to include our changes.

Add a fragment using a <FrameLayout> whenever you need to replace fragments programmatically, such as when you need to add fragment changes to the back stack.

```xml
<?xml version="1.0" encoding="utf-8"?>
<LinearLayout xmlns:android="http://schemas.android.com/apk/res/android"
    android:orientation="horizontal"
    android:layout_width="match_parent"
    android:layout_height="match_parent">

    <fragment
        android:name="com.hfad.workout.WorkoutListFragment"
        android:id="@+id/list_frag"
        android:layout_width="0dp"
        android:layout_weight="2"
        android:layout_height="match_parent"/>
```

Workout
└ app/src/main
  └ res
    └ layout-large
      └ activity_main.xml

```xml
    <fragment
    <FrameLayout                        We're going to display the
                                        fragment inside a FrameLayout.
        android:name="com.hfad.workout.WorkoutDetailFragment"       We'll add the fragment
        android:id="@+id/detail_frag"                               to the frame layout
        android:id="@+id/fragment_container"                        programmatically.
        android:layout_width="0dp"      We'll give the FrameLayout an ID
        android:layout_weight="3"       of fragment_container so we can
        android:layout_height="match_parent"/>   refer to it in our activity code.

</LinearLayout>
```

Use layout differences to tell which layout the device is using

We want `MainActivity` to perform different actions when the user clicks on a workout depending on whether the device is running on a phone or a tablet. We can tell which version of the layout's being used by checking whether or not the layout includes the frame layout we added on the previous page.

If the app is running on a tablet, the device will be using the version of *activity_main.xml* that's in the *layout-large* folder. This layout includes a frame layout with an ID of `fragment_container`. When the user clicks on a workout, we want to display a new instance of `WorkoutDetailFragment` in the frame layout.

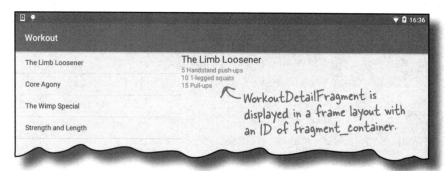

WorkoutDetailFragment is displayed in a frame layout with an ID of fragment_container.

If the app's running on a phone, the device will be using *activity_main.xml* in the *layout* folder. This layout doesn't include the frame layout. If the user clicks on a workout, we want `MainActivity` to start `DetailActivity` as it does currently.

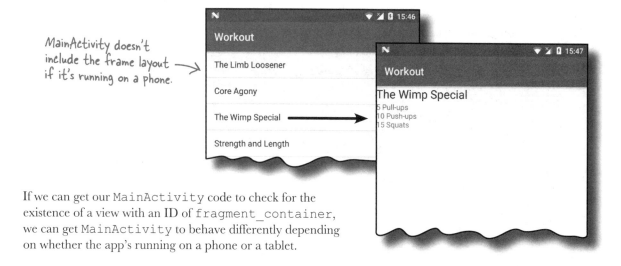

MainActivity doesn't include the frame layout if it's running on a phone.

If we can get our `MainActivity` code to check for the existence of a view with an ID of `fragment_container`, we can get `MainActivity` to behave differently depending on whether the app's running on a phone or a tablet.

The revised MainActivity code

We've updated MainActivity so that the itemClicked()
method looks for a view with an ID of fragment_
container. We can then perform different actions depending
on whether or not the view is found.

Here's our full code for *MainActivity.java*; update your version of
the code to match ours:

```
package com.hfad.workout;

import android.support.v7.app.AppCompatActivity;
import android.os.Bundle;
import android.view.View;
import android.content.Intent;

public class MainActivity extends AppCompatActivity
                        implements WorkoutListFragment.Listener {

    @Override
    protected void onCreate(Bundle savedInstanceState) {
        super.onCreate(savedInstanceState);
        setContentView(R.layout.activity_main);
    }

    @Override
    public void itemClicked(long id) {
        View fragmentContainer = findViewById(R.id.fragment_container);
        if (fragmentContainer != null) {
            //Add the fragment to the FrameLayout
        } else {
            Intent intent = new Intent(this, DetailActivity.class);
            intent.putExtra(DetailActivity.EXTRA_WORKOUT_ID, (int) id);
            startActivity(intent);
        }
    }
}
```

We've not changed this method.

Get a reference to the frame layout that will contain WorkoutDetailFragment. This will only exist if the app is being run on a device with a large screen.

We need to write code that will run if the frame layout exists.

If the frame layout doesn't exist, the app must be running on a device with a smaller screen. In that case, start DetailActivity and pass it the ID of the workout as before.

Folder hierarchy:
Workout
└ **app/src/main**
  └ **java**
    └ **com.hfad.workout**
      └ **MainActivity.java**

The next thing we need to do is see how we can add
WorkoutDetailFragment to the frame layout programmatically.

Using fragment transactions

You can programmatically add a fragment to an activity's layout so long as the activity's running. All you need is a view group in which to place the fragment, such as a frame layout.

You add, replace, or remove fragments at runtime using a **fragment transaction**. A fragment transaction is a set of changes relating to the fragment that you want to apply, all at the same time.

When you create a fragment transaction, you need to do three things:

1 **Begin the transaction.**
This tells Android that you're starting a series of changes that you want to record in the transaction.

2 **Specify the changes.**
These are all the actions you want to group together in the transaction. This can include adding, replacing, or removing a fragment, updating its data, and adding it to the back stack.

3 **Commit the transaction.**
This finishes the transaction and applies the changes.

1. Begin the transaction

You begin the transaction by first getting a reference to the activity's fragment manager. As you may remember from the previous chapter, the fragment manager is used to manage any fragments used by the activity. If you're using fragments from the Support Library as we are here, you get a reference to the fragment manager using the following method:

```
getSupportFragmentManager();
```

← This returns the fragment manager that deals with fragments from the Support Library.

Once you have a reference to the fragment manager, you call its `beginTransaction()` method to begin the transaction:

```
FragmentTransaction transaction = getSupportFragmentManager().beginTransaction();
```

↑
The start of the fragment transaction

That's all you need to do to begin the transaction. On the next page we'll look at how you specify the changes you want to make.

2. Specify the changes

After beginning the transaction, you need to say what changes the transaction should include.

If you want to add a fragment to your activity's layout, you call the fragment transaction's add() method. This takes two parameters, the resource ID of the view group you want to add the fragment to, and the fragment you want to add. The code looks like this:

```
WorkoutDetailFragment fragment = new WorkoutDetailFragment();
transaction.add(R.id.fragment_container, fragment);
```
← Create the fragment.

← Add the fragment to the ViewGroup.

To replace the fragment, you use the replace() method:

```
transaction.replace(R.id.fragment_container, fragment);
```
← Replace the fragment.

To remove the fragment completely, you use the remove() method:

```
transaction.remove(fragment);
```
← Remove the fragment.

You can optionally use the setTransition() method to say what sort of transition animation you want for this transaction:

```
transaction.setTransition(transition);
```
← You don't have to set a transition.

transition is the type of animation. Options for this are TRANSIT_FRAGMENT_CLOSE (a fragment is being removed from the stack), TRANSIT_FRAGMENT_OPEN (a fragment is being added), TRANSIT_FRAGMENT_FADE (the fragment should fade in and out), and TRANSIT_NONE (no animation). By default, there are no animations.

Once you've specified all the actions you want to take as part of the transaction, you can use the addToBackStack() method to add the transaction to the back stack. This method takes one parameter, a String name you can use to label the transaction. This parameter is needed if you need to programmatically retrieve the transaction. Most of the time you won't need to do this, so you can pass in a null value like this:

```
transaction.addToBackStack(null);
```
← Most of the time you won't need to retrieve the transaction, so it can be set to null.

3. Commit the transaction

Finally, you need to commit the transaction. This finishes the transaction, and applies the changes you specified. You commit the transaction by calling the transaction's commit() method like this:

```
transaction.commit();
```

That's everything we need to know in order to create fragment transactions, so let's put it into practice by getting our MainActivity code to display an updated version of WorkoutDetailFragment every time the user clicks on a workout.

 **Activity Magnets**

We want to write a new version of the MainActivity's itemClicked() method. It needs to change the workout details that are displayed in WorkoutDetailFragment each time the user clicks on a new workout. See if you can finish the code below.

```
public void itemClicked(long id) {
    View fragmentContainer = findViewById(R.id.fragment_container);
    if (fragmentContainer != null) {
        WorkoutDetailFragment details = new WorkoutDetailFragment();

        FragmentTransaction ft = getSupportFragmentManager()..................................................;
        details.setWorkout(id);

        ft.............................(R.id.fragment_container, ...............................);

        ft..........................................(FragmentTransaction.TRANSIT_FRAGMENT_FADE);

        ft...........................................(null);

        ft...........................;
    } else {
        Intent intent = new Intent(this, DetailActivity.class);
        intent.putExtra(DetailActivity.EXTRA_WORKOUT_ID, (int) id);
        startActivity(intent);
    }
}
```

You won't need to use all of the magnets.

replace

commit()

beginTransaction()   setTransition

startTransaction()

details   endTransaction()   addToBackStack

Activity Magnets Solution

We want to write a new version of the MainActivity's itemClicked() method. It needs to change the workout details that are displayed in WorkoutDetailFragment each time the user clicks on a new workout. See if you can finish the code below.

```java
public void itemClicked(long id) {
    View fragmentContainer = findViewById(R.id.fragment_container);
    if (fragmentContainer != null) {
        WorkoutDetailFragment details = new WorkoutDetailFragment();

        FragmentTransaction ft = getSupportFragmentManager().beginTransaction();
        details.setWorkout(id);

        ft.replace(R.id.fragment_container, details);
        ft.setTransition(FragmentTransaction.TRANSIT_FRAGMENT_FADE);
        ft.addToBackStack(null);
        ft.commit();
    } else {
        Intent intent = new Intent(this, DetailActivity.class);
        intent.putExtra(DetailActivity.EXTRA_WORKOUT_ID, (int) id);
        startActivity(intent);
    }
}
```

This begins the transaction. → `beginTransaction()`

This is a new instance of WorkoutDetailFragment. It displays details of the workout the user selected. → `details`

Each time the user clicks on a workout, we'll replace the fragment with a new instance of it. → `replace`

Set the fragment to fade in and out. → `setTransition`

Add the transaction to the back stack. → `addToBackStack`

Commit the transaction. → `commit()`

`endTransaction()` ← *You didn't need to use these magnets.* → `startTransaction()`

The updated MainActivity code

We're going to get a new instance of `WorkoutDetailFragment`
(one that displays the correct workout), display the fragment in the
activity, and then add the transaction to the back stack. Here's the full
code. Update your version of *MainActivity.java* to reflect our changes:

```java
package com.hfad.workout;

import android.support.v4.app.FragmentTransaction;
...
```

We're using a FragmentTransaction from the Support Library as we're using Support Library Fragments.

```java
public class MainActivity extends AppCompatActivity
                        implements WorkoutListFragment.Listener {
```

We haven't changed this method.

```java
    @Override
    protected void onCreate(Bundle savedInstanceState) {
        super.onCreate(savedInstanceState);
        setContentView(R.layout.activity_main);
    }
```

Workout
app/src/main
java
com.hfad.workout
MainActivity.java

```java
    @Override
    public void itemClicked(long id) {
        View fragmentContainer = findViewById(R.id.fragment_container);
        if (fragmentContainer != null) {
            WorkoutDetailFragment details = new WorkoutDetailFragment();
            FragmentTransaction ft = getSupportFragmentManager().beginTransaction();
            details.setWorkout(id);
            ft.replace(R.id.fragment_container, details);
            ft.setTransition(FragmentTransaction.TRANSIT_FRAGMENT_FADE);
            ft.addToBackStack(null);
            ft.commit();
        } else {
            Intent intent = new Intent(this, DetailActivity.class);
            intent.putExtra(DetailActivity.EXTRA_WORKOUT_ID, (int) id);
            startActivity(intent);
        }
    }
}
```

Start the fragment transaction.

Add the transaction to the back stack.

← Replace the fragment.

← Get the new and old fragments to fade in and out.

← Commit the transaction.

On the next page we'll see what happens when the code runs.

What happens when the code runs

Here's a runthrough of what happens when we run the app.

1 **The app is launched on a tablet and MainActivity starts.**
WorkoutListFragment is attached to MainActivity, and MainActivity is registered as a listener on WorkoutListFragment.

Tablet   MainActivity   WorkoutListFragment

2 **When an item is clicked in WorkoutListFragment, the fragment's onListItemClick() method is called.**
This calls MainActivity's itemClicked() method, passing it the ID of the workout that was clicked; in this example, the ID is 1.

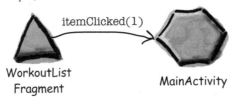

WorkoutList Fragment   MainActivity

3 **MainActivity's itemClicked() method sees that the app is running on a tablet.**
It creates a new instance of WorkoutDetailFragment, and begins a new fragment transaction.

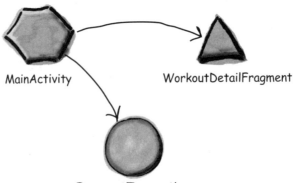

MainActivity   WorkoutDetailFragment

FragmentTransaction

The story continues...

④ **As part of the transaction, WorkoutDetailFragment's views are updated with details of the workout that was selected, in this case the one with ID 1.**
The fragment is added to the `FrameLayout fragment_container` in `MainActivity`'s layout, and the whole transaction is added to the back stack.

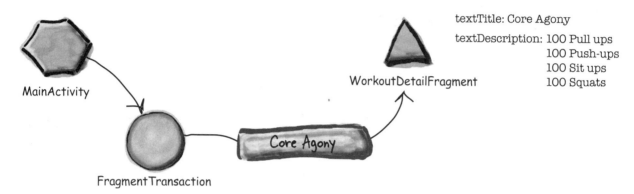

MainActivity

FragmentTransaction

Core Agony

WorkoutDetailFragment

textTitle: Core Agony

textDescription: 100 Pull ups
100 Push-ups
100 Sit ups
100 Squats

⑤ **MainActivity commits the transaction.**
All of the changes specified in the transaction take effect, and the `WorkoutDetailFragment` is displayed next to `WorkoutListFragment`.

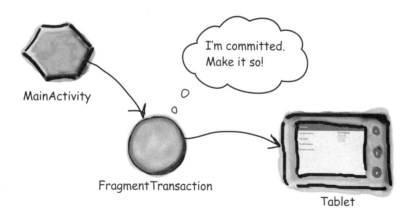

MainActivity

I'm committed. Make it so!

FragmentTransaction

Tablet

Let's take the app for a test drive.

Create AVD
Create layout
Show workout

When we run the app, a list of the workouts appears on the left side of the screen. When we click on one of the workouts, details of that workout appear on the right. If we click on another workout and then click on the Back button, details of the workout we chose previously appear on the screen.

The app seems to be working fine as long as we don't rotate the screen. If we change the screen orientation, there's a problem. Let's see what happens.

Rotating the tablet breaks the app

When you run the app on a phone and rotate the device, the app works as you'd expect. Details of the workout the user selected continue to be displayed on the screen:

When we run the app on a phone and rotate it, the app continues to display details of the workout we selected.

But when you run the app on a tablet, there's a problem. Regardless of which workout you've chosen, when you rotate the device, the app displays details of the first workout in the list:

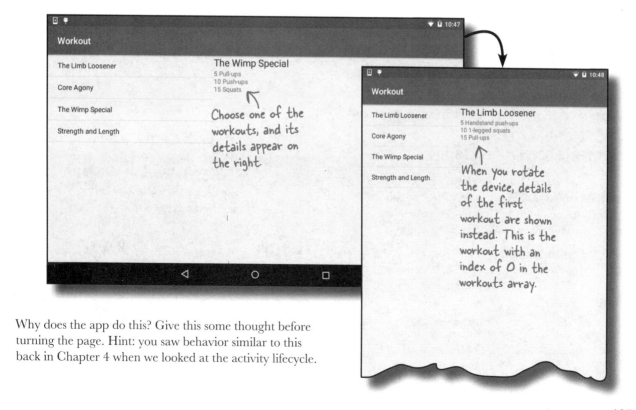

Choose one of the workouts, and its details appear on the right.

When you rotate the device, details of the first workout are shown instead. This is the workout with an index of 0 in the workouts array.

Why does the app do this? Give this some thought before turning the page. Hint: you saw behavior similar to this back in Chapter 4 when we looked at the activity lifecycle.

Saving an activity's state (revisited)

When we first looked at the activity lifecycle back in Chapter 4, you saw how when you rotate the device, Android destroys and recreates the activity. When this happens, local variables used by the activity can get lost. To prevent this from happening, we saved the state of our local variables in the activity's onSaveInstanceState() method:

```
public void onSaveInstanceState(Bundle savedInstanceState) {
    savedInstanceState.putInt("seconds", seconds);
    savedInstanceState.putBoolean("running", running);
}
```

Earlier in the book, we used the onSaveInstanceState() method to save the state of these two variables.

We then restored the state of the variables in the activity's onCreate() method:

```
protected void onCreate(Bundle savedInstanceState) {
    ...
    if (savedInstanceState != null) {
        seconds = savedInstanceState.getInt("seconds");
        running = savedInstanceState.getBoolean("running");
    }
    ...
}
```

We restored the state of the variables in the onCreate() method.

So what does this have to do with our current problem?

Fragments can lose state too

If the activity uses a fragment, **the fragment gets destroyed and recreated along with the activity**. This means that any local variables used by the fragment can also lose their state.

In our WorkoutDetailFragment code, we use a local variable called workoutId to store the ID of the workout the user clicks on in the WorkoutListFragment list view. When the user rotates the device, workoutId loses its current value and it's set to 0 by default. The fragment then displays details of the workout with an ID of 0—the first workout in the list.

When you rotate the tablet, WorkoutDetailFragment loses the value of workoutId, and sets it back to its default value of 0.

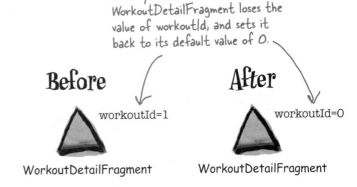

Before

workoutId=1

WorkoutDetailFragment

After

workoutId=0

WorkoutDetailFragment

Save the fragment's state...

You deal with this problem in a fragment in a similar way to how you deal with it in an activity.

You first override the fragment's `onSaveInstanceState()` method. This method works in a similar way to an activity's `onSaveInstanceState()` method. It gets called before the fragment gets destroyed, and it has one parameter: a `Bundle`. You use the `Bundle` to save the values of any variables whose state you need to keep.

In our case, we want to save the state of our `workoutId` variable, so we'd use code like this:

```java
public void onSaveInstanceState(Bundle savedInstanceState) {
    savedInstanceState.putLong("workoutId", workoutId);
}
```

The onSaveInstanceState() method gets called before the fragment is destroyed.

Once you've saved the state of any variables, you can restore it when the fragment is recreated.

...then use onCreate() to restore the state

Just like an activity, a fragment has an `onCreate()` method that has one parameter, a `Bundle`. This is the `Bundle` to which you saved the state of your variables in the fragment's `onSaveInstanceState()` method, so you can use it to restore the state of those variables in your fragment's `onCreate()` method.

In our case, we want to restore the state of the `workoutId` variable, so we can use code like this:

```java
public void onCreate(Bundle savedInstanceState){
    super.onCreate(savedInstanceState);
    if (savedInstanceState != null) {
        workoutId = savedInstanceState.getLong("workoutId");
    }
}
```

We can use this Bundle to get the previous state of the workoutId variable.

We'll show you the full code on the next page.

The updated code for
WorkoutDetailFragment.java

We've updated our code for *WorkoutDetailFragment.java* to save
the state of the `workoutId` variable before the fragment is
destroyed, and restore it if the fragment is recreated. Here's our
code; update your version of *WorkoutDetailFragment.java* to reflect
our changes.

```java
package com.hfad.workout;

import android.support.v4.app.Fragment;
import android.os.Bundle;
import android.view.LayoutInflater;
import android.view.View;
import android.view.ViewGroup;
import android.widget.TextView;

public class WorkoutDetailFragment extends Fragment {
    private long workoutId;

    @Override
    public void onCreate(Bundle savedInstanceState){
        super.onCreate(savedInstanceState);
        if (savedInstanceState != null) {
            workoutId = savedInstanceState.getLong("workoutId");
        }
    }

    @Override
    public View onCreateView(LayoutInflater inflater, ViewGroup container,
                             Bundle savedInstanceState) {
        return inflater.inflate(R.layout.fragment_workout_detail, container, false);
    }
```

Add the onCreate() method.

Set the value of the workoutId.

```
Workout
  └ app/src/main
      └ java
          └ com.hfad.workout
              └ WorkoutDetail
                Fragment.java
```

The code continues
on the next page.

WorkoutDetailFragment.java (continued)

```java
@Override
public void onStart() {
    super.onStart();
    View view = getView();
    if (view != null) {
        TextView title = (TextView) view.findViewById(R.id.textTitle);
        Workout workout = Workout.workouts[(int) workoutId];
        title.setText(workout.getName());
        TextView description = (TextView) view.findViewById(R.id.textDescription);
        description.setText(workout.getDescription());
    }
}

@Override
public void onSaveInstanceState(Bundle savedInstanceState) {
    savedInstanceState.putLong("workoutId", workoutId);
}

public void setWorkout(long id) {
    this.workoutId = id;
}
```

Save the value of the workoutId in the savedInstanceState Bundle before the fragment gets destroyed. We're retrieving it in the onCreate() method.

Workout

app/src/main

java

com.hfad.workout

WorkoutDetail
Fragment.java

Test drive the app

Now, when you run the app on a tablet and rotate the device, details of
the workout the user selected continue to be displayed on the screen.

When you click on one of the workouts, its details continue to be displayed when you rotate the device.

431

Your Android Toolbox

You've got Chapter 10 under your belt and now you've added fragments for larger interfaces to your toolbox.

You can download the full code for the chapter from https://tinyurl.com/ HeadFirstAndroid.

BULLET POINTS

- Make apps look different on different devices by putting separate layouts in device-appropriate folders.

- Android keeps track of places you've visited within an app by adding them to the back stack as separate transactions. Pressing the Back button pops the last transaction off the back stack.

- Use a frame layout to add, replace, or remove fragments programmatically using fragment transactions.

- Begin the transaction by calling the `FragmentManager beginTransaction()` method. This creates a `FragmentTransaction` object.

- Add, replace, and delete fragments using the `FragmentTransaction add()`, `replace()`, and `remove()` methods.

- Add a transaction to the back stack using the `FragmentTransaction addToBackStack()` method.

- Commit a transaction using the `FragmentTransaction commit()` method. This applies all the updates in the transaction.

- Save the state of a fragment's variables in the `Fragment onSaveInstanceState()` method.

- Restore the state of a fragment's variables in the `Fragment onCreate()` method.

11 dynamic fragments

Nesting Fragments

The Back button was going crazy, transactions everywhere. So I hit them with the getChildFragmentManager() method and BAM! Everything went back to normal.

So far you've seen how to create and use static fragments.

But what if you want your fragments to be more **dynamic**? Dynamic fragments have a lot in common with dynamic activities, but there are crucial differences you need to be able to deal with. In this chapter you'll see how to **convert dynamic activities** into **working dynamic fragments**. You'll find out how to use **fragment transactions** to help **maintain your fragment state**. Finally, you'll discover how to **nest one fragment inside another**, and how the **child fragment manager** helps you control unruly back stack behavior.

Adding dynamic fragments

In Chapters 9 and 10, you saw how to create fragments, how to include them in activities, and how to connect them together. To do this, we created a list fragment displaying a list of workouts, and a fragment displaying details of a single workout.

These fragments we've created so far have both been static. Once the fragments are displayed, their contents don't change. We may completely replace the fragment that's displayed with a new instance, but we can't update the contents of the fragment itself.

In this chapter we're going to look at how you deal with a fragment that's more dynamic. By this, we mean a fragment whose views gets updated after the fragment is displayed. To learn how to do, we're going to change the stopwatch *activity* we created in Chapter 4 into a stopwatch *fragment*. We're going to add our new stopwatch fragment to `WorkoutDetailFragment` so that it's displayed underneath the details of the workout.

We're only showing the tablet version of the app here, but the new stopwatch fragment will appear in the phone version too.

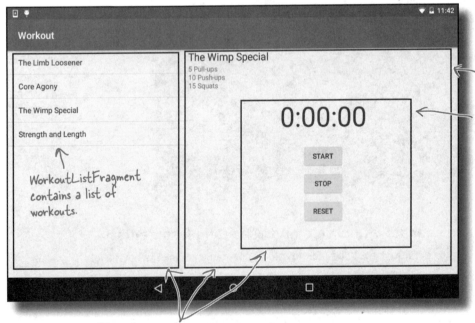

WorkoutDetailFragment displays details of the workout the user clicks on.

We're going to add a stopwatch fragment to WorkoutDetailFragment.

WorkoutListFragment contains a list of workouts.

These lines won't appear in the actual app. We've added them here to show you each of the fragments.

Here's what we're going to do

There are a number of steps we'll go through to change the
app to display the stopwatch:

1 **Convert StopwatchActivity into StopwatchFragment.**
We'll take the `StopwatchActivity` code we created in
Chapter 4, and change it into fragment code. We'll also display
it in a new temporary activity called `TempActivity` so that
we can check that it works. We'll temporarily change the app
so that `TempActivity` starts when the app gets launched.

2 **Test StopwatchFragment.**
The `StopwatchActivity` included Start, Stop, and Reset
buttons. We need to check that these still work when the
stopwatch code is in a fragment.

We also need to test what happens to `StopwatchFragment`
when the user rotates the device.

We'll start by adding
StopwatchFragment
to a new activity
called TempActivity.

3 **Add StopwatchFragment to WorkoutDetailFragment.**
Once we're satisfied that `StopwatchFragment` works, we'll
add it to `WorkoutDetailFragment`.

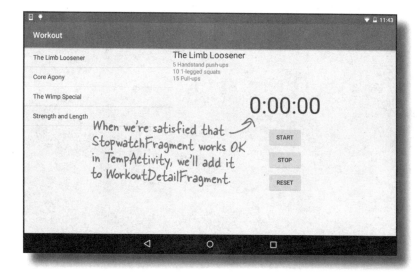

When we're satisfied that
StopwatchFragment works OK
in TempActivity, we'll add it
to WorkoutDetailFragment.

Let's get started.

Do this!

**We're going to update the Workout
app in this chapter, so open your
original Workout project from
Chapter 9 in Android Studio.**

The new version of the app

We're going to change our app to get StopwatchFragment working in a new temporary activity called TempActivity. This will enable us to confirm that StopwatchFragment works before we add it to WorkoutDetailFragment later in the chapter.

Here's how the new version of the app will work:

1 **When the app gets launched, it starts TempActivity.**
TempActivity uses *activity_temp.xml* for its layout, and contains a fragment, StopwatchFragment.

2 **StopwatchFragment displays a stopwatch with Start, Stop, and Reset buttons.**

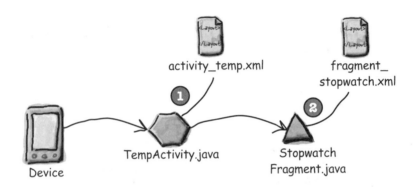

activity_temp.xml

fragment_
stopwatch.xml

TempActivity.java

Stopwatch
Fragment.java

Device

All of the other activities and fragments we created in Chapters 9 and 10 will still exist in the project, but we're not going to do anything with them until later in the chapter.

Create TempActivity

We'll start by creating `TempActivity`. Create a new empty activity by switching to the Project view of Android Studio's explorer, highlighting the *com.hfad.workout* package in the *app/src/main/java* folder, going to the File menu and choosing New...→Activity→Empty Activity. Name the activity "TempActivity", name the layout "activity_temp", make sure the package name is `com.hfad.workout`, and **check the Backwards Compatibility (AppCompat) checkbox**.

If prompted for the activity's source language, select the option for Java.

We're going to change our app so that, when it's launched, it starts `TempActivity` instead of `MainActivity`. To do this, we need to move `MainActivity`'s launcher intent filter to `TempActivity` instead. Open the file *AndroidManifest.xml* in the *app/src/main* folder, then make the following changes:

```xml
<?xml version="1.0" encoding="utf-8"?>
<manifest xmlns:android="http://schemas.android.com/apk/res/android"
    package="com.hfad.workout">

    <application
        ...
        <activity android:name=".MainActivity">
            <intent-filter>
                <action android:name="android.intent.action.MAIN" />
                <category android:name="android.intent.category.LAUNCHER" />
            </intent-filter>
        </activity>
        <activity android:name=".DetailActivity" />
        <activity android:name=".TempActivity">
            <intent-filter>
                <action android:name="android.intent.action.MAIN" />
                <category android:name="android.intent.category.LAUNCHER" />
            </intent-filter>
        </activity>
    </application>

</manifest>
```

Workout
app/src/main
AndroidManifest.xml

This bit specifies that it's the main activity of the app.

This says the activity can be used to launch the app.

We'll update `TempActivity` on the next page.

TempActivity needs to extend AppCompatActivity

☐ **Convert stopwatch**
☐ **Test stopwatch**
☐ **Add to fragment**

All of the fragments we're using in this app come from the Support Library. As we said back in Chapter 9, all activities that use Support Library fragments must extend the `FragmentActivity` class or one of its subclasses such as `AppCompatActivity`. If they don't, the code will break.

All of the other activities we've created in this app extend `AppCompatActivity`, so we'll make `TempActivity` extend this class too. Here's our code for *TempActivity.java*. Update your version of the code so that it matches ours below:

```java
package com.hfad.workout;

import android.support.v7.app.AppCompatActivity;
import android.os.Bundle;

public class TempActivity extends AppCompatActivity {

    @Override
    protected void onCreate(Bundle savedInstanceState) {
        super.onCreate(savedInstanceState);
        setContentView(R.layout.activity_temp);
    }
}
```

The activity extends AppCompatActivity.

Workout

└ app/src/main

└ java

└ com.hfad.workout

└ TempActivity.java

We'll add a new stopwatch fragment

We're going to add a new stopwatch fragment called *StopwatchFragment.java* that uses a layout called *fragment_stopwatch.xml*. We're going to base the fragment on the stopwatch activity we created back in Chapter 4.

We already know that activities and fragments behave in similar ways, but we also know that a fragment is a distinct type of object—a fragment is not a subclass of activity. **Is there some way we could rewrite that stopwatch activity code so that it works like a fragment?**

Fragments and activities have similar lifecycles...

To understand how to rewrite an activity as a fragment, we need to think a little about the similarities and differences between them. If we look at the lifecycles of fragments and activities, we'll see that they're very similar:

Lifecycle method	Activity	Fragment
onAttach()		✓
onCreate()	✓	✓
onCreateView()		✓
onActivityCreated()		✓
onStart()	✓	✓
onPause()	✓	✓
onResume()	✓	✓
onStop()	✓	✓
onDestroyView()		✓
onRestart()	✓	
onDestroy()	✓	✓
onDetach()		✓

...but the methods are slightly different

Fragment lifecycle methods are almost the same as activity lifecycle methods, but there's one major difference: activity lifecycle methods are **protected** and fragment lifecycle methods are **public**. And we've already seen that the ways that activities and fragments create a layout from a layout resource file are different.

Also, in a fragment, we can't call methods like findViewById() directly. Instead, we need to find a reference to a View object, and then call the view's findViewById() method.

With these similarities and differences in mind, it's time you started to write some code...

Sharpen your pencil

This is the code for `StopwatchActivity` we wrote earlier. You're going to convert this code into a fragment called `StopwatchFragment`. With a pencil, make the changes you need. Keep the following things in mind:

- Instead of a layout file called *activity_stopwatch.xml*, it will use a layout called *fragment_stopwatch.xml*.

- Make sure the access restrictions on the methods are correct.

- How will you specify the layout?

- The `runTimer()` method won't be able to call `findViewById()`, so you might want to pass a `View` object into `runTimer()`.

```
public class StopwatchActivity extends Activity {
    //Number of seconds displayed on the stopwatch.
    private int seconds = 0;    ←——The number of seconds that have passed
    //Is the stopwatch running?
    private boolean running;    ←——running says whether the stopwatch is running.
    private boolean wasRunning;  ←  wasRunning says whether the stopwatch was running
                                      before the stopwatch was paused.

    @Override
    protected void onCreate(Bundle savedInstanceState) {
        super.onCreate(savedInstanceState);
        setContentView(R.layout.activity_stopwatch);
        if (savedInstanceState != null) {
            seconds = savedInstanceState.getInt("seconds");
            running = savedInstanceState.getBoolean("running");
            wasRunning = savedInstanceState.getBoolean("wasRunning");
        }
        runTimer();    ←——Start the runTimer() method.
    }


    @Override
    protected void onPause() {    ←——Stop the stopwatch if the activity is paused.
        super.onPause();
        wasRunning = running;
        running = false;
    }
```

If the activity was destroyed and recreated, restore the state of the variables from the savedInstanceState Bundle.

```
    @Override
    protected void onResume() {          ← Start the stopwatch if the activity is resumed.
        super.onResume();
        if (wasRunning) {
            running = true;
        }
    }
                                Save the activity's state before
                                the activity is destroyed.
    @Override
    public void onSaveInstanceState(Bundle savedInstanceState) {
        savedInstanceState.putInt("seconds", seconds);
        savedInstanceState.putBoolean("running", running);
        savedInstanceState.putBoolean("wasRunning", wasRunning);
    }

    public void onClickStart(View view) {
        running = true;
    }

    public void onClickStop(View view) {    ← Start, stop, or reset the stopwatch
        running = false;                       depending on which button is clicked.
    }

    public void onClickReset(View view) {
        running = false;
        seconds = 0;                    Use a Handler to post code to
    }                                   increment the number of seconds and
                                        update the text view every second.
    private void runTimer() {
        final TextView timeView = (TextView)findViewById(R.id.time_view);
        final Handler handler = new Handler();
        handler.post(new Runnable() {
            @Override
            public void run() {
                int hours = seconds/3600;
                int minutes = (seconds%3600)/60;
                int secs = seconds%60;
                String time = String.format(Locale.getDefault(),
                        "%d:%02d:%02d", hours, minutes, secs);
                timeView.setText(time);
                if (running) {
                    seconds++;
                }
                handler.postDelayed(this, 1000);
            }
        });
    }
}
```

Sharpen your pencil
Solution

This is the code for `StopwatchActivity` we wrote earlier. You're going to convert this code into a fragment called `StopwatchFragment`. With a pencil, make the changes you need. Keep the following things in mind:

- Instead of a layout file called *activity_stopwatch.xml*, it will use a layout called *fragment_stopwatch.xml*.

- Make sure the access restrictions on the methods are correct.

- How will you specify the layout?

- The `runTimer()` method won't be able to call `findViewById()`, so you might want to pass a `View` object into `runTimer()`.

This is the new name. ↓

```
public class ~~StopwatchActivity~~ StopwatchFragment extends ~~Activity~~ Fragment
    //Number of seconds displayed on the stopwatch.
    private int seconds = 0;
    //Is the stopwatch running?
    private boolean running;
    private boolean wasRunning;
```
We're extending Fragment, not Activity.

← This method needs to be public.

```
    @Override
    ~~protected~~ public void onCreate(Bundle savedInstanceState) {
        super.onCreate(savedInstanceState);
        ~~setContentView(R.layout.activity_stopwatch);~~
        if (savedInstanceState != null) {
            seconds = savedInstanceState.getInt("seconds");
            running = savedInstanceState.getBoolean("running");
            wasRunning = savedInstanceState.getBoolean("wasRunning");
        }
        ~~runTimer();~~
    }
```
← You don't set a fragment's layout in its onCreate() method.

← We're not calling runTimer() yet because we've not set the layout—we don't have any views yet.

We can leave this code in the onCreate() method.

We set the fragment's layout in the onCreateView() method.

```
    @Override
    public View onCreateView(LayoutInflater inflater, ViewGroup container,
                    Bundle savedInstanceState) {
        View layout = inflater.inflate(R.layout.fragment_stopwatch, container, false);
        runTimer(layout);
        return layout;
    }
```
← Pass the layout view to the runTimer() method.

← This method needs to be public.

```
    @Override
    ~~protected~~ public void onPause() {
        super.onPause();
        wasRunning = running;
        running = false;
    }
```

```
@Override                ← This method needs to be public.
protected public  void onResume() {
    super.onResume();
    if (wasRunning) {
        running = true;
    }
}

@Override
public void onSaveInstanceState(Bundle savedInstanceState) {
    savedInstanceState.putInt("seconds", seconds);
    savedInstanceState.putBoolean("running", running);
    savedInstanceState.putBoolean("wasRunning", wasRunning);
}

public void onClickStart(View view) {
    running = true;
}

public void onClickStop(View view) {
    running = false;
}

public void onClickReset(View view) {
    running = false;
    seconds = 0;
}
                              The runTimer() method now takes a View.
private void runTimer( View view ) {
    final TextView timeView = (TextView) view.findViewById(R.id.time_view);
    final Handler handler = new Handler();  ← Use the view parameter to call findViewById().
    handler.post(new Runnable() {
        @Override
        public void run() {
            int hours = seconds/3600;
            int minutes = (seconds%3600)/60;
            int secs = seconds%60;
            String time = String.format(Locale.getDefault(),
                    "%d:%02d:%02d", hours, minutes, secs);
            timeView.setText(time);
            if (running) {
                seconds++;
            }
            handler.postDelayed(this, 1000);
        }
    });
}
}
```

The StopwatchFragment.java code

Convert stopwatch
Test stopwatch
Add to fragment

We'll add `StopwatchFragment` to our Workout project so that we can use it in our app. You do this in the same way you did in Chapter 9. Highlight the *com.hfad.workout* package in the *app/src/main/java* folder, then go to File→New...→Fragment→Fragment (Blank). Give the fragment a name of "StopwatchFragment", give it a layout name of "fragment_stopwatch", and uncheck the options for including fragment factory methods and interface callbacks. ← *If prompted for the fragment's source language, select the option for Java.*

When you click on the Finish button, Android Studio creates a new fragment for you in a file called *StopwatchFragment.java* in the *app/src/main/java* folder. Replace the fragment code Android Studio gives you with the following code (this is the code you updated in the exercise on the previous page):

```java
package com.hfad.workout;

import android.os.Bundle;
import android.os.Handler;
import android.support.v4.app.Fragment;
import android.view.LayoutInflater;
import android.view.View;
import android.view.ViewGroup;
import android.widget.TextView;
import java.util.Locale;
```

Workout

app/src/main

java

com.hfad.workout

Stopwatch Fragment.java

```java
public class StopwatchFragment extends Fragment {
    //Number of seconds displayed on the stopwatch.
    private int seconds = 0;   //← The number of seconds that have passed
    //Is the stopwatch running?
    private boolean running;   //← running says whether the stopwatch is running.
    private boolean wasRunning;  //← wasRunning says whether the stopwatch was running
                                 //   before the stopwatch was paused.

    @Override
    public void onCreate(Bundle savedInstanceState) {
        super.onCreate(savedInstanceState);
        if (savedInstanceState != null) {      //← Restore the state of the variables
                                               //   from the savedInstanceState Bundle.
            seconds = savedInstanceState.getInt("seconds");
            running = savedInstanceState.getBoolean("running");
            wasRunning = savedInstanceState.getBoolean("wasRunning");
        }
    }
```

The code continues on the next page.

StopwatchFragment.java (continued)

```java
@Override
public View onCreateView(LayoutInflater inflater, ViewGroup container,
                         Bundle savedInstanceState) {
    View layout = inflater.inflate(R.layout.fragment_stopwatch, container, false);
    runTimer(layout);
    return layout;
}
```

← Set the fragment's layout and start the runTimer() method, passing in the layout.

```java
@Override
public void onPause() {
    super.onPause();
    wasRunning = running;
    running = false;
}
```

If the fragment's paused, record whether the stopwatch was running and stop it.

Workout
└ **app/src/main**
  └ **java**
    └ **com.hfad.workout**
      └ **Stopwatch Fragment.java**

```java
@Override
public void onResume() {
    super.onResume();
    if (wasRunning) {
        running = true;
    }
}
```

← If the stopwatch was running before it was paused, set it running again.

```java
@Override
public void onSaveInstanceState(Bundle savedInstanceState) {
    savedInstanceState.putInt("seconds", seconds);
    savedInstanceState.putBoolean("running", running);
    savedInstanceState.putBoolean("wasRunning", wasRunning);
}
```

Put the values of the variables in the Bundle before the activity is destroyed. These are used when the user turns the device.

```java
public void onClickStart(View view) {
    running = true;
}
```

This code needs to run when the user clicks on the Start button.

The code continues on the next page. →

StopwatchFragment.java (continued)

Workout

app/src/main

java

com.hfad.workout

Stopwatch
Fragment.java

```java
public void onClickStop(View view) {
    running = false;
}
```
This code needs to run when the user clicks on the Stop button.

```java
public void onClickReset(View view) {
    running = false;
    seconds = 0;
}
```
This code needs to run when the user clicks on the Reset button.

```java
private void runTimer(View view) {
    final TextView timeView = (TextView) view.findViewById(R.id.time_view);
    final Handler handler = new Handler();
    handler.post(new Runnable() {
        @Override
        public void run() {
            int hours = seconds/3600;
            int minutes = (seconds%3600)/60;
            int secs = seconds%60;
            String time = String.format(Locale.getDefault(),
                    "%d:%02d:%02d", hours, minutes, secs);
            timeView.setText(time);
            if (running) {
                seconds++;
            }
            handler.postDelayed(this, 1000);
        }
    });
}
```

Putting the code in a Handler means it can run in the background thread.

Display the number of seconds that have passed in the stopwatch.

If the stopwatch is running, increment the number of seconds.

Run the Handler code every second.

That's all the Java code we need for our
StopwatchFragment. The next thing we need to do is say
what the fragment should look like by updating the layout code
Android Studio gave us.

The StopwatchFragment layout

We'll use the same layout for StopwatchFragment as we used in our original Stopwatch app. To do so, replace the contents of *fragment_stopwatch.xml* with the code below:

```xml
<?xml version="1.0" encoding="utf-8"?>
<LinearLayout xmlns:android="http://schemas.android.com/apk/res/android"
    xmlns:tools="http://schemas.android.com/tools"
    android:layout_width="match_parent"
    android:layout_height="match_parent"
    android:orientation="vertical"
    android:padding="16dp">

    <TextView
        android:id="@+id/time_view"
        android:layout_width="wrap_content"
        android:layout_height="wrap_content"
        android:layout_gravity="center_horizontal"
        android:textAppearance="@android:style/TextAppearance.Large"
        android:textSize="56sp" />

    <Button
        android:id="@+id/start_button"
        android:layout_width="wrap_content"
        android:layout_height="wrap_content"
        android:layout_gravity="center_horizontal"
        android:layout_marginTop="20dp"
        android:onClick="onClickStart"
        android:text="@string/start" />

    <Button
        android:id="@+id/stop_button"
        android:layout_width="wrap_content"
        android:layout_height="wrap_content"
        android:layout_gravity="center_horizontal"
        android:layout_marginTop="8dp"
        android:onClick="onClickStop"
        android:text="@string/stop" />
```

The number of hours, minutes, and seconds that have passed.

The Start button

The Stop button

Workout

app/src/main

res

layout

fragment_stopwatch.xml

0:00:00

START

STOP

RESET

The Reset button code is on the next page.

The StopwatchFragment layout (continued)

```
<Button
    android:id="@+id/reset_button"
    android:layout_width="wrap_content"
    android:layout_height="wrap_content"
    android:layout_gravity="center_horizontal"
    android:layout_marginTop="8dp"
    android:onClick="onClickReset"
    android:text="@string/reset" />
</LinearLayout>
```

← The Reset button

The StopwatchFragment layout uses String values

The XML code in *fragment_stopwatch.xml* uses string values for the text on the Start, Stop, and Reset buttons. We need to add these to *strings.xml*:

```
...
    <string name="start">Start</string>
    <string name="stop">Stop</string>
    <string name="reset">Reset</string>
...
```

These are the button labels.

The Stopwatch fragment looks just like it did when it was an activity. The difference is that we can now use it in other activities and fragments.

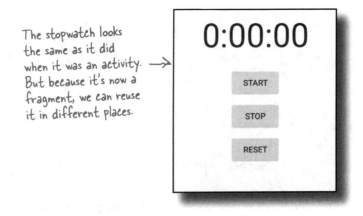

The stopwatch looks the same as it did when it was an activity. → But because it's now a fragment, we can reuse it in different places.

The next thing we need to do is display it in `TempActivity`'s layout.

Add StopwatchFragment to TempActivity's layout

The simplest way of adding `StopwatchFragment` to TempActivity's layout is to use the `<fragment>` element. Using the `<fragment>` element means that we can add the fragment directly into the layout instead of writing fragment transaction code.

Here's our code for *activity_temp.xml*. Replace the code that's currently in that file with this updated code:

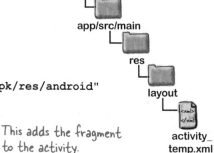

```xml
<?xml version="1.0" encoding="utf-8"?>
<fragment xmlns:android="http://schemas.android.com/apk/res/android"
    android:name="com.hfad.workout.StopwatchFragment"
    android:layout_width="match_parent"
    android:layout_height="match_parent"/>
```

This adds the fragment to the activity.

Workout
app/src/main
res
layout
activity_temp.xml

That's everything we need to see `StopwatchFragment` running. Let's take it for a test drive.

Test drive the app

When we run the app, `TempActivity` is displayed. It contains `StopwatchFragment`. The stopwatch is set to 0.

When we run the app, TempActivity starts, not MainActivity. TempActivity displays StopwatchFragment as expected.

The next thing we'll do is check that `StopwatchFragment`'s buttons work OK.

The app crashes if you click on a button

Convert stopwatch
Test stopwatch
Add to fragment

When you click on any one of the buttons in the Workout app's new stopwatch, the app crashes:

This is what happened →
when we clicked on
the Start button in
StopwatchFragment.

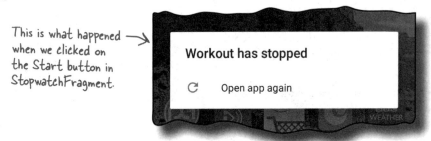

Workout has stopped

C   Open app again

When we converted the stopwatch activity into a fragment, we didn't change any of the code relating to the buttons. We know this code worked great when the stopwatch was in an activity, so why should it cause the app to crash in a fragment?

Here's the error output from Android Studio. Can you see what may have caused the problem?

Yikes.

```
04-13 11:56:43.623 10583-10583/com.hfad.workout E/AndroidRuntime: FATAL EXCEPTION: main
    Process: com.hfad.workout, PID: 10583
    java.lang.IllegalStateException: Could not find method onClickStart(View) in a
    parent or ancestor Context for android:onClick attribute defined on view class
    android.support.v7.widget.AppCompatButton with id 'start_button'
        at android.support.v7.app.AppCompatViewInflater$DeclaredOnClickListener.
            resolveMethod(AppCompatViewInflater.java:327)
        at android.support.v7.app.AppCompatViewInflater$DeclaredOnClickListener.
            onClick(AppCompatViewInflater.java:284)
        at android.view.View.performClick(View.java:5609)
        at android.view.View$PerformClick.run(View.java:22262)
        at android.os.Handler.handleCallback(Handler.java:751)
        at android.os.Handler.dispatchMessage(Handler.java:95)
        at android.os.Looper.loop(Looper.java:154)
        at android.app.ActivityThread.main(ActivityThread.java:6077)
        at java.lang.reflect.Method.invoke(Native Method)
        at com.android.internal.os.ZygoteInit$MethodAndArgsCaller.
            run(ZygoteInit.java:865)
        at com.android.internal.os.ZygoteInit.main(ZygoteInit.java:755)
```

Let's look at the StopwatchFragment layout code

In the layout code for the StopwatchFragment, we're binding the
buttons to methods in the same way that we did for an activity, by
using the android:onClick attribute to say which method should
be called when each button is clicked:

We're using the same layout for the stopwatch now that it's a fragment as we did when it was an activity.

```xml
<?xml version="1.0" encoding="utf-8"?>
<LinearLayout xmlns:android="http://schemas.android.com/apk/res/android"
    ...
    <Button
        android:id="@+id/start_button"
        android:layout_width="wrap_content"
        android:layout_height="wrap_content"
        android:layout_gravity="center_horizontal"
        android:layout_marginTop="20dp"
        android:onClick="onClickStart"
        android:text="@string/start" />

    <Button
        android:id="@+id/stop_button"
        android:layout_width="wrap_content"
        android:layout_height="wrap_content"
        android:layout_gravity="center_horizontal"
        android:layout_marginTop="8dp"
        android:onClick="onClickStop"
        android:text="@string/stop" />

    <Button
        android:id="@+id/reset_button"
        android:layout_width="wrap_content"
        android:layout_height="wrap_content"
        android:layout_gravity="center_horizontal"
        android:layout_marginTop="8dp"
        android:onClick="onClickReset"
        android:text="@string/reset" />
</LinearLayout>
```

Workout
app/src/main
res
layout
fragment_stopwatch.xml

We're using the android:onClick attributes in the layout to say which methods should be called when each button is clicked.

This worked OK when we were using an activity, so why should we
have a problem now that we're using a fragment?

The onClick attribute calls methods in the activity, not the fragment

There's a big problem with using the `android:onClick` attribute to say which method should be called when a view is clicked. The attribute specifies which method should be called in the **current activity**. This is fine when the views are in an *activity*'s layout. But when the views are in a *fragment*, this leads to problems. Instead of calling methods in the fragment, Android calls methods in the parent activity. If it can't find the methods in this activity, the app crashes. That's what Android Studio's error message was trying to tell us.

It's not just buttons that have this problem. The `android:onClick` attribute can be used with any views that are subclasses of the `Button` class. This includes checkboxes, radio buttons, switches, and toggle buttons.

Now we *could* move the methods out of the fragment and into the activity, but that approach has a major disadvantage. It would mean that the fragment is no longer self-contained—if we wanted to reuse the fragment in another activity, we'd need to include the code in *that* activity too. Instead, we'll deal with it in the fragment.

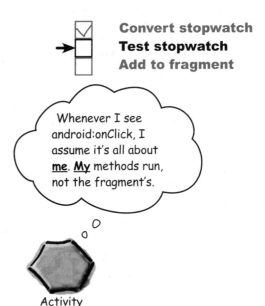

Convert stopwatch
Test stopwatch
Add to fragment

Whenever I see android:onClick, I assume it's all about **me**. **My** methods run, not the fragment's.

Activity

How to make button clicks call methods in the fragment

There are three things you need to do in order to get buttons in a fragment to call methods in the fragment instead of the activity:

1 Remove references to android:onClick in the fragment layout.
Buttons attempt to call methods in the activity when the `onClick` attribute is used, so these need to be removed from the fragment layout.

2 Optionally, change the onClick method signatures. ← *This step's optional, but it's a good opportunity to tidy up our code.*
When we created our `onClickStart()`, `onClickStop()`, and `onClickReset()` methods, we made them public and gave them a single `View` parameter. This was so they'd get called when the user clicked on a button. As we're no longer using the `android:onClick` attribute in our layout, we can set our methods to private and remove the `View` parameter.

3 Bind the buttons to methods in the fragment by implementing an OnClickListener.
This will ensure that the right methods are called when the buttons are clicked.

Let's do this now in our `StopwatchFragment`.

1. Remove the onClick attributes from the fragment's layout

The first thing we'll do is remove the `android:onClick` lines of code from the fragment's layout. This will stop Android from trying to call methods in the activity when the buttons are clicked:

```xml
<?xml version="1.0" encoding="utf-8"?>

<LinearLayout xmlns:android="http://schemas.android.com/apk/res/android"

    ...

    <Button
        android:id="@+id/start_button"
        android:layout_width="wrap_content"
        android:layout_height="wrap_content"
        android:layout_gravity="center_horizontal"
        android:layout_marginTop="20dp"
        android:onClick="onClickStart"
        android:text="@string/start" />


    <Button
        android:id="@+id/stop_button"
        android:layout_width="wrap_content"
        android:layout_height="wrap_content"
        android:layout_gravity="center_horizontal"
        android:layout_marginTop="8dp"
        android:onClick="onClickStop"
        android:text="@string/stop" />


    <Button
        android:id="@+id/reset_button"
        android:layout_width="wrap_content"
        android:layout_height="wrap_content"
        android:layout_gravity="center_horizontal"
        android:layout_marginTop="8dp"
        android:onClick="onClickReset"
        android:text="@string/reset" />

</LinearLayout>
```

Workout
└─ app/src/main
   └─ res
      └─ layout
         └─ fragment_
            stopwatch.xml

Remove the onClick attributes for each of the buttons in the stopwatch.

The next thing we'll do is tidy up our `onClickStart()`, `onClickStop()`, and `onClickReset()` code.

2. Change the onClick... method signatures

Back in Chapter 4, when we created our `onClickStart()`, `onClickStop()`, and `onClickReset()` methods in `StopwatchActivity`, we had to give them a specific method signature like this:

The methods had to be public. ⟶
```
public void onClickStart(View view) {

}
```
The methods had to have a void return value.

The methods had to have a single parameter of type View.

The methods had to take this form so that they'd respond when the user clicked on a button. Behind the scenes, when you use the `android:onClick` attribute, Android looks for a public method with a void return value, and with a name that matches the method specified in the layout XML.

Now that our code is in a fragment and we're no longer using the `android:onClick` attribute in our layout code, we can change our method signatures like this:

Our methods no longer need to be public, so we can make them private. ⟶
```
private void onClickStart() {

}
```
We no longer need the View parameter.

So let's update our fragment code. Change the `onClickStart()`, `onClickStop()`, and `onClickReset()` methods in *StopwatchFragment.java* to match ours:

```
    . . .
        ~~public~~ private void onClickStart(~~View view~~) {
            running = true;
        }

        ~~public~~ private void onClickStop(~~View view~~) {
            running = false;
        }

        ~~public~~ private void onClickReset(~~View view~~) {
            running = false;
            seconds = 0;
        }
    . . .
```

Change the methods to private.

Remove the View parameters.

```
Workout
  └ app/src/main
      └ java
          └ com.hfad.workout
              └ Stopwatch
                Fragment.java
```

3. Make the fragment implement OnClickListener

To make the buttons call methods in StopwatchFragment when they are clicked, we'll make the fragment implement the View. OnClickListener interface like this:

This turns the fragment into an OnClickListener.

```
public class StopwatchFragment extends Fragment implements View.OnClickListener {
    ...
}
```

This turns StopwatchFragment into a type of View. OnClickListener so that it can respond when views are clicked.

You tell the fragment how to respond to clicks by implementing the View.OnClickListener onClick() method. This method gets called whenever a view in the fragment is clicked.

```
@Override
public void onClick(View v) {
    ...
}
```

You must override the onClick() method in your fragment code.

The onClick() method has a single View parameter. This is the view that the user clicks on. You can use the view's getId() method to find out which view the user clicked on, and then decide how to react.

Code Magnets

See if you can complete the StopwatchFragment onClick() method. You need to call the onClickStart() method when the Start button is clicked, the onClickStop() method when the Stop button is clicked, and the onClickReset() method when the Reset button is clicked.

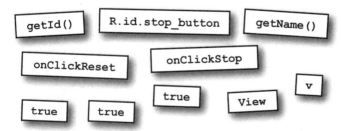

```
@Override
public void onClick(View v) {

    switch (........ ..................) {
        case R.id.start_button:
            onClickStart();
            break;

        case ........................ :

            ........................ ();
            break;
        case R.id.reset_button:

            ........................ ();
    }

}
```

Code Magnets Solution

See if you can complete the `StopwatchFragment onClick()` method. You need to call the `onClickStart()` method when the Start button is clicked, the `onClickStop()` method when the Stop button is clicked, and the `onClickReset()` method when the Reset button is clicked.

You didn't need to use these magnets.

`getName()`

`true`   `true`   `true`   `View`

```
@Override
public void onClick(View v) {

    switch ( v . getId() ) {
        case R.id.start_button:
            onClickStart();
        break;

        case R.id.stop_button :
            onClickStop ();
        break;
        case R.id.reset_button:
            onClickReset ();

    }

}
```

The StopwatchFragment onClick() method

We need to make a few changes to *StopwatchFragment.java*; we'll show you the changes one at a time, then the fully updated code a couple of pages ahead.

Here's the code to implement the `StopwatchFragment onClick()` method so that the correct method gets called when each button is clicked:

```
@Override
public void onClick(View v) {            ← This is the View the user clicked on.
    switch (v.getId()) {                 ← Check which View was clicked.
        case R.id.start_button:
            onClickStart();              ← If the Start button was clicked,
            break;                         call the onClickStart() method.
        case R.id.stop_button:           ← If the Stop button was clicked,
            onClickStop();                 call the onClickStop() method.
            break;
        case R.id.reset_button:          ← If the Reset button was clicked,
            onClickReset();                call the onClickReset() method.
            break;
    }
}
```

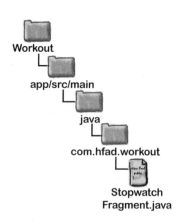

Workout

app/src/main

java

com.hfad.workout

Stopwatch
Fragment.java

There's just one more thing we need to do to get our buttons working: attach the listener to the buttons in the fragment.

Attach the OnClickListener to the buttons

To make views respond to clicks, you need to call each view's setOnClickListener() method. The setOnClickListener() method takes an OnClickListener object as a parameter. Because StopwatchFragment implements the OnClickListener interface, we can use the keyword this to pass the fragment as the OnClickListener in the setOnClickListener() method.

As an example, here's how you attach the OnClickListener to the Start button:

Get a reference to the button.

```
Button startButton = (Button) layout.findViewById(R.id.start_button);
startButton.setOnClickListener(this);
```
← *Attach the listener to the button.*

The call to each view's setOnClickListener() method needs to be made after the fragment's views have been created. This means they need to go in the StopwatchFragment onCreateView() method like this:

```
@Override
public View onCreateView(LayoutInflater inflater, ViewGroup container,
                         Bundle savedInstanceState) {
    View layout = inflater.inflate(R.layout.fragment_stopwatch, container, false);
    runTimer(layout);
    Button startButton = (Button) layout.findViewById(R.id.start_button);
    startButton.setOnClickListener(this);
    Button stopButton = (Button) layout.findViewById(R.id.stop_button);
    stopButton.setOnClickListener(this);
    Button resetButton = (Button) layout.findViewById(R.id.reset_button);
    resetButton.setOnClickListener(this);
    return layout;
}
```
This attaches the listener to each of the buttons.

We'll show you the full StopwatchFragment code on the next page.

Workout
   app/src/main
      java
         com.hfad.workout
            Stopwatch Fragment.java

The StopwatchFragment code

Here's the revised code for *StopwatchFragment.java*; update your
version to match ours:

Workout

app/src/main

java

com.hfad.workout

Stopwatch
Fragment.java

```java
package com.hfad.workout;

import java.util.Locale;
import android.os.Bundle;
import android.os.Handler;
import android.support.v4.app.Fragment;
import android.view.LayoutInflater;
import android.view.View;
import android.view.ViewGroup;
import android.widget.TextView;
import android.widget.Button;
```
← We're using the Button class, so we'll import it.

```java
public class StopwatchFragment extends Fragment implements View.OnClickListener {
    //Number of seconds displayed on the stopwatch.
    private int seconds = 0;
    //Is the stopwatch running?
    private boolean running;
    private boolean wasRunning;
```

The fragment needs to implement
the View.OnClickListener interface.

We're not changing the onCreate() method.

```java
    @Override
    public void onCreate(Bundle savedInstanceState) {
        super.onCreate(savedInstanceState);
        if (savedInstanceState != null) {
            seconds = savedInstanceState.getInt("seconds");
            running = savedInstanceState.getBoolean("running");
            wasRunning = savedInstanceState.getBoolean("wasRunning");
        }
    }
```

Update the onCreateView() method to
attach the listener to the buttons.

```java
    @Override
    public View onCreateView(LayoutInflater inflater, ViewGroup container,
                        Bundle savedInstanceState) {
        View layout = inflater.inflate(R.layout.fragment_stopwatch, container, false);
        runTimer(layout);
        Button startButton = (Button)layout.findViewById(R.id.start_button);
        startButton.setOnClickListener(this);
        Button stopButton = (Button)layout.findViewById(R.id.stop_button);
        stopButton.setOnClickListener(this);
        Button resetButton = (Button)layout.findViewById(R.id.reset_button);
        resetButton.setOnClickListener(this);
        return layout;
    }
```

The code continues
on the next page.

458   Chapter 11

The StopwatchFragment code (continued)

- [x] Convert stopwatch
- [ ] **Test stopwatch**
- [ ] Add to fragment

```
@Override
public void onClick(View v) {
    switch (v.getId()) {
        case R.id.start_button:
            onClickStart();
            break;
        case R.id.stop_button:
            onClickStop();
            break;
        case R.id.reset_button:
            onClickReset();
            break;
    }
}

@Override
public void onPause() {
    super.onPause();
    wasRunning = running;
    running = false;
}

@Override
public void onResume() {
    super.onResume();
    if (wasRunning) {
        running = true;
    }
}

@Override
public void onSaveInstanceState(Bundle savedInstanceState) {
    savedInstanceState.putInt("seconds", seconds);
    savedInstanceState.putBoolean("running", running);
    savedInstanceState.putBoolean("wasRunning", wasRunning);
}
```

As we're implementing the OnClickListener interface, we need to override the onClick() method.

Call the appropriate method in the fragment for the button that was clicked.

We've not changed these methods.

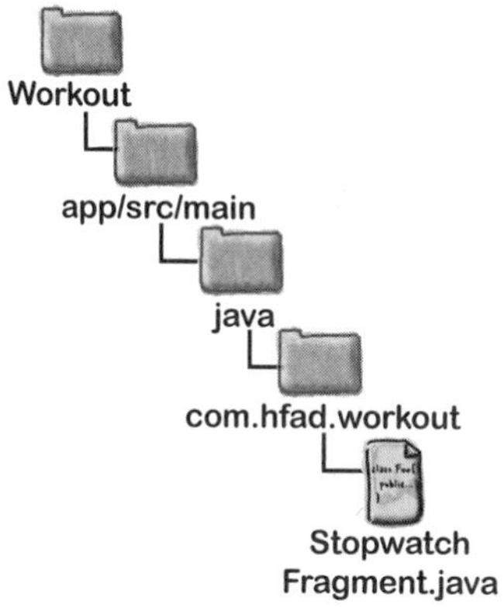

Workout
app/src/main
java
com.hfad.workout
Stopwatch Fragment.java

The code continues on the next page.

Convert stopwatch
Test stopwatch
Add to fragment

The StopwatchFragment code (continued)

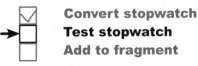

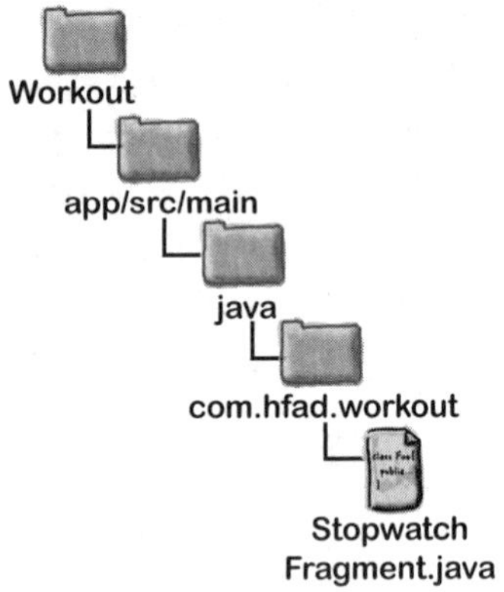

Workout
app/src/main
java
com.hfad.workout
Stopwatch
Fragment.java

```
    private void onClickStart() {
        running = true;
    }

    private void onClickStop() {
        running = false;
    }

    private void onClickReset() {
        running = false;
        seconds = 0;
    }

    private void runTimer(View view) {
        final TextView timeView = (TextView) view.findViewById(R.id.time_view);
        final Handler handler = new Handler();
        handler.post(new Runnable() {
            @Override
            public void run() {
                int hours = seconds/3600;
                int minutes = (seconds%3600)/60;
                int secs = seconds%60;
                String time = String.format(Locale.getDefault(),
                        "%d:%02d:%02d", hours, minutes, secs);
                timeView.setText(time);
                if (running) {
                    seconds++;
                }
                handler.postDelayed(this, 1000);
            }
        });
    }
}
```

We've changed these methods so they're private. We've also removed the View parameter, as we no longer needed it.

We've not changed this method.

Those are all the code changes needed for *StopwatchFragment.java*.
Let's see what happens when we run the app.

Test drive the app

When we run the app, the stopwatch is displayed as before.
This time, however, the Start, Stop, and Reset buttons work.

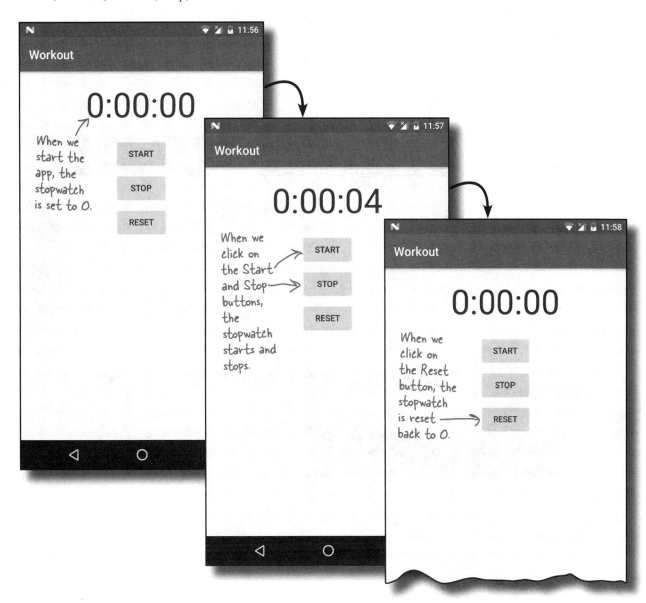

When we start the app, the stopwatch is set to 0.

When we click on the Start and Stop buttons, the stopwatch starts and stops.

When we click on the Reset button, the stopwatch is reset back to 0.

Now that we've got the buttons working, the next thing we
need to test is what happens when we rotate the device.

Rotating the device resets the stopwatch

☑ Convert stopwatch
☐ **Test stopwatch**
☐ Add to fragment

There's still one more problem we need to sort out. When we rotate our device, the stopwatch gets reset back to 0.

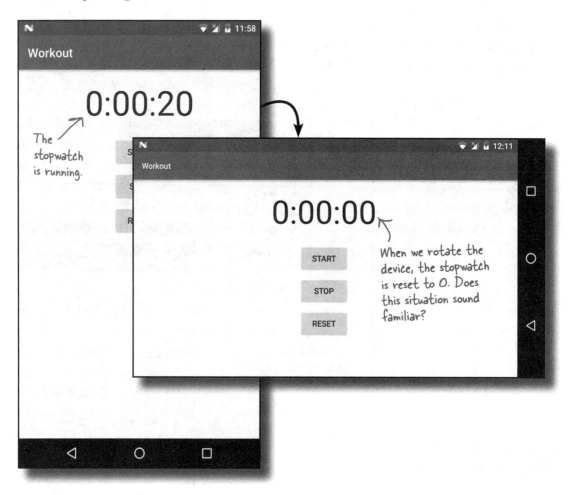

The stopwatch is running.

When we rotate the device, the stopwatch is reset to 0. Does this situation sound familiar?

We encountered a similar problem when we first created `StopwatchActivity` back in Chapter 4. `StopwatchActivity` lost the state of any instance variables when it was rotated because activities are destroyed and recreated when the device is rotated. We solved this problem by saving and restoring the state of any instance variables used by the stopwatch.

This time, the problem isn't due to the code in `StopwatchFragment`. Instead, it's because of how we're adding `StopwatchFragment` to `TempActivity`.

Use <fragment> for static fragments...

When we added StopwatchFragment to TempActivity, we did it by adding a <fragment> element to its layout like this:

```xml
<?xml version="1.0" encoding="utf-8"?>
<fragment xmlns:android="http://schemas.android.com/apk/res/android"
    android:name="com.hfad.workout.StopwatchFragment"
    android:layout_width="match_parent"
    android:layout_height="match_parent"/>
```

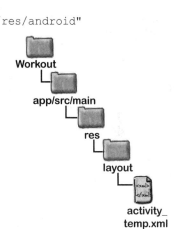

Workout

app/src/main

res

layout

activity_
temp.xml

We did this because it was the simplest way to display our fragment in an activity and see it working.

As we said back in Chapter 9, the <fragment> element is a placeholder for where the fragment's layout should be inserted. When Android creates the activity's layout, it replaces the <fragment> element with the fragment's user interface.

When you rotate the device, Android recreates the activity. If your activity contains a <fragment> element, *it reinserts a new version of the fragment each time the activity is recreated.* The old fragment is discarded, and any instance variables are set back to their original values. In this particular example, this means that the stopwatch is set back to 0.

...but dynamic fragments need a fragment transaction

The <fragment> element works well for fragments that display static data. If you have a fragment that's dynamic, like our stopwatch, you need to add the fragment using a fragment transaction instead.

We're going to change TempActivity so that we no longer display StopwatchFragment using a <fragment>. Instead, we'll use a fragment transaction. To do this, we need to make changes to *activity_temp.xml* and *TempActivity.java*.

Change activity_temp.xml to use a FrameLayout

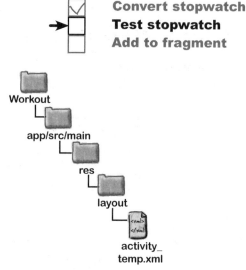

Convert stopwatch
Test stopwatch
Add to fragment

As you learned back in Chapter 10, when you want to add a fragment to an activity using a fragment transaction, you first need to add a placeholder for the fragment in the activity's layout. We did this in Chapter 10 by adding a frame layout to the layout, and giving it an ID so we could refer to it in our Java code.

We need to do the same thing with *activity_temp.xml*. We'll replace the `<fragment>` element with a frame layout, and give the frame layout an ID of `stopwatch_container`. Update your version of *activity_temp.xml* so that it reflects ours:

```xml
<?xml version="1.0" encoding="utf-8"?>
<fragment FrameLayout xmlns:android="http://schemas.android.com/apk/res/android"
    android:name="com.hfad.workout.StopwatchFragment"
    android:id="@+id/stopwatch_container"
    android:layout_width="match_parent"
    android:layout_height="match_parent"/>
```

Replace the fragment with a FrameLayout.

← Delete this line.

Add a fragment transaction to TempActivity.java

Once you've added the frame layout to your activity's layout, you can create the fragment transaction that will add the fragment to the frame layout.

We want to add `StopwatchFragment` to `TempActivity` as soon as `TempActivity` gets created. We only want to add a new fragment, however, if one hasn't previously been added to it. We don't want to override any existing fragment.

To do this, we'll add code to `TempActivity`'s `onCreate()` method that checks whether the `savedInstanceState` `Bundle` parameter is null.

If `savedInstanceState` is null, this means that `TempActivity` is being created for the first time. In that case, we need to add `StopwatchFragment` to the activity.

If `savedInstanceState` is not null, that means that `TempActivity` is being recreated after having been destroyed. In that situation, we don't want to add a new instance of `StopwatchFragment` to the activity, as it would overwrite an existing fragment.

Pool Puzzle

Your **job** is to take code snippets from the pool and place them into the blank lines in *TempActivity.java*. You may **not** use the same code snippet more than once, and you won't need to use all the code snippets. Your **goal** is to create a fragment transaction that will add an instance of StopwatchFragment to TempActivity.

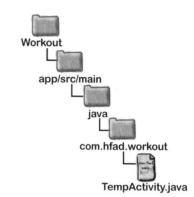

Workout

app/src/main

java

com.hfad.workout

TempActivity.java

```java
@Override
protected void onCreate(Bundle savedInstanceState) {
    super.onCreate(savedInstanceState);
    setContentView(R.layout.activity_temp);
    if (savedInstanceState == null) {
        StopwatchFragment stopwatch = new StopwatchFragment();
        FragmentTransaction ft = ....................................................................................;
        ft.add(R.id.stopwatch_container, .........................);
        ft.........................(null);
        ft.setTransition(FragmentTransaction.TRANSIT_FRAGMENT_FADE);
        ft. .........................;
    }
}
```

Note: each snippet from the pool can only be used once!

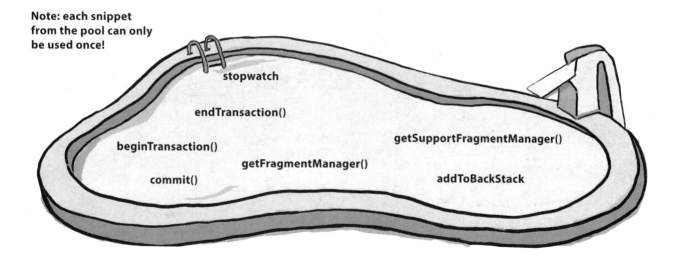

stopwatch

endTransaction()

beginTransaction()

getFragmentManager()

commit()

getSupportFragmentManager()

addToBackStack

Pool Puzzle Solution

Your **job** is to take code snippets from the pool and place them into the blank lines in *TempActivity.java*. You may **not** use the same code snippet more than once, and you won't need to use all the code snippets. Your **goal** is to create a fragment transaction that will add an instance of StopwatchFragment to TempActivity.

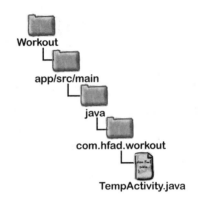

Workout
app/src/main
java
com.hfad.workout
TempActivity.java

```
@Override
protected void onCreate(Bundle savedInstanceState) {
    super.onCreate(savedInstanceState);
    setContentView(R.layout.activity_temp);
    if (savedInstanceState == null) {
        StopwatchFragment stopwatch = new StopwatchFragment();
        FragmentTransaction ft = getSupportFragmentManager() . beginTransaction() ;
        ft.add(R.id.stopwatch_container, stopwatch );
        ft. addToBackStack (null);
        ft.setTransition(FragmentTransaction.TRANSIT_FRAGMENT_FADE);
        ft. commit() ;
    }
}
```

This begins the fragment transaction. We need to use getSupportFragmentManager(), not getFragmentManager(), as we're using fragments from the Support Library.

Add the transaction to the back stack.

Add an instance of StopwatchFragment to TempActivity's layout.

Commit the transaction.

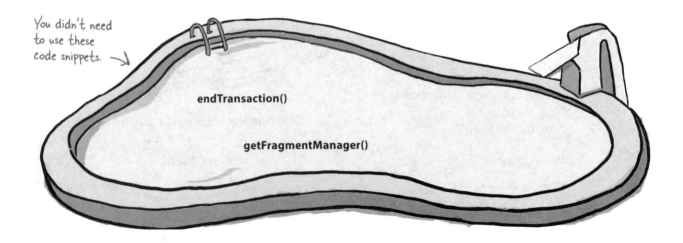

You didn't need to use these code snippets.

endTransaction()

getFragmentManager()

The full code for TempActivity.java

We've added a fragment transaction to *TempActivity.java* that adds StopwatchFragment to TempActivity. Our full code is below. Update your version of *TempActivity.java* so that it matches ours.

You need to import the FragmentTransaction class from the Support Library.

```java
package com.hfad.workout;

import android.support.v4.app.FragmentTransaction;
import android.support.v7.app.AppCompatActivity;
import android.os.Bundle;

public class TempActivity extends AppCompatActivity {

    @Override
    protected void onCreate(Bundle savedInstanceState) {
        super.onCreate(savedInstanceState);
        setContentView(R.layout.activity_temp);
        if (savedInstanceState == null) {
            StopwatchFragment stopwatch = new StopwatchFragment();
            FragmentTransaction ft = getSupportFragmentManager().beginTransaction();
            ft.add(R.id.stopwatch_container, stopwatch);
            ft.addToBackStack(null);
            ft.setTransition(FragmentTransaction.TRANSIT_FRAGMENT_FADE);
            ft.commit();
        }
    }
}
```

Workout

app/src/main

java

com.hfad.workout

TempActivity.java

Begin the fragment transaction.

We only want to add the fragment if the activity isn't being recreated after having been destroyed.

Add the stopwatch, and add the transaction to the back stack.

Set the fragment transition to fade in and out.

Commit the transaction. This applies the changes.

Those are all the code changes we need to add StopwatchFragment to TempActivity using a fragment transaction. Let's see what happens when we run the code.

Test drive the app

When we run the app, the stopwatch is displayed as before. The Start, Stop, and Reset buttons all work, and when we rotate the app, the stopwatch keeps running.

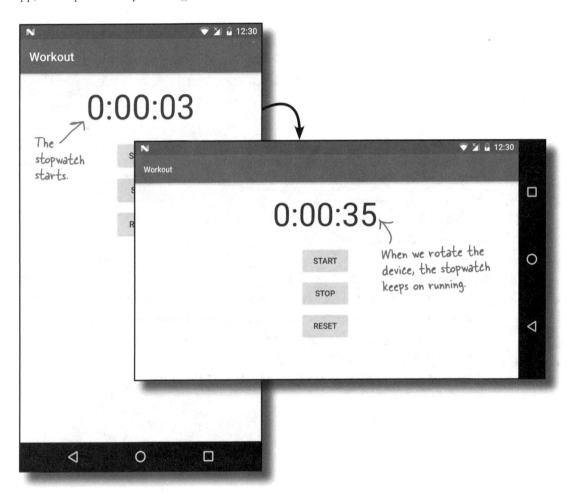

The stopwatch starts.

When we rotate the device, the stopwatch keeps on running.

At the beginning of the chapter, we said we'd first focus on getting StopwatchFragment working in a new temporary activity so that we could confirm it works OK. Now that we've achieved that, we can reuse it in WorkoutDetailFragment.

Add the stopwatch to WorkoutDetailFragment

We're going to add `StopwatchFragment` to
`WorkoutDetailFragment` so that a stopwatch is displayed
underneath details of the workout. The stopwatch will appear along
with the workout details whenever the user chooses one of the workouts.

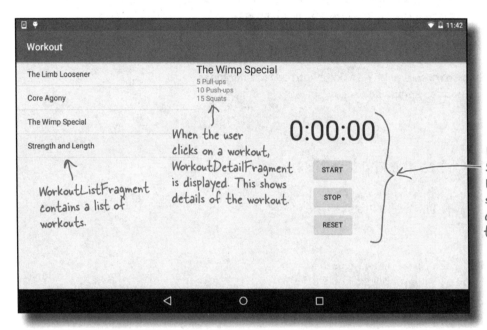

WorkoutListFragment
contains a list of
workouts.

When the user
clicks on a workout,
WorkoutDetailFragment
is displayed. This shows
details of the workout.

We're going to add
StopwatchFragment to
WorkoutDetailFragment
so a stopwatch is
displayed underneath
the workout details.

Here's how the app will work:

1 **When the app gets launched, it starts MainActivity.**
`MainActivity` includes `WorkoutListFragment`, which
displays a list of workouts.

2 **The user clicks on a workout and WorkoutDetailFragment is displayed.**
`WorkoutDetailFragment` displays details of the workout, and contains
`StopwatchFragment`.

3 **StopwatchFragment displays a stopwatch.**

We've simplified the
app structure here, but
these are the key points.

Device → MainActivity.java → WorkoutList Fragment.java → WorkoutDetail Fragment.java → Stopwatch Fragment.java

We'll go through the steps on the next page.

What we're going to do

There are just a couple of steps we need to go through in order to get the new version of the app up and running.

1 **Make the app start MainActivity when it launches.**
Earlier in the chapter, we temporarily changed the app so that it would start TempActivity. We need to change the app so that it starts MainActivity again.

2 **Add StopwatchFragment to WorkoutDetailFragment.**
We'll do this using a fragment transaction.

Let's get started.

Start MainActivity when the app launches

Earlier in the chapter, we updated *AndroidManifest.xml* to make the app start TempActivity. This was so that we could get StopwatchFragment working before adding it to WorkoutDetailFragment.

Now that StopwatchFragment is working, we need to start MainActivity again when the app launches. To do this, update *AndroidManifest.xml* with the following changes:

```
...
    <application
        ...
        <activity android:name=".MainActivity">
            <intent-filter>
                <action android:name="android.intent.action.MAIN" />
                <category android:name="android.intent.category.LAUNCHER" />
            </intent-filter>
        </activity>
        <activity android:name=".DetailActivity" />
        <activity android:name=".TempActivity">
            <intent-filter>
                <action android:name="android.intent.action.MAIN" />
                <category android:name="android.intent.category.LAUNCHER" />
            </intent-filter>
        </activity>
    </application>
...
```

Workout

app/src/main

AndroidManifest.xml

Add an intent filter to start MainActivity when the app is launched.

Remove the intent filter from TempActivity.

Add a FrameLayout where the fragment should appear

Next we need to add StopwatchFragment to WorkoutDetailFragment. We'll do this by adding a frame layout to *fragment_workout_detail.xml*, just as we did in *activity_temp.xml*. We'll then be able to add StopwatchFragment to WorkoutDetailFragment using a fragment transaction.

Here's our code for *fragment_workout_detail.xml*; update your code so that it matches ours:

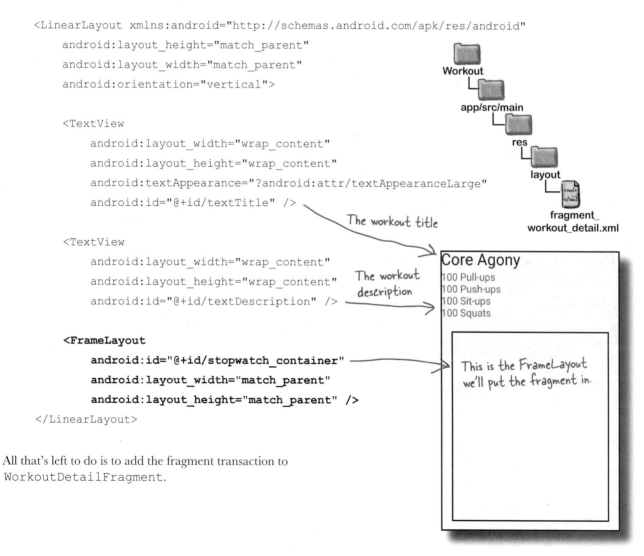

```
<LinearLayout xmlns:android="http://schemas.android.com/apk/res/android"
    android:layout_height="match_parent"
    android:layout_width="match_parent"
    android:orientation="vertical">

    <TextView
        android:layout_width="wrap_content"
        android:layout_height="wrap_content"
        android:textAppearance="?android:attr/textAppearanceLarge"
        android:id="@+id/textTitle" />

    <TextView
        android:layout_width="wrap_content"
        android:layout_height="wrap_content"
        android:id="@+id/textDescription" />

    <FrameLayout
        android:id="@+id/stopwatch_container"
        android:layout_width="match_parent"
        android:layout_height="match_parent" />
</LinearLayout>
```

Workout
app/src/main
res
layout
fragment_workout_detail.xml

The workout title

The workout description

Core Agony
100 Pull-ups
100 Push-ups
100 Sit-ups
100 Squats

This is the FrameLayout we'll put the fragment in.

All that's left to do is to add the fragment transaction to WorkoutDetailFragment.

So far, we've only used fragment transactions in activities

Earlier in the chapter, we added the following code to TempActivity to add StopwatchFragment to its layout:

```java
protected void onCreate(Bundle savedInstanceState) {
    super.onCreate(savedInstanceState);
    setContentView(R.layout.activity_temp);
    if (savedInstanceState == null) {
        StopwatchFragment stopwatch = new StopwatchFragment();
        FragmentTransaction ft = getSupportFragmentManager().beginTransaction();
        ft.add(R.id.stopwatch_container, stopwatch);
        ft.addToBackStack(null);
        ft.setTransition(FragmentTransaction.TRANSIT_FRAGMENT_FADE);
        ft.commit();
    }
}
```

This code adds StopwatchFragment to TempActivity when TempActivity is created.

The above code worked well when we wanted to add StopwatchFragment to an activity. How will it need to change now that we want to add StopwatchFragment to a *fragment?*

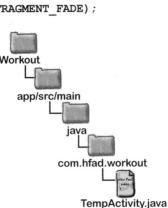

Workout

app/src/main

java

com.hfad.workout

TempActivity.java

Using fragment transactions in fragments uses most of the same code

The good news is that you can use nearly all of the same code when you want to use a fragment transaction inside a fragment. There's just one key difference: fragments don't have a method called getSupportFragmentManager(), so we need to edit this line of code:

```java
FragmentTransaction ft = getSupportFragmentManager().beginTransaction();
```

In order to create the fragment transaction, we need to get a reference to a fragment manager. Fragments have *two* methods you can use for this purpose: **getFragmentManager()** and **getChildFragmentManager()**. So what's the difference between these two methods, and which one should we use in our app?

Using getFragmentManager() creates extra transactions on the back stack

The getFragmentManager() method gets the fragment manager associated with the fragment's *parent activity*. Any fragment transaction you create using this fragment manager is added to the back stack as a separate transaction.

In our case, when someone clicks on a workout, we want the app to display the details of the workout and the stopwatch. MainActivity creates a transaction that displays WorkoutDetailFragment. If we use getFragmentManager() to create a transaction to display StopwatchFragment, this will be added to the back stack as a separate transaction.

The problem with using two transactions to display the workout and stopwatch is what happens when the user presses the Back button.

Suppose the user clicks on a workout. Details of the workout will be displayed, along with the stopwatch. If the user then clicks on the Back button, they will expect the screen to go back to how it looked before they selected a workout. But **the Back button simply pops the last transaction on the back stack**. That means if we create two transactions to add the workout detail and the stopwatch, when the user clicks the Back button, only the stopwatch will be removed. They have to click the Back button again to remove the workout details.

A transaction for WorkoutDetailFragment is added to the back stack, followed by a separate transaction for StopwatchFragment.

When the user hits the Back button, the StopwatchFragment transaction is popped off the back stack. The transaction for WorkoutDetailFragment stays on the back stack.

The user clicks an item in the list just once to display the workout details and stopwatch.

The user has to click the Back button twice to get back to where they started. Clicking the Back button once only removes the stopwatch.

Clearly this behavior is less than ideal. So what about getChildFragmentManager()?

☑ **Convert stopwatch**
☑ **Test stopwatch**
→ ☐ **Add to fragment**

Using getChildFragmentManager() creates nested transactions instead

The getChildFragmentManager() method gets the fragment manager associated with the fragment's *parent fragment*. Any fragment transaction you create using this fragment manager is added to the back stack inside the parent fragment transaction, not as a separate transaction.

In our particular case, this means that the fragment transaction that displays WorkoutDetailFragment contains a second transaction that displays StopwatchFragment.

> I display workout details, and I also display the stopwatch.

The transaction to add StopwatchFragment is nested inside the transaction to add → WorkoutDetailFragment.

Workout Details | Stopwatch

WorkoutDetailFragment and StopwatchFragment are still displayed when the user clicks on a workout, but the behavior is different when the user clicks on the Back button. As the two transactions are nested, *both* transactions are popped off the back stack when the user presses the Back button. The workout details and the stopwatch are both removed if the user presses the Back button once. That's what we want, so we'll use this method in our app.

This time the user has to press the Back button just once to undo both the workout detail and stopwatch transactions.

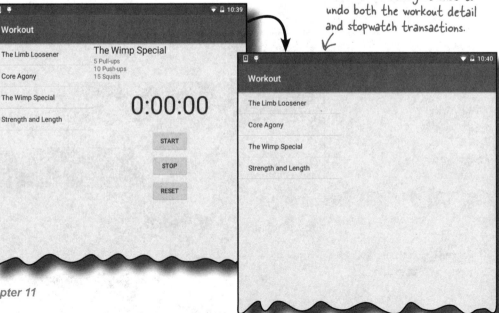

What getChildFragmentManager() fragment transaction code looks like

We've written code that will add `StopwatchFragment` to `WorkoutDetailFragment`. It creates a fragment transaction using the fragment manager returned by `getChildFragmentManager()`. Here's the code:

Workout
app/src/main
java
com.hfad.workout
WorkoutDetail
Fragment.java

```java
public void onCreate(Bundle savedInstanceState) {
    super.onCreate(savedInstanceState);
    if (savedInstanceState == null) {
        StopwatchFragment stopwatch = new StopwatchFragment();
        FragmentTransaction ft = getChildFragmentManager().beginTransaction();
        ft.add(R.id.stopwatch_container, stopwatch);
        ft.addToBackStack(null);
        ft.setTransition(FragmentTransaction.TRANSIT_FRAGMENT_FADE);
        ft.commit();
    } else {
        workoutId = savedInstanceState.getLong("workoutId");
    }
}
```

We're using getChildFragmentManager() instead of getSupportFragmentManager(). Apart from that, the code is the same as we had earlier.

We need to add this code to *WorkoutDetailFragment.java*. We'll show you the full code on the next page.

there are no Dumb Questions

Q: I can see that the child fragment manager handles the case where I put one fragment inside another. But what if I put one fragment inside another, inside another, inside another...?

A: The transactions will all be nested within each other, leaving just a single transaction at the activity level. So the nested set of child transactions will be undone by a single Back button click.

Q: Fragments seem more complicated than activities. Should I use fragments in my apps?

A: That depends on your app and what you want to achieve. One of the major benefits of using fragments is that you can use them to support a wide range of different screen sizes. You can, say, choose to display fragments side by side on tablets and on separate screens on smaller devices. You'll also see in the next chapter that some UI designs require you to use fragments.

The full WorkoutDetailFragment.java code

☑ Convert stopwatch
☑ Test stopwatch
→ ☐ **Add to fragment**

Here's the full code for *WorkoutDetailFragment.java*. Update
your version of the code to include our changes.

```java
package com.hfad.workout;

import android.support.v4.app.Fragment;
import android.support.v4.app.FragmentTransaction;
import android.os.Bundle;
import android.view.LayoutInflater;
import android.view.View;
import android.view.ViewGroup;
import android.widget.TextView;

public class WorkoutDetailFragment extends Fragment {
    private long workoutId;

    @Override
    public void onCreate(Bundle savedInstanceState) {
        super.onCreate(savedInstanceState);
        if (savedInstanceState != null) {
        if (savedInstanceState == null) {
            StopwatchFragment stopwatch = new StopwatchFragment();
            FragmentTransaction ft = getChildFragmentManager().beginTransaction();
            ft.add(R.id.stopwatch_container, stopwatch);
            ft.addToBackStack(null);
            ft.setTransition(FragmentTransaction.TRANSIT_FRAGMENT_FADE);
            ft.commit();
        } else {
            workoutId = savedInstanceState.getLong("workoutId");
        }
    }
}
```

You need to import the FragmentTransaction class from the Support Library.

Workout
app/src/main
java
com.hfad.workout
WorkoutDetail Fragment.java

← Delete this line.

Begin the fragment transaction.

We only want to add the fragment if the activity isn't being recreated after having been destroyed.

← Add the stopwatch, and add the transaction to the back stack.

Set the fragment transition to fade in and out.

← Commit the transaction.

The code continues on the next page.

The full code (continued)

```java
@Override
public View onCreateView(LayoutInflater inflater, ViewGroup container,
                         Bundle savedInstanceState) {
    return inflater.inflate(R.layout.fragment_workout_detail, container, false);
}

@Override
public void onStart() {
    super.onStart();
    View view = getView();
    if (view != null) {
        TextView title = (TextView) view.findViewById(R.id.textTitle);
        Workout workout = Workout.workouts[(int) workoutId];
        title.setText(workout.getName());
        TextView description = (TextView) view.findViewById(R.id.textDescription);
        description.setText(workout.getDescription());
    }
}

@Override
public void onSaveInstanceState(Bundle savedInstanceState) {
    savedInstanceState.putLong("workoutId", workoutId);
}

public void setWorkout(long id) {
    this.workoutId = id;
}
}
```

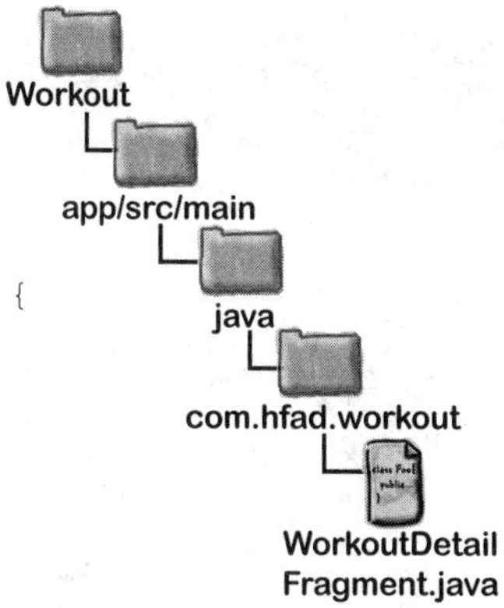

We didn't change any of the methods on this page.

Workout

app/src/main

java

com.hfad.workout

WorkoutDetail
Fragment.java

That's everything we need for our app. Let's take it for a test
drive and check that it works OK.

We'll start by testing the app on a tablet.

When we start the app, `MainActivity` is displayed.

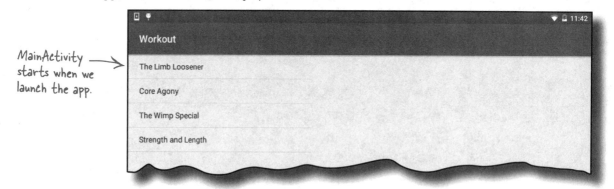

MainActivity starts when we launch the app.

When we click on one of the workouts, details of that workout are displayed along with a stopwatch. If we click on a second workout and then click on the Back button, details of the first workout are displayed.

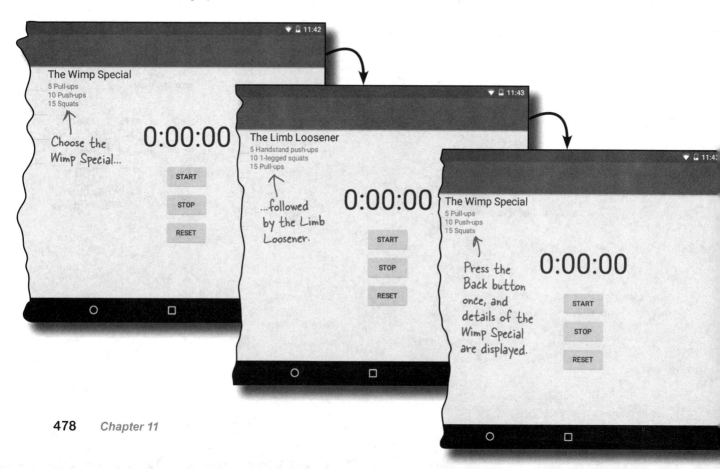

Choose the Wimp Special...

...followed by the Limb Loosener.

Press the Back button once, and details of the Wimp Special are displayed.

Test drive (continued)

When we click on the stopwatch buttons, they all work as expected.
When we rotate the app, the stopwatch maintains its state.

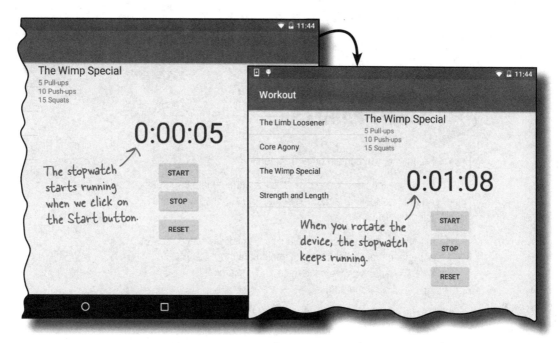

The stopwatch starts running when we click on the Start button.

When you rotate the device, the stopwatch keeps running.

When we run the app on a phone, `WorkoutDetailFragment`
is displayed inside a separate activity, `DetailActivity`. The
stopwatch is still displayed underneath the workout details, and
functions as expected.

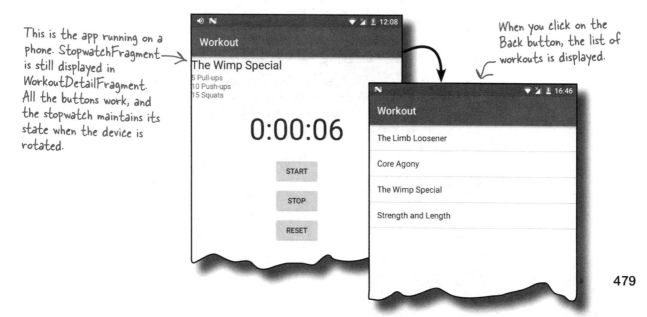

This is the app running on a phone. StopwatchFragment is still displayed in WorkoutDetailFragment. All the buttons work, and the stopwatch maintains its state when the device is rotated.

When you click on the Back button, the list of workouts is displayed.

Your Android Toolbox

You've got Chapter 11 under your belt and now you've added dynamic fragments to your toolbox.

You can download the full code for the chapter from https://tinyurl.com/ HeadFirstAndroid.

BULLET POINTS

- Fragments can contain other fragments.

- If you use the `android:onClick` attribute in a fragment, Android will look for a method of that name in the fragment's parent activity.

- Instead of using the `android:onClick` attribute in a fragment, make the fragment implement the `View.OnClickListener` interface and implement its `onClick()` method.

- If you use the `<fragment>` element in your layout, the fragment gets recreated when you rotate the device. If your fragment is dynamic, use a fragment transaction instead.

- Fragments contain two methods for getting a fragment manager, `getFragmentManager()` and `getChildFragmentManager()`.

- `getFragmentManager()` gets a reference to the fragment manager associated with the fragment's parent activity. Any fragment transactions you create using this fragment manager are added to the back stack as extra transactions.

- `getChildFragmentManager()` gets a reference to the fragment manager associated with the fragment's parent fragment. Any fragment transactions you create using this fragment manager are nested inside the parent fragment transaction.

12 design support library

Swipe Right

> This new snackbar's awesome; it does so much more than toast.

Ever wondered how to develop apps with a rich, slick UI?

With the release of the **Android Design Support Library**, it became much easier to create apps with an intuitive UI. In this chapter, we'll show you around some of the highlights. You'll see how to add *tabs* so that your users can *navigate around your app more easily*. You'll discover how to *animate your toolbars* so that they can *collapse or scroll on a whim*. You'll find out how to add *floating action buttons* for common user actions. Finally, we'll introduce you to *snackbars*, a way of displaying short, informative messages to the user that they can interact with.

The Bits and Pizzas app revisited

In Chapter 8, we showed you a sketch of the top-level screen of the Bits and Pizzas app. It contained a list of places in the app the user could go to. The first three options linked to category screens for pizzas, pasta, and stores, and the final option linked to a screen where the user could create an order.

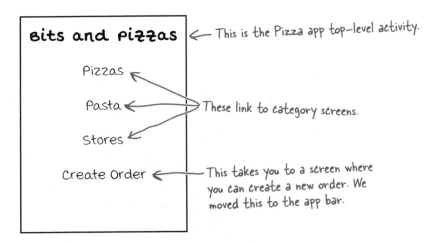

Bits and Pizzas ← This is the Pizza app top-level activity.

Pizzas
Pasta ⟷ These link to category screens.
Stores

Create Order ← This takes you to a screen where you can create a new order. We moved this to the app bar.

So far you've seen how to add actions to the app bar. These are used for simple commands, such as Create Order or Send Feedback. But what about the category screens? As we want to use these for navigating through the app rather than taking an action, we'll take a different approach.

We're going to change the Bits and Pizzas app so that it uses **tab navigation**. We'll display a set of tabs underneath the toolbar, with each option on a different tab. When the user clicks on a tab, the screen for that option will be displayed. We'll also let the user swipe left and right between the different tabs.

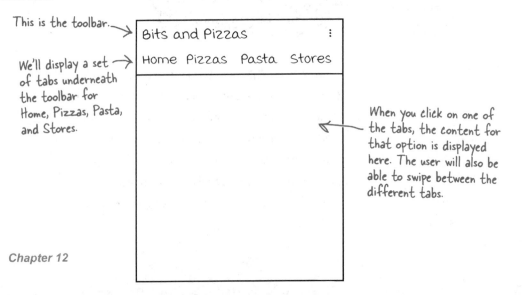

This is the toolbar.

Bits and Pizzas ⋮

We'll display a set of tabs underneath the toolbar for Home, Pizzas, Pasta, and Stores.

Home Pizzas Pasta Stores

When you click on one of the tabs, the content for that option is displayed here. The user will also be able to swipe between the different tabs.

The app structure

We're going to change MainActivity so that it uses tabs. The tabs will include options for Home, Pizzas, Pasta, and Stores, so that the user can easily navigate to the main sections of the app.

We'll create fragments for these different options; when the user clicks on one of the tabs, the fragment for that option will be displayed:

This is what the new version of → the app will look like.

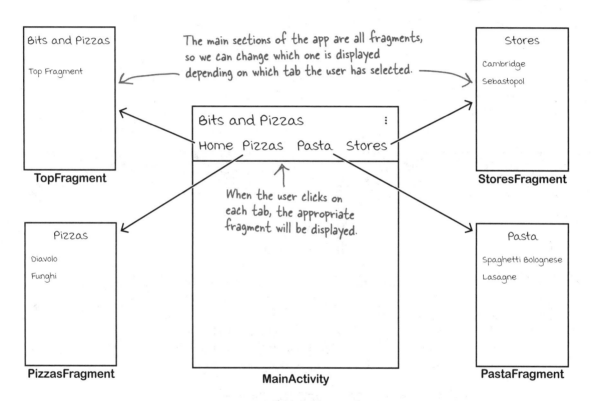

The main sections of the app are all fragments, so we can change which one is displayed depending on which tab the user has selected.

TopFragment

StoresFragment

When the user clicks on each tab, the appropriate fragment will be displayed.

PizzasFragment

MainActivity

PastaFragment

We'll go through the steps for how to do this on the next page.

Here's what we're going to do

There are three main steps we'll go through to get tabs working:

1 **Create the fragments.**
We'll create basic versions of `TopFragment`, `PizzaFragment`, `PastaFragment`, and `StoresFragment` so that we can easily tell which fragment is displayed on each of the tabs.

We'll create these fragments. →

2 **Enable swipe navigation between the fragments.**
We'll update `MainActivity` so that the user can swipe between the different fragments.

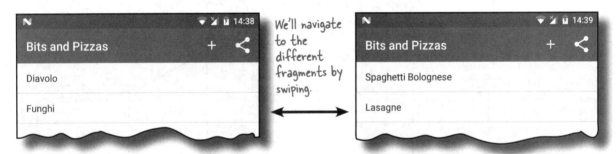

We'll navigate to the different fragments by swiping.

3 **Add the tab layout.**
Finally, we'll add a tab layout to `MainActivity` that will work in conjunction with the swipe navigation. The user will be able to navigate to each fragment by clicking on a tab, or swiping between them.

We'll add a tab layout to MainActivity, but the user will still be able to swipe between the fragments if they want to. →

Do this!

We're going to update the Bits and Pizzas app in this chapter, so open your original Bits and Pizzas project from Chapter 8 in Android Studio.

We'll start by creating the fragments.

Create TopFragment

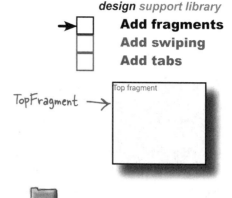

We'll use `TopFragment` to display content that will appear on the Home tab. For now, we'll display the text "Top fragment" so that we know which fragment is displayed. Highlight the *com.hfad.bitsandpizzas* package in the *app/src/main/java* folder, then go to File→New...→Fragment→Fragment (Blank). Name the fragment "TopFragment" and name its layout "fragment_top". Then replace the code for *TopFragment.java* with the code below:

```
package com.hfad.bitsandpizzas;

import android.os.Bundle;
import android.support.v4.app.Fragment;
import android.view.LayoutInflater;
import android.view.View;
import android.view.ViewGroup;

public class TopFragment extends Fragment {

    @Override
    public View onCreateView(LayoutInflater inflater, ViewGroup container,
                             Bundle savedInstanceState) {
        return inflater.inflate(R.layout.fragment_top, container, false);
    }

}
```

TopFragment.java is a fragment from the Support Library.

BitsAndPizzas
app/src/main
java
com.hfad.bitsandpizzas
TopFragment.java

Add the following string resource to *strings.xml*; we'll use this in our fragment layout:

```
<string name="title_top">Top fragment</string>
```

Add this to strings.xml. We'll use it in the layout so we know when TopFragment is being displayed.

Then update the code for *fragment_top.xml* as follows:

```
<LinearLayout xmlns:android="http://schemas.android.com/apk/res/android"
    xmlns:tools="http://schemas.android.com/tools"
    android:layout_width="match_parent"
    android:layout_height="match_parent"
    android:orientation="vertical"
    tools:context="com.hfad.bitsandpizzas.TopFragment">

    <TextView
        android:layout_width="match_parent"
        android:layout_height="match_parent"
        android:text="@string/title_top" />
</LinearLayout>
```

BitsAndPizzas
app/src/main
res
layout
fragment_top.xml

Create PizzaFragment

Add fragments
Add swiping
Add tabs

We'll use a `ListFragment` called `PizzaFragment` to display the list of pizzas. Highlight the *com.hfad.bitsandpizzas* package in the *app/src/main/java* folder, then go to File→New...→Fragment→Fragment (Blank). Name the fragment "PizzaFragment", and uncheck the option to create a layout. Why? Because list fragments don't need a layout—they use their own.

Don't choose the Fragment (List) option, as this generates more complex code.

PizzaFragment →

Diavolo
Funghi

Next, add a new string array resource called `"pizzas"` to *strings. xml* (this contains the names of the pizzas):

```xml
<string-array name="pizzas">
    <item>Diavolo</item>
    <item>Funghi</item>
</string-array>
```

Add the array of pizzas to strings.xml.

BitsAndPizzas
app/src/main
res
values
strings.xml

Then change the code for *PizzaFragment.java* so that it's a `ListFragment`. Its list view needs to be populated with the pizza names. Here's the updated code:

```java
package com.hfad.bitsandpizzas;

import android.os.Bundle;
import android.support.v4.app.ListFragment;
import android.view.LayoutInflater;
import android.view.View;
import android.view.ViewGroup;
import android.widget.ArrayAdapter;

public class PizzaFragment extends ListFragment {

    @Override
    public View onCreateView(LayoutInflater inflater, ViewGroup container,
                             Bundle savedInstanceState) {
        ArrayAdapter<String> adapter = new ArrayAdapter<>(
                inflater.getContext(),
                android.R.layout.simple_list_item_1,
                getResources().getStringArray(R.array.pizzas));
        setListAdapter(adapter);
        return super.onCreateView(inflater, container, savedInstanceState);
    }
}
```

We'll use a ListFragment to display the list of pizzas.

The ArrayAdapter populates the ListFragment's ListView with the pizza names.

BitsAndPizzas
app/src/main
java
com.hfad.bitsandpizzas
PizzaFragment.java

Create PastaFragment

We'll use a `ListFragment` called `PastaFragment` to display the list of pasta. Highlight the *com.hfad.bitsandpizzas* package in the *app/src/main/java* folder and create a new blank fragment named "PastaFragment". You can uncheck the option to create a layout, as list fragments use their own layouts.

PastaFragment →

Spaghetti Bolognese
Lasagne

Next, add a new string array resource called `"pasta"` to *strings.xml* (this contains the names of the pasta):

```xml
<string-array name="pasta">
    <item>Spaghetti Bolognese</item>   ← Add the array of
    <item>Lasagne</item>                  pasta to strings.xml.
</string-array>
```

BitsAndPizzas
  app/src/main
    res
      values
        strings.xml

Then change the code for *PastaFragment.java* so that it's a `ListFragment` that displays a list of the pasta names. Here's the updated code:

```java
package com.hfad.bitsandpizzas;

import android.os.Bundle;
import android.support.v4.app.ListFragment;
import android.view.LayoutInflater;
import android.view.View;
import android.view.ViewGroup;
import android.widget.ArrayAdapter;

public class PastaFragment extends ListFragment {

    @Override
    public View onCreateView(LayoutInflater inflater, ViewGroup container,
                             Bundle savedInstanceState) {
        ArrayAdapter<String> adapter = new ArrayAdapter<>(
                inflater.getContext(),
                android.R.layout.simple_list_item_1,
                getResources().getStringArray(R.array.pasta));
        setListAdapter(adapter);
        return super.onCreateView(inflater, container, savedInstanceState);
    }
}
```

BitsAndPizzas
  app/src/main
    java
      com.hfad.bitsandpizzas
        PastaFragment.java

Create StoresFragment

We'll use a ListFragment called StoresFragment to display the list of stores. Highlight the *com.hfad.bitsandpizzas* package in the *app/src/main/java* folder and create a new blank fragment named "StoresFragment." Uncheck the option to create a layout, as list fragments define their own layouts.

StoresFragment →

Cambridge
Sebastopol

Next, add a new string array resource called "stores" to *strings. xml* (this contains the names of the stores):

BitsAndPizzas

```
<string-array name="stores">
    <item>Cambridge</item>    ← Add the array of
    <item>Sebastopol</item>      stores to strings.xml.
</string-array>
```

app/src/main

res

values

strings.xml

Then change the code for *StoresFragment.java* so that it's a ListFragment. Its list view needs to be populated with the store names. Here's the updated code:

```java
package com.hfad.bitsandpizzas;

import android.os.Bundle;
import android.support.v4.app.ListFragment;
import android.view.LayoutInflater;
import android.view.View;
import android.view.ViewGroup;
import android.widget.ArrayAdapter;

public class StoresFragment extends ListFragment {

    @Override
    public View onCreateView(LayoutInflater inflater, ViewGroup container,
                             Bundle savedInstanceState) {
        ArrayAdapter<String> adapter = new ArrayAdapter<>(
                inflater.getContext(),
                android.R.layout.simple_list_item_1,
                getResources().getStringArray(R.array.stores));
        setListAdapter(adapter);
        return super.onCreateView(inflater, container, savedInstanceState);
    }
}
```

We'll use a ListFragment to display the list of stores.

BitsAndPizzas

app/src/main

java

com.hfad.bitsandpizzas

StoresFragment.java

We've now added all the fragments we need, so let's move on to the next step.

Use a view pager to swipe through fragments

We want to be able to swipe through the different fragments
we've just created. To do this, we'll use a **view pager**, which is
a view group that allows you to swipe through different pages in
a layout, each page containing a separate fragment.

The view pager will let us swipe between the different fragments.

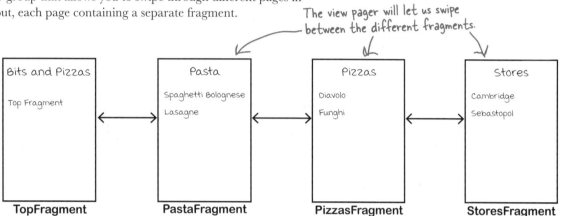

You use a view pager by adding it to your layout, then writing
activity code to control which fragments should be displayed. The
`ViewPager` class comes from the v4 Support Library, which
is included in the v7 AppCompat Support Library, so you also
need to make sure you add one of these libraries to your project
as a dependency. In our particular case, we already added the v7
AppCompat Support Library to our project in Chapter 8.

You can check which Support Libraries are included in your project in Android Studio by choosing Project Structure from the File menu, clicking on the app module, and then choosing Dependencies.

What view pager layout code looks like

You add a view pager to your layout using code like this:

The ViewPager class is found in the v4 Support Library (which is included in the v7 AppCompat Support Library).

```
<android.support.v4.view.ViewPager
    android:id="@+id/pager"
    android:layout_width="match_parent"
    android:layout_height="match_parent" />
```

You need to give the ViewPager an ID so that you can control its behavior in your activity code.

The above code defines the view pager, and gives it an ID of
`pager`. Every view pager you create *must* have an ID so that
you can get a reference to it in your activity code. Without this
ID, you can't specify which fragments should appear on each
page of the view pager.

We're going to add a view pager to `MainActivity`. We'll
look at the full code for its layout on the next page.

Add a view pager to MainActivity's layout

We're going to add a view pager to `MainActivity`'s layout, and remove the text view that's already there. Open the file *activity_main.xml*, then update your code so that it matches ours below (we've bolded our changes):

```xml
<?xml version="1.0" encoding="utf-8"?>
<LinearLayout
    xmlns:android="http://schemas.android.com/apk/res/android"
    xmlns:tools="http://schemas.android.com/tools"
    android:layout_width="match_parent"
    android:layout_height="match_parent"
    android:orientation="vertical"
    tools:context="com.hfad.bitsandpizzas.MainActivity">

    <include
        layout="@layout/toolbar_main"
        android:id="@+id/toolbar" />

    <android.support.v4.view.ViewPager
        android:id="@+id/pager"
        android:layout_width="match_parent"
        android:layout_height="match_parent" />

    <TextView
        android:layout_width="wrap_content"
        android:layout_height="wrap_content"
        android:text="Hello World!" />

</LinearLayout>
```

← Add the ViewPager below the Toolbar.

We're no longer displaying a TextView in MainActivity, so delete these lines of code.

BitsAndPizzas

app/src/main

res

layout

activity_main.xml

That's everything we need to add a view pager to our layout. To get our new view pager to display fragments, we need to write some activity code. We'll do that next.

Tell a view pager about its pages using a fragment pager adapter

To get a view pager to display a fragment on each of its pages, there are two key pieces of information you need to give it: the number of pages it should have, and which fragment should appear on each page. You do this be creating a **fragment pager adapter**, and adding it to your activity code.

A fragment pager adapter is a type of adapter that specializes in adding fragments to pages in a view pager. You generally use one when you want to have a small number of pages that are fairly static, as each fragment the user visits is kept in memory. ←

*If you want your view pager to have a large number of pages, you would use a **fragment state pager adapter** instead. We're not covering it here, but the code is almost identical.*

Fragment pager adapter code looks like this:

```java
private class SectionsPagerAdapter extends FragmentPagerAdapter {

    public SectionsPagerAdapter(FragmentManager fm) {
        super(fm);
    }

    @Override
    public int getCount() {
        //The number of pages in the ViewPager
    }

    @Override
    public Fragment getItem(int position) {
        //The fragment to be displayed on each page
    }
}
```

We're setting this to private, as we're going to add it to MainActivity as an inner class.

You need to extend the FragmentPagerAdapter class.

You must have a constructor that takes a FragmentManager parameter.

You need to override the getCount() method to specify the number of pages in the view pager.

You need to say which fragment should appear on each page. The position gives the page number, starting at 0.

When you create a fragment pager adapter, there are two key methods you ***must*** override: getCount() and getItem(). You use getCount() to specify how many pages there should be in the view pager, and the getItem() to say which fragment should be displayed on each page.

We'll show you the code for the Bits and Pizzas fragment pager adapter on the next page.

The code for our fragment pager adapter

We want our view pager to have four pages. We'll display
`TopFragment` on the first page, `PizzaFragment`
on the second, `PastaFragment` on the third, and
`StoresFragment` on the fourth.

To accomplish this, we're going to create a fragment pager
adapter called `SectionsPagerAdapter`. Here's the code
(we'll add it to *MainActivity.java* in a couple of pages):

```java
private class SectionsPagerAdapter extends FragmentPagerAdapter {

    public SectionsPagerAdapter(FragmentManager fm) {
        super(fm);
    }

    @Override
    public int getCount() {
        return 4;
    }

    @Override
    public Fragment getItem(int position) {
        switch (position) {
            case 0:
                return new TopFragment();
            case 1:
                return new PizzaFragment();
            case 2:
                return new PastaFragment();
            case 3:
                return new StoresFragment();
        }
        return null;
    }

}
```

We'll have four pages in our ViewPager, one for each of the fragments we want to be able to swipe through.

BitsAndPizzas
└ **app/src/main**
　└ **java**
　　└ **com.hfad.bitsandpizzas**
　　　└ **MainActivity.java**

The getCount() method specifies 4 pages, so the getItem() method should only request the fragments for these 4 page positions.

We want to display TopFragment first, so we'll return a new instance of it for position 0 of the ViewPager.

That's all the code we need for our
`SectionsPagerAdapter`. Next we need to get our view
pager to use it.

Attach the fragment pager adapter to the view pager

Finally, we need to attach our `SectionsPagerAdapter` to the view pager so that the view pager can use it. You attach a fragment pager adapter to a view pager by calling the `ViewPager setAdapter()` method, and passing it a reference to an instance of the fragment pager adapter.

Here's the code to attach the fragment pager adapter we created to the view pager:

```
@Override
protected void onCreate(Bundle savedInstanceState) {
    super.onCreate(savedInstanceState);
    ...
    //Attach the SectionsPagerAdapter to the ViewPager
    SectionsPagerAdapter pagerAdapter =
                    new SectionsPagerAdapter(getSupportFragmentManager());
    ViewPager pager = (ViewPager) findViewById(R.id.pager);
    pager.setAdapter(pagerAdapter);
}
```

BitsAndPizzas

app/src/main

java

com.hfad.bitsandpizzas

MainActivity.java

This attaches the FragmentPagerAdapter we created to the ViewPager.

We're using support fragments, so we need to pass our adapter a reference to the support fragment manager.

That's everything we need to be able to swipe through our fragments. We'll show you the full code for `MainActivity` on the next page.

there are no Dumb Questions

Q: When should I use tabs in my app?

A: Tabs work well when you want to give the user a quick way of navigating between a small number of sections or categories. You would generally put each one on a separate tab.

Q: What if I have a large number of categories? Can I still use tabs?

A: You can, but you may want to consider other forms of navigation such as navigation drawers. These are panels that slide out from the side of the screen. We'll show you how to create them in Chapter 14.

Q: You mentioned the fragment state pager adapter. What's that?

A: It's very similar to a fragment pager adapter, except that it also handles saving and restoring a fragment's state. It uses less memory than a fragment pager adapter, as when pages aren't visible, the fragment it displays may be destroyed. It's useful if your view pager has a large number of pages.

The full code for MainActivity.java

Here's our full code for *MainActivity.java*. Update your version of the code to match our changes (in bold):

```java
package com.hfad.bitsandpizzas;

import android.support.v7.app.AppCompatActivity;
import android.os.Bundle;
import android.support.v7.widget.Toolbar;
import android.view.Menu;
import android.view.MenuItem;
import android.content.Intent;
import android.support.v7.widget.ShareActionProvider;
import android.support.v4.view.MenuItemCompat;
import android.support.v4.view.ViewPager;
import android.support.v4.app.Fragment;
import android.support.v4.app.FragmentManager;
import android.support.v4.app.FragmentPagerAdapter;
```

We're using these extra classes so we need to import them.

```java
public class MainActivity extends AppCompatActivity {

    private ShareActionProvider shareActionProvider;

    @Override
    protected void onCreate(Bundle savedInstanceState) {
        super.onCreate(savedInstanceState);
        setContentView(R.layout.activity_main);
        Toolbar toolbar = (Toolbar) findViewById(R.id.toolbar);
        setSupportActionBar(toolbar);

        //Attach the SectionsPagerAdapter to the ViewPager
        SectionsPagerAdapter pagerAdapter =
                    new SectionsPagerAdapter(getSupportFragmentManager());
        ViewPager pager = (ViewPager) findViewById(R.id.pager);
        pager.setAdapter(pagerAdapter);
    }
```

BitsAndPizzas

app/src/main

java

com.hfad.bitsandpizzas

MainActivity.java

Attach the FragmentPagerAdapter to the ViewPager.

The code continues on the next page. →

- [x] Add fragments
- [ ] **Add swiping** ←
- [ ] Add tabs

The MainActivity.java code (continued)

None of the code on this page has changed.

```
@Override
public boolean onCreateOptionsMenu(Menu menu) {
    getMenuInflater().inflate(R.menu.menu_main, menu);
    MenuItem menuItem = menu.findItem(R.id.action_share);
    shareActionProvider =
            (ShareActionProvider) MenuItemCompat.getActionProvider(menuItem);
    setShareActionIntent("Want to join me for pizza?");
    return super.onCreateOptionsMenu(menu);
}

@Override
public boolean onOptionsItemSelected(MenuItem item) {
    switch (item.getItemId()) {
        case R.id.action_create_order:
            Intent intent = new Intent(this, OrderActivity.class);
            startActivity(intent);
            return true;
        default:
            return super.onOptionsItemSelected(item);
    }
}

private void setShareActionIntent(String text) {
    Intent intent = new Intent(Intent.ACTION_SEND);
    intent.setType("text/plain");
    intent.putExtra(Intent.EXTRA_TEXT, text);
    shareActionProvider.setShareIntent(intent);
}
```

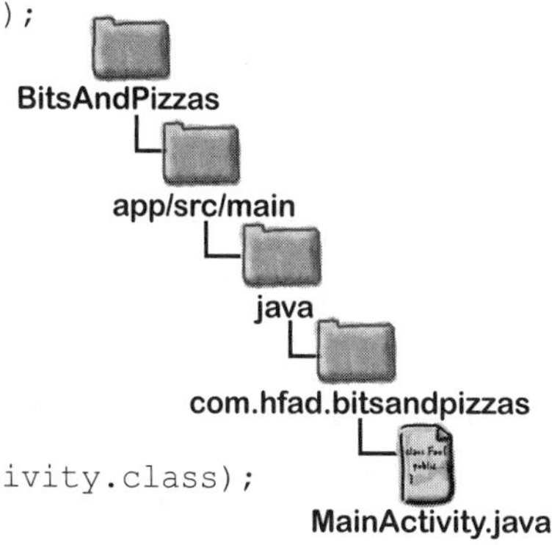

BitsAndPizzas
app/src/main
java
com.hfad.bitsandpizzas
MainActivity.java

The code continues on the next page. →

The MainActivity.java code (continued)

Add fragments
Add swiping
Add tabs

```java
private class SectionsPagerAdapter extends FragmentPagerAdapter {

    public SectionsPagerAdapter(FragmentManager fm) {
        super(fm);
    }

    @Override
    public int getCount() {
        return 4;
    }

    @Override
    public Fragment getItem(int position) {
        switch (position) {
            case 0:
                return new TopFragment();
            case 1:
                return new PizzaFragment();
            case 2:
                return new PastaFragment();
            case 3:
                return new StoresFragment();
        }
        return null;
    }
}
}
```

The FragmentPagerAdapter passes information to the ViewPager.

Say how many pages the ViewPager should contain.

Specify which fragment should appear on each page.

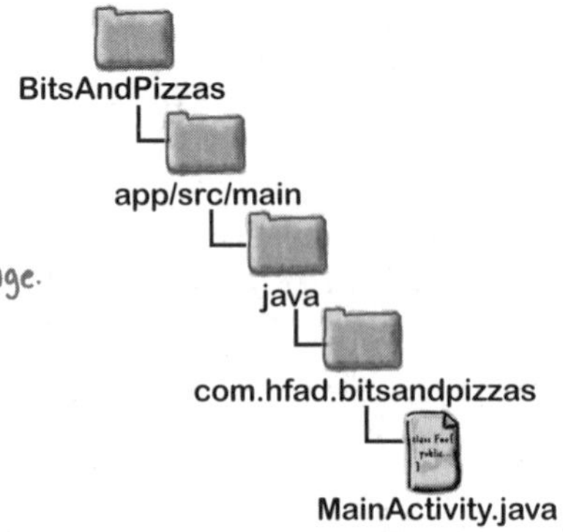

BitsAndPizzas

app/src/main

java

com.hfad.bitsandpizzas

MainActivity.java

Now that we've updated our MainActivity code,
let's take our app for a test drive and see what happens.

Test drive the app

When we run the app, `TopFragment` is displayed. When we swipe the screen to the left, `PizzaFragment` is displayed, followed by `PastaFragment` and `StoresFragment`. When we swipe the screen in the opposite direction starting from `StoresFragment`, `PastaFragment` is displayed, followed by `PizzaFragment` and `TopFragment`.

This is TopFragment. It's displayed first.

PizzaFragment is shown next...

...followed by PastaFragment.

The ViewPager displays the fragments in this order as we swipe through them.

StoresFragment is last. There are no more pages in the ViewPager after this.

Now that we can swipe through the fragments in `MainActivity`, let's add tabs.

Add tab navigation to MainActivity

☑ **Add fragments**
☑ **Add swiping**
→ ☐ **Add tabs**

We're going to add tabs to `MainActivity` as an additional way of navigating through our fragments. Each fragment will be displayed on a separate tab, and clicking on each tab will show that fragment. We'll also be able to swipe through the tabs using the existing view pager.

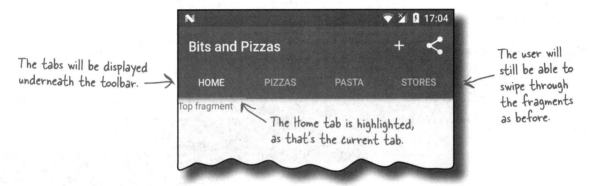

The tabs will be displayed underneath the toolbar. →

The Home tab is highlighted, as that's the current tab.

The user will still be able to swipe through the fragments as before.

You use tabs by adding them to your layout, then writing activity code to link the tabs to the view pager. The classes we need to do this come from the **Android Design Support Library**, so you need to add this library to your project as a dependency. To do this, choose File→Project Structure in Android Studio, click on the app module, then choose Dependencies. When you're presented with the project dependencies screen, click on the "+" button at the bottom or right side of the screen. When prompted, choose the Library Dependency option, then select the Design Library from the list of possible libraries. Finally, use the OK buttons to save your changes.

We'll look at the Design Support Library in more detail later in the chapter.

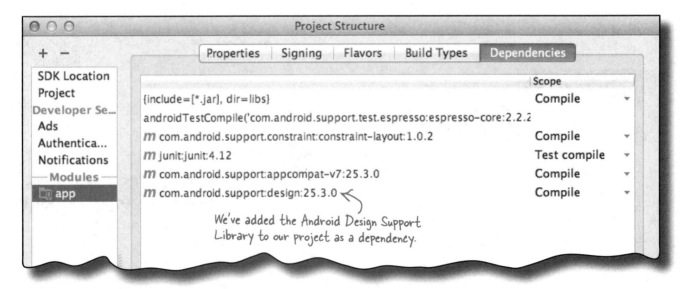

We've added the Android Design Support Library to our project as a dependency.

How to add tabs to your layout

You add tabs to your layout using two components from
the Design Support Library: a **TabLayout** and an
AppBarLayout. You use a TabLayout to add the tabs, and
the AppBarLayout to group the tabs and your toolbar together.

The code to add tabs to your layout looks like this:

```
<android.support.design.widget.AppBarLayout
    android:layout_width="match_parent"
    android:layout_height="wrap_content"
    android:theme="@style/ThemeOverlay.AppCompat.Dark.ActionBar" >

    <android.support.v7.widget.Toolbar
        android:id="@+id/toolbar"
        android:layout_width="match_parent"
        android:layout_height="?attr/actionBarSize" />

    <android.support.design.widget.TabLayout
        android:id="@+id/tabs"
        android:layout_width="match_parent"
        android:layout_height="wrap_content" />

</android.support.design.widget.AppBarLayout>
```

The AppBarLayout comes from the Design Support Library.

This line applies a theme to the Toolbar and TabLayout so that they have a consistant appearance.

You include the Toolbar inside the AppBarLayout.

The TabLayout comes from the DesignSupportLibrary. You add it to the AppBarLayout.

The Toolbar and TabLayout elements both have IDs
because you need to be able to reference them in your activity
code in order to control their behavior.

The AppBarLayout contains both the Toolbar and the
TabLayout. It's a type of vertical linear layout that's designed
to work with app bars. The android:theme attribute is used
to style the Toolbar and TabLayout. We've given ours a
theme of ThemeOverlay.AppCompat.Dark.ActionBar.

On the next page we'll show you the code to add tabs to
MainActivity's layout.

Add fragments
Add swiping
Add tabs

Add tabs to MainActivity's layout

Here's our code for *activity_main.xml*. Update your version of the code to match our changes (in bold):

```xml
<?xml version="1.0" encoding="utf-8"?>
<LinearLayout
    xmlns:android="http://schemas.android.com/apk/res/android"
    xmlns:tools="http://schemas.android.com/tools"
    android:layout_width="match_parent"
    android:layout_height="match_parent"
    android:orientation="vertical"
    tools:context="com.hfad.bitsandpizzas.MainActivity">

    <android.support.design.widget.AppBarLayout
        android:layout_width="match_parent"
        android:layout_height="wrap_content"
        android:theme="@style/ThemeOverlay.AppCompat.Dark.ActionBar" >
```

⟵ Add an AppBarLayout.

BitsAndPizzas
app/src/main
res
layout
activity_main.xml

```xml
        <include
            layout="@layout/toolbar_main"
            android:id="@+id/toolbar" />
        <android.support.v7.widget.Toolbar
            android:id="@+id/toolbar"
            android:layout_width="match_parent"
            android:layout_height="?attr/actionBarSize" />
```

We've decided to put our Toolbar code in activity_main.xml instead of including it from a separate file. This is so that we can show you the full code in one place. In practice, using the <include> still works.

The Toolbar goes inside the AppBarLayout.

```xml
        <android.support.design.widget.TabLayout
            android:id="@+id/tabs"
            android:layout_width="match_parent"
            android:layout_height="wrap_content" />
    </android.support.design.widget.AppBarLayout>

    <android.support.v4.view.ViewPager
        android:id="@+id/pager"
        android:layout_width="match_parent"
        android:layout_height="match_parent" />
</LinearLayout>
```

⟵ Add a TabLayout inside the AppBarLayout.

Link the tab layout to the view pager

Once you've added the tab layout, you need to write some activity code to control it. Most of the tab layout's behavior (such as which fragment appears on which tab) comes from the view pager you've already created. All you need to do is implement a method in the view pager's fragment pager adapter to specify the text you want to appear on each tab, then link the view pager to the tab layout.

We're going to add the text we want to appear on each of the tabs as String resources. Open the file *strings.xml*, then add the following Strings:

```
<string name="home_tab">Home</string>
<string name="pizza_tab">Pizzas</string>
<string name="pasta_tab">Pasta</string>
<string name="store_tab">Stores</string>
```

These Strings will be displayed on the tabs.

BitsAndPizzas
app/src/main
res
values
strings.xml

To add the text to each of the tabs, you need to implement the fragment pager adapter's `getPageTitle()` method. This takes one parameter, an `int` for the tab's position, and needs to return the text that should appear on that tab. Here's the code we need to add the above String resources to our four tabs (we'll add it to *MainActivity.java* on the next page):

```
@Override
public CharSequence getPageTitle(int position) {
    switch (position) {
        case 0:
            return getResources().getText(R.string.home_tab);
        case 1:
            return getResources().getText(R.string.pizza_tab);
        case 2:
            return getResources().getText(R.string.pasta_tab);
        case 3:
            return getResources().getText(R.string.store_tab);
    }
    return null;
}
```

This is a new method in the fragment pager adapter we created earlier.

These lines of code add the String resources to the tabs.

BitsAndPizzas
app/src/main
java
com.hfad.bitsandpizzas
MainActivity.java

Finally, you need to attach the view pager to the tab layout. You do this by calling the `TabLayout` object's `setupWithViewPager()` method, and passing in a reference to the `ViewPager` object as a parameter:

```
TabLayout tabLayout = (TabLayout) findViewById(R.id.tabs);
tabLayout.setupWithViewPager(pager);
```

This line attaches the ViewPager to the TabLayout. The TabLayout uses the ViewPager to determine how many tabs there should be, and what should be on each tab.

That's everything we need to get our tabs working. We'll show you the full code for `MainActivity` on the next page.

The full code for MainActivity.java

Here's our full code for *MainActivity.java*. Update your version of
the code to match our changes (in bold):

```java
package com.hfad.bitsandpizzas;

import android.support.v7.app.AppCompatActivity;
import android.os.Bundle;
import android.support.v7.widget.Toolbar;
import android.view.Menu;
import android.view.MenuItem;
import android.content.Intent;
import android.support.v7.widget.ShareActionProvider;
import android.support.v4.view.MenuItemCompat;
import android.support.v4.view.ViewPager;
import android.support.v4.app.Fragment;
import android.support.v4.app.FragmentManager;
import android.support.v4.app.FragmentPagerAdapter;
import android.support.design.widget.TabLayout;
```

We're using the TabLayout
class, so we need to import it.

BitsAndPizzas
app/src/main
java
com.hfad.bitsandpizzas
MainActivity.java

```java
public class MainActivity extends AppCompatActivity {

    private ShareActionProvider shareActionProvider;

    @Override
    protected void onCreate(Bundle savedInstanceState) {
        super.onCreate(savedInstanceState);
        setContentView(R.layout.activity_main);
        Toolbar toolbar = (Toolbar) findViewById(R.id.toolbar);
        setSupportActionBar(toolbar);

        //Attach the SectionsPagerAdapter to the ViewPager
        SectionsPagerAdapter pagerAdapter =
                    new SectionsPagerAdapter(getSupportFragmentManager());
        ViewPager pager = (ViewPager) findViewById(R.id.pager);
        pager.setAdapter(pagerAdapter);

        //Attach the ViewPager to the TabLayout
        TabLayout tabLayout = (TabLayout) findViewById(R.id.tabs);
        tabLayout.setupWithViewPager(pager);
    }
```

This links the ViewPager to the TabLayout.

The code continues
on the next page. →

The MainActivity.java code (continued)

design *support library*

☑ **Add fragments**
☑ **Add swiping**
→ **Add tabs**

None of the code on this page has changed.

```java
@Override
public boolean onCreateOptionsMenu(Menu menu) {
    getMenuInflater().inflate(R.menu.menu_main, menu);
    MenuItem menuItem = menu.findItem(R.id.action_share);
    shareActionProvider =
            (ShareActionProvider) MenuItemCompat.getActionProvider(menuItem);
    setShareActionIntent("Want to join me for pizza?");
    return super.onCreateOptionsMenu(menu);
}


@Override
public boolean onOptionsItemSelected(MenuItem item) {
    switch (item.getItemId()) {
        case R.id.action_create_order:
            Intent intent = new Intent(this, OrderActivity.class);
            startActivity(intent);
            return true;
        default:
            return super.onOptionsItemSelected(item);
    }
}


private void setShareActionIntent(String text) {
    Intent intent = new Intent(Intent.ACTION_SEND);
    intent.setType("text/plain");
    intent.putExtra(Intent.EXTRA_TEXT, text);
    shareActionProvider.setShareIntent(intent);
}
```

BitsAndPizzas

app/src/main

java

com.hfad.bitsandpizzas

MainActivity.java

The code continues on the next page. →

The MainActivity.java code (continued)

```java
    private class SectionsPagerAdapter extends FragmentPagerAdapter {

        public SectionsPagerAdapter(FragmentManager fm) {
            super(fm);
        }

        @Override
        public int getCount() {
            return 4;
        }

        @Override
        public Fragment getItem(int position) {
            switch (position) {
                case 0:
                    return new TopFragment();
                case 1:
                    return new PizzaFragment();
                case 2:
                    return new PastaFragment();
                case 3:
                    return new StoresFragment();
            }
            return null;
        }

        @Override
        public CharSequence getPageTitle(int position) {
            switch (position) {
                case 0:
                    return getResources().getText(R.string.home_tab);
                case 1:
                    return getResources().getText(R.string.pizza_tab);
                case 2:
                    return getResources().getText(R.string.pasta_tab);
                case 3:
                    return getResources().getText(R.string.store_tab);
            }
            return null;
        }
    }
}
```

BitsAndPizzas

app/src/main

java

com.hfad.bitsandpizzas

MainActivity.java

This method adds the text to the tabs.

Test drive the app

design *support library*

☑ **Add fragments**
☑ **Add swiping**
→ ☑ **Add tabs**

When we run the app, `MainActivity` includes a tab layout.
We can swipe through the fragments as before, and we can also
navigate to each fragment by clicking on the appropriate tab.

Here's the
TabLayout.

You can navigate to each fragment
by swiping through them as before,
or clicking on the appropriate tab.

That's all the code you need to implement
tab and swipe navigation. So what's next?

The Design Support Library helps you implement material design

So far, we've added tabs to our app to help the user navigate around the app. To do this, we've used two components from the Design Support Library: the `TabLayout` and `AppBarLayout`.

The Design Support Library was introduced as a way of making it easier for developers to use **material design** components in their apps. Material design was introduced with Lollipop as a way of giving a consistent look and feel to all Android apps. The idea is that a user can switch from a Google app like the Play Store to an app designed by a third-party developer and instantly feel comfortable and know what to do. It's inspired by paper and ink, and uses print-based design principles and movement to reflect how real-world objects (such as index cards and pieces of paper) look and behave.

The Design Support Library lets you do more than add tabs to your apps.

Material Design

You can find the full (and evolving) specs for material design here:

https://material.io/guidelines/

⭐ **It lets you add floating action buttons (FABs).**
These are special action buttons that float above the main screen.

This is a FAB.

⭐ **It includes snackbars, a way of displaying interactive short messages to the user as an alternative to toasts.**
Unlike a toast (which you learned about in Chapter 5), you can add actions to snackbars so that the user can interact with them.

Closed Home - BBC News   UNDO

This is a snackbar. It's like a toast, but more interactive.

⭐ **You can use it to animate your toolbars.**
You can make your toolbar scroll off the screen, or collapse, if the user scrolls content in another view.

⭐ **It includes a navigation drawer layout.**
This is a slide-out drawer you can use as an alternative to using tabs. We'll look at this feature in Chapter 14.

For the rest of this chapter, we're going to show you how to implement some of these features in the Bits and Pizzas app.

Here's what we'll do

We're going to add more goodness from the Design Support Library to the Bits and Pizzas app. Here are the steps we'll go through:

① Enable MainActivity's toolbar to scroll.
We'll change `MainActivity` so that the toolbar scrolls up and down when the user scrolls the contents of the view pager we added earlier. To see this working, we'll add content we can scroll to `TopFragment`.

When the user scrolls this content, →
the toolbar will scroll up too.

② Add a collapsing toolbar to OrderActivity.
We'll start by adding a plain collapsing toolbar to `OrderActivity`. The toolbar will collapse when the user scrolls `OrderActivity`'s contents. After we've got the plain collapsing toolbar working, we'll add an image to it.

This is a toolbar with an image. →
When the user scrolls the main content, we'll get it to collapse.

③ Add a FAB to OrderActivity.
We'll display a floating action button to the bottom-right corner.

This is the FAB we'll →
add to OrderActivity.

④ Make the FAB display a snackbar.
The snackbar will appear at the bottom of the screen when the user clicks on the FAB. The FAB will move up when the snackbar appears, and move back down when the snackbar is no longer there.

This is the snackbar.
←

We'll start by getting our toolbar to scroll in response to the user scrolling the content in the view pager.

Make the toolbar respond to scrolls

We're going to change our app so that MainActivity's toolbar scrolls whenever the user scrolls content in TopFragment. To enable this, there are two things we need to do:

1 **Change MainActivity's layout to enable the toolbar to scroll.**

2 **Change TopFragment to include scrollable content.**

We'll start by changing MainActivity's layout.

Use a CoordinatorLayout to coordinate animations between views

To get the toolbar to move when content in the fragment is scrolled, we'll add a **coordinator layout** to MainActivity. A coordinator layout is like a souped-up frame layout that's used to coordinate animations and transitions between different views. In this case, we'll use the coordinator layout to coordinate scrollable content in TopFragment and MainActivity's toolbar.

You add a coordinator layout to an activity's layout using code like this:

```
<android.support.design.widget.CoordinatorLayout
    android:layout_width="match_parent"
    android:layout_height="match_parent">

        ...

</android.support.design.widget.CoordinatorLayout>
```

The CoordinatorLayout comes from the Design Support Library.

You add any views whose behavior you want to coordinate inside the CoordinatorLayout.

Any views in your layout whose animations you want to coordinate must be included in the <CoordinatorLayout> element. In our case, we want to coordinate animations between the toolbar and the contents of the view pager, so these views need to be included in the coordinator layout.

Scrolling toolbar
Collapsing toolbar
FAB
Snackbar

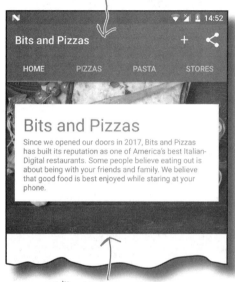

We'll get the toolbar to scroll when the user scrolls the content in TopFragment.

We'll add this scrollable content to TopFragment.

A CoordinatorLayout allows the behavior of one view to affect the behavior of another.

Add a coordinator layout to MainActivity's layout

We're going to replace the linear layout in *activity_main.xml* with a coordinator layout. Here's our code; update your version to match our changes (in bold):

> We're replacing the LinearLayout with a CoordinatorLayout.

```xml
<?xml version="1.0" encoding="utf-8"?>
<android.support.design.widget.CoordinatorLayout
<LinearLayout
    xmlns:android="http://schemas.android.com/apk/res/android"
    xmlns:app="http://schemas.android.com/apk/res-auto"
    xmlns:tools="http://schemas.android.com/tools"
    android:layout_width="match_parent"
    android:layout_height="match_parent"
    android:orientation="vertical"
    tools:context="com.hfad.bitsandpizzas.MainActivity">

    <android.support.design.widget.AppBarLayout
        android:layout_width="match_parent"
        android:layout_height="wrap_content"
        android:theme="@style/ThemeOverlay.AppCompat.Dark.ActionBar">

        <android.support.v7.widget.Toolbar
            android:id="@+id/toolbar"
            android:layout_width="match_parent"
            android:layout_height="?attr/actionBarSize" />

        <android.support.design.widget.TabLayout
            android:id="@+id/tabs"
            android:layout_width="match_parent"
            android:layout_height="wrap_content" />
    </android.support.design.widget.AppBarLayout>

    <android.support.v4.view.ViewPager
        android:id="@+id/pager"
        android:layout_width="match_parent"
        android:layout_height="match_parent" />
</android.support.design.widget.CoordinatorLayout>
</LinearLayout>
```

Add the app namespace, as we'll need to use attributes from it over the next few pages.

Delete this line, as we're no longer using a LinearLayout.

BitsAndPizzas

app/src/main

res

layout

activity_main.xml

We're replacing the LinearLayout with a CoordinatorLayout.

How to coordinate scroll behavior

As well as adding views to the coordinator layout, you need to say how you want them to behave. In our case, we want the toolbar to scroll in response to another view's scroll event. This means that we need to **mark the view the user will scroll**, and **tell the toolbar to respond to it**.

Mark the view the user will scroll

You mark the view the user will scroll by giving it an attribute of **app:layout_behavior** and setting it to the built-in String "@string/appbar_scrolling_view_behavior". This tells the coordinator layout that you want views in the app bar layout to be able to respond when the user scrolls this view. In our case, we want the toolbar to scroll in response to the user scrolling the view pager's content, so we need to add the app:layout_behavior attribute to the ViewPager element:

```
<android.support.v4.view.ViewPager
    ...
    app:layout_behavior="@string/appbar_scrolling_view_behavior" />
```

You add this line to the ViewPager to tell the CoordinatorLayout you want to react to the user scrolling its content.

Tell the toolbar to respond to scroll events

You tell views in the app bar layout how to respond to scroll events using the **app:layout_scrollFlags** attribute. In our case, we're going to set the toolbar to scroll upward off the screen when the user scrolls the view pager content up, and quickly return to its original position when the user scrolls down. To do this, we need to set the Toolbar app:layout_scrollFlags attribute to "scroll|enterAlways".

The scroll value allows the view to scroll off the top of screen. Without this, the toolbar would stay pinned to the top of the screen. The enterAlways value means that the toolbar quickly scrolls down to its original position when the user scrolls the corresponding view. The toolbar will still scroll down without this value, but it will be slower.

Here's the code we need to add to the toolbar to enable it to scroll:

```
<android.support.v7.widget.Toolbar
    ...
    app:layout_scrollFlags="scroll|enterAlways" />
```

This line tells the CoordinatorLayout (and AppBarLayout) how you want the Toolbar to react to the user scrolling content.

We'll look at the full code for MainActivity's layout on the next page.

Scrolling toolbar
Collapsing toolbar
FAB
Snackbar

The toolbar MUST be contained within an app bar layout in order for it to scroll. The app bar layout and coordinator layout work together to enable the toolbar to scroll.

The code to enable to toolbar to scroll

Here's our updated code for *activity_main.xml*. Update your
version of the code to match our changes (in bold):

```xml
<?xml version="1.0" encoding="utf-8"?>
<android.support.design.widget.CoordinatorLayout
    xmlns:android="http://schemas.android.com/apk/res/android"
    xmlns:app="http://schemas.android.com/apk/res-auto"
    xmlns:tools="http://schemas.android.com/tools"
    android:layout_width="match_parent"
    android:layout_height="match_parent"
    tools:context="com.hfad.bitsandpizzas.MainActivity">

    <android.support.design.widget.AppBarLayout
        android:layout_width="match_parent"
        android:layout_height="wrap_content"
        android:theme="@style/ThemeOverlay.AppCompat.Dark.ActionBar" >

        <android.support.v7.widget.Toolbar
            android:id="@+id/toolbar"
            android:layout_width="match_parent"
            android:layout_height="?attr/actionBarSize"
            app:layout_scrollFlags="scroll|enterAlways" />

        <android.support.design.widget.TabLayout
            android:id="@+id/tabs"
            android:layout_width="match_parent"
            android:layout_height="wrap_content" />
    </android.support.design.widget.AppBarLayout>

    <android.support.v4.view.ViewPager
        android:id="@+id/pager"
        android:layout_width="match_parent"
        android:layout_height="match_parent"
        app:layout_behavior="@string/appbar_scrolling_view_behavior" />
</android.support.design.widget.CoordinatorLayout>
```

BitsAndPizzas
app/src/main
res
layout
activity_
main.xml

← Add this line to enable the
Toolbar to scroll. If you
wanted the TabLayout to
scroll too, you'd add the
code to that element as well.

↑
This line marks the view whose
content you expect the user to scroll.

Those are all the changes we need to make to MainActivity.
Next we'll add scrollable content to TopFragment.

Add scrollable content to TopFragment

We're going to change `TopFragment`'s layout so that it contains scrollable content. We'll add an image of one of the Bits and Pizzas restaurants, along with some text describing the company ethos.

Here's what the new version of `TopFragment` will look like:

← We'll change TopFragment to include an image and some text. We want the user to be able to scroll the entire contents of the fragment.

We'll start by adding the String and image resources to our project.

Add String and image resources

We'll add the String resources first. Open *strings.xml*, then add the following:

```
<string name="company_name">Bits and Pizzas</string>
<string name="restaurant_image">Restaurant image</string>
<string name="home_text">Since we opened our doors in 2017, Bits and Pizzas
    has built its reputation as one of America's best Italian-Digital
    restaurants. Some people believe eating out is about being with your
    friends and family. We believe that good food is best enjoyed while
    staring at your phone.</string>
```

Next we'll add the restaurant image to the *drawable-nodpi* folder. First, switch to the Project view of Android Studio's explorer and check whether the *app/src/main/res/drawable-nodpi* folder exists in your project. If it's not already there, highlight the *app/src/main/res* folder, go to the File menu, choose the New... option, then click on the option to create a new Android resource directory. When prompted, choose a resource type of "drawable", name it "drawable-nodpi" and click on OK.

Once you have a *drawable-nodpi* folder, download the file *restaurant.jpg* from *https://git.io/v9oet*, and add it to the *drawable-nodpi* folder.

You need to add this image → to the drawable-nodpi folder.

Use a nested scroll view to make layout content scrollable

We'll allow the user to scroll the contents of `TopFragment` using a **nested scroll view**. This kind of view works just like a normal scroll view, except that it enables *nested scrolling*. This is important because the coordinator layout *only* listens for nested scroll events. If you use a normal scroll view in your layout, the toolbar won't scroll when the user scrolls the content.

← Another view that enables nested scrolling is the recycler view. You'll find out how to use this in the next chapter.

You add a nested scroll view to your layout using code like this:

```
<android.support.v4.widget.NestedScrollView
    android:layout_width="match_parent"
    android:layout_height="match_parent" >
```

← The NestedScrollView comes from the Design Support Library.

```
    ...
```

← You add any views you want the user to be able to scroll to the NestedScrollView.

```
</android.support.v4.widget.NestedScrollView >
```

You add any views you want the user to be able to scroll to the nested scroll view. If you just have one view, you can add this to the nested scroll view directly. If you want to scroll multiple views, however, these must be added to a separate layout inside the scroll view. This is because a nested scroll view can only have one direct child. As an example, here's how you'd add two text views to a nested scroll view with the help of a linear layout:

```
<android.support.v4.widget.NestedScrollView
    android:layout_width="match_parent"
    android:layout_height="match_parent" >

    <LinearLayout
        ... >

        <TextView
            ... />

        <TextView
            ... />
    </LinearLayout>

</android.support.v4.widget.NestedScrollView >
```

← We're just using a LinearLayout as an example—it could be some other sort of layout instead. The key point is that the NestedScrollView can only have one direct child. If you want to put more than one view in the NestedScrollView, in this case two TextViews, you must put them in another layout first.

Next we'll update `TopFragment`'s layout so it uses a nested scroll view.

How we'll structure TopFragment's layout

Scrolling toolbar
Collapsing toolbar
FAB
Snackbar

We're going to add a restaurant image and some text to
`TopFragment`'s layout. Before we write the code, here's a
breakdown of how we'll structure it.

1 We want the entire fragment to be scrollable. This means we need to
put all the views in a nested scroll view.

2 We'll use two text views for the Bits and Pizzas company name and text.
We'll put these in a vertical linear layout with a white background.

3 We want to display the linear layout containing the two text views on
top of the image. We'll do this by putting them both in a frame layout.

Putting this together, we'll use a nested scroll view for our layout,
and this will contain a frame layout. The frame layout will include
two elements, an image view and a linear layout. The linear layout
will contain two text views to display the company name and ethos.

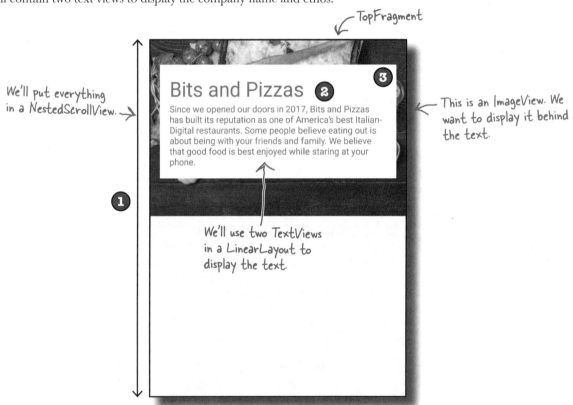

← TopFragment

We'll put everything
in a NestedScrollView. →

This is an ImageView. We
want to display it behind
the text.

We'll use two TextViews
in a LinearLayout to
display the text.

On the next page we'll show you the full code for *fragment_top.xml*.
Once you've updated your code, we'll take the app for a test drive.

The full code for fragment_top.xml

Here's the full code for *fragment_top.xml*; update your code to match ours:

```xml
<android.support.v4.widget.NestedScrollView        ← We want the whole fragment to be able to scroll.
    xmlns:android="http://schemas.android.com/apk/res/android"
    xmlns:tools="http://schemas.android.com/tools"
    android:layout_width="match_parent"
    android:layout_height="match_parent"
    tools:context="com.hfad.bitsandpizzas.TopFragment">

                     ┌── We're using a FrameLayout because we want to
    <FrameLayout  ←──    position the text on top of the image.
        android:layout_width="match_parent"
        android:layout_height="wrap_content" >

        <ImageView android:id="@+id/info_image"
            android:layout_width="match_parent"
            android:layout_height="wrap_content"
            android:scaleType="centerCrop"
            android:src="@drawable/restaurant"
            android:contentDescription="@string/restaurant_image" />

        <LinearLayout
            android:layout_width="match_parent"
            android:layout_height="wrap_content"
            android:layout_marginTop="40dp"
            android:layout_marginLeft="16dp"
            android:layout_marginRight="16dp"
            android:padding="16dp"
            android:background="#FFFFFF"
            android:orientation="vertical">

            <TextView
                android:textSize="32sp"
                android:layout_width="match_parent"
                android:layout_height="wrap_content"
                android:text="@string/company_name" />

            <TextView
                android:layout_width="match_parent"
                android:layout_height="wrap_content"
                android:text="@string/home_text" />
        </LinearLayout>
    </FrameLayout>
</android.support.v4.widget.NestedScrollView>
```

We're using a LinearLayout to contain the text. We're giving it a white background, and the margins will add space around the edges.

BitsAndPizzas
app/src/main
res
layout
fragment_top.xml

Test drive the app

When we run the app, `TopFragment` displays the new
layout. When we scroll the content, the toolbar scrolls too.

☑ **Scrolling toolbar**
☐ **Collapsing toolbar**
☐ **FAB**
☐ **Snackbar**

*When you scroll the content up,
the toolbar scrolls up too.*

This is TopFragment's scrollable content.

By allowing the toolbar to scroll, you free up more space for
content. An added bonus is that you don't have to write any
activity or fragment code to control the toolbar's behavior.
All of the functionality came from using widgets from the
Design Support Library.

Add a collapsing toolbar to OrderActivity

A variant of allowing your toolbar to scroll is the **collapsing toolbar**. A collapsing toolbar is one that starts off large, shrinks when the user scrolls the screen content up, and grows again when the user scrolls the screen content back down. You can even add an image to it, which disappears when the toolbar reaches its minimum height, and becomes visible again as the toolbar expands:

These are both collapsing toolbars, one plain and one with an image.

As you scroll the main content, the collapsing toolbar shrinks and grows.

Over the next few pages, we're going to change OrderActivity to include a collapsing toolbar.

First add some String resources

Before we get started, we need to add some String resources to *strings.xml* that we'll use in OrderActivity's layout. Open *strings.xml*, then add the following resources:

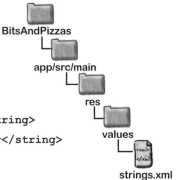

BitsAndPizzas
app/src/main
res
values
strings.xml

```xml
<string name="order_name_hint">Please enter your name</string>
<string name="order_details_hint">Please enter your order</string>
```

We'll start updating the layout on the next page.

How to create a plain collapsing toolbar

You add a collapsing toolbar to your activity's layout using the collapsing toolbar layout from the Design Support Library. In order for it to work, you need to add the collapsing toolbar layout to an app bar layout that's included within a coordinator layout. The collapsing toolbar layout should contain the toolbar you want to collapse.

As the collapsing toolbar needs to respond to scroll events in a separate view, you also need to add scrollable content to the coordinator layout, for example using a nested scroll view.

Here's an overview of how you need to structure your layout file in order to use a collapsing toolbar:

```
<android.support.design.widget.CoordinatorLayout
    ... >

    <android.support.design.widget.AppBarLayout
        ... >

        <android.support.design.widget.CollapsingToolbarLayout
            ... >

            <android.support.v7.widget.Toolbar
                ... />

        </android.support.design.widget.CollapsingToolbarLayout>
    </android.support.design.widget.AppBarLayout>

    <android.support.v4.widget.NestedScrollView
        ...>

        ...

    </android.support.v4.widget.NestedScrollView>
</android.support.design.widget.CoordinatorLayout>
```

You add the CollapsingToolbarLayout to an AppBarLayout, which sits inside a CoordinatorLayout. The CollapsingToolbarLayout contains the Toolbar.

The scrollable content goes here.

In addition to structuring your layout in a particular way, there are some key attributes you need to use to get your collapsing toolbar to work properly. We'll look at these next.

Nested scroll view attributes

As before, you need to tell the coordinator layout which view you expect the user to scroll. You do this by setting the nested scroll view's `layout_behavior` attribute to `"@string/appbar_scrolling_view_behavior"`:

```
<android.support.v4.widget.NestedScrollView
    ...
    app:layout_behavior="@string/appbar_scrolling_view_behavior" >
```

This is the same as when we created a scrolling toolbar.

Collapsing toolbar layout attributes

You want the collapsing toolbar layout to collapse and expand in response to scroll events, so you need to set its `layout_scrollFlags` attribute to control this behavior. In our case, we want the collapsing toolbar layout to collapse until it's the size of a standard toolbar, so we'll set the attribute to a value of `"scroll|exitUntilCollapsed"`:

```
<android.support.design.widget.CollapsingToolbarLayout
    ...
    app:layout_scrollFlags="scroll|exitUntilCollapsed" >
```

This means we want the toolbar to collapse until it's done collapsing.

App bar layout attributes

As before, you apply a theme to your app bar layout to control the appearance of its contents. You also need to specify a height for the contents of the app bar layout. This is the maximum height the collapsing toolbar will be able to expand to. In our case, we'll apply a theme of `"@style/ThemeOverlay.AppCompat.Dark.ActionBar"` as before and set the height to 300dp:

```
<android.support.design.widget.AppBarLayout
    android:layout_width="match_parent"
    android:layout_height="300dp"
    android:theme="@style/ThemeOverlay.AppCompat.Dark.ActionBar" >
```

This is the maximum height of the collapsing toolbar.

Toolbar attributes

If you have items on your toolbar such as an Up button, these may scroll off the screen as the toolbar collapses. You can prevent this from happening by setting the `layout_collapseMode` attribute to `"pin"`:

```
<android.support.v7.widget.Toolbar
    android:id="@+id/toolbar"
    android:layout_width="match_parent"
    android:layout_height="?attr/actionBarSize"
    app:layout_collapseMode="pin" />
```

This pins anything that's on the toolbar, such as the Up button, to the top of the screen.

The full code to add a collapsing toolbar to activity_order.xml

Here's how to add a collapsing toolbar to `OrderActivity`'s layout. Replace your existing code for *activity_order.xml* with the code below:

```xml
<?xml version="1.0" encoding="utf-8"?>
<android.support.design.widget.CoordinatorLayout
    xmlns:android="http://schemas.android.com/apk/res/android"
    xmlns:app="http://schemas.android.com/apk/res-auto"
    android:id="@+id/coordinator"
    android:layout_width="match_parent"
    android:layout_height="match_parent" >
```

We've added an ID to the CoordinatorLayout, as we'll need it later in the chapter.

```xml
    <android.support.design.widget.AppBarLayout
        android:layout_width="match_parent"
        android:layout_height="300dp"
        android:theme="@style/ThemeOverlay.AppCompat.Dark.ActionBar" >
```

```xml
        <android.support.design.widget.CollapsingToolbarLayout
            android:layout_width="match_parent"
            android:layout_height="match_parent"
            app:layout_scrollFlags="scroll|exitUntilCollapsed" >
```

This is the CollapsingToolbarLayout. It needs to be within an AppBarLayout.

```xml
            <android.support.v7.widget.Toolbar
                android:id="@+id/toolbar"
                android:layout_width="match_parent"
                android:layout_height="?attr/actionBarSize"
                app:layout_collapseMode="pin" />
```

The CollapsingToolbarLayout contains a toolbar.

```xml
        </android.support.design.widget.CollapsingToolbarLayout>
    </android.support.design.widget.AppBarLayout>
```

Scrolling toolbar
Collapsing toolbar
FAB
Snackbar

BitsAndPizzas
app/src/main
res
layout
activity_order.xml

The code continues on the next page. →

The activity_order.xml code (continued)

```xml
<android.support.v4.widget.NestedScrollView
    android:layout_width="match_parent"
    android:layout_height="match_parent"
    app:layout_behavior="@string/appbar_scrolling_view_behavior" >

    <LinearLayout
        android:layout_width="match_parent"
        android:layout_height="wrap_content"
        android:orientation="vertical"
        android:padding = "16dp" >

        <EditText
            android:layout_width="match_parent"
            android:layout_height="wrap_content"
            android:hint="@string/order_name_hint" />

        <EditText
            android:layout_width="match_parent"
            android:layout_height="wrap_content"
            android:hint="@string/order_details_hint" />

    </LinearLayout>

</android.support.v4.widget.NestedScrollView>

</android.support.design.widget.CoordinatorLayout>
```

← The NestedScrollView contains the content we want the user to be able to scroll.

We're using a LinearLayout to position the scrollable content.

BitsAndPizzas
app/src/main
res
layout
activity_order.xml

We're using EditTexts to add some content we can scroll to the layout.

Let's see what happens when we run the app.

Test drive the app

When we run the app, `OrderActivity` displays the new layout,
including the collapsing toolbar. The collapsing toolbar starts off
large, and collapses as we scroll the content.

Scrolling toolbar
Collapsing toolbar
FAB
Snackbar

This is the toolbar when it's collapsed.

This is the
toolbar
when it's
expanded.

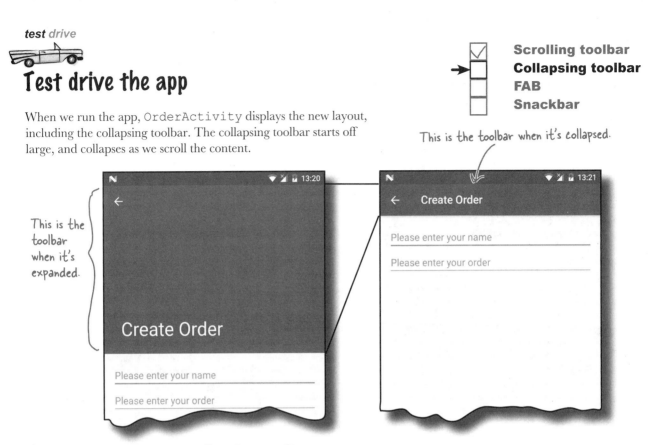

You can add images to collapsing toolbars too

The collapsing toolbar we've created so far is quite plain. It has
a plain background, which grows and shrinks as we scroll the
content in the activity.

We can improve this by adding an image to the collapsing toolbar.
We'll display the image when the collapsing toolbar is large, and
when it shrinks we'll display a standard toolbar instead:

This is the
same collapsing
toolbar,
except we're
going to add
an image to it.

How to add an image to a collapsing toolbar

We're going to update the collapsing toolbar we just created so that it includes an image. For convenience, we'll use the same image that we added to `TopFragment`.

You add an image to a collapsing toolbar by adding an `ImageView` to the `CollapsingToolBarLayout`, specifying the image you want to use. As an optional extra, you can add a parallax effect to the `ImageView` so that the image scrolls at a different rate than the rest of the toolbar. You do this by adding a `layout_collapseMode` attribute to the `ImageView` with a value of `"parallax"`.

We want to use a drawable named "restaurant" for our image. Here's the code we need:

```
<android.support.design.widget.CollapsingToolbarLayout
    ... >

    <ImageView
        android:layout_width="match_parent"
        android:layout_height="match_parent"
        android:scaleType="centerCrop"          ← We're cropping the image to fit inside the AppBarLayout.
        android:src="@drawable/restaurant"
        android:contentDescription="@string/restaurant_image"
        app:layout_collapseMode="parallax" />
                    ↖ This line is optional. It adds parallax animation so the image moves at a different rate than the scrollable content.

    <Toolbar
        ... >

</android.support.design.widget.CollapsingToolbarLayout>
```

BitsAndPizzas
app/src/main
res
layout
activity_order.xml

By default, when the toolbar is collapsed, it will continue to display the image as its background. To get the toolbar to revert to a plain background color when it's collapsed, you add a `contentScrim` attribute to the `CollapsingToolbarLayout`, setting it to the value of the color. We want our toolbar to have the same background color as before, so we'll set it to `"?attr/colorPrimary"`:

```
<android.support.design.widget.CollapsingToolbarLayout
    ...
    app:layout_scrollFlags="scroll|exitUntilCollapsed"
    app:contentScrim="?attr/colorPrimary" >       ← This line changes the toolbar back to its default color when it's collapsed.
```

Those are all the changes we need, so we'll update the code on the next page, and then take it for a test drive.

The updated code for activity_order.xml

Scrolling toolbar
Collapsing toolbar
FAB
Snackbar

Here's the updated code for *activity_order.xml* to add an image to the
collapsing toolbar (update your version to match our changes in bold):

```xml
<?xml version="1.0" encoding="utf-8"?>
<android.support.design.widget.CoordinatorLayout
    xmlns:android="http://schemas.android.com/apk/res/android"
    xmlns:app="http://schemas.android.com/apk/res-auto"
    android:id="@+id/coordinator"
    android:layout_width="match_parent"
    android:layout_height="match_parent" >

    <android.support.design.widget.AppBarLayout
        android:layout_width="match_parent"
        android:layout_height="300dp"
        android:theme="@style/ThemeOverlay.AppCompat.Dark.ActionBar" >

        <android.support.design.widget.CollapsingToolbarLayout
            android:layout_width="match_parent"
            android:layout_height="match_parent"
            app:layout_scrollFlags="scroll|exitUntilCollapsed"
            app:contentScrim="?attr/colorPrimary" >
```

BitsAndPizzas

app/src/main

res

layout

activity_order.xml

This line changes the toolbar background when it's collapsed.

These lines add an image to the collapsing toolbar. It uses snazzy parallax animation.

```xml
            <ImageView
                android:layout_width="match_parent"
                android:layout_height="match_parent"
                android:scaleType="centerCrop"
                android:src="@drawable/restaurant"
                android:contentDescription="@string/restaurant_image"
                app:layout_collapseMode="parallax" />

            <android.support.v7.widget.Toolbar
                android:id="@+id/toolbar"
                android:layout_width="match_parent"
                android:layout_height="?attr/actionBarSize"
                app:layout_collapseMode="pin" />

        </android.support.design.widget.CollapsingToolbarLayout>
    </android.support.design.widget.AppBarLayout>
```

The code continues on the next page. →

The activity_order.xml code (continued)

```
<android.support.v4.widget.NestedScrollView
    android:layout_width="match_parent"
    android:layout_height="match_parent"
    app:layout_behavior="@string/appbar_scrolling_view_behavior" >

    ...

</android.support.v4.widget.NestedScrollView>
</android.support.design.widget.CoordinatorLayout>
```

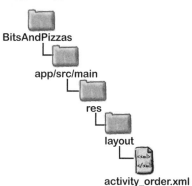

BitsAndPizzas
app/src/main
res
layout
activity_order.xml

Let's see what the app looks like when we run it.

Test drive the app

When we run the app, `OrderActivity`'s collapsing toolbar includes an image. As the toolbar collapses, the image fades, and the toolbar's background changes to its original color. When the toolbar is expanded again, the image reappears.

The toolbar changes color when it's collapsed.

The image appears on the toolbar.

FABs and snackbars

There are two final additions we're going to make to `OrderActivity` from the Design Support Library: a FAB and a snackbar.

A **FAB** is a **floating action button**. It's a circled icon that floats above the user interface, for example in the bottom-right corner of the screen. It's used to promote actions that are so common or important that you want to make them obvious to the user.

A **snackbar** is like a toast except that you can interact with it. It's a short message that appears at the bottom of the screen that's used to give the user information about an operation. Unlike with a toast, you can add actions to a snackbar, such as an action to undo an operation.

We'll add a FAB and snackbar to OrderActivity

We're going to add a FAB to `OrderActivity`. When the user clicks on the FAB, we'll display a snackbar that shows a message to the user. In the real world, you'd want to use the FAB to perform an action such as saving the user's pizza order, but we're just going to focus on showing you how to add the widgets to your app.

Here's what the new version of `OrderActivity` will look like:

Scrolling toolbar
Collapsing toolbar
FAB
Snackbar

This is a FAB that appears in the Google Calendar app. It floats in the bottom-right corner of the screen, and you use it to add events.

This is the snackbar that appears in the Chrome app when you've just closed a web page. You can reopen the page by clicking on the Undo action in the snackbar.

Here's the FAB we're going to add.

When we click on the FAB, a snackbar gets displayed. When it appears, the FAB moves up out of the way.

Add the icon for the FAB

design *support library*

Scrolling toolbar
Collapsing toolbar
FAB
Snackbar

We'll start by adding an icon to our project to display on the FAB. You can either create your own icon from scratch or use one of the icons provided by Google: *https://design.google.com/icons/*.

We're going to use the "done" icon `ic_done_white_24dp`, and we'll add a version of it to our project's *drawable** folders, one for each screen density. Android will decide at runtime which version of the icon to use depending on the screen density of the device.

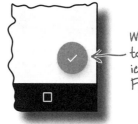

We're going to use this icon on our FAB.

First, switch to the Project view of Android Studio's explorer, highlight the *app/src/main/res* folder in your project, then create folders called *drawable-hdpi*, *drawable-mdpi*, *drawable-xhdpi*, *drawable-xxhdpi*, and *drawable-xxxhdpi* if they don't already exist. Then go to *http://tinyurl.com/HeadFirstAndroidDoneIcons*, and download *ic_done_white_24dp.png* Bits and Pizzas images. Add the image in the *drawable-hdpi* folder to the *drawable-hdpi* folder in your project, then repeat this process for the other folders.

How to add a FAB to your layout

You add a FAB to your layout using code like this:

```
<android.support.design.widget.CoordinatorLayout ...>

    ...

    <android.support.design.widget.FloatingActionButton
        android:layout_width="wrap_content"
        android:layout_height="wrap_content"
        android:layout_gravity="end|bottom"
        android:layout_margin="16dp"
        android:src="@drawable/ic_done_white_24dp"
        android:onClick="onClickDone" />

</android.support.design.widget.CoordinatorLayout>
```

The code for adding a FAB is similar to the code for adding an ImageButton. That's because FloatingActionButton is a subclass of ImageButton.

If you're using the FAB in an activity, you can use the onClick attribute to specify which method should be called when it's clicked.

The above code adds a FAB to the bottom-end corner of the screen, with a margin of 16dp. It uses the `src` attribute to set the FAB's icon to the `ic_done_white_24dp` drawable. We're also using the FAB's `onClick` attribute to specify that the `onClickDone()` method in the layout's activity will get called when the user clicks on the FAB. We'll create this method later.

You usually use a FAB inside a `CoordinatorLayout`, as this means that you can coordinate movement between the different views in your layout. In our case, it means that the FAB will move up when the snackbar appears.

On the next page we'll show you the code for `OrderActivity`'s layout.

The material design guidelines recommend using no more than one FAB per screen.

The updated code for activity_order.xml

Scrolling toolbar
Collapsing toolbar
FAB
Snackbar

Here's the updated code for *activity_order.xml* (update your version to match our changes in bold):

We've not changed any of the code on this page.

```xml
<?xml version="1.0" encoding="utf-8"?>
<android.support.design.widget.CoordinatorLayout
    xmlns:android="http://schemas.android.com/apk/res/android"
    xmlns:app="http://schemas.android.com/apk/res-auto"
    android:id="@+id/coordinator"
    android:layout_width="match_parent"
    android:layout_height="match_parent" >

    <android.support.design.widget.AppBarLayout
        android:layout_width="match_parent"
        android:layout_height="300dp"
        android:theme="@style/ThemeOverlay.AppCompat.Dark.ActionBar" >

        <android.support.design.widget.CollapsingToolbarLayout
            android:layout_width="match_parent"
            android:layout_height="match_parent"
            app:layout_scrollFlags="scroll|exitUntilCollapsed"
            app:contentScrim="?attr/colorPrimary" >

            <ImageView
                android:layout_width="match_parent"
                android:layout_height="match_parent"
                android:scaleType="centerCrop"
                android:src="@drawable/restaurant"
                android:contentDescription="@string/restaurant_image"
                app:layout_collapseMode="parallax" />

            <android.support.v7.widget.Toolbar
                android:id="@+id/toolbar"
                android:layout_width="match_parent"
                android:layout_height="?attr/actionBarSize"
                app:layout_collapseMode="pin" />

        </android.support.design.widget.CollapsingToolbarLayout>
    </android.support.design.widget.AppBarLayout>
```

BitsAndPizzas
app/src/main
res
layout
activity_order.xml

The code continues on the next page. →

The activity_order.xml code (continued)

```xml
<android.support.v4.widget.NestedScrollView
    android:layout_width="match_parent"
    android:layout_height="match_parent"
    app:layout_behavior="@string/appbar_scrolling_view_behavior" >

    <LinearLayout
        ...
    </LinearLayout>

</android.support.v4.widget.NestedScrollView>

<android.support.design.widget.FloatingActionButton
    android:layout_width="wrap_content"
    android:layout_height="wrap_content"
    android:layout_gravity="end|bottom"
    android:layout_margin="16dp"
    android:src="@drawable/ic_done_white_24dp"
    android:onClick="onClickDone" />

</android.support.design.widget.CoordinatorLayout>
```

We're adding the FAB to the CoordinatorLayout so that it will move out the way when a snackbar gets displayed.

BitsAndPizzas
app/src/main
res
layout
activity_order.xml

Add the onClickDone() method to OrderActivity

Now that we've added a FAB to OrderActivity's layout, we need to write some activity code to make the FAB do something when it's clicked. You do this in the same way that you would for a button, by adding the method described by the FAB's onClick attribute to your activity code.

In our case, we've given the onClick attribute a value of "onClickDone", so this means we need to add an onClickDone() method to *OrderActivity.java*:

```java
public void onClickDone(View view) {
    //Code that runs when the FAB is clicked
}
```

You don't have to add this method now; you can wait until we show you the full code a few pages ahead.

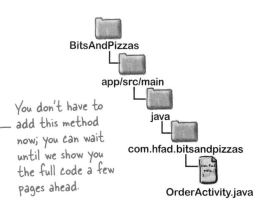

BitsAndPizzas
app/src/main
java
com.hfad.bitsandpizzas
OrderActivity.java

Now we're going to write some code to display a snackbar when the user clicks on the FAB.

How to create a snackbar

As we said earlier in the chapter, a snackbar is a bar that appears at the bottom of the screen that displays a short message to the user. It's similar to a toast, except that you can interact with it.

To create a snackbar, you call the `Snackbar.make()` method. This method takes three parameters: the `View` you want to hold the snackbar, the text you want to display, and an `int` duration. As an example, here's the code for a snackbar that appears on the screen for a short duration:

```
CharSequence text = "Hello, I'm a Snackbar!";
int duration = Snackbar.LENGTH_SHORT;
Snackbar snackbar = Snackbar.make(findViewById(R.id.coordinator, text, duration);
```

If you want to display a String resource, you can pass in the resource ID instead of the text.

In the above code, we've used a view called `coordinator` to hold the snackbar. This view will usually be your activity's coordinator layout so that it can coordinate the snackbar with other views.

We've set the snackbar's duration to `LENGTH_SHORT`, which shows the snackbar for a short period of time. Other options are `LENGTH_LONG` (which shows it for a long duration) and `LENGTH_INDEFINITE` (which shows it indefinitely). With any of these options, the user is able to swipe away the snackbar so that it's no longer displayed.

You can add an action to the snackbar by calling its `setAction()` method. This can be useful if, for example, you want the user to be able to undo an operation they've just performed. The `setAction()` method takes two parameters: the text that should appear for the action, and a `View.onClickListener()`. Any code you want to run when the user clicks on the action should appear in the listener's `onClick()` event:

You pass the setAction() method the text that should appear for the action, and a View.OnClickListener.

```
snackbar.setAction("Undo", new View.OnClickListener() {
    @Override
    public void onClick(View view) {
        //Code to run when the user clicks on the Undo action
    }
});
```

You need to specify what should happen if the user clicks on the Undo action.

Once you've finished creating the snackbar, you display it using its `show()` method:

```
snackbar.show();
```

Pool Puzzle

Your **goal** is to make OrderActivity's
onClickDone() method display a
snackbar. The snackbar should include
an action, "Undo", which shows a toast
when clicked. Take code snippets from
the pool and place them into the blank
lines in the code. You may **not** use the
same snippet more than once, and you
won't need to use all the snippets.

```java
public void onClickDone(View view) {
    CharSequence text = "Your order has been updated";
    int duration =........................................;
    Snackbar snackbar = Snackbar.................(findViewById(R.id.coordinator),.............,.............);
    snackbar.setAction("Undo", new View.OnClickListener() {
        @Override
        public void onClick(View view) {
            Toast toast = Toast................. OrderActivity.this, "Undone!",....................................);
            toast..................;
        }
    });
    snackbar..................;
}
```

**Note: each thing from
the pool can only be
used once!**

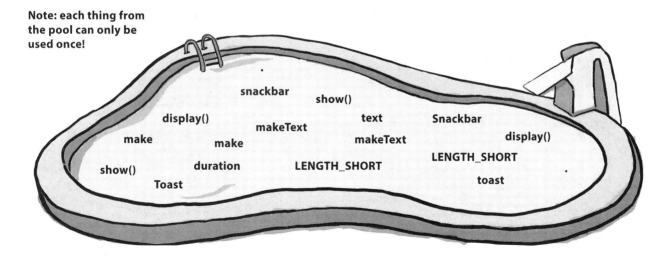

snackbar

show()

display()

makeText

text

Snackbar

make

make

makeText

display()

show()

duration

LENGTH_SHORT

LENGTH_SHORT

Toast

toast

Pool Puzzle Solution

Your **goal** is to make OrderActivity's onClickDone() method display a snackbar. The snackbar should include an action, "Undo", which shows a toast when clicked. Take code snippets from the pool and place them into the blank lines in the code. You may **not** use the same snippet more than once, and you won't need to use all the snippets.

```java
public void onClickDone(View view) {
    CharSequence text = "Your order has been updated";
    int duration = Snackbar . LENGTH_SHORT ;
    Snackbar snackbar = Snackbar. make (findViewById(R.id.coordinator), text , duration );
    snackbar.setAction("Undo", new View.OnClickListener() {
        @Override
        public void onClick(View view) {
            Toast toast = Toast. makeText OrderActivity.this, "Undone!", Toast . LENGTH_SHORT );
            toast. show() ;
        }
    });
    snackbar. show() ;
}
```

You didn't need to use these snippets.

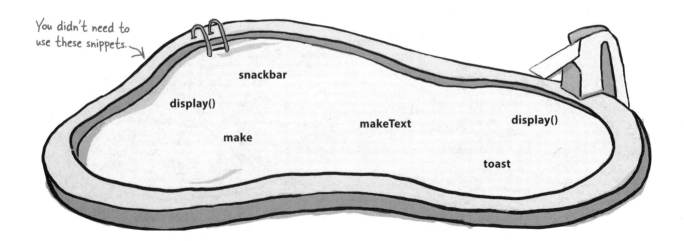

snackbar

display()

make

makeText

display()

toast

The full code for OrderActivity.java

Here's our full code for *OrderActivity.java*, including the code to add a snackbar with an action. Update your version of the code to match our changes (in bold):

```java
package com.hfad.bitsandpizzas;

import android.support.v7.app.AppCompatActivity;
import android.os.Bundle;
import android.support.v7.widget.Toolbar;
import android.support.v7.app.ActionBar;
import android.view.View;
import android.support.design.widget.Snackbar;
import android.widget.Toast;
```
We're using these new classes, so you need to import them.

```java
public class OrderActivity extends AppCompatActivity {

    @Override
    protected void onCreate(Bundle savedInstanceState) {
        super.onCreate(savedInstanceState);
        setContentView(R.layout.activity_order);
        Toolbar toolbar = (Toolbar) findViewById(R.id.toolbar);
        setSupportActionBar(toolbar);
        ActionBar actionBar = getSupportActionBar();
        actionBar.setDisplayHomeAsUpEnabled(true);
    }
```

BitsAndPizzas
app/src/main
java
com.hfad.bitsandpizzas
OrderActivity.java

This method gets called when the user clicks on the FAB.

```java
    public void onClickDone(View view) {
        CharSequence text = "Your order has been updated";
        int duration = Snackbar.LENGTH_SHORT;
        Snackbar snackbar = Snackbar.make(findViewById(R.id.coordinator), text, duration);
        snackbar.setAction("Undo", new View.OnClickListener() {
            @Override
            public void onClick(View view) {
                Toast toast = Toast.makeText(OrderActivity.this, "Undone!", Toast.LENGTH_SHORT);
                toast.show();
            }
        });
        snackbar.show();
    }
}
```
Create the snackbar.

Add an action to the snackbar.

If the user clicks on the snackbar's action, display a toast.

Display the snackbar.

Test drive the app

When we run the app, a FAB is displayed in `OrderActivity`. When we click on the FAB, a snackbar is displayed and the FAB moves up to accommodate it. When we click on the Undo action on the snackbar, a toast is displayed.

Here's the FAB we created.

When you click on the FAB, a snackbar is displayed. The FAB moves up out of the way.

When we click on the snackbar's Undo action, a toast is displayed.

As you can see, snackbars have a lot in common with toasts, as they're both used to display messages to the user. But if you want the user to be able to *interact* with the information you're showing them, choose a snackbar.

Your Android Toolbox

You've got Chapter 12 under your belt and now you've added the Design Support Library to your toolbox.

You can download the full code for the chapter from https://tinyurl.com/HeadFirstAndroid.

BULLET POINTS

- Enable swipe navigation using a **view pager**.

- You tell a view pager about its pages by implementing a **fragment pager adapter**.

- Use the fragment pager adapter's `getCount()` method to tell the view pager how many pages it should have. Use its `getItem()` method to tell it which fragment should appear on each page.

- Add tab navigation by implementing a **tab layout**. Put the toolbar and tab layout inside an **app bar layout** in your layout code, then attach the tab layout to the view pager in your activity code.

- The tab layout comes from the **Android Design Support Library**. This library helps you implement the **material design guidelines** in your app.

- Use a **coordinator layout** to coordinate animations between views.

- Add scrollable content the coordinator layout can coordinate using a **nested scroll view**.

- Use a **collapsing toolbar layout** to add a toolbar that collapses and grows in response to user scroll actions.

- Use a **FAB** (floating action button) to promote common or important user actions.

- A **snackbar** lets you display short messages that the user can interact with.

13 recycler views and card views

Get Recycling

You've already seen how the humble list view is a key part of most apps. But compared to some of the *material design* components we've seen, it's somewhat plain. In this chapter, we'll introduce you to the **recycler view**, a more advanced type of list that gives you *loads more flexibility* and *fits in with the material design ethos*. You'll see how to create **adapters** tailored to your data, and how to completely change the look of your list with *just two lines of code*. We'll also show you how to use **card views** to give your data a *3D material design* appearance.

There's still work to do on the Bits and Pizzas app

In Chapter 12, we updated the Bits and Pizzas app to include components from the Design Support Library, including a tab layout, FAB, and collapsing toolbar. We added these to help users navigate to places in the app more easily, and to implement a consistent material design look and feel. If you recall, material design is inspired by paper and ink, and uses print-based design principles and movement to reflect how real-world objects (such as index cards and pieces of paper) look and behave. But there's one key area we didn't look at: lists.

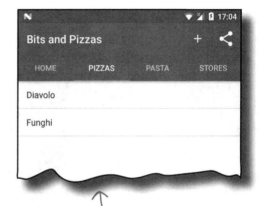

We're currently using list views in `PizzaFragment`, `PastaFragment`, and `StoresFragment` to display the available pizzas, pasta, and stores. These lists are very plain compared with the rest of the app, and could do with some work to give them the same look and feel.

This is the current PizzaFragment. It includes a list of pizzas, but it looks quite plain.

Another disadvantage of list views is that they don't implement nested scrolling. In Chapter 12, we made `MainActivity`'s toolbar scroll in response to the user scrolling content in the activity's fragments. This currently works for `TopFragment`, as it uses a nested scroll view. As none of the other fragments use nested scrolling, however, the toolbar remains fixed when the user tries to scroll their content.

To address these issues, we're going to change `PizzaFragment` to use a **recycler view**. This is a more advanced and flexible version of a list view that implements nested scrolling. Instead of displaying just the names of each pizza in a list view, we'll use a recycler view to display its name and image:

This is the recycler view we're going to add to PizzaFragment.

When you scroll the recycler view, the toolbar moves up. This matches the behavior of TopFragment.

Recycler views from 10,000 feet

Before we dive into the code, let's take a look at how recycler views work. As a recycler view is more flexible than a list view, it takes a lot more setting up.

Like list views, recycler views efficiently manage a small number of views to give the appearance of a large collection of views that extend beyond the screen. They allow you greater flexibility about how the data is displayed than list views do.

A recycler view accesses its data using an **adapter**. Unlike a list view, however, it doesn't use any of the built-in Android adapters such as array adapters. Instead, *you have to write an adapter of your own that's tailored to your data*. This includes specifying the type of data, creating views, and binding the data to the views.

Items are positioned in a recycler view using a **layout manager**. There are a number of built-in layout managers you can use that allow you to position items in a linear list or grid.

Here's a diagram of all those elements put together:

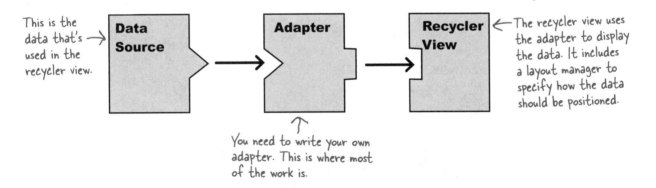

This is the data that's used in the recycler view.

Data Source

Adapter

You need to write your own adapter. This is where most of the work is.

Recycler View

The recycler view uses the adapter to display the data. It includes a layout manager to specify how the data should be positioned.

In our particular case, we're going to create a recycler view to display pizza names and images. We'll go through the steps for how to do this on the next page.

Here's what we're going to do

There are five main steps we'll go through to get the recycler view working:

① **Add the pizza data to the project.**
We'll add images of the pizzas to the app, along with a new `Pizza` class. This class will be the recycler view's data source.

② **Create a card view for the pizza data.**
We're going to make each pizza in the recycler view look as though it's displayed on a separate card. To do this, we'll use a new type of view called a *card view*.

③ **Create a recycler view adapter.**
As we said on the previous page, when you use a recycler view you need to write your own adapter for it. Our adapter needs to take the pizza data and bind each item to a card view. Each card will then be able to be displayed in the recycler view.

④ **Add a recycler view to PizzaFragment.**
After we've created the adapter, we'll add the recycler view to `PizzaFragment`. We'll make it use the adapter, and use a layout manager to display pizza data in a two-column grid.

⑤ **Make the recycler view respond to clicks.**
We'll create a new activity, `PizzaDetailActivity`, and get it to start when the user clicks on one of the pizzas. We'll display details of the pizza in the activity.

These are card views displaying pizza data.

This → is the recycler view.

This is PizzaDetailActivity. →

The first thing we'll do is add the pizza data.

Do this!

We're going to update the Bits and Pizzas app in this chapter, so open your Bits and Pizzas project in Android Studio.

Add the pizza data

We'll start by adding the pizza images to the Bits and Pizzas project. Download the files *diavolo.jpg* and *funghi.jpg* from *https://git.io/v9oet*, then add them to the folder *app/src/main/res/drawable-nodpi*. This folder should already exist in your project, as we added an image to it in Chapter 12.

These are the → pizza images.

Add the Pizza class

We'll get our data from a Pizza class, which we need to add. The ⟵ In a real app, class defines an array of two pizzas, where each pizza has a name and image resource ID. Switch to the Project view of Android Studio's explorer, highlight the com.hfad.bitsandpizzas package in the *app/src/main/java* folder, then go to File→New...→Java class. When prompted, name the class "Pizza" and make sure the package name is com.hfad.bitsandpizzas. Finally, replace the code in *Pizza.java* with the following:

In a real app, we might use a database for this. We're using a Java class here for simplicity.

```java
package com.hfad.bitsandpizzas;

public class Pizza {
    private String name;
    private int imageResourceId;

    public static final Pizza[] pizzas = {
            new Pizza("Diavolo", R.drawable.diavolo),
            new Pizza("Funghi", R.drawable.funghi)
    };

    private Pizza(String name, int imageResourceId) {
        this.name = name;
        this.imageResourceId = imageResourceId;
    }

    public String getName() {
        return name;
    }

    public int getImageResourceId() {
        return imageResourceId;
    }
}
```

Each Pizza has a name and image resource ID. The image resource ID refers to the pizza images we added to the project above.

— The Pizza constructor

→ These are getters for the private variables.

BitsAndPizzas
└ app/src/main
  └ java
    └ com.hfad.bitsandpizzas
      └ Pizza.java

Display the pizza data in a card

☑ Pizza data
→ ☐ **Card view**
☐ **Adapter**
☐ **Recycler view**
☐ **Clicks**

The next thing we need to do is define a layout for the pizza data. This layout will be used by the recycler view's adapter to determine how each item in the recycler view should look. We're going to use a **card view** for this layout.

A card view is a type of frame layout that lets you display information on virtual cards. Card views can have rounded corners and shadows to make it look as though they're positioned above their background. If we use a card view for our pizza data, each pizza will look as though it's displayed on a separate card in the recycler view.

← These are card views. We'll use cards to display the pizza data in the recycler view. →

Add the CardView and RecyclerView Support Libraries

Card views and recycler views come from the CardView and RecyclerView v7 Support Libraries, respectively, so before we can go any further, you need to add them to your project as dependencies.

In Android Studio go to File→Project Structure. In the Project Structure window, click on the "app" option and switch to the Dependencies tab. Then click on the "+" button at the bottom or right side of the screen, choose the "Library dependency" option, and add the CardView Library. Repeat these steps to add the RecyclerView-v7 Library, then click on the OK button to save your changes.

Make sure you add both libraries. ↙

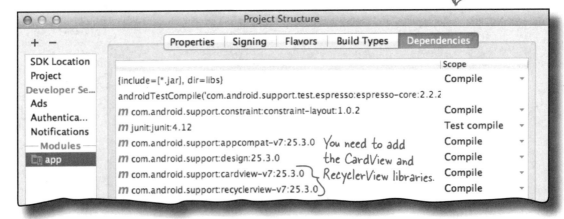

Now that you've added the Support Libraries, we'll create a card view that we can use for our pizza data.

recycler views *and card views*

Pizza data
Card view
Adapter
Recycler view
Clicks

How to create a card view

We're going to create a card view that displays an image with a caption. We'll use it here for the name and image of individual pizzas, but you could also use the same layout for different categories of data such as pasta or stores.

You create a card view by adding a `<CardView>` element to a layout. If you want to use the card view in a recycler view (as we do here), you need to create a new layout file for the card view. Do this by highlighting the *app/src/main/res/layout* folder, and choosing File→New→Layout resource file. When prompted, name the layout "card_captioned_image".

You add a card view to your layout using code like this:

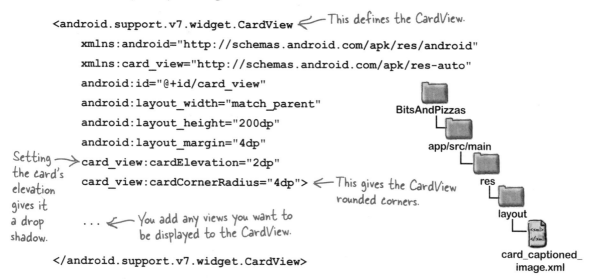

```
<android.support.v7.widget.CardView          ← This defines the CardView.
    xmlns:android="http://schemas.android.com/apk/res/android"
    xmlns:card_view="http://schemas.android.com/apk/res-auto"
    android:id="@+id/card_view"
    android:layout_width="match_parent"
    android:layout_height="200dp"
    android:layout_margin="4dp"
    card_view:cardElevation="2dp"
    card_view:cardCornerRadius="4dp">   ← This gives the CardView
                                          rounded corners.
    ...   ← You add any views you want to
           be displayed to the CardView.
</android.support.v7.widget.CardView>
```

Setting the card's elevation gives it a drop shadow.

BitsAndPizzas
app/src/main
res
layout
card_captioned_
image.xml

In the above code, we've added an extra namespace of:

```
xmlns:card_view="http://schemas.android.com/apk/res-auto"
```

so that we can give the card rounded corners and a drop shadow to make it look higher than its background. You add rounded corners using the `card_view:cardCornerRadius` attribute, and the `card_view:cardElevation` attribute sets its elevation and adds drop shadows.

Once you've defined the card view, you need to add any views you want to display to it. In our case, we'll add a text view and image view to display the name and image of the pizza. We'll show you the full code for this on the next page.

The full card_captioned_image.xml code

Pizza data
Card view
Adapter
Recycler view
Clicks

BitsAndPizzas

app/src/main

res

layout

card_captioned_image.xml

Here's the full code for *card_captioned_image.xml* (update your version of the file to match ours):

```xml
<?xml version="1.0" encoding="utf-8"?>
<android.support.v7.widget.CardView
    xmlns:android="http://schemas.android.com/apk/res/android"
    xmlns:card_view="http://schemas.android.com/apk/res-auto"
    android:id="@+id/card_view"
    android:layout_width="match_parent"
    android:layout_height="200dp"
    android:layout_margin="5dp"
    card_view:cardElevation="2dp"
    card_view:cardCornerRadius="4dp">
```

← The card view will be as wide as its parent allows, and 200dp high.

```xml
    <LinearLayout
        android:layout_width="match_parent"
        android:layout_height="match_parent"
        android:orientation="vertical">
```

← We've put the ImageView and TextView in a LinearLayout, as the CardView can only have one direct child.

```xml
        <ImageView android:id="@+id/info_image"
            android:layout_height="0dp"
            android:layout_width="match_parent"
            android:layout_weight="1.0"
            android:scaleType="centerCrop"/>
```

The image will be as wide as the CardView allows. We're using centerCrop to make sure the image scales uniformly.

The CardView contains an ImageView and a TextView.

```xml
        <TextView
            android:id="@+id/info_text"
            android:layout_marginLeft="4dp"
            android:layout_marginBottom="4dp"
            android:layout_height="wrap_content"
            android:layout_width="match_parent"/>
    </LinearLayout>
</android.support.v7.widget.CardView>
```

Diavolo

This is what the CardView will look like when data's been added to it. We'll do this via the recycler view's adapter.

Note that the above layout doesn't explicitly mention pizza data. This means we can use the same layout for any data items that consist of a caption and an image, such as pasta.

Now that we've created a layout for the card views, we'll move on to creating the recycler view's adapter.

recycler views and card views
☑ **Pizza data**
☑ **Card view**
→ ☐ **Adapter**
☐ **Recycler view**
☐ **Clicks**

How our recycler view adapter will work

As we said earlier, when you use a recycler view in your app, you need to create a recycler view adapter. That's because unlike a list view, recycler views don't use any of the built-in adapters that come with Android. While writing your own adapter may seem like hard work, on the plus side it gives you more flexibility than using a built-in one.

The adapter has two main jobs: to create each of the views that are visible within the recycler view, and to bind each view to a piece of data. In our case, the recycler view needs to display a set of cards, each containing a pizza image and caption. This means that the adapter needs to create each card and bind data to it.

We'll create the recycler view adapter over the next few pages. Here are the steps we'll go through to create it:

① **Specify what data the adapter should work with.**
We want the adapter to work with the pizza data. Each pizza has a name and image resource ID, so we'll pass the adapter an array of pizza names, and an array of image resource IDs.

② **Define the views the adapter should populate.**
We want to use the data to populate a set of pizza cards defined by *card_captioned_image.xml*. We then need to create a set of these cards that will be displayed in the recycler view, one card per pizza.

③ **Bind the data to the cards.**
Finally, we need to display the pizza data in the cards. To make that happen, we need to populate the info_text text view with the name of the pizza, and the info_image image view with the pizza's image.

We'll start by adding a RecyclerView.Adapter class to our project.

---
there are no
Dumb Questions

Q: Why doesn't Android provide ready-made adapters for recycler views?

A: Because recycler view adapters don't just specify the data that will appear. They also specify the views that will be used for each item in the collection. That means that recycler view adapters are both more powerful, and less general, than list view adapters.

Add a recycler view adapter

Pizza data
Card view
Adapter
Recycler view
Clicks

You create a recycler view adapter by extending the `RecyclerView.Adapter` class and overriding various methods; we'll cover these over the next few pages. You also need to define a `ViewHolder` as an inner class, which tells the adapter which views to use for the data items.

We're going to create a recycler view adapter called `CaptionedImagesAdapter`. In Android Studio, highlight the `com.hfad.bitsandpizzas` package in the *app/src/main/java* folder, then go to File→New...→Java class. When prompted, name the class "CaptionedImagesAdapter" and make sure the package name is `com.hfad.bitsandpizzas`. Then replace the code in *CaptionedImagesAdapter.java* with the following:

BitsAndPizzas

app/src/main

java

com.hfad.bitsandpizzas

CaptionedImages
Adapter.java

```
package com.hfad.bitsandpizzas;

import android.support.v7.widget.RecyclerView;
```
← We're extending the RecyclerView class, so we need to import it.

```
class CaptionedImagesAdapter extends
        RecyclerView.Adapter<CaptionedImagesAdapter.ViewHolder>{
```
The ViewHolder is used to specify which views should be used for each data item.

```
    public static class ViewHolder extends RecyclerView.ViewHolder {
        //Define the view to be used for each data item
    }
}
```
You define the ViewHolder as an inner class. We'll complete this later in the chapter.

As you can see, the `ViewHolder` inner class you define is a key part of the adapter. We've left the `ViewHolder` class empty for now, but we'll come back to it later in the chapter.

Before we look in more detail at view holders, we'll tell the adapter what sort of data it should use by adding a constructor.

Relax

Don't worry if Android Studio gives you error messages when you add the above code to your project.

It's just warning you that the code isn't complete yet. We still need to override various methods in our adapter code to tell it how to behave, and we'll do this over the next few pages.

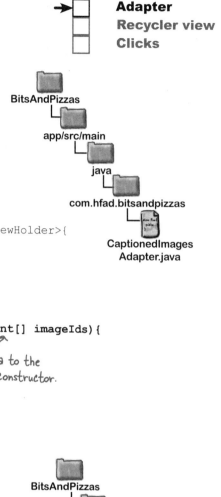

recycler views *and card views*

Pizza data
Card view
Adapter
Recycler view
Clicks

Tell the adapter
what data it should work with...

When you define a recycler view adapter, you need to tell it what sort of data it should use. You do this by defining a constructor that includes the data types you want the adapter to use as parameters.

In our case, we want the adapter to take String captions and int image IDs. We'll therefore add String[] and int[] parameters to the constructor, and save the arrays as private variables. Here's the code that does this; you can either update your version of *CaptionedImagesAdapter.java* now, or wait until we show you the full adapter code later in the chapter.

BitsAndPizzas
app/src/main
java
com.hfad.bitsandpizzas
CaptionedImages
Adapter.java

```
class CaptionedImagesAdapter extends
        RecyclerView.Adapter<CaptionedImagesAdapter.ViewHolder>{

    private String[] captions;      We'll use these variables
    private int[] imageIds;         to hold the pizza data.
    ...

    public CaptionedImagesAdapter(String[] captions, int[] imageIds){
        this.captions = captions;
        this.imageIds = imageIds;       We'll pass the data to the
    }                                   adapter using its constructor.
}
```

...and implement the getItemCount() method

We also need to tell the adapter how many data items there are. You do this by overriding the RecyclerViewAdapter getItemCount() method. This returns an int value, the number of data items. We can derive this from the number of captions we pass the adapter. Here's the code:

BitsAndPizzas
app/src/main
java
com.hfad.bitsandpizzas
CaptionedImages
Adapter.java

```
class CaptionedImagesAdapter extends
        RecyclerView.Adapter<CaptionedImagesAdapter.ViewHolder>{
    ...

    @Override
    public int getItemCount(){
        return captions.length;     The length of the captions array equals the
    }                               number of data items in the recycler view.
}
```

Next we'll define the adapter's view holder.

Define the adapter's view holder

The view holder is used to define what view or views the recycler view should use for each data item it's given. You can think of it as a holder for the views you want the recycler view to display. In addition to views, the view holder contains extra information that's useful to the recycler view, such as its position in the layout.

In our case, we want to display each item of pizza data on a card, which means we need to specify that the adapter's view holder uses a card view. Here's the code to do this (we'll show you the full adapter code later in the chapter):

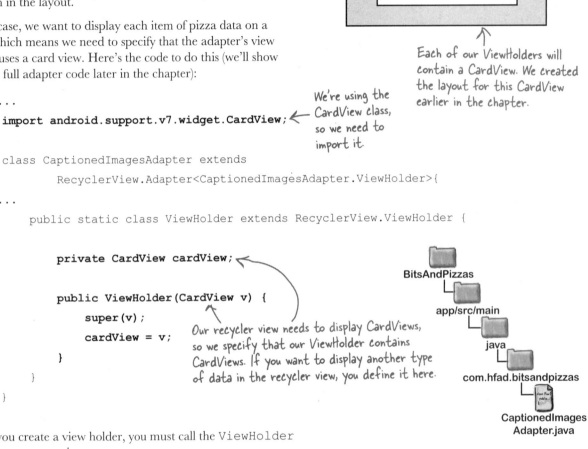

ViewHolder

CardView

Each of our ViewHolders will contain a CardView. We created the layout for this CardView earlier in the chapter.

```
...
import android.support.v7.widget.CardView;
```

We're using the CardView class, so we need to import it.

```
class CaptionedImagesAdapter extends
        RecyclerView.Adapter<CaptionedImagesAdapter.ViewHolder>{
...
    public static class ViewHolder extends RecyclerView.ViewHolder {

        private CardView cardView;

        public ViewHolder(CardView v) {
            super(v);
            cardView = v;
        }
    }
}
```

Our recycler view needs to display CardViews, so we specify that our ViewHolder contains CardViews. If you want to display another type of data in the recycler view, you define it here.

BitsAndPizzas

app/src/main

java

com.hfad.bitsandpizzas

CaptionedImages
Adapter.java

When you create a view holder, you must call the `ViewHolder` super constructor using:

```
super(v);
```

This is because the `ViewHolder` superclass includes metadata such as the item's position in the recycler view, and you need this information for the adapter to work properly.

Now that we've defined our view holders, we need to tell the adapter how to construct one. We'll do this by overriding the adapter's `onCreateViewHolder()` method.

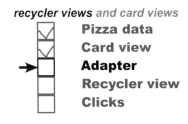

Override the onCreateViewHolder() method

The `onCreateViewHolder()` method gets called when the recycler view requires a new view holder. The recycler view calls the method repeatedly when the recycler view is first constructed to build the set of view holders that will be displayed on the screen.

The method takes two parameters: a `ViewGroup` parent object (the recycler view itself) and an `int` parameter called `viewType`, which is used if you want to display different kinds of views for different items in the list. It returns a view holder object. Here's what the method looks like:

```
@Override
public CaptionedImagesAdapter.ViewHolder onCreateViewHolder(
        ViewGroup parent, int viewType){
    //Code to instantiate the ViewHolder
}
```

This method gets called when the recycler view needs to create a view holder.

BitsAndPizzas

app/src/main

java

com.hfad.bitsandpizzas

CaptionedImages Adapter.java

We need to add code to the method to instantiate the view holder. To do this, we need to call the `ViewHolder`'s constructor, which we defined on the previous page. The constructor takes one parameter, a `CardView`. We'll create the `CardView` from the *card_captioned_image.xml* layout we created earlier in the chapter using this code:

```
CardView cv = (CardView) LayoutInflater.from(parent.getContext())
        .inflate(R.layout.card_captioned_image, parent, false);
```

Get a LayoutInflater object.

Use the LayoutInflator to turn the layout into a CardView. This is nearly identical to code you've already seen in the onCreateView() of fragments.

Here's the full code for the `onCreateViewHolder()` method (we'll add this to the adapter later):

```
@Override
public CaptionedImagesAdapter.ViewHolder onCreateViewHolder(
                ViewGroup parent, int viewType){
    CardView cv = (CardView) LayoutInflater.from(parent.getContext())
            .inflate(R.layout.card_captioned_image, parent, false);
    return new ViewHolder(cv);
}
```

Specify what layout to use for the contents of the ViewHolder.

Now that the adapter can create view holders, we need to get it to populate the card views they contain with data.

Add the data to the card views

You add data to the card views by implementing the adapter's `onBindViewHolder()` method. This gets called whenever the recycler view needs to display data in a view holder. It takes two parameters: the view holder the data needs to be bound to, and the position in the data set of the data that needs to be bound.

Our card view contains two views, an image view with an ID of `info_image`, and a text view with an ID of `info_text`. We'll populate these with data from the `captions` and `imageIds` arrays. Here's the code that will do that:

Pizza data
Card view
Adapter
Recycler view
Clicks

id: info_text

TextView

id: info_image

CardView

ImageView

Each CardView contains a TextView and ImageView. We need to populate these with the caption and image of each pizza.

```
...
import android.widget.ImageView;
import android.widget.TextView;
import android.graphics.drawable.Drawable;
import android.support.v4.content.ContextCompat;
```

We're using these extra classes, so we need to import them.

```
class CaptionedImagesAdapter extends
        RecyclerView.Adapter<CaptionedImagesAdapter.ViewHolder>{

    private String[] captions;
    private int[] imageIds;
```

We added these variables earlier. They contain the captions and image resource IDs of the pizzas.

BitsAndPizzas

app/src/main

java

com.hfad.bitsandpizzas

CaptionedImages
Adapter.java

```
    ...

    @Override
    public void onBindViewHolder(ViewHolder holder, int position){
        CardView cardView = holder.cardView;
        ImageView imageView = (ImageView)cardView.findViewById(R.id.info_image);
        Drawable drawable =
                ContextCompat.getDrawable(cardView.getContext(), imageIds[position]);
        imageView.setImageDrawable(drawable);
        imageView.setContentDescription(captions[position]);
        TextView textView = (TextView)cardView.findViewById(R.id.info_text);
        textView.setText(captions[position]);
    }
}
```

The recycler view calls this method when it wants to use (or reuse) a view holder for a new piece of data.

Display the image in the ImageView.

Display the caption in the TextView.

That's all the code we need for our adapter. We'll show you the full code over the next couple of pages.

The full code for CaptionedImagesAdapter.java

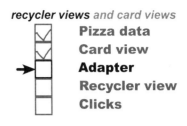

Here's our complete code for the adapter. Update your version of *CaptionedImagesAdapter.java* so that it matches ours.

```java
package com.hfad.bitsandpizzas;

import android.support.v7.widget.RecyclerView;
import android.support.v7.widget.CardView;
import android.view.ViewGroup;
import android.view.LayoutInflater;
import android.widget.ImageView;
import android.widget.TextView;
import android.graphics.drawable.Drawable;
import android.support.v4.content.ContextCompat;
```

These are the classes we're using, so we need to import them.

BitsAndPizzas
└ **app/src/main**
   └ **java**
      └ **com.hfad.bitsandpizzas**
         └ **CaptionedImages Adapter.java**

```java
class CaptionedImagesAdapter extends
        RecyclerView.Adapter<CaptionedImagesAdapter.ViewHolder>{

    private String[] captions;
    private int[] imageIds;
```

We're using these variables for the captions and image resource IDs.

```java
    public static class ViewHolder extends RecyclerView.ViewHolder {

        private CardView cardView;

        public ViewHolder(CardView v) {
            super(v);
            cardView = v;
        }
    }
```

Each ViewHolder will display a CardView.

```java
    public CaptionedImagesAdapter(String[] captions, int[] imageIds){
        this.captions = captions;
        this.imageIds = imageIds;
    }
```

Pass data to the adapter in its constructor.

The code continues on the next page.

The full CaptionedImagesAdapter.java code (continued)

Pizza data
Card view
Adapter
Recycler view
Clicks

BitsAndPizzas
app/src/main
java
com.hfad.bitsandpizzas
CaptionedImages
Adapter.java

```java
@Override
public int getItemCount(){     ← The number of data items
    return captions.length;
}

@Override
public CaptionedImagesAdapter.ViewHolder onCreateViewHolder(
        ViewGroup parent, int viewType){
    CardView cv = (CardView) LayoutInflater.from(parent.getContext())
            .inflate(R.layout.card_captioned_image, parent, false);
    return new ViewHolder(cv);
}
```

Use the layout we created earlier for the CardViews.

```java
@Override
public void onBindViewHolder(ViewHolder holder, int position){
    CardView cardView = holder.cardView;
    ImageView imageView = (ImageView)cardView.findViewById(R.id.info_image);
    Drawable drawable =
            ContextCompat.getDrawable(cardView.getContext(), imageIds[position]);
    imageView.setImageDrawable(drawable);
    imageView.setContentDescription(captions[position]);
    TextView textView = (TextView)cardView.findViewById(R.id.info_text);
    textView.setText(captions[position]);
}
```

Populate the CardView's ImageView and TextView with data.

That's all the code we need for our adapter. So what's next?

Create the recycler view

So far we've created a card view layout that displays captioned images, and an adapter that creates the cards and populates them with data. The next thing we need to do is create the recycler view, which will pass pizza data to the adapter so that it can populate the cards with the pizza images and captions. The recycler view will then display the cards.

We're going to add the recycler view to our existing `PizzaFragment`. Whenever the user clicks on the Pizzas tab in `MainActivity`, the pizzas will be displayed:

This is what the recycler → view in PizzaFragment will look like. It will display the pizza cards in a two-column grid.

Add a layout for PizzaFragment

Before we can add the recycler view, we need to add a new layout file to our project for `PizzaFragment` to use. This is because we intially created `PizzaFragment` as a `ListFragment`, and these define their own layout.

To add the layout file, highlight the *app/src/main/res/layout* folder in Android Studio, and choose File→New→Layout resource file. When prompted, name the layout "fragment_pizza".

Add the RecyclerView to PizzaFragment's layout

Pizza data
Card view
Adapter
Recycler view
Clicks

BitsAndPizzas

app/src/main

res

layout

fragment_
pizza.xml

You add a recycler view to a layout using the `<RecyclerView>` element from the RecyclerView Support Library.

Our `PizzaFragment` layout only needs to display a single recycler view, so here's the full code for *fragment_pizza.xml* (update your version of the code to match ours):

```
<android.support.v7.widget.RecyclerView          ←—This defines the RecyclerView.
    xmlns:android="http://schemas.android.com/apk/res/android"
    android:id="@+id/pizza_recycler"          ←—  We've given the recycler view an ID so
    android:layout_width="match_parent"            that we can refer to it in our Java code.
    android:layout_height="match_parent"
    android:scrollbars="vertical" />          ←—This adds a vertical scrollbar.
```

You add scrollbars to the recycler view using the `android:scrollbars` attribute. We've set this to `"vertical"` because we want our recycler view to be able to scroll vertically. We've also given the recycler view an ID so that we can get a reference to it in our `PizzaFragment` code; we need this in order to control its behavior.

Now that we've added a recycler view to `PizzaFragment`'s layout, we need to update our fragment code to get the recycler view to use the adapter we created.

Get the recycler view to use the adapter

To get the recycler view to use the adapter, there are two things we need to do: tell the adapter what data to use, then attach the adapter to the recycler view. We can tell the adapter what data to use by passing it the pizza names and image resource IDs via its constructor. We'll then use the `RecyclerView` `setAdapter()` method to assign the adapter to the recycler view.

The code to do this is all code that you've seen before, so we'll show you the full `PizzaFragment` code on the next page.

The full PizzaFragment.java code

Here's our full code for *PizzaFragment.java* (update your
version of the code to match our changes):

```
package com.hfad.bitsandpizzas;

import android.os.Bundle;
import android.support.v4.app.ListFragment;
import android.view.LayoutInflater;
import android.view.View;
import android.view.ViewGroup;
import android.widget.ArrayAdapter;
import android.support.v7.widget.RecyclerView;

public class PizzaFragment extends ListFragment {

    @Override
    public View onCreateView(LayoutInflater inflater, ViewGroup container,
                             Bundle savedInstanceState) {
        ArrayAdapter<String> adapter = new ArrayAdapter<>(
            inflater.getContext(),
            android.R.layout.simple_list_item_1,
            getResources().getStringArray(R.array.pizzas));
        setListAdapter(adapter);
        return super.onCreateView(inflater, container, savedInstanceState);
        RecyclerView pizzaRecycler = (RecyclerView)inflater.inflate(
                        R.layout.fragment_pizza, container, false);

        String[] pizzaNames = new String[Pizza.pizzas.length];
        for (int i = 0; i < pizzaNames.length; i++) {
            pizzaNames[i] = Pizza.pizzas[i].getName();
        }

        int[] pizzaImages = new int[Pizza.pizzas.length];
        for (int i = 0; i < pizzaImages.length; i++) {
            pizzaImages[i] = Pizza.pizzas[i].getImageResourceId();
        }

        CaptionedImagesAdapter adapter = new CaptionedImagesAdapter(pizzaNames, pizzaImages);
        pizzaRecycler.setAdapter(adapter);
        return pizzaRecycler;
    }
}
```

*We're changing PizzaFragment to be
a Fragment, not a ListFragment.*

*We're no longer using an
ArrayAdapter, so delete this line.*

*We need to import the
RecyclerView class.*

Change this from ListFragment to Fragment.

BitsAndPizzas
— **app/src/main**
— — **java**
— — — **com.hfad.bitsandpizzas**
— — — — **Pizza
Fragment.java**

*Delete these lines,
as they're no longer
necessary.*

*Use the layout we updated
on the previous page.*

*Add the pizza names to an array
of Strings, and the pizza images
to an array of ints.*

Pass the arrays to the adapter.

There's just one more thing we need to do: specify how the
views in the recycler view should be arranged.

Pizza data
Card view
Adapter
Recycler view
Clicks

A recycler view uses a layout manager to arrange its views

One of the ways in which a recycler view is more flexible than a list view is in how it arranges its views. A list view displays its views in a single vertical list, but a recycler view gives you more options. You can choose to display views in a linear list, a grid, or a staggered grid.

You specify how to arrange the views using a **layout manager**. The layout manager positions views inside a recycler view: the type of layout manager you use determines how items are positioned. Here are some examples:

We don't cover how to do it, but you can also write your own layout managers. If you search for "android recyclerview layoutmanager" you'll find many third-party ones you can use in your code, from carousels to circles.

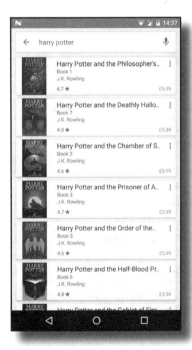

Linear layout manager

This arranges items in a vertical or horizontal list.

Grid layout manager

This arranges items in a grid.

Staggered grid layout manager

This arranges unevenly sized items in a staggered grid.

On the next page, we'll show you how to specify which layout manager to use in your recycler view.

recycler views and card views

Pizza data
Card view
Adapter
Recycler view
Clicks

Specify the layout manager

You tell the recycler view which layout manager it should use by creating a new instance of the type of layout manager you want to use, then attaching it to the recycler view.

Linear layout manager

To tell the recycler view that you want it to display its views in a linear list, you'd use the following code:

```
LinearLayoutManager layoutManager = new LinearLayoutManager(getActivity());
pizzaRecycler.setLayoutManager(layoutManager);
```

This needs to be a Context. If you use this code in an activity, you use "this" instead of getActivity().

The `LinearLayoutManager` constructor takes one parameter, a `Context`. If you're using the code in an activity, you'd normally use `this` to pass it the current activity (a context). The above code uses `getActivity()` instead, as our recycler view is in a fragment.

Grid layout manager

You use similar code to specify a grid layout manager, except that you need to create a new `GridLayoutManager` object instead. The `GridLayoutManager` takes two parameters in its constructor: a `Context`, and an `int` value specifying the number of columns the grid should have.

This says that the GridLayoutManager should be two columns wide.

```
GridLayoutManager layoutManager = new GridLayoutManager(getActivity(), 2);
```

You can also change the orientation of the grid. To do this, you add two more parameters to the constructor: the orientation, and whether you want the views to appear in reverse order.

Gives the GridLayoutManager a horizontal orientation.

```
GridLayoutManager layoutManager =
        new GridLayoutManager(getActivity(), 1, GridLayoutManager.HORIZONTAL, false);
```

If you wanted to display the list in reverse order, you'd set this to true.

Staggered grid layout manager

You tell the recycler view to use a staggered grid layout manager by creating a new `StaggeredGridLayoutManager` object. Its constructor takes two parameters: an `int` value for the number of columns or rows, and an `int` value for its orientation. As an example, here's how you'd specify a staggered grid layout oriented vertically with two rows:

This gives the staggered grid layout a vertical orientation.

```
StaggeredGridLayoutManager layoutManager =
        new StaggeredGridLayoutManager(2, StaggeredGridLayoutManager.VERTICAL);
```

Let's add a layout manager to our recycler view.

The full PizzaFragment.java code

We're going to use a GridLayoutManager to display the pizza data in a grid. Here's the full code for *PizzaFragment.java*, update your version of the code to match our changes (in bold):

```java
package com.hfad.bitsandpizzas;

import android.os.Bundle;
import android.support.v4.app.Fragment;
import android.view.LayoutInflater;
import android.view.View;
import android.view.ViewGroup;
import android.support.v7.widget.RecyclerView;
import android.support.v7.widget.GridLayoutManager;

public class PizzaFragment extends Fragment {

    @Override
    public View onCreateView(LayoutInflater inflater, ViewGroup container,
                             Bundle savedInstanceState) {
        RecyclerView pizzaRecycler = (RecyclerView)inflater.inflate(
                R.layout.fragment_pizza, container, false);

        String[] pizzaNames = new String[Pizza.pizzas.length];
        for (int i = 0; i < pizzaNames.length; i++) {
            pizzaNames[i] = Pizza.pizzas[i].getName();
        }

        int[] pizzaImages = new int[Pizza.pizzas.length];
        for (int i = 0; i < pizzaImages.length; i++) {
            pizzaImages[i] = Pizza.pizzas[i].getImageResourceId();
        }

        CaptionedImagesAdapter adapter = new CaptionedImagesAdapter(pizzaNames, pizzaImages);
        pizzaRecycler.setAdapter(adapter);
        GridLayoutManager layoutManager = new GridLayoutManager(getActivity(), 2);
        pizzaRecycler.setLayoutManager(layoutManager);
        return pizzaRecycler;
    }
}
```

We're using this class, so we need to import it.

Pizza data
Card view
Adapter
Recycler view
Clicks

BitsAndPizzas
app/src/main
java
com.hfad.bitsandpizzas
Pizza Fragment.java

We're going to display the CardViews in a grid with two columns, so we're using a GridLayoutManager.

Next we'll examine what happens when the code runs, then take our app for a test drive.

What happens when the code runs

recycler views and card views
Pizza data
Card view
Adapter
Recycler view
Clicks

① **The user clicks on the Pizzas tab in MainActivity.**
PizzaFragment is displayed, and its onCreateView() method runs.

② **The PizzaFragment onCreateView() method creates a new CaptionedImagesAdapter.**
The method passes the names and images of the pizzas to the adapter using the adapter's constructor, and sets the adapter to the recycler view.

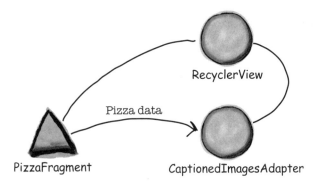

③ **The PizzaFragment onCreateView() method creates a GridLayoutManager and assigns it to the recycler view.**
The GridLayoutManager means that the views will be displayed in a grid. As the recycler view has a vertical scrollbar, the list will be displayed vertically.

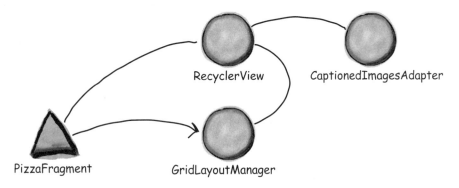

The story continues

Pizza data
Card view
Adapter
Recycler view
Clicks

4 The adapter creates a view holder for each of the CardViews the recycler view needs to display.

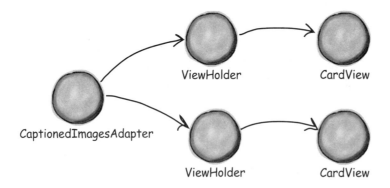

5 The adapter then binds the pizza names and images to the text view and image view in each card view.

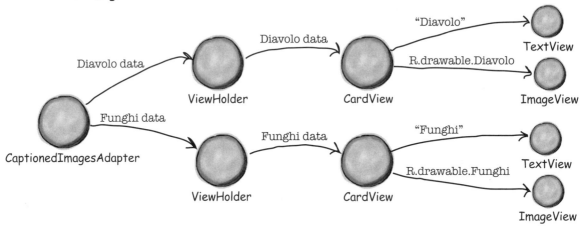

Let's run the app and see how it looks.

Test drive the app

When we run the app, `MainActivity` is displayed.
When we click on or swipe to the Pizzas tab, the pizzas
are displayed in a grid. When we scroll the pizza data,
`MainActivity`'s toolbar responds.

When you click on the Pizzas
tab, PizzaFragment is displayed.
It contains this grid of card
views populated with pizza data.

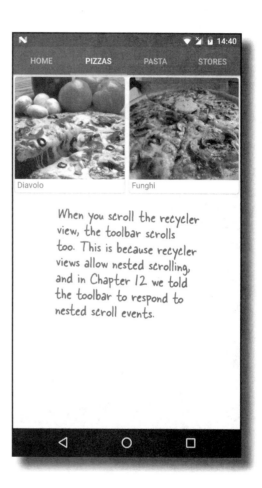

When you scroll the recycler
view, the toolbar scrolls
too. This is because recycler
views allow nested scrolling,
and in Chapter 12 we told
the toolbar to respond to
nested scroll events.

As you can see, adding a recycler view is more involved
than adding a list view, but it gives you a lot more flexibility.
Most of the work comes from having to write a bespoke
recycler view adapter, but you can reuse it elsewhere in
your app. As an example, suppose you wanted to display
pasta cards in a recycler view. You would use the same
adapter we created earlier, but pass it pasta data instead of
pizzas.

Before we move on, have a go at the following exercise.

RecyclerView Magnets

Use the magnets on this page and the next to create a new recycler
view for the pasta dishes. The recycler view should contain a grid of card
views, each one displaying the name and image of a pasta dish.

This is the code for the Pasta class.

```java
package com.hfad.bitsandpizzas;

public class Pasta {
    private String name;
    private int imageResourceId;

    public static final...............[] pastas = {
            new Pasta("Spaghetti Bolognese", R.drawable.spag_bol),
            new Pasta("Lasagne", R.drawable.lasagne)
    };

    private Pasta(String name, int imageResourceId) {
        this.name = name;
        this.imageResourceId = imageResourceId;
    }

    public String ........................ {
        return name;
    }

    public int ......................................... {
        return imageResourceId;
    }
}
```

BitsAndPizzas
app/src/main
java
com.hfad.bitsandpizzas
Pasta.java

```
getName()        Pasta

android:scrollbars      RecyclerView

android.support.v7.widget.RecyclerView

=

"vertical"        getImageResourceId()
```

This is the code for the layout.

```xml
< .................................................
    xmlns:android="http://schemas.android.com/apk/res/android"
    android:id="@+id/pasta_recycler"

    ..................................................
    android:layout_width="match_parent"
    android:layout_height="match_parent"/>
```

BitsAndPizzas
app/src/main
res
layout
fragment_
pasta.xml

...
← This is the code for PastaFragment.java.

```java
public class PastaFragment extends Fragment {

    @Override
    public View onCreateView(LayoutInflater inflater, ViewGroup container,
                             Bundle savedInstanceState) {
        RecyclerView pastaRecycler = (RecyclerView)inflater.inflate(

        ................................................., container, false);

        String[] pastaNames = new String[Pasta.pastas.length];
        for (int i = 0; i < pastaNames.length; i++) {
            pastaNames[i] = Pasta.pastas[i].getName();
        }

        int[] pastaImages = new int[Pasta.pastas.length];
        for (int i = 0; i < pastaImages.length; i++) {
            pastaImages[i] = Pasta.pastas[i].getImageResourceId();
        }

        ................................................. adapter =

                new ................................................. (pastaNames, .............................);
        pastaRecycler.setAdapter(adapter);

        ................................................. layoutManager = new ................................................. (getActivity(), 2);
        pastaRecycler.setLayoutManager(layoutManager);
        return pastaRecycler;
    }
}
```

BitsAndPizzas
└ **app/src/main**
    └ **java**
        └ **com.hfad.bitsandpizzas**
            └ **Pasta Fragment.java**

CaptionedImagesAdapter

ArrayAdapter

CaptionedImagesAdapter

GridLayout

GridLayoutManager

R.layout.fragment_pasta

pastaImages

GridLayout

ArrayAdapter

GridLayoutManager

RecyclerView Magnets Solution

Use the magnets on this page and the next to create a new recycler
view for the pasta dishes. The recycler view should contain a grid of card
views, each one displaying the name and image of a pasta dish.

```
package com.hfad.bitsandpizzas;

public class Pasta {
    private String name;
    private int imageResourceId;           It's an array of Pasta objects.

    public static final   Pasta   [] pastas = {
            new Pasta("Spaghetti Bolognese", R.drawable.spag_bol),
            new Pasta("Lasagne", R.drawable.lasagne)
    };

    private Pasta(String name, int imageResourceId) {
        this.name = name;
        this.imageResourceId = imageResourceId;
    }

    public String   getName()   {            These methods are used by
        return name;                          PastaFragment.java.
    }

    public int   getImageResourceId()   {
        return imageResourceId;
    }
}
```

BitsAndPizzas
└ **app/src/main**
  └ **java**
    └ **com.hfad.bitsandpizzas**
      └ **Pasta.java**

RecyclerView

This is a spare magnet.

Add the recycler view to the layout.

```
<   android.support.v7.widget.RecyclerView
        xmlns:android="http://schemas.android.com/apk/res/android"
        android:id="@+id/pasta_recycler"
        android:scrollbars   =   "vertical"          Add vertical scrollbars.
        android:layout_width="match_parent"
        android:layout_height="match_parent"/>
```

BitsAndPizzas
└ **app/src/main**
  └ **res**
    └ **layout**
      └ **fragment_
pasta.xml**

...

```
public class PastaFragment extends Fragment {

    @Override
    public View onCreateView(LayoutInflater inflater, ViewGroup container,
                             Bundle savedInstanceState) {
        RecyclerView pastaRecycler = (RecyclerView)inflater.inflate(
```

Use this layout. ——→ `R.layout.fragment_pasta` ..., container, false);

```
        String[] pastaNames = new String[Pasta.pastas.length];
        for (int i = 0; i < pastaNames.length; i++) {
            pastaNames[i] = Pasta.pastas[i].getName();
        }

        int[] pastaImages = new int[Pasta.pastas.length];
        for (int i = 0; i < pastaImages.length; i++) {
            pastaImages[i] = Pasta.pastas[i].getImageResourceId();
        }
```

We're using the
CaptionedImagesAdapter
we wrote earlier.

Pass the pasta names and
images to the adapter.

`CaptionedImagesAdapter` adapter =

new `CaptionedImagesAdapter` (pastaNames, `pastaImages`);
```
        pastaRecycler.setAdapter(adapter);
```

`GridLayoutManager` layoutManager = new `GridLayoutManager` (getActivity(), 2);
```
        pastaRecycler.setLayoutManager(layoutManager);
        return pastaRecycler;
    }
}
```

Use the GridLayoutManager to
display the card views in a grid.

BitsAndPizzas
└ app/src/main
  └ java
    └ com.hfad.bitsandpizzas
      └ Pasta
        Fragment.java

You didn't need to use
these magnets.

`GridLayout`

`GridLayout`   `ArrayAdapter`   `ArrayAdapter`

Make the recycler view respond to clicks

Pizza data
Card view
Adapter
Recycler view
Clicks

So far, we've added a recycler view to `PizzaFragment`, and created an adapter to populate it with pizza data.

The next thing we need to do is get the recycler view to respond to clicks. We'll create a new activity, `PizzaDetailActivity`, which will start when the user clicks on one of the pizzas. The name and image of the pizza the user selects will be displayed in the activity:

When the user clicks on one of the pizzas in the recycler view, we'll display details of that pizza in PizzaDetailActivity.

Before we can get the recycler view to respond to clicks, we need to create `PizzaDetailActivity`.

Create PizzaDetailActivity

To create `PizzaDetailActivity`, click on the `com.hfad.bitsandpizzas` package in the Bits and Pizzas folder structure, then go to File→New...→Activity→Empty Activity. Name the activity "PizzaDetailActivity", name the layout "activity_pizza_detail", make sure the package name is `com.hfad.bitsandpizzas`, and **check the Backwards Compatibility (AppCompat) option**.

If prompted for the activity's source language, select the option for Java.

Now let's update `PizzaDetailActivity`'s layout. Open *activity_pizza_detail.xml*, and update it with the code below, which adds a text view and image view to the layout that we'll use to display details of the pizza:

```xml
<?xml version="1.0" encoding="utf-8"?>
<LinearLayout xmlns:android="http://schemas.android.com/apk/res/android"
    xmlns:tools="http://schemas.android.com/tools"
    android:layout_width="match_parent"
    android:layout_height="match_parent"
    android:orientation="vertical"
    tools:context="com.hfad.bitsandpizzas.PizzaDetailActivity">

    <include
        layout="@layout/toolbar_main"
        android:id="@+id/toolbar" />

    <TextView
        android:id="@+id/pizza_text"
        android:layout_width="wrap_content"
        android:layout_height="wrap_content"
        android:textAppearance="?android:attr/textAppearanceLarge" />

    <ImageView
        android:id="@+id/pizza_image"
        android:layout_height="wrap_content"
        android:layout_width="match_parent"
        android:adjustViewBounds="true"/>
</LinearLayout>
```

We'll add a toolbar to the activity.

We'll put the name of the pizza in the TextView.

We'll put the pizza image in the ImageView.

BitsAndPizzas
app/src/main
res
layout
activity_pizza_detail.xml

We'll look at what we need the code for *PizzaDetailActivity.java* to do on the next page.

Pizza data
Card view
Adapter
Recycler view
Clicks

What PizzaDetailActivity needs to do

There are a couple of things that we need
`PizzaDetailActivity` to do:

★ `PizzaDetailActivity`'s main purpose is to display the name
and image of the pizza the user has selected. To do this, we'll get
the selected pizza's ID from the intent that starts the activity. We'll
pass this to `PizzaDetailActivity` from `PizzaFragment`
when the user clicks on one of the pizzas in the recycler view.

★ We'll enable the `PizzaDetailActivity`'s Up button so that
when the user clicks on it, they'll get returned to `MainActivity`.

Update AndroidManifest.xml to give
PizzaDetailActivity a parent

We'll start by updating *AndroidManifest.xml* to specify that
`MainActivity` is the parent of `PizzaDetailActivity`.
This means that when the user clicks on the Up button in
`PizzaDetailActivity`'s app bar, `MainActivity` will be
displayed. Here's our version of *AndroidManifest.xml* (update your
version to match our changes in bold):

```
<manifest ...>
    <application
        ...>
        <activity
            android:name=".MainActivity">
            ...
        </activity>
        <activity
            android:name=".OrderActivity"
            ...
        </activity>
        <activity
            android:name=".PizzaDetailActivity"
            android:parentActivityName=".MainActivity">
        </activity>
    </application>
</manifest>
```

BitsAndPizzas

app/src/main

AndroidManifest.xml

This sets MainActivity as
PizzaDetailActivity's parent.

Next, we'll update *PizzaDetailActivity.java*. You've already seen how to
do everything we need, so we're just going to show you the full code.

recycler views *and card views*
Pizza data
Card view
Adapter
Recycler view
Clicks

The code for PizzaDetailActivity.java

Here's the full code for *PizzaDetailActivity.java*; update your version of the code to match ours:

BitsAndPizzas

app/src/main

java

com.hfad.bitsandpizzas

PizzaDetailActivity.java

```java
package com.hfad.bitsandpizzas;

import android.support.v7.app.ActionBar;
import android.support.v7.app.AppCompatActivity;
import android.os.Bundle;
import android.support.v7.widget.Toolbar;
import android.widget.ImageView;
import android.widget.TextView;
import android.support.v4.content.ContextCompat;
```

We're using these classes, so we need to import them.

```java
public class PizzaDetailActivity extends AppCompatActivity {

    public static final String EXTRA_PIZZA_ID = "pizzaId";
```

We'll use this constant to pass the ID of the pizza as extra information in the intent.

```java
    @Override
    protected void onCreate(Bundle savedInstanceState) {
        super.onCreate(savedInstanceState);
        setContentView(R.layout.activity_pizza_detail);

        //Set the toolbar as the activity's app bar
        Toolbar toolbar = (Toolbar) findViewById(R.id.toolbar);
        setSupportActionBar(toolbar);
        ActionBar actionBar = getSupportActionBar();
        actionBar.setDisplayHomeAsUpEnabled(true);
```

← Enable the Up button.

```java
        //Display details of the pizza
        int pizzaId = (Integer)getIntent().getExtras().get(EXTRA_PIZZA_ID);
        String pizzaName = Pizza.pizzas[pizzaId].getName();
        TextView textView = (TextView)findViewById(R.id.pizza_text);
        textView.setText(pizzaName);
        int pizzaImage = Pizza.pizzas[pizzaId].getImageResourceId();
        ImageView imageView = (ImageView)findViewById(R.id.pizza_image);
        imageView.setImageDrawable(ContextCompat.getDrawable(this, pizzaImage));
        imageView.setContentDescription(pizzaName);
    }
}
```

Use the pizza ID to populate the TextView and ImageView.

From the intent, get the pizza the user chose.

Get a recycler view to respond to clicks

Pizza data
Card view
Adapter
Recycler view
Clicks

Next, we need to get items in the recycler view to respond to clicks so that we can start `PizzaDetailActivity` when the user clicks on a particular pizza.

When you create a navigation list with a list view, you can respond to click events within the list by giving the list view an `OnItemClickListener`. The list view then listens to each of the views that it contains, and if any of them are clicked, the list view calls its `OnItemClickListener`. That means that you can respond to list item clicks with very little code.

List views are able to do this because they inherit a bunch of functionality from a deep hierarchy of superclasses. Recycler views, however, don't have such a rich set of built-in methods, as they don't inherit from the same superclasses. Here's a class hierarchy diagram for the `ListView` and `RecyclerView` classes:

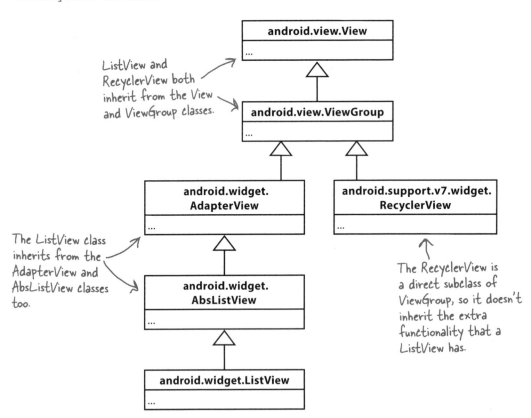

While this gives recycler views more flexibility, it also means that with a recycler view you have to do a lot more of the work yourself. So how do we get our recycler view to respond to clicks?

You can listen for view events from the adapter

To get your recycler view to respond to click events, you need access to the views that appear inside it. These views are all created inside the recycler view's adapter. When a view appears onscreen, the recycler view calls the `CaptionedImagesAdapter`'s `onBindViewHolder()` method to make the card view match the details of the list item.

When the user clicks on one of the pizza cards in the recycler view, we want to start `PizzaDetailActivity`, passing it the position of the pizza that was clicked. That means you *could* put some code inside the adapter to start an activity like this:

BitsAndPizzas

app/src/main

java

com.hfad.bitsandpizzas

CaptionedImages
Adapter.java

```java
class CaptionedImagesAdapter extends
        RecyclerView.Adapter<CaptionedImagesAdapter.ViewHolder>{
...
    @Override
    public void onBindViewHolder(ViewHolder holder, final int position){
        final CardView cardView = holder.cardView;
        ImageView imageView = (ImageView)cardView.findViewById(R.id.info_image);
        Drawable drawable =
                ContextCompat.getDrawable(cardView.getContext(), imageIds[position]);
        imageView.setImageDrawable(drawable);
        imageView.setContentDescription(captions[position]);
        TextView textView = (TextView)cardView.findViewById(R.id.info_text);
        textView.setText(captions[position]);
        cardView.setOnClickListener(new View.OnClickListener(){
            @Override
            public void onClick(View v) {
                Intent intent = new Intent(cardView.getContext(), PizzaDetailActivity.class);
                intent.putExtra(PizzaDetailActivity.EXTRA_PIZZA_ID, position);
                cardView.getContext().startActivity(intent);
            }
        });
    }
}
```

Don't update the adapter code just yet. This is just an example.

Adding this code to the adapter would start PizzaDetailActivity when a CardView is clicked.

But just because you *could* write this code, it doesn't necessarily mean that you should.

You *could* respond to a click event by adding code to your adapter class. But can you think of a reason why you *wouldn't* want to do that?

Pizza data
Card view
Adapter
Recycler view
Clicks

Keep your adapters reusable

If you deal with click events in the `CaptionedImagesAdapter`
class, *you'll limit how that adapter can be used.* Think about the app we're
building. We want to display lists of pizzas, pasta, and stores. In each
case, we'll probably want to display a list of captioned images. If we
modify the `CaptionedImagesAdapter` class so that clicks always
send the user to an activity that displays details of a single pizza, we
won't be able to use the `CaptionedImagesAdapter` for the pasta
and stores lists. We'll have to create a separate adapter for each one.

Decouple your adapter with an interface

Instead of that approach, we'll keep the code that starts the activity
outside of the adapter. When someone clicks on an item in the list,
we want the adapter to call the fragment that contains the list, and
then the fragment code can fire off an intent to the next activity. That
way we can reuse `CaptionedImagesAdapter` for the pizzas,
pasta, and stores lists, and in each case leave it to the fragments to
decide what happens in response to a click.

We're going to use a similar pattern to the one that allowed us to
decouple a fragment from an activity in Chapter 9. We'll create a
`Listener` interface inside `CaptionedImagesAdapter` like this:

```
interface Listener {
    void onClick(int position);
}
```

We'll call the listener's `onClick()` method whenever one of the
card views in the recycler view is clicked. We'll then add code to
`PizzaFragment` so that it implements the interface; this will allow
the fragment to respond to clicks and start an activity.

This is what will happen at runtime:

1 A user will click on a card view in the recycler view.

2 The `Listener`'s `onClick()` method will be called.

3 The `onClick()` method will be implemented in `PizzaFragment`. Code
in this fragment will start `PizzaDetailActivity`.

Let's start by adding code to *CaptionedImagesAdapter.java*.

Add the interface to the adapter

We've updated our *CaptionedImagesAdapter.java* code to add the `Listener` interface and call its `onClick()` method whenever one of the card views is clicked. Apply the changes below (in bold) to your code, then save your work:

```
package com.hfad.bitsandpizzas;

import android.support.v7.widget.RecyclerView;
import android.support.v7.widget.CardView;
import android.view.ViewGroup;
import android.view.LayoutInflater;
import android.widget.ImageView;
import android.widget.TextView;
import android.graphics.drawable.Drawable;
import android.support.v4.content.ContextCompat;
import android.view.View;
```
← We're using this extra class, so we need to import it.

```
class CaptionedImagesAdapter extends
        RecyclerView.Adapter<CaptionedImagesAdapter.ViewHolder>{

    private String[] captions;
    private int[] imageIds;
    private Listener listener;
```
← Add the Listener as a private variable.

```
    interface Listener {
```
← Add the interface.
```
        void onClick(int position);
    }

    public static class ViewHolder extends RecyclerView.ViewHolder {

        private CardView cardView;

        public ViewHolder(CardView v) {
            super(v);
            cardView = v;
        }
    }

    public CaptionedImagesAdapter(String[] captions, int[] imageIds){
        this.captions = captions;
        this.imageIds = imageIds;
    }
```

BitsAndPizzas

app/src/main

java

com.hfad.bitsandpizzas

CaptionedImages
Adapter.java

The code continues →
on the next page.

The CaptionedImagesAdapter.java code (continued)

Pizza data
Card view
Adapter
Recycler view
Clicks

```java
@Override
public int getItemCount(){
    return captions.length;
}
```

Activityies and fragments will use this
method to register as a listener.

```java
public void setListener(Listener listener){
    this.listener = listener;
}
```

BitsAndPizzas

app/src/main

java

com.hfad.bitsandpizzas

```java
@Override
public CaptionedImagesAdapter.ViewHolder onCreateViewHolder(
        ViewGroup parent, int viewType){
    CardView cv = (CardView) LayoutInflater.from(parent.getContext())
            .inflate(R.layout.card_captioned_image, parent, false);
    return new ViewHolder(cv);
}
```

CaptionedImages
Adapter.java

You need to change the position variable
to final, as it's used in an inner class.

```java
@Override
public void onBindViewHolder(ViewHolder holder, final int position){
    CardView cardView = holder.cardView;
    ImageView imageView = (ImageView)cardView.findViewById(R.id.info_image);
    Drawable drawable =
            ContextCompat.getDrawable(cardView.getContext(), imageIds[position]);
    imageView.setImageDrawable(drawable);
    imageView.setContentDescription(captions[position]);
    TextView textView = (TextView)cardView.findViewById(R.id.info_text);
    textView.setText(captions[position]);
    cardView.setOnClickListener(new View.OnClickListener() {
        @Override
        public void onClick(View v) {
            if (listener != null) {
                listener.onClick(position);
            }
        }
    });
}
```

Add the
listener
to the
CardView.

When the CardView is clicked, call
the Listener onClick() method.

Now that we've added a listener to the adapter, we need to
implement it in PizzaFragment.

recycler views *and card views*

Pizza data
Card view
Adapter
Recycler view
Clicks

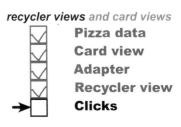

Implement the listener in PizzaFragment.java

We'll implement CaptionedImagesAdapter's Listener interface in PizzaFragment so that when a card view in the recycler view is clicked, PizzaDetailActivity will be started. Here's the updated code; update your version of the code to match ours (our changes are in bold):

```java
package com.hfad.bitsandpizzas;

import android.os.Bundle;
import android.support.v4.app.Fragment;
import android.view.LayoutInflater;
import android.view.View;
import android.view.ViewGroup;
import android.support.v7.widget.RecyclerView;
import android.support.v7.widget.GridLayoutManager;
import android.content.Intent;
```

← We're using an Intent to start the activity, so import this class.

BitsAndPizzas
└ app/src/main
  └ java
    └ com.hfad.bitsandpizzas
      └ Pizza Fragment.java

```java
public class PizzaFragment extends Fragment {

    @Override
    public View onCreateView(LayoutInflater inflater, ViewGroup container,
                            Bundle savedInstanceState) {
        RecyclerView pizzaRecycler = (RecyclerView)inflater.inflate(
                R.layout.fragment_pizza, container, false);

        String[] pizzaNames = new String[Pizza.pizzas.length];
        for (int i = 0; i < pizzaNames.length; i++) {
            pizzaNames[i] = Pizza.pizzas[i].getName();
        }

        int[] pizzaImages = new int[Pizza.pizzas.length];
        for (int i = 0; i < pizzaImages.length; i++) {
            pizzaImages[i] = Pizza.pizzas[i].getImageResourceId();
        }
```

*The code continues →
on the next page.*

The PizzaFragment.java code (continued)

Pizza data
Card view
Adapter
Recycler view
Clicks

```java
CaptionedImagesAdapter adapter =
                new CaptionedImagesAdapter(pizzaNames, pizzaImages);
pizzaRecycler.setAdapter(adapter);
GridLayoutManager layoutManager = new GridLayoutManager(getActivity(), 2);
pizzaRecycler.setLayoutManager(layoutManager);

adapter.setListener(new CaptionedImagesAdapter.Listener() {
    public void onClick(int position) {
        Intent intent = new Intent(getActivity(), PizzaDetailActivity.class);
        intent.putExtra(PizzaDetailActivity.EXTRA_PIZZA_ID, position);
        getActivity().startActivity(intent);
    }
});
    return pizzaRecycler;
    }
}
```

This implements the Listener
onClick() method. It starts
PizzaDetailActivity, passing it the
ID of the pizza the user chose.

That's all the code we need to make views in the recycler view respond to clicks. By taking this approach, we can use the same adapter and card view for different types of data that is composed of an image view and text view.

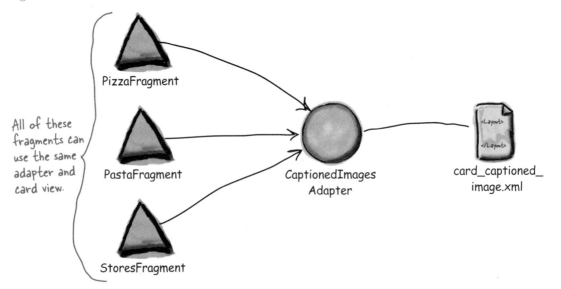

All of these fragments can use the same adapter and card view.

PizzaFragment

PastaFragment

StoresFragment

CaptionedImages Adapter

card_captioned_ image.xml

Let's see what happens when we run the code.

Test drive the app

When we run the app and click on the Pizzas tab, `PizzaFragment` is displayed. When we click on one of the pizzas, `PizzaDetailActivity` starts, and details of that pizza are displayed.

When you click on the Pizzas tab, PizzaFragment is displayed.

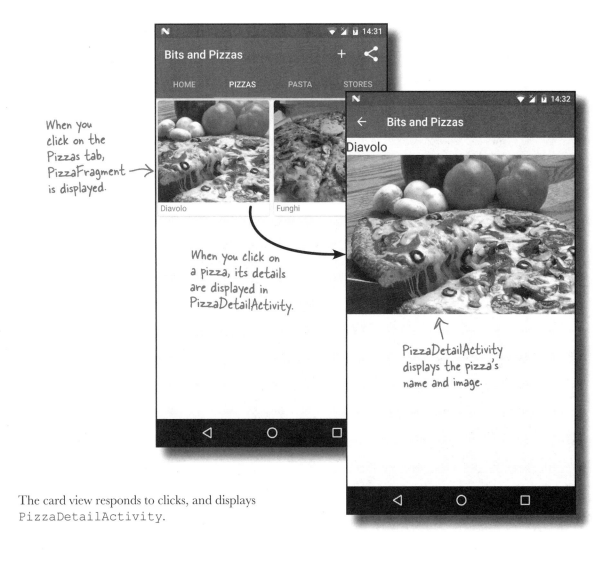

When you click on a pizza, its details are displayed in PizzaDetailActivity.

PizzaDetailActivity displays the pizza's name and image.

The card view responds to clicks, and displays `PizzaDetailActivity`.

Your Android Toolbox

You've got Chapter 13 under your belt and now you've added recycler views and card views to your toolbox.

You can download the full code for the chapter from https://tinyurl.com/HeadFirstAndroid.

BULLET POINTS

- Card views and recycler views have their own Support Libraries.

- Add a card view to a layout using the `<android.support.v7.widget.CardView>` element.

- Give the card view rounded corners using the `cardCornerRadius` attribute. This requires a namespace of `"http://schemas.android.com/apk/res-auto"`.

- Give the card view a drop shadow using the `cardElevation` attribute. This requires a namespace of `"http://schemas.android.com/apk/res-auto"`.

- Recycler views work with adapters that are subclasses of `RecyclerView.Adapter`.

- When you create your own `RecyclerView.Adapter`, you must define the view holder and implement the `onCreateViewHolder()`, `onBindViewHolder()`, and `getItemCount()` methods.

- You add a recycler view to a layout using the `<android.support.v7.widget.RecyclerView>` element. You give it a scrollbar using the `android:scrollbars` attribute.

- Use a layout manager to specify how items in a recycler view should be arranged. A `LinearLayoutManager` arranges items in a linear list, a `GridLayoutManager` arranges items in a grid, and a `StaggeredGridLayoutManager` arranges items in a staggered grid.

14 navigation drawers

Going Places

> I know I'll never get lost so long as I have my lucky navigation drawers.

You've already seen how tabs help users navigate your apps.

But if you need a *large number* of them, or want to *split them into sections*, the **navigation drawer** is your new BFF. In this chapter, we'll show you how to create a navigation drawer that *slides out from the side of your activity at a single touch*. You'll learn how to give it a header using a **navigation view**, and provide it with a **structured set of menu items** to take the user to all the major hubs of your app. Finally, you'll discover how to set up a **navigation view listener** so that the drawer *responds to the slightest touch and swipe*.

Tab layouts allow easy navigation...

In Chapter 12, we introduced you to the tab layout as a way of making it easy for users to navigate around your app. In that chapter we added a Home screen tab to the Bits and Pizzas app, along with tabs for the Pizzas, Pasta, and Stores categories:

These are the tabs we created in Chapter 12. →

Tab layouts work well if you have a small number of category screens that are all at the same level in the app hierarchy. But what if you want to use a large number of tabs, or group the tabs into sections?

...but navigation drawers let you show more options

If you want users to be able to navigate through a large number of options, or group them into sections, you might prefer to use a **navigation drawer**. This is a slide-out panel that contains links to other parts of the app that you can group into different sections. As an example, the Gmail app uses a navigation drawer that contains sections such as email categories, recent labels, and all labels:

The main email categories are at the top of the drawer.

Labels that have recently been clicked on are displayed in a separate section.

Finally, here's a long list of all the email labels.

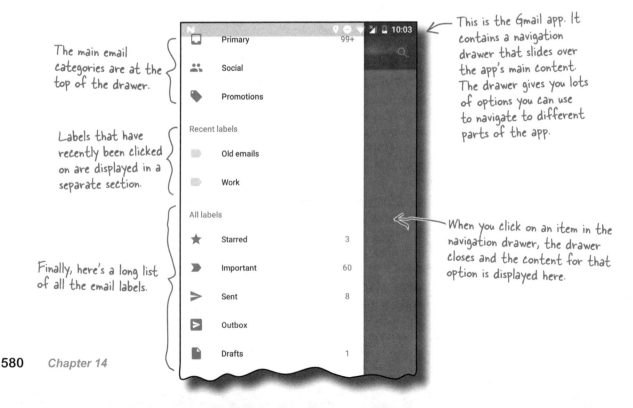

This is the Gmail app. It contains a navigation drawer that slides over the app's main content. The drawer gives you lots of options you can use to navigate to different parts of the app.

When you click on an item in the navigation drawer, the drawer closes and the content for that option is displayed here.

We're going to create a navigation drawer for a new email app

We're going to create a navigation drawer for a new email app called CatChat. The navigation drawer will contain a header (including an image and some text) and a set of options. The main options will be for the user's inbox, draft messages, sent items, and trash. We'll also include a separate support section for help and feedback options:

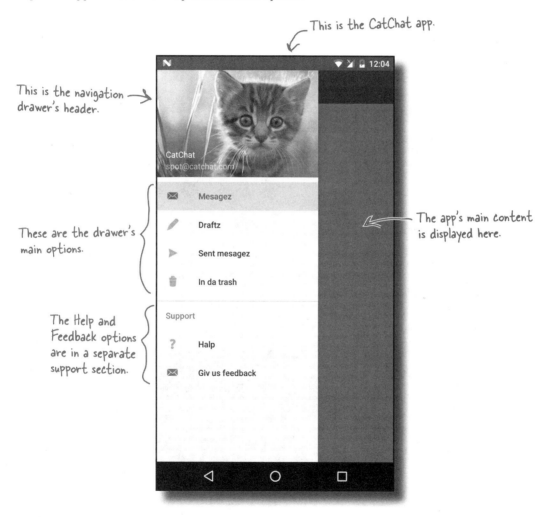

This is the CatChat app.

This is the navigation drawer's header.

These are the drawer's main options.

The Help and Feedback options are in a separate support section.

The app's main content is displayed here.

The navigation drawer is composed of several different components. We'll go through these on the next page.

Navigation drawers deconstructed

You implement a navigation drawer by adding a **drawer layout** to your activity's layout. This defines a drawer you can open and close, and it needs to contain two views:

① **A view for the main content.**
This is usually a layout containing a toolbar and a frame layout, which you use to display fragments.

② **A view for the drawer contents.**
This is usually a navigation view, which controls most of the drawer's behavior.

When the drawer's closed, the drawer layout looks just like a normal activity. It displays the layout for its main content:

Here the drawer's closed, so it looks like a plain old activity.

The main content of the activity usually is composed of a toolbar and a frame layout that's used to display fragments.

When you open the navigation drawer, it slides over the activity's main content to display the drawer's contents. This is usually a navigation view, which displays a drawer header image and a list of options. When you click on one of these options, it either starts a new activity or displays a fragment in the activity's frame layout:

The drawer's contents are defined by a navigation view.

The drawer slides over the main content when it opens.

Here's what we're going to do

We're going to create a navigation drawer for the CatChat app.
There are four main steps we'll go through to do this:

1 **Create basic fragments and activities for the app's contents.**
When the user clicks on one of the options in the navigation drawer, we want
to display the fragment or activity for that option. We'll create the fragments
InboxFragment, DraftsFragment, SentItemsFragment, and
TrashFragment, and activities HelpActivity and FeedbackActivity.

These are
~~ the activities.

These
are the →
fragments.

2 **Create the drawer's header.**
We'll build a layout, *nav_header.xml*, for the drawer's header. It will
contain an image and text.

3 **Create the drawer's options.**
We'll build a menu, *menu_nav.xml*, for the options the
drawer will display.

4 **Create the navigation drawer.**
We'll add the navigation drawer to the app's main activity,
and get it to display the header and options. We'll then
write activity code to control the drawer's behavior.

The drawer's
header and
← options

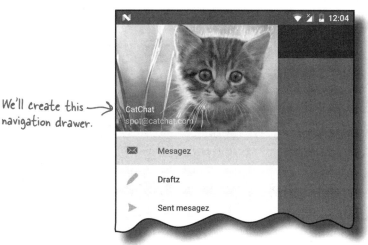

We'll create this →
navigation drawer.

Let's get started.

Fragments/activities
Header
Options
Drawer

Create the CatChat project

Before we begin, we need a new project for the CatChat app. Create a new Android project with an empty activity for an application named "CatChat" with a company domain of "hfad. com", making the package name com.hfad.catchat. The minimum SDK should be API level 19 so that it works with most devices. Specify an activity called "MainActivity" and a layout called "activity_main", and **make sure that you check the Backwards Compatibility (AppCompat) option.**

Add the v7 AppCompat and Design Support Libraries

We're going to use components and themes from the v7 AppCompat and Design Support Libraries in this chapter, so we need to add them to our project as dependencies. To do this, choose File→Project Structure in Android Studio, click on the app module, then choose Dependencies. When you're presented with the project dependencies screen, click on the "+" button at the bottom or right side of the screen. When prompted, choose the Library Dependency option, then select the Design Library from the list of possible libraries. Repeat these steps for the v7 AppCompat Support Library if Android Studio hasn't already added it for you. Finally, use the OK buttons to save your changes.

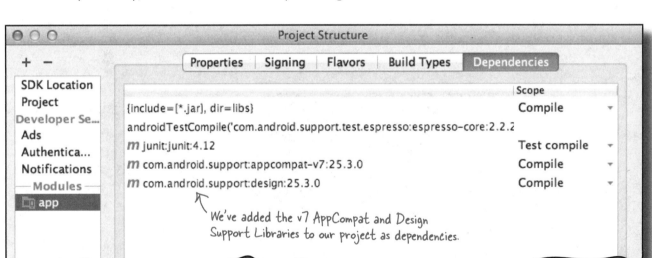

We've added the v7 AppCompat and Design Support Libraries to our project as dependencies.

Next, we'll create four basic fragments for the app's inbox, drafts, sent messages, and trash. We'll use these fragments later in the chapter when we write the code for the navigation drawer.

Create InboxFragment

We'll display InboxFragment when the user clicks on the inbox option in the navigation drawer. Highlight the com.hfad. catchat package in the *app/src/main/java* folder, then go to File→New...→Fragment→Fragment (Blank). Name the fragment "InboxFragment" and name its layout "fragment_inbox". Then update the code for *InboxFragment.java* to match our code below:

This is what InboxFragment → looks like.

```java
package com.hfad.catchat;

import android.os.Bundle;
import android.support.v4.app.Fragment;
import android.view.LayoutInflater;
import android.view.View;
import android.view.ViewGroup;

public class InboxFragment extends Fragment {

    @Override
    public View onCreateView(LayoutInflater inflater, ViewGroup container,
                             Bundle savedInstanceState) {
        return inflater.inflate(R.layout.fragment_inbox, container, false);
    }

}
```

All the fragments use the Fragment class from the Support Library.

CatChat
app/src/main
java
com.hfad.catchat
InboxFragment.java

And here's the code for *fragment_inbox.xml* (update your version of this code too):

```xml
<LinearLayout xmlns:android="http://schemas.android.com/apk/res/android"
    xmlns:tools="http://schemas.android.com/tools"
    android:layout_width="match_parent"
    android:layout_height="match_parent"
    android:orientation="vertical"
    tools:context="com.hfad.catchat.InboxFragment">

    <TextView
        android:layout_width="match_parent"
        android:layout_height="match_parent"
        android:text="Inbox" />

</LinearLayout>
```

CatChat
app/src/main
res
layout
fragment_inbox.xml

InboxFragment's layout just contains a TextView. We're adding this text so we can easily tell when it's displayed.

Create DraftsFragment

When the user clicks on the drafts option in the navigation drawer, we'll show `DraftsFragment`. Select the `com.hfad.catchat` package in the *app/src/main/java* folder, and create a new blank fragment named "DraftsFragment" with a layout called of "fragment_drafts". Then replace the code for *DraftsFragment.java* with ours below:

DraftsFragment ⟶ Drafts

```java
package com.hfad.catchat;


import android.os.Bundle;
import android.support.v4.app.Fragment;
import android.view.LayoutInflater;
import android.view.View;
import android.view.ViewGroup;


public class DraftsFragment extends Fragment {

    @Override
    public View onCreateView(LayoutInflater inflater, ViewGroup container,
                             Bundle savedInstanceState) {
        return inflater.inflate(R.layout.fragment_drafts, container, false);
    }

}
```

CatChat
app/src/main
java
com.hfad.catchat
DraftsFragment.java

Next replace the code for *fragment_drafts.xml* too:

```xml
<LinearLayout xmlns:android="http://schemas.android.com/apk/res/android"
    xmlns:tools="http://schemas.android.com/tools"
    android:layout_width="match_parent"
    android:layout_height="match_parent"
    android:orientation="vertical"
    tools:context="com.hfad.catchat.DraftsFragment">

    <TextView
        android:layout_width="match_parent"
        android:layout_height="match_parent"
        android:text="Drafts" />

</LinearLayout>
```

CatChat
app/src/main
res
layout
fragment_drafts.xml

Create SentItemsFragment

We'll show SentItemsFragment when the user clicks on the
sent items option in the navigation drawer. Highlight the com.
hfad.catchat package in the *app/src/main/java* folder, and
create a new blank fragment named "SentItemsFragment" with
a layout called "fragment_sent_items". Then update the code for
SentItemsFragment.java to match our code below:

SentItemsFragment → Sent items

```java
package com.hfad.catchat;

import android.os.Bundle;
import android.support.v4.app.Fragment;
import android.view.LayoutInflater;
import android.view.View;
import android.view.ViewGroup;

public class SentItemsFragment extends Fragment {

    @Override
    public View onCreateView(LayoutInflater inflater, ViewGroup container,
                             Bundle savedInstanceState) {
        return inflater.inflate(R.layout.fragment_sent_items, container, false);
    }
}
```

CatChat
app/src/main
java
com.hfad.catchat
SentItemsFragment.java

And here's the code for *fragment_sent_items.xml* (update your version):

```xml
<LinearLayout xmlns:android="http://schemas.android.com/apk/res/android"
    xmlns:tools="http://schemas.android.com/tools"
    android:layout_width="match_parent"
    android:layout_height="match_parent"
    android:orientation="vertical"
    tools:context="com.hfad.catchat.SentItemsFragment">

    <TextView
        android:layout_width="match_parent"
        android:layout_height="match_parent"
        android:text="Sent items" />

</LinearLayout>
```

CatChat
app/src/main
res
layout
fragment_sent_items.xml

Create TrashFragment

When the user clicks on the trash option in the navigation drawer, we'll show `TrashFragment`. Highlight the `com.hfad.catchat` package in the *app/src/main/java* folder, and create a new blank fragment named "TrashFragment" with a layout called of "fragment_trash". Then replace the code for *TrashFragment.java* with ours below:

TrashFragment → [Trash]

```java
package com.hfad.catchat;

import android.os.Bundle;
import android.support.v4.app.Fragment;
import android.view.LayoutInflater;
import android.view.View;
import android.view.ViewGroup;

public class TrashFragment extends Fragment {

    @Override
    public View onCreateView(LayoutInflater inflater, ViewGroup container,
                             Bundle savedInstanceState) {
        return inflater.inflate(R.layout.fragment_trash, container, false);
    }

}
```

CatChat
app/src/main
java
com.hfad.catchat
TrashFragment.java

Next replace the code for *fragment_trash.xml* too:

```xml
<LinearLayout xmlns:android="http://schemas.android.com/apk/res/android"
    xmlns:tools="http://schemas.android.com/tools"
    android:layout_width="match_parent"
    android:layout_height="match_parent"
    android:orientation="vertical"
    tools:context="com.hfad.catchat.TrashFragment">

    <TextView
        android:layout_width="match_parent"
        android:layout_height="match_parent"
        android:text="Trash" />

</LinearLayout>
```

CatChat
app/src/main
res
layout
fragment_trash.xml

We've now created all the fragments we need. Next, we'll create a toolbar we can include in our activities.

Create a toolbar layout

We're going to add a toolbar in a separate layout so that we can include it in each activity's layout (we'll create our activities soon). Switch to the Project view of Android Studio's explorer, select the *app/src/res/main/layout* folder, then go to the File menu and choose New → Layout resource file. When prompted, name the layout file "toolbar_main", then click on OK.

Next, open *toolbar_main.xml*, and replace the code Android Studio has created for you with the following:

This is the same toolbar code we've used in previous chapters.

```xml
<android.support.v7.widget.Toolbar
    xmlns:android="http://schemas.android.com/apk/res/android"
    android:layout_width="match_parent"
    android:layout_height="?attr/actionBarSize"
    android:background="?attr/colorPrimary"
    android:theme="@style/ThemeOverlay.AppCompat.Dark.ActionBar" />
```

CatChat

app/src/main

res

layout

toolbar_
main.xml

Before we can use the toolbar in any of our activities, we need to change the theme used by your activity. We'll do this in app's style resource.

First, open *AndroidManifest.xml*, and make sure that the value of the theme attribute is set to `"@style/AppTheme"`. Android Studio may have set this value for you; if not, you'll need to update it to match ours below:

```xml
<?xml version="1.0" encoding="utf-8"?>
<manifest ...>
    <application
        android:allowBackup="true"
        android:icon="@mipmap/ic_launcher"
        android:label="@string/app_name"
        android:roundIcon="@mipmap/ic_launcher_round"
        android:supportsRtl="true"
        android:theme="@style/AppTheme">
        <activity android:name=".MainActivity">
            ...
        </activity>
    </application>
</manifest>
```

CatChat

app/src/main

AndroidManifest.xml

Android Studio may have already added this value for you.

We'll update the AppTheme style on the next page.

Update the app's theme

Fragments/activities
Header
Options
Drawer

Next, we'll update the `AppTheme` style so that it uses a theme of `"Theme.AppCompat.Light.NoActionBar"`. We'll also override some of the colors that are used in the original theme.

First, open the *app/src/main/res/values* folder and check that Android Studio has created a file for you called *styles.xml*. If this file doesn't exist, you'll need to create it. To do this, select the *values* folder, then go to the File menu and choose New → "Values resource file". When prompted, name the file "styles", then click on OK.

Next, update *styles.xml* so that it matches ours:

This theme removes the default app bar (we're replacing it with a toolbar).

CatChat
app/src/main
res
values
styles.xml

```
<resources>
    <style name="AppTheme" parent="Theme.AppCompat.Light.NoActionBar">
        <item name="colorPrimary">@color/colorPrimary</item>
        <item name="colorPrimaryDark">@color/colorPrimaryDark</item>
        <item name="colorAccent">@color/colorAccent</item>
    </style>
</resources>
```

Android Studio may have added these colors for you.

The `AppTheme` style uses color resources, and these need to be included in *colors.xml*. First, make sure that Android Studio has created this file for you in the *app/src/main/res/values* folder (if it hasn't, you'll need to create it yourself). Then update *colors.xml* so that it matches our code below:

CatChat
app/src/main
res
values
colors.xml

```
<?xml version="1.0" encoding="utf-8"?>
<resources>
    <color name="colorPrimary">#3F51B5</color>
    <color name="colorPrimaryDark">#303F9F</color>
    <color name="colorAccent">#FF4081</color>
</resources>
```

Add these colors if Android Studio hasn't already done it for you.

Now that we've set up a style so that we can use a toolbar, we'll create two activities for the help and feedback options in the navigation drawer. We'll display these activities when the user selects the appropriate option.

Create HelpActivity

We'll start by creating `HelpActivity`. Select the `com.hfad.catchat` package in Android Studio, then go to the File menu and choose New. Select the option to create a new empty activity, and give it a name of "HelpActivity", with a layout name of "activity_help". Make sure the package name is `com.hfad.catchat`, and **check the Backwards Compatibility (AppCompat) checkbox.** Then update *activity_help.xml* so that it matches ours below:

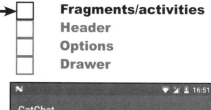

```xml
<?xml version="1.0" encoding="utf-8"?>
<LinearLayout xmlns:android="http://schemas.android.com/apk/res/android"
    xmlns:tools="http://schemas.android.com/tools"
    android:layout_width="match_parent"
    android:layout_height="match_parent"
    android:orientation="vertical"
    tools:context="com.hfad.catchat.HelpActivity">

    <include
        layout="@layout/toolbar_main"
        android:id="@+id/toolbar" />

    <TextView
        android:layout_width="match_parent"
        android:layout_height="match_parent"
        android:text="Help" />
</LinearLayout>
```

> We're adding a toolbar and "Help" text to HelpActivity.

CatChat
└ app/src/main
  └ res
    └ layout
      └ activity_help.xml

Next update *HelpActivity.java* to match our version:

```java
package com.hfad.catchat;

import android.support.v7.app.AppCompatActivity;
import android.os.Bundle;
import android.support.v7.widget.Toolbar;

public class HelpActivity extends AppCompatActivity {

    @Override
    protected void onCreate(Bundle savedInstanceState) {
        super.onCreate(savedInstanceState);
        setContentView(R.layout.activity_help);
        Toolbar toolbar = (Toolbar) findViewById(R.id.toolbar);
        setSupportActionBar(toolbar);
    }
}
```

> The activity needs to extend AppCompatActivity because we're using an AppCompat theme.

CatChat
└ app/src/main
  └ java
    └ com.hfad.catchat
      └ HelpActivity.java

Create FeedbackActivity

Finally, select the com.hfad.catchat package again and create an
empty activity called "FeedbackActivity", with a layout name of "activity_
feedback". Make sure the package name is com.hfad.catchat, and
check the Backwards Compatibility (AppCompat) checkbox.
Then update *activity_feedback.xml* so that it matches ours below:

```xml
<?xml version="1.0" encoding="utf-8"?>
<LinearLayout xmlns:android="http://schemas.android.com/apk/res/android"
    xmlns:tools="http://schemas.android.com/tools"
    android:layout_width="match_parent"
    android:layout_height="match_parent"
    android:orientation="vertical"
    tools:context="com.hfad.catchat.FeedbackActivity">

    <include
        layout="@layout/toolbar_main"
        android:id="@+id/toolbar" />

    <TextView
        android:layout_width="match_parent"
        android:layout_height="match_parent"
        android:text="Feedback" />
</LinearLayout>
```

CatChat

app/src/main

res

layout

activity_feedback.xml

Then update *FeedbackActivity.java* to match this version:

```java
package com.hfad.catchat;

import android.support.v7.app.AppCompatActivity;
import android.os.Bundle;
import android.support.v7.widget.Toolbar;

public class FeedbackActivity extends AppCompatActivity {

    @Override
    protected void onCreate(Bundle savedInstanceState) {
        super.onCreate(savedInstanceState);
        setContentView(R.layout.activity_feedback);
        Toolbar toolbar = (Toolbar) findViewById(R.id.toolbar);
        setSupportActionBar(toolbar);
    }
}
```

This activity needs to extend
AppCompatActivity as well.

CatChat

app/src/main

java

com.hfad.catchat

FeedbackActivity.java

We need to build a navigation drawer

We've now added all the fragments and activities to our project that the options in the navigation drawer will link to. Next, we'll create the navigation drawer itself.

The navigation drawer comprises two separate components:

 A navigation drawer header.
This is a layout that appears at the top of the navigation drawer. It usually consists of an image with some text, for example a photo of the user and their email account.

This is the header we'll create. It consists of an image and two pieces of text.

CatChat
spot@catchat.com

 A set of options.
You define a set of options to be displayed in the navigation drawer underneath the header. When the user clicks on one of these options, the screen for that option is displayed as a fragment within the navigation drawer's activity, or as a new activity.

The navigation drawer will contain these options.

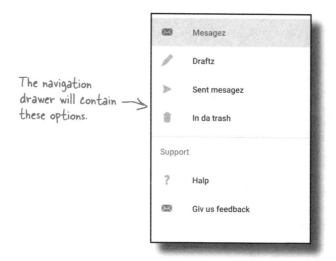

We're going to build these components, then use them in `MainActivity` to build a navigation drawer. We'll start with the navigation drawer header.

Create the navigation drawer's header

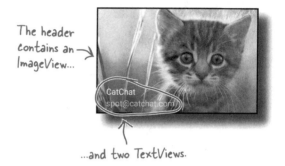

The header contains an ImageView...

...and two TextViews.

The navigation drawer's header comprises a simple layout that you add to a new layout file. We're going to use a new file called *nav_header.xml*. Create this file by selecting the *app/src/main/res/layout* folder in Android Studio, and choosing File→New→Layout resource file. When prompted, name the layout "nav_header".

Our layout is composed of an image and two text views. This means we need to add an image file to our project as a drawable, and two String resources. We'll start with the image file.

Add the image file

To add the image file, first switch to the Project view of Android Studio's explorer if you haven't already done so, and check whether the *app/src/main/res/drawable* folder exists in your project. If it's not already there, select the *app/src/main/res* folder in your project, go to the File menu, choose the New... option, and then click on the option to create a new Android resource directory. When prompted, choose a resource type of drawable, name it "drawable", and click on OK.

Once you've created the *drawable* folder, download the file *kitten_small.jpg* from *https://git.io/v9oet*, and add it to the *drawable* folder.

Add the String resources

Next, we'll add two String resources, which we'll use for the text views. Open the file *app/src/main/res/values/strings.xml*, then add the following resource:

```
<resources>
    ...
    <string name="app_name">CatChat</string>
    <string name="user_name">spot@catchat.com</string>
</resources>
```

Android Studio may have already added this String by default.

Now that you've added the resources, we can write the layout code. You're already familiar with the code we need to do this, so we're going to give you the full code on the next page.

The full nav_header.xml code

Here's our full code for *nav_header.xml*; update your version of the file to match ours:

```xml
<?xml version="1.0" encoding="utf-8"?>
<FrameLayout xmlns:android="http://schemas.android.com/apk/res/android"
    android:layout_width="match_parent"
    android:layout_height="180dp"
    android:theme="@style/ThemeOverlay.AppCompat.Dark" >

    <ImageView
        android:layout_width="wrap_content"
        android:layout_height="wrap_content"
        android:scaleType="centerCrop"
        android:src="@drawable/kitten_small" />

    <LinearLayout
        android:layout_width="wrap_content"
        android:layout_height="match_parent"
        android:orientation="vertical"
        android:gravity="bottom|start"
        android:layout_margin="16dp" >

        <TextView
            android:layout_width="wrap_content"
            android:layout_height="wrap_content"
            android:text="@string/app_name"
            android:textAppearance="@style/TextAppearance.AppCompat.Body1" />

        <TextView
            android:layout_width="wrap_content"
            android:layout_height="wrap_content"
            android:text="@string/user_name" />
    </LinearLayout>

</FrameLayout>
```

We're explicitly setting the height of the layout to 180dp so that it doesn't take up too much space in the drawer.

The image background is quite dark, so we're using this line to make the text light.

CatChat
app/src/main
res
layout
nav_header.xml

This LinearLayout will appear on top of the ImageView. We're using it to display text at the bottom of the image.

This is a built-in style that makes the text look slightly bolder. It comes from the AppCompat Support Library.

Now that we've created the drawer's header, we'll create its list of options.

The drawer gets its options from a menu

Fragments/activities
Header
Options
Drawer

The navigation drawer gets its list of options from a menu resource file. The code to do this is similar to that needed to add a set of options to an app bar.

Before we look at the code to add the options to the navigation drawer, we need to add a menu resource file to our project. To do this, select the *app/src/main/res* folder in Android Studio, go to the File menu, and choose New. Then select the option to create a new Android resource file. You'll be prompted for the name of the resource file and the type of resource. Give it a name of "menu_nav", give it a resource type of "Menu", and make sure that the Directory name is "menu". When you click on OK, Android Studio will create the file for you.

Next we'll add String resources for the titles of our menu items so that we can use them later in the chapter. Open *strings.xml* and add the following resources:

```
<resources>
    ...
    <string name="nav_inbox">Mesagez</string>
    <string name="nav_drafts">Draftz</string>
    <string name="nav_sent">Sent mesagez</string>
    <string name="nav_trash">In da trash</string>
    <string name="nav_support">Support</string>
    <string name="nav_help">Halp</string>
    <string name="nav_feedback">Giv us feedback</string>
</resources>
```

CatChat

app/src/main

res

values

strings.xml

Next we can start constructing our menu code.

We need to create a menu with two sections

As we said earlier, we want to split the items in our navigation drawer into two sections. The first section will contain options for the main places in the app the user will want to visit: her inbox, draft messages, sent items, and trash. We'll then add a separate support section for help and feedback options.

Let's start by adding the main options.

These are the app's main options.

	Mesagez
	Draftz
	Sent mesagez
	In da trash

This is the support section.

Support

	Halp
	Giv us feedback

Add items in the order you want them to appear in the drawer

When you design a set of options for a navigation drawer, you generally put the items the user is most likely to want to click on at the top of the list. In our case, these options are for the inbox, draft messages, sent items, and trash.

You add items to the menu resource file in the order in which you want them to appear in the drawer. For each item, you specify an ID so you can refer to it in your Java code, and a title for the text you want to appear. You can also specify an icon that will appear alongside the item's text. As an example, here's the code to add an "inbox" item:

CatChat

app/src/main

res

menu

menu_nav.xml

```xml
<?xml version="1.0" encoding="utf-8"?>
<menu xmlns:android="http://schemas.android.com/apk/res/android">

    <item
        android:id="@+id/nav_inbox"
        android:icon="@android:drawable/sym_action_email"
        android:title="@string/nav_inbox" />

    ...

</menu>
```

You need to give the item an ID so that your activity code can respond to it being clicked.

This is the text that appears in the navigation drawer.

This is a built-in drawable you can use to display an email icon.

In the above code, we're using one of Android's built-in icons: `"@android:drawable/sym_action_email"`. Android comes with a set of built-in icons that you can use in your apps. The `"@android:drawable"` part tells Android you want to use one of these icons. You can see the full list of available icons when you start typing the icon name in Android Studio:

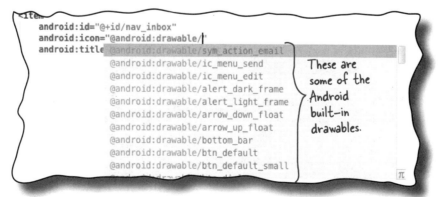

These are some of the Android built-in drawables.

Fragments/activities
Header
Options
Drawer

How to group items together

As well as adding menu items individually, you can add them as part
of a group. You define a group using the <group> element like this:

```
<menu xmlns:android="http://schemas.android.com/apk/res/android">

    <group>
        . . .   ← Any items you want to
    </group>        include in the group go here.

</menu>
```

This is useful if you want to apply an attribute to an entire
group of items. As an example, you can highlight which item
in the drawer the user has selected by setting the group's
android:checkableBehavior attribute to "single". This
behavior is helpful when you intend to display screens for the items
as fragments inside the navigation drawer's activity (in our case
MainActivity), as it makes it easy to tell which option is currently
selected:

```
<menu xmlns:android="http://schemas.android.com/apk/res/android">

    <group android:checkableBehavior="single">

        . . .
                        This means that a single item in the group will
    </group>            be highlighted (the option the user selects).

</menu>
```

You can highlight an item in the navigation drawer by default by
setting its android:checked attribute to "true". As an example,
here's how you highlight the inbox item:

```
<menu xmlns:android="http://schemas.android.com/apk/res/android">

    <group android:checkableBehavior="single">

        <item
            android:id="@+id/nav_inbox"
            android:icon="@android:drawable/sym_action_email"
            android:title="@string/nav_inbox"
            android:checked="true" />

        . . .            This highlights the item in the
    </group>             navigation drawer by default.

</menu>
```

We'll show you the full code for the first four menu items on the next page.

We'll use a group for the first section

We're going to add the inbox, drafts, sent messages, and trash options to our menu resource file as a group, and highlight the first item by default. We're using a group for these items because the screen for each option is a fragment, which we'll display in `MainActivity`.

The code on this page adds these four items.

Here's our code; update your version of *menu_nav.xml* to match ours.

```xml
<?xml version="1.0" encoding="utf-8"?>
<menu xmlns:android="http://schemas.android.com/apk/res/android">

    <group android:checkableBehavior="single">
        <item
            android:id="@+id/nav_inbox"
            android:icon="@android:drawable/sym_action_email"
            android:title="@string/nav_inbox"
            android:checked="true" />
        <item
            android:id="@+id/nav_drafts"
            android:icon="@android:drawable/ic_menu_edit"
            android:title="@string/nav_drafts" />
        <item
            android:id="@+id/nav_sent"
            android:icon="@android:drawable/ic_menu_send"
            android:title="@string/nav_sent" />
        <item
            android:id="@+id/nav_trash"
            android:icon="@android:drawable/ic_menu_delete"
            android:title="@string/nav_trash" />
    </group>

</menu>
```

← Add this group and the four items it contains to your menu resource file so they'll appear in the navigation drawer.

CatChat
app/src/main
res
menu
menu_nav.xml

That's the first group of items sorted. We'll deal with the remaining items next.

Add the support section as a submenu

The second set of items in the navigation drawer forms a separate section. There's a heading of "Support," along with help and feedback options for the user to click on.

To create this section, we'll start by adding the Support heading as a separate item. As it's a heading, we only need to give it a title; it doesn't need an icon, and we're not assigning it an ID as we don't need it to respond to clicks:

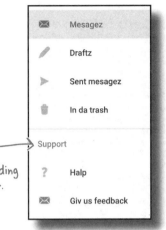

```
...
    <item android:title="@string/nav_support">
    </item>
...
```

This adds a Support heading to the navigation drawer.

We want the help and feedback options to appear within the Support section, so we'll add them as separate items in a submenu inside the support item:

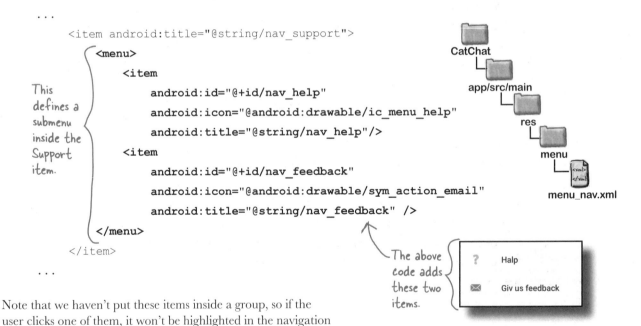

```
...
        <item android:title="@string/nav_support">
            <menu>
                <item
                    android:id="@+id/nav_help"
                    android:icon="@android:drawable/ic_menu_help"
                    android:title="@string/nav_help"/>
                <item
                    android:id="@+id/nav_feedback"
                    android:icon="@android:drawable/sym_action_email"
                    android:title="@string/nav_feedback" />
            </menu>
        </item>
...
```

This defines a submenu inside the Support item.

The above code adds these two items.

Note that we haven't put these items inside a group, so if the user clicks one of them, it won't be highlighted in the navigation drawer. This is because the help and feedback options will be displayed in new activities, not as fragments in the navigation drawer's activity.

We'll show you the full menu code on the next page.

The full menu_nav.xml code

Here's the full code for *menu_nav.xml*; update your version of the code to match ours:

The code on this page creates the full menu.

```xml
<?xml version="1.0" encoding="utf-8"?>
<menu xmlns:android="http://schemas.android.com/apk/res/android">
    <group android:checkableBehavior="single">
        <item
            android:id="@+id/nav_inbox"
            android:icon="@android:drawable/sym_action_email"
            android:title="@string/nav_inbox" />
        <item
            android:id="@+id/nav_drafts"
            android:icon="@android:drawable/ic_menu_edit"
            android:title="@string/nav_drafts" />
        <item
            android:id="@+id/nav_sent"
            android:icon="@android:drawable/ic_menu_send"
            android:title="@string/nav_sent" />
        <item
            android:id="@+id/nav_trash"
            android:icon="@android:drawable/ic_menu_delete"
            android:title="@string/nav_trash" />
    </group>

    <item android:title="@string/nav_support">
        <menu>
            <item
                android:id="@+id/nav_help"
                android:icon="@android:drawable/ic_menu_help"
                android:title="@string/nav_help"/>
            <item
                android:id="@+id/nav_feedback"
                android:icon="@android:drawable/sym_action_email"
                android:title="@string/nav_feedback" />
        </menu>
    </item>
</menu>
```

These are the main options.

This is the support section.

CatChat
app/src/main
res
menu
menu_nav.xml

Now that we've added a menu and navigation drawer header layout, we can create the actual drawer.

Fragments/activities
Header
Options
Drawer

How to create a navigation drawer

You create a navigation drawer by adding a drawer layout to your activity's
layout as its root element. The drawer layout needs to contain two things:
a view or view group for the activity's content as its first element, and a
navigation view that defines the drawer as its second:

```xml
<?xml version="1.0" encoding="utf-8"?>
<android.support.v4.widget.DrawerLayout
    xmlns:android="http://schemas.android.com/apk/res/android"
    xmlns:app="http://schemas.android.com/apk/res-auto"
    android:id="@+id/drawer_layout"
    android:layout_width="match_parent"
    android:layout_height="match_parent" >

    <LinearLayout
        android:layout_width="match_parent"
        android:layout_height="match_parent"
        android:orientation="vertical" >
        . . .
    </LinearLayout>

    <android.support.design.widget.NavigationView
        android:id="@+id/nav_view"
        android:layout_width="wrap_content"
        android:layout_height="match_parent"
        android:layout_gravity="start"
        app:headerLayout="@layout/nav_header"
        app:menu="@menu/menu_nav" />
</android.support.v4.widget.DrawerLayout>
```

← The DrawerLayout defines the drawer.

← You give it an ID so you can refer to it in your activity code.

The DrawerLayout's first view is a layout for the activity's main content. You see it when the drawer is closed.

The NavigationView defines the drawer's contents.

This attaches the drawer to the start edge of the activity (the left for left-to-right languages).

This is the layout for the drawer's header.

This is the menu resource file containing the drawer's options.

There are two key `<NavigationView>` attributes that you use to control
the drawer's appearance: `headerLayout` and `menu`.

The `app:headerLayout` attribute specifies the layout that should be
used for the navigation drawer's header (in this case *nav_header.xml*). This
attribute is optional.

You use the `app:menu` attribute to say which menu resource file contains
the drawer's options (in this case *menu_drawer.xml*). If you don't include this
attribute, your navigation drawer won't include any items.

The full code for activity_main.xml

We're going to add a navigation drawer to `MainActivity`'s layout that uses the header layout and menu we created earlier in the chapter. The layout's main content will comprise a toolbar and frame layout. We'll use the frame layout later in the chapter to display fragments.

Here's our full code for *activity_main.xml*; update your code to match ours:

```xml
<?xml version="1.0" encoding="utf-8"?>
<android.support.v4.widget.DrawerLayout    ← The layout's root element is a DrawerLayout.
    xmlns:android="http://schemas.android.com/apk/res/android"
    xmlns:app="http://schemas.android.com/apk/res-auto"
    android:id="@+id/drawer_layout"    ← It has an ID so we can refer to
    android:layout_width="match_parent"       it in our activity code later.
    android:layout_height="match_parent" >

    <LinearLayout    ← This is for the drawer's main content.
        android:layout_width="match_parent"
        android:layout_height="match_parent"
        android:orientation="vertical" >

        <include
            layout="@layout/toolbar_main"
            android:id="@+id/toolbar" />

        <FrameLayout
            android:id="@+id/content_frame"
            android:layout_width="match_parent"
            android:layout_height="match_parent" />
    </LinearLayout>

    <android.support.design.widget.NavigationView
        android:id="@+id/nav_view"
        android:layout_width="wrap_content"
        android:layout_height="match_parent"
        android:layout_gravity="start"
        app:headerLayout="@layout/nav_header"
        app:menu="@menu/menu_nav" />
</android.support.v4.widget.DrawerLayout>
```

The activity's main content is composed of a Toolbar, and a FrameLayout in which we'll display fragments.

CatChat
app/src/main
res
layout
activity_main.xml

The NavigationView defines the drawer's appearance and much of its behavior. We're giving it an ID, as we'll need to refer to it in our activity code.

We're using the layout we created earlier as the drawer's header, and the menu resource file for the list of options.

Before we run the app to see how the navigation drawer's looking, we'll update `MainActivity` to display `InboxFragment` in the frame layout when the activity gets created.

Fragments/activities
Header
Options
Drawer

Add InboxFragment to MainActivity's frame layout

When we created our menu resource file, we set the inbox option to be highlighted by default. We'll therefore display `InboxFragment` in `MainActivity`'s frame layout when the activity is created so that it matches the drawer's contents. We'll also set the toolbar as the activity's app bar so that it displays the app's title.

Here's our code for *MainActivity.java*; replace your version of the code to match ours:

CatChat
└ **app/src/main**
  └ **java**
    └ **com.hfad.catchat**
      └ **MainActivity.java**

```java
package com.hfad.catchat;

import android.support.v7.app.AppCompatActivity;
import android.os.Bundle;
import android.support.v7.widget.Toolbar;
import android.support.v4.app.Fragment;
import android.support.v4.app.FragmentTransaction;


public class MainActivity extends AppCompatActivity {
```

Make sure the activity extends the AppCompatActivity class, as we're using an AppCompat theme and support fragments.

```java
    @Override
    protected void onCreate(Bundle savedInstanceState) {
        super.onCreate(savedInstanceState);
        setContentView(R.layout.activity_main);
        Toolbar toolbar = (Toolbar) findViewById(R.id.toolbar);
        setSupportActionBar(toolbar);
```

← *Set the Toolbar as the activity's app bar.*

Use a fragment transaction to display an instance of InboxFragment.

```java
        Fragment fragment = new InboxFragment();
        FragmentTransaction ft = getSupportFragmentManager().beginTransaction();
        ft.add(R.id.content_frame, fragment);
        ft.commit();
    }
}
```

Let's see what happens when we run the app.

Test drive the app

When we run the app, `InboxFragment` is displayed in `MainActivity`. When you swipe the app from the left side of the screen (in left-to-right languages like English) the navigation drawer is displayed. The navigation drawer contains a header layout, and the list of options we defined in our menu resource file. The first option is automatically highlighted:

 In right-to-left languages, the drawer will appear on the right side of the screen instead.

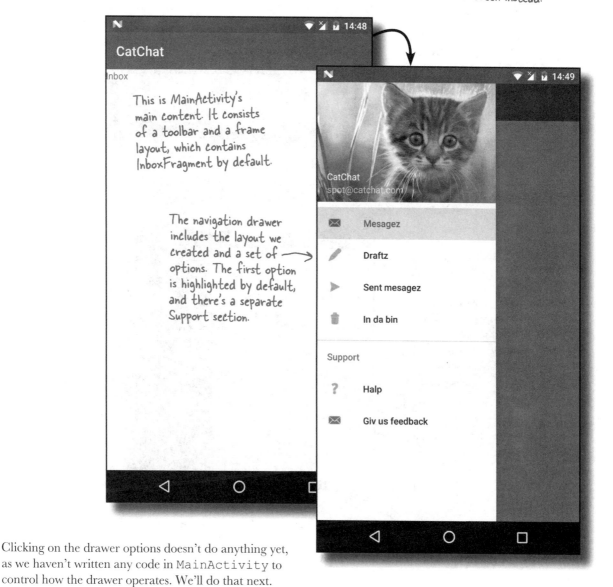

This is MainActivity's main content. It consists of a toolbar and a frame layout, which contains InboxFragment by default.

The navigation drawer includes the layout we created and a set of options. The first option is highlighted by default, and there's a separate Support section.

Clicking on the drawer options doesn't do anything yet, as we haven't written any code in `MainActivity` to control how the drawer operates. We'll do that next.

What the activity code needs to do

Fragments/activities
Header
Options
Drawer

There are three things we need our activity code to do:

1 **Add a drawer toggle.**
This provides a visual sign to the user that the activity contains a navigation drawer. It adds a "burger" icon to the toolbar, and you can click on this icon to open the drawer.

This is the "burger" icon. Clicking on it opens the navigation drawer.

2 **Make the drawer respond to clicks.**
When the user clicks on one of the options in the navigation drawer, we'll display the appropriate fragment or activity and close the drawer.

When the user clicks on one of the main options, we'll display the fragment for that option and close the drawer. The option will be highlighted in the navigation drawer the next time we open it.

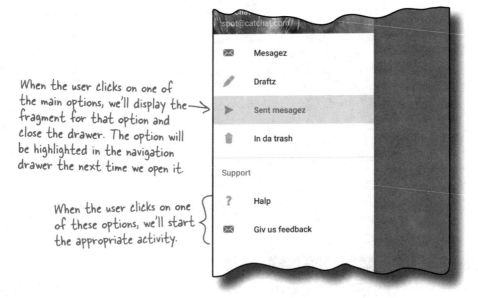

When the user clicks on one of these options, we'll start the appropriate activity.

3 **Close the drawer when the user presses the Back button.**
If the drawer's open, we'll close it when the user clicks on the Back button. If the drawer's already closed, we'll get the Back button to function as normal.

We'll start by adding the drawer toggle.

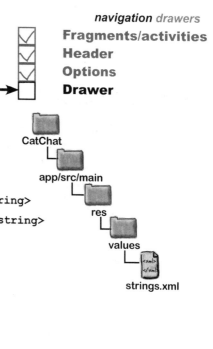

Add a drawer toggle

The first thing we'll do is add a drawer toggle so that we can open the navigation drawer by clicking on an icon in the toolbar.

We'll start by creating two String resources to describe the "open drawer" and "close drawer" actions; these are required for accessibility purposes. Add the two Strings below to *strings.xml*:

```
<string name="nav_open_drawer">Open navigation drawer</string>
<string name="nav_close_drawer">Close navigation drawer</string>
```

You create the drawer toggle in the activity's `onCreate()` method by creating a new instance of the **ActionBarDrawerToggle** class and adding it to the drawer layout. We'll show you the code for this first, then add it to `MainActivity` later in the chapter.

The `ActionBarDrawerToggle` constructor takes five parameters: the current activity, the drawer layout, the toolbar, and the IDs of two String resources for opening and closing the drawer (the String resources we added above):

```
Toolbar toolbar = (Toolbar) findViewById(R.id.toolbar);
...

DrawerLayout drawer = (DrawerLayout) findViewById(R.id.drawer_layout);
ActionBarDrawerToggle toggle = new ActionBarDrawerToggle(this,      <-- The current activity
                                          The activity's DrawerLayout --> drawer,
                                                                  toolbar,   <-- The activity's toolbar
                               These Strings are needed for accessibility. { R.string.nav_open_drawer,
                                                                            { R.string.nav_close_drawer);
```

↑ This adds the burger icon to your toolbar.

Once you've created the drawer toggle, you add it to the drawer layout by calling the `DrawerLayout addDrawerListener()` method, passing the toggle as a parameter:

```
drawer.addDrawerListener(toggle);
```

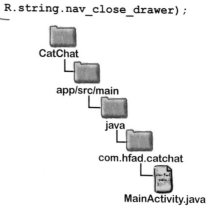

Finally, you call the toggle's `syncState()` method to synchronize the icon on the toolbar with the state of the drawer. This is because the icon changes when you click on it to open the drawer:

```
toggle.syncState();
```

We'll add the drawer toggle to `MainActivity`'s `onCreate()` method in a few pages.

Fragments/activities
Header
Options
Drawer

Respond to the user clicking items in the drawer

Next, we'll get `MainActivity` to respond to items in the
navigation drawer being clicked by getting the activity to implement a
NavigationView.OnNavigationItemSelectedListener
interface. Doing this means that whenever an item is
clicked, a new method we'll create in `MainActivity`,
`onNavigationItemSelected()`, will get called. We'll use this
method to display the screen for the appropriate option.

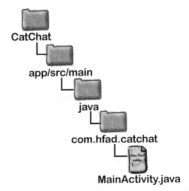

CatChat

app/src/main

java

com.hfad.catchat

MainActivity.java

First, we'll get `MainActivity` to implement the interface using the
code below. This code turns `MainActivity` into a listener for the
navigation view:

```
...
import android.support.design.widget.NavigationView;


public class MainActivity extends AppCompatActivity
                        implements NavigationView.OnNavigationItemSelectedListener {

    ...

}
```

*Implementing this interface means that your activity can
respond to the user clicking options in the navigation drawer.*

Next we need to register the listener, `MainActivity`, with the
navigation view so that it will be notified when the user clicks on one
of the options in the drawer. We'll do this by getting a reference to the
navigation view in the activity's `onCreate()` method, and calling its
`setNavigationItemSelectedListener()` method:

```
@Override
protected void onCreate(Bundle savedInstanceState) {

    ...

    NavigationView navigationView = (NavigationView) findViewById(R.id.nav_view);
    navigationView.setNavigationItemSelectedListener(this);

}
```

*This registers the activity as a listener
on the navigation view so it will be
notified if the user clicks on an item.*

Finally, we need to implement the
`onNavigationItemSelected()` method.

Implement the onNavigationItemSelected() method

The onNavigationItemSelected() method gets called when the user clicks on one of the items in the navigation drawer. It takes one parameter, the MenuItem that was clicked, and returns a boolean to indicate whether the item in the drawer should be highlighted:

This method gets called whenever an item in the drawer is clicked. Its parameter is the clicked item.

```
@Override
public boolean onNavigationItemSelected(MenuItem item) {
    //Code to handle navigation clicks
}
```

The code in this method needs to display the appropriate screen for the clicked item. If the item is an activity, the code needs to start it with an intent. If the item is a fragment, it needs to be displayed in MainActivity's frame layout using a fragment transaction.

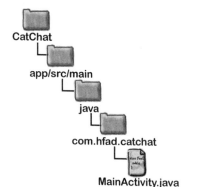

When you display fragments by clicking on an item in a navigation drawer, you don't generally add the transaction to the back stack as we did previously. This is because when the user clicks on the Back button, they don't expect to revisit every option they clicked on in the drawer. Instead, you use code like this:

```
FragmentTransaction ft = getSupportFragmentManager().beginTransaction();
ft.replace(R.id.content_frame, fragment);
ft.commit();
```

This is the same fragment transaction code you've seen before except that we're not adding the transaction to the activity's back stack.

Finally, you need to close the drawer. To do this, you get a reference to the drawer layout, and call its closeDrawer() method:

```
DrawerLayout drawer = (DrawerLayout) findViewById(R.id.drawer_layout);
drawer.closeDrawer(GravityCompat.START);
```

We're using GravityCompat.START because we've attached the drawer to the activity's start edge. If we'd attached it to the end edge, we'd use GravityCompat.END instead.

This closes the drawer so that it slides back to the activity's start edge.

You now know everything you need in order to write the code for the onNavigationItemSelected() method, so have a go at the following exercise.

Code Magnets

When the user clicks on an item in the navigation drawer, we need to display the appropriate screen for that item. If it's a fragment, we need to display it in the `content_frame` frame layout. If it's an activity, we need to start it. Finally, we need to close the navigation drawer.

See if you can complete the code below and on the next page. You won't need to use all of the magnets.

```
@Override
public boolean onNavigationItemSelected(MenuItem item) {

    int id = item. ........................ ;
    Fragment fragment = null;
    Intent intent = null;

    switch( ............. ){
        case R.id.nav_drafts:

            fragment = .................................................... ;


            .................... ;
        case R.id.nav_sent:

            fragment = .................................................... ;


            .................... ;
        case R.id.nav_trash:

            fragment = .................................................... ;


            .................... ;
        case R.id.nav_help:

            intent = new Intent( ...................... , .................................... );


            .................... ;
```

```
    case R.id.nav_feedback:

        intent = new Intent(................,................................);

            ................;
    default:

        fragment = ................................;
}

if (........................ != null) {

    FragmentTransaction ft = getSupportFragmentManager()........................;

    ft.replace(R.id.content_frame, ........................);

    ft. ........................;
} else {

    startActivity(........................);
}

DrawerLayout drawer = (DrawerLayout) findViewById(R.id.drawer_layout);

drawer. ........................ (................................);
return true;
}
```

closeDrawer	GravityCompat.START	fragment	FeedbackActivity.class

beginTransaction()	break	break	intent	DraftsFragment()	new	this
HelpActivity.class	TrashFragment()	break	InboxFragment()	break	break
id	HelpActivity	SentItemsFragment()	new	START	getItemId()
commit()	new	FeedbackActivity	fragment	new	this

Code Magnets Solution

When the user clicks on an item in the navigation drawer, we need to display the appropriate screen for that item. If it's a fragment, we need to display it in the `content_frame` frame layout. If it's an activity, we need to start it. Finally, we need to close the navigation drawer.

See if you can complete the code below and on the next page. You won't need to use all of the magnets.

```
@Override
public boolean onNavigationItemSelected(MenuItem item) {

    int id = item. getItemId() ;              ← Get the ID of the item that was selected.
    Fragment fragment = null;
    Intent intent = null;

    switch( id ){
        case R.id.nav_drafts:

            fragment = new DraftsFragment() ;

            break ;
        case R.id.nav_sent:

            fragment = new SentItemsFragment() ;        ← Save an instance of the
                                                          fragment we want to display
            break ;                                       in the fragment variable.
        case R.id.nav_trash:

            fragment = new TrashFragment() ;

            break ;
        case R.id.nav_help:

            intent = new Intent( this , HelpActivity.class );
                                                 ↑
            break ;              Construct an intent to start
                                 HelpActivity if the Help option's clicked.
```

```
case R.id.nav_feedback:

    intent = new Intent( .... this .... , .... FeedbackActivity.class .... );

        break ;
    default:
```

If the feedback option is clicked, we need to start FeedbackActivity.

```
        fragment = .... new .... InboxFragment() .... ;
}
```

Display InboxFragment by default, as it's the first option in the drawer.

```
if ( .... fragment .... != null) {
```

If we need to display a fragment, use a fragment transaction.

```
    FragmentTransaction ft = getSupportFragmentManager(). .... beginTransaction() .... ;

    ft.replace(R.id.content_frame, .... fragment .... );

    ft. .... commit() .... ;
} else {

    startActivity( .... intent .... );
}
```

If we need to display an activity, use the intent we constructed to start it.

```
DrawerLayout drawer = (DrawerLayout) findViewById(R.id.drawer_layout);

drawer. .... closeDrawer .... ( .... GravityCompat.START .... );
return true;
}
```

Finally, close the drawer.

We'll add this code to MainActivity.java in a couple of pages.

You didn't need to use these magnets.

```
HelpActivity          FeedbackActivity          START
```

Close the drawer when the user presses the Back button

Fragments/activities
Header
Options
Drawer

Finally, we'll override what happens when the Back button's pressed. If the user presses the Back button when the navigation drawer's open, we'll close the drawer. If the drawer's already closed we'll get the Back button to function as normal.

CatChat
app/src/main
java
com.hfad.catchat
MainActivity.java

To do this, we'll implement the activity's `onBackPressed()` method, which gets called whenever the user clicks on the Back button. Here's the code:

This gets called when the Back button gets pressed.

```
@Override
public void onBackPressed() {
    DrawerLayout drawer = (DrawerLayout) findViewById(R.id.drawer_layout);
    if (drawer.isDrawerOpen(GravityCompat.START)) {
        drawer.closeDrawer(GravityCompat.START);
    } else {
        super.onBackPressed();
    }
}
```

If the drawer is currently open, close it.

Otherwise, call up to the superclass onBackPressed() method.

That's everything we need for `MainActivity`. We'll show you the full code over the next couple of pages, and then take it for a test drive.

---

there are no
Dumb Questions

Q: Do you have to use a navigation view for your drawer contents?

A: No, but it's *much* easier if you do. Before the Android Design Library came out, it was common practice to use a list view instead. This approach is still possible, but it requires a lot more code.

Q: Can your activity contain more than one navigation drawer?

A: Your activity can have one navigation drawer per vertical edge of its layout. To add a second navigation drawer, add an extra navigation view to your drawer layout underneath the first.

The full MainActivity.java code

Here's the full code for *MainActivity.java*; update your version of the code to match ours:

```java
package com.hfad.catchat;

import android.support.v7.app.AppCompatActivity;
import android.os.Bundle;
import android.support.v7.widget.Toolbar;
import android.support.v4.app.Fragment;
import android.support.v4.app.FragmentTransaction;
import android.support.v4.widget.DrawerLayout;
import android.support.v7.app.ActionBarDrawerToggle;
import android.support.design.widget.NavigationView;
import android.view.MenuItem;
import android.content.Intent;
import android.support.v4.view.GravityCompat;
```

We're using these extra classes so we need to import them.

CatChat
└── app/src/main
    └── java
        └── com.hfad.catchat
            └── MainActivity.java

```java
public class MainActivity extends AppCompatActivity
                          implements NavigationView.OnNavigationItemSelectedListener {
```

Implementing this interface means the activity can listen for clicks.

```java
    @Override
    protected void onCreate(Bundle savedInstanceState) {
        super.onCreate(savedInstanceState);
        setContentView(R.layout.activity_main);
        Toolbar toolbar = (Toolbar) findViewById(R.id.toolbar);
        setSupportActionBar(toolbar);

        DrawerLayout drawer = (DrawerLayout) findViewById(R.id.drawer_layout);
        ActionBarDrawerToggle toggle = new ActionBarDrawerToggle(this,
                                                    drawer,
                                                    toolbar,
                                                    R.string.nav_open_drawer,
                                                    R.string.nav_close_drawer);
        drawer.addDrawerListener(toggle);
        toggle.syncState();
```

Add a drawer toggle.

The code continues on the next page. →

you are here ▸ **615**

MainActivity.java (continued)

Fragments/activities
Header
Options
Drawer

```java
NavigationView navigationView = (NavigationView) findViewById(R.id.nav_view);
navigationView.setNavigationItemSelectedListener(this);
```

Register the activity with the navigation view as a listener.

```java
    Fragment fragment = new InboxFragment();
    FragmentTransaction ft = getSupportFragmentManager().beginTransaction();
    ft.add(R.id.content_frame, fragment);
    ft.commit();
}
```

This method gets called when the user clicks on one of the items in the drawer.

```java
@Override
public boolean onNavigationItemSelected(MenuItem item) {
    int id = item.getItemId();
    Fragment fragment = null;
    Intent intent = null;

    switch(id){
        case R.id.nav_drafts:
            fragment = new DraftsFragment();
            break;
        case R.id.nav_sent:
            fragment = new SentItemsFragment();
            break;
        case R.id.nav_trash:
            fragment = new TrashFragment();
            break;
        case R.id.nav_help:
            intent = new Intent(this, HelpActivity.class);
            break;
        case R.id.nav_feedback:
            intent = new Intent(this, FeedbackActivity.class);
            break;
        default:
            fragment = new InboxFragment();
    }
```

CatChat

app/src/main

java

com.hfad.catchat

MainActivity.java

The code continues on the next page. →

- [x] **Fragments/activities**
- [x] **Header**
- [x] **Options**
- [ ] **Drawer**

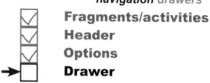

MainActivity.java (continued)

```
        if (fragment != null) {
            FragmentTransaction ft = getSupportFragmentManager().beginTransaction();
            ft.replace(R.id.content_frame, fragment);
            ft.commit();
        } else {
            startActivity(intent);
        }
```

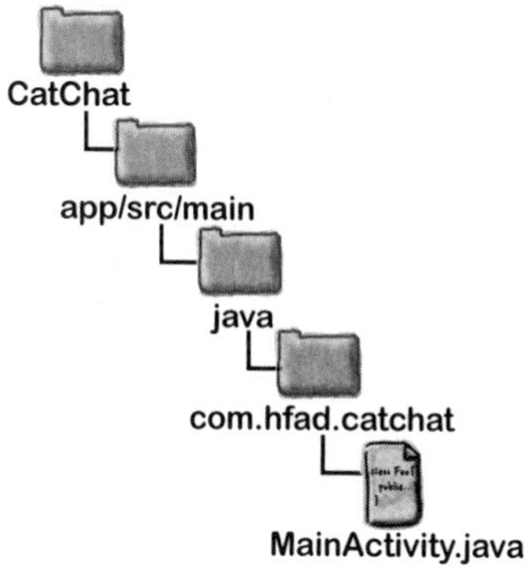

Display the appropriate fragment or activity, depending on which option in the drawer the user selects.

```
        DrawerLayout drawer = (DrawerLayout) findViewById(R.id.drawer_layout);
        drawer.closeDrawer(GravityCompat.START);
        return true;
    }
```

Close the drawer when the user selects one of the options.

When the user presses the Back button, close the drawer if it's open.

```
    @Override
    public void onBackPressed() {
        DrawerLayout drawer = (DrawerLayout) findViewById(R.id.drawer_layout);
        if (drawer.isDrawerOpen(GravityCompat.START)) {
            drawer.closeDrawer(GravityCompat.START);
        } else {
            super.onBackPressed();
        }
    }
}
```

CatChat
app/src/main
java
com.hfad.catchat
MainActivity.java

Let's see what happens when we run the code.

Test drive the app

When we run the app, a drawer toggle icon is displayed in the toolbar. Clicking on this icon opens the navigation drawer. When we click on one of the first four options, the fragment for that option is displayed in `MainActivity` and the drawer closes; the option for that item is highlighted the next time we open the drawer. When we click on one of the last two options, the activity for that option is started.

MainActivity includes a drawer toggle. Clicking on it opens the drawer.

When we click on the Sent mesagez option, SentItemsFragment gets displayed and the drawer closes. The option is highlighted in the drawer the next time we open it.

When we click on the Halp option, HelpActivity gets displayed and the drawer closes.

We've created a fully operational navigation drawer.

Your Android Toolbox

You've got Chapter 14 under your belt and now you've added navigation drawers to your toolbox.

> You can download the full code for the chapter from https://tinyurl.com/HeadFirstAndroid.

BULLET POINTS

- Use a navigation drawer if you want to provide the user with a large number of shortcuts, or group them into sections.

- Create a navigation drawer by adding a **drawer layout** to your activity's layout. The drawer layout's first element needs to be a view that defines the activity's main content, usually a layout containing a `Toolbar` and `FrameLayout`. Its second element defines the contents of the drawer, usually a `NavigationView`.

- The **NavigationView** comes from the Design Support Library. It controls most of the drawer's behavior.

- You add a header to your drawer by creating a layout for it, and adding the header's resource ID to the navigation view's `headerLayout` attribute.

- You add items to the drawer by creating a menu resource, and adding the menu's resource ID to the navigation view's `menu` attribute.

- Add items to the menu resource in the order in which you want them to appear in the drawer.

- If you want to highlight which item in the drawer the user selects, add the menu items to a group and set the group's `checkableBehavior` attribute to `"single"`.

- Use an **ActionBarDrawerToggle** to display a "burger" icon in the activity's toolbar. This provides a visual sign that the activity has a navigation drawer. Clicking on it opens the drawer.

- Respond to the user clicking on items in the drawer by making your activity implement the **NavigationView.OnNavigation ItemSelectedListener** interface. Register the activity with the navigation view as a listener, then implement the `onNavigationItemSelected()` method.

- Close the navigation drawer using the `DrawerLayout closeDrawer()` method.

15 SQLite databases

Fire Up the Database

When I said I wanted persistence, I was talking about the database.

If you're recording high scores or saving tweets, your app will need to store data. And on Android you usually keep your data safe inside a **SQLite database**. In this chapter, we'll show you how to **create a database, add tables to it, and prepopulate it with data**, all with the help of the friendly **SQLite helper**. You'll then see how you can cleanly roll out **upgrades** to your database structure, and how to **downgrade** it if you need to undo any changes.

Back to Starbuzz

Back in Chapter 7, we created an app for Starbuzz Coffee.
The app allows the user to navigate through a series of
screens so that she can see the drinks available at Starbuzz.

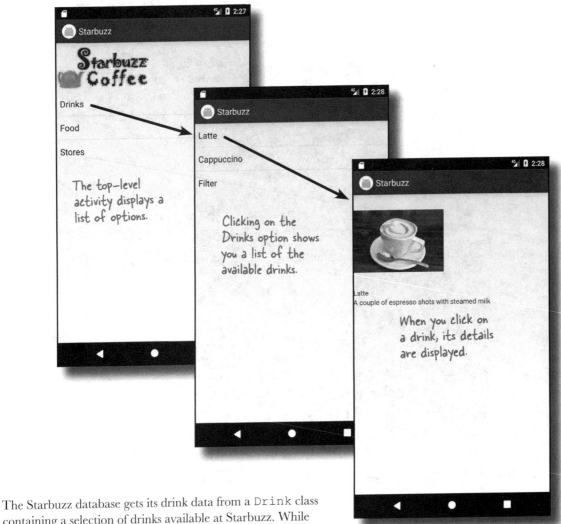

The top-level activity displays a list of options.

Clicking on the Drinks option shows you a list of the available drinks.

When you click on a drink, its details are displayed.

The Starbuzz database gets its drink data from a `Drink` class
containing a selection of drinks available at Starbuzz. While
this made building the first version of the app easier, there's a
better way of storing and persisting data.

Over the next two chapters, we're going to change the
Starbuzz app so that it gets its data from a SQLite database.
In this chapter, we'll see how to create the database, and in
the next chapter, we'll show you how to connect activities to it.

Android uses SQLite databases to persist data

All apps need to store data, and the main way you do that in Androidville is with a **SQLite database**. Why SQLite?

⭐ **It's lightweight.**
Most database systems need a special database server process in order to work. SQLite doesn't; a SQLite database is just a file. When you're not using the database, it doesn't use up any processor time. That's important on a mobile device, because we don't want to drain the battery.

⭐ **It's optimized for a single user.**
Our app is the only thing that will talk to the database, so we shouldn't have to identify ourselves with a username and password.

⭐ **It's stable and fast.**
SQLite databases are amazingly stable. They can handle database transactions, which means if you're updating several pieces of data and mess up, SQLite can roll the data back. Also, the code that reads and writes the data is written in optimized C code. Not only is it fast, but it also reduces the amount of processor power it needs.

> **We're going to go through the <u>basics</u> of SQLite in this chapter.**
>
> **If you plan on doing a lot of database heavy lifting in your apps, we suggest you do more background reading on SQLite and SQL.**

Where's the database stored?

Android automatically creates a folder for each app where the app's database can be stored. When we create a database for the Starbuzz app, it will be stored in the following folder on the device:

/data/data/com.hfad.starbuzz/databases

An app can store several databases in this folder. Each database consists of two files.

The first file is the **database file** and has the same name as your database—for example, "starbuzz". This is the main SQLite database file. All of your data is stored in this file.

The second file is the **journal file**. It has the same name as your database, with a suffix of "-journal"—for example, "starbuzz-journal". The journal file contains all of the changes made to your database. If there's a problem, Android will use the journal to undo your latest changes.

com.hfad.starbuzz is the app's unique identifier.

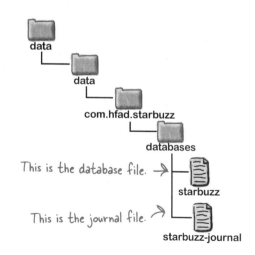

data

data

com.hfad.starbuzz

databases

This is the database file. → starbuzz

This is the journal file. → starbuzz-journal

Android comes with SQLite classes

Android uses a set of classes that allows you to manage a SQLite database. There are three types of object that do the bulk of this work:

The SQLite Helper

A SQLite helper enables you to create and manage databases. You create one by extending the `SQLiteOpenHelper` class.

The SQLite Database

The `SQLiteDatabase` class gives you access to the database. It's like a `SQLConnection` in JDBC.

Cursors

A `Cursor` lets you read from and write to the database. It's like a `ResultSet` in JDBC.

We're going to use these objects to show you how to create a SQLite database your app can use to persist data by replacing the `Drink` class with a SQLite database.

---

there are no
Dumb Questions

Q: If there's no username and password on the database, how is it kept secure?

A: The directory where an app's databases are stored is only readable by the app itself. The database is secured down at the operating system level.

Q: Can I write an Android app that talks to some other kind of external database, such as Oracle?

A: There's no reason why you can't access other databases over a network connection, but be careful to conserve the resources used by Android. For example, you might use less battery power if you access your database via a web service. That way, if you're not talking to the database, you're not using up any resources.

Q: Why doesn't Android use JDBC to access SQLite databases?

A: We know we're going to be using a SQLite database, so using JDBC would be overkill. Those layers of database drivers that make JDBC so flexible would just drain the battery on an Android device.

Q: Is the database directory inside the app's directory?

A: No. It's kept in a separate directory from the app's code. That way, the app can be overwritten with a newer version, but the data in the database will be kept safe.

The current Starbuzz app structure

Here's a reminder of the current structure of the Starbuzz app:

1 **TopLevelActivity displays a list of options: Drinks, Food, and Stores.**

2 **When the user clicks on the Drinks option, it launches DrinkCategoryActivity.**
This activity displays a list of drinks that it gets from the Java `Drink` class.

3 **When the user clicks on a drink, its details get displayed in DrinkActivity.**
`DrinkActivity` gets details of the drink from the Java `Drink` class.

The app currently gets its data from the Drink class.

activity_top_level.xml · activity_drink_category.xml · Drink.java · activity_drink.xml

Device → **1** TopLevelActivity.java → **2** DrinkCategoryActivity.java → **3** DrinkActivity.java

How does the app structure need to change if we're to use a SQLite database?

Do this!

We're going to update the Starbuzz app in this chapter, so open your original Starbuzz project in Android Studio.

Let's change the app to use a database

We'll use a SQLite helper to create a SQLite database we can use with our Starbuzz app. We're going to replace our Drink Java class with a database, so we need our SQLite helper to do the following:

① **Create the database.**
Before we can do anything else, we need to get the SQLite helper to create version 1 (the first version) of our Starbuzz database.

② **Create the Drink table and populate it with drinks.**
Once we have a database, we can create a table in it. The table's structure needs to reflect the attributes in the current Drink class, so it needs to be able to store the name, description, and image resource ID of each drink. We'll then add three drinks to it.

The app has the same structure as before except that we're replacing the file *Drink.java* with a SQLite helper and a SQLite Starbuzz database. The SQLite helper will maintain the Starbuzz database, and provide access to it for the other activities. We'll change the activities to use the database in the next chapter.

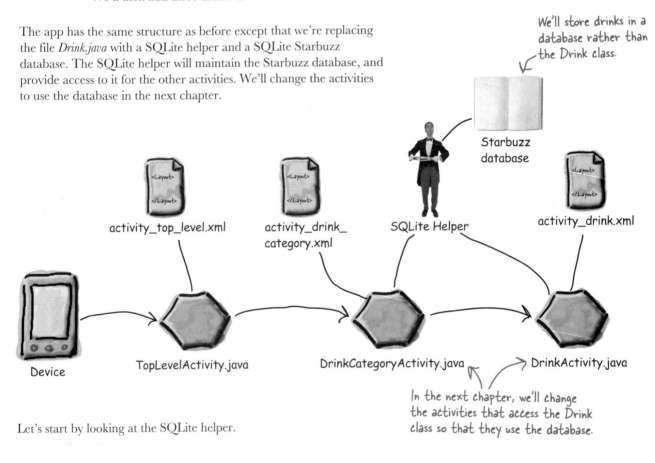

We'll store drinks in a database rather than the Drink class.

Starbuzz database

activity_top_level.xml

activity_drink_category.xml

SQLite Helper

activity_drink.xml

Device

TopLevelActivity.java

DrinkCategoryActivity.java

DrinkActivity.java

In the next chapter, we'll change the activities that access the Drink class so that they use the database.

Let's start by looking at the SQLite helper.

The SQLite helper manages your database

The **SQLiteOpenHelper** class is there to help you create and maintain your SQLite databases. Think of it as a personal assistant who takes care of the general database housekeeping.

Let's look at some typical tasks that the SQLite helper can assist you with:

Creating the database

When you first install an app, the database file won't exist. The SQLite helper will make sure the database file is created with the correct name and with the correct table structures installed.

Getting access to the database

Our app shouldn't need to know all of the details about where the database file is, so the SQLite helper can serve us with an easy-to-use database object whenever we need it. At all hours, day or night.

The SQLite helper

Keeping the database shipshape

The structure of the database will probably change over time, and the SQLite helper can be relied upon to convert an old version of a database into a shiny, spiffy new version, with all the latest database structures it needs.

Create the SQLite helper

You create a SQLite helper by writing a class that extends the **SQLiteOpenHelper** class. When you do this, you ***must*** override the onCreate() and onUpgrade() methods. These methods are mandatory.

The onCreate() method gets called when the database first gets created on the device. The method should include all the code needed to create the tables you need for your app.

The onUpgrade() method gets called when the database needs to be upgraded. As an example, if you need to modify the structure of the database after it's been released, this is the method to do it in.

In our app, we're going to use a SQLite helper called StarbuzzDatabaseHelper. Create this class in your Starbuzz project by switching to the Project view of Android Studio's explorer, selecting the com.hfad.starbuzz package in the *app/src/main/ java* folder, and navigating to File→New...→Java Class. Name the class "StarbuzzDatabaseHelper", make sure the package name is com. hfad.starbuzz and then replace its contents with the code below:

This is the full path of the
SQLiteOpenHelper class.

```
package com.hfad.starbuzz;

import android.database.sqlite.SQLiteOpenHelper;
import android.content.Context;
import android.database.sqlite.SQLiteDatabase;


class StarbuzzDatabaseHelper extends SQLiteOpenHelper {

    StarbuzzDatabaseHelper(Context context) {
    }

    @Override
    public void onCreate(SQLiteDatabase db) {
    }

    @Override
    public void onUpgrade(SQLiteDatabase db, int oldVersion, int newVersion) {
    }

}
```

SQLite helpers must extend
the SQLiteOpenHelper class.

Starbuzz
app/src/main
java
com.hfad.starbuzz
StarbuzzDatabase
Helper.java

We'll write the code for the
constructor on the next page.

The onCreate() and onUpgrade() methods are
mandatory. We've left them empty for now, and we'll
look at them in more detail throughout the chapter.

To get the SQLite helper to do something, we need to add code to its methods. The first thing to do is tell the SQLite helper what database it needs to create.

Specify the database

There are two pieces of information the SQLite helper needs in order to create the database.

First, we need to give the database a name. By giving the database a name, we make sure that the database remains on the device when it's closed. If we don't, the database will only be created in memory, so once the database is closed, it will disappear.

Creating databases that are only held in memory can be useful when you're testing your app.

The second piece of information we need to provide is the version of the database. The database version needs to be an integer value, starting at 1. The SQLite helper uses this version number to determine whether the database needs to be upgraded.

You specify the database name and version by passing them to the constructor of the SQLiteOpenHelper superclass. We're going to give our database a name of "starbuzz", and as it's the first version of the database, we'll give it a version number of 1. Here's the code we need (update your version of *StarbuzzDatabaseHelper.java* to match the code below):

Name: "starbuzz"
Version: 1

SQLite database

```
...
class StarbuzzDatabaseHelper extends SQLiteOpenHelper {

    private static final String DB_NAME = "starbuzz"; // the name of our database
    private static final int DB_VERSION = 1; // the version of the database

    StarbuzzDatabaseHelper(Context context) {
        super(context, DB_NAME, null, DB_VERSION);
    }
    ...
}
```

We're calling the constructor of the SQLiteOpenHelper superclass, and passing it the database name and version.

This parameter is an advanced feature relating to cursors. We'll cover cursors in the next chapter.

The constructor specifies details of the database, but the database doesn't get created at that point. The SQLite helper waits until the app needs to access the database, and then creates the database.

We've now done everything we need to tell the SQLite helper what database to create. The next step is to tell it what tables to create.

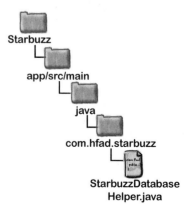

Starbuzz

app/src/main

java

com.hfad.starbuzz

StarbuzzDatabase
Helper.java

Inside a SQLite database

The data inside a SQLite database is stored in tables. A table contains several rows, and each row is split into columns. A column contains a single piece of data, like a number or a piece of text.

You need to create a table for each distinct piece of data that you want to record. In the Starbuzz app, for example, we'll need to create a table for the drink data. It will look something like this:

The columns in the table are _id, NAME, DESCRIPTION, and IMAGE_RESOURCE_ID. The Drink class contained similarly named attributes.

_id	NAME	DESCRIPTION	IMAGE_RESOURCE_ID
1	"Latte"	"Espresso and steamed milk"	54543543
2	"Cappuccino"	"Espresso, hot milk and steamed-milk foam"	654334453
3	"Filter"	"Our best drip coffee"	44324234

Some columns can be specified as **primary keys**. A primary key uniquely identifies a single row. If you say that a column is a primary key, then the database won't allow you to store rows with duplicate keys.

We recommend that your tables have a single column called _id to hold the primary key that contains integer values. This is because Android code is hardwired to expect a numeric _id column, so not having one can cause you problems later on.

Storage classes and data types

Each column in a table is designed to store a particular type of data. For example, in our DRINK table, the DESCRIPTION column will only ever store text data. Here are the main data types you can use in SQLite, and what they can store:

INTEGER	Any integer type
TEXT	Any character type
REAL	Any floating-point number
NUMERIC	Booleans, dates, and date-times
BLOB	Binary Large Object

Unlike most database systems, you don't need to specify the column size in SQLite. Under the hood, the data type is translated into a much broader storage class. This means you can say very generally what kind of data you're going to store, but you're not forced to be specific about the size of data.

> It's an Android convention to call your primary key columns _id. Android code expects there to be an _id column on your data. Ignoring this convention will make it harder to get the data out of your database and into your user interface.

You create tables using Structured Query Language (SQL)

Every application that talks to SQLite needs to use a standard database language called Structured Query Language (SQL). SQL is used by almost every type of database. If you want to create the DRINK table, you will need to do it in SQL.

This is the SQL command to create the table: *The _id column is the primary key.*

```
CREATE TABLE DRINK (_id INTEGER PRIMARY KEY AUTOINCREMENT,
                    NAME TEXT,
                    DESCRIPTION TEXT,
                    IMAGE_RESOURCE_ID INTEGER)
```

The table name

These are table columns.

The `CREATE TABLE` command says what columns you want in the table, and what the data type is of each column. The `_id` column is the primary key of the table, and the special keyword `AUTOINCREMENT` means that when we store a new row in the table, SQLite will automatically generate a unique integer for it.

The onCreate() method is called when the database is created

The SQLite helper is in charge of creating the SQLite database. An empty database is created on the device the first time it needs to be used, and then the SQLite helper's `onCreate()` method is called. The `onCreate()` method has one parameter, a `SQLiteDatabase` object that represents the database that's been created.

You can use the `SQLiteDatabase execSQL()` method to execute SQL on the database. This method has one parameter, the SQL you want to execute.

`execSQL(String sql);`   *Execute the SQL in the String on the database.*

We'll use the `onCreate()` method to create the DRINK table. Here's the code (we'll add the code in a few pages):

```java
public void onCreate(SQLiteDatabase db){
    db.execSQL("CREATE TABLE DRINK ("
        + "_id INTEGER PRIMARY KEY AUTOINCREMENT, "
        + "NAME TEXT, "
        + "DESCRIPTION TEXT, "
        + "IMAGE_RESOURCE_ID INTEGER);");
}
```

This gives us an empty DRINK table. We want to prepopulate it with drink data, so let's look at how you do that.

> ## The SQLiteDatabase class gives you access to the database.

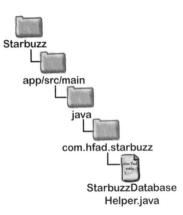

Starbuzz

app/src/main

java

com.hfad.starbuzz

StarbuzzDatabase
Helper.java

Insert data using the insert() method

To insert data into a table in a SQLite database, you start by specifying what values you want to insert into the table. To do this, you first create a **ContentValues** object:

```
ContentValues drinkValues = new ContentValues();
```

A ContentValues object describes a set of data. You usually create a new ContentValues object for each row of data you want to create.

You add data to the ContentValues object using its **put()** method. This method adds name/value pairs of data: NAME is the column you want to add data to, and value is the data:

```
contentValues.put("NAME", "value");
```
← *NAME is the column you want to add data to. value is the value you want it to have.*

As an example, here's how you'd use the put() method to add the name, description, and image resource ID of a latte to a ContentValues object called drinkValues:

This is a single row of data.
```
drinkValues.put("NAME", "Latte");
```
← *Put the value "Latte" in the NAME column.*
```
drinkValues.put("DESCRIPTION", "Espresso and steamed milk");
```
← *Put "Espresso and steamed milk" in the DESCRIPTION column.*
```
drinkValues.put("IMAGE_RESOURCE_ID", R.drawable.latte);
```
← *You need a separate call to the put() method for each value you want to enter.*

Once you've added a row of data to the ContentValues object, you insert it into the table using the SQLiteDatabase insert() method. This method inserts data into a table, and returns the ID of the record once it's been inserted. If the method is unable to insert the record, it returns a value of −1. As an example, here's how you'd insert the data from drinkValues into the DRINK table:

```
db.insert("DRINK", null, drinkValues);
```
← *This inserts a single row into the table.*

The middle parameter is usually set to null, as in the above code. It's there in case the ContentValues object is empty, and you want to insert an empty row into your table. It's unlikely you'd want to do this, but if you did you'd replace the null value with the name of one of the columns in your table.

Running the lines of code above will insert a Latte row into the DRINK table:

_id	NAME	DESCRIPTION	IMAGE_RESOURCE_ID
1	"Latte"	"Espresso and steamed milk"	54543543

← *A shiny new record gets inserted into the table.*

The insert() methods inserts one row of data at a time. But what if you want to insert multiple records?

Insert multiple records

To insert multiple rows into a table, you need to make repeat calls to the insert() method. Each call to the method inserts a separate row.

To insert multiple rows, you usually create a new method that inserts a single row of data, and call it each time you want to add a new row. As an example, here's an insertDrink() method we wrote to insert drinks into the DRINK table:

```
private static void insertDrink(SQLiteDatabase db,
                                String name,
                                String description,
                                int resourceId) {
    ContentValues drinkValues = new ContentValues();
    drinkValues.put("NAME", name);
    drinkValues.put("DESCRIPTION", description);
    drinkValues.put("IMAGE_RESOURCE_ID", resourceId);
    db.insert("DRINK", null, drinkValues);
}
```

This is the database we want to add records to.

We're passing the data to the method as parameters.

Construct a ContentValues object with the data.

Then insert the data.

To add three drinks to the DRINK table, each one a separate row of data, you'd call the method three times:

```
insertDrink(db, "Latte", "Espresso and steamed milk", R.drawable.latte);
insertDrink(db, "Cappuccino", "Espresso, hot milk and steamed-milk foam",
                R.drawable.cappuccino);
insertDrink(db, "Filter", "Our best drip coffee", R.drawable.filter);
```

That's everything you need to know to insert data into tables. On the next page we'll show you the revised code for *StarbuzzDatabaseHelper.java*.

Create database
Create table

The StarbuzzDatabaseHelper code

Here's the complete code for *StarbuzzDatabaseHelper.java* (update your
code to reflect our changes):

Starbuzz

app/src/main

java

com.hfad.starbuzz

StarbuzzDatabase
Helper.java

You need to add this
extra import statement.

```java
package com.hfad.starbuzz;

import android.content.ContentValues;
import android.content.Context;
import android.database.sqlite.SQLiteDatabase;
import android.database.sqlite.SQLiteOpenHelper;

class StarbuzzDatabaseHelper extends SQLiteOpenHelper{

    private static final String DB_NAME = "starbuzz"; // the name of our database
    private static final int DB_VERSION = 1; // the version of the database

    StarbuzzDatabaseHelper(Context context){
        super(context, DB_NAME, null, DB_VERSION);
    }

    @Override
    public void onCreate(SQLiteDatabase db){
        db.execSQL("CREATE TABLE DRINK (_id INTEGER PRIMARY KEY AUTOINCREMENT, "
                    + "NAME TEXT, "
                    + "DESCRIPTION TEXT, "
                    + "IMAGE_RESOURCE_ID INTEGER);");
        insertDrink(db, "Latte", "Espresso and steamed milk", R.drawable.latte);
        insertDrink(db, "Cappuccino", "Espresso, hot milk and steamed-milk foam",
                    R.drawable.cappuccino);
        insertDrink(db, "Filter", "Our best drip coffee", R.drawable.filter);
    }

    @Override
    public void onUpgrade(SQLiteDatabase db, int oldVersion, int newVersion) {
    }

    private static void insertDrink(SQLiteDatabase db, String name,
                                    String description, int resourceId) {
        ContentValues drinkValues = new ContentValues();
        drinkValues.put("NAME", name);
        drinkValues.put("DESCRIPTION", description);
        drinkValues.put("IMAGE_RESOURCE_ID", resourceId);
        db.insert("DRINK", null, drinkValues);
    }
}
```

Say what the database name and
version is. It's the first version of the
database, so the version should be 1.

onCreate() gets called when the database first gets created,
so we're using it to create the table and insert data.

Create the DRINK table.

Insert each
drink in a
separate row.

onUpgrade() gets called when the database
needs to be upgraded. We'll look at this next.

We need to insert several
drinks, so we created a
separate method to do this.

What the SQLite helper code does

1 **The user installs the app and launches it.**
When the app needs to access the database, the SQLite helper checks to see if
the database already exists.

> You need a database,
> sir? Let me see if it's
> already there for you.

SQLite helper

2 **If the database doesn't exist, it gets created.**
It's given the name and version number specified in the SQLite helper.

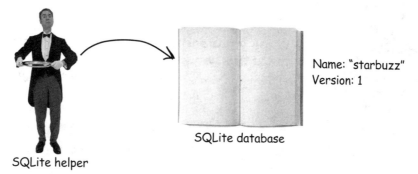

Name: "starbuzz"
Version: 1

SQLite database

SQLite helper

3 **When the database is created, the onCreate() method in the
SQLite helper is called.**
It adds a DRINK table to the database, and populates it with records.

> Your database,
> sir. Will that
> be all?

onCreate()

DRINK

Name: "starbuzz"
Version: 1

SQLite database

SQLite helper

What if you need to make changes to the database?

So far, you've seen how to create a SQLite database that your app will be able to use to persist data. But what if you need to make changes to the database at some future stage?

As an example, suppose lots of users have already installed your Starbuzz app on their devices, and you want to a add a new FAVORITE column to the DRINK table. How would you distribute this change to new and existing users?

Well, we could change the CREATE TABLE statement in the onCreate() method, but that doesn't feel entirely right to me. I mean, what if a device already has the old version of the database installed?

When you need to change an app's database, there are two key scenarios you have to deal with.

The first scenario is that the user has never installed your app before, and doesn't have the database installed on their device. In this case, the SQLite helper creates the database the first time the database needs to be accessed, and runs its `onCreate()` method.

The second scenario is where the user installs a new version of your app that includes a different version of the database. If the SQLite helper spots that the database that's installed is out of date, it will call either the `onUpgrade()` or `onDowngrade()` method.

So how can the SQLite helper tell if the database is out of date?

SQLite databases have a version number

The SQLite helper can tell whether the SQLite database needs updating by looking at its version number. You specify the version of the database in the SQLite helper by passing it to the `SQLiteOpenHelper` superclass in its constructor.

Earlier on, we specified the version number of the database like this:

```
...
    private static final String DB_NAME = "starbuzz";
    private static final int DB_VERSION = 1;

    StarbuzzDatabaseHelper(Context context) {
        super(context, DB_NAME, null, DB_VERSION);
    }
...
```

When the database gets created, its version number gets set to the version number in the SQLite helper, and the SQLite helper `onCreate()` method gets called.

When you want to update the database, you change the version number in the SQLite helper code. To *upgrade* the database, specify a number that's larger than you had before, and to *downgrade* your database, specify a number that's lower:

```
...
    private static final int DB_VERSION = 2;
...
```

Here we're increasing the version number, so the database will get upgraded.

Most of the time, you'll want to upgrade the database, so specify a number that's larger. You usually only downgrade your database when you want to undo changes you made in a previous upgrade.

When the user installs the latest version of the app on their device, the first time the app needs to use the database, the SQLite helper checks its version number against that of the database on the device.

If the version number in the SQLite helper code is **higher** than that of the database, it calls the SQLite helper **onUpgrade()** method. If the version number in the SQLite helper code is **lower** than that of the database, it calls the **onDowngrade()** method instead.

Once it's called either of these methods, it changes the version number of the database to match the version number in the SQLite helper.

Geek Bits

SQLite databases support a version number that's used by the SQLite helper, and an internal schema version. Whenever a change is made to the database schema, such as the table structure, the database increments the schema version by 1. You have no control over this value, it's just used internally by SQLite.

What happens when you change the version number

Let's look at what happens when you release a new version of the app where you've changed the SQLite helper version number from 1 to 2. We'll consider two scenarios: where a first-time user installs the app, and when an existing user installs it.

Scenario 1: A first-time user installs the app

① The first time the user runs the app, the database doesn't exist, so the SQLite helper creates it.

The SQLite helper gives the database the name and version number specified in the SQLite helper code.

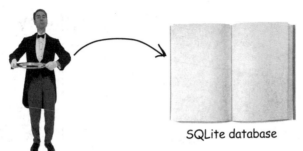

Name: "starbuzz"
Version: 2

The SQLite helper gives the database a version number of 2 if this is the version number specified in the SQLite helper code.

SQLite database

SQLite helper

② When the database is created, the onCreate() method in the SQLite helper is called.

The onCreate() method includes code to populate the database.

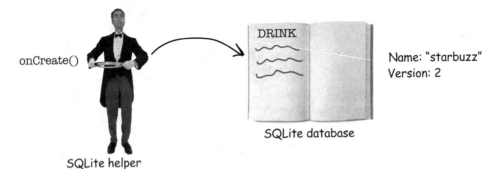

onCreate()

DRINK

Name: "starbuzz"
Version: 2

SQLite database

SQLite helper

That's what happens when a first-time user installs the app. What about when an existing user installs the new version?

Scenario 2: an existing user installs the new version

1 **When the user runs the new version of the app, the database helper checks whether the database exists.**

If the database already exists, the SQLite helper doesn't recreate it.

Very good, sir, I see you already have version 1 of the database.

SQLite helper

SQLite database

Name: "starbuzz"
Version: 1

2 **The SQLite helper checks the version number of the existing database against the version number in the SQLite helper code.**

If the SQLite helper version number is higher than the database version, it calls the onUpgrade() method. If the SQLite helper version number is lower than the database version, it calls the onDowngrade() method. It then changes the database version number to reflect the version number in the SQLite helper code.

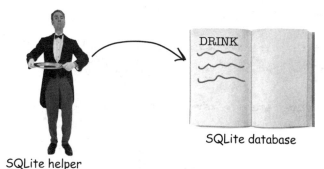

SQLite helper

SQLite database

Name: "starbuzz"
Version: ✗ 2

The SQLite helper runs the onUpgrade() method (if the new version number is higher) and updates the database version number.

Now that you've seen under what circumstances the onUpgrade() and onDowngrade() methods get called, let's find out more about how you use them.

Upgrade your database with onUpgrade()

The onUpgrade() method has three parameters—the
SQLite database, the user's version number of the database,
and the new version of the database that's passed to the
SQLiteOpenHelper superclass:

*The user's version of the
database, which is out of date*

*The new version
described in the
SQlite helper code*

```
@Override
public void onUpgrade(SQLiteDatabase db, int oldVersion, int newVersion) {
    //Your code goes here
}
```

*Remember, to upgrade the database,
the new version must be higher than
the user's existing version.*

The version numbers are important, as you can use them to say
what database changes should be made depending on which
version of the database the user already has. As an example,
suppose you needed to run code if the user has version 1 of the
database, and the SQLite helper version number is higher. Your
code would look like this:

```
@Override
public void onUpgrade(SQLiteDatabase db, int oldVersion, int newVersion) {
    if (oldVersion == 1) {
        //Code to run if the database version is 1
    }
}
```

*This code will only run if the
user has version 1 of the
database, and the SQLite
helper version number is higher.*

You can also use the version numbers to apply successive updates
like this:

```
@Override
public void onUpgrade(SQLiteDatabase db, int oldVersion, int newVersion) {
    if (oldVersion == 1) {
        //Code to run if the database version is 1
    }
    if (oldVersion < 3) {
        //Code to run if the database version is 1 or 2
    }
}
```

*This code will only run if the
user's database is at version 1.*

*This code will run if the user's
database is at version 1 or 2.*

Using this approach means that you can make sure that the user
gets all the database changes applied that they need, irrespective
of which version they have installed.

The onDowngrade() method works in a similar way to the
onUpgrade() method. Let's take a look on the next page.

Downgrade your database with onDowngrade()

The onDowngrade() method isn't used as often as the onUpgrade() method, as it's used to revert your database to a previous version. This can be useful if you release a version of your app that includes database changes, but you then discover that there are bugs. The onDowngrade() method allows you to undo the changes and set the database back to its previous version.

Just like the onUpgrade() method, the onDowngrade() method has three parameters—the SQLite database you want to downgrade, the version number of the database itself, and the new version of the database that's passed to the SQLiteOpenHelper superclass:

```
@Override
public void onDowngrade(SQLiteDatabase db, int oldVersion, int newVersion) {
    //Your code goes here
}
```

To downgrade the database, the new version must be lower than the user's exisiting version.

Just as with the onUpgrade() method, you can use the version numbers to revert changes specific to a particular version. As an example, if you needed to make changes to the database when the user's database version number is 3, you'd use code like following:

```
@Override
public void onDowngrade(SQLiteDatabase db, int oldVersion, int newVersion) {
    if (oldVersion == 3) {
        //Code to run if the database version is 3
    }
}
```

This code will run if the user has version 3 of the database, but you want to downgrade it to a lower version.

Now that you know how to upgrade and downgrade a database, let's walk through the more common scenario: upgrading.

Let's upgrade the database

Suppose we need to upgrade our database to add a new column to the DRINK table. As we want all new and existing users to get this change, we need to make sure that it's included in both the onCreate() and onUpgrade() methods. The onCreate() method will make sure that all new users get the new column, and the onUpgrade() method will make sure that all existing users get it too.

Rather than put similar code in both the onCreate() and onUpgrade() methods, we're going to create a separate updateMyDatabase() method, called by both the onCreate() and onUpgrade() methods. We'll move the code that's currently in the onCreate() method to this new updateMyDatabase() method, and we'll add extra code to create the extra column. Using this approach means that you can put all of your database code in one place, and more easily keep track of what changes you've made each time you've updated the database.

Here's the full code for *StarbuzzDatabaseHelper.java* (update your code to reflect our changes):

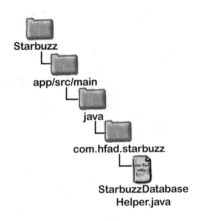

Starbuzz
app/src/main
java
com.hfad.starbuzz
StarbuzzDatabase
Helper.java

```
package com.hfad.starbuzz;

import android.content.ContentValues;
import android.content.Context;
import android.database.sqlite.SQLiteDatabase;
import android.database.sqlite.SQLiteOpenHelper;

class StarbuzzDatabaseHelper extends SQLiteOpenHelper{

    private static final String DB_NAME = "starbuzz"; // the name of our database
    private static final int DB_VERSION = 2; // the version of the database
```

Changing the version number to a larger integer means the SQLite helper will know that you want to upgrade the database.

```
    StarbuzzDatabaseHelper(Context context){
        super(context, DB_NAME, null, DB_VERSION);
    }


    @Override
    public void onCreate(SQLiteDatabase db){
        updateMyDatabase(db, 0, DB_VERSION);
    }
```

← *Replace the existing onCreate() code with this call to updateMyDatabase().*

The code continues on the next page.

The SQLite helper code (continued)

```
@Override
public void onUpgrade(SQLiteDatabase db, int oldVersion, int newVersion) {
    updateMyDatabase(db, oldVersion, newVersion);
}
```
← Call the updateMyDatabase() method from onUpgrade(), passing along the parameters.

```
private static void insertDrink(SQLiteDatabase db, String name,
                                String description, int resourceId) {
    ContentValues drinkValues = new ContentValues();
    drinkValues.put("NAME", name);
    drinkValues.put("DESCRIPTION", description);
    drinkValues.put("IMAGE_RESOURCE_ID", resourceId);
    db.insert("DRINK", null, drinkValues);
}


private void updateMyDatabase(SQLiteDatabase db, int oldVersion, int newVersion) {
    if (oldVersion < 1) {
        db.execSQL("CREATE TABLE DRINK (_id INTEGER PRIMARY KEY AUTOINCREMENT, "
                        + "NAME TEXT, "
                        + "DESCRIPTION TEXT, "
                        + "IMAGE_RESOURCE_ID INTEGER);");
        insertDrink(db, "Latte", "Espresso and steamed milk", R.drawable.latte);
        insertDrink(db, "Cappuccino", "Espresso, hot milk and steamed-milk foam",
                        R.drawable.cappuccino);
        insertDrink(db, "Filter", "Our best drip coffee", R.drawable.filter);
    }
    if (oldVersion < 2) {
        //Code to add the extra column
    }
}
}
```

This is the code we previously had in our onCreate() method.

This code will run if the user already has version 1 of the database. We need to write this code next.

Starbuzz
app/src/main
java
com.hfad.starbuzz
StarbuzzDatabase
Helper.java

The next thing we need to do is write the code to upgrade the database. Before we do that, try the exercise on the next page.

BE the SQLite Helper

On the right, you'll see some SQLite helper code. Your job is to play like you're the SQLite helper and say which code will run for each of the users below. We've labeled the code we want you to consider. We've done the first one to start you off.

User 1 runs the app for the first time.

Code segment A. The user doesn't have the database, so the onCreate() method runs.

User 2 has database version 1.

User 3 has database version 2.

User 4 has database version 3.

User 5 has database version 4.

User 6 has database version 5.

```
...

class MyHelper extends SQLiteOpenHelper{

    StarbuzzDatabaseHelper(Context context){
        super(context, "fred", null, 4);
    }

    @Override
    public void onCreate(SQLiteDatabase db){
     A  //Run code A
        ...
    }

    @Override
    public void onUpgrade(SQLiteDatabase db,
                          int oldVersion,
                          int newVersion){
        if (oldVersion < 2) {
         B  //Run code B
            ...
        }
        if (oldVersion == 3) {
         C  //Run code C
            ...
        }
     D  //Run code D
        ...
    }

    @Override
    public void onDowngrade(SQLiteDatabase db,
                            int oldVersion,
                            int newVersion){
        if (oldVersion == 3) {
         E  //Run code E
            ...
        }
        if (oldVersion < 6) {
         F  //Run code F
            ...
        }
    }
}
```

Answers on page 654.

Upgrade an existing database

When you need to upgrade your database, there are two types of actions you might want to perform:

⭐ **Change the database records.**
Earlier in the chapter, you saw how to insert records in your database using the `SQLiteDatabase insert()` method. You may want to add more records when you upgrade the database, or update or delete the records that are already there.

⭐ **Change the database structure.**
You've already seen how you can create tables in the database. You may also want to add columns to existing tables, rename tables, or remove tables completely.

We'll start by looking at how you change database records.

How to update records

You update records in a table in a similar way to how you insert them.

You start by creating a new `ContentValues` object that specifies what you want to update values to. As an example, suppose you wanted to update the Latte data in the DRINK table so that the value of the DESCRIPTION field is "Tasty":

_id	NAME	DESCRIPTION	IMAGE_RESOURCE_ID
1	"Latte"	~~"Espresso and steamed milk"~~ "Tasty"	54543543

To do this, you'd create a new `ContentValues` object that describes the data that needs to be updated:

```
ContentValues drinkValues = new ContentValues();
drinkValues.put("DESCRIPTION", "Tasty");
```

We want to change the value of the DESCRIPTION column to Tasty, so we give the name "DESCRIPTION" a value of "Tasty".

Notice that when you're updating records, you only need to specify the data you want to change in the `ContentValues` object, not the entire row of data.

Once you've added the data you want to change to the `ContentValues` object, you use the `SQLiteDatabase update()` method to update the data. We'll look at this on the next page.

Update records with the update() method

The update() method lets you update records in the database, and returns the number of records it's updated. To use the update() method, you specify the table you want to update records in, the ContentValues object that contains the values you want to update, and the conditions for updating them.

As an example, here's how you'd change the value of the DESCRIPTION column to "Tasty" where the name of the drink is "Latte":

```
ContentValues drinkValues = new ContentValues();
drinkValues.put("DESCRIPTION", "Tasty");
db.update("DRINK",
          drinkValues,
          "NAME = ?",
          new String[] {"Latte"});
```

db.update("DRINK", ⟵—— This is the name of the table whose records you want to update.

drinkValues, ⟵—This is the ContentValues object that contains the new values.

The conditions for updating the data, in this case where NAME = "Latte". { "NAME = ?",

new String[] {"Latte"}); ⟵—The value "Latte" is substituted for the ? in the "NAME = ?" statement above.

The first parameter of the update() method is the name of the table you want to update (in this case, the DRINK table).

The second parameter is the ContentValues object that describes the values you want to update. In the example above, we've added "DESCRIPTION" and "Tasty" to the ContentValues object, so it updates the value of the DESCRIPTION column to "Tasty".

The last two parameters specify which records you want to update by describing conditions for the update. Together, they form the WHERE clause of a SQL statement.

The third parameter specifies the name of the column in the condition. In the above example, we want to update records where the value of the NAME column is "Latte", so we use "NAME = ?"; it means that we want the value in the NAME column to be equal to some value. The ? symbol is a placeholder for this value.

The last parameter is an array of Strings that says what the value of the condition should be. In our particular case we want to update records where the value of the NAME column is "Latte", so we use:

```
new String[] {"Latte"});
```

We'll look at more complex conditions on the next page.

Watch it!

If you set the last two parameters of the update() method to null, ALL records in the table will be updated.

As an example, the code:

```
db.update("DRINK",
          drinkValues,
          null, null);
```

will update all records in the DRINK table.

Apply conditions to multiple columns

You can also specify conditions that apply to multiple columns. As an example, here's how you'd update all records where the name of the drink is "Latte", or the drink description is "Our best drip coffee":

```
db.update("DRINK",
          drinkValues,
          "NAME = ? OR DESCRIPTION = ?",
          new String[] {"Latte", "Our best drip coffee"});
```

This means: Where NAME = "Latte" or DESCRIPTION = "Our best drip coffee".

Each ? placeholder is replaced with a value from this array. The number of values in the array must match the number of ?'s.

If you want to apply conditions that cover multiple columns, you specify the column names in the update() method's third parameter. As before, you add a placeholder ? for each value you want to add as part of each condition. You then specify the condition values in the update() method's fourth parameter.

The condition values must be Strings, even if the column you're applying the condition to contains some other type of data. As an example, here's how you'd update DRINK records where the _id (numeric) is 1:

```
db.update("DRINK",
          drinkValues,
          "_id = ?",
          new String[] {Integer.toString(1)});
```

Convert the int 1 to a String value.

Delete records with the delete() method

You delete records using the SQLiteDatabase delete() method. It works in a similar way to the update() method you've just seen. You specify the table you want to delete records from, and conditions for deleting the data. As an example, here's how you'd delete all records from the DRINK table where the name of the drink is "Latte":

```
db.delete("DRINK",
          "NAME = ?",
          new String[] {"Latte"});
```

See how similar this is to the update() method.

The entire row is deleted.

_id	NAME	DESCRIPTION	IMAGE_RESOURCE_ID
1	"Latte"	"Espresso and steamed milk"	54543543

The first parameter is the name of the table you want to delete records from (in this case, DRINK). The second and third arguments allow you to describe conditions to specify exactly which records you wish to delete (in this case, where NAME = "Latte").

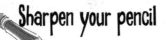

Sharpen your pencil

Here's the `onCreate()` method of a `SQLiteOpenHelper` class. Your job is to say what values have been inserted into the NAME and DESCRIPTION columns of the DRINK table when the `onCreate()` method has finished running.

```java
@Override
public void onCreate(SQLiteDatabase db) {
    ContentValues espresso = new ContentValues();
    espresso.put("NAME", "Espresso");
    ContentValues americano = new ContentValues();
    americano.put("NAME", "Americano");
    ContentValues latte = new ContentValues();
    latte.put("NAME", "Latte");
    ContentValues filter = new ContentValues();
    filter.put("DESCRIPTION", "Filter");
    ContentValues mochachino = new ContentValues();
    mochachino.put("NAME", "Mochachino");

    db.execSQL("CREATE TABLE DRINK ("
            + "_id INTEGER PRIMARY KEY AUTOINCREMENT, "
            + "NAME TEXT, "
            + "DESCRIPTION TEXT);");
    db.insert("DRINK", null, espresso);
    db.insert("DRINK", null, americano);
    db.delete("DRINK", null, null);
    db.insert("DRINK", null, latte);
    db.update("DRINK", mochachino, "NAME = ?", new String[] {"Espresso"});
    db.insert("DRINK", null, filter);
}
```

You don't → need to enter the value of the _id column.

_id	NAME	DESCRIPTION

→ Answers on page 655.

Change the database structure

In addition to creating, updating, or deleting database records, you may want to make changes to the database structure. As an example, in our particular case we want to add a new FAVORITE column to the DRINK table.

Add new columns to tables using SQL

Earlier in the chapter, you saw how you could create tables using the SQL CREATE TABLE command like this:

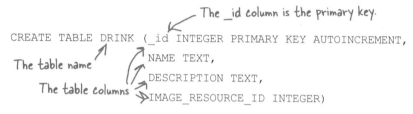

```
                                  The _id column is the primary key.
CREATE TABLE DRINK (_id INTEGER PRIMARY KEY AUTOINCREMENT,
     The table name         NAME TEXT,
                            DESCRIPTION TEXT,
          The table columns IMAGE_RESOURCE_ID INTEGER)
```

You can also use SQL to change an existing table using the ALTER TABLE command. As an example, here's what the command looks like to add a column to a table:

```
ALTER TABLE DRINK          The table name
ADD COLUMN FAVORITE NUMERIC    The column you want to add
```

In the example above, we're adding a column to the DRINK table called FAVORITE that holds numeric values.

Renaming tables

You can also use the ALTER TABLE command to rename a table. As an example, here's how you'd rename the DRINK table to FOO:

```
ALTER TABLE DRINK      The current table name
RENAME TO FOO      The new name of the table
```

On the next page, we'll show you how to remove a table from the database.

Delete tables by dropping them

If you want to delete a table from the database, you use the DROP
TABLE command. As an example, here's how you'd delete the
DRINK table:

      DROP TABLE DRINK ← The name of the table you want to remove

This command is useful if you have a table in your database schema
that you know you don't need anymore, and want to remove it in
order to save space. Make sure you only use the DROP TABLE
command if you're absolutely sure you want to get rid of the table and
all of its data.

Execute the SQL using execSQL()

As you saw earlier in the chapter, you execute SQL commands using
the SQLiteDatabase execSQL() method:

      SQLiteDatabase.execSQL(String sql);

You use the execSQL() method any time you need to execute SQL
on the database. As an example, here's how you'd execute SQL to
add a new FAVORITE column to the DRINK table:

      db.execSQL("ALTER TABLE DRINK ADD COLUMN FAVORITE NUMERIC;");

Now that you've seen the sorts of actions you might want to
perform when upgrading your database, let's apply this to
StarbuzzDatabaseHelper.java.

The full SQLite helper code

Here's the full code for *StarbuzzDatabaseHelper.java* that will add a new FAVORITE column to the DRINK table. Update your code to match ours (the changes are in bold):

```java
package com.hfad.starbuzz;

import android.content.ContentValues;
import android.content.Context;
import android.database.sqlite.SQLiteDatabase;
import android.database.sqlite.SQLiteOpenHelper;

class StarbuzzDatabaseHelper extends SQLiteOpenHelper{

    private static final String DB_NAME = "starbuzz"; // the name of our database
    private static final int DB_VERSION = 2; // the version of the database

    StarbuzzDatabaseHelper(Context context){
        super(context, DB_NAME, null, DB_VERSION);
    }

    @Override
    public void onCreate(SQLiteDatabase db){
        updateMyDatabase(db, 0, DB_VERSION);
    }

    @Override
    public void onUpgrade(SQLiteDatabase db, int oldVersion, int newVersion) {
        updateMyDatabase(db, oldVersion, newVersion);
    }
```

Changing the version number to a larger integer enables the SQLite helper to spot that you want to upgrade the database.

The code to create any database tables is in the updateMyDatabase() method.

The code to upgrade the database is in our updateMyDatabase() method.

Starbuzz
app/src/main
java
com.hfad.starbuzz
StarbuzzDatabase
Helper.java

The code continues over the page.

The SQLite helper code (continued)

```java
    private static void insertDrink(SQLiteDatabase db, String name,
                                    String description, int resourceId) {
        ContentValues drinkValues = new ContentValues();
        drinkValues.put("NAME", name);
        drinkValues.put("DESCRIPTION", description);
        drinkValues.put("IMAGE_RESOURCE_ID", resourceId);
        db.insert("DRINK", null, drinkValues);
    }

    private void updateMyDatabase(SQLiteDatabase db, int oldVersion, int newVersion) {
        if (oldVersion < 1) {
            db.execSQL("CREATE TABLE DRINK (_id INTEGER PRIMARY KEY AUTOINCREMENT, "
                    + "NAME TEXT, "
                    + "DESCRIPTION TEXT, "
                    + "IMAGE_RESOURCE_ID INTEGER);");
            insertDrink(db, "Latte", "Espresso and steamed milk", R.drawable.latte);
            insertDrink(db, "Cappuccino", "Espresso, hot milk and steamed-milk foam",
                    R.drawable.cappuccino);
            insertDrink(db, "Filter", "Our best drip coffee", R.drawable.filter);
        }
        if (oldVersion < 2) {
            db.execSQL("ALTER TABLE DRINK ADD COLUMN FAVORITE NUMERIC;");
        }
    }
}
```

Add a numeric FAVORITE column to the DRINK table.

Starbuzz
└ app/src/main
  └ java
    └ com.hfad.starbuzz
      └ StarbuzzDatabase
        Helper.java

The new code in the SQLite helper means that existing users will get the new FAVORITE column added to the DRINK table the next time they access the database. It also means that any new users will get the complete database created for them, including the new column.

We'll go through what happens when the code runs on the next page. Then in the next chapter, you'll see how to use the database data in your activities.

What happens when the code runs

1 When the database first needs to be accessed, the SQLite helper checks whether the database already exists.

You need a database, sir? Let me see if it's already there for you.

SQLite helper

2a If the database doesn't exist, the SQLite helper creates it and runs its onCreate() method.

Our onCreate() method code calls the updateMyDatabase() method. This creates the DRINK table (including the new FAVORITE column) and populates the table with records.

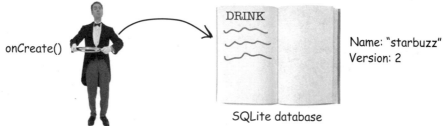

onCreate()

SQLite helper

DRINK

Name: "starbuzz"
Version: 2

SQLite database

2b If the database already exists, the SQLite helper checks the version number of the database against the version number in the SQLite helper code.

If the SQLite helper version number is higher than the database version, it calls the onUpgrade() method. If the SQLite helper version number is lower than the database version, it calls the onDowngrade() method. Our SQLite helper version number is higher than that of the existing database, so the onUpgrade() method is called. It calls the updateMyDatabase() method, and this adds the new FAVORITE column to the DRINK table.

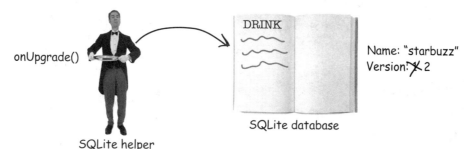

onUpgrade()

SQLite helper

DRINK

Name: "starbuzz"
Version: ~~1~~ 2

SQLite database

BE the SQLite Helper Solution

On the right you'll see some SQLite helper code. Your job is to play like you're the SQLite helper and say which code will run for each of the users below. We've labeled the code we want you to consider. We've done the first one to start you off.

User 1 runs the app for the first time.

Code segment A. The user doesn't have the database, so the onCreate() method runs.

User 2 has database version 1.

Code segment B, then D. The database needs to be upgraded with oldVersion == 1.

User 3 has database version 2.

Code segment D. The database needs to be upgraded with oldVersion == 2.

User 4 has database version 3.

Code segment C then D. The database needs to be upgraded with oldVersion == 3.

User 5 has database version 4.

None. The user has the correct version of the database.

User 6 has database version 5.

Code segment F. The database needs to be downgraded with oldVersion == 5.

```
...

class MyHelper extends SQLiteOpenHelper{

    StarbuzzDatabaseHelper(Context context){
        super(context, "fred", null, 4);
    }

    @Override
    public void onCreate(SQLiteDatabase db){
        A  //Run code A
        ...
    }

    @Override
    public void onUpgrade(SQLiteDatabase db,
                            int oldVersion,
                            int newVersion){
        if (oldVersion < 2) {
            B  //Run code B
            ...
        }
        if (oldVersion == 3) {
            C  //Run code C
            ...
        }
        D  //Run code D
        ...
    }

    @Override
    public void onDowngrade(SQLiteDatabase db,
                            int oldVersion,
                            int newVersion){
        if (oldVersion == 3) {
            E  //Run code E
            ...
        }
        if (oldVersion < 6) {
            F  //Run code F
            ...
        }
    }

}
```

The new version of the database is 4.

The onCreate() method will only run if the user doesn't have the database.

This will run if the user has version 1.

This will run if the user has version 3.

This will run if the user has version 1, 2, or 3.

This will never run. If the user has version 3, their database needs to be upgraded, not downgraded.

This will run if the user has version 5. For onDowngrade() to run, the user must have a version greater than 4, as that's the current version number of the helper.

Sharpen your pencil
Solution

Here's the onCreate() method of a SQLiteOpenHelper class. Your job is to say what values have been inserted into the NAME and DESCRIPTION columns of the DRINK table when the onCreate() method has finished running.

```
@Override
public void onCreate(SQLiteDatabase db) {
    ContentValues espresso = new ContentValues();
    espresso.put("NAME", "Espresso");
    ContentValues americano = new ContentValues();
    americano.put("NAME", "Americano");
    ContentValues latte = new ContentValues();
    latte.put("NAME", "Latte");
    ContentValues filter = new ContentValues();
    filter.put("DESCRIPTION", "Filter");
    ContentValues mochachino = new ContentValues();
    mochachino.put("NAME", "Mochachino");
```

Create the table, adding _id, NAME, and DESCRIPTION columns.

```
    db.execSQL("CREATE TABLE DRINK ("
            + "_id INTEGER PRIMARY KEY AUTOINCREMENT, "
            + "NAME TEXT, "
            + "DESCRIPTION TEXT);");
    db.insert("DRINK", null, espresso);
    db.insert("DRINK", null, americano);
    db.delete("DRINK", null, null);
    db.insert("DRINK", null, latte);
    db.update("DRINK", mochachino, "NAME = ?", new String[] {"Espresso"});
    db.insert("DRINK", null, filter);
}
```

← Insert Espresso in the NAME column.
← Insert Americano in the NAME column.
← Delete all the drinks.
← Insert Latte in the NAME column.
Set NAME to Mochachino where NAME is Espresso. No records get updated.

Insert Filter in the DESCRIPTION column.

Here's the final result of running the above code. →

_id	NAME	DESCRIPTION
	Latte	
		Filter

Your Android Toolbox

You've got Chapter 15 under your belt and now you've added creating, updating, and upgrading databases to your toolbox.

You can download the full code for the chapter from https://tinyurl.com/HeadFirstAndroid.

BULLET POINTS

- Android uses SQLite as its backend database to persist data.

- The `SQLiteDatabase` class gives you access to the SQLite database.

- A SQLite helper lets you create and manage SQLite databases. You create a SQLite helper by extending the `SQLiteOpenHelper` class.

- You must implement the `SQLiteOpenHelper onCreate()` and `onUpgrade()` methods.

- The database gets created the first time it needs to be accessed. You need to give the database a name and version number, starting at 1. If you don't give the database a name, it will just get created in memory.

- The `onCreate()` method gets called when the database first gets created.

- The `onUpgrade()` method gets called when the database needs to be upgraded.

- Execute SQL using the `SQLiteDatabase execSQL(String)` method.

- Use the SQL `ALTER TABLE` command to change an existing table. Use `RENAME TO` to rename the table, and `ADD COLUMN` to add a column.

- Use the SQL `DROP TABLE` command to delete a table.

- Add records to tables using the `insert()` method.

- Update records using the `update()` method.

- Remove records from tables using the `delete()` method.

16 basic cursors

Getting Data Out

Charles gave me a cursor that returned everything from the EXPENSIVE_GIFT table.

So how do you connect your app to a SQLite database?

So far you've seen how to create a SQLite database using a SQLite helper. The next step is to get your activities to access it. In this chapter, we'll focus on how you read data from a database. You'll find out **how to use cursors to get data from the database**. You'll see **how to navigate cursors,** and **how to get access to their data**. Finally, you'll discover how to use **cursor adapters** to bind cursors to list views.

The story so far...

In Chapter 15, you created a SQLite helper for Starbuzz Coffee. The SQLite helper creates a Starbuzz database, adds a DRINK table to it, and populates the table with drinks.

The activities in the Starbuzz app currently get their data from the Java Drink class. We're going to change the app so the activities get data from the SQLite database instead.

Here's a reminder of how the app currently works:

① **TopLevelActivity displays a list of options for Drinks, Food, and Stores.**

② **When the user clicks on the Drinks option, it launches DrinkCategoryActivity.**
This activity displays a list of drinks that it gets from the Java Drink class.

③ **When the user clicks on a drink, its details get displayed in DrinkActivity.**
DrinkActivity gets details of the drink from the Java Drink class.

We've created the SQLite helper and added code so it can create the Starbuzz database. It's not being used by any activities yet.

Starbuzz database

SQLite Helper

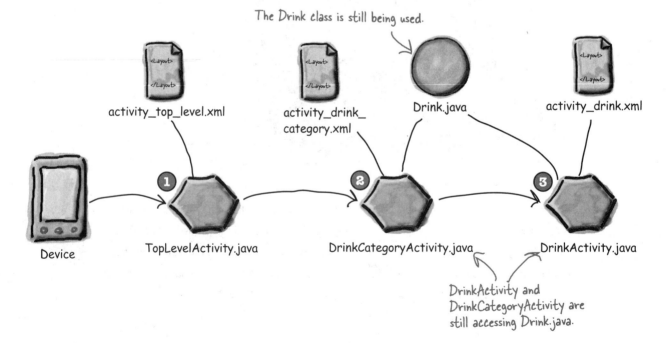

The Drink class is still being used.

activity_top_level.xml

activity_drink_category.xml

Drink.java

activity_drink.xml

Device

TopLevelActivity.java

DrinkCategoryActivity.java

DrinkActivity.java

DrinkActivity and DrinkCategoryActivity are still accessing Drink.java.

The new Starbuzz app structure

There are two activities that use the `Drink` class:
`DrinkActivity` and `DrinkCategoryActivity`.
We need to change these activities so that they read data
from the SQLite database with assistance from the SQLite
helper.

Here's what the new structure of the Starbuzz app will look
like:

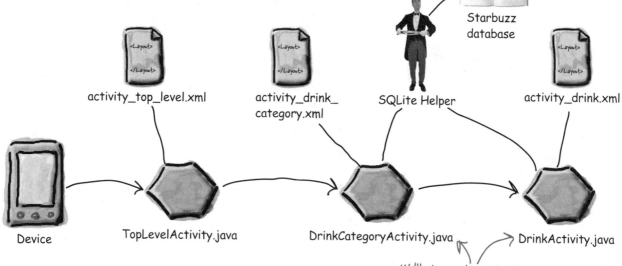

activity_top_level.xml   activity_drink_
category.xml

Starbuzz
database

SQLite Helper

activity_drink.xml

Device   TopLevelActivity.java   DrinkCategoryActivity.java   DrinkActivity.java

We'll change the activities that
access the Drink class so that they
use the database instead.

We will no longer be
using the Drink class. →

Drink.java

We'll start by updating `DrinkActivity`, and we'll
change `DrinkCategoryActivity` later on in the
chapter.

Do this!

**We're going to update the
Starbuzz app in this chapter,
so open your Starbuzz
project in Android Studio.**

What we'll do to change DrinkActivity to use the Starbuzz database

There are a number of steps we need to go through to change `DrinkActivity` so that it uses the Starbuzz database:

1 **Get a reference to the Starbuzz database.**
We'll do this using the Starbuzz SQLite helper we created in Chapter 15.

DrinkActivity.java   SQLite Helper   Starbuzz database

2 **Create a cursor to read drink data from the database.**
We need to read the data held in the Starbuzz database for the drink the user selects in `DrinkCategoryActivity`. The cursor will give us access to this data. (We'll explain cursors soon.)

3 **Navigate to the drink record.**
Before we can use the data retrieved by the cursor, we need to explicitly navigate to it.

4 **Display details of the drink in DrinkActivity.**
Once we've navigated to the drink record in the cursor, we need to read the data and display it in `DrinkActivity`.

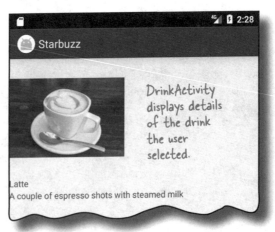

DrinkActivity displays details of the drink the user selected.

Before we begin, let's remind ourselves of the *DrinkActivity.java* code we created in Chapter 7.

The current DrinkActivity code

Below is a reminder of the current *DrinkActivity.java* code. The
onCreate() method gets the drink ID selected by the user, gets
the details of that drink from the Drink class, and then populates
the activity's views using the drink attributes. We need to change
the code in the onCreate() method to get the data from the
Starbuzz database.

```
package com.hfad.starbuzz;

... ← We're not showing you
         the import statements.
public class DrinkActivity extends Activity {

    public static final String EXTRA_DRINKID = "drinkId";

    @Override
    protected void onCreate(Bundle savedInstanceState) {
        super.onCreate(savedInstanceState);
        setContentView(R.layout.activity_drink);

        //Get the drink from the intent
        int drinkId = (Integer)getIntent().getExtras().get(EXTRA_DRINKID);
        Drink drink = Drink.drinks[drinkId];

        //Populate the drink name
        TextView name = (TextView)findViewById(R.id.name);
        name.setText(drink.getName());

        //Populate the drink description
        TextView description = (TextView)findViewById(R.id.description);
        description.setText(drink.getDescription());

        //Populate the drink image
        ImageView photo = (ImageView)findViewById(R.id.photo);
        photo.setImageResource(drink.getImageResourceId());
        photo.setContentDescription(drink.getName());
    }

}
```

Starbuzz

app/src/main

java

com.hfad.starbuzz

DrinkActivity.java

This is the drink the user selected.

*Use the drink ID from the intent to get the
drink details from the Drink class. We'll need to
change this so the drink comes from the database.*

We need to
populate the
views in the
layout with
values from
the database,
not from the
Drink class.

Get a reference to the database

Database reference
Create cursor
Navigate to record
Display drink

The first thing we need is to get a reference to the Starbuzz database using the SQLite helper we created in the last chapter. To do that, you start by getting a reference to the SQLite helper:

```
SQLiteOpenHelper starbuzzDatabaseHelper = new StarbuzzDatabaseHelper(this);
```

This is a Context, in this case the current activity.

You then call the SQLite helper's getReadableDatabase() or getWritableDatabase() to get a reference to the database. You use the getReadableDatabase() method if you need read-only access to the database, and the getWritableDatabase() method if you need to perform any updates. Both methods return a SQLiteDatabase object that you can use to access the database:

```
SQLiteDatabase db = starbuzzDatabaseHelper.getReadableDatabase();
```

or:

```
SQLiteDatabase db = starbuzzDatabaseHelper.getWritableDatabase();
```

If Android fails to get a reference to the database, a SQLiteException is thrown. This can happen if, for example, you call the getWritableDatabase() to get read/write access to the database, but you can't write to the database because the disk is full.

In our particular case, we only need to read data from the database, so we'll use the getReadableDatabase() method. If Android can't get a reference to the database and a SQLiteException is thrown, we'll use a Toast (a pop-up message) to tell the user that the database is unavailable:

```
SQLiteOpenHelper starbuzzDatabaseHelper = new StarbuzzDatabaseHelper(this);
try {
    SQLiteDatabase db = starbuzzDatabaseHelper.getReadableDatabase();
    //Code to read data from the database
} catch(SQLiteException e) {
    Toast toast = Toast.makeText(this,
                        "Database unavailable",
                        Toast.LENGTH_SHORT);
    toast.show();
}
```

These lines create a Toast that will display the message "Database unavailable" for a few seconds.

This line displays the toast.

Database unavailable

Once you have a reference to the database, you can get data from it using a cursor. We'll look at cursors next.

Get data from the database with a cursor

As we said in Chapter 15, a **cursor** lets you read from and write to the database. You specify what data you want access to, and the cursor brings back the relevant records from the database. You can then navigate through the records supplied by the cursor.

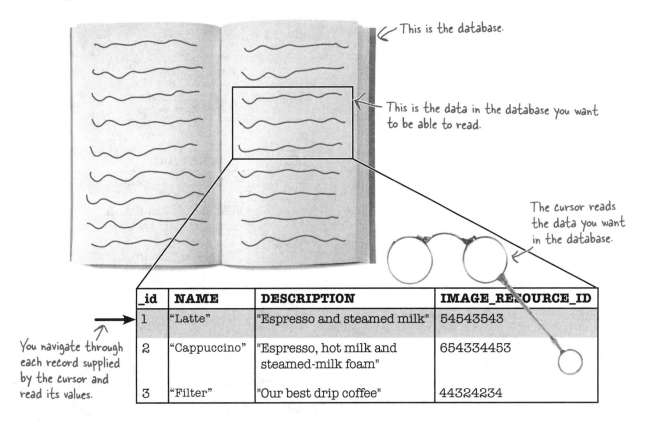

← This is the database.

← This is the data in the database you want to be able to read.

The cursor reads the data you want in the database.

_id	NAME	DESCRIPTION	IMAGE_RESOURCE_ID
1	"Latte"	"Espresso and steamed milk"	54543543
2	"Cappuccino"	"Espresso, hot milk and steamed-milk foam"	654334453
3	"Filter"	"Our best drip coffee"	44324234

You navigate through each record supplied by the cursor and read its values.

You create a cursor using a **database query**. A database query lets you specify which records you want access to from the database. As an example, you can say you want to access all the records from the DRINK table, or just one particular record. These records are then returned in the cursor.

You create a cursor using the SQLiteDatabase query() method:

The query() method returns a Cursor object. → `Cursor cursor = db.query(...);`

The query() method parameters go here. We'll look at them over the next few pages.

There are many overloaded versions of this method with different parameters, so rather than go into each variation, we're only going to show you the most common ways of using it.

Return all the records from a table

The simplest type of database query is one that returns all the records from a particular table in the database. This is useful if, for instance, you want to display all the records in a list in an activity. As an example, here's how you'd return the values in the _id, NAME, and DESCRIPTION columns for every record in the DRINK table:

This is the name of the table.

We want to return the values in these columns.

```
Cursor cursor = db.query("DRINK",
                    new String[] {"_id","NAME", "DESCRIPTION"},
                    null, null, null, null, null);
```

Set these parameters to null when you want to return all records from a table.

The query returns all the data from the _id, NAME, and DESCRIPTION columns in the DRINK table.

_id	NAME	DESCRIPTION
1	"Latte"	"Espresso and steamed milk"
2	"Cappuccino"	"Espresso, hot milk and steamed-milk foam"
3	"Filter"	"Our best drip coffee"

To return all the records from a particular table, you pass the name of the table as the query() method's first parameter, and a String array of the column names as the second. You set all of the other parameters to null, as you don't need them for this type of query.

```
Cursor cursor = db.query("TABLE_NAME",
                    new String[] {"COLUMN1","COLUMN2"},
                    null, null, null, null, null);
```

You specify each column whose value you want to return in an array of Strings.

There are five extra parameters you need to set to null.

Next we'll look at how you can return the records in a particular order.

Behind the scenes, Android uses the query() method to construct an SQL SELECT statement.

Return records in a particular order

If you want to display data in your app in a particular order, you use the query to sort the data by a particular column. This can be useful if, for example, you want to display drink names in alphabetical order.

By default, the data in the table appears in _id order, as this was the order in which data was entered:

_id	NAME	DESCRIPTION	IMAGE_RESOURCE_ID	FAVORITE
1	"Latte"	"Espresso and steamed milk"	54543543	0
2	"Cappuccino"	"Espresso, hot milk and steamed-milk foam"	654334453	0
3	"Filter"	"Our best drip coffee"	44324234	1

If you wanted to retrieve data from the _id, NAME, and FAVORITE column in ascending NAME order, you would use the following:

```
Cursor cursor = db.query("DRINK",
        new String[] {"_id", "NAME", "FAVORITE"},
        null, null, null, null,
        "NAME ASC");
```
← Order by NAME in ascending order.

_id	NAME	FAVORITE
2	"Cappuccino"	0
3	"Filter"	1
1	"Latte"	0

The ASC keyword means that you want to order that column in ascending order. Columns are ordered in ascending order by default, so if you want you can omit the ASC. To order the data in descending order instead, you'd use DESC.

You can sort by multiple columns too. As an example, here's how you'd order by FAVORITE in descending order, followed by NAME in ascending order:

```
Cursor cursor = db.query("DRINK",
        new String[] {"_id", "NAME", "FAVORITE"},
        null, null, null, null,
        "FAVORITE DESC, NAME");
```
← Order by FAVORITE in descending order, then NAME in ascending order.

_id	NAME	FAVORITE
3	"Filter"	1
2	"Cappuccino"	0
1	"Latte"	0

Next we'll look at how you return selected records from the database.

Return selected records

Database reference
Create cursor
Navigate to record
Display drink

You can filter your data by declaring conditions the data must meet, just as you did in Chapter 15. As an example, here's how you'd return records from the DRINK table where the name of the drink is "Latte":

```
Cursor cursor = db.query("DRINK",
                new String[] {"_id", "NAME", "DESCRIPTION"},
                "NAME = ?",
                new String[] {"Latte"},
                null, null, null);
```

These are the columns we want to return.

We want to return records where the value of the NAME column is "Latte".

The third and fourth parameters in the query describe the conditions the data must meet.

The third parameter specifies the column in the condition. In the above example we want to return records where the value of the NAME column is "Latte", so we use "NAME = ?". We want the value in the NAME column to be equal to some value, and the ? symbol is a placeholder for this value.

The fourth parameter is an array of Strings that specifies what the value of the condition should be. In the above example we want to update records where the value of the NAME column is "Latte", so we use:

```
new String[] {"Latte"};
```

_id	NAME	DESCRIPTION
1	"Latte"	"Espresso and steamed milk"

The query returns all the data from the NAME and DESCRIPTION columns in the DRINK table where the value of the NAME column is "Latte".

The value of the condition must be an array of Strings, even if the column you're applying the condition to contains some other type of data. As an example, here's how you'd return records from the DRINK table where the drink _id is 1:

```
Cursor cursor = db.query("DRINK",
                new String[] {"_id", "NAME", "DESCRIPTION"},
                "_id = ?",
                new String[] {Integer.toString(1)},
                null, null, null);
```

Convert the int 1 to a String value.

You've now seen the most common ways of using the query() method to create a cursor, so try the following exercise to construct the cursor we need for *DrinkActivity.java*.

To find out more ways of using the query() method, visit the SQLiteDatabase documentation:

https://developer.android.com/reference/android/database/sqlite/SQLiteDatabase.html

Code Magnets

In our code for DrinkActivity, we want to get the name, description, and image resource ID for the drink ID passed to it in an intent. Can you create a cursor that will do that?

```
...
int drinkId = (Integer)getIntent().getExtras().get(EXTRA_DRINKID);

//Create a cursor
SQLiteOpenHelper starbuzzDatabaseHelper = new StarbuzzDatabaseHelper(this);
try {
    SQLiteDatabase db = starbuzzDatabaseHelper.getReadableDatabase();

    Cursor cursor = db.query(................,

            new String[] {........................, ......................, ............................},

                "........................",

            new String[] {................................................},

        null, null, null);
} catch(SQLiteException e) {
    Toast toast = Toast.makeText(this, "Database unavailable", Toast.LENGTH_SHORT);
    toast.show();
}
...
```

You won't need to use all of the magnets.

drinkId

toString

"NAME"

"DRINK"

"IMAGE_RESOURCE_ID"

"DESCRIPTION"

?

=

.

)

_id

Integer

(

id

Code Magnets Solution

In our code for `DrinkActivity` we want to get the name, description, and image resource ID for the drink passed to it in an intent. Can you create a cursor that will do that?

```
...
int drinkId = (Integer)getIntent().getExtras().get(EXTRA_DRINKID);

//Create a cursor
SQLiteOpenHelper starbuzzDatabaseHelper = new StarbuzzDatabaseHelper(this);
try {
    SQLiteDatabase db = starbuzzDatabaseHelper.getReadableDatabase();
    Cursor cursor = db.query( "DRINK" ,
            new String[] { "NAME" , "DESCRIPTION" , "IMAGE_RESOURCE_ID" },
            " _id = ? ",
            new String[] { Integer . toString ( drinkId ) },
            null, null, null);
} catch (SQLiteException e) {
    Toast toast = Toast.makeText(this, "Database unavailable", Toast.LENGTH_SHORT);
    toast.show();
}
...
```

← We want to access the DRINK table.

Get the NAME, DESCRIPTION, and IMAGE_RESOURCE_ID.

← Where _id matches the drinkId

drinkId is an int, so needed to be converted to a String.

You didn't need to use this magnet.

`id`

The DrinkActivity code so far

We want to change *DrinkActivity.java*'s onCreate() method so
that DrinkActivity gets its drink data from the Starbuzz
database instead of from the Drink Java class. Here's the code
so far (we suggest you wait until we show you the *full* code—a few
pages ahead—before you update your version of *DrinkActivity.java*):

```java
package com.hfad.starbuzz;
...
public class DrinkActivity extends Activity {

    public static final String EXTRA_DRINKID = "drinkId";

    @Override
    protected void onCreate(Bundle savedInstanceState) {
        super.onCreate(savedInstanceState);
        setContentView(R.layout.activity_drink);

        //Get the drink from the intent
        int drinkId = (Integer)getIntent().getExtras().get(EXTRA_DRINKID);
        Drink drink = Drink.drinks[drinkId];

        //Create a cursor
        SQLiteOpenHelper starbuzzDatabaseHelper = new StarbuzzDatabaseHelper(this);
        try {
            SQLiteDatabase db = starbuzzDatabaseHelper.getReadableDatabase();
            Cursor cursor = db.query ("DRINK",
                new String[] {"NAME", "DESCRIPTION", "IMAGE_RESOURCE_ID"},
                "_id = ?",
                new String[] {Integer.toString(drinkId)},
                null, null, null);
        } catch(SQLiteException e) {
            Toast toast = Toast.makeText(this, "Database unavailable", Toast.LENGTH_SHORT);
            toast.show();
        }
        ...
    }
}
```

Our Starbuzz code uses the Activity class,
but we could have changed the code to
use AppCompatActivity if we'd wanted to.

Starbuzz

app/src/main

java

com.hfad.starbuzz

DrinkActivity.java

We'll add the code to the onCreate() method.

We're no longer getting
the drinks from Drink.java.

Get a
reference
to the
database.

Create a cursor to get
the name, description,
and image resource ID
of the drink the user
selected.

Display a pop-up message if a
SQLiteException is thrown.

There's more code we
haven't changed yet,
but you don't need to
see it right now.

Now that we've created our cursor, the next thing we need to do
is get the drink name, description, and image resource ID from
the cursor so that we can update DrinkActivity's views.

To read a record from a cursor, you first need to navigate to it

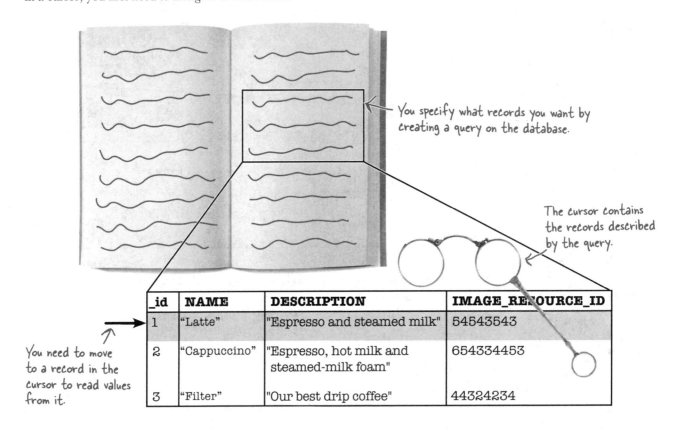

Database reference
Create cursor
Navigate to record
Display drink

You've now seen how to create a cursor; you get a reference to a SQLiteDatabase, and then use its query() method to say what data you want the cursor to return. But that's not the end of the story—once you have a cursor, you need to read values from it.

Whenever you need to retrieve values from a particular record in a cursor, you first need to navigate to that record.

You specify what records you want by creating a query on the database.

The cursor contains the records described by the query.

_id	NAME	DESCRIPTION	IMAGE_RESOURCE_ID
1	"Latte"	"Espresso and steamed milk"	54543543
2	"Cappuccino"	"Espresso, hot milk and steamed-milk foam"	654334453
3	"Filter"	"Our best drip coffee"	44324234

You need to move to a record in the cursor to read values from it.

In our particular case, we have a cursor that's composed of a single record that contains details of the drink the user selected. We need to navigate to that record in order to read details of the drink.

Navigate cursors

There are four main methods you use to navigate through the records in a cursor: moveToFirst(), moveToLast(), moveToPrevious(), and moveToNext().

To go to the first record in a cursor, you use its moveToFirst() method. This method returns a value of true if it finds a record, and false if the cursor hasn't returned any records):

```
if (cursor.moveToFirst()) {
    //Do something
};
```

To go to the last record, you use the moveToLast() method. Just like the moveToFirst() method, it returns a value of true if it finds a record, and false if it doesn't:

```
if (cursor.moveToLast()) {
    //Do something
};
```

To move through the records in the cursor, you use the moveToPrevious() and moveToNext() methods.

The moveToPrevious() method moves you to the previous record in the cursor. It returns true if it succeeds in moving to the previous record, and false if it fails (for example, if it's already at the first record):

```
if (cursor.moveToPrevious()) {
    //Do something
};
```

The moveToNext() method works in a similar way to the moveToPrevious() method, except that it moves you to the next record in the cursor instead:

```
if (cursor.moveToNext()) {
    //Do something
};
```

In our case, we want to read values from the first (and only) record in the cursor, so we'll use the moveToFirst() method to navigate to this record.

Once you've navigated to a record in your cursor, you can access its values. We'll look at how to do that next.

Move to the first row.

NAME	DESCRIPTION
"Latte"	"Espresso and steamed milk"
Cappuccino	"Espresso, hot milk and steamed-milk foam"
Filter	"Our best drip coffee"

NAME	DESCRIPTION
"Latte"	"Espresso and steamed milk"
Cappuccino	"Espresso, hot milk and steamed-milk foam"
Filter	"Our best drip coffee"

Move to the last row.

NAME	DESCRIPTION
"Latte"	"Espresso and steamed milk"
Cappuccino	"Espresso, hot milk and steamed-milk foam"
Filter	"Our best drip coffee"

Move to the previous row.

NAME	DESCRIPTION
"Latte"	"Espresso and steamed milk"
Cappuccino	"Espresso, hot milk and steamed-milk foam"
Filter	"Our best drip coffee"

Move to the next row.

Get cursor values

Database reference
Create cursor
Navigate to record
Display drink

You retrieve values from a cursor's current record using the cursor's get*() methods: getString(), getInt(), and so on. The exact method you use depends on the type of value you want to retrieve. To get a String value, for example, you'd use the getString() method, and to get an int value you'd use getInt(). Each of the methods takes a single parameter: the index of the column whose value you want to retrieve, starting at 0.

As an example, we're using the following query to create our cursor:

```
Cursor cursor = db.query ("DRINK",
                          new String[] {"NAME", "DESCRIPTION", "IMAGE_RESOURCE_ID"},
                          "_id = ?",
                          new String[] {Integer.toString(1)},
                          null, null, null);
```

The cursor has three columns: NAME, DESCRIPTION, and IMAGE_RESOURCE_ID. The first two columns, NAME and DESCRIPTION, contain Strings, and the third column, IMAGE_RESOURCE_ID, contains int values.

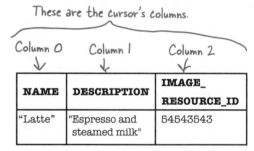

These are the cursor's columns.

NAME	DESCRIPTION	IMAGE_RESOURCE_ID
"Latte"	"Espresso and steamed milk"	54543543

Column 0 → NAME, Column 1 → DESCRIPTION, Column 2 → IMAGE_RESOURCE_ID

Suppose you wanted to get the value of the NAME column for the current record. NAME is the first column in the cursor, and contains String values. You'd therefore use the getString() method, passing it a parameter of 0 for the column index:

```
String name = cursor.getString(0);
```
← NAME is column 0 and contains Strings.

Similarly, suppose you wanted to get the contents of the IMAGE_RESOURCE_ID column. This has a column index of 2 and contains int values, so you'd use the code:

```
int imageResource = cursor.getInt(2);
```
← IMAGE_RESOURCE_ID is column 2 and contains ints.

Finally, close the cursor and the database

Once you've finished retrieving values from the cursor, you need to close the cursor and the database in order to release their resources. You do this by calling the cursor and database **close()** methods:

```
cursor.close();
db.close();
```
These lines close the cursor and the database.

You can find details of all the cursor get methods in http://developer.android.com/reference/android/database/Cursor.html.

We've now covered all the code you need to replace the code in DrinkActivity so that it gets its data from the Starbuzz database. Let's look at the revised code in full.

The DrinkActivity code

Here's the full code for *DrinkActivity.java* (apply the changes in bold to
your code, then save your work):

```java
package com.hfad.starbuzz;

import android.app.Activity;
import android.os.Bundle;
import android.widget.ImageView;
import android.widget.TextView;
import android.widget.Toast;
import android.database.Cursor;
import android.database.sqlite.SQLiteDatabase;
import android.database.sqlite.SQLiteException;
import android.database.sqlite.SQLiteOpenHelper;
```

We're using these extra classes in the code.

Starbuzz
app/src/main
java
com.hfad.starbuzz
DrinkActivity.java

```java
public class DrinkActivity extends Activity {

    public static final String EXTRA_DRINKID = "drinkId";

    @Override
    protected void onCreate(Bundle savedInstanceState) {
        super.onCreate(savedInstanceState);
        setContentView(R.layout.activity_drink);

        //Get the drink from the intent
        int drinkId = (Integer)getIntent().getExtras().get(EXTRA_DRINKID);
        Drink drink = Drink.drinks[drinkId];

        //Create a cursor
        SQLiteOpenHelper starbuzzDatabaseHelper = new StarbuzzDatabaseHelper(this);
        try {
            SQLiteDatabase db = starbuzzDatabaseHelper.getReadableDatabase();
            Cursor cursor = db.query ("DRINK",
                            new String[] {"NAME", "DESCRIPTION", "IMAGE_RESOURCE_ID"},
                            "_id = ?",
                            new String[] {Integer.toString(drinkId)},
                            null, null, null);
```

This is the ID of the drink the user chose.

We're no longer getting our data from the drinks array, so we need to delete this line.

Create a cursor that gets the NAME, DESCRIPTION, and IMAGE_RESOURCE_ID data from the DRINK table where _id matches drinkId.

The code continues on the next page.

The DrinkActivity code (continued)

Database reference
Create cursor
Navigate to record
Display drink

```java
//Move to the first record in the Cursor
if (cursor.moveToFirst()) {
```
There's only one record in the cursor, but we still need to move to it.

The name of the drink is the first item in the cursor, the description is the second column, and the image resource ID is the third. That's because we told the cursor to use the NAME, DESCRIPTION, and IMAGE_RESOURCE_ID columns from the database in that order.

```java
    //Get the drink details from the cursor
    String nameText = cursor.getString(0);
    String descriptionText = cursor.getString(1);
    int photoId = cursor.getInt(2);

    //Populate the drink name
    TextView name = (TextView)findViewById(R.id.name);
    name.setText(drink.getName());
    name.setText(nameText);
```
Set the drink name to the value from the database.

```java
    //Populate the drink description
    TextView description = (TextView)findViewById(R.id.description);
    description.setText(drink.getDescription());
    description.setText(descriptionText);
```
Use the drink description from the database.

```java
    //Populate the drink image
    ImageView photo = (ImageView)findViewById(R.id.photo);
    photo.setImageResource(drink.getImageResourceId());
    photo.setContentDescription(drink.getName());
    photo.setImageResource(photoId);
    photo.setContentDescription(nameText);
}
```
Set the image resource ID and description to the values from the database.

```java
    cursor.close();
    db.close();
```
Close the cursor and database.

```java
} catch(SQLiteException e) {
    Toast toast = Toast.makeText(this,
                        "Database unavailable",
                        Toast.LENGTH_SHORT);
    toast.show();
    }
}
}
```
If a SQLiteException is thrown, this means there's a problem with the database. In this case, we'll use a toast to display a message to the user.

Starbuzz
└ **app/src/main**
   └ **java**
      └ **com.hfad.starbuzz**
         └ **DrinkActivity.java**

So that's the complete `DrinkActivity` code. Let's review where we've got to, and what we need to do next.

Connecting your activities to a database takes more code than using a Java class.

But if you take your time working through the code in this chapter, you'll be fine.

What we've done so far

Now that we've finished updating the *DrinkActivity.java* code, let's look at the app structure diagram to see what we've done, and what we need to do next.

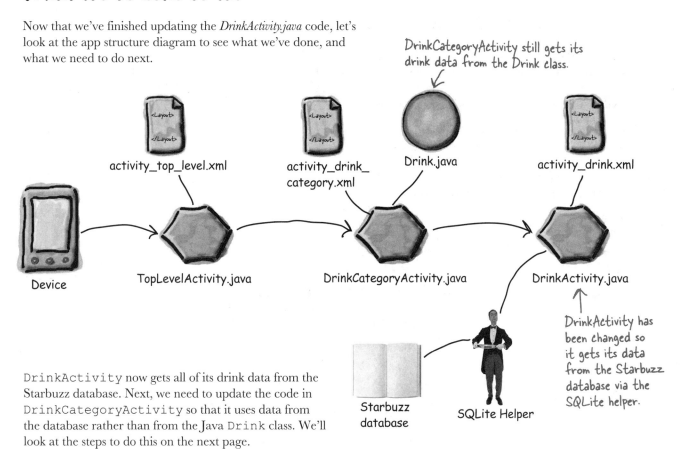

DrinkCategoryActivity still gets its drink data from the Drink class.

activity_top_level.xml

activity_drink_category.xml

Drink.java

activity_drink.xml

Device

TopLevelActivity.java

DrinkCategoryActivity.java

DrinkActivity.java

DrinkActivity has been changed so it gets its data from the Starbuzz database via the SQLite helper.

Starbuzz database

SQLite Helper

`DrinkActivity` now gets all of its drink data from the Starbuzz database. Next, we need to update the code in `DrinkCategoryActivity` so that it uses data from the database rather than from the Java `Drink` class. We'll look at the steps to do this on the next page.

---

there are no Dumb Questions

Q: How much SQL do I need to know to create cursors?

A: It's useful to have an understanding of SQL `SELECT` statements, as behind the scenes the `query()` method translates to one. In general, your queries probably won't be too complex, but SQL knowledge is a useful skill.

If you want to learn more about SQL, we suggest getting a copy of *Head First SQL* by Lynn Beighley.

Q: You said that if the database can't be accessed, a `SQLiteException` is thrown. How should I deal with it?

A: First, check the exception details. The exception might be caused by an error in SQL syntax, which you can then rectify.

How you handle the exception depends on the impact it has on your app. As an example, if you can get read access to the database but can't write to it, you can still give the user read-only access to the database, but you might want to tell the user that you can't save their changes. Ultimately, it all depends on your app.

What we'll do to change DrinkCategoryActivity to use the Starbuzz database

When we updated `DrinkActivity` to get it to read data from the Starbuzz database, we created a cursor to read data for the drink the user selected, and then we used the values from the cursor to update `DrinkActivity`'s views.

The steps we need to go through to update `DrinkCategoryActivity` are slightly different. This is because `DrinkCategoryActivity` displays a list view that uses the drink data as its source. We need to switch the source of this data to be the Starbuzz database.

Here are the steps we need to go through to change `DrinkCategoryActivity` so that it uses the Starbuzz database:

① Create a cursor to read drink data from the database.
As before, we need to get a reference to the Starbuzz database. Then we'll create a cursor to retrieve the drink names from the DRINK table.

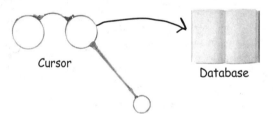

Cursor

Database

② Replace the list view's array adapter with a cursor adapter.
The list view currently uses an array adapter to get its drink names. This is because the data's held in an array in the `Drink` class. Because we're now accessing the data using a cursor, we'll use a cursor adapter instead.

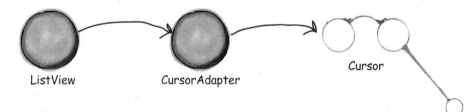

ListView   CursorAdapter   Cursor

Before we get started on these tasks, let's remind ourselves of the *DrinkCategoryActivity.java* code we created in Chapter 7.

The current DrinkCategoryActivity code

Here's a reminder of what the current *DrinkCategoryActivity.java* code looks
like. The onCreate() method populates a list view with drinks using an
array adapter. The onListItemClick() method adds the drink the
user selects to an intent, and then starts DrinkActivity:

```java
package com.hfad.starbuzz;

...

public class DrinkCategoryActivity extends Activity {

    @Override
    protected void onCreate(Bundle savedInstanceState) {
        super.onCreate(savedInstanceState);
        setContentView(R.layout.activity_drink_category);
        ArrayAdapter<Drink> listAdapter = new ArrayAdapter<>(
                this,
                android.R.layout.simple_list_item_1,
                Drink.drinks);
        ListView listDrinks = (ListView) findViewById(R.id.list_drinks);
        listDrinks.setAdapter(listAdapter);

        //Create a listener to listen for clicks in the list view
        AdapterView.OnItemClickListener itemClickListener =
                new AdapterView.OnItemClickListener(){
                    public void onItemClick(AdapterView<?> listDrinks,
                                            View itemView,
                                            int position,
                                            long id) {
                        //Pass the drink the user clicks on to DrinkActivity
                        Intent intent = new Intent(DrinkCategoryActivity.this,
                                DrinkActivity.class);
                        intent.putExtra(DrinkActivity.EXTRA_DRINKID, (int) id);
                        startActivity(intent);
                    }
                };

        //Assign the listener to the list view
        listDrinks.setOnItemClickListener(itemClickListener);
    }
}
```

> DrinkCategoryActivity
> displays a list of drinks.

Starbuzz

app/src/main

java

com.hfad.starbuzz

DrinkCategory
Activity.java

At the
moment, we're
using an
ArrayAdapter
to bind an
array to the
ListView.
We need to
replace this
code so that
the data
comes from
a database
instead.

Create cursor
Cursor adapter

Get a reference to the Starbuzz database...

We need to change `DrinkCategoryActivity` so that it gets its data from the Starbuzz database. Just as before, this means that we need to create a cursor to return the data we need.

We start by getting a reference to the database. We only need to read the drink data and not update it, so we'll use the `getReadableDatabase()` method as we did before:

```
SQLiteOpenHelper starbuzzDatabaseHelper = new StarbuzzDatabaseHelper(this);
SQLiteDatabase db = starbuzzDatabaseHelper.getReadableDatabase();
```

We get a reference to the database in exactly the same way that we did earlier in this chapter.

...then create a cursor that returns the drinks

To create the cursor, we need to specify what data we want it to contain. We want to use the cursor to display a list of drink names, so the cursor needs to include the NAME column. We'll also include the _id column to get the ID of the drink: we need to pass the ID of the drink the user chooses to `DrinkActivity` so that `DrinkActivity` can display its details. Here's the cursor:

```
cursor = db.query("DRINK",
                  new String[]{"_id", "NAME"},
                  null, null, null, null, null);
```

This cursor returns the _id and NAME of every record in the DRINK table.

Putting this together, here's the code to get a reference to the database and create the cursor (you'll add this code to *DrinkCategoryActivity.java* later when we show you the full code listing):

```
SQLiteOpenHelper starbuzzDatabaseHelper = new StarbuzzDatabaseHelper(this);
try {
    SQLiteDatabase db = starbuzzDatabaseHelper.getReadableDatabase();
    cursor = db.query("DRINK",
                      new String[]{"_id", "NAME"},
                      null, null, null, null, null);
    //Code to use data from the database
} catch(SQLiteException e) {
    Toast toast = Toast.makeText(this,
                        "Database unavailable",
                        Toast.LENGTH_SHORT);
    toast.show();
}
```

If the database is unavailable, a SQLiteException gets thrown. If this happens, we'll use a toast to display a pop-up message as before.

Next we'll use the cursor's data to populate `DrinkCategoryActivity`'s list view.

How do we replace the array data in the list view?

When we wanted `DrinkCategoryActivity`'s list view to display data from the `Drink.drinks` array, we used an array adapter. As you saw back in Chapter 7, an array adapter is a type of adapter that works with arrays. It acts as a bridge between the data in an array and a list view:

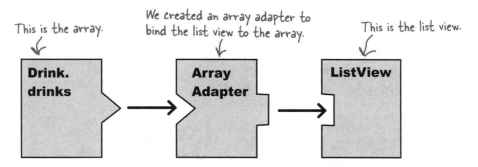

This is the array.

We created an array adapter to bind the list view to the array.

This is the list view.

Now that we're getting our data from a cursor, we'll use a **cursor adapter** to bind the data to our list view. A cursor adapter is just like an array adapter, except that instead of getting its data from an array, it reads the data from a cursor:

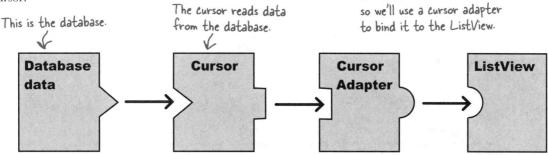

This is the database.

The cursor reads data from the database.

Our data comes from a cursor, so we'll use a cursor adapter to bind it to the ListView.

We'll look at this in more detail on the next page.

> **ListViews and Spinners can use any subclass of the Adapter class for their data. This includes ArrayAdapter, CursorAdapter, and SimpleCursorAdapter (a subclass of CursorAdapter).**

A simple cursor adapter maps cursor data to views

We're going to create a simple cursor adapter, a type of cursor adapter that can be used in most cases where you need to display cursor data in a list view. It takes columns from a cursor, and maps them to text views or image views, for example in a list view.

In our case, we want to display a list of drink names. We'll use a simple cursor adapter to map the name of each drink returned by our cursor to `DrinkCategoryActivity`'s list view.

Here's how it will work:

1 **The list view asks the adapter for data.**

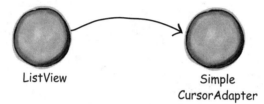

ListView   Simple
                  CursorAdapter

2 **The adapter asks the cursor for data from the database.**

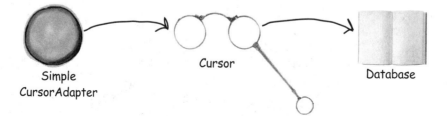

Simple   Cursor   Database
CursorAdapter

3 **The adapter returns the data to the list view.**
The name of each drink is displayed in the list view as a separate text view.

Each of the drinks is displayed in the list view as a separate text view.

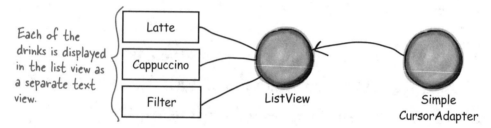

| Latte |
| Cappuccino |
| Filter |

ListView   Simple
                  CursorAdapter

Let's construct the simple cursor adapter.

How to use a simple cursor adapter

You use a simple cursor adapter in a similar way to how you use an array adapter: you initialize the adapter, then attach it to the list view.

We're going to create a simple cursor adapter to display a list of drink names from the DRINK table. To do this, we'll create a new instance of the `SimpleCursorAdapter` class, passing in parameters to tell the adapter what data to use and how it should be displayed. Finally, we'll assign the adapter to the list view.

Here's the code (you'll add it to *DrinkCategoryActivity.java* later in the chapter):

```
SimpleCursorAdapter listAdapter = new SimpleCursorAdapter(this,
                    android.R.layout.simple_list_item_1,
                    cursor,
                    new String[]{"NAME"},
                    new int[]{android.R.id.text1},
                    0);
    listDrinks.setAdapter(listAdapter);
```

"this" is the current activity.

This is the cursor. →

← This is the same layout we used with the array adapter. It displays a single value for each row in the list view.

Display the contents of the NAME column in the ListView text views.

← Use setAdapter() to connect the adapter to the list view.

The general form of the `SimpleCursorAdapter` constructor looks like this:

```
SimpleCursorAdapter adapter = new SimpleCursorAdapter(Context context,
                    int layout,
                    Cursor cursor,
                    String[] fromColumns,
                    int[] toViews,
                    int flags)
```

This is usually the current activity.

← How to display the data

The cursor you create. → The cursor should include the _id column, and the data you want to appear.

Which columns in the cursor to match to which views

Used to determine the behavior of the cursor

The `context` and `layout` parameters are exactly the same ones you used when you created an array adapter: `context` is the current context, and `layout` says how you want to display the data. Instead of saying which array we need to get our data from, we need to specify which cursor contains the data. You then use `fromColumns` to specify which columns in the cursor you want to use, and `toViews` to say which views you want to display them in.

The `flags` parameter is usually set to `0`, which is the default. The alternative is to set it to `FLAG_REGISTER_CONTENT_OBSERVER` to register a content observer that will be notified when the content changes. We're not covering this alternative here, as it can lead to memory leaks (you'll see how to deal with changing content in the next chapter).

Any cursor you use with a cursor adapter MUST include the _id column or it won't work.

Close the cursor and database

When we introduced you to cursors earlier in the chapter, we said that you needed to close the cursor and database after you'd finished with it in order to release their resources. In our `DrinkActivity` code, we used a cursor to retrieve drink details from the database, and once we'd used these values with our views, we immediately closed the cursor and database.

When you use a cursor adapter, (including a simple cursor adapter) it works slightly differently; the cursor adapter needs the cursor to stay open in case it needs to retrieve more data from it. Let's look in more detail at how cursor adapters work to see why this might happen.

① The list view gets displayed on the screen.

When the list is first displayed, it will be sized to fit the screen. Let's say it has space to show five items.

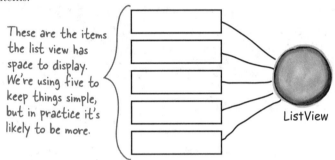

These are the items the list view has space to display. We're using five to keep things simple, but in practice it's likely to be more.

ListView

② The list view asks its adapter for the first five items.

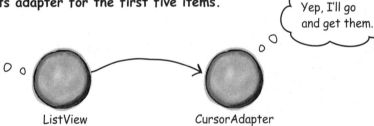

Hey, Adapter, can I have the first five data items?

Yep, I'll go and get them.

ListView   CursorAdapter

③ The cursor adapter asks its cursor to read five rows from the database.

No matter how many rows the database table contains, the cursor only needs to read the first five rows.

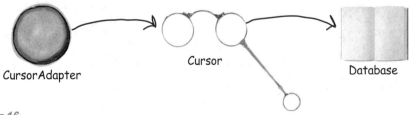

CursorAdapter   Cursor   Database

The story continues

 The user scrolls the list.

As the user scrolls the list, the adapter asks the cursor to read more rows from the database. This works fine if the cursor's still open. But if the cursor's already been closed, the cursor adapter can't get any more data from the database.

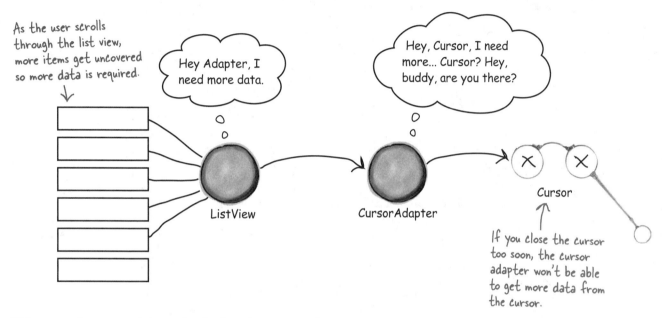

As the user scrolls through the list view, more items get uncovered so more data is required.

Hey Adapter, I need more data.

Hey, Cursor, I need more... Cursor? Hey, buddy, are you there?

ListView

CursorAdapter

Cursor

If you close the cursor too soon, the cursor adapter won't be able to get more data from the cursor.

This means that you can't immediately close the cursor and database once you've used the setAdapter() method to connect the cursor adapter to your list view. Instead, we'll close the cursor and database in the activity's onDestroy() method, which gets called just before the activity is destroyed. Because the activity's being destroyed, there's no further need for the cursor or database connection to stay open, so they can be closed:

```java
public void onDestroy(){
    super.onDestroy();
    cursor.close();
    db.close();
}
```

Close the cursor and database when the activity is destroyed.

That's everything you need to know in order to update the code for DrinkCategoryActivity, so have a go at the exercise on the next page.

Pool Puzzle

Your **job** is to take code segments from the pool and place them into the blank lines in *DrinkCategoryActivity.java*. You may **not** use the same code segment more than once, and you won't need to use all the code segments. Your **goal** is to populate the list view with a list of drinks from the database.

```java
public class DrinkCategoryActivity extends Activity {

    private SQLiteDatabase db;
    private Cursor cursor;

    @Override
    protected void onCreate(Bundle savedInstanceState) {
        super.onCreate(savedInstanceState);
        setContentView(R.layout.activity_drink_category);
        ListView listDrinks = (ListView) findViewById(R.id.list_drinks);

        ........................................ starbuzzDatabaseHelper = new StarbuzzDatabaseHelper(this);
        try {
            db = starbuzzDatabaseHelper. ................................................ ;
            cursor = db.query("DRINK",
                    new String[]{ ................................................................ },
                    null, null, null, null, null);
```

Starbuzz
└─ **app/src/main**
   └─ **java**
      └─ **com.hfad.starbuzz**
         └─ **DrinkCategory Activity.java**

The code continues → on the next page

Note: each segment in the pool can only be used once!

getWritableDatabase()

SimpleCursorAdapter   "NAME"

db

cursor   cursor   SQLiteOpenHelper

cursor   "NAME"   getReadableDatabase()

"DESCRIPTION"   "_id"   SQLiteException

,   DatabaseException

```
        SimpleCursorAdapter listAdapter = new ............................................. (this,
                android.R.layout.simple_list_item_1,
                ............... ,
                new String[]{............... },
                new int[]{android.R.id.text1},
                0);
        listDrinks.setAdapter(listAdapter);
    } catch(............................................. e) {
        Toast toast = Toast.makeText(this, "Database unavailable", Toast.LENGTH_SHORT);
        toast.show();
    }


    //Create the listener
    AdapterView.OnItemClickListener itemClickListener =
            new AdapterView.OnItemClickListener(){
                public void onItemClick(AdapterView<?> listDrinks,
                                        View itemView,
                                        int position,
                                        long id) {
                    //Pass the drink the user clicks on to DrinkActivity
                    Intent intent = new Intent(DrinkCategoryActivity.this,
                            DrinkActivity.class);
                    intent.putExtra(DrinkActivity.EXTRA_DRINKID, (int) id);
                    startActivity(intent);
                }
            };


    //Assign the listener to the list view
    listDrinks.setOnItemClickListener(itemClickListener);
}

@Override
public void onDestroy(){
    super.onDestroy();
    ............... .close();
    ............... .close();
}
}
```

Starbuzz

app/src/main

java

com.hfad.starbuzz

DrinkCategory
Activity.java

Pool Puzzle Solution

Your **job** is to take code segments from the pool and place them into the blank lines in *DrinkCategoryActivity.java*. You may **not** use the same code segment more than once, and you won't need to use all the code segments. Your **goal** is to populate the list view with a list of drinks from the database.

```
public class DrinkCategoryActivity extends Activity {

    private SQLiteDatabase db;
    private Cursor cursor;

    @Override
    protected void onCreate(Bundle savedInstanceState) {
        super.onCreate(savedInstanceState);
        setContentView(R.layout.activity_drink_category);
        ListView listDrinks = (ListView) findViewById(R.id.list_drinks);
```

← You get a reference to the database using a SQLiteOpenHelper.

```
        SQLiteOpenHelper    starbuzzDatabaseHelper = new StarbuzzDatabaseHelper(this);
        try {
            db = starbuzzDatabaseHelper. getReadableDatabase() ;
            cursor = db.query("DRINK",
                new String[]{ "_id",  "NAME"                    },
                null, null, null, null, null);
```

We're reading from the database, so we just need read-only access.

The cursor must include the _id and NAME columns. We want to pass the drink ID to DrinkActivity, and we need to display the drink names.

Starbuzz
└ app/src/main
  └ java
    └ com.hfad.starbuzz
      └ **DrinkCategory Activity.java**

These code snippets were not needed. ↘

getWritableDatabase()

,

"DESCRIPTION"

DatabaseException

← We're using a SimpleCursorAdapter.

```
        SimpleCursorAdapter listAdapter = new  SimpleCursorAdapter  (this,
                android.R.layout.simple_list_item_1,
                cursor ,
                new String[]{ "NAME" },
                new int[]{android.R.id.text1},
                0);
        listDrinks.setAdapter(listAdapter);
    } catch( SQLiteException    e) {
        Toast toast = Toast.makeText(this, "Database unavailable", Toast.LENGTH_SHORT);
        toast.show();
    }


    //Create the listener
    AdapterView.OnItemClickListener itemClickListener =
            new AdapterView.OnItemClickListener(){
                public void onItemClick(AdapterView<?> listDrinks,
                                        View itemView,
                                        int position,
                                        long id) {
                    //Pass the drink the user clicks on to DrinkActivity
                    Intent intent = new Intent(DrinkCategoryActivity.this,
                            DrinkActivity.class);
                    intent.putExtra(DrinkActivity.EXTRA_DRINKID, (int) id);
                    startActivity(intent);
                }
            };


    //Assign the listener to the list view
    listDrinks.setOnItemClickListener(itemClickListener);
}

@Override
public void onDestroy(){
    super.onDestroy();
    cursor  .close();
    db  .close();
}

}
```

Use the cursor → **cursor** , we just created.

Display the contents of the NAME column.

If the database is unavailable, we'll catch the SQLiteException.

Starbuzz
app/src/main
java
com.hfad.starbuzz
DrinkCategory Activity.java

Close the cursor before you close the database.

The revised code for DrinkCategoryActivity

Create cursor
Cursor adapter

Here's the full code for *DrinkCategoryActivity.java*, with the array adapter replaced by a cursor adapter (the changes are in bold); update your code to match ours:

```
package com.hfad.starbuzz;

import android.app.Activity;
import android.os.Bundle;
import android.widget.ListView;
import android.view.View;
import android.content.Intent;
import android.widget.AdapterView;
import android.database.Cursor;
import android.database.sqlite.SQLiteDatabase;
import android.database.sqlite.SQLiteException;
import android.database.sqlite.SQLiteOpenHelper;
import android.widget.SimpleCursorAdapter;
import android.widget.Toast;
```

We're using these extra classes, so you need to import them.

```
public class DrinkCategoryActivity extends Activity {

    private SQLiteDatabase db;
    private Cursor cursor;
```

We're adding these as private variables so we can close the database and cursor in our onDestroy() method.

```
    @Override
    protected void onCreate(Bundle savedInstanceState) {
        super.onCreate(savedInstanceState);
        setContentView(R.layout.activity_drink_category);
        ArrayAdapter<Drink> listAdapter = new ArrayAdapter<>(
                this,
                android.R.layout.simple_list_item_1,
                Drink.drinks);
```

We're no longer using an array adapter, so delete these lines of code.

```
        ListView listDrinks = (ListView) findViewById(R.id.list_drinks);
        SQLiteOpenHelper starbuzzDatabaseHelper = new StarbuzzDatabaseHelper(this);
        try {
            db = starbuzzDatabaseHelper.getReadableDatabase();
            cursor = db.query("DRINK",
                    new String[]{"_id", "NAME"},
                    null, null, null, null, null);
```

← Get a reference to the database.

Create the cursor.

The code continues on the next page.

The DrinkCategoryActivity code (continued)

```java
                SimpleCursorAdapter listAdapter = new SimpleCursorAdapter(this,
                        android.R.layout.simple_list_item_1,
                        cursor,
                        new String[]{"NAME"},
                        new int[]{android.R.id.text1},
                        0);
            listDrinks.setAdapter(listAdapter);
        } catch(SQLiteException e) {
            Toast toast = Toast.makeText(this, "Database unavailable", Toast.LENGTH_SHORT);
            toast.show();
        }

        //Create a listener to listen for clicks in the list view
        AdapterView.OnItemClickListener itemClickListener =
                new AdapterView.OnItemClickListener(){
                    public void onItemClick(AdapterView<?> listDrinks,
                                            View itemView,
                                            int position,
                                            long id) {
                        //Pass the drink the user clicks on to DrinkActivity
                        Intent intent = new Intent(DrinkCategoryActivity.this,
                                DrinkActivity.class);
                        intent.putExtra(DrinkActivity.EXTRA_DRINKID, (int) id);
                        startActivity(intent);
                    }
                };

        //Assign the listener to the list view
        listDrinks.setOnItemClickListener(itemClickListener);
    }

    @Override
    public void onDestroy(){
        super.onDestroy();
        cursor.close();
        db.close();
    }
}
```

Map the contents of the NAME column to the text in the ListView.

Create the cursor adapter.

Set the adapter to the ListView.

Display a message to the user if a SQLiteException gets thrown.

We didn't need to change any of the listener code.

Starbuzz

app/src/main

java

com.hfad.starbuzz

DrinkCategory Activity.java

We're closing the database and cursor in the activity's onDestroy() method. The cursor will stay open until the cursor adapter no longer needs it.

Let's try running our freshly updated app.

Test drive the app

When you run the app, `TopLevelActivity` gets displayed.

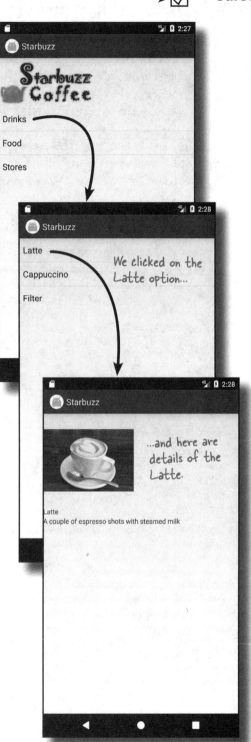

When you click on the Drinks item, `DrinkCategoryActivity` is launched. It displays all the drinks from the Starbuzz database.

When you click on one of the drinks, `DrinkActivity` is launched and details of the selected drink are displayed.

The app looks exactly the same as before, but now the data is being read from the database. In fact, you can now delete the *Drink.java* code, because we no longer need the array of drinks. Every piece of data we need is now coming from the database.

Your Android Toolbox

You've got Chapter 16 under your belt and now you've added basic cursors to your toolbox.

You can download the full code for the chapter from https://tinyurl.com/HeadFirstAndroid.

CHAPTER 16

BULLET POINTS

- A **cursor** lets you read from and write to the database.

- You create a cursor by calling the `SQLiteDatabase query()` method. Behind the scenes, this builds a SQL `SELECT` statement.

- The `getWritableDatabase()` method returns a `SQLiteDatabase` object that allows you to read from and write to the database.

- The `getReadableDatabase()` returns a `SQLiteDatabase` object. This gives you read-only access to the database. It *may* also allow you to write to the database, but this isn't guaranteed.

- Navigate through a cursor using the `moveTo*()` methods.

- Get values from a cursor using the `get*()` methods. Close cursors and database connections after you've finished with them.

- A **cursor adapter** is an adapter that works with cursors. Use `SimpleCursorAdapter` to populate a list view with the values returned by a cursor.

17 cursors and asynctasks

Staying in the Background

My doInBackground() method's awesome. If I left it all to Mr. Main Event, can you imagine how slow he'd be?

In most apps, you'll need your app to update its data.

So far you've seen how to create apps that read data from a SQLite database. But what if you want to update the app's data? In this chapter you'll see how to get your app to **respond to user input** and **update values in the database**. You'll also find out how to **refresh the data that's displayed** once it's been updated. Finally, you'll see how writing efficient **multithreaded code** with **AsyncTask**s will keep your app speedy.

We want our Starbuzz app to update database data

In Chapter 16, you learned how to change your app to read its data from a SQLite database. You saw how to read an individual record (a drink from the Starbuzz data) and display that record's data in an activity. You also learned how to populate a list view with database data (in this case drink names) using a cursor adapter.

In both of these scenarios, you only needed to *read* data from the database. But what if you want users to be able to update the data?

We're going to change the Starbuzz app so that users can record which drinks are their favorites. We'll do this by adding a checkbox to `DrinkActivity`; if it's checked, it means the current drink is one of the user's favorites:

> Users can say which drinks are their favorites by checking a checkbox. We need to add this checkbox to DrinkActivity and get it to update the database.

We'll also add a new list view to `TopLevelActivity`, which contains the user's favorite drinks:

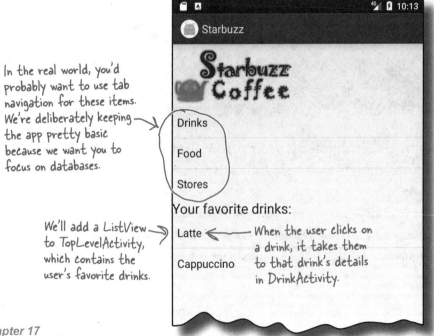

> In the real world, you'd probably want to use tab navigation for these items. We're deliberately keeping the app pretty basic because we want you to focus on databases.

> We'll add a ListView to TopLevelActivity, which contains the user's favorite drinks.

> When the user clicks on a drink, it takes them to that drink's details in DrinkActivity.

We'll update DrinkActivity first

In Chapter 15, we added a FAVORITE column to the DRINK table in the Starbuzz database. We'll use this column to let users indicate whether a particular drink is one of their favorites. We'll display its value in the new checkbox we're going to add to `DrinkActivity`, and when the user clicks on the checkbox, we'll update the FAVORITE column with the new value.

Here are the steps we'll go through to update `DrinkActivity`:

1 **Update DrinkActivity's layout to add a checkbox and text label.**

We'll add this checkbox and label to activity_drink.xml. →

2 **Display the value of the FAVORITE column in the checkbox.**
To do this, we'll need to retrieve the value of the FAVORITE column from the Starbuzz database.

3 **Update the FAVORITE column when the checkbox is clicked.**
We'll update the FAVORITE column with the value of the checkbox so that the data in the database stays up to date.

Let's get started.

Do this!

We're going to update the Starbuzz app in this chapter, so open your Starbuzz project in Android Studio.

Add a checkbox to DrinkActivity's layout

We'll start by adding a new checkbox to DrinkActivity's layout to indicate whether the current drink is one of the user's favorites. We're using a checkbox, as it's an easy way to display true/false values.

First, add a String resource called `"favorite"` to *strings.xml* (we'll use this as a label for the checkbox):

```xml
<string name="favorite">Favorite</string>
```

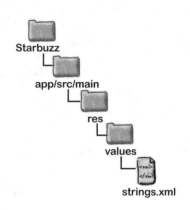

Then add the checkbox to *activity_drink.xml*. We'll give the checkbox an ID of `favorite` so that we can refer to it in our activity code. We'll also set its `android:onClick` attribute to `"onFavoriteClicked"` so that it calls the `onFavoriteClicked()` method in DrinkActivity when the user clicks on the checkbox. Here's the layout code; update your code to reflect our changes (they're in bold):

```xml
<LinearLayout ... >
    <ImageView
        android:id="@+id/photo"
        android:layout_width="190dp"
        android:layout_height="190dp" />

    <TextView
        android:id="@+id/name"
        android:layout_width="wrap_content"
        android:layout_height="wrap_content" />

    <TextView
        android:id="@+id/description"
        android:layout_width="match_parent"
        android:layout_height="wrap_content" />

    <CheckBox android:id="@+id/favorite"
        android:layout_width="wrap_content"
        android:layout_height="wrap_content"
        android:text="@string/favorite"
        android:onClick="onFavoriteClicked" />
</LinearLayout>
```

These are the photo, name, and description views we added when we first created the activity.

The checkbox has an ID of favorite.

We're giving the checkbox a label.

When the checkbox is clicked, the onFavoriteClicked() method in DrinkActivity will get called. We need to write this method.

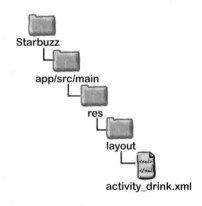

Next we'll change the DrinkActivity code to get the checkbox to reflect the value of the FAVORITE column from the database.

Display the value of the FAVORITE column

In order to update the checkbox, we first need to retrieve the value of the FAVORITE column from the database. We can do this by updating the cursor we're using in DrinkActivity's onCreate() method to read drink values from the database.

Starbuzz

app/src/main

java

com.hfad.starbuzz

DrinkActivity.java

Here's the cursor we're currently using to return data for the drink the user has selected:

```
Cursor cursor = db.query("DRINK",
        new String[]{"NAME", "DESCRIPTION", "IMAGE_RESOURCE_ID"},
        "_id = ?",
        new String[]{Integer.toString(drinkId)},
        null, null, null);
```

To include the FAVORITE column in the data that's returned, we simply add it to the array of column names returned by the cursor:

Add the FAVORITE column to the cursor.

```
Cursor cursor = db.query("DRINK",
        new String[]{"NAME", "DESCRIPTION", "IMAGE_RESOURCE_ID", "FAVORITE"},
        "_id = ?",
        new String[]{Integer.toString(drinkId)},
        null, null, null);
```

You don't need to update your version of the code yet. We'll show you the full set of changes for DrinkActivity.java soon.

Once we have the value of the FAVORITE column, we can update the favorite checkbox accordingly. To get this value, we first navigate to the first (and only) record in the cursor using:

```
cursor.moveToFirst();
```

We can then get the value of the column for the current drink. The FAVORITE column contains numeric values, where 0 is false and 1 is true. We want the favorite checkbox to be ticked if the value is 1 (true), and unticked if the value is 0 (false), so we'll use the following code to update the checkbox:

Get the value of the FAVORITE column. It's stored in the database as 1 for true, 0 for false.

```
boolean isFavorite = (cursor.getInt(3) == 1);
CheckBox favorite = (CheckBox) findViewById(R.id.favorite);
favorite.setChecked(isFavorite);
```

Set the value of the favorite checkbox.

That's all the code we need to reflect the value of the FAVORITE column in the favorite checkbox. Next, we need to get the checkbox to respond to clicks so that it updates the database when its value changes.

Respond to clicks to update the database

When we added the `favorite` checkbox to *activity_drink.xml*, we set its `android:onClick` attribute to `onFavoriteClicked()`. This means that whenever the user clicks on the checkbox, the `onFavoriteClicked()` method in the activity will get called. We'll use this method to update the database with the current value of the checkbox. If the user checks or unchecks the checkbox, the `onFavoriteClicked()` method will save the user's change to the database.

In Chapter 15, you saw how to use SQLiteDatabase methods to change the data held in a SQLite database: the `insert()` method to insert data, the `delete()` method to delete data, and the `update()` method to update existing records.

You can use these methods to change data from within your activity. As an example, you could use the `insert()` method to add new drink records to the **DRINK** table, or the `delete()` method to delete them. In our case, we want to update the **DRINK** table's FAVORITE column with the value of the checkbox using the `update()` method.

As a reminder, the `update()` method looks like this:

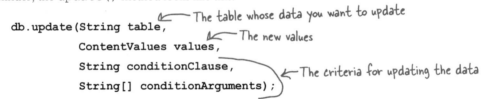

```
db.update(String table,
          ContentValues values,
          String conditionClause,
          String[] conditionArguments);
```

where `table` is the name of the table you want to update, and `values` is a `ContentValues` object containing name/value pairs of the columns you want to update and the values you want to set them to. The `conditionClause` and `conditionArguments` parameters lets you specify which records you want to update.

You already know everything you need to get `DrinkActivity` to update the FAVORITE column for the current drink when the checkbox is clicked, so have a go at the following exercise.

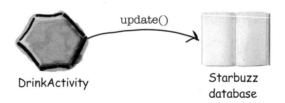

Code Magnets

In our code for `DrinkActivity` we want to update the FAVORITE column in the database with the value of the `favorite` checkbox. Can you construct the `onFavoriteClicked()` method so that it will do that?

```java
public class DrinkActivity extends Activity {
...
    //Update the database when the checkbox is clicked

    public void onFavoriteClicked(........................){

        int drinkId = (Integer) getIntent().getExtras().get(EXTRA_DRINKID);
        CheckBox favorite = (CheckBox) findViewById(R.id.favorite);

        ............................ drinkValues = new ...................................;

        drinkValues.put(........................, favorite.isChecked());

        SQLiteOpenHelper starbuzzDatabaseHelper = new StarbuzzDatabaseHelper(this);
        try {

            SQLiteDatabase db = starbuzzDatabaseHelper.............................................;

            db.update(...................,...............................,

                                ......................., new String[] {Integer.toString(drinkId)});
            db.close();
        } catch(SQLiteException e) {
            Toast toast = Toast.makeText(this, "Database unavailable", Toast.LENGTH_SHORT);
            toast.show();
        }
    }
}
```

You won't need to use all the magnets.

`drinkValues`

`"FAVORITE"`

`View view`

`"_id = ?"`

`ContentValues`

`"DRINK"`

`ContentValues()`

`getReadableDatabase()`

`favorite`

`getWritableDatabase()`

Code Magnets Solution

In our code for `DrinkActivity` we want to update the FAVORITE column in the database with the value of the `favorite` checkbox. Can you construct the `onFavoriteClicked()` method so that it will do that?

```java
public class DrinkActivity extends Activity {
...
    //Update the database when the checkbox is clicked

    public void onFavoriteClicked( View view ) {

        int drinkId = (Integer) getIntent().getExtras().get(EXTRA_DRINKID);
        CheckBox favorite = (CheckBox) findViewById(R.id.favorite);

        ContentValues drinkValues = new ContentValues();

        drinkValues.put( "FAVORITE" , favorite.isChecked());

        SQLiteOpenHelper starbuzzDatabaseHelper = new StarbuzzDatabaseHelper(this);
        try {

            SQLiteDatabase db = starbuzzDatabaseHelper. getWritableDatabase() ;

            db.update( "DRINK" , drinkValues ,
```

> We need read/write access to the database to update it.

```java
                    "_id = ?" , new String[] {Integer.toString(drinkId)});
            db.close();
        } catch(SQLiteException e) {
            Toast toast = Toast.makeText(this, "Database unavailable", Toast.LENGTH_SHORT);
            toast.show();
        }
    }
}
```

> You didn't need to use these magnets.

`getReadableDatabase()`

`favorite`

The full DrinkActivity.java code

We've now done everything we need to change `DrinkActivity` so that it reflects the contents of the FAVORITE column in the `favorite` checkbox. It then updates the value of the column in the database if the user changes the value of the checkbox.

Here's the full code for *DrinkActivity.java*, so update your version of the code so that it reflects ours (our changes are in bold):

```java
package com.hfad.starbuzz;

import android.app.Activity;
import android.os.Bundle;
import android.widget.ImageView;
import android.widget.TextView;
import android.widget.Toast;
import android.database.Cursor;
import android.database.sqlite.SQLiteDatabase;
import android.database.sqlite.SQLiteException;
import android.database.sqlite.SQLiteOpenHelper;
import android.view.View;
import android.widget.CheckBox;
import android.content.ContentValues;
```

We're using these extra classes, so you need to import them.

```java
public class DrinkActivity extends Activity {

    public static final String EXTRA_DRINKID = "drinkId";

    @Override
    protected void onCreate(Bundle savedInstanceState) {
        super.onCreate(savedInstanceState);
        setContentView(R.layout.activity_drink);

        //Get the drink from the intent
        int drinkId = (Integer) getIntent().getExtras().get(EXTRA_DRINKID);
```

Starbuzz
  └ *app/src/main*
        └ *java*
            └ *com.hfad.starbuzz*
                  └ **DrinkActivity.java**

The code continues →
on the next page.

DrinkActivity.java (continued)

Update layout
Show favorite
Update favorite

```java
//Create a cursor
SQLiteOpenHelper starbuzzDatabaseHelper = new StarbuzzDatabaseHelper(this);
try {
    SQLiteDatabase db = starbuzzDatabaseHelper.getReadableDatabase();
    Cursor cursor = db.query("DRINK",
            new String[]{"NAME", "DESCRIPTION", "IMAGE_RESOURCE_ID", "FAVORITE"},
            "_id = ?",
            new String[]{Integer.toString(drinkId)},
            null, null, null);

    //Move to the first record in the Cursor
    if (cursor.moveToFirst()) {
        //Get the drink details from the cursor
        String nameText = cursor.getString(0);
        String descriptionText = cursor.getString(1);
        int photoId = cursor.getInt(2);
        boolean isFavorite = (cursor.getInt(3) == 1);

        //Populate the drink name
        TextView name = (TextView) findViewById(R.id.name);
        name.setText(nameText);

        //Populate the drink description
        TextView description = (TextView) findViewById(R.id.description);
        description.setText(descriptionText);

        //Populate the drink image
        ImageView photo = (ImageView) findViewById(R.id.photo);
        photo.setImageResource(photoId);
        photo.setContentDescription(nameText);

        //Populate the favorite checkbox
        CheckBox favorite = (CheckBox)findViewById(R.id.favorite);
        favorite.setChecked(isFavorite);
    }
```

Add the FAVORITE column to the cursor.

If the FAVORITE column has a value of 1, this indicates a true value.

Starbuzz
└ app/src/main
  └ java
    └ com.hfad.starbuzz
      └ DrinkActivity.java

If the drink is a favorite, put a checkmark in the favorite checkbox.

The code continues on the next page.

DrinkActivity.java (continued)

```
            cursor.close();
            db.close();
        } catch (SQLiteException e) {
            Toast toast = Toast.makeText(this,
                    "Database unavailable",
                    Toast.LENGTH_SHORT);
            toast.show();
        }
    }
```

Starbuzz
app/src/main
java
com.hfad.starbuzz
DrinkActivity.java

```
    //Update the database when the checkbox is clicked
    public void onFavoriteClicked(View view){
        int drinkId = (Integer) getIntent().getExtras().get(EXTRA_DRINKID);

        //Get the value of the checkbox
        CheckBox favorite = (CheckBox) findViewById(R.id.favorite);
        ContentValues drinkValues = new ContentValues();
        drinkValues.put("FAVORITE", favorite.isChecked());
```

Add the value of the favorite checkbox to the drinkValues ContentValues object.

```
        //Get a reference to the database and update the FAVORITE column
        SQLiteOpenHelper starbuzzDatabaseHelper = new StarbuzzDatabaseHelper(this);
        try {
            SQLiteDatabase db = starbuzzDatabaseHelper.getWritableDatabase();
            db.update("DRINK",
                    drinkValues,
                    "_id = ?",
                    new String[] {Integer.toString(drinkId)});
            db.close();
        } catch(SQLiteException e) {
            Toast toast = Toast.makeText(this, "Database unavailable", Toast.LENGTH_SHORT);
            toast.show();
        }
    }
}
```

Update the drink's FAVORITE column in the database to the value of the checkbox.

Display a message if there's a problem with the database.

Let's check what happens when we run the app.

Test drive the app

When we run the app and navigate to a drink, the new
`favorite` checkbox is displayed (unchecked):

Here's the new checkbox
we added with its label. →

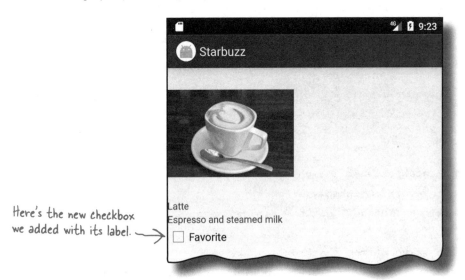

When we click on the checkbox, a checkmark appears to
indicate that the drink is one of our favorites:

When we click on the checkbox, a
checkmark appears, and the value
gets written to the database. →

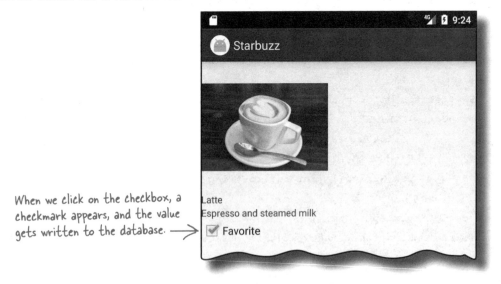

When we close the app and navigate back to the drink, the checkmark
remains. The value of the checkbox has been written to the database.

That's everything we need to display the value of the FAVORITE column
from the database, and update the database with any changes to it.

Display favorites in TopLevelActivity

The next thing we need to do is display the user's favorite drinks in
TopLevelActivity. Here are the steps we'll go through to do
this:

① **Add a list view and text view to TopLevelActivity's layout.**

② **Populate the list view and get it to respond to clicks.**
We'll create a new cursor that retrieves the user's favorite drinks from
the database, and attach it to the list view using a cursor adapter.
We'll then create an onItemClickListener so that we can get
TopLevelActivity to start DrinkActivity when the user clicks
on one of the drinks.

③ **Refresh the list view data when we choose a new favorite
drink.**
If we choose a new favorite drink in DrinkActivity, we want it to
be displayed in TopLevelActivity's list view when we navigate
back to it.

Applying all of these changes will enable us to display
the user's favorite drinks in TopLevelActivity.

The favorites list view will
get its data from the
database using a cursor.

Cursor

Starbuzz
database

When you click
on a drink in the
favorites list view,
DrinkActivity will
start, displaying
details of the
drink.

We'll go through these steps over the next few pages.

705

Display the favorite drinks in activity_top_level.xml

As we said on the previous page, we're going to add a list view to *activity_top_level.xml*, which we'll use to display a list of the user's favorite drinks. We'll also add a text view to display a heading for the list.

First, add the following String resource to *strings.xml* (we'll use this for the text view's text):

```
<string name="favorites">Your favorite drinks:</string>
```

Next, we'll add the new text view and list view to the layout. Here's our code for *activity_top_level.xml*; update your version of the code to match our changes:

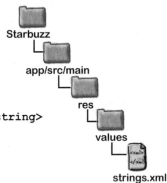

```
<LinearLayout ... >
    <ImageView
        android:layout_width="200dp"
        android:layout_height="100dp"
        android:src="@drawable/starbuzz_logo"
        android:contentDescription="@string/starbuzz_logo" />

    <ListView
        android:id="@+id/list_options"
        android:layout_width="match_parent"
        android:layout_height="wrap_content"
        android:entries="@array/options" />

    <TextView
        android:layout_width="wrap_content"
        android:layout_height="wrap_content"
        android:textAppearance="?android:attr/textAppearanceLarge"
        android:text="@string/favorites" />

    <ListView
        android:id="@+id/list_favorites"
        android:layout_width="match_parent"
        android:layout_height="wrap_content" />
</LinearLayout>
```

The layout already contains the Starbuzz logo and list view.

We'll add a text view to display the text "Your favorite drinks." We'll put this in a String called favorites.

The list_favorites ListView will display the user's favorite drinks.

Those are all the changes we need to make to *activity_top_level.xml*. Next, we'll update *TopLevelActivity.java*.

cursors *and asynctasks*
Update layout
Populate list view
Refresh data

Refactor TopLevelActivity.java

Before we write any code for our new list view, we're going to refactor our existing TopLevelActivity code. This will make the code a lot easier to read later on. We'll move the code relating to the options list view into a new method called setupOptionsListView(). We'll then call this method from the onCreate() method.

Here's our code for *TopLevelActivity.java* (update your version of the code to reflect our changes).

```java
package com.hfad.starbuzz;
...
public class TopLevelActivity extends Activity {

    @Override
    protected void onCreate(Bundle savedInstanceState) {
        super.onCreate(savedInstanceState);
        setContentView(R.layout.activity_top_level);
        setupOptionsListView();
    }
```

← Call the new setupOptionsListView() method.

Starbuzz
app/src/main
java
com.hfad.starbuzz
TopLevel Activity.java

```java
    private void setupOptionsListView() {
        //Create an OnItemClickListener
        AdapterView.OnItemClickListener itemClickListener =
                                    new AdapterView.OnItemClickListener(){
            public void onItemClick(AdapterView<?> listView,
                                    View itemView,
                                    int position,
                                    long id) {
                if (position == 0) {
                    Intent intent = new Intent(TopLevelActivity.this,
                                        DrinkCategoryActivity.class);
                    startActivity(intent);
                }
            }
        };
        //Add the listener to the list view
        ListView listView = (ListView) findViewById(R.id.list_options);
        listView.setOnItemClickListener(itemClickListener);
    }
}
```

All of this code was in the onCreate() method. We're putting it in a new method to make the code tidier.

If the Drink option in the list_options list view is clicked, start DrinkCategoryActivity.

What changes are needed for TopLevelActivity.java

We need to display the user's favorite drinks in the `list_favorites` list view we added to the layout, and get it to respond to clicks. To do this, we need to do the following:

1 **Populate the list_favorites list view using a cursor.**
The cursor will return all drinks where the FAVORITE column has been set to 1—all drinks that the user has flagged as being a favorite. Just as we did in our code for `DrinkCategoryActivity`, we can connect the cursor to the list view using a cursor adapter.

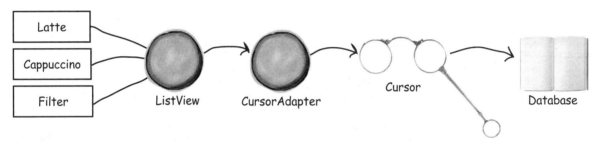

2 **Create an onItemClickListener so that the list_favorites list view can respond to clicks.**
If the user clicks on one of their favorite drinks, we can create an intent that starts `DrinkActivity`, passing it the ID of the drink that was clicked. This will show the user details of the drink they've just chosen.

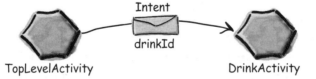

You've already seen all the code that's needed to do this. In fact, it's almost identical to the code we wrote in earlier chapters to control the list of drinks in `DrinkCategoryActivity`. The only difference is that this time, we only want to display drinks with a value of 1 in the FAVORITE column.

We've decided to put the code that controls a list view in a new method called `setupFavoritesListView()`. We'll show you this method on the next page before adding it to *TopLevelActivity.java*.

Ready Bake Code

The `setupFavoritesListView()` method populates the `list_favorites` list view with the names of the user's favorite drinks. Make sure you understand the code below before turning the page.

```java
private void setupFavoritesListView() {
    //Populate the list_favorites ListView from a cursor
    ListView listFavorites = (ListView) findViewById(R.id.list_favorites);
    try{
        SQLiteOpenHelper starbuzzDatabaseHelper = new StarbuzzDatabaseHelper(this);
        db = starbuzzDatabaseHelper.getReadableDatabase();
        favoritesCursor = db.query("DRINK",
            new String[] { "_id", "NAME"},
            "FAVORITE = 1",
            null, null, null, null);
        CursorAdapter favoriteAdapter =
            new SimpleCursorAdapter(TopLevelActivity.this,
            android.R.layout.simple_list_item_1,
            favoritesCursor,
            new String[]{"NAME"},
            new int[]{android.R.id.text1}, 0);
        listFavorites.setAdapter(favoriteAdapter);
    } catch(SQLiteException e) {
        Toast toast = Toast.makeText(this, "Database unavailable", Toast.LENGTH_SHORT);
        toast.show();
    }


    //Navigate to DrinkActivity if a drink is clicked
    listFavorites.setOnItemClickListener(new AdapterView.OnItemClickListener() {
        @Override
        public void onItemClick(AdapterView<?> listView, View v, int position, long id) {
            Intent intent = new Intent(TopLevelActivity.this, DrinkActivity.class);
            intent.putExtra(DrinkActivity.EXTRA_DRINKID, (int)id);
            startActivity(intent);
        }
    });
}
```

Get the list_favorites list view.

Create a cursor that gets the values of the _id and NAME columns where FAVORITE=1.

Get the names of the user's favorite drinks.

Create a new cursor adapter.

Use the cursor in the cursor adapter.

Display the names of the drinks in the list view.

Display a message if there's a problem with the database.

Starbuzz
app/src/main
java
com.hfad.starbuzz
TopLevel Activity.java

This will get called if an item in the list view is clicked.

If the user clicks on one of the items in the list_favorites list view, create an intent to start DrinkActivity, including the ID of the drink as extra information.

The new TopLevelActivity.java code

Update layout
Populate list view
Refresh data

We've updated TopLevelActivity to populate the
list_favorites list view and make it respond to clicks.
Update your version of *TopLevelActivity.java* to match ours
(there's a lot of new code, so go through it carefully and
take your time):

```
package com.hfad.starbuzz;

import android.app.Activity;
import android.os.Bundle;
import android.content.Intent;
import android.widget.AdapterView;
import android.widget.ListView;
import android.view.View;
import android.database.Cursor;
import android.database.sqlite.SQLiteOpenHelper;
import android.database.sqlite.SQLiteException;
import android.database.sqlite.SQLiteDatabase;
import android.widget.SimpleCursorAdapter;
import android.widget.CursorAdapter;
import android.widget.Toast;
```

We're using all these
extra classes, so we
need to import them.

Starbuzz
└ app/src/main
  └ java
    └ com.hfad.starbuzz
      └ TopLevel
        Activity.java

```
public class TopLevelActivity extends Activity {
```

We're adding the database and cursor as private
variables so that we can access them in the
setUpFavoritesListView() and onDestroy() methods.

```
    private SQLiteDatabase db;
    private Cursor favoritesCursor;

    @Override
    protected void onCreate(Bundle savedInstanceState) {
        super.onCreate(savedInstanceState);
        setContentView(R.layout.activity_top_level);
        setupOptionsListView();
        setupFavoritesListView();
    }
```

Call the setupFavoritesListView()
method from the onCreate() method.

The code continues
on the next page.

The TopLevelActivity.java code (continued)

We don't need to change this method.

```java
private void setupOptionsListView() {
    //Create an OnItemClickListener
    AdapterView.OnItemClickListener itemClickListener =
                            new AdapterView.OnItemClickListener(){
        public void onItemClick(AdapterView<?> listView,
                            View itemView,
                            int position,
                            long id) {
            if (position == 0) {
                Intent intent = new Intent(TopLevelActivity.this,
                                    DrinkCategoryActivity.class);
                startActivity(intent);
            }
        }
    };

    //Add the listener to the list view
    ListView listView = (ListView) findViewById(R.id.list_options);
    listView.setOnItemClickListener(itemClickListener);
}
```

This is the method we created to populate the list_favorites list view and make it respond to clicks.

```java
private void setupFavoritesListView() {
    //Populate the list_favorites ListView from a cursor
    ListView listFavorites = (ListView) findViewById(R.id.list_favorites);
    try{
        SQLiteOpenHelper starbuzzDatabaseHelper = new StarbuzzDatabaseHelper(this);
        db = starbuzzDatabaseHelper.getReadableDatabase();  ← Get a reference to the database.
        favoritesCursor = db.query("DRINK",
                new String[] { "_id", "NAME"},
                "FAVORITE = 1",
                null, null, null, null);
```

The list_favorites list view will use this cursor for its data.

Starbuzz

app/src/main

java

com.hfad.starbuzz

TopLevel
Activity.java

The code continues on the next page.

The TopLevelActivity.java code (continued)

```java
        CursorAdapter favoriteAdapter =
                new SimpleCursorAdapter(TopLevelActivity.this,
                        android.R.layout.simple_list_item_1,
                        favoritesCursor,
                        new String[]{"NAME"},
                        new int[]{android.R.id.text1}, 0);
        listFavorites.setAdapter(favoriteAdapter);
    } catch (SQLiteException e) {
        Toast toast = Toast.makeText(this, "Database unavailable", Toast.LENGTH_SHORT);
        toast.show();
    }


    //Navigate to DrinkActivity if a drink is clicked
    listFavorites.setOnItemClickListener(new AdapterView.OnItemClickListener() {
        @Override
        public void onItemClick(AdapterView<?> listView, View v, int position, long id) {
            Intent intent = new Intent(TopLevelActivity.this, DrinkActivity.class);
            intent.putExtra(DrinkActivity.EXTRA_DRINKID, (int)id);
            startActivity(intent);
        }
    });
}


    //Close the cursor and database in the onDestroy() method
    @Override
    public void onDestroy(){
        super.onDestroy();
        favoritesCursor.close();
        db.close();
    }

}
```

Use the cursor in a cursor adapter.

← Set the cursor adapter to the list view.

Get the list_favorites list view to respond to clicks.

← Start DrinkActivity, passing it the ID of the drink that was clicked on.

The onDestroy() method gets called just before the activity is destroyed. We'll close the cursor and database in this method, as we no longer need them if the activity's being destroyed.

Starbuzz
app/src/main
java
com.hfad.starbuzz
TopLevel
Activity.java

The above code populates the list_favorites list view with the user's favorite drinks. When the user clicks on one of these drinks, an intent starts DrinkActivity and passes it the ID of the drink. Let's take the app for a test drive and see what happens.

cursors and asynctasks
☑ Update layout
☑ **Populate list view**
☐ Refresh data

Test drive the app

When you run the app, the new text view and `list_favorites` list view are displayed in `TopLevelActivity`. If you've marked a drink as being a favorite, it appears in the list view.

If you click on that drink, `DrinkActivity` starts and details of the drink are displayed.

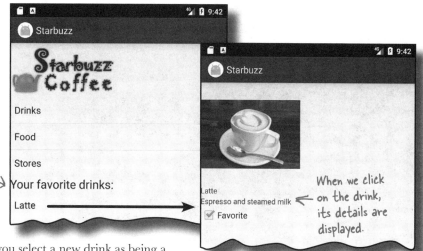

Here's the new list_favorites list view we created. It displays a latte, as we marked this as a favorite drink earlier in the chapter.

When we click on the drink, its details are displayed.

But there's a problem. If you select a new drink as being a favorite, when you go back to `TopLevelActivity` the `list_favorites` list view doesn't include the new drink. The new drink is only included in the list view if you rotate the device.

We've marked a cappuccino as a favorite, but it's not appearing in the list view.

When we rotate the device, the cappuccino appears in the list view. Why's that?

Why do you think the new drink we chose as a favorite doesn't appear in the list view until we rotate the device? Give this some thought before turning the page.

Cursors don't automatically refresh

If the user chooses a new favorite drink by navigating through
the app to `DrinkActivity`, the new favorite drink isn't
automatically displayed in the `list_favorites` list view in
`TopLevelActivity`. This is because ***cursors retrieve data
when the cursor gets created***.

In our case, the cursor is created in the activity `onCreate()`
method, so it gets its data when the activity is created. When the
user navigates through the other activities, `TopLevelActivity` is
stopped. It's not destroyed and recreated, so neither is the cursor.

When you start a second activity,
the second activity is stacked
on top of the first. The first
activity isn't destroyed. Instead,
it's paused and then stopped, as
it loses the focus and stops being
visible to the user.

Cursors don't automatically keep track of whether the underlying
data in the database has changed. So if the underlying data changes
after the cursor's been created, the cursor doesn't get updated: it still
contains the original records, and none of the changes. That means
that if the user marks a new drink as being a favorite after the cursor
is created, the cursor will be out of date.

If you update the data
in the database...

...the cursor won't
see the new data if
the cursor's already
been created.

_id	NAME	DESCRIPTION	IMAGE_RESOURCE_ID	FAVORITE
1	"Latte"	"Espresso and steamed milk"	54543543	1
2	"Cappucc			
3	"Filter"			

_id	NAME	DESCRIPTION	IMAGE_RESOURCE_ID	FAVORITE
1	"Latte"	"Espresso and steamed milk"	54543543	0
2	"Cappuccino"	"Espresso, hot milk and steamed-milk foam"	654334453	0
3	"Filter"	"Our best drip coffee"	44324234	0

So how do we get around this?

Change the cursor with changeCursor()

cursors and asynctasks
☑ **Update layout**
☑ **Populate list view**
→ **Refresh data**

The solution is to change the underlying cursor used by the list_favorites list view to an updated version. To do this, you define a new version of the cursor, get a reference to the list view's cursor adapter, and then call the cursor adapter's changeCursor() method to change the cursor. Here are the details:

1. Define the cursor

You define the cursor in exactly the same way as you did before. In our case, we want the query to return the user's favorite drinks, so we use:

```
Cursor newCursor = db.query("DRINK",
                    new String[] { "_id", "NAME"},
                    "FAVORITE = 1",
                    null, null, null, null);
```

This is the same query that we had before.

2. Get a reference to the cursor adapter

You get a reference to the list view's cursor adapter by calling the list view's getAdapter() method. This method returns an object of type Adapter. As our list view is using a cursor adapter, we can cast the adapter to a CursorAdapter:

```
ListView listFavorites = (ListView) findViewById(R.id.list_favorites);
CursorAdapter adapter = (CursorAdapter) listFavorites.getAdapter();
```

You get the ListView's adapter using the getAdapter() method.

3. Change the cursor using changeCursor()

You change the cursor used by the cursor adapter by calling its changeCursor() method. This method takes one parameter, the new cursor:

```
adapter.changeCursor(newCursor);
```
← *Change the cursor used by the cursor adapter to the new one.*

The changeCursor() method replaces the cursor adapter's current cursor with the new one. It then closes the old cursor, so you don't need to do this yourself.

We're going to change the cursor used by the list_favorites list view in TopLevelActivity's onRestart() method. This means that the data in the list view will get refreshed when the user returns to TopLevelActivity. Any new favorite drinks the user has chosen will be displayed, and any drinks that are no longer flagged as favorites will be removed from the list.

We'll show you the full code for *TopLevelActivity.java* over the next few pages.

The revised TopLevelActivity.java code

☑ Update layout
☑ Populate list view
→ ☐ **Refresh data**

Here's the full *TopLevelActivity.java* code; update your code to reflect our changes (in bold).

```java
package com.hfad.starbuzz;

import android.app.Activity;
import android.os.Bundle;
import android.content.Intent;
import android.widget.AdapterView;
import android.widget.ListView;
import android.view.View;
import android.database.Cursor;
import android.database.sqlite.SQLiteOpenHelper;
import android.database.sqlite.SQLiteException;
import android.database.sqlite.SQLiteDatabase;
import android.widget.SimpleCursorAdapter;
import android.widget.CursorAdapter;
import android.widget.Toast;

public class TopLevelActivity extends Activity {

    private SQLiteDatabase db;
    private Cursor favoritesCursor;

    @Override
    protected void onCreate(Bundle savedInstanceState) {
        super.onCreate(savedInstanceState);
        setContentView(R.layout.activity_top_level);
        setupOptionsListView();
        setupFavoritesListView();
    }
```

Starbuzz
app/src/main
java
com.hfad.starbuzz
TopLevel Activity.java

You don't need to change any of the code on this page.

The code continues on the next page.

The TopLevelActivity.java code (continued)

```java
private void setupOptionsListView() {
    //Create an OnItemClickListener
    AdapterView.OnItemClickListener itemClickListener =
                                    new AdapterView.OnItemClickListener(){
        public void onItemClick(AdapterView<?> listView,
                                View itemView,
                                int position,
                                long id) {
            if (position == 0) {
                Intent intent = new Intent(TopLevelActivity.this,
                                        DrinkCategoryActivity.class);
                startActivity(intent);
            }
        }
    };

    //Add the listener to the list view
    ListView listView = (ListView) findViewById(R.id.list_options);
    listView.setOnItemClickListener(itemClickListener);
}


private void setupFavoritesListView() {
    //Populate the list_favorites ListView from a cursor
    ListView listFavorites = (ListView) findViewById(R.id.list_favorites);
    try{
        SQLiteOpenHelper starbuzzDatabaseHelper = new StarbuzzDatabaseHelper(this);
        db = starbuzzDatabaseHelper.getReadableDatabase();
        favoritesCursor = db.query("DRINK",
                                new String[] { "_id", "NAME"},
                                "FAVORITE = 1",
                                null, null, null, null);

        CursorAdapter favoriteAdapter =
                new SimpleCursorAdapter(TopLevelActivity.this,
                        android.R.layout.simple_list_item_1,
                        favoritesCursor,
                        new String[]{"NAME"},
                        new int[]{android.R.id.text1}, 0);
        listFavorites.setAdapter(favoriteAdapter);
```

You don't need to change any of the code on this page.

Starbuzz
app/src/main
java
com.hfad.starbuzz
TopLevel
Activity.java

The code continues on the next page.

The TopLevelActivity.java code (continued)

☑ Update layout
☑ Populate list view
Refresh data

```java
    } catch(SQLiteException e) {
        Toast toast = Toast.makeText(this, "Database unavailable", Toast.LENGTH_SHORT);
        toast.show();
    }

    //Navigate to DrinkActivity if a drink is clicked
    listFavorites.setOnItemClickListener(new AdapterView.OnItemClickListener() {
        @Override
        public void onItemClick(AdapterView<?> listView, View v, int position, long id) {
            Intent intent = new Intent(TopLevelActivity.this, DrinkActivity.class);
            intent.putExtra(DrinkActivity.EXTRA_DRINKID, (int)id);
            startActivity(intent);
        }
    });
}
```

Add the onRestart() method. This will get called when the user navigates back to TopLevelActivity.

```java
@Override
public void onRestart() {
    super.onRestart();
    Cursor newCursor = db.query("DRINK",
                                new String[] { "_id", "NAME"},
                                "FAVORITE = 1",
                                null, null, null, null);
```

Create a new version of the cursor.

Starbuzz
└ **app/src/main**
  └ **java**
    └ **com.hfad.starbuzz**
      └ **TopLevel Activity.java**

```java
    ListView listFavorites = (ListView) findViewById(R.id.list_favorites);
    CursorAdapter adapter = (CursorAdapter) listFavorites.getAdapter();
    adapter.changeCursor(newCursor);
    favoritesCursor = newCursor;
}
```

Switch the cursor being used by the list_favorites list view to the new cursor.

Change the value of favoritesCursor to the new cursor so we can close it in the activity's onDestroy() method.

```java
//Close the cursor and database in the onDestroy() method
@Override
public void onDestroy(){
    super.onDestroy();
    favoritesCursor.close();
    db.close();
}
}
```

Let's see what happens when we run the app now.

Test drive the app

When we run the app, our favorite drinks are displayed in
`TopLevelActivity` as before. When we click on one of the
drinks, its details are displayed in `DrinkActivity`. If we
uncheck the `favorite` checkbox for that drink and return to
`TopLevelActivity`, the data in the `list_favorites` list view
is refreshed and the drink is no longer displayed.

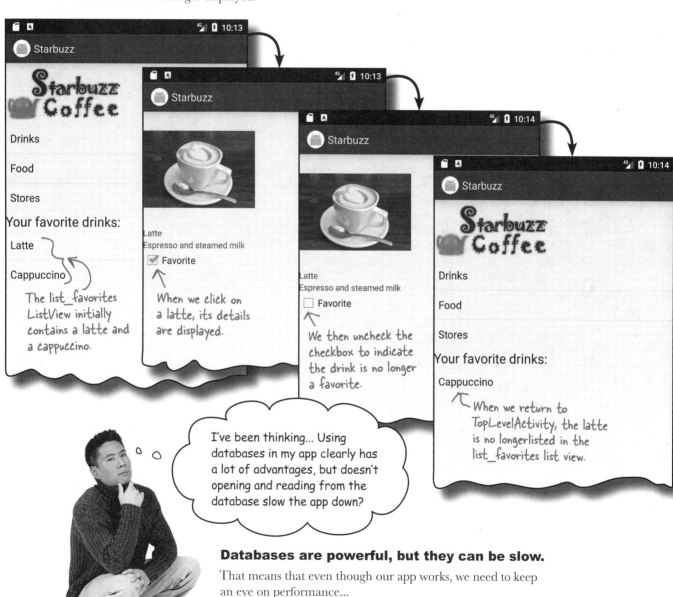

The list_favorites ListView initially contains a latte and a cappuccino.

When we click on a latte, its details are displayed.

We then uncheck the checkbox to indicate the drink is no longer a favorite.

When we return to TopLevelActivity, the latte is no longerlisted in the list_favorites list view.

I've been thinking... Using databases in my app clearly has a lot of advantages, but doesn't opening and reading from the database slow the app down?

Databases are powerful, but they can be slow.

That means that even though our app works, we need to keep
an eye on performance...

Databases can make your app go in sloooow-moooo....

Think about what your app has to do when it opens a database. It first needs to go searching for the database file. If the database file isn't there, it needs to create a blank database. Then it needs to run all of the SQL commands to create tables inside the database and any initial data it needs. Finally, it needs to fire off some queries to get the data out of there.

That all takes time. For a tiny database like the one used in the Starbuzz app, it's not a lot of time. But as a database gets bigger and bigger, that time will increase and increase. Before you know it, your app will lose its mojo and will be slower than YouTube on Thanksgiving.

There's not a lot you can do about the speed of creating and reading from a database, but you *can* prevent it from slowing down your interface.

Life is better when threads work together

The big problem with accessing a slow database is that can make your app feel unresponsive. To understand why, you need to think about how threads work in Android. Since Lollipop, there are three kinds of threads you need to think about:

⭐ **The main event thread**
This is the real workhorse in Android. It listens for intents, it receives touch messages from the screen, and it calls all of the methods inside your activities.

⭐ **The render thread**
You don't normally interact with this thread, but it reads a list of requests for screen updates and then calls the device's low-level graphics hardware to repaint the screen and make your app look pretty.

⭐ **Any other threads that you create**

If you're not careful, your app will do almost all of its work on the main event thread because this thread runs your event methods. If you just drop your database code into the `onCreate()` method (as we did in the Starbuzz app), then the main event thread will be busy talking to the database, instead of rushing off to look for any events from the screen or other apps. If your database code takes a long time, users will feel like they're being ignored or wonder if the app has crashed.

So the trick is to **move your database code off the main event thread and run it in a custom thread in the background**. We'll go through how you do this using the `DrinkActivity` code we wrote earlier in the chapter. As a reminder, the code updates the FAVORITE column in the Starbuzz database when the user clicks on the `favorite` checkbox, and displays a message if the database is unavailable.

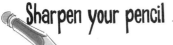

Sharpen your pencil

We're going to run the `DrinkActivity` code to update the database in a background thread, but before we rush off and start hacking code, let's think about what we need to do.

The code that we have at the moment does three different things. Choose the type of thread you think each should run on. We've completed the first one to start you off.

A Set up the interface.

```
int drinkId = (Integer) getIntent().getExtras().get(EXTRA_DRINKID);
CheckBox favorite = (CheckBox) findViewById(R.id.favorite);
ContentValues drinkValues = new ContentValues();
drinkValues.put("FAVORITE", favorite.isChecked());
```

Main event thread	A background thread
✓	

This code must run on the main event thread, as it needs to access the activity's views.

B Talk to the database.

```
SQLiteOpenHelper starbuzzDatabaseHelper = new StarbuzzDatabaseHelper(this);
SQLiteDatabase db = starbuzzDatabaseHelper.getWriteableDatabase();
db.update("DRINK",...);
```

Main event thread	A background thread

C Update what's displayed on the screen.

```
Toast toast = Toast.makeText(...);
toast.show();
```

Main event thread	A background thread

Sharpen your pencil
Solution

We're going to run the DrinkActivity code to update the database in a background thread, but before we rush off and start hacking code, let's think about what we need to do.

The code that we have at the moment does three different things. Choose the type of thread you think each should run on. We've completed the first one to start you off.

(A) **Set up the interface.**

```
int drinkId = (Integer) getIntent().getExtras().get(EXTRA_DRINKID);
CheckBox favorite = (CheckBox) findViewById(R.id.favorite);
ContentValues drinkValues = new ContentValues();
drinkValues.put("FAVORITE", favorite.isChecked());
```

Main event thread	A background thread
✓	

(B) **Talk to the database.**

```
SQLiteOpenHelper starbuzzDatabaseHelper = new StarbuzzDatabaseHelper(this);
SQLiteDatabase db = starbuzzDatabaseHelper.getWriteableDatabase();
db.update("DRINK",...);
```

We want to run the database code in the background.

Main event thread	A background thread
	✓

(C) **Update what's displayed on the screen.**

```
Toast toast = Toast.makeText(...);
toast.show();
```

← We must run the code to display a message on the screen on the main event thread; otherwise, we'll get an exception.

Main event thread	A background thread
✓	

What code goes on which thread?

When you use databases in your app, it's a good idea to run database code in a background thread, and update views with the database data in the main event thread. We're going to work through the onFavoritesClicked() method in the DrinkActivity code so that you can see how to approach this sort of problem.

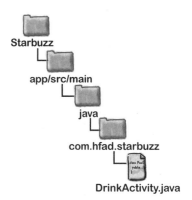

Starbuzz
└ app/src/main
  └ java
    └ com.hfad.starbuzz
      └ DrinkActivity.java

Here's the code for the method (we've split it into sections, which we'll describe below):

```java
//Update the database when the checkbox is clicked
public void onFavoriteClicked(View view){
```

1
```java
    int drinkId = (Integer) getIntent().getExtras().get(EXTRA_DRINKID);
    CheckBox favorite = (CheckBox) findViewById(R.id.favorite);
    ContentValues drinkValues = new ContentValues();
    drinkValues.put("FAVORITE", favorite.isChecked());
```

2
```java
    SQLiteOpenHelper starbuzzDatabaseHelper = new StarbuzzDatabaseHelper(this);
    try {
        SQLiteDatabase db = starbuzzDatabaseHelper.getWritableDatabase();
        db.update("DRINK", drinkValues,
                            "_id = ?", new String[] {Integer.toString(drinkId)});
        db.close();
    } catch(SQLiteException e) {
```

3
```java
        Toast toast = Toast.makeText(this, "Database unavailable", Toast.LENGTH_SHORT);
        toast.show();
    }
}
```

1 **Code that needs to be run before the database code**
The first few lines of code get the value of the favorite checkbox, and put it in the drinkValues ContentValues object. This code must be run before the database code.

2 **Database code that needs to be run on a background thread**
This updates the DRINK table.

3 **Code that needs to be run after the database code**
If the database is unavailable, we want to display a message to the user. This must run on the main event thread.

We're going to implement the code using an **AsyncTask**. What's that, you ask?

AsyncTask performs asynchronous tasks

An `AsyncTask` lets you perform operations in the background. When they've finished running, it then allows you to update views in the main event thread. If the task is repetitive, you can even use it to publish the progress of the task while it's running.

You create an `AsyncTask` by extending the `AsyncTask` class, and implementing its `doInBackground()` method. The code in this method runs in a background thread, so it's the perfect place for you to put database code. The `AsyncTask` class also has an `onPreExecute()` method that runs before `doInBackground()`, and an `onPostExecute()` method that runs afterward. There's an `onProgressUpdate()` method if you need to publish task progress.

Here's what an `AsyncTask` looks like:

You add your AsyncTask class as an inner class to the activity that needs to use it.

```
private class MyAsyncTask extends AsyncTask<Params, Progress, Result>

    protected void onPreExecute() {
        //Code to run before executing the task
    }

    protected Result doInBackground(Params... params) {
        //Code that you want to run in a background thread
    }

    protected void onProgressUpdate(Progress... values) {
        //Code that you want to run to publish the progress of your task
    }

    protected void onPostExecute(Result result) {
        //Code that you want to run when the task is complete
    }
}
```

This method is optional. It runs before the code you want to run in the background.

You must implement this method. It contains the code you want to run in the background.

This method is optional. It lets you publish progress of the code running in the background.

This method is also optional. It runs after the code has finished running in the background.

`AsyncTask` is defined by three generic parameters: `Params`, `Progress`, and `Results`. `Params` is the type of object used to pass any task parameters to the `doInBackground()` method, `Progress` is the type of object used to indicate task progress, and `Result` is the type of the task result. You can set any of these to `Void` if you're not going to use them.

We'll go through this over the next few pages by creating a new `AsyncTask` called `UpdateDrinkTask` we can use to update drinks in the background. Later on, we'll add this to our `DrinkActivity` code as an inner class.

The onPreExecute() method

We'll start with the onPreExecute() method. This gets called before the background task begins, and it's used to set up the task. It's called on the main event thread, so it has access to views in the user interface. The onPreExecute() method takes no parameters, and has a void return type.

In our case, we're going to use the onPreExecute() method to get the value of the favorite checkbox, and put it in the drinkValues ContentValues object. This is because we need access to the checkbox view in order to do this, and it must be done before any of our database code can be run. We're using a separate attribute outside the method for the drinkValues ContentValues object so that other methods in the class can access the ContentValues object (we'll look at these methods over the next few pages).

Here's the code:

```java
private class UpdateDrinkTask extends AsyncTask<Params, Progress, Result> {

    private ContentValues drinkValues;

    protected void onPreExecute() {
        CheckBox favorite = (CheckBox)findViewById(R.id.favorite);
        drinkValues = new ContentValues();
        drinkValues.put("FAVORITE", favorite.isChecked());
    }

    ...

}
```

Before we run the database code, we need to get the value of the favorite checkbox.

Next, we'll look at the doInBackground() method.

onPreExecute()

The doInBackground() method

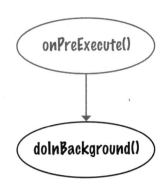

The doInBackground() method runs in the background immediately after onPreExecute(). You define what type of parameters the task should receive, and what the return type should be.

We're going to use the doInBackground() method for our database code so that it runs in a background thread. We'll pass it the ID of the drink we need to update; because the drink ID is an int value, we need to specify that the doInBackground() method receives Integer objects. We'll use a Boolean return value so we can tell whether the code ran successfully:

```java
private class UpdateDrinkTask extends AsyncTask<Integer, Progress, Boolean> {

    private ContentValues drinkValues;
```

You change this to Integer to match the parameter of the doInBackground() method.

You change this to Boolean to match the return type of the doInBackground() method.

```java
    ...

    protected Boolean doInBackground(Integer... drinks) {
        int drinkId = drinks[0];
        SQLiteOpenHelper starbuzzDatabaseHelper =
                            new StarbuzzDatabaseHelper(DrinkActivity.this);
        try {
            SQLiteDatabase db = starbuzzDatabaseHelper.getWritableDatabase();
            db.update("DRINK", drinkValues,
                        "_id = ?", new String[] {Integer.toString(drinkId)});
            db.close();
            return true;
        } catch(SQLiteException e) {
            return false;
        }
    }

    ...

}
```

This code runs in a background thread.

This is an array of Integers, but we'll just include one item, the drink ID.

The update() method uses the drinkValues object that the onPreExecute() method created.

Next, we'll look at the onProgressUpdate() method.

The onProgressUpdate() method

The onProgressUpdate() method is called on the main event thread, so it has access to views in the user interface. You can use this method to display progress to the user by updating views on the screen. You define what type of parameters the method should have.

The onProgressUpdate() method runs if a call to publishProgress() is made by the doInBackground() method like this:

```
protected Boolean doInBackground(Integer... count) {
    for (int i = 0; i < count; i++) {
        publishProgress(i);    ← This calls the onProgressUpdate()
    }                              method, passing in a value of i.
}


protected void onProgressUpdate(Integer... progress) {
    setProgress(progress[0]);
}
```

In our app, we're not publishing the progress of our task, so we don't need to implement this method. We'll indicate that we're not using any objects for task progress by changing the signature of UpdateDrinkTask:

We're not using the onProgressUpdate() method, so this is Void.

```
private class UpdateDrinkTask extends AsyncTask<Integer, Void, Boolean> {

    ...

}
```

Finally, we'll look at the onPostExecute() method.

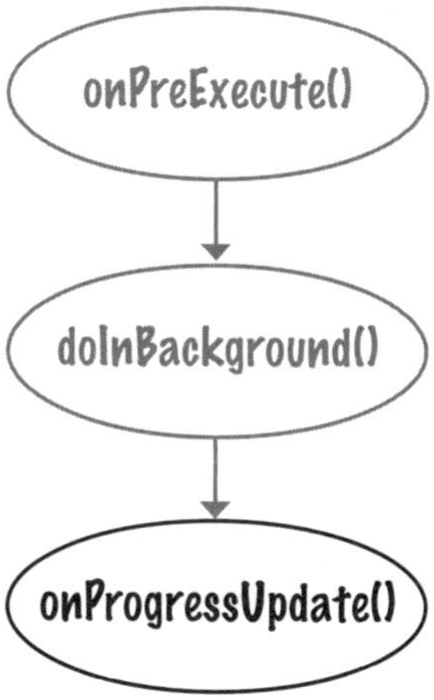

onPreExecute()

doInBackground()

onProgressUpdate()

The onPostExecute() method

The onPostExecute() method is called after the
background task has finished. It's called on the main event
thread, so it has access to views in the user interface. You can
use this method to present the results of the task to the user.
The onPostExecute() method gets passed the results of the
doInBackground() method, so it must take parameters that
match the doInBackground() return type.

We're going to use the onPostExecute() method to check
whether the database code in the doInBackground()
method ran successfully. If it didn't, we'll display a message
to the user. We're doing this in the onPostExecute()
method, as this method can update the user interface; the
doInBackground() method runs in a background thread, so
it can't update views.

Here's the code:

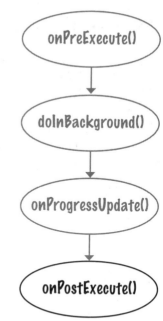

```java
private class UpdateDrinkTask extends AsyncTask<Integer, Void, Boolean> {
```

This is set to Boolean, as our
doInBackground() method returns a Boolean.

```java
    ...

    protected void onPostExecute(Boolean success) {
        if (!success) {
            Toast toast = Toast.makeText(DrinkActivity.this,
                                "Database unavailable", Toast.LENGTH_SHORT);
            toast.show();
        }
    }
}
```

Pass the toast the
DrinkActivity context.

Now that we've written the code for our AsyncTask methods,
let's revisit the AsyncTask class parameters.

The AsyncTask class parameters

When we first introduced the `AsyncTask` class, we said it was defined by three generic parameters: `Params`, `Progress`, and `Results`. You specify what these are by looking at the type of parameters used by your `doInBackground()`, `onProgressUpdate()`, and `onPostExecute()` methods. `Params` is the type of the `doInBackground()` parameters, `Progress` is the type of the `onProgressUpdate()` parameters, and `Result` is the type of the `onPostExecute()` parameters:

```
private class MyAsyncTask extends AsyncTask<Params, Progress, Result>

    protected void onPreExecute() {
        //Code to run before executing the task
    }

    protected Result doInBackground(Params... params) {
        //Code that you want to run in a background thread
    }

    protected void onProgressUpdate(Progress... values) {
        //Code that you want to run to publish the progress of your task
    }

    protected void onPostExecute(Result result) {
        //Code that you want to run when the task is complete
    }
}
```

In our example, `doInBackground()` takes `Integer` parameters, `onPostExecute()` takes a `Boolean` parameter, and we're not using the `onProgressUpdate()` method. This means that in our example, `Params` is `Integer`, `Progress` is `Void`, and `Result` is `Boolean`:

This is Void because we didn't implement the onProgressUpdate() method.

```
private class UpdateDrinkTask extends AsyncTask<Integer, Void, Boolean> {
    ...
    protected Boolean doInBackground(Integer... drinks) {
        ...
    }

    protected void onPostExecute(Boolean... success) {
        ...
    }
}
```

We'll show you the full `UpdateDrinkTask` class on the next page.

The full UpdateDrinkTask class

Here's the full code for the UpdateDrinkTask class. It needs
to be added to DrinkActivity as an inner class, but we
suggest you wait to do that until we show you how to execute it
and show you the full *DrinkActivity.java* code listing.

```java
private class UpdateDrinkTask extends AsyncTask<Integer, Void, Boolean> {
    private ContentValues drinkValues;

    protected void onPreExecute() {
        CheckBox favorite = (CheckBox) findViewById(R.id.favorite);
        drinkValues = new ContentValues();
        drinkValues.put("FAVORITE", favorite.isChecked());
    }

    protected Boolean doInBackground(Integer... drinks) {
        int drinkId = drinks[0];
        SQLiteOpenHelper starbuzzDatabaseHelper =
                new StarbuzzDatabaseHelper(DrinkActivity.this);
        try {
            SQLiteDatabase db = starbuzzDatabaseHelper.getWritableDatabase();
            db.update("DRINK", drinkValues,
                    "_id = ?", new String[] {Integer.toString(drinkId)});
            db.close();
            return true;
        } catch(SQLiteException e) {
            return false;
        }
    }

    protected void onPostExecute(Boolean success) {
        if (!success) {
            Toast toast = Toast.makeText(DrinkActivity.this,
                    "Database unavailable", Toast.LENGTH_SHORT);
            toast.show();
        }
    }
}
```

We've defined drinkValues as a private variable, as it's used by the onExecute() and doInBackground() methods.

Before we run the database code, we need to put the value of the favorite checkbox in the drinkValues ContentValues object.

Our database code goes in the doInBackground() method.

After the database code has run in the background, check whether it ran successfully. If it didn't, display a message.

We have to put the code to display a message in the onPostExecute() method, as it needs to be run on the main event thread to update the screen.

Execute the AsyncTask...

You run the `AsyncTask` by calling the `AsyncTask execute()`
method and passing it any parameters required by the
`doInBackground()` method. As an example, we want to pass the
drink the user chose to our `AsyncTask`'s `doInBackground()`
method, so we call it using:

```
int drinkId = (Integer) getIntent().getExtras().get(EXTRA_DRINKID);
new UpdateDrinkTask().execute(drinkId);  ← Execute the AsyncTask and pass it the drink ID.
```

The type of parameter you pass with the `execute()` method
must match the type of parameter expected by the `AsyncTask`
`doInBackground()` method. We're passing an integer value (the
drink ID), which matches the type of parameter expected by our
`doInBackground()` method:

```
protected Boolean doInBackground(Integer... drinks) {

    ...

}
```

...in DrinkActivity's onFavoritesClicked() method

Our `UpdateDrinkTask` class (the `AsyncTask` we created) needs to
update the FAVORITE column in the Starbuzz database whenever the
`favorite` checkbox in `DrinkActivity` is clicked. We therefore need
to execute it in `DrinkActivity`'s `onFavoritesClicked()` method.
Here's what the new version of the method looks like:

```
//Update the database when the checkbox is clicked
public void onFavoriteClicked(View view){
    int drinkId = (Integer)getIntent().getExtras().get(EXTRA_DRINKID);
    new UpdateDrinkTask().execute(drinkId);  ←── The new version of the
}                                                onFavoritesClicked() method no
                                                 longer contains code to update the
                                                 FAVORITE column. Instead, it calls
                                                 the AsyncTask, which performs the
                                                 update in the background.
```

We'll show you the new *DrinkActivity.java* code over the next few pages.

The full DrinkActivity.java code

Here's the complete code for *DrinkActivity.java*; update your
version of the code to reflect our changes:

```
package com.hfad.starbuzz;

import android.app.Activity;
import android.os.Bundle;
import android.widget.ImageView;
import android.widget.TextView;
import android.widget.Toast;
import android.database.Cursor;
import android.database.sqlite.SQLiteDatabase;
import android.database.sqlite.SQLiteException;
import android.database.sqlite.SQLiteOpenHelper;
import android.view.View;
import android.widget.CheckBox;
import android.content.ContentValues;
import android.os.AsyncTask;
```
← We're using the AsyncTask class, so we need to import it.

```
public class DrinkActivity extends Activity {

    public static final String EXTRA_DRINKID = "drinkId";
```
We don't need to change the onCreate() method, we're just showing it for completeness.
```
    @Override
    protected void onCreate(Bundle savedInstanceState) {
        super.onCreate(savedInstanceState);
        setContentView(R.layout.activity_drink);

        //Get the drink from the intent
        int drinkId = (Integer) getIntent().getExtras().get(EXTRA_DRINKID);

        //Create a cursor
        SQLiteOpenHelper starbuzzDatabaseHelper = new StarbuzzDatabaseHelper(this);
        try {
            SQLiteDatabase db = starbuzzDatabaseHelper.getReadableDatabase();
            Cursor cursor = db.query("DRINK",
                    new String[]{"NAME", "DESCRIPTION", "IMAGE_RESOURCE_ID", "FAVORITE"},
                    "_id = ?",
                    new String[]{Integer.toString(drinkId)},
                    null, null, null);
```
The code continues →
on the next page.

The full DrinkActivity.java code (continued)

```java
        //Move to the first record in the Cursor
        if (cursor.moveToFirst()) {
            //Get the drink details from the cursor
            String nameText = cursor.getString(0);
            String descriptionText = cursor.getString(1);
            int photoId = cursor.getInt(2);
            boolean isFavorite = (cursor.getInt(3) == 1);

            //Populate the drink name
            TextView name = (TextView) findViewById(R.id.name);
            name.setText(nameText);

            //Populate the drink description
            TextView description = (TextView) findViewById(R.id.description);
            description.setText(descriptionText);

            //Populate the drink image
            ImageView photo = (ImageView) findViewById(R.id.photo);
            photo.setImageResource(photoId);
            photo.setContentDescription(nameText);

            //Populate the favorite checkbox
            CheckBox favorite = (CheckBox)findViewById(R.id.favorite);
            favorite.setChecked(isFavorite);
        }
        cursor.close();
        db.close();
    } catch (SQLiteException e) {
        Toast toast = Toast.makeText(this,
                "Database unavailable",
                Toast.LENGTH_SHORT);
        toast.show();
    }
}
```

Starbuzz
app/src/main
java
com.hfad.starbuzz
DrinkActivity.java

None of the code on this page needs to change.

The code continues on the next page.

The full DrinkActivity.java code (continued)

```java
//Update the database when the checkbox is clicked
public void onFavoriteClicked(View view){
    int drinkId = (Integer) getIntent().getExtras().get(EXTRA_DRINKID);

    //Get the value of the checkbox
    CheckBox favorite = (CheckBox) findViewById(R.id.favorite);
    ContentValues drinkValues = new ContentValues();
    drinkValues.put("FAVORITE", favorite.isChecked());

    //Get a reference to the database and update the FAVORITE column
    SQLiteOpenHelper starbuzzDatabaseHelper =
            new StarbuzzDatabaseHelper(this);
    try {
        SQLiteDatabase db = starbuzzDatabaseHelper.getWritableDatabase();
        db.update("DRINK",
                drinkValues,
                "_id = ?",
                new String[] {Integer.toString(drinkId)});
        db.close();
    } catch(SQLiteException e) {
        Toast toast = Toast.makeText(this, "Database unavailable", Toast.LENGTH_SHORT);
        toast.show();
    }

    new UpdateDrinkTask().execute(drinkId);   ← Execute the task.
}
```

Starbuzz
app/src/main
java
com.hfad.starbuzz
DrinkActivity.java

Delete all these lines of code, as we're now using an AsyncTask for these actions.

The code continues → on the next page.

The full DrinkActivity.java code (continued)

```java
//Inner class to update the drink.
private class UpdateDrinkTask extends AsyncTask<Integer, Void, Boolean> {
    private ContentValues drinkValues;

    protected void onPreExecute() {
        CheckBox favorite = (CheckBox) findViewById(R.id.favorite);
        drinkValues = new ContentValues();
        drinkValues.put("FAVORITE", favorite.isChecked());
    }

    protected Boolean doInBackground(Integer... drinks) {
        int drinkId = drinks[0];
        SQLiteOpenHelper starbuzzDatabaseHelper =
                new StarbuzzDatabaseHelper(DrinkActivity.this);
        try {
            SQLiteDatabase db = starbuzzDatabaseHelper.getWritableDatabase();
            db.update("DRINK", drinkValues,
                    "_id = ?", new String[] {Integer.toString(drinkId)});
            db.close();
            return true;
        } catch(SQLiteException e) {
            return false;
        }
    }

    protected void onPostExecute(Boolean success) {
        if (!success) {
            Toast toast = Toast.makeText(DrinkActivity.this,
                    "Database unavailable", Toast.LENGTH_SHORT);
            toast.show();
        }
    }
}
```

Add the AsyncTask to the activity as an inner class.

Before the database code runs, put the value of the checkbox in the drinkValues ContentValues object.

Run the database code in a background thread.

Update the value of the FAVORITE column.

If the database code didn't run correctly, display a message to the user.

Starbuzz
app/src/main
java
com.hfad.starbuzz
DrinkActivity.java

That's everything you need in order to create an `AsyncTask`.
Let's check what happens when we run the app.

Test drive the app

When we run the app and navigate to a drink, we can indicate that the drink is a favorite drink by checking the "favorite" checkbox. Clicking on the checkbox still updates the FAVORITE column in the database with its value, but this time the code is running on a background thread.

In an ideal world, all of your database code should run in the background. We're not going to change our other Starbuzz activities to do this, but why not make this change yourself?

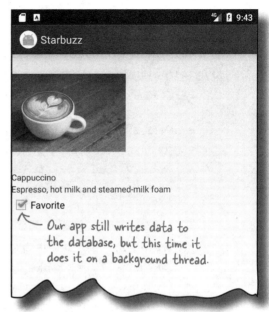

Our app still writes data to the database, but this time it does it on a background thread.

---

there are no Dumb Questions

Q: I've written code before that just ran the database code and it was fine. Do I really need to run it in the background?

A: For really small databases, like the one in the Starbuzz app, you probably won't notice the time it takes to access the database. But that's just because the database is small. If you use a larger database, or if you run an app on a slower device, the time it takes to access the database will be significant. So yes, you should *always* run database code in the background.

Q: Remind me—why is it bad to update a view from the background thread?

A: The short answer is that it will throw an exception if you try. The longer answer is that multithreaded user interfaces are hugely buggy. Android avoided the problem by simply banning them.

Q: Which part of the database code is slowest: opening the database, or reading data from it?

A: There's no general way of knowing. If your database has a complex data structure, opening the database for the first time will take a long time because it will need to create all the tables. If you're running a complex query, that might take a very long time. In general, play it safe and run everything in the background.

Q: If it take a few seconds to read data from the database, what will the user see?

A: The user will see blank views until the database code sets the values.

Q: Why have we put the database code for just one activity in an `AsyncTask`?

A: We wanted to show you how to use `AsyncTask`s in one activity as an example. In the real world, you should do this for the database code in all your activities.

Your Android Toolbox

You've got Chapter 17 under your belt and now you've added writing to SQLite databases to your toolbox.

You can download the full code for the chapter from https://tinyurl.com/ HeadFirstAndroid.

■ BULLET POINTS

- The `CursorAdapter` `changeCursor()` method replaces the cursor currently used by a cursor adapter with a new cursor that you provide. It then closes the old cursor.

- Run your database code in a background thread using `AsyncTask`.

A summary of the AsyncTask steps

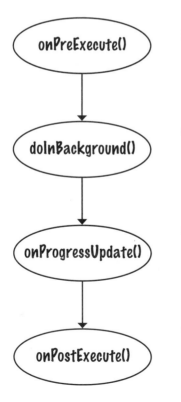

1 **onPreExecute() is used to set up the task.**
It's called before the background task begins, and runs on the main event thread.

2 **doInBackground() runs in the background thread.**
It runs immediately after `onPreExecute()`. You can specify what type of parameters it has, and what its return type is.

3 **onProgressUpdate() is used to display progress.**
It runs in the main event thread when the `doInBackground()` method calls `publishProgress()`.

4 **onPostExecute() is used to display the task outcome to the user when doInBackground has finished.**
It runs in the main event thread and takes the return value of `doInBackground()` as a parameter.

18 started services

At Your Service

Did I mention I've started a ProtectionRacketService?

There are some operations you want to keep on running, irrespective of which app has the focus. If you start downloading a file, for instance, *you don't want the download to stop when you switch to another app.* In this chapter we'll introduce you to **started services**, components that *run operations in the background*. You'll see how to create a started service using the `IntentService` class, and find out how its lifecycle fits in with that of an activity. Along the way, you'll discover how to **log messages**, and *keep users informed* using Android's built-in **notification service**.

Services work in the background

An Android app is a collection of activities and other components. The bulk of your app's code is there to interact with the user, but sometimes you need to do things in the background, such as download a large file, stream a piece of music, or listen for a message from the server.

These kinds of tasks aren't what activities are designed to do. In simple cases, you can create a thread, but if you're not careful your activity code will start to get complex and unreadable.

That's why **services** were invented. A service is an application component like an activity but without a user interface. They have a simpler lifecycle than activities, and they come with a bunch of features that make it easy to write code that will run in the background while the user is doing something else.

In addition to writing your own services, you can use Android's built-in ones.

Built-in services include the notification service, location service, alarm service, and download service.

There are three types of service

Services come in three main flavors:

⭐ **Started services**
A started service can run in the background indefinitely, even when the activity that started it is destroyed. If you wanted to download a large file from the Internet, you would probably create it as a started service. Once the operation is done, the service stops.

⭐ **Bound services**
A bound service is bound to another application component such as an activity. The activity can interact with it, send requests, and get results. A bound service runs as long as components are bound to it. When the components are no longer bound, the service is destroyed. If you wanted to create an odometer to measure the distance traveled by a vehicle, for example, you'd probably use a bound service. This way, any activities bound to the service could keep asking the service for updates on the distance traveled.

⭐ **Scheduled services**
A scheduled service is one that's scheduled to run at a particular time. As an example, from API 21, you can schedule jobs to run at an appropriate time.

In this chapter, we're going to look at how you create a started service.

We'll create a STARTED service

We're going to create a new project that contains an activity called `MainActivity`, and a started service called `DelayedMessageService`. Whenever `MainActivity` calls `DelayedMessageService`, it will wait for 10 seconds and then display a piece of text.

1...2..3...4...5...6...7 ...8...9...10... Here's the text.

← MainActivity will use this layout.

activity_main.xml

The activity will pass → text to the service.

Text

The service will ← display the text after 10 seconds.

MainActivity.java   **DelayedMessageService.java**

We're going to do this in two stages:

① **Display the message in Android's log.**
We'll start by displaying the message in Android's log so that we can check that the service works OK. We can look at the log in Android Studio.

② **Display the message in a notification.**
We'll get `DelayedMessageService` to use Android's built-in notification service to display the message in a notification.

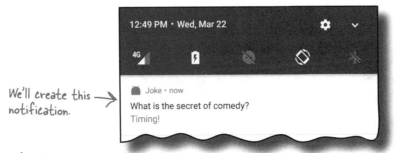

We'll create this → notification.

12:49 PM · Wed, Mar 22

Joke · now
What is the secret of comedy?
Timing!

Create the project

We'll start by creating the project. Create a new Android project for an application named "Joke" with a company domain of "hfad.com", making the package name `com.hfad.joke`. The minimum SDK should be API 19 so that it will work with most devices. You'll need an empty activity named "MainActivity" and a layout named "activity_main" so that your code matches ours. **Make sure that you uncheck the Backwards Compatibility (AppCompat) option when you create the activity.**

The next thing we need to do is create the service.

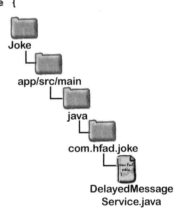

Log
Display notification

Use the IntentService class to create a basic started service

The simplest way of creating a started service is to extend the **IntentService** class, as it provides you with most of the functionality you need. You start it with an intent, and it runs the code that you specify in a separate thread.

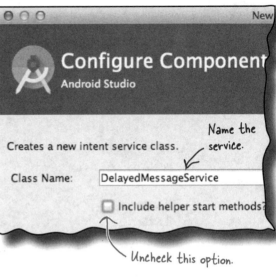

Creates a new intent service class.

Name the service.

Class Name: DelayedMessageService

☐ Include helper start methods?

Uncheck this option.

We're going to add a new intent service to our project. To do this, switch to the Project view of Android Studio's explorer, click on the `com.hfad.joke` package in the *app/src/main/java* folder, go to File→New..., and select the Service option. When prompted, choose the option to create a new Intent Service. Name the service "DelayedMessageService" and uncheck the option to include helper start methods to minimize the amount of code that Android Studio generates for you. Click on the Finish button, then replace the code in *DelayedMessageService.java* with the code here:

```java
package com.hfad.joke;

import android.app.IntentService;
import android.content.Intent;

public class DelayedMessageService extends IntentService {

    public DelayedMessageService() {
        super("DelayedMessageService");
    }

    @Override
    protected void onHandleIntent(Intent intent) {
        //Code to do something
    }
}
```

Extend the IntentService class.

Put the code you want the service to run in the onHandleIntent() method.

Some versions of Android Studio may ask you what the source language should be. If prompted, select the option for Java.

Joke
└ app/src/main
  └ java
    └ com.hfad.joke
      └ DelayedMessage
        Service.java

The above code is all you need to create a basic intent service. You extend the `IntentService` class, add a public constructor, and implement the `onHandleIntent()` method.

The `onHandleIntent()` method should contain the code you want to run each time the service is passed an intent. It runs in a separate thread. If it's passed multiple intents, it deals with them one at a time.

We want `DelayedMessageService` to display a message in Android's log, so let's look at how you log messages.

How to log messages

Adding messages to a log can be a useful way of checking that your code works the way you want. You tell Android what to log in your Java code, and when the app's running, you check the output in Android's log (a.k.a. logcat).

You log messages using one of the following methods in the Android.util.Log class:

Log.v(String tag, String message)   Logs a verbose message.

Log.d(String tag, String message)   Logs a debug message.

Log.i(String tag, String message)   Logs an information message.

Log.w(String tag, String message)   Logs a warning message.

Log.e(String tag, String message)   Logs an error message.

Each message is composed of a String tag you use to identify the source of the message, and the message itself. As an example, to log a verbose message that's come from DelayedMessageService, you use the Log.v() method like this:

```
Log.v("DelayedMessageService", "This is a message");
```

You can view the logcat in Android Studio and filter by the different types of message. To see the logcat, select the Android Monitor option at the bottom of your project screen in Android Studio and then select the logcat tab:

There's also a Log.wtf() method you can use to report exceptions that should never happen. According to the Android documentation, wtf means "What a Terrible Failure." We know it really means "Welcome to Fiskidagurinn," which refers to the Great Fish Day festival held annually in Dalvik, Iceland. Android developers can often be heard to say, "My AVD just took 8 minutes to boot up. WTF??" as a tribute to the small town that gave its name to the standard Android executable bytecode format.

Select the logcat tab.

You can filter on the type of message here.

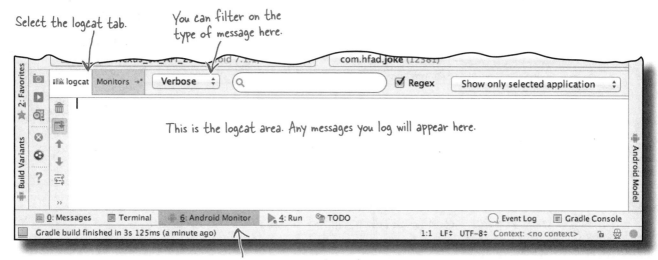

This is the logcat area. Any messages you log will appear here.

Select the Android Monitor option.

Log
Display notification

The full DelayedMessageService code

We want our service to get a piece of text from an intent, wait for 10 seconds, then display the piece of text in the log. To do this, we'll add a showText() method to log the text, and then call it from the onHandleIntent() method after a delay of 10 seconds.

Here's the full code for *DelayedMessageService.java* (update your version of the code to reflect our changes):

```
package com.hfad.joke;

import android.app.IntentService;
import android.content.Intent;
import android.util.Log;     ← We're using the Log class, so we need to import it.

public class DelayedMessageService extends IntentService {

                                                            Use a constant to pass
    public static final String EXTRA_MESSAGE = "message";   ← a message from the
                                                            activity to the service.

    public DelayedMessageService() {
        super("DelayedMessageService");     ← Call the super constructor.
    }
                            This method contains the code you want to
                            run when the service receives an intent.
    @Override                        ↓
    protected void onHandleIntent(Intent intent) {
        synchronized (this) {
            try {
                wait(10000);     ← Wait 10 seconds.
            } catch (InterruptedException e) {
                e.printStackTrace();
            }
        }                        Get the text from the intent
                                      ↓
        String text = intent.getStringExtra(EXTRA_MESSAGE);
        showText(text);
    }                    ⌐ Call the showText() method.
                        ↙
    private void showText(final String text) {
        Log.v("DelayedMessageService", "The message is: " + text);
    }                    ↖
}                This logs a piece of text so we can see it in
                the logcat through Android Studio.
```

Joke

app/src/main

java

com.hfad.joke

DelayedMessage
Service.java

You declare services in AndroidManifest.xml

Just like activities, each service needs to be declared in *AndroidManifest.xml* so that Android can call it; if a service isn't declared in this file, Android won't know it's there and won't be able to call it.

Android Studio should update *AndroidManifest.xml* for you automatically whenever you create a new service by adding a new `<service>` element. Here's what our *AndroidManifest.xml* code looks like:

```xml
<?xml version="1.0" encoding="utf-8"?>
<manifest xmlns:android="http://schemas.android.com/apk/res/android"
    package="com.hfad.joke">

    <application
        android:allowBackup="true"
        android:icon="@mipmap/ic_launcher"
        android:label="@string/app_name"
        android:roundIcon="@mipmap/ic_launcher_round"
        android:supportsRtl="true"
        android:theme="@style/AppTheme">
        <activity android:name=".MainActivity">
            <intent-filter>
                <action android:name="android.intent.action.MAIN" />
                <category android:name="android.intent.category.LAUNCHER" />
            </intent-filter>
        </activity>

        <service
            android:name=".DelayedMessageService"
            android:exported="false">
        </service>
    </application>
</manifest>
```

Don't worry if this code looks different than yours.

Joke
⌊ app/src/main
⌊ AndroidManifest.xml

You declare a service in AndroidManifest.xml like this. Android Studio should do this for you automatically.

The service name has a "." in front of it so that Android can combine it with the package name to derive the fully qualified class name.

The `<service>` element contains two attributes: `name` and `exported`. The `name` attribute tells Android what the name of the service is—in our case, `DelayedMessageService`. The `exported` attribute tells Android whether the service can be used by other apps. Setting it to `false` means that the service will only be used within the current app.

Now that we have a service, let's get `MainActivity` to start it.

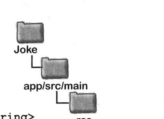

Log
Display notification

Add a button to activity_main.xml

We're going to get `MainActivity` to start
`DelayedMessageService` whenever a button is clicked, so
we'll add the button to `MainActivity`'s layout.

First, add the following values to *strings.xml*:

```xml
<string name="question">What is the secret of comedy?</string>
<string name="response">Timing!</string>
```

Then, replace your *activity_main.xml* code with ours below so
that `MainActivity` displays a button:

```xml
<?xml version="1.0" encoding="utf-8"?>
<LinearLayout
    xmlns:android="http://schemas.android.com/apk/res/android"
    xmlns:tools="http://schemas.android.com/tools"
    android:layout_width="match_parent"
    android:layout_height="match_parent"
    android:orientation="vertical"
    android:padding="16dp"
    tools:context="com.hfad.joke.MainActivity">

    <Button
        android:layout_width="wrap_content"
        android:layout_height="wrap_content"
        android:layout_gravity="center_horizontal"
        android:text="@string/question"
        android:id="@+id/button"
        android:onClick="onClick"/>

</LinearLayout>
```

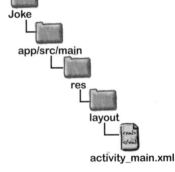

This creates a button. When it's
clicked, the onClick() method in
the activity will get called.

The button will call an `onClick()` method whenever the
user clicks it, so we'll add this method to `MainActivity`.

Log
Display notification

You start a service using startService()

We'll use `MainActivity`'s `onClick()` method to start `DelayedMessageService` whenever the user clicks on the button. You start a service from an activity in a similar way to how you start an activity. You create an explicit intent that's directed at the service you want to start, then use the **startService()** method in your activity to start it:

```
Intent intent = new Intent(this, DelayedMessageService.class);
startService(intent);
```

Starting a service is just like starting an activity, except you use startService() instead of startActivity().

Here's our code for *MainActivity.java*; update your version to match ours:

```java
package com.hfad.joke;

import android.app.Activity;
import android.content.Intent;
import android.os.Bundle;
import android.view.View;
```

We're using these classes, so we need to import them.

```java
public class MainActivity extends Activity {
```

We're using Activity here, but you could use AppCompatActivity instead.

```java
    @Override
    protected void onCreate(Bundle savedInstanceState) {
        super.onCreate(savedInstanceState);
        setContentView(R.layout.activity_main);
    }

    public void onClick(View view) {
        Intent intent = new Intent(this, DelayedMessageService.class);
        intent.putExtra(DelayedMessageService.EXTRA_MESSAGE,
                                getResources().getString(R.string.response));
        startService(intent);
    }
}
```

This will run when the button gets clicked.

Create the intent.

Add text to the intent.

Start the service.

Joke

app/src/main

java

com.hfad.joke

MainActivity.java

That's all the code we need to get our activity to start the service. Before we take it for a test drive, let's go through what happens when the code runs.

What happens when you run the app

Here's what the code does when we run the app:

1 **MainActivity starts DelayedMessageService by calling startService() and passing it an intent.**

The intent contains the message `MainActivity` wants `DelayedMessageService` to display, in this case "Timing!".

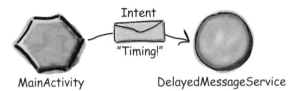

2 **When DelayedMessageService receives the intent, its onHandleIntent() method runs.**

`DelayedMessageService` waits for 10 seconds.

3 **DelayedMessageService logs the message.**

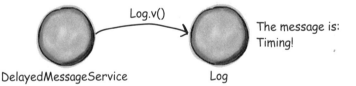

4 **When DelayedMessageService has finished running, it's destroyed.**

Let's take the app for a test drive so we can see it working.

Test drive the app

When you run the app, `MainActivity` is displayed. It contains a
single button:

Here's the button. ⟶ **What is the secret of comedy?**

Press the button, switch back to Android Studio, and watch the
logcat output in the bottom part of the IDE. After 10 seconds, the
message "Timing!" should appear in the logcat.

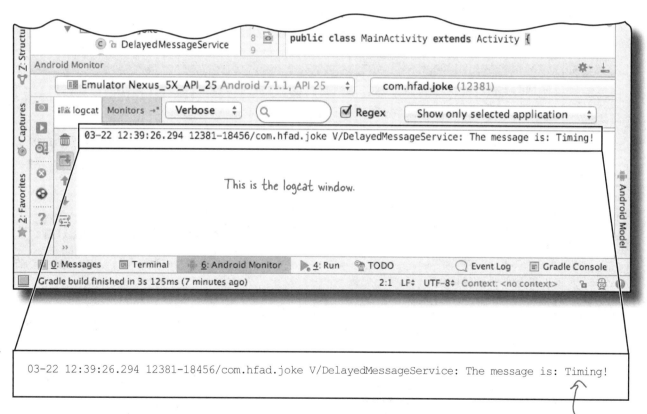

```
8    public class MainActivity extends Activity {
C  DelayedMessageService    9
```

Android Monitor

```
Emulator Nexus_5X_API_25 Android 7.1.1, API 25  ⇕    com.hfad.joke (12381)
```

logcat   Monitors →*   Verbose ⇕   (Q   ) ☑ Regex   Show only selected application ⇕

```
03-22 12:39:26.294 12381-18456/com.hfad.joke V/DelayedMessageService: The message is: Timing!
```

This is the logcat window.

0: Messages   Terminal   6: Android Monitor   4: Run   TODO   Event Log   Gradle Console

Gradle build finished in 3s 125ms (7 minutes ago)   2:1 LF⇕ UTF-8⇕ Context: <no context>

```
03-22 12:39:26.294 12381-18456/com.hfad.joke V/DelayedMessageService: The message is: Timing!
```

Now that you've seen `DelayedMessageService` running, let's
look in more detail at how started services work.

After a 10-second delay, the
message is displayed in the log.

The states of a started service

When an application component (such as an activity) starts a service, the service moves from being created to running to being destroyed.

A started service spends most of its life in a ***running*** state; it's been started by another component such as an activity, and it runs code in the background. It continues to run even if the component that started it is destroyed. When the service has finished running code, it's ***destroyed***.

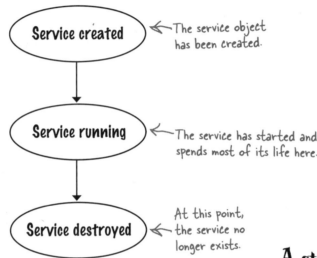

Service created ← The service object has been created.

Service running ← The service has started and spends most of its life here.

Service destroyed ← At this point, the service no longer exists.

Just like an activity, when a service moves from being created to being destroyed, it triggers key service lifecycle methods, which it inherits.

When the service is created, its `onCreate()` method gets called. You override this method if you want to perform any tasks needed to set up the service.

When the service is ready to start, its `onStartCommand()` method is called. If you're using an `IntentService` (which is usually the case for a started service), you don't generally override this method. Instead, you add any code you want the service to run to its `onHandleIntent()` method, which is called after `onStartCommand()`.

The `onDestroy()` method is called when the started service is no longer running and it's about to be destroyed. You override this method to perform any final cleanup tasks, such as freeing up resources.

We'll take a closer look at how these methods fit into the service states on the next page.

A started service runs after it's been started.

onCreate() gets called when the service is first created, and it's where you do any service setup.

onDestroy() gets called just before the service gets destroyed.

The started service lifecycle: from create to destroy

Here's an overview of the started service lifecycle from birth to death.

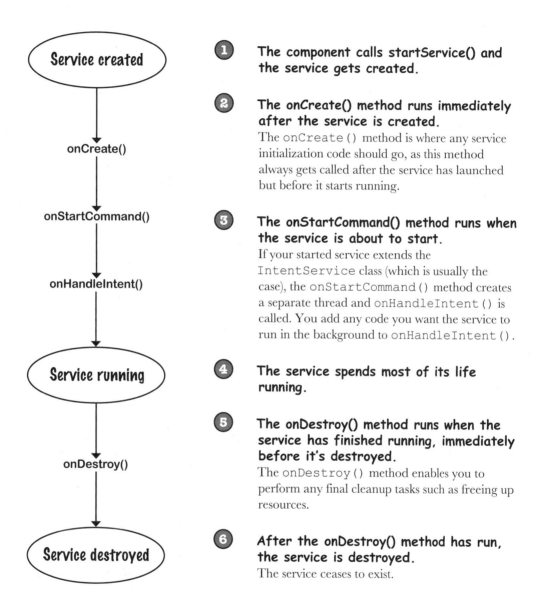

1 The component calls startService() and the service gets created.

2 The onCreate() method runs immediately after the service is created.

The onCreate() method is where any service initialization code should go, as this method always gets called after the service has launched but before it starts running.

3 The onStartCommand() method runs when the service is about to start.

If your started service extends the IntentService class (which is usually the case), the onStartCommand() method creates a separate thread and onHandleIntent() is called. You add any code you want the service to run in the background to onHandleIntent().

4 The service spends most of its life running.

5 The onDestroy() method runs when the service has finished running, immediately before it's destroyed.

The onDestroy() method enables you to perform any final cleanup tasks such as freeing up resources.

6 After the onDestroy() method has run, the service is destroyed.

The service ceases to exist.

The onCreate(), onStartCommand(), and onDestroy() methods are three of the main service lifecycle methods. So where do these methods come from?

Your service inherits the lifecycle methods

As you saw earlier in the chapter, the started service you created extends the `android.app.IntentService` class. This class gives your service access to the Android lifecycle methods. Here's a diagram showing the class hierarchy:

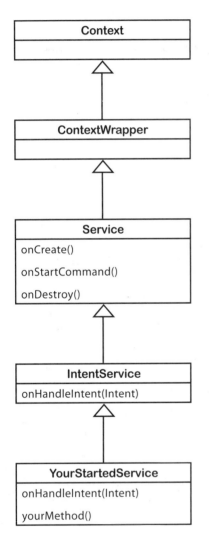

Context abstract class

(android.content.Context)

An interface to global information about the application environment. Allows access to application resources, classes, and operations.

ContextWrapper class

(android.content.ContextWrapper)

A proxy implementation for the `Context`.

Service class

(android.app.Service)

The `Service` class implements default versions of the lifecycle methods. You'll find out more about it in the next chapter.

IntentService class

(android.app.IntentService)

The `IntentService` class gives you an easy way of creating started services. It includes a method, `onHandleIntent()`, which handles any intents it's given on a background thread.

YourStartedService class

(com.hfad.foo)

Most of the behavior of your started service is handled by superclass methods your service inherits. All you do is override the methods you need and add a public constructor.

Now that you understand more about how started services work behind the scenes, have a go at the following exercise. After that, we'll look at how we can make `DelayedMessageService` display its message in a notification.

Service Magnets

Below is most of the code needed to create a started service called
WombleService that plays a *.mp3* file in the background, and an
activity that uses it. See if you can finish off the code.

← This is the service.

```java
public class WombleService extends ................................. {

    public WombleService() {
        super("WombleService");
    }


    @Override
    protected void ..................................... (Intent intent) {
        MediaPlayer mediaPlayer =
                MediaPlayer.create(getApplicationContext(), R.raw.wombling_song);
        mediaPlayer.start();
    }
}
```

This uses the Android MediaPlayer class to play a file called
wombling_song.mp3. The file is located in the res/raw folder.

← This is the activity.

```java
public class MainActivity extends Activity {

    @Override
    protected void onCreate(Bundle savedInstanceState) {
        super.onCreate(savedInstanceState);
        setContentView(R.layout.activity_main);
    }


    public void onClick(View view) {
        Intent intent = new Intent(this, ...............................................);

        ............................... (intent);
    }
}
```

You won't need to use
all of these magnets.

| IntentService | onHandleIntent | startActivity | startService |
| WombleService.class | Underground | Overground | WombleService |

Service Magnets Solution

Below is most of the code needed to create a started service called
WombleService that plays a *.mp3* file in the background, and an
activity that uses it. See if you can finish off the code.

This is the service. It extends the IntentService class.

```java
public class WombleService extends  IntentService  {

    public WombleService() {
        super("WombleService");
    }
```
The code needs to run in the onHandleIntent() method.
```java
    @Override
    protected void  onHandleIntent  (Intent intent) {
        MediaPlayer mediaPlayer =
                MediaPlayer.create(getApplicationContext(), R.raw.wombling_song);
        mediaPlayer.start();
    }
}
```

This is the activity.

```java
public class MainActivity extends Activity {

    @Override
    protected void onCreate(Bundle savedInstanceState) {
        super.onCreate(savedInstanceState);
        setContentView(R.layout.activity_main);
    }
```
Create an explicit intent directed at WombleService.class.
```java
    public void onClick(View view) {
        Intent intent = new Intent(this,  WombleService.class );
         startService  (intent);
    }
}
```
Start the service.

You didn't need to use these magnets.

`startActivity`

`Underground`   `Overground`   `WombleService`

Android has a built-in notification service

We're going to change our Joke app so that our message gets displayed in a **notification**. Notifications are messages that are displayed outside the app's user interface. When a notification gets issued, it's displayed as an icon in the notification area of the status bar. You can see details of the notification in the notification drawer, which you access by swiping down from the top of the screen:

Heads—up notifications are temporarily displayed in a floating window at the top of the screen.

These are notification icons.

This is the notification drawer.

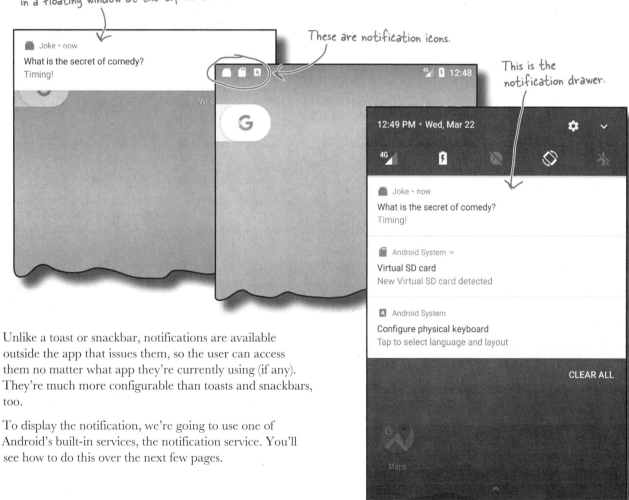

Unlike a toast or snackbar, notifications are available outside the app that issues them, so the user can access them no matter what app they're currently using (if any). They're much more configurable than toasts and snackbars, too.

To display the notification, we're going to use one of Android's built-in services, the notification service. You'll see how to do this over the next few pages.

We'll use notifications from the AppCompat Support Library

We're going to create notifications using classes from the AppCompat Support Library so that our notifications will work consistently across a wide range of Android versions. While it's possible to create notifications using classes from the main release of Android, recent changes to these classes mean that the newest features won't be available on older versions.

Before we can use the notification classes from the Support Library, we need to add it to our project as a dependency. To do this, choose File→Project Structure, then click on the app module and choose Dependencies. Android Studio may have already added the AppCompat Support Library for you automatically. If so, you will see it listed as appcompat-v7. If it hasn't been added, you will need to add it yourself. Click on the "+" button at the bottom or right side of the screen, choose the Library Dependency option, select the appcompat-v7 library, and then click on the OK button. Click on OK again to save your changes and close the Project Structure window.

> Use notifications from the AppCompat Support Library to allow apps running on older versions of Android to include the newest features.

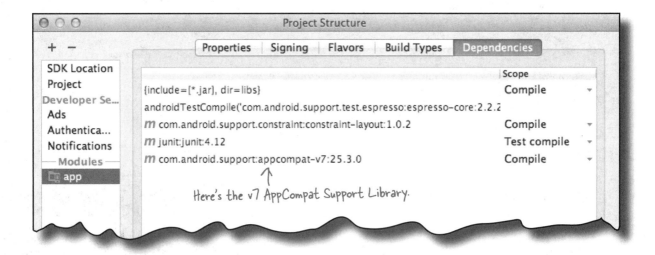

Here's the v7 AppCompat Support Library.

To get `DelayedMessageService` to display a notification, there are three things we need to do: create a notification builder, tell the notification to start `MainActivity` when it's clicked, and issue the notification. We'll build up the code over the next few pages, then show you the full code at the end.

First create a notification builder

The first thing we need to do is create a notification builder. This enables you to build a notification with specific content and features.

The NotificationCompat class comes from the AppCompat Support Library.

Each notification you create must include a small icon, a title, and some text as a bare minimum. Here's the code to do that:

```
NotificationCompat.Builder builder = new NotificationCompat.Builder(this)
    .setSmallIcon(android.R.drawable.sym_def_app_icon)
    .setContentTitle(getString(R.string.question))
    .setContentText(text);
```

This displays a small icon, in this case a built-in Android icon.

Set the title and text.

To add more features to the notification, you simply add the appropriate method call to the builder. As an example, here's how you additionally specify that the notification should have a high priority, vibrate the device when it appears, and disappear when the user clicks on it:

```
NotificationCompat.Builder builder = new NotificationCompat.Builder(this)
    .setSmallIcon(android.R.drawable.sym_def_app_icon)
    .setContentTitle(getString(R.string.question))
    .setContentText(text)
    .setPriority(NotificationCompat.PRIORITY_HIGH)
    .setVibrate(new long[] {0, 1000})
    .setAutoCancel(true);
```

Make it a high priority and vibrate the device.

Simply chain the method calls together to add more features to the notification.

This makes the notification disappear when the user clicks on it.

Wait for 0 milliseconds before vibrating the device for 1,000 milliseconds.

These are just some of the properties that you can set. You can also set properties such as the notification's visibility to control whether it appears on the device lock screen, a number to display in case you want to send many notifications from the same app, and whether it should play a sound. You can find out more about these properties (and many others) here:

https://developer.android.com/reference/android/support/v4/app/NotificationCompat.Builder.html

Next, we'll add an action to the notification to tell it which activity to start when it's clicked.

> **You create a heads-up notification (one that appears in a small floating window) by setting its priority to high, and making it vibrate the device or play a sound.**

Add an action to tell the notification which activity to start when clicked

When you create a notification, it's a good idea to add an action to it, specifying which activity in your app should be displayed when the user clicks on the notification. As an example, an email app might issue a notification when the user receives a new email, and display the contents of that email when the user clicks on it. In our particular case, we're going to start MainActivity.

You add an action by creating a **pending intent** to start an activity, which you then add to the notification. A pending intent is an intent that your app can pass to other applications. The application can then submit the intent on your app's behalf at a later time.

To create a pending intent, you first create an explicit intent directed to the activity you want to start when the notification is clicked. In our case, we want to start MainActivity, so we use:

This is a normal intent that starts MainActivity.

```
Intent actionIintent = new Intent(this, MainActivity.class);
```

We then use that intent to create a pending intent using the PendingIntent.getActivity() method.

```
PendingIntent actionPendingIntent = PendingIntent.getActivity(
    this,
    0,
    actionIntent,
    PendingIntent.FLAG_UPDATE_CURRENT);
```

This is a flag that's used if you ever need to retrieve the pending intent. We don't need to, so we're setting it to 0.

A context, in this case the current service.

This is the intent we created above.

This means that if there's a matching pending intent, it will be updated.

The getActivity() method takes four parameters: a context (usually this), an int request code, the explicit intent we defined above, and a flag that specifies the pending intent's behavior. In the above code, we've used a flag of FLAG_UPDATE_CURRENT. This means that if a matching pending intent already exists, its extra data will be updated with the contents of the new intent. Other options are FLAG_CANCEL_CURRENT (cancel any existing matching pending intents before generating a new one), FLAG_NO_CREATE (don't create the pending intent if there's no matching existing one), and FLAG_ONE_SHOT (you can only use the pending intent once).

Once you've created the pending intent, you add it to the notification using the notification builder setContentIntent() method:

```
builder.setContentIntent(actionPendingIntent);
```

This adds the pending intent to the notification.

This tells the notification to start the activity specified in the intent when the user clicks on the notification.

Issue the notification using the built-in notification service

Finally, you issue the notification using Android's notification service.

To do this, you first need to get a **NotificationManager**. You do this by calling the getSystemService() method, passing it a parameter of NOTIFICATION_SERVICE:

```
NotificationManager notificationManager =
                (NotificationManager) getSystemService(NOTIFICATION_SERVICE);
```

This gives you access to Android's notification service.

You then use the notification manager to issue the notification by calling its **notify()** method. This takes two parameters: a notification ID and a Notification object.

The notification ID is used to identify the notification. If you send another notification with the same ID, it will replace the current notification. This is useful if you want to update an existing notification with new information.

You create the Notification object by calling the notification builder's **build()** method. The notification it builds includes all the content and features you've specified via the notification builder.

Here's the code to issue the notification:

```
public static final int NOTIFICATION_ID = 5453;

...

NotificationManager notificationManager =
                (NotificationManager) getSystemService(NOTIFICATION_SERVICE);
notificationManager.notify(NOTIFICATION_ID, builder.build());
```

This is an ID we'll use for the notification. It's a random number we made up.

Use the notification service to display the notification we created.

That's everything we need to create and issue notifications. We'll show you the full code for DelayedMessageService on the next page.

The full code for DelayedMessageService.java

Here's the full code for *DelayedMessageService.java*. It
now uses a notification to display a message to the user.
Update your code to match ours:

```
package com.hfad.joke;

import android.app.IntentService;
import android.content.Intent;
import android.util.Log;          ← Delete this line.
import android.support.v4.app.NotificationCompat;
import android.app.PendingIntent;
import android.app.NotificationManager;
```

> We're using these extra classes,
> so we need to import them.

Joke

app/src/main

java

com.hfad.joke

**DelayedMessage
Service.java**

```
public class DelayedMessageService extends IntentService {

    public static final String EXTRA_MESSAGE = "message";
    public static final int NOTIFICATION_ID = 5453;

    public DelayedMessageService() {
        super("DelayedMessageService");
    }
```

> This is used to identify the
> notification. It could be any number;
> we just decided on 5453.

```
    @Override
    protected void onHandleIntent(Intent intent) {
        synchronized (this) {
            try {
                wait(10000);
            } catch (InterruptedException e) {
                e.printStackTrace();
            }
        }
        String text = intent.getStringExtra(EXTRA_MESSAGE);
        showText(text);
    }
```

The code continues →
on the next page.

The DelayedMessageService.java code (continued)

Joke

app/src/main

java

com.hfad.joke

DelayedMessage
Service.java

```java
private void showText(final String text) {
    Log.v("DelayedMessageService", "The message is: " + text);

    //Create a notification builder
    NotificationCompat.Builder builder =
            new NotificationCompat.Builder(this)
                    .setSmallIcon(android.R.drawable.sym_def_app_icon)
                    .setContentTitle(getString(R.string.question))
                    .setContentText(text)
                    .setPriority(NotificationCompat.PRIORITY_HIGH)
                    .setVibrate(new long[] {0, 1000})
                    .setAutoCancel(true);

    //Create an action
    Intent actionIntent = new Intent(this, MainActivity.class);
    PendingIntent actionPendingIntent = PendingIntent.getActivity(
                    this,
                    0,
                    actionIntent,
                    PendingIntent.FLAG_UPDATE_CURRENT);
    builder.setContentIntent(actionPendingIntent);

    //Issue the notification
    NotificationManager notificationManager =
            (NotificationManager) getSystemService(NOTIFICATION_SERVICE);
    notificationManager.notify(NOTIFICATION_ID, builder.build());
}
}
```

Use a notification builder to specify the content and features of the notification.

Create an intent.

Use the intent to create a pending intent.

Add the pending intent to the notification.

Display the notification using a notification manager.

That's all the code we need for our started service. Let's go through what happens when the code runs.

What happens when you run the code

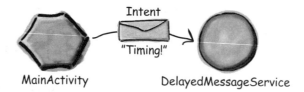

Before you try running the updated app, let's go through what
happens when the code runs:

1 **MainActivity starts DelayedMessageService by calling startService()
and passing it an intent.**

The intent contains the message `MainActivity` wants
`DelayedMessageService` to display.

Intent

"Timing!"

MainActivity   DelayedMessageService

2 **DelayedMessageService waits for 10 seconds.**

1...2...3...4...

DelayedMessageService

3 **DelayedMessageService creates a notification builder and sets
details of how the notification should be configured.**

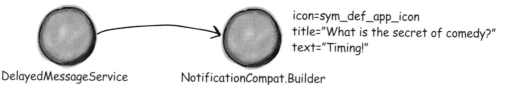

icon=sym_def_app_icon
title="What is the secret of comedy?"
text="Timing!"

DelayedMessageService   NotificationCompat.Builder

4 **DelayedMessageService creates an intent for MainActivity, which it
uses to create a pending intent.**

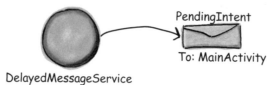

PendingIntent

To: MainActivity

DelayedMessageService

Log
Display notification

The story continues

⑤ **DelayedMessageService adds the pending intent to the notification builder.**

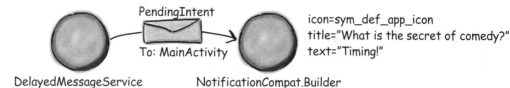

⑥ **DelayedMessageService creates a NotificationManager object and calls its notify() method.**
The notification service displays the notification built by the notification builder.

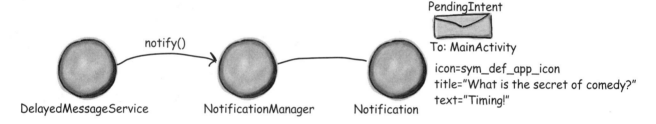

⑦ **When the user clicks on the notification, the notification uses its pending intent to start MainActivity.**

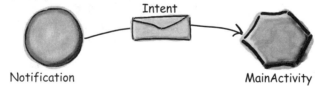

Now that we've gone through what the code does, let's take the app for a test drive.

Test drive the app

When you click on the button in MainActivity, a notification is displayed after 10 seconds. You'll receive the notification irrespective of which app you're in.

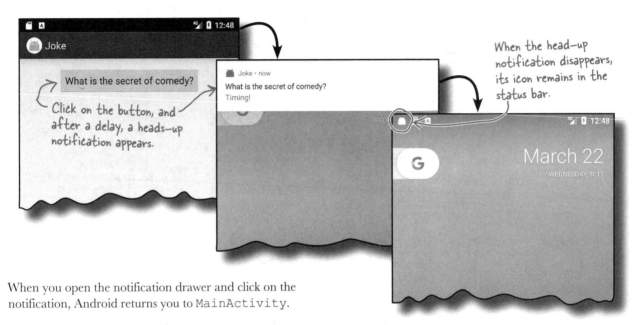

Click on the button, and after a delay, a heads-up notification appears.

When the head-up notification disappears, its icon remains in the status bar.

When you open the notification drawer and click on the notification, Android returns you to MainActivity.

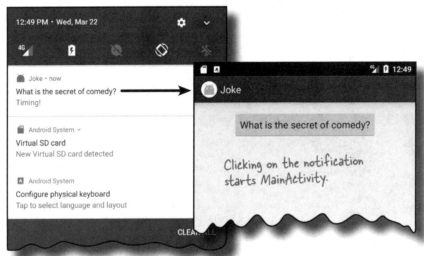

Clicking on the notification starts MainActivity.

You now know how to create a started service that displays a notification using the Android notification service. In the next chapter, we'll look at how you create a bound service.

Your Android Toolbox

You've got Chapter 18 under your belt and now you've added started services to your toolbox.

BULLET POINTS

- A **service** is an application component that can perform tasks in the background. It doesn't have a user interface.

- A **started service** can run in the background indefinitely, even when the activity that started it is destroyed. Once the operation is done, it stops itself.

- A **bound service** is bound to another component such as an activity. The activity can interact with it and get results.

- A **scheduled service** is one that's scheduled to run at a particular time.

- You can create a simple started service by extending the **IntentService** class, overriding its onHandleIntent() method and adding a public constructor.

- You declare services in *AndroidManifest.xml* using the **<service>** element.

- You start a started service using the **startService()** method.

- When a started service is created, its onCreate() method gets called, followed by onStartCommand(). If the service is an IntentService, onHandleIntent() is then called in a separate thread. When the service has finished running, onDestroy() gets called before the service is destroyed.

- The IntentService class inherits lifecycle methods from the **Service** class.

- You log messages using the **Android.util.Log** class. You can view these messages in the logcat in Android Studio.

- You create a notification using a **notification builder**. Each notification must include a small icon, a title, and some text as a bare minimum.

- A **heads-up** notification has its priority set to high, and vibrates the device or plays a sound when it's issued.

- You tell the notification which activity to start when it's clicked by creating a **pending intent** and adding it to the notification as an action.

- You issue the notification using a **notification manager**. You create a notification manager using Android's notification service.

> You can download the full code for the chapter from https://tinyurl.com/HeadFirstAndroid.

19 bound services and permissions

Bound Together

Today, CALL_PHONE permission. Tomorrow, complete world domination. Bwahaha...

Started services are great for background operations, but what if you need a service that's more interactive? In this chapter you'll discover how to create a **bound service**, *a type of service your activity can interact with*. You'll see how to **bind** to the service when you need it, and how to **unbind** from it when you're done to save resources. You'll find out how to use **Android's Location Services** to get *location updates from your device GPS*. Finally, you'll discover how to use **Android's permission model**, including *handling runtime permission requests*.

Bound services are bound to other components

As you saw in Chapter 18, a started service is one that starts when it's passed an intent. It runs code in the background, and stops when the operation is complete. It continues running even if the component that starts it gets destroyed.

A **bound service** is one that's bound to another application component, such as an activity. Unlike a started service, the component can interact with the bound service and call its methods.

To see this in action, we're going to create a new odometer app that uses a bound service. We'll use Android's location service to track the distance traveled:

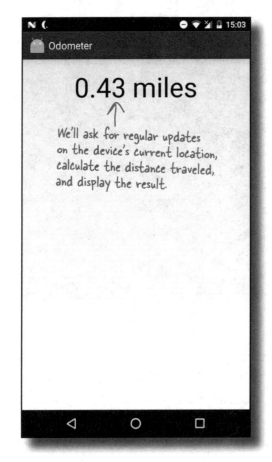

We'll ask for regular updates on the device's current location, calculate the distance traveled, and display the result.

On the next page we'll look at the steps we'll go through to create the app.

Here's what we're going to do

We're going to build the app in three main steps:

1 **Create a basic version of a bound service called OdometerService.**
We'll add a method to it, `getDistance()`, which will return a random number.

OdometerService

2 **Get an activity, MainActivity, to bind to OdometerService and call its getDistance() method.**
We'll call the method every second, and update a text view in `MainActivity` with the results.

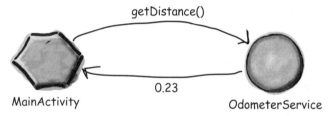

getDistance()

MainActivity   0.23   OdometerService

3 **Update OdometerService to use Android's Location Services.**
The service will get updates on the user's current location, and use these to calculate the distance traveled.

Are we nearly there yet?

OdometerService

Create a new Odometer project

We'll start by creating the project. Create a new Android project for an application named "Odometer" with a company domain of "hfad.com", making the package name `com.hfad.odometer`. The minimum SDK should be API 19 so that it will work with most devices. You'll need an empty activity named "MainActivity" and a layout named "activity_main" so that your code matches ours. **Make sure that you uncheck the Backwards Compatibility (AppCompat) option when you create the activity.**

Create a new service

OdometerService
MainActivity
Location Services

You create a bound service by extending the **Service** class. This class is more general than the `IntentService` class we used in Chapter 18, which is used for started services. Extending `Service` gives you more flexibility, but requires more code.

We're going to add a new bound service to our project, so switch to the Project view of Android Studio's explorer, click on the `com.hfad.odometer` package in the *app/src/main/java* folder, go to File→New..., and select the Service option. When prompted, choose the option to create a new Service (not an Intent Service), and name the service "OdometerService". Uncheck the "Exported" option, as this only needs to be true if you want services outside this app to access the service. Make sure that the "checkednabled" option is checked; if it isn't, the activity won't be able to run the app. Then replace the code in *OdometerService.java* with this (shown here in bold):

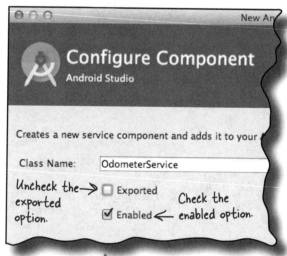

Some versions of Android Studio may ask you what the source language should be. If prompted, select the option for Java.

```
package com.hfad.odometer;

import android.app.Service;
import android.content.Intent;
import android.os.IBinder;

public class OdometerService extends Service {

    @Override
    public IBinder onBind(Intent intent) {
        //Code to bind the service
    }

}
```

The class extends the Service class.

The onBind() method is called when a component wants to bind to the service.

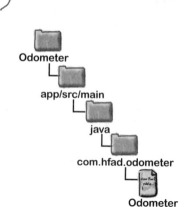

The above code implements one method, `onBind()`, which gets called when a component, such as an activity, wants to bind to the service. It has one parameter, an `Intent`, and returns an `IBinder` object.

`IBinder` is an interface that's used to bind your service to the activity, and you need to provide an implementation of it in your service code. We'll look at how you do this next.

Implement a binder

You implement the `IBinder` by adding a new inner class to your
service code that extends the `Binder` class (which implements the
`IBinder` interface). This inner class needs to include a method
that activities can use to get a reference to the bound service.

We're going to define a binder called `OdometerBinder`
that `MainActivity` can use to get a reference to
`OdometerService`. Here's the code we'll use to define it:

```
public class OdometerBinder extends Binder {
    OdometerService getOdometer() {
        return OdometerService.this;
    }
}
```

When you create a bound service, you need to provide a Binder implementation.

The activity will use this method to get a reference to the OdometerService.

We need to return an instance of the `OdometerBinder` in
`OdometerService`'s `onBind()` method. To do this, we'll create
a new private variable for the binder, instantiate it, and return it in
the `onBind()` method. Update your *OdometerService.java* code to
include our changes below:

```
...
import android.os.Binder;

public class OdometerService extends Service {

    private final IBinder binder = new OdometerBinder();

    public class OdometerBinder extends Binder {
        OdometerService getOdometer() {
            return OdometerService.this;
        }
    }

    @Override
    public IBinder onBind(Intent intent) {
        return binder;
    }
}
```

We're using this extra class, so we need to import it.

We're using a private final variable for our IBinder object

This is our IBinder implementation.

Return the IBinder.

Odometer
app/src/main
java
com.hfad.odometer
Odometer
Service.java

We've now written all the service code we need to allow
`MainActivity` to bind to `OdometerService`. Next, we'll add
a new method to the service to make it return a random number.

Add a getDistance() method to the service

We're going to add a method to OdometerService called getDistance(), which our activity will call. We'll get it to return a random number for now, and later on we'll update it to use Android's location services.

Here's the full code for *OdometerService.java* including this change; update your version to match ours:

```
package com.hfad.odometer;

import android.app.Service;
import android.content.Intent;
import android.os.IBinder;
import android.os.Binder;
import java.util.Random;
```
← We're using this extra class, so we need to import it.

Odometer
└ app/src/main
  └ java
    └ com.hfad.odometer
      └ Odometer
        Service.java

```
public class OdometerService extends Service {

    private final IBinder binder = new OdometerBinder();
    private final Random random = new Random();
```
← We'll use a Random() object to generate random numbers.

```
    public class OdometerBinder extends Binder {
        OdometerService getOdometer() {
            return OdometerService.this;
        }
    }


    @Override
    public IBinder onBind(Intent intent) {
        return binder;
    }
```
← Add the getDistance() method.

```
    public double getDistance() {
        return random.nextDouble();
    }
}
```
← Return a random double.

Next we'll update MainActivity so that it uses OdometerService.

Update MainActivity's layout

The next step in creating our app is to get MainActivity to
bind to OdometerService and call its getDistance()
method. We're going to start by adding a text view to
MainActivity's layout. This will display the number
returned by OdometerService's getDistance() method.

Update your version of *activity_main.xml* to reflect our changes:

```xml
<?xml version="1.0" encoding="utf-8"?>
<LinearLayout
    xmlns:android="http://schemas.android.com/apk/res/android"
    xmlns:tools="http://schemas.android.com/tools"
    android:layout_width="match_parent"
    android:layout_height="match_parent"
    tools:context="com.hfad.odometer.MainActivity"
    android:orientation="vertical"
    android:padding="16dp">

    <TextView
        android:id="@+id/distance"
        android:layout_width="wrap_content"
        android:layout_height="wrap_content"
        android:textSize="48sp"
        android:layout_gravity="center_horizontal"
        android:textAppearance="?android:attr/textAppearanceLarge" />

</LinearLayout>
```

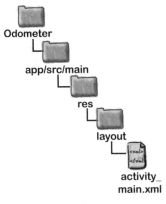

Odometer
app/src/main
res
layout
activity_
main.xml

We'll use the TextView to display
the number returned by the
OdometerService getDistance() method.

Now that we've added a text view to MainActivity's layout,
we'll update its activity code. Let's go through the changes we
need to make.

Odometer

0.43 miles

What MainActivity needs to do

To get an activity to connect to a bound service and call its methods,
there are a few steps you need to perform:

1   **Create a ServiceConnection.**
This uses the service's `IBinder` object to form a connection with the service.

2   **Bind the activity to the service.**
Once you've bound it to the service, you can call the service's methods directly.

3   **Interact with the service.**
In our case, we'll use the service's `getDistance()` method to
update the activity's text view.

When your activity is bound
to the service, you can use it
to update your activity.

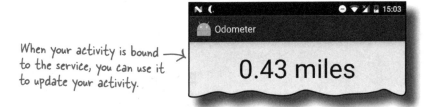

4   **Unbind from the service when you've finished with it.**
When the service is no longer used, Android destroys the service to free up resources.

We'll go through these steps with `MainActivity`, starting with
creating the `ServiceConnection`.

Create a ServiceConnection

A **ServiceConnection** is an interface that enables your activity to bind to a service. It has two methods that you need to define: onServiceConnected() and onServiceDisconnected(). The onServiceConnected() method is called when a connection to the service is established, and onServiceDisconnected() is called when it disconnects.

We need to add a ServiceConnection to MainActivity. Here's what the basic code looks like; update your version of *MainActivity.java* to matches ours:

```java
package com.hfad.odometer;

import android.app.Activity;
import android.os.Bundle;
import android.content.ServiceConnection;
import android.os.IBinder;
import android.content.ComponentName;

public class MainActivity extends Activity {

    private ServiceConnection connection = new ServiceConnection() {
        @Override
        public void onServiceConnected(ComponentName componentName, IBinder binder) {
            //Code that runs when the service is connected
        }
        @Override
        public void onServiceDisconnected(ComponentName componentName) {
            //Code that runs when the service is disconnected
        }
    };

    @Override
    protected void onCreate(Bundle savedInstanceState) {
        super.onCreate(savedInstanceState);
        setContentView(R.layout.activity_main);
    }
}
```

We're using these classes, so we need to import them.

We're using an Activity here, but you could use AppCompatActivity instead.

Create a Service Connection object.

You need to define these methods.

Add MainActivity's onCreate() method.

Odometer
app/src/main
java
com.hfad.odometer
Main
Activity.java

We'll update the onServiceConnected() and onServiceDisconnected() methods on the next page.

The onServiceConnected() method

As we said on the previous page, the `onServiceConnected()`
method is called when a connection is established between
the activity and the service. It takes two parameters: a
`ComponentName` object that describes the service that's been
connected to, and an `IBinder` object that's defined by the service:

> *The ComponentName identifies
> the service. It includes the
> service package and class names.*

```java
@Override
public void onServiceConnected(ComponentName componentName, IBinder binder) {
    //Code that runs when the service is connected

}
```

> *This is an IBinder defined by
> the service. We added one to
> OdometerService earlier.*

There are two things we need the `onServiceConnected()`
method to do:

⭐ Use its `IBinder` parameter to get a reference to the service we're connected to,
in this case `OdometerService`. We can do this by casting the `IBinder` to an
`OdometerService.OdometerBinder` (as this is the type of `IBinder` we
defined in `OdometerService`) and calling its `getOdometer()` method.

⭐ Record that the activity is bound to the service.

Here's the code to do these things (update your version of
MainActivity.java to include our changes):

```java
public class MainActivity extends Activity {

    private OdometerService odometer;
    private boolean bound = false;

    private ServiceConnection connection = new ServiceConnection() {
        @Override
        public void onServiceConnected(ComponentName componentName, IBinder binder) {
            OdometerService.OdometerBinder odometerBinder =
                    (OdometerService.OdometerBinder) binder;
            odometer = odometerBinder.getOdometer();
            bound = true;
        }
        ...
    };

    ...
}
```

> *Add these variables to record
> a reference to the service, and
> whether the activity is bound to it.*

> *Use the IBinder to get a
> reference to the service.*

> *The activity is bound to the service,
> so set the bound variable to true.*

Odometer
app/src/main
java
com.hfad.odometer
**Main
Activity.java**

The onServiceDisconnected() method

The onServiceDisconnected() method is called when the
service and the activity are disconnected. It takes one parameter, a
ComponentName object that describes the service:

```
@Override
public void onServiceDisconnected(ComponentName componentName) {
    //Code that runs when the service is disconnected
}
```

There's only one thing we need the
onServiceDisconnected() method to do when it's called:
record that the activity is no longer bound to the service. Here's
the code to do that; update your version of *MainActivity.java* to
match ours:

```
public class MainActivity extends Activity {

    private OdometerService odometer;
    private boolean bound = false;

    private ServiceConnection connection = new ServiceConnection() {
        @Override
        public void onServiceConnected(ComponentName componentName, IBinder binder) {
            OdometerService.OdometerBinder odometerBinder =
                    (OdometerService.OdometerBinder) binder;
            odometer = odometerBinder.getOdometer();
            bound = true;
        }
        @Override
        public void onServiceDisconnected(ComponentName componentName) {
            bound = false;
        }
    };
    ...
}
```

*Set bound to false, as MainActivity is
no longer bound to OdometerService.*

Odometer

app/src/main

java

com.hfad.odometer

**Main
Activity.java**

Next we'll look at how you bind to and unbind from the service.

Use bindService() to bind the service

When you bind your activity to a service, you usually do it in one of two places:

⭐ In the activity's `onStart()` method when the activity becomes visible. This is appropriate if you only need to interact with the service when it's visible.

⭐ In the activity's `onCreate()` method when the activity gets created. Do this if you need to receive updates from the service even when the activity's stopped.

You don't usually bind to a service in the activity's onResume() method in order to keep the processing done in this method to a minimum.

In our case, we only need to display updates from `OdometerService` when `MainActivity` is visible, so we'll bind to the service in its `onStart()` method.

To bind to the service, you first create an explicit intent that's directed at the service you want to bind to. You then use the activity's `bindService()` method to bind to the service, passing it the intent, the `ServiceConnection` object defined by the service, and a flag to describe how you want to bind.

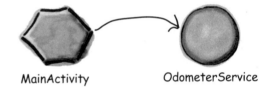

MainActivity   OdometerService

To see how you do this, here's the code you'd use to bind `MainActivity` to `OdometerService` (we'll add this code to *MainActivity.java* a few pages ahead):

```java
@Override
protected void onStart() {
    super.onStart();
    Intent intent = new Intent(this, OdometerService.class);
    bindService(intent, connection, Context.BIND_AUTO_CREATE);
}
```

This is an intent directed to the OdometerService.

This is the ServiceConnection object.

The bindService() method uses the intent and service connection to bind the activity to the service.

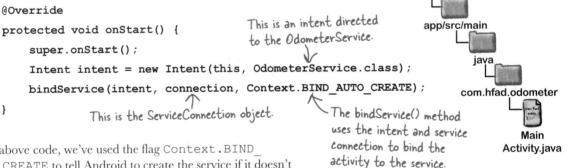

Odometer
app/src/main
java
com.hfad.odometer
Main Activity.java

In the above code, we've used the flag `Context.BIND_AUTO_CREATE` to tell Android to create the service if it doesn't already exist. There are other flags you can use instead; you can see all the available ones in the Android documentation here:

https://developer.android.com/reference/android/content/Context.html

Next, we'll look at how you unbind the activity from the service.

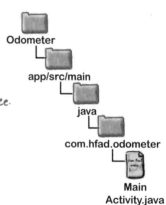

Use unbindService() to unbind from the service

When you unbind your activity from a service, you usually add the code to do so to your activity's onStop() or onDestroy() method. The method you use depends on where you put your bindService() code:

⭐ If you bound to the service in your activity's onStart() method, unbind from it in the onStop() method.

⭐ If you bound to the service in your activity's onCreate() method, unbind from it in the onDestroy() method.

In our case, we used MainActivity's onStart() method to bind to OdometerService, so we'll unbind from it in the activity's onStop() method.

You unbind from a service using the unbindService() method. The method takes one parameter, the ServiceConnection object. Here's the code that we need to add to MainActivity (we'll add this code to *MainActivity.java* a few pages ahead):

```java
@Override
protected void onStop() {
    super.onStop();
    if (bound) {
        unbindService(connection);
        bound = false;
    }
}
```

This uses the ServiceConnection object to unbind from the service.

When we unbind, we'll set bound to false.

Odometer
└ app/src/main
  └ java
    └ com.hfad.odometer
      └ Main
        Activity.java

In the above code we're using the value of the bound variable to test whether or not we need to unbind from the service. If bound is true, this means MainActivity is bound to OdometerService. We need to unbind the service, and set the value of bound to false.

So far we have an activity that binds to the service when the activity starts, and unbinds from it when the activity stops. The final thing we need to do is get MainActivity to call OdometerService's getDistance() method, and display its value.

Call OdometerService's getDistance() method

Once your activity is bound to the service, you can call its methods. We're going to call the OdometerService's getDistance() method every second, and update MainActivity's text view with its value.

To do this, we're going to write a new method called displayDistance(). This will work in a similar way to the runTimer() code we used in Chapters 4 and 11.

Here's our displayDistance() method. We'll add it to *MainActivity.java* a couple of pages ahead:

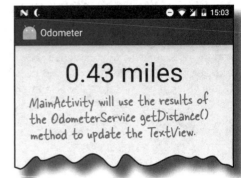

MainActivity will use the results of the OdometerService getDistance() method to update the TextView.

```java
private void displayDistance() {
    final TextView distanceView = (TextView) findViewById(R.id.distance);    ← Get the TextView.
    final Handler handler = new Handler();    ← Create a new Handler.
    handler.post(new Runnable() {    ← Call the Handler's post() method, passing in a new Runnable.
        @Override
        public void run() {
            double distance = 0.0;
            if (bound && odometer != null) {        If we've got a reference to the OdometerService
                distance = odometer.getDistance();   and we're bound to it, call getDistance().
            }
            String distanceStr = String.format(Locale.getDefault(),
                                    "%1$,.2f miles", distance);
            distanceView.setText(distanceStr);         You could use a String resource for "miles",
            handler.postDelayed(this, 1000);           but we've hardcoded it here for simplicity.
        }
    });
}
```

Post the code in the Runnable to be run again after a delay of 1 second. As this line of code is included in the Runnable run() method, it will run every second (with a slight lag).

We'll call the displayDistance() method in MainActivity's onCreate() method so that it starts running when the activity gets created (we'll add this code to *MainActivity.java* on the next page):

```java
@Override
protected void onCreate(Bundle savedInstanceState) {
    ...
    displayDistance();    ← Call displayDistance() in MainActivity's
}                            onCreate() method to kick it off.
```

We'll show you the full code for MainActivity on the next page.

The full MainActivity.java code

Here's the complete code for *MainActivity.java*; make sure your
version of the code matches ours:

```java
package com.hfad.odometer;

import android.app.Activity;
import android.os.Bundle;
import android.content.ServiceConnection;
import android.os.IBinder;
import android.content.ComponentName;
import android.content.Context;
import android.content.Intent;
import android.os.Handler;
import android.widget.TextView;
import java.util.Locale;
```

We're using these extra classes,
so we need to import them.

Odometer
└ app/src/main
  └ java
    └ com.hfad.odometer
      **Main
      Activity.java**

```java
public class MainActivity extends Activity {

    private OdometerService odometer;
```
← Use this for the OdometerService.
```java
    private boolean bound = false;
```
← Use this to store whether or not the
activity's bound to the service.
```java
    private ServiceConnection connection = new ServiceConnection() {
```
← We need to
define a
ServiceConnection.
```java
        @Override
        public void onServiceConnected(ComponentName componentName, IBinder binder) {
            OdometerService.OdometerBinder odometerBinder =
                    (OdometerService.OdometerBinder) binder;
            odometer = odometerBinder.getOdometer();
```
← Get a reference to the
OdometerService when the
service is connected.
```java
            bound = true;
        }
        @Override
        public void onServiceDisconnected(ComponentName componentName) {
            bound = false;
        }
    };

    @Override
    protected void onCreate(Bundle savedInstanceState) {
        super.onCreate(savedInstanceState);
        setContentView(R.layout.activity_main);
        displayDistance();
```
← Call the displayDistance() method
when the activity is created.
```java
    }
```

The code continues →
on the next page.

The MainActivity.java code (continued)

OdometerService
MainActivity
Location Services

```java
@Override
protected void onStart() {
    super.onStart();
    Intent intent = new Intent(this, OdometerService.class);
    bindService(intent, connection, Context.BIND_AUTO_CREATE);
}
```
Bind the service when the activity starts.

```java
@Override
protected void onStop() {
    super.onStop();
    if (bound) {
        unbindService(connection);
        bound = false;
    }
}
```
Unbind the service when the activity stops.

Display the value returned by the service's getDistance() method.

```java
private void displayDistance() {
    final TextView distanceView = (TextView) findViewById(R.id.distance);
    final Handler handler = new Handler();
    handler.post(new Runnable() {
        @Override
        public void run() {
            double distance = 0.0;
            if (bound && odometer != null) {
                distance = odometer.getDistance();
            }
            String distanceStr = String.format(Locale.getDefault(),
                                               "%1$,.2f miles", distance);
            distanceView.setText(distanceStr);
            handler.postDelayed(this, 1000);
        }
    });
}
```
Call OdometerService's getDistance() method.

Update the TextView's value every second.

Odometer
└─ **app/src/main**
   └─ **java**
      └─ **com.hfad.odometer**
         └─ **Main Activity.java**

That's all the code you need to get `MainActivity` to use
`OdometerService`. Let's go through what happens when
you run the code.

What happens when you run the code

Before you see the app up and running, let's walk through what the code does.

1 When MainActivity is created, it creates a ServiceConnection object and calls the displayDistance() method.

2 MainActivity calls bindService() in its onStart() method.

The bindService() method includes an intent meant for OdometerService, and a reference to the ServiceConnection.

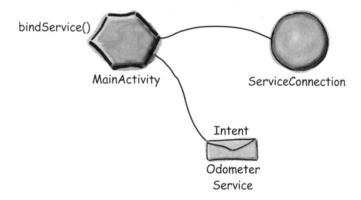

3 Android creates an instance of the OdometerService, and passes it the intent by calling its onBind() method.

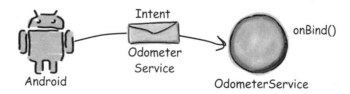

The story continues

OdometerService
MainActivity
Location Services

4 **OdometerService's onBind() method returns a Binder.**
The Binder is passed to MainActivity's ServiceConnection.

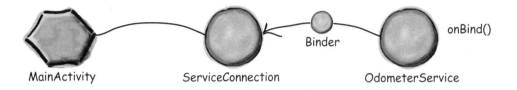

5 **The ServiceConnection uses the Binder to give MainActivity a reference to OdometerService.**

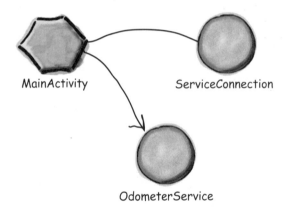

6 **MainActivity's displayDistance() method calls OdometerService's getDistance() method every second.**
OdometerService returns a random number to MainActivity, in this case 0.56.

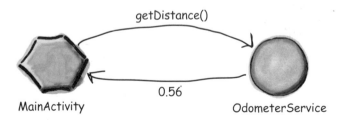

The story continues

7 When MainActivity stops, it disconnects from OdometerService by calling unbindService().

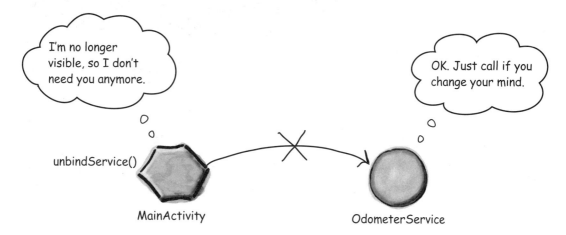

8 OdometerService is destroyed when MainActivity is no longer bound to it.

Now that you understand what happens when the code runs, let's take the app for a test drive.

Test drive the app

When we run the app, a random number is displayed in
MainActivity. This number changes every second.

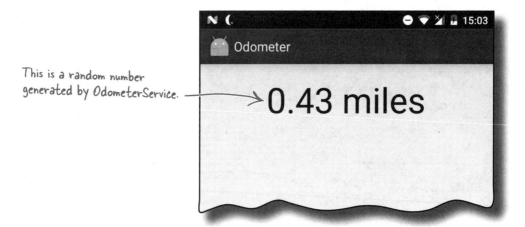

This is a random number
generated by OdometerService. → **0.43 miles**

We now have a working service that MainActivity
can bind to. We still need to change the service so that
the getDistance() method returns the distance
traveled instead of a random number. Before we do that,
however, we're going to take a closer look at how bound
services work behind the scenes.

there are no Dumb Questions

Q: What's the difference between a started service and a bound service again?

A: A started service is created when an activity (or some other component) calls startService(). It runs code in the background, and when it finishes running, the service is destroyed.

A bound service is created when the activity calls bindService(). The activity can interact with the service by calling its methods. The service is destroyed when no components are bound to it.

Q: Can a service be both started and bound?

A: Yes. In such cases, the service is created when startService() or bindService() is called. It's only destroyed when the code it was asked to run in the background has stopped running, and there are no components bound to it.

Creating this kind of started-and-bound service is more complicated than creating a service that's only started or bound. You can find out how to do it in the Android documentation: *https://developer.android. com/guide/components/services.html*.

Q: What's the difference between a Binder and an IBinder?

A: An IBinder is an *interface*. A Binder is a class that *implements* the IBinder interface.

Q: Can other apps use a service I create?

A: Yes, but only if you set its exported attribute to true in *AndroidManifest.xml*.

The states of a bound service

When an application component (such as an activity) binds to a service, the service moves between three states: being created, being bound, and being destroyed. A bound service spends most of its time in a bound state.

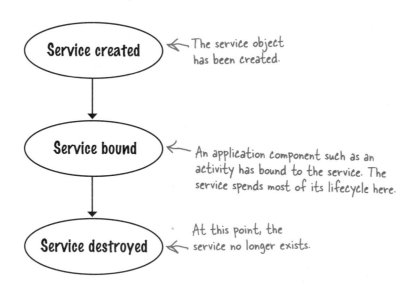

The service object has been created.

An application component such as an activity has bound to the service. The service spends most of its lifecycle here.

At this point, the service no longer exists.

Just like a started service, when a bound service is created, its onCreate() method gets called. As before, you override this method if you want to perform any tasks needed to set up the service.

The onBind() method runs when a component binds to the service. You override this method to return an IBinder object to the component, which it uses to get a reference to the service.

When all components have unbound from the service, its onUnbind() method is called.

Finally, the onDestroy() method is called when no components are bound to the service and it's about to be destroyed. As before, you override this method to perform any final cleanup tasks and free up resources.

We'll take a closer look at how these methods fit into the service states on the next page.

A bound service is destroyed when no components are bound to it.

The bound service lifecycle: from create to destroy

Here's a more detailed overview of the bound service lifecycle from birth to death.

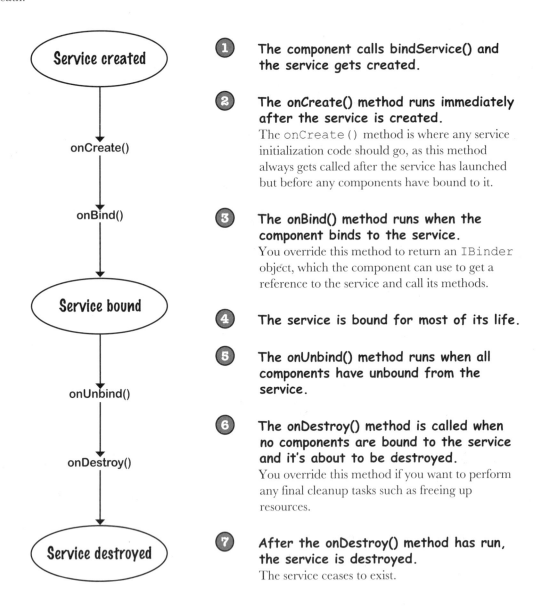

1 The component calls bindService() and the service gets created.

2 The onCreate() method runs immediately after the service is created.
The onCreate() method is where any service initialization code should go, as this method always gets called after the service has launched but before any components have bound to it.

3 The onBind() method runs when the component binds to the service.
You override this method to return an IBinder object, which the component can use to get a reference to the service and call its methods.

4 The service is bound for most of its life.

5 The onUnbind() method runs when all components have unbound from the service.

6 The onDestroy() method is called when no components are bound to the service and it's about to be destroyed.
You override this method if you want to perform any final cleanup tasks such as freeing up resources.

7 After the onDestroy() method has run, the service is destroyed.
The service ceases to exist.

Now that you have a better understanding of how bound services work, let's change our Odometer app so that it displays the actual distance traveled by the user.

We'll use Android's Location Services to return the distance traveled

We need to get our `OdometerService` to return the distance traveled in its `getDistance()` method. To do this, we'll use Android's Location Services. These allow you to get the user's current location, request periodic updates, and ask for an intent to be fired when the user comes within a certain radius of a particular location.

In our case, we're going to use the Location Services to get periodic updates on the user's current location. We'll use these to calculate the distance the user has traveled.

To do this, we'll perform the following steps:

1 **Declare we need permission to use the Location Services.**
Our app can only use the Location Services if the user grants our app permission to do so.

2 **Set up a location listener when the service is created.**
This will be used to `listen` for updates from the Location Services.

3 **Request location updates.**
We'll create a location manager, and use it to request updates on the user's current location.

4 **Calculate the distance traveled.**
We'll keep a running total of the distance traveled by the user, and return this distance in the `OdometerService`'s `getDistance()` method.

5 **Remove location updates just before the service is destroyed.**
This will free up system resources.

Before we start, we'll add the AppCompat Support Library to our project, as we'll need to use it in our code.

Add the AppCompat Support Library

OdometerService
MainActivity
Location Services

To get our location code working properly, there are a couple of classes we need to use from the AppCompat Support Library, so we'll add it to our project as a dependency. You do this in the same way that you did in earlier chapters. Choose File→Project Structure, then click on the app module and choose Dependencies. You'll be presented with the following screen:

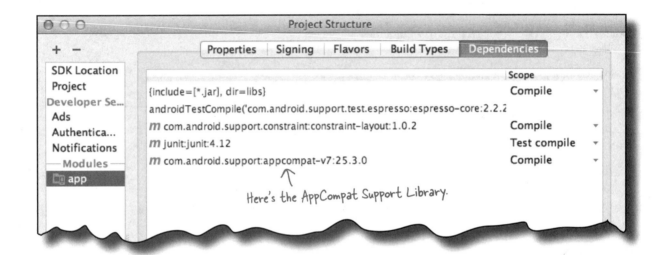

Here's the AppCompat Support Library.

Android Studio may have already added the AppCompat Support Library automatically. If so, you will see it listed as appcompat-v7, as shown above.

If the AppCompat Library isn't listed, you will need to add it yourself. To do this, click on the "+" button at the bottom or right side of the screen, choose the Library Dependency option, select the appcompat-v7 library, then click on the OK button. Click on OK again to save your changes and close the Project Structure window.

Next, we'll look at how to declare we need permission to use Android's Location Services.

Declare the permissions you need

Android allows you to perform many actions by default, but there are some that the user needs to give permission for in order for them to work. This can be because they use the user's private information, or could affect stored data or the way in which other apps function. Location Services is one of those things that the user needs to grant your app permission to use.

You declare the permissions your app requires in *AndroidManifest.xml* using the `<uses-permission>` element, which you add to the root `<manifest>` element. In our case, we need to access the user's precise location in order to display the distance traveled, so we need to declare the ACCESS_FINE_LOCATION permission. To do this, you add the following declaration to *AndroidManifest.xml* (update your version of the file to reflect this change):

```xml
<?xml version="1.0" encoding="utf-8"?>
<manifest xmlns:android="http://schemas.android.com/apk/res/android"
    package="com.hfad.odometer">
```

Declare we need a permission.

We need to know the user's precise location.

```xml
<uses-permission android:name="android.permission.ACCESS_FINE_LOCATION" />

    <application
        ...
    </application>
</manifest>
```

Odometer

app/src/main

AndroidManifest.xml

How the app uses the above declaration depends on your app's target SDK (usually the most recent version of Android) and the API level of the user's device:

⭐ If your target SDK is API level 23 or above, *and* the user's device is running 23 or above, **the app requests permission at runtime**. The user can deny or revoke permission, so whenever your code wants to use the thing that requires permission, it needs to check that permission is still granted. You'll find out how to do this later in the chapter.

⭐ If your target SDK is API level 22 or below, *or* the user's device is running 22 or below, **the app requests permission when it's installed**. If the user denies permission, the app isn't installed. Once granted, permission can't be revoked except by uninstalling the app.

Now that we've declared that our app needs to know the user's location, let's get to work on OdometerService.

Add a location listener to OdometerService

You create a location listener by implementing the
LocationListener interface. It has four methods that you need
to define: onLocationChanged(), onProviderEnabled(),
onProviderDisabled(), and onStatusChanged().
onLocationChanged() gets called when the user's location has changed.
We'll use this method later in the chapter to track the distance the user has
traveled. The onProviderEnabled(), onProviderDisabled(), and
onStatusChanged() methods are called when the location provider is ⟵ *We'll look at location*
enabled, when it is disabled, or when its status has changed, respectively. *providers on the next page.*

We need to set up a location listener when OdometerService is first created,
so we'll implement the interface in OdometerService's onCreate()
method. Update your version of *OdometerService.java* to include our changes below:

```
. . .
import android.os.Bundle;
import android.location.LocationListener;        We're using these
import android.location.Location;                extra classes, so we
                                                 need to import them.

public class OdometerService extends Service {
    . . .
    private LocationListener listener; ⟵  We're using a private variable
                                          for the LocationListener so
                                          other methods can access it.
    @Override
    public void onCreate() {
        super.onCreate();          Set up the LocationListener.
        listener = new LocationListener() {   The Location parameter describes the
            @Override                          current location. We'll use this later.
            public void onLocationChanged(Location location) {
                //Code to keep track of the distance
            }
                                We'll complete this code
            @Override           later in the chapter.
            public void onProviderDisabled(String arg0) {}
                                                              We won't use any of
            @Override                                         these methods in our
            public void onProviderEnabled(String arg0) {}     OdometerService code,
                                                              but we still need to
            @Override                                         declare them.
            public void onStatusChanged(String arg0, int arg1, Bundle bundle) {}
        };
    }
    . . .
}
```

app/src/main

java

com.hfad.odometer

*Odometer
Service.java*

We need a location manager and location provider

To get location updates, we need to do three things: create a location manager to get access to Android's Location Services, specify a location provider, and request that the location provider sends regular updates on the user's current location to the location listener we added on the previous page. We'll start by getting a location manager.

Create a location manager

You create a location manager in a similar way to how you created a notification manager in Chapter 18: using the getSystemService() method. Here's the code to create a location manager that you can use to access Android's Location Services (we'll add the code to OdometerService's onCreate() method later on):

This is how you access the Android location service.

```
LocationManager locManager = (LocationManager)getSystemService(Context.LOCATION_SERVICE);
```

We used the getSystemService() method in Chapter 18 to get access to Android's notification service.

Specify the location provider

Next, we need to specify the location provider, which is used to determine the user's location. There are two main options: GPS or network. The GPS option uses the device's GPS sensor to establish the user's location, whereas the network option looks at Wi-Fi, Bluetooth, or mobile networks.

Not all devices have both types of location provider, so you can use the location manager's getBestProvider() method to get the most accurate location provider on the device. This method takes two parameters: a Criteria object you can use to specify criteria such as power requirements, and a flag to indicate whether it should currently be enabled on the device.

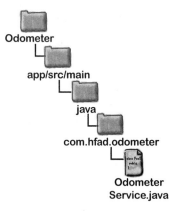

Odometer
↓
app/src/main
↓
java
↓
com.hfad.odometer
↓
Odometer
Service.java

We want to use the location provider on the device with the greatest accuracy, so we'll use the following (we'll add it to OdometerService later):

```
String provider = locManager.getBestProvider(new Criteria(), true);
```

This gets the most accurate location provider that's available on the device.

Next we'll get the location provider to send location updates to the location listener.

OdometerService
MainActivity
Location Services

Request location updates...

You get the location provider to send updates to the location listener using the location manager's requestLocationUpdates() method. It takes takes four parameters: the location provider, the minimum time interval between updates in milliseconds, the minimum distance between location updates in meters, and the location listener you want to receive the updates. As an example, here's how you'd request location updates from the location provider every second when the device has moved more than a meter:

The location provider

The distance in meters

```
locManager.requestLocationUpdates(provider, 1000, 1, listener);
```
← *The LocationListener you want to receive updates*

The time in milliseconds

...but first check that your app has permission

If your app's target SDK is API level 23 or above, you need to check at runtime whether the user has granted you permission to get their current location. (As we said earlier in the chapter, if your target SDK is API level 23 or above, and the user's device is running one of these versions, the user may have installed the app without granting Location Services permission. You therefore have to check whether permission's been granted before running any code that requires Location Services, or your code won't compile.)

You can check your app's target SDK version by choosing File -> Project Structure, clicking on the app option, and then choosing Flavors.

You check whether permission's been granted using the ContextCompat. checkSelfPermission() method. ContextCompat is a class from the AppCompat Support Library that provides backward compatibility with older versions of Android. Its checkSelfPermission() method takes two parameters: the current Context (usually this) and the permission you want to check. It returns a value of PackageManager.PERMISSION_ GRANTED if permission has been granted.

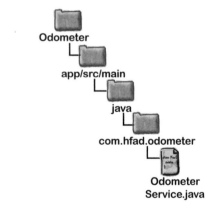

In our case, we want to check whether the app's been granted ACCESS_ FINE_LOCATION permission. Here's the code to do that:

Check if the ACCESS_FINE_LOCATION permission has been granted...

```
if (ContextCompat.checkSelfPermission(this,
            android.Manifest.permission.ACCESS_FINE_LOCATION)
        == PackageManager.PERMISSION_GRANTED) {
    locManager.requestLocationUpdates(provider, 1000, 1, listener);
}
```
...before requesting location updates.

On the next page we'll show you all the code you need to add to *OdometerService.java* to request location updates.

Here's the updated OdometerService code

Here's the full code to request location updates (update
your version of *OdometerService.java* to include our changes):

```
...
import android.content.Context;
import android.location.LocationManager;
import android.location.Criteria;
import android.support.v4.content.ContextCompat;
import android.content.pm.PackageManager;


public class OdometerService extends Service {
    ...
    private LocationManager locManager;
    public static final String PERMISSION_STRING
            = android.Manifest.permission.ACCESS_FINE_LOCATION;

    ...


    @Override
    public void onCreate() {
        super.onCreate();
        listener = new LocationListener() {
            ...
        };
        locManager = (LocationManager) getSystemService(Context.LOCATION_SERVICE);
        if (ContextCompat.checkSelfPermission(this, PERMISSION_STRING)
                        == PackageManager.PERMISSION_GRANTED) {
            String provider = locManager.getBestProvider(new Criteria(), true);
            if (provider != null) {
                locManager.requestLocationUpdates(provider, 1000, 1, listener);
            }
        }
    }
    ...
}
```

We're using
these extra
classes, so
import them.

We're using a private variable for
the LocationManager so we can
access it from other methods.

We're adding the permission String as a constant.

Get the LocationManager.

Check
whether
we have
permission.

Get the most
accurate location
provider.

Request updates from the location provider.

Odometer
app/src/main
java
com.hfad.odometer
Odometer
Service.java

Next we'll get our location listener to deal with the location updates.

Calculate the distance traveled

So far, we've requested that the location listener be notified when the user's current location changes. When this happens, the listener's `onLocationChanged()` method gets called.

This method has one parameter, a `Location` object representing the user's current location. We can use this object to calculate the distance traveled by keeping a running total of the distance between the user's current location and their last.

You find the distance in meters between two locations using the `Location` object's `distanceTo()` method. As an example, here's how you'd find the distance between two locations called `location` and `lastLocation`:

```
double distanceInMeters = location.distanceTo(lastLocation);
```

This gets the distance between location and lastLocation.

Here's the code we need to add to `OdometerService` to record the distance traveled by the user (update your version of *OdometerService.java* to match ours):

```
public class OdometerService extends Service {
    private static double distanceInMeters;
    private static Location lastLocation = null;
    ...


    @Override
    public void onCreate() {
        super.onCreate();
        listener = new LocationListener() {
            @Override
            public void onLocationChanged(Location location) {
                if (lastLocation == null) {
                    lastLocation = location;
                }
                distanceInMeters += location.distanceTo(lastLocation);
                lastLocation = location;
            }
            ...
        }
        ...
    }
    ...
}
```

We're using static variables to store the distance traveled and the user's last location so that their values are retained when the service is destroyed.

Set the user's starting location.

Update the distance traveled and the user's last location.

We'll use this code to return the distance traveled to `MainActivity`.

Return the miles traveled

To tell `MainActivity` how far the user has traveled, we need to update `OdometerService`'s `getDistance()` method. It currently returns a random number, so we'll change it to convert the value of the `distanceInMeters` variable to miles and return that value. Here's the new version of the `getDistance()` method; update your version of it to match ours:

```
public double getDistance() {
    return random.nextDouble();

    return this.distanceInMeters / 1609.344;
}
```

Delete this line.

This converts the distance traveled in meters into miles. We could make this calculation more precise if we wanted to, but it's accurate enough for our purposes.

Odometer
app/src/main
java
com.hfad.odometer
Odometer Service.java

Finally, we'll stop the listener getting location updates when the service is about to be destroyed.

Stop the listener getting location updates

We're going to stop the location listener getting updates using the `OdometerService`'s `onDestroy()` method, as this gets called just before the service is destroyed.

You stop the updates by calling the location manager's `removeUpdates()` method. It takes one parameter, the listener you wish to stop receiving the updates:

`locManager.removeUpdates(listener);` ← *This stops the location listener getting updates.*

If your app's target SDK is API level 23 or above, you need to check whether the user has granted `ACCESS_FINE_LOCATION` permission before calling the `removeUpdates()` method. This is because you can only use this method if the user's granted this permission, and Android Studio will complain if you don't check first. You check whether permission's been granted in the same way we did earlier, by checking the return value of the `ContextCompat.checkSelfPermission()` method:

We can only remove the updates if we have permission.

```
if (ContextCompat.checkSelfPermission(this, PERMISSION_STRING)
        == PackageManager.PERMISSION_GRANTED) {
    locManager.removeUpdates(listener);
}
```

Over the next few pages we'll show you the full code for `OdometerService`, including the new `onDestroy()` method.

The full OdometerService.java code

OdometerService
MainActivity
Location Services

We've now done everything we need to get OdometerService
to return the distance traveled. Update your version of
OdometerService.java to match ours.

```java
package com.hfad.odometer;


import android.app.Service;
import android.content.Context;
import android.content.Intent;
import android.os.Bundle;
import android.os.IBinder;
import android.os.Binder;
import java.util.Random;
import android.location.LocationListener;
import android.location.Location;
import android.location.LocationManager;
import android.location.Criteria;
import android.support.v4.content.ContextCompat;
import android.content.pm.PackageManager;



public class OdometerService extends Service {

    private final IBinder binder = new OdometerBinder();
    private final Random random = new Random();
    private LocationListener listener;
    private LocationManager locManager;
    private static double distanceInMeters;
    private static Location lastLocation = null;
    public static final String PERMISSION_STRING
            = android.Manifest.permission.ACCESS_FINE_LOCATION;

    public class OdometerBinder extends Binder {
        OdometerService getOdometer() {
            return OdometerService.this;
        }
    }
```

We're no longer returning a random number, so you can delete this import.

Delete the Random() object, as we're no longer using it.

The code continues on the next page.

Odometer

app/src/main

java

com.hfad.odometer

Odometer
Service.java

The OdometerService.java code (continued)

```java
@Override
public void onCreate() {                    None of the code on
    super.onCreate();                       this page has changed.
    listener = new LocationListener() {
        @Override
        public void onLocationChanged(Location location) {
            if (lastLocation == null) {
                lastLocation = location;
            }
            distanceInMeters += location.distanceTo(lastLocation);
            lastLocation = location;
        }

        @Override
        public void onProviderDisabled(String arg0) {
        }

        @Override
        public void onProviderEnabled(String arg0) {
        }

        @Override
        public void onStatusChanged(String arg0, int arg1, Bundle bundle) {
        }
    };

    locManager = (LocationManager) getSystemService (Context.LOCATION_SERVICE);
    if (ContextCompat.checkSelfPermission(this, PERMISSION_STRING)
                    == PackageManager.PERMISSION_GRANTED) {
        String provider = locManager.getBestProvider(new Criteria(), true);
        if (provider != null) {
            locManager.requestLocationUpdates(provider, 1000, 1, listener);
        }
    }
}
```

Odometer
app/src/main
java
com.hfad.odometer
**Odometer
Service.java**

The code continues →
on the next page.

The OdometerService.java code (continued)

Odometer
└ app/src/main
  └ java
    └ com.hfad.odometer
      └ Odometer
        Service.java

```java
@Override
public IBinder onBind(Intent intent) {
    return binder;
}

@Override                          ← Add the onDestroy() method.
public void onDestroy() {
    super.onDestroy();
    if (locManager != null && listener != null) {
        if (ContextCompat.checkSelfPermission(this, PERMISSION_STRING)
                == PackageManager.PERMISSION_GRANTED) {
            locManager.removeUpdates(listener);   ← Stop getting locations updates (if
        }                                            we have permission to remove them).
        locManager = null;    ⎫ Set the LocationManager and
        listener = null;      ⎭ LocationListener variables to null.
    }
}


public double getDistance() {
    return this.distanceInMeters / 1609.344;
}
}
```

Let's take the app for a test drive.

---

there are no
Dumb Questions

Q: I noticed I can call `checkSelfPermission()` directly in my service without using `ContextCompat`. Why do I have to use the `ContextCompat` version?

A: Because it's simpler to use. A `checkSelfPermission()` method was added to the `Context` class in API level 23, but this means it's not available on devices running an older version of Android.

Test drive the app

When we launch the app, 0.0 miles is initially displayed. When we check the app permissions, permission hasn't been granted to use Location Services. You can check this on your device by opening the device settings, choosing Apps, selecting the Odometer app, and opening the Permissions section:

Location Services permission for the app may be granted on your device by default. If this is the case, see what happens when you switch it off.

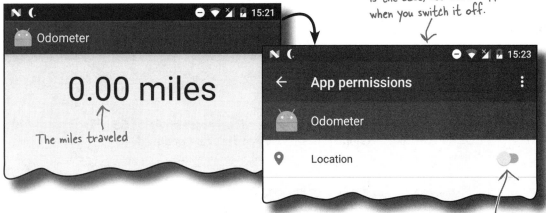

The miles traveled

The app hasn't been granted permission to use Location Services.

When we grant Location permission for the Odometer app and return to the app, the location icon is displayed in the status bar, and the number of miles traveled increases when we take the device for a walk. The location icon disappears when we leave the app:

The location icon indicates our device GPS is being used.

The icon disappears when we leave the app.

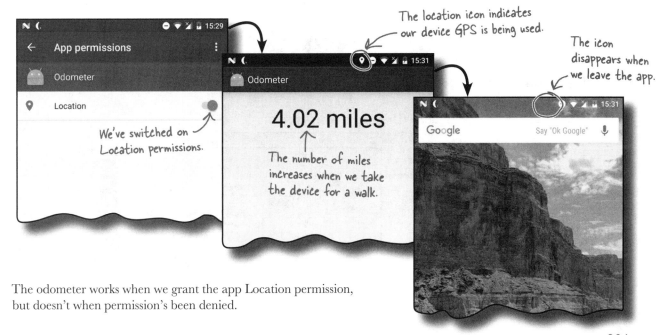

We've switched on Location permissions.

The number of miles increases when we take the device for a walk.

The odometer works when we grant the app Location permission, but doesn't when permission's been denied.

Get the app to request permission

So far, we've made `OdometerService` check whether it has permission to get the user's precise location. If permission's been granted, it uses the Android Location Services to track the distance the user travels. But what if permission *hasn't* been granted?

If the app doesn't have permission to get the user's precise location, `OdometerService` can't use the Location Services we require. Rather than just accepting this, the app would work better if it were to ask the user to grant the permission.

We're going to change `MainActivity` so that if the user hasn't granted the permission we need, we'll request it. To achieve this, we'll get `MainActivity` to do three things:

① **Before MainActivity binds to the service, request ACCESS_FINE_ LOCATION permission if it's not already been granted.**
This will present the user with a permission request dialog.

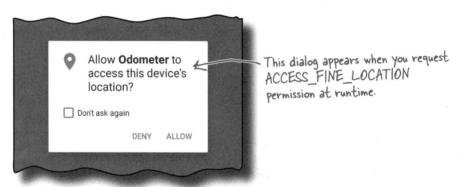

This dialog appears when you request ACCESS_FINE_LOCATION permission at runtime.

② **Check the response, and bind to the service if permission is granted.**

③ **If permission is denied, issue a notification.**

We'll issue this notification if the user doesn't grant the permission we need.

Let's start by looking at how you make an activity request permissions at runtime.

Check permissions at runtime

Earlier in the chapter, you saw how to check whether the user has granted a particular permission using the ContextCompat.checkSelfPermission() method:

This code checks whether the user has granted a permission.

```
if (ContextCompat.checkSelfPermission(this, PERMISSION_STRING)
        == PackageManager.PERMISSION_GRANTED) {
    //Run code that needs the user's permission
}
```

If the user has granted permission, the method returns a value of PackageManager.PERMISSION_GRANTED, and the code requiring the permission will run successfully. But what if permission has been denied?

Ask for permissions you don't have

If the user hasn't granted one or more permissions needed by your code, you can use the **ActivityCompat. requestPermissions()** method to request permission at runtime. ActivityCompat is a class from the AppCompat Support Library that provides backward compatibility with older versions of Android. Its requestPermissions() method takes three parameters: a Context (usually this), a String array of permissions you want to check, and an int request code for the permission request. As an example, here's how you'd use the method to request the ACCESS_FINE_LOCATION permission:

> # The requestPermissions() method can only be called by an activity. It can't be called from a service.

Use this method to request permissions at runtime.

This is the request code for the permissions request. It can be any int. You'll see where this gets used in a couple of pages.

```
ActivityCompat.requestPermissions(this,
    new String[]{android.Manifest.permission.ACCESS_FINE_LOCATION}, 6854);
```

When the requestPermissions() method is called, it displays one or more dialogs asking the user for each permission. The dialog gives the user a choice between denying or allowing the permission, and there's also a checkbox they can check if they don't want to be asked about the permission again. If they check the checkbox and deny the permission, subsequent calls to the requestPermissions() method won't display the dialog.

Note that the requestPermissions() method can only be called from an activity. You can't request permissions from a service.

We're going to update MainActivity so that it requests permission to get the device's location if it hasn't already been granted.

This is the permissions request dialog.

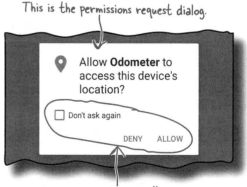

The user can deny or allow permissions using these options.

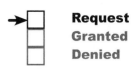

Check for Location Services permissions in MainActivity's onStart() method

We're currently using MainActivity's onStart() method to bind the activity to OdometerService. We're going to change the code so that MainActivity only binds to the service if the user has granted the permission specified by the PERMISSION_STRING constant we defined in OdometerService. If permission's not been granted, we'll ask for it.

Here's the updated code for *MainActivity.java*; update your version of the code with our changes:

We're using these extra classes, so we need to import them.

```
...
import android.content.pm.PackageManager;
import android.support.v4.app.ActivityCompat;
import android.support.v4.content.ContextCompat;


public class MainActivity extends Activity {

    ...

    private final int PERMISSION_REQUEST_CODE = 698;


    ...
    @Override
    protected void onStart() {
        super.onStart();
        if (ContextCompat.checkSelfPermission(this, OdometerService.PERMISSION_STRING)
                != PackageManager.PERMISSION_GRANTED) {
            ActivityCompat.requestPermissions(this,
                    new String[]{OdometerService.PERMISSION_STRING},
                    PERMISSION_REQUEST_CODE);
        } else {
            Intent intent = new Intent(this, OdometerService.class);
            bindService(intent, connection, Context.BIND_AUTO_CREATE);
        }
    }
}
```

We'll use this int for the permission request code.

If permission hasn't already been granted...

...request it at runtime.

If permission has already been granted, bind to the service.

Once you've requested permission from the user, you need to check the user's response. We'll do that next.

Check the user's response to the permission request

When you ask the user to grant a permission using the `requestPermissions()` method, you can't determine whether permission was granted by checking its return value. That's because the permission request happens asynchronously so that the current thread isn't blocked while you wait for the user to respond.

Instead, you check the user's response by overriding the activity's **onRequestPermissionsResult()** method. This has three parameters: an int request code to identify the permissions request, a String array of permissions, and an int array for the results of the requests.

To use this method, you first check whether the int request code matches the one you used in the `requestPermissions()` method. If it does, you then check whether the permission has been granted.

The code below checks whether the user granted the permission we requested using the `requestPermissions()` method on the previous page. If permission's been granted, it binds to `OdometerService`. Add this method to your version of *MainActivity.java*:

> *The onRequestPermissionsResult() method returns the results of your permissions requests.*

```java
@Override
public void onRequestPermissionsResult(int requestCode,
                                       String permissions[], int[] grantResults) {
    switch (requestCode) {
        case PERMISSION_REQUEST_CODE: {
            if (grantResults.length > 0
                    && grantResults[0] == PackageManager.PERMISSION_GRANTED) {
                Intent intent = new Intent(this, OdometerService.class);
                bindService(intent, connection, Context.BIND_AUTO_CREATE);
            } else {
                //Code to run if permission was denied
            }
        }
    }
}
```

> *Check whether the code matches the one we used in our requestPermissions() method.*

> *If the request was cancelled, no results will be returned.*

> *We still need to write this code.*

> *If permission was granted, bind to the service.*

Odometer

└ app/src/main

  └ java

    └ com.hfad.odometer

      └ MainActivity.java

Finally, if the user doesn't give us permission to use their current location, we need to inform them that the odometer won't work.

Issue a notification if we're denied permission

Request
Granted
Denied

If the user decides not to grant permission to use their current location, the OdometerService won't be able to tell how far they've traveled. If this happens, we'll issue a notification to inform the user. We're going to use a notification because it will remain in the notification area until the user has decided what to do. Another advantage of using a notification is that we can get it to start MainActivity when it's clicked. Doing this means that MainActivity's onStart() method will run, which will again prompt the user to grant the permission (unless the user has previously selected the option not to be asked again).

We'll issue this notification if the user denies permission.

> ◈ Odometer · now
> Odometer
> Location permission required

See if you can build the notification we require by having a go at the exercise on the next page.

---

there are no
Dumb Questions

Q: I tried turning off Location permissions for the Odometer app when I was in the middle of using it, and the number of miles displayed went back to 0. Why?

A: When you switch off the Location permissions for the app, Android may kill the process the app is running in. This resets all of the variables.

Q: That sounds drastic. Are there any other times when Android might kill a process?

A: Yes, when it's low on memory, but it will always try to keep alive any processes that are actively being used.

Q: Why aren't we calling the requestPermissions() method from OdometerService?

A: Because the requestPermissions() method is only available for activities, not services.

Q: Can I change the text that's displayed in the requestPermissions() dialog?

A: No. The text and options it displays are fixed, so Android won't let you change them.

Q: But I want to give the user more information about why I need a particular permission. Can I do that?

A: One option is to call the ActivityCompat. shouldShowRequestPermissionRationale() method before calling requestPermissions(). This returns a true value if the user has previously denied the permission request, and hasn't checked the checkbox to say they don't want to be asked again. If this is the case, you can give the user more information outside the permission request before requesting the permission again.

Q: What other permissions do I have to declare and ask permission for?

A: Generally, you need the user's permission for any actions that use private data or may affect the way in which other apps function. The online documentation for each class should indicate whether a permission is needed, and Android Studio should highlight this too. You can find a full list of actions requiring permissions here:

https://developer.android.com/guide/topics/permissions/requesting. html#normal-dangerous

Q: What if I design an app that performs these kinds of actions and don't ask for permission?

A: If your target SDK is API level 23 or above and you don't request permission, your code won't compile.

Pool Puzzle

Your **goal** is to build and issue a heads-up notification. The notification should start MainActivity when it's clicked, then disappear. Take code snippets from the pool, and place them in the blank lines in the code. You may **not** use the same snippet more than once, and you won't need to use all the snippets.

Write the code to create this notification.

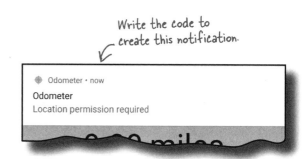

```java
NotificationCompat.Builder builder = new NotificationCompat.Builder(this)
            .setSmallIcon(android.R.drawable.ic_menu_compass)
            .setContentTitle("Odometer")
            .setContentText("Location permission required")
            .setPriority(NotificationCompat.........................)
            .setVibrate(new long[] {0, 1000})
            ...................................(true);

Intent actionIntent = new Intent(this, MainActivity.class);
PendingIntent actionPendingIntent = PendingIntent....................(this, 0,
                    actionIntent, PendingIntent.FLAG_UPDATE_CURRENT);
builder.setContentIntent(...................................);

NotificationManager notificationManager =
            (NotificationManager) getSystemService(.................................);
notificationManager.notify(43,.........................);
```

A built-in drawable to display a compass icon.

Note: each thing from the pool can only be used once!

NOTIFICATION

getService

setVanishWhenClicked

actionPendingIntent

builder.build()

setAutoCancel

actionIntent

getActivity

HIGH

PRIORITY_HIGH

getAction

NOTIFICATION_SERVICE

builder

PRIORITY_LOW

LOW

Pōōl Puzzle Solution

Your **goal** is to build and issue a heads-up notification. The notification should start MainActivity when it's clicked, then disappear. Take code snippets from the pool, and place them in the blank lines in the code. You may **not** use the same snippet more than once, and you won't need to use all the snippets.

```
NotificationCompat.Builder builder = new NotificationCompat.Builder(this)
                .setSmallIcon(android.R.drawable.ic_menu_compass)
                .setContentTitle("Odometer")
                .setContentText("Location permission required")
                .setPriority(NotificationCompat. PRIORITY_HIGH )
                .setVibrate(new long[] {0, 1000})
                .   setAutoCancel   (true);

    Intent actionIntent = new Intent(this, MainActivity.class);
    PendingIntent actionPendingIntent = PendingIntent. getActivity (this, 0,
                actionIntent, PendingIntent.FLAG_UPDATE_CURRENT);
    builder.setContentIntent( actionPendingIntent );
    NotificationManager notificationManager =
                (NotificationManager) getSystemService( NOTIFICATION_SERVICE );
    notificationManager.notify(43, builder.build() );
```

← Heads-up notifications need to have a high priority.

This makes the notification disappear → when it's clicked.

Create a PendingIntent using the getActivity() method.

← Add the PendingIntent to the notification so that it starts MainActivity when it's clicked.

Use the notification service.

↖ Build the notification.

You didn't need to use these snippets. ↘

NOTIFICATION

setVanishWhenClicked

getService

actionIntent

HIGH

getAction

builder

PRIORITY_LOW

LOW

Request ✓
Granted ✓
Denied →

Add notification code to onRequestPermissionsResults()

We'll update our `MainActivity` code so that if the user denies our permission request, it issues a heads-up notification.

First, add the following Strings to *Strings.xml*; we'll use these for the notification's title and text:

```
<string name="app_name">Odometer</string>  ← Android Studio may have
                                              already added this String.
<string name="permission_denied">Location permission required</string>
```

Then update your version of *MainActivity.java* with the following code:

```
...
import android.support.v4.app.NotificationCompat;
import android.app.NotificationManager;
import android.app.PendingIntent;
                                         We're using these extra classes,
                                         so we need to import them.
public class MainActivity extends Activity {

    ...
    private final int NOTIFICATION_ID = 423;  ← We'll use this constant
                                                 for the notification ID.

    ...
    @Override
    public void onRequestPermissionsResult(int requestCode,
                                   String permissions[], int[] grantResults) {
        switch (requestCode) {
            case PERMISSION_REQUEST_CODE: {
                if (grantResults.length > 0
                        && grantResults[0] == PackageManager.PERMISSION_GRANTED) {

                    ...
                } else {
                    //Create a notification builder
                    NotificationCompat.Builder builder = new NotificationCompat.Builder(this)
                        .setSmallIcon(android.R.drawable.ic_menu_compass)
                        .setContentTitle(getResources().getString(R.string.app_name))
                        .setContentText(getResources().getString(R.string.permission_denied))
                        .setPriority(NotificationCompat.PRIORITY_HIGH)
                        .setVibrate(new long[] {1000, 1000})
                        .setAutoCancel(true);
```

These settings are needed for all notifications.

Add these to make it a heads-up notification.

.setAutoCancel(true); ←This line makes the notification disappear when it's clicked.

The code continues on the next page. →

The notification code (continued)

Request
Granted
Denied

```java
//Create an action
Intent actionIntent = new Intent(this, MainActivity.class);
PendingIntent actionPendingIntent = PendingIntent.getActivity(
        this,
        0,
        actionIntent,
        PendingIntent.FLAG_UPDATE_CURRENT);
builder.setContentIntent(actionPendingIntent);
```

Adding a PendingIntent to the notification means that it will start MainActivity when it's clicked.

```java
//Issue the notification
NotificationManager notificationManager =
        (NotificationManager) getSystemService(NOTIFICATION_SERVICE);
notificationManager.notify(NOTIFICATION_ID, builder.build());
        }
    }
}
```

Build the notification and issue it.

```
    ...
}
```

Odometer

app/src/main

java

com.hfad.odometer

Main Activity.java

That's all the code we need to display a notification if the user decides to deny us ACCESS_FINE_LOCATION permission. We'll show you the full MainActivity code over the next few pages, then take the app for a final test drive.

Request
Granted
Denied

The full code for MainActivity.java

Here's our complete code for *MainActivity.java*; make sure your version of the code matches ours:

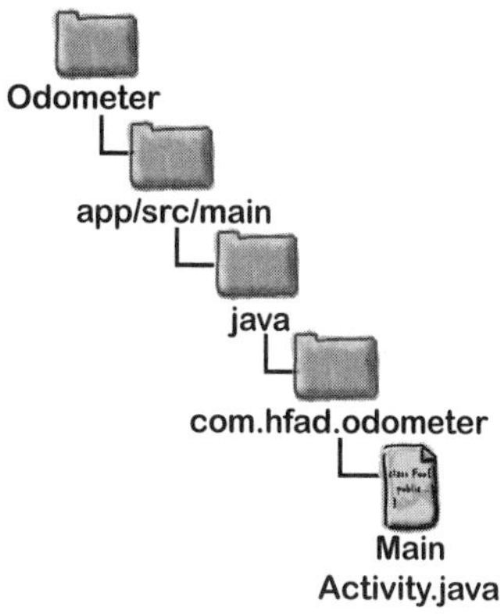

```java
package com.hfad.odometer;

import android.app.Activity;
import android.os.Bundle;
import android.content.ServiceConnection;
import android.os.IBinder;
import android.content.ComponentName;
import android.content.Context;
import android.content.Intent;
import android.os.Handler;
import android.widget.TextView;
import java.util.Locale;
import android.content.pm.PackageManager;
import android.support.v4.app.ActivityCompat;
import android.support.v4.content.ContextCompat;
import android.support.v4.app.NotificationCompat;
import android.app.NotificationManager;
import android.app.PendingIntent;

public class MainActivity extends Activity {

    private OdometerService odometer;
    private boolean bound = false;
    private final int PERMISSION_REQUEST_CODE = 698;
    private final int NOTIFICATION_ID = 423;

    private ServiceConnection connection = new ServiceConnection() {
        @Override
        public void onServiceConnected(ComponentName componentName, IBinder binder) {
            OdometerService.OdometerBinder odometerBinder =
                    (OdometerService.OdometerBinder) binder;
            odometer = odometerBinder.getOdometer();
            bound = true;
        }
        @Override
        public void onServiceDisconnected(ComponentName componentName) {
            bound = false;
        }
    };
```

These are all classes from the AppCompat Support Library.

We've been using the Activity class, but you can use AppCompatActivity if you prefer.

We need a ServiceConnection in order to bind MainActivity to OdometerService.

The folder structure shown: Odometer → app/src/main → java → com.hfad.odometer → Main Activity.java

The code continues on the next page.

The MainActivity.java code (continued)

Request

Granted

Denied

```java
@Override
protected void onCreate(Bundle savedInstanceState) {
    super.onCreate(savedInstanceState);
    setContentView(R.layout.activity_main);
    displayDistance();
}

@Override
public void onRequestPermissionsResult(int requestCode,
                            String permissions[], int[] grantResults) {
    switch (requestCode) {
        case PERMISSION_REQUEST_CODE: {
            if (grantResults.length > 0
                    && grantResults[0] == PackageManager.PERMISSION_GRANTED) {
                Intent intent = new Intent(this, OdometerService.class);
                bindService(intent, connection, Context.BIND_AUTO_CREATE);
            } else {
                //Create a notification builder
                NotificationCompat.Builder builder = new NotificationCompat.Builder(this)
                        .setSmallIcon(android.R.drawable.ic_menu_compass)
                        .setContentTitle(getResources().getString(R.string.app_name))
                        .setContentText(getResources().getString(R.string.permission_denied))
                        .setPriority(NotificationCompat.PRIORITY_HIGH)
                        .setVibrate(new long[] { 1000, 1000})
                        .setAutoCancel(true);
                //Create an action
                Intent actionIntent = new Intent(this, MainActivity.class);
                PendingIntent actionPendingIntent = PendingIntent.getActivity(this, 0,
                        actionIntent, PendingIntent.FLAG_UPDATE_CURRENT);
                builder.setContentIntent(actionPendingIntent);
                //Issue the notification
                NotificationManager notificationManager =
                        (NotificationManager) getSystemService(NOTIFICATION_SERVICE);
                notificationManager.notify(NOTIFICATION_ID, builder.build());
            }
        }
    }
}
```

If we've asked the user for permissions at runtime, check the result.

Bind to the service if the user has granted permission.

Issue a notification if permission's been denied.

Odometer

app/src/main

java

com.hfad.odometer

Main Activity.java

The code continues on the next page.

The MainActivity.java code (continued)

```java
@Override
protected void onStart() {
    super.onStart();
    if (ContextCompat.checkSelfPermission(this,
                        OdometerService.PERMISSION_STRING)
                        != PackageManager.PERMISSION_GRANTED) {
        ActivityCompat.requestPermissions(this,
                new String[]{OdometerService.PERMISSION_STRING},
                PERMISSION_REQUEST_CODE);
    } else {
        Intent intent = new Intent(this, OdometerService.class);
        bindService(intent, connection, Context.BIND_AUTO_CREATE);
    }
}
```

Request ACCESS_FINE_LOCATION permission if we don't have it already.

Bind to OdometerService if we've been granted the permission it requires.

We're binding to OdometerService in two different places, so you could put this code in a separate method.

```java
@Override
protected void onStop() {
    super.onStop();
    if (bound) {
        unbindService(connection);
        bound = false;
    }
}
```

Unbind from OdometerService when MainActivity stops.

Odometer
app/src/main
java
com.hfad.odometer
Main
Activity.java

Display the distance traveled.

```java
private void displayDistance() {
    final TextView distanceView = (TextView)findViewById(R.id.distance);
    final Handler handler = new Handler();
    handler.post(new Runnable() {
        @Override
        public void run() {
            double distance = 0.0;
            if (bound && odometer != null) {
                distance = odometer.getDistance();
            }
            String distanceStr = String.format(Locale.getDefault(),
                                            "%1$,.2f miles", distance);
            distanceView.setText(distanceStr);
            handler.postDelayed(this, 1000);
        }
    });
}
```

Test drive the app

When we run the app with its Location permission switched off,
a permission request dialog is displayed. If we click on the Deny
option, a notification is issued:

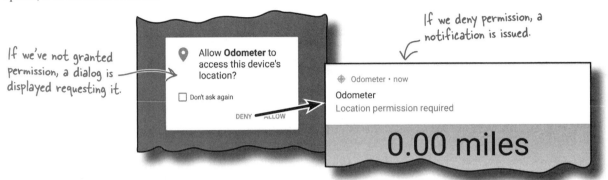

If we've not granted
permission, a dialog is
displayed requesting it.

If we deny permission, a
notification is issued.

When we click on the notification, the permission request dialog is
displayed again. If we click on the option to allow permission, the
Location icon appears in the status bar and the number of miles
increases when we take the device on a road trip:

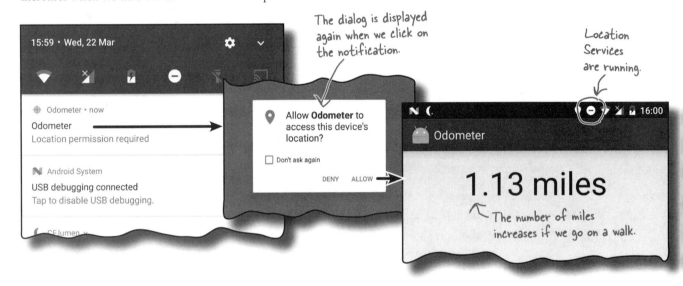

The dialog is displayed
again when we click on
the notification.

Location
Services
are running.

The number of miles
increases if we go on a walk.

We know you're full of great ideas for improving
the Odometer app, so why not try them out? As an
example, try adding Start, Stop, and Reset buttons
to start, stop, and reset the distance traveled.

Your Android Toolbox

You've got Chapter 19 under your belt and now you've added bound services to your toolbox.

You can download the full code for the chapter from https://tinyurl.com/HeadFirstAndroid.

BULLET POINTS

- You create a bound service by extending the **Service** class. You define your own **Binder** object, and override the **onBind()** method.

- Bind a component to a service using the **bindService()** method.

- Use a **ServiceConnection** so that your activity can get a reference to the service when it's bound.

- Unbind a component from a service using the **unbindService()** method.

- When a bound service is created, its onCreate() method is called. onBind() gets called when a component binds to the service.

- When all components have unbound from the service, its onUnbind() method is called.

- A bound service is destroyed when no components are bound to it. Its onDestroy() method is called just before the service is destroyed.

- Use the **Android Location Services** to determine the current location of the device.

- To get the current location of the device, you need to declare that the app requires **ACCESS_FINE_LOCATION** permission in *AndroidManifest.xml*.

- Get location updates using a **LocationListener**.

- A **LocationManager** gives you access to Android's Location Services. Get the best location provider available on the device using its **getBestProvider()** method. Request location updates from the provider using **requestLocationUpdates()**.

- Use **removeUpdates()** to stop getting location updates.

- If your target SDK is API level 23 or above, check at runtime whether your app has been granted a permission using the **ContextCompat.checkSelfPermission()** method.

- Request permissions at runtime using **ActivityCompat.requestPermissions()**.

- Check the user's response to a permission request by implementing the activity's **onRequestPermissionsResult()** method.

Leaving town...

It's been great having you here in Androidville

We're sad to see you leave, but there's nothing like taking what you've learned and putting it to use. There are still a few more gems for you in the back of the book and a handy index, and then it's time to take all these new ideas and put them into practice. Bon voyage!

Meet the Relatives

There are two more layouts you will often meet in Androidville.

In this book we've concentrated on using simple *linear and frame layouts*, and introduced you to *Android's new constraint layout*. But there are two more layouts we'd like you to know about: **relative layouts** and **grid layouts**. They've largely been superseded by the constraint layout, but we have a soft spot for them, and we think they'll stay around for a few more years.

A relative layout displays views in relative positions

A relative layout allows you to position views relative to their parent layout, or relative to other views in the layout.

You define a relative layout using the `<RelativeLayout>` element like this:

```
<RelativeLayout xmlns:android="http://schemas.android.com/apk/res/android"
    android:layout_width="match_parent"
    android:layout_height="match_parent"
```

The layout_width and layout_height specify what size you want the layout to be.

```
    ...>
```
← *There may be other attributes too.*

```
    ...
```
← *This is where you add any views.*

```
</RelativeLayout>
```

Positioning views relative to the parent layout

If you want a view to always appear in a particular position on the screen, irrespective of the screen size or orientation, you need to position the view relative to its parent. As an example, here's how you'd make sure a button always appears in the top-center of the layout:

```
<RelativeLayout ... >
    <Button
        android:layout_width="wrap_content"
        android:layout_height="wrap_content"
        android:text="@string/click_me"
        android:layout_alignParentTop="true"
        android:layout_centerHorizontal="true" />
</RelativeLayout>
```

The layout contains the button, so the layout is the button's parent.

layout_alignParentTop

The parent layout

The child view.

layout_centerHorizontal

The lines of code:

```
android:layout_alignParentTop="true"
android:layout_centerHorizontal="true"
```

mean that the top edge of the button is aligned to the top edge of the layout, and the button is centered horizontally in the parent layout. This will be the case no matter what the screen size, language, or orientation of your device:

Positioning views to the left or right

You can also position a view to the left or right of the parent layout. There are two ways of doing this.

The first way is to explicitly position the view on the left or right using:

android:layout_alignParentLeft="true"

or:

android:layout_alignParentRight="true"

These lines of code mean that the left (or right) edge of the view is aligned to the left (or right) edge of the parent layout, regardless of the screen size, orientation, or language being used on the device.

layout_alignParentLeft="true"

The child view.

The child view.

android:layout_alignParentRight="true"

Use start and end to take language direction into account

For apps where the minimum SDK is *at least* API 17, you can position views on the left or right depending on the language setting on the device. As an example, you might want views to appear on the left for languages that are read from left to right such as English. For languages that are read from right to left, you might want them to appear on the right instead so that their position is mirrored.

To do this, you use:

android:layout_alignParentStart="true"

or:

android:layout_alignParentEnd="true"

android:layout_alignParentStart="true" aligns the start edge of the view with that of its parent. The start edge is on the left for languages that are read from left to right, and the right edge for languages that are read from right to left.

android:layout_alignParentEnd="true" aligns the end edge of the view with that of its parent. The end edge is on the right for languages that are read from left to right, and the left edge for languages that are read from right to left.

android:layout_alignParentStart="true"

For left-to-right languages.

For right-to-left languages.

The view appears on the left or the right depending on the direction of the language used on the device.

android:layout_alignParentEnd="true"

For left-to-right languages.

For right-to-left languages.

Attributes for positioning views relative to the parent layout

Here are some of the most common attributes for positioning views relative to their parent layout. Add the attribute you want to the view you're positioning, then set its value to `"true"`:

```
android:attribute="true"
```

Attribute	What it does
layout_alignParentBottom	Aligns the bottom edge of the view to the bottom edge of the parent.
layout_alignParentLeft	Aligns the left edge of the view to the left edge of the parent.
layout_alignParentRight	Aligns the right edge of the view to the right edge of the parent.
layout_alignParentTop	Aligns the top edge of the view to the top edge of the parent.
layout_alignParentStart	Aligns the start edge of the view to the start edge of the parent.
layout_alignParentEnd	Aligns the end edge of the view to the end edge of the parent.
layout_centerInParent	Centers the view horizontally and vertically in the parent.
layout_centerHorizontal	Centers the view horizontally in the parent.
layout_centerVertical	Centers the view vertically in the parent.

The view is aligned to the parent's left and bottom edges.

CLICK ME

The view is aligned to the parent's right and top edges.

CLICK ME

CLICK ME

The start is on the left and the end is on the right for left-to-right languages. This is reversed for right-to-left languages.

CLICK ME

CLICK ME

CLICK ME

CLICK ME

Positioning views relative to other views

In addition to positioning views relative to the parent layout, you can also position views *relative to other views*. You do this when you want views to stay aligned in some way, irrespective of the screen size or orientation.

In order to position a view relative to another view, the view you're using as an anchor must be given an ID using the `android:id` attribute:

android:id="@+id/button_click_me"

The syntax "`@+id`" tells Android to include the ID as a resource in its resource file *R.java*. You must include the "+" whenever you define a new view in the layout. If you don't, Android won't add the ID as a resource and you'll get errors in your code. You can omit the "+" when the ID has already been added as a resource.

Here's how you create a layout with two buttons, with one button centered in the middle of the layout, and the second button positioned underneath the first:

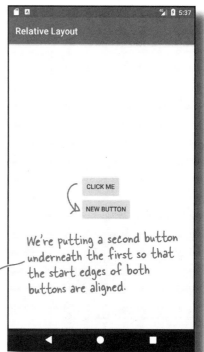

```
<RelativeLayout ... >          We're using this button as an anchor
    <Button                     for the second one, so it needs an ID.
        android:id="@+id/button_click_me"
        android:layout_width="wrap_content"
        android:layout_height="wrap_content"
        android:layout_centerInParent="true"
        android:text="Click Me" />

    <Button
        android:layout_width="wrap_content"
        android:layout_height="wrap_content"
        android:layout_alignStart="@id/button_click_me"
        android:layout_below="@id/button_click_me"
        android:text="New Button" />
</RelativeLayout>
```

We're putting a second button underneath the first so that the start edges of both buttons are aligned.

The lines:

```
    android:layout_alignStart="@id/button_click_me"
    android:layout_below="@id/button_click_me"
```

When you're referring to views that have already been defined in the layout, you can use @id instead of @+id.

ensure that the second button has its start edge aligned to the start edge of the first button, and is always positioned beneath it.

Attributes for positioning views relative to other views

Here are attributes you can use when positioning views relative to another view. Add the attribute to the view you're positioning, and set its value to the view you're positioning relative to:

```
android:attribute="@+id/view_id"
```

Remember, you can leave out the "+" if you've already defined the view ID in your layout.

Attribute	What it does
layout_above	Puts the view above the view you're anchoring it to.
layout_below	Puts the view below the view you're anchoring it to.
layout_alignTop	Aligns the top edge of the view to the top edge of the view you're anchoring it to.
layout_alignBottom	Aligns the bottom edge of the view to the bottom edge of the view you're anchoring it to.
layout_alignLeft, layout_alignStart	Aligns the left (or start) edge of the view to the left (or start) edge of the view you're anchoring it to.
layout_alignRight, layout_alignEnd	Aligns the right (or end) edge of the view to the right (or end) edge of the view you're anchoring it to.
layout_toLeftOf, layout_toStartOf	Puts the right (or end) edge of the view to the left (or start) of the view you're anchoring it to.
layout_toRightOf, layout_toEndOf	Puts the left (or start) edge of the view to the right (or end) of the view you're anchoring it to.

Your view goes above.

CLICK ME

The view you're anchoring it to

Your view goes below.

CLICK ME

CLICK ME

Align the view's top edges.

Align the view's bottom edges.

CLICK ME

CLICK ME

Align the view's left or start edges.

CLICK ME

Align the view's right or end edges.

CLICK ME

CLICK ME

Your view goes to the left or start.

CLICK ME

Your view goes to the right or end.

A grid layout displays views in a grid

A grid layout splits the screen up into a grid of rows and columns, and allocates views to cells:

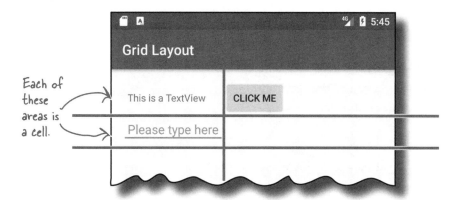

Each of these areas is a cell.

How you define a grid layout

You define a grid layout in a similar way to how you define the other types of layout, this time using the **<GridLayout>** element:

```
<GridLayout xmlns:android="http://schemas.android.com/apk/res/android"
        android:layout_width="match_parent"
        android:layout_height="match_parent"
        android:columnCount="2"
        ... >

        ...

</GridLayout>
```

These are the same attributes we used for our other layouts.

How many columns you want your layout to have (in this case, 2)

This is where you add any views.

You specify how many columns you want the grid layout to have using:

android:columnCount="number"

where number is the number of columns. You can also specify a maximum number of rows using:

android:rowCount="number"

but in practice you can usually let Android figure this out based on the number of views in the layout. Android will include as many rows as is necessary to display the views.

Adding views to the grid layout

You add views to a grid layout in a similar way to how you add views to a linear layout:

```
<GridLayout ... >

    <TextView
        android:layout_width="wrap_content"
        android:layout_height="wrap_content"
        android:text="@string/textview" />

    <Button
        android:layout_width="wrap_content"
        android:layout_height="wrap_content"
        android:text="@string/click_me" />

    <EditText
        android:layout_width="wrap_content"
        android:layout_height="wrap_content"
        android:hint="@string/edit" />

</GridLayout>
```

Just as with a linear layout, there's no need to give your views IDs unless you're explicitly going to refer to them in your activity code. The views don't need to refer to each other within the layout, so they don't need to have IDs for this purpose.

By default, the grid layout positions your views in the order in which they appear in the XML. So if you have a grid layout with two columns, the grid layout will put the first view in the first position, the second view in the second position, and so on.

The downside of this approach is that if you remove one of your views from the layout, it can drastically change the appearance of the layout. To get around this, you can specify where you want each view to appear, and how many columns you want it to span.

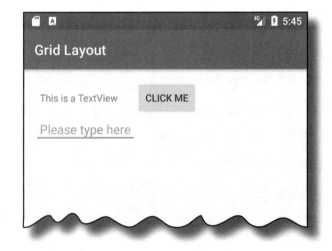

Let's create a new grid layout

To see this in action, we'll create a grid layout that specifies which cells we want views to appear in, and how many columns they should span. The layout is composed of a text view containing the text "To", an editable text field that contains hint text of "Enter email address", an editable text field that contains hint text of "Message", and a button labeled "Send":

Here's what we're going to do

① **Sketch the user interface, and split it into rows and columns.**
This will make it easier for us to see how we should construct our layout.

② **Build up the layout row by row.**

We'll start with a sketch

The first thing we'll do to create our new layout is sketch it out. That way we can see how many rows and columns we need, where each view should be positioned, and how many columns each view should span.

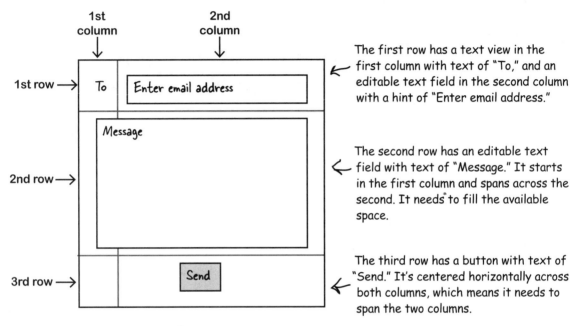

1st column

2nd column

1st row →

To | Enter email address

The first row has a text view in the first column with text of "To," and an editable text field in the second column with a hint of "Enter email address."

Message

2nd row →

The second row has an editable text field with text of "Message." It starts in the first column and spans across the second. It needs to fill the available space.

3rd row →

Send

The third row has a button with text of "Send." It's centered horizontally across both columns, which means it needs to span the two columns.

The grid layout needs two columns

We can position our views how we want if we use a grid layout with two columns:

```
<GridLayout xmlns:android="http://schemas.android.com/apk/res/android"
    xmlns:tools="http://schemas.android.com/tools"
    android:layout_width="match_parent"
    android:layout_height="match_parent"
    android:padding="16dp"
    android:columnCount="2"
    tools:context="com.hfad.gridlayout.MainActivity" >
</GridLayout>
```

Now that we have the basic grid layout defined, we can start adding views.

Row 0: add views to specific rows and columns

The first row of the grid layout is composed of a text view in the first column, and an editable text field in the second column. You start by adding the views to the layout:

```
<GridLayout...>
    <TextView
        android:layout_width="wrap_content"
        android:layout_height="wrap_content"
        android:text="@string/to" />

    <EditText
        android:layout_width="wrap_content"
        android:layout_height="wrap_content"
        android:layout_gravity="fill_horizontal"
        android:hint="@string/to_hint" />
</GridLayout>
```

You can use android:gravity and android:layout_gravity attributes with grid layouts.

You can use layout_gravity in grid layouts too. We're using fill_horizontal because we want the editable text field to fill the remaining horizontal space.

Then you use the `android:layout_row` and `android:layout_column` attributes to say which row and column you want each view to appear in. The row and column indices start from 0, so if you want a view to appear in the first column and first row, you use:

```
android:layout_row="0"
android:layout_column="0"
```

Columns and rows start at 0, so this refers to the first row and first column.

Row and column indices start at 0. layout_column="n" refers to column n+1 in the display.

Let's apply this to our layout code by putting the text view in column 0, and the editable text field in column 1.

```
<GridLayout...>
    <TextView
        ...
        android:layout_row="0"
        android:layout_column="0"
        android:text="@string/to" />

    <EditText
        ...
        android:layout_row="0"
        android:layout_column="1"
        android:hint="@string/to_hint" />
</GridLayout>
```

Column 0   Column 1

Row 0 → To | Enter email address

Row 1: make a view span multiple columns

The second row of the grid layout is composed of an editable text field that starts in the first column and spans across the second. The view takes up all the available space.

To get a view to span multiple columns, you start by specifying which row and column you want the view to start in. We want the view to start in the first column of the second row, so we need to use:

```
android:layout_row="1"
android:layout_column="0"
```

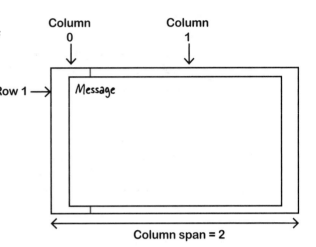

Column span = 2

We want our view to go across two columns, and we can do this using the android:layout_columnSpan attribute like this:

```
android:layout_columnSpan="number"
```

where number is the number of columns we want the view to span across. In our case, this is:

```
android:layout_columnSpan="2"
```

Putting it all together, here's the code for the message view:

```
<GridLayout...>
    <TextView... />
    <EditText.../>
    <EditText
        android:layout_width="wrap_content"
        android:layout_height="wrap_content"
        android:layout_gravity="fill"
        android:gravity="top"
        android:layout_row="1"
        android:layout_column="0"
        android:layout_columnSpan="2"
        android:hint="@string/message" />
</GridLayout>
```

These are the views we added on the last page for row 0.

We want the view to fill the available space, and for the text to appear at the top.

The view starts in column 0, and spans two columns.

Now that we've added the views for the first two rows, all we need to do is add the button.

Row 2: make a view span multiple columns

We need the button to be centered horizontally across the two columns like this:

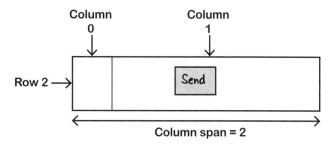

 **Layout Magnets**

We wrote some code to center the Send button in the third row of the grid layout, but a sudden breeze blew some of it away. See if you can reconstruct the code using the magnets below.

```
<GridLayout...>
    <TextView... />
    <EditText.../>
    <EditText.../>
```
These are the views we've already added.

```
    <Button
        android:layout_width="wrap_content"
        android:layout_height="wrap_content"

        android:layout_row=
                          ...............

        android:layout_column=
                          ...............

        android:layout_gravity=
                          ...................................

        android:layout_columnSpan=
                          ...............

        android:text="@string/send" />

</GridLayout>
```

You won't need to use all of these magnets.

```
fill_horizontal
```

```
"0"
```
```
"2"
```
```
"0"
```
```
"1"
```
```
"1"
```
```
"2"
```
```
center_horizontal
```

Layout Magnets Solution

We wrote some code to center the Send button in the third row of the grid layout, but a sudden breeze blew some of it away. See if you can reconstruct the code using the magnets below.

```
<GridLayout...>
    <TextView... />
    <EditText.../>
    <EditText.../>

    <Button
        android:layout_width="wrap_content"
        android:layout_height="wrap_content"

        android:layout_row=        "2"          The button starts at row 2, column 0.

        android:layout_column=     "0"          We want to center it horizontally.

        android:layout_gravity=    center_horizontal

        android:layout_columnSpan= "2"          It spans two columns.

        android:text="@string/send" />

</GridLayout>
```

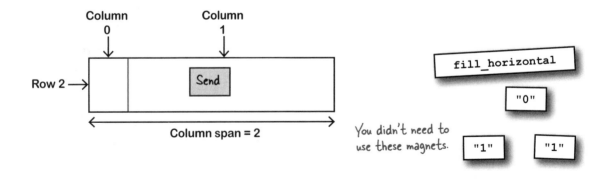

You didn't need to use these magnets.

`fill_horizontal` `"0"` `"1"` `"1"`

The full code for the grid layout

Here's the full code for the grid layout.

```xml
<?xml version="1.0" encoding="utf-8"?>
<GridLayout xmlns:android="http://schemas.android.com/apk/res/android"
    xmlns:tools="http://schemas.android.com/tools"
    android:layout_width="match_parent"
    android:layout_height="match_parent"
    android:padding="16dp"
    android:columnCount="2"
    tools:context="com.hfad.gridlayout.MainActivity">

    <TextView
        android:layout_width="wrap_content"
        android:layout_height="wrap_content"
        android:layout_row="0"
        android:layout_column="0"
        android:text="@string/to" />

    <EditText
        android:layout_width="wrap_content"
        android:layout_height="wrap_content"
        android:layout_gravity="fill_horizontal"
        android:layout_row="0"
        android:layout_column="1"
        android:hint="@string/to_hint" />
```

The To text view.

The email address text field.

The code for the Message text field and the Send button is on the next page.

The grid layout code (continued)

```
<EditText
    android:layout_width="wrap_content"
    android:layout_height="wrap_content"
    android:layout_gravity="fill"
    android:gravity="top"
    android:layout_row="1"
    android:layout_column="0"
    android:layout_columnSpan="2"
    android:hint="@string/message" />

<Button
    android:layout_width="wrap_content"
    android:layout_height="wrap_content"
    android:layout_row="2"
    android:layout_column="0"
    android:layout_gravity="center_horizontal"
    android:layout_columnSpan="2"
    android:text="@string/send" />
</GridLayout>
```

The Message text field

The button spans two columns, starting from row 2 column 0. It's centered horizontally.

appendix ii: gradle

The Gradle Build Tool

Take one SDK, add a sprinkling of libraries, mix well, then bake for two minutes.

Most Android apps are created using a build tool called Gradle.

Gradle works behind the scenes to find and download libraries, compile and deploy your code, run tests, clean the grouting, and so on. Most of the time you *might not even realize it's there* because Android Studio provides a graphical interface to it. Sometimes, however, it's helpful to dive into Gradle and **hack it manually**. In this appendix we'll introduce you to some of Gradle's many talents.

has Gradle
What ~~have the Romans~~ ever done for us?
∧

When you click the run button in Android Studio, most of the actual work
is done by an external build tool called **Gradle**. Here are some of the
things that Gradle does:

★ Locates and downloads the correct versions of any third-party libraries you need.

★ Calls the correct build tools in the correct sequence to turn all of your source code and
resources into a deployable app.

★ Installs and runs your app on an Android device.

★ A whole bunch of other stuff, like running tests and checking the quality of your code.

It's hard to list all of the things that Gradle does because it's designed to
be easily extensible. Unlike other XML-based build tools like Maven or
Ant, Gradle is written in a procedural language (Groovy), which is used
for both configuring a build and adding extra functionality.

Your project's Gradle files

Every time you create a new project, Android Studio creates two files
called *build.gradle*. One of these files is in your project folder, and contains
a small amount of information that specifies the basic settings of your app,
such as what version of Gradle to use, and which online repository:

```
buildscript {
    repositories {
        jcenter()
    }
    dependencies {
        classpath 'com.android.tools.build:gradle:2.3.0'
    }
}

allprojects {
    repositories {
        jcenter()
    }
}

task clean(type: Delete) {
    delete rootProject.buildDir
}
```

MyProject

└─ **build.gradle**

You will normally only need to change the code in this file if you want to
install a third-party plug-in, or need to specify another place that contains
downloadable libraries.

Your app's main Gradle file

The second *build.gradle* file lives inside the *app* folder within your project. This file tells Gradle how to build all of the code in your main Android module. It's where the majority of your application's properties are set, such as the level of the API that you're targeting, and the specifics of which external libraries your app will need:

```
apply plugin: 'com.android.application'

android {
    compileSdkVersion 25
    buildToolsVersion "25.0.1"
    defaultConfig {
        applicationId "com.hfad.example"
        minSdkVersion 19
        targetSdkVersion 25
        versionCode 1
        versionName "1.0"
        testInstrumentationRunner "android.support.test.runner.AndroidJUnitRunner"
    }
    buildTypes {
        release {
            minifyEnabled false
            proguardFiles getDefaultProguardFile('proguard-android.txt'), 'proguard-rules.pro'
        }
    }
}


dependencies {
    compile fileTree(dir: 'libs', include: ['*.jar'])
    androidTestCompile('com.android.support.test.espresso:espresso-core:2.2.2', {
        exclude group: 'com.android.support', module: 'support-annotations'
    })
    compile 'com.android.support:appcompat-v7:25.1.1'
    compile 'com.android.support.constraint:constraint-layout:1.0.2'
    testCompile 'junit:junit:4.12'
}
```

MyProject

app

build.gradle

Gradle comes built in to your project

Every time you create a new application, Android Studio includes an install of the Gradle build tool. If you look in the project directory, you will see two files called *gradlew* and *gradlew.bat*. These files contains scripts that allow you to build and deploy your app from the command line.

To get more familiar with Gradle, open a command prompt or terminal on your development machine and change into the top-level directory of your project. Then run one of the *gradlew* scripts with the parameter `tasks`. Gradle will tell you some of the tasks that it can perform for you:

We've cut down the actual output, because there are many, many tasks that you can run by default.

```
File Edit Window Help EmacsFTW
$ ./gradlew tasks
Build tasks
-----------
assemble - Assembles all variants of all applications and
         secondary packages.
build - Assembles and tests this project.
clean - Deletes the build directory.
compileDebugSources
mockableAndroidJar - Creates a version of android.jar that's
         suitable for unit tests.

Install tasks
-------------
installDebug - Installs the Debug build.
uninstallAll - Uninstall all applications.
uninstallDebug - Uninstalls the Debug build.

Verification tasks
------------------
check - Runs all checks.
connectedAndroidTest - Installs and runs instrumentation tests
         for all flavors on connected devices.
lint - Runs lint on all variants.
test - Run unit tests for all variants.

To see all tasks and more detail, run gradlew tasks --all

BUILD SUCCESSFUL

Total time: 6.209 secs
$
```

Let's take a quick tour of some of the most useful ones.

The check task

The check task performs static analysis on the source code in your application. Think of it as your coding buddy, who at a moment's notice can scoot through your files looking for coding errors. By default, the check task uses the *lint* tool to look for common Android programming errors. It will generate a report in *app/build/reports/lint-results.html*:

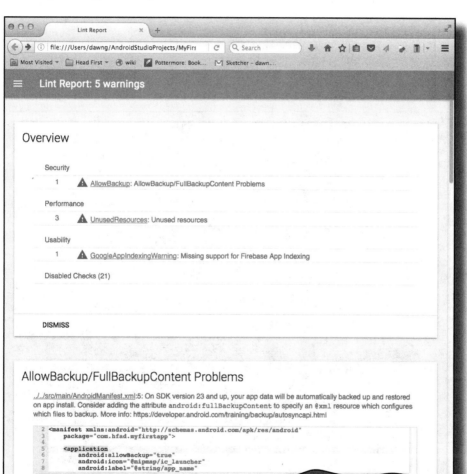

The clean installDebug task

This task will do a complete compile and install of your application on your connected device. You can obviously do this from the IDE, but it can be useful to do this from the command line if, for example, you want to automatically build your application on an Integration Server.

The androidDependencies task

For this task, Gradle will automatically pull down any libraries your application requires, and some of those libraries will automatically pull down other libraries, which might pull down other libraries and... well, you get the idea.

Even though your *app/build.gradle* file might only mention a couple of libraries, your application might need to install many dependent libraries for your app. So it's sometimes useful to see which libraries your application requires, and why. That's what the `androidDependencies` task is for: it displays a tree of all of the libraries in your app:

```
File Edit Window Help EmacsFTW
$ ./gradlew androidDependencies

Incremental java compilation is an incubating feature.
:app:androidDependencies
debug
+--- com.android.support:appcompat-v7:25.1.1@aar
|    +--- com.android.support:support-annotations:25.1.1@jar
|    +--- com.android.support:support-v4:25.1.1@aar
|    |    +--- com.android.support:support-compat:25.1.1@aar
|    |    |    \--- com.android.support:support-annotations:25.1.1@jar
|    |    +--- com.android.support:support-media-compat:25.1.1@aar
|    |    |    +--- com.android.support:support-annotations:25.1.1@jar
|    |    |    \--- com.android.support:support-compat:25.1.1@aar
|    |    |         \--- com.android.support:support-annotations:25.1.1@jar
|    |    +--- com.android.support:support-core-utils:25.1.1@aar
|    |    |    +--- com.android.support:support-annotations:25.1.1@jar
|    |    |    \--- com.android.support:support-compat:25.1.1@aar
...
```

gradlew <your-task-goes-here>

The real reason that Android apps are commonly built with Gradle is because it's easily extended. All Gradle files are written in Groovy, which is a general-purpose language designed to be run by Java. That means you can easily add your own custom tasks.

As an example, add the following code to the end of your *app/build.gradle* file:

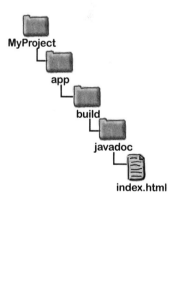

```
task javadoc(type: Javadoc) {
    source = android.sourceSets.main.java.srcDirs
    classpath += project.files(android.getBootClasspath().join(File.pathSeparator))
    destinationDir = file("$project.buildDir/javadoc/")
    failOnError false
}
```

This code creates a new task called `javadoc`, which generates javadoc for your source code. You can run the task with:

```
./gradlew javadoc
```

The generated files will be published in *app/build/javadoc*:

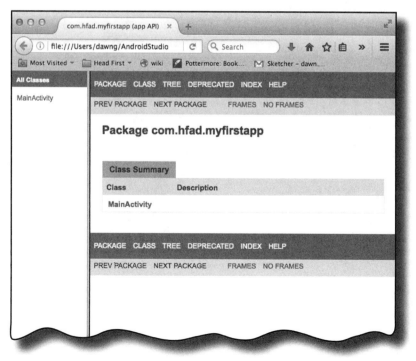

Gradle plug-ins

As well as writing your own tasks, you can also install Gradle plug-ins. A plug-in can greatly extend your build environment. Want to write Android code in Clojure? Want your build to automatically interact with source control systems like Git? How about spinning up entire servers in Docker and then testing your application on them?

You can do these things, and many, many more by using Gradle plug-ins. For details on what plug-ins are available, see *https:// plugins.gradle.org*.

appendix iii: art

The Android Runtime

Ever wonder how Android apps can run on so many kinds of devices? Android apps run in a virtual machine called the **Android runtime (ART)**, not the Oracle Java Virtual Machine (JVM). This means that your apps are quicker to start on small, low-powered devices and run more efficiently. In this appendix, we'll look at how ART works.

What is the Android runtime?

The Android Runtime (ART) is the system that runs your compiled code on an Android device. It first appeared on Android with the release of KitKat and became the standard way of running code in Lollipop.

ART is designed to run your compiled Android apps quickly and efficiently on small, low-powered devices. Android Studio uses the Gradle build system to do all the work of creating and installing apps for you, but it can be useful to understand what happens behind the scenes when you click the Run button. Let's see what really goes on.

> You don't need to understand the info in this appendix in order to create cool Android apps. So if you're not into the nitty-gritty of what's going on behind the scenes when an Android device runs an app, feel free to skip this appendix.

Previously, Java code ran on the Oracle JVM

Java has been around for a very long time, and compiled Java applications have almost always been run on the Oracle Java Virtual Machine (JVM). In that scenario, Java source code gets compiled down to *.class* files. One *.class* file gets created for every Java class, interface, or enum in your source code:

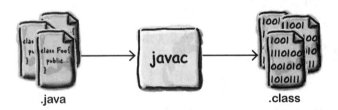

.java   javac   .class

The *.class* files contain Java bytecodes, which can be read and executed by the JVM. The JVM is a software emulation of a Central Processing Unit (CPU), like the chip at the heart of your development machine. But because it's emulated, it can be made to work on almost any device. That's why Java code is designed to be written once, run anywhere.

So is that what happens on Android devices? Well…not quite. The Android Runtime performs the same kind of job as the JVM, but it does it in a very different way.

ART compiles code into DEX files

When you do Android development, your Java source code is compiled down into *.dex* files. A *.dex* file serves a similar purpose to a *.class* file, because it contains executable bytecodes. But instead of being JVM bytecodes, they are in a different format called **Dalvik**. DEX stands for **D**alvik **EX**ecutable.

Rather than creating a *.dex* file for each and every class file, your app will normally be compiled down into a single file called *classes.dex*. That single *.dex* file will contain bytecodes for all of your source code, and for every library in your app.

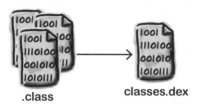

.class → classes.dex

The DEX format can only cope with 65,535 methods, so if your app contains a lot of code or some large libraries, your file might need to be converted into multiple *.dex* files:

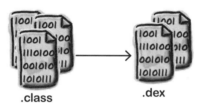

.class → .dex

You can find out more about creating multi-DEX apps here:

https://developer.android.com/studio/build/multidex.html.

How DEX files get created

When Android builds your app, it uses a tool called dx, which stitches `.class` files into a DEX file:

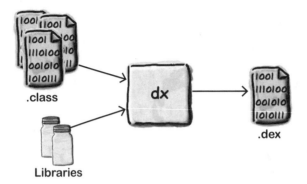

It may seem a bit weird that the compilation process involves two stages of compilation: first to *.class* files, and then from *.class* files to the DEX format. Why doesn't Google just create a single tool that goes straight from `.java` source code to DEX bytecodes?

For a while Google was developing a compiler called JACK and an associated linker called JILL that could create DEX code straight from Java code, but there was a problem. Some Java tools don't just work at the source code level; they work directly with *.class* files, and modify the code that those files contain.

For example, if you use a code coverage tool to see which code your tests are actually running, the coverage tool will likely want to modify the contents of the generated *.class* files to add in additional bytecodes to keep track of the code as it's executed. If you used the JACK compiler, no *.class* files were generated.

So back in March 2017, Google announced that it was shelving JACK, and was putting all of its efforts into making the dx tool work really well with the latest Java *.class* formats. This has the additional advantage that any new Java language features—so long as they don't require new Java byte codes—will automatically be supported by Android.

DEX files are zipped into APK files

But Android apps aren't shipped around as *.dex* files. There's a whole bunch of other files that make up your app: images, sounds, metadata, and so on. All of these resources and your DEX bytecode is wrapped up into a single zip file called an Android Package or *.apk* file. The *.apk* file is created by another tool called the Android Asset Packing Tool, or aapt.

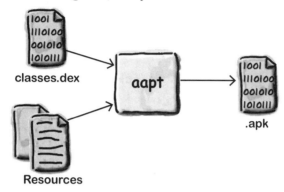

When you download an app from the Google Play Store, what actually gets downloaded is an APK file. In fact, when you run your app from Android Studio, the build system will first build an *.apk* file and then install it onto your Android device.

You may need to sign the .apk file

If you're going to distribute your app through the Google Play Store, you will need to sign it. Signing an app package means that you store an additional file in the *.apk* that is based on a checksum of the contents of the *.apk* and a separately generated private key. The *.apk* file uses the standard jarsigner tool that comes as part of Oracle's Java Development Kit. The jarsigner tool was created to sign *.jar* files, but it will also work with *.apk* files.

If you sign the *.apk* file, you will then also need to run it through a tool called zipalign, which will make sure that the compressed parts of the file are lined up on byte boundaries. Android wants them byte-aligned so it can read them easily without needing to uncompress the file.

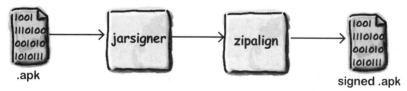

Android Studio will do all of this for you if you choose Generate Signed APK from the Build menu.

So that's how your app gets converted from Java source code into an installable file. But how does it get installed and run on your device?

Say hello to the Android Debug Bridge (adb)

All communication between your development machine and your Android device takes place over the Android Debug Bridge. There are two sides to the bridge: a command-line tool on your dev machine called adb, and a daemon process on your Android device called adbd (the Android Debug Bridge Daemon).

The `adb` command on your development machine will run a copy of itself in the background, called the ADB server. The server receives commands over network port 5037, and sends them to the adbd process on the device. If you want to copy or read a file, install an app, or look at the logcat information for an app, then all of this information passes back and forth across the debug bridge.

So when the build system wants to install your APK file, it does so by sending a command like this to the debug bridge:

```
adb install bitsandpizzas.apk
```

The file will then be transferred to a virtual device, or over a USB cable to a real device, and be installed into the */data/app/* directory, where it will sit waiting for the app to be run.

How apps come alive: running your APK file

When your app is run, whether it's been started by a user pressing its launch icon or because the IDE has started it, the Android device needs to turn that *.apk* file into a process running in memory.

It does this using a process called Zygote. Zygote is like a half-started process. It's allocated some memory and already contains the main Android libraries. It has everything it needs, in fact, except for the code that's specific to your app.

When Android runs your app, it first creates a copy (a.k.a. fork) of the Zygote process, and then tells the copied process to load your application code. So why does Android leave this half-started process hanging around? Why not just start a fresh process from scratch for each app? It's because of performance. It can take Android a long time to create a new process from scratch, but it can fork a copy of an existing process in a split second.

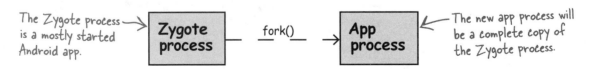

The Zygote process is a mostly started Android app.

Zygote process — fork() → App process

The new app process will be a complete copy of the Zygote process.

Android converts the .dex code to OAT format

The new app process now needs to load the code that's specific to your app. Remember, your app code is stored in the *classes.dex* file inside your *.apk* package. So the *classes.dex* file is extracted from the *.apk* and placed into a separate directory. But rather than simply use the *classes.dex* file, Android will convert the Dalvik byte codes in *classes.dex* into native machine code. Technically, the *classes.dex* will be converted into an ELF shared object. Android calls this library format OAT, and calls the tool that converts the *classes.dex* file dex2oat.

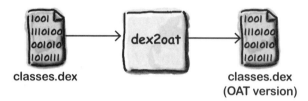

classes.dex → **dex2oat** → **classes.dex (OAT version)**

The converted file is stored into a directory named something like this:

/data/dalvik-cache/data@app@com.hfad.bitsandpizzas@base.apk@classes.dex

This file can then be loaded as a native library by the application process, and the app appears on the screen.

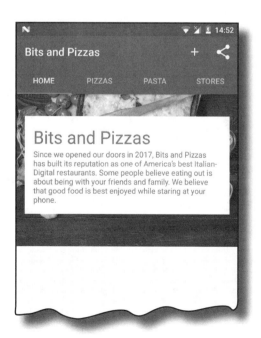

appendix iv: adb

The Android Debug Bridge

In this book, we've focused on using an IDE for all your Android needs. But there are times when using a command-line tool can be plain useful, like those times when Android Studio can't see your Android device but you just *know* it's there. In this chapter, we'll introduce you to the **Android Debug Bridge (or adb)**, a command-line tool you can use to communicate with the emulator or Android devices.

adb: your command-line pal

Every time your development machine needs to talk to an Android device, whether it's a real device connected with a USB cable, or a virtual device running in an emulator, it does so by using the **Android Debug Bridge (adb)**. The adb is a process that's controlled by a command that's also called `adb`.

The `adb` command is stored in the *platform-tools* directory of the Android System Developer's Kit on your computer. If you add the *platform-tools* directory to your `PATH`, you will be able to run adb from the command line.

In a terminal or at a command prompt, you can use it like this:

```
Interactive Session
$ adb devices
List of devices attached
emulator-5554        device
$
```

The `adb devices` command means "Tell me which Android devices you are connected to." The `adb` command works by talking to an adb server process, which runs in the background. The adb server is sometimes called the *adb dæmon* or *adbd*. When you enter an `adb` command in a terminal, a request is sent to network port 5037 on your machine. The adbd listens for commands to come in on this port. When Android Studio wants to run an app, or check the log output, or do anything else that involves talking to an Android device, it will do it via port 5037.

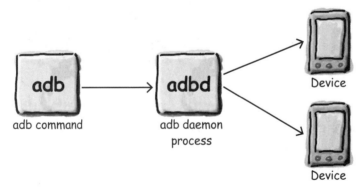

When the adbd receives a command, it will forward it to a separate adbd process that's running in the relevant Android device. This process will then be able to make changes to the Android device or return the requested information.

Sometimes, if the adb server isn't running, the `adb` command will
need to start it:

```
Interactive Session
$ adb devices
* daemon not running. starting it now on port 5037 *
* daemon started successfully *
List of devices attached
emulator-5554      device
$
```

Likewise, if ever you plug in an Android device and Android
Studio can't see it, you can manually kill the adb server and restart
it:

```
Interactive Session
$ adb devices
List of devices attached
$ adb kill-server
$ adb start-server
* daemon not running. starting it now on port 5037 *
* daemon started successfully *
$ adb devices
List of devices attached
emulator-5554      device
$
```

By killing and restarting the server, you force adb to get back in
touch with any connected Android devices.

Running a shell

Most of the time you won't use adb directly; you'll let an IDE like Android Studio do the work for you. But there are times when it can be useful to go to the command line and interact with your devices directly.

One example is if you want to run a shell on your device:

```
Interactive Session
$ adb shell
root@generic_x86:/ #
```

The adb shell command will open up an interactive shell directly on the Android device. If you have more than one device attached, you can indicate which device you mean with the -s option, followed by the name given by the adb devices command. For example, adb -s emulator-5554 shell will open a shell on the emulator.

Once you open a shell to your device, you can run a lot of the standard Linux commands:

```
Interactive Session
$ adb shell
root@generic_x86:/ # ls
acct
cache
charger
config
d
data
default.prop
dev
etc
file_contexts
....
1|root@generic_x86:/ # df
Filesystem              Size     Used     Free     Blksize
/dev                  439.8M    60.0K   439.8M    4096
/mnt/asec             439.8M     0.0K   439.8M    4096
/mnt/obb              439.8M     0.0K   439.8M    4096
/system               738.2M   533.0M   205.2M    4096
/data                 541.3M   237.8M   303.5M    4096
/cache                 65.0M     4.3M    60.6M    4096
/mnt/media_rw/sdcard  196.9M     4.5K   196.9M    512
/storage/sdcard       196.9M     4.5K   196.9M    512
root@generic_x86:/ #
```

Useful shell commands

If you open a shell to Android, you have access to a whole bunch of command line tools. Here are just a few:

Command	Description	Example (and what it does)
pm	Package management tool.	`pm list packages` (this lists all installed apps)
		`pm path com.hfad.bitzandpizzas` (find where an app is installed)
		`pm -help` (show other options)
ps	Process status.	`ps` (lists all processes and their IDs)
dexdump	Display details of an APK.	`dexdump -d /data/app/com.hfad.bitzandpizzas-2/base.apk` (disassemble an app)
lsof	List a process's open files and other connections.	`lsof -p 1234` (show what process with id 1234 is doing)
screencap	Take a screenshot.	`screencap -p /sdcard/screenshot.png` (save current screenshot to *sdcard/screenshot.png*, and get it off the device with `adb pull /sdcard/screenshot.png`)
top	Show busiest processes.	`top -m 5` (show the top five processes)

Each of these examples works from an interactive shell prompt, but you can also pass them direct to the shell command from your development machine. For example, this command will show the apps installed on your device:

```
Interactive Session
$ adb shell pm list packages
```

Kill the adb server

Sometimes the connection can fail between your development machine and your device. If this happens, you can reset the connection by killing the adb server:

```
Interactive Session
$ adb kill-server
```

The next time you run an adb command, the server will restart and a fresh connection will be made.

Get the output from logcat

All of the apps running on your Android device send their output to a central stream called the logcat. You can see the live output from the logcat by running the adb logcat command:

```
Interactive Session
$ adb logcat
--------- beginning of system
I/Vold    (  936): Vold 2.1 (the revenge) firing up
D/Vold    (  936): Volume sdcard state changing -1
(Initializing) -> 0 (No-Media)
W/DirectVolume(  936): Deprecated implied prefix pattern
detected, please use '/devices/platform/goldfish_mmc.0*'
instead
...
```

The logcat output will keep streaming until you stop it. It can be useful to run adb logcat if you want to store the output in a file. The adb logcat command is used by Android Studio to produce the output you see in the Devices/logcat panel.

Copying files to/from your device

The adb pull and adb push commands can be used to transfer files back and forth. For example, here we are copying the */default.prop/* properties file into a local file called *1.txt*:

```
Interactive Session
$ adb pull /default.prop 1.txt
28 KB/s (281 bytes in 0.009s)
$ cat 1.txt
#
# ADDITIONAL_DEFAULT_PROPERTIES
#
ro.secure=0
ro.allow.mock.location=1
ro.debuggable=1
ro.zygote=zygote32
dalvik.vm.dex2oat-Xms=64m
dalvik.vm.dex2oat-Xmx=512m
dalvik.vm.image-dex2oat-Xms=64m
dalvik.vm.image-dex2oat-Xmx=64m
ro.dalvik.vm.native.bridge=0
persist.sys.usb.config=adb
$
```

And much, much more...

There are many, many commands that you can run using adb: you can back up and restore databases (very useful if you need to debug a problem with a database app), start the adb server on a different port, reboot machines, or just find out a lot of information about the running devices. To find out all the options available, just type adb on the command line:

```
Interactive Session
$ adb
Android Debug Bridge version 1.0.32
 -a                         - directs adb to listen on all
interfaces for a connection
 -d                         - directs command to the only
connected USB device
                              returns an error if more than
one USB device is present.
 -e                         - directs command to the only
running emulator.
returns an error if more than one emulator is ....
```

appendix v: the android emulator

Speeding Things Up

Ever felt like you were spending all your time waiting for the emulator? There's no doubt that using the Android emulator is useful. It allows you to see how your app will run on devices other than the physical ones you have access to. But at times it can feel a little...sluggish. In this appendix, we'll explain why the emulator can seem slow. Even better, we'll give you a few tips we've learned for **speeding it up**.

Why the emulator is so slow

When you're writing Android apps, you'll spend a lot of time waiting for the Android emulator to start up or deploy your code. Why is that? Why is the Android emulator so slooooooow? If you've ever written iPhone code, you know how fast the iPhone simulator is. If it's possible for the iPhone, then why not for Android?

There's a clue in the names: the iPhone *simulator* and the Android *emulator*.

The iPhone simulator simulates a device running the iOS operating system. All of the code for iOS is compiled to run natively on the Mac and the iPhone simulator runs at Mac-native speed. That means it can simulate an iPhone boot-up in just a few seconds.

The Android emulator works in a completely different way. It uses an open source application called QEMU (or Quick Emulator) to emulate the entire Android hardware device. It runs code that interprets machine code that's intended to be run by the device's processor. It has code that emulates the storage system, the screen, and pretty much every other piece of physical equipment on an Android device.

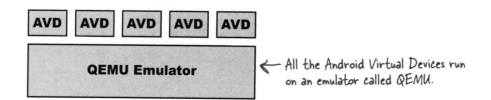

← All the Android Virtual Devices run on an emulator called QEMU.

An emulator like QEMU creates a much more realistic representation of a virtual device than something like the iPhone simulator does, but the downside is that it has to do far more work for even simple operations like reading from disk or displaying something on a screen. That's why the emulator takes so long to boot up a device. It has to pretend to be every little hardware component inside the device, and it has to interpret every single instruction.

How to speed up your Android development

1. Use a real device

The simplest way to speed up your development process is by using a real device. A real device will boot up much faster than an emulated one, and it will probably deploy and run apps a lot more quickly. If you want to develop on a real device, you may want to go into "Developer options" and check the Stay Awake option. This will prevent your device from locking the screen, which is useful if you are repeatedly deploying to it.

2. Use an emulator snapshot

Booting up is one of the slowest things the emulator does. If you save a snapshot of the device while it's running, the emulator will be able to reset itself to this state without having to go through the boot-up process. To use a snapshot with your device, open the AVD manager from the Android Studio menu by selecting Tools→Android→AVD Manager, edit the AVD by clicking on the Edit symbol, and then check the "Store a snapshot for faster startup" option.

This will save a snapshot of what the memory looks like when the device is running. The emulator will be able to restore the memory in this state without booting the device.

3. Use hardware acceleration

By default, the QEMU emulator will have to interpret each machine code instruction on the virtual device. That means it's very flexible because it can pretend to be lots of different CPUs, but it's one of the main reasons why the emulator is slow. Fortunately, there's a way to get your development machine to run the machine code instructions directly. There are two main types of Android Virtual Device: ARM machines and x86 machines. If you create an x86 Android device and your development machine is using a particular type of Intel x86 CPU, then you can configure your emulator to run the Android machine code instructions directly on your Intel CPU.

You will need to install Intel's Hardware Accelerated Execution Manager (HAXM). At the time of writing , you can find HAXM here:

https://software.intel.com/en-us/android/articles/intel-hardware-accelerated-execution-manager ← If it's moved, a quick web search should track it down.

HAXM is a hypervisor. That means it can switch your CPU into a special mode to run virtual machine instructions directly. However, HAXM will only run on Intel processors that support Intel Virtualization Technology. But if your development machine is compatible, then HAXM will make your AVD run much faster.

4. Use Instant Run

Since Android Studio 2.3, it's been possible to redeploy apps much more quickly using the Instant Run utility. This utility allows Android Studio to recompile just the files that have changed, and then patch the application currently running on the device. This means that instead of waiting for a minute or so while the application is recompiled and deployed, you can see your changes running in just a few seconds.

To use Instant Run, click on the Apply Changes option in the Run menu, or click on the lightning bolt icon in the toolbar:

Click on this button in the toolbar to apply changes using Instant Run.

There are a couple of conditions on using Instant Run. First, your app's target needs to be at least API 15. Second, you need to deploy to a device that runs API 21 or above. So long as you satisfy both these conditions, you'll find that Instant Run is by far the fastest way of getting your code up and running.

appendix vi: leftovers

The Top Ten Things (we didn't cover)

Oh my, look at the tasty treats we have left...

Even after all that, there's still a little more.

There are just a few more things we think you need to know. We wouldn't feel right about ignoring them, and we really wanted to give you a book you'd be able to lift without extensive training at the local gym. Before you put down the book, **read through these tidbits**.

1. Distributing your app

Once you've developed your app, you'll probably want to make it available to other users. You'll likely want to do this by releasing your app through an app marketplace such as Google Play.

There are two stages to this process: preparing your app for release, and then releasing it.

Preparing your app for release

Before you can release your app, you need to configure, build, and test a release version of it. This includes tasks such as deciding on an icon for your app and modifying *AndroidManifest.xml* so that only devices that are able to run your app are able to download it.

Before you release your app, make sure that you test it on at least one tablet and one phone to check that it looks the way you expect and its performance is acceptable.

You can find further details of how to prepare your app for release here:

http://developer.android.com/tools/publishing/preparing.html

Releasing your app

This stage includes publicizing your app, selling it, and distributing it.

To release your app on the Play Store, you need to register for a publisher account and use the Developer Console to publish your app. You can find further details here:

http://developer.android.com/distribute/googleplay/start.html

For ideas on how to best target your app to your users and build a buzz about it, we suggest you explore the documents here:

http://developer.android.com/distribute/index.html

2. Content providers

You've seen how to use intents to start activities in other apps. As an example, you can start the Messaging app to send the text you pass to it. But what if you want to use another app's data in your own app? For example, what if you want to use Contacts data in your app to perform some task, or insert a new Calendar event?

You can't access another app's data by interrogating its database. Instead, you use a **content provider**, which is an interface that allows apps to share data in a controlled way. It allows you to perform queries to read the data, insert new records, and update or delete existing records.

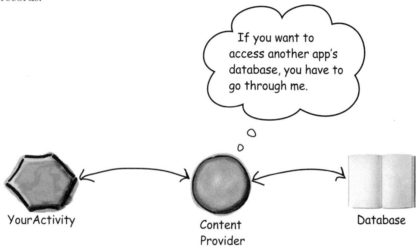

If you want to access another app's database, you have to go through me.

YourActivity   Content Provider   Database

If you want other apps to use your data, you can create your own content provider.

You can find out more about the concept of content providers here:

http://developer.android.com/guide/topics/providers/content-providers.html

Here's a guide on using Contacts data in your app:

http://developer.android.com/guide/topics/providers/contacts-provider.html

And here's a guide on using Calendar data:

http://developer.android.com/guide/topics/providers/calendar-provider.html

3. Loaders

If you do a lot of work with databases or content providers, sooner or later you'll encounter **loaders**. A loader helps you load data so that it can be displayed in an activity or fragment.

Loaders run on separate threads in the background, and make it easier to manage threads by providing callback methods. They persist and cache data across configuration changes so that if, for example, the user rotates their device, the app doesn't create duplicate queries. You can also get them to notify your app when the underlying data changes so that you can deal with the change in your views.

The Loader API includes a generic `Loader` class, which is the base class for all loaders. You can create your own loader by extending this class, or you can use one of the built-in subclasses: `AsyncTaskLoader` or `CursorLoader`. `AsyncTaskLoader` uses an `AsyncTask`, and `CursorLoader` loads data from a content provider.

You can find out more about loaders here:

https://developer.android.com/guide/components/loaders.html

4. Sync adapters

Sync adapters allow you to synchronize data between an Android device and a web server. This allows you to do things like back up the user's data to a web server, for instance, or transfer data to a device so that it can be used offline.

Sync adapters have a number of advantages over designing your own data transfer mechanism.

- ⭐ They allow you to automate data transfer based on specific criteria—for example, time of day or data changes.

- ⭐ They automatically check for network connectivity, and only run when the device has a network connection.

- ⭐ Sync adapter–based data transfers run in batches, which helps improve battery performance.

- ⭐ They let you add user credentials or a server login to the data transfer.

You can find out how to use sync adapters here:

https://developer.android.com/training/sync-adapters/index.html

5. Broadcasts

Suppose you want your app to react in some way when a system event occurs. You may, for example, have built a music app, and you want it to stop playing music if the headphones are removed. How can your app tell when these events occur?

Android broadcasts system events when they occur, including things like the device running low on power, a new incoming phone call, or the system getting booted. You can listen for these events by creating a **broadcast receiver**. Broadcast receivers allow you to subscribe to particular broadcast messages so that your app can respond to particular system events.

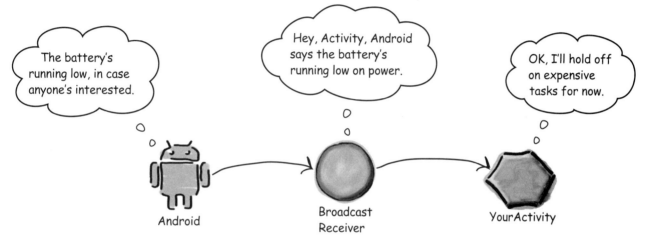

Your app can also send custom broadcast messages to notify other apps of events.

You can find out more about broadcasts here:

https://developer.android.com/guide/components/broadcasts.html

6. The WebView class

If you want to provide your users with access to web content, you have two options. The first option is to open the web content with an external app like Chrome or Firefox. The second option is to display the content inside your app using the `WebView` class.

The `WebView` class allows you to display the contents of a web page inside your activity's layout. You can use it to deliver an entire web app as a client application, or to deliver individual web pages. This approach is useful if there's content in your app you might need to update, such as an end-user agreement or user guide.

You add a `WebView` to your app by including it in your layout:

```
<WebView  xmlns:android="http://schemas.android.com/apk/res/android"
    android:id="@+id/webview"
    android:layout_width="match_parent"
    android:layout_height="match_parent" />
```

You then tell it which web page it should load by calling its `loadUrl()` method:

```
WebView webView = (WebView) findViewById(R.id.webview);
webView.loadUrl("http://www.oreilly.com/");
```

You also need to specify that the app must have Internet access by adding the `INTERNET` permission to *AndroidManifest.xml*:

```
<manifest ... >
    <uses-permission android:name="android.permission.INTERNET" />
    ...
</manifest>
```

You can find out more about using web content in your apps here:

http://developer.android.com/guide/webapps/index.html

7. Settings

Many apps include a settings screen so that the user can record their preferences. As an example, an email app may allow the user to specify whether they want to see a confirmation dialog before sending an email:

This is the settings screen for the Gmail app.

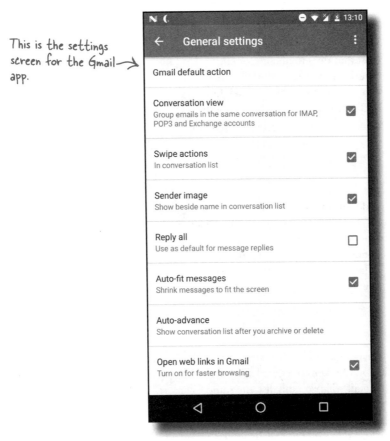

You build a settings screen for your app using the Preferences API. This allows you to add individual preferences, and record a value for each preference. These values are recorded in a shared preferences file for your app.

You can find out more about creating settings screens here:

https://developer.android.com/guide/topics/ui/settings.html

8. Animation

As Android devices increasingly take advantage of the power of their built-in graphics hardware, animation is being used more and more to improve the user's app experience.

There are several types of animation that you can perform in Android:

Property animation

Property animation relies on the fact that the visual components in an Android app use a lot of numeric properties to describe their appearance. If you change the value of a property like the height or the width of a view, you can make it animate. That's what property animation is: smoothly animating the properties of visual components over time.

View animations

A lot of animations can be created declaratively as XML resources. So you can have XML files that use a standard set of animations (like scaling, translation, and rotation) to create effects that you can call from your code. The wonderful thing about declarative view animations is that they are decoupled from your Java code, so they are very easy to port from one app project to another.

Activity transitions

Let's say you write an app that displays a list of items with names and images. You click on an item and you're taken to a detail view of it. The activity that shows you more detail will probably use the same image that appeared in the previous list activity.

Activity transitions allow you to animate a view from one activity that will also appear in the next activity. So you can make an image from a list smoothly animate across the screen to the position it takes in the next activity. This will give your app a more seamless feel.

To learn more about Android animations see:

https://developer.android.com/guide/topics/graphics/index.html

To learn about activity transitions and material design, see:

https://developer.android.com/training/material/animations.html

9. App widgets

An app widget is a small application view that you can add to other apps or your home screen. It gives you direct access to an app's core content or functionality from your home screen without you having to launch the app.

Here's an example of an app widget:

This is an app widget. It gives you direct access to the app's core functionality without you having to launch the app.

To find out how you create your own app widgets, look here:

http://developer.android.com/guide/topics/appwidgets/index.html

10. Automated testing

All modern development relies heavily on automated testing. If you create an app that's intended to be used by thousands or even millions of people, you will quickly lose users if it's flaky or keeps crashing.

There are many ways to automatically test your app, but they generally fall into two categories: **unit testing** and **on-device testing** (sometimes called *instrumentation testing*).

Unit tests

Unit tests run on your development machine, and they check the individual pieces—or units—of your code. The most popular unit testing framework is **JUnit**, and Android Studio will probably bundle JUnit into your project. Unit tests live in the *app/src/tes*t folder of your project, and a typical test method looks something like this:

```
@Test
public void returnsTheCorrectAmberBeers() {
    BeerExpert beerExpert = new BeerExpert();
    assertArrayEquals(new String[]{"Jack Amber", "Red Moose"},
            beerExpert.getBrands("amber").toArray());
}
```

You can find more out about JUnit here:

http://junit.org

On-device tests

On-device tests run inside an emulator or physical device and check the fully assembled app. They work by installing a separate package alongside your app that uses a software layer called *instrumentation* to interact with your app in the same way as a user. An increasingly popular framework for on-device testing is called **Espresso**, and Android Studio will probably bundle it in to your project. On-device tests live in the *app/src/androidTest* folder, and Espresso tests look something like this:

```
@Test
public void ifYouDoNotChangeTheColorThenYouGetAmber() {
    onView(withId(R.id.find_beer)).perform(click());
    onView(withId(R.id.brands)).check(matches(withText(
            "Jail Pale Ale\nGout Stout\n")));
}
```

When you run an on-device test, you will see the app running on your phone or tablet and responding to keypresses and gestures just as if a person were using it.

You can find out more about Espresso testing here:

https://developer.android.com/training/testing/ui-testing/espresso-testing.html

Index

A

action bar, 314. *See also* app bar
ActionBarActivity class, 298
ActionBar class, 306, 314
ActionBarDrawerToggle class, 607
actions
  about, 100
  in app bar
    adding, 315–317, 319–325
    icons for, 320, 322
    menu for, 321, 323
    method for, 324–325
    title for, 320, 322
  category specified with, 106, 117
  determining activities for, 105–106
  share actions, 332–335
  specifying in an intent, 100–104
  types of, 101
activities
  about, 2, 12, 31, 38, 120–121
  backward compatibility for, 295, 298
  calling custom Java classes from, 71–74
  calling methods from, 59–62
  class hierarchy for, 139, 297
  class name for, 85
  converting to fragments, 438–449
  creating, 13–14, 61, 67–68
  declaring in manifest file, 85
  default, 41
  editing. *See* code editor; design editor
  location in project, 17
  main, specifying, 84, 120
  multiple
    chaining, 78
    creating, 78–83
    passing text to, 90–95
    retrieving text from, 96–97
    starting with intents, 86–89

  navigating. *See* navigation
  organizing, 249–255, 290–291
    category activities, 249–250, 252–255, 267–268, 277–278
    detail/edit activities, 249–250, 253–255, 279–283
    top-level activities, 249–250, 252–255
  in other apps
    determining from actions, 105–106
    none available, 117
    starting with intents, 99–104
    users always choosing, 112–117
    users choosing default, 111
    users choosing if multiple, 100, 104, 111
  parent activity, 328
  states of. *See* activity lifecycle
Activity class, 61, 139, 297
activity lifecycle
  about, 137–138, 146–147
  class hierarchy for, 139
  compared to fragment lifecycle, 439
  methods associated with, 137–139, 147, 167, 439
  states in
    based on app's focus, 154–157
    based on app's visibility, 146–147
    list of, 137–138, 146–147
    saving and restoring, 140–141, 145
ActivityNotFoundException, 103, 117
activity transitions, 868
adapters
  array. *See* ArrayAdapter class
  decoupling, with interface, 572–574
  recycler view. *See* recycler view adapter
  sync adapters, 864
AdapterView class, 261, 269
adb (Android Debug Bridge)
  about, 846, 850–851
  copying files, 855
  killing adb server, 854
  logcat output, 854
  running a shell, 852–853

Argenteus leo, in scuti area, sexies auro & cyano tæniata, est familiæ PARTICIPATAE Venetijs.

Andreas de Ryes

In eadem octies argento & cyano virgata, puniceus leo, ex eodem colore diadematus, est BIERSEORVM in Belgio.

Iacob. Héricourt.

Aut in ea, totidem fascijs argenteis puniceisque sulcata, leo sabuleus, auro numellatus, est familiæ TOV- *Philibert. Monet.* TEVILLAE in Gallia.

In scuti pagina verò sexies oblique, argento atque ostro exarata, leo aureus, est BADOERIAE familiæ Ve- *M. S. ex Musais Romanis.* netijs.

Aut in ea denis ijsdem fascijs descripta, coccineus leo, auro redimitus & vngulatus, linguatus autem cyano, cum cauda bifida & decussata, est regia tessera CYPRI.

Io. Iacob. Chifflet.

Vel in eadem, totidem balteis argenteis & cyaneis referta, leo puniceus,
cum

WAPPEN-BILDER-LEXIKON

OTTFRIED NEUBECKER / WILHELM RENTZMANN

WAPPEN BILDER LEXIKON

DICTIONNAIRE HERALDIQUE
ENCYCLOPAEDIA OF HERALDRY

BATTENBERG VERLAG MÜNCHEN

Cooke's Ordinary, um 1340, Schilde Nr. 435−490
Das älteste Wappenbilderregister der Welt
Privatbesitz des Chefs des englischen Heroldsamts, Sir Anthony Wagner, Garter King of Arms

Vorwort

Zwei verschiedenartige Ursachen rücken ein vor etwa hundert Jahren konzipiertes und erschienenes Sammelwerk wieder in den Blickpunkt; das eine ist die Zunahme der Freunde des Münzensammelns, das andere die stürmische Entwicklung der öffentlichen Heraldik, d. h. der Wappen der Staaten und mehr noch der Gemeinden. Es ist hier nicht der Raum, die Gründe für beide Erscheinungen zu untersuchen; hier darf die getroffene Feststellung genügen.

Das *Numismatische Wappen-Lexicon des Mittelalters und der Neuzeit* von Wilhelm Rentzmann, zu Lebzeiten Rendant am Königlich Preußischen Joachimsthalschen Gymnasium zu Berlin, trägt zwar die Eierschalen einer ungenügend durchdachten Darbietung, ist aber dennoch der gegebene Stamm für eine Weiterarbeit, eine Arbeit, die fortzuführen dem früh verstorbenen Autor nicht mehr gegönnt war. Er starb am 30. Mai 1880, also nur vier Jahre nach der Veröffentlichung seines zweiten numismatischen Werkes[1], an dessen Vervollständigung er unermüdlich weitergearbeitet haben soll. Sein Nachlaß ist verschollen. Rentzmanns Materialkenntnis ist bewundernswert, aber die Bewältigung des Stoffes kann nicht als gelungen betrachtet werden. Er schloß zutreffend von sich auf andere, indem er meinte, Numismatiker seien keine Heraldiker. Folglich könne man Numismatikern nicht zumuten, Wappenbilder heraldisch geordnet aufzufinden; so griff er zu einer alphabetischen Ordnung, deren Tücken die Benützung seiner Tafeln äußerst mühsam gestalteten.

Wie schwierig sich das Problem der systematischen Ordnung von Wappenbildern durch die Jahrhunderte gestaltete, wird auf den folgenden Seiten geschildert werden.

Im vorliegenden Werk ist Rentzmanns Material unter Verwendung der inzwischen gewonnenen Erkenntnisse neu geordnet worden. Rentzmann hat den Unterschied zwischen Münz- und Wappenbild geflissentlich verwischt, so daß zwar der Numismatiker in einem Wappenbilderlexikon auch Münzbilder findet, die weit vor der Zeit der ersten Wappen geprägt worden sind. Der Heraldiker allerdings wird im Unklaren gelassen, ob das aufgefundene Bild als Wappen anzusehen ist oder nicht.

Die Ergänzung, die wir vorgenommen haben, erstreckt sich auf alle[2] Staatswappen, die seit etwa 1850 bis zur Gegenwart entstanden sind, und schließt Hunderte von wichtigen städtischen Wappen aus aller Welt ein, besonders auch solcher Städte, die bereits mit anderen Bildern oder mit ungenau dargestellten Wappen vertreten sind. Die neu eingefügten Wappen sind daran kenntlich, daß sie mit den konventionellen heraldischen Schraffuren versehen sind. Auf diese Schraffuren hatte Rentzmann mit der Begründung verzichtet, die Münzen hätten ohnehin keine echten Farben, sondern nur die ihres Werkmetalls.

Die meisten Ergänzungen sind Wiedergaben der Zeichnungen, die der Verfasser Neubecker in den letzten Jahren für die *Brockhaus Enzyklopädie* nach ausschließlich amtlichen, zur Zeit gültigen Vorlagen gezeichnet hatte. Dem Verlag F. A. Brockhaus, Wiesbaden, sei hiermit für seine Großzügigkeit, die Weiterverwendung jener Wappenzeichnungen zu gestatten, aufrichtig gedankt. Darüber hinaus sind mehrere Hundert wieder erloschene Wappen gezeichnet worden von den Herren Alfred Dochtermann, Stuttgart, Adolf F. J. Karlovský, Birsfelden bei Basel, Karl Ulrich Neeb, Offenbach, Joachim von Roebel, Bonn-Bad Godesberg, Anton Sched, München, und vor allem Alfred Znamierowski, München.

Zur Geschichte der Wappenbildersystematisierung

Die Zahl der heraldischen Leitfäden ist groß; diese Art Literatur gibt es seit etwa drei Jahrhunderten, und das in vielen verschiedenen Sprachen; und in allen steht zu lesen, Wappen seien Erkennungszeichen. Das ist auch richtig.

Man sollte daher meinen, daß folglich im Laufe der über acht Jahrhunderte, in denen es Wappen gibt, mehrere Übersichten entstanden seien, um das Erkennen der heraldischen Zeichen zu erleichtern oder überhaupt erst zu ermöglichen. Dem ist aber durchaus nicht so. Nur in einem einzigen abendländischen Lande sind dahinzielende Überlegungen schon in der Blütezeit des Wappenwesens (diese bis etwa 1500 gerechnet) angestellt worden; nämlich in England. Die dortige ständische Ordnung war – und ist eigentlich noch immer – mit heraldischer Denkweise so eng verknüpft, daß Kontrollmaßnahmen durch einen wichtigen Gesichtspunkt erfordert wurden, und zwar durch den Grundsatz, kein Wappen dürfe einem andern Wappen verwechselbar ähnlich sein. Eine solche Kontrolle ist nur möglich an Hand einer Bilderregistratur.

Auf dem europäischen Kontinent wurde dieser Gesichtspunkt zwar vertreten, aber sehr lässig beobachtet; jedenfalls sind hier Bilderregister während des Mittelalters nicht entstanden. In Frankreich hat das zur Folge, daß es unzählige sich gleichende Wappen nicht verwandter Familien gibt; in Deutschland wurden anläßlich obrigkeitlicher Verleihung aus dem offenbar gleichen Grunde so viele überladene Wappen geschaffen, die mangels einer verläßlichen Prüfmöglichkeit mit Figuren und Farbanordnungen ausgestattet wurden, von denen man hoffen durfte, daß sich niemand mit Prioritätsrechten melden würde. Vorsichtshalber aber salvierten sich die Verleiher mit einem Vorbehaltsvermerk, z. B. *Unschedlich doch andern die villeicht der gemelten Wappen und cleinetten gleich furtten an iren Wappen und Rechten.*

Diese mangelnde Prüfmöglichkeit auf graphischer – sei es bildlicher oder schriftlicher – Grundlage trug mit dazu bei, aus der Wappenkenntnis ein Spezialwissen, aber auch ein Art Geheimwissenschaft zu machen, zu der nur besondere Kenner Zugang hatten. Daß diese Kennerschaft sich bei den beruflich mit Personenkenntnis ausgerüsteten Herolden konzentrierte, ergab sich sozusagen von selbst; daher heißt auch alles, was mit Wappen zusammenhängt, Heraldik, also: Wappenwesen, Wappenkunst, Wappenlehre, in Italien sogar Adelswesen.

---

[1] Das erste Werk ist das Numismatische Legenden-Lexicon des Mittelalters und der Neuzeit, 1864, Reprint 1969.

[2] Aus technischen Gründen kommen leider das gültige Staatsemblem von Bangladesch, das Wappen von Grenada (seit 7. 2. 1964) und das Wappen von Westsamoa nicht, und das Wappen der Virgin Islands (Jungfern-Inseln) nur als Teil des Wappens der Leeward-Inseln vor.

Die Wappenkenner des europäischen Mittelalters waren zumeist Berufs-Herolde; soweit wir schriftliche oder bildliche Zeugnisse ihres wappenkundlichen Interesses besitzen, sind diese ständisch orientiert, d. h. sie gliedern ihre Sammlungen zunächst regional und innerhalb der regionalen Gruppen hierarchisch. Auf diese Weise war es immerhin möglich, ohne zu großen Aufwand Wappenähnlichkeiten innerhalb eines gewissen Gebietes zu verhindern, bzw., wie am Niederrhein, das Beizeichenwesen auszubauen. Alles, was darüber hinaus zu beachten gewesen wäre, mußte dem Erinnerungsvermögen überlassen werden, also zu einem Privileg der Gedächtniskünstler geraten. In Portugal ging das so weit, daß das künstlerisch hervorragende »Große Wappenbuch« als Geheimsache galt.

Wer nun eine optisch erfaßbare Kontrollmöglichkeit schaffen will, muß ein Ordnungssystem ersinnen. Seltsamerweise hatte das jahrhundertelang seine Schwierigkeiten. Das erste der englischen Figurenregister, die der angestrebten Ordnung halber ein »Ordinary« genannt werden, faßt zwar ganze Gruppen zusammen, aber die Abfolge der Gruppen scheint doch ziemlich zufällig zu sein; jedenfalls sind schon die sogenannten gemeinen Figuren und die sogenannten Heroldstücke nicht auseinandergehalten. Auch eine alphabetische Ordnung oder eine Berücksichtigung der Quantitäten ist nicht erkennbar.

Das erste, nach seinem Vorbesitzer Robert Cooke, dem Clarenceux Herold des Jahres 1576, benannte Ordinary (Abb. S. 6) läßt das ständische Interesse dadurch erkennen, daß jede Gruppe − soweit betroffen − mit einem als Fahne an der Lanze gemalten rechteckigen Feld für einen Bannerherrn statt eines Wappenschildes beginnt, übrigens eine Methode, die auch die etwa gleichzeitige Wappenrolle von Zürich auf ihren ersten Tafeln für die Territorien anwendet.

Sodann schließen die 646 Schilde in nachstehender − bezifferter − Weise an:
1−23 Kreuze; 29−96 Löwen; 97−112 Adler; 113−119 mit Scheiben belegte Balken; 120−130 Taschenärmel; 131−171 ein Sparren; 172−176 zwei Sparren; 177−182 drei Sparren; 183−238 ein Schrägbalken; 239−248 zwei und mehr Schrägbalken; 249−273 gegittert; 274−303 Schildhaupt; 304−333 mehrere Balken; 334−386 ein Balken; 372−379 Balken zwischen Sparren; 387−396 Rautenbalken; 397−415 Schrägkreuze; 416−419 Scheiben; 420−427 Freiviertel; 428−431 geschacht; 432−438 gerautet; 439−441 Halbmonde; 442−458 hersehende und schreitende Löwen; 459−479 geviert; 480−485 mit Spitzenteilung geviert; 486−496 Fünf- und Sechsblätter; 497−508 Pfähle; 509−512 wellengeteilt; 513−519 Feh; 520−525 Ringe; 526−536 Zickzackbalken; 537−538 mit Figuren belegte Ringe; 539 Gürtelschnallen; 540−543 Wassersäcke; 544−546 Kelche; 547−549 Fische; 550−551 Schindeln; 552−553 Sterne; 554−559 geständert; 560 Keil; 561−563 (nochmals) Schildhäupter; 564−567 Innenbord; 568 Helme; 569−570 Schildchen; 571−572 Muscheln; 573−574 (nochmals) Sechsblätter; 575−580 quergestreift; 581−586 zwei Balken; 587−588 Rauten; 589−593 Lilien; 594−595 Trompeten; 596−597 Merletten; 598−644 Verschiedenes.

Wissenschaftlich von erheblicher Bedeutung ist das etwa gleichzeitige Cotgrave's Ordinary, von dem es nur noch eine mit 219 Wappenskizzen am Rande illustrierte Kopie aus dem Jahre 1562 gibt. Diese hat damals Hugh Cotgrave of Sermes nach dem ihm von Hugh Fitzwilliam of Sprotborough (in der Grafschaft Lincoln) als Erbstück vorgelegten Original mühsam unter Weglassung dessen, was er nicht entziffern konnte, angefertigt. Sie ist deswegen so wichtig, weil sie Wappenbeschreibungen in einer ausgebildeten Fachsprache zu einem Zeitpunkt bietet, zu dem in Mitteleuropa an eine Terminologie bei weitem nicht zu denken war. Der Inhalt hat zwar große Ähnlichkeit mit Cooke's Ordinary, ist aber als unter dem Einfluß der sprachlichen Formulierungen genauer gegliedert anzusehen. Die so erkennbaren Gruppen sind:
1−9 Dornenkreuze; 10−25 Tatzenkreuze; 26−30 Ankerkreuze; 31−35 Lilienkreuze; 36−94 springende Löwen; 95−104 Löwen; 105−116 Adler; 117−151 einzelne Sparren; 152−164 zwei und mehr Sparren; 165−187 Gitter; 188−220 Schildhäupter; 221−249 mehrere Balken; 250−309 einzelne Balken; 310−383 einzelne Schrägbalken; 384−393 mehrere Schrägbalken; 394−399 Scheiben; 400−403 Wassersäcke; 404−419 geviert; 420−425 mit Spitzenteilung geviert; 426−429 wellengeteilt; 430−437 Feh; 438−442 Ringe; 443−444 mit Figuren belegte Ringe; 445 Gürtelschnallen; 446−457 Zickzackbalken; 458−459 Halbmonde; 460−476 hersehende und schreitende Löwen; 477−487 Fünfblätter und Rosen; 488−489 Rauten; 490−493 fenstergerautet; 494−504 längsgestreift; 505−511 Taschenärmel; 512−515 Keile; 516 geständert; 517−518 mit Münzen bestreut; 519−521 geständert; 522−523 Schindeln; 524−525 Sterne; 526−527 Merletten; 528−529 Fische; 530−531 Trompeten; 532−534 Schildchen; 535−537 Freiviertel; 538 Lilien; 539−541 quergestreift; 542 mehrere Pfähle; 543−547 Kelche; 548−549 Greifen; 550−551 mehrere Löwen; 552−555 Greifen; 556 Fische.

Etwa 40 Jahre später wurde ein Ordinary auf den ersten Blättern in gleicher Weise angereichert, wie dies auch auf dem Kontinent üblich war, d. h. mit dem Wappen fremder Herrscher und einheimischer Prinzen.

In dem Hauptteil dieses Codex, *William Jenyns' Ordinary,* fällt ungeachtet der auf 1611 angestiegenen Zahl der gemalten Wappen das Fehlen der Gruppe »Kreuze« und eine weniger komprimierte Zusammenfassung der Bildgruppen auf. Löwen und Adler eröffnen nunmehr den Reigen und betonen somit ihre Rolle als Könige ihrer Tiergattungen, die Löwen in weitaus größerer Anzahl als die Adler. Die Vielfalt der zu gruppierenden Figuren nimmt zu und erschwert die Klassifizierung.

Die Bilder sind inzwischen angesichts ihrer Menge schon nach Seitenzahlen und nicht mehr nach einzelnen Nummern zu zitieren:
Blatt 4b−14 Löwen; 14b Adler; 15−16b Pfähle und Keile; 16b Muscheln; 17−20b einzelne und mehrere Balken; 21 und 22 Schrägkreuze; 22b Garben; 23−23b Wassersäcke; 23b Sterne; 24−25 Halbmonde; 25b−26 Scheiben; 26−26b Ringe und dergl.; 27 und 27b einzelne und mehrere Balken; 28−29 Gitter; 29b Taschenärmel; 30−32b einzelne und mehrere Balken; 33−34b Schildchen und Schildränder; 34b Fische; 35−35b Feuerstähle; 36 Fünfblätter; 36b−37 Schach; 37b−38 schräggestreift; 38−38b Fünfblätter; 39 Taschenärmel; 39−45 Sparren; 45−45b Schachroche, Kastelle u. dergl.; 46−51b Schrägbalken.

Nach William Jenyns, Lancaster Herold 1516−1527, ist dieses Ordinary deswegen benannt, weil sein Wappen zweimal in diesen Kodex eingemalt ist. Der jetzige Eigentümer, seit etwa 1880−1890 College of Arms in London, unterscheidet diese Sammlung von dem in der Literatur öfter hiermit verwechselten *Thomas Jenyns' Book;* von

Überschriften zu den ersten vier Schilden:

Le Counte darindell porte de goules oue vn leon rampant dor

Le Counte de Lincolne port dor a vn leon rampant de purpre

Le Counte de Northfolk mons^r Roger & Bigod porte parte dor & de vert a vn leon rampāt de goules

Le Counte de Cornewaille port dargēt a vn Leon ramp̄ de goules corone dor a vn bordo^{ur} de sable besantee

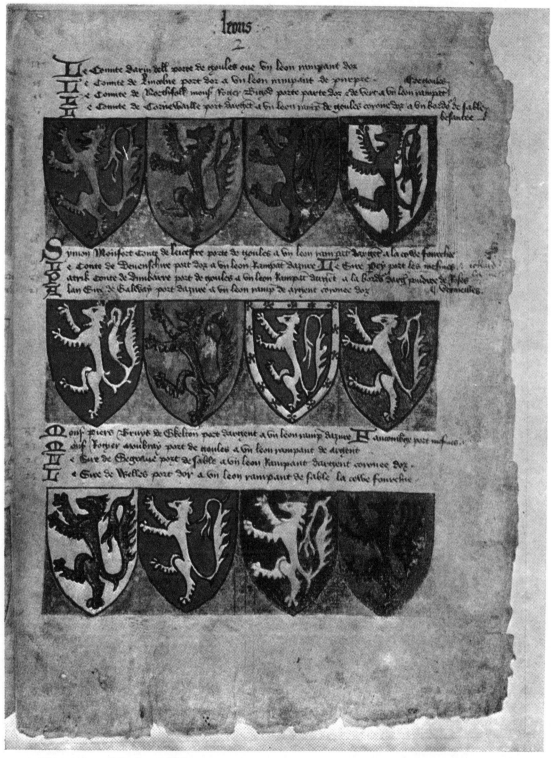

Thomas Jenyns' Book, um 1410
Eine der 14 Seiten mit Löwenwappen, dabei das des Römischen Königs Richard von Cornwall
Nach dem Exemplar der Königin Margarete von Anjou im Besitz des British Museum Add. 40851

letzterem gibt es zahlreiche Kopien die in zwei Gruppen zerfallen. Die eine wird als Gruppe der Königin Margarete angesehen; die andere als die Fassung des Thomas Jenyns selbst. Königin Margarete aus dem Hause Anjou war die Gemahlin König Heinrichs VI. (1445–1482) und leiht dieser Gruppe ihren Namen, weil vorne in dem Original (British Museum MS. Add. 40851, aus dem Handel erworben 1923) ihr Wappen eingemalt ist.

Thomas Jenyns, ein Edler aus dem Hause oder dem Haushalt des Grafen Henry von Huntingdon, hatte den inzwischen verlorenen Band im Jahre 1578 von dem Vorbesitzer, Robert Glover aus Somerset erhalten. Diese Sammlung bedeutet (in beiden Fassungen) insofern einen Fortschritt, als zu je vier nebeneinanderstehenden Schildchen in vier darübergeschriebenen Zeilen die Beschreibung in französischer Sprache steht (Abb. S. 9), ein Beleg mehr dafür, daß die französische Kunstsprache die Mutter der heraldischen Terminologien aller anderen Sprachen ist. Ein neues Problem der Anordnung taucht durch die noch immer neue Methode auf, Wappen durch Quadrierung zu verbinden; die Frage ist dann, welches der vier Felder das Leitmotiv liefert. In *Thomas Jenyns' Book,* das auf etwa 1410 datiert wird, weist bereits das erste Wappen auf dieses Problem hin; es ist das Wappen des Königs von Spanien, das bei den Löwen steht, obwohl darin das Löwenwappen von León erst den 2. und 3. Platz hinter dem Wappen von Kastilien einnimmt.

Weiterhin zeichnet sich ein neuer Ordnungsgedanke ab, indem nach den privilegierten Tieren Löwe und Adler zunächst Heroldsbilder und erst danach gemeine Figuren kommen. Die Ordnung der insgesamt 1208 Schilde sieht so aus:

Seite 5b–12 Löwen; 12b–13b hersehende schreitende Löwen (sogen. Leoparden); 14–14b Adler; 15–19 Schrägbalken; 19b–21 Schrägbalken; 21b–22 Zickzackbalken; 22b–25 einzelne Balken; 25b–29 mehrere Balken; 29b quergestreift; 30 wellengeteilt; 30b–31 Feh; 31b–32 Dornenbalken oder Feuerstähle; 32b–36 Sparren; 36b–37 gegittert; 37b–39 Schildhäupter; 40–43b Kreuze; 44 Wassersäcke; 44b–45b geviert; 45b–46 Ringe; 46b Rosen; mit Figuren belegte Ringe, Gürtelschnallen, Halbmonde; 47–47b Fünfblätter, Rosen, Gürtelschnallen; 48–48b Rauten; 48b–49 Taschenärmel; 49b Keile, Pfähle, Ständer; 50–51 Schildchen; 51b–52 Schach; 52b Kelche, Trompeten; 53 Scheiben; 53b Sterne (Sporenräder); 54 Garben; 54b–55 Lilien; 55 Keile, Fische; 55b Muscheln, Hasen. Die anschließenden Schilde bis Nr. 1595 sind nicht mehr nach Bildern geordnet, fallen daher für unsere Betrachtung aus.

Der Kontinent hat nichts Gleichwertiges aufzuweisen, obwohl auch hier regional Wappengruppen entstehen; diese aber gründen sich auf Vasallenverhältnisse oder gemeinsame Stammväter, sind also ständisch oder genealogisch zu verstehen (Abb. S. 10).

Mit den englischen Wappenbüchern haben die europäischen nunmehr gemeinsam, daß sie mit den Wappen der abendländischen Fürsten, apokryphen Wappen von Heiligen und Herrschern des Altertums und des fernen Orients beginnen und sich dann dem einheimischen Adel zuwenden. Zu den großen Ausnahmen gehören im Mittelalter Wappenbücher, die unpersönliche Wappen verzeichnen. Hier ist in erster Linie auf Jörg *Rugenn's Wappenbuch* (Universitätsbibliothek Innsbruck MS 545) aus der Zeit um 1492 hinzuweisen, da es von Blatt 231 an eine große Zahl von Stadtwappen bietet, darin viele erstmals in Farben darstellt, z. B. das Wappen von Berlin. Aber auch Jörg Rugenn bleibt hierbei in den gewohnten Bahnen der regionalen Zusammenfassung.

Den entscheidenden Schritt in Richtung auf eine durchdachte Ordnung hat erst der Römer Jesuit Silvester Petra Sancta 1638 mit seinem Werke *Tesserae gentilitiae* getan,[3] indem er in den Kapiteln 19–66 folgende Klassifikation[4] vorgenommen hat:

19. Zu den Metallen und Farben kommen zwei Wappenpelzwerke hinzu – 20. Die innere Einteilung des Wappenschildes wird beschrieben – 21. Über die mit dem bloßen Metall oder leuchtender Farbe versehenen Schilde – 22. Über das in zwei Hälften aufgeteilte Schildfeld – 23. Über das in zwei ungleiche Teile aufgeteilte Schildfeld – 24. Über das dreigeteilte Wappenschildfeld – 25. Über das viergeteilte Wappenschildfeld – 26. Über das in mehrere Felder aufgeteilte Wappenschildfeld – 27. Über den Wappenbalken und dessen verschiedenen Gebrauch – 28. Über den Pfosten oder Wappenpfahl – 29. Über die Wappenschärpe (= Schrägbalken) – 30. Über den Schrägstreifen, der von der linken Schildecke zur oberen geführt zu werden pflegt. – 31. Über Wappensparren – 32. Über Wappenwolkenbild – 33. Über wellenförmigen Geschlechterwappen – 34. Über die gestreiften oder röhrenüberzogenen Geschlechterwappen – 35. Über die gekrümmten und bogenförmigen Wappen – 36. Über die gezahnten Geschlechterwappen – 37. Über Gebrauch der Mauerzinnen in Wappenschilden – 38. Über die dreieckigen Wappenflügel (= Ständer) – 39. Über die Schildchen oder symbolischen Kärtchen (= Schach, Rauten, Wecken) – 40. Über die Wappenschindeln – 41. Über die Wappenspindeln – 42. Über die Byzantinischen Münzen – 43. Über Wappenkuchen – 44. Über Wappenfladen – 45. Über durchkreuzte Geschlechterschildchen – 46. Über Wappenkarfunkel (= Lilienhaspel) – 47. Über Schildmarken oder mit einem Buchstaben oder einem Wort beschriftete Schilde – 48. Über das symbolische Kreuz und über seine verschiedene Gestaltung – 49. Über den Schild-Zehner und über dessen verschiedene Gestaltung (Schrägkreuz) – 50. Über Kreuzchen und deren verschiedenen Gebrauch – 51. Über den Fellüberzug des Schildes – 52. Über das Hermelinfell – 53. Über den Löwen – 54. Andere, teils wilde, teils zahme Lebewesen, werden vorgeführt – 55. Über die Wappenschlangen – 56. Über die Wappenfische – 57. Über den Adler – 58. Über andere symbolische Vögel – 59. Über Sonne, Mond

---

[3] *Tesserae gentilitiae.* A Silvestro Petra Sancta Romano, Societatis Jesu, ex legibus fecialium descriptae, Romae, typis haered. Francisci Corbeletti Superiorum permissu MDCXXXVIII. (Geschlechter-Wappen. Von Silvester Petra Sancta aus den Heroldsgesetzen beschrieben, Rom, Druck Erben des Francesco Corbeletti, mit Erlaubnis der Oberen, 1638, (678 Seiten folio.)

[4] Wiedergabe im lateinischen Urtext bei Gustav Ad. Seyler, *Geschichte der Heraldik* = J. Siebmacher's Großes Wappenbuch, Band A, Nürnberg 1890, Reprint Neustadt a. d. Aisch 1970, S. 588. Wir geben eine wörtliche Übersetzung, die u.a. erkennen läßt, welche drolligen Verrenkungen erforderlich sind, um antike Wörter auf die Heraldik anwendbar zu machen.

Liste der Burgmannen der Burg des Erzbischofs von Trier zu Mayen
S. 12 (= 6v) des *Balduineums,* Codex im Besitz des Staatsarchivs Koblenz, Bildzeile 2 bis 6
Das erste Wappen ist im Original gänzlich rot übermalt; auf der Photographie scheint ein Zickzackschrägbalken durch.

und andere Sterne in Wappen – 60. Über Wappenblumen – 61. Über Wappenbienen[5] – 62. Über Früchte und Bäume in Wappen – 63. Einige Werkzeuge, die in unserm Wappenwesen vorkommen, werden vorgeführt – 64. Über Wappenbauwerke – 65. Über das Menschenbild und die Darstellung der Teile davon in Wappen – 66. Über Mittelschilde.

Petra Sancta steht im Rufe, die heraldischen Schraffierungen erfunden zu haben[6]; inzwischen weiß man aber, daß sie sich seit etwa 1600 von den Niederlanden aus verbreitet haben. Das stimmt damit überein, daß Petra Sancta selbst darauf hinweist, wieviel Material zur Sache er gerade in Deutschland und den Niederlanden gefunden habe; in seinem Werk gibt er auch den sogen. »Alten Siebmacher« vielfach als Belegstelle an[7].

[5] Daß die Bienen ein eigenes Kapitel erhielten, dürfte wohl darauf zurückzuführen sein, daß damals ein Papst aus dem Hause Barberini, Urban VIII. (1623–1644), regierte. Das Wappen dieses Geschlechts zeigt in Blau drei goldene Bienen.

[6] Seyler a.a.O. – S. 592

[7] Vgl. unser Vorsatzpapier, das diesem Werk entnommen ist.

Petra Sancta handelt von Wappen immer nur als Adelsmarken; die Berücksichtigung öffentlicher Wappen kommt auch ihm nur in den Sinn, wenn er von fürstlicher Prunkentfaltung handelt.

So ist tatsächlich das Werk von Rentzmann das erste, das sich von der Verflechtung der Heraldik mit der Genealogie[8] freimacht, allerdings eine neue, die mit der Numismatik eingeht.

Um die Benützung dieser gänzlich neugeordneten Ausgabe zu erleichtern, geben wir folgende Hinweise, die sich teils auf Eigentümlichkeiten der Rentzmannschen Arbeitsweise, teils auf die von uns vorgenommenen Ergänzungen beziehen.

[8] So auch Jürgen Arndt, *Zur Ordnung der Wappen nach Bildern in historischer und systematischer Betrachtung*, in: Herold-Jahrbuch, 1. Band, Berlin 1972, S. 5–24, bes. S. 12

Hinweise für die Benützung

Zweck dieses Buches ist vornehmlich, Identifizierung von Wappen zu ermöglichen, die dem Suchenden vorliegen, deren Benennung er aber nicht kennt.

Voraussetzung für den Erfolg ist, daß es sich um das Wappen eines Staates, einer größeren Stadt oder eines Münzberechtigten handelt. Für Vorlagen aus der Zeit vor etwa 1800 können statt eigentlicher Wappen auch Münzbilder aufgefunden werden. Münzbilder sind als solche nicht besonders gekennzeichnet, sondern auch in Wappenschilde eingezeichnet.

Handelt es sich bei dem aufzusuchenden Bild um eine einfache Schildteilung oder um nur ein Wappenfeld, so ist die Auffindung mit Hilfe der Übersichten auf den Seiten 16, 117, 131, 274 und 303 ziemlich leicht möglich. Die Zuhilfenahme des alphabetischen Stichwortregisters im Anschluß an diese Hinweise kann dabei nützlich sein.

Da es oft schwer zu beurteilen ist, was auf einer Münze Vorder- oder Rückseite ist, hat W. Rentzmann seinerzeit beide Bilder in einem Wappenschild nebeneinander stehend dargestellt und durch daruntergesetzte Buchstaben V und R angegeben, was er für die Vorder- und die Rückseite hielt. Die mit V gekennzeichnete Abbildung liefert dann das Leitmotiv.

Sind auf einer Münze zwei Wappenschilde nebeneinander gestellt, so sieht das ebenso aus, ist jedoch nicht mit V und R versehen und unterscheidet sich nicht von Wappen, die selbst »gespalten« sind.

Entsprechendes gilt für Münzen mit drei oder vier Schilden, wie die nachstehenden Abbildungen näher erläutern.

Münze von Uri, Schwyz und Unterwalden mit den Wappen in drei einzelnen, 1 : 2 gestellten Schilden
Foto HMZ

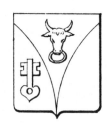

Zusammenziehung der Wappen von Uri, Schwyz und Unterwalden in einem Wappenschild nach Rentzmanns Methode, wenn in der Vorlage 1 : 2 gestellt
Bild 200, **4**, 1

Goldmünze der rheinischen Kurfürsten Trier, Mainz und Pfalz mit den Wappen in drei einzelnen, 2 : 1 gestellten Schilden
Foto Staatl. Münzsammlung, München

Zusammenziehung der Wappen von Kurtrier, Kurmainz und Kurpfalz in einem Wappenschild nach Rentzmanns Methode, wenn in der Vorlage 2 : 1 gestellt
Bild 99, **3**, 4

Zusammenziehung der Wappen von Kurtrier, Kurmainz und Kurpfalz im gültigen Wappen des Landes Rheinland-Pfalz
Bild 101, **4**, 2

Taler der Reichsstadt Schwäbisch Hall, 1749 Ihre drei Wappenschilde 1 : 2 gestellt

Zusammenziehung der drei 1 : 2 gestellten Wappenschilde der Reichsstadt Schwäbisch Hall nach Rentzmanns Methode
Bild 249, **3**, 5

Taf. 11.

1.	Saalfeld Abtei.	36.	Schlesien.	77.	Camenz.
2.	Mümpelgard.	37.	Fischingen.	78.	do.
3.	Salm.		Koepenick.	79.	Schlesien.
4.	Bar.		Rheinau.	80.	do.
	Chiny.	38.	Schlesien,	81.	Usenberg.
5.	Bar.	39.	Sulz.	82.	Schlesien.
6.	do.	40.	Bar.	83.	Beckum.
7.	Salm-Neuburg.	41.	Weissensee.	84.	Tarnowitz.
8.	Saalfeld Stadt.	42.	Gengenbach (Abtei).	85.	Baden-Durlach.
9.	Saalfeld Abtei.	43.	Gengenbach (Stadt).	86.	Heilbronn.
10.	Saalfeld Abtei, Stadt.		Rheinau.	87.	Biberach.
11.	Mümpelgard.	44.	Rheinau.	88.	Californien.
	Pfirt	45.	Ost-Indien.	89.	Castorland.
	Saalfeld Abtei, Stadt.	46.	Perpignan.		Montreal.
	Stolberg (Werniger.)	47.	Schlesien.	90.	Wesel.
	Weisensee.	48.	Ost-Indien.	91	Cochinchina.
12.	Mümpelgard	49.	Audh.	92.	Schlesien.
13.	Weisensee.	50.	do.	93.	Ardebil.
14.	do.	51.	do.	94.	Hulaguiden.
15.	do.	52.	Schlesien.	95.	Cincinati (Ohio).
16.	Schlesien.	53.	do.	96.	Persien (Koway).
17.	Weissensee.	54.	Weissensee.	97.	Sari.
18.	Wernigerode.	55.	Sicilien.	98.	Bretagne.
19.	Weissensee.	56.	Eriwan.	99.	do.
	Wernigerode.	57.	Georgien.	100.	do
20.	Glogau Herzogth.	58.	Schlesien.	101.	Persien (Koway)
21.	Oestreich.	59.	Dschudschiden.	102.	Bayern.
	Weissensee.		(Gulistan).	103.	Castiglione delle Stiviere.
22.	Schlesien.	60.	Oswego (New-York).		
	Stolberg Stadt.	61.	Youghal (1646).	104.	Persien (Schiraz).
	Weissensee.	62.	Magdalenen-Insel.	105.	Mantua, Herzogthum.
23.	Schlesien.	63.	Prinz Edwards-Insel.	106.	do. do.
24.	Stolberg Grfsch.	64.	Mohamed - Abad - Be-	107.	Murbach und Lüders.
	Weissensee.		nares.	108.	Aquila (bei Mantua).
25.	Cochinchina.	65.	Mirepoix.	109.	Castiglione delle Stiviere.
26.	Schlesien.	66.	Pittsburg (Virginien)		
	Stolberg Grfsch.	67.	Prenzlau. ?	110.	Oettingen.
	Wernigerode Grfsch.	68.	Ortenburg (Fam. Wid-	111.	Reuss.
	Weissensee.		mann.)	112.	Oettingen.
27.	Stolberg Grfsch.	69.	Ortenburg (Fam. Por-	113.	do.
28.	Ost-Indien.		tia).	114.	Nürnberg, Burggraf.
29.	Fischingen.	70.	Schlesien	115.	do. do.
30.	Meinau.	71.	Brandenburg (Mrkgr.)	116.	Bolivia.
31.	Reichenau.	72.	do.	117.	Paraguay.
32.	Weissensee.	73.	Ungarn.	118.	Lima
33.	Hindostan (Baberiden)	74.	do.	119.	Ayacucho.
34.	Khoi.	75.	do.		Cazamarca.
35.	Weissensee.	76.	Usenberg.		Cuzco.

Zu den Tafeln des Bildbandes hatte Rentzmann einen Registerband mit dem Titel

NUMISMATISCHES
WAPPEN-LEXICON
JNDEX

verfaßt.

Dieser Index zerfällt in zwei Abtheilungen:

1) Tafel-Nachweis (S. 1—78)
2) Verzeichniss der Staaten- und Städte-Wappen (S. 79—113)

Abt. 2 unterscheidet sich von unserm Namensverzeichnis nicht grundsätzlich; wir haben uns vor allem bemüht, die geographischen Angaben teils genauer zu fassen, teils zu berichtigen.

Abt. 1 sollte dem Benutzer ermöglichen, anhand der Nummern auf den Bildtafeln die richtige Bezeichnung zu ermitteln. Dieses umständliche Verfahren wird durch unsere Umarbeitung vermieden.

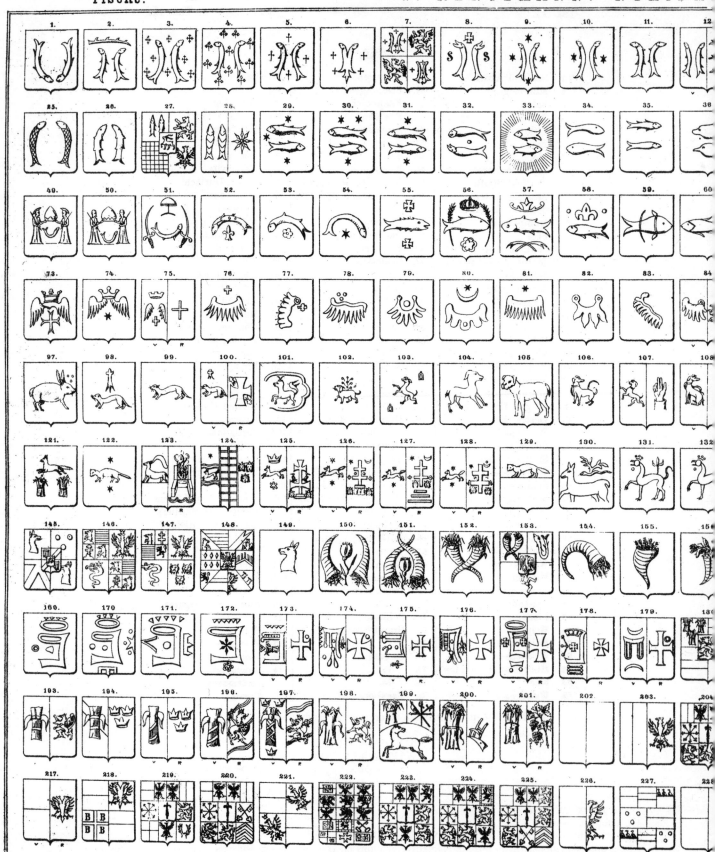

Tafel 11 aus W. Rentzmann, Numismatisches
WAPPEN-LEXICON
des Mittelalters und der Neuzeit
Staaten und Städtewappen
Berlin 1876
bzw. Anastatischer Neudruck, Halle (Saale) 1924
(auf etwa die Hälfte verkleinerte Wiedergabe)

Betr. Fische (Nr. 1−65), Flasche (66), Flügel (67−85), Fontaine (86), Fuchs (87−149, zerfallend in: Biber 87−89,
Fuchs, recte Wiesel 90, Hase 91−97, Hermelin 98−100, Hund 101−115, Lama 116−120, Marder, recte Wolf 121,
Marder 122−129, Panther 130−137, Wolf 138−149), Füllhorn (150−157), Gabel (158), Gesicht (!, 159−179),
Garbe (180−201), Gespalten 202−208), Getheilt (209−240).

Unter diesem Begriff sind alle
Wappen und Münzbilder zusammengefaßt worden, die in der Heraldik
als Heroldstücke, Heroldsbilder,
Ehrenstücke bezeichnet werden.
In dem nachstehenden Inhaltsverzeichnis dieser Gruppe geben die
links stehenden Ziffern an, unter
welchem Ordnungsstichwort die
verschiedenen Motive eingeordnet
sind. Die Ziffern rechts geben die
aufzuschlagende Seite an.

Die Tinkturen
Ledige Schilde

Les Émaux
Écus plains

Tinctures
Plain shields

Regalienschild (Bluthann),
bes. bei Kurpfalz, Sachsen,
Brandenburg und Preußen,
Schwyz, Kanton, Urform,
bis ins 17. Jahrhundert

Metall: Gold = Gelb
or / or

Metall: Silber = Weiß
argent / argent

Farbe: Rot
gueules / gules

Uri,
Schwyz und Unterwalden

Farbe: Blau
azur / azure

Farbe: Schwarz
sable / sable

Farbe: Grün
sinople / vert

Farbe: Purpur
pourpre / purple

Pelzwerk

Fourrures

Furs

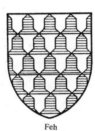

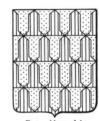

Hermelin
hermine / ermine
Bretagne, Herzogtum

Feh
vair / vair
Camerino (Marchesi Varani)

Rot-golden gefeht
Vairé de gueules et d'or
Vairy gules and or

Kürsch
pannes de vair
Fur

Teilungen
Geteilt

Partitions
Coupé

Divisions
Per fesse

Ferrara, Stadt
Freiburg, Kanton
Höxter, Stadt (Westfalen)
Kampen, Stadt (Overijssel)
Lausanne, Stadt
Lübeck, Stadt
Magdeburg, Erzbistum
Megen, Grafschaft
(Nordbrabant)
Monferrat, Markgrafschaft
(Oberitalien)

Münster, Stadt
Neapel, Stadt
Nördlingen
Obwalden
Saluzzo
Siena
Solothurn
Ulm
Unterwalden

Corvey, Abtei (Westfalen)
Desana

Halberstadt, Magdeburg
und Mainz

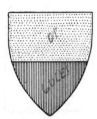

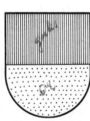

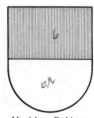

Corvey, Abtei
Neapel, Stadt
Liechtenstein, Fürstentum

Schwerin, Grafschaft
Herren von Münzenberg-
Falkenstein (Hessen)

Hohenberg, Grafschaft
Lucca, Stadt - Lübeck, Stadt
Haigerloch – Horb (Neckar)

Magdeburg, Erzbistum
Obwalden
Solothurn

Kampen, Stadt (Overijssel)
Herren von Breitenstein,
† 1666

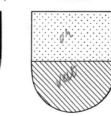

Grafen von Lupfen
Schloß bei Tuttlingen
(Württemberg)

Siena

Ferrara
Freiburg, Kanton

Rolle, Stadt (Waadt)

Ulm, Überlingen und
Ravensburg

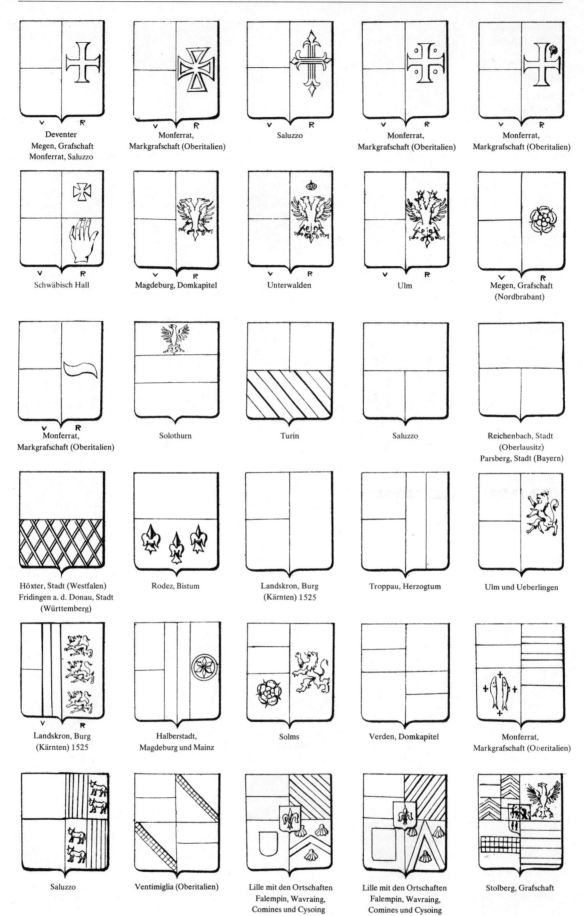

Deventer
Megen, Grafschaft
Monferrat, Saluzzo

Monferrat,
Markgrafschaft (Oberitalien)

Saluzzo

Monferrat,
Markgrafschaft (Oberitalien)

Monferrat,
Markgrafschaft (Oberitalien)

Schwäbisch Hall

Magdeburg, Domkapitel

Unterwalden

Ulm

Megen, Grafschaft
(Nordbrabant)

Monferrat,
Markgrafschaft (Oberitalien)

Solothurn

Turin

Saluzzo

Reichenbach, Stadt
(Oberlausitz)
Parsberg, Stadt (Bayern)

Höxter, Stadt (Westfalen)
Fridingen a. d. Donau, Stadt
(Württemberg)

Rodez, Bistum

Landskron, Burg
(Kärnten) 1525

Troppau, Herzogtum

Ulm und Ueberlingen

Landskron, Burg
(Kärnten) 1525

Halberstadt,
Magdeburg und Mainz

Solms

Verden, Domkapitel

Monferrat,
Markgrafschaft (Oberitalien)

Saluzzo

Ventimiglia (Oberitalien)

Lille mit den Ortschaften
Falempin, Wavraing,
Comines und Cysoing

Lille mit den Ortschaften
Falempin, Wavraing,
Comines und Cysoing

Stolberg, Grafschaft

Herren von Lobkowicz

Monferrat,
Markgrafschaft (Oberitalien)

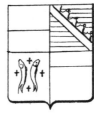

Lille mit den Ortschaften
Falempin, Wavraing,
Comines und Cysoing

Monferrat,
Markgrafschaft (Oberitalien)

Lille mit den Ortschaften
Falempin, Wavraing,
Comines und Cysoing

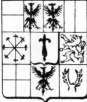

Lucca, Herzogtum, 1824

Corvey, Abtei (Westfalen)
Münster, Bistum 1611

Solms-Hohensolms-Lich
Solms-Laubach-Rödelheim

Solms-Braunfels

Solms-Braunfels

Brandenburg,
Kurfürstentum

Brandenburg,
Kurfürstentum

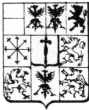

Brandenburg,
Kurfürstentum

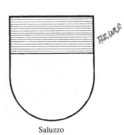

Brandenburg,
Kurfürstentum

Brandenburg,
Kurfürstentum

Preußen, Königreich,
1701

Brandenburg-Ansbach,
1673

Schildhaupt

Chef

Chief

Monferrat
Herren von Münzenberg
Saluzzo

Asti
Monferrat,
Markgrafschaft (Oberitalien)

Monferrat,
Markgrafschaft (Oberitalien)

Saluzzo

Lausanne, Stadt

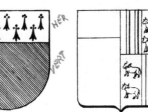
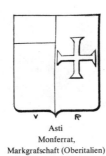

Herren von Bruchhausen
(Niederrhein)

Saluzzo

Münsterberg und Oels,
Herzogtümer

Desana, Grafschaft
(bei Vercelli)

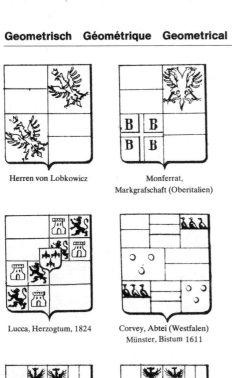

Teilungen
Gespalten

Partitions
Parti

Divisions
Per pale

Bergamo, Stadt (Italien)
Böhmisch-Kamenitz
(Grafen von Wartenberg)
Burgdorf (Kanton Bern)
Desana, Grafschaft
Gandersheim, Abtei
Halberstadt, Bistum

Hildesheim, Bistum
Luzern
Metz, Bistum
Metz, Stadt
Reckheim
Tessin

Augsburg, Bistum

Reckheim

Hildesheim, Bistum
Bergamo, Stadt (Italien)

Aubonne, Stadt (Waadt)

Halberstadt, Bistum
Payerne, Stadt (Waadt)
Insel Malta

Augsburg, Bistum
Buchloe, Stadt (Bayr. Schwaben)
Sursee, Stadt (Kanton Luzern)

Corner (Venedig) · Vevey, Ballei
Vevey, Stadt, 16. Jahrh.
Herren von Plettenberg

Herren von Plettenberg

Cossonay, Stadt (Waadt)

Luzern

Gandersheim, Abtei

Herren von Wartenberg
Böhmisch-Kamenitz, Stadt

Metz, Stadt

Burgdorf, Stadt
(Kanton Bern)
Battenberg, Stadt (Hessen)

Tessin
Gersau (Kanton Schwyz)

Troppau, Herzogtum
(Dynastie Liechtenstein)

Troppau, Herzogtum

Luzern
Passerano

Luzern

Graubünden

Herren von Rantzau

Brandenburg,
Kurfürstentum
Preußen, Königreich, 1701

Madagaskar

Dahome

Räzüns, Herrschaft
(Graubünden)

Leisnig

Desana, Grafschaft
(bei Vercelli)

**Zweimal geteilt
und Balken**

**Tiercé en fasce
et fasce**

**Tierced fesswise
and fess**

Aire (1710)

Beichlingen
Béthune
Bouillon
Brabant und Limburg
Dendermonde (Termonde)
Gazoldo
Groningen
Henrichemont
Leuchtenberg
Löwen

Lucca
Mailand
Münster, Bistum
Münster i. W., Stadt
Österreich
Herren von Trčka von Dub
und Lípa
Werne an der Lippe
(Westfalen)
Zug (Schweiz)

Reutlingen, Stadt
Zofingen (Schweiz)

Österreich
Freiburg im Breisgau, Stadt

Maasdam (Südholland)

Münster i. W., Bistum
Werne, Stadt (Westfalen)
Lahr und Geroldseck

Lothier, Herzogtum
Löwen, Stadt · Österreich
Vianen, Herrschaft

Béthune, Herzogtum
Herford, Stift

Cajetan Anton von Nothaft,
Propst von Berchtesgaden
1732–57

Münster i. W., Fürstentum,
seit 1804 im preuß. Staatswappen

Zug (Schweiz)
Leuchtenberg, Landgrafschaft

Vinstingen, Herrschaft
Muiden (Nordholland)
Grafschaft Hals (Bayern)

Mörs, Grafschaft,
seit 6. 4. 1706 Fürstentum

Prag, Erzbistum

Gelnhausen, Stadt

Herren van Borssele (Seeland)
Herren von Waldsee
(Württemberg)

Groningen

Oude-Tonge (Südholland)

Norddeutscher Bund,
30. 11. 1867 bis 1871

Reutlingen, Stadt

Münster i. W., Stadt

Helgoland

**Balken in geometrisch
gemustertem Feld**

**Fasce dans champ
subdivisé**

**Fess on geometrically
designed field**

Reutlingen, Stadt

Herren von Brakel
(Westfalen), 1384 ausgestorben
Herren von Regensberg
(Kanton Zürich)

Kuinre, Grafschaft
(Overijssel)

Greifswald

Im ersten von drei Wappenschilden

Au premier de trois écussons

On the first of three escutcheons

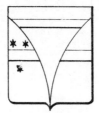

Leuchtenberg, Landgrafschaft

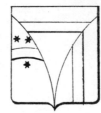

Leuchtenberg, Landgrafschaft

Oberelsaß

Oberelsaß und Breisach

Murbach und Lüders, Abtei (Oberelsaß)

Artois

Kempten, Stadt

Kempten, Stadt

Tirol

Kärnten

Oberelsaß

Minden, Münster und Osnabrück, Bistümer

Minden, Münster und Osnabrück, Bistümer

Reckheim

Im ersten von vier Wappenschilden

Au premier de quatre écussons

On the first of four escutcheons

Österreich

Österreich

Tirol

Württemberg

Österreich
Wien, Stadt 1529

Tirol

Tirol

Tirol

Moers, Grafschaft

Mecheln, Antwerpen, Brüssel und Herzogenbusch

Mecheln, Antwerpen, Brüssel und Herzogenbusch

Im gespaltenen Schilde oder auf Avers

Dans écu parti ou sur avers

On shield per pale or on obverse

Leuchtenberg, Landgrafschaft

Österreich

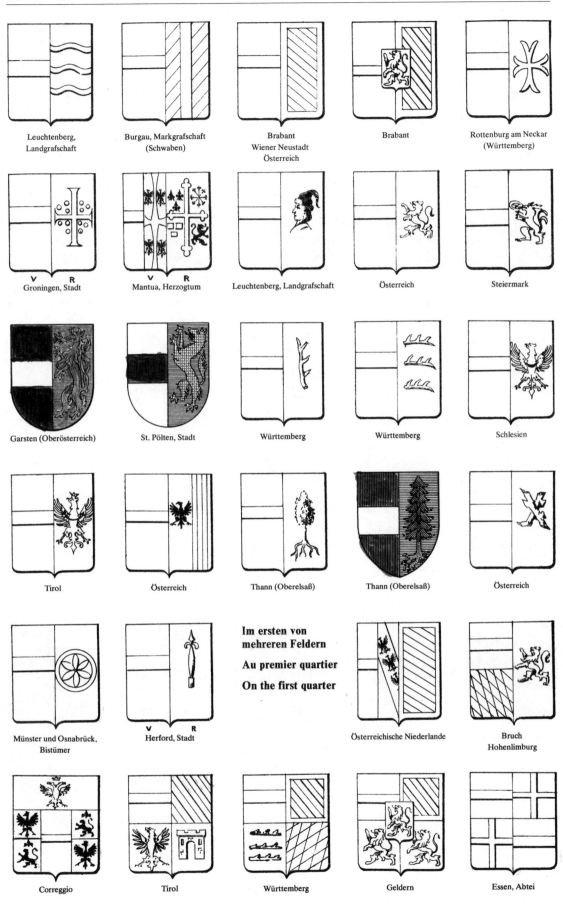

Leuchtenberg,
Landgrafschaft

Burgau, Markgrafschaft
(Schwaben)

Brabant
Wiener Neustadt
Österreich

Brabant

Rottenburg am Neckar
(Württemberg)

Groningen, Stadt

Mantua, Herzogtum

Leuchtenberg, Landgrafschaft

Österreich

Steiermark

Garsten (Oberösterreich)

St. Pölten, Stadt

Württemberg

Württemberg

Schlesien

Tirol

Österreich

Thann (Oberelsaß)

Thann (Oberelsaß)

Österreich

Münster und Osnabrück,
Bistümer

Herford, Stadt

**Im ersten von
mehreren Feldern**

Au premier quartier

On the first quarter

Österreichische Niederlande

Bruch
Hohenlimburg

Correggio

Tirol

Württemberg

Geldern

Essen, Abtei

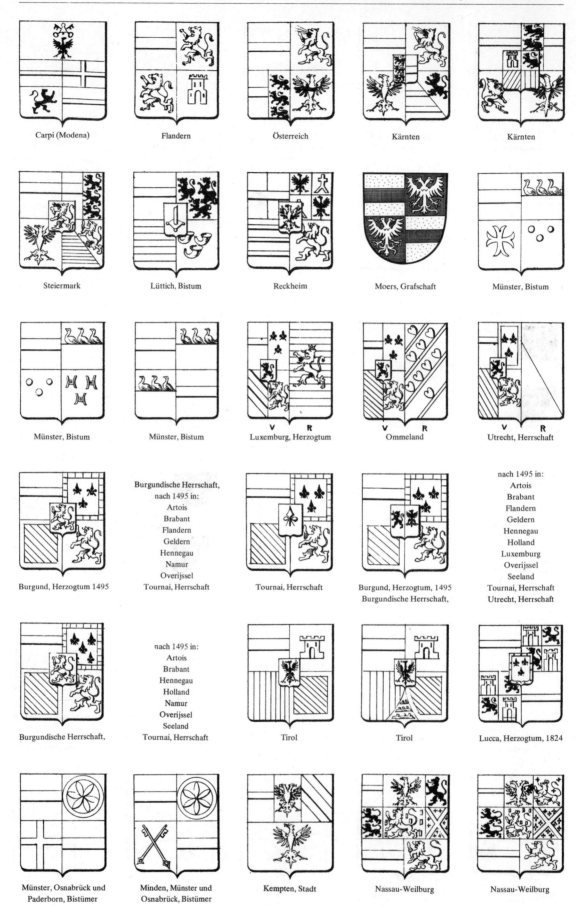

Carpi (Modena)

Flandern

Österreich

Kärnten

Kärnten

Steiermark

Lüttich, Bistum

Reckheim

Moers, Grafschaft

Münster, Bistum

Münster, Bistum

Münster, Bistum

Luxemburg, Herzogtum

Ommeland

Utrecht, Herrschaft

Burgund, Herzogtum 1495

Burgundische Herrschaft,
nach 1495 in:
Artois
Brabant
Flandern
Geldern
Hennegau
Namur
Overijssel
Tournai, Herrschaft

Tournai, Herrschaft

Burgund, Herzogtum, 1495
Burgundische Herrschaft,

nach 1495 in:
Artois
Brabant
Flandern
Geldern
Hennegau
Holland
Luxemburg
Overijssel
Seeland
Tournai, Herrschaft
Utrecht, Herrschaft

Burgundische Herrschaft,

nach 1495 in:
Artois
Brabant
Hennegau
Holland
Namur
Overijssel
Seeland
Tournai, Herrschaft

Tirol

Tirol

Lucca, Herzogtum, 1824

Münster, Osnabrück und
Paderborn, Bistümer

Minden, Münster und
Osnabrück, Bistümer

Kempten, Stadt

Nassau-Weilburg

Nassau-Weilburg

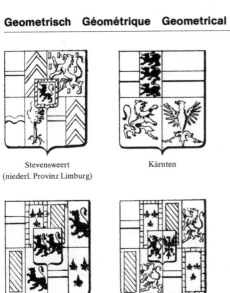

Stevensweert
(niederl. Provinz Limburg)

Kärnten

Mirandola, Herzogtum

Mirandola, Herzogtum

Correggio

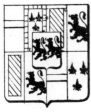

Geldern

Flandern · Geldern
Namur

Château-Regnault (Ardennes)

Mailand, Herzogtum

Kombiniert mit kleinen Figuren

Combinée avec de petits meubles

Combined with lesser charges

Wien, Erzbistum

Wien, Erzbistum

Wien, Erzbistum

Meppen, Stadt (Westfalen)

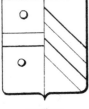

Nördlingen

Haldenstein, Herrschaft (Bez.
Imboden, Graubünden), Besitz
der Freiherrn Buol von Schauenstein

Gembloux (Belgien)

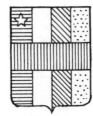

Zentralafrikanische Republik

Reims, Stadt

Rochefort

Reckheim

Reckheim

Reckheim

Reckheim

Nevers

Strahow, Prämonstratenserstift (Prag)

Strahow,
Prämonstratenserstift (Prag)

Haldenstein, Herrschaft

(Bez. Imboden,
Graubünden),
Besitz der Freiherrn
Buol von Schauenstein

Wellenbalken

Fasce ondée

Fess wavy

Stargard in Pommern

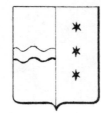

Aargau, Variante 1805

Aargau, 1803

Aargau, 1803

Stevensweert
(niederl. Provinz Limburg)

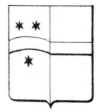

Leuchtenberg, Landgrafschaft

Zickzackbalken

Fasce vivrée

Fess dancetty

Krakau, Bistum
Haus Wittelsbach, um 1220

Pfaffenhofen a. d. Ilm, Stadt
(Bayern)

Manderscheid

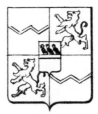

Reckheim

Reckheim

Reckheim

Reckheim

Zinnenbalken

Fasce enclavée

Fess embattled

Büren, Grafschaft
(Gelderland)

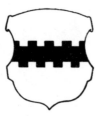

Opladen, Stadt (Niederrhein)

**Weitere Sonder-
formen**

**Autres formes
extraordinaires**

**Other special
shapes**

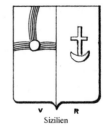

Sizilien

Klosterneuburg,
Chorherrenstift

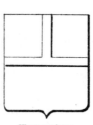

Klosterneuburg,
Chorherrenstift

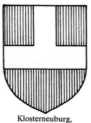

Klosterneuburg,
Chorherrenstift

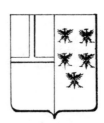

Klosterneuburg,
Chorherrenstift

Schachbalken

Fasce échiquetée

Fess checky

Dinslaken
Jametz 1588

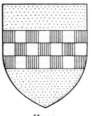

Hamm
Mark, Grafschaft

Hamm
Mark, Grafschaft

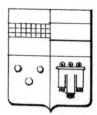

Bouillon und Sedan

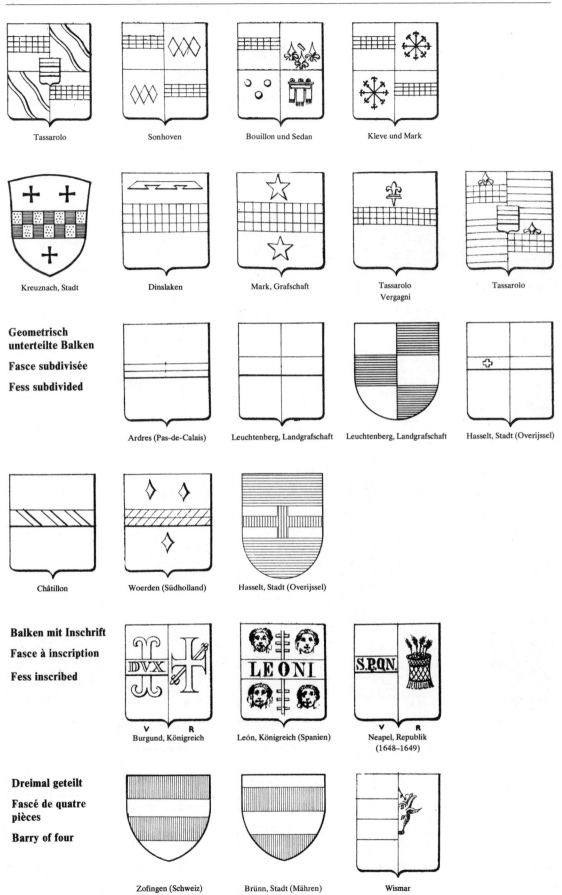

Tassarolo   Sonhoven   Bouillon und Sedan   Kleve und Mark

Kreuznach, Stadt   Dinslaken   Mark, Grafschaft   Tassarolo Vergagni   Tassarolo

Geometrisch unterteilte Balken

Fasce subdivisée

Fess subdivided

Ardres (Pas-de-Calais)   Leuchtenberg, Landgrafschaft   Leuchtenberg, Landgrafschaft   Hasselt, Stadt (Overijssel)

Châtillon   Woerden (Südholland)   Hasselt, Stadt (Overijssel)

Balken mit Inschrift

Fasce à inscription

Fess inscribed

Burgund, Königreich   León, Königreich (Spanien)   Neapel, Republik (1648–1649)

Dreimal geteilt

Fascé de quatre pièces

Barry of four

Zofingen (Schweiz)   Brünn, Stadt (Mähren)   Wismar

**Zwei Balken
(viermal geteilt)**

**Deux fasces
(fascé de cinq
pièces)**

**Two bars
(barry of five)**

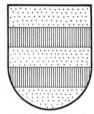

Oldenburg, Grafschaft
Haselünne, Stadt
(Niedersachsen)

Isenburg

Herren von Bicken (Hessen)
ausgestorben 1732

Béziers (Languedoc)

Nevers und Rethel

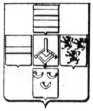

Lüttich, Bistum

Norwegen

Dänemark

Togo

Schweden

Rudolstadt (Thüringen)

Mansfeld, Grafschaft

**Zwei Balken im
gevierten Schilde**

**Deux fasces dans
écu écartelé**

**Two bars on
quartered shield**

Vianen (Südholland)

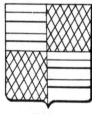

Eisleben
Mansfeld, Grafschaft

Mansfeld, Grafschaft

Oldenburg, Grafschaft

Oldenburg, Land

Oldenburg, Herzogtum

Oldenburg, Großherzogtum,
27. 11. 1821

Cilli, Grafschaft
(Südsteiermark)

Oldenburg, Herzogtum

Ungarn, Dynastie Hunyadi

Böhmen
Ungarn

Château-Regnault
(Ardennes)

Haldenstein, Herrschaft (Bez.
Imboden, Graubünden), Besitz der
Freiherrn Buol von Schauenstein

Ungarn

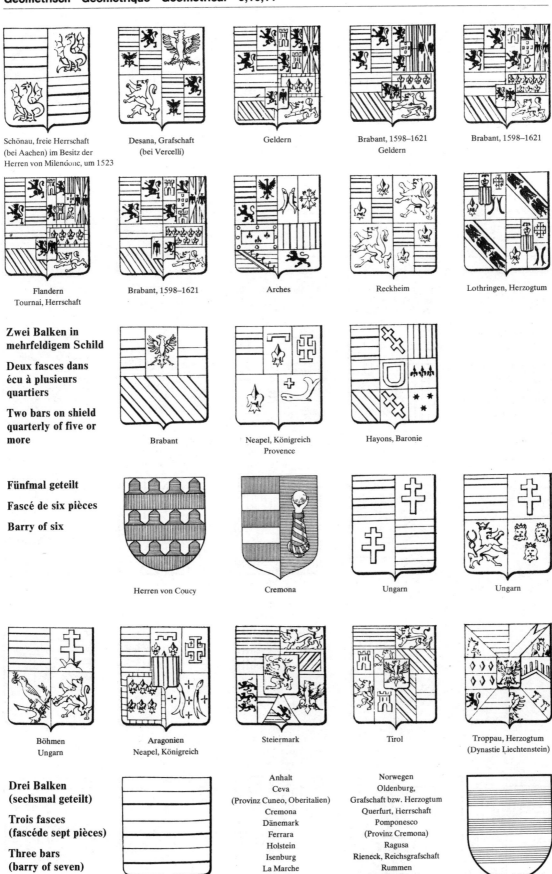

Schönau, freie Herrschaft
(bei Aachen) im Besitz der
Herren von Milendonc, um 1523

Desana, Grafschaft
(bei Vercelli)

Geldern

Brabant, 1598–1621
Geldern

Brabant, 1598–1621

Flandern
Tournai, Herrschaft

Brabant, 1598–1621

Arches

Reckheim

Lothringen, Herzogtum

Zwei Balken in mehrfeldigem Schild

Deux fasces dans écu à plusieurs quartiers

Two bars on shield quarterly of five or more

Brabant

Neapel, Königreich
Provence

Hayons, Baronie

Fünfmal geteilt

Fascé de six pièces

Barry of six

Herren von Coucy

Cremona

Ungarn

Ungarn

Böhmen
Ungarn

Aragonien
Neapel, Königreich

Steiermark

Tirol

Troppau, Herzogtum
(Dynastie Liechtenstein)

Drei Balken (sechsmal geteilt)

Trois fasces (fascéde sept pièces)

Three bars (barry of seven)

	Anhalt	Norwegen
	Ceva	Oldenburg,
	(Provinz Cuneo, Oberitalien)	Grafschaft bzw. Herzogtum
	Cremona	Querfurt, Herrschaft
	Dänemark	Pomponesco
	Ferrara	(Provinz Cremona)
	Holstein	Ragusa
	Isenburg	Rieneck, Reichsgrafschaft
	La Marche	Rummen
	Loos	Sachsen
Alpen, Herrschaft	Mainz, Domkapitel	Ungarn
(Kreis Moers)	Mansfeld, Grafschaft	Zofingen (Schweiz)
Ampurias (Spanien)	Mantua, Herzogtum	

Herrschaft Eisenberg
(Thüringen)

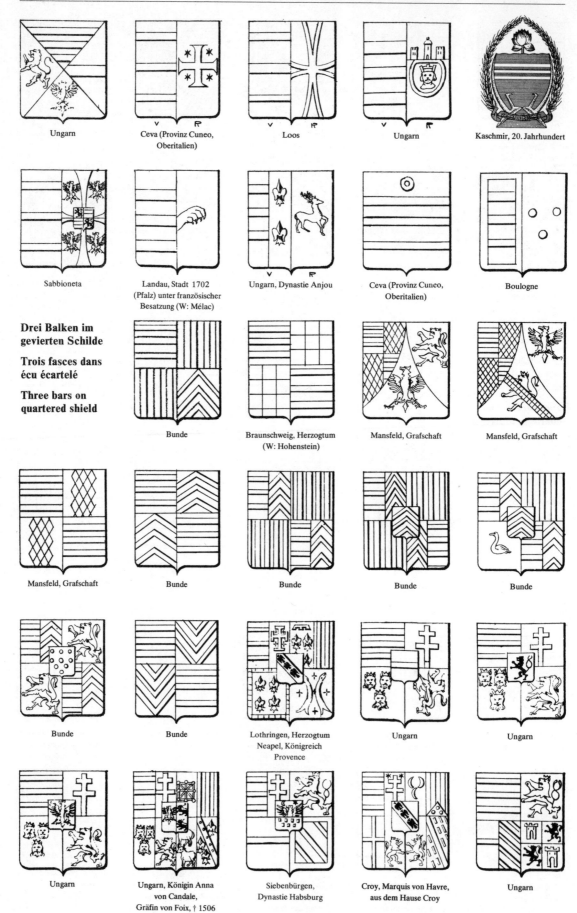

Ungarn

Ceva (Provinz Cuneo, Oberitalien)

Loos

Ungarn

Kaschmir, 20. Jahrhundert

Sabbioneta

Landau, Stadt 1702 (Pfalz) unter französischer Besatzung (W: Mélac)

Ungarn, Dynastie Anjou

Ceva (Provinz Cuneo, Oberitalien)

Boulogne

Drei Balken im gevierten Schilde

Trois fasces dans écu écartelé

Three bars on quartered shield

Bunde

Braunschweig, Herzogtum (W: Hohenstein)

Mansfeld, Grafschaft

Mansfeld, Grafschaft

Mansfeld, Grafschaft

Bunde

Bunde

Bunde

Bunde

Bunde

Bunde

Lothringen, Herzogtum Neapel, Königreich Provence

Ungarn

Ungarn

Ungarn

Ungarn, Königin Anna von Candale, Gräfin von Foix, † 1506

Siebenbürgen, Dynastie Habsburg

Croy, Marquis von Havre, aus dem Hause Croy

Ungarn

Ungarn

Ungarn

Böhmen

Schlesien
Tirol

Ungarn

Jägerndorf, Herzogtum
(vor 1490)
Ungarn, Dynastie Hunyadi

Schlesien
Ungarn

Ungarn

Ungarn

Ungarn, Dynastie Hunyadi

Ungarn, Dynastie Hunyadi

Ungarn, Dynastie Hunyadi

Mansfeld, Grafschaft

Ungarn

Kessenich

Rummen

Heinsberg, Herrschaft
(Niederrhein)

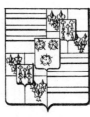

Rheidt und Well

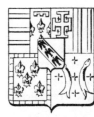

Namur (Belgien)

Lothringen, Herzogtum
Neapel, Königreich
Provence

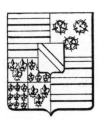

Chimay, Fürstentum
(W: Ligne-Arschott-
Arenberg, 1590)

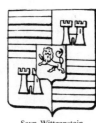

Sayn-Wittgenstein

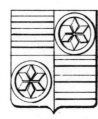

Kessenich

Mainz, Erzbistum

Chimay, Fürstentum
Croy, Herzöge, 1354
Megen, Grafschaft

Havré

Drei Balken in mehrfeldigem Schild

Trois fasces dans écu à cinq quartiers

Three bars on shield quarterly of five

Deutschland
Österreich
Tirol

Deutschland
Österreich
Tirol

Deutschland
Österreich

Drei Balken in vielfeldigem Schild

Trois fasces dans écu à plus de six quartiers

Three bars on shield quartered of six or more

Kärnten

Kärnten

Kärnten

Oberelsaß

Tassarolo

Château-Regnault (Ardennes)

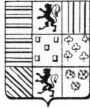
Hayons, Baronie

Steiermark

Deutschland-Österreich

Siebenmal geteilt

Fascé huit pièces

Barry of eight

Alt-Ungarn

Herren von Querfurt

Vereinigte Staaten von Amerika

Ungarn

Siebenmal geteilt in geviertem Schild

Fascé de huit pièces dans écu écartelé

Barry of eight on quartered shield

Brogel Bunde

Ungarn, Dynastie Hunyadi

Ungarn

Ungarn

Tirol

Tirol

Tirol

Tirol

Mailand, Herzogtum

Tirol

Lothringen, Herzogtum Neapel, Königreich Provence

Lothringen, Herzogtum Pfalzburg (Lothringen) und Lixheim

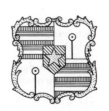
Hawaii, Republik, 25. 5. 1896

Hawaii, Königreich

Siebenmal geteilt in mehrfeldigem Schild

Fascé de huit pièces dans écu à plus de six quartiers

Barry of eight on shield quartered of six or more

Deutschland-Österreich

Deutschland-Österreich

Vier Balken

Quatre fasces

Four bars

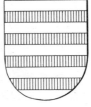

Mainz, Domkapitel

Vier Balken im ersten von mehreren Schilden

Quatre fasces au premier de plusieurs écussons

Four bars on the first of many escutcheons

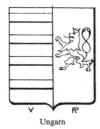

Ungarn

Ungarn

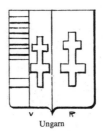

Mansfeld, Grafschaft

Tirol

Vier Balken in gespaltenem Schild oder auf Avers

Quatre fasces dans écu parti ou sur avers

Four bars on shield per pale or on obverse

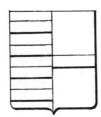

Lüttich für Loos und Bouillon

Vinstingen (Diana von Havre)

Ungarn

Walachei

Vier Balken in geviertem Schild

Quatre fasces dans écu écartelé

Four bars on quartered shield

Siebenbürgen, Dynastie Zapolya Ungarn

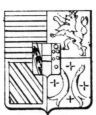

Toskana

Ungarn

Ungarn

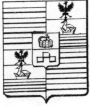

Grafen von Sinzendorf

Reckheim

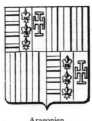

Lothringen, Herzogtum

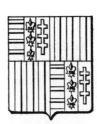

Aragonien
Neapel, Königreich
Sizilien

Neapel, Königreich

Toskana

Kessenich

Neunmal geteilt

Burelé de dix pièces

Barry of ten

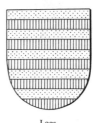

Loos
Herren von Rieneck

Loos und Chiny

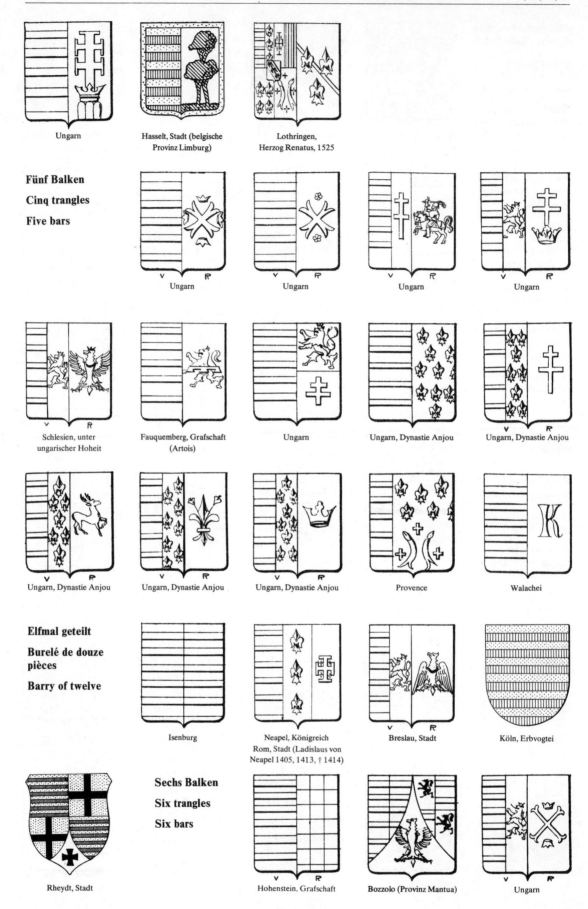

Ungarn

Hasselt, Stadt (belgische Provinz Limburg)

Lothringen, Herzog Renatus, 1525

Fünf Balken

Cinq trangles

Five bars

Ungarn

Ungarn

Ungarn

Ungarn

Schlesien, unter ungarischer Hoheit

Fauquemberg, Grafschaft (Artois)

Ungarn

Ungarn, Dynastie Anjou

Ungarn, Dynastie Anjou

Ungarn, Dynastie Anjou

Ungarn, Dynastie Anjou

Ungarn, Dynastie Anjou

Provence

Walachei

Elfmal geteilt

Burelé de douze pièces

Barry of twelve

Isenburg

Neapel, Königreich Rom, Stadt (Ladislaus von Neapel 1405, 1413, † 1414)

Breslau, Stadt

Köln, Erbvogtei

Rheydt, Stadt

Sechs Balken

Six trangles

Six bars

Hohenstein, Grafschaft

Bozzolo (Provinz Mantua)

Ungarn

Sayn

Kessenich

Dreizehnmal geteilt

Burelé de quatorze pièces

Barry of fourteen

Loos

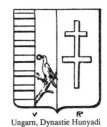

Ungarn, Dynastie Hunyadi

Mehr als dreizehn-mal geteilt

Burelé sans nombre

Striped fesswise

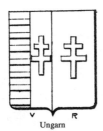

Ungarn

Ungarn

Vereinigte Staaten von Amerika

Zwei Wellenbalken

Deux fasces ondées

Two bars wavy

Gerona

Lyme Regis, Stadt (Dorsetshire, England)

Stevensweert (niederl. Provinz Limburg)

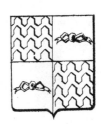

Camerino, Herzogtum (Provinz Marche, Italien, Marchesi Varani)

Drei Wellenbalken

Trois fasces ondées

Three bars wavy

Guayana, 21. 1. 1966

Botswana

Agde (Languedoc)

Padua
Ragusa
Stolp (Pommern)
Xerez de la Fontera

Mehrfach wellen-oder zinnengeteilt

Fascé ondé ou enclavé

Barry wavy or embattled

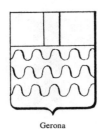

Gerona

Penang, 11. 9. 1949

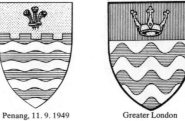

Greater London

Tschad, 1970

Zwei Zinnenbalken

Deux fasces enclavées

Two bars embattled

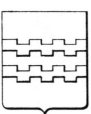

Gorinchem
Heukelum (Südholland)

Heukelum (Südholland)

Verkürzte Balken

Hamaïdes

Bars couped

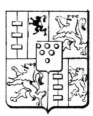

Elsloo

Pfahl allein

Pal seul

Pal only

Medemblik (Nordholland)
Savona (Italien)

Leuchtenberg, Landgrafschaft

Medemblik, Hoorn und
Enkhuisen

Medemblik, Stadt

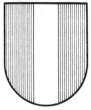

Dordrecht, Stadt

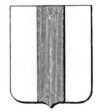

Brielle, Stadt (Südholland)

Turnhout, Herrschaft
(Belgien)

Unter Schildhaupt

Sous chef

Under chief

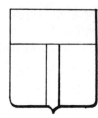

Baden im Aargau, Stadt

Baden, Grafschaft (Aargau)

Savona, Stadt (Italien)

Mit Innenzeichnung

Chargé de dessins

Charged with design

Delft, Stadt (Niederlande)

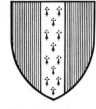

Bregenz, Grafschaft

**Belegt mit
Heroldsbildern**

**Chargé de pièces
honorables**

**Charged with
subordinaries**

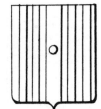

Barcelona, Grafschaft

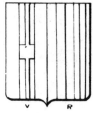

Gerona

Herren von Erlach (Schweiz)

Neuenburg
Troppau, Stadt

Troppau, Stadt

Troppau, Stadt

Neuenburg, Grafschaft

Badenweiler, Herrschaft
Valangin, Herrschaft
(Schweiz)

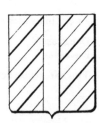

Neuenburg,
Fürstentum (1806–1814)

**Begleitet und
überdeckt**

**Accompagné et à
autre pièce brochant**

**between or sur-
mounted by other
charges**

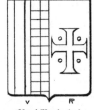

Urgel (Katalonien)
unter aragonesischer Hoheit

Gouda, Stadt (Niederlande)

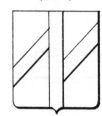

Sultana (Labuan)

Burgau, Markgrafschaft
(Schwaben)

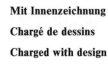

Zwei Phähle

Deux pals

Two pallets

Wittgenstein

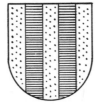
Landsberg, Markgrafschaft

Sizilien

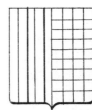...

Puigcerda (Katalonien)

Piombino

Piombino

Amboise (Touraine)

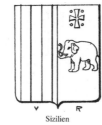
Urgel (Katalonien)
unter aragonesischer Hoheit

Chemnitz, Stadt

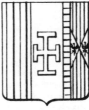
Erfurt

Barcelona

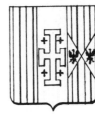
Barcelona

Barcelona

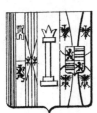
Sabbioneta

Zwei Pfähle in geviertem Schild

Deux pals dans écu écartelé

Two pallets on quartered shield

Barcelona

Viglevano

Erfurt, großes Stadtwappen,
17. Jahrhundert

Desana, Grafschaft
(bei Vercelli)

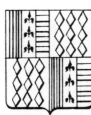
Piombino

Sizilien, Königreich

Sizilien, Königreich

Sayn-Wittgenstein

Fünfmal gespalten

Palé de six pièces

Paly of six

Trivulzio (Misox, Musocco)

Trivulzio (Misox, Musocco)

Rennes, Stadt (Bretagne)

Herzöge von Atri, Fürsten
von Teramo a. d. Hause
der Acquaviva d'Aragon

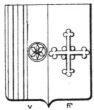

Auf Avers

Sur Avers

On obverse

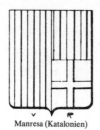
Manresa (Katalonien)

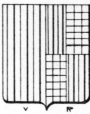
Tarrega (Katalonien)

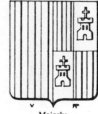
Majorka

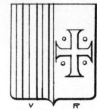
Sardinien, Königreich

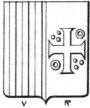
Argentona (Katalonien)

Cervera (Katalonien)
Gerona (Katalonien)
Granollers (Katalonien)
Igualada (Katalonien)
Manresa (Katalonien)
Mataró (Katalonien)
Villafranca del Panadés
(Katalonien)

Besalú (Katalonien)
Olot (Katalonien)

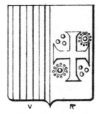
Sardinien, Königreich

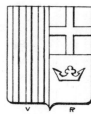
Solsona (Katalonien)

Barcelona · Caldas
Tagamanent · Tarrasa

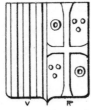
Agramunt (Katalonien)

Argentona (Katalonien)
Balaguer (Katalonien)
Bañolas (Katalonien)
Barcelona (Katalonien)
Berga (Katalonien)
Besalú (Katalonien)
Cervera (Katalonien)
Figueras (Katalonien)
Gerona (Katalonien)
Granollers (Katalonien)

Igualada (Katalonien)
La Bisbál (Katalonien)
Manresa (Katalonien)
Olot (Katalonien)
Puigcerda (Katalonien)
Tarrasa (Katalonien)
Tarrega (Katalonien)
Vich (Katalonien)
Villafranca del Panadés
(Katalonien)

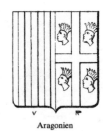
Aragonien

Aragonien

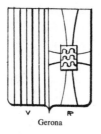
Gerona

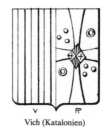
La Bisbál (Katalonien)

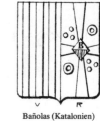
Vich (Katalonien)

Bañolas (Katalonien)

Besalú (Katalonien)

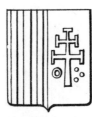
Besalú (Katalonien)

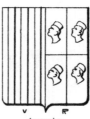
Aragonien

Meißen-Thüringen

Aragonien

Im ersten von drei Schilden

Au premier de trois écussons

On the first of three escutcheons

Sayn-Wittgenstein

Mit Farbangabe

Aux émaux indiqués

The tinctures shown

Foix, Grafschaft

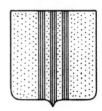
Vietnam (Süd), 1963

In gespaltenem Schilde

Dans écu parti

On shield per pale

Sayn

Oberösterreich

Desana, Grafschaft
(bei Vercelli)

Musocco und Musso
(Dynastie Trivulzio)

In geviertem oder mehrfeldigem Schild

Dans écu écartelé on à plusieurs quartiers

On shield quarterly of four or more

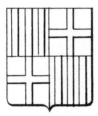
Bunde

Aragonien
Neapel und Sizilien

Neapel, Königreich

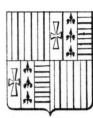
Sizilien

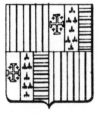
Aragonien
Neapel und Sizilien

Katalonien

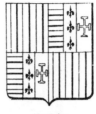
Klettgau (Grafen von
Schwarzenberg)

Bunde

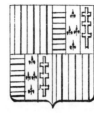
Bunde

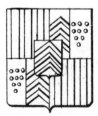
Bunde

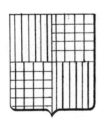
Tarrega (Katalonien)

Schwarzenberg

Kirchberg

Foix, Grafschaft

Bracciano, Stadt (Provinz
Rom), Besitz der Orsini

Granollers (Katalonien)

Aragonien
Majorka

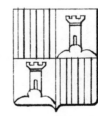
Schwarzenberg

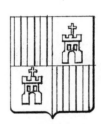
Balearen

Saragossa

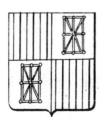
Aragonien

Neapel, Königreich

Monferrat, Markgrafschaft
(Oberitalien)

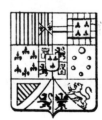
La Habana·Mexiko
Nicaragua · Potosí (Bolivien)
Spanien nach 1759

Vier Phähle

Quatre pals

Four pallets

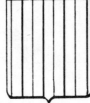

Desana, Grafschaft
Foix, Grafschaft
Granollers (Katalonien)
Katalonien
Landsberg, Markgrafschaft
Musocco und Musso
Perpignan
Provence
Schwarzenberg
Valencia (Spanien)
Vigliano

Aragonien
Béthune (Pas-de-Calais)

Kreta 1646–1647

Katalonien
Roussillon

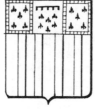

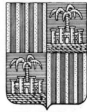

Valencia (Spanien)

Paderborn, Stadt

Aix-en-Provence

Olot (Katalonien)

Palma de Mallorca

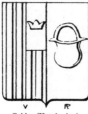

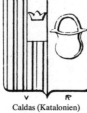

Murano, 1741–1752 (1743).

V.   Petro Grimani, Doge
     Matteo Moratta, Consul
     Sebastian Piz, Proconsul
R.   Girolanno Gazabin
     Peleg Ongaro
     Antonio Rosseto
     Nicolao Ferro

Caldas (Katalonien)

Murano, Insel

**Mehrere Pfähle
in schräggeviertem
Grunde**

**Plusieurs pals dans
fond écartelé**

**Any pallets on
quartered field**

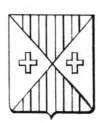

Vich (Katalonien)

Sizilien

Neapel und Sizilien

Neapel und Sizilien

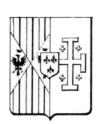

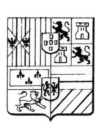

Neapel und Sizilien

Neapel und Sizilien

Barcelona

Spanien

**Mehrere Pfähle in
geteiltem Schild**

**Plusieurs pals dans
écu coupé**

**Any pallets on
shield per fess**

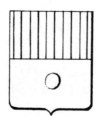

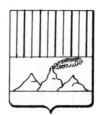

Montpellier, Stadt
(Languedoc)

Guatemala, 31. 5. 1858

Frauenberg an der Moldau
(Böhmen)

Pfahlweise gestreift

Palé sans nombre

Striped palewise

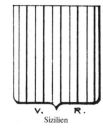

Sizilien

Vereinigte Staaten von
Amerika

Greenpoint (New York)

Desana, Grafschaft
(bei Vercelli)

New-York

Cohoes (New-York)

Constantine (Michigan)
Cooperstown (New York)
Detroit (Michigan)
Galion (Ohio)
Ionia (Michigan)
New-York
Warren (Ohio)

Chicago (Illinois)

Wellenpfähle

Pals ondés

Pallets wavy

Yukon (Kanada)

Tarragona (Spanien)

Tarragona (Spanien)

Sambia, 19. 2. 1965

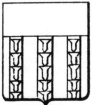

Nordrhodesien, 16. 8. 1939

Fehpfähle

Pals vairés

Pallets vairy

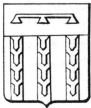

Blois, Grafschaft
Château Porcien
St.-Paul, Grafschaft

St.-Paul, Grafschaft

St.-Paul, Grafschaft

Verkürzte Pfähle

Pals retraits

Pallets retracted

Piombino

Piombino

Piombino

Piombino

Piombino

**Pfähle von Balken
überdeckt**

**Pals, à fasce(s)
brochant**

**Pallets surmounted
by bars**

Val di Taro (Provinz Parma)

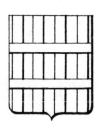

Val di Taro (Provinz Parma)

Béthune (Pas-de-Calais)

Aufrechte Gitter

Grillage

Grill

Elsloo

Falun (Schweden)

Bellpuig (Katalonien)

Schräggeteilt

Tranché et taeillé

Per bend and per bend sinister

Reckheim
Utrecht, Stadt
Zürich

Utrecht, Stadt

Utrecht, Stadt

Zürich

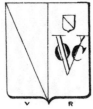

Java (unter holländischer Herrschaft)

Zürich (zwei gegeneinander gelehnte Schilde)

Zürich

Utrecht, Stadt

Zürich

Zürich

Gezahnt schräg-geteilt

Tranché denché

Per bend danccettly

Bologna, Herrschaft

Bologna, Herrschaft

Schrägbalken

Bande

Bend

Baden, Markgrafschaft

Bossu
Charenton
Freies Gebiet
in Österreichisch-Flandern
Ligne, Fürstentum
Regensburg, Bistum
Straßburg, Bistum

Schleusingen (Thüringen)

Straßburg, Stadt

Baden-Durlach,
Markgrafschaft

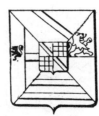

Baden, 1500

Baden, 1500

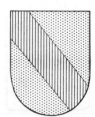

Bossu oder Boussu, Herrschaft
(Hennegau)

Chalon, Dynastie (Burgund)

Baden, Stammwappen
Baden-Baden, Stadt

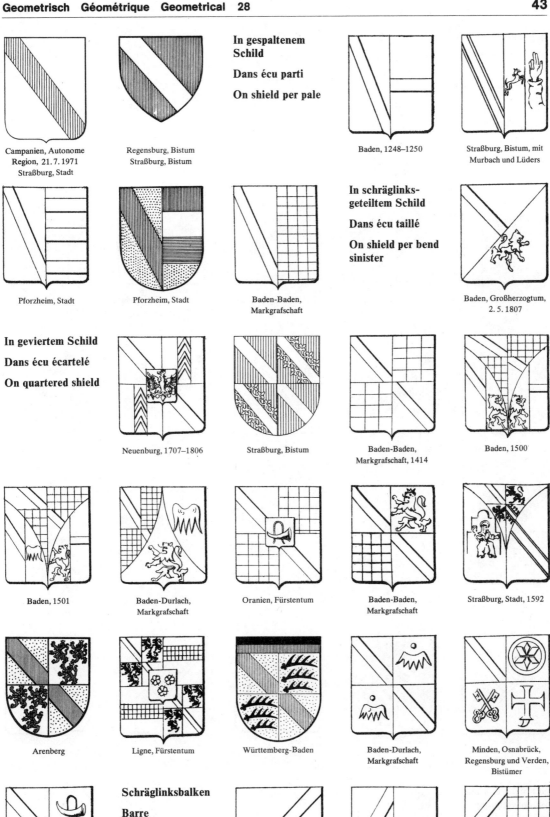

In gespaltenem
Schild

Dans écu parti

On shield per pale

Campanien, Autonome
Region, 21.7.1971
Straßburg, Stadt

Regensburg, Bistum
Straßburg, Bistum

Baden, 1248–1250

Straßburg, Bistum, mit
Murbach und Lüders

Pforzheim, Stadt

Pforzheim, Stadt

Baden-Baden,
Markgrafschaft

In schräglinks-
geteiltem Schild

Dans écu taillé

On shield per bend
sinister

Baden, Großherzogtum,
2.5.1807

In geviertem Schild

Dans écu écartelé

On quartered shield

Neuenburg, 1707–1806

Straßburg, Bistum

Baden-Baden,
Markgrafschaft, 1414

Baden, 1500

Baden, 1501

Baden-Durlach,
Markgrafschaft

Oranien, Fürstentum

Baden-Baden,
Markgrafschaft

Straßburg, Stadt, 1592

Arenberg

Ligne, Fürstentum

Württemberg-Baden

Baden-Durlach,
Markgrafschaft

Minden, Osnabrück,
Regensburg und Verden,
Bistümer

Schräglinksbalken

Barre

Bend sinister

Oranien, Fürstentum

Regensburg, Bistum

Baden, 1248–1250

Baden-Baden,
Markgrafschaft, 1414

44

**Schrägbalken,
belegt mit kleinen
Figuren**

**Bande chargée de
meubles**

Bend charged

Arlay, Herrschaft
(Dynastie Chalon)
Rochefort

Thun, Stadt (Schweiz)

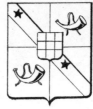
Oranien, Fürstentum

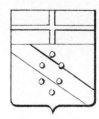
Massa und Carrara,
um 1529

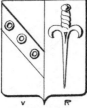
Masserano, Fürstentum
(Piemont)

Bern

Lothringen, Herzogtum

Lothringen, Herzogtum

Metz, Stadt, 1552

Lothringen, Herzogtum

Lothringen, Herzogtum

Lothringen, Herzogtum

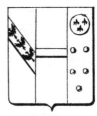
Toskana

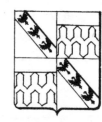
Lothringen, Herzogtum

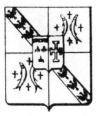
Lothringen, Herzogtum

Spalato
Vauvillars

Vauvillars

Rethel

Galloway, Landschaft in
Südwestschottland

Karlsruhe, Stadt

Karlsruhe, Stadt

Siena

Lucca
Pistoja

Lucca

**Schrägbalken mit
Innenzeichnung**

**Bandes et barres
chargées de dessins**

**Bends charged with
design**

Straßburg, Stadt

Brandenburg, Markgrafschaft

Ebrach, Kloster

Dalmatien

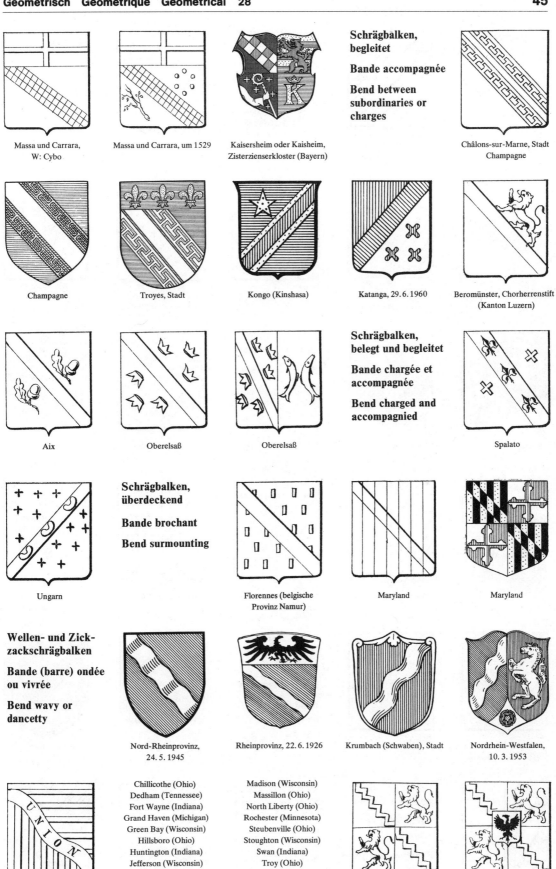

Massa und Carrara,
W: Cybo

Massa und Carrara, um 1529

Kaisersheim oder Kaisheim,
Zisterzienserkloster (Bayern)

**Schrägbalken,
begleitet**

Bande accompagnée

**Bend between
subordinaries or
charges**

Châlons-sur-Marne, Stadt
Champagne

Champagne

Troyes, Stadt

Kongo (Kinshasa)

Katanga, 29. 6. 1960

Beromünster, Chorherrenstift
(Kanton Luzern)

Aix

Oberelsaß

Oberelsaß

**Schrägbalken,
belegt und begleitet**

**Bande chargée et
accompagnée**

**Bend charged and
accompagnied**

Spalato

Ungarn

**Schrägbalken,
überdeckend**

Bande brochant

Bend surmounting

Florennes (belgische
Provinz Namur)

Maryland

Maryland

**Wellen- und Zick-
zackschrägbalken**

**Bande (barre) ondée
ou vivrée**

**Bend wavy or
dancetty**

Nord-Rheinprovinz,
24. 5. 1945

Rheinprovinz, 22. 6. 1926

Krumbach (Schwaben), Stadt

Nordrhein-Westfalen,
10. 3. 1953

Belmont (New-York)
Camden (Ohio)
Charlotte (Michigan)

Chillicothe (Ohio)
Dedham (Tennessee)
Fort Wayne (Indiana)
Grand Haven (Michigan)
Green Bay (Wisconsin)
Hillsboro (Ohio)
Huntington (Indiana)
Jefferson (Wisconsin)
Kendalville (Indiana)
Laureville (Ohio)
Ligonier (Indiana)
Lima (Ohio)

Madison (Wisconsin)
Massillon (Ohio)
North Liberty (Ohio)
Rochester (Minnesota)
Steubenville (Ohio)
Stoughton (Wisconsin)
Swan (Indiana)
Troy (Ohio)
Vereinigte Staaten von Amerika
West Unity (Ohio)
Wheeling (West Virginia)
Woodsfield (Ohio)

Reckheim

Reckheim

Schräggestreift

Bandé

Bendy

Abbeville (Somme)
Atri · Blois, Grafschaft

Burgund, Herzogtum
Gubbio (Italien)
Kuinre, Grafschaft (Overijssel)
Lavagna (Ligurien)
Masserano und Crevacuore
Nevers, Grafschaft
Padua
Sémur (Côte-d'Or)
Turenne (Corrèze)
Herren von Vargula
(Thüringen)
Urbino (Italien)

Kempten, Stadt

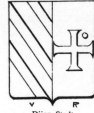

Dijon, Stadt

Treviso (Venetien)

Burgund, Grafschaft
Burgund, Herzogtum

Urbino (Italien)

Gubbio
(Prov. Reggio nell'Emilia)

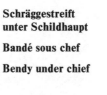

Gubbio
(Prov. Reggio nell'Emilia)

Landau a. d. Isar, Stadt
(Bayern)

Schelklingen, Grafschaft
(Schwaben)
Ehingen (Donau), Stadt

**Schräggestreift
unter Schildhaupt**

Bandé sous chef

Bendy under chief

Abbeville (Somme)

Manchester

**Schräggestreift in
gespaltenem Schilde**

**Bandé dans écu
parti**

**Bendy on shield per
pale**

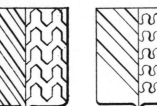

Camerino, Herzogtum
(Provinz Marche, Italien,
Marchesi Varani)

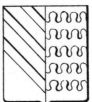

Camerino, Herzogtum
(Provinz Marche, Italien,
Marchesi Varani)

Auxonne, Stadt (Côte d'Or)

Glatz, im Besitz der
Freiherren von Pernstein,
1537–1548

Musocco und Musso
(Dynastie Trivulzio)

Lille, Stände

**Schräggestreift
innerhalb Schild-
randes**

Bandé à bordure

**Bendy within
bordure**

Burgund, Herzogtum, um 1200

Nivernais, Herzogtum

Brescia

**Schräggestreift in
geviertem Schilde**

**Bandé dans écu
écartelé**

**Bendy on quartered
shield**

Masserano, Fürstentum
(Piemont)

Vicenza (Oberitalien)

Solder und Sonhoven

Paar, Reichsgrafen
1. 7. 1629

Masserano, Fürstentum
(Piemont)

Masserano, Fürstentum
(Piemont)

Hoorn, Grafschaft
Kessenich

Schräggestreift in mehrfeldigem Schild

Bandé dans écu de plus de quatre quartiers

Bendy on shield quarterly of more then four quarters

Tirol

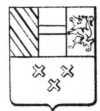

Breda, Herrschaft

Urbino (Italien)
Gubbio
(Prov. Reggio nell'Emilia)

Urbino (Italien)

Schräglinksgestreift

Barré

Bendy sinister

Glatz, Grafschaft

Glatz, Grafschaft

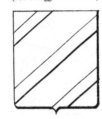

Avesnes · Gubbio
Hennegau · Savoyen

Kempten, Stadt

Camerino, Herzogtum
(Provinz Marche, Italien,
Marchesi Varani)

Erfurt

Kuba, 24. 1. 1906

Savoyen

Münsterberg und Oels,
Herzogtümer

Schrägflüsse

Bandes ondées

Bendlets wavy

Beckum, Stadt, um 1580

Beckum, Stadt (Westfalen)

Billerbeck, Stadt (Westfalen)

Mit Spitzen geteilt

Coupé émanché

Per fess dancetty

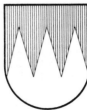

Franken, Herzogtum
Sulz
Würzburg, Bistum

Klettgau (Herren von Sulz)

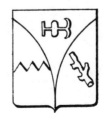

Klettgau (Herren von Sulz)

Klettgau (Herren von Sulz)

Bahrain, 1965

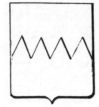

Büren, Stadt (Westfalen)
Würzburg, Bistum

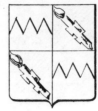

Würzburg, Bistum

Klettgau (Herren von Sulz)

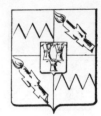

Klettgau (Herren von Sulz)

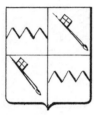

Würzburg, Bistum

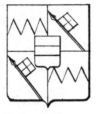

Würzburg, Großherzogtum
1806–1814

Würzburg, Bistum

Spitzen und Keile
Pointes et piles
Piles

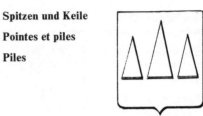

Pesaro

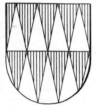

Hotzenplotz, Stadt, 1415

Olmütz, Bistum (Mähren)

Olmütz, Bistum (Mähren)

Valladolid

Sparren
Chevron
Chevron

Courtrai (Kortrijk)
Pont de Vaux (Bresse), Kapitel

Büren, Stadt (Westfalen)

Murano, Insel

Murano, 1779–1788 (1787).

V.   Paulo Renier, Doge
     Paulo Ongaro, Consul
     Antonio Pisani, Proconsul
R.   Angelo Barbin
     Giovanni Batiste Rioda
     Vincenzo Motta
     Francesco Ferri

Courtrai (Kortrijk)

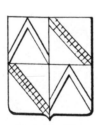

Heyde und ter Blyt

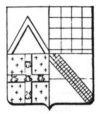

Heyde und ter Blyt

Courtrai (Kortrijk),
Burggrafschaft, 17. Jahrhundert

Courtrai (Kortrijk),
Burggrafschaft,
17. Jahrhundert

Zwei und drei
Sparren
Chevrons
Chevrons and
chevronels

Ravensberg

Beaumont, Herrschaft

Bouchain, Stadt, 1711
Flandern
Hanau, Grafschaft
Hennegau
's-Heerenberg, Herrschaft
Hessen-Hanau
Perche, Grafschaft
Ravensberg

Ravensberg

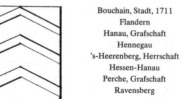

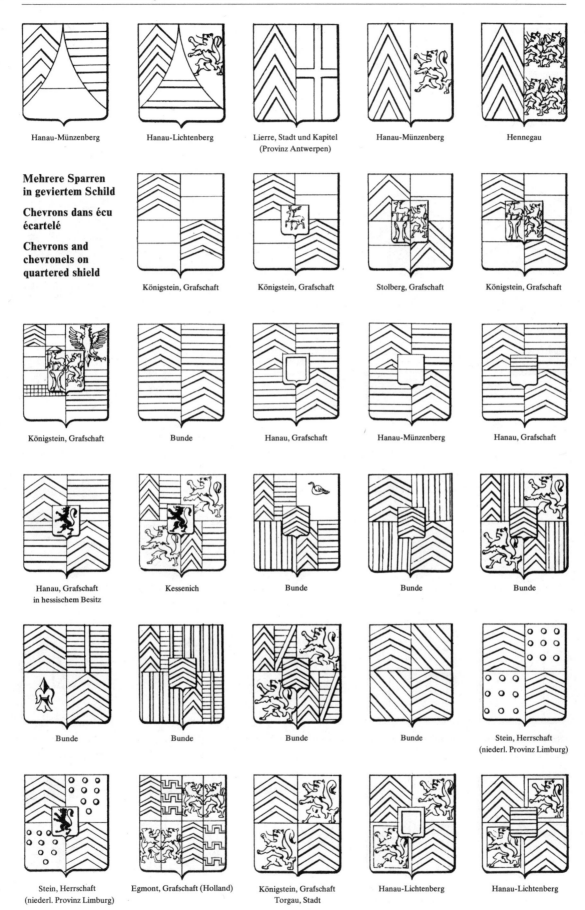

Hanau-Münzenberg

Hanau-Lichtenberg

Lierre, Stadt und Kapitel
(Provinz Antwerpen)

Hanau-Münzenberg

Hennegau

**Mehrere Sparren
in geviertem Schild**

**Chevrons dans écu
écartelé**

**Chevrons and
chevronels on
quartered shield**

Königstein, Grafschaft

Königstein, Grafschaft

Stolberg, Grafschaft

Königstein, Grafschaft

Königstein, Grafschaft

Bunde

Hanau, Grafschaft

Hanau-Münzenberg

Hanau, Grafschaft

Hanau, Grafschaft
in hessischem Besitz

Kessenich

Bunde

Bunde

Bunde

Bunde

Bunde

Bunde

Bunde

Stein, Herrschaft
(niederl. Provinz Limburg)

Stein, Herrschaft
(niederl. Provinz Limburg)

Egmont, Grafschaft (Holland)

Königstein, Grafschaft
Torgau, Stadt

Hanau-Lichtenberg

Hanau-Lichtenberg

Drei Sparren in sechsfeldigem Schild

Trois chevrons dans écu à six quartiers

Three chevronels on shield quarterly of six

Hanau, Grafschaft

Sparren, begleitet

Chevron(s) accompagné(s)

Chevron and chevronels accompagnied

Courtrai (Kortrijk)

Tournai, Herrschaft

Bunde

Gloucester

Sturzsparren

Chevrons renversés

Chevronels reversed

Bunde

Westindische Föderation, 1. 8. 1957

Geviert (quadriert)

Ecartelé

Quarterly

Brandenburg, Kurfürstentum

Brandenburg-Ansbach
Brandenburg-Bayreuth
Castell, Grafschaft
Hildesheim, Stadt
Hohenzollern
Neustadt a. d. Aisch
Pesaro
Piacenza, Stadt
Vierzon (Cher)

Brandenburg, Kurfürstentum

Preußen, Herzogtum

Castell, Grafschaft

Hohenzollern, Dynastie
Hohenzollernsche Lande,
22. 9. 1880

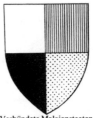

Verbündete Malaienstaaten, 1929

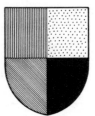

Windward-Inseln, 16. 8. 1939

Hohenzollernsche Lande, 19. 11. 1928

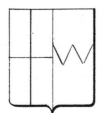

Nürnberg und Würzburg

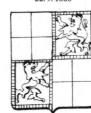

Brandenburg, Kurfürstentum

Brandenburg, Kurfürstentum

Brandenburg, Kurfürstentum

Hohenzollern-Hechingen

Hohenzollern-Sigmaringen

Jägerndorf, Herzogtum
unter brandenburgischer
Herrschaft (ab 1523)

Hohenzollern

Brandenburg, Kurfürstentum

Brandenburg, Kurfürstentum

Geschacht

Echiqueté

Checky

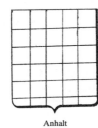

Anhalt

Aschersleben
Bretagne
Ellrich (Grafschaft Hohenstein)
Greußen (Thüringen)
Hohenstein, Grafschaft
Jauer, Stadt
Mirandola, Fürstentum
Nordhausen, Stadt
Pistoja
Sponheim
Urgel (Katalonien)

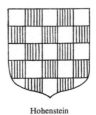

Hohenstein
Jauer
Kroatien
Sponheim, hintere Grafschaft

Kroatien,
Sozialistische Volksrepublik

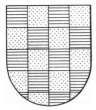

Sponheim, vordere Grafschaft

Kinsale (Irland)

Pistoja

Askanien, Grafschaft
Aschersleben, Grafschaft

Genevois, Grafschaft

Geschacht in geteiltem Schild

Echiqueté dans écu coupé

Checky on shield per fess

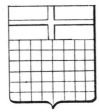

Belgiojoso (Prov. Pavia)

Mirandola und Concordia

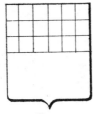

Hamm

Hohenstein, Grafschaft

Geschacht in gespaltenem Schild

Echiqueté dans écu parti

Checky on shield per pale

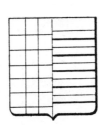

Hohenstein, Grafschaft

Limoges

Jauer (Schlesien)

Hohenstein, Grafschaft

Brieg, Herzogtum
Schlesische evangelische
Stände

Urgel (Katalonien) unter
aragonesischer Hoheit

Urgel (Katalonien) unter
aragonesischer Hoheit

Brosse

Geschacht mit Freiviertel

Echiqueté à franc-quartier

Checky with canton

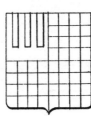

Châteaumeillant (Cher)

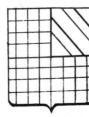

St.-Paul, Grafschaft

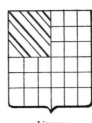

Limoges
St.-Paul, Grafschaft

Bretagne · Brosse
Limoges

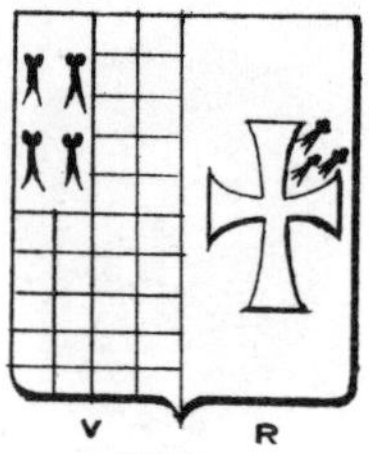

Bretagne

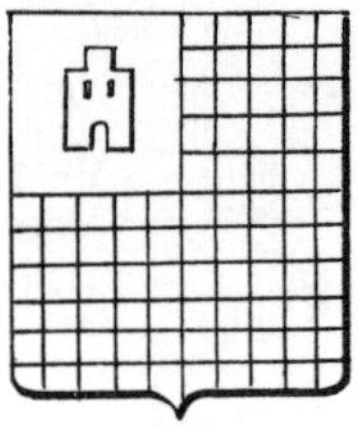
Limoges

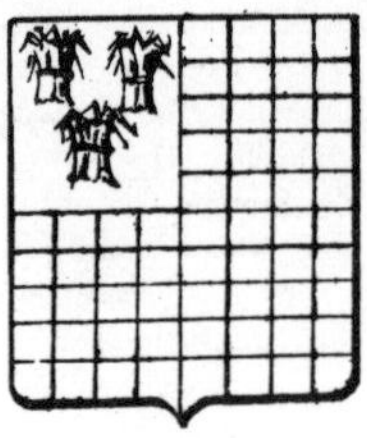
Brosse

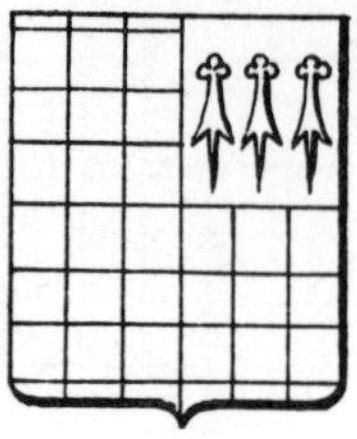
Limoges

Geschacht in vier oder mehrfeldigem Schild

Echiqueté dans écusson à quatre ou plusieurs quartiers

Checky on shield quarterly of four or more

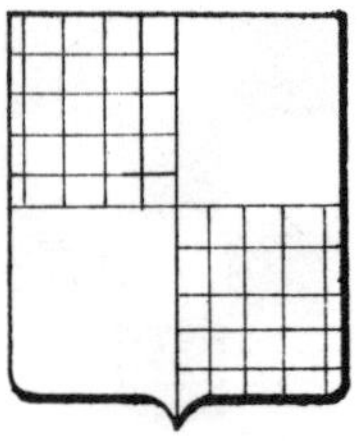
Baden-Baden, Markgrafschaft, 1414

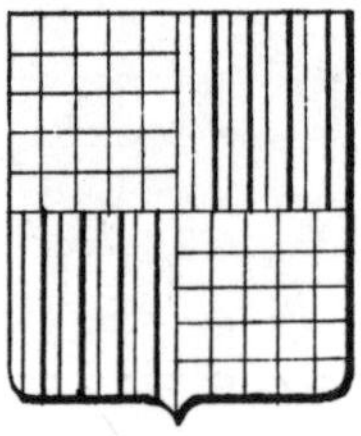
Barcelona, Stadt

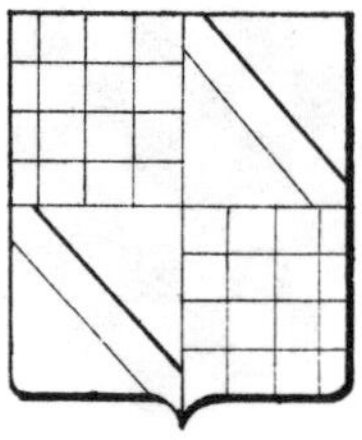
Baden-Baden, Markgrafschaft, 1414

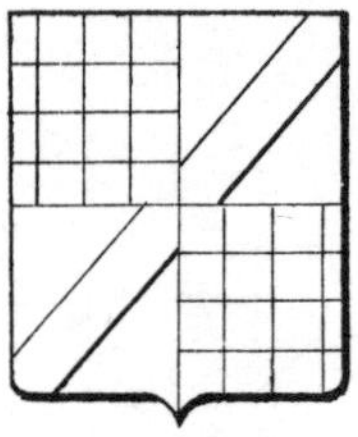
Baden-Baden, Markgrafschaft, 1414

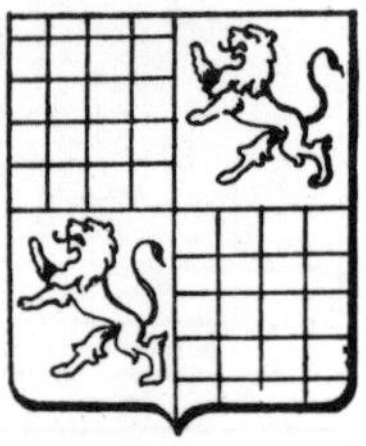
Herren von Schoonvorst (Brabant)

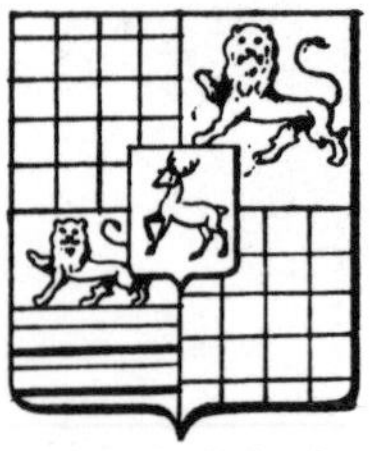
Hohenstein, Grafschaft

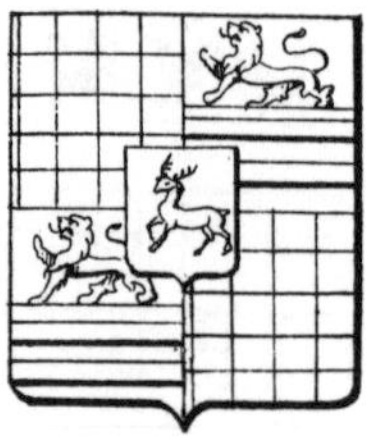
Hohenstein, Grafschaft

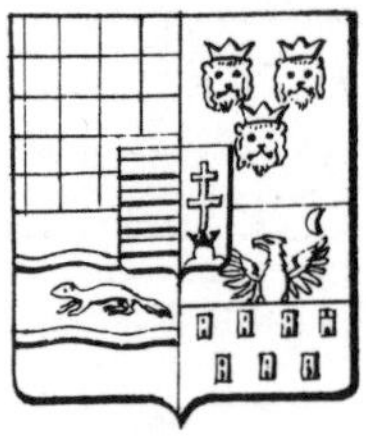
Ungarn

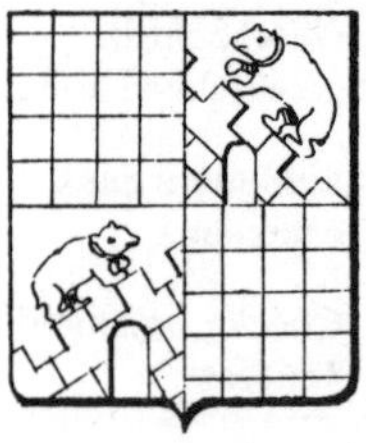
Anhalt

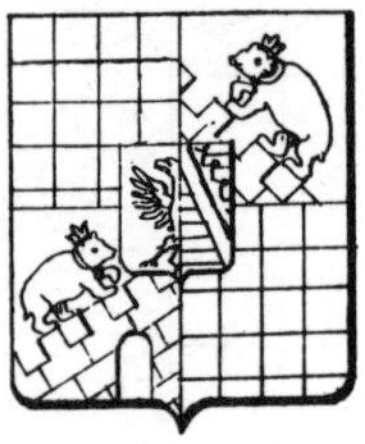
Anhalt, circa 1529

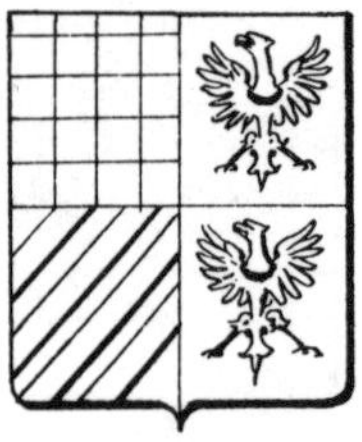
Münsterberg und Oels

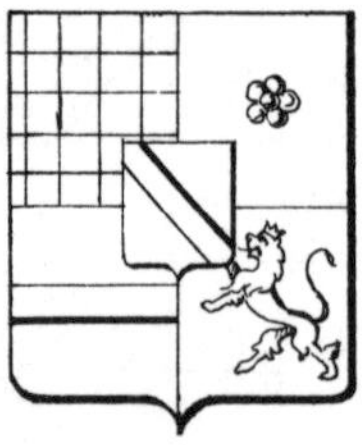
Baden, Markgrafschaft, 1527

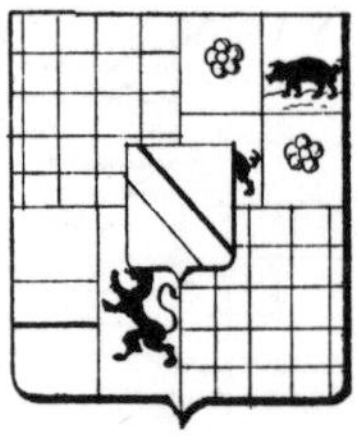
Baden-Baden, Markgrafschaft, 1527

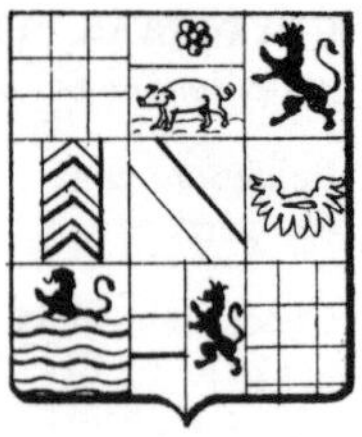
Baden-Baden, Markgrafschaft, 1622

Pfahlweise gerautet

Losangé

Lozengy

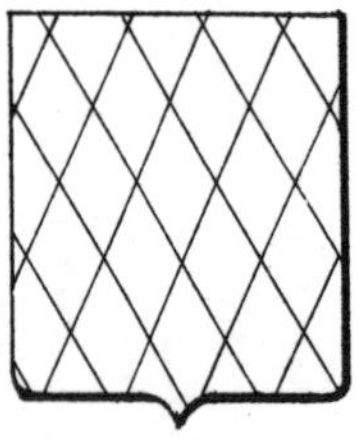
Almelo (Overijssel)
Monaco, Fürstentum
Stein, Herrschaft

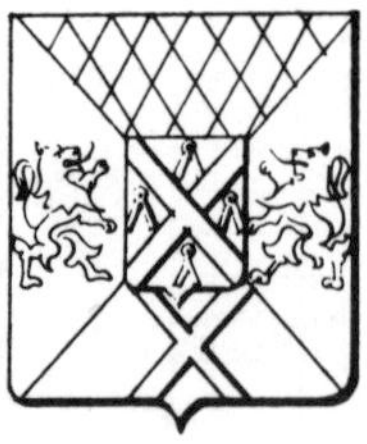
Batenburg

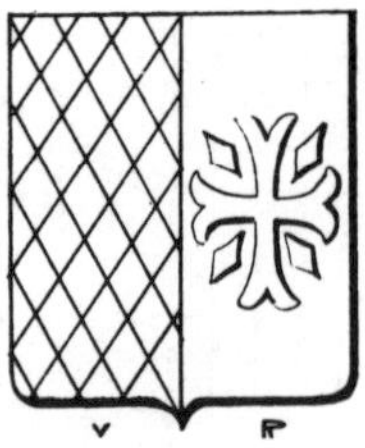

Monaco, Fürstentum

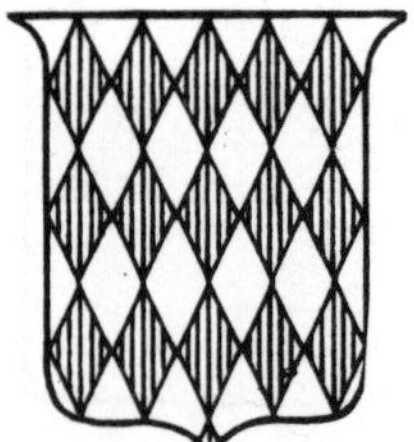
Monaco, Fürstentum

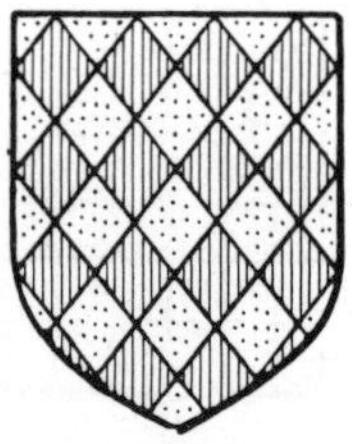
Angoumois, französische Provinz

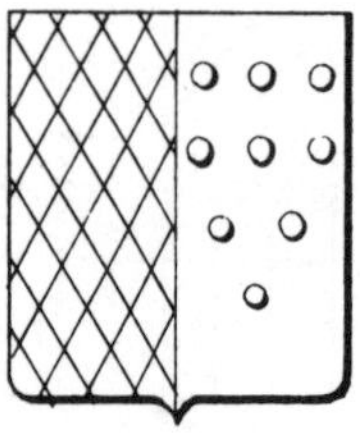
Stein, Herrschaft (niederl. Provinz Limburg)

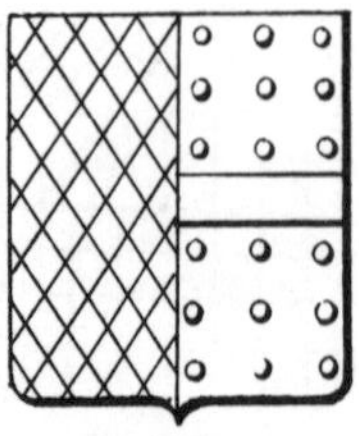
Stein, Herrschaft (niederl. Provinz Limburg)

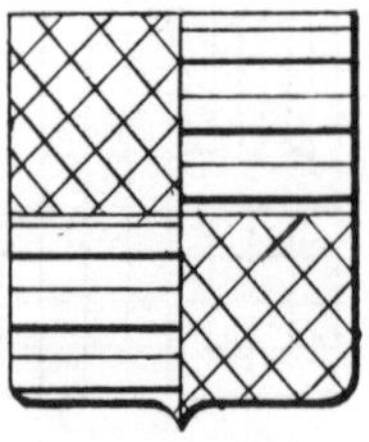
Mansfeld, Grafschaft

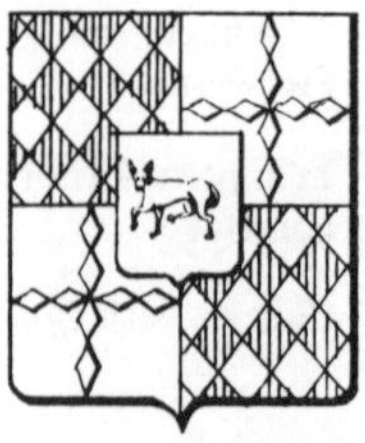
Desana, Grafschaft (bei Vercelli)

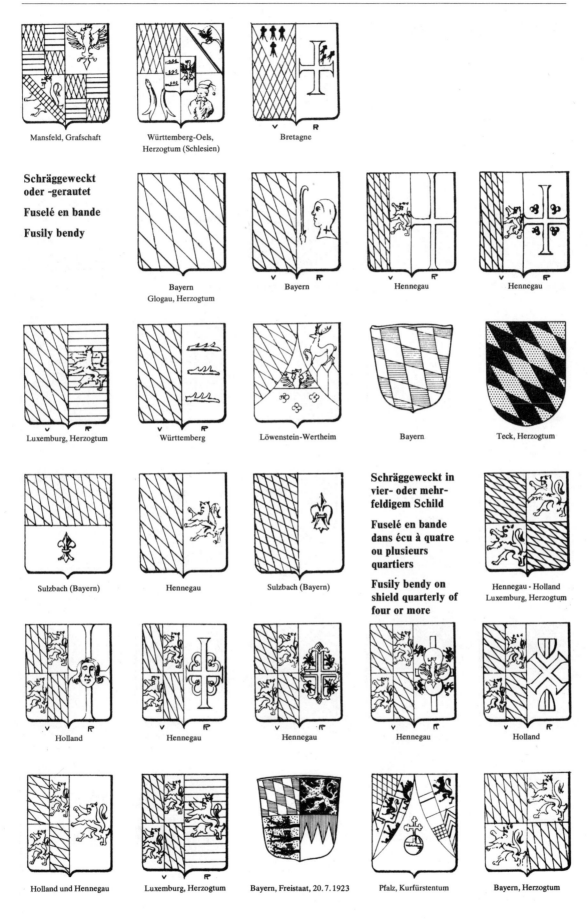

Mansfeld, Grafschaft

Württemberg-Oels,
Herzogtum (Schlesien)

Bretagne

**Schräggeweckt
oder -gerautet**

Fuselé en bande

Fusily bendy

Bayern
Glogau, Herzogtum

Bayern

Hennegau

Hennegau

Luxemburg, Herzogtum

Württemberg

Löwenstein-Wertheim

Bayern

Teck, Herzogtum

Sulzbach (Bayern)

Hennegau

Sulzbach (Bayern)

**Schräggeweckt in
vier- oder mehr-
feldigem Schild**

**Fuselé en bande
dans écu à quatre
ou plusieurs
quartiers**

**Fusily bendy on
shield quarterly of
four or more**

Hennegau - Holland
Luxemburg, Herzogtum

Holland

Hennegau

Hennegau

Hennegau

Holland

Holland und Hennegau

Luxemburg, Herzogtum

Bayern, Freistaat, 20. 7. 1923

Pfalz, Kurfürstentum

Bayern, Herzogtum

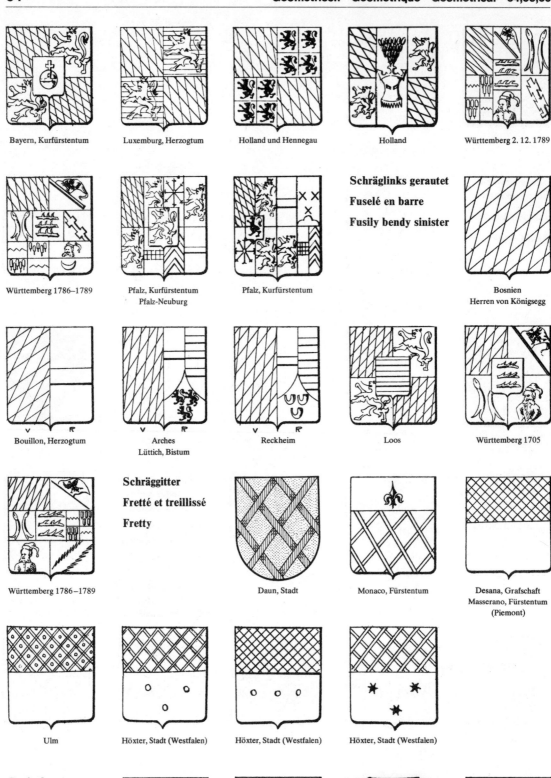

Bayern, Kurfürstentum

Luxemburg, Herzogtum

Holland und Hennegau

Holland

Württemberg 2. 12. 1789

Württemberg 1786–1789

Pfalz, Kurfürstentum
Pfalz-Neuburg

Pfalz, Kurfürstentum

Schräglinks gerautet
Fuselé en barre
Fusily bendy sinister

Bosnien
Herren von Königsegg

Bouillon, Herzogtum

Arches
Lüttich, Bistum

Reckheim

Loos

Württemberg 1705

Württemberg 1786–1789

Schräggitter
Fretté et treillissé
Fretty

Daun, Stadt

Monaco, Fürstentum

Desana, Grafschaft
Masserano, Fürstentum
(Piemont)

Ulm

Höxter, Stadt (Westfalen)

Höxter, Stadt (Westfalen)

Höxter, Stadt (Westfalen)

Dreiecke
Triangle
Triangle

Frankenthal, Stadt
(Rheinpfalz), 1570

Frankenthal, Stadt
(Rheinpfalz)

Nauru

Loos

Lille, Stadt

Béthune (Pas-de-Calais)
Lille, Stadt

Béthune (Pas-de-Calais)

Schlesien

Hermannstadt
(Siebenbürgen)

Rechtecke

Rectangles

Rectangles

Piacenza, Stadt

Grafen von Sinzendorf

Athen, Herzogtum

Jametz, Stadt (Meuse)

Northwest Territories
(Kanada)

**Rauten oder
Wecken**

Losanges

Lozenges

Gerona

Valencia (Spanien)

Hennegau

Hennegau

Sachsen, Herzogtum
(Dynastie Ballenstedt)

Béthune (Pas-de-Calais)

Salm-Niedersalm

Att(e)l, Benediktinerkloster
bei Wasserburg

Braunau, Stadt
(Oberösterreich)

Ebersberg,
Benediktinerkloster
(Oberbayern)

Monaco, Fürstentum

Reckheim

Châteauroux (Indre,
Geschlecht de Chauvigny)

Mansfeld, Grafschaft

Brandenburg, Markgrafschaft

Virneburg, Grafschaft

Pentagramm

Pentalpha

Pentacle

Marokko, Königreich

Marokko, Königreich, 1957

Eine Scheibe

Un Disque

One Roundle

Lenzburg (Schweiz)

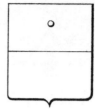

Saluzzo

Anhalt

Drei Scheiben

Trois Disques

Three Roundles

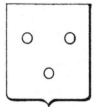

Alsleben an der Saale.
Boulogne · Brehna
Gronsfeld · Valentinois

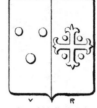

Gronsfeld, Grafschaft
(niederl. Provinz Limburg)

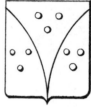

Brehna

Gronsfeld, Grafschaft
(niederl. Provinz Limburg)

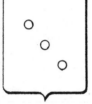

Hildesheim, Bistum

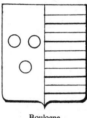

Boulogne

Gronsfeld, Grafschaft
(niederl. Provinz Limburg)

Gronsfeld, Grafschaft
(niederl. Provinz Limburg)

Gronsfeld, Grafschaft
(niederl. Provinz Limburg)

Fünf Scheiben

Cinq Disques

Five Roundles

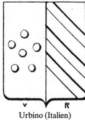

Urbino (Italien)

Tripolis (Libyen)

**Sechs/sieben
Scheiben**

Six/sept Disques

Six/seven Roundles

Castiglione del Lago
Pesaro · Toskana
Urbino

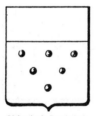

Valentinois, Landschaft
(Südfrankreich)

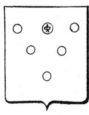

Pesaro · Toskana
Urbino

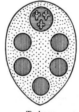

Toskana

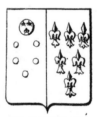

Etrurien, Königreich,
1800–1803

England, Königreich

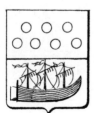

Lorient, Stadt (Morbihan)

**Neun und mehr
Scheiben**

**Neuf disques ou
davantage**

**Nine roundles or
more**

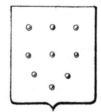

Herren von Schoonvorst
und zu Zichem (Brabant)

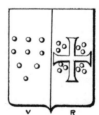

Herren von Schoonvorst
(Brabant)

Stein, Herrschaft
(niederl. Provinz Limburg)

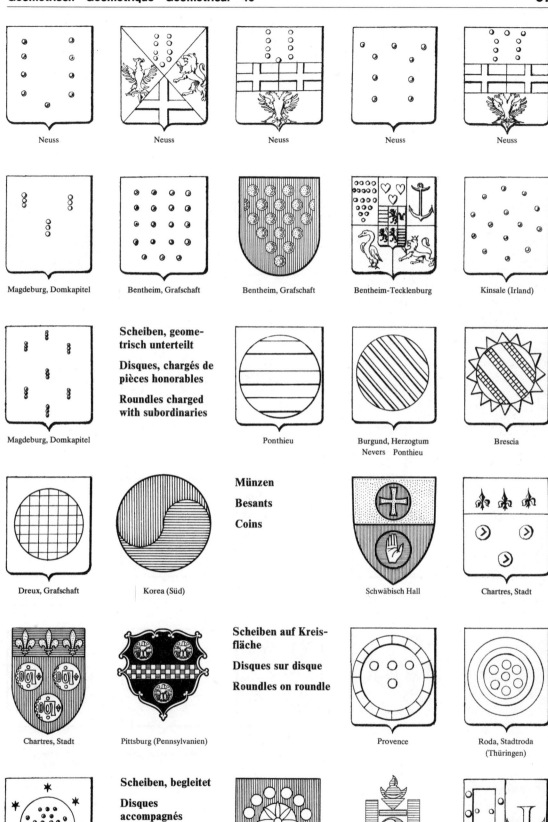

Neuss

Neuss

Neuss

Neuss

Neuss

Magdeburg, Domkapitel

Bentheim, Grafschaft

Bentheim, Grafschaft

Bentheim-Tecklenburg

Kinsale (Irland)

Magdeburg, Domkapitel

Scheiben, geometrisch unterteilt

Disques, chargés de pièces honorables

Roundles charged with subordinaries

Ponthieu

Burgund, Herzogtum
Nevers   Ponthieu

Brescia

Dreux, Grafschaft

Korea (Süd)

Münzen

Besants

Coins

Schwäbisch Hall

Chartres, Stadt

Chartres, Stadt

Pittsburg (Pennsylvanien)

Scheiben auf Kreisfläche

Disques sur disque

Roundles on roundle

Provence

Roda, Stadtroda
(Thüringen)

Portugiesisch Indien (Goa)

Scheiben, begleitet

Disques accompagnés

Roundles accompagnied

Sikkim

Mongolische Volksrepublik
26. 11. 1924

Portugiesisch Indien (Goa)

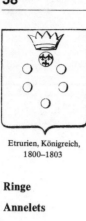

Etrurien, Königreich,
1800–1803

Zofingen (Schweiz)

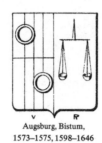

Zofingen (Schweiz)

Zofingen (Schweiz)

Ringe

Annelets

Annulets

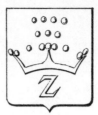

Augsburg, Bistum,
1573–1575, 1598–1646

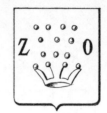

Kastilien

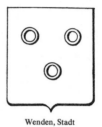

Wenden, Stadt

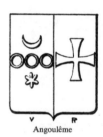

Mâcon (Saône-et-Loire)

Chalon-sur-Saône, Stadt

Grafen von Schlick

Grafen von Schlick

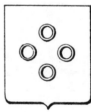

La Marche

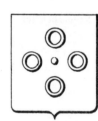

Angoulême

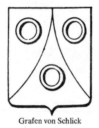

Perleberg
(Mark Brandenburg)

Cremona (Familie Fonduli)

Korsika 1736

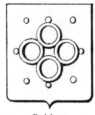

Narbonne, Vicomté

Maguelone,
Bistum (Languedoc)

Northumberland

Kent

Angoulême

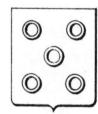

Perleberg
(Mark Brandenburg)

England, Königreich
Pérogord,
Landschaft (Guyenne)

Navarra

Kreuzchen, gerad-armig

Croisette

Crosslet couped

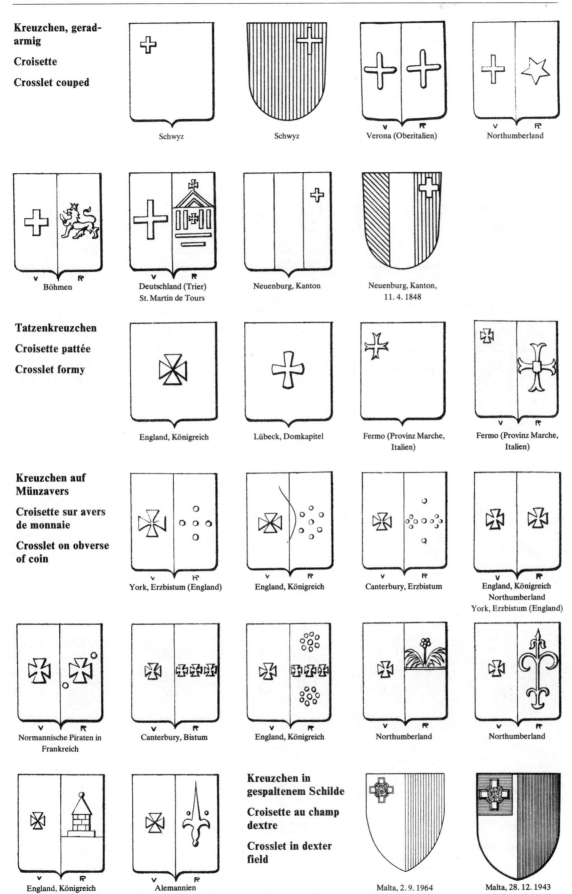

Schwyz

Schwyz

Verona (Oberitalien)

Northumberland

Böhmen

Deutschland (Trier)
St. Martin de Tours

Neuenburg, Kanton

Neuenburg, Kanton,
11. 4. 1848

Tatzenkreuzchen

Croisette pattée

Crosslet formy

England, Königreich

Lübeck, Domkapitel

Fermo (Provinz Marche,
Italien)

Fermo (Provinz Marche,
Italien)

Kreuzchen auf Münzavers

Croisette sur avers de monnaie

Crosslet on obverse of coin

York, Erzbistum (England)

England, Königreich

Canterbury, Erzbistum

England, Königreich
Northumberland
York, Erzbistum (England)

Normannische Piraten in
Frankreich

Canterbury, Bistum

England, Königreich

Northumberland

Northumberland

England, Königreich

Alemannien

Kreuzchen in gespaltenem Schilde

Croisette au champ dextre

Crosslet in dexter field

Malta, 2. 9. 1964

Malta, 28. 12. 1943

Kreuzchen in geteiltem Schilde bzw. begleitet

Croisette dans écu coupé ou accompagnée

Crosslet in shield per fesse resp. "and in base"

Elbing, Stadt (Westpreußen)

Schwäbisch Hall

Elbing, Stadt (Westpreußen)

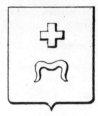

Venedig

Zwei Kreuzchen

Deux croisettes

Two crosslets

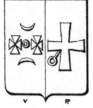

Angoulême, Stadt

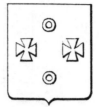

Mantes, Stadt (Yvelines)

Aquitanien

Danzig, 25.5.1457

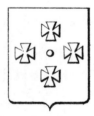

Danzig

Drei Kreuzchen

Trois croisettes

Three crosslets

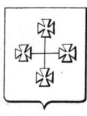

Tournon (Ardèche)

Xaintes (Charente-Inférieure)
Herrschaft

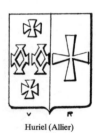

Aquitanien

Angoulême, Stadt

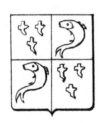

Desana, Grafschaft
(bei Vercelli)

Vier Kreuzchen

Quatre croisettes

Four crosslets

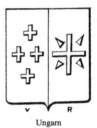

Ungarn

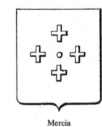

Mercia

Aquitanien

Dänemark

Aquitanien
Limoges

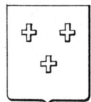
Turenne (Corrèze)

Huriel (Allier)
Limoges

Fünf und mehr Kreuzchen

Cinq croisettes ou davantage

Five crosslets or more

England, Königreich

Brandenburg, Markgrafschaft

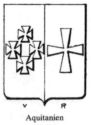

Brandenburg, Markgrafschaft

Lille (Belagerungsmünze)

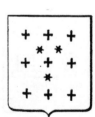

Halbe (abgeledigte) Kreuze

Demi-croix alésées

Half-crosses couped

Schweden

Schlesien

Oppeln, Stadt (Oberschlesien)

Schlesien

Schwebendes Kreuz

Croix alésée

Cross couped

Griechenland, Königreich
Schweiz

Zürich

Alemannien

Saluzzo

Schweiz

Griechenland, Königreich

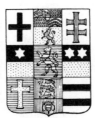

Hessen-Kassel 1815

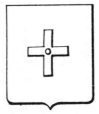

Navarra (Nord)

Sizilien

Tatzenkreuz

Croix pattée

Cross formy

Acqui · Albi (Tarn)
Alessandria · Aquitanien

Asti · Bourges
Bretagne
Burgund, Herzogtum
Cambrai, Stadt
Châlons-sur-Marne, Bistum
Clermont, Bistum
Deutschland · Frankreich
Hennegau · Kastilien
Lyon, Grafschaft
Magdeburg, Erzbistum
Metz, Bistum
Monferrat · Navarra

Novara, Stadt · Penthièvre
Poitou · Rimini
Rodez (Aveyron)
Salzburg, Erzbistum
Toul, Bistum
Treviso (Venetien)
Vendôme (Loir-et-Cher)
Vercelli (Oberitalien)
Vienne (Südfrankreich)
Viterbo (Italien)
Viviers (Ardèche)
Walcourt (Belgien)

Rzeszów

Asti · Auxonne
Oberlothringen
Sachsen · Tortona

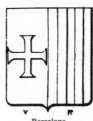

Solsona (Katalonien)

Barcelona

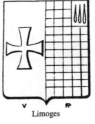

Limoges

Kreuzchen auf Revers

Revers à croisettes

Crosslets on reverse

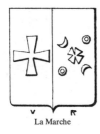

La Marche

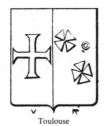

Toulouse

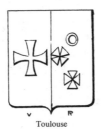

Toulouse

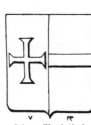

Xaintes (Charente-Inférieure)

Turenne (Corrèze)

Schwebendes Kreuz auf Revers

Revers à croix alésée

Couped cross on reverse

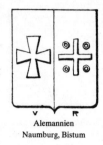
Alemannien
Naumburg, Bistum

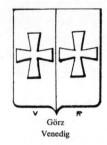
Görz
Venedig

St. Nazaire

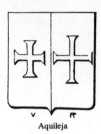
Aquileja

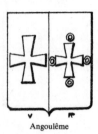
Angoulême

England, Königreich

Bretagne

Mâcon (Saône-et-Loire)

Normandie

Variiertes Kreuz auf Revers

Croix déformée et flanchis sur le revers

Varied crosses on reverse

León und Kastilien

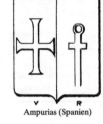
Ampurias (Spanien)

Schweden

Geometrische Zeichen auf Revers

Signes géometriques sur le revers

Geometrical signs on reverse

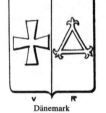
Narbonne, Erzbistum

Dänemark

Châteauroux (Indre,

Mond und/oder Sterne auf Revers

Revers à croissant(s) et/ou étoile(s)

Crescent(s) and/or mullet(s) on reverse

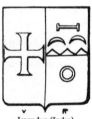
Issoudun (Indre)

Dänemark

Tripolis, Grafschaft (Libanon)

Béziers (Languedoc)

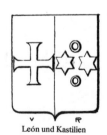
León und Kastilien

Lebewesen, hier Löwe, auf Revers

Animaux (lions) sur revers

Beasts (lions) on reverse

Brabant · Cambrai, Bistum
Hoorn, Grafschaft · Rethel

Bretagne

Bretagne

Hennegau

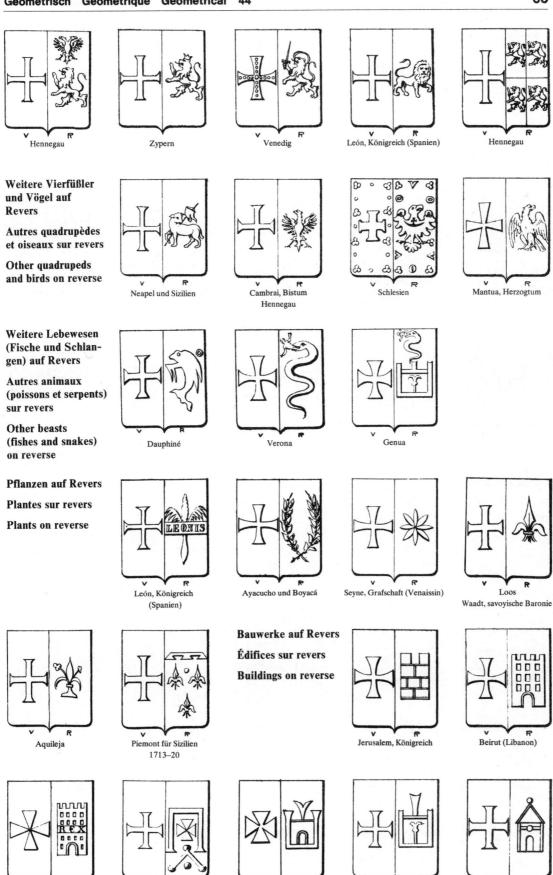

Hennegau   Zypern   Venedig   León, Königreich (Spanien)   Hennegau

Weitere Vierfüßler und Vögel auf Revers

Autres quadrupèdes et oiseaux sur revers

Other quadrupeds and birds on reverse

Neapel und Sizilien   Cambrai, Bistum Hennegau   Schlesien   Mantua, Herzogtum

Weitere Lebewesen (Fische und Schlangen) auf Revers

Autres animaux (poissons et serpents) sur revers

Other beasts (fishes and snakes) on reverse

Dauphiné   Verona   Genua

Pflanzen auf Revers

Plantes sur revers

Plants on reverse

León, Königreich (Spanien)   Ayacucho und Boyacá   Seyne, Grafschaft (Venaissin)   Loos   Waadt, savoyische Baronie

Aquileja   Piemont für Sizilien 1713–20

Bauwerke auf Revers

Édifices sur revers

Buildings on reverse

Jerusalem, Königreich   Beirut (Libanon)

Zypern   Vendôme (Loir-et-Cher)   Zypern   Genua   Toron, Herrschaft (Königreich Jerusalem)

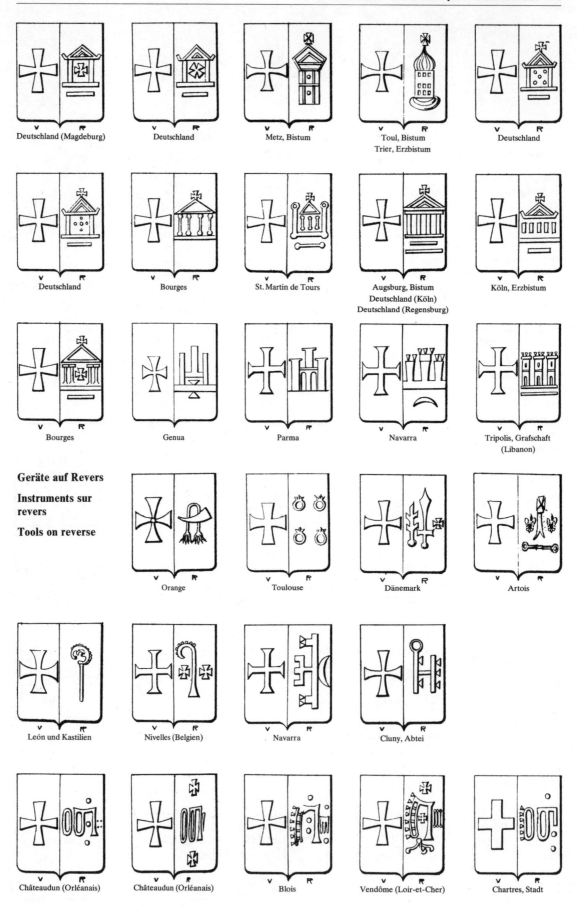

Deutschland (Magdeburg)

Deutschland

Metz, Bistum

Toul, Bistum
Trier, Erzbistum

Deutschland

Deutschland

Bourges

St. Martin de Tours

Augsburg, Bistum
Deutschland (Köln)
Deutschland (Regensburg)

Köln, Erzbistum

Bourges

Genua

Parma

Navarra

Tripolis, Grafschaft
(Libanon)

Geräte auf Revers

Instruments sur revers

Tools on reverse

Orange

Toulouse

Dänemark

Artois

León und Kastilien

Nivelles (Belgien)

Navarra

Cluny, Abtei

Châteaudun (Orléanais)

Châteaudun (Orléanais)

Blois

Vendôme (Loir-et-Cher)

Chartres, Stadt

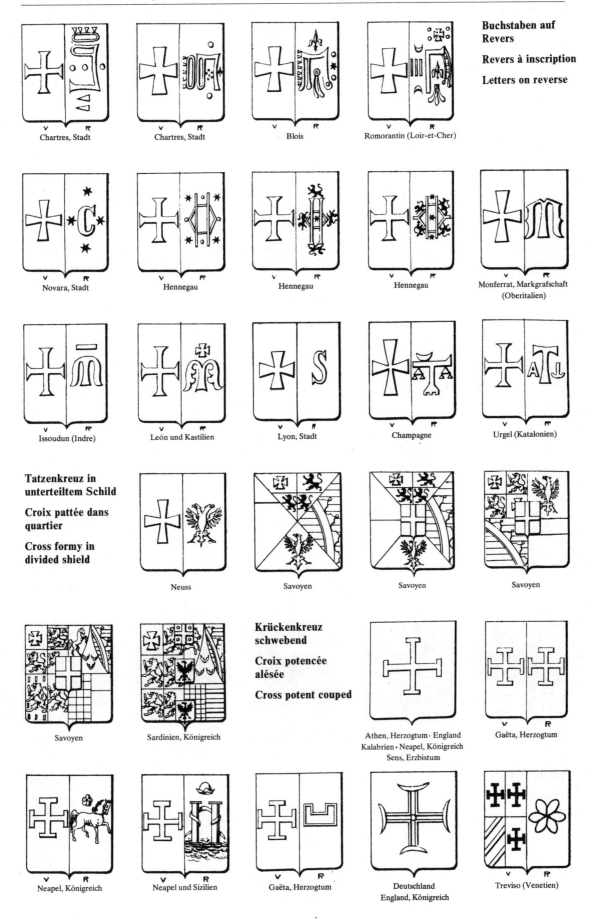

Buchstaben auf Revers

Revers à inscription

Letters on reverse

Chartres, Stadt

Chartres, Stadt

Blois

Romorantin (Loir-et-Cher)

Novara, Stadt

Hennegau

Hennegau

Hennegau

Monferrat, Markgrafschaft (Oberitalien)

Issoudun (Indre)

León und Kastilien

Lyon, Stadt

Champagne

Urgel (Katalonien)

Tatzenkreuz in unterteiltem Schild

Croix pattée dans quartier

Cross formy in divided shield

Neuss

Savoyen

Savoyen

Savoyen

Savoyen

Sardinien, Königreich

Krückenkreuz schwebend

Croix potencée alésée

Cross potent couped

Athen, Herzogtum · England
Kalabrien · Neapel, Königreich
Sens, Erzbistum

Gaëta, Herzogtum

Neapel, Königreich

Neapel und Sizilien

Gaëta, Herzogtum

Deutschland
England, Königreich

Treviso (Venetien)

Krückenkreuz, Varianten

Croix potencée variée

Cross potent, varieties

England, Königreich

Venedig

Longobarden

Valence (Drôme)

Ankerkreuz

Croix ancrée

Cross moline

Autun
Auxonne, Stadt (Côte d'Or)

Bentinck
Brescia
Gubbio (Prov. Reggio
nell'Emilia)
Macerata (Italien)
Pesaro
Pyrmont
Saint Vaast
(Seine-Inférieure)
Sizilien
Ungarn
Utrecht, Bistum

Pyrmont

Cambrai, Bistum
Holland

Northumberland

St. Sévère, Herrschaft
(Berry)

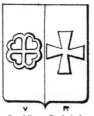
Penthièvre, Grafschaft
(Bretagne)
Vierzon (Cher)

Savoyen

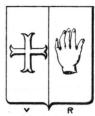
Schwäbisch Hall

Cambrai, Bistum

Cambrai, Bistum

Zütphen (Gelderland)

Nürnberg, Stadt

Paderborn, Stadt

Waldeck und Pyrmont

Waldeck und Pyrmont

Waldeck und Pyrmont

Waldeck und Pyrmont

Waldeck und Pyrmont

Johanniterkreuz

Croix de Malte

Maltese cross

Johanniter-Orden

Monferrat, Markgrafschaft
(Oberitalien)

Monferrat, Markgrafschaft
(Oberitalien)

Insel Malta

Verden, Bistum

León und Kastilien

Verden, Domkapitel

Lüneburg, St. Michaelis

Göttweih, Kloster
(Niederösterreich)

**Mit ein bis drei
Kügelchen besetztes
Kreuz**

Croix pommetées

Cross pommy

Parma

Verdun, Bistum

Bretagne

Augsburg, Bistum

Deutschland (Regensburg)

Dänemark

Brandenburg,
Markgrafschaft

Herstal (Belgien)
Sizilien und Calabrien

Lüttich, Bistum
Niederlothringen

Schlüsselkreuz

Croix cléchée vidée

Cross of Toulouse

Metz, Bistum

Pisa

Pisa

Venedig

Frinco
(Provinz Alessandria)

Frinco
(Provinz Alessandria)

Asti
Saluzzo

Languedoc

La Bisbál (Katalonien)
Toulouse, Grafschaft

Toulouse, Grafschaft

Languedoc

Dänemark

**Rautenförmig ausge-
brochenes Kreuz**

**Croix vidée en
forme de losange**

**Cross voided
lozengewise**

Angoulême

Kleeblatt- und Lilienkreuz

Croix tréflée et fleurdelisée

Cross botonny and flory

Asti
Brescia

Desana, Grafschaft
(bei Vercelli)
Dülmen, Stadt (Westfalen),
Ende 16. Jahrhundert
Masserano, Fürstentum
(Piemont)
Passerano
(Provinz Alessandria)
San Benigno di Fruttuario
(Provinz Turin)
Schivelbein (Pommern)
Stendal (Altmark)
Ungarn

Bozzolo
Flandern

Masserano
Novara
Radicati
San Benigno di Fruttuario
Ungarn
Utrecht, Bistum
Verona

Mailand

Kessenich

Masserano und Crevacuore

Novara, Stadt

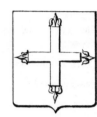

Bretagne

Brabant
Neapel, Königreich

Saluzzo

Orange

San Benigno di Fruttuario
Masserano, Piemont

Hennegau

Auxerre (Yonne)

Geldern

León, Königreich (Spanien)

Apulien

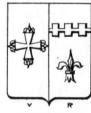

Neapel, Königreich

Deutschland (Straßburg)

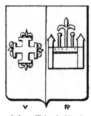

Arleux (Dép. du Nord, Frankreich)

León und Kastilien

Chieti, Stadt, 1494–1495

Toul, Bistum

Savoyen

Savoyen

Tonnerre (Yonne)

Fußspitzkreuz

Croix au pied fiché

Cross fitchy

Oldenburg
Verden, Bistum

Mâcon (Saône-et-Loire)

Mâcon (Saône-et-Loire)

Wiederkreuz

Croix recroisettée

Cross crosslet

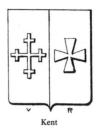

Mercia

Kent

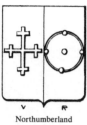

Northumberland

Clermont, Bistum

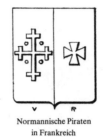

Mercia

Normannische Piraten
in Frankreich

Mercia

Mercia

Mercia

Byzanz

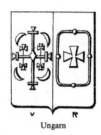

Byzanz

Ungarn

Hochkreuz

Croix latine

Long cross

Salerno

Werl, Stadt (Westfalen)

León und Kastilien

Bergerac (Périgord)

Bretagne

Bretagne

Bretagne

Viviers (Ardèche),Bistum

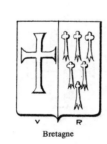

Cambrai, Bistum

Hennegau

Hennegau

**Kreuze,
Sonderformen**

**Croix,
formes extra-
ordinaires**

**Crosses, special
shapes**

Rimini

Châteauroux (Indre)

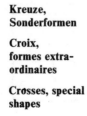

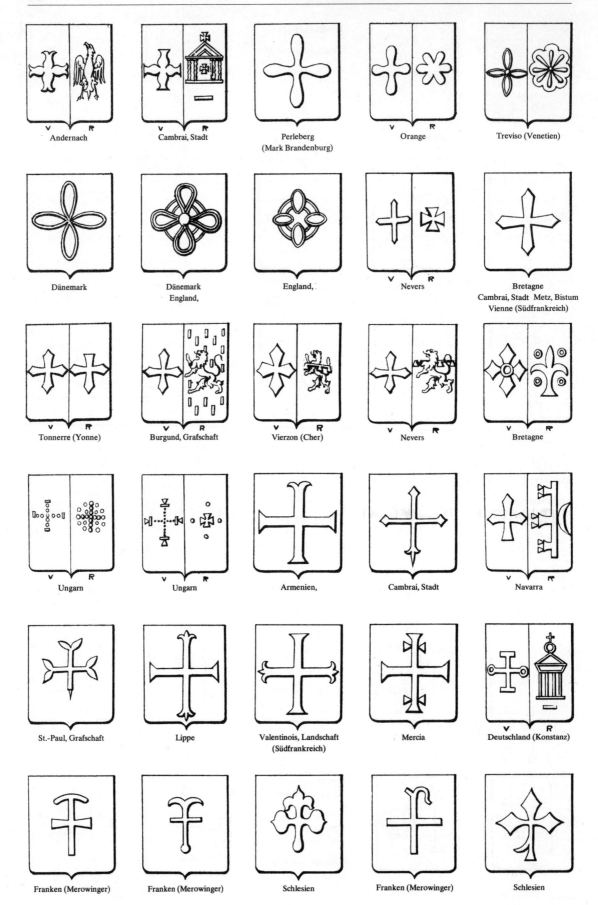

Andernach

Cambrai, Stadt

Perleberg
(Mark Brandenburg)

Orange

Treviso (Venetien)

Dänemark

Dänemark
England,

England,

Nevers

Bretagne
Cambrai, Stadt Metz, Bistum
Vienne (Südfrankreich)

Tonnerre (Yonne)

Burgund, Grafschaft

Vierzon (Cher)

Nevers

Bretagne

Ungarn

Ungarn

Armenien,

Cambrai, Stadt

Navarra

St.-Paul, Grafschaft

Lippe

Valentinois, Landschaft
(Südfrankreich)

Mercia

Deutschland (Konstanz)

Franken (Merowinger)

Franken (Merowinger)

Schlesien

Franken (Merowinger)

Schlesien

**Kreuz und Schräg-
kreuz kombiniert**

**Croix et santoir
combinés**

**Cross and saltire
combined**

England,
Sizilien

Aquileja

Tirol

Tirol

Ivrea (Prov. Aosta)
Tirol

Aquileja · Cortemillia
Incisa · Ivrea
Tirol · Cortemillia

Crevacuore, Markgrafschaft
(Provinz Novara)

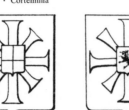

Tirol

Metz, Bistum

**Idem, mit Mittel-
schildchen belegt**

**Idem, chargés en
abîme d'un sur-le-
tout**

**Idem, surmounted
by an inescutcheon**

Nürnberg, Burggrafschaft

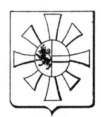

Böhmen

Salzburg, Erzbistum

Gotteshausbund

Gotteshausbund

Rottweil
Tirol

Zwei Kreuze

Deux croix

Two crosses

Elbing, Stadt (Westpreußen)

Danzig
24. 5. 1457

**Kreuz mit behäng-
ten Querarmen**

**Croix, les bras
latéraux festonnés**

**Cross, the lateral
arms festoovned**

Dol (Bretagne,
Ille-et-Vilaine)

Maine, Grafschaft
(Frankreich)

Gaëta, Herzogtum

Toul, Stadt

Anjou

Orléans

León und Kastilien

**Kreuze, diagonal
durchkreuzt**

**Croix traversées
diagonalement**

**Crosses diagonally
traversed**

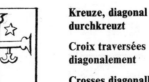

Deutschland (Otto III.,
reg. 983–1002, und Adelheid)

Clermont, Bistum

Ravenna

Champagne

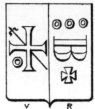

Chalon-sur-Saône, Stadt

St.-Paul, Grafschaft

León, Königreich (Spanien)

**Kreuz, mit Krumm-
stab gekreuzt**

**Croix brochant sur
crosse**

**Cross surmounting
crozier**

Osnabrück, Bistum

Münster, Bistum

Cahors, Bistum

**Kreuz, mit Stäben
gekreuzt**

**Croix brochant sur
flanchis**

**Cross surmounting
rods**

Armenien

Metz, Bistum

Norwegen

**Kreuz, bewinkelt
von Kreuzchen oder
Kreuzstäben**

**Croix cantonnée de
flanchis ou de
bâtons croisettés**

**Cross cantoned with
crosslets or crossed
rods**

Ungarn

Brandenburg, Markgrafschaft

**Kreuz, bewinkelt
von beknopften oder
ringendigen Stäben**

**Croix cantonnée de
bourdons (aussi à
annelets)**

**Cross cantoned with
bourdons (also with
annulets on top)**

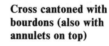
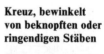

England, Königreich

Mende (Lozère)

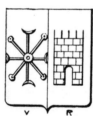

Kastilien

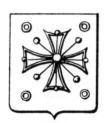

Tripolis, Grafschaft (Libanon)

Brabant
Straßburg, Bistum

Norwegen

**Kreuz, bewinkelt
von Kleeblattstäben**

**Croix cantonnée de
bâtons tréflés**

**Cross cantoned with
rods botonny**

England, Königreich

Mailand
Verona   Vertus

Verona (Oberitalien)

Deutschland (Friedrich II.,
reg. 1212–1250)

Clermont, Bistum

Arles, Erzbistum
Orange

Aquileja

**Kreuz, bewinkelt
von Lilienstäben**

**Croix cantonnée de
bâtons fleurdelisés**

**Cross cantoned with
rods flory**

Deutschland (Goslar)
Lüttich, Bistum

León, Königreich (Spanien)

Norwegen

England, Königreich

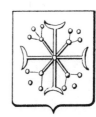

Namur (Belgien)

Norwegen

**Kreuz, bewinkelt
von Blättern**

**Croix cantonnée de
feuilles**

**Cross cantoned with
leaves**

Armenien

Namur (Belgien)

Aquileja

**Kreuz, bewinkelt
von verschieden-
artigen Stäben**

**Croix cantonné de
bâtons différents**

**Cross cantoned with
different rods**

Chalon-sur-Saône,
Grafschaft

St.-Paul, Grafschaft

Flandern

Goslar, Stadt

**Kreuz, Rechteck
überdeckend**

**Croix brochant sur
rectangle**

**Cross debruising
rectangle**

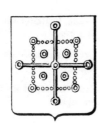

Norwegen

England

Dänemark
England

**Kreuz, Bögen
überdeckend**

**Croix brochant sur
arcs**

**Cross debruising
bows**

Alemannien
Breisach

England, Königreich

Lille, Stadt

Corvey, Abtei (Westfalen)

Kreuz, von ein bis drei Dreiecken bewinkelt

Croix cantonnée d' un à trois triangles

Cross cantoned with one to three triangles

Montluçon (Allier)

Augsburg, Bistum

Bayern (Salzburg)
Bayern (Tettnang)

Flandern

Deutschland (Augsburg)
Deutschland (Canosa, Apulien)
Deutschland (Civitavecchia)
Deutschland (Regensburg)
Deutschland (Salzburg)

Augsburg, Bistum

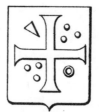

Augsburg, Bistum
Deutschland (Regensburg)
Deutschland (Salzburg)

Augsburg, Bistum
Bayern (Neuburg)
Deutschland (Cham)

Augsburg, Bistum

Augsburg, Bistum
Deutschland (Regensburg)

Deutschland (Regensburg)

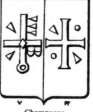

Armenien

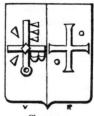

Champagne

Champagne

Kreuz, bewinkelt von vier Dreiecken

Croix cantonnée de quatre triangles

Cross between four triangles

Brioude (Auvergne) · England
Gascogne · Kent, Königreich
Mercia · Ostangeln (England) · Wessex

England, Königreich

England, Königreich

Deutschland (Freising)

Venedig

Metz, Bistum

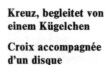

York, Erzbistum (England)

Kreuz, begleitet von Wecken

Croix cantonnée de losanges

Cross cantoned with lozenges

Augsburg, Bistum

Mainz (Heiligenstadt)

Venedig

Urgel (Katalonien)

Kreuz, begleitet von einem Kügelchen

Croix accompagnée d'un disque

Cross accompagnied by one roundle

Verdun, Bistum

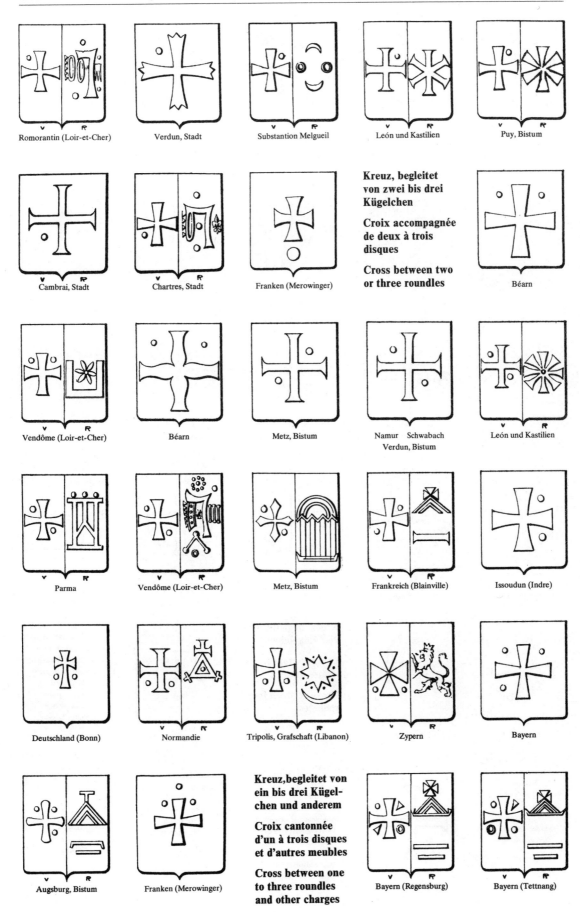

Romorantin (Loir-et-Cher)

Verdun, Stadt

Substantion Melgueil

León und Kastilien

Puy, Bistum

Cambrai, Stadt

Chartres, Stadt

Franken (Merowinger)

Kreuz, begleitet von zwei bis drei Kügelchen

Croix accompagnée de deux à trois disques

Cross between two or three roundles

Béarn

Vendôme (Loir-et-Cher)

Béarn

Metz, Bistum

Namur   Schwabach
Verdun, Bistum

León und Kastilien

Parma

Vendôme (Loir-et-Cher)

Metz, Bistum

Frankreich (Blainville)

Issoudun (Indre)

Deutschland (Bonn)

Normandie

Tripolis, Grafschaft (Libanon)

Zypern

Bayern

Augsburg, Bistum

Franken (Merowinger)

Kreuz, begleitet von ein bis drei Kügelchen und anderem

Croix cantonnée d'un à trois disques et d'autres meubles

Cross between one to three roundles and other charges

Bayern (Regensburg)

Bayern (Tettnang)

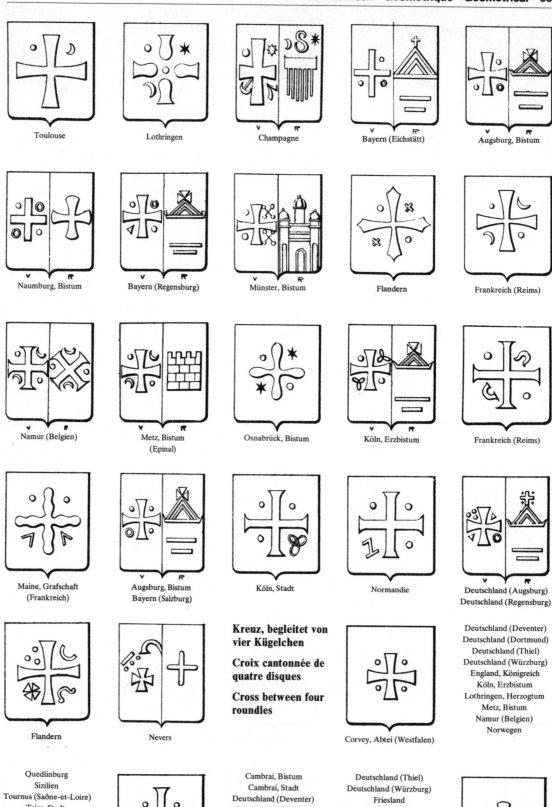

Toulouse

Lothringen

Champagne

Bayern (Eichstätt)

Augsburg, Bistum

Naumburg, Bistum

Bayern (Regensburg)

Münster, Bistum

Flandern

Frankreich (Reims)

Namur (Belgien)

Metz, Bistum
(Epinal)

Osnabrück, Bistum

Köln, Erzbistum

Frankreich (Reims)

Maine, Grafschaft
(Frankreich)

Augsburg, Bistum
Bayern (Salzburg)

Köln, Stadt

Normandie

Deutschland (Augsburg)
Deutschland (Regensburg)

**Kreuz, begleitet von
vier Kügelchen**

**Croix cantonnée de
quatre disques**

**Cross between four
roundles**

Deutschland (Deventer)
Deutschland (Dortmund)
Deutschland (Thiel)
Deutschland (Würzburg)
England, Königreich
Köln, Erzbistum
Lothringen, Herzogtum
Metz, Bistum
Namur (Belgien)
Norwegen

Flandern

Nevers

Corvey, Abtei (Westfalen)

Quedlinburg
Sizilien
Tournus (Saône-et-Loire)
Trier, Stadt
Utrecht, Bistum
Verdun, Bistum
Westfriesland

Cambrai, Bistum
Cambrai, Stadt
Deutschland (Deventer)
Deutschland (Dinant)
Deutschland (Dortmund)
Deutschland (Fritzlar)
Deutschland (Köln)
Deutschland (Masstricht)
Deutschland (Minden)
Deutschland (Speyer)

Deutschland (Thiel)
Deutschland (Würzburg)
Friesland
Lyon, Grafschaft
Metz, Bistum
Quedlinburg
Sachsen
Toul, Bistum
Utrecht, Bistum

Bergh-St.-Winnoc

Alemannien
Carcassonne

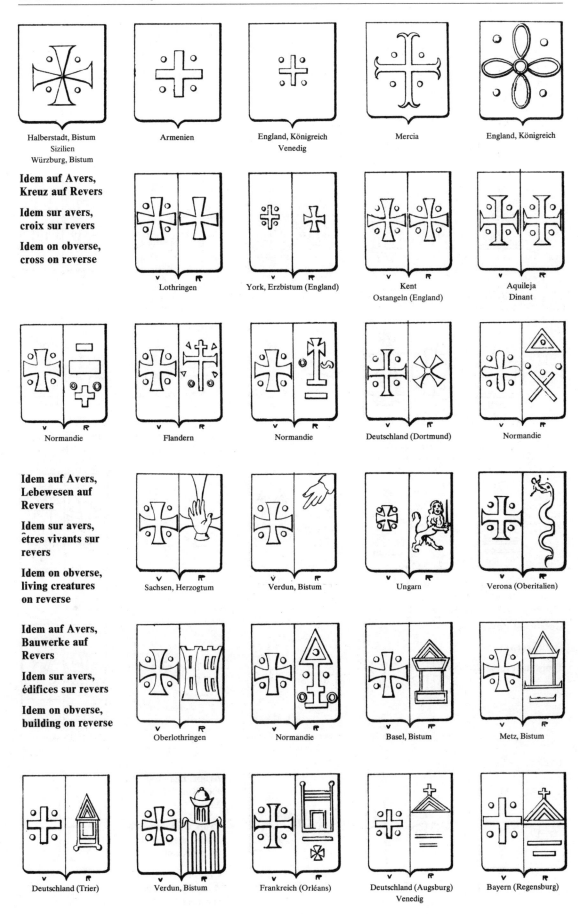

Halberstadt, Bistum Sizilien Würzburg, Bistum	Armenien	England, Königreich Venedig	Mercia	England, Königreich

**Idem auf Avers,
Kreuz auf Revers**

**Idem sur avers,
croix sur revers**

**Idem on obverse,
cross on reverse**

Lothringen	York, Erzbistum (England)	Kent Ostangeln (England)	Aquileja Dinant

Normandie	Flandern	Normandie	Deutschland (Dortmund)	Normandie

**Idem auf Avers,
Lebewesen auf
Revers**

**Idem sur avers,
êtres vivants sur
revers**

**Idem on obverse,
living creatures
on reverse**

Sachsen, Herzogtum	Verdun, Bistum	Ungarn	Verona (Oberitalien)

**Idem auf Avers,
Bauwerke auf
Revers**

**Idem sur avers,
édifices sur revers**

**Idem on obverse,
building on reverse**

Oberlothringen	Normandie	Basel, Bistum	Metz, Bistum

Deutschland (Trier)	Verdun, Bistum	Frankreich (Orléans)	Deutschland (Augsburg) Venedig	Bayern (Regensburg)

Bayern (Nabburg)
Metz, Bistum

Normandie

Alemannien
Deutschland (Basel)

Deutschland (Köln)

Alemannien

Basel, Bistum
Deutschland (Mainz)
Deutschland (Regensburg)

Bayern

Deutschland (Mainz)

Münster, Bistum

Lüttich, Bistum

Erfurt

Deutschland (Esslingen,
Mainz, Speyer)
Venedig

Deutschland (Mainz)

Deutschland (Mergentheim)

Deutschland (Worms)
Italien

Deutschland (Dürstede/
Konstanz/Mainz)
Frankreich (Blainville/Bordeaux)

Metz, Bistum

Normandie

Normandie

Normandie

Geräte auf Revers

Outils sur revers

Tools on reverse

Deutschland (Wertheim)

Dänemark, Königreich, und
Odense, Bistum

Akkon

Urgel (Katalonien)

Tournus (Saône-et-Loire)

Flandern

Savoyen

**Kreuz, begleitet von
vier Kügelchen und
Mond**

**Croix cantonnée de
quatre disques et
un croissant**

**Cross between four
roundles and one
crescent**

Deutschland (Worms)

Kreuz, begleitet von mehr als fünf Kügelchen

Croix accompagnée de plus de cinq disques

Cross between more then five roundles

Valentinois, Landschaft (Südfrankreich)

Mainz, Stadt

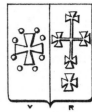
Venedig

Northumberland

Kastilien

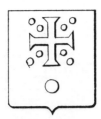
Toul, Stadt

Deutschland (Augsburg)

Agramunt (Katalonien)

Aquitanien · Arleux
Bar · Brabant
Calais
Cambrai, Bistum
Deutschland (Heinrich VII.)
Flandern · Florennes
Geldern
Heinsberg (Niederrhein)
Helmershausen (Thüringen)
Hennegau

Herstal (Belgien)
Holland
Hoorn, Grafschaft
Isenburg
Köln, Erzbistum
Kuinre, Grafschaft
(Overijssel)
Ligny · Lippe
Loos und Chiny
Lothringen · Lüttich

Luxemburg
Mainz · Moers
Namur · Poilvache
Porcien (Ardennes)
Portugal
Ravensberg
Rethel · Rummen
Sancerre (Cher)
Schöneck · Toul
Trier · Werden

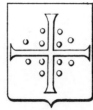

Deutschland (Regensburg)

Perleberg (Mark Brandenburg)

England · Flandern
Hennegau

Normannische Piraten in Frankreich

Normannische Piraten in Frankreich

Wendische Münze

Caracas (Venezuela)

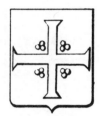
Verona (Oberitalien)

Flandern

Frinco (Provinz Alessandria)

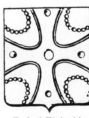
England, Königreich

Idem, und andere Figuren

Idem, et d'autres meubles

Idem, and other charges

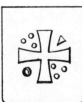
Deutschland (Augsburg)
Deutschland (Regensburg)
Deutschland (Salzburg)

Deutschland (Acino)
Deutschland (Canosa)
Deutschland (Civitavecchia)

Agramunt (Katalonien)

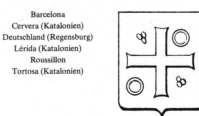
Barcelona
Cervera (Katalonien)
Deutschland (Regensburg)
Lérida (Katalonien)
Roussillon
Tortosa (Katalonien)

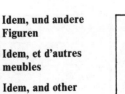
Barcelona
Roussillon

Urgel (Katalonien)

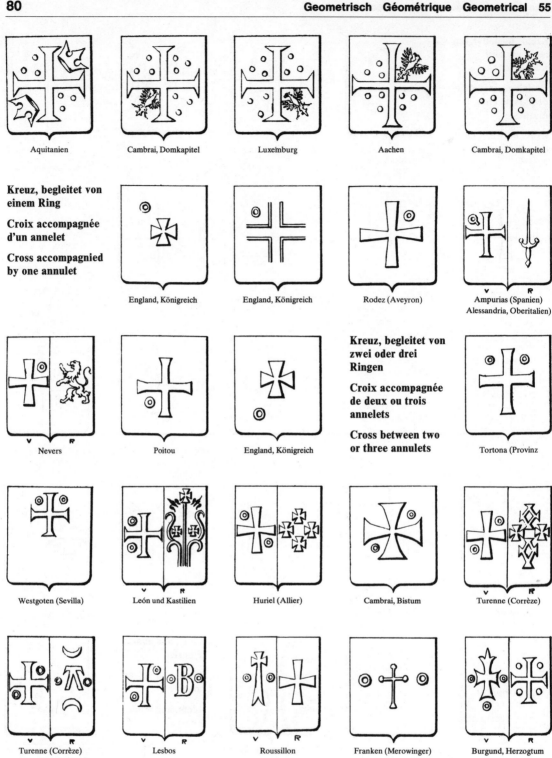

| | Aquitanien | Cambrai, Domkapitel | Luxemburg | Aachen | Cambrai, Domkapitel |

Kreuz, begleitet von einem Ring

Croix accompagnée d'un annelet

Cross accompagnied by one annulet

England, Königreich | England, Königreich | Rodez (Aveyron) | Ampurias (Spanien) Alessandria, Oberitalien)

Nevers | Poitou | England, Königreich

Kreuz, begleitet von zwei oder drei Ringen

Croix accompagnée de deux ou trois annelets

Cross between two or three annulets

Tortona (Provinz

Westgoten (Sevilla) | León und Kastilien | Huriel (Allier) | Cambrai, Bistum | Turenne (Corrèze)

Turenne (Corrèze) | Lesbos | Roussillon | Franken (Merowinger) | Burgund, Herzogtum

Kreuz, begleitet von vier Ringen

Croix accompagnée de quatre annelets

Cross between four annulets

Dogliani (Provinz Cuneo)

Kastilien
Lüttich, Bistum
Mercia
Navarra
Norwegen
Piemont
Ponthieu
Utrecht, Bistum
Venedig

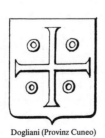

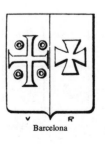

Barcelona

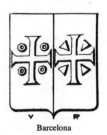

Barcelona

Naumburg, Bistum

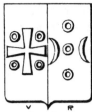

Angoulême

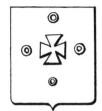

Halberstadt, Bistum

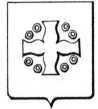

Mâcon (Saône-et-Loire), Stadt

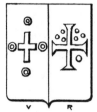

Tripolis, Grafschaft (Libanon)

Kreuz, begleitet von acht Ringen

Croix accompagnée de huit annelets

Cross between eight annulets

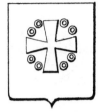

Châteaumeillant (Cher)

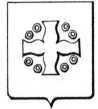

Kastilien

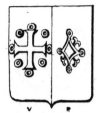

Béthune (Pas-de-Calais)

Kreuz, begleitet von einem Ring und anderen Figuren

Croix accompagnée d'un annelet et d'autres meubles

Cross between one annulet and other charges

Bayern (Neuburg)

Bayern (Nabburg)

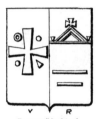

Bayern (Neuburg)
Bayern (Tettnang)
Bayern (Regensburg)

Deutschland (Augsburg)

Augsburg, Bistum
Deutschland (Augsburg/
Canosa, Apulien/Civitavecchia)

Roussillon

Augsburg, Bistum·Bayern
(Neuburg/Novum Cativinum/
Regensburg) Deutschland

Freising, Bistum

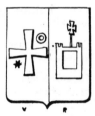

Riom (Puy-de-Dôme)

Cahors, Bistum

Kreuz, begleitet von zwei Ringen und anderen Figuren

Croix accompagnée de deux annelets et d'autres meubles

Cross between two annulets and other charges

Flandern

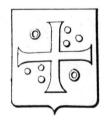

Deutschland (Augsburg)

Bamberg, Bistum

Flandern

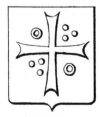

Barcelona
Oliana
Roussillon

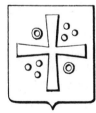

Oliana·Solsona
Tortosa·Vich (Katalonien)
Olot

Mâcon (Saône-et-Loire), Stadt

Barcelona

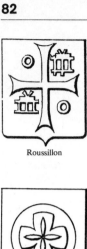

Kreuz, begleitet von vier Ringen und andern Figuren

Croix accompagnée de quatre annelets et d'autres meubles

Cross between four annulets and other charges

Roussillon

Köln, Erzbistum

Kreuz im Kreise

Croix sur disque

Cross on roundle

Georgien

Norwegen

Norwegen

Roda, Stadtroda (Thüringen)

Roda, Stadtroda (Thüringen)

Georgien

Ostangeln (England)

Schlesien

Norwegen

Brandenburg, Kurfürstentum

Kreuz, begleitet von Kreuzchen

Croix accompagnée de flanchis

Cross accompagnied by crosslets

Arles

Savoyen- Achaja, Fürstentum (14. Jahrh.)

Troyes

Corbie, Abtei (Somme)

Cambrai, Domkapitel

Cambrai, Bistum

Brandenburg, Markgrafschaft

England, Königreich Venedig

León und Kastilien

Venedig

Hennegau

Kreuz, begleitet von Kreuzchen und andern Figuren

Croix accompagnée de flanchis et d'autres meubles

Cross between crosslets and other charges

Normandie

Frankreich (Reims)

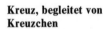

Flandern

Flandern

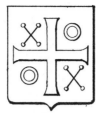

Hildesheim, Bistum

Normandie

Brandenburg, Kurfürstentum

Kreuz, begleitet von Sonne

Croix accompagnée de soleil

Cross between sun and annulet

Fauquemberg, Grafschaft (Artois)

Kreuz, begleitet von Mond(en)

Croix accompagnée de croissant(s)

Cross accompagnied by crescent(s)

Antiochien

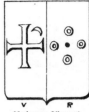

Narbonne, Vicomté

Bourbon

Issoudun (Indre)

Bourbon

Beaumont · Cambrai, Bistum England · Hennegau

Wessex

Ostangeln (England) Wessex

León und Kastilien

Dänemark

Kreuz, begleitet von Mond(en) und anderen Figuren

Croix accompagnée de croissant(s) et d'autres meubles

Cross between crescent(s) and other charges

Vienne (Südfrankreich)

Deutschland (Worms)

Werben an der Elbe (Altmark)

Carcassonne, Bistum

Normandie

Lausanne, Bistum Neuenburg, Grafschaft

Carcassonne, Grafschaft

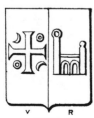

Zypern

Reims, Erzbistum

Zypern

**Kreuz, begleitet von
einem Stern**

**Croix accompagnée
d'une étoile**

**Cross accompagnied
by one mullet**

Verdun, Bistum

Penthièvre, Grafschaft
(Bretagne)

Savoyen-Achaja,
Fürstentum (14. Jahrh.)

Neapel, Königreich

Angoulême

Metz, Bistum

Châteauroux (Indre,
Geschlecht de Chauvigny)

**Kreuz, begleitet von
zwei Sternen**

**Croix accompagnée
de deux étoiles**

**Cross between two
mullets**

León und Kastilien
Kastilien

Kastilien

Pesaro

Cremona

Penthièvre,
Grafschaft (Bretagne)

Stargard in Pommern

Treviso (Venetien)

Verdun, Bistum

Tortona
(Provinz Alessandria, Oberitalien)

León und Kastilien

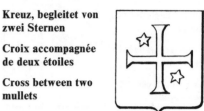

Navarra

**Kreuz, begleitet von
vier Sternen**

**Croix accompagnée
de quatre étoiles**

**Cross between four
mullets**

Armenien

Bremen, Erzbistum

Deutschland (Dortmund)
Genua
Gollnow (Pommern)
Köln, Erzbistum
Masserano (Piemont)
Schottland
Stargard in Pommern
Treviso (Venetien)
Venedig

Metz, Bistum

Treviso (Venetien)

Merseburg

Halberstadt, Bistum

Helmershausen
(Thüringen)

Schlesien

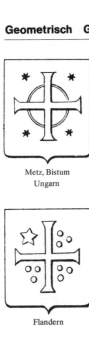

Metz, Bistum
Ungarn

Münster, Bistum

Tonnerre (Yonne)

**Kreuz, begleitet
von Stern(en) und
anderen Figuren**

**Croix accompagnée
d'étoile(s) et
d'autres meubles**

**Cross between
mullet(s) and other
charges**

Franken (Merowinger)

Flandern

Metz, Bistum

Parma

Laon, Bistum

Münster, Bistum

Utrecht, Bistum

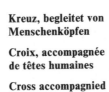

Genua

**Kreuz, begleitet von
Menschenköpfen**

**Croix, accompagnée
de têtes humaines**

**Cross accompagnied
by human heads**

Saluzzo

Österreich (Steiermark)

Deutschland
(Friedrich I., reg. 1152–1190)

Griechenland, Republik, 1926

Meißen, Bistum

Ungarn

Deutschland (Friedrich I.,
reg. 1152–1190, und
Heinrich II., reg. 1169–1197)

Ungarn

**Kreuz, begleitet
von Vierfüßlern und
Teilen davon**

**Croix accompagnée
de quadrupèdes et
de parties de
ceux-ci.**

**Cross between
quadrupeds and
parts thereof**

Kessenich

Cambrai, Bistum

Hennegau

Bretagne

Bozzolo   Elincourt
Masserano   Sabbioneta

Aquitanien

Lima (Peru)

San Benigno di Fruttuario
(Provinz Turin)

Kreuz, begleitet von Vögeln und Teilen davon

Croix accompagnée d'oiseaux et de parties de ceux-ci

Cross accompagnied by birds and parts thereof

Stendal (Altmark)

Hennegau

Aachen, Stadt
Cambrai, Bistum

Cambrai, Bistum

Cambrai, Bistum

Recanati

Maccagno (Provinz Como)

Cambrai, Bistum

San Benigno di Fruttuario
(Provinz Turin)

Poilvache

Deutschland

Kreuz, begleitet von Wassertieren

Croix accompagnée d'animaux aquatiques

Cross accompagnied by aquatic animals

Lüttich

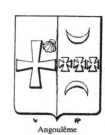

Angoulême

Kreuz, begleitet von Rose(tte)n

Croix accompagnée de rose(tte)s

Cross accompagnied by roses

Monferrat,
Markgrafschaft (Oberitalien)

Tonnerre (Yonne)

Metz, Bistum

Sizilien

Sizilien

Saint Lucia, 16. 8. 1939

Holland

Aquileja

Berg
Brabant
Deutschland
England
Holland
Lippe
Navarra
Norwegen
Stein

Geldern

Tirol

Mantua, Herzogtum

Luzern

Flandern

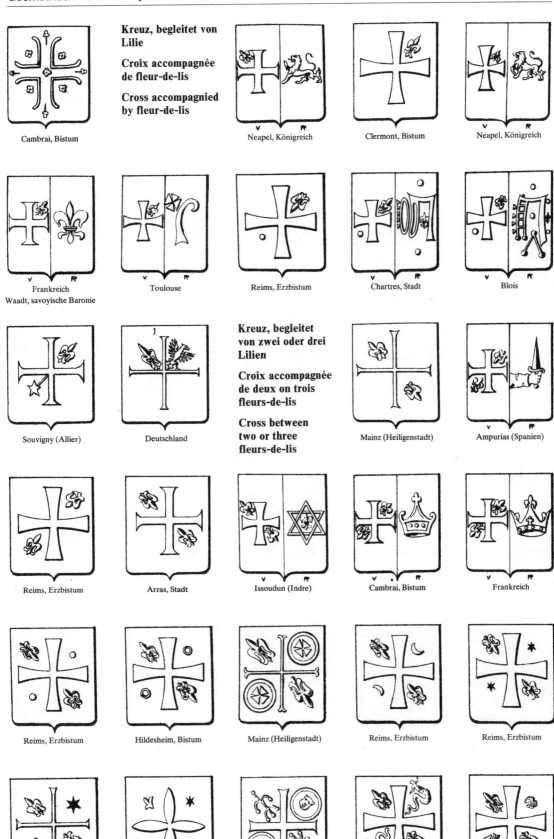

Kreuz, begleitet von Lilie

Croix accompagnée de fleur-de-lis

Cross accompagnied by fleur-de-lis

Cambrai, Bistum

Neapel, Königreich

Clermont, Bistum

Neapel, Königreich

Frankreich
Waadt, savoyische Baronie

Toulouse

Reims, Erzbistum

Chartres, Stadt

Blois

Souvigny (Allier)

Deutschland

Kreuz, begleitet von zwei oder drei Lilien

Croix accompagnée de deux on trois fleurs-de-lis

Cross between two or three fleurs-de-lis

Mainz (Heiligenstadt)

Ampurias (Spanien)

Reims, Erzbistum

Arras, Stadt

Issoudun (Indre)

Cambrai, Bistum

Frankreich

Reims, Erzbistum

Hildesheim, Bistum

Mainz (Heiligenstadt)

Reims, Erzbistum

Reims, Erzbistum

Mainz (Heiligenstadt)

Armenien

Mainz (Heiligenstadt)

Asti

Souvigny (Allier)

Deutschland

**Kreuz, begleitet von
vier Lilien**

**Croix accompagnée
de quatre
fleurs-de-lis**

**Cross between four
fleurs-de-lis**

Sizilien
Venedig

Reims, Erzbistum

Norwegen

**Kreuz, begleitet von
Klee-(Drei-)blättern**

**Croix accompagnée
de trèfles**

**Cross between
trefoils**

Deutschland (Köln)

Cambrai, Bistum

Bar
Cambrai, Bistum

Brandenburg, Markgrafschaft

Cambrai, Bistum

Deutschland (Köln)

Deutschland (Köln)

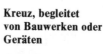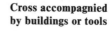

Mailand
Verona   Vertus

Holland

**Kreuz, begleitet
von Blättern oder
Zweigen**

**Croix accompagnée
de feuilles ou de
rameaux**

**Cross between
leaves or twigs**

Armenien

St. Pölten, Bistum

**Kreuz, begleitet
von Bauwerken oder
Geräten**

**Croix accompagnée
d'édifices ou d'in-
struments**

**Cross accompagnied
by buildings or tools**

Brandenburg
an der Havel, Neustadt

Spanien

Navarra

Navarra

Toulouse

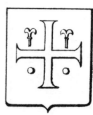

Sens, Grafschaft

Orange

Mainz (Heiligenstadt)

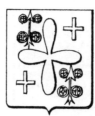

Padua

Padua

Roussillon

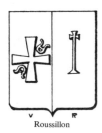

Roussillon

Brandenburg, Markgrafschaft

Salerno

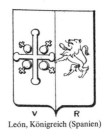

Steiermark

León, Königreich (Spanien)

Deutschland (Worms)

Lübeck, Bistum

Arles

Ungarn

Luxemburg, Herzogtum

Aquitanien
Navarra

England, Königreich

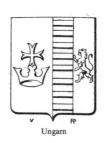

Navarra

Navarra

**Kreuz, begleitet von
Buchstaben**

**Croix accompagnée
de lettres**

**Cross accompanied
by letters**

Nivelles (Belgien)

Mainz (Heiligenstadt)

Deutschland (Otto III.,
reg. 983–1002, und Adelheid)

Grenoble

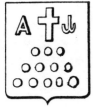

Toul, Stadt

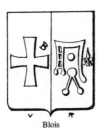

Blois

Béarn

Troyes, Stadt

Franken (Merowinger)

Grenoble

Massa Marittima

Deutschland (Breisach)

Provins (Seine-et-Marne)

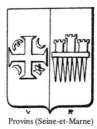

Frankreich (Reims)

Toulouse

Santa Marta, 1820

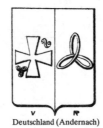
Celles

Tonnerre (Yonne)

Angoulême

Sancerre (Cher)

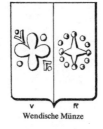
Deutschland (Andernach)

Eutin, Stadt

Toul, Stadt

Frankreich (Reims)

Franken (Merowinger)

Wendische Münze

Gien (Loiret)

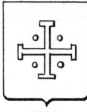
Mailand
Verona
Vertus

León und Kastilien

Krückenkreuz, begleitet von Strichen

Croix potencée accompagnée de traits

Cross potent accompagnied by lines

Neapel, Herzogtum

Byzanz

Krückenkreuz, begleitet von geometrischen Zeichen

Croix potencée accompagnée de signes géométriques

Cross potent accompagnied by geometrical signs

Zähringen

England, Königreich

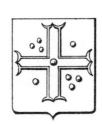
England, Königreich

Cambrai, Bistum

England, Königreich

Franken (Merowinger)

England, Königreich

England, Königreich

England, Königreich

Ungarn

**Krückenkreuz, be-
gleitet von Kreuz-
chen**

**Croix potencée
accompagnée de
croisettes**

**Cross potent accom-
pagnied by crosslets**

Pegau, Benediktinerabtei
(Sachsen)

Athen, Herzogtum
Neapel, Königreich · Provence
Savoyen · Zypern · Spanien

Zypern

Portugal

Neapel, Königreich
Provence

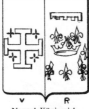

Neapel, Königreich
Provence

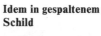

Brasilien

**Idem in gespaltenem
Schild**

Idem dans écu parti

**Idem on shield per
pale**

Neapel, Königreich
Provence

Zypern

Neapel, Königreich
Provence

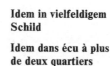

Neapel, Königreich

**Idem in vielfeldigem
Schild**

**Idem dans écu à plus
de deux quartiers**

**Idem on shield quar-
tered of four or more**

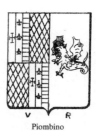

Piombino

Murano, 1709–1722 (1713).

V. Joan Cornaro, Doge
   Pasquale A. Dolfino, Proconsul
   Joan Fontana, Consul
R. Giacomo Pizzo
   Victorio Nich.
   Antonio Ferra
   Agosto Zuffo

Savoyen

Savoyen

Sardinien, Königreich
30. 12. 1814

**Krückenkreuz, be-
gleitet von Monden,
auch mit Sternen**

**Croix potencée
accompagnée de
croissant(s) aussi
avec des étoiles**

**Cross potent accom-
pagnied by crescents
even with mullets**

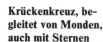

England

England,
Schweden

Dänemark

Gollnow, Stadt (Pommern)

**Krückenkreuz,
begleitet von Lebe-
wesen**

**Croix potencée
accompagnée d'êtres
vivants**

**Cross potent
accompagnied by
living beings**

Pegau, Benediktinerabtei
(Sachsen)

Pegau, Benediktinerabtei

Pegau, Benediktinerabtei

Caracas (Venezuela)

Krückenkreuz, begleitet von Pflanzen

Croix potencée accompagnée de plantes

Cross potent accompagnied by plants

Mainz, Erzbistum

Vandalen

Krückenkreuz, begleitet von Bauwerken oder Geräten

Croix potencée accompagnée d'édifices ou d'instruments

Cross potent accompagnied by buildings or tools

Lima (Peru)
Potosí (Bolivien)
Spanien

Lima (Peru)

Caracas (Venezuela)

Pegau, Benediktinerabtei
(Sachsen)

Pegau, Benediktinerabtei
(Sachsen)

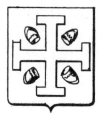

Burgund, Herzogtum

England, Königreich

England, Königreich

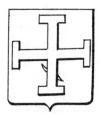

Georgien

England, Königreich

Neapel und Sizilien

Malteser- und Ankerkreuz, begleitet von Kügelchen

Croix de Malte ou croix ancrée accompagnée de disques

Maltese cross or cross moline between roundles

Frankfurt an der Oder

Vorderösterreich

Toskana

Tonnerre (Yonne)

Geldern
Kleve, Kuinre,
Lippe

England, Königreich

Lippe

England, Münster, Bistum
Osnabrück, Bistum

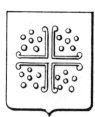

Lippe

Cervera (Katalonien)

Ankerkreuz, begleitet von Kreuzchen

Croix ancrée accompagnée de flanchis

Cross moline between crosslets

Mark

Corvey, Abtei (Westfalen)
Deutschland (Köln)
Lippe
Mark
Münster, Bistum
Osnabrück, Bistum
Schwalenberg

Waldeck

Ankerkreuz, begleitet von Mond und Sternen

Croix ancrée accompagnée de croissant et d'étoiles

Cross moline accompagnied by crescent and mullets

Mainz (Heiligenstadt)

Knyphausen und Varel

Armenien

Venedig

Utrecht, Bistum

Armenien

Bremen, Erzbistum
Köln, Erzbistum
Münster, Bistum
Osnabrück, Bistum
Ravensberg
Schottland
Schwalenberg

Helmershausen (Thüringen)
Köln, Erzbistum

Mainz (Heiligenstadt)

Ankerkreuz, begleitet von weiteren Figuren

Croix ancrée accompagnée d'autres meubles

Cross moline accompagnied by other charges

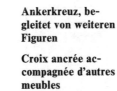

Ungarn

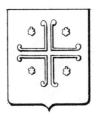

Münster, Bistum

Ephesus

Armenien

Brandenburg

Mexiko, Königreich
(span. Vizekönigreich)

Dillingen

Toskana

Kreuz mit deichselförmigen Armen

Croix aux bras terminés en pairle

Cross with pall-shaped limbs

Mercia

Armenien

Armenien

Kleeblatt- und Lilienkreuze, begleitet

Croix tréflée et fleurdelisée accompagnées

Crosses botony and flory accompagnied

Maccagno (Provinz Como)
Masserano, Fürstentum (Piemont)

England, Königreich

Jerusalem

Béarn

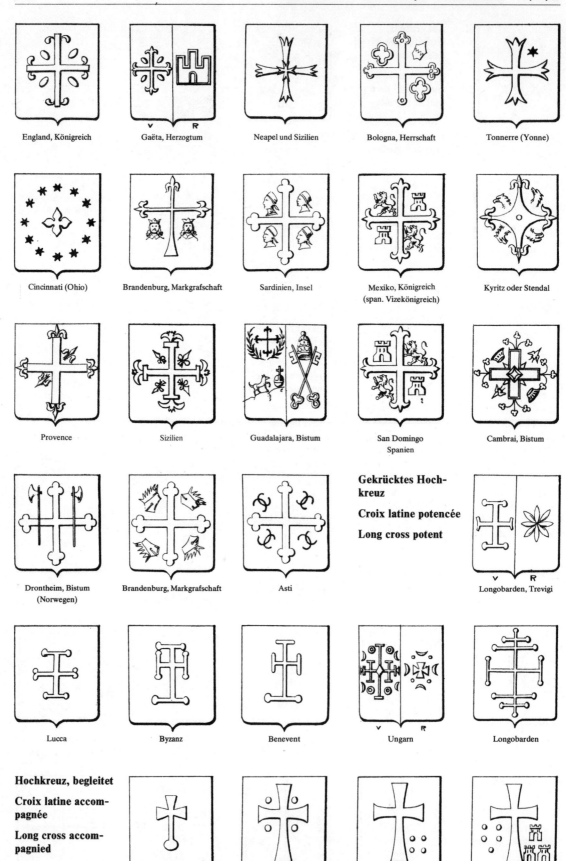

England, Königreich

Gaëta, Herzogtum

Neapel und Sizilien

Bologna, Herrschaft

Tonnerre (Yonne)

Cincinnati (Ohio)

Brandenburg, Markgrafschaft

Sardinien, Insel

Mexiko, Königreich
(span. Vizekönigreich)

Kyritz oder Stendal

Provence

Sizilien

Guadalajara, Bistum

San Domingo
Spanien

Cambrai, Bistum

Drontheim, Bistum
(Norwegen)

Brandenburg, Markgrafschaft

Asti

**Gekrücktes Hoch-
kreuz**

Croix latine potencée

Long cross potent

Longobarden, Trevigi

Lucca

Byzanz

Benevent

Ungarn

Longobarden

Hochkreuz, begleitet

**Croix latine accom-
pagnée**

**Long cross accom-
pagnied**

Franken (Merowinger)

Majorka

Majorka

Majorka

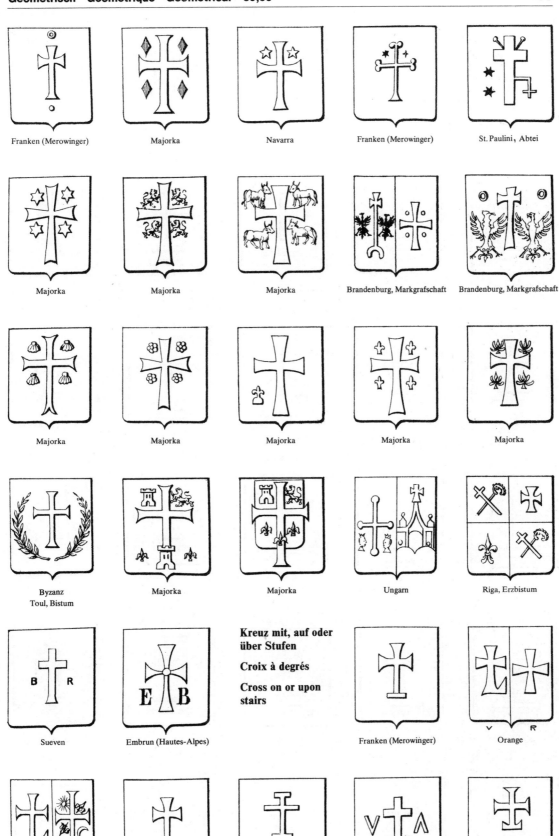

Franken (Merowinger)   Majorka   Navarra   Franken (Merowinger)   St. Paulini, Abtei

Majorka   Majorka   Majorka   Brandenburg, Markgrafschaft   Brandenburg, Markgrafschaft

Majorka   Majorka   Majorka   Majorka   Majorka

Byzanz
Toul, Bistum   Majorka   Majorka   Ungarn   Riga, Erzbistum

**Kreuz mit, auf oder
über Stufen**

Croix à degrés

**Cross on or upon
stairs**

Sueven   Embrun (Hautes-Alpes)   Franken (Merowinger)   Orange

Lyon, Erzbistum   Franken (Merowinger)   Franken (Merowinger)   Metz, Stadt   Toul, Stadt

Franken (Merowinger)	Franken (Merowinger)	Westgoten	Lyon, Erzbistum	Lyon, Erzbistum
Byzanz	Byzanz	Franken (Merowinger)	Franken (Merowinger)	Byzanz
Longobarden	Franken (Merowinger)	Salerno	Westgoten	Byzanz
Westgoten	Salerno	Byzanz	Longobarden	Benevent
Mainz, Stadt	Franken (Merowinger)	Benevent	Byzanz	Franken (Merowinger)
Westgoten	Franken (Merowinger)	Westgoten	Byzanz	Byzanz

Kreuz mit geradlinig erweitertem Fuß

Croix à pied élargi à lignes droites

Cross with rectilineally enlarged foot

Franken (Merowinger)

Norwegen

Kreuz mit krumm erweitertem Fuß

Croix à pied élargi courbé

Cross with bently enlarged foot

Kastilien

Ostangeln (England)

Franken (Merowinger)

Franken (Merowinger)

Schlesien

Franken (Merowinger)

Antiochien

Sizilien

Ostangeln (England)

Reims, Stadt

Schwebendes Kreuz, belegt

Croix alésée chargée

Cross couped surmounted

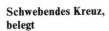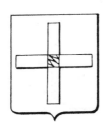
Griechenland, Königreich, 1832–1862

Ungarn

Alemannien

Hennegau

Schlesien

Toul, Bistum

Heiligenkreuz, Kloster (Niederösterreich)

Heiligenkreuz, Kloster (Niederösterreich)

Toul, Bistum

Kessenich

Roussillon

Schwebendes Kreuz, belegt mit Mittelschild

Croix alésée avec sur-le-tout

Cross couped with inescutcheon

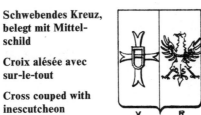
Tirol

Cambrai, Domkapitel

Schaffhausen

Aachen

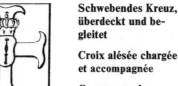

St. Gallen, Abtei

Deutscher Orden nebst Worms, Breslau und Ellwangen,
Hochmeister Franz Ludwig von der Pfalz (1694–1732)

Schweden

Brandenburg, Markgrafschaft

Schwebendes Kreuz, überdeckt und be-gleitet

Croix alésée chargée et accompagnée

Cross couped, surmounted and accompagnied

Böhmen

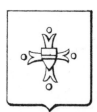

Saint Lucia, 1. 3. 1970

Lippe

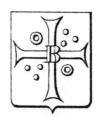

Barcelona

Nottingham

Schwebendes Kreuz, belegt mit Mittel-schild und begleitet

Croix alésée avec sur-le-tout et accompagnée

Cross couped, sur-mounted by inescut-cheon and accom-pagnied

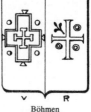

Vorderösterreich

Correggio

Masserano, Fürstentum
(Piemont)

Majorka

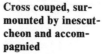

Spanien

Mexiko, Königreich
(span. Vizekönigreich)

Gemeines Kreuz

Croix pleine

Plain cross

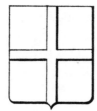

Alessandria
Amersfoort
Aspermont
Castiglione delle Stiviere
Como
Dahlen
Deutscher Orden
Fermo
Fulda, Abtei
Geldern
Genua
Johanniter-Orden

Konstanz, Stadt
Languedoc
Livland · Lodi
Mersburg, Bistum
Modena Novara ·Padua
Parma · Pavia
Pettau (Steiermark)
Reckheim · Reggio
Riga, Erzbistum
Sardinien, Königreich
Savoyen · Schweiz ·Siegburg
Speyer, Bistum

Treviso (Venetien)
Trier, Erzbistum
Toulon, Stadt
Utrecht, Bistum
Valence (Drôme)
Vercelli (Oberitalien) 1638
Verdun, Bistum
Verona (Oberitalien)
Vicenza (Oberitalien)
Werden, Abtei
Wien, Stadt
Zwolle (Overijssel)

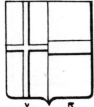

Freiburg im Breisgau, Stadt

Bologna, Herrschaft

England und Irland,
Commonwealth, 1649–1653

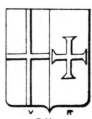

Geldern

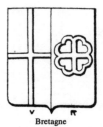

Bretagne

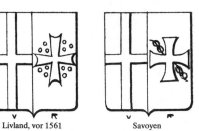

Livland, vor 1561

Savoyen

Savoyen

Konstanz, Stadt

Trier, Erzbistum

Sizilien

Konstanz, Bistum

England und Irland,
Commonwealth, 1649–1653

Gemeines Kreuz im ersten von drei Schilden

Croix pleine au premier de trois écussons

Plain cross on the first of three escutcheons

Werden und Helmstedt, Abtei

Trier, Köln und Pfalz

Murbach und Lüders,
Abtei (Oberelsaß)

Reckheim

Mainz, Pfalz und Trier

Kopenhagen

Kampen, Deventer und Zwolle

Neuss

Kampen, Deventer und Zwolle

Werden, Abtei

Marsberg, Stadt
(jetzt Obermarsberg, Westfalen)

Marsberg, Stadt
(jetzt Obermarsberg, Westfalen)

Bologna, Herrschaft

Gemeines Kreuz im ersten von vier Schilden

Croix pleine au premier de quatre écussons

Plain cross on the first of four escutcheons

Werden, Abtei

Werden, Abtei

Mainz, Köln, Pfalz und Trier

Werden, Abtei

Savoyen

Gemeines Kreuz im ersten von fünf Schilden

Croix pleine au premier de cinq écussons

Plain cross on the first of five escutcheons

Amersfoort mit Reene,
Montfoort, Wyck und Utrecht

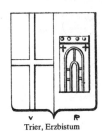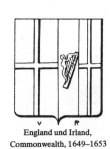

Gemeines Kreuz mit Farbangabe

Croix pleine, les émaux indiqués

Plain cross, the tinctures shown

Fermo
Johanniter-Orden
Metz, Bistum
Novara, Stadt

Messina
Reckheim

Freiburg i. Br., Erzbistum
Lodi, Stadt (Provinz Mailand)

Aspermont, Herrschaft
Como
Dänemark

England
Freiburg i. Br., Stadt
Genua, Stadt
Konstanz, Bistum
Ligurische Republik
1798–1805
Mailand, Stadt
Padua, Stadt
Reichenau, Abtei
St. Georg
Trier, Erzbistum

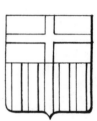

Alessandria
Amersfoort

Toulon, Stadt
Verona, Stadt

Modena, Stadt
Parma, Stadt

Griechenland
Hünfeld, Stadt
Speyer, Bistum · Zwolle, Stadt

Marseille, Stadt
Portugal, ursprünglich

Rottenburg, Bistum

Aachen, Bistum, 1930
Merseburg, Bistum

Deutscher Orden
Fulda, Abtei
Köln, Erzbistum

Gemeines Kreuz in außergewöhnlicher Farbstellung

Croix pleine aux émaux disposés d'une manière extra-ordinaire

Plain cross, the tinctures unusually marshalled

Gemeines Kreuz in geteiltem Schild

Croix pleine dans écu coupé

Plain cross on shield per fess

Davos
Zehngerichtebund
(Graubünden)

Saarland, 13. 12. 1948–1956

Paderborn, Stadt
Sanahuja
Solsona (Katalonien)

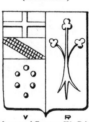

Massa und Carrara,
W: Cybo und Malaspina

Massa und Carrara, W: Cybo,
Medici und Malaspina 1529

Massa und Carrara, W: Cybo,
Medici und Malaspina 1529

Massa und Carrara, um 1529

Bonn, Stadt,
vor 1939, 1952–1971

Gemeines Kreuz in gespaltenem Schild

Croix pleine dans écu parti

Plain cross on shield per pale

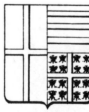

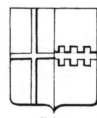

Bonn

Reckheim

Siegburg

Soignies, Kapitel zu St.-Vincent,
und Stadt (Belgien)

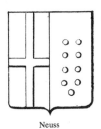

Neuss

Neuss

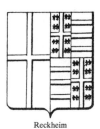

Savoyen

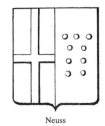

Reckheim

Schwäbisch Hall

Spoleto, Stadt (Italien)

Reckheim

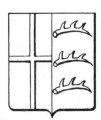

Konstanz und Württemberg,

als ausschreibende
Fürsten des Schwäbischen
Kreises

Schwäbischer Kreis

Fulda, Abtei und Kapitel

Fulda, Stadt (Hessen)

Speyer, Bistum,
und Abtei Weißenburg

Werden und Helmstedt, Abtei

England und Irland,
Commonwealth, 1649–1653

**Gemeines Kreuz in
dreiteiligem Schild**

**Croix pleine
chargeant chapé**

**Per pale and per
chevron, a plain
cross in the first
quarter**

Rheinland-Pfalz,
24. 5. 1947/10. 5. 1948

**Gemeines Kreuz in
geviertem Schild**

**Croix pleine dans
écu écartelé**

**Plain cross on
quartered shield**

Trier mit Augsburg und Prüm

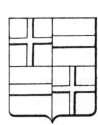

Baer, Bannerherrschaft
Essen, Abtei

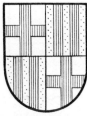

Barcelona, Stadt

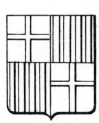

Barcelona
Valls (Katalonien)
Vich (Katalonien)

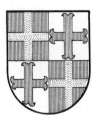

Reckheim

Paderborn, Bistum

England, Schottland und
Irland, Commonwealth,
1654–1660

Trier mit Freising,
Regensburg und Prüm

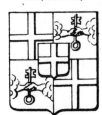

Konstanz, Bistum

Utrecht, Provinz

Utrecht, Stadt

Trier und Luxemburg

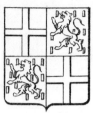

Reckheim · Utrecht, Provinz · Reckheim · Reckheim · Reckheim

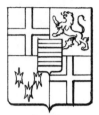

Reckheim / Utrecht, Provinz · Reckheim · Reckheim · Reckheim · Köln, Erzbistum

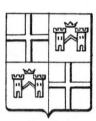
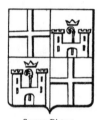
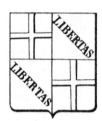

Neuss · Speyer, Bistum, und Abtei Weißenburg · Speyer, Bistum, und Abtei Weißenburg · Bologna, Stadt

Gemeines Kreuz in mehrfeldigem Schild

Croix pleine dans écu de plus de quatre quartiers

Plain cross on shield of more then four quarters

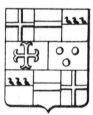

Ferdinand, Fürst von Lobkowicz verm. 1769 Gabriele Prinzessin von Savoyen-Carignan · Münster und Paderborn, Bistümer · Hessen-Kassel, 1815

Tatzenkreuz

Croix pattée

Cross formy

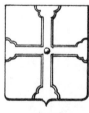

Monferrat, Markgrafschaft (Oberitalien) · Görz · Venedig · Irland

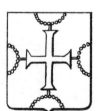

England, Königreich

Kreuz, gesäumt

Croix liserée

Cross fimbriated

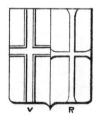
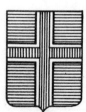

England · Schottland Schweden · Utrecht, Bistum · Island, 12. 2. 1919

**Gemeines Kreuz
unter Schildhaupt**

**Croix pleine sous
chef**

**Plain cross under
chief**

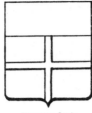

Konstanz, Stadt
Passerano

Konstanz, Stadt
1417

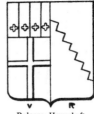

Bologna, Herrschaft

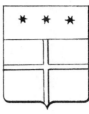

Bologna, Stadt

Konstanz, Stadt

Bologna, Stadt

Konstanz, Stadt

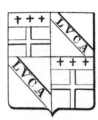

Schwäbisch Hall

Lucca, Stadt

Bologna, Stadt

Bologna, Stadt

Carpi (Modena)

Dornenkreuz

Croix engrêlée

Cross engrailed

Eupen

Sarawak, Fürstentum,
bis 1946

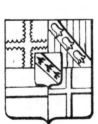

Vauvillars

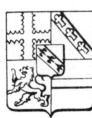

Vauvillars

**Kreuz, in der Mitte
belegt oder über-
deckt**

**Croix chargée en
abîme**

**Cross surmounted
on fess point**

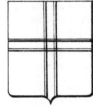

Norwegen

England, Königreich

England, Königreich

Gronsfeld, Grafschaft
(niederl. Provinz Limburg)

Nordirland, 2. 8. 1924

England, Königreich

Lincoln

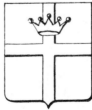

Koblenz, Stadt

Koblenz, Stadt

Sarawak, Staat (Nordborneo),
10. 3. 1947

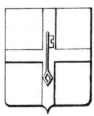

Werl, Stadt (Westfalen)

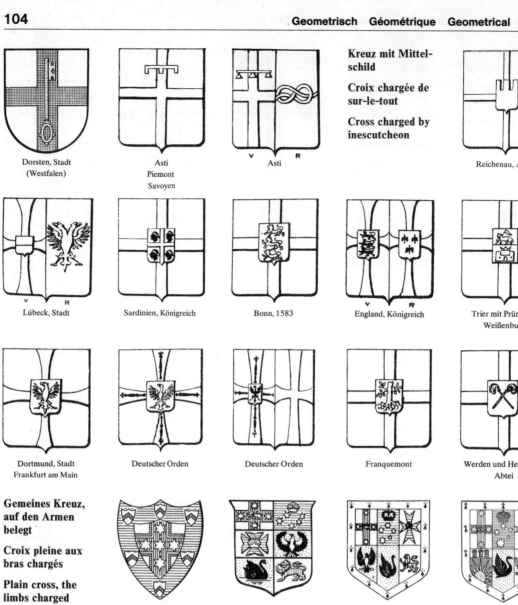

Dorsten, Stadt
(Westfalen)

Asti
Piemont
Savoyen

Asti

**Kreuz mit Mittel-
schild**

**Croix chargée de
sur-le-tout**

**Cross charged by
inescutcheon**

Reichenau, Abtei

Lübeck, Stadt

Sardinien, Königreich

Bonn, 1583

England, Königreich

Trier mit Prüm und
Weißenburg

Dortmund, Stadt
Frankfurt am Main

Deutscher Orden

Deutscher Orden

Franquemont

Werden und Helmstedt,
Abtei

**Gemeines Kreuz,
auf den Armen
belegt**

**Croix pleine aux
bras chargés**

**Plain cross, the
limbs charged**

Australien, 7. 5. 1908

Australien, Variante der
Commonwealth Bank

Australien, 19. 9. 1912

Australien, Variante auf
Münzen, 1937

Jamaika
Kingston (Jamaika)

Jamaika, 3. 2. 1661

**Gemeines Kreuz,
im ersten Feld
begleitet**

**Croix pleine can-
tonnée au premier
quartier**

**Plain cross cantoned
in the dexter chief
corner**

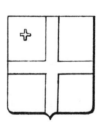

Trier, Erzbistum

Chambéry (Savoie)

Kreta 1898–1913

Mantua, Stadt

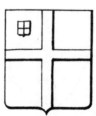

Ostindien-Kompanie
St. Helena

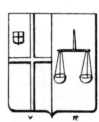

Bombay (Ostindische
Kompanie), 1698

Cirkars (Ostindische
Kompanie)

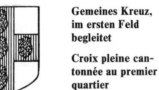

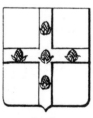

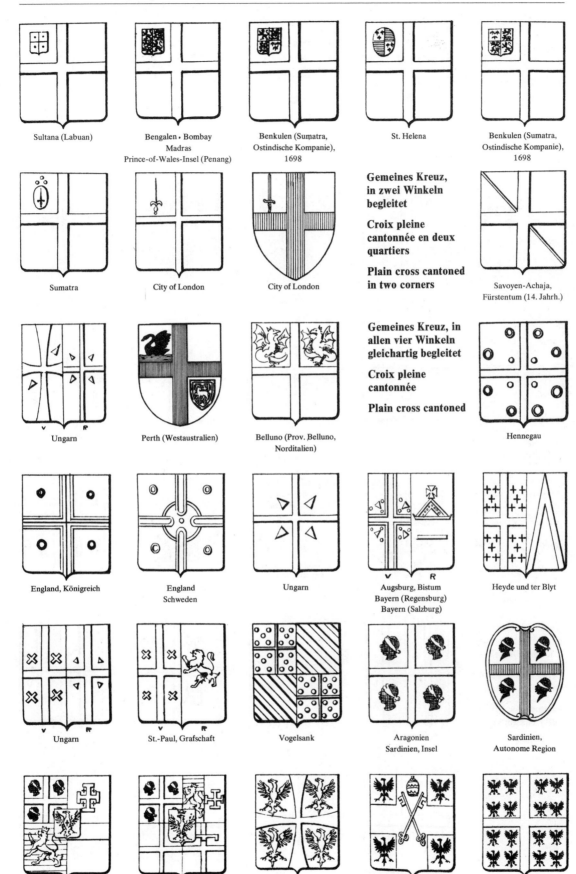

Sultana (Labuan)

Bengalen · Bombay
Madras
Prince-of-Wales-Insel (Penang)

Benkulen (Sumatra,
Ostindische Kompanie),
1698

St. Helena

Benkulen (Sumatra,
Ostindische Kompanie),
1698

Sumatra

City of London

City of London

**Gemeines Kreuz,
in zwei Winkeln
begleitet**

**Croix pleine
cantonnée en deux
quartiers**

**Plain cross cantoned
in two corners**

Savoyen-Achaja,
Fürstentum (14. Jahrh.)

Ungarn

Perth (Westaustralien)

Belluno (Prov. Belluno,
Norditalien)

**Gemeines Kreuz, in
allen vier Winkeln
gleichartig begleitet**

**Croix pleine
cantonnée**

Plain cross cantoned

Hennegau

England, Königreich

England
Schweden

Ungarn

Augsburg, Bistum
Bayern (Regensburg)
Bayern (Salzburg)

Heyde und ter Blyt

Ungarn

St.-Paul, Grafschaft

Vogelsank

Aragonien
Sardinien, Insel

Sardinien,
Autonome Region

Sardinien, Königreich

Sardinien, Königreich

Mantua, Herzogtum
Novellara (Provinz Reggio)

Mantua, Herzogtum

Hoorn, Grafschaft

Hoorn, Grafschaft

Hoorn, Grafschaft

Weert (niederländ. Provinz Limburg)

England, Königreich

Grafen von Rabenswald (Thüringen)

Deutschland

Châlons-sur-Marne, Bistum

St. Wendel, Stadt (Saarland)

Clermont-Ferrand

Apulien Provence

Norwegen

England, Königreich

Brescia
Cambrai, Bistum
Ivrea (Prov. Aosta)

Werden und Helmstedt, Abtei

Andernach, Stadt

Avignon
Kirchenstaat

Le Mans

Serbien bis 1882

Jugoslawien, Dynastie
Karadjordjevitch, 1.12.1918

Lesbos, Thasos und Phokaea

Gemeines Kreuz, in allen Winkeln verschieden begleitet

Croix pleine cantonnée différemment

Plain cross differently cantoned

Ungarn

Roussillon

Roussillon

Ungarn

Neufundland, 1.1.1637

Mailand

Toronto (Kanada)

Virginien (Nordamerika)

Melbourne
(Victoria, Australien)

Armenien, Republik,
Juli 1919

Neusüdwales, 11. 10. 1906

Flandern

Jamberoo, seit 1954
Stadtteil von Kiame
(Neusüdwales)

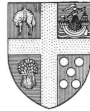

Wellington (Neuseeland),
6. 6. 1951

Canada Company

Adelaide (Südaustralien)

Brisbane (Australien,
Neusüdwales, seit 1859
Queensland)

Aiglehawk (Australien)
Castlemaine
(Victoria, Australien)

Ballarat
(Victoria, Australien)

Port Albert
(Victoria, Australien)

Melbourne
(Victoria, Australien)

Melbourne,
(Victoria, Australien)

Richmond (Neusüdwales)
Sandridge (Victoria,
Australien),
jetzt Port Melbourne
South Yarra
(Victoria, Australien)

Australien

Dominica, 21. 7. 1961

Fidschi, 4. 7. 1908

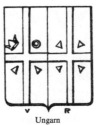

Ghana, 4. 3. 1957

Ungarn

Reggio (Emilia)

**Idem, mit Mittel-
schild**

**Idem, avec sur-le-
tout**

**Idem, with
inescutcheon**

Mergentheim, Stadt

Mergentheim, Stadt

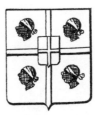

Cagliari (W: Sardinien)

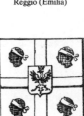

Sardinien, Königreich

Castiglione delle Stiviere
(Provinz Mantua)

Bulgarien,
Fürst Alexander I. (1879–86)

Dänemark, 16. 11. 1972

Mantua, Herzogtum

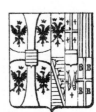

Monferrat, Markgrafschaft
(Oberitalien)

Bozzolo (Provinz Mantua)

Sabbioneta

Novellara (Provinz Reggio)

Arches · Guastalla
Mantua, Herzogtum
Solferino

Nevers

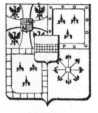

Nevers

Nevers

Arches, Fürstentum
Mantua, Herzogtum
Nevers, Grafschaft

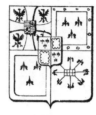

Bozzolo

Castiglione delle Stiviere
Guastalla
Mantua, Herzogtum
Sabbioneta
Solferino

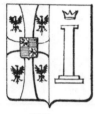

Sabbioneta

Sabbioneta

Castiglione delle Stiviere
(Provinz Mantua)

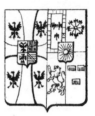

Nevers

Castiglione delle Stiviere
(Provinz Mantua)

Mantua, Herzogtum

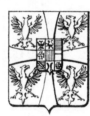

Mantua, Herzogtum

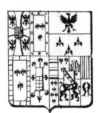

Nevers

Hoorn, Grafschaft
Weert (niederländ.
Provinz Limburg)

Schweden

Schrägkreuz, schwebend

Flanchis

Saltire couped

England, Königreich

Bretagne
Sizilien
Deutschland (Speyer)

Böhmen

Schweden

Meißen, Markgrafschaft

Dänemark

Brabant
Zypern

Neapel und Sizilien

Alemannien

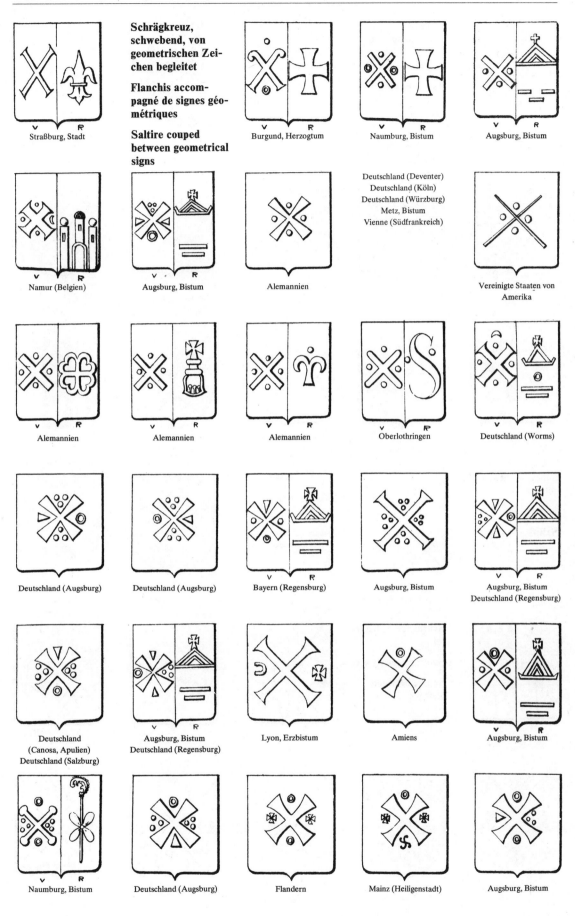

Schrägkreuz, schwebend, von geometrischen Zeichen begleitet

Flanchis accompagné de signes géométriques

Saltire couped between geometrical signs

Straßburg, Stadt

Burgund, Herzogtum

Naumburg, Bistum

Augsburg, Bistum

Namur (Belgien)

Augsburg, Bistum

Alemannien

Deutschland (Deventer)
Deutschland (Köln)
Deutschland (Würzburg)
Metz, Bistum
Vienne (Südfrankreich)

Vereinigte Staaten von Amerika

Alemannien

Alemannien

Alemannien

Oberlothringen

Deutschland (Worms)

Deutschland (Augsburg)

Deutschland (Augsburg)

Bayern (Regensburg)

Augsburg, Bistum

Augsburg, Bistum
Deutschland (Regensburg)

Deutschland
(Canosa, Apulien)
Deutschland (Salzburg)

Augsburg, Bistum
Deutschland (Regensburg)

Lyon, Erzbistum

Amiens

Augsburg, Bistum

Naumburg, Bistum

Deutschland (Augsburg)

Flandern

Mainz (Heiligenstadt)

Augsburg, Bistum

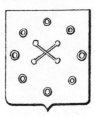

Vereinigte Staaten von Amerika

Schrägkreuz, schwebend, von anderen Figuren begleitet

Flanchis accompagné d'autres meubles

Saltire couped between other charges

Brabant

Mainz, Erzbistum

Mainz (Heiligenstadt)

Nevers, Grafschaft

Verona (Oberitalien)

Mehrere Schrägkreuzchen

Plusieurs flanchis

Several saltires couped

Breda
Vianen (Südholland)

Breda

Breda

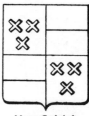

Megen, Grafschaft (Nordbrabant)

Bergen-op-Zoom

Bergen-op-Zoom

Amsterdam

Schrägkreuz, durchgehend

Sautoir

Saltire

Disentis, Gemeinde (Graubünden)

Disentis, Kloster (Graubünden)
Freyburg in Thüringen, Burggrafschaft
Meißen, Bistum
Meißen, Burggrafschaft
Schottland

Disentis, Kloster (Graubünden)

Disentis, Gemeinde (Graubünden)
Schottland

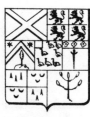

St. George del Mina

Schrägkreuz, begleitet

Sautoir accompagné

Saltire between charges

Oettingen

Oettingen

Oettingen

Seraing (Belgien)

Ellwangen, Stadt

Norwegen

Langres, Bistum

Montreal (Kanada)

Florennes
(belgische Provinz Namur)

Plymouth

Batenburg

Batenburg

Gronsfeld, Grafschaft
(niederl. Provinz Limburg)

Gronsfeld, Grafschaft
(niederl. Provinz Limburg)

Gronsfeld, Grafschaft
(niederl. Provinz Limburg)

Wien, Stadt

Byzanz

Neuschottland, 19. 1. 1929

Krückenschrägkreuz

Sautoir potencé

Saltire potent

Dänemark

Namur (Belgien)

Savoyen-Achaja,
(Fürstentum 14. Jahrh.)

Pegau, Benediktinerabtei
(Sachsen)

Pegau, Benediktinerabtei
(Sachsen)

Pegau, Benediktinerabtei

Pegau, Benediktinerabtei

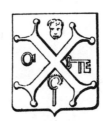

Pegau, Benediktinerabtei

Pegau, Benediktinerabtei

Pegau, Benediktinerabtei
(Sachsen)

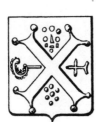

Pegau, Benediktinerabtei

Brehna

Pegau, Benediktinerabtei

Pegau, Benediktinerabtei

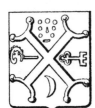

Pegau, Benediktinerabtei
(Sachsen)

Pegau, Benediktinerabtei

Pegau, Benediktinerabtei

Pegau, Benediktinerabtei

Pegau, Benediktinerabtei

Pegau, Benediktinerabtei
(Sachsen)

Pegau, Benediktinerabtei

Pegau, Benediktinerabtei

Pegau, Benediktinerabtei

Pegau, Benediktinerabtei

Pegau, Benediktinerabtei
(Sachsen)

Pegau, Benediktinerabtei

Pegau, Benediktinerabtei

Ungarn

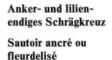

Pegau, Benediktinerabtei

Pegau, Benediktinerabtei
(Sachsen)

Böhmen

**Anker- und lilien-
endiges Schrägkreuz**

**Sautoir ancré ou
fleurdelisé**

**Saltire moline or
flory**

Altenburg, Stadt

Brabant

Lippe

Quedlinburg, Abtei

Pegau, Benediktinerabtei

Pegau, Benediktinerabtei

Pegau, Benediktinerabtei

Pegau, Benediktinerabtei
(Sachsen)

Pegau, Benediktinerabtei

Pegau, Benediktinerabtei

Pegau, Benediktinerabtei

Ungarn

Holland

Ungarn

Ungarn

Namslau (Niederschlesien)
Ungarn

Doppel- oder Patriarchenkreuz

Croix patriarcale

Patriarchal cross

Aragonien

Hersfeld, Abtei
Majorka
Neapel, Königreich
St. Omer, Stadt
(Frankreich)
Polen
Provence
Solsona (Katalonien)
Ungarn

St. Omer, Stadt
(Frankreich)

Hersfeld, Abtei

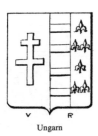

Ungarn

Ungarn

Ungarn

Ungarn

Ungarn

Ungarn

Ungarn

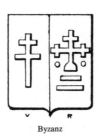

Byzanz

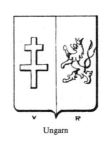

Ungarn

Ungarn

Ungarn

Ungarn

Ungarn

St. Omer (Frankreich)

Anjou

Ungarn

Ungarn

Dalmatien

Patriarchenkreuz in geteiltem Schild

Croix patriarcale dans écu coupé

Patriarchal cross on shield per fess

Ypern (Belgien)

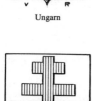

Ypern (Belgien)

Patriarchenkreuz in gespaltenem Schild

Croix patriarcale dans écu parti

Patriarchal cross on shield per pale

Ungarn

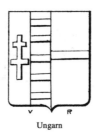

Ungarn

Hersfeld

Patriarchenkreuz in geviertem Schild

Croix patriarcale dans écu écartelé

Patriarchal cross on quartered shield

Ungarn

Ungarn

Ungarn, Dynastie Hunyadi

Ungarn

Ungarn

Ungarn, König Johann Zápolya 1526–1540

Ungarn

Ungarn, Dynastie Hunyadi

Ungarn, Dynastie Hunyadi

Patriarchenkreuz in vielfeldigem Schild

Croix patriarcale dans écu de plus de cinq quartiers

Patriarchal cross on shield of more then five quarters

Hessen-Darmstadt

Hessen-Homburg, 1815

Hessen-Kassel 1736

Hessen-Kassel 1803–1815

Patriarchenkreuz mit verbreitertem Fuß oder Stufen

Croix patriarcale au pied élargi ou à degrés

Patriarchal cross with enlarged foot or upon stairs

Armenien

Ungarn

Norwegen

Johanniter-Orden

Byzanz

Amalfi

Patriarchenkreuz, begleitet

Croix patriarcale accompagnée

Patriarchal cross accompagnied

Norwegen

Ungarn

Fraustadt (Wschowa, jetzt Wojwodschaft Grünberg)

Fraustadt (Wschowa, jetzt Wojwodschaft Grünberg)

England, York

Normannische Piraten in Frankreich

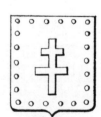

Norwegen, Geistliche Münzen

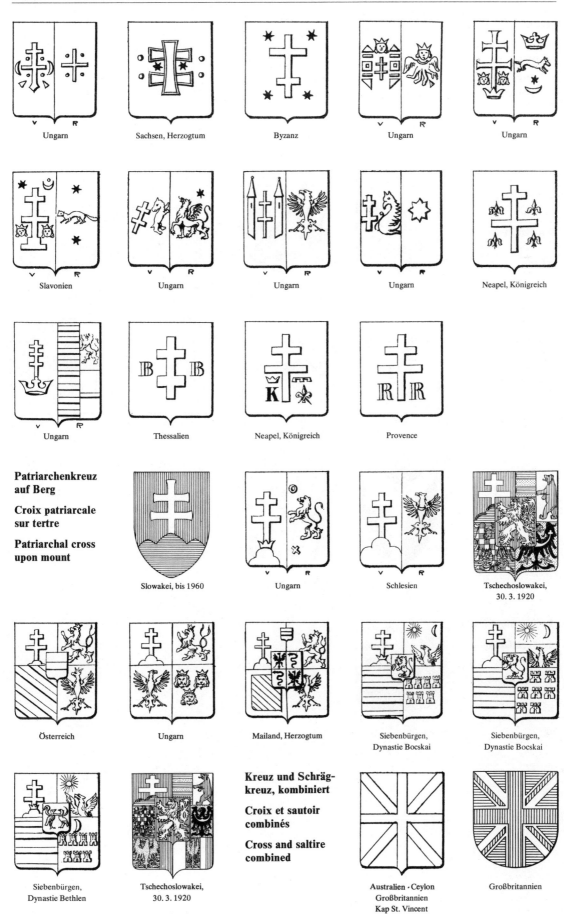

Ungarn

Sachsen, Herzogtum

Byzanz

Ungarn

Ungarn

Slavonien

Ungarn

Ungarn

Ungarn

Neapel, Königreich

Ungarn

Thessalien

Neapel, Königreich

Provence

Patriarchenkreuz auf Berg

Croix patriarcale sur tertre

Patriarchal cross upon mount

Slowakei, bis 1960

Ungarn

Schlesien

Tschechoslowakei, 30. 3. 1920

Österreich

Ungarn

Mailand, Herzogtum

Siebenbürgen, Dynastie Bocskai

Siebenbürgen, Dynastie Bocskai

Siebenbürgen, Dynastie Bethlen

Tschechoslowakei, 30. 3. 1920

Kreuz und Schrägkreuz, kombiniert

Croix et sautoir combinés

Cross and saltire combined

Australien · Ceylon Großbritannien Kap St. Vincent

Großbritannien

Hakenkreuz

Swastika ou croix gammée

Swastika or fylfot or cross gammadion or cross potent rebated

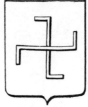

Kotschinchina   Franken (Merowinger)

Windmühlenkreuz

Volants de moulin à vent

Windmill's sails

New-York, Stadt   New-York, Stadt

Schächerkreuz, schwebend

Pairle alésée

Pall couped

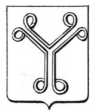

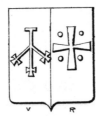

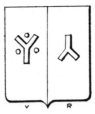

Canterbury, Erzbistum   Ostangeln (England)   Kent   Böhmen

Schächerkreuz, durchgehend

Pairle

Pall

Nigeria, 23. 4. 1960   Schweden und Norwegen, 1818

Rechtshalbes Kreuz

Croix défaillant à senestre

Cross without sinister limb

Schweden und Norwegen, 1842

Mit diesem Abschnitt beginnen die sogenannten gemeinen Figuren.
In dem nachstehenden Inhaltsverzeichnis dieser Gruppe geben die links stehenden Ziffern an, unter welchem Ordnungsstichwort die verschiedenen Motive eingeordnet sind. Die Ziffern rechts geben die aufzuschlagende Seite an.

Sonne, auch belegt

Soleil, aussi chargé

Sun, even charged

Córdoba (Argentinien)
Cuzco (Peru)
Lima (Peru)
Murschidabad (Bengalen)
Neapel und Sizilien
Potosí (Bolivien)
Uruguay

Argentinien　　　　　　　　Hamadan (Iran)　　　　　Eriwan (Kaukasus)

Castiglione delle Stiviere
Mantua, Herzogtum
Masserano
Schirwan (Kaukasus)
Solferino
Solis
Solsona (Katalonien)
Täbris (Persien)
Uruguay

Bozzolo　　　　　　Bozzolo (Provinz Mantua)　　　Pavia　　　　Ispahan

Bugginesen (Engl.
Ostindien-Kompanie)　　Kotschinchina　　Durango (Mexiko)　　Córdoba (Argentinien)　　Mohammedabad (Benares)

Sakankpur　　　Japan　　China, Republik, 17. 12. 1928　　Padua　　Rimini, Herrschaft
　　　　　　　　　　　　Taiwan (Formosa)

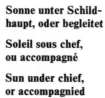

**Sonne unter Schild-
haupt, oder begleitet**

**Soleil sous chef,
ou accompagné**

**Sun under chief,
or accompagnied**

Rimini, Herrschaft　　Irak, Republik, 14. 7. 1959　　　　　　　Guadeloupe　　Saarlouis

Osmanisches Reich,
vor 1922　　　Guastalla　　Mantua, Herzogtum　　Japan　　Cuzco (Peru)
　　　　　　　　　　　　Masserano, Fürstentum　　　　　　Lima (Peru)
　　　　　　　　　　　　(Piemont)　　　　　　　　　　Südperu 20. 3. 1836

Truchseß von Waldburg
für Sonnenberg

Uganda, 9. 10. 1962

Niger, 1. 12. 1962

Aufgehende Sonne

Soleil mouvant

Sun rising

Lettland, Republik,
15. 6. 1921

Biafra, 1967

Querétaro (Mexiko)

Britisch Kolumbien,
31. 3. 1906

Südaustralien, Wappen,
20. 11. 1936

Gilbert- und Ellice-Inseln,
. 1. 5. 1937

Mond

Croissant

Crescent

Bagdad

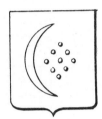

Dalmatien

Ostindien

Sizilien

Mondsee (Oberösterreich)

Frankreich

Perak (Malaya)

Schlesien

Schlesien

Brunei

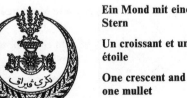

Perak (Malaya)

Ein Mond mit einem Stern

Un croissant et une étoile

One crescent and one mullet

Toulouse

Türkei

Köln, Stadt, mit W. der
heiligen drei Könige

Türkei

Gollnow, Stadt (Pommern)

Triest, Bistum und Stadt

Navarra
Schlesien

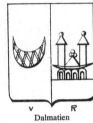

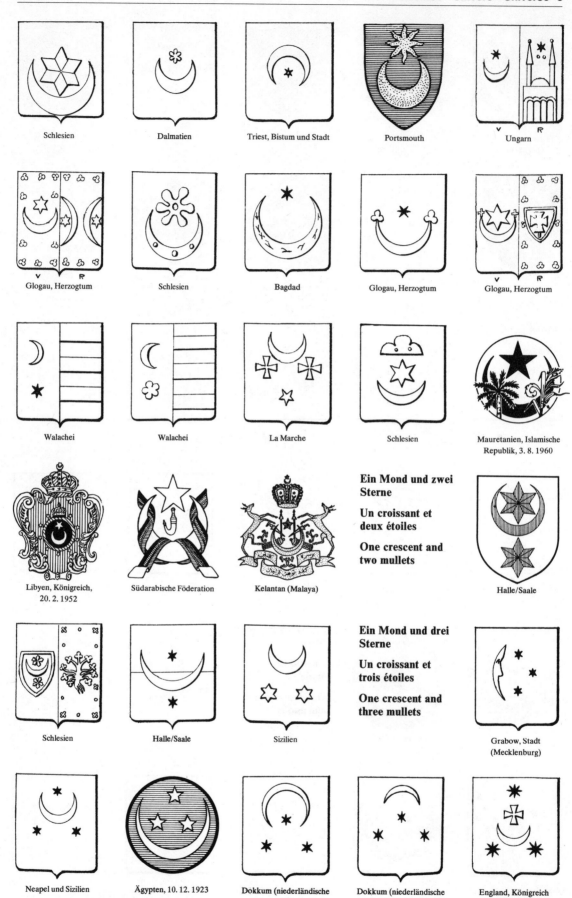

Schlesien

Dalmatien

Triest, Bistum und Stadt

Portsmouth

Ungarn

Glogau, Herzogtum

Schlesien

Bagdad

Glogau, Herzogtum

Glogau, Herzogtum

Walachei

Walachei

La Marche

Schlesien

Mauretanien, Islamische
Republik, 3. 8. 1960

Libyen, Königreich,
20. 2. 1952

Südarabische Föderation

Kelantan (Malaya)

**Ein Mond und zwei
Sterne**

**Un croissant et
deux étoiles**

**One crescent and
two mullets**

Halle/Saale

Schlesien

Halle/Saale

Sizilien

**Ein Mond und drei
Sterne**

**Un croissant et
trois étoiles**

**One crescent and
three mullets**

Grabow, Stadt
(Mecklenburg)

Neapel und Sizilien

Ägypten, 10. 12. 1923

Dokkum (niederländische
Provinz Friesland)

Dokkum (niederländische
Provinz Friesland)

England, Königreich

Ein Mond und vier bis fünf Sterne

Un croissant et quatre à cinq étoiles

One crescent and four to five mullets

England, Königreich

Dschohor (Johore)

Dschohor (Johore)

Singapur, Republik, 7. 11. 1959

Zwei Monde, auch mit Sternen

Deux croissants, aussi avec des étoiles

Two crescents, even with mullets

Angoulême und la Marche

Britannien

Glogau, Herzogtum

Gollnow, Stadt (Pommern)

Drei Monde, auch mit Sternen

Trois croissants, aussi avec des étoiles

Three crescents, even with mullets

Hedel, Stadt (Prov. Gelderland)

Ägypten, bis 1923

Châteaudun (Orléanais)
Monster (Südholland)
Stevensweert (niederl. Provinz Limburg)

Hedel, Stadt (Prov. Gelderland)

Châteaudun (Orléanais)

Lund, Stadt (Schweden)

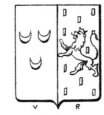

's-Heerenberg, Herrschaft (Grafschaft Zütphen)

Bentheim-Tecklenburg, Graf Adolf † 1622 verm. 1606 Margarete von Nassau-Weilburg

Kessenich

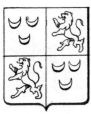

's-Heerenberg, Herrschaft (Grafschaft Zütphen)

Vier Monde, auch mit Sternen

Quatre croissants, aussi avec des étoiles

Four crescents, even with mullets

Perleberg oder Werben

England, Königreich

Ein Stern, fünfzackig, auch begleitet

Une étoile à cinq rais, aussi accompagnée

One mullet of five points, even accompagnied

Madeira
Montenegro
Orange

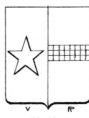

Dinslaken

Maastricht

Maastricht

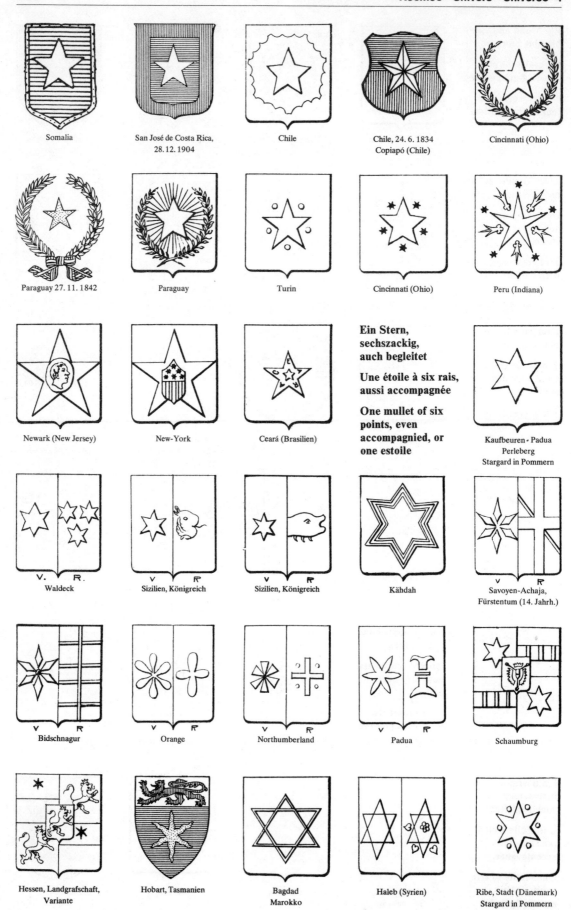

Somalia

San José de Costa Rica,
28.12.1904

Chile

Chile, 24. 6. 1834
Copiapó (Chile)

Cincinnati (Ohio)

Paraguay 27. 11. 1842

Paraguay

Turin

Cincinnati (Ohio)

Peru (Indiana)

Newark (New Jersey)

New-York

Ceará (Brasilien)

**Ein Stern,
sechszackig,
auch begleitet**

**Une étoile à six rais,
aussi accompagnée**

**One mullet of six
points, even
accompagnied, or
one estoile**

Kaufbeuren - Padua
Perleberg
Stargard in Pommern

Waldeck

Sizilien, Königreich

Sizilien, Königreich

Kähdah

Savoyen-Achaja,
Fürstentum (14. Jahrh.)

Bidschnagur

Orange

Northumberland

Padua

Schaumburg

Hessen, Landgrafschaft,
Variante

Hobart, Tasmanien

Bagdad
Marokko

Haleb (Syrien)

Ribe, Stadt (Dänemark)
Stargard in Pommern
Waldeck

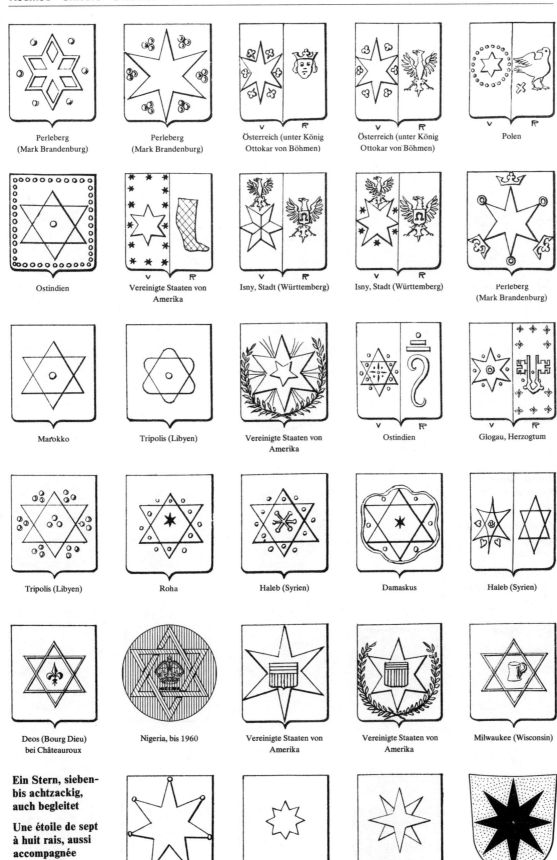

Perleberg (Mark Brandenburg)	Perleberg (Mark Brandenburg)
Österreich (unter König Ottokar von Böhmen)	Österreich (unter König Ottokar von Böhmen)
Polen	

Ostindien

Vereinigte Staaten von Amerika

Isny, Stadt (Württemberg)

Isny, Stadt (Württemberg)

Perleberg (Mark Brandenburg)

Marokko

Tripolis (Libyen)

Vereinigte Staaten von Amerika

Ostindien

Glogau, Herzogtum

Tripolis (Libyen)

Roha

Haleb (Syrien)

Damaskus

Haleb (Syrien)

Deos (Bourg Dieu) bei Châteauroux

Nigeria, bis 1960

Vereinigte Staaten von Amerika

Vereinigte Staaten von Amerika

Milwaukee (Wisconsin)

Ein Stern, sieben- bis achtzackig, auch begleitet

Une étoile de sept à huit rais, aussi accompagnée

One mullet of seven to eight points, even accompagnied

Venezuela

Hakeborn (bei Staßfurt)
Pomponesco
Waldeck

Pomponesco

Waldeck

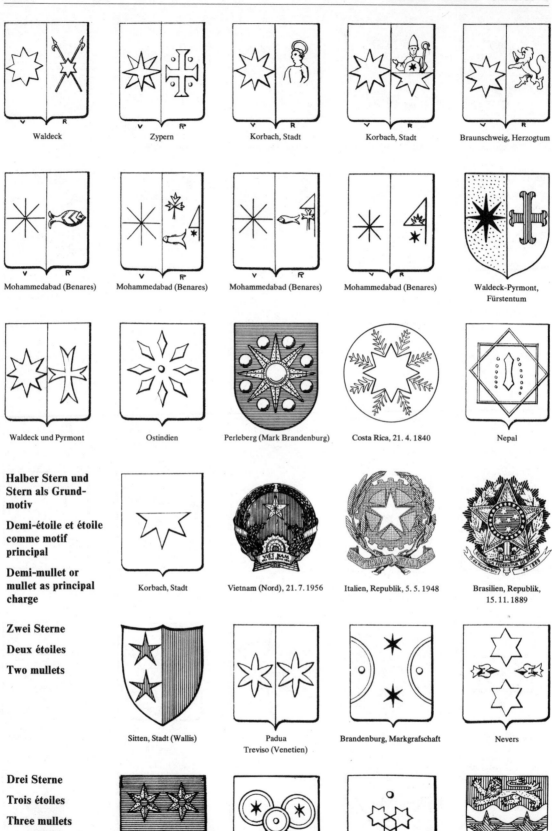

Waldeck

Zypern

Korbach, Stadt

Korbach, Stadt

Braunschweig, Herzogtum

Mohammedabad (Benares)

Mohammedabad (Benares)

Mohammedabad (Benares)

Mohammedabad (Benares)

Waldeck-Pyrmont, Fürstentum

Waldeck und Pyrmont

Ostindien

Perleberg (Mark Brandenburg)

Costa Rica, 21. 4. 1840

Nepal

Halber Stern und Stern als Grundmotiv

Demi-étoile et étoile comme motif principal

Demi-mullet or mullet as principal charge

Korbach, Stadt

Vietnam (Nord), 21. 7. 1956

Italien, Republik, 5. 5. 1948

Brasilien, Republik, 15. 11. 1889

Zwei Sterne

Deux étoiles

Two mullets

Sitten, Stadt (Wallis)

Padua
Treviso (Venetien)

Brandenburg, Markgrafschaft

Nevers

Drei Sterne

Trois étoiles

Three mullets

Norden (Ostfriesland)

Waldeck

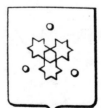

Perleberg (Mark Brandenburg)

Caymans-Inseln, 14. 5. 1958

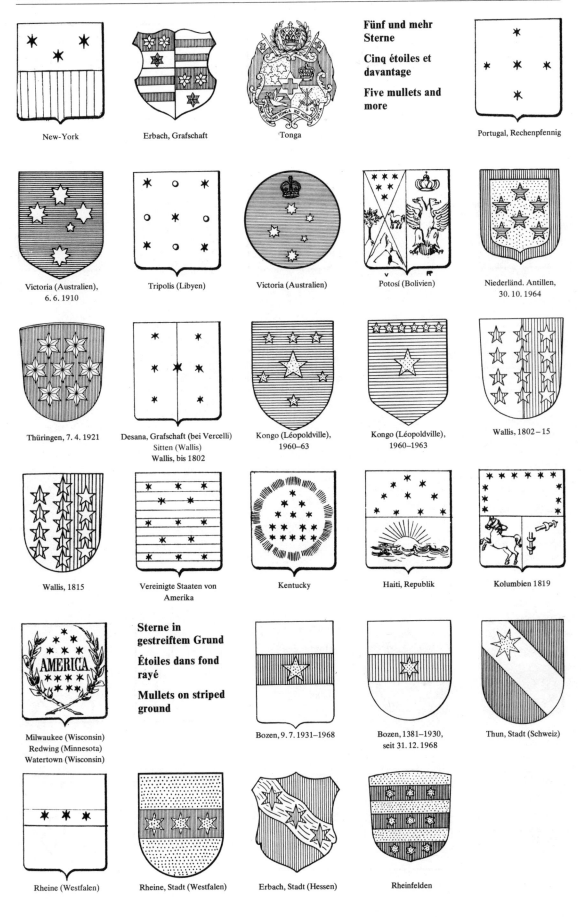

New-York

Erbach, Grafschaft

Tonga

Fünf und mehr Sterne

Cinq étoiles et davantage

Five mullets and more

Portugal, Rechenpfennig

Victoria (Australien),
6. 6. 1910

Tripolis (Libyen)

Victoria (Australien)

Potosí (Bolivien)

Niederländ. Antillen,
30. 10. 1964

Thüringen, 7. 4. 1921

Desana, Grafschaft (bei Vercelli)
Sitten (Wallis)
Wallis, bis 1802

Kongo (Léopoldville),
1960–63

Kongo (Léopoldville),
1960–1963

Wallis, 1802–15

Wallis, 1815

Vereinigte Staaten von
Amerika

Kentucky

Haiti, Republik

Kolumbien 1819

Milwaukee (Wisconsin)
Redwing (Minnesota)
Watertown (Wisconsin)

Sterne in gestreiftem Grund

Étoiles dans fond rayé

Mullets on striped ground

Bozen, 9. 7. 1931–1968

Bozen, 1381–1930,
seit 31. 12. 1968

Thun, Stadt (Schweiz)

Rheine (Westfalen)

Rheine, Stadt (Westfalen)

Erbach, Stadt (Hessen)

Rheinfelden

Berge

Montagnes et tertres

Mounts

Goldberg, Stadt (Schlesien)

Goldberg, Stadt (Schlesien)

Goldberg, Stadt (Schlesien)

Schaffhausen

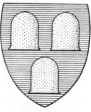

Gubbio

Gubbio

Breisach

Breisach

Monferrat, Markgrafschaft (Oberitalien)

Bühl, Stadt (Baden)

Landkarten

Cartes géographiques

Maps

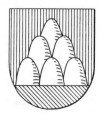

Bangladesch

Birma, 1947

Birma, 4. 1. 1974

Landschaften ohne Architektur

Paysage sans bâtiment

Landscape without buildings

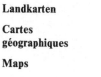

Alberta, Provinz (Kanada), 30. 5. 1907

Nepal, vor 1962

Lima (Peru)
Peru, Republik

La Paz (Bolivien)

Victoria (Australien)

Nepal, 16. 12. 1962

Gebirge

Montagnes rocheuses

Mountains and rocks

Guatemala
San Salvador

Sombrerete (Mexiko)

Potosí (Bolivien)

Potosí (Bolivien)

Chuquisaca (Bolivien), heute: Sucre
Yngavi (Bolivien)

Berge, besetzt und überhöht

Montagnes sommées ou surmontées

Mountains over-topped

Zacatecas (Mexiko)

Falun (Schweden)

Argentinische Republik

Famatima, Departement
in der Provinz La Rioja
La Rioja, argentinische
Provinz

San Salvador

San Salvador

San Salvador

Sachsen-Weimar-Eisenach

Sachsen-Weimar-Eisenach

Potosí (Bolivien)

Potosí (Bolivien)

**Berglandschaft mit
Tieren**

**Paysage
montagneux
avec des animaux**

**Landscape with
beasts**

Santiago de Chile

León de Nicaragua

Bolivien

Potosí (Bolivien)

Bolivien
Callao

Potosí (Bolivien)

Bolivien (Potosí)

La Paz

Cobija (bis 1883
Bolivien, seitdem Chile)

Socabaya (Peru)
Yanacocha

Bolivien, 26. 7. 1826

Bolivien
Socabaya (Peru)

Bolivien (Potosí)

Abtao (Bolivien)
Bolivien
Papudo (Chile)

Bolivien, 14. 7. 1888

Bolivien

Paraguay

Zwei Berge

Deux montagnes

Two rocks

Guatemala

Quezaltenango
(Guatemala)

Ecuador, 19. 9. 1830

**Drei Berge oder
Bergkette**

**Trois rochers et
chaine de
montagnes**

**Three rocks or
range of mountains**

Quito (Ecuador)

Costa Rica
Guatemala

Costa Rica

San Marino

Afghanistan, 1928

Costa Rica · Guatemala
Honduras · Nicaragua

Mittelamerika

Nicaragua

Guatemala, 17. 5. 1851

Huancavelica (Peru)

Vulkane

Volcans

Volcanoes

Coquimbo (Chile)
Santiago de Chile

San Salvador

San Salvador

San Salvador

Costa Rica
Guatemala
Valparaiso (Chile)

Chile, 9. 6. 1817

Chile, 9. 6. 1817

Chile, 9. 6. 1817

**Landschaft mit
Bauwerk**

**Paysage avec
bâtiments**

**Landscape with
buildings**

Yngavi (Bolivien)

Paucartambo

Mexiko, Stadt, 4. 7. 1523

Oruro (Bolivien)

Potosí (Bolivien)

Potosí (Bolivien)

Popayán (Kolumbien),
10. 11. 1558

Popayán (Kolumbien)

Honduras

Rumänien 10. 3. 1948

Rumänien 24. 9. 1952

Rumänien 21. 8. 1965

Geräte vor Gebirge im Hintergrund

Instruments sur fond montagneux

Tools surmounting mountainous background

Vermont (USA)

Irak, Königreich, 3. 3. 1931

Argentinien

Argentinien

Bolivien
Cobija (bis 1883 Bolivien, seitdem Chile)

Bolivien (Potosí)

Potosí (Bolivien)

Landschaft mit Wasser im Vordergrund

Paysage avec de l'eau au premier plan

Landscape with water in the foreground

New-York

Peru, Republik

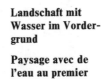

Lima (Peru)

Puerto Rico, 23. 12. 1901

New York, Staat

Ecuador, 6. 11. 1845

Ecuador, 6. 11. 1845

Sabah (Nordborneo), 1963

Nordborneo, 13. 9. 1948

Trinidad und Tobago, 13. 10. 1958

Trinidad und Tobago

Antigua (Westindien), bis 1967

Málaga, Stadt

Honduras

Tunis, 1536

St. Lucia, 1889–1907

Málaga, Stadt

Réunion, 7. 1. 1925

Korea (Nord)

**Wasser im Hinter-
grund, im Vorder-
grund Strand oder Kai**

**Eau dans le fond,
plage ou quai au
premier plan**

**Water in the back-
ground, strand or
quay in the fore-
ground**

Guam

Liberia

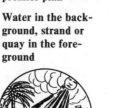

Tobago, 1880

Leeward-Inseln

Tobago, 1815

Liberia, 16. 7. 1847

Buenos Aires

Buenos Aires

Turks- & Caicos-Inseln

Hongkong

Falkland-Inseln

Seychellen

Cuzco (Peru)

Arequipa
Cuzco (Peru)

**Gebirge zwischen
Wasser**

**Montagnes entre
mers**

**Range of mountains
between seas**

Nicaragua, 5. 9. 1908
Nicaragua, 18. 8. 1971

El Salvador, 27. 5. 1912

Honduras

Costa Rica

Costa Rica, 27. 11. 1906

Costa Rica, 23. 10. 1964

Bogotá, Stadt
Kolumbien 9. 5. 1834
Medellín · Neugranada · Popayán

Panama, Republik 1904

Inseln

Iles

Isles

St. Helena

Kanarische Inseln

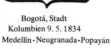

In dem umfangreichen Abschnitt, der den Lebewesen gewidmet ist, wird mit dem Menschen begonnen, worauf die Vierfüßler, vornean der Löwe mit seiner Variante, dem Leoparden, dann die Vögel, vornean der heraldische Adler, schließlich die niederen Tiere folgen.
In dem nachstehenden Inhaltsverzeichnis dieser Gruppe geben die links stehenden Ziffern an, unter welchem Ordnungsstichwort die verschiedenen Motive eingeordnet sind. Die Ziffern rechts geben die aufzuschlagende Seite an.

Mensch, stark stilisiert

Personne, fort stylisée

Person, deformed

Madras

Madras

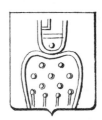
Schadragiri

Negapatam (Indien)

Mensch, aufrecht, ohne Attribut

Personne, debout, sans attribut

Person, upright, without attribute

New-York

Mensch aufrecht, Lebewesen tragend

Personne, debout, portant être vivant

Person upright, supporting living being

Wilna

Minsk

Glogau, Stadt

Perpignan
(Pyrénées Orientales)

Mensch, Stab haltend

Personne, tenant bâton

Person, bearing rod

Loccum, Abtei
(Niedersachsen)

Breslau, Bistum

Schlesien

Glarus, Kanton

Glarus, Kanton

St. Urban

Abuschehr

Hindustan
(Timuriden, Großmoguln)

Allenstein

Allenstein

Schlesien

Monnikendam
(Nordholland)

Mensch, Pflanze tragend

Personne, tenant plante

Person, bearing plant

Hannover,
Kurfürstentum, nach 1788

Hannover,
Kurfürstentum, vor 1788

Schlesien

Bolívar, Provinz
(Kolumbien), 1813

Mensch, Waffe(n) haltend

Personne, tenant arme(s)

Person, bearing weapon(s)

Chihuahua (Mexiko)

Callao

Monaco, Stadt

Kolumbien

Mensch, Fahne haltend

Personne, tenant drapeau

Person, holding flag

Eisenach, Stadt

Odense, Stadt (Dänemark)

Glückstadt

Glückstadt, 1617

Appleton (Wisconsin)

Beaver Dam (Wisconsin)
East Troy (Wisconsin)
Fond du Lac (Wisconsin)
Freeport (Illinois)
Mayfield (Wisconsin)
Milwaukee (Wisconsin)
Racine (Wisconsin)
Redwing (Minnesota)
Watertown (Wisconsin)

Mensch mit stabförmigem Gerät

Personne, tenant instrument en forme de bâton

Person, holding staffshaped tool

St. Christopher-Nevis-Anguilla,
4. 6. 1957

Montserrat (Westindien)

Trier, Stadt

Beuthen, Stadt (Oberschlesien)

Beuthen, Stadt (Oberschlesien)

Kap der Guten Hoffnung, Kapprovinz, 4. 5. 1911

Südafrika, Dominion, Republik, 17. 9. 1910

Mensch mit kleinem Attribut

Personne, portant attribut menu

Person, bearing tiny attribute

Hindustan
(Timuriden, Großmoguln)

Schlesien

München, Stadt

München, Stadt

München, Stadt

Mensch, tänzelnd

Personne, sautillant

Person, skipping

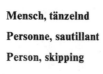

Bidschnagur

Bidschnagur

Mahiswar

Hindustan
(Timuriden, Großmoguln)

Hindustan
(Timuriden, Großmoguln)

**Mensch auf
Fußgestell**

Personne, soutenue

**Person, staying on
pedestal**

San Luis Potosí (Mexiko)

Barbados

Mensch, sitzend

Personne assise

Person seated

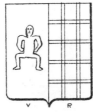

Bidschnagur

Ostindien

Lesotho
4. 10. 1966

Kolumbien

Kongo (Brazzaville), 1960

Norrköping (Schweden)

Drenthe
(niederländische Provinz)

Gotha, Stadt

Oslo

Guipuzcoa, Provinz (Spanien)

Sierra Leone, 30. 7. 1914

Holland

Mexiko, Erzbistum

Londonderry, Stadt
(Nordirland)

Reiter, unbewaffnet

Cavalier, sans armes

Rider, unarmed

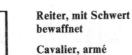

Neapel, Königreich
1555–59

**Reiter, mit Schwert
bewaffnet**

**Cavalier, armé
d'épée**

**Rider, provided
with sword**

Castiglione delle Stiviere
(Provinz Mantua)

Desana, Grafschaft
(bei Vercelli)

Schlesien

Münsterberg
(Schlesien), Herzogtum

Litauen

Litauen, Republik

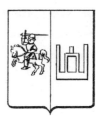

Litauen

Glogau,
Herzogtum, Poln. Anteil
Litauen

Ancona

Reiter mit Fahne

**Cavalier, tenant
drapeau**

**Rider, holding
standard**

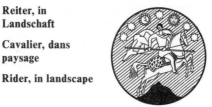

Wenden, Fürst Pribislav

Schwerin, Stadt
(Mecklenburg)

Marburg an der Lahn, Stadt
(Hessen)

Köslin, Stadt (Pommern)

**Reiter, in
Landschaft**

**Cavalier, dans
paysage**

Rider, in landscape

Georgien, Republik,
27. 12. 1918

Guatemala, 1532

Mongolische Volksrepublik
6. 7. 1960

Mongolische Volksrepublik
30. 6. 1940

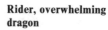

Zara (Zadar)

**Reiter, Drachen
tötend**

**Cavalier, foulant
dragon**

**Rider, overwhelming
dragon**

Moskau

Stein am Rhein, Stadt
(Kanton Schaffhausen)

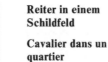

Rußland

**Reiter in einem
Schildfeld**

**Cavalier dans un
quartier**

**Rider on one
quarter**

Guatemala, 28. 7. 1532

Ancona

Polen

Isny, Stadt (Württemberg)

Rußland

Westfriesland

Polen

Oberhalber Mensch

Personne, naissant

Person, issuant

Schadragiri

Madras

Ikari (Mysore)

Tschad, Republik

Waldeck

Mutter mit Kind
Mère avec enfant
Mother with child

Gabun

Glogau, Stadt

Glogau, Herzogl. Anteil

Glogau, Stadt

Glogau, Stadt

Mensch mit Gerät
Personne, tenant instrument
Person, bearing tool

Bayern, Herzogtum

Guanajuato (Mexiko)

Salzburg, Domkapitel

Ungarn

Münster, Domkapitel

Münster, Domkapitel

Münster, Domkapitel

Mensch, etwas haltend, aus Figur hervorkommend
Personne, tenant meuble, issant de meuble
Person, bearing charge, issuant from charge

Korbach, Stadt

Korbach, Stadt

Lüben, Stadt (Schlesien)

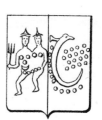

Lüdenscheid, Stadt (Westfalen)

Vereinigte Staaten von Amerika

St. Veit

Mensch, etwas tragend, aus Schildrand hervorkommend
Personne, portant meuble, mouvant de la pointe
Person, bearing charge, issuant from base

Österreich (Steiermark)

Zwei und mehr Personen
Deux personnes et davantage
Two and more persons

Hindustan
(Timuriden, Großmoguln)

Hindustan
(Timuriden, Großmoguln)

Mysore, Fürstentum (Indien)

Ikari (Mysore)

Neufundland

St. Vincent, 1889

St. Vincent, 1907

St. Vincent, 29. 11. 1912

Audh (Britisch-Indien)

Audh (Britisch-Indien)

Graubünden, 1803

Portonovo

Schadragiri

Araukanien und Patagonien

Menschengesicht

Tête humaine en face

Human head affronté

Indore

Weißensee (Thüringen)

Buchara

Halberstadt, Domkapitel

Glogau, Herzogtum

Glogau, Herzogtum

Glogau, Herzogtum

Breslau, Stadt

(missing label)
Breslau, Stadt

Breslau, Stadt

Breslau, Stadt

Breslau, Bistum

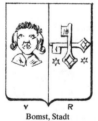
Bomst, Stadt
(ehem. Provinz Posen)

Köslin, Stadt (Pommern)

Kopf im Profil

Tête humaine de profil

Human head in profile

Coburg, Stadt   Gotha
Korsika · Weißenfels
Weißensee

Coburg, Stadt

Coburg, Pflege

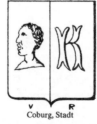
Coburg, Stadt

Gotha
Weißenfels

Kopf im Profil mit Stirnbinde oder Laubkranz

Tête humaine de profil tortillée ou couronnée de feuillage

Human head in profile, wreathed about the temples

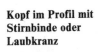

Glogau und Krossen

Pistoja

Korsika

Kopf mit Hut

Tête avec chapeau

Head with hat

Pfalz

Eisenach, Stadt

Meißen, Markgrafschaft

Eisenach, Stadt

Eisenach, Stadt

Heidenheim an der Brenz (Württemberg)

Leuchtenberg, Landgrafschaft

Leuchtenberg, Landgrafschaft

Eisenach, Stadt

Kopf mit Kapuze

Tête capuchonnée

Head with hood

München, Stadt

München, Stadt

Sagan für Posen

Nimbierter Kopf

Tête nimbée

Head with nimbus

Höxter, Stadt (Westfalen)

Breslau, Stadt

Halberstadt, Bistum
Metz, Stadt

Halberstadt, Domkapitel

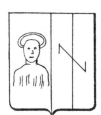

Halberstadt, Stadt

Breslau, Stadt

Halberstadt, Bistum

Haupt in Schüssel

Tête sur assiette

Head on dish

Künzelsau, Stadt
(Württemberg)
Teplitz (Böhmen)

Köslin, Stadt (Pommern)

Köslin, Stadt (Pommern)

Breslau, Stadt,
Johanniter-Orden
Köslin, Stadt (Pommern)

**Kopf, gekrönt,
hersehend**

**Tête en face,
couronnée**

**Human head
affronté, crowned**

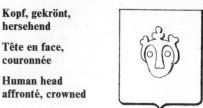

Greifswald

Nordhausen, Abtei

Königsberg/Neumark

Stockholm, Stadt

Stockholm, Oberstatthalteramt,
bis 1937

Stockholm, Oberstatthalteramt,
seit 28. 1. 1938

Kempten, Abtei

Kempten, Abtei

Schlesien

Ungarn

Schmalkalden (Thüringen)

Idem, im Profil

Idem, de profil

Idem, in profile

Lauingen/Donau,
Stadt (Bayern)
Weißensee (Thüringen)

München-Freising, Erzbistum

Barbados, Coburg, Stadt
Freising, Bistum, Lauingen

Schlesien

Barbados

Barbados

Tanger, 19. 8. 1938

**Menschenkopf,
begleitet**

**Tête humaine,
accompagnée**

**Human head,
accompagnied**

Konstanz, Bistum

Schlesien

Sancerre (Cher)

Coburg, Pflege

Erfurt

Schlesien

Österreich

Böhmen

St. Quentin, Stadt (Aisne)

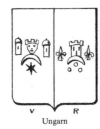

Kamerun, Republik

Ungarn

Brandenburg (Salzwedel)

Salzwedel, Grafschaft

Limoges

Tiengen im Klettgau

Doppelte und drei-fache Köpfe

Têtes, double et triple

Double and triple head

Lyck, Stadt (Ostpreußen)

Basel, Bistum

Österreich

Musocco und Musso
(Dynastie Trivulzio)

Trivulzio (Misox, Musocco)

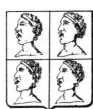

Sardinien, Königreich

Kopf in einem Schildfeld

Tête dans un quartier

Head on a quarter

Freising, Regensburg
und Lüttich, Bistümer

Musocco und Musso
(Dynastie Trivulzio)

Hand, leer

Main, nue

Hand, empty

Brandenburg, Markgrafschaft

Brandenburg, Markgrafschaft

Corvey, Abtei (Westfalen)
Deutschland (Esslingen)
Konstanz, Stadt
Langres, Bistum
Sens, Stadt (Yonne)

Belley (Ain)
Besançon, Stadt   Böhmen

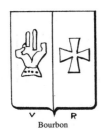

Bourbon

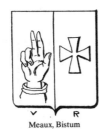

Meaux, Bistum

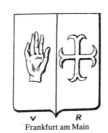

Frankfurt am Main

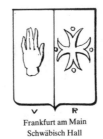

Frankfurt am Main
Schwäbisch Hall

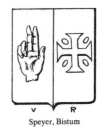

Speyer, Bistum

Besançon, Erzbistum

Rottenburg am Neckar
(Württemberg)

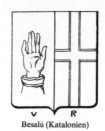

Besalú (Katalonien)

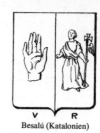

Besalú (Katalonien)

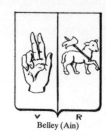

Belley (Ain)

Verdun, Bistum

Verdun, Bistum

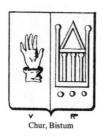

Chur, Bistum

Gascogne

York, Erzbistum (England)

Verdun, Bistum

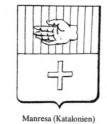

Manresa (Katalonien)

**Hand, aus Wolken
hervorkommend**

**Main, mouvant de
nuée ou arc-en-ciel**

**Hand, issuant from
clouds or rainbow**

York, Erzbistum (England)

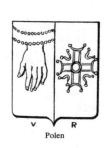

Polen

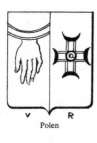

Polen

Berg, Herzogtum
Deutschland (Augsburg)

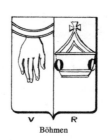

Böhmen

Deutschland (Deventer)

Deutschland (Deventer)

Böhmen

**Arm, mit leerer
Hand**

Bras, la main nue

**Arm, the hand
empty**

Seckau, Bistum (Österreich)

Graz-Seckau, Bistum

Costa Rica, 2.11.1824

Offene Hand, belegt

**Main ouverte,
chargée**

Open hand, charged

Kaufbeuren

Kaufbeuren

Schwäbisch Hall

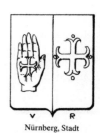

Nürnberg, Stadt

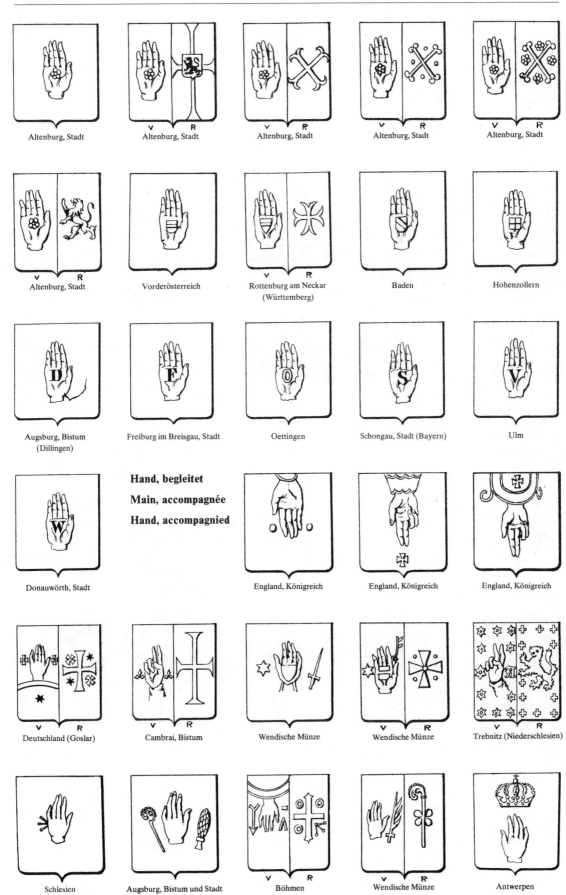

Altenburg, Stadt

Altenburg, Stadt

Altenburg, Stadt

Altenburg, Stadt

Altenburg, Stadt

Altenburg, Stadt

Vorderösterreich

Rottenburg am Neckar
(Württemberg)

Baden

Hohenzollern

Augsburg, Bistum
(Dillingen)

Freiburg im Breisgau, Stadt

Oettingen

Schongau, Stadt (Bayern)

Ulm

Hand, begleitet

Main, accompagnée

Hand, accompagnied

Donauwörth, Stadt

England, Königreich

England, Königreich

England, Königreich

Deutschland (Goslar)

Cambrai, Bistum

Wendische Münze

Wendische Münze

Trebnitz (Niederschlesien)

Schlesien

Augsburg, Bistum und Stadt

Böhmen

Wendische Münze

Antwerpen

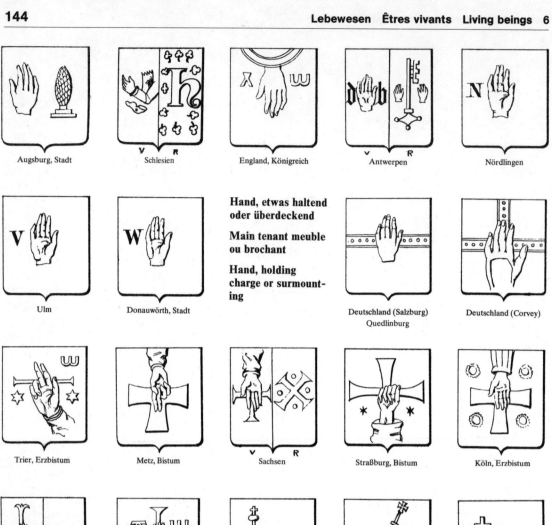

Augsburg, Stadt | Schlesien | England, Königreich | Antwerpen | Nördlingen

Ulm | Donauwörth, Stadt

Hand, etwas haltend oder überdeckend

Main tenant meuble ou brochant

Hand, holding charge or surmounting

Deutschland (Salzburg) Quedlinburg | Deutschland (Corvey)

Trier, Erzbistum | Metz, Bistum | Sachsen | Straßburg, Bistum | Köln, Erzbistum

Nürnberg, Stadt | Metz, Bistum | Michelsberg | Metz, Bistum / Trier, Erzbistum | Savigny, Abtei (Frankreich)

Venedig | Metz, Bistum | Deutschland (Quedlinburg) | Köln, Erzbistum | Metz, Bistum

Chur, Bistum | Meaux, Bistum | Cambrai, Bistum | Toul, Bistum | Cambrai, Bistum

Savigny, Abtei (Frankreich)

Böhmen

São Paulo, Stadt (Brasilien)

St.-Médard-de-Soissons, Abtei

Savoyen

Bosnien und Herzegowina

Massachusetts

Monferrat, Markgrafschaft (Oberitalien)

Spalato

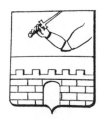

Elbogen, Stadt (Nordwestböhmen)

Siebenbürgen, Dynastie Barcsai

Siebenbürgen 1605–1683

Böhmen

Detroit (Michigan)

El Paso (Illinois)
Freeport (Illinois)
Grand Rapids (Michigan)
Hartford (Connecticut)
Illinois
Jackson (Michigan)
Kalamazoo (Michigan)
New-York
Peru (Illinois)
Racine (Wisconsin)
Ypsilanti (Michigan)

Mount Washington (New Hampshire)

Bolivien

Passau, Domkapitel

Louisville (Kentucky)

Zwei Hände
Deux mains
Two hands

Vereinigte Staaten von Amerika

Philadelphia (Pennsylvanien)

Córdoba (Argentinien)

Rio Grande, Stadt (Brasilien)

Buenos Aires
La Plata
La Rioja · Yanacocha

Argentinien

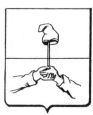

Argentinien

Salta (Argentinien)

Córdoba (Argentinien)

Potosí (Bolivien)

Sachsen-Lauenburg

Guanajuato (Mexiko)

Trier, Erzbistum

Trier, Erzbistum

Beine

Jambes

Legs

Schlesien

Füssen, Stadt (Bayern)

Sizilien

Insel Man

Insel Man

Sizilien

Auge

Oeil

Eye

Utah   Vereinigte Staaten von Amerika

Herz

Cœur

Heart

Ostindien

Elsaß

Toluca (Mexiko)

Potosí (Bolivien)

Potosí (Bolivien)

Pontianak (West-Borneo)

Java (unter holländischer
Herrschaft)

Benkulen (Sumatra,
Ostindische Kompanie), 1685

Pontianak (West-Borneo)

Pontianak (West-Borneo)

Rummen

Brehna

Rummen
Tecklenburg

Braunschweig,

Bentheim-Tecklenburg

Bentheim-Tecklenburg

Bentheim-Tecklenburg

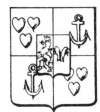

Bentheim-Tecklenburg

Bentheim-Tecklenburg

Bentheim-Tecklenburg

Bentheim-Tecklenburg

Bentheim-Tecklenburg

Wiborg, Bistum (Finnland)

Brehna

Bogenschießender Kentaur

Centaure sagittaire

Sagittary

England, König Stephan
(reg. 1135–1154),
apokryphes W.

Ortokiden zu Mardin

Hindustan
(Timuriden, Großmoguln)

Engel, ohne Attribut

Ange, sans attribut

Angel, without attribute

Trier, Erzbistum

Engelberg, Benediktinerkloster
(Kanton Unterwalden)

Brandenburg, Markgrafschaft

Liegnitz, Herzogtum

Brandenburg, Markgrafschaft

Hindustan
(Timuriden, Großmoguln)

Barby

Barby

Engel, Attribut haltend

Ange, tenant attribut

Angel, bearing attribute

Trier, Erzbistum

Straßburg, Bistum

Engelberg, Benediktinerkloster
(Kanton Unterwalden)

Polen

Hindustan
(Timuriden, Großmoguln)

Tabago

Engel, Drachen niedertretend

Ange, foulant dragon

Angel, overwhelming dragon

Brüssel, Stadt

Brüssel, Stadt

Brüssel, Stadt

Jena, Stadt

Zeitz, Stadt

Zwei Engel

Deux anges

Two angels

Äthiopien

Sirene (Seejungfer, Meerweib)

Sirène

Mermaid

Warschau, Stadt

Warschau, Stadt

Anguilla (Westindien), Juli 1967

Löwe, aufrecht

Lion rampant

Lion (rampant)

Aquitanien

Arnheim (Arnhem)
Arras
Artois
Atri
Audenarde (Oudenaarde),
Belgien
Batenburg
Belgien
Birma
Bologna, Stadt
Born, Herrschaft
Bozzolo

Brabant
Braunschweig, Stadt
Brescello
Bretagne
Burgund
Cambrai, Bistum
Coevorden, Stadt (Drenthe)
Desana
Diepholz
Elincourt
Elsloo
Fauquemont

Flandern
Franeker (Friesland)
Geldern
Gronsfeld
Guastalla
Guatemala
's-Heerenberg
Heinsberg
Henneberg
Herstal (Belgien)
Hessen
Hohenlimburg

Holland, Grafschaft
Hoorn
Jever, Herrschaft
Jülich, Herzogtum
Kastilien
Kleve
Kuinre, Grafschaft (Overijssel)
Kurland
Laufenburg (Oberrhein)
Leeuwarden
Ligny
Limbricht

Löwenberg (Schlesien)
Lohra
(spätere Grafschaft Hohenstein)
Loos
Lüneburg, Stadt
Luxemburg
Megen
Meißen-Sachsen
Mexiko
Mirandola
Mittweida, Stadt (Sachsen)
Namur (Belgien)

Nevers
Orange
Herren von
Randerad oder Randerath
Recanati
Reckheim
Rheda
Rummen
St.-Paul
San Benigno di Fruttuario
(Provinz Turin)
Schwarzburg (Thüringen)

Serbien
Sorau
Spanien
Stevensweert
Ueberlingen
Vorst
Weißensee (Thüringen)
Ypern
Zierikzee
Zütphen

Holland Laufenburg (Oberrhein)
Südholland, Provinz
Willisau, Kanton Luzern

Braunschweig, Stadt,
15. 10. 1438

Chioggia, Stadt
(Provinz Venedig)

Leeuwarden

Brescia, Stadt

Belgien
Brabant

Flandern
Jülich, Herzogtum
Meißen, Markgrafschaft

Bulgarien, Volksrepublik,
6. 12. 1947

Hessen, Bundesland
4. 8. 1948

Culemborg (Gelderland)

Diepholz
Geldern
Jülich, Stadt 1543
Loos
St.-Paul

Lünen, Stadt (Westfalen)

Gera, Stadt (Thüringen)
Vogtland

Leonberg, Stadt (Württemberg)

Broich

Diepholz
Flandern
Glatz
Hohenlimburg
Jülich, Herzogtum
Loos

Arnstadt, Stadt

Batenburg
Berg, Herzogtum
Desana, Grafschaft
(bei Vercelli)
Elsloo
Flandern
Geldern
Gronsfeld
's-Heerenberg
Herstal
Hessen
Hohenlimburg

Jever, Herrschaft
Laufenburg (Oberrhein)
Luxemburg
Mansfeld
Metz, Bistum
Namur
Pfalz, Kurfürstentum
Reuß
Rheda
Schmalkalden (Thüringen)
Schönau, freie Herrschaft
(bei Aachen)

Schwarzburg (Thüringen)
Stevensweert
Ueberlingen
Ungarn
Veldenz
Weert
(niederländ. Provinz Limburg)
Weißensee (Thüringen)
Zütphen (Gelderland)
Zypern

Saragossa, Stadt (Spanien)
Ventimiglia, Stadt (Italien)

Bulgarien,
Königreich, bis 1946

León, Königreich (Spanien)
León, Stadt (Spanien)
Wasserburg, Stadt

Habsburg, Grafschaft

Neustadt a. d. Weinstraße
Pfalz

Zypern

Hessen

's-Heerenberg, Herrschaft
(Grafschaft Zütphen)
Heidelberg · Pfalz, Kurfürstentum

Limburg, belgische Provinz

Rudolstadt (Thüringen)

Hessen
Thüringen, Landgrafschaft

Aspern

Böhmen
Chotieborsch, Stadt
(bei Pardubitz, Böhmen)
Diepholz
Falkenberg
Geldern
Görlitz
's-Heerenberg
Heinsberg
Jung Bunzlau
Limburg, Grafschaft
Loos · Sagan

Böhmen
Glatz, Stadt

Protektorat Böhmen und
Mähren, 19. 9. 1939
Tschechoslowakei, 19. 5. 1919

Geldern
Perwez (Belgien)

Gent, Stadt

Namur, Stadt (Belgien)

Bentheim-Rheda

**Löwe, im ersten von
drei Schilden**

**Lion, au premier de
trois écussons**

**Lion, on first of
three escutcheons**

Ueberlingen,
Ulm und Ravensburg

Pfalz-Simmern

Batenburg

Hessen

Geldern

Brabant,
Limburg und Luxemburg

Solms

Schwarzburg (Thüringen)

Breslau, Stadt

Böhmen

Böhmen

Pfalz-Veldenz

Batenburg

Batenburg

Pfalz- Zweibrücken

Gronsfeld, Grafschaft
(niederl. Provinz Limburg)

Gronsfeld, Grafschaft
(niederl. Provinz Limburg)

Geldern

Franquemont

Artois

Ueberlingen,
Ulm und Ravensburg

Schweden (für Finnland)

Breslau, Stadt

**Löwe, im ersten von
vier Schilden**

**Lion, au premier de
quatre écussons**

**Lion, on first of
four escutcheons**

Wien, Stadt 1529

Sachsen, Herzogtum

Essen, Abtei
Werden, Abtei

Hohenlimburg

Wien, Stadt 1529

Essen, Abtei
Werden, Abtei

Essen, Abtei
Werden, Abtei

Pfalz und Köln

Köln, Erzbistum (Hermann
von Hessen 1473/80–1508)

Pfalz und Köln

's-Heerenberg, Herrschaft
(Grafschaft Zütphen)
Jülich und Berg

's-Heerenberg, Herrschaft
(Grafschaft Zütphen)

Broich

Wien, Stadt 1529

Werden und Helmstedt, Abtei

**Löwe, im ersten von
fünf Schilden**

**Lion, au premier de
cinq écussons**

**Lion, on first of
five escutcheons**

Stevensweert
(niederl. Provinz Limburg)

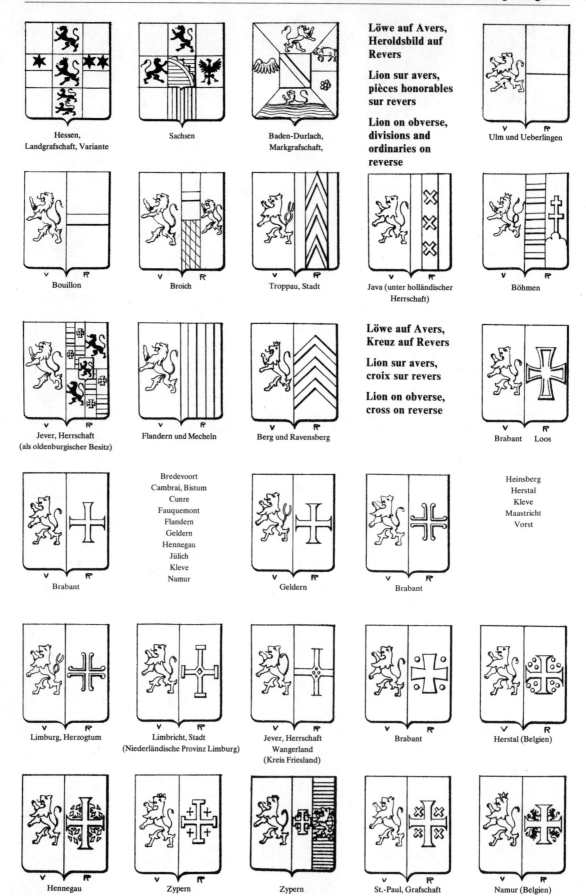

Hessen,
Landgrafschaft, Variante

Sachsen

Baden-Durlach,
Markgrafschaft,

**Löwe auf Avers,
Heroldsbild auf
Revers**

**Lion sur avers,
pièces honorables
sur revers**

**Lion on obverse,
divisions and
ordinaries on
reverse**

Ulm und Ueberlingen

Bouillon

Broich

Troppau, Stadt

Java (unter holländischer
Herrschaft)

Böhmen

Jever, Herrschaft
(als oldenburgischer Besitz)

Flandern und Mecheln

Berg und Ravensberg

**Löwe auf Avers,
Kreuz auf Revers**

**Lion sur avers,
croix sur revers**

**Lion on obverse,
cross on reverse**

Brabant   Loos

Brabant

Bredevoort
Cambrai, Bistum
Cunre
Fauquemont
Flandern
Geldern
Hennegau
Jülich
Kleve
Namur

Geldern

Brabant

Heinsberg
Herstal
Kleve
Maastricht
Vorst

Limburg, Herzogtum

Limbricht, Stadt
(Niederländische Provinz Limburg)

Jever, Herrschaft
Wangerland
(Kreis Friesland)

Brabant

Herstal (Belgien)

Hennegau

Zypern

Zypern

St.-Paul, Grafschaft

Namur (Belgien)

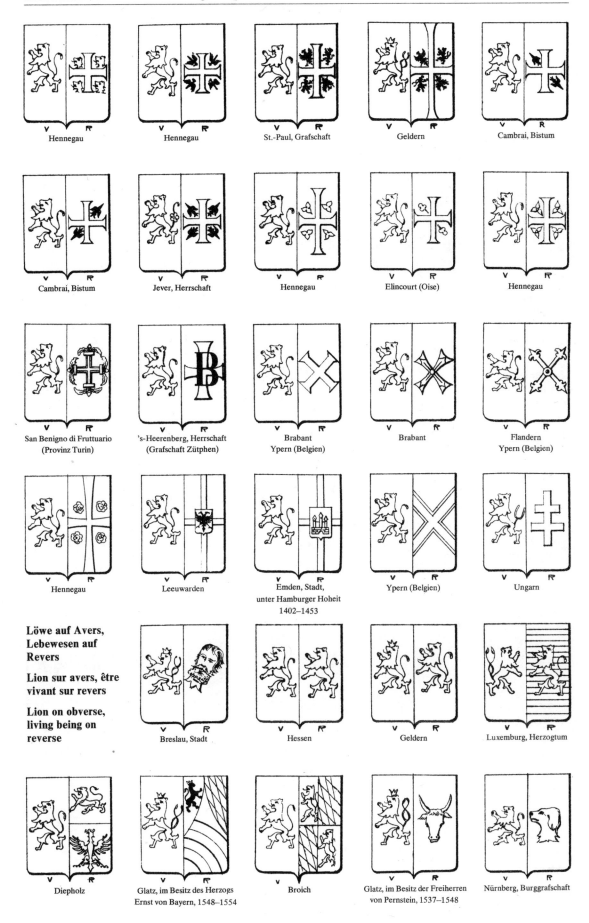

Hennegau

Hennegau

St.-Paul, Grafschaft

Geldern

Cambrai, Bistum

Cambrai, Bistum

Jever, Herrschaft

Hennegau

Elincourt (Oise)

Hennegau

San Benigno di Fruttuario
(Provinz Turin)

's-Heerenberg, Herrschaft
(Grafschaft Zütphen)

Brabant
Ypern (Belgien)

Brabant

Flandern
Ypern (Belgien)

Hennegau

Leeuwarden

Emden, Stadt,
unter Hamburger Hoheit
1402–1453

Ypern (Belgien)

Ungarn

**Löwe auf Avers,
Lebewesen auf
Revers**

**Lion sur avers, être
vivant sur revers**

**Lion on obverse,
living being on
reverse**

Breslau, Stadt

Hessen

Geldern

Luxemburg, Herzogtum

Diepholz

Glatz, im Besitz des Herzogs
Ernst von Bayern, 1548–1554

Broich

Glatz, im Besitz der Freiherren
von Pernstein, 1537–1548

Nürnberg, Burggrafschaft

Diepholz
Geldern

Hulhuisen
Jülich, Herzogtum
Nassau
Schwarzburg (Thüringen)
Ueberlingen

Diepholz

Glogau, Stadt

Breslau, Stadt

Kuinre, Grafschaft
(Overijssel)
St.-Paul, Grafschaft

Löwenberg (Schlesien)

Batenburg und Anholt
Leeuwarden
Namur (Belgien)

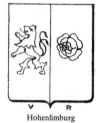

Böhmen

**Löwe auf Avers,
weitere Figuren auf
Revers**

**Lion sur avers,
d'autres meubles sur
revers**

**Lion on obverse,
other charges on
reverse**

Hohenlimburg

Guatemala
Mexiko, Königreich
Nicaragua · Potosí

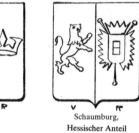

Lima (Peru)

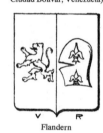

Guayana (Spanisch)
Angostura, Stadt (jetzt
Ciudad Bolívar, Venezuela)

Kastilien

Schweden

Böhmen

Schaumburg,
Hessischer Anteil

Flandern

Hessen-Kassel

Leiden

San Benigno di Fruttuario
(Provinz Turin)

Nürnberg, Burggrafschaft

Java
(unter holländischer Herrschaft)

Breslau, Stadt

**Löwe in geteiltem
Schild, oben**

**Lion, au 1 d'écu
coupé**

**Lion in chief of
shield per fess**

Braunschweig, Herzogtum
(W: Lauterberg)

Braunschweig, Herzogtum
(W: Hohenstein)

Zütphen (Gelderland)

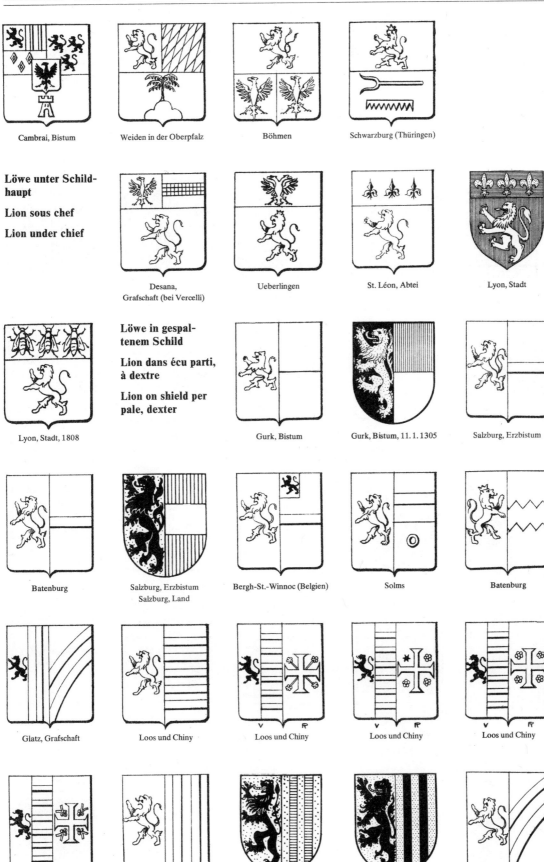

Cambrai, Bistum

Weiden in der Oberpfalz

Böhmen

Schwarzburg (Thüringen)

**Löwe unter Schild-
haupt**

Lion sous chef

Lion under chief

Desana,
Grafschaft (bei Vercelli)

Ueberlingen

St. Léon, Abtei

Lyon, Stadt

Lyon, Stadt, 1808

**Löwe in gespal-
tenem Schild**

**Lion dans écu parti,
à dextre**

**Lion on shield per
pale, dexter**

Gurk, Bistum

Gurk, Bistum, 11. 1. 1305

Salzburg, Erzbistum

Batenburg

Salzburg, Erzbistum
Salzburg, Land

Bergh-St.-Winnoc (Belgien)

Solms

Batenburg

Glatz, Grafschaft

Loos und Chiny

Loos und Chiny

Loos und Chiny

Loos und Chiny

Brabant

Dresden, Stadt
Leipzig, Stadt
Sachsen, Herzogtum

Leipzig, Stadt

Dresden, Stadt

Glatz, Grafschaft

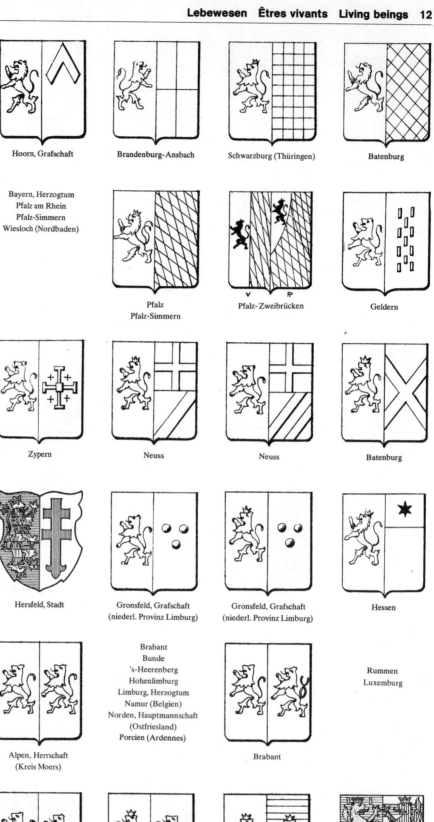

Masserano,
Fürstentum (Piemont)

Hoorn, Grafschaft

Brandenburg-Ansbach

Schwarzburg (Thüringen)

Batenburg

Amberg, Stadt

Bayern, Herzogtum
Pfalz am Rhein
Pfalz-Simmern
Wiesloch (Nordbaden)

Pfalz
Pfalz-Simmern

Pfalz-Zweibrücken

Geldern

Geldern

Zypern

Neuss

Neuss

Batenburg

Batenburg

Hersfeld, Stadt

Gronsfeld, Grafschaft
(niederl. Provinz Limburg)

Gronsfeld, Grafschaft
(niederl. Provinz Limburg)

Hessen

Altenburg, Stadt

Alpen, Herrschaft
(Kreis Moers)

Brabant
Bunde
's-Heerenberg
Hohenlimburg
Limburg, Herzogtum
Namur (Belgien)
Norden, Hauptmannschaft
(Ostfriesland)
Porcien (Ardennes)

Brabant

Rummen
Luxemburg

Gelderland

Luxemburg, Herzogtum

Geldern
Jülich und Berg

Luxemburg, Herzogtum

Luxemburg,
Erbgroßherzog Jean, 1953

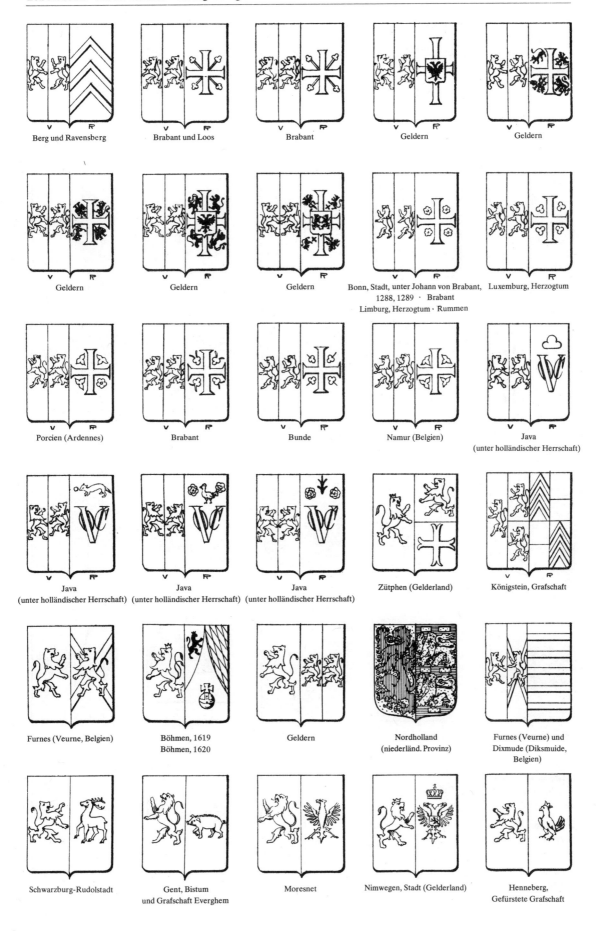

Berg und Ravensberg

Brabant und Loos

Brabant

Geldern

Geldern

Geldern

Geldern

Geldern

Bonn, Stadt, unter Johann von Brabant,
1288, 1289 · Brabant
Limburg, Herzogtum · Rummen

Luxemburg, Herzogtum

Porcien (Ardennes)

Brabant

Bunde

Namur (Belgien)

Java
(unter holländischer Herrschaft)

Java
(unter holländischer Herrschaft)

Java
(unter holländischer Herrschaft)

Java
(unter holländischer Herrschaft)

Zütphen (Gelderland)

Königstein, Grafschaft

Furnes (Veurne, Belgien)

Böhmen, 1619
Böhmen, 1620

Geldern

Nordholland
(niederländ. Provinz)

Furnes (Veurne) und
Dixmude (Diksmuide,
Belgien)

Schwarzburg-Rudolstadt

Gent, Bistum
und Grafschaft Everghem

Moresnet

Nimwegen, Stadt (Gelderland)

Henneberg,
Gefürstete Grafschaft

Henneberg,
Gefürstete Grafschaft

Senegal, 1965

Hohenlimburg
Solms

Jülich, Stadt

Ipswich

Pfalz und Mainz

Schwarzburg (Thüringen)

Franeker, Stadt
(niederländische Provinz
Friesland)

Scheer (Württemberg)

Henneberg,
Gefürstete Grafschaft

Solms

**Löwe neben
Spitzenteilung**

**Lion chargeant
chapé**

**Lion on shield per
pale and per
chevron**

Pfalz, Kurfürstentum

Glatz, im Besitz des
Herzogs Ernst von Bayern,
1548–1554

Pfalz-Simmern

Bayern, Kurfürstentum

Pfalz, Kurfürstentum

Hessen-Nassau,
preuß. Provinz

**Löwe in anders
dreigeteiltem
Schilde**

Lion dans écu tiercé

**Lion on tierced
shield**

Geldern

Jülich, Kleve und Berg

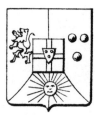

Gronsfeld, Grafschaft
(niederl. Provinz Limburg)

Gronsfeld, Grafschaft
(niederl. Provinz Limburg)

Correggio

Modena, 1814–1860

**Löwe in geviertem
Schild, in Feld 2:
Heroldsbild**

**Lion dans écu
écartelé, au 2: pièce
honorable**

**Lion on quartered
shield, on second
quarter: ordinary**

Kampen, Stadt (Overijssel)
Solms-Lich
Solms-Hohensolms-Lich

Solms-Lich

Löwenstein, Grafschaft

Herford, Abtei, Äbtissin Anna II.
Gräfin von Limburg 1520–1565
Salzburg, Erzbistum

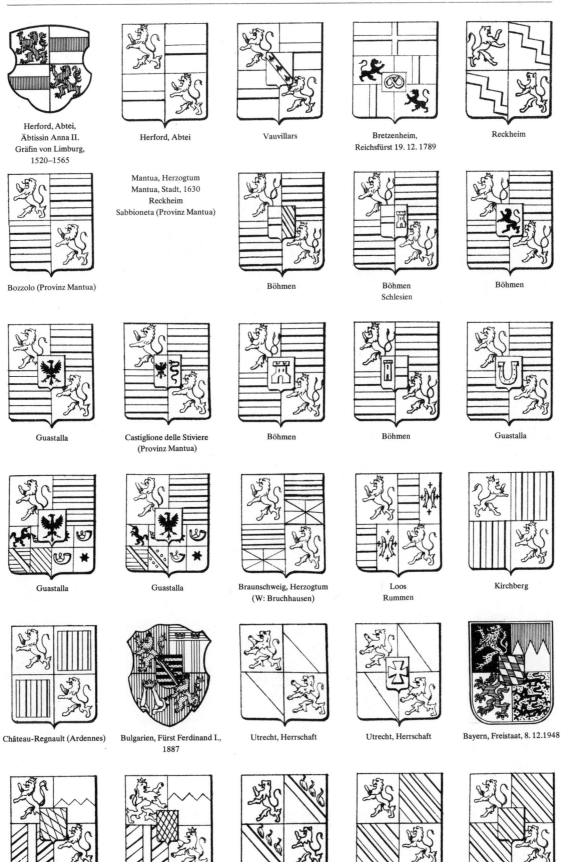

Herford, Abtei,
Äbtissin Anna II.
Gräfin von Limburg,
1520–1565

Herford, Abtei

Vauvillars

Bretzenheim,
Reichsfürst 19. 12. 1789

Reckheim

Mantua, Herzogtum
Mantua, Stadt, 1630
Reckheim
Sabbioneta (Provinz Mantua)

Bozzolo (Provinz Mantua)

Böhmen

Böhmen
Schlesien

Böhmen

Guastalla

Castiglione delle Stiviere
(Provinz Mantua)

Böhmen

Böhmen

Guastalla

Guastalla

Guastalla

Braunschweig, Herzogtum
(W: Bruchhausen)

Loos
Rummen

Kirchberg

Château-Regnault (Ardennes)

Bulgarien, Fürst Ferdinand I.,
1887

Utrecht, Herrschaft

Utrecht, Herrschaft

Bayern, Freistaat, 8. 12. 1948

Bayern, Königreich,
18. 10. 1835

Bayern, Königreich, 1835
Variante

Reckheim

Masserano,
Fürstentum (Piemont)

Masserano,
Fürstentum (Piemont)
Pomponesco

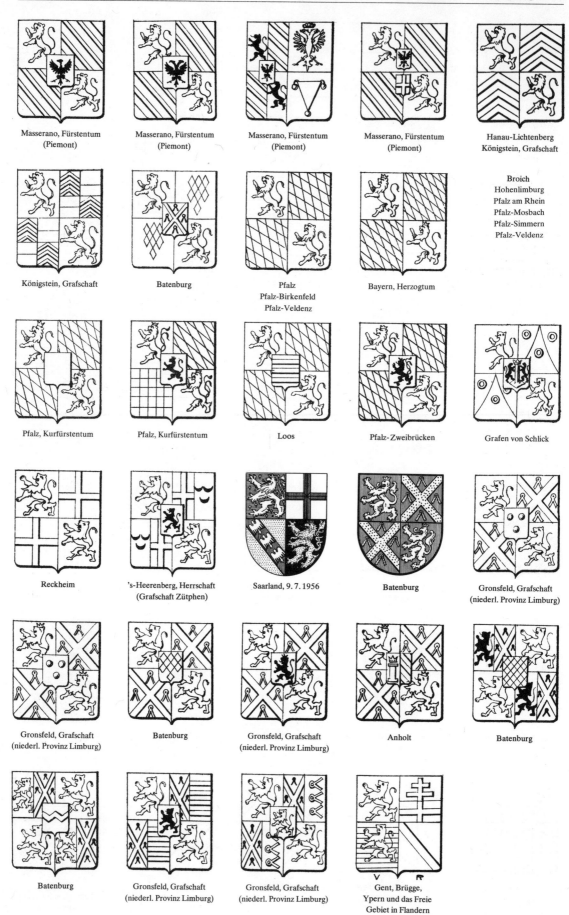

Masserano, Fürstentum (Piemont)

Masserano, Fürstentum (Piemont)

Masserano, Fürstentum (Piemont)

Masserano, Fürstentum (Piemont)

Hanau-Lichtenberg Königstein, Grafschaft

Broich
Hohenlimburg
Pfalz am Rhein
Pfalz-Mosbach
Pfalz-Simmern
Pfalz-Veldenz

Königstein, Grafschaft

Batenburg

Pfalz
Pfalz-Birkenfeld
Pfalz-Veldenz

Bayern, Herzogtum

Pfalz, Kurfürstentum

Pfalz, Kurfürstentum

Loos

Pfalz-Zweibrücken

Grafen von Schlick

Reckheim

's-Heerenberg, Herrschaft (Grafschaft Zütphen)

Saarland, 9. 7. 1956

Batenburg

Gronsfeld, Grafschaft (niederl. Provinz Limburg)

Gronsfeld, Grafschaft (niederl. Provinz Limburg)

Batenburg

Gronsfeld, Grafschaft (niederl. Provinz Limburg)

Anholt

Batenburg

Batenburg

Gronsfeld, Grafschaft (niederl. Provinz Limburg)

Gronsfeld, Grafschaft (niederl. Provinz Limburg)

Gent, Brügge, Ypern und das Freie Gebiet in Flandern

Löwe in geviertem Schild, in Feld 2: Sterne

Lion dans écu écartelé, au 2: étoiles

Lion on quartered shield, on second quarter: mullets

Château-Regnault (Ardennes)

Hessen

Hessen, Landgrafschaft bis 1567
Hessen-Darmstadt, 1567–1642

Hessen, Landgrafschaft, Variante

Löwe in geviertem Schild, in Feld 2: Herzen

Lion dans écu écartelé, au 2: cœurs

Lion on quartered shield, on second quarter: hearts

Braunschweig, Herzogtum

Löwe in geviertem Schild, in Feld 2: Vierfüßler und deren Teile

Lion dans écu écartelé, au 2: quadrupèdes et leurs parties

Lion on quartered shield, on second quarter: quadrupeds and parts thereof

Solms-Hohensolms-Lich
Solms

Hanau, Grafschaft

Jülich und Berg

Baden, Kurfürstentum,
2. 5. 1803

Gent, Brügge,
Ypern und das Freie
Gebiet in Flandern

Braunschweig, Herzogtum

Nassau

Berg
Brabant

Frankfurt an der Oder
Friedland und Sagan,
Geldern
's-Heerenberg
Heinsberg
Hennegau
Herstal
Holland
Holland und Hennegau

Franeker
Jülich, Herzogtum
Mainz, Erzbistum
Mons
Namur
Rummen
St.-Paul
Thoren, Abtei
Veldenz

Hennegau, Belgische Provinz

Jülich und Berg

Berg, Herzogtum
Brabant und Limburg
Heinsberg, Herrschaft

Heinsberg, Herrschaft
(Niederrhein)

Anholt · Geldern
Heinsberg, Herrschaft (Niederrhein)
Luxemburg, Herzogtum

Heinsberg, Herrschaft
(Niederrhein)
Loos

Wallenstein

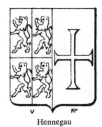

Hennegau

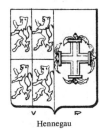

Hennegau

Hennegau

Ravenstein

Jülich und Berg

Löwenstein, Grafschaft

Thoren, Abtei

Braunschweig,
Herzogtum, 1419

Brabant

's-Heerenberg, Herrschaft
(Grafschaft Zütphen)

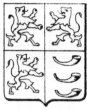

Hoorn, Grafschaft

Sachsen-Coburg und Gotha

Sachsen-Weimar-Eisenach

Sachsen-Weimar-Eisenach

Hoorn, Grafschaft

Limburg,
niederländ. Provinz

Hoorn, Grafschaft
Weert (niederländ.
Provinz Limburg)

Luxemburg, Herzogtum

Böhmen-Luxemburg

Vianen (Südholland)

Armagnac, Grafschaft

Österreich

Ungarn

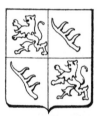

Braunschweig, Herzogtum

Kurland

Bretagne

Iglau (Mähren)

**Löwe in geviertem
Schild, in Feld 2:
Vögel und deren Teile**

**Lion dans écu
écartelé, au 2:
oiseaux et leurs
parties**

**Lion on quartered
shield, on second
quarter: birds and
parts thereof**

Castiglione delle Stiviere
(Provinz Mantua)

Sachsen

Sachsen

Westfriesland (Statthalter
aus dem Hause Sachsen)

Westfriesland (Statthalter
aus dem Hause Sachsen)

Westfriesland (Statthalter
aus dem Hause Sachsen)

Jägerndorf, Herzogtum
unter brandenburgischer
Herrschaft (ab 1523)

Bozzolo · Elincourt
Kuinre, Grafschaft (Overijssel)
Luxemburg · St.-Paul

Protektorat Böhmen und
Mähren, 19. 9. 1939

Elincourt (Oise)
St.-Paul, Grafschaft

Sachsen-Coburg-Saalfeld

Zittau ·

Breslau, Stadt, 1530

Correggio

Batenburg

Masserano, Fürstentum
(Piemont)

Löwenstein-Wertheim-
Virneburg, Grafschaft

Reuß, Fürstentum

Reuß, Fürstentum

Reuß, Fürstentum

Reuß, Fürstentum

Sachsen-Meiningen

Baden-Durlach,
Markgrafschaft

Baden-Durlach,
Markgrafschaft, 1527

Baden-Durlach,
Markgrafschaft, 1527

**Löwe in geviertem
Schild, in Feld 2:
Pflanzen**

**Lion dans écu
écartelé, au 2:
plantes**

**Lion on quartered
shield, on second
quarter: plants**

Desana, Grafschaft
(bei Vercelli)

Baden-Durlach,
Markgrafschaft

Solms

Zaltbommel
(Prov. Gelderland)

Aquitanien

Namur (Belgien)

Flandern, unter
burgundischer Herrschaft,
1404

Gascogne

**Löwe in geviertem
Schild, in Feld 2:
Bauwerke**

**Lion dans écu
écartelé, au 2:
édifices**

**Lion on quartered
shield, on second
quarter: buildings**

Caracas (Venezuela),
1811–1820
Spanien

Sagan, Stadt

Löwe in geviertem Schild, in Feld 2: Geräte

Lion dans écu écartelé, au 2: instruments

Lion on quartered shield, on second quarter: tools

Tegucigalpa (Honduras)

Guatemala, nach 1701
Mexiko, Königreich (span. Vizekönigreich)
Nicaragua

Manila

Schweden

Franeker, Stadt (niederländische Provinz Friesland)

Hoorn, Grafschaft

Gronsfeld, Grafschaft
(niederl. Provinz Limburg)

Sachsen-Coburg

Mainz und Pfalz

Löwe in schräg-geviertem Grund

Lion dans fond écartelé en sautoir

Lion on ground per saltire

Löwe innerhalb Bordes

Lion entouré de bordure

Lion between bordure

Hennegau

Brescello

Soissons

Brandenburg-Ansbach

Brandenburg-Ansbach

Nürnberg, Burggrafschaft

Jägerndorf, Herzogtum
unter brandenburgischer
Herrschaft (ab 1523)

Jägerndorf, Herzogtum
unter brandenburgischer
Herrschaft (ab 1523)

Boxmèer (Nordbrabant)
Stevensweert
(niederl. Provinz Limburg)

's-Heerenberg, Herrschaft
(Grafschaft Zütphen)
Stevensweert (niederl. Provinz Limburg)

Stevensweert
(niederl. Provinz Limburg)

Richard von Cornwall,
zum römischen König gewählt
1257, † 1272.

's-Heerenberg, Herrschaft
(Grafschaft Zütphen)

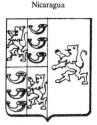

's-Heerenberg, Herrschaft
(Grafschaft Zütphen)

's-Heerenberg, Herrschaft
(Grafschaft Zütphen)

's-Heerenberg, Herrschaft
(Grafschaft Zütphen)

's-Heerenberg, Herrschaft
(Grafschaft Zütphen)

's-Heerenberg, Herrschaft
(Grafschaft Zütphen)

Poitiers, Stadt

Oaxaca, Stadt
(Mexiko) (1812)

Cartago (Costa Rica),
17. 8. 1565

Cochabamba (Bolivien)

Mecheln, Erzbistum
Schottland

Schottland

Schottland

Schottland 1515–1524

Hohenzollern-Hechingen

**Löwe in mit Kugeln
bestreutem Felde**

**Lion dans écu semé
de disques**

**Lion on shield semé
of roundles**

Desana, Grafschaft
(bei Vercelli)

Desana, Grafschaft
(bei Vercelli)

Orlamünde

s-Heerenberg, Herrschaft
(Grafschaft Zütphen)

's-Heerenberg, Herrschaft
(Grafschaft Zütphen)

Desana, Grafschaft
(bei Vercelli)

**Löwe in mit Schin-
deln bestreutem
Feld**

**Lion dans écu
billetté**

**Lion on shield
billety**

Burgund, Grafschaft
Geldern 1202–1326

Nevers, Stadt

Burgund, Grafschaft
Nassau

Franche Comté

Nassau, Herzogtum

Nevers, Stadt

Geldern

Burgund, Grafschaft

Nevers, Stadt

Nassau

Geldern

Geldern

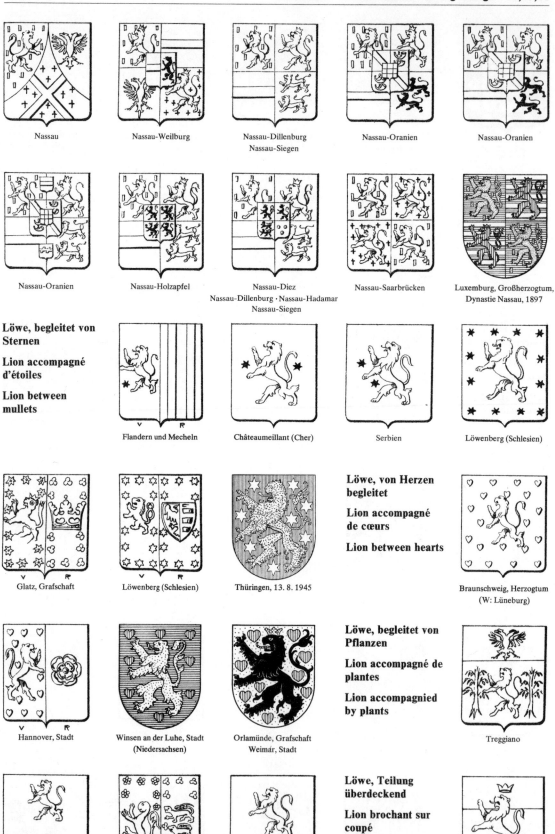

Nassau

Nassau-Weilburg

Nassau-Dillenburg
Nassau-Siegen

Nassau-Oranien

Nassau-Oranien

Nassau-Oranien

Nassau-Holzapfel

Nassau-Diez
Nassau-Dillenburg · Nassau-Hadamar
Nassau-Siegen

Nassau-Saarbrücken

Luxemburg, Großherzogtum,
Dynastie Nassau, 1897

**Löwe, begleitet von
Sternen**

**Lion accompagné
d'étoiles**

**Lion between
mullets**

Flandern und Mecheln

Châteaumeillant (Cher)

Serbien

Löwenberg (Schlesien)

Glatz, Grafschaft

Löwenberg (Schlesien)

Thüringen, 13. 8. 1945

**Löwe, von Herzen
begleitet**

**Lion accompagné
de cœurs**

Lion between hearts

Braunschweig, Herzogtum
(W: Lüneburg)

Hannover, Stadt

Winsen an der Luhe, Stadt
(Niedersachsen)

Orlamünde, Grafschaft
Weimár, Stadt

**Löwe, begleitet von
Pflanzen**

**Lion accompagné de
plantes**

**Lion accompagnied
by plants**

Treggiano

Tarma (Peru)

Glogau, Herzogin Mechtild
von Braunschweig, † 1318

Hannover, Stadt

**Löwe, Teilung
überdeckend**

**Lion brochant sur
coupé**

**Lion surmounting
per fess**

Desana, François de Mareuil,
Seigneur de Montereau,
Verwalter

Löwe, Querstreifung überdeckend

Lion, brochant sur burelé

Lion, surmounting barry

Audenarde (Oudenaarde), Belgien	Luxemburg, Herzogtum	Luxemburg, Großherzogtum	Gent, Stadt

Brügge, Stadt	Luxemburg, Herzogtum	Luxemburg, Herzogtum	Brügge, Stadt (Belgien)	Luxemburg, Herzogtum

Luxemburg, Herzogtum Mähren	Luxemburg, Erbgroßherzog Jean, 1948	Luxemburg, Herzogtum	Luxemburg und Bar, gemeinschaftlich	Brescello

Löwe, von Schräg-balken überdeckt

Lion, à la bande brochante

Lion surmounted by bend

Bamberg, Bistum Namur, belgische Provinz	Bamberg, Bistum	Namur, belgische Provinz	Bamberg, Bistum

Namur, Grafschaft	Gennep (niederl. Provinz Limburg)	Namur (Belgien)	Namur (Belgien)	Castiglione delle Stiviere (Provinz Mantua)

  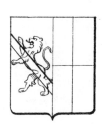 

Friedberg, Burggrafschaft (Hessen)	Mansfeld, Grafschaft	Mansfeld, Grafschaft	Bamberg, Bistum, und Nürnberg, Burggrafschaft	Bamberg und Würzburg, Bistümer

Bamberg, Bistum, und
Nürnberg, Burggrafschaft

Bamberg, Würzburg, Bistümer,
und
Nürnberg, Burggrafschaft

Bamberg und Würzburg,
Bistümer

Fränkischer (Reichs-)Kreis

**Löwe und Wellen-
balken**

**Lion et fasce
(barres) ondées**

**Lion and fess
(bends) wavy**

Overijssel, niederl. Provinz

Overijssel, niederl. Provinz

Overijssel, niederl. Provinz

Schweden

**Löwe und Turnier-
kragen**

Lion et lambel

Lion and label

Geldern
Nevers, Grafschaft
Vierzon (Cher)

Zweibrücken, Stadt
(Rheinland-Pfalz)

Ligny, Grafschaft (Frankreich)

Brederode

Manderscheid und
Blankenheim

Vianen (Südholland)

Vianen (Südholland)

Vianen (Südholland)

Vianen (Südholland)

**Löwe mit Brust-
schild**

**Lion avec écusson
sur l'épaule**

**Lion bearing
escutcheon on chest**

Elsloo

Zwolle, Stadt (Overijssel)

Emden, Häuptlingschaft

Tschechoslowakei,
30. 3. 1920

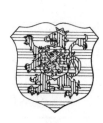

Heinsberg, Herrschaft
(Niederrhein)

Bulgarien, König Ferdinand I.
(1908–18)

Tschechoslowakei,
17. 11. 1960

Luxemburg, Großherzogtum,
Dynastie Nassau, 1890–1897

Böhmen 1619, 1620

Luxemburg, Herzogtum

Reckheim

Rummen

Luxemburg, Herzogtum

Luxemburg, Herzogtum

Hohenlimburg

Arras, Stadt
Artois

Arras, Stadt

Bulgarien, König Ferdinand I.
(1908–18)

Löwe und Sonne

Lion et soleil

Lion and sun

Sievas

Seldschuken (Iconium)

Penahabad

Hindustan (Timuriden,
Großmoguln)

Hindustan (Timuriden,
Großmoguln)
Ispahan · Täbris

Eriwan (Kaukasus)
Schemachá

Ispahan

Penahabad

Täbris

Schiras

Ispahan
Kabul

Ispahan

Thairan

Persien (Eriwan)

Persien (Eriwan)
Persien (Teheran)

Persien

Iran

Iran, 1955

Löwe und zweiter Vierfüßler

Lion et autre quadrupède

Lion and other quadruped

Herat (Afghanistan)

Tiflis (Kaukasus)

Kaschan (Persien)

Ispahan
Qom oder Kum (Persien)

Qom oder Kum (Persien)

Qom oder Kum (Persien)

Löwe und Adler

Lion et aigle

Lion and eagle

Flandern und Brabant
Holland
Luxemburg, Herzogtum

Namur (Belgien)

Holland

Kujavien, Landschaft

Kujavien, Landschaft

Löwe und Ring

Lion et annelet

Lion and annulet

Weißenau, Abtei
(Württemberg)

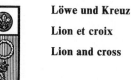

Kapland, Kap der Guten
Hoffnung, Kapkolonie,
22. 5. 1876

Löwe und Kreuz

Lion et croix

Lion and cross

Batenburg

Äthiopien nach europäischer
Vorstellung 19. Jh.

Äthiopien nach europäischer
Vorstellung seit 17. Jh.

Hersfeld, Stadt

Thüringen, 15. 8. 1933

Löwe und Pflanze

Lion et plante

Lion and plant

Pesaro

Hannover, Stadt

Serbien

Löwe und Bauwerk

Lion et édifice

Lion and buiding

Göttingen , Stadt

Grafen von Schlick

Grafen von Schlick

Grafen von Schlick

Lüneburg, Stadt

Meißen, Stadt

Saulgau, Stadt (Württemberg)

Saulgau, Stadt (Württemberg)

Löwe und Krone

Lion et couronne

Lion and crown (coronet)

Schaumburg,
Hessischer Anteil

Castiglione delle Stiviere
(Provinz Mantua)

Hessen-Kassel

Elbing,
unter schwedischer Herrschaft

Löwe, Stock haltend

Lion tenant bâton

Lion bearing rod

St.-Paul, Grafschaft

Mirandola, Fürstentum

Holland

Holland

Löwe, Schildchen haltend

Lion, tenant écusson

Lion, holding escutcheon

Lüttich, Bistum

Kampen, Stadt (Overijssel)

Braunschweig, Herzogtum
Meißen, Markgrafschaft

Pfalz

Frankenthal, Stadt
(Rheinpfalz), 27. 11. 1954

Caracas (Venezuela)

San Giorgio und Polistina
(Kalabrien)

Caracas (Venezuela)

Caracas (Venezuela)

Sagan, Herzogtum
(Herzogin Mathilde von
Braunschweig, † 1318)

Sagan, Herzogtum
(Herzogin Elisabeth
von Braunschweig)

Hessen, Schildchen: Nidda

Vianen (Südholland)

's-Heerenberg, Herrschaft
(Grafschaft Zütphen)

's-Heerenberg, Herrschaft
(Grafschaft Zütphen)

Neckargemünd

Nimwegen, Stadt (Gelderland)

Rosenheim

Broich

Arras, Stadt

Kampen, Stadt (Overijssel)

Lüttich, Bistum

San Benigno di Fruttuario
(Provinz Turin)

Abertham

Königgrätz, Stadt (Böhmen)

Löwe, Fahne haltend

Lion tenant drapeau

Lion bearing flag

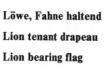

Brederode
Guastalla
Novellara (Provinz Reggio)
St.-Paul, Grafschaft
Solferino
Venedig

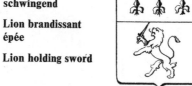

Bologna, Stadt und Herrschaft

Bologna, Erzbistum

**Löwe, Schwert
schwingend**

**Lion brandissant
épée**

Lion holding sword

Venedig

Lyon, Stadt

Castiglione delle Stiviere
(Provinz Mantua) · Flandern
Zaltbommel (Prov. Gelderland)

Ueberlingen

Geldern

Ueberlingen

Ueberlingen

Hessen, Großherzogtum,
29. 7. 1808

Hessen, Großherzogtum,
9. 12. 1902

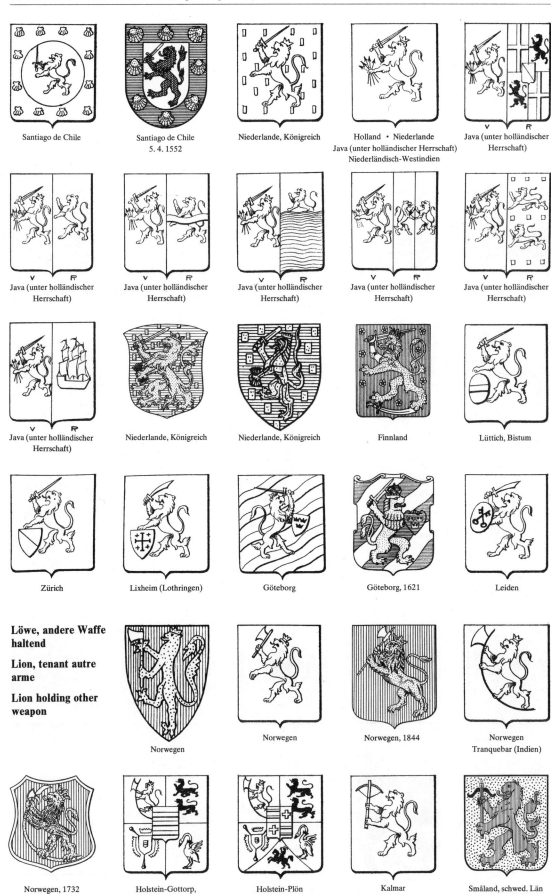

Santiago de Chile	Niederlande, Königreich
Santiago de Chile 5. 4. 1552	Holland · Niederlande / Java (unter holländischer Herrschaft) / Niederländisch-Westindien
	Java (unter holländischer Herrschaft)

Java (unter holländischer Herrschaft)

Java (unter holländischer Herrschaft)

Java (unter holländischer Herrschaft)

Java (unter holländischer Herrschaft)

Java (unter holländischer Herrschaft)

Java (unter holländischer Herrschaft)

Niederlande, Königreich

Niederlande, Königreich

Finnland

Lüttich, Bistum

Zürich

Lixheim (Lothringen)

Göteborg

Göteborg, 1621

Leiden

Löwe, andere Waffe haltend

Lion, tenant autre arme

Lion holding other weapon

Norwegen

Norwegen

Norwegen, 1844

Norwegen Tranquebar (Indien)

Norwegen, 1732

Holstein-Gottorp, Herzogtum 1490

Holstein-Plön Holstein-Sonderburg Holstein-Gottorp, Herzogtum

Kalmar

Småland, schwed. Län

**Löwe, weitere
Geräte haltend**

**Lion, tenant d'autres
instruments**

**Lion holding further
tools**

Mainz, Erzbistum

Broich

Broich

Düsseldorf, Stadt

Düsseldorf, Stadt

Wuppertal, Stadt

Ostflandern

Melk, Stadt
(Niederösterreich)

Melk, Stadt
(Niederösterreich)

Liegnitz, Stadt

Liegnitz, Stadt

Kongo (Brazzaville),
12.8.1963

Bulgarien, Volksrepublik,
30.3.1948

Bulgarien, Volksrepublik,
14.5.1971

Kuttenberg, Stadt (Böhmen)

**Löwe mit Buch-
staben**

Lion et lettre

Lion and letter

Glatz, Stadt

Görlitz

Königgrätz, Stadt (Böhmen)

Hohenstein, Grafschaft

Ueberlingen

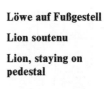
Ueberlingen

Löwe auf Fußgestell

Lion soutenu

**Lion, staying on
pedestal**

Bologna, Stadt

Murten, Stadt
(Kanton Freiburg)

Heidelberg

Löwenberg (Schlesien)

Holland

Leitmeritz, Stadt (Böhmen)

Löwe, auf Gerät stehend

Lion soutenu d'instrument

Lion, staying on tool

Barmen, Stadt
(jetzt Wuppertal)

Barmen, Stadt
(jetzt Wuppertal)

Bremgarten, Stadt
(Kanton Aargau)

Hondschote (Belgien) 1582

Zwei Löwen

Deux lions rampants

Two lions rampant

Batenburg · Geldern
Gronsfeld, Grafschaft
(niederl. Provinz Limburg) · Hessen

Château-Regnault (Ardennes)

Château-Regnault (Ardennes)

Cambrai, Bistum

Anholt, Herrschaft

Eisenach, Stadt

Delft, Stadt (Niederlande)

Winterthur, Stadt

Ungarn

Hohenlimburg
Luxemburg, Herzogtum

Lüttich, Bistum

Deutschland

Armenien

Armenien

Cartagena (Kolumbien)

Cartagena (Kolumbien),
23. 12. 1574

Armenien

Deutschland

Mirandola und Concordia

Weißensee (Thüringen)

Österreich (unter König
Ottokar von Böhmen)

Österreich (unter König
Ottokar von Böhmen)

's-Heerenberg, Herrschaft
(Grafschaft Zütphen)

Deutschland

Siebenbürgen,
Woiwode Moses Székel, 1603

Zaltbommel (Prov. Gelderland)

Tibet

's-Heerenberg, Herrschaft
(Grafschaft Zütphen)

**Drei bis vier (auf-
rechte) Löwen**

**Trois à quatre lions
rampants**

**Three to four lions
rampant**

Cambrai, Bistum

Périgord, Landschaft (Guyenne)

Lüttich, Bistum

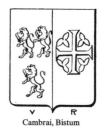

Cambrai, Bistum

Cambrai, Domkapitel

Cambrai, Bistum

Périgord, Landschaft (Guyenne)

Hennegau

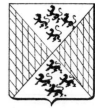

Hennegau

Löwenkopf

Tête de lion

Lion's head

Arnstadt
Laufenburg (Oberrhein)

Laufenburg (Oberrhein)

Schlesien

Schlesien

Arnstadt
Schwarzburg (Thüringen)

Löwenberg (Schlesien)

Löwenberg (Schlesien)

Laufenburg (Oberrhein)

Laufenburg (Oberrhein)

Laufenburg (Oberrhein)

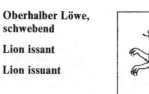

Hessen

**Oberhalber Löwe,
schwebend**

Lion issant

Lion issuant

Laufenburg (Oberrhein)

Laufenburg (Oberrhein)

Bad Tölz

Arnstadt
Schwarzburg (Thüringen)

Brabant

Brabant

Hennegau

Löwe, wachsend (hervorkommend)

Lion issant

Lion issuant from partition

Luxemburg, Herzogtum

Grafen von Schlick

Mexiko, Königreich
(span. Vizekönigreich)

Piacenza

Pfalz

Amberg, Stadt

Amberg, Stadt

Bildhausen, Zisterzienserstift
(Bayr. Franken)

Lumey, Baronie der Grafen
von der Marck

Lüttich, Wilhelm von der Mark,
»der große Eber der
Ardennen« († 1484)

Java (unter holländischer
Herrschaft) · Reckheim
Seeland (niederländ. Provinz)

Seeland
(niederländ. Provinz)

Java (unter holländischer
Herrschaft)

Middelburg (niederländische
Provinz Seeland)

Middelburg (niederländische
Provinz Seeland)

Middelburg (niederländische
Provinz Seeland)

Grafen von Batthyany

Löwe, aus Gegenstand hervorkommend

Lion mouvant de meuble

Lion issuant from charge

Alsleben an der Saale,
Herrschaft

Amberg, Stadt

Bayern, Herzogtum

Rügen

Rügen

Hessen

Hessen

Wellington (Neuseeland),
13. 6. 1878–1951

**Zwei oberhalbe
Löwen**

Deux lions issants

Two lions issuant

Hessen

**Löwe in fünf- und
mehrfeldigem Schild**

**Lion dans écu de
cinq quartiers et
davantage**

**Lion on shield
quartered of five
and more**

Spanien

Böhmen

Österreich

Jülich, Kleve und Berg

Jülich, Kleve und Berg

Brandenburg für Jülich,
Kleve, Berg, Mark und
Ravensberg, 1609

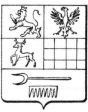

Schwarzburg (Thüringen)

Geldern

Niederländ. Provinzen

Böhmen, 1619, 1620

Braunschweig,
Herzogtum, 1582

Holstein-Gottorp,
Herzogtum 1585

Château-Regnault (Ardennes)

Jülich, Kleve und Berg

Nassau-Diez

Böhmen, 1619, 1620

Böhmen, 1619, 1620

Sayn-Wittgenstein

Holstein-Gottorp,
Herzogtum 1698

Jülich, Kleve und Berg

Niederländ. Provinzen

Batenburg

Löwenstein-Wertheim-Virneburg,
Grafschaft

Bozzolo
(Provinz Mantua)

Solms-Laubach-Rödelheim

Solms-Laubach-Wildenfels

Batenburg

Pfalz- Zweibrücken

Batenburg

Gronsfeld. Johann II. Graf von
Bronkhorst und zu Gronsfeld, † 1617,
verm. Sibylla Gräfin von Eberstein

Salm zu Anholt

Hennegau
Ligny und St. Paul

Hennegau
Ligny und St. Paul

Stolberg, Grafschaft

Nassau-Idstein
Nassau-Saarbrücken
Nassau-Weilburg

Spanische Niederlande, unter der
Regierung des Kurfürsten Max
Emanuel von Bayern 1691–1713

Pfalz, Kurfürstentum
Pfalz-Neuburg

Pfalz, Kurfürstentum

Mailand, Herzogtum

Anholt-Bronkhorst

Sachsen, Herzogtum

Desana, Grafschaft (bei Vercelli)

Correggio

Stolberg, Grafschaft

Stolberg, Grafschaft

Löwenstein-Wertheim

Löwenstein-Wertheim-
Rochefort, Grafschaft

Löwenstein-Wertheim

Löwenstein-Wertheim-
Rochefort, Grafschaft

Löwenstein-Wertheim

Löwenstein-Wertheim-
Rochefort, Grafschaft

Westfriesland

Hessen, Großherzogtum,
9. 12. 1902

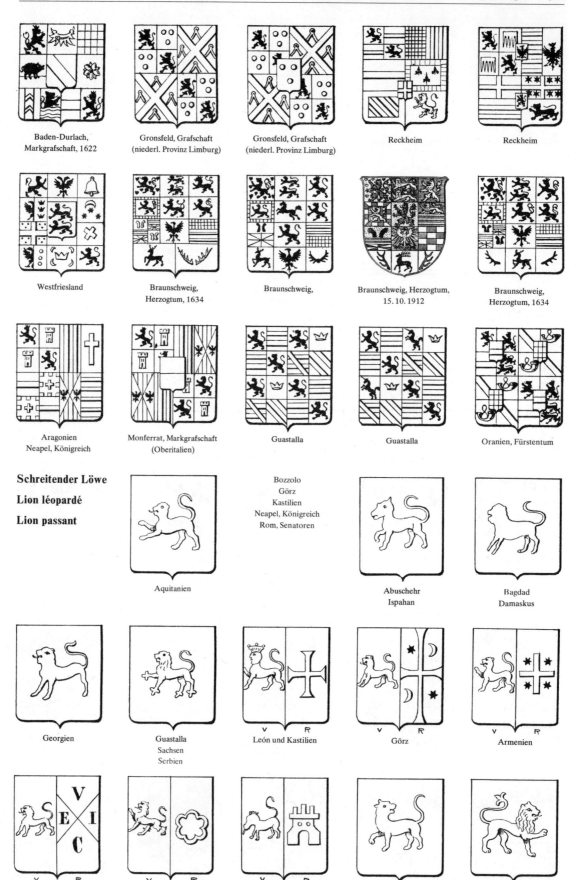

Baden-Durlach,
Markgrafschaft, 1622

Gronsfeld, Grafschaft
(niederl. Provinz Limburg)

Gronsfeld, Grafschaft
(niederl. Provinz Limburg)

Reckheim

Reckheim

Westfriesland

Braunschweig,
Herzogtum, 1634

Braunschweig,

Braunschweig, Herzogtum,
15. 10. 1912

Braunschweig,
Herzogtum, 1634

Aragonien
Neapel, Königreich

Monferrat, Markgrafschaft
(Oberitalien)

Guastalla

Guastalla

Oranien, Fürstentum

Schreitender Löwe

Lion léopardé

Lion passant

Bozzolo
Görz
Kastilien
Neapel, Königreich
Rom, Senatoren

Aquitanien

Abuschehr
Ispahan

Bagdad
Damaskus

Georgien

Guastalla
Sachsen
Serbien

León und Kastilien

Görz

Armenien

Bombay

Görz

Guayana (Spanisch)

Polen

Lemberg

Rescht

Deutschland (Otto IV.,
reg. 1198–1218)

Diepholz, Stadt

**Schreitender Löwe
in einem Schildfeld**

**Lion léopardé dans
un quartier**

**Lion passant on part
of a shield**

Bonn

Lyon, Stadt

Braunschweig, Herzogtum
(W: Lauterberg)

Eritrea, italienische Kolonie,
8. 6. 1919

Rom, Senatoren, 1326

Braunschweig, Herzogtum

Rom, Senatoren

Alsleben an der Saale,
Herrschaft

Rom, Senatoren

Zütphen (Gelderland)

Zütphen (Gelderland)

Reckheim

Löwenstein-Wertheim-
Rochefort, Grafschaft

Meranien, Herzogtum

Rom, Senatoren, 1291

Dünkirchen

Dünkirchen

Roermond, Stadt
(Niederl. Provinz Limburg)

Schwarzburg (Thüringen)

Schwarzburg (Thüringen)

Diepholz

Rotterdam

Rotterdam

Görz

Görz

Görz

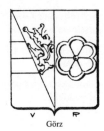

Görz

Görz

Görz

Görz

Görz

Görz und Gradiska

Pfalz, Kurfürstentum

Thurgau

Thurgau, 13. 4. 1803

Föderation von
Rhodesien und Nyassaland,
24. 8. 1954

Malawi, 30. 6. 1964

Sierra Leone, 1. 4. 1961

**Schreitender Löwe
auf Fußgestell**

**Lion léopardé
soutenu**

**Lion passant on
pedestal**

Holland

Birma

Calw, Stadt (Württemberg)

Calw, Stadt (Württemberg)

Löwenstein-Wertheim

Löwenstein-Wertheim

Löwenstein-Wertheim-
Rochefort, Grafschaft

Nyassaland, 11. 5. 1914

Braunschweig, Stadt

Hannover, Stadt

Boulogne, Grafschaft

Braunschweig, Stadt
Deutschland (Otto IV.,
reg. 1198–1218)

Braunschweig, Stadt

Maastricht

Schreitender Löwe, begleitet

Lion léopardé accompagné

Lion passant accompagnied

Beromünster, Chorherrenstift
(Kanton Luzern)

Beromünster, Chorherrenstift
(Kanton Luzern)

Ueberlingen

Lüttich, Bistum

Serbien

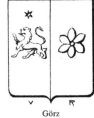

Braunschweig, Stadt

Görz

Senegal, bis 1965

Serbien

Armenien

Kärnten

Meranien, Herzogtum

Rom, Senatoren

China

Rescht

Gandscha (1804–1924
Jelisavetpol, Aserbaidshan)

Abuschehr

Braunschweig, Stadt

Hannover, Stadt

Sachsen

Schlesien

Göttingen, Stadt

Pamplona, Stadt (Spanien)

Böhmen, Ottokar II., 1252

Rom, Senatoren
(Karl I. von Anjou)

Ceylon, April 1953
Sri Lanka

Schwarzburg (Thüringen)

Deutschland
(Otto IV., reg. 1198–1218)

Tiflis (Kaukasus)

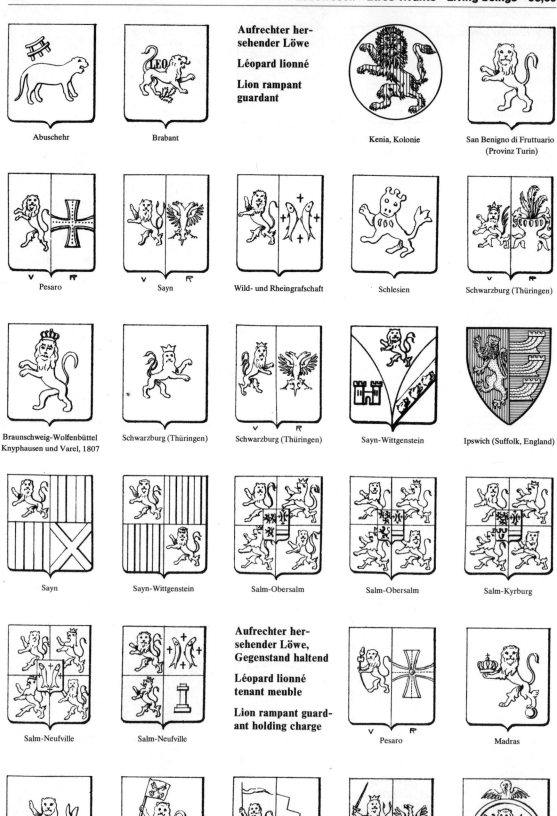

Abuschehr

Brabant

**Aufrechter her-
sehender Löwe**

Léopard lionné

**Lion rampant
guardant**

Kenia, Kolonie

San Benigno di Fruttuario
(Provinz Turin)

Pesaro

Sayn

Wild- und Rheingrafschaft

Schlesien

Schwarzburg (Thüringen)

Braunschweig-Wolfenbüttel
Knyphausen und Varel, 1807

Schwarzburg (Thüringen)

Schwarzburg (Thüringen)

Sayn-Wittgenstein

Ipswich (Suffolk, England)

Sayn

Sayn-Wittgenstein

Salm-Obersalm

Salm-Obersalm

Salm-Kyrburg

Salm-Neufville

Salm-Neufville

**Aufrechter her-
sehender Löwe,
Gegenstand haltend**

**Léopard lionné
tenant meuble**

**Lion rampant guard-
ant holding charge**

Pesaro

Madras

Österreich

Masserano, Fürstentum
(Piemont)

Bologna, Herrschaft

Böhmen

Grafen von Batthyany

**Schreitender her-
sehender Löwe**

Léopard

**Lion passant
guardant**

Braunschweig, Stadt

Guyenne (französ. Provinz)

Mysore, Fürstentum (Indien)

Mysore, Fürstentum (Indien)

Mysore, Fürstentum (Indien)

Mysore, Fürstentum (Indien)

Cincinnati (Ohio)

Rom, Senatoren
(Karl I. von Anjou)

Allah-Abad

Aire, Stadt (Landes)

Sierra Leone

Bordeaux

Armenien

León und Kastilien

Braunschweig, Herzogtum
Braunschweig, Stadt
Ueberlingen

Uppsala, Stadt (Schweden)

Mysore, Fürstentum (Indien)

Diepholz

Armenien

Äthiopien
(Kaiser Johannes, 1872–89)

Mysore, Fürstentum (Indien)

Mysore, Fürstentum (Indien)

**Schreitender her-
sehender Löwe in
einem Schildfeld**

**Léopard dans un
quartier**

**Lion passant
guardant on part of
a shield**

Lyme Regis, Stadt
(Dorsetshire, England)

Italienisch Somaliland,
3. 4. 1919

Bonn, 1939–52

Bonn, 1973

Lucca, Stadt

Peru (Indiana)

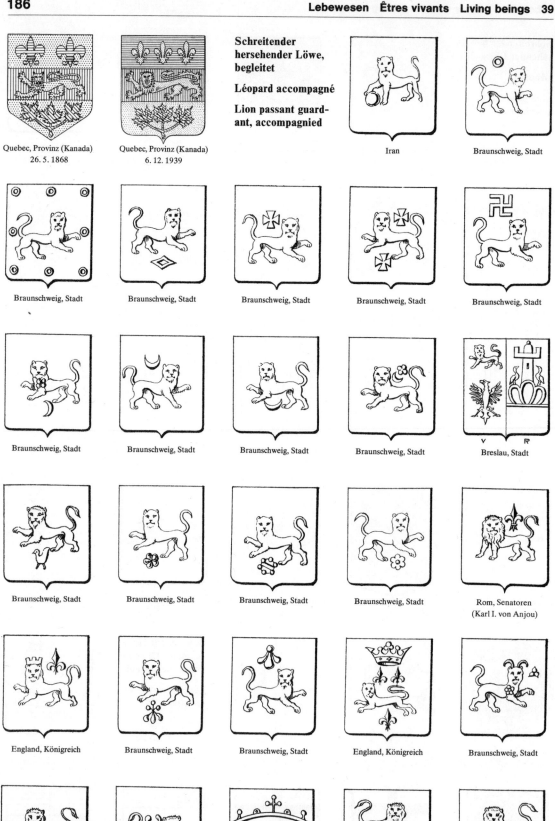

Quebec, Provinz (Kanada)
26. 5. 1868

Quebec, Provinz (Kanada)
6. 12. 1939

**Schreitender
hersehender Löwe,
begleitet**

Léopard accompagné

**Lion passant guard-
ant, accompagnied**

Iran

Braunschweig, Stadt

Braunschweig, Stadt

Braunschweig, Stadt

Braunschweig, Stadt

Braunschweig, Stadt

Braunschweig, Stadt

Braunschweig, Stadt

Braunschweig, Stadt

Braunschweig, Stadt

Braunschweig, Stadt

Breslau, Stadt

Braunschweig, Stadt

Braunschweig, Stadt

Braunschweig, Stadt

Braunschweig, Stadt

Rom, Senatoren
(Karl I. von Anjou)

England, Königreich

Braunschweig, Stadt

Braunschweig, Stadt

England, Königreich

Braunschweig, Stadt

Braunschweig, Stadt

Braunschweig, Stadt

Braunschweig, Herzogtum

Braunschweig, Stadt

Braunschweig, Stadt

Braunschweig, Stadt	Hannover, Stadt	Braunschweig, Stadt	Braunschweig, Stadt	Aquitanien
Braunschweig, Stadt	Braunschweig, Stadt	Braunschweig, Stadt	Melbourne (Victoria, Australien)	Rom, Stadt
Viterbo (Italien), 1316	León, Königreich (Spanien)	Braunschweig, Stadt	Braunschweig, Stadt	Braunschweig, Stadt
Braunschweig, Stadt	Braunschweig, Stadt	Braunschweig, Stadt	Braunschweig, Stadt	Braunschweig, Stadt
Braunschweig, Stadt	Braunschweig, Stadt	Braunschweig, Stadt	Braunschweig, Stadt	Braunschweig, Stadt
Braunschweig, Stadt	Braunschweig, Stadt	Braunschweig, Stadt	Braunschweig, Stadt	Braunschweig, Stadt

Braunschweig, Stadt

Braunschweig, Stadt

Braunschweig, Stadt

Braunschweig, Stadt

Braunschweig, Stadt

Braunschweig, Stadt

Braunschweig, Stadt

Braunschweig, Stadt

Braunschweig, Stadt

Braunschweig, Stadt

**Schreitender
hersehender Löwe,
begleitet von Buch-
staben**

**Léopard accompagné
de lettre**

**Lion passant guard-
ant with letter**

Braunschweig, Stadt

Braunschweig, Stadt

Hessen (Frankenberg)

Braunschweig, Stadt

Braunschweig, Stadt

Braunschweig, Stadt

Braunschweig, Stadt

Braunschweig, Stadt

Braunschweig, Stadt

Braunschweig, Stadt

Braunschweig, Stadt

**Zwei schreitende
(auch hersehende)
Löwen**

**Deux léopards et
lions léopardés**

**Two lions passant,
even guardant ones**

Braunschweig, Herzogtum

Flensburg (Schleswig)
Gronsfeld
Hohenlohe
Öhringen, Stadt
Reckheim
Schleswig, Herzogtum
Stevensweert
Sülzburg

Braunschweig, Herzogtum
Diez an der Lahn,
Duderstadt · Normandie

Zypern, seit 1910–1960

Hohenlohe

Hohenlohe

Reckheim
Westfriesland

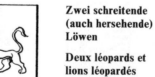

Java (unter
holländischer Herrschaft)

Java (unter
holländischer Herrschaft)

Friesland, niederländ. Provinz

Hohenlohe 1623

Schleswig-Holstein,
Herzogtümer

Braunschweig, Herzogtum,
19. Jahrhundert

Braunschweig, Herzogtum

Hohenlohe

Schleswig-Holstein.

Schleswig-Holstein,
Bundesland, 5. 3. 1947

Zwei schreitende Löwen, auch hersehende, in geviertem Schild

Deux léopards ou lions léopardés dans écu écartelé

Two lions passant on quartered shield

Hessen, Landgrafschaft,
Variante

Braunschweig, Herzogtum,
1419

Braunschweig, Herzogtum

Braunschweig, Herzogtum

Braunschweig, Herzogtum

Braunschweig, Herzogtum,
1585

Hohenlohe 1558

Hohenlohe 1623–1764

Schleswig-Holstein,
vor 1864

Idem, in mehrfeldigem Schild

Idem, dans écu de plus de quatre quartiers

Idem, on shield quartered of five and more

Braunschweig, Herzogtum,
1596

Braunschweig, Herzogtum,
1582

Hohenlohe-Bartenstein 1774

Braunschweig, Herzogtum,
1585

Drei schreitende (auch hersehende) Löwen

Trois léopards et lions léopardés

Three lions passant, even guardant ones

Dänemark

Eichstätt, Domkapitel
England
Maccagno (Provinz Como)
Reval, Stadt
Schwäbischer Kreis

Eichstätt, Domkapitel

Baden-Württemberg,
3. 5. 1954

Dänemark

Jersey, Kanalinsel

Jersey, Kanalinsel

Estland, Republik, 11. 7. 1925

Reval

Dänemark
Tranquebar (Indien)

Kärnten

Kärnten

Kärnten

Kärnten

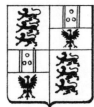

Kärnten

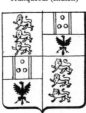

Dänemark (W: Dänemark
und Pfalz-Bayern)

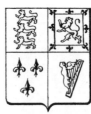

England, 1340–1603

Eichstätt, Domkapitel

Schwäbischer Kreis

Schwäbischer Kreis
(Konstanz und Württemberg)

Dänemark
Dänisch-Westindien
Tranquebar (Indien)

Dänemark

Dänemark (sog.
Kabinettswappen), 1662
Schleswig-Holstein, Herzogtümer

Dänemark (W: Dänemark,
Norwegen, Holstein)

Maccagno (Provinz Como)

Maccagno (Provinz Como)

Großbritannien,
Variante vor 1707

Dunedin (Neuseeland,
W: Großbritannien und
Irland, 1837)

Großbritannien seit 1837

Großbritannien,
1689–1702, Variante

Großbritannien, 1801–1837
Hannover, Königreich,
1815–1837, 1848–1866

Hannover, Königreich,
1848–1866

Hannover, Königreich,
1837–1848

Mauritius

Kanada

Dänemark

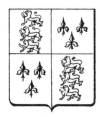

Dänemark

England, 1340–1603

Dänemark

Dänemark

Großbritannien, 1707–1714

Großbritannien, 1714–1801

Südsee-Kompanie
(Großbritannien)

**Vier und fünf schrei-
tende (auch herse-
hende) Löwen**

**Quatre et cinq
léopards et lions
léopardés**

**Four and five lions
passant, even guard-
ant ones**

Hennegau

York, Stadt (England)

**Halbe schreitende
hersehende Löwen**

Demi-léopards

**Demi-lions passant
guardant**

Dover

Dover

**Löwen- und
Leopardenkopf
im Visier**

Tête de léopard

Lion's face

Arnstadt

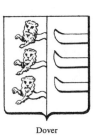

Burundi, 1962

Schwarzburg (Thüringen)

Neapel und Sizilien

Neapel und Sizilien

Ungarn

Armenien

Samos, Fürstentum,
bis 1912

Kongo (Kinshasa)

Kongo (Kinshasa)
Saire (Zaïre)

Dalmatien, Königreich

Ungarn, 8. 11. 1868

Ungarn, 9. 2. 1874

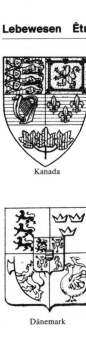

Ungarn, 15. 10. 1915

Löwe, hockend

Lion accroupi

Lion sejant

Schlesien

Bruch
Hohenlimburg

Ungarn

Flandern
Geldern
Holland
Solder und Anholt
Stein

Namur (Belgien)

Florennes
(belgische Provinz Namur)

Megen, Grafschaft
(Nordbrabant)

Cambrai, Bistum

Flandern

Perwez (Belgien)

Rummen

Florennes
(belgische Provinz Namur)
Namur (Belgien)

Geldern

Hennegau

Jever, Herrschaft
Leeuwarden

Bolsward (niederländische
Provinz Friesland)

Bermuda, 4. 10. 1910

Schottland

Siebenbürgen,
Dynastie Bocskai

Paraguay
(Finanzverwaltung),
27. 11. 1842

Löwe, ruhend

Lion couché

Lion couchant

Treggiano

Cincinnati (Ohio)

Lacrosse (Wisconsin)
Laureville (Ohio)

Iran

León, Königreich (Spanien)

Mailand

Transvaal, 18. 2. 1858

Löwe mit Stab oder Kreuzstab, stehend oder schreitend

Léopard (aussi lionné) avec bâton

Lion passant or statant with rod

Armenien

Armenien

Armenien

Armenien

Armenien

Äthiopien
(Kaiser Menelik, 1889)

Äthiopien

Äthiopien 1932

Paraguay, 27. 11. 1842

Geflügelter Löwe

Léopard (et lion) ailé

Winged lion

Kärnten

Deutschland

Reichenau, Abtei

Reichenau, Abtei

Bayern

Cattaro (Kotor)

Sebenico (Šibenik)
Spalato (Split)
Tornese (Peloponnes)
Treviso (Venetien)
Venedig

Italien, Republik
W. der Marine, 9. 11. 1947

Ungarn
Venedig

Venedig

Palma
Venedig

Famagusta (Zypern) 1570

Rovigo, Stadt
Ungarn
Venedig
Zypern,
unter venezianischer Herrschaft

Frinco

Frinco

Frinco

Frinco · Masserano,
Fürstentum (Piemont)
Radicati und Passerano

Savoyen

Venedig

Zypern

Ionische Republik

Gießen

Gießen, 29. 4. 1916

Dalmatien und Albanien
unter
venezianischer Herrschaft

Panther

Panthère

Heraldic panther

Venedig

Venedig

Venedig

Steiermark

Steiermark

Steiermark

Steiermark

Steiermark

Steyr, Stadt

Bär

Ours

Bear

Ingolstadt, Stadt

Graz

Graz

Appenzell
Appenzell (Innerrhoden)

Berlin

St. Gallen, Abtei

St. Gallen, Abtei

Anhalt

Rietberg (Ostfriesland)

Ostfriesland

Appenzell

Appenzell (Innerrhoden)

Appenzell (Außerrhoden)

Appenzell (Außerrhoden)

Berlin St. Gallen Desana, Grafschaft	St. Gallen, Stadt	Berlin	Berlin und Kölln	Appenzell
Grönland	St. Gallen, Abtei	Ostkarelien	Berlin Bern Desana, Grafschaft	Bern
Bern	Bern	Bern	Bern	Bern
St. Gallen, Abtei	Anhalt, Freistaat, 4. 4. 1924	Anhalt-Bernburg	Anhalt, circa 1550	Anhalt-Zerbst, 1667
Bern	Bern	Bern	Ungarn	Sieradz

Bärenpranken

Pattes d'ours

Bear's paws

Hoya, Grafschaft	Hoya, Grafschaft	Hoya, Grafschaft	Hoya, Grafschaft

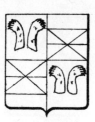

Braunschweig, Herzogtum
(W: Hoya und Bruchhausen)

Braunschweig, Herzogtum
(W: Hoya und Bruchhausen)

Elefant

Eléphant

Elephant

Siam

Siam

Ostindien

Bidschnagur

Ostindien

Bidschnagur

Bidschnagur

Bidschnagur

Ceylon

Eriwan (Kaukasus)
Helfenstein, Grafschaft
(Württemberg)
Mysore, Fürstentum (Indien)
Siam

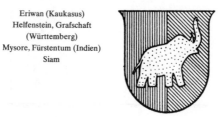

Guinea, 1958

Mysore, Fürstentum
(Indien)

Dhaffer-Abad

Ferkhab Hissar
Khalak-Abad
Khurschid Suard
Ostindien

Feiz Hissar · Ferrokhi
Kalikut · Khalak-Abad

Albany (New York)

Mysore, Fürstentum
(Indien)

Mysore, Fürstentum
(Indien)

Ferrokhi
Mysore, Fürstentum (Indien)
Nagar

Selem Abad

Mysore, Fürstentum (Indien)

Bidschnagur

Nagar

Bidschnagur

Österreich

Österreich

Trànquebar (Indien)

Ceylon

Ferkhab Hissar

Mysore, Fürstentum (Indien)

Carolina
Ceylon
Neu-England

Rescht

Radschputana

Elfenbeinküste, 17. 8. 1960

Ceylon, 17. 12. 1906

Helfenstein, Grafschaft
(Württemberg)

Helfenstein, Grafschaft
Besitz der Grafen Fugger auf
Adelshofen und Zinnenburg

Helfenstein, Grafschaft
(Württemberg)

Elfenbeinküste, 26. 6. 1964

Zentralafrikanische Republik,
17. 5. 1963

Laos

Siam

Ostindien

Rinder

Race bovine

Horned cattle

Turin, Stadt

Béarn

Buenos Aires
Desana
Frinco
Navarra
Parma
Persien (Täbris)
Schleiz, Stadt (Thüringen)
Wohlau (Niederschlesien)
Ziegenrück (Thüringen)

Parma

Vereinigte Staaten von Amerika

Cincinnati · Hillsboro (Ohio)
Tippecanoe (Ohio)
Vereinigte Staaten von Amerika

Britannien

Ceylon

Radschputana

Schleiz, Stadt (Thüringen)

Oxford, Stadt (England)

Manitoba, 10. 5. 1905

Béarn

Ostindien

Hindustan
(Timuriden, Großmoguln)

Hindustan
(Timuriden, Großmoguln)

Edam, Stadt (Nordholland)

Schleiz, Stadt (Thüringen)

Schleiz, Stadt (Thüringen)

Schleiz, Stadt (Thüringen)

Schleiz, Stadt (Thüringen)

Schleiz, Stadt (Thüringen)

Schleiz, Stadt (Thüringen)

Tiflis (Kaukasus)

Schleiz, Stadt (Thüringen)

Täbris

Eriwan (Kaukasus)

Schemachá

Britannien

Parma
Desana, Grafschaft (bei Vercelli)

Béarn

Schleiz, Stadt (Thüringen)

Auersperg, 1630

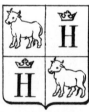

Navarra (Nord)

Béarn

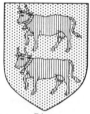

Béarn

Navarra (Nord)

Oberhalbes Zebu

**Taureau des Indes,
naissant**

Indian bull issuant

Ceylon

Mahiswar

Halber Stierkopf

**Demi-rencontre de
taureau**

**Half of bull's head
caboshed**

Wismar

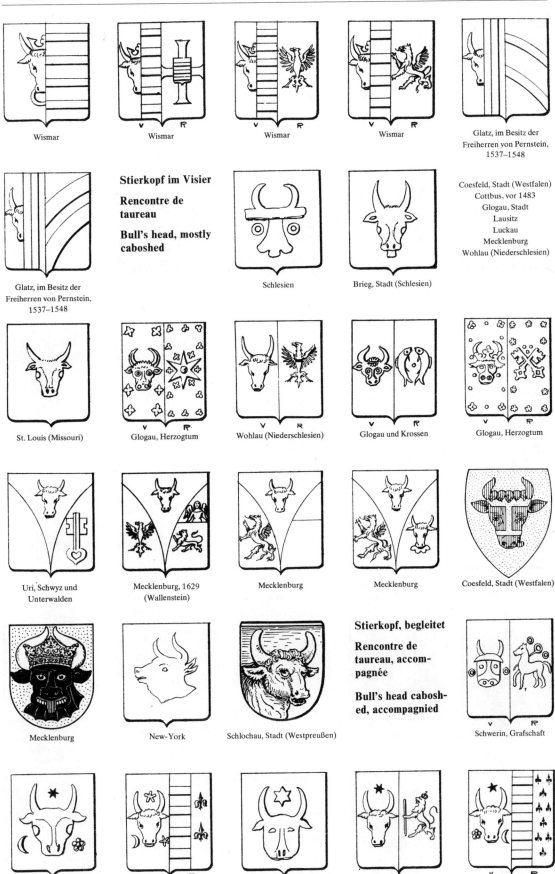

Wismar

Wismar

Wismar

Wismar

Glatz, im Besitz der
Freiherren von Pernstein,
1537–1548

Glatz, im Besitz der
Freiherren von Pernstein,
1537–1548

Stierkopf im Visier

Rencontre de taureau

Bull's head, mostly caboshed

Schlesien

Brieg, Stadt (Schlesien)

Coesfeld, Stadt (Westfalen)
Cottbus, vor 1483
Glogau, Stadt
Lausitz
Luckau
Mecklenburg
Wohlau (Niederschlesien)

St. Louis (Missouri)

Glogau, Herzogtum

Wohlau (Niederschlesien)

Glogau und Krossen

Glogau, Herzogtum

Uri, Schwyz und
Unterwalden

Mecklenburg, 1629
(Wallenstein)

Mecklenburg

Mecklenburg

Coesfeld, Stadt (Westfalen)

Stierkopf, begleitet

Rencontre de taureau, accompagnée

Bull's head caboshed, accompagnied

Mecklenburg

New-York

Schlochau, Stadt (Westpreußen)

Schwerin, Grafschaft

Moldau, Fürstentum

Moldau, Fürstentum

Schlesien

Moldau, Fürstentum

Moldau, Fürstentum

Moldau, Fürstentum

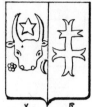

Moldau, Fürstentum

Moldau, Fürstentum

Bukowina, 9. 12. 1862

Mecklenburg
Wismar

Luckau, Stadt

Chicago (Illinois)

**Stierkopf in gespal-
tenem Schild**

**Rencontre de
taureau dans écu
parti**

**Bull's head caboshed
on shield per pale**

Glatz, im Besitz der
Freiherren von Pernstein,
1537–1548

Moldau und Walachei,
Fürstentümer

**Stierkopf mit Nasen-
ring**

**Rencontre de
taureau bouclée**

**Bull's head cabosh-
ed, ringed through
the nose**

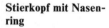

Schlesien

Bromberg
Glatz, Grafschaft

Uri (Schweiz)

Uri (Schweiz)

Uri, Schwyz und
Unterwalden

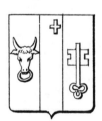

Friedland (W: Mecklenburg,
Sagan, Friedland),
16. 6. 1629

Uri, Schwyz und
Unterwalden

Glatz, im Besitz der
Freiherren von Pernstein,
1537–1548

Uri (Schweiz)

Uri (Schweiz)

Glatz, im Besitz der
Freiherren von Pernstein,
1537–1548

Idem, gekrönt

Idem, couronnée

Idem, crowned

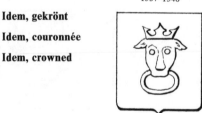

Glatz, im Besitz der
Freiherren von Pernstein,
1537–1548

Castiglione delle Stiviere
(Provinz Mantua)
Mecklenburg

Mecklenburg

Großpolen, Landschaft
Kalisch, Woiwodschaft

**Stierkopf in mehr-
feldigem Schild**

**Recontre de
taureau dans un
quartier**

**Bull's head cabosh-
ed, on one quarter**

Mecklenburg

Mecklenburg

Mecklenburg, nach Ende
15. Jahrhundert bis 1658

Mecklenburg, nach Ende
15. Jahrhundert bis 1658

Lobkowicz, Fürsten, 1646

Mecklenburg, Herzogtümer
und Großherzogtümer
seit 1658

Mecklenburg-Schwerin,
Freistaat, 15. 12. 1921

Mecklenburg,
16. 6. 1629–1632
(Wallenstein)

Transkei, 15. 1. 1971

**Geweihträger
(Hirsch und dergl.)**

Cerf et famille

**Deer and kindred
animals**

Basra (Persischer Golf)

Hohenstein, Grafschaft
Klettenberg
Sayn-Wittgenstein für
Klettenberg 1647
Sorau
Stolberg, Grafschaft

Sachsen-Eisenberg

Hirschberg in Schlesien, Stadt

Hirschberg in Schlesien, Stadt

Ålands-Inseln

Tromsö, Stadt (Norwegen)

Sigmaringen, Stadt

St. Blasien, Abtei (Schwarzwald)
Hirschberg in Schlesien, Stadt
Stolberg, Grafschaft

Schneidemühl, Stadt

Sayn-Wittgenstein

Hirschberg in Schlesien,
Stadt

Pommern

Stolberg-Stolberg

Hessen-Darmstadt

China

Ungarn

Monferrat, Markgrafschaft
(Oberitalien)

Stolberg, Grafschaft

Stolberg, Grafschaft

Stolberg, Grafschaft

Sorau

Gästrikland, Landschaft
(Schweden)

Anchin, Benediktinerabtei
(bei Douai)

Aragonien

Nordhausen, Stadt

Stolberg, Grafschaft

Stolberg, Grafschaft

Stolberg, Grafschaft

Stolberg, Grafschaft

Stolberg, Grafschaft

Stolberg, Grafschaft

Stolberg, Grafschaft

Stolberg, Grafschaft

Stolberg, Grafschaft

Hohenzollern-Sigmaringen

Sorau, Stadt

Stolberg, Grafschaft

Stolberg, Grafschaft

Stolberg, Grafschaft

Stolberg, Grafschaft

Stolberg, Grafschaft

Stolberg, Grafschaft

Stolberg, Grafschaft

Stolberg, Grafschaft

Mehrere Hirsche

Plusieurs cerfs

Several stags

Massa (Italien)

**Hirsch- und Elch-
kopf**

**Tête et rencontre de
cerf et d'élan**

**Stag's and elk's
head, even casboshed**

New-York

Ronsdorf

Mitau, Stadt

Mecklenburg

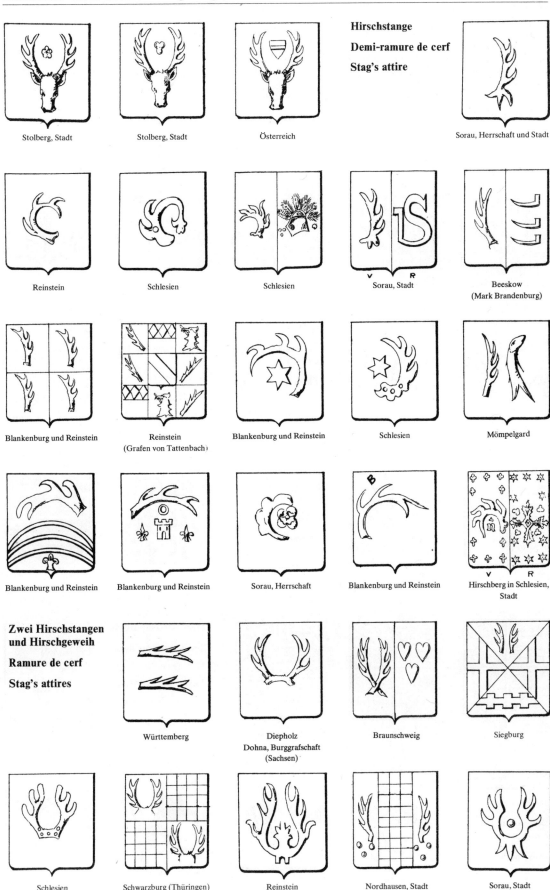

Stolberg, Stadt

Stolberg, Stadt

Österreich

Hirschstange

Demi-ramure de cerf

Stag's attire

Sorau, Herrschaft und Stadt

Reinstein

Schlesien

Schlesien

Sorau, Stadt

Beeskow
(Mark Brandenburg)

Blankenburg und Reinstein

Reinstein
(Grafen von Tattenbach)

Blankenburg und Reinstein

Schlesien

Mömpelgard

Blankenburg und Reinstein

Blankenburg und Reinstein

Sorau, Herrschaft

Blankenburg und Reinstein

Hirschberg in Schlesien,
Stadt

**Zwei Hirschstangen
und Hirschgeweih**

Ramure de cerf

Stag's attires

Württemberg

Diepholz
Dohna, Burggrafschaft
(Sachsen)

Braunschweig

Siegburg

Schlesien

Schwarzburg (Thüringen)

Reinstein

Nordhausen, Stadt

Sorau, Stadt

204

Sorau, Herrschaft   Sorau, Herrschaft   Blankenburg und Reinstein   Braunschweig, Herzogtum (W: Wölpe)   Sigmaringen, Grafschaft

Blankenburg und Reinstein   Braunschweig   Blankenburg und Reinstein   Blankenburg und Reinstein   Blankenburg und Reinstein

Drei Hirschstangen

Trois demi-ramures de cerf

Three stag's attires

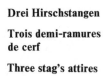
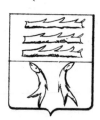

Schlesien   Brandenburg, Kurfürstentum   Württemberg   Mömpelgard

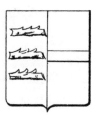
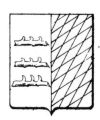

Württemberg   Württemberg   Württemberg, Königreich   Württemberg, Königreich, 30.12.1817   Württemberg, Volksstaat, 20.2.1922

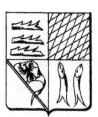

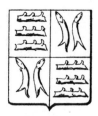

Drei Hirschgeweihe

Trois ramures de cerf

Three stag's antlers

Mömpelgard Württemberg   Württemberg-Oels, Herzogtum (Schlesien)   Württemberg   Tepl (Böhmen)

Steinbock, Ziegenbock, Widder, springend

Bouquetin, bouc, bélier, rampant

Ibex, buck, ram, rampant

Chur, Bistum und Stadt   Gotteshausbund   Gotteshausbund   Schaffhausen

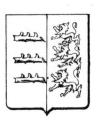

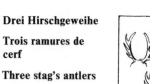

Schaffhausen, Kanton

Desana, Grafschaft
(bei Vercelli)

Lublin (Polen)

Wallmoden-Gimborn

**Idem, stehend oder
schreitend**

**Idem, passant ou
arrêté**

**Idem, passant or
statant**

Chur, Bistum

Chur, Bistum

Istrien

Schlesien

Georgien

Eriwan (Kaukasus)

Boxmeer (Nordbrabant)

Schaffhausen

Schaffhausen

Schiras

Schemachá

Schaffhausen

Hindustan
(Timuriden, Großmoguln)

Hindustan
(Timuriden, Großmoguln)

Schaf, stehend

Mouton, arrêté

Sheep, statant

Sydney (Australien)

Färöer

Quimper (Finistère)

Falkland-Inseln, 29. 9. 1948

Bourges, Stadt

Bourges, Stadt

Osterlamm

Agneau pascal

Paschal lamb

Meißen, Bistum
St. Gallen, Abtei
Ungarn

Kärnten
Lüttich, Bistum

Audenarde
(Oudenaarde, Belgien)

Breslau, Bistum
Cambrai, Bistum
England
Ermland, Bistum
Gotland
Johanniter-Orden
Kastilien
Loos
Meißen, Bistum

Namur
Neapel und Sizilien
Posen, Erzbistum
Rouen, Stadt
St. Omer (Frankreich), Stadt
St. Gallen, Abtei
Tirlemont (Tienen, Belgien)
Ungarn
Wisby (Gotland)

Namur (Belgien)

Tirlemont (Belgien)

Lesbos

Hennegau

Meißen, Bistum

Prüm

Perth (Schottland)

Rouen, Stadt

Brixen, Bistum und Domkapitel

Brixen, Bistum und Domkapitel

Toulouse, Stadt

Puerto Rico,
8. 11. 1511, 9. 3. 1905

Bockskopf

Tête de bouc

Buck's head

Colocz
Cosel (Oberschlesien)
Schlochau, Stadt (Westpreußen)

Chur, Bistum

Britisch Somaliland

Cosel (Oberschlesien)

Cosel (Oberschlesien)

Cosel (Oberschlesien)

Queensland 29. 4. 1893

Südwestafrika, 1962

Schaffhausen

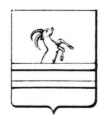

Garsten (Oberösterreich)

Goldenes Vlies

Toison d'or

Golden fleece

Colonia
Hobart Town, Tasmanien
Neapel und Sizilien

Leeds (England)

Goulburn (Neusüdwales)

Brisbane (Australien, Neusüdwales, seit 1859 Queensland)

Ipswich (Queensland)
Queensland
Rockhampton (Queensland)
Sydney (Australien)
Toowoomba (Queensland)
Wollongong (Neusüdwales)

Kamel

Chameau

Camel

Eriwan (Kaukasus)

Lama (Vicuña)

Lama

Llama

Lima (Peru)

Potosí (Bolivien)

Ayacucho (Peru)

Caxamarca (Peru)
Cuzco (Peru)
Lima (Peru)
Pasco (Peru)
Peru, Republik, 25. 2. 1825

Pferd und Esel

Cheval et âne

Horse and donkey

Kent, Grafschaft

Westfalen, Provinz

Haag, Grafschaft (Oberbayern)
Schwerin, Grafschaft

Stuttgart

Braunschweig, Herzogtum

China
(Dynastie Ming, 1368–1644)
Großbritannien
Hannover, Königreich
Lauenburg, Herzogtum
Westfalen, Herzogtum

Niedersachsen, 13. 10. 1952

Hannover, preuß. Provinz

Bidschnagur

China

St. Alban

China (Dynastie Ming,
1368–1644)

Bidschnagur

Vereinigte Staaten von
Amerika

Ceylon

Pferd auf Fußgestell

Cheval soutenu

Horse on pedestal

Braunschweig, Herzogtum,
1918 Land (Freistaat)

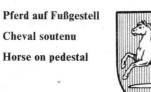

Lavagna und Masserano

Sabbioneta

Lavagna (Ligurien)

Persien (Kanjah)

Uri, Schwyz und Unterwalden für die Grafschaft Bellinzona 1500–1503

Pferd, aufgezäumt

Cheval caparaçonné

Horse caparisoned

Mirandola, Herzogtum

Bidschnagur

Pferd und Esel, begleitet

Cheval et âne, accompagnés

Horse and donkey, accompagnied

Ungarn

Neapel, Königreich

Britannien

Neapel, Königreich

Persien (Bagdad)

Bagdad

Gandscha (1804–1924 Jelisavetpol, Aserbaidshan)

Gandscha (1804–1924 Jelisavetpol, Aserbaidshan)

England, Königreich

Braunschweig, Herzogtum

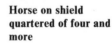

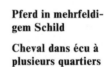

Wolfenbüttel, Stadt, 7. 8. 1570

Pferd in mehrfeldigem Schild

Cheval dans écu à plusieurs quartiers

Horse on shield quartered of four and more

Savoyen

Savoyen

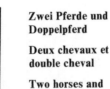

Westphalen, Königreich 1807–1813

Zwei Pferde und Doppelpferd

Deux chevaux et double cheval

Two horses and double-horse

Stuttgart

China

Pferdekopf

Tête de cheval

Horse's head

Vandalen

Lauenburg, Herzogtum, 22. 10. 1819

Lauenburg, Herzogtum 12. 12. 1866

Vandalen

New Jersey

Halbes Pferd
Demi-cheval
Demi-horse

Ostindien

Hlinsko (Böhmen)

Einhorn
Licorne
Unicorn

Schwäbisch Gmünd

Ferrara

Bayern

Giengen an der Brenz, Stadt
Schwäbisch Gmünd

Ferrara

Urbino (Italien)

Bayern

Reggio

Pegasus
Pégase
Pegasus

Britannien

Exotische Vierfüßler
Quadrupèdes exoti-
ques
Exotic quadrupeds

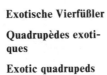

Sudan, Republik, bis 1971

Orange River Colony,
10.12.1904

Ostindien

Tipperah (Bengalen)

Tipperah (Bengalen)

Natal, Kolonie, 10.6.1907

Natal, Provinz, 4.5.1911

Tanganjika-Territorium

Melbourne (Victoria, Australien)
Port Phillip (Victoria, Australien)

Greif
Griffon
Griffin

Anklam, Stadt (Pommern)

Dalarne (Schweden)
Demmin (Pommern)
Garz (Pommern)
Gollnow (Pommern)
Greifswald
Holzapfel, Grafschaft, 7.9.1643
Mecklenburg
Pommern
Pyritz (Pommern)
Rostock

Schweidnitz, Stadt
Stargard in Pommern
Stettin
Stolp (Pommern)
Stralsund
Treptow an der Rega
(Pommern)
Usedom, Insel (Pommern)
Wolgast (Pommern)
Montalban

Rostock
Ungarn

Pommern

Södermanland

Mecklenburg, nach Ende
15. Jahrhundert bis 1658

Greif auf Münzavers

Griffon sur avers de monnaie

Griffin on obverse of coin

Stargard in Pommern

Ungarn

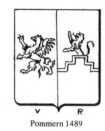

Mecklenburg

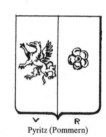

Pommern 1489

Mecklenburg

Schweidnitz, Stadt

Rostock

Garz (Pommern)

Pyritz (Pommern)

Greif, gekrönt

Griffon, couronné

Griffin, crowned

Stralsund

Nyköping (W: von Södermanland)

Perugia (Italien)

Perugia (Italien)

Greif, begleitet

Griffon, accompagné

Griffin, accompagnied

Kahla

Alexandrien

Polen

Wartenberg
(Niederschlesien)

Holzapfel, Grafschaft,
7. 9. 1643

Greifswald

Greifswald

Stargard in Pommern

Livland

Swinemünde

Anklam, Stadt (Pommern)

Bialystok (Polen)

Greif in zweiteiligem Schild

Griffon dans écu à deux quartiers

Griffin in one of two quarters

Rostock

Rostock

Stargard in Pommern

Greif in geviertem Schild

Griffon dans écu écartelé

Griffin on quartered shield

Xabon

Pommern

Pommern 1523

Pommern 1489–1499

Pommern 1489–1499

Esterházy, Grafen

Pommern

Pommern 1523

Pommern

Pommern 1523

Idem, in neunfeldigem Schild

Idem, au premier de neuf quartiers

Idem, on shield quartered of nine

Pommern 1524

Greifenkopf

Tête de griffon

Griffin's head

Stettin

Pasewalk, Stadt (Pommern)
Stettin

Schonen (Südschweden)

Malmö, Stadt, 23. 4. 1437

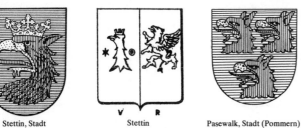

Stettin, Stadt

Stettin

Pasewalk, Stadt (Pommern)

Greif, wachsend

Griffon issant et naissant

Griffin issuant

Greifenhagen, Stadt
(Pommern)

Stolp (Pommern)

Grimmen, Stadt (Pommern)

Altdamm (Pommern)

Grafen von Sprinzenstein
(Österreich)

Grafen von Sprinzenstein
(Österreich)

Eber

Sanglier

Boar

Novara, Stadt

New-York
Taunton (Massachusetts)
Vereinigte Staaten von Amerika

Schweidnitz, Stadt

Bermuda

Schweidnitz, Stadt

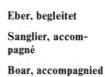

Georgien

Eber, begleitet

**Sanglier, accom-
pagné**

Boar, accompagnied

Britannien

Britannien

Ebersberg, Benediktinerkloster
(Oberbayern)

Ungarn

Britannien

Pruntrut (Berner Jura)

Frankreich

Frankreich, König Ludwig XII.
(reg. 1498–1514)

Asti
Frankreich
Mailand, Herzogtum

Ebrach, Kloster

Zwei Eber

Deux sangliers

Two boars

Britannien

Eberkopf

Hure de sanglier

Boar's head

Schweidnitz, Stadt

Nevers, Stadt

Schweidnitz, Stadt

Schlesien

Sayn (Freusberg)

Sayn

Wolf und Fuchs

Loup et renard

Wolf and fox

Passau, Bistum

Passau, Bistum
Wolfhagen (Hessen)

Passau, Bistum und Stadt

Passau, Bistum

Peine, Stadt (Niedersachsen)

Peine, Stadt (Niedersachsen)

Kent · Montalcino
(Toskana), 1555–1559
Rom, Republik 1849 · Siena

Byzanz, Kaiserreich

Wolf, wachsend

Loup issant

Wolf issuant

Siebenbürgen, Dynastie Zapolya
Ungarn, König Johann Zápolya
1526–1540

Siebenbürgen, Dynastie Zapolya
Ungarn, König Johann Zápolya
1526–1540

Ungarn

Wolf, wachsend in geviertem Schild

Loup issant dans écu écartelé

Wolf issuant, on quartered shield

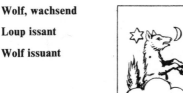

Ungarn, Königin Isabella,

Tochter König Sigismunds I.
von Polen, aus seiner 2. Ehe
mit Bona Sforza (Mailand)
† 1559, ∞ 1539,
Johann Zápolya, 1526–40

Oppeln und Ratibor, Herzogtum
Siebenbürgen, Dynastie Zapolya
Ungarn, König Johann Zápolya

Ungarn, König Johann
Zápolya 1526–1540

Wolfskopf

Tête de loup

Wolf's head

Serbien

Grafen von Windisch-
Graetz (Österreich)

Wolfszähne

Dents de loup

Wolf's teeth

Kinsky

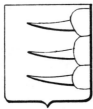

Siebenbürgen,
Dynastie Báthori

Polen (König Stephan
Bathory 1574–1586)
Siebenbürgen, Dynastie Báthori

Polen (König Stephan
Bathory 1574–1586)

Polen (König Stephan
Bathory 1574–1586)

Hund (Bracke, Windspiel)

Chien (braque et lévrier)

Hound (talbot and greyhound)

Castiglione delle Stiviere (Provinz Mantua)

Mantua, Herzogtum

Persien (Schiras)

Mantua, Herzogtum

Aquila bei Mantua

Murbach und Lüders, Abtei (Oberelsaß)

Castiglione delle Stiviere (Provinz Mantua)

Bayern

Persien (Koway)

Brackenkopf

Tête de chien braque

Talbot's head

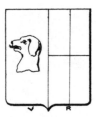

Reuß, Fürstentum

Oettingen

Oettingen

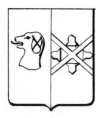

Oettingen

Nürnberg, Burggrafschaft

Nürnberg, Burggrafschaft

Hase

Lièvre

Hare

Hulagiden, Ilchane von Transoxanien, Mitte 15. Jahrh.

Ardebil (pers. Aserbaidshan)

Schlesien

Cincinnati (Ohio)

Persien (Koway)

Sari

Haßfurt, Stadt (Unterfranken)

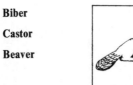

Kotschinchina

Biber

Castor

Beaver

Castorland (Kanada) Montreal (Kanada)

Kalifornien

Biberach an der Riß, Stadt

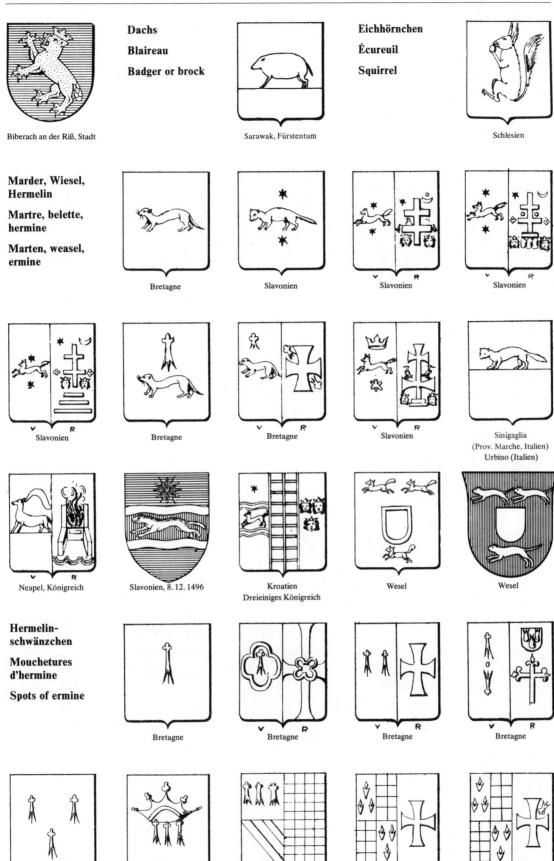

Dachs

Blaireau

Badger or brock

Biberach an der Riß, Stadt

Sarawak, Fürstentum

Eichhörnchen

Écureuil

Squirrel

Schlesien

Marder, Wiesel, Hermelin

Martre, belette, hermine

Marten, weasel, ermine

Bretagne

Slavonien

Slavonien

Slavonien

Slavonien

Bretagne

Bretagne

Slavonien

Sinigaglia
(Prov. Marche, Italien)
Urbino (Italien)

Neapel, Königreich

Slavonien, 8. 12. 1496

Kroatien
Dreieiniges Königreich

Wesel

Wesel

Hermelin-schwänzchen

Mouchetures d'hermine

Spots of ermine

Bretagne

Bretagne

Bretagne

Bretagne

Bretagne

Bretagne

Bretagne
Limoges

Bretagne
Limoges

Bretagne
Limoges

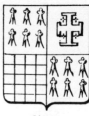

Bretagne
Limoges

Bretagne
Limoges

Bretagne

Bretagne

Limoges

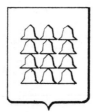

Bretagne

Penthièvre, Grafschaft
(Bretagne)

Köln, Stadt

Roubaix, Stadt
(Dép. du Nord)

Roubaix, Stadt
(Dép. du Nord)

Eisenhutfeh

Vair, vairé

Vair, vairy

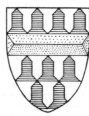

Camerino, Herzogtum
(Provinz Marche, Italien,
Marchesi Varani)

Tongern, Stadt (Belgien)

Kürsch

Pannes de vair

Fur

Bregenz, Stadt, 24. 2. 1529

Vorarlberg, 20. 8. 1864

Krokodil

Crocodile

Crocodile

Schildkröte

Tortue

Turtle, tortoise

Lesotho 4. 10. 1966

Basutoland, 10. 3. 1951

Vereinigte Staaten von
Amerika

Tierrachen

Gueule de monstre

Monster's mouth

Britische Salomon-Inseln
10. 3. 1947

Kastilien

Francisco Franco,
Generalissimus,
Staatschef von Spanien

Lynn oder King's Lynn,
Stadt (England)

Adler (heraldisch), ungekrönt

Aigle héraldique sans couronne

Eagle, not crowned

Aquila

Aachen · Altenburg · Aquileja
Arboga · Arleux · Arnsberg
Arnstein · Baer, Bannerherrschaft
Bayern · Besançon, Stadt
Bozzolo
Brandenburg, Markgrafschaft
Burgund, Herzogtum
Cagliari · Cambrai, Bistum
Como · Crevacuore
Desana · Deventer
Diepholz · Donauwörth
Dortmund · Drossen

Elincourt · Esslingen
Florennes · Freiburg, Grafschaft
Goslar · Görz · Gronsfeld
Guastalla · Heilbronn
Hersfeld (Abtei)
Jever, Herrschaft
Kölln an der Spree · Krain
L'-Aquila, Abruzzen
Lausitz (Brandenburg.Anteil)
Lavagna (Ligurien)
Lenzen · Lobdeburg
Loos · Lothringen · Lüttich

Mantua, Herzogtum
Massa Lombarda
Mirandola
Mirecourt (Vosges)
Neapel, Königreich
Neckargemünd
Neuenahr
Nordhausen, Stadt
Nördlingen · Novellara
Österreich · Ostfriesland
Pisa · Reckheim
Rietberg (Ostfriesland)

Rottweil · St. Bavo
San Benigno di Fruttuario
Schongau · Savoyen
Herren von Schoonvorst
Schweinfurt
Siebenbürgen, Fürstin
Katharina von Brandenburg,
1630
Sizilien · Solferino · Steiermark
Stein, Herrschaft
Stevensweert
Terceira (Azoren)
Teschen, Herzogtum

Thoren, Abtei · Tirol
Trient, Bistum · Ueberlingen
Ungarn · Urbino
Valence (Drôme)
Valentinois, Landschaft
(Südfrankreich)
Vaudemont
Verona · Vicenza (Oberitalien)
Walcourt (Belgien)
Werben an der Elbe
(Altmark)
Wertheim
Windsheim, Stadt (Bayern)

Idem, im ersten von drei bis fünf Schilden

Idem, au premier de trois à cinq écussons

Idem, on first of three to five escutcheons

Münsterberg und Oels, Herzogtümer

Ungarn

Brandenburg, Kurfürstentum

Brandenburg-Ansbach

Cambrai, Bistum

Megen, Grafschaft
(Nordbrabant)

Brandenburg, Kurfürstentum
Preußen, Herzogtum

Tirol

Bozzolo (Provinz Mantua)
Sabbioneta

Masserano, Fürstentum (Piemont)

Tirol

Kampen, Deventer und Zwolle

Friedland (W: Friedland,
Stargard, Sagan), 16. 6. 1629

Masserano, Fürstentum
(Piemont)

Bozzolo (Provinz Mantua)
Sabbioneta

Brandenburg-Ansbach
Brandenburg-Bayreuth

Friedland (W: Friedland,
Mecklenburg, Sagan), 16. 6. 1629

Schwarzburg (Thüringen)

Murbach und Lüders,
Abtei (Oberelsaß)

Murbach und Lüders,
Abtei (Oberelsaß)

Utrecht, Bistum

Nürnberg, Stadt

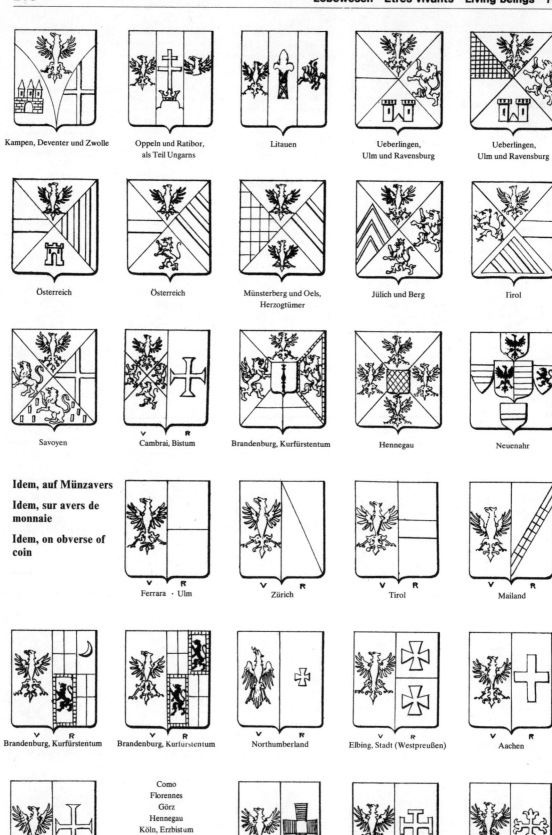

Kampen, Deventer und Zwolle

Oppeln und Ratibor,
als Teil Ungarns

Litauen

Ueberlingen,
Ulm und Ravensburg

Ueberlingen,
Ulm und Ravensburg

Österreich

Österreich

Münsterberg und Oels,
Herzogtümer

Jülich und Berg

Tirol

Savoyen

Cambrai, Bistum

Brandenburg, Kurfürstentum

Hennegau

Neuenahr

Idem, auf Münzavers

**Idem, sur avers de
monnaie**

**Idem, on obverse of
coin**

Ferrara · Ulm

Zürich

Tirol

Mailand

Brandenburg, Kurfürstentum

Brandenburg, Kurfurstentum

Northumberland

Elbing, Stadt (Westpreußen)

Aachen

Aachen
Cambrai, Bistum

Como
Florennes
Görz
Hennegau
Köln, Erzbistum
Lüttich, Bistum
Parma
Savoyen

Loos

Cambrai, Bistum
Lüttich, Bistum

Lavagna (Ligurien)

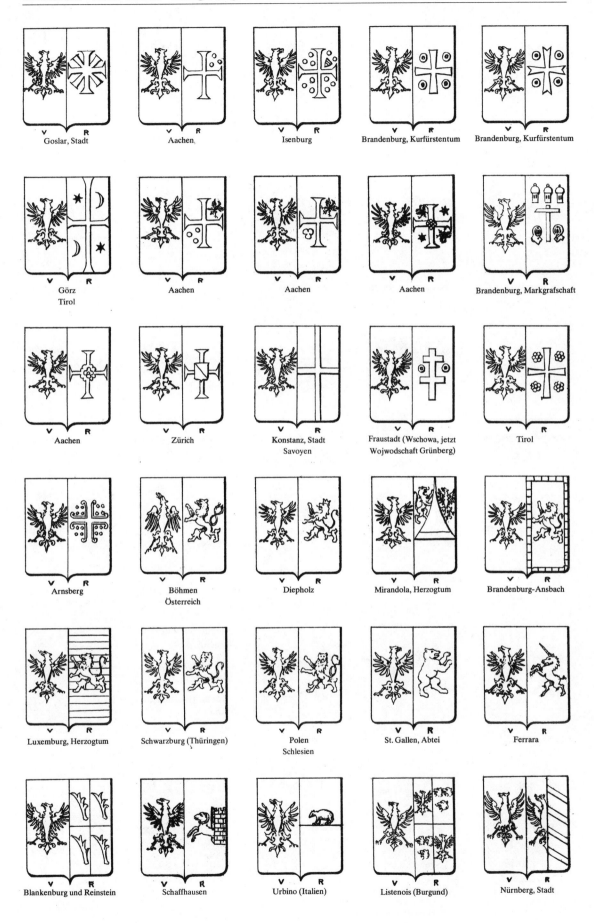

Goslar, Stadt

Aachen

Isenburg

Brandenburg, Kurfürstentum

Brandenburg, Kurfürstentum

Görz
Tirol

Aachen

Aachen

Aachen

Brandenburg, Markgrafschaft

Aachen

Zürich

Konstanz, Stadt
Savoyen

Fraustadt (Wschowa, jetzt
Wojwodschaft Grünberg)

Tirol

Arnsberg

Böhmen
Österreich

Diepholz

Mirandola, Herzogtum

Brandenburg-Ansbach

Luxemburg, Herzogtum

Schwarzburg (Thüringen)

Polen
Schlesien

St. Gallen, Abtei

Ferrara

Blankenburg und Reinstein

Schaffhausen

Urbino (Italien)

Listenois (Burgund)

Nürnberg, Stadt

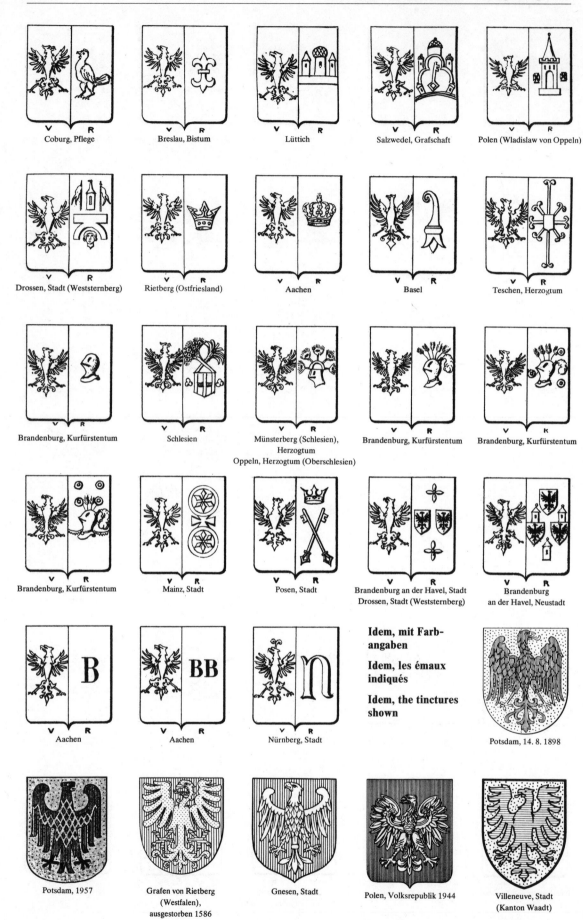

Coburg, Pflege

Breslau, Bistum

Lüttich

Salzwedel, Grafschaft

Polen (Wladislaw von Oppeln)

Drossen, Stadt (Weststernberg)

Rietberg (Ostfriesland)

Aachen

Basel

Teschen, Herzogtum

Brandenburg, Kurfürstentum

Schlesien

Münsterberg (Schlesien),
Herzogtum
Oppeln, Herzogtum (Oberschlesien)

Brandenburg, Kurfürstentum

Brandenburg, Kurfürstentum

Brandenburg, Kurfürstentum

Mainz, Stadt

Posen, Stadt

Brandenburg an der Havel, Stadt
Drossen, Stadt (Weststernberg)

Brandenburg
an der Havel, Neustadt

Aachen

Aachen

Nürnberg, Stadt

**Idem, mit Farb-
angaben**

**Idem, les émaux
indiqués**

**Idem, the tinctures
shown**

Potsdam, 14. 8. 1898

Potsdam, 1957

Grafen von Rietberg
(Westfalen),
ausgestorben 1586

Gnesen, Stadt

Polen, Volksrepublik 1944

Villeneuve, Stadt
(Kanton Waadt)

Oppeln, Herzogtum
Teschen, Herzogtum

Arnsberg, Stadt

Schweinfurt

Deutschland (Römischer
König) ab 1175 bezeugt
Goslar, Stadt

Aachen, Stadt

Deutsches Reich
11. 11. 1919

Deventer

Oppenheim, Stadt
(Rheinland-Pfalz)

Arnstadt, Stadt

Dortmund, Stadt
24. 9. 1946

Deutschland,
Bundesrepublik, 20. 1. 1950
Deutsches Reich, bis 15. 11. 1935

Oron-le-Châtel
(Kanton Waadt)

Dortmund, Stadt,
um 1500-1946

Deutsches Reich, bis 5. 11. 1935
Bundesrepublik Deutschland
20. 1. 1950

Villingen, Stadt, 10. 8. 1530

**Adler (heraldisch),
gekrönt**

**Aigle héraldique,
couronnée**

Eagle, crowned

Aachen

Alten burg
Aquileja
Arnstadt
Castiglione delle Stiviere
Como
Correggio
Crevacuore
Deventer
Ferrara
Frankfurt am Main
Guastalla
Modena

Nordhausen
Nördlingen
Novellara
Piacenza
Pisa
Reckheim
Sachsen-Lauenburg
Schongau
Sizilien
Teschen
Tirol
Verona

Soldin (Mark Brandenburg

Brescello
Castiglione delle Stiviere

Desana
Deventer
Dortmund, Stadt
Guastalla
Mantua
Pesaro
Saluzzo
Tassarolo
Triest, Bistum
Triest, Stadt
Urbino

Mähren

**Idem, im ersten von
drei Schilden**

**Idem, au premier de
trois écussons**

**Idem, on first of
three escutcheons**

Utrecht, Bistum

Murano, Insel

Murano, 1694–1700.

V. Silvester Valieri, Doge
    Benito Balbi
    Giovanni Maria Licini
R. Antonio Briati
    Paulo Zimi
    Nian. Maria Marinet
    Pietro Santini

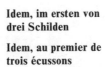
Polen
(Dynastie Wettin 1697–1763)

Polen (König Stephan
Bathory 1574–1586)
Siebenbürgen, Dynastie Báthori

Polen (König Stephan
Bathory 1574–1586)
Siebenbürgen, Dynastie Báthori

Polen (König Johann III.
Sobieski 1674–1696)

Polen (Dynastie Wasa
1587–1672)

Posen, Stadt (z. Zt. der Dynastie
Wasa 1587–1672)

Rietberg (Ostfriesland)

Polen (Dynastie Wasa
1587–1672)

Polen (König Stephan
Bathory 1574–1586)

Idem, auf Münzavers

**Idem, sur avers de
monnaie**

**Idem, on obverse of
coin**

Ungarn

Elbing (W: Polen und Elbing)

Danzig (W: Polen und Danzig)

Brokmerland

Crevacuore, Markgrafschaft
(Provinz Novara)

Norden (Ostfriesland)

Masserano, Fürstentum
(Piemont)

Teschen, Herzogtum

Donauwörth, Stadt
Fraustadt
Polen

Fraustadt (Wschowa,
jetzt Wojwodschaft Grünberg)

Glogau, Herzogtum. 1476–1524
Kurland · Polen

Castiglione delle Stiviere
(Provinz Mantua)

Teschen, Herzogtum

Castiglione delle Stiviere
(Provinz Mantua)

Radicati

Böhmen

Namslau (Niederschlesien)
Polen
Rietberg (Ostfriesland)
Schweidnitz, Stadt
Ungarn

Lobsens (Lobzenica,
Wojewodschaft Bromberg) als
Besitz der Familie Krotowski

Tournai, Herrschaft

Posen, Stadt

Brandenburg, Kurfürstentum
Teschen, Herzogtum

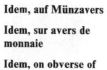

Teschen, Herzogtum

**Idem, mit Farb-
angaben**

**Idem, les émaux
indiqués**

**Idem, the tinctures
shown**

Frankfurt am Main

Polen, Republik 1. 8. 1919

Polen, Republik 13. 12. 1927

Germersheim, Stadt
(Rheinland-Pfalz)

Nördlingen

Mähren;
W – Besserung 7. 12. 1462

Mähren

**Adler, belegt mit
Halbmond oder Klee-
stengeln**

**Aigle chargée de
croissant ou de demi-
cercle tréflé**

**Eagle charged with
crescent or similar
figures**

Acqui

Cortemillia (Provinz Cuneo)
Incisa (Provinz Allessandria)
Ivrea (Provinz Aosta)
Mantua, Herzogtum
Tirol

Brandenburg, Markgrafschaft
Drossen, Stadt
(Weststernberg), berichtigt 1930

Ostpreußen

Tirol
Verona (Oberitalien)

Trient, Bistum

Glogau, Stadt

Krossen an der Oder,
Herzogtum
Liegnitz und Brieg,
Herzogtum
Münsterberg und Schweidnitz,
Herzogtümer
Oppeln und Ratibor,
Herzogtum
Schlesien

Liegnitz und Brieg

Krain

Jägerndorf, Herzogtum

Krossen an der Oder,
Herzogtum
Liegnitz, Brieg und Wohlau,
Herzogtümer
Schlesien

Schlesien

Goldberg, Stadt (Schlesien)

Liegnitz und Brieg
Löwenberg (Schlesien)

Münsterberg, Stadt (Schlesien)

Idem, auf Münzavers

**Idem, sur avers de
monnaie**

**Idem, on obverse of
coin**

Acqui, Bistum

Cortemillia (Provinz Cuneo)
Crevacuore, Markgrafschaft
(Provinz Novara)
Uri, Schwyz und Unterwalden

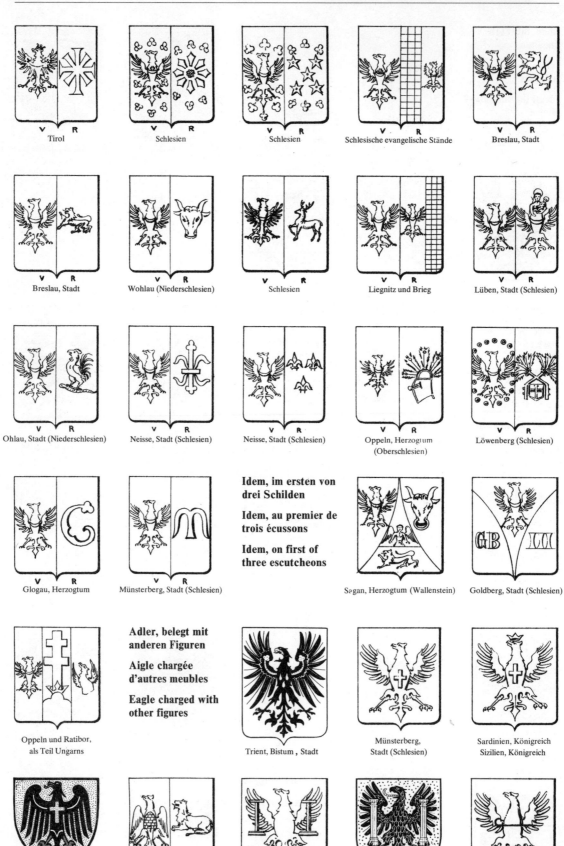

Tirol

Schlesien

Schlesien

Schlesische evangelische Stände

Breslau, Stadt

Breslau, Stadt

Wohlau (Niederschlesien)

Schlesien

Liegnitz und Brieg

Lüben, Stadt (Schlesien)

Ohlau, Stadt (Niederschlesien)

Neisse, Stadt (Schlesien)

Neisse, Stadt (Schlesien)

Oppeln, Herzogtum (Oberschlesien)

Löwenberg (Schlesien)

Idem, im ersten von drei Schilden

Idem, au premier de trois écussons

Idem, on first of three escutcheons

Glogau, Herzogtum

Münsterberg, Stadt (Schlesien)

Sagan, Herzogtum (Wallenstein)

Goldberg, Stadt (Schlesien)

Adler, belegt mit anderen Figuren

Aigle chargée d'autres meubles

Eagle charged with other figures

Oppeln und Ratibor, als Teil Ungarns

Trient, Bistum , Stadt

Münsterberg, Stadt (Schlesien)

Sardinien, Königreich Sizilien, Königreich

Rottweil

Deseret (Utah)

Besançon, Stadt Masserano, Fürstentum (Piemont)

Besançon, Stadt

Brixen, Domkapitel

Erfurt, Stadt

Mühlhausen in Thüringen

Mühlhausen in Thüringen

Mühlhausen in Thüringen

Frankfurt am Main

Polen

Ravensburg

Polen

Wangen im Allgäu
Windsheim, Stadt (Bayern)

Windsheim, Stadt (Bayern)

Wetzlar, Stadt

**Adler mit Brust-
schild**

**Aigle chargée d'un
écusson sur l'esto-
mac**

**Eagle charged with
inescutcheon on
body**

Föderation Arabischer
Republiken

Ägypten, 21. 2. 1973

Libysche Arabische Republik,
1. 1. 1972

Monferrat, Markgrafschaft
(Oberitalien)

Saluzzo

Saluzzo

Esslingen, Stadt

Österreich

Oberösterreich

Heilbronn

Gelnhausen, Stadt

Heilbronn

Reutlingen, Stadt

Olmütz, Stadt (Mähren)

Österreich, Republik,
8. 5. 1919

Österreich, Republik,
1. 5. 1945

Münsterberg und Oels,
Herzogtümer

Zürich

Libysche Arabische Republik,
6. 11. 1969

Jemen, Republik

Ägypten, 1958

Syrien 1958–1971

Irak, Republik, 2. 6. 1965

Südjemen , Volksrepublik

Burgenland, 1. 8. 1922

Vereinigte Staaten
von Amerika

Brandenburg-Ansbach, Markgrafschaft
Brandenburg-Bayreuth, Markgrafschaft
Jägerndorf, Herzogtum , Neustadt a. d. Aisch
Preußen, Herzogtum

Preußen,
Herzogtum

Preußen, Herzogtum

Hohenzollern 1849

Brieg, Herzogtum

Löwenberg (Schlesien)

Teschen, Herzogtum

Bayern, Herzogtum

Schongau, Stadt (Bayern)

Lavagna und Masserano

Sardinien, Königreich

Alessandria   1646

Sardinien, Königreich

Wien, Stadt und Bundesland
13. 2. 1925

Ostpreußen, 1941

Nürnberg, Stadt

Ägypten, 1953

Syrien bis 1958

San Benigno di Fruttuario
(Provinz Turin)

Ueberlingen,
Stadt, 12. 2. 1528

Böhmen
Luxemburg, Herzogtum

Ueberlingen

Gotteshausbund

Polen (König Stephan
Bathory 1574–1586)

Polen (König Stephan
Bathory 1574–1586)

Tirol

Deutsches Reich, 1871

Deutsches Reich
27. 4. 1871

Deutsches Reich
3. 8. 1871

Deutsches Reich
6. 12. 1888

Kempten, Stadt

Aalen, Stadt (Württemberg)

Mittenwalde, Stadt
(Mark Brandenburg)

Liberia

Dinkelsbühl

Rietberg (Ostfriesland)

Quedlinburg , Stadt

Jemen, Republik

Jemen, Republik

Vereinigte Arabische Emirate

Iglau (Mähren)

Königsberg in Preußen,
2. 8. 1724

Brandenburg, Kurfürstentum
Krossen an der Oder,
Herzogtum

Brandenburg, Kurfürstentum

Brandenburg, Kurfürstentum

Brandenburg, Kurfürstentum

Brandenburg, Kurfürstentum

Kleve und Mark als Teile
von Kurbrandenburg

Mark, Brandenburg, Provinz

Colmar im Elsaß, Stadt

Spandau
(Mark Brandenburg)

Belleville

Oberschlesien, 19. 6. 1942

Isny, Stadt (Württemberg)

Polen (Dynastie
Wasa 1587–1672)

Polen (Dynastie Wasa
1587–1672)

Hennegau

Esslingen, Stadt

Chrudim, Stadt (Böhmen)

Frankfurt am Main

Heilbronn

Iglau (Mähren)

Mosbach, Stadt (Nordbaden)

Nürnberg, Stadt

Preußen, Herzogtum

Elbing (W: Polen und Elbing)

Znaim (Mähren)

Znaim (Mähren)

Cincinnati (Ohio)

Dekalb (Tennessee)
Detroit (Michigan)
East Troy (Wisconsin)
Fond du Lac (Wisconsin)
Fort Washington (Wisconsin)
Hillsdale (Michigan)
Milwaukee (Wisconsin)
Newbourg (Wisconsin)
New-Orleans (Louisiana)
New-York
Oskosh (Wisconsin)

Palatine (Illinois)
Parrysbourg (Ohio)
Philadelphia (Pennsylvanien)
Racine (Wisconsin)
Vereinigte Staaten von Amerika

New-York

Appleton (Wisconsin)

Barton (Wisconsin)
Beaver Dam (Wisconsin)
Manitowac (Wisconsin)
Marshall (Wisconsin)
Mayfield (Wisconsin)
Milwaukee (Wisconsin)
Oconto County (Wisconsin)
North Prairie (U.S.A.)
Sauk City (Wisconsin)

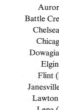

Adrian (Michigan)
Albion (Michigan)
Ann Arbor (Michigan)

Aurora (Illinois)
Battle Creek (Michigan)
Chelsea (Michigan)
Chicago (Illinois)
Dowagiac (Michigan)
Elgin (Illinois)
Flint (Michigan)
Janesville (Wisconsin)
Lawton (Michigan)
Lena (Michigan)
Lowell (Michigan)

Madison (Wisconsin)
Marshall (Wisconsin)
Milwaukee (Wisconsin)
New-Lisbon (Wisconsin)
Racine (Wisconsin)
Rockford (Illinois)
Saginaw City (Michigan)
Salina (Michigan)
South Bend (Indiana)
Sycamore (Illinois)
Ypsilanti (Michigan)

Vereinigte Staaten
von Amerika

Kalifornien

Kalifornien

Kalifornien

New-York · Trenton (New Jersey)
Vereinigte Staaten von Amerika

Albion (Michigan)

Kalifornien
Niles (Michigan)
Paw-Paw (Michigan)
Racine (Wisconsin)

Hillsdale (Michigan)
Hudson (Michigan)

Hillsdale (Michigan)

Chicago (Illinois)
Vereinigte Staaten von Amerika

Hennegau

Troppau, Herzogtum
(Dynastie Liechtenstein)

Kärnten

Oberösterreich

Österreich

Elsaß-Lothringen, 29. 12. 1891

Österreich

Doria, Geschlecht in Genua

Fürstenberg,
Landgrafschaft und Fürstentum

Österreich

Ungarn

Val di Taro (Provinz Parma)

Brandenburg, Markgrafschaft

Hennegau

Österreich

Luxemburg, Herzogtum

Friedland, Fürstentum,
12. 3. 1624,
Herzogtum, 4. 1. 1627

Kurland

Indonesien 11. 2. 1950

Rumänien 23. 6. 1921

Spanien, 2. 2. 1938

Fürstenberg, Landgrafschaft
und Fürstentum

Friedland und Sagan,
Herzogtum, 16. 2. 1628

Friedland und Sagan,
Herzogtum, 16. 2. 1628

Italien, Königreich 1805–1814

**Adler mit Nimbus
oder Kranz um Kopf**

**Aigle, la tête nimbée
ou ornée de feuillage**

**Eagle, with halo or
wreath about head**

Coburg

Tirol

Tirol, 8. 11. 1921

Tirol, 8. 3. 1949

**Adler innerhalb
Schildrandes**

**Aigle entourée de
bordure**

**Eagle between
bordure**

Bayern

Fürstenberg,
Landgrafschaft und Fürstentum

Bogotà, 3. 12. 1548

**Adler, begleitet von
Ringen**

**Aigle, tenant ou
accompagnant annelets**

Eagle and annulets

Fraustadt (Wschowa, jetzt
Wojwodschaft Grünberg)

Brandenburg, Kurfürstentum

Brandenburg, Kurfürstentum

Perleberg (Mark Brandenburg)
Werben an der Elbe (Altmark)

Brandenburg, Kurfürstentum

**Adler, begleitet von
Mond und Stern**

**Aigle, accompagnée de
croissant et étoile**

**Eagle under crescent
and mullet**

Örebro, Stadt (Schweden)

Werben an der Elbe (Altmark)

Österreich

**Adler, begleitet von
Stern(en)**

**Aigle accompagnée
d'étoile(s)**

Eagle and mullet(s)

Ostfriesland
Rietberg (Ostfriesland)

Arnstein

Brandenburg, Kurfürstentum

Stendal (Altmark)

Schlesien

Bayern

**Adler, begleitet von
Kreuz(en)**

**Aigle accompagnée de
croisette(s)**

**Eagle accompagnied
by crosslet(s)**

Wetzlar, Stadt

Trebnitz (Niederschlesien)

Adler auf Weltkugel oder Berg

Aigle soutenue de globe terrestre ou tertre

Eagle upon terrestrial globe or mount

Brooklyn (New York)

Elisabeth Port (New Jersey)
Greenpoint (New York)
Honesdale (Pennsylvanien)
Jersey City (New Jersey)
Mansfield (Ohio)
Newark (New Jersey)
New-York
Vereinigte Staaten von Amerika

Vereinigte Staaten von Amerika

Vereinigte Staaten von Amerika

Neapel und Sizilien

Nizza

New-York

Goldberg, Stadt (Schlesien)

Bolivien
Vereinigte Staaten von Amerika

Adler, begleitet von Vierfüßler

Aigle accompagnée de quadrupède

Eagle accompagnied by quadruped

Brandenburg, Markgrafschaft

Brandenburg, Markgrafschaft

Brandenburg, Kurfürstentum

Kallies, Stadt (Pommern)

Adler, begleitet von Pflanze(n)

Aigle accompagnée de plante(s)

Eagle and plants

Glogau, Herzogtum

Breslau, Bistum

Schweidnitz, Stadt

Breslau, Stadt

Vereinigte Staaten von Amerika

Tegucigalpa (Honduras)

Mexiko, 5. 2. 1934

Mexiko, 16. 9. 1968

Mexiko, Republik

Chiapas
Mexiko, Kaiserreich, 1865-67

Durango
Mexiko, Kaiserreich, Republik
San Luis Potosí
Sonora
Tuxpango
Uruachic
Uruapan

Guanajuato (Mexiko)

Zamora (Mexiko)

Mexiko, Kaiserreich, 1863-1865
Veracruz (Mexiko)

Las Chiapas (Mexiko)
Mexiko, Kaiserreich, 1822–1823

Mexiko, Kaiserreich,
1822–1823

Columbus (Ohio)

Columbus (Wisconsin)
Cooperstown (New York)
Fond du Lac (Wisconsin)
Gallipolis (Ohio)

Bologna, Herrschaft

Ofen-Pest

Vereinigte Staaten von Amerika

Vereinigte Staaten von Amerika

Seneca Falls (New York)

Vereinigte Staaten von Amerika

Potosí (Bolivien)

Iles de France (Mauritius)
et Bourbon (Réunion), 1804
Isle Bonaparte (1806–1810)

Alleghany (Pennsylvanien)

Bellaire (Ohio)
Bethel (Indiana)
Cambridge (Ohio)
Chillicothe (Ohio)
Circleville (Ohio)
Lawrenceville (Pennsylvanien)
Massachusetts
Oskosh (Wisconsin)
Oxford (Ohio)
Piqua (Ohio)
Pittsburg (Pennsylvanien)
Steubenville (Ohio)

Stoughton (Wisconsin)
Toledo (Ohio)
Troy (Ohio)
Vereinigte Staaten von Amerika
Wapakoneta (Ohio)
Wellsville (Ohio)
Wheeling (Westvirginia)
Wilmington (Ohio)
Woodstock (Illinois)
Wooster (Ohio)
Zanesville (Ohio)

Adler auf Bauwerk stehend

Aigle soutenue d'édifice

Eagle upon building

Abu Dhabi, Streitkräfte, 1968

Schlesien

Aquileja

Polen

Mexiko, Kaiserreich,
1822–1823

Mexiko, Kaiserreich,
1822–1823

Adler, Schwert schwingend oder haltend

Aigle brandissant ou tenant glaive

Eagle holding sword

Westpreußen

Westpreußen

Westpreußen

Elbing (W: Westpreußen
und Elbing)

Danzig (W: Westpreußen
und Danzig)

Grenzmark Posen –
Westpreußen, 28. 7. 1929

Grenzmark Posen –
Westpreußen, 10. 2. 1925

Preußen, 2. 10. 1933

Siebenbürgen,
Dynastie Rákóczi

Adler, Szepter haltend

Aigle tenant sceptre

Eagle holding sceptre

Preußen, Königreich

Preußen, Königreich,
Modell 1889

Hohenzollern, 1849

**Adler mit weiteren
Hoheitszeichen**

**Aigle tenant d'autres
signes de souveraineté**

**Eagle holding other
emblems of
sovereignty**

Georgien

Deutsches Reich, Hoheits-
abzeichen der Wehrmacht, 1935

Deutsches Reich,
5. 11. 1935 / 7. 3. 1936

**Adler, begleitet von
Schildchen und
anderen Geräten**

**Aigle accompagnée
d'écussons et d'autres
meubles**

**Eagle with escutch-
eons and other charges**

Luzern

Nördlingen

Pomponesco

Forlí, Stadt
(Provinz Forlí, Italien)

Danzig – Westpreußen,
Januar 1942

Brandenburg, Kurfürstentum

Schwarzburg (Thüringen)

Brandenburg, Kurfürstentum

Wimpfen am Neckar

Wimpfen am Neckar

Polen

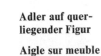

Trier, Erzbistum

**Adler auf quer-
liegender Figur**

**Aigle sur meuble
horizontal**

**Eagle upon horizontal
object**

Bolivien

Desana, Dynastie Tizzone

Rom, Republik

Cincinnati (Ohio)

Greenville (Ohio)
Kendalville (Indiana)
Kylburn City (Wisconsin)
Tomah (Wisconsin)
Two Rivers (Wisconsin)
Vereinigte Staaten von Amerika
Waterloo (Wisconsin)
Watertown (Wisconsin)

Vereinigte Staaten von Amerika

Kalifornien

Cleveland (Ohio)

Ungarn

New-York

Frankreich, Kaiserreich

Syrakus

Zara (Dalmatien) 1813

Appleton (Wisconsin)

East Troy (Wisconsin)
Fond du Lac (Wisconsin)
Manitowac (Wisconsin)
Mayfield (Wisconsin)
Milwaukee (Wisconsin)
Vereinigte Staaten von Amerika

Rom, Republik

Zacatecas (Mexiko)

Verona (Oberitalien)

Adler, auf Waffen-gruppe stehend

Aigle soutenue de groupe d'armes

Eagle upon group of weapons

Jordanien, Königreich, 1921

Abu Dhabi, 1968

Mexiko, Kaiserreich, 1822–1823

Preußen, Königreich

Chuquisaca (Bolivien), heute: Sucre

Adler mit Spruchband oder Buchstaben

Aigle sur listel ou avec lettre(s)

Eagle upon scroll or with letter(s)

Vereinigte Staaten von Amerika

Kalkutta

Oesel

Oels , Stadt

St. Léon

Dortmund, Stadt
Drossen, Stadt (Weststernberg)

Dortmund, Stadt
Drossen, Stadt (Weststernberg)

Frankfurt an der Oder

Nordhausen, Stadt

Schweinfurt

Karlsburg, Stadt
(Siebenbürgen)

**Adler in geteiltem
Schild**

Aigle dans écu coupé

**Eagle on shield
per fess**

Ulm

Deventer

Beichlingen

Neuenburg,
Fürstentum (1806–1814)

Musocco und Musso

Breslau, 19. 10. 1938

Düren

Prenzlau, Stadt (Uckermark),
21. 10. 1705

**Adler in gespaltenem
Schild**

Aigle dans écu parti

**Eagle on shield
per pale**

Deventer

Schlesien

Oberösterreich

Oberösterreich

Neuenahr

Holland

Nördlingen

Brandenburg-Ansbach

Posen, Stadt

Holland

Breslau, Stadt

Sayn-Altenkirchen

Teschen, Herzogtum

Pesaro

Rietberg (Ostfriesland)

Braunschweig, Herzogtum

Blankenburg und Reinstein

Württemberg-Oels,
Herzogtum (Schlesien)

Trient und Brixen

Savona (Italien)

Savona (Italien)

Fürstenwalde

Teschen, Herzogtum

Teschen, Herzogtum

Chiemsee, Bistum

Brandenburg, Kurfürstentum

Lothringen, Herzogtum

Posen, Stadt
(z. Zt. der Dynastie Wasa
1587–1672)

Krossen an der Oder, Stadt

Teschen, Herzogtum

Adler in dreiteiligem Schild

Aigle dans écu tiercé

Eagle on tierced shield

Polen
(Aufstandsregierung 1863)

Polen (König Stanislaus II.
Poniatowski 1764–1795)

Polen
(W: Polen, Litauen, Radolin)

Riga, Stadt
(unter polnischer Oberhoheit)

Desana, Grafschaft
(bei Vercelli)

Lobsens (Lobzenica,
Wojewodschaft Bromberg)
als Besitz der Familie Krotowski

Posen, Stadt
(z. Zt. der Dynastie Wasa
1587–1672)

Megen, Grafschaft
(Nordbrabant)

Sudetenland, Reichsgau,
9. 9. 1940

Adler in zweiteiligem Schild, unten

Aigle dans écu divisé en deux pièces, en pointe

Eagle on shield divided in two parts, in base

Aigle

Reckheim

Adler in geviertem Schild, Feld 2: Heroldstücke

Aigle dans écu écartelé, quartier 2: pièces honorables

Eagle on quartered shield, quarter 2: geometrical charges

Deventer   Preußen, Königreich   Bologna, Herrschaft   Bologna, Herrschaft

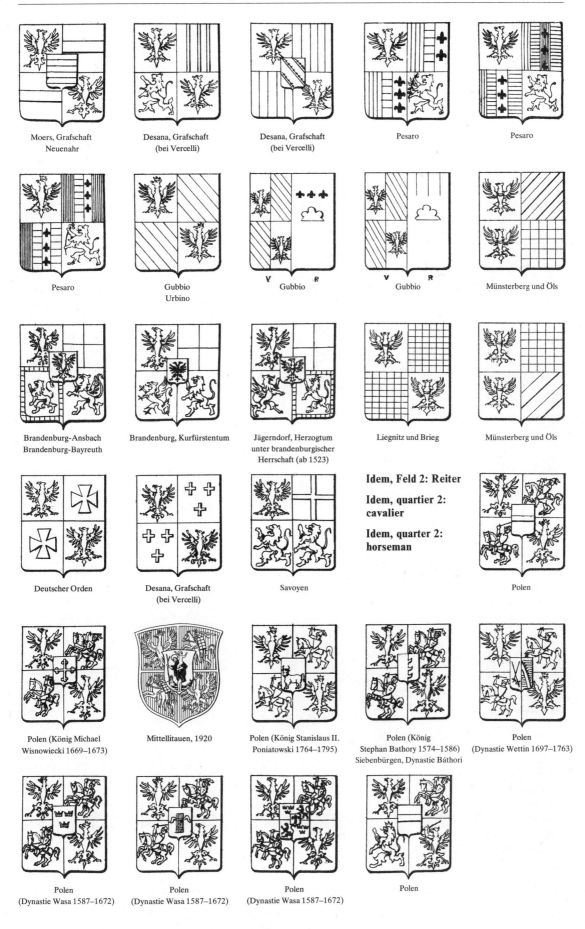

Moers, Grafschaft
Neuenahr

Desana, Grafschaft
(bei Vercelli)

Desana, Grafschaft
(bei Vercelli)

Pesaro

Pesaro

Pesaro

Gubbio
Urbino

Gubbio

Gubbio

Münsterberg und Öls

Brandenburg-Ansbach
Brandenburg-Bayreuth

Brandenburg, Kurfürstentum

Jägerndorf, Herzogtum
unter brandenburgischer
Herrschaft (ab 1523)

Liegnitz und Brieg

Münsterberg und Öls

Idem, Feld 2: Reiter

**Idem, quartier 2:
cavalier**

**Idem, quarter 2:
horseman**

Deutscher Orden

Desana, Grafschaft
(bei Vercelli)

Savoyen

Polen

Polen (König Michael
Wisnowiecki 1669–1673)

Mittellitauen, 1920

Polen (König Stanislaus II.
Poniatowski 1764–1795)

Polen (König
Stephan Bathory 1574–1586)
Siebenbürgen, Dynastie Báthori

Polen
(Dynastie Wettin 1697–1763)

Polen
(Dynastie Wasa 1587–1672)

Polen
(Dynastie Wasa 1587–1672)

Polen
(Dynastie Wasa 1587–1672)

Polen

Idem, Feld 2: Löwe

Idem, quartier 2: lion

Idem, quarter 2: lion

Stolberg, Grafschaft

Sachsen-Altenburg-Weimar

Sachsen, Herzogtum

Desana, Grafschaft
(bei Vercelli)

Hennegau

Holland
Massa (Italien)
Masserano, Fürstentum
(Piemont)
Ostfriesland

Correggio

Neuenahr

Mirandola, Herzogtum

Ostfriesland

Mirandola, Fürstentum

Luxemburg, Herzogtum

Brandenburg-Ansbach

Lixheim (Lothringen)

Brandenburg, Kurfürstentum

Stolberg, Grafschaft

Brandenburg, Kurfürstentum

Friedland, Herrschaft,
15. 9. 1622

Listenois (Burgund)

**Idem, Feld 2:
andere Vierfüßler**

**Idem, quartier 2:
autre quadrupède**

**Idem, quarter 2:
other quadruped**

Rumänien 1867–1872

Rumänien 8. 3. 1872

Glogau, Stadt

Schwarzburg (Thüringen)

Oesel

Idem, Feld 2: Greif

**Idem, quartier 2:
griffon**

**Idem, quarter 2:
griffin**

Brandenburg-Bayreuth,
1486

Preußen, Königreich

Brandenburg, Kurfürstentum

Idem, Feld 2: Vogel

Idem, quartier 2: oiseau

Idem, quarter 2: bird

Brandenburg, Kurfürstentum

Castiglione delle Stiviere
(Provinz Mantua)

Brandenburg, Kurfürstentum
Preußen, Herzogtum

Brandenburg, Kurfürstentum
Preußen, Herzogtum

Brandenburg, Kurfürstentum
Preußen, Herzogtum

Münsterberg
(Haus Podiebrad) 1456–1569

Brandenburg-Ansbach
Brandenburg-Bayreuth

Brandenburg, Kurfürstentum
Preußen, Herzogtum

Brandenburg, Kurfürstentum
Preußen, Herzogtum

V   R
Böhmen

Brandenburg, Kurfürstentum

Frankfurt am Main

Bozzolo (Provinz Mantua)
Castiglione delle Stiviere
(Provinz Mantua)

Oppeln, Herzogtum
(Oberschlesien)
Siebenbürgen, Dynastie Bethlen

Siebenbürgen

Idem, Feld 2: andere Lebewesen

Idem, quartier 2: autre être vivant

Idem, quarter 2: other living being

Stolberg, Grafschaft

Leiningen

Desana, Grafschaft
(bei Vercelli)
Mailand, Herzogtum

Castiglione delle Stiviere
(Provinz Mantua)
Mailand, Herzogtum

Castiglione delle Stiviere
(Provinz Mantua)
Mailand, Herzogtum

Mailand

Idem, Feld 2: Pflanze

Idem, quartier 2: plante

Idem, quarter 2: plant

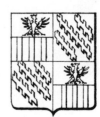

Urbino (Italien)

Camerino, Herzogtum

Radicati

Solferino

Radicati
(Provinz Marche, Italien,
Dynastie Rovere)

Desana, Grafschaft
(bei Vercelli)

Barby, Grafschaft

Savona
(König Ludwig XI.
von Frankreich)

Desana,
unter französischer Herrschaft,
1515–1529

Breslau, Bistum

Liechtenstein
Troppau, Herzogtum
Troppau und Jägerndorf

Liechtenstein, Fürstentum

**Idem, Feld 2:
Bauwerk**

**Idem, quartier 2:
édifice**

**Idem, quarter 2:
building**

Westfriesland

**Idem, Feld 2:
Geräte**

**Idem, quartier 2:
instruments**

**Idem, quarter 2:
tools**

Litauen
Polen (Dynastie Wasa
1587–1672)

Oppeln und Ratibor,
als Teil Polens

Polen (Dynastie Wasa
1587–1672)

Polen (Dynastie Wasa
1587–1672)

Frankfurt, Großherzogtum,
1810–13

Geldern, als Teil Preußens

Frinco
(Provinz Alessandria)

Frinco
(Provinz Alessandria)

**Idem, Feld 2:
Buchstaben**

**Idem, quartier 2:
lettres**

**Idem, quarter 2:
letters**

Goldberg, Stadt (Schlesien)

Gubbio

**Adler in mehrfeldigem
Schild**

**aigle dans écu de plus
de quatre quartiers**

**Eagle on shield
quartered of five or
more**

Münsterberg
(Haus Podiebrad) 1456–1569

Pesaro
Urbino (Italien)

Pesaro
Urbino (Italien)

Pesaro
Urbino (Italien)

Pesaro
Urbino (Italien)

Mirandola, Herzogtum

Polen (Königin
Bona Sforza 1518–1558)

Solferino

Auersperg, 1664
Münsterberg (Schlesien),
Herzogtum

Castiglione delle Stiviere
(Provinz Mantua)

Liegnitz und Brieg,
Ehewappen mit Anhalt
(16. und 17. Jahrhundert)

Polen
(Dynastie Wettin 1697–1763)

Schwarzburg (Thüringen)

Stolberg, Grafschaft

Nevers und Rethel

Brandenburg, Kurfürstentum
Preußen, Herzogtum

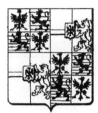

Mirandola, Fürstentum

Desana, Grafschaft
(bei Vercelli)

Masserano, Fürstentum
(Piemont)

Preußen, Königreich,
mittleres Wappen, 9.1.1817

Gestümmelter Adler
Alérion
Alerion

Brandenburg, Kurfürstentum

Schlesien

Lothringen, Herzogtum

Zwei Adler
Deux aigles
Two eagles

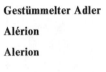

Preußen, Herzogtum

Drei Adler
Trois aigles
Three eagles

Leiningen
Megen, Grafschaft (Nordbrabant)
Wezemaal (Belgien)

Megen, Grafschaft
(Nordbrabant)

Megen, Grafschaft
(Nordbrabant)

Megen, Grafschaft
(Nordbrabant)

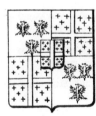

Leiningen-Westerburg

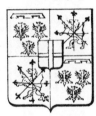

Leiningen-Dagsburg

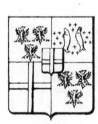

Leiningen-Westerburg

Drossen, Stadt
(Weststernberg)

Weert
(niederländ. Provinz Limburg)

Vier Adler
Quatre aigles
Four eagles

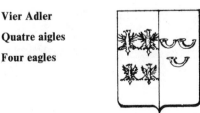

Eggenberg, 1467

Salzwedel, Stadt

Fünf Adler

Cinq aigles

Five eagles

Österreich

Kärnten

Niederösterreich

Tirol

16 Adler

16 aigles

16 eagles

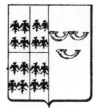
Hoorn, Grafschaft
Weert
(niederländ. Provinz Limburg)

Hoorn, Grafschaft
Weert
(niederländ. Provinz Limburg)

Oberhalber Adler

Aigle naissant

Eagle issuant

Österreich

**Adler, aus Figur
hervorkommend**

**Aigle mouvant de
meuble**

**Eagle issuant from
charge**

Ungarn

Schlesien

Chios, Insel
(W: Marchesi Giustiniani,
Genua, vor 1566)

Mantanzas

Anhalt-Plötzkau, 1603

Brandenburg, Markgrafschaft

Oberschlesien, 1.6.1926

Mühlhausen in Thüringen

Wertheim

Verona (Oberitalien)

Rietberg (Ostfriesland)

**Adler, wachsend in
geteiltem Schild**

**Aigle issant dans
écu coupé**

**Eagle issuant on shield
per fess**

Savona (Italien)

Finale (Provinz Savona)

Hildesheim, Stadt

Hildesheim, Stadt

Hildesheim, Stadt

Eger, Stadt (Böhmen)

Eger, Stadt (Böhmen)

Breslau, Stadt

Breslau, Stadt

Breslau, Stadt

Chios, Insel
(W: Marchesi Giustiniani,
Genua, vor 1566)

Siebenbürgen

Siebenbürgen,
Dynastie Habsburg

Siebenbürgen, Großfürstentum,
2. 11. 1765

Siebenbürgen,
Dynastie Báthori

Löwenstein-Wertheim,
Grafschaft

Wertheim

Mühlhausen in Thüringen

Diepholz

**Adler im ersten von
drei oder mehr Feldern
oder Schilden**

**Aigle au premier de
plusieurs quartiers ou
écussons**

**Eagle on first of three
or more quarters or
escutcheons**

Siebenbürgen,
Dynastie Rákóczi

Siebenbürgen,
Dynastie Báthori

Siebenbürgen,
Dynastie Rákóczi

Siebenbürgen,
Fürst Johann Kemény, 1661

Siebenbürgen,
Dynastie Barcsai

Siebenbürgen,
Dynastie Rákóczi

Siebenbürgen,
Fürstin Katharina von
Brandenburg, 1630

Rechtshalber Adler

**Demi-aigle mouvant
de trait de partition**

**Demi-eagle on shield
per pale**

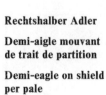

Ratibor, Fürstentum

Beichlingen

Werdenfels, Grafschaft
Garmisch-Partenkirchen
3. 12. 1935

Horschowitz (Böhmen)

Anhalt
Beichlingen
Sachsen-Lauenburg

Rom, Senatoren

Kaufbeuren

Kaufbeuren

Nürnberg, Stadt

Nürnberg, Stadt

Nürnberg, Augsburg und Regensburg

Troppau, Stadt

Stendal (Altmark)

St. Ghislain (Hennegau)

Memmingen, Stadt

Oppeln, Stadt (Oberschlesien)

Oppeln, Stadt (Oberschlesien)

Memmingen, Stadt

Schlesien

Perleberg (Mark Brandenburg)

Polička, Stadt (Böhmen) 1478 Rom, Senatoren

Brandenburg, Markgrafschaft

Brandenburg, Markgrafschaft

Brzesc Kujawski, Wojwodschaft

Ungarn

Deutschland

Kujavien, Landschaft

Deutschland

Mohrin (Neumark)

Küstrin, Stadt

Küstrin, Stadt

Desana, Grafschaft (bei Vercelli)

Desana, Grafschaft (bei Vercelli)

Schlesien

Wusterhausen a. d. Dosse

Workum (niederländ. Provinz Friesland)

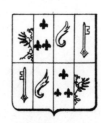

St. Emmeram, Benediktinerabtei, Regensburg, 1561

Anhalt

Anhalt, Herzogtum

Anhalt

Anhalt

Anhalt

Anhalt
Ohlau, Herzogtum
(Niederschlesien)

Anhalt

Kempten, Stadt

Brandenburg, Kurfürstentum

Schlesien

Schlesien

Nordhausen, Stadt

Sneek
(niederl. Provinz Friesland)

Sneek
(niederl. Provinz Friesland)

Liegnitz, Herzogtum

Genf

Schlesien

Genf
Passerano

Genf

Salzwedel, Stadt

Genf

Salzwedel, Stadt

Mülhausen im Elsaß

Ratibor, Stadt
(Oberschlesien)

Ratibor, Stadt
(Oberschlesien)

Nürnberg, Stadt

Phönix

Phénix

Phoenix

Haiti, Kaiserreich
Hohenlohe-Schillingsfürst
Mailand
Potosí (Bolivien)
Vereinigte Staaten von Amerika

Buenos Aires

Griechenland, Republik,
1. 6. 1973

Cirencester, Stadt
(Gloucestershire)

Mailand

Cirencester, Gazoldo
Mirandola,
Neapel und Sizilien

Griechenland, Präsidentschaft
von Kapo d'Istrias, 1827–1831

Haiti, Kaiserreich

Griechenland, Republik,
9. 4. 1932

Exotische Vögel in Adlerhaltung

Oiseaux exotiques en attitude d'aigle

Exotic birds on eagle's attitude

Ostindien

Bolivien

Siam
Thailand

Sudan, Republik, seit 1971

Sarawak (Malaysia),
1. 9. 1973

Papua-Neuguinea 24. 6. 1971

Neukaledonien

Südaustralien, Badge

Adler mit Helm oder Helmzier

Aigle heaumée ou munie de cimier

Eagle helmeted or crested

Prenzlau, Stadt (Uckermark)

Nancy (Lothringen)

Lixheim (Lothringen)

Neuruppin

Prenzlau, Stadt (Uckermark)

Norden (Ostfriesland)

Neuruppin

Harpyie oder Jungfrauenadler

Harpie

Harpy

Ungarn

Nürnberg, Stadt

Ostfriesland

Deutschland

Nürnberg, Stadt

Nürnberg, Stadt

Ostfriesland

Ostfriesland

Ostfriesland

Ostfriesland

Ostfriesland

Emden, Stadt

Emden, Stadt

Emden, Stadt

Eule

Hibou

Owl

Bolivien

Doppeladler

Aigle bicéphale

Two-headed eagle

Atabeck-Zenkide
von Sindsbar

Quedlinburg

Dschudschiden (Gulistan)

Ortokiden zu Keyfa

Ortokiden zu Amid

Rußland,
Republik,1917

Aachen

Arnheim
Arnstadt
Bayeux
Bolsward
Brandenburg,
Markgrafschaft
Cambrai, Stadt und Bistum
Koevorden
Desana
Düren
Flandern
Heinsberg

Loos
Lübeck, Stadt
Luxemburg
Mailand
Neuss
Orange
Randerad
Schwarzburg, (Thüringen)
Werden und Helmstedt
Zaltbommel (Prov. Gelderland)

Brandenburg, Markgrafschaft

Arnheim
(Arnhem), Niederlande

Albanien, 20. 1. 1920
Albanien, 20. 10. 1943

Albanien, 8. 8. 1929

Brandenberg

Desana, Grafschaft
Diedenhofen, Luxemburg,
Herzogtum · Neuss

Essen, Stadt, rechter Schild

Correggio , Mailand ,
Mirandola, Rußland ,
Walachei

Wien, 26. 9. 1461

Krems, Stadt

Albanien, 28. 9. 1939

Maccagno (Provinz Como)

Albanien, 14. 3. 1946

**Idem, mit Hoheits-
zeichen in den Fängen**

**Idem, tenant des
signes de souveraineté**

**Idem, holding insignia
of sovereignty**

Albanien, 20. 2. 1914

Georgien

Rußland

Rußland

**Doppeladler auf
Münzavers**

**Aigle bicéphale sur
avers de monnaie**

**Two-headed eagle on
obverse of coin**

Lübeck, Stadt

Ulm

Megen, Grafschaft
(Nordbrabant)

Megen, Grafschaft
(Nordbrabant)

Ferrara

Österreich

Deutschland-Österreich

Loos

Halen

Herren von Randerad
oder Randerath,
(Niederrhein)

Heinsberg, Herrschaft
(Niederrhein)
Moers. Grafschaft

Crevacuore, Markgrafschaft
(Provinz Novara)

Carmagnola (Provinz Turin)

Lübeck, Stadt

Halen

Österreich
Steiermark

Böhmen

Tirol

Kempten, Stadt

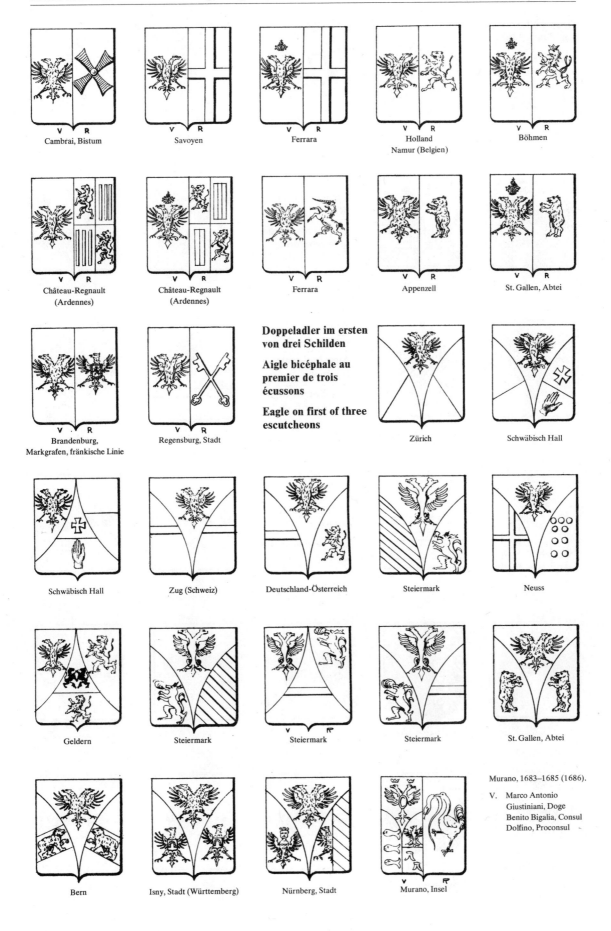

Cambrai, Bistum

Savoyen

Ferrara

Holland
Namur (Belgien)

Böhmen

Château-Regnault
(Ardennes)

Château-Regnault
(Ardennes)

Ferrara

Appenzell

St. Gallen, Abtei

Brandenburg,
Markgrafen, fränkische Linie

Regensburg, Stadt

**Doppeladler im ersten
von drei Schilden**

**Aigle bicéphale au
premier de trois
écussons**

**Eagle on first of three
escutcheons**

Zürich

Schwäbisch Hall

Schwäbisch Hall

Zug (Schweiz)

Deutschland-Österreich

Steiermark

Neuss

Geldern

Steiermark

Steiermark

Steiermark

St. Gallen, Abtei

Bern

Isny, Stadt (Württemberg)

Nürnberg, Stadt

Murano, Insel

Murano, 1683–1685 (1686).

V.   Marco Antonio
     Giustiniani, Doge
     Benito Bigalia, Consul
     Dolfino, Proconsul

Doppeladler im ersten von vier Schilden

Aigle bicéphale au premier de quatre écussons

Two-headed eagle on first of four escutcheons

Neuss

Geldern

Geldern

Ostfriesland

Geldern

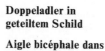

Isny, Stadt (Württemberg)

Doppeladler, begleitet

Aigle bicéphale accompagnée

Two-headed eagle accompagnied

Neuss

Leeuwarden

Westfriesland

Schwarzburg (Thüringen)

Doppeladler in geteiltem Schild

Aigle bicéphale dans écu coupé

Two-headed eagle on shield per fess

Groningen, Stadt

Sabbioneta

Desana, Grafschaft (bei Vercelli)

Correggio

Doppeladler in gespaltenem Schild

Aigle bicéphale dans écu parti

Two-headed eagle on shield per pale

Lübeck, Stadt
Unterwalden

Neuss

Neuss

Neuß, Stadt, 2.9.1475

Neuss

Geldern

Deutschland-Holland

Görlitz

Görlitz, Stadt, 29.8.1433

Steiermark

Schlesien

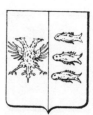

Reichenau und Tamins

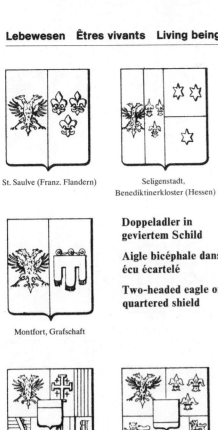

St. Saulve (Franz. Flandern)

Seligenstadt,
Benediktinerkloster (Hessen)

Hamburg

Essen, Stadt

Minden, Stadt

Montfort, Grafschaft

Doppeladler in geviertem Schild

Aigle bicéphale dans écu écartelé

Two-headed eagle on quartered shield

Desana, Grafschaft
(bei Vercelli)

Groningen, Stadt
Moers, Grafschaft

Masserano,
Fürstentum (Piemont)

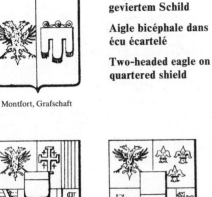

Monferrat,
Markgrafschaft (Oberitalien)

Hohenlohe 1764

Heinsberg,
Herrschaft (Niederrhein)

Geldern

Batenburg

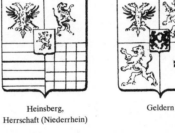

Anholt
Batenburg

Geldern

Leeuwarden

Masserano,
Fürstentum (Piemont)

Görlitz, Stadt, 2.10.1536

Soragna (Provinz Parma)

Grafen von Trautson
und zu Falkenstein, 1598

Ferrara
Modena, Herzogtum

Burg Friedberg

Wiener Neustadt

Wiener Neustadt

Doppeladler in mehrfeldigem Schild

Aigle bicéphale dans écu de plus de quatre quartiers

Two-headed eagle on shield quartered of five or more

Brescello · Ferrara
Modena, Herzogtum
Reggio

Modena, Herzogtum

Ferrara
Modena, Herzogtum
Reggio

Ferrara
Modena, Herzogtum

Mantua, Herzogtum
Nevers und Rethel

Doppeladler belegt

Aigle bicéphale chargée

Two-headed eagle surmounted

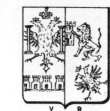

Chuquisaca (Bolivien),
heute: Sucre · La Plata
Sucre (Bolivien)

Albanien, 25. 1. 1925

Ravensburg

Doppeladler mit Brustschild

Aigle bicéphale portant écusson sur l'estomac

Two-headed eagle bearing escutcheon on breast

Desana, Grafschaft
(bei Vercelli)

San Benigno di Fruttuario
(Provinz Turin)

Monferrat,
Markgrafschaft (Oberitalien)

Obwalden

Lübeck, Stadt

Lübeck, Stadt

Lübeck,
Freie und Hansestadt

Metz, Stadt

Friedberg, Stadt (Hessen)

Burg Friedberg

Utrecht, Provinz
Zürich

Utrecht, Provinz und Stadt

Cambrai, Stadt
Groningen, Stadt

Groningen, Stadt

Österreich

Österreich,
Bundesstaat, 1. 5. 1934

Groningen und Ommelanden

Groningen, Provinz

Arquata
Ronco und Roccaforte
Tassarolo

Masserano, Fürstentum
(Piemont)

Haldenstein, Herrschaft
(Bez. Imboden, Graubünden)

Lavagna und Masserano

Desana, Grafschaft (bei Vercelli)
Lavagna und Masserano

Desana, Grafschaft
(bei Vercelli)

Wien, Stadt

Wien, 1942

Wien, 15. 2. 1934

Serbien , Königreich
1882–1918

Serbien, Königreich
Dynastie Karadjordjević

Batenburg

Desana, Grafschaft
(bei Vercelli)

Deutschland-Bayern

Rußland

Batenburg
Nimwegen, Stadt
(Gelderland)

Nimwegen, Stadt (Gelderland)

Nimwegen, Stadt (Gelderland)

Böhmen

Westfriesland

Cambrai, Bistum

St. Gallen, Abtei

Gotteshausbund

Rußland

Siebenbürgen,
Dynastie Báthori

Tirol

Besançon, Stadt
Masserano, Fürstentum (Piemont)

Fosdinovo
(Provinz Massa-Carrara)

Desana,
Grafschaft (bei Vercelli)

Desana, Grafschaft
(bei Vercelli)

Desana, Dynastie Tizzone

Haldenstein, Herrschaft
(Bez. Imboden, Graubünden)

Lima (Peru)

Kempten, Stadt

Nimwegen, Stadt (Gelderland)

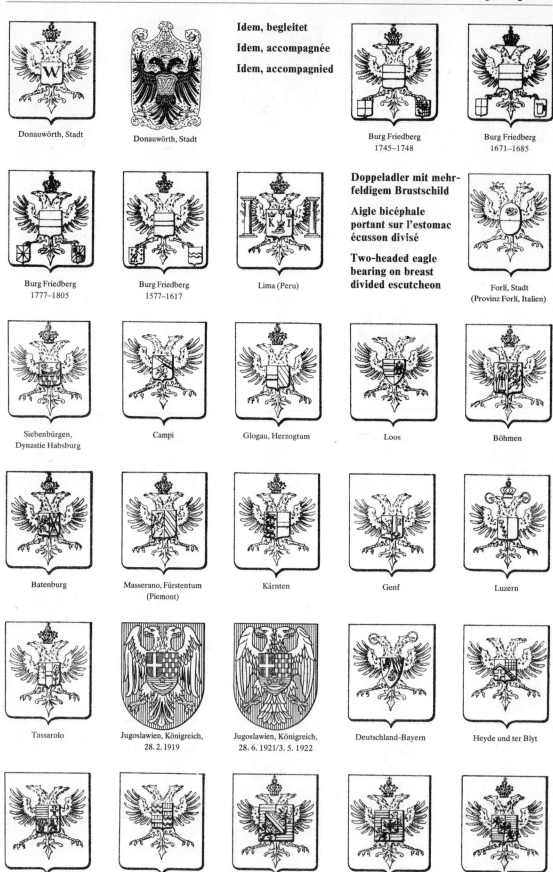

Donauwörth, Stadt

Donauwörth, Stadt

Idem, begleitet

Idem, accompagnée

Idem, accompagnied

Burg Friedberg
1745–1748

Burg Friedberg
1671–1685

Burg Friedberg
1777–1805

Burg Friedberg
1577–1617

Lima (Peru)

**Doppeladler mit mehr-
feldigem Brustschild**

**Aigle bicéphale
portant sur l'estomac
écusson divisé**

**Two-headed eagle
bearing on breast
divided escutcheon**

Forlí, Stadt
(Provinz Forlí, Italien)

Siebenbürgen,
Dynastie Habsburg

Campi

Glogau, Herzogtum

Loos

Böhmen

Batenburg

Masserano, Fürstentum
(Piemont)

Kärnten

Genf

Luzern

Tassarolo

Jugoslawien, Königreich,
28. 2. 1919

Jugoslawien, Königreich,
28. 6. 1921/3. 5. 1922

Deutschland-Bayern

Heyde und ter Blyt

Ungarn

Val di Taro (Provinz Parma)

Oberelsaß

Mähren
Tirol

Mähren
Tirol

Böhmen

Deutschland-Österreich

Toledo
Spanien

Doppeladler mit Brustschild und weiteren Hoheitszeichen

Aigle bicéphale avec écusson et d'autres emblèmes

Two-headed eagle with inescutcheon and other insignia

Deutschland-Österreich

Österreich, Kaisertum,
10. 10. 1915

Deutschland-Bayern

Rußland

Rußland, 8. 12. 1856–1917

Sizilien

Böhmen

Finnland, Großfürstentum
in Personalunion mit Rußland

Montenegro, Fürstentum
Königreich

Perth (Schottland)

Schlesien

Polen (Kongreßpolen 1815)

Albanien, 20. 2. 1914

Schwarzburg (Thüringen)

Schwarzburg-Rudolstadt

Deutschland-Österreich, 1764

Deutschland-Österreich, 1745

Toskana

Böhmen

Deutschland-Bayern

Deutschland-Bayern

Steiermark

Tirol

Moldau und Walachei,
Fürstentümer

Doppeladler, wachsend

Aigle bicéphale issant

Two-headed eagle issuant

Potosí (Bolivien)

Catanzaro (Kalabrien)

Würzburg, Burggrafschaft

Henneberg,
Gefürstete Grafschaft
Schmalkalden (Thüringen)

Henneberg,
Gefürstete Grafschaft

Thurn und Taxis

Versailles

Duisburg

Außergewöhnlicher Doppeladler

Aigle bicéphale extraordinaire

Extraordinary two-headed eagle

Ortokiden zu Amid

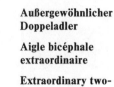

Laibach, Bistum

Laibach, Bistum

Schlesien

Breslau, Stadt, 1262, 1948

Fiume, 1659–1919

Stelzvögel

Échassiers

Stilt-birds

Franken (Merowinger)

Reuß, Fürstentum
(W. Kranichfeld)

Gubbio
Urbino (Italien)

Greyerz (Gruyères),
Landschaft
(Westschweiz)

Greyerz (Gruyères),
Landschaft
(Westschweiz)

Brisbane (Australien,
Neusüdwales, seit 1859
Queensland)

Bendigo (Victoria, 1840–1891:
Sandhurst) • Melbourne
Richmond (Neusüdwales)

Bathurst (Neusüdwales)

Deloraine (Tasmanien)
Hobart Town,
(Name 1804–1881,
seitdem Hobart, Tasmanien)
Melbourne
(Victoria, Australien)
South Yarra
(Victoria, Australien)
Sydney (Australien)
Westbury (Tasmanien)

China

Den Haag

Den Haag

Isenburg

Uganda

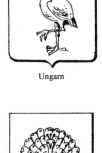

Melbourne
(Victoria, Australien)

Ungarn

Leoben, Stadt (Österreich)

Strausberg, Stadt
(Mark Brandenburg)

Pfau

Paon

Peacock

Wied

Birma, 1825

Birma

Georgien

Georgien

Masenderan, Landschaft
(Persien)

Ostindien

Asterabads
Masenderan, Landschaft
(Persien)

Eriwan (Kaukasus)

Georgien

Neuwied, Stadt

Wied

Hahn und Huhn

Coq et poule

Cock and hen

Henneberg,
Gefürstete Grafschaft

Schlesien

Persien (Koway)

Schlesien

Kambodscha

New-York

Frankfurt an der Oder
Montalban
Singapur

Nikobaren

Pondichéry (nach 1674)

Singapur

Singapur

Singapur

Henneberg,
Gefürstete Grafschaft

Bidschnagur

Henneberg,
Gefürstete Grafschaft

Henneberg,
Gefürstete Grafschaft

Assam

Bugginesen

Ohlau, Stadt (Niederschlesien)

Gaillac (Tarn)

Kenia, 15. 10. 1963

Henneberg,
Gefürstete Grafschaft

Henneberg,
Gefürstete Grafschaft

Henneberg,
Gefürstete Grafschaft

Henneberg,
Gefürstete Grafschaft

Sachsen
(Alt-Weimarer Linie)

Sachsen-Gotha-Henneberg

Frankfurt an der Oder

Ohlau, Stadt (Niederschlesien)

Ohlau, Stadt (Niederschlesien)

Murano, Insel

Hannover, Stadt

Persien (Eriwan)

Ohlau, Stadt (Niederschlesien)

Mirandola und Concordia

Frankfurt an der Oder

Schwan und Gans
Cygne et oie
Swan and goose

Kaisheim oder Kaisersheim
(Kloster), Abt Elias Götz
1681–1696

Braunau, Stadt (Böhmen)

Stormarn

Fremantle (Westaustralien)

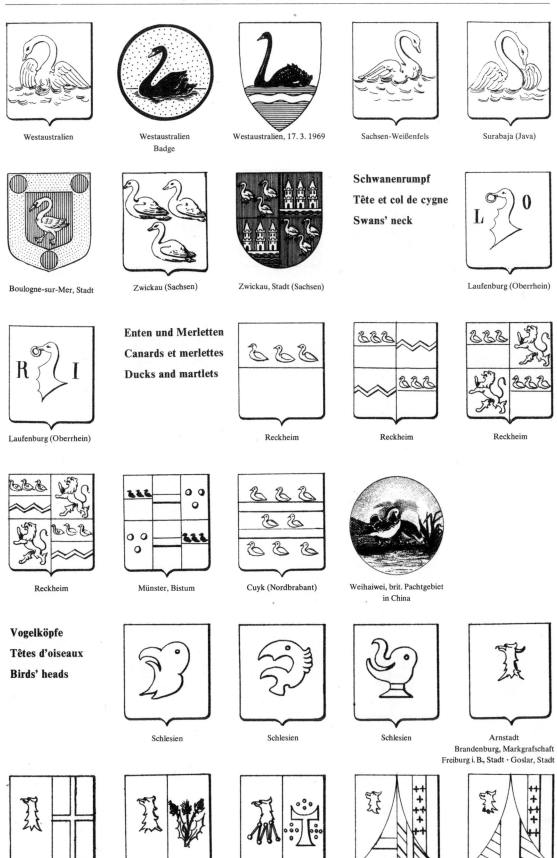

Westaustralien

Westaustralien
Badge

Westaustralien, 17. 3. 1969

Sachsen-Weißenfels

Surabaja (Java)

Boulogne-sur-Mer, Stadt

Zwickau (Sachsen)

Zwickau, Stadt (Sachsen)

Schwanenrumpf
Tête et col de cygne
Swans' neck

Laufenburg (Oberrhein)

Laufenburg (Oberrhein)

Enten und Merletten
Canards et merlettes
Ducks and martlets

Reckheim

Reckheim

Reckheim

Reckheim

Münster, Bistum

Cuyk (Nordbrabant)

Weihaiwei, brit. Pachtgebiet
in China

Vogelköpfe
Têtes d'oiseaux
Birds' heads

Schlesien

Schlesien

Schlesien

Arnstadt
Brandenburg, Markgrafschaft
Freiburg i. B., Stadt · Goslar, Stadt

Freiburg im Breisgau, Stadt

Arbeca

Arbeca

Vorderösterreich

Vorderösterreich

Schlesien

Schlesien

Schlesien

Freiburg, Grafschaft

Freiburg, Grafschaft

Schlesien

Schlesien

Schlesien

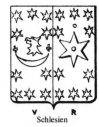
Schlesien

Rathenow, Stadt

Sorau

Schlesien

Brandenburg, Markgrafschaft

Schlesien

Ungarn

Schlesien
Schwarzburg (Thüringen)

Nordhausen, Stadt

Ungarn

Schlesien

Schlesien

Schlesien

Arnstadt
Schwarzburg (Thüringen)

Perleberg (Mark Brandenburg)

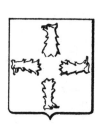
Brandenburg, Markgrafschaft

Flügel

Demi-vols

Wings

Schlesien

Beckum, Stadt.

Tarnowitz (Niederschlesien)

Baden-Durlach,
Markgrafschaft

Schlesien

Kamenz, Herrschaft (Lausitz)

Usenberg (Baden)

Kamenz, Herrschaft (Lausitz)

Schlesien

Usenberg (Baden)

Schlesien

Ungarn

Ungarn

Ungarn

Ungarn

Prenzlau, Stadt (Uckermark)

Brandenburg, Markgrafschaft

Brandenburg, Markgrafschaft

Ortenburg, Grafschaft
(Kärnten) im Besitz der
Grafen Widman 1640–1662

Ortenburg, Grafschaft
(Kärnten) im Besitz der
Fürsten von Portia

**Adlerbein und
Klauflügel**

**Membres et main
d'aigle**

Eagle's legs

Kamenz, Herrschaft (Lausitz)

Schlesien

Villach, Stadt

Tarnowitz (Niederschlesien)

Grafen von Dietrichstein

Federbusch

Panache

Plume of feathers

Großbritannien
Prince of Wales

Großbritannien

Prince of Wales

Malaiischer Bund, 19. 3. 1952

Malaysia, 19. 3. 1963–1965

Malaysia, seit 1965

Ungarn

Vogel, stehend, die Flügel angelegt

Oiseau arrêté, les ailes pliées

Bird closed

Mekka

Island, 5. 10. 1903

Polen

Kermed

Aachen

Terceira (Azoren)

Granollers (Katalonien)

Idem, begleitet

Idem, accompagné

Idem, accompagnied

Neapel und Sizilien

Granollers (Katalonien)

Abuschehr

Glogau, Herzogtum

Glogau, Herzogtum

Lüttich

Lüttich, Bistum

Birma

Vogel, stehend oder schreitend, Flügel angehoben

Oiseau, arrêté ou passant, essorant

Bird rising

Freiburg im Breisgau, Stadt

Lüttich, Bistum Schlesien

Deutschland (Quedlinburg)

Aquileja

Obermünster, Damenstift in Regensburg

Lüttich, Bistum

Ungarn

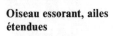

Ungarn

Vogel, stehend oder schreitend, Flügel gespreizt

Oiseau essorant, ailes étendues

Bird rising, wings displayed

Urbino (Italien)

Britannien

Drossen, Stadt (Weststernberg)

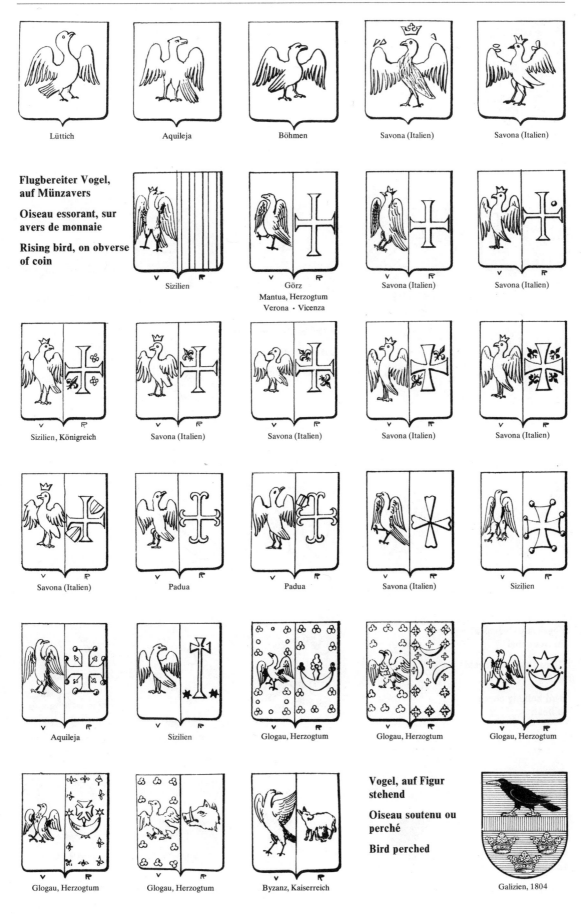

Lüttich

Aquileja

Böhmen

Savona (Italien)

Savona (Italien)

**Flugbereiter Vogel,
auf Münzavers**

**Oiseau essorant, sur
avers de monnaie**

**Rising bird, on obverse
of coin**

Sizilien

Görz
Mantua, Herzogtum
Verona · Vicenza

Savona (Italien)

Savona (Italien)

Sizilien, Königreich

Savona (Italien)

Savona (Italien)

Savona (Italien)

Savona (Italien)

Savona (Italien)

Padua

Padua

Savona (Italien)

Sizilien

Aquileja

Sizilien

Glogau, Herzogtum

Glogau, Herzogtum

Glogau, Herzogtum

Glogau, Herzogtum

Glogau, Herzogtum

Byzanz, Kaiserreich

**Vogel, auf Figur
stehend**

**Oiseau soutenu ou
perché**

Bird perched

Galizien, 1804

Britische Salomon-Inseln
24. 9. 1956

Surinam

Surinam

Ungarn, Dynastie Hunyadi

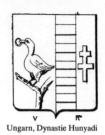

Ungarn, Dynastie Hunyadi

Ungarn

Grafen von Sprinzenstein
(Österreich)

Walachei

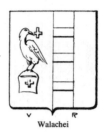

Walachei

Insel Man

Siebenbürgen,
Dynastie Rákóczi

Urbino (Italien)

Vogel als Schildhalter

Oiseau comme tenant

Bird as supporter

Urbino (Italien)

Kalifornien

Kalifornien

Bolsward (niederländische
Provinz Friesland)

Urbino (Italien)

Hoorn, Grafschaft

**Vogel mit Gegenstand
im Schnabel**

**Oiseau portant meuble
au bec**

**Bird holding charge
in beak**

Walachei

Mexiko, Königreich

England, Königreich

Sydney (Australien)

Kabul

Liverpool

Griquatown (Südafrika)

Fidschi, Königreich,
12. 1. 1873 – Sept. 1874

Zypern, Republik 1960

La Paz

Vereinigte Staaten von Amerika

Providence (Rhode Island)

Urbino (Italien)

Vogel auf Rücken eines anderen Tieres

Oiseau sur le dos d'une autre bête

Bird on back of other beast

Ungarn

Kallies, Stadt (Pommern)

Georgien

Persien (Hamadan)

Zoppot

Vogel, sonstwie begleitet

Oiseau accompagné autrement

Bird otherwise accompagnied

Pesaro

Walachei

Siebenbürgen, Dynastie Barcsai

Siebenbürgen, Dynastie Rákóczi

Siebenbürgen, Dynastie Bethlen

Siebenbürgen, Fürst Michael Apafi, 1661–1690

China (Dynastie Kin)

Schlesien

Georgien

Siebenbürgen, Dynastie Rákóczi

Vogel, fliegend

Oiseau volant

Bird volant

Château Porcien

Lörrach

Kendalville (Indiana)
Ligonier (Indiana)
Lima (Ohio)

Zacatecas (Mexiko)

Aquileja

Preußen, Republik, 11.7.1921

Vogel, gegen die Sonne oder zwischen Sternen fliegend

Oiseau volant vers le soleil ou parmi des étoiles

Bird volant towards the sun or between stars

Preußen, Königreich
(König Friedrich Wilhelm I.)

Bolivien

Adamsville (Ohio)

Vereinigte Staaten von Amerika

Bellaire (Ohio)
Cambridge (Ohio)

Charlotte (Michigan)
Cincinnati (Ohio)
Cleveland (Ohio)
Dedham (Tennessee)
Eaton Rapids (Michigan)
Fond du Lac (Wisconsin)
Fortville (Indiana)
Green Bay (Wisconsin)
Huntington (Indiana)
Kentucky
Lancaster (Ohio)

Lansing (Michigan)
Madison (Wisconsin)
Massillon (Ohio)
Monroeville (Ohio)
Oskosh (Wisconsin)
Richmond (Indiana)
Rochester (Minnesota)
Steubenville (Ohio)
Vereinigte Staaten von Amerika
Watertown (Wisconsin)
Wheeling (Westvirginia)

Vogel, fliegend, etwas haltend

Oiseau volant, tenant meuble

Bird volant, holding charge

Vereinigte Staaten von Amerika

Chicago (Illinois)

Unkers Hill (Massachusetts)

Alleghany (Pennsylvanien)

Cincinnati (Ohio)
Massachusetts
Springfield (Massachusetts)
Vereinigte Staaten von Amerika

Vereinigte Staaten von Amerika

Columbus (Ohio)

Como (Indiana)
New-London (Ohio)
Peru (Indiana)
Pittsburg (Pennsylvanien)
Pittsburg (Virginia)

Preußen, 2. 10. 1933

Vogel, abwärts fliegend

Oiseau, volant vers la pointe

Bird volant downwards

Castiglione delle Stiviere
(Provinz Mantua)

Socabaya (Peru)

Bolivien (Potosí)

Socybaya (Peru)

Bogotá, Stadt (Kolumbien)
Neugranada
Popayán (Kolumbien)

Zwei Vögel

Deux oiseaux

Two birds

Schlesien

Plauen, Vogtei

Schlesien

Schlesien

Hagenau, (Unterelsaß)

Kyritz

Ungarn

Oppeln und Ratibor,
unter der Regierung von
Gabriel Bethlen 1622–1629

Deutschland

Fisch

Poisson

Fish

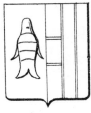

Einsiedeln,
Benediktinerabtei
(Kanton Schwyz)

Einsiedeln, Benediktinerkloster
(Kanton Schwyz)

Gengenbach, Stadt
Rheinau, Benediktiner-
Reichsabtei (Kanton Zürich)

Rheinau,
Benediktiner-Reichsabtei
(Kanton Zürich)

Gengenbach, Stadt

Dauphiné
Frinco (Provinz Alessandria)

Navarra (Nord)

Perpignan
(Pyrénées Orientales)

Ostindien

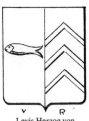

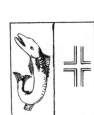

Rheinau,
Benediktiner-Reichsabtei
(Kanton Zürich)

Dauphiné
Desana, Grafschaft
Frinco (Provinz Alessandria)

Desana, Grafschaft
(bei Vercelli)

Rheinau,
Benediktiner-Reichsabtei
(Kanton Zürich)

Oswego (New York)

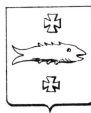

Levis Herzog von
Mirepoix, 1751

Youghal (Irland) 1646

Dschudschiden (Gulistan)

Pillau (Ostpreußen)

Nyon, Stadt (Kanton Waadt)

Magdalenen-Insel (Kanada)

Gengenbach, Abtei

Sizilien

Weißensee (Thüringen)

Weißensee (Thüringen)

Schlesien

Schlesien

Dauphiné

Schlesien

Schlesien

Schlesien

Georgien

Eriwan (Kaukasus)

Audh (Britisch-Indien)

Sulz

Bar

Neuschottland, 26. 5. 1868

Kaiserslautern, Stadt
(Rheinpfalz)

Neapel, König Joseph
Napoleon (1806–1808)

's-Heerenberg, Herrschaft
(Grafschaft Zütphen)

Dauphiné

Zwei Fische

Deux poissons

Two fishes

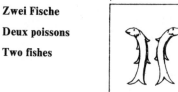

Mömpelgard

Pfirt
Saalfeld, Abtei
Saalfeld, Stadt
Stolberg, Grafschaft
Weißensee (Thüringen)
Wernigerode, Grafschaft

Orbe, Stadt (Waadt)
Mömpelgard, Herrschaft
Pfirt, Grafschaft

Wernigerode, Grafschaft

Saalfeld, Abtei

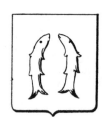

Schlesien · Stolberg, Grafschaft
Weißensee (Thüringen)
Wernigerode, Grafschaft

Kotschinchina

Ostindien

Mömpelgard

Saalfeld, Stadt

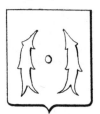

Weißensee (Thüringen)
Wernigerode am Harz

Glogau, Herzogtum

Wernigerode am Harz

Weißensee (Thüringen)

Bar

Bar

Salm

Bar
Chiny

Stolberg, Grafschaft
Weißensee (Thüringen)

Saalfeld, Abtei
Saalfeld, Stadt

Saalfeld, Abtei

Mömpelgard

Mömpelgard

Schlesien

Schlesien
Stolberg, Stadt
Weißensee (Thüringen)

Österreich
Weißensee (Thüringen)

Weißensee (Thüringen)

Schlesien

Schlesien

Audh (Britisch-Indien)

Audh (Britisch-Indien)

Audh (Britisch-Indien)

Pegu, Landschaft in Birma

Weißensee (Thüringen)

Saalfeld, Stadt

Weißensee (Thüringen)

Bar-le-Duc, Stadt

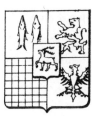

Stolberg, Grafschaft

Salm-Neuburg

Schlesien

Forchheim, Stadt (Bayern)

Weißensee (Thüringen)

Fischingen, Benediktinerabtei
Köpenick
Rheinau, Benediktiner-Reichsabtei

Fischingen,
Benediktinerabtei
(Kanton Thurgau)

Hindustan
(Timuriden, Großmoguln)

Khoi

Weißensee (Thüringen)

Reichenau, Abtei

Fischingen
Fischingen, Benediktinerabtei
(Kanton Thurgau)

Mainau, Benediktinerkloster
(Bodenseeinsel)

Gdingen

Narva, Stadt (Estland)

Narva, Stadt (Estland)

Drei Fische

Trois poissons

Three fishes

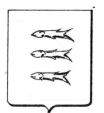

Enkhuizen , Stadt (Nordholland)
Haldenstein, Herrschaft (Graubünden)
Reichenau und Tamins

Asch, Stadt (Böhmen)
Kingston upon Thames

Enkhuizen , Stadt
(Nordholland)

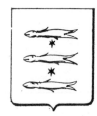

Enkhuizen , Stadt
(Nordholland)

Enkhuizen , Stadt
(Nordholland)

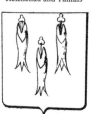

Lynn oder King's Lynn,
Stadt (England)

Wernigerode am Harz

Asch, Stadt (Böhmen)

Halber Fisch

Demi-poisson

Demi-fish

Mohammedabad (Benares)

Stockfisch

Morue séchée

Stock-fish

James Milner, Charlottetown
Prinz-Edwards-Insel (Kanada)

Island, bis 1903

Fischmonster

Monstre à queue de
poisson

Fish-tailed monsters

Ceylon

Wolgast (Pommern)

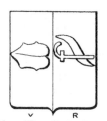

Jezd

Hindustan
(Timuriden, Großmoguln)

Krebs
Écrevisse
Crayfish

Cottbus

Cottbus

Hindustan
(Timuriden, Großmoguln)

Hindustan
(Timuriden, Großmoguln)

Hindustan
(Timuriden, Großmogul)

Cottbus

Muschel
Coquille
Escallop

England, Königreich

Schlesien

Pistoja

Pistoja

Aragonien

Turks- und Caicos-Inseln,
28. 9. 1965

Guadalajara, Bistum

Schlange und Aal
Serpent et anguille
Snake and eel

Italienische Landvogteien
unter der Herrschaft von
Uri und Unterwalden

Aalen, Stadt (Württemberg)

Mailand
Verona

Mailand

Castiglione delle Stiviere
(Provinz Mantua)

Cremona, Herrschaft
Mailand, Herzogtum
Masserano, Fürstentum
(Piemont)

Genua

Fermo
(Provinz Marche, Italien)

Bologna, Herrschaft

Ostindien

Gwalior (Indien)

Rimini, Herrschaft

Ahlen, Stadt (Westfalen)

Ahlen, Stadt (Westfalen)

Ahlen, Stadt (Westfalen)

China (Dynastie Ta Ts'ing, 1636–1912)

China (Dynastie Ta Ts'ing, 1636–1912)

China (Dynastie Ming, 1368–1644)

China (Dynastie Pe Tscheu)

Pavia, Grafschaft

Lombardisch-Venetianisches Königreich

Lombardisch-Venetianisches Königreich nach 1815

Drache mit zwei Beinen, ungeflügelt

Dragon à deux jambes, sans ailes

Dragon with two legs, without wings

Georgien

Österreich

Polen

Laibach, Stadt

Idem, mit vier Beinen

Idem, à quatre jambes

Idem, with four legs

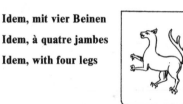

Ungarn

Böhmen

Namur (Belgien)

Ungarn

China

China, Kaiserreich bis 1911

Vietnam (Süd), 1954-1955

Drache ohne Beine, geflügelt

Dragon sans jambes, ailé

Dragon without legs, winged

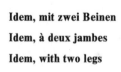

Kotschinchina

Idem, mit zwei Beinen

Idem, à deux jambes

Idem, with two legs

Schlesien

Schlesien

Norrköping (Schweden)

Basel, Stadt
Laibach, Stadt

Malmedy

Schlesien

Cincinnati (Ohio)
Peru·(Indiana) Pittsburg
Sycamore (Illinois)

Polen

Giengen an der Brenz

Verona (Oberitalien)

Polen

Idem, mit vier Beinen

Idem, à quatre jambes

Idem, with four legs

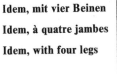

China (Dynastie Ming,
1368–1644)

Assam

Wales

Östergötland, Herzogtum
(Schweden)

Zwei Drachen

Deux dragons

Two dragones

Madrid, 13.9.1850

Ungarn

Bhutan

Cisterna dal Pozzo,
Fürsten della Cisterna
(Piemont)

Der Abschnitt »Pflanzen« umfaßt
alle Gewächse, vom Baum bis zum
Kleeblatt; wegen ihrer Häufigkeit
sind den Rosen und den Lilien
eigene Gruppierungen zugewiesen.
In dem nachstehenden Inhaltsverzeichnis dieser Gruppe geben die
links stehenden Ziffern an, unter
welchem Ordnungsstichwort die
verschiedenen Motive eingeordnet
sind. Die Ziffern rechts geben die
aufzuschlagende Seite an.

Laubbaum, unbegleitet

Arbre à feuilles, seul

Tree with foliage, single

Lindau, Stadt

Telgte, Stadt (Westfalen)

Lindau, Abtei

Schlesien

Arboree
Costa Rica

Franquemont

Bologna, Herrschaft
(Papst Julius II. aus dem
Hause della Rovere)

Gubbio
Pesaro
Sinigaglia (Prov. Marche)
Urbino

Zerega

Bocholt, Stadt (Westfalen)
Lindau, Stadt
Wimpfen am Neckar

Santa Rosa

Hartford (Connecticut)

Urariche (Mexiko)

Montalcino (Toskana)

Schlesien

Hagen in Westfalen, Stadt

Offenbach, Stadt (Hessen)

Bocholt, Stadt (Westfalen)

Lindau, Stadt

Homburg, Stadt (Saarland)

Telgte, Stadt (Westfalen)

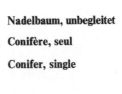
Äquatorial-Guinea,
12. 10. 1968

Nadelbaum, unbegleitet

Conifère, seul

Conifer, single

Wollin (Pommern)

Massachusetts

Palmen

Palmiers

Palm-trees

Antigua (Westindien)

Ceylon
Charlestown
(Westindien, Insel Nevis)
Olancho (Honduras)

Auckland (Neuseeland)

Cardona

Potosí (Bolivien)

Apulien

Baum auf Münzavers

Arbre sur avers de monnaie

Tree on obverse of coin

Urbino (Italien)

Schlesien

Costa Rica

San José de Costarica

Costa Rica

Baum unter Schildhaupt

Arbre sous chef

Tree under chief

Bolivien, 1825, Variante

Bolivien, 17. 8. 1825

Herzogenbusch (Nordbrabant)

Herzogenbusch (Nordbrabant)

Amiens, Stadt

Malakka, 4. 5. 1961

Baum in geteiltem Schild

Arbre dans écu coupé

Tree on shield per fess

Franquemont

Haldenstein, Herrschaft (Bez. Imboden, Graubünden), Besitz der Familie von Salis

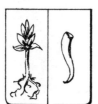

Haldenstein, Herrschaft (Bez. Imboden, Graubünden), Besitz der Familie von Salis

Haldenstein, Herrschaft (Bez. Imboden, Graubünden), Besitz der Familie von Salis

Baum in gespaltenem Schild

Arbre dans écu parti

Tree on shield per pale

Thann (Oberelsaß)

Fosdinovo (Provinz Massa-Carrara)

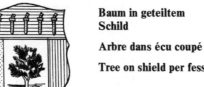

Buchhorn, Stadt (seit 1811 Friedrichshafen, Bodensee)

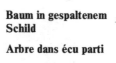

Friedrichshafen, bis 1811 Buchhorn

Baum in dreiteiligem Schild

Arbre dans écu tiercé

Tree on tierced shield

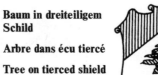

Libanon

Franquemont

Baum in geviertem Schild

Arbre dans écu écartelé

Tree on quartered shield

Solferino

Mehrere Bäume

Plusieurs arbres

Several trees

Kotschinchina

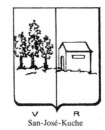

San-José-Kuche

Tlazasalca

Olten, Stadt
(Kanton Solothurn)

Prinz-Edwards-Insel
(Kanada), 30. 5. 1905

Baum, begleitet

Arbre, accompagné

Tree, accompanied

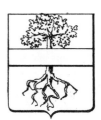

Bocholt, Stadt (Westfalen)

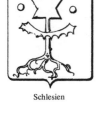

Schlesien

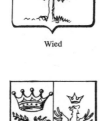

Wied

Grootebroek, Stadt
(Nordholland)

New-York

Barbados, 21. 12. 1965

Pesaro

Gubbio, Pesaro
Urbino

Treggiano

...

Urbino (Italien)

Tangermünde (Altmark)

Brandenburg, Land
15. 12. 1945

Brandenburg

Fürstenwalde

Fürstenwalde

Saudi-Arabien

Schardschah

Malediven

Oranje-Freistaat

Pointe à Pitre (Guadeloupe)

Costa Rica, 10. 5. 1823

Haiti, Republik

Haiti, Republik

Haiti, Republik, 21. 6. 1964

Fürstenwalde

Baum und ein Tier
Arbre et un animal
Tree and one animal

Kristiansand, Stadt
(Norwegen)

Ostindien

Deutsch-Ostafrikanische
Gesellschaft, 1885

Brabant
Lothringen, Herzogtum

Schemachá

Lindau, Stadt

Andover, Stadt (Hampshire)

Bernau, Stadt
(Mark Brandenburg)

Persien (Tiflis)

Madrid

Britisch Westafrika

Polen

Madagaskar

Eriwan (Kaukasus)

Bagdad

Nîmes (Südfrankreich)

Haiti, Kaiser Faustin I.,
1849-1858

Haiti, Kaiser Faustin I.,
1849-1858

Hamar, Stadt (Norwegen)

Brandenburg-Bayreuth

Baum und zwei Tiere
Arbre et deux animaux
Tree and two animals

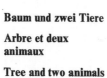

Pirna, Stadt (Sachsen)
Ravenna, Stadt

Pirna, Stadt (Sachsen)

Ravenna, Stadt

Oranje-Freistaat, 23. 2. 1857

Eberswalde, Neustadt

Eberswalde, Stadt
(Mark Brandenburg)

Guadalajara, 8. 11. 1539

Biscaya
Neu-Biscaya (Durango)

Hessen

Sydney (Australien)

Bolivien

Sydney (Australien)

Sydney (Australien)

Rangun, Stadt (Birma)

Brandenburg

Brandenburg, Markgrafschaft

Baumstumpf

Tronc d'arbre

Trunk

Wimpfen am Neckar

Baumäste

Chicots

Ragged staffs

Siebenbürgen,
Dynastie Báthori

Břevnov,
jetzt Stadtteil von Prag

Schlesien

Klettgau (Herren von Sulz)

Österreich

Desana, Grafschaft
(bei Vercelli)

Desana, Grafschaft
(bei Vercelli)

Desana, Grafschaft
(bei Vercelli)

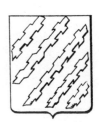

Desana, Grafschaft
(bei Vercelli)

Beblätterte Zweige

Rameaux feuillés

Twigs with leaves

Herschmanmiestetz

Herschmanmiestetz

Jagadhari

Bidschnagur

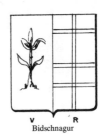

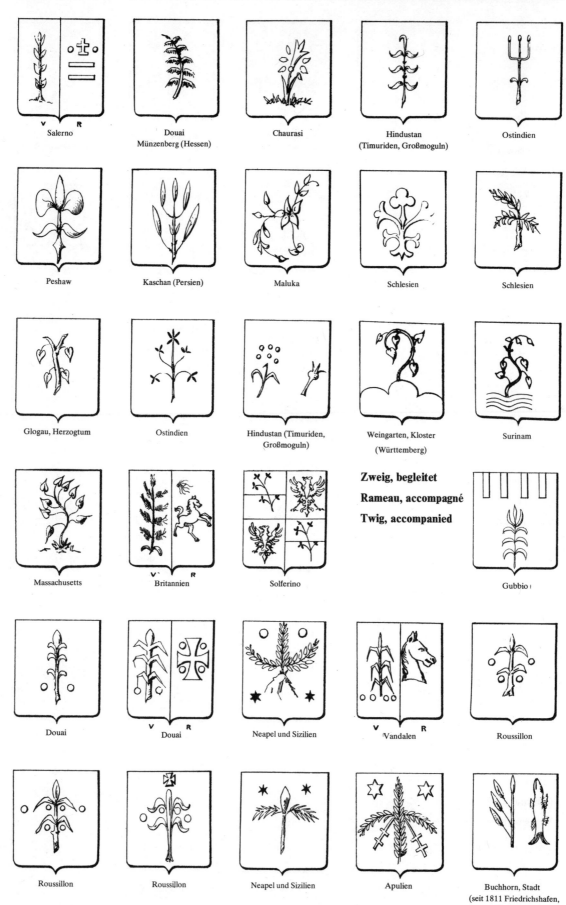

Salerno

Douai
Münzenberg (Hessen)

Chaurasi

Hindustan
(Timuriden, Großmogul)

Ostindien

Peshaw

Kaschan (Persien)

Maluka

Schlesien

Schlesien

Glogau, Herzogtum

Ostindien

Hindustan (Timuriden,
Großmogul)

Weingarten, Kloster
(Württemberg)

Surinam

Massachusetts

Britannien

Solferino

Zweig, begleitet
Rameau, accompagné
Twig, accompanied

Gubbio

Douai

Douai

Neapel und Sizilien

Vandalen

Roussillon

Roussillon

Roussillon

Neapel und Sizilien

Apulien

Buchhorn, Stadt
(seit 1811 Friedrichshafen,
Bodensee)

Annapolis (Maryland, USA)

Bidschnagur

St. Omer, Stadt (Frankreich)

Bauni

Douai

Neapel und Sizilien

Dschaipur, Indien

Floreffe
(belgische Provinz Namur)

Mehrere Zweige

Plusieurs rameaux

Several twigs

Casale

Penahabad
Tiflis (Kaukasus)

St. Étienne, Stadt
(Frankreich)

Evreux (Eure, Normandie)

Krossen an der Oder,
Herzogtum

Eritrea, 1952

**Zweige unter
Schildhaupt**

Rameaux sous chef

Twigs under chief

Rijswijk, Stadt (Südholland)

Amiens, Stadt

Ontario, Provinz, 26. 5. 1868

Kanada, 25. 11. 1869

Blattranken

Feuilles tigées

Leaves slipped

Reims, Stadt

Schlesien

Frinco (Provinz Alessandria)

Schlesien

Eichenreis

Branche de chêne

Oak-leaves acorned

Rijswijk, Stadt (Südholland)

Khevenhüller

Khevenhüller

Khevenhüller

Rautenkranz

Couronne de rue

Crown of rue

Sachsen, Herzogtümer, Königreich
Westfriesland (Statthalter aus dem
Hause Sachsen)

Sachsen-Land

Sachsen, Provinz,
22. 9. 1880/1945–48

Sachsen-Anhalt, 14. 12. 1948

Sachsen, Herzogtum

Sachsen, Herzogtum

Sachsen, Herzogtum

Sachsen, Herzogtum

Sachsen, Herzogtümer, Königreich
Westfriesland (Statthalter
aus dem Hause Sachsen)

Würzburg, Herzogtum

Sachsen, Herzogtum

Sachsen, Kurfürstentum

Sachsen, Provinz, 27. 6. 1927

Sachsen-Weißenfels

Sachsen, Kurfürstentum

Sachsen-Eisenach
Sayn-Altenkirchen

Westfriesland (Statthalter
aus dem Hause Sachsen)

Sachsen (Neu-Gothaer Linie)

Troppau, Herzogtum
(Dynastie Liechtenstein)

Troppau und Jägerndorf
Troppau, Herzogtum
(Dynastie Liechtenstein)

Sachsen, Kurfürstentum

Savoyen

Sachsen, Kurfürstentum

Sachsen, Kurfürstentum

Sachsen, Kurfürstentum

Sachsen, Kurfürstentum

Sachsen-Lauenburg

Sachsen-Lauenburg

Thüringen, 15. 8. 1933

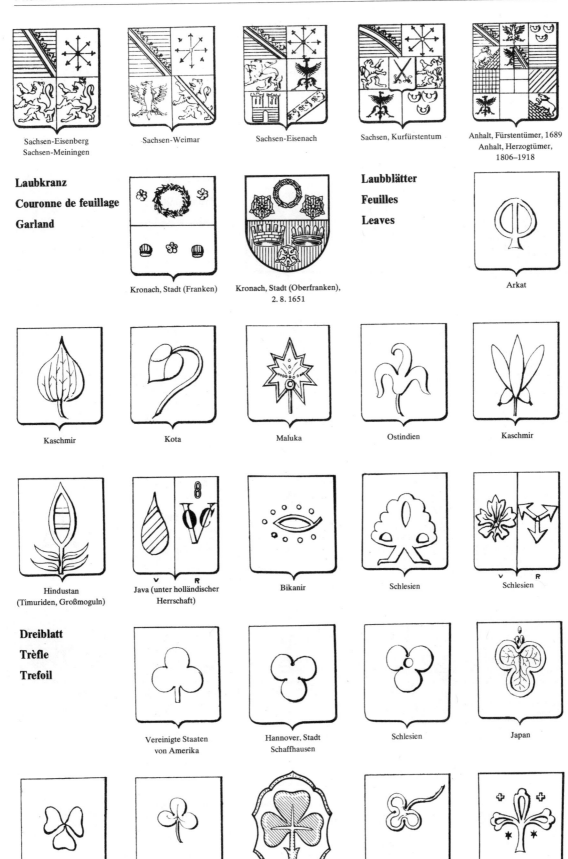

Sachsen-Eisenberg
Sachsen-Meiningen

Sachsen-Weimar

Sachsen-Eisenach

Sachsen, Kurfürstentum

Anhalt, Fürstentümer, 1689
Anhalt, Herzogtümer,
1806–1918

Laubkranz

Couronne de feuillage

Garland

Kronach, Stadt (Franken)

Kronach, Stadt (Oberfranken),
2. 8. 1651

Laubblätter

Feuilles

Leaves

Arkat

Kaschmir

Kota

Maluka

Ostindien

Kaschmir

Hindustan
(Timuriden, Großmoguln)

Java (unter holländischer
Herrschaft)

Bikanir

Schlesien

Schlesien

Dreiblatt

Trèfle

Trefoil

Vereinigte Staaten
von Amerika

Hannover, Stadt
Schaffhausen

Schlesien

Japan

Schlesien

Lixheim (Lothringen)

Fürth in Bayern, Stadt

Kota

Garz (Pommern)

Schlesien

Hannover, Stadt

Zwei Blätter

Deux feuilles

Two leaves

Almora

Pesaro

Pesaro

Rietberg (Ostfriesland)

Montreal (Kanada)

Drei Blätter

Trois feuilles

Three leaves

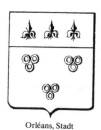

Bühl, Stadt (Baden)

Irsee, Abtei (Bayr. Schwaben)

Irsee, Abtei (Bayr. Schwaben)
Abt Thomas Hofmann,
1565–96

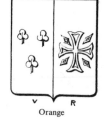

St. Omer (Frankreich) , Stadt

Orange

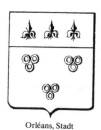

Orléans, Stadt

Orléans, Stadt

Orléans, Stadt

Orléans, Stadt

Blätter im Drei- oder Sechspaß

Feuilles posées en pairle

Leaves in pall

Seehausen in der Altmark

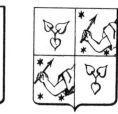

Seehausen in der Altmark

Burg Milching,
Reichsfreiherrn 1569

Brandenburg, Markgrafschaft

Perleberg
(Mark Brandenburg)

Perleberg
(Mark Brandenburg)

Perleberg
(Mark Brandenburg)

Brandenburg, Markgrafschaft

Vier und mehr Blätter

Plus de trois feuilles

Four leaves and more

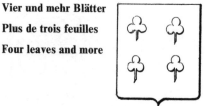

Orange

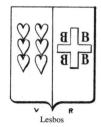

Lesbos

Kassel, Stadt (Hessen)

Seeblätter

Feuilles de nénuphar ou bouterolles

Water-lily leaves

Brehna

Friesack (Mark Brandenburg)

Brehna

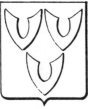

Brehna

Wiborg, Bistum (Finnland)

Baumfrüchte

Fruits

Fruits

Augsburg, Stadt

Augsburg, Stadt

Augsburg, Stadt

Augsburg, Stadt

Barbados

Bogotá, (Kolumbien)
Neugranada
Popayán (Kolumbien)

Neugranada

Grenada

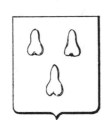

Toul, Domkapitel

Weinstock

Cep de vigne

Vine

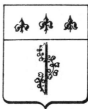

Amiens, Stadt (Frankreich)

Connecticut (U.S.A.)

Weintraube

Grappe de raisin

Grapes

Jena
Weimar

Hobart Town, (Name 1804–1881,
seitdem Hobart, Tasmanien)

New-York

Neapel, Republik
(1648–1649)

Jena

Ballarat (Victoria, Australien)
Melbourne (Victoria, Australien)
Sandhurst, 1840–1891 = Bendigo

Getreideähren

Épis

Ears

Herat (Afghanistan)

Irak, Republik, 14. 7. 1959

Dinkelsbühl

Dinkelsbühl , Stadt

Neapel und Sizilien

Negri Sembilan (Malaya)

Bahawalpur (jetzt Pakistan)

Garben

Gerbes

Sheaves

Cincinnati (Ohio)
Philadelphia (Pennsylvanien)

Mailand
Neapel und Sizilien

Brosse

Melbourne
(Victoria, Australien)

Addison (Michigan)

Stockholm

Livland

Göteborg

Melbourne
(Victoria, Australien)

Schweden

James Milner, Charlottetown
(Kanada)
Prinz-Edwards-Insel

Norrköping (Schweden)

Schweden

Södermanland (Schweden)

Polen
(Dynastie Wasa, 1587–1672)
Schweden

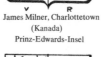

Schweden

Huriel (Allier)

Neapel, Republik (1648–1649)

Fernöstliche Republik,
27. 4. 1921

Venezuela

Venezuela, 28. 3. 1905 – 1930

Venezuela, 20. 4. 1836 – 1905
Venezuela, 15. 7. 1930

Tasmanien, 21. 5. 1917

Saskatschewan (Kanada),
25. 8. 1906

Freiherren von Puchheim
(Oberösterreich)

Freiherren von Puchheim
(Oberösterreich)

Grafen von Puchheim,
26.3.1613

Grafen von Puchheim,
26.3.1613

Verbündete Malaienstaaten, 1914

Halmpflanzen

Plantes culmifères

Stalked plants

Mauritius

The Island of St. John in
Canada (heute: Prinz-
Edwards-Insel) 14.7.1769

Dänisch-Westindien

Vietnam (Süd), 1955-1957

Vietnam (Süd), 1955-1957

Vietnam (Süd), 1957-1963

Nutzpflanzen

Plantes économiques

Kitchen-plants

Madagaskar, Republik,
24.12.1959

Pakistan, 1955

Französische Südsee- und
Antarktis-Gebiete

Außergewöhnliche Zweige

Branches extra-ordinaires

Extraordinary twigs

Hindustan
(Timuriden, Großmoguln)

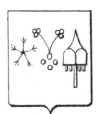

Hindustan
(Timuriden, Großmoguln)

Hindustan
(Timuriden, Großmoguln)

Topfpflanzen

Plantes en pot

Potted plants

Ostindien

Neapel und Sizilien

Mexiko, Stadt

Dundee, Stadt (Schottland)

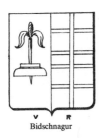

Bidschnagur

England, Königreich
Northumberland

Blütenzweig

Fleur tigée

Flower slipped

Bareli (Indien)

Treptow an der Rega
(Pommern)

Neuschottland
Pittsburg (Pennsylvanien)
Schottland
Watertown (New York)
Waukegan (Illinois)
Wooster (Ohio)

Nancy (Lothringen)
Rëus, Stadt (Spanien)
Rosas

Detroit (Michigan)

Melbourne
(Victoria, Australien)

Melbourne
(Victoria, Australien)

Nancy, Stadt (Lothringen)

Florida

Wettingen,
Zisterzienserabtei (Aargau)

Zacatecas (Mexiko)

Schottland

Blühende Zweige
Tiges fleuries
Blooming twigs

Großbritannien

Ballarat
(Victoria, Australien)

Lérida (Katalonien)

Lérida (Katalonien)

Cardona

Lérida (Katalonien)

Cardona

Lérida (Katalonien)

Port of Spain (Trinidad)

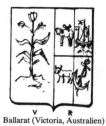

Auckland (Neuseeland)

Halifax (Neuschottland)
Montreal (Kanada)
Neuschottland

Großbritannien

Ballarat (Victoria, Australien)

Schottland

Zwei Blütenzweige
Deux tiges fleuries
Two blooming twigs

Halbe Rose
Demi-rose
Demi-rose

Rapperswil, Stadt
(Kanton St. Gallen)

Mailand

Schlesien

Rose und Rosette

Rose et rosette

Roses

Arkat

Arkat

Sari

Rimini

Altenburg (Thüringen)

Garz (Pommern)
Gochsheim (Baden)
Hagenau, Stadt (Unterelsaß)
Lippe
Pyritz (Pommern)
Wildenfels (Vogtland, Solms)

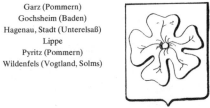

Japan

Großbritannien
Lippe

Lippe

Hagenau, Stadt (Unterelsaß)

Ottweiler, Stadt (Saarland)

Lemgo, Stadt (Westfalen)

Leicester, Stadt (England)

Haleb (Syrien)

England, Königreich
Hohenlimburg

Vereinigte Staaten von Amerika

Rosenheim, Stadt (Bayern)

Gochsheim (Baden)

Mandschukuo, 1934

Schlesien

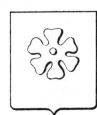

Schlesien

Rosas

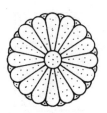

Rëus, Stadt (Spanien)

Japan

Rose auf Münzavers

Rose sur avers de monnaie

Rose on obverse of coin

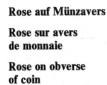

Utrecht, Stadt

Gap (Hautes-Alpes)

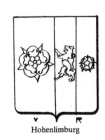

Hohenlimburg

Hagenau, Stadt (Unterelsaß)

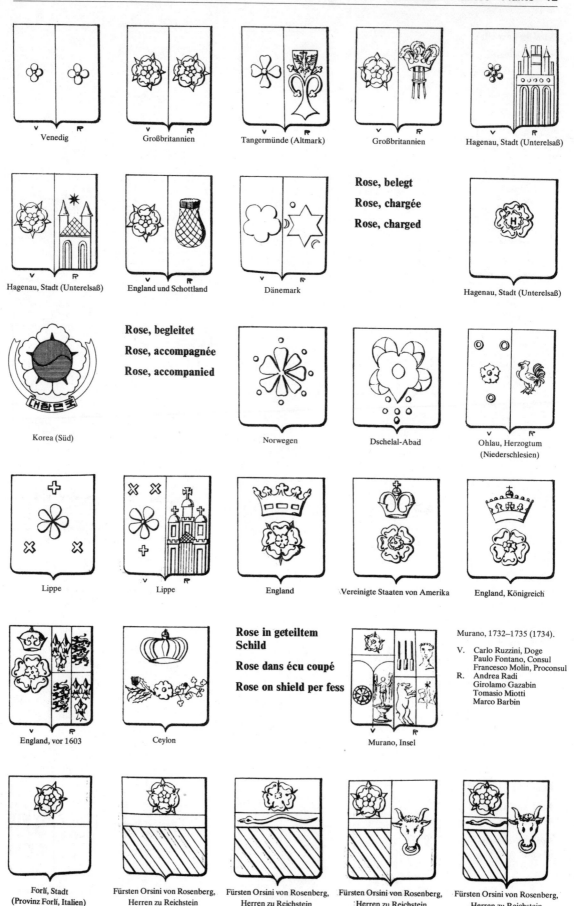

Venedig

Großbritannien

Tangermünde (Altmark)

Großbritannien

Hagenau, Stadt (Unterelsaß)

Hagenau, Stadt (Unterelsaß)

England und Schottland

Dänemark

Rose, belegt
Rose, chargée
Rose, charged

Hagenau, Stadt (Unterelsaß)

Korea (Süd)

Rose, begleitet
Rose, accompagnée
Rose, accompanied

Norwegen

Dschelal-Abad

Ohlau, Herzogtum
(Niederschlesien)

Lippe

Lippe

England

Vereinigte Staaten von Amerika

England, Königreich

England, vor 1603

Ceylon

Rose in geteiltem
Schild

Rose dans écu coupé

Rose on shield per fess

Murano, Insel

Murano, 1732–1735 (1734).

V.   Carlo Ruzzini, Doge
     Paulo Fontano, Consul
     Francesco Molin, Proconsul
R.   Andrea Radi
     Girolamo Gazabin
     Tomasio Miotti
     Marco Barbin

Forlí, Stadt
(Provinz Forlí, Italien)

Fürsten Orsini von Rosenberg,
Herren zu Reichstein
(1581–1599)

Fürsten Orsini von Rosenberg,
Herren zu Reichstein
(1581–1599)

Fürsten Orsini von Rosenberg,
Herren zu Reichstein
(1581–1599)

Fürsten Orsini von Rosenberg,
Herren zu Reichstein
(1581–1599)

Rose in gespaltenem Schild

Rose dans écu parti

Rose on shield per pale

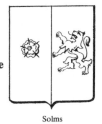

Solms

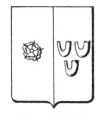

St.-Paul-Trois-Châteaux (Drôme)

Hoorn, Grafschaft Weert (niederländ. Provinz Limburg)

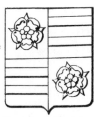

Weert (niederländ. Provinz Limburg)

Rose in geviertem Schild

Rose dans écu écartelé

Rose on quartered shield

Braunschweig, Herzogtum

Sachsen-Altenburg

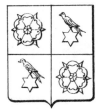

Gronsfeld, Grafschaft (niederl. Provinz Limburg)

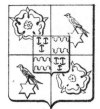

Gronsfeld, Grafschaft (niederl. Provinz Limburg)

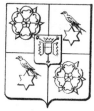

Barby, Grafschaft

Barby, Grafschaft

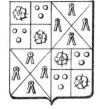

Lippe

Schaumburg-Lippe

Lippe-Detmold 1687

Rose in mehrfeldigem Schild

Rose dans écu de plus de quatre quartiers

Rose on shield quartered of five or more

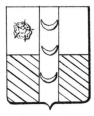

Rom, Senatoren

Rom, Senatoren (Ursini und Stephani)

Rose innerhalb Schildrandes

Rose entourée de bordure

Rose between bordure

Schaumburg-Lippe

Zwei Rosen

Deux roses

Two roses

Murano, Insel

Murano, 1762–1779 (1762).

V.   Giovanni Mocenigo, Doge
     Aloisio Bertoni, Consul
     Zuan Antonio Barozzi,
     Proconsul
R.   Giovanni Marcereto
     Jacomo Mazzola
     Rainiero Rosseti
     Aloisio Ravanello

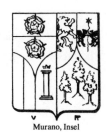

Murano, Insel

Murano, 1763–1779 (1768).

V.   Giovanni Mocenigo, Doge
     Paulo Colonna, Consul
     Aloisio Corner, Proconsul
R.   Danielo Dorico
     Vettino Mestre
     Giovanni Morato

Murano, Insel

Murano, 1783–1779 (1769).

V.   Giovanni Mocenigo, Doge
     Antonio Balbi, Consul
     Giorgio Bertoni, Proconsul
R.   Aloisio Bertoni
     Francesco Zanetti
     Andrea Antonio Mestre
     Domenico Ferrari

Murano, Insel

Murano, 1700–1709 (1701).

V.   Aloisio Mocenigo, Doge
     Giorgio Barbaro
     Giorgio Zuffo
R.   Victorio Miotti
     Fernando Bigag
     Domenico Palada
     Liberio Motta

Murano, 1722–1732 (1731).

V.   Sebastian Mocenigo, Doge
     Zuan Mestre
     Domenico Marini
R.   Gierolamo Rosseti
     Domenico Zanoni
     Zuan Barbin
     Victorio Moro

Murano, Insel

Murano, 1722–1732 (1722).

V.   Sebastian Mocenigo, Doge
     Zuan Fontana, Consul
     Luigi Tiepolo, Proconsul
R.   Domenico Obici
     Antonio Ferro
     Francesco Briatti
     Zuan Mestre

Murano, Insel

Rapperswil, Stadt
(Kanton St. Gallen)

Drei Rosen

Trois roses

Three roses

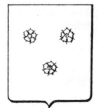

Zaltbommel
(Prov. Gelderland)

Zaltbommel
(Prov. Gelderland)

Sydney (Australien)

Arenberg
Geldern
Lippe

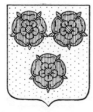
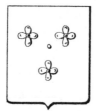
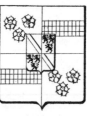

Grenoble, Stadt

Cugnon,
Herrschaft (Belgien)

Schlesien

Arenberg

Southampton, Stadt
(England)

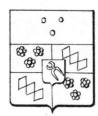
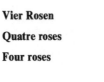

Vier Rosen

Quatre roses

Four roses

Fünf Rosen

Cinq roses

Five roses

Gronsfeld, im Besitz
der Grafen von Törring, 1719

Närke,
Landschaft (Schweden)

Eggenberg,
als Herzöge von Krumau 1628

Sechs und mehr Rosen

Six roses et davantage

Six roses and more

Murano, 1752–1762 (1752).

V.   Francesco Loredano, Doge
     Bartolomeo Bertoni, Consul
     Defendi Zeno, Proconsul
R.   Paolo Rosseto
     Francesco Santini
     Gastone Ferro
     Domenico Gastaldello

Eggenberg,
als Fürsten von Gradiska
und Aquileja 1647

Murano, Insel

Halberstadt, Stadt

Halbe Lilie

Demi-fleur-de-lis

Demi-fleur-de-lis

Schlesien

Schlesien

Schlesien

Mantes, Stadt (Yvelines)

Mantes, Stadt (Yvelines)

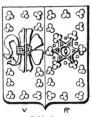

Schlesien

Poitou

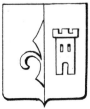

Poitou

Poitou

Eine Lilie

Une fleur-de-lis

One fleur-de-lis

Agramunt (Katalonien)

Aquileja
Arles, Erzbistum
Bergh-St.-Winnoc (Belgien)
Cayenne, Französische Kolonie
Demmin (Pommern)
Desana, Grafschaft
Florenz
Frankreich
Französisch-Guayana
Fuligno
Geertruidenberg
(Provinz Nordbrabant)

Houffalize (Belgien)
Kammin
Kessenich (Rheinland)
Kyritz
Lille, Stadt
Neisse (Schlesien)
Odense (Dänemark)
Reckheim
Reggio
Riga, Domkapitel
Rummen
St. Venant (Pas-de-Calais)

Herren von Schoonvorst
(Brabant)
Soissons
Straßburg, Stadt
Toskana
Ungarn
Warburg (Westfalen)
Weißensee (Thüringen)

Lille, Stadt

Florenz, Stadt

Schlesien

Treptow an der Rega
(Pommern)

Cambrai, Bistum

Pondichéry (nach 1674)

Eine Lilie auf Münzavers

Une fleur-de-lis sur avers de monnaie

One fleur-de-lis on obverse of coin

Straßburg, Stadt

Straßburg, Stadt

Meaux, Stadt

Agramunt (Katalonien)

Agramunt (Katalonien)

Barcelona

Straßburg, Stadt

Vendée, Landschaft und
Départment 1793–1796

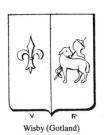

Wisby (Gotland)

Demmin (Pommern)

Neisse, Stadt (Schlesien)

Ungarn

Ungarn

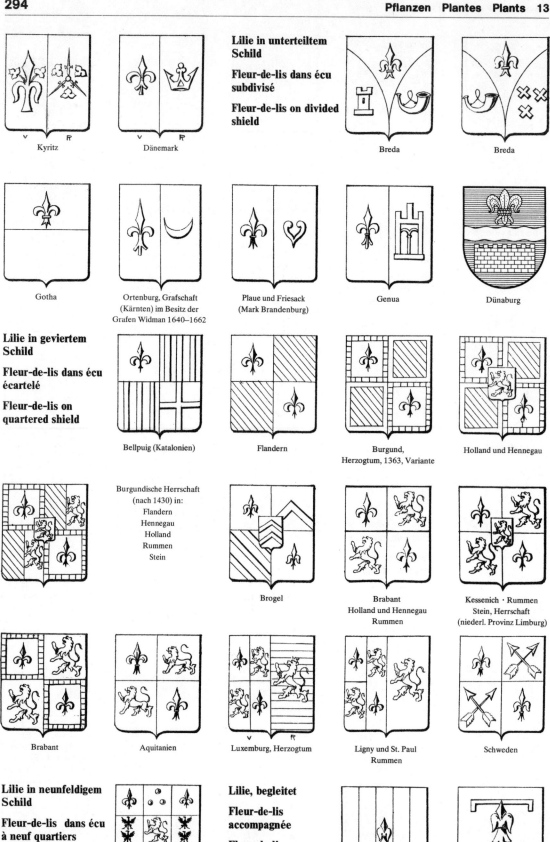

Kyritz

Dänemark

Lilie in unterteiltem Schild

Fleur-de-lis dans écu subdivisé

Fleur-de-lis on divided shield

Breda

Breda

Gotha

Ortenburg, Grafschaft (Kärnten) im Besitz der Grafen Widman 1640–1662

Plaue und Friesack (Mark Brandenburg)

Genua

Dünaburg

Lilie in geviertem Schild

Fleur-de-lis dans écu écartelé

Fleur-de-lis on quartered shield

Bellpuig (Katalonien)

Flandern

Burgund, Herzogtum, 1363, Variante

Holland und Hennegau

Burgundische Herrschaft (nach 1430) in:
Flandern
Hennegau
Holland
Rummen
Stein

Brogel

Brabant
Holland und Hennegau
Rummen

Kessenich · Rummen
Stein, Herrschaft
(niederl. Provinz Limburg)

Brabant

Aquitanien

Luxemburg, Herzogtum

Ligny und St. Paul
Rummen

Schweden

Lilie in neunfeldigem Schild

Fleur-de-lis dans écu à neuf quartiers

Fleur-de-lis on shield quartered of nime

Maccagno (Provinz Como)

Lilie, begleitet

Fleur-de-lis accompagnée

Fleur-de-lis accompanied

Perpignan
(Pyrénées Orientales)

Provence

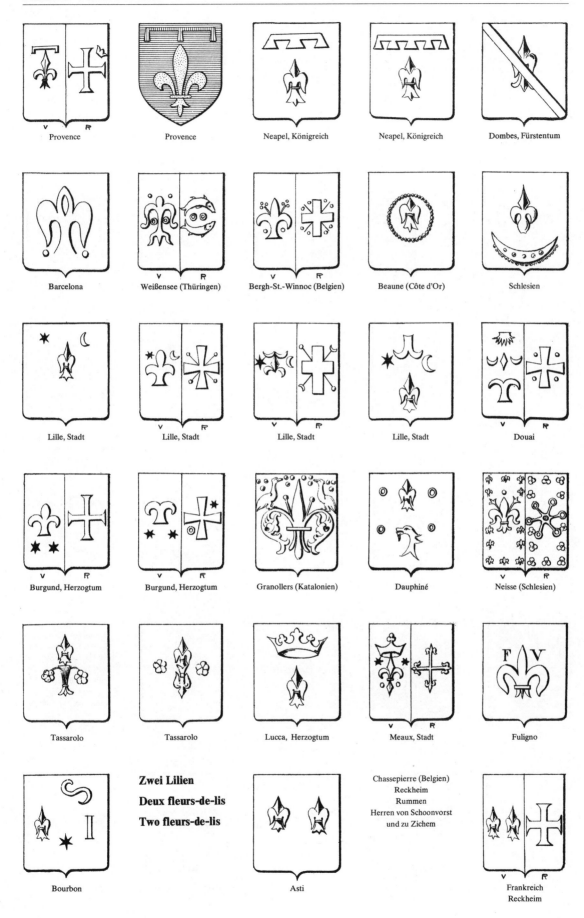

Provence	Provence	Neapel, Königreich	Neapel, Königreich	Dombes, Fürstentum
Barcelona	Weißensee (Thüringen)	Bergh-St.-Winnoc (Belgien)	Beaune (Côte d'Or)	Schlesien
Lille, Stadt	Lille, Stadt	Lille, Stadt	Lille, Stadt	Douai
Burgund, Herzogtum	Burgund, Herzogtum	Granollers (Katalonien)	Dauphiné	Neisse (Schlesien)
Tassarolo	Tassarolo	Lucca, Herzogtum	Meaux, Stadt	Fuligno

Zwei Lilien

Deux fleurs-de-lis

Two fleurs-de-lis

Chassepierre (Belgien)
Reckheim
Rummen
Herren von Schoonvorst
und zu Zichem

Bourbon		Asti	Frankreich Reckheim

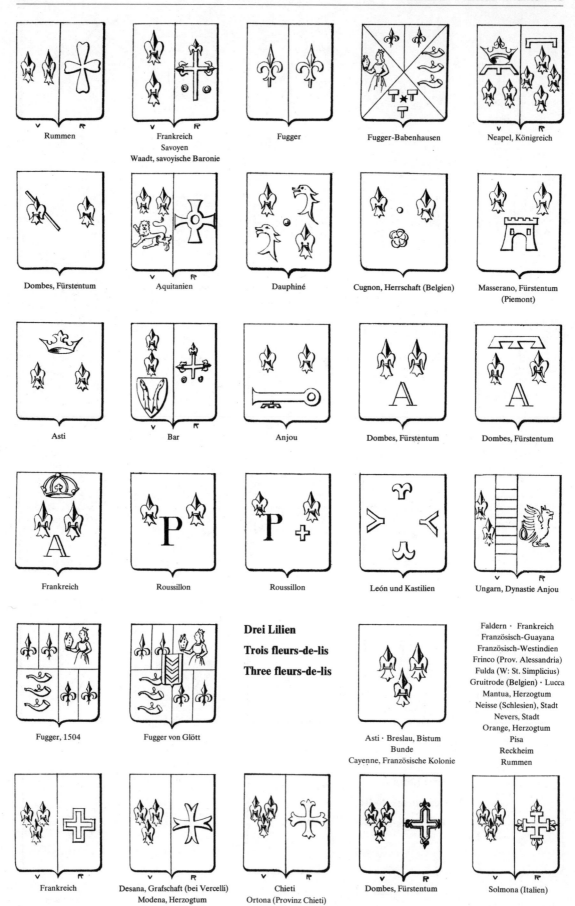

Rummen

Frankreich
Savoyen
Waadt, savoyische Baronie

Fugger

Fugger-Babenhausen

Neapel, Königreich

Dombes, Fürstentum

Aquitanien

Dauphiné

Cugnon, Herrschaft (Belgien)

Masserano, Fürstentum
(Piemont)

Asti

Bar

Anjou

Dombes, Fürstentum

Dombes, Fürstentum

Frankreich

Roussillon

Roussillon

León und Kastilien

Ungarn, Dynastie Anjou

Fugger, 1504

Fugger von Glött

Drei Lilien

Trois fleurs-de-lis

Three fleurs-de-lis

Faldern · Frankreich
Französisch-Guayana
Französisch-Westindien
Frinco (Prov. Alessandria)
Fulda (W: St. Simplicius)
Gruitrode (Belgien) · Lucca
Mantua, Herzogtum
Neisse (Schlesien), Stadt
Nevers, Stadt
Orange, Herzogtum
Pisa
Reckheim
Rummen

Asti · Breslau, Bistum
Bunde
Cayenne, Französische Kolonie

Frankreich

Desana, Grafschaft (bei Vercelli)
Modena, Herzogtum

Chieti
Ortona (Provinz Chieti)

Dombes, Fürstentum

Solmona (Italien)

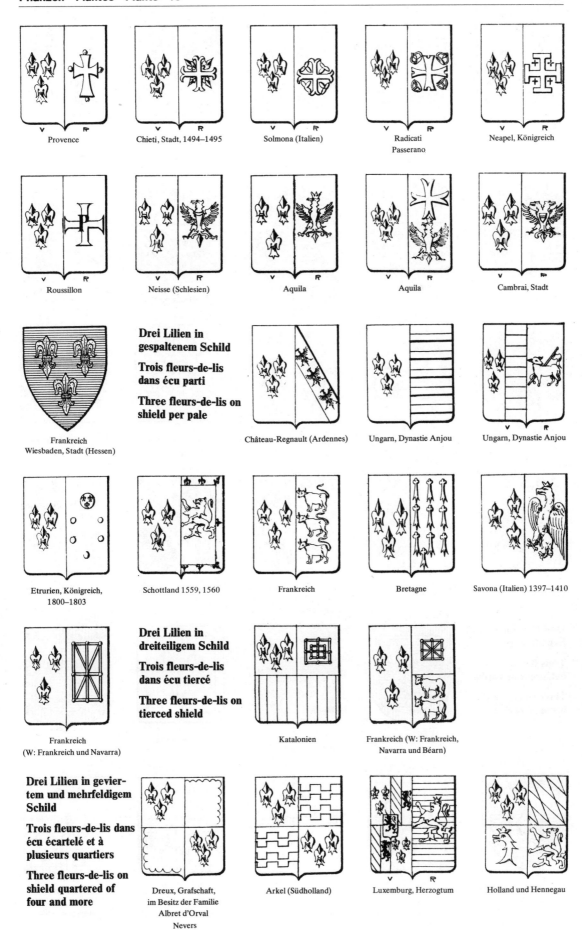

Provence

Chieti, Stadt, 1494–1495

Solmona (Italien)

Radicati
Passerano

Neapel, Königreich

Roussillon

Neisse (Schlesien)

Aquila

Aquila

Cambrai, Stadt

Drei Lilien in gespaltenem Schild

Trois fleurs-de-lis dans écu parti

Three fleurs-de-lis on shield per pale

Frankreich
Wiesbaden, Stadt (Hessen)

Château-Regnault (Ardennes)

Ungarn, Dynastie Anjou

Ungarn, Dynastie Anjou

Etrurien, Königreich,
1800–1803

Schottland 1559, 1560

Frankreich

Bretagne

Savona (Italien) 1397–1410

Drei Lilien in dreiteiligem Schild

Trois fleurs-de-lis dans écu tiercé

Three fleurs-de-lis on tierced shield

Frankreich
(W: Frankreich und Navarra)

Katalonien

Frankreich (W: Frankreich,
Navarra und Béarn)

Drei Lilien in geviertem und mehrfeldigem Schild

Trois fleurs-de-lis dans écu écartelé et à plusieurs quartiers

Three fleurs-de-lis on shield quartered of four and more

Dreux, Grafschaft,
im Besitz der Familie
Albret d'Orval
Nevers

Arkel (Südholland)

Luxemburg, Herzogtum

Holland und Hennegau

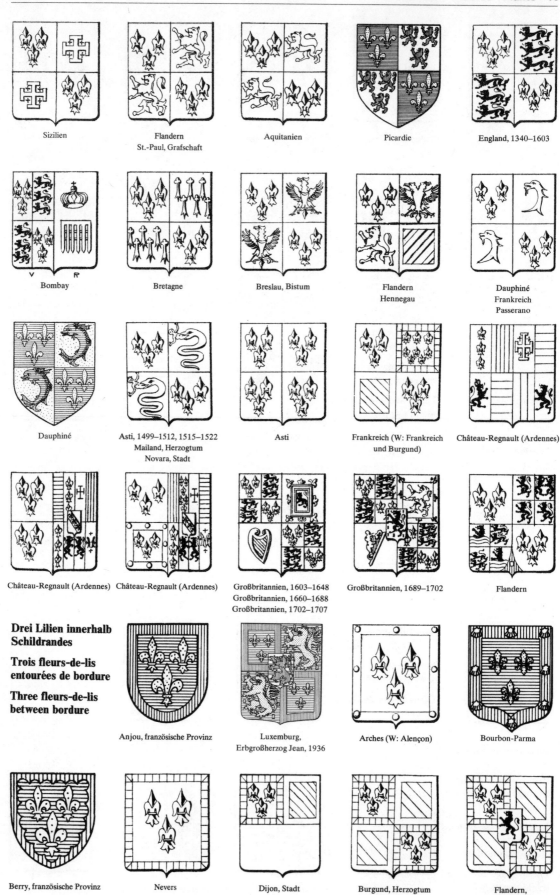

Sizilien

Flandern
St.-Paul, Grafschaft

Aquitanien

Picardie

England, 1340–1603

Bombay

Bretagne

Breslau, Bistum

Flandern
Hennegau

Dauphiné
Frankreich
Passerano

Dauphiné

Asti, 1499–1512, 1515–1522
Mailand, Herzogtum
Novara, Stadt

Asti

Frankreich (W: Frankreich
und Burgund)

Château-Regnault (Ardennes)

Château-Regnault (Ardennes)

Château-Regnault (Ardennes)

Großbritannien, 1603–1648
Großbritannien, 1660–1688
Großbritannien, 1702–1707

Großbritannien, 1689–1702

Flandern

**Drei Lilien innerhalb
Schildrandes**

**Trois fleurs-de-lis
entourées de bordure**

**Three fleurs-de-lis
between bordure**

Anjou, französische Provinz

Luxemburg,
Erbgroßherzog Jean, 1936

Arches (W: Alençon)

Bourbon-Parma

Berry, französische Provinz

Nevers

Dijon, Stadt

Burgund, Herzogtum
Flandern, unter
burgundischer Herrschaft

Flandern,
unter burgundischer
Herrschaft, 1404

Burgund, Herzogtum, 1430

Burgundische Herrschaft in:
Flandern
Geldern
Hennegau
Holland und Hennegau
Namur (Belgien)

Hennegau

Hennegau

Flandern, unter burgundischer
Herrschaft, 1430
Hennegau

Lothringen

Ferrara

Drei Lilien unter Schildhaupt

Trois fleurs-de-lis sous chef

Three fleurs-de-lis under chief

Versailles, Stadt, 15. 9. 1789

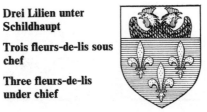

Eton College

Drei Lilien, begleitet

Trois fleurs-de-lis, accompagnées

Three fleurs-de-lis, accompanied

Casale
Desana, Grafschaft (bei Vercelli)
Passerano - Tassarolo

Radicati
Passerano

Chieti
Como, 1494–1495

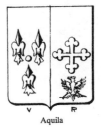

Aquila

Vianen (Südholland)

Bourbon, französische Provinz

Vianen (Südholland)

Vianen (Südholland)

Château-Regnault (Ardennes)

Arquata
(Provinz Marche, Italien)

Asti
Dombes, Fürstentum
Neapel, Königreich
Provence
Rom, Karl I. von Anjou,
Senator
Rummen

Frankreich, 13. 8. 1830

Orléanais

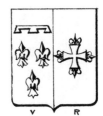

Neapel, Königreich

Neuenburg, 1543–1707

Neuenburg, 1543–1707

Asti, 1490–1498

Neapel, Königreich
Provence

Asti, 1490–1498

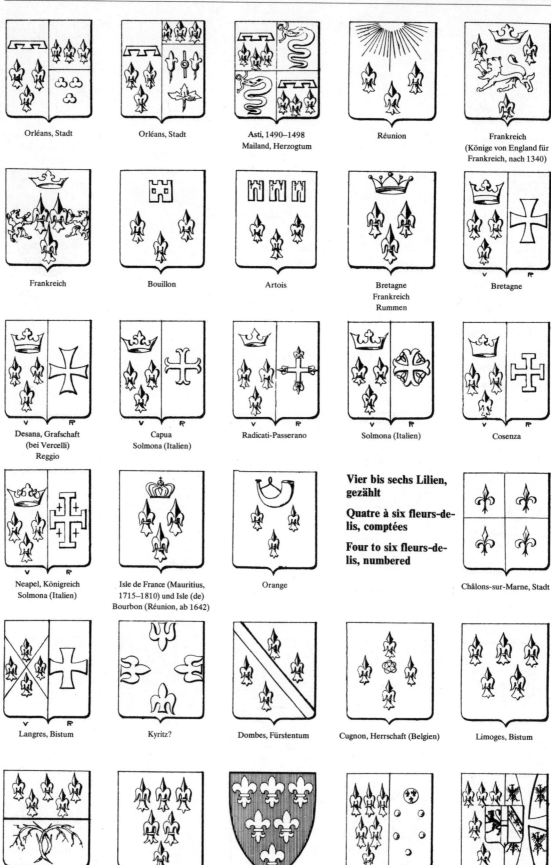

Orléans, Stadt

Orléans, Stadt

Asti, 1490–1498
Mailand, Herzogtum

Réunion

Frankreich
(Könige von England für
Frankreich, nach 1340)

Frankreich

Bouillon

Artois

Bretagne
Frankreich
Rummen

Bretagne

Desana, Grafschaft
(bei Vercelli)
Reggio

Capua
Solmona (Italien)

Radicati-Passerano

Solmona (Italien)

Cosenza

Neapel, Königreich
Solmona (Italien)

Isle de France (Mauritius,
1715–1810) und Isle (de)
Bourbon (Réunion, ab 1642)

Orange

**Vier bis sechs Lilien,
gezählt**

**Quatre à six fleurs-de-
lis, comptées**

**Four to six fleurs-de-
lis, numbered**

Châlons-sur-Marne, Stadt

Langres, Bistum

Kyritz?

Dombes, Fürstentum

Cugnon, Herrschaft (Belgien)

Limoges, Bistum

Reims, Stadt

Castro (Parma)
Frankreich · Neisse (Schlesien)
Novara, Stadt

Neisse, Stadt (Schlesien)
Sulzbach-Rosenberg,
Stadt (Bayern) Grafen von
Sulzbach (apokryphes W.)

Etrurien, Königreich,
1800–1803

Parma und Piacenza,
Herzogtum

Parma und Piacenza,
Herzogtum

Breslau, Bistum

Castro (Parma)
Novara, Stadt
Parma und Piacenza, Herzogtum

Breslau, Bistum

Breslau, Bistum

Parma und Piacenza,
Herzogtum

Parma und Piacenza,
Herzogtum

Parma und Piacenza,
Herzogtum

Parma, Piacenza und Guastalla
Herzogtum, 1814–1859

Königreich beider Sizilien,
1816–1861

Lilien ohne bestimmte Anzahl

Fleurs-de-lis, sans nombre

Fleurs-de-lis sans nombre

Frankreich, vor Karl VI. (1380–1422)
Neapel, Königreich
Pfalzburg und Lixheim (Lothringen)

Frankreich (»France ancien«)
Ile de France
St.-Denis

Französische Ostindische
Handelskompanie
Madagaskar, Ile Bourbon, Réunion

Meaux, Stadt

Ungarn, Dynastie Anjou

Touraine

Dijon, Stadt

Auxonne, Stadt (Côte d'Or)

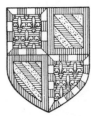

Burgund, Herzogtum, 1363

Riom (Puy-de-Dôme)

Maine, Grafschaft (Frankreich)

Marche, Landschaft
(Frankreich)

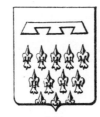

Artois
Neapel, Königreich
Pfalzburg und Lixheim (Lothringen)

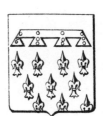

Artois

Artois

Neapel, Königreich
Provence

Provence

Provence

Bologna, Stadt

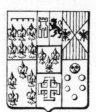

Artois, Flandern, Hennegau,
Valenciennes, Lille, Tournai
und Mecheln, gemeinsam

Neapel und Sizilien

Neapel und Sizilien

Exotische Pflanzen

Plantes exotiques

Exotic plants

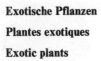
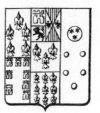

Japan

Japan

Japan (Kiri-Mon)

Ahmed-Schahi

In dem Abschnitt »Leblose
Figuren« sind folgende Gruppen
zusammengefaßt:

1. die Bauwerke, sowie die Schiffe
2. die spezifisch heraldischen
   Zusammenstellungen und
   Figuren
3. Gebrauchsgegenstände, auch
   zeremonielle
4. schwer deutbare Figuren bis hin
   zu konventionellen Zeichen, wie
   Buchstaben und durch vielfache
   Nachahmung unkenntlich
   gewordene Münzbilder.

Alle Figuren sind, um ihre Auffindung zu erleichtern, grundsätzlich nach ihrer äußeren Gestalt
und nicht nach ihrem Zweck eingeordnet.

In dem nachstehenden Inhaltsverzeichnis dieser Gruppen geben
die links stehenden Ziffern an,
unter welchem Ordnungsstichwort
die verschiedenen Motive eingeordnet sind. Die Ziffern rechts
geben die aufzuschlagende Seite
an.

Mauer

Mur

Wall

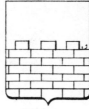

Bautzen, Stadt

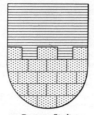

Bautzen, Stadt
Oberlausitz, Markgrafschaft

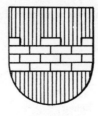

Muri, Benediktinerkloster
(Kanton Aargau)

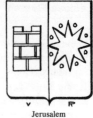

Jerusalem

Jerusalem

Jemen, Königreich

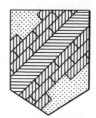

England

Ingermanland

Säule, oben begleitet

Colonne, sommée ou surmontée

Column, accompanied in chief

Dschaja Nagara

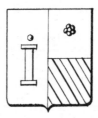

Rom, Senatoren

Yngavi (Bolivien)

Chile, 23. 9. 1819

Indien 1949

Anholt

La Paz

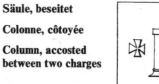

La Paz   La Paz

Potosí (Bolivien)

Potosí (Bolivien)

Säule, beseitet

Colonne, côtoyée

Column, accosted between two charges

Byzanz

Bayern

Gollnow, Stadt (Pommern)

Schlesien

Chile

Weißensee (Thüringen)

Lüttich, Bistum.

Lüttich, Bistum

Schlesien

Mêhun (Cher)

Lüttich, Bistum

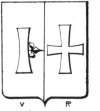

Lüttich, Stadt

Säule in geviertem Schild

Colonne dans écu écartelé

Column on quartered shield

Lüttich, Bistum

Lüttich, Bistum

Lüttich, belgische Provinz

Zwei Säulen

Deux colonnes

Two columns

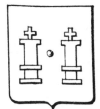

Neapel und Sizilien

Neapel und Sizilien

Reykjavík, 17.6.1957

Spanien

Neapel und Sizilien

Neapel und Sizilien

Neaoel und Sizilien

Kap St. Vincent

Mailand

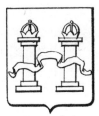

Besançon, Stadt

Grönland, Island und Färöer

Besançon, Stadt

Altar

Autel

Altar

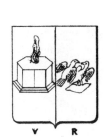

Potosí (Bolivien)

Mühlenturm

Tour de moulin

Mill-tower

Antigua (Westindien), 16.2.1967

Pyramide

Pyramide

Pyramid

Kairo

Honduras, 3.10.1825

Giebelbau

Édifice à pignon

Gable

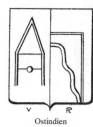

Ostindien

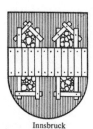

Schlesien

Hamburg

Lobsens (Lobzenica, Wojewodschaft
Bromberg) als Besitz der
Familie Krotowski

Brücke

Pont

Bridge

Innsbruck

Bienenkorb

Ruche d'abeilles

Beehive

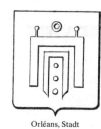

Vereinigte Staaten
von Amerika

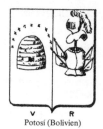

Potosí (Bolivien)

Fortville (Indiana)
Kendalville (Indiana)
Milwaukee (Wisconsin)

Springbrunnen

Fontaine

Fountain

Heilbronn

Tor

Porte

Portal

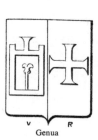

Portenau

Rimini, Stadt

Stadttor, stark stilisiert

**Porte de ville, fort
stylisée**

**Gateway, considerably
conventionalized**

Orléans

Parma, Stadt

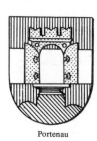

Orléans, Stadt

Vendôme (Loir-et-Cher)

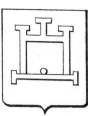

Vendôme (Loir-et-Cher)

Genua

Genua

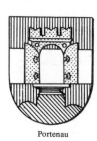

Genua

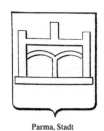

Genua

Parma, Stadt

Genua

Genua

Genua

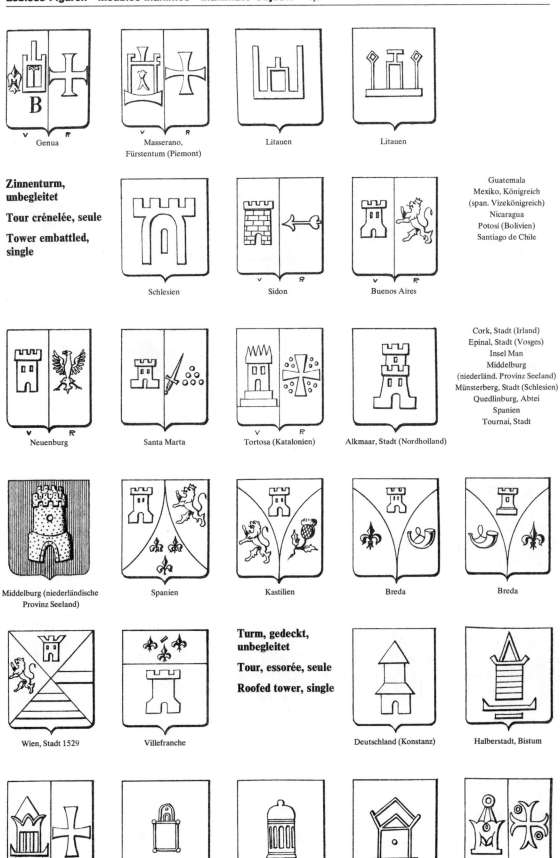

Genua

Masserano,
Fürstentum (Piemont)

Litauen

Litauen

**Zinnenturm,
unbegleitet**

Tour crénelée, seule

**Tower embattled,
single**

Schlesien

Sidon

Buenos Aires

Guatemala
Mexiko, Königreich
(span. Vizekönigreich)
Nicaragua
Potosí (Bolivien)
Santiago de Chile

Neuenburg

Santa Marta

Tortosa (Katalonien)

Alkmaar, Stadt (Nordholland)

Cork, Stadt (Irland)
Epinal, Stadt (Vosges)
Insel Man
Middelburg
(niederländ. Provinz Seeland)
Münsterberg, Stadt (Schlesien)
Quedlinburg, Abtei
Spanien
Tournai, Stadt

Middelburg (niederländische
Provinz Seeland)

Spanien

Kastilien

Breda

Breda

Wien, Stadt 1529

Villefranche

**Turm, gedeckt,
unbegleitet**

Tour, essorée, seule

Roofed tower, single

Deutschland (Konstanz)

Halberstadt, Bistum

Metz, Bistum

Niederlothringen

Meißen, Markgrafschaft
?

Deutschland (Würzburg)

Johanniter-Orden

Frohnleithen, Stadt (Steiermark)

Jerusalem

Nyköping (Schweden)

England

Deutschland (Konstanz)

Magdeburg, Erzbistum

Montreuil

Metz, Bistum

Oberlothringen

Franken (Merowinger)

Mainz, Erzbsitum

Stablo, Abtei

Tournai, Stadt

Mecklenburg-Strelitz, 6.1.1921

Giebelbau, Kreuz einschließend

Édifice à pignon, enfermant croisette

Building with gable, enclosing crosslet

Oberlothringen

Quentovic (Niederlande)

Metz, Bistum

Deutschland (Andernach)

Erfurt

Deutschland (Regensburg)

Straßburg, Bistum

Flandern

Giebelbau, mit Kreuz besetzt, unbegleitet

Édifice à pignon, sommé de croisette, seul

Building with gable, topped with crosslet, single

Hennegau

Böhmen

Oberlothringen

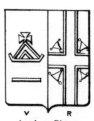
Augsburg, Bistum

Deutschland (Neuffen)

Straßburg, Bistum

Niederlothringen

Metz, Bistum

Würzburg, Bistum

Metz, Bistum

Deutschland (Regensburg)

Deutschland (Augsburg)
Deutschland (Regensburg)

Köln, Erzbistum
Xanten

Augsburg, Bistum

Chur, Bistum

Straßburg, Bistum

Idem, begleitet

Idem, accompagné

Idem, accompanied

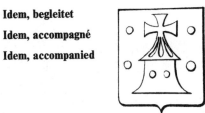

Schlesien

Alemannien

Schlesien

Loos

Schlesien

Schlesien

Ungarn

Giebelbau, Kreuz tragend und einschließend

Édifice à pignon, supportant et enfermant crosslets

Building with gable, topped and filled with crosslets

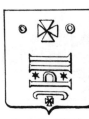

Deutschland (Köln)

Deutschland (Köln)

Novara, Bistum

Tours

Aquitanien

Trier, Erzbistum

Deutschland (Köln)

Deutschland (Straßburg)

Deutschland (Straßburg)

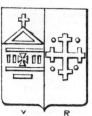

England, Königreich

Köln, Erzbistum

Giebelbau zwischen kleinen Figuren

Édifice à pignon, accompagné de menus meubles

Building with gable, between small charges

Deutschland (Quedlinburg)

Normandie

Mauerwerk mit Mittel- oder seitlichem Turm

Muraille avec tour centrale ou latérale

Masonry with central or lateral tower

England

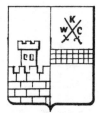

Klattau, Stadt (Böhmen)

Freiburg im Üchtland, Stadt (Schweiz)

Freiburg im Üchtland, Stadt (Schweiz)

Gedeckter Turm mit seitlichem Mauerwerk

Tour avec muraille latérale

Roofed tower with lateral walls

Deutschland

Lüttich, Bistum

Gedeckter Turm zwischen Gestirnen

Tour essorée, accompagnée d'astres

Roofed tower between celestial bodies

Schlesien

Schlesien

Stargard in Pommern

Ungarn

Ungarn

Mauer mit zwei Türmen, unbegleitet

Mur ou courtine avec deux tours, seuls

Wall with two towers, single

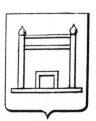

Arles, Stadt
Sens, Stadt (Yonne)

Niederlothringen

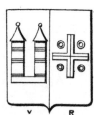

Brandenburg, Markgrafschaft

Brandenburg, Markgrafschaft

Brugg

Weißenburg im Elsaß

Rothenburg ob der Tauber

Linz, Stadt (Niederösterreich)

Trier, Erzbistum

Offenburg, Stadt

Ravensburg
Rothenburg ob der Tauber

Deutschland (Regensburg)

Deutschland (Köln)

Höxter, Stadt (Westfalen)

**Idem, von Kreuz über-
höht, auch begleitet**

**Idem, surmonté de
croisette, aussi
accompagné**

**Idem, accompanied
with crosslets in chief
and eventually with
other charges**

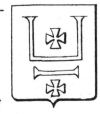

Toulouse

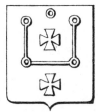

Vendôme (Loir-et-Cher)

Vendôme (Loir-et-Cher)

Vendôme (Loir-et-Cher)

Châteaudun (Orléanais)

Châteaudun (Orléanais)

Vendôme (Loir-et-Cher)

Vendôme (Loir-et-Cher)

Aquileja

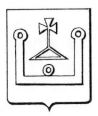

Mainz, (Erfurt)

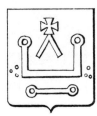

Genua

**Idem, mit Giebel
zwischen den Türmen**

**Idem, avec pignon sur
la courtine**

**Idem, with gable
between the towers**

Burgund, Herzogtum

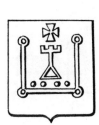

Blois

Aquitanien

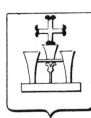

Epirus

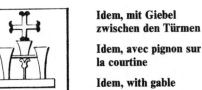

Burgund, Herzogtum

Lüttich

Riom (Puy-de-Dôme)

Epirus

Campobasso
Frankreich

Bergerac (Périgord)

Bretagne
Frankreich
Savoyen-Achaja
Toulouse

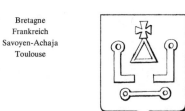

Savoyen-Achaja,
Fürstentum (14. Jahrh.)

Epirus

Savoyen-Achaja,
Fürstentum (14. Jahrh.)

Perwez (Belgien)

Athen, Herzogtum

Karytaina
(Arkadien)
Neopatras (Neapatra,
Griechenland)
Salona (Griechenland)
Savoyen-Achaja
Fürstentum (14. Jahrh.)

Aquitanien

Arkel (Südholland)
Berg, Herzogtum
Bergheim
Blankenberg
Borkelo
Bretagne
Burgund, Herzogtum
Campobasso
Epirus
Essen, Abtei
Evreux (Normandie)

Fauquemont
Fivelgo, Grafschaft
Florennes (Provinz Namur)
Frankreich
Gerisheim, Abtei
Heinsberg (Niederrhein)
Hekeren
Hennegau
Herstal
Hohenlimburg
Holland

Hoorn, Grafschaft
Jever, Herrschaft
Jülich, Herzogtum
Köln, Erzbistum
Kuinre, Grafschaft (Overijssel)
Ligny
Loos
Luxemburg
Namur
Nassau-Weilburg
Navarra

Oldenburg
Herren von
Randerad oder Randerath
St. Dié
Savoyen-Achaja, Fürstentum
Schaumburg
Stein und Limbricht
Toul, Bistum
Toulouse, Grafschaft
Werden und Helmstedt, Abtei
Xaintes (Charente-Inférieure)

Epirus

Savoyen-Achaja,
Fürstentum (14. Jahrh.)

Navarra

Brugg
Ungarn

Offenburg, Stadt

Loos

St.-Paul, Grafschaft

Brabant
Maastricht
Namur (Belgien)

Brabant
Maastricht
Namur (Belgien)

Aquileja

Kastilien

Kastilien

Aquileja

Maastricht

Verdun, Bistum

Toul, Bistum

Aquileja

Speyer, Stadt

Magdeburg, Erzbistum

Metz, Bistum

Savoyen-Achaja,
Fürstentum (14. Jahrh.)

Veracruz (Mexiko)

Savoyen-Achaja,
Fürstentum (14. Jahrh.)

Bergamo, Stadt (Italien)

Brabant
Flandern · Loos

Deutschland (Eichstätt)

Trier, Erzbistum

Deutschland

Speyer, Bistum

Corvey, Abtei (Westfalen)

Deutschland (Mainz)

Köln, Erzbistum

Brabant
Namur (Belgien)

Vendôme (Loir-et-Cher)

St. Aignan (Loir-et-Cher)

Hennegau

Hennegau

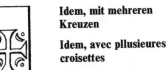

**Idem, mit mehreren
Kreuzen**

**Idem, avec pllusieures
croisettes**

**Idem, with several
crosslets**

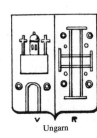

Köln, Erzbistum

Ungarn

Mainz, Erzbistum

Vilvorde

Lüttich

Straßburg, Bistum

Deutschland (Goslar)

Deutschland (Mainz)

Metz, Bistum

Ein Turm, begleitet

Une tour, accompagnée

**One tower,
accompanied**

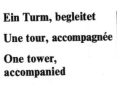

Schlesien

Schlesien

Dreux, Stadt

Schlesien

Lüttich, Bistum

Hamburg

Stargard in Pommern
?

Solsona (Katalonien)

Valparaiso, 9.3.1802/7.8.1811

Oudewater, Stadt
(niederl. Provinz Seeland)

Singapur,
13.9.1948

Northampton

Nowgorod

Schlesien

Rabenswald,
Grafen von (Thüringen)

Polen

Bolkenhayn, Stadt (Schlesien)

Klagenfurt

Klagenfurt

Laibach, Stadt

Lüttich, Bistum

Nienburg, Kloster

Tortosa (Katalonien)

Sedan , Stadt
Tournai, Stadt

Basel, Stadt

Deutschland (Straßburg)

Frankreich

Epinal, Stadt (Vosges)

Ungarn

Sedan
Sens, Stadt (Yonne)

Sedan

Schlesien

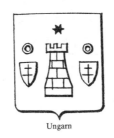

Schlesien

Oldenburg in Holstein

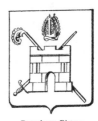

Ungarn

Ratzeburg, Bistum

Tournai, Bistum

Trujillo

Cattaro (Kotor)

Córdoba (Argentinien)

Madrid

Callao

Córdoba (Argentinien)

Meißen, Markgrafschaft
?

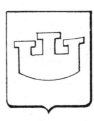

Chur, Bistum

Montfoort, Stadt
(Provinz Utrecht)

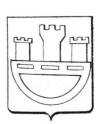

Alkmaar, Stadt (Nordholland)

**Bauwerk mit drei
Zinnentürmen**

**Édifice avec trois tours
crénelées**

**Building with three
embattled towers**

Gaëta, Herzogtum

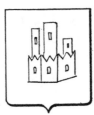

Kastilien

Capua

Schlesien

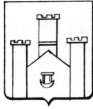

Bouillon

Hagenau, Stadt (Unterelsaß)

Antiochien

Spanien

Aquileja

Pesaro

Aquileja

Brescello
Elburg (Gelderland)
Hamburg
Kampen (Overijssel)
Kastilien
Lenzburg (Schweiz)
Middelburg (Seeland)
Roda, Stadtroda (Thüringen)
Speyer, Stadt
Thorn, Stadt
Trocki
Zaltbommel (Gelderland)

Aquileja
Pontefract, Stadt
(Yorkshire), 1584

Bergen in Norwegen

Thorn, Stadt

Amalfi

Idem, auf Münzavers

Idem, sur avers de monnaie

Idem, on obverse of coin

Ampurias (Spanien)

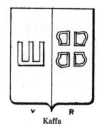
Kaffa

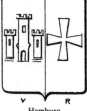
Hamburg

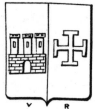
Cambrai, Bistum

Spanien

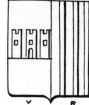
Namur (Belgien)

Kastilien

Kastilien

Spanien

Kastilien

Kastilien

Bauwerk mit drei gedeckten Türmen

Édifice avec trois tours essorées

Building with three roofed towers

Kastilien   Kastilien   Kastilien

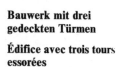

Ungarn

Brandenburg, Kurfürstentum

Brandenburg (Przibislav)

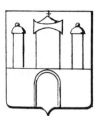
Schlesien

Köthen, Stadt (Anhalt)

Deutschland   Ungarn   Merseburg, Bistum   Naumburg, Bistum   Trier, Erzbistum

Preßburg

Quedlinburg

Münster, Bistum

Ungarn

Ragusa

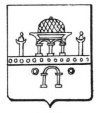

Sachsen, Herzogtum

Brandenburg
an der Havel, Altstadt

Prag (Altstadt)

Ungarn

Berg, Herzogtum
Köln, Erzbistum (Neuß)

Aquileja

Schlesien

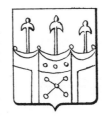

Polen

Norwegen

Köln, Erzbistum

Deutschland (Magdeburg)
Magdeburg, Erzbistum

Idem, auf Münzavers

**Idem, sur avers de
monnaie**

**Idem, on obverse of
coin**

Hamburg und Lübeck

Dänemark

Hamburg

Mark

Polen

Quedlinburg, Abtei

Friedberg, Burggrafschaft
(Hessen)

Teschen, Stadt

Hamburg

Prsg (Altstadt)

Idem, mit Farbangabe

**Idem, les émaux
indiqués**

**Idem, the tinctures
shown**

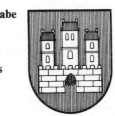

Preßburg

Salzburg, Stadt

Lund, Stadt (Schweden)

Bromberg, Stadt

**Bauwerk mit ein oder
zwei Türmen, oben
von kleinen Figuren
begleitet**

**Édifice avec une ou
deux tours, surmonté
de menus meubles**

**Building with one or
two towers, and in
chief small charges**

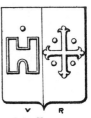

Gaëta, Herzogtum

Schlesien

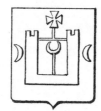

Mainz, Stadt
Namur (Belgien)

Verdun, Bistum

Provence

Schweden

Metz, Bistum

Riom (Puy-de-Dôme)

Lüttich

Bautzen, Stadt

Ungarn

Ungarn

Ascoli Piceno

Deutschland (Dortmund)

Porto, Stadt (Portugal)

Böhmen

Magdeburg, Stadt

Magdeburg, Stadt

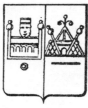

Isny, Stadt (Württemberg)

Reichenbach im Vogtland,
Stadt

Beraun (Beroun),
Stadt (Böhmen)

Prag (Neustadt)

Ungarn

Ungarn

Ungarn

Ungarn

Luxemburg, Herzogtum

Reichenberg, Stadt
(Nordböhmen)

Pirmasens, Stadt
(Rheinpfalz)

Châteaudun (Orléanais)

Cambrai, Bistum

Luxemburg, Herzogtum

Aquitanien

Einbeck, Stadt
(Niedersachsen)

Einbeck, Stadt
(Niedersachsen)

Lauban, Stadt (Schlesien)

Schleiz, Stadt (Thüringen)

Schleiz, Stadt (Thüringen)

Schleiz, Stadt (Thüringen)

Blankenburg und Reinstein

Blankenburg und Reinstein

Blankenburg und Reinstein

Blankenburg und Reinstein

Blankenburg und Reinstein

Blankenburg und Reinstein

Schivelbein (Pommern)

Herren von Arnstein,
unter Vögten von Quedlinburg

Burgund, Herzogtum

Goslar, Stadt

Namur (Belgien)

La Spezia, Stadt (Italien)

Lüttich

Marburg an der Drau, Stadt

Goslar, Vogtei

Falkenstein,
Grafschaft (Harz)

Dinant

Brandenburg (Neumark)

Brandenburg, Markgrafschaft

Friaul-Julisch Venetien,
Autonome Region, 8. 12. 1967

Mexiko, Stadt, um 1924

Cuzco (Peru)

Ascoli Piceno

Baumburg, Augustiner-
Chorherren-Stift bei Altenmarkt
(Oberbayern), 1488

Münzenberg (Hessen)

Schlesien

Lippstadt, Stadt (Westfalen)

Flandern

Stendal (Altmark)

Kronach, Stadt
(Franken) vor 1651

La Marche

Angoulême

La Marche

Stein, Herrschaft
(niederl. Provinz Limburg)

Bretagne
Stein, Herrschaft
(niederl. Provinz Limburg)

Neapel, Königreich

Solmona (Italien)

Bretagne · Frankreich
Provence

Piemont

Warburg (Westfalen)

Lüttich

Warburg (Westfalen)

Demmin (Pommern)

Namur (Belgien)

Namur (Belgien)

Angoulême, Stadt
(Frankreich)
Périgueux (Landschaft)

Bretagne

Savoyen
Waadt, savoyische Baronie

Frankreich

Cambrai, Bistum
Frankreich

Frankreich
Waadt, savoyische Baronie

Bretagne

Weißenburg im Nordgau
(heute:
Weißenburg in Bayern)

Toskana

Jeßnitz, Stadt (Anhalt)

Jeßnitz, Stadt (Anhalt)

Huy (Belgien)

Lüttich, Bistum

Lüttich

Roda, Stadtroda (Thüringen)

Linz, Stadt (Niederösterreich)

Linz, Stadt (Niederösterreich)

Linz, Stadt (Niederösterreich)
7. 2. 1966

Ravensburg, Stadt

Urgel (Katalonien)

Lauf an der Pegnitz, Stadt
(vor 1505)

Görlitz

Plauen im Vogtland, Stadt

Demmin (Pommern)

Offenburg, Stadt
Weißenburg im Nordgau
(heute: Weißenburg in Bayern)

Weißenburg im Nordgau
(heute:
Weißenburg in Bayern)

Drossen, Stadt
(Weststernberg)

Meißen, Markgrafschaft
?

Colchester (Essex) 1648

Cattaro (Kotor)

Callao

Peru, Republik

Köln, Erzbistum

Brandenburg, Kurfürstentum

Bonn

Brandenburg, Kurfürstentum

Brandenburg, Markgrafschaft

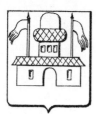

Köln, Erzbistum

Lüttich

Unna (Westfalen)

Unna (Westfalen)

Sachsen

Afghanistan, 1928

Afghanistan, 1929

Auschwitz

Ungarn

Lüttich

Namur (Belgien)

Ragusa

Salerno, Stadt

Weißenburg im Nordgau
(heute:
Weißenburg in Bayern)

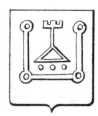

Riom (Puy-de-Dôme)

Waadt, savoyische Baronie

**Dreitürmiges Bau-
werk, oben begleitet**

**Édifice à trois tours,
surmonté**

**Building with three
towers, accompanied
in chief**

Parma

Capua

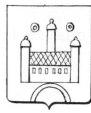

Ungarn

Namur (Belgien)

Brandenburg, Kurfürstentum

Ungarn

Kastilien

Hamburg

Hamburg

Kastilien

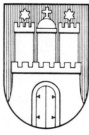

Kambodscha, Republik
8.10.1970

Freystadt in Schlesien, Stadt
(Regierungsbezirk Liegnitz)

Ungarn

Antwerpen, Stadt

Antwerpen, Stadt

Neapel und Sizilien

Neapel und Sizilien

Blankenburg und Reinstein

Blankenburg und Reinstein

Chios, Insel (W: Marchesi
Giustiniani, Genua, vor 1566)

Kastilien

Deutschland (Köln)

Ungarn

Ungarn

Hennegau

Budweis, Stadt (Böhmen)

Salzwedel, Stadt

Rhenen, Stadt
(Provinz Utrecht)

Bridgewater

Edinburgh, Stadt (Schottland)

Pontefract, Stadt (Yorkshire)

Tschaslau (Böhmen)

Grünberg, Stadt (Schlesien)

Rotenburg (Wümme), Stadt
(Niedersachsen)

Pontefract, Stadt
(Yorkshire), 1584

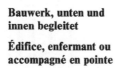

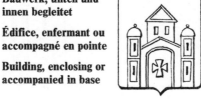

**Bauwerk, unten und
innen begleitet**

**Édifice, enfermant ou
accompagné en pointe**

**Building, enclosing or
accompanied in base**

Mainz, Erzbistum

Metz, Bistum

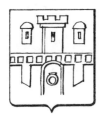

Brandenburg, Markgrafschaft

Löwen, Grafschaft

Lüttich

Champagne

Schlesien

Schlesien

Hedel, Stadt
(Prov. Gelderland)

Lüttich

Waldeck

Hamburg

Hamburg

Hamburg

Ungarn

Parma, Stadt

Schlesien

Trier, Erzbistum

Nimwegen, Stadt (Gelderland)

Ascoli Piceno

Ibiza (Insel)

Cartagena, Stadt
(Spanien, Provinz Murcia)

Wellur

Helmstedt, Stadt (Niedersachsen)

Brandenburg an der Havel,
Neustadt

Kopenhagen, 1661

Montpellier, Stadt
(Languedoc)

Århus

Puebla de los Ángeles
(heute Puebla de Zaragoza,
Mexiko)

Brandenburg, Markgrafschaft

Aquileja

Halberstadt, Bistum

Brandenburg,
Markgrafschaft

Halberstadt, Bistum

Halberstadt, Bistum

Ungarn

Ungarn

Brandenburg

Sachsen

Ungarn

Prag (Altstadt)

Prag (Altstadt)

Köln, Erzbistum

Komotau, Stadt (Böhmen)

Diepholz

Álborg (Dänemark)

Lemberg, Stadt (Galizien)

Elburg, Stadt (Gelderland)

Elburg, Stadt (Gelderland)

Norwich, Stadt (England)

Norwich, Stadt (England)

Norwich, Stadt (England)

Osterode am Harz, Stadt

Hoya, Stadt

Schleiz, Stadt (Thüringen)

Blankenburg und Reinstein

Blankenburg und Reinstein

Blankenburg und Reinstein

Chur, Stadt

Chur, Stadt

Chur, Stadt

Stargard in Pommern

Stargard in Pommern

Brandenburg an der Havel, Neustadt

Brandenburg an der Havel, Neustadt

Brandenburg an der Havel, Neustadt

Brandenburg an der Havel, Neustadt

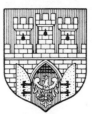

Krakau, Stadt

Krakau, Republik

Schlesien

Brandenburg an der Havel, Neustadt

Brandenburg an der Havel, Neustadt

Schlesien

Stendal (Altmark)

Stendal (Altmark)

Schivelbein (Pommern) Stendal (Altmark)

Stendal (Altmark)

Hessen

Weißensee (Thüringen)

Wernigerode am Harz, Stadt

Langensalza

Parma, Stadt

Schlesien

Lippe

Wildeshausen (Oldenburg) ?

Goslar, Stadt

Schlesien

Hessen

Warburg (Westfalen)

Warburg (Westfalen)

Demmin (Pommern)

Tournai, Stadt

Memel

Kampen, Stadt (Overijssel)

Oldenburg, Stadt

Oldenburg, Stadt

Oldenburg, Stadt

Tilsit, Stadt (Ostpreußen),
2. 11. 1552

Freiberg, Stadt (Sachsen)

Lüneburg, Stadt

Lüneburg, Stadt

Diepholz

Schmalkalden (Thüringen)

Brandenburg an der Havel,
Neustadt

Lippe

Cham, Stadt (Bayern)
1809

Dorchester
(Grafschaft Dorset, England)

Brandenburg an der Havel,
Neustadt

Spandau (Mark Brandenburg)

Schivelbein (Pommern)

Spandau (Mark Brandenburg)

Spandau
(Mark Brandenburg)

Spandau
(Mark Brandenburg)

Brandenburg, Markgrafschaft

Goslar, Stadt

Osnabrück, Bistum

Osnabrück, Bistum

Osnabrück, Bistum
Wiedenbrück, Stadt
(Westfalen)

Hofgeismar

Hamburg

Hamburg

Marsberg, Stadt
(jetzt Obermarsberg,
Westfalen)

Marsberg, Stadt
(jetzt Obermarsberg,
Westfalen)

Trier, Münzstätte Koblenz

Salzwedel, Stadt

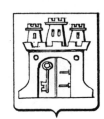

Gibraltar

Brandenburg,
Markgrafschaft

Salzwedel, Grafschaft

Gibraltar

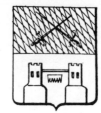

Gibraltar, 10. 7. 1502

Cham, Stadt (Bayern)

Hameln

Goslar, Stadt

Bauwerk, oben und unten begleitet

Édifice surmonté et accompagné en pointe

Building, accompanied in chief and in base

Ungarn

Ungarn

Bolkenhayn, Stadt (Schlesien)

Vendôme (Loir-et-Cher)

Vendôme (Loir-et-Cher)

Vendôme (Loir-et-Cher)

Brandenburg, Kurfürstentum

Brandenburg, Markgrafschaft

Châteaudun (Orléanais)

Châteaudun (Orléanais)

Châteaudun (Orléanais)

Vendôme (Loir-et-Cher)

Vendôme (Loir-et-Cher)

Glogau, Stadt

Posen, Stadt

Drontheim, Stadt (Norwegen)

Ungarn

Klagenfurt

Ungarn

Brandenburg an der Havel, Neustadt

Brandenburg an der Havel, Neustadt

Brandenburg an der Havel, Neustadt

Deutschland (Goslar)

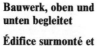

Altenburg, Stadt

Halberstadt, Bistum

Neuburg an der Donau, Stadt
(Bayern)

Hannover, Stadt

Hannover, Stadt

Einbeck, Stadt
(Niedersachsen)

Hannover, Stadt

München, 25. 2. 1835

Pyritz (Pommern)

München, 2. 11. 1936

Goslar, Vogt Otto von
Braunschweig

Goslar,
Vogt Pfalzgraf Heinrich

Hochberg

Havelberg, Stadt
(Mark Brandenburg)

Havelberg, Stadt
(Mark Brandenburg)

Schlesien

Schlesien

Mexiko, Königreich

Spandau (Mark Brandenburg)

Brandenburg,
Markgrafschaft

Hagenau, Stadt (Unterelsaß)

Metz, Bistum

Marsberg, Stadt
(jetzt Obermarsberg,
Westfalen)

Brandenburg, Markgrafschaft

Ungarn

Frankfurt an der Oder

Linz, Stadt (Niederösterreich)

Veere (Seeland, Niederlande)

Brandenburg, Markgrafschaft

Brandenburg an der Havel,
Neustadt

Spandau
(Mark Brandenburg)

Spandau, Stadt, 1289, 1861
Spandau, Bezirk von Berlin

Osnabrück, Bistum

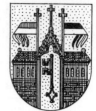

Herford, Stadt

Dorpat, Stadt

Riga, Stadt

Riga, Stadt

Riga und Reval

Suhl, Stadt (Thüringen)

Veere
(Seeland, Niederlande)

Vier- und mehrtürmige Bauwerke, auch begleitet

Édifices à plus de trois tours, aussi accompagnés

Buildings with four towers or more, also accompanied ones

Scarborough, Stadt
(England) 1645

Erfurt

Magdeburg, Erzbistum

Brandenburg,
Markgrafschaft

Brandenburg an der Havel,
Stadt, 1950

Trier, Erzbistum

Graudenz

Graudenz

Brandenburg an der Havel,
Neustadt

Brandenburg an der Havel,
Neustadt

Brandenburg an der Havel,
Neustadt

Sachsen, Herzogtum

Helmstedt, Stadt
(Niedersachsen)

Merseburg, Stadt

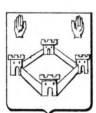

Antwerpen, Stadt

Bordeaux

Bordeaux

Freiberg, Stadt (Sachsen)

Northeim

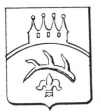

Blankenburg und Reinstein

Stendal (Altmark)

Meiningen, Stadt (Thüringen)

Brehna

Brehna

Brandenburg an der Havel,
Neustadt

Brandenburg an der Havel,
Neustadt

Mons (Belgien)

Brandenburg an der Havel,
Altstadt

Zerbst, Stadt (Anhalt)

Erfurt

Brandenburg an der Havel,
Altstadt

Kirchenbauten
Église à clocher
Church with tower

Augsburg, Bistum

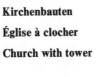

Regensburg, Bistum

Lüttich, Bistum

Deutschland (Regensburg)

Leutkirch, Stadt (Württemberg)

Arkaden und
Säulenhallen
Arcades et portiques
Arcades and porticoes

Ålborg (Dänemark)

Segovia, Stadt (Spanien)

Segovia, Stadt (Spanien)

Genua

Halberstadt, Bistum

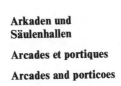

China, Volksrepublik,
20.9.1950

Burganlage
Château fort ou ville
fortifiée
Fortified place

Deutschland (Regensburg)

Verdun, Stadt

Recklinghausen, Stadt
(Westfalen)

Tournai, Stadt

Bauwerk mit seitlich hervorkommender Figur

Édifice avec un meuble mouvant latéralement

Building with charge issuant laterally

Flensburg, Stadt (Schleswig)

Ribe, Stadt (Dänemark)

Schaffhausen

Schaffhausen

Schaffhausen

Schaffhausen, Stadt

Bristol

Bristol, Stadt (England)

Bauwerk in geteiltem Schild

Édifice dans écu coupé

Building in shield per fess

Manila, 20. 3. 1596

Kolberg, Stadt

Bauwerk innerhalb Schildrandes

Édifice entouré de bordure

Building between bordure

Cartago (Costa Rica)

Mexiko, Stadt

Mexiko, Stadt, 4. 7. 1523

Quito (Ecuador) 15. 3. 1541

Veracruz (Mexiko)

Veracruz (Mexiko), 4. 7. 1523

Bauwerk in gespalte- nem Schild

Édifice dans écu parti

Building in shield per pale

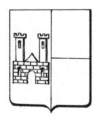

Ravensburg und Ulm

Landeshut, Stadt (Schlesien)

Sayn-Wittgenstein

Borja

Quedlinburg

San Miguel el Grande, Heute: San Miguel Allende (Mexiko)

Rovigo, Stadt

Antwerpen, belgische Provinz

Britisch-Somaliland, Protektorat, 18. 12. 1950

Bauwerk in dreiteiligem Grund

Édifice dans fond tiercé

Building on tierced ground

Kampen, Deventer und Zwolle

Kampen, Deventer und Zwolle

Sayn-Wittgenstein

Bauwerk in geviertem Schild

Édifice dans écu écartelé

Building on quartered shield

Sedan und Raucourt

Sedan und Raucourt

Sedan und Raucourt

Steiermark

Tirol

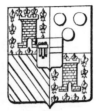

Siebenbürgen, Dynastie Habsburg

Spanien

Spanien, 1868–71, 1931–37

Spanien, 1871–73

Spanien, 6. 1. 1875–1931
Puerto Rico, 1886–98

Caracas, Stadt (Venezuela), 1811–1820

Costa Rica
Kastilien
Mexiko, Königreich
(span. Vizekönigreich)
Nicaragua
Oran (Algerien), 1691–1692
Potosí (Bolivien)
Spanien

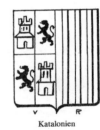

Kastilien

Katalonien

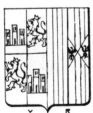

Kastilien

Katalonien

Trinidad

Thurn und Taxis

Mailand, Herzogtum
Parma, Herzogtum

Actopan (Mexiko)
Catorce (Mexiko)

Chiapa de los Indios (Mexiko)
Jalapa (Mexiko)
Manila (Philippinen)
Mexiko, Königreich
(span. Vizekönigreich)
Oaxaca (Mexiko) (1812)
Orizaba (Mexiko)
Parma (Italien)
Pasquara
Philippinen
Popayán (Kolumbien)

Puebla de los Ángeles (heute
Puebla de Zaragoza, Mexiko)
Quarta de Amilpas
(später Ciudad Morelos)
San Luis Potosí (Mexiko)
Santa Maria del Rosario (Kuba)
Santiago de Chile
Sombrerete (Mexiko)
Spanien 1701
Tacuba (Mexiko)
Valladolid (Spanien)

Manila

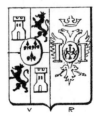

Santa Cruz de la Sierra
(Bolivien)

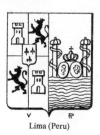

Lima (Peru)

Etrurien, Königreich,
1803–1807

Neapel und Sizilien
Spanien

Neapel und Sizilien
Spanien

Friedberg, Burggrafschaft
(Hessen)

Mexiko, Königreich
(span. Vizekönigreich)
Potosí (Bolivien) · Spanien

Mexiko, Königreich
(span. Vizekönigreich)
Spanien nach 1701

Zütphen, Stadt (Gelderland)

Vasto und Pescara

Vasto und Pescara

Vasto und Pescara

Sizilien

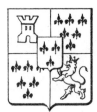

Quedlinburg

Quedlinburg, Abtei

Quedlinburg

Westfriesland

Moldau, Fürstentum

Moldau, Fürstentum

Straits Settlements,
25. 3. 1911

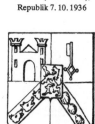

Euzkadi (Baskenland),
Republik 7. 10. 1936

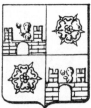

Magdeburg, Stadt

Brabant, unter spanischer
Herrschaft, 1504

Parma und Piacenza,
Herzogtum

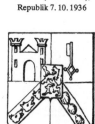

Campeche, Mexiko

Sayn-Sayn

Dahome, 9. 12. 1964

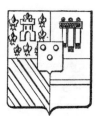

Sedan und Raucourt

Idem, Feld 1 geteilt

**Idem, le premier
quartier coupé**

**Idem, the first quarter
per fess**

Mexiko, Königreich
(span. Vizekönigreich)
Spanien

Guanajuato (Mexiko)

Bauwerk in fünf- bis sechsteiligem Schild

Édifice dans écu de cinq ou six quartiers

Building in shield quartered of five or more

Neapel und Sizilien

Spanien, König
Joseph Napoleon

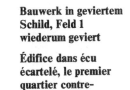

Bauwerk in geviertem Schild, Feld 1 wiederum geviert

Édifice dans écu écartelé, le premier quartier contre-écartelé

Building on quartered shield, the first grand quarter quarterly

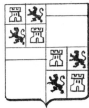

Lucca, Fürstentum

Spanien

Reckheim

Tirol

Barcelona · Majorka
Neapel und Sizilien
Valencia (Spanien)

Neapel und Sizilien
Overijssel · Spanien
Seeland (niederländ. Provinz)

Neapel und Sizilien
Spanien

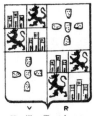

Spanien, 2. 2. 1938

Kastilien (Beatrix von
Portugal, 14. Jahrhundert)

Spanische Herrschaft in:

Artois, Grafschaft
Brabant
Flandern
Geldern
Hennegau
Holland
Luxemburg
Overijssel
Seeland
Utrecht, Herrschaft

Artois

Brabant
Flandern
Geldern
Luxemburg
Mexiko, Königreich
(span. Vizekönigreich)
Overijssel
Spanien
Tournai, Herrschaft
Utrecht, Herrschaft

Geldern
Hennegau

Mexiko, Königreich
(span. Vizekönigreich)
Spanien

Mexiko, Königreich
(span. Vizekönigreich)
Spanien 1580–1640

Mailand, Herzogtum

Spanische Herrschaft

nach 1580 in:
Artois, Grafschaft
Brabant
Burgund, Herzogtum
Flandern
Hennegau
Luxemburg
Tournai, Herrschaft

Mexiko, Königreich
(span. Vizekönigreich)
Spanien

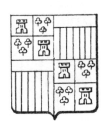

Mailand, Herzogtum

Brabant, unter spanischer
Herrschaft, 1701
Limburg · Namur

Aragonien
Neapel und Sizilien

Spanien

Mailand, Herzogtum

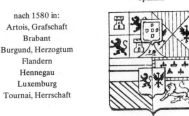

Werden, Abtei

Zwei bis drei Bauwerke

Deux à trois édifices

Two to three buildings

Guanabacoa (Kuba),
14. 8. 1743

Budapest, 1873

Budapest, 1964

Newcastle-upon-Tyne, Stadt
(England)

Dublin

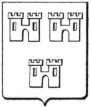

Dublin

Camerino, Herzogtum
(Provinz Marche, Italien)

Camerino, Herzogtum
(Provinz Marche, Italien)

Kampen, Stadt (Overijssel)

Brabant
Loos

Tournai, Herrschaft

Deutschland (Straßburg)

San Marino

Puno (Peru)

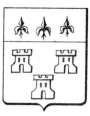

La Habana (Kuba)

La Habana (Kuba)
San Antonio-Abad (Insel Ibiza)

La Habana (Kuba)

La Habana (Kuba)

Perleberg
(Mark Brandenburg)
?

Tours, Stadt

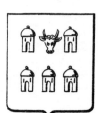

Tours, Stadt

Vier bis fünf Bauwerke

Quatre à cinq édifices

Four to five buildings

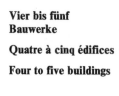

Brandenburg, Markgrafschaft

Poitou

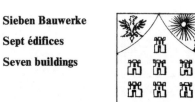

Winchester, Stadt (England)   Schleiz, Stadt (Thüringen)

Sieben Bauwerke

Sept édifices

Seven buildings

Siebenbürgen

Siebenbürgen,
Dynastie Rákóczi

Boot

Canot

Boat

Schweden

Lodsch

Kiel

Helsingfors-Helsinki

Kiel

Åbo (Finnland)

Deutschland (Speyer)

Illyrien

Veere (Seeland, Niederlande)
Vlissingen
(Seeland, Niederlande)

Einmaster

Bâtiment avec un seul mât

Onemasted ship

St. Barthélemy

Deutschland (Celles)

Duurstede (heute amtlich:
Dorestad) (Provinz Utrecht)
Quentovic (Niederlande)

Youghal (Irland)

Sansibar,
britisches Protektorat

Dubai

Oberkanada

Oberkanada

Mauritius, 25. 8. 1906

Lissabon

Nordborneo, 20. 7. 1882

Neubraunschweig, 26. 5. 1868

Paris

Mindanao und Sulu
(Philippinen)

Großes Segelschiff, frontal

Grand voilier, vu de front

Sailing vessel, frontally

Panamakanalzone, 8. 6. 1915

Surinam, 1959

Zweimaster

Bâtiment à deux mâts

Twomasted ship

Grenada

Réunion

Aden, brit. Protektorat
(Südarabien)

Kuwait

Tunesien, 21. 6. 1956

Tunesien, 30. 5. 1963

Malakka, 14. 8. 1951

St. Christopher, Nevis und
Anguilla, 16. 2. 1967

Dreimaster

Voilier à trois mâts

Ship with three masts

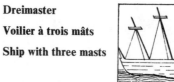

Vereinigte Staaten von Amerika   Vereinigte Staaten von Amerika

Hobart Town, (Name
1804–1881, seitdem
Hobart, Tasmanien)

Guinea (Brandenburgisch)

Halifax (Neuschottland)

Asiatische Kompanie

Potosí (Bolivien)

Bermuda

Halifax (Neuschottland)
Kanada
Montreal (Kanada)
Neubraunschweig
New-York
Pittsburg (Pennsylvanien)
Prinz-Edwards-Insel (Kanada)
Queenston (Provinz Ontario)

Bahama-Inseln
Cartagena (Kolumbien)

Chile

Dänisch-Westindien

Falkland-Inseln, 16. 10. 1925

Britisch Guiana, 8. 12. 1954

Britisch Guiana

San Sebastian, Stadt
(Spanien)

Gabun, 1963

. Lorient, Stadt (Morbihan)

Bahama-Inseln, 7. 12. 1971

Kalkutta, Stadt, 26. 12. 1896

Nantes, Stadt (Bretagne)

Nantes, Stadt (Bretagne)

Paris

La Rochelle, Stadt
(Frankreich)

Bahama-Inseln, 5. 6. 1959

Quebec, Stadt (Kanada),
20. 12. 1967

Royal African Company
(Goldküste)

Auckland (Neuseeland),
23. 10. 1911

Britisch Honduras, 28. 1. 1907
Belize

Sydney (Australien)
5. 11. 1872

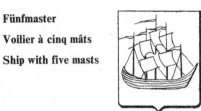

Fünfmaster

Voilier à cinq mâts

Ship with five masts

Philadelphia (Pennsylvanien)

Mastbaum

Mât de vaisseau

Mast

Melbourne (Victoria, Australien)

Dampfer

Bateau à vapeur

Steamer

New-York

Vereinigte Staaten von
Amerika

Mehrere Schiffe

Plusieurs navires

Several ships

Panama, Stadt 15. 9. 1521

Panama, Stadt 15. 9. 1521

Hongkong, 21. 1. 1959

Bombay, 20. 9. 1877

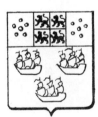

Bombay (Ostindische
Kompanie), 1600

Bombay (Ostindische
Kompanie), 1600

Bombay (Ostindische
Kompanie), 1600

Trinidad und Tobago, 9. 8. 1962

Britische Südafrika-Kompanie
Chartered 15. 10. 1889

Neuseeland, 26. 8. 1911

**Schiff neben
Bauwerken**

Navire et édifices

Ship with buildings

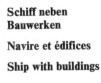

Santander, Stadt (Spanien)

Cork, Stadt (Irland)

Cork, Stadt (Irland)

Schild als Münzbild

Ecu ou bouclier comme thème de monnaie

Shield as theme on coin

Schlesien

Schlesien

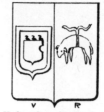
Harbour Grace (Neufundland)
St. Johns (Neufundland)

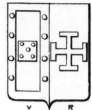
Portugiesisch Indien (Goa)

Cincinnati (Ohio)

Vereinigte Staaten von Amerika

Schild als Wappenbild in geometrischem Grund

Ecusson comme meuble dans fond géométrique

Escutcheon as charge on geometrical ground

Belgisch Kongo,
23. 10. 1886

Isenburg

Isenburg

Isenburg, Fürst Carl
(1806–1813)

Gerona

Mecheln, Stadt

Mecheln, Stadt

Mecheln, Stadt

Hohenzollern-Hechingen

Baden, Großherzogtum,
2. 5. 1807

Bayern, Königreich,
20. 12. 1806

Bayern, Königreich,
4. 1. 1806

Westflandern,
belgische Provinz

Philippinen
1905

Philippinen, 6. 11. 1935

Philippinen, 4. 7. 1946

Schild als Münzbild, begleitet von kleinen Figuren

Ecusson comme thème de monnaie, accompagné de menus meubles

Escutcheon as theme on coin between small objects

Zierikzee
(niederländ. Provinz Seeland)

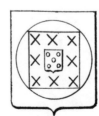
Portugiesisch Indien (Goa)

Werben an der Elbe
(Altmark)

Vereinigte Staaten von Amerika

Cincinnati (Ohio)

Idem, begleitet von Lebewesen

Idem, accompagné d'êtres vivants

Idem, with living beings

Graubünden

Weißensee (Thüringen)

Thorn, Stadt

Masserano, Fürstentum
(Piemont)

Masserano, Fürstentum
(Piemont)

Altenburg, Stadt
Herren von Rosenberg

Cattaro (Kotor),
unter venezianischer Herrschaft

Cattaro (Kotor),
unter venezianischer Herrschaft

Cattaro (Kotor),
unter venezianischer Herrschaft

Cattaro (Kotor),
unter venezianischer Herrschaft

Schwyz

San Benigno di Fruttuario
(Provinz Turin)

Masserano, Fürstentum
(Piemont)

Solothurn
Ulm

Saluzzo

Lavagna (Ligurien)

Saluzzo

Saluzzo

Solothurn

Luzern

Zürich

New-York

Vereinigte Staaten von Amerika

South Bend (Indiana)
Vereinigte Staaten von Amerika

Vereinigte Staaten von Amerika

Masserano, Fürstentum
(Piemont)

Masserano, Fürstentum
(Piemont)

Konstanz, Stadt

Konstanz, Stadt

Konstanz, Stadt

Schwäbisch Hall

Desana, Grafschaft
(bei Vercelli)
Sitten (Wallis) · Wallis

Vereinigte Staaten von Amerika

New-York

Newark (New Jersey)
New-York

Bangor (Maine)
Bridgeport (Connecticut)
Jackson (Michigan)
Kalamazoo (Michigan)

Colmar im Elsaß, Stadt

Ueberlingen

Bologna, Herrschaft

Schwyz

Solothurn
Ulm

Mirandola und Concordia

Masserano, Fürstentum
(Piemont)

Masserano, Fürstentum
(Piemont)

Monferrat, Markgrafschaft
(Oberitalien)

Monferrat, Markgrafschaft
(Oberitalien)

Monferrat, Markgrafschaft
(Oberitalien)

Luzern

Desana, Grafschaft
(bei Vercelli)

Desana, Grafschaft
(bei Vercelli)

Lavagna (Ligurien)
Masserano und Crevacuore

Ueberlingen

Bern

Uri (Schweiz)

Luzern

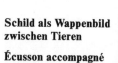

Vereinigte Staaten von Amerika

**Schild als Wappenbild
zwischen Tieren**

**Écusson accompagné
d'animaux**

**Escutcheon as charge
between animals**

Togo, 14. 3. 1962

Blois, Stadt

Wesel, Stadt (Niederrhein)

China, Republik, 1912

Schild begleitet von Pflanzen

Écusson, accompagné de plantes

Escutcheon accompanied by plants

Guernsey, Kanalinsel

Kleve, Stadt (Niederrhein)

Cincinnati (Ohio)

Newark (New Jersey)
New-York
Peru (Indiana)
Vereinigte Staaten von Amerika

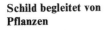

Vereinigte Staaten von Amerika

New-York

Vereinigte Staaten von Amerika

Vereinigte Staaten von Amerika

Ungarn, Volksrepublik
12. 5. 1957

Schild unter Bauwerk als Münzbild

Écusson sous édifice comme thème de monnaie

Escutcheon under building as theme on coin

Reckheim
Rummen

Aachen

Millen, Gangelt und Vucht,
Herrschaft (ehem. Selfkantkreis)
Löwen, Stadt

Geldern

Heinsberg, Herrschaft
(Niederrhein)

Moers, Grafschaft

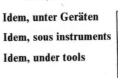

Aachen

Idem, unter Geräten

Idem, sous instruments

Idem, under tools

Audenarde (Oudenaarde),
Belgien

Audenarde (Oudenaarde),
Belgien

Gerona

Polen

Mecheln, Stadt

Masserano, Fürstentum
(Piemont)

Castiglione delle Stiviere
(Provinz Mantua)

Maastricht

Vereinigte Staaten von Amerika

Schild als Wappenbild, begleitet von Geräten

Bouclier ou écusson accompagné d'instruments

Shield or escutcheon and tools

Swasiland, 30. 4. 1968

Bloemfontein, Stadt
(W: Oranje-Freistaat)

Schild unter Buchstaben als Münzbild

Écusson sous lettre comme thème de monnaie

Escutcheon under letter as theme of coin

Konstanz, Stadt

Cham, Stadt (Bayern)

Höxter, Stadt (Westfalen)

Helfenstein, Grafschaft
(Württemberg)

Thoren, Abtei

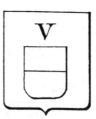

Ulm

Ueberlingen

Wien, Stadt

Mehrere Schilde als Münz- oder als Wappenbild

Plusieurs écussons comme thème de monnaie ou comme meuble

Several shields as theme of coin or as charge

Drossen, Stadt
(Weststernberg)

Dachau, Stadt

Brandenburg, Markgrafschaft

Brandenburg, Markgrafschaft

Brandenburg, Markgrafschaft

Fünf Schildchen

Cinq écussons

Five ecutcheons

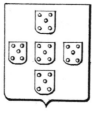

Azoren
Portugal

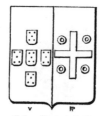

Guinea (Portugiesisch)

Guinea (Portugiesisch)

Idem, innerhalb Schildrandes

Idem, entourés de bordure

Idem, between bordure

Azoren

Ilha do Principe
(Golf von Guinea)
Madeira
Portugal
Portugiesisch-Guinea
Portugiesisch Indien (Goa)
São Tomé

Portugal

Céuta, Stadt (Nordafrika)

Idem, auf Münzavers

Idem, sur avers de monnaie

Idem, on obverse of coin

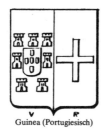

Guinea (Portugiesisch)

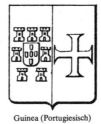

Guinea (Portugiesisch)

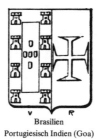

Brasilien
Portugiesisch Indien (Goa)

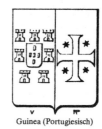

Guinea (Portugiesisch)

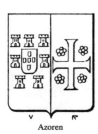

Azoren

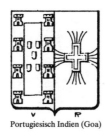

Portugiesisch Indien (Goa)

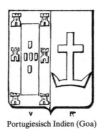

Brasilien

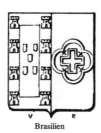

Portugiesisch Indien (Goa)

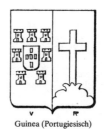

Guinea (Portugiesisch)

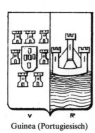

Guinea (Portugiesisch)

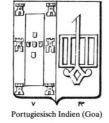

Portugiesisch Indien (Goa)

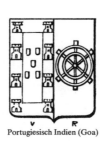

Portugiesisch Indien (Goa)

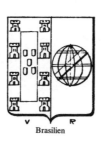

Brasilien

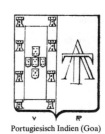

Portugiesisch Indien (Goa)

Fünf Schildchen in einem Schilddrittel

Cinq écussons dans écu tiercé

Five escutcheons on tierced shield

Timor, 8. 5. 1935

Goa, vor 1935

Angola, 8. 5. 1935

Macao, 8. 5. 1935

Portugiesisch Indien (Goa),
8. 5. 1935

Kap Verde, 8. 5. 1935

(Portugiesisch) Guinea,
8. 5. 1935

São Tomé e Principe,
8. 5. 1935

Moçambique, 8. 5. 1935

Moçambique, vor 1935

Fünf bis sechs Schildchen in Wellengrund

Cinq à six écussons dans fond ondé

Five to six escutcheons on ground wavy

Leeward-Inseln
nach dem Ausscheiden
von Dominica

Leeward-Inseln, 10. 4. 1909

Vollwappen als Münz-bild

Armoiries complètes comme thème de monnaie

Complete achievements as theme on coin

Monferrat, Markgrafschaft
(Oberitalien)

Monferrat, Markgrafschaft
(Oberitalien)

Hohenstein, Grafschaft

Neustadt a. d. Aisch

Brandenburg an der Havel,
Neustadt

Zofingen (Schweiz)

Geldern

's-Heerenberg, Herrschaft
(Grafschaft Zütphen)

Mailand, Herzogtum
Verona · Vertus

Helm

Heaume, casque

Helm

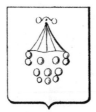
Monteil

Eisenach, Stadt

Landshut, Stadt (Bayern)

Landshut, Stadt (Bayern)

Landshut, Stadt (Bayern)

Schlesien

Seeland (niederländ. Provinz)

Helm gekrönt oder mit Zier

Casque couronné ou avec cimier

Helm crowned or crested

Frankfurt an der Oder

Brandenburg, Kurfürstentum

Frankfurt an der Oder

Halle/Saale

Savoyen-Achaja, Fürstentum
(14. Jahrh.)

Savoyen-Achaja, Fürstentum
(14. Jahrh.)

England, Königreich

Verona (Oberitalien)

Schlesien

Schlesien

Anhalt

Anhalt

Anhalt

Querfurt, Stadt

Ratibor, Stadt (Oberschlesien)

Batenburg

Hessen · Thüringen
Weißensee (Thüringen)

Sachsen

Braunschweig

Gandersheim, Stadt
(Niedersachsen)

Glogau, Herzogtum

Ellrich
(Grafschaft Hohenstein)

Schmalkalden (Thüringen)

Saluzzo

Ungarn

Laufenburg (Oberrhein)

Laufenburg (Oberrhein)

Ungarn

Schlesien

Schlesien

Brandenburg, Kurfürstentum

Schlesien

Schlesien

Brandenburg, Kurfürstentum

Brandenburg, Kurfürstentum

Brandenburg, Kurfürstentum

Schlesien

Frankfurt an der Oder

Spandau (Mark Brandenburg)

Österreich

Eisleben

Eisleben

Schlesien

Laufenburg (Oberrhein)

Schlesien
Usedom, (Pommern)

Schlesien

Rügen

Schlesien

Oppeln, Herzogtum
(Oberschlesien)

Beuthen (Oberschlesien)

Kujavien

Schlesien

Zofingen (Schweiz)

Wied

Usenberg (Baden)

Usenberg (Baden)

Todtnau (Kreis Lörrach)

Vorderösterreich

Vorderösterreich

Zofingen (Schweiz)

Neuenburg

Weißensee (Thüringen)

Thüringen

Schlesien

Siebenbürgen,
Fürst Michael Apafi,
1661–1690

Schlesien

Schlesien

Schweidnitz, Stadt

Schweidnitz, Herzogtum

Oldenburg

Sachsen

Geldern

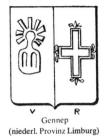

Gennep
(niederl. Provinz Limburg)

Geldern und Zütphen
's-Heerenberg, Herrschaft
(Grafschaft Zütphen)

's-Heerenberg, Herrschaft
(Grafschaft Zütphen)

Geldern

Serbien

Orange

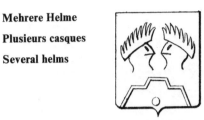

Ellrich
(Grafschaft Hohenstein)

Mehrere Helme

Plusieurs casques

Several helms

Brandenburg
an der Havel, Stadt

Valladolid (Morélia, Spanien)

Königsberg/Neumark

Landshut, Stadt (Bayern)

Landshut, Stadt (Bayern)

Landshut, Stadt (Bayern)

Perleberg (Mark Brandenburg)

Brandenburg, Markgrafschaft

Gatter, Gitter, Netz

Grillage, réseau, herse

Fretty, net, portcullis

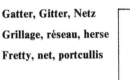

Herren von Brakel
(Westfalen), 1384 ausgestorben

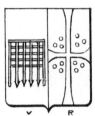

England, Königreich

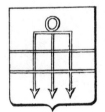

Warendorf, Stadt (Westfalen)

England, Königreich
Kinsale (Irland)

England, Königreich

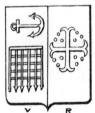

England, Königreich

St. Maximin

Norwegen

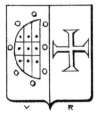

Portugiesisch Indien (Goa)

Pau , Stadt

Schlesien

Bolivien

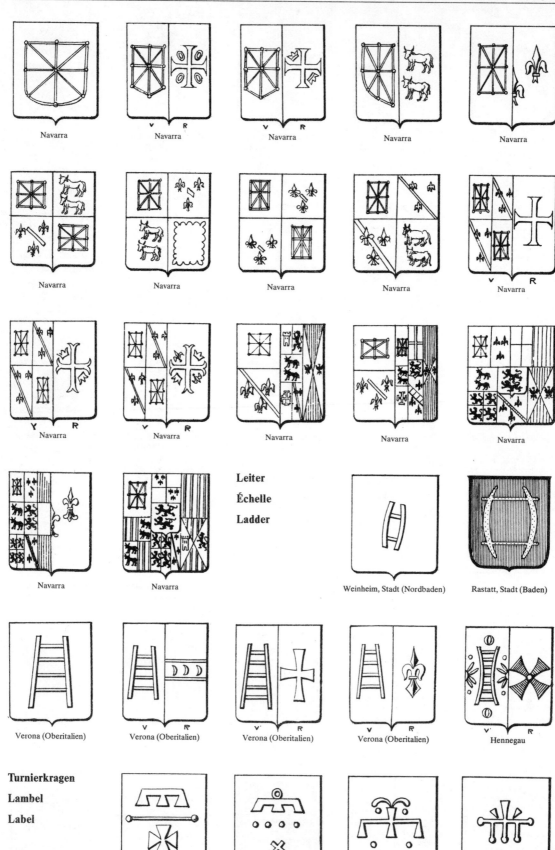

Navarra   Navarra   Navarra   Navarra   Navarra

Navarra   Navarra   Navarra   Navarra   Navarra

Navarra   Navarra   Navarra   Navarra   Navarra

Leiter
Échelle
Ladder

Navarra   Navarra   Weinheim, Stadt (Nordbaden)   Rastatt, Stadt (Baden)

Verona (Oberitalien)   Verona (Oberitalien)   Verona (Oberitalien)   Verona (Oberitalien)   Hennegau

Turnierkragen
Lambel
Label

Montluçon (Allier)   Etampes (Seine-et-Oise)   Franken (Merowinger)   Franken (Merowinger)

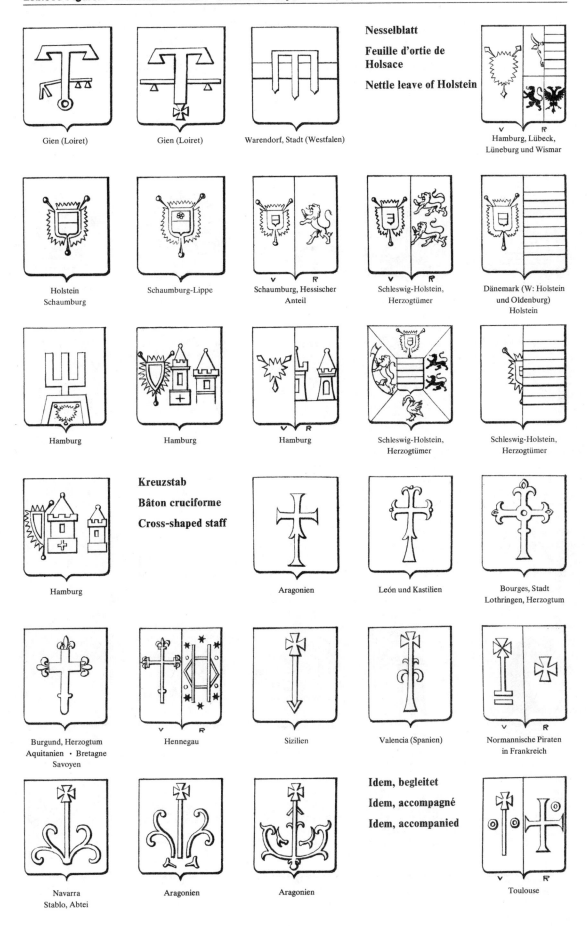

Nesselblatt

Feuille d'ortie de Holsace

Nettle leave of Holstein

Gien (Loiret)

Gien (Loiret)

Warendorf, Stadt (Westfalen)

Hamburg, Lübeck, Lüneburg und Wismar

Holstein Schaumburg

Schaumburg-Lippe

Schaumburg, Hessischer Anteil

Schleswig-Holstein, Herzogtümer

Dänemark (W: Holstein und Oldenburg) Holstein

Hamburg

Hamburg

Hamburg

Schleswig-Holstein, Herzogtümer

Schleswig-Holstein, Herzogtümer

Kreuzstab

Bâton cruciforme

Cross-shaped staff

Hamburg

Aragonien

León und Kastilien

Bourges, Stadt Lothringen, Herzogtum

Burgund, Herzogtum Aquitanien · Bretagne Savoyen

Hennegau

Sizilien

Valencia (Spanien)

Normannische Piraten in Frankreich

Idem, begleitet

Idem, accompagné

Idem, accompanied

Navarra Stablo, Abtei

Aragonien

Aragonien

Toulouse

Barcelona , Grafschaft

León und Kastilien

Lüttich, Bistum

Navarra

Memel
Schlesien

Lüttich, Bistum

Sachsen

Ungarn

Spanische Klostermünze

Lüttich, Bistum

Riga, Erzbistum

Riga, Erzbistum

Riga, Domkapitel

Riga, Stift

Riga, Erzbistum

Krummstab

Crosse

Crozier

Besançon, Erzbistum

Rewa

Eichstätt, Bistum
Viviers (Ardèche)

Basel, Bistum und Stadt

Basel-Stadt

Basel-Land

Utrecht, Bistum

Arles, Erzbistum

Naumburg, Bistum

Cambrai, Bistum

Trier, Erzbistum

Urgel (Katalonien)

Wendische Münze

Naumburg, Bistum

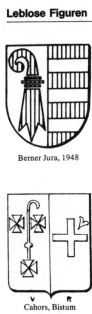
Berner Jura, 1948

Kusel, Stadt (Rheinpfalz)

Thérouanne (Pas-de-Calais)

Toulouse, Grafschaft

Kastilien

Cahors, Bistum

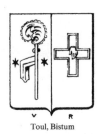
Wendische Münze

Thérouanne (Pas-de-Calais)

Langres, Bistum

Corbie, Abtei (Somme)

Cahors, Bistum

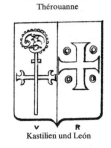
Münster, Bistum
Osnabrück, Bistum
Thérouanne

Toul, Bistum

St. Eure

Meaux, Bistum

Kastilien

Kastilien und León

Laon, Bistum

Aire, Bistum (Landes)

Augsburg, Bistum und Stadt

Erfurt

Erfurt

Wendische Münze

Oberaltaich, Benediktinerabtei
(Niederbayern)

Tournai, Bistum

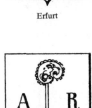
Roth, Kloster

Utrecht, Bistum

Vandalen

Benediktbeuren, Abtei

Helmstedt
Kolberg, Stadt
Konstanz, Bistum
Naumburg, Bistum
Thérouanne (Pas-de-Calais)

Werden, Abtei
(Konrad von Gleichen)

Kolberg, Stadt

Konstanz, Bistum

Konstanz, Bistum

Konstanz, Bistum

Erfurt

Cambrai, Bistum

Kolberg, Stadt

Benediktbeuern, Abtei

Stans

Gars, Propstei (Oberbayern)

Werden und Helmstedt, Abtei

Erfurt · Kolberg, Stadt
Konstanz, Bistum
Naumburg, Bistum

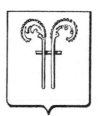

Dänemark

Tournai, Bistum

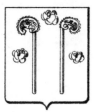

Konstanz, Bistum

Tournai, Bistum

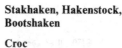

Noyon, Bistum

**Stakhaken, Hakenstock,
Bootshaken**

Croc

Boat-hook

Kolberg, Stadt

Konstanz, Bistum

Kolberg, Stadt

**Lilienstab, Szepter,
Lanze**

**Bâton fleurdelisé,
sceptre, lance**

**Staff flory, sceptre,
lance**

Triest, Stadt

Perleberg
(Mark Brandenburg) ?

Valdivia (Chile)

Ungarn

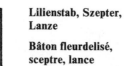

Kyritz

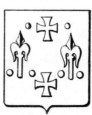

Meißen, Bistum

Lérida (Katalonien)
1808-1814

Brandenburg, Kurfürstentum
Preußen, Herzogtum

Brandenburg, Kurfürstentum

Preußen, Herzogtum

Geldern, als Teil Preußens,
1718
Neuenburg, 1707

Preußen, Königreich

Preußen, Königreich

Brandenburg, Kurfürstentum

Brandenburg, Kurfürstentum

Bayern, Königreich, 1807

Pahang (Malaya)

Tansania, 1964

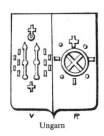

Ungarn

Pahang (Malaya)

**Idem, gekreuzt oder
radial, Glevenrad,
Lilienhaspel**

**Idem, passés en sautoir,
rais d'escarboucle**

**Idem, crossed, or
carbuncle, escarbuncle**

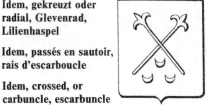

Triest, Bistum und Stadt

Kyritz

Kyritz

Murschidabad (Bengalen)

Ahmad-Abad

Perleberg
(Mark Brandenburg)

Österreich
(unter König Ottokar von Böhmen)

Marchiennes

Ciney (Belgien) • Cysoing, Abtei
(Französisch Flandern)
Kleve, Herzogtum

Kleve, Herzogtum

St. Bertin

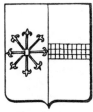

Kleve, Herzogtum
Mark

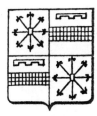

Utrecht, Bistum,
Engelbert von Cleve,
Gouverneur 1481–1483

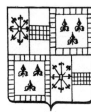

Nevers, Herzogtum

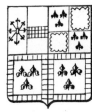

Nevers, Herzogtum

Nevers, Herzogtum

Kleve, Mark und Ravensberg

Jülich, Kleve und Berg

Sachsen-Eisenach

Sachsen (Alt-Coburger Linie)

Sachsen (Alt-Coburger Linie)

Jülich, Kleve und Berg

Jülich, Kleve und Berg

Merkurstab und Donnerkeil

Caducée et foudre

Caduceus and thunderbolt

Curaçao

Lima (Peru)

Sabbioneta

Gabel, Dreizack und Sonnenschirm

Fourche, trident et parasol

Fork, trident and parasol

Schwarzburg (Thüringen)

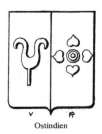

Ostindien

Canterbury, Erzbistum

Arkat
Masulipatam (Indien)

Hindustan (Timuriden)
Kadsch · Ostindien

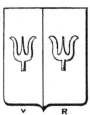

Mohammedabad (Benares)

Ukraine

Nepal

Adhim-Abad

Saröndsch

Delhi

Leuchter, Kandelaber
Chandelier
Candlestick, chandelier

Java

Hacke
Houe
Pick

Israel 11. 2. 1949

Südrhodesien, 11. 8. 1924,
seit 24. 10. 1964 Rhodesien

Homburg vor der Höhe,
Stadt (Hessen)

Gambia, 10. 11. 1964

Schaufel, Spaten, Spatenblatt

Bêche, pelle, fer de pelle

Shovel, spade, spade-blade

Algier 1848

J. Shaw & Co, Importers of Hardwares, Upper Town, Quebec, 1837

T. S. Brown & Co, Importers of Hardwares, Montreal (Quebec), um 1837

Brandenburg, Markgrafschaft

Kolben, Ruder

Masse, rame

Mace, oar

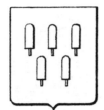

Schenken von Limburg

Riedlingen, Stadt (Württemberg)

Colmar im Elsaß, Stadt

Colmar im Elsaß, Stadt

Rutenbündel

Faisceau de licteur

Fasces

Haiti, Republik

Mantua, Stadt
Römische Republik, 1798–99
St. Gallen, Kanton, S. 4. 1803
Sarine und Broye, Département (West-Schweiz)
20. 3. 1798 – 20. 11. 1800

St. Gallen, Kanton, 5. 4. 1803

Mainz, Stadt, 1793

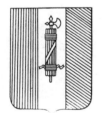

Italienische Sozialrepublik, 23. 1. 1944

Italien, Königreich, W. des Faschismus, 12. 12. 1926

Rom, Republik, 1848-1849

Sarine und Broye, Département (West-Schweiz) 20. 3. 1798 – 20. 11. 1800

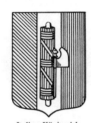

Rom, Republik 1798–1800

Haiti, Republik

Albany (New York)

Frankreich, Republik, 1929

Montluçon (Allier)

Vandalen

Venezuela, 14. 10. 1830

Bogotá, (Kolumbien)
Kolumbien, 6. 10. 1821
Popayán (Kolumbien)

Ecuador, 19. 9. 1830

Hammer

Marteau

Hammer

York, Erzbistum (England)

Deutsche Demokratische
Republik, 12. 1. 1950

Frinco (Provinz Alessandria)

Frinco (Provinz Alessandria)

Frinco (Provinz Alessandria)

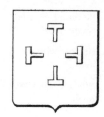

Frinco (Provinz Alessandria)

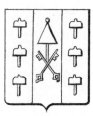

Frinco (Provinz Alessandria)

Deutsche Demokratische
Republik, 21. 8. 1952

Deutsche Demokratische
Republik, 27. 9. 1955

Ungarn, Volksrepublik
14. 9. 1949

Abertham

Kongo (Brazzaville),
31. 12. 1969

Russische Sozialistische
Föderative Sowjetrepublik,
26. 7. 1918

Ukrainische Sozialistische
Sowjetrepublik, 1. 1. 1950

Litauische Sozialistische
Sowjetrepublik, 10. 9. 1940

Estnische Sozialistische
Sowjetrepublik, 21. 10. 1940

Lettische Sozialistische
Sowjetrepublik, 25. 8. 1940

Weißrussische Sozialistische
Sowjetrepublik, 1937

Weißrussische Sozialistische
Sowjetrepublik

Sowjetunion, 1924

Sowjetunion, 15. 12. 1936

Sowjetunion 12. 9. 1956

Sowjetunion, Okt. 1945

Anker

Ancre

Anchor

Århus
Stadt und Bistum

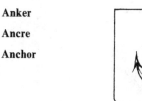

Byzanz

Ludwigshafen am Rhein,
Stadt, 14. 9. 1937

Chile

Canton (Ohio)

Cincinnati (Ohio)
Fredericktown (Ohio)
Green Bay (Wisconsin)
Providence (Rhode Island)
Vereinigte Staaten von Amerika

Englische Besitzungen

New-York

Pitcairn-Inseln, 4. 11. 1969

Pointe à Pitre (Guadeloupe)

Brieg, Stadt (Schlesien)

Brieg, Stadt (Schlesien)

Solingen, Stadt

Kapstadt, 12. 6. 1804

Rieneck (Grafen Nostiz
zu Rieneck 1673)

Rieneck (Grafen Nostiz
zu Rieneck 1673)

Fackel

Torche, flambeau

Torch

Falkland Islands'
Dependencies, 11. 3. 1952
Brit. Antarkt. Geb. 1. 8. 1963

Tanganjika, 1962

Jugoslawien, Mai 1945

Jugoslawien, 7. 4. 1963

Pfeil

Flèche

Arrow

Stralsund

Schlesien

Stralsund

Dänemark

Anklam, Stadt (Pommern)

Sidon

Stralsund

Stralsund

Stralsund

Anklam, Stadt (Pommern)

Nyköping (Schweden)
Sorau

Sorau

Sonora (Mexiko)

Hohenfriedeberg, Stadt
(Schlesien)

San Luis Potosí (Mexiko)

Louisville (Kentucky)

Närke, Landschaft (Schweden)
Schweden

Schweden

Bahía

Pfeilbündel

Faisceau de flèches

Sheaf of arrows

Geldern
Kastilien und León
St. Martin

Sheffield, Stadt (England)

Pfeil und Bogen

Flèche et arc

Arrow and bow

Mexiko 1811–1813
Oaxaca, Stadt (Mexiko) (1812)

Dschudschiden (Gulistan)

Dahome, 1958

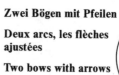

Ruanda

Zwei Bögen mit Pfeilen

Deux arcs, les flèches ajustées

Two bows with arrows

Mali

Dolch und Schwert

Poignard, épée, glaive

Dagger and sword

Batavia · Béarn
Lothringen, Herzogtum

Atschin

Ägypten · Peshaw
Schemaché

Niederlothringen

Narwar (Indien)

Ostindien

Böhmen

Schweden

Lothringen, Herzogtum
Toul (Liverdun)
Trier, Erzbistum · Vaudemont

Kalpi

Bidschnagur

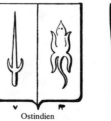

Hennegau

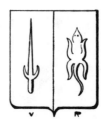

Ostindien

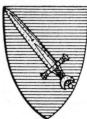

Essen, Stadt, linker Schild

Hindustan
(Tímuriden, Großmogul)

Schemachá

Northumberland

St. Martin, Abtei (England)

St. Peter, Abtei (England)

St. Peter, Abtei (England)

Bhartpur

Nadschpur

Béarn

Nepal

Kabul

Ahmed-Schahi

Dänemark

Haarlem, Stadt
(Nordholland)

Haarlem, Stadt
(Nordholland)

Béarn

Lothringen, Herzogtum

Vaudemont (Lothringen)

Brandenburg, Markgrafschaft

Batavia

Batavia

Batavia

Zaltbommel
(Prov. Gelderland)

Zaltbommel
(Prov. Gelderland)

St. Amand, Stadt
(Franz. Flandern)

Lothringen, Herzogtum

Bath, Stadt (England)

Reckheim

Aalst (Alost),
Grafschaft (Flandern)

Boulogne

Toul, Stadt

Dänemark

Schwert mit anderer Figur gekreuzt

Épée, passée en croix ou en sautoir avec autre meuble

Sword crossed with other charge

Naumburg, Bistum

Naumburg, Bistum

Dorpat, Bistum

Naumburg, Bistum
Striegau, Stadt
(Niederschlesien)
Trier, Erzbistum
Weißenau, Abtei
(Württemberg)

Dorpat, Bistum
Striegau, Stadt (Niederschlesien)
Trier, Erzbistum

Cattaro, 1813

Großbritannien

Mantua, Herzogtum

Zwei Schwerter

Deux épées

Two swords

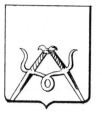

Pesaro

China (Dynastie Pe Tscheu)

Sachsen, Kurfürstentum

Sachsen, Kurfürstentum

Sachsen, Kurfürstentum

Sachsen, Kurfürstentum

Sachsen, Kurfürstentum

Sachsen, Kurfürstentum

Sachsen, Kurfürstentum

Sachsen, Kurfürstentum

Sachsen, Kurfürstentum

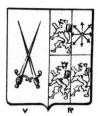

Sachsen, Kurfürstentum

Sachsen, Kurfürstentum

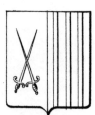

Sachsen, Kurfürstentum

Sachsen, Kurfürstentum

Essen, Bistum

Quedlinburg, Abtei

Hermannstadt (Siebenbürgen)

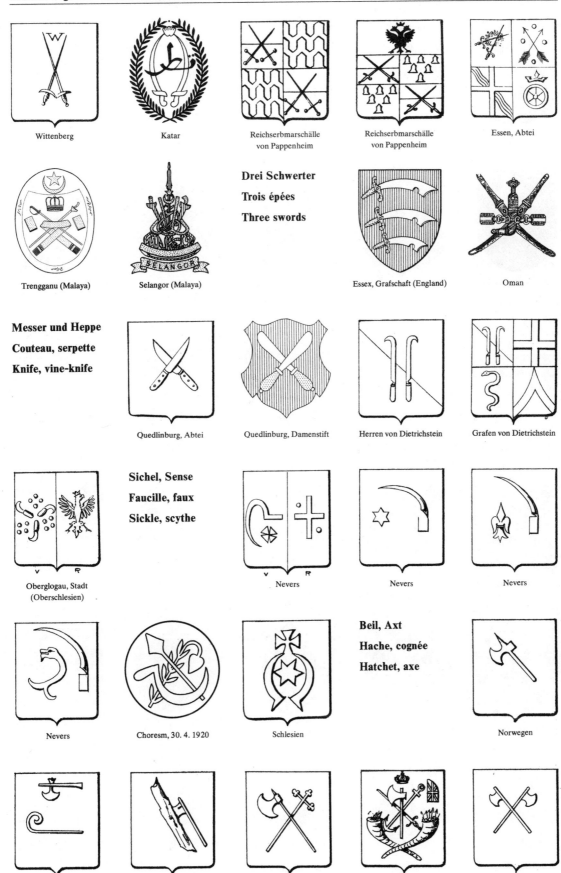

Wittenberg

Katar

Reichserbmarschälle von Pappenheim

Reichserbmarschälle von Pappenheim

Essen, Abtei

Trengganu (Malaya)

Selangor (Malaya)

Drei Schwerter
Trois épées
Three swords

Essex, Grafschaft (England)

Oman

Messer und Heppe
Couteau, serpette
Knife, vine-knife

Quedlinburg, Abtei

Quedlinburg, Damenstift

Herren von Dietrichstein

Grafen von Dietrichstein

Oberglogau, Stadt
(Oberschlesien)

Sichel, Sense
Faucille, faux
Sickle, scythe

Nevers

Nevers

Nevers

Nevers

Choresm, 30. 4. 1920

Schlesien

Beil, Axt
Hache, cognée
Hatchet, axe

Norwegen

Deutschland (Bonn)

Vereinigte Staaten von Amerika

Drontheim, Bistum
(Norwegen)

Oberkanada
1850-1867

Biel, Stadt (Schweiz)

Biel, Stadt (Schweiz)

Fahne, Flagge

Drapeau

Flag

Miesbach, Stadt (Bayern)

Magdeburg, Erzbistum

Würzburg, Bistum

Würzburg, Stadt

Würzburg, Stadt

Tunesien, bis 1956

Ludwigsburg, Stadt
(Württemberg)

Herstal (Belgien)

Demmin (Pommern)

Jalisco (Teilstaat von Mexiko)

Mompos (Kolumbien)

Kalifornien

Vereinigte Staaten von Amerika

South Bend (Indiana)
Utica (New York)

Kenton (Ohio)
Vereinigte Staaten von Amerika

Vereinigte Staaten von Amerika

Umm-al-Qiwain

Philadelphia (Pennsylvanien)

Adschman, 1969

Ras-el-Khaimah

Fudschairah

Algerien, Republik

Audh (Britisch-Indien)

Audh (Britisch-Indien)

Maryland

Württemberg

Württemberg

Würzburg, Großherzogtum

Fahnengruppe

Drapeaux groupés

Flags grouped

China, Politische Konsultative
Nationalkonferenz, 28.9.1949

La Guaira (Venezuela)

Dominikanische Republik,
Modell 12.6.1896

**Gonfanon,
Kirchenfahne**

Gonfanon

Gonfanon

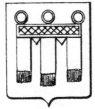

Montfort, Grafschaft

Tübingen, Stadt
(Württemberg)

Böblingen, Stadt
(Württemberg)

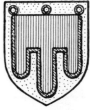

Auvergne,
französische Provinz

Vorarlberg, 3.12.1918

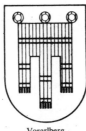

Vorarlberg
18.6.1936

Feldkirch (Vorarlberg)

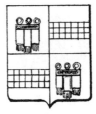

Sedan

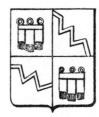

Fürstenberg, Landgrafschaft
und Fürstentum

Reichsapfel

Monde

Mound, orb

Pfalz, Kurfürstentum

Bad Soden, Stadt (Hessen)

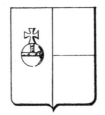

Lübeck, Stadt

Pfalz, Kurfürstentum

Hamburg

Bayern, Kurfürstentum

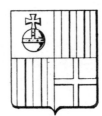

Bellpuig (Katalonien),
1641–1643

Georgien,
Könige aus dem Hause
Bagration

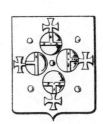

Meißen, Markgrafschaft

**Himmelsglobus,
Armillarsphäre**

Sphère armillaire

Armillary sphere

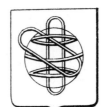

Mirandola, Fürstentum
Padua
Urbino (Italien)

Guinea (Portugiesisch)
São Tomé e Principe

Brasilien

Brasilien, Königreich,
dann Kaiserreich, 18.9.1822

Brasilien und Portugal,
18.5.1816
Guinea (Portugiesisch)

Portugal

Guanabara, Staat
(Brasilien)

**Andere kreisförmige
Figuren**

**Autres meubles
circulaires**

Other circular charges

Schlesien

Schlesien

Ostindien

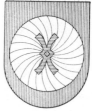

Hameln

Hameln

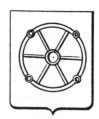

Amalfi

Rad

Roue

Wheel

Roda, Stadtroda
(Thüringen)

Battenberg, Stadt
Erfurt, Stadt

Frankfurt, Großherzogtum
1810–1814
Fürst Primas 1806–1814
Hofgeismar · Lobdeburg
Macerata (Italien)
Mainz, Erzbistum
Miltenberg,Stadt
Molsheim, Stadt (Unterelsaß)
Osnabrück, Bistum
Osnabrück, Stadt
Radkersburg, Stadt (Steiermark)
Weißensee (Thüringen)
Wiedenbrück, Stadt (Westfalen)

Roda, Stadtroda
(Thüringen)

Heusden (Nordbrabant)
Roda, Stadtroda (Thüringen)

St. Bertin
Treffurt (Thüringen)

Erfurt, Stadt
Mainz, Erzbistum

Osnabrück, Bistum

Osnabrück, Stadt

Donaueschingen, Stadt

Erfurt

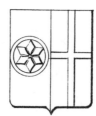

Osnabrück und Paderborn

Mainz und Pfalz

Mainz und Worms

Halberstadt,
Magdeburg und Mainz

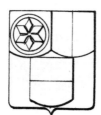

Halberstadt,
Magdeburg und Mainz

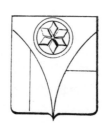

Halberstadt,
Magdeburg und Mainz

Mainz, Köln und Trier

Mainz, Köln, Pfalz und Trier

Minden, Münster und
Osnabrück, Bistümer

Halberstadt (Dompropstei),
Osnabrück und Verden

**Rad im ersten von vier
Feldern**

**Roue au premier de
quatre champs**

**Wheel on first of four
fields**

Mainz, Hessen, Köln,
Pfalz, Speyer und Trier

Mainz, Köln,
Speyer und Trier

**Rad in geviertem oder
mehrfeldigem Schild**

**Roue dans écu à quatre
quartiers ou davantage**

**Wheel on shield quart-
ered of four or more**

Mainz, Domkapitel

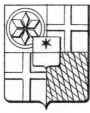

Mainz, Bayern,
Köln und Trier

Mainz, Hessen, Köln,
Pfalz und Trier

Mainz, Bayern,
Köln und Trier

Mainz, Köln, Pfalz und Trier

Osnabrück und Paderborn

Mainz und Pfalz

Mainz, Pfalz und Trier

Mainz, Frankfurt a. M.,
Hessen und Nassau

Cysoing, Abtei
(Französisch Flandern)

Miltenberg, Stadt

Miltenberg, Stadt

Mainz, Bayern, Köln,
Pfalz und Trier

Münster, Osnabrück
und Paderborn, Bistümer

**Rad begleitet oder über-
deckt**

**Roue accompagnée ou
avec autre meuble
brochant**

**Wheel accompanied or
surmounted**

Erfurt

Erfurt

Molsheim, Stadt (Unterelsaß)

Erfurt

Erfurt

Erfurt

Erfurt

Zwei Räder

Deux roues

Two wheels

Erfurt

Brehna

Erfurt

Mainz, Stadt, 12. 6. 1915

Fritzlar, Stadt (Hessen)

Mainz, Stadt, 1815–1915

Zahnrad

Roue à dents, roue de moulin

Cog wheel, pinion

Ribe, Stadt (Dänemark)

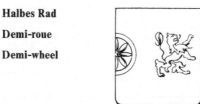

Mülhausen im Elsaß

Mülhausen im Elsaß

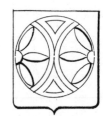

Mühldorf am Inn, Stadt (Bayern)

Saargebiet, 28. 7. 1920–1935

Halbes Rad

Demi-roue

Demi-wheel

Mainz, Erzbistum

Erfurt

Erfurt

Wagengestell

Train de chariot

Carriage-frame

Carrara
Padua

Wagen

Char

Carriage

Hamilton (Ohio)
New-York

Melbourne
(Victoria, Australien)

Melbourne
(Victoria, Australien)

Melbourne
(Victoria, Australien)

Neue Republik (Südafrika)

Pflug

Charrue

Plough

Port Albert
(Victoria, Australien)

Antigua (Guatemala)

Dundas (Ontario)
East Saginaw (Michigan)
Janesville (Wisconsin)
Kingston (Jamaika)
Lansing (New York)
Troy (New York)
Toronto
York (Kanada), seit 1834

Straubing, Stadt (Bayern)

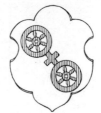

Straubing, Stadt (Bayern)

Wagga Wagga (Neusüdwales)

Philadelphia (Pennsylvanien)

Philadelphia (Pennsylvanien)

Pennsylvanien

Pennsylvanien

Straubing, Stadt (Bayern)

New Jersey

Kanone und Kanonenrohr

Canon, tube de canon

Gun, gun-barrel

Vereinigte Staaten von Amerika

Smolensk

Vereinigte Staaten von Amerika

Vereinigte Staaten von Amerika

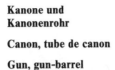

Anguilla (Westindien), Oktober 1967

Vereinigte Staaten von Amerika

Maschine

Machine, engin

Machine, engine

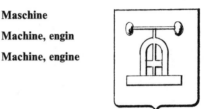

New-York

Kattowitz, Stadt (Oberschlesien)

Grenada, 1889–1903

Kamm

Peigne

Comb

Provins (Seine-et-Marne)

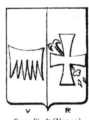

Sens, Stadt (Yonne)

Provins (Seine-et-Marne)

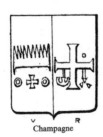

Champagne

Rethel

Sari

Rethel

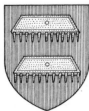

Rethel

Rechen, Harke

Râteau

Rake

Rethel Stadt

Tuwa, 1921–1944

Päpstliche Tiara

Tiare papale

Papal tiara

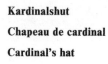

Fermo (Provinz Marche, Italien)

Venaissin, Grafschaft
(Südfrankreich)

Kardinalshut

Chapeau de cardinal

Cardinal's hat

Windische Mark

Mitra

Mitre épiscopale

Episcopal mitre

Ellwangen, Abtei
Kolberg, Stadt
St.-Paul-Trois-Châteaux

Thérouanne (Pas-de-Calais)

Thérouanne (Pas-de-Calais)

Aire, Bistum (Landes)

Ellwangen, Abtei

Paderborn, Domkapitel

Ellwangen, Abtei

Aire, Bistum (Landes)

Dänemark

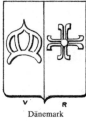

Dänemark

Dänemark

Lyon, Erzbistum

Aquileja

Koblenz, Stadt

Arras, Bistum

Andorra

Saintonge, Provinz
(Frankreich)

Schlesien

St. Honorat de Lérins,
Abtei (Insel, Alpes-Maritimes)

Andorra, ursprüngliche Form

Andorra

Andorra

Thérouanne (Pas-de-Calais)

Cambrai, Bistum

Nuchuy (Aserbaidshan)

Italien
Palmanova (Provinz Udine)

Gubbio (Prov. Reggio nell'Emilia)

Maine, Grafschaft
(Frankreich)
Neapel, Königreich

Quedlinburg, Stadt

Norwegen

Deutscher Orden

Böhmen

Bretagne
Dänemark
Eisenach
Frankreich
Görlitz
Gotha
Navarra
Neapel, Königreich
Norwegen

Provence
Sabbioneta
Schlesien
Schweden
Schweidnitz, Stadt
Ungarn

Bombay

Adelaide (Südaustralien)
Neusüdwales
Sydney (Australien)

Melbourne (Victoria, Australien)

Bombay

Dänemark

Navarra
Parma

Cambrai, Bistum

Navarra

Mailand

Evreux (Eure, Normandie)
Navarra

Sizilien

Navarra

Aquitanien

Sizilien

Johanniter-Orden

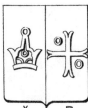

Johanniter-Orden

Maine, Grafschaft (Frankreich)

England, Königreich

Ungarn

Ungarn

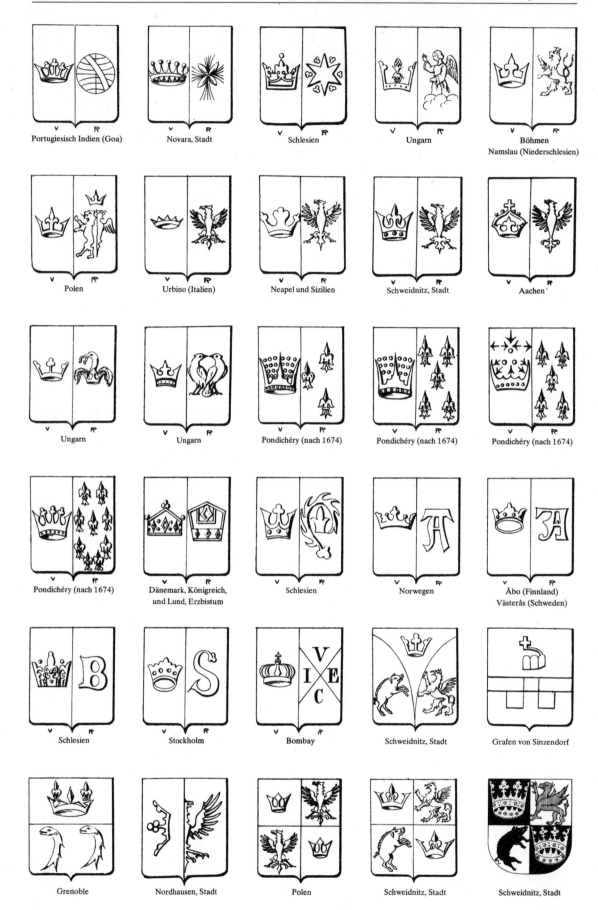

Portugiesisch Indien (Goa)

Novara, Stadt

Schlesien

Ungarn

Böhmen
Namslau (Niederschlesien)

Polen

Urbino (Italien)

Neapel und Sizilien

Schweidnitz, Stadt

Aachen

Ungarn

Ungarn

Pondichéry (nach 1674)

Pondichéry (nach 1674)

Pondichéry (nach 1674)

Pondichéry (nach 1674)

Dänemark, Königreich,
und Lund, Erzbistum

Schlesien

Norwegen

Åbo (Finnland)
Västerås (Schweden)

Schlesien

Stockholm

Bombay

Schweidnitz, Stadt

Grafen von Sinzendorf

Grenoble

Nordhausen, Stadt

Polen

Schweidnitz, Stadt

Schweidnitz, Stadt

Dauphiné

Königsberg/Neumark

Schlesien

Brandenburg, Markgrafschaft

Schlesien

Nuchuy (Aserbaidshan)

Brandenburg, Markgrafschaft

Schlesien

Vereinigte Staaten von Amerika

Maine, Grafschaft (Frankreich)

Maine, Grafschaft (Frankreich) Neapel, Königreich Provence

Neapel, Königreich Provence

Sizilien

Neapel, Königreich Provence

Kronstadt, Stadt (Siebenbürgen)

Toskana

Neapel und Sizilien

Großbritannien

Großbritannien

Großbritannien

Kielce, Stadt (Polen)

Gotha, Stadt

Gotha, Stadt

Wittenberg

Gotha, Stadt

Brandenburg, Markgrafschaft

Norwegen

Norwegen

Schweden

Irland

Kingston upon Hull

Schweden

England und Irland, vor 1603

Åbo (Finnland)
Västerås (Schweden)

Stockholm 1512–1520

Schweden

Schweden

Köln, Stadt

Köln, Stadt, mit W.
der heiligen drei Könige

Köln, Stadt

Köln, Stadt

Östergötland, Herzogtum
(Schweden)
Schweden

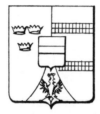

Galizien und Lodomerien, 1772

Galizien und Lodomerien,
27. 1. 1782

Schweden

Schweden

Elbing (W: Schweden
und Elbing)

Södermanland

Schweden

Schweden

Tegernsee

Bremen, Herzogtum,
1648–1715

Schweden

Lima, 7. 12. 1537

Köln, Stadt

Schweden

Schweden

Schweden

Königsberg/Neumark

Åbo (Finnland)

Schweden

Köln, Stadt

Straits Settlements

Murcia (span. Königreich)

Murcia, Stadt

Hut

Chapeau

Hat

Windische Mark

Korsika

Phrygische Mütze

Bonnet phrygien

Phrygian cap

Nantes
Valenciennes (Französ. Flandern)

Guanajuato (Mexiko)

Mexiko, Republik
Neugranada
Vereinigte Staaten
von Amerika

Jalisco (Teilstaat von Mexiko)

Newbourg (New-York)

Mittelamerika

Lyon, Stadt, 1793

Kolumbien 9. 5. 1834

Neugranada

Jagdhorn, Hiefhorn

Cor de chasse

Bugle

Hoorn, Stadt (Nordholland)
Württemberg (Urach)

Breda

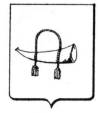

Orange
Württemberg (Urach)

Orange

Orange

Breda

Hindustan
(Timuriden, Großmoguln)

Orange

Haldenstein, Herrschaft (Bez.
Imboden, Graubünden), Besitz der
Freiherrn Buol von Schauenstein

Orange

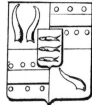

Haldenstein, Herrschaft (Bez.
Imboden, Graubünden), Besitz
Freiherrn Buol v. Schauenstein

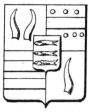

Haldenstein, Herrschaft (Bez.
Imboden, Graubünden), Besitz
der Freiherrn Buol v. Schauenstein

Orange

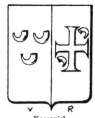

Kessenich

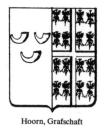

Hoorn, Grafschaft
Weert
(niederländ. Provinz Limburg)

Kessenich

Weert
(niederländ. Provinz Limburg)

Weißenhorn, Stadt (Bayern)

Hoorn, Grafschaft
Wessem
(niederländ. Provinz Limburg)

Orange

Jägerndorf, Stadt

Lüttich, Bistum

Kessenich

Orange

Füllhorn

Corne d'abondance

Cornucopia

Bogotá, (Kolumbien)
Popayán (Kolumbien)

Caracas (Venezuela)

Neapel und Sizilien

Neapel und Sizilien

Bloemfontein, Stadt
(Oranje-Freistaat)

Neapel, Königreich

Neugranada

'Bogotá, (Kolumbien)
Neugranada
Popayán (Kolumbien)

Neapel, König Joseph
Napoleon (1806–1808)

Tonne, Faß

Tonneau

Tun, barrel

Halifax (Neuschottland)
Milwaukee (Wisconsin)
Wapakoneta (Ohio)
West Jefferson (Ohio)

Philadelphia (Pennsylvanien)

Milwaukee (Wisconsin)

Cincinnati (Ohio)

W. A. & S. Black, Eisen-
warenhändler, Halifax
(Neuschottland), 1816

Korb

Corbeille

Basket

Neapel, Republik (1648–1649)

Cincinnati (Ohio)

Sabbioneta

Kessel und Eimer

Chaudron, seau

Kettle, pail

Caldas (Katalonien)

Emmerich, Stadt
(Niederrhein)

Bottich

Cuve

Tub

Milwaukee (Wisconsin)

Vase, Flammentopf

**Vase, pot jaillissant des
flammes**

Vase, blazing pot

Veere (Seeland, Niederlande)
Vlissingen (Seeland, Niederlande)

Mirandola, Fürstentum

Öllampe

Lampe à huile

Oil-lamp

Woburn (Massachusetts)

Kiste

Caisse

Chest

Grand Rapids (Michigan)

Alleghany (Pennsylvanien)

Circleville (Ohio)
MacConnelsville (Ohio)
Peru (Indiana)
Vereinigte Staaten von Amerika

Flasche

Bouteille

Bottle

Pittsburg (Virginia)

Krug, Kanne

Cruche, canette

Jug, pitcher

Brandenburg, Kurfürstentum

Badgastein (Land Salzburg, Österreich)

Milwaukee (Wisconsin)

Cincinnati (Ohio)
Watertown (Wisconsin)

New-York

Cincinnati (Ohio)
Ohio (U.S.A.)

Milwaukee (Wisconsin)

Kelch, Becher, Pokal, Henkeltopf

Calice, gobelet, hanap, bocal, pot à anse

Cup, goblet, pot with a handle

New-York

New-York

Santan Marta

Quedlinburg, Abtei

Puebla de los Ángeles
(heute Puebla de Zaragoza, Mexiko)

Ägypten, 1461–1517

Kuttenberg, Stadt (Böhmen)

Kambodscha, Königreich

Belmonte, Herzogtum
des Geschlechts Pignatelli

Sack

Sac

Sack

Säckingen, Stadt (Südbaden)

Waage

Balance

Balance, scales

Bombay, Präsidentschaft

Jezd

Pontianak (West-Borneo)

Mompos (Kolumbien)
Montero
New-York

New-York

New-York

New-York

China

Georgien

Georgien

Frankreich
San Domingo

Hindustan
(Timuriden, Großmoguln)

Kamerun
1960

Uruguay

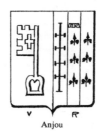

Uruguay 14. 3. 1829

Schlüssel

Clé

Key

Saumur (Maine-et-Loire)

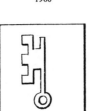

Bremen, Stadt

Cluny, Abtei
Grafen von Frohberg (Elsaß)
Narbonne, Vicomté
Soest, Stadt (Westfalen)
Stade, Stadt
Trier, Erzbistum
Worms, Stadt

Schlesien

Anjou

Stade, Stadt

Soest, Stadt (Westfalen)

Dorsten, Stadt (Westfalen)
Maastricht
Stade, Stadt

Bremen, Stadt

Alcalá la Real (Andalusien)
Avignon
Cluny, Abtei

Alcalá la Real (Andalusien)
Bremen, Stadt · Stade, Stadt
Worms, Stadt

Bremen, Stadt

Bremen, Stadt

Obwalden

Öhringen, Stadt
(Württemberg)

Uri, Schwyz und Unterwalden

Nidwalden (Unterwalden
nid dem Wald)
Unterwalden

**Schlüssel mit Doppel-
schaft**

Clé à double tige

Key with double shank

Meißen, Bistum

Nidwalden (Unterwalden nid
dem Wald)

Nidwalden (Unterwalden
nid dem Wald)

Meißen, Bistum

Benevent

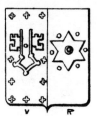

Glogau, Herzogtum

Schlüssel, begleitet

Clé, accompagnée

Key, accompanied

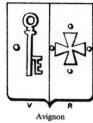

Avignon

Dänemark

Worms, Bistum

Worms, Stadt

Trier, Erzbistum

Anjou
Neapel, Königreich

Anjou

Anjou

Schlesien

Brandenburg, Markgrafschaft

Schlesien

Cluny, Abtei

Trier, Erzbistum

**Schlüssel in unter-
teiltem Schild**

Clé dans écu divisé

Key on divided shield

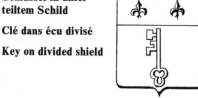
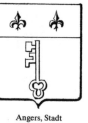

Angers, Stadt

Angers, Stadt

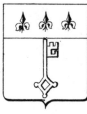

Angers, Stadt

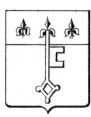

Angers, Stadt

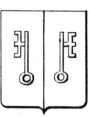

Genf

Vich (Katalonien)

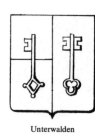

Unterwalden

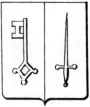

Cluny, Abtei

Narbonne, Stadt

Genf

Zwei Schlüssel

Deux clés

Two keys

Kirchenstaat

Anjou

Avignon
Herren von Gittelde
(Braunschweig)
Kirchenstaat
Salzwedel, Stadt
Trier, Erzbistum
Vich, Bistum (Katalonien)

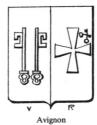

Avignon

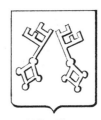

Avignon

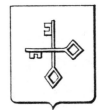

Meißen, Bistum

Salzwedel, Stadt

Vich (Katalonien)

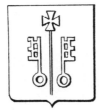

Salzwedel, Stadt

Trier, Erzbistum

Sagan, Herzogtum

Bremen, Erzbistum

Kirchenstaat
Leiden
Liegnitz, Stadt
Minden, Bistum
Minden, Stadt
Posen, Stadt
Regensburg, Stadt
Trier, Erzbistum
Wyschehrad (Prag)

Regensburg, Stadt

Leiden, Stadt

Venaissin, Grafschaft
(Südfrankreich)

Venaissin, Grafschaft
(Südfrankreich)

Liegnitz, Stadt

Wyschehrad (Prag)

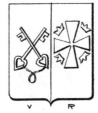

Frinco (Provinz Alessandria)

Venaissin, Grafschaft
(Südfrankreich)

Glogau, Herzogtum

Leiden

Bremen, Erzbistum
Bremen, Herzogtum
Riga, Stadt

Lübbecke, Stadt (Westfalen)

Bologna, Erzbistum

Kirchenstaat

Desana, Grafschaft (bei Vercelli)
Frinco (Provinz Alessandria)
Kirchenstaat

Vatikanstadt, 7. 6. 1929

Urbano, Fort, 1706–1709

Aquila

Leiden

Liegnitz, Stadt

Cluny, Abtei

Idem, in mehrfeldigem Schild

Idem, dans écu à plusieurs champs

Idem, on shield with several fields

Xanten, Stadt (Niederrhein)

Bremen und Lübeck

Bremen und Verden

Bremen, Osnabrück und Paderborn

Minden, Münster und Osnabrück, Bistümer

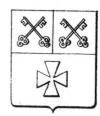

Bremen, Minden und Verden

Pilsen, Stadt

Pilsen, Stadt

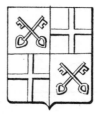

Bremen und Verden

Schlüssel, gekreuzt mit anderer Figur

Clé passée en sautoir ou en croix avec autre meuble

Key crossed with other charge

Oberaltaich, Benediktinerabtei (Niederbayern)

Loccum, Abtei (Niedersachsen)

Naumburg, Bistum

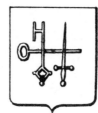

Naumburg, Bistum

Sachsen-Zeitz

Drei Schlüssel

Trois clés

Three keys

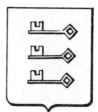

Avignon, Stadt

Avignon, Stadt

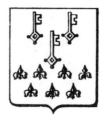

Le Mans, Stadt

Ostende, Stadt (Belgien)

Vorhängeschloß, Hufeisen

Cadenas, fer à cheval

Padlock, horseshoe

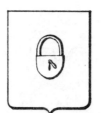

Grand Rapids (Michigan) Janesville (Wisconsin)

Isny, Stadt (Württemberg)

Brandenburg, Kurfürstentum

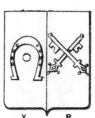

Glogau, Herzogtum

Schlesien

Gars, Propstei (Oberbayern)

Mercia

Dachau, Stadt

Dachau, Stadt

Glocke

Cloche

Bell

Oedenburg

Franeker, Stadt
Lüdinghausen, Stadt
Puigcerda (Katalonien)

Lüdinghausen, Stadt
(Westfalen)

Franeker, Stadt
(niederländische Provinz
Friesland)

Mindelheim, Stadt
(Württemberg)

Harfe

Harpe

Harp

Irland, Republik

Irland

England und Irland,
Commonwealth, 1649–1653

Irland

Irland

**Doppelhaken,
Zainhaken**

Crampon

Cramp

Halberstadt, Stadt

Halberstadt, Stadt

Wolfach, Stadt (Südbaden)

Mannheim, Stadt (Nordbaden)

Purmerend, Stadt (Nordholland)

Purmerend, Stadt
(Nordholland)

Köslin, Stadt (Pommern)

Rüsselsheim, Stadt (Hessen)

Maueranker, Mühleisen

Anille

Millrind

Hatzfeld, Herrschaft (Hessen)

Hatzfeld, Herrschaft (Hessen)

Bad Dürkheim, Stadt
(Rheinpfalz)

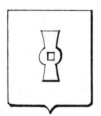

Mühlhausen in Thüringen

Hameln

Mühlhausen (Thüringen)

Vianen (Südholland)

Culemborg, Stadt
(Gelderland)
Vianen, Stadt (Südholland)

Culemborg, Stadt
(Gelderland)

Vianen, Stadt (Südholland)

Culemborg, Grafschaft
(Gelderland)

Culemborg, Grafschaft
(Gelderland)

Lippe-Detmold 1789

Beschläge

Bris d'huis, vertenelles

Hinge-pins

Herren von Schlotheim
(Thüringen)

Herren von Schlotheim
(Thüringen)

Schlesien

Schlesien

Ortokiden

Schlesien

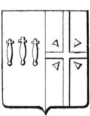

Château-Landon
(Seine-et-Marne)

Ungarn

Werkzeugbesteck

Garniture d'outils

Set of tools

Indianapolis (Indiana)

Faenza (Provinz Ravenna)

Faenza (Provinz Ravenna)

Hobart Town, (Name
1804–1881, seitdem
Hobart, Tasmanien)

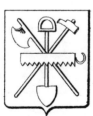

Milwaukee (Wisconsin)

Hobart Town, (Name
1804–1881, seitdem
Hobart, Tasmanien)

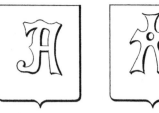

Gotha, Stadt

Schlesien

Obermarsberg,
Stadt (Westfalen), 12. 3. 1911

St. Eadmund, König der
Ostangeln, † 870
Verona (Oberitalien)

Ostangeln (England)

Sizilien

Marsberg, Stadt
(jetzt Obermarsberg, Westfalen)

Cosel (Oberschlesien)

Augsburg, Stadt

Norwegen

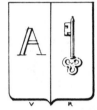

St. Edmundsbury

Dänemark

Amiens, Grafschaft

Åbo (Finnland)
Västerås (Schweden)

Monaco, Fürstentum

Åbo (Finnland)

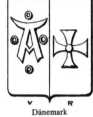

Västerås (Schweden)

Amiens, Grafschaft

Åbo-Turku, Stadt (Finnland)

Navarra (Nord)

Kurland

Beuthen (Oberschlesien)

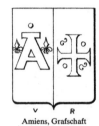

Bañolas (Katalonien)

Norwegen

Quedlinburg

Bayern

Anduze (Languedoc, Gard)

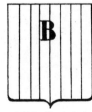

Schweden

Schlesien

Beuthen (Oberschlesien)

Batenburg

Byzanz

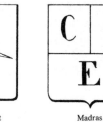

Aachen

Bañolas (Katalonien)

Krossen an der Oder,
Herzogtum

Wartenberg (Niederschlesien)

Korbach, Stadt

Madras

Schemnitz (Slowakei)

Demerara (Brit. Guayana)

Dänische Asiatische
Kompanie

Dänische Ostindische
Kompanie

Tranquebar (Indien)

Gotha, Stadt

Krossen an der Oder,
Herzogtum

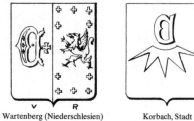

Eger, Stadt (Böhmen)
Einbeck, Stadt (Niedersachsen)

Einbeck, Stadt
(Niedersachsen)

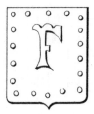

Einbeck, Stadt
(Niedersachsen)

Bombay

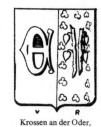

Eisenach, Stadt
Freystadt in Schlesien, Stadt
(Regierungsbezirk Liegnitz)

Sagan, Herzogtum

Schlesien

Freiburg im Breisgau, Stadt

Trient, Bistum

Eisenach, Stadt

Sagan, Herzogtum

Freystadt in Schlesien, Stadt
(Regierungsbezirk Liegnitz)

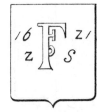

Jülich, Stadt 1621

Schlesien

Goslar, Stadt

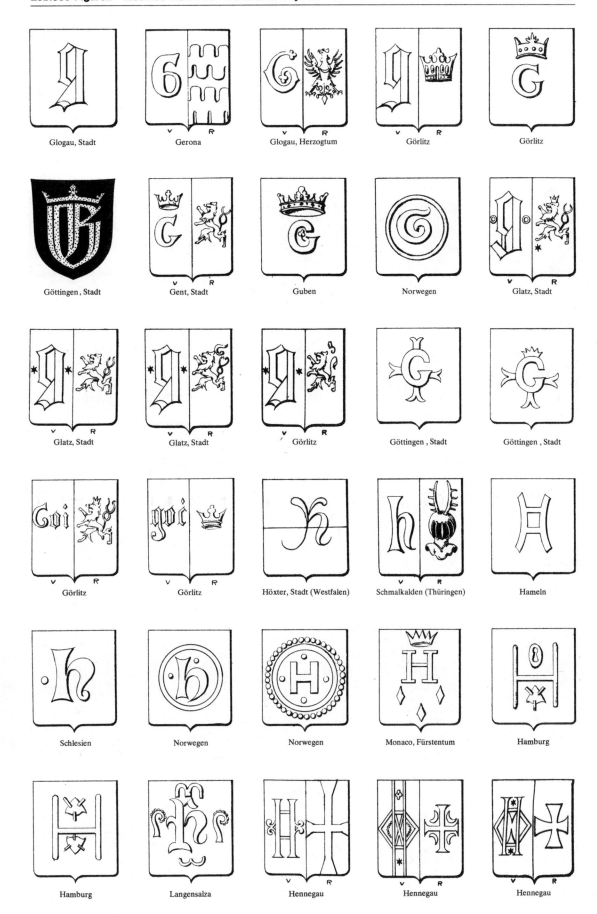

Glogau, Stadt	Gerona	Glogau, Herzogtum	Görlitz	Görlitz
Göttingen, Stadt	Gent, Stadt	Guben	Norwegen	Glatz, Stadt
Glatz, Stadt	Glatz, Stadt	Görlitz	Göttingen, Stadt	Göttingen, Stadt
Görlitz	Görlitz	Höxter, Stadt (Westfalen)	Schmalkalden (Thüringen)	Hameln
Schlesien	Norwegen	Norwegen	Monaco, Fürstentum	Hamburg
Hamburg	Langensalza	Hennegau	Hennegau	Hennegau

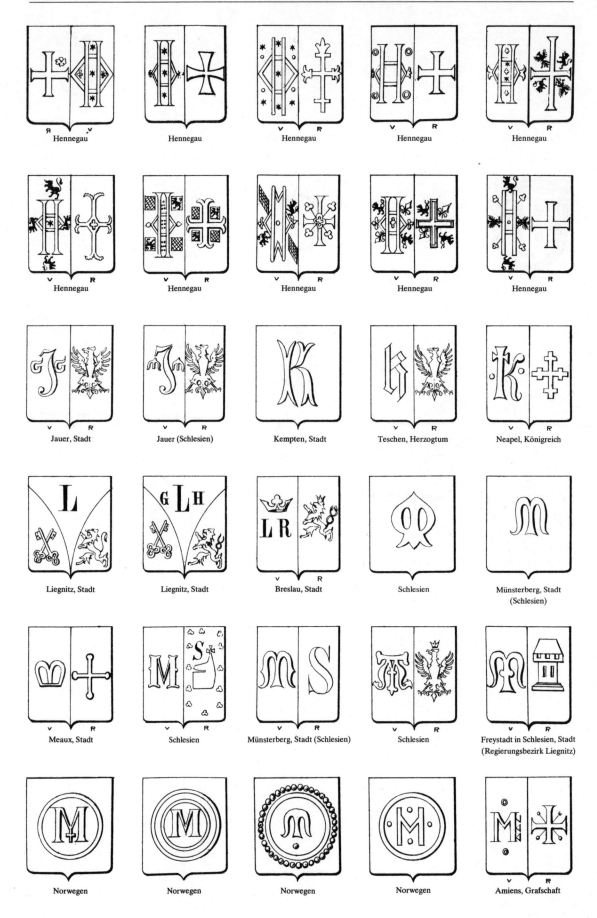

Hennegau   Hennegau   Hennegau   Hennegau   Hennegau

Hennegau   Hennegau   Hennegau   Hennegau   Hennegau

Jauer, Stadt   Jauer (Schlesien)   Kempten, Stadt   Teschen, Herzogtum   Neapel, Königreich

Liegnitz, Stadt   Liegnitz, Stadt   Breslau, Stadt   Schlesien   Münsterberg, Stadt (Schlesien)

Meaux, Stadt   Schlesien   Münsterberg, Stadt (Schlesien)   Schlesien   Freystadt in Schlesien, Stadt (Regierungsbezirk Liegnitz)

Norwegen   Norwegen   Norwegen   Norwegen   Amiens, Grafschaft

Münsterberg, Stadt (Schlesien)

Meaux, Stadt

Münsterberg, Stadt (Schlesien)

Meaux, Stadt

Mantua, Herzogtum

Meaux, Stadt

Meaux, Stadt

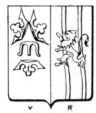

Schweden

Desana, Grafschaft
(bei Vercelli)

Meaux, Stadt

Issoudun (Indre)

Issoudun (Indre)

Monferrat, Markgrafschaft
(Oberitalien)

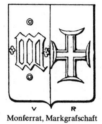

Massow, Stadt (Pommern)

Meaux, Stadt

Meaux, Stadt

Majorka 1808–1814

Münsterberg, Stadt (Schlesien)

Wiener Neustadt

Wiener Neustadt

Nürnberg, Stadt

Nürnberg, Stadt

Namslau (Niederschlesien)

Navarra (Süd)

Northeim

Norwegen

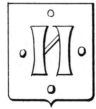

Novara, Stadt

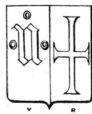

Namur (Belgien)

Nördlingen

Niedermünster.
Benediktinernonnenkloster
(Regensburg)

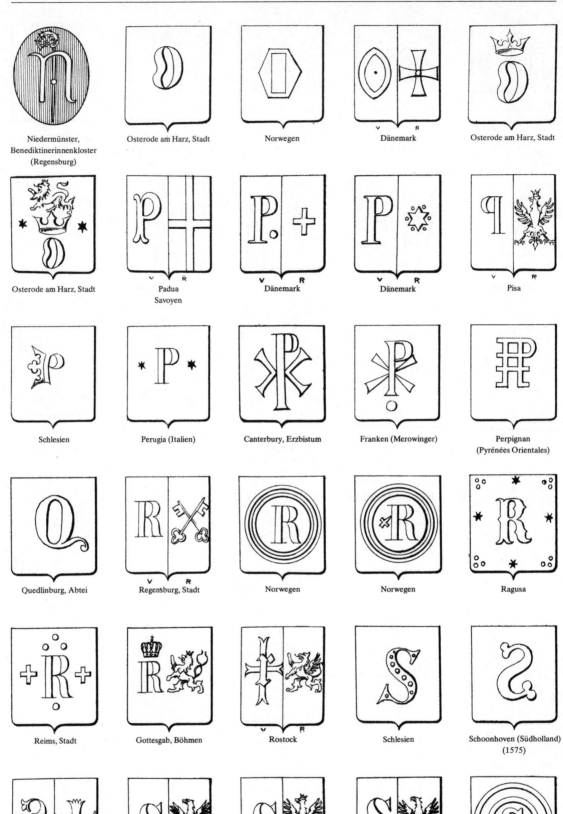

Niedermünster,
Benediktinerinnenkloster
(Regensburg)

Osterode am Harz, Stadt

Norwegen

Dänemark

Osterode am Harz, Stadt

Osterode am Harz, Stadt

Padua
Savoyen

Dänemark

Dänemark

Pisa

Schlesien

Perugia (Italien)

Canterbury, Erzbistum

Franken (Merowinger)

Perpignan
(Pyrénées Orientales)

Quedlinburg, Abtei

Regensburg, Stadt

Norwegen

Norwegen

Ragusa

Reims, Stadt

Gottesgab, Böhmen

Rostock

Schlesien

Schoonhoven (Südholland)
(1575)

Siena

Plock (Polen)

Sagan, Stadt

Sagan, Stadt

Norwegen

Norwegen

Wendische Münze

Mâcon (Saône-et-Loire)

Wendische Münze

Wendische Münze

Siena

Wendische Münze

Schweden

Chur, Bistum

Stockholm

Schmalkalden (Thüringen)

Stockholm

Schemnitz (Slowakei)

Landeshut, Stadt (Schlesien)

Zittau (Sachsen)

Solmona (Italien)

Rom, Stadt

Périgord, Landschaft
(Guyenne)

Sorau, Stadt

Sorau, Stadt

Sorau, Stadt

Litauen

Riga, Stadt

Polen
(Dynastie Wasa 1587–1672)

Polen (König Stephan
Bathory 1574–1586)

Kurland

Henneberg,
Gefürstete Grafschaft

Rimini

Tarragona
Tortona, Toul

Toul, Stadt

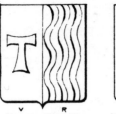

Tarragona (Spanien)

Monferrat, Markgrafschaft
(Oberitalien)

Tarragona (Spanien)

Teschen, Stadt

Bosnien

Trebnitz (Niederschlesien)

Österreich

Tarragona (Spanien), 1640–43

Todtnau (Kreis Lörrach)

Breslau, Stadt

Norwegen

Byzanz

Java (unter holländischer
Herrschaft)

Prince-of-Wales-Insel
(Penang)

Prince-of-Wales-Insel
(Penang)

Bombay

Java (unter holländischer
Herrschaft)

Bandjermasin (Borneo;
Vereinigte Ostindische
Kompanie, Niederlande) Ceylon

Ceylon, unter der niederländischen Vereinigten
Ostindischen Kompanie, 1632

Negapatam (Indien)

Pallikat

Pallikat

Pallikat

Pallikat

Bandjermasin (Borneo;
Vereinigte Ostindische
Kompanie, Niederlande)

Vevey, Stadt (Waadt), 1603

Breslau, Stadt

Breslau, Stadt

Breslau, Stadt

Vevey, Stadt (Kanton Waadt)
Waadt,

Breslau, Stadt

Breslau, Stadt

Wieck
(Westliches Estland)

Urbino (Italien)

Audenarde (Oudenaarde),
Belgien

St. Walburg, Kloster in Eichstätt

Brasilien

Wilhering, Zisterzienserkloster
(Oberösterreich)

Wilhering, Zisterzienserkloster
(Oberösterreich)

Dänemark und Wiborg

Köslin, Stadt (Pommern)
Zittau (Sachsen)

Dänemark und Århus

Dänemark und Ribe

Dänemark und Wiborg

Trebnitz (Niederschlesien)

Dänemark

Sorau, Stadt

Zwettl, Zisterzienserstift
(Niederösterreich)

Zwettl, Zisterzienserstift
(Niederösterreich)

Inschriften

Inscriptions

Inscriptions

Frankreich, Königreich,
18. 2. 1831

Ecuador, 19. 6. 1843

Waadt, Kanton, 16. 4. 1803

Waadt, Kanton, 16. 4. 1803

Guatemala, 18. 11. 1871

Guatemala, 12. 9. 1968

Zacatecas (Mexiko)

Arabische Schrift

Ecriture arabe

Arabic script

Tughra, sansibarischer Typ
Hier: Sultan Seyyid
Dschamschid (reg. bis 1964)

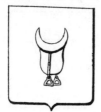

Tughra, türkischer Typ. Hier:
Kg. v. Afghanistan Mohammed
Zahir Schah (reg. 1933-73)

Perlis (Malaya)

Hedschas und Nedschd

Schlingen, Riemen

Lacets, courroies

Knots, laces, straps

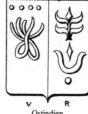

Wellington, Stadt

Haltern, Stadt (Westfalen)

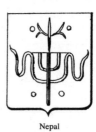

Haltern, Stadt (Westfalen)

Straßburg, Bistum

Boulogne, Grafschaft

Norwegen

Northumberland

Savoyen

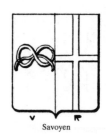

Savoyen

Kaschmir

Ostindien

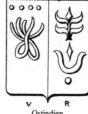

Nepal

Nepal

Rehfährte

Passée de chevreuil

Track of roe

Gars, Propstei (Oberbayern)

Abstrakte Zeichen

Signes abstraits

Abstract signs

Châteaudun (Orléanais)

Châteaudun (Orléanais)

Vendôme (Loir-et-Cher)

Blois

Vendôme (Loir-et-Cher)

Vendôme (Loir-et-Cher)

Châteaudun (Orléanais)

Châteaudun (Orléanais)

Châteaudun (Orléanais)

Châteaudun (Orléanais)

Châteaudun (Orléanais)

Blois

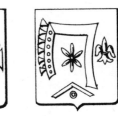
Blois

Vendôme (Loir-et-Cher)

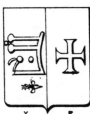
Blois

Huriel (Allier)

Châteaumeillant (Cher)

Charenton

Porcien (Ardennes)

Porcien (Ardennes)

Vendôme (Loir-et-Cher)

Dorpat, Bistum
Riga, Erzbistum

Jedes Wappen steht − von wenigen Ausnahmen abgesehen − nur an einer Stelle. Als Leitmotiv dient ein Bild normalerweise dann, wenn es heraldisch rechts (= links vom Beschauer), oben oder auch zentral steht. Letzteres gilt vor allem für besonders markante Bilder, die auffälliger sind als die Begleitfiguren rechts oder oben. Pragmatische Anordnung hat den Vorrang vor dogmatischer Placierung. So sind z. B. alle Wappen, die durch ein Schildhaupt bereichert sind, bei der Hauptfigur eingeordnet, z. B. die Wappen der Städte Amiens, Lille und Reims.

Zu den schwierigsten Problemen der Heraldik gehört u. a. die Beantwortung der Frage, um was für einen Gegenstand es sich jeweils handelt; so sind in den oben besprochenen englischen Ordinaries die Schachroche und die Kastelle zusammengefaßt; und auch in unserm Werk gilt der Augenschein mehr als die Sachkenntnis, die beim Suchenden nicht vorausgesetzt werden darf.

So findet man die Fünf Wunden Christi bei den Muscheln (Guadalajara Seite 252, Zeile 3, Platz 5) oder den Thron von Nowgorod bei den Türmen. Liegt der Fehler mehr in der Wiedergabe der Wappen selbst, wie z. B. beim Brustschild des russischen Doppeladlers auf S. 253, Zeile 4, Platz 4, dann ist er, soweit erkannt, im Stichwortregister aufspürbar, nämlich unter dem Stichwort Einhorn (von Turkestan) statt Pferd. Aus dem gleichen Grunde ist beim Stichwort »Garbe« die »Wasa-Garbe« ausgegliedert. Verwechselbar sind auch die Wolfszähne mit Baumästen, Berge mit Blättern, sogar Hörner mit Fischen. Manche Wappen haben im Lauf der Zeit ihre Interpretation geändert; so nennt man in Köln die Hermelinschwänzchen »Funken«, und der Gegenstand zwischen den Türmen von Jeßnitz wird als Komet, als Szepter oder als Spindel mit Garnknäuel gedeutet. Im Rahmen des Möglichen bietet das Stichwortregister für Wißbegierige eine Fundgrube; hierin sind vor allem solche Bilder verzeichnet, die an versteckter Stelle, z. B. in mehrfeldigen Schilden, vorkommen. Wegen ihrer Massenhaftigkeit sind Kreuze, Löwen, Adler, Rosen, Lilien u. dgl. nur dann nachgewiesen, wenn sie besonders interessante Eigenschaften haben, wie die geschachten und die schwertschwingenden Adler.

Die Häufigkeit mancher Bilder erklärt sich aus mehrfachen Erbgängen; das gilt z. B. für die Hörner bei Hoorn, Weert oder Oranien, für die Fische von Bar, Salm oder Wernigerode, auch für den Rautenkranz von Sachsen und Küenring bei Sachsen, Liechtenstein und Monferrat.

Wenn unter dem Namen eines Wappens eine Zeitangabe mit Tagesdatum steht, so bedeutet das den Entstehungstag dieses Wappens; eine Jahreszahl allein bedeutet das frühestmögliche Vorkommen.

In dem nun folgenden Stichwortverzeichnis ist der Platz jedes Wappens durch Seitenzahl, Zeile (fette Ziffer) und Platz innerhalb der Zeile angegeben.

Stichwortverzeichnis

Namensregister

GROSSER DEUTSCHER ORDENSKATALOG
Orden und Ehrenzeichen bis 1918

Von Arnhard Graf Klenau
1974, 225 Seiten, mit ca. 3.000 Nummern, Bewertungen
und 350 Abbildungen, Paperback DM 48,–
ISBN 3-87045-082-7

Deutschland ist das Land mit der größten Anzahl an verschiedenen Orden. Der *Große deutsche Ordenskatalog* erfaßt den gesamten Komplex an Orden und Ehrenzeichen etwa vom Beginn des 18. Jahrhunderts bis zum Ende des Deutschen Kaiserreichs 1918. Dieser Zeitraum ist mit Sicherheit der interessanteste der deutschen Ordensgeschichte. Die davorliegenden Bereiche sind nur für den Historiker von Bedeutung, da sammlungsfähige Realien kaum existieren. – Nachdem in den letzten Jahren das Sammeln von Orden und Ehrenzeichen der deutschen Staaten ständig neue Liebhaber gefunden hat, wurde immer häufiger der Wunsch geäußert, einen auf den praktischen Gebrauch ausgerichteten Katalog zusammenzustellen. Arnhard Graf Klenau hat erstmals diesen Versuch unternommen und seine Aufgabe mit viel Sachkenntnis gelöst und ein vorzügliches und in seiner Art einmaliges Buch geschaffen. Die Orden wurden in bisher unbekannter Vollständigkeit dokumentiert. 350 Abbildungen in Originalgröße ermöglichen ein rasches und bequemes Arbeiten. Die Numerierung, die reiche Bebilderung und die auktionalen Preisauszeichnungen sind für den Anfänger, den fortgeschrittenen Sammler, aber auch den Händler von größtem Nutzwert.

BATTENBERG VERLAG · 8 MÜNCHEN 71

NUMISMATIK
HERALDIK
ORDENSKUNDE

BATTENBERG
VERLAG
8 MÜNCHEN 71

Marcus Gilbert.

vngues linguam & diadema inornaueris, est BONAYORVM perinde in Gallia. Vel si leoni eidem puniceo substernas aurum, in scuti regione laxiore, atque in apice vellus cymbalite, est LIGNIERESIORVM item in Gallia.

De sable au chef cousù de gueulles au lion d'argent brochant sur le tout.

Argenteus leo, in area scuti sabulea, cum sutili eius apice puniceo, est BERNAVSIORVM in Belgio.

Iacob. Hēricourt.

Pinguntur quoque integri leones, in parmulis aut bipartitis, aut lemniscatis, aut icone aliqua minore signatis.

Vel puniceus leo, cum aurata lingua, in solo partim argenteo, partim cyaneo: atque est FOLOIGNEORVM in Belgio.

Iacob. Hemricourtius in speculo nobilitatis Hasban.

In parmula autem intercisa, ab læuo angulo, partitione diagonia, & supernè cyanea, infernè coccinea, leo aureus, est ROSINGENIORVM in Imp.

Quod attinet ad parmulas lemniscatas;

VVappenbuch, seu liber tesserar. Gentilitiar. Imperij ac totius Germ.

Vti aureus leo, puniceam linguam exserens, in valuulo superne sapphirino, & inferne argenteolo; est autem HESSENIORVM in Silesia.

VVappenbuch, seu liber tesserar Gētilitiar Imperij, ac totius Germ.

Argen-